Ask Me Smarter!

Brain Questions for Kids that are **FUN**-da-men-tal in Helping Them SOAR to Scholastic Success

Preschool – 5th Grade

By: Donna M. Roszak

Ask Me Smarter!

Brain Questions for Kids that are **FUN**-da-men-tal in Helping Them SOAR to Scholastic Success

Preschool – 5th Grade

Copyright © 2015 by Donna M. Roszak
All rights reserved

Published in the United States by: Zebra Print Press, LLC

Cover design by Donna M. Roszak
Cover creation by www.jimandzetta.com
Interior layout and typesetting by www.jimandzetta.com
Ebook conversion by www.jimandzetta.com

No part of this book or the related files may be reproduced or transmitted in any form, by any means (electronic, photocopying, recording, or otherwise) without the prior written permission of the publisher. The information in this book is meant to supplement and enhance, not replace, all other educational teaching methods. While best efforts have been used in preparing this book, the author and publisher make no representations or warranties with respect to the accuracy or completeness of the contents of this book. The author and publisher have checked with sources believed to be reliable in their efforts to provide information that is complete and generally in accord with the standards accepted at the time of publication. However, in view of the possibility of human error, neither nor any other party who has been involved in the preparation or publication of this work warrants that the information contained herein is in every respect accurate or complete, and they are not responsible for any errors or omissions or for the results obtained from the use of such information. Readers are encouraged to confirm the information contained herein with other sources.

Library of Congress Control Number: 2014945333

ISBN:978-0-9860801-1-1 (Trade Paperback)
       978-0-9860801-8-0 (eBook)
       978-0-9860801-9-7 (Hardcover)

Trademark and Sources Referenced Disclaimer: All trademarks and trade names used or mentioned are the property of their respective owners and are used only to describe and provide specific examples. Every effort has been made to properly capitalize, punctuate, and attribute trademarks and trade names to their respective owners. Further, every effort has been made to cite all sources used in the compilation of this book. If the author and publisher were remiss in any regard, the author and publisher would be happy to insert the appropriate acknowledgement in any subsequent edition of this book.

Printed in the United States of America

First Edition

Website: **www.askmesmarter.com**

To my sons Joey and Lucas, who have always believed in this book, to my mother Dorothy, whom I hope would be proud, and to my-mother-in law Joan, who has encouraged me throughout this endeavor.

Table of Contents

A Note to Parents, Guardians, and Teachers 11
Preface 12
How to Use This Book 13

Chapter 1 – Language Arts 17
    Language Arts – Pre-School 17
    Language Arts – Kindergarten 25
    Language Arts – 1st Grade 32
    Language Arts – 2nd Grade 41
    Language Arts – 3rd Grade 48
    Language Arts – 4th Grade 80
    Language Arts – 5th Grade 94

Chapter 2 – Notable Literary Works Through the Ages 120
    Arranged chronologically by date of publication

Chapter 3 – Math 159
    Math – Pre-School 159
    Math – Kindergarten 161
    Math – 1st Grade 166
    Math – 2nd Grade 179
    Math – 3rd Grade 192
    Math – 4th Grade 210
    Math – 5th Grade 229

Chapter 4 – Science 253
    Science – Pre-School 253
    Science – Kindergarten 258
    Science – 1st Grade 266
    Science – 2nd Grade 272
    Science – 3rd Grade 279
    Science – 4th Grade 306
    Science – 5th Grade 331

Chapter 5 – Social Studies 361
    Social Studies – Pre-School 361
    Social Studies – Kindergarten 362
    Social Studies – 1st Grade 367
    Social Studies – 2nd Grade 371
    Social Studies – 3rd Grade 386
    Social Studies – 4th Grade 416
    Social Studies – 5th Grade 459

Chapter 6 – Government and Civics **514**
    Government and Civics – Pre-School 514
    Government and Civics – Kindergarten 515
    Government and Civics – 1st Grade 516
    Government and Civics – 2nd Grade 517
    Government and Civics – 3rd Grade 517
    Government and Civics – 4th Grade 521
    Government and Civics – 5th Grade 523
    Practice Citizenship Test 531

Chapter 7 – Economics **535**
    Economics – Pre-School 535
    Economics – Kindergarten 535
    Economics – 1st Grade 536
    Economics – 2nd Grade 536
    Economics – 3rd Grade 538
    Economics – 4th Grade 539
    Economics – 5th Grade 540

Chapter 8 – Physical Education **548**
    Physical Education – Pre-School 548
    Physical Education – Kindergarten 548
    Physical Education – 1st Grade 554
    Physical Education – 2nd Grade 558
    Physical Education – 3rd Grade 561
    Physical Education – 4th Grade 563
    Physical Education – 5th Grade 566

Chapter 9 – Health and Safety **569**
    Health and Safety – Pre-School 569
    Health and Safety – Kindergarten 570
    Health and Safety – 1st Grade 572
    Health and Safety – 2nd Grade 574
    Health and Safety – 3rd Grade 575
    Health and Safety – 4th Grade 579
    Health and Safety – 5th Grade 584

Chapter 10 – The Arts **589**
    The Arts – Pre-School 589
    The Arts – Kindergarten 590
    The Arts – 1st Grade 594
    The Arts – 2nd Grade 600
    The Arts – 3rd Grade 608
    The Arts – 4th Grade 614
    The Arts – 5th Grade 618

Chapter 11 – Environment 629
Environment – Pre-School 629
Environment – Kindergarten 630
Environment – 1st Grade 630
Environment – 2nd Grade 631
Environment – 3rd Grade 631
Environment – 4th Grade 632
Environment – 5th Grade 632

Chapter 12 – Technology and Information Skills 636
Technology and Information Skills – Pre School 636
Technology and Information Skills – Kindergarten 636
Technology and Information Skills – 1st Grade 639
Technology and Information Skills – 2nd Grade 641
Technology and Information Skills – 3rd Grade 644
Technology and Information Skills – 4th Grade 649
Technology and Information Skills – 5th Grade 653

Chapter 13 – Current Events 664
Pre-School – 5th Grade 664

Chapter 14 – Timelines 665
U. S. History Timeline 665
Timeline of Inventions, Theories, Innovations, and Discoveries 683
Timeline of American Presidents 709
Timeline of African-American History 710
Native American Facts 718
Indian Tribes 718
Famous Indian Leaders: 718
Native American Indian Tribes by Region 718
Timeline of Native Americans 720
Timeline of Prehistoric Eras and Periods 726
Timeline of World Civilizations 727
Timeline of Historical Periods 730
Notable American and World Tragedies 732
Wonders of the World 734
The Seven Wonders of the Ancient World 734
The Seven New Wonders of the World 734
The Seven Natural Wonders of the World 734
The Seven Wonders of the Underwater World 734
The Seven Wonders of the Industrial World 735

APPENDICES – Answers to Questions **736**
　APPENDIX 1: Chapter 1 – Language Arts 736
　APPENDIX 2: Chapter 2 – Notable Literary Works through the Ages 759
　APPENDIX 3: Chapter 3 – Math 762
　APPENDIX 4: Chapter 4 – Science 777
　APPENDIX 5: Chapter 5 – Social Studies 792
　APPENDIX 6: Chapter 6 – Government and Civics 809
　APPENDIX 7: Chapter 7 – Economics 813
　APPENDIX 8: Chapter 8 – Physical Education 815
　APPENDIX 9: Chapter 9 – Health and Safety 819
　APPENDIX 10: Chapter 10 – The Arts 823
　APPENDIX 11: Chapter 11 – Environment 829
　APPENDIX 12: Chapter 12 – Technology and Information Skills 831
　APPENDIX 13: Chapter 13 – Current Events 836
Bibliography **837**

A Note to Parents, Guardians, and Teachers

This book is based on the premise that parents/guardians are their children's greatest and most influential teachers!

This book is designed as a **one-source tool** to help parents/guardians empower their children with a solid knowledge foundation, *based on traditional state content standards per grade level*, as they progress through their elementary school years. It is intended to enhance and reinforce the facts, ideas, and concepts that children are learning in school. A local or state curriculum guide available for parents/guardians may read: "Third grade students will name and identify two and three dimensional figures," or, "By the end of grade four, students will explain the basic purpose of government in society, recognizing the three levels of government." So what do those listed standards really mean? This book serves to take away the guesswork, and to provide concrete questions that relate to the listed content standards per grade level. It is an oral approach to disseminating primarily rote information, and knowledge of various academic and non-academic disciplines. It is a book based on the notion that learning is a life-long process, and that children learn differently and at different rates. Leaning is not always aligned with chronological age. It is a book that is sensitive to the fact that children come from diverse cultural upbringings and have diverse educational backgrounds and experiences.

What it is NOT: This book is *not* a school curriculum guide. It is *not* intended to be a quiz, a trivia game of random questions, or a competition venue. It is *not* a school textbook or workbook. It is *not* a manual for homeschoolers. It is *not* intended to be a substitute for fulfilling all school grade objectives and outcomes. It is *not* intended to promote the higher level thinking skills as outlined in Bloom's taxonomy. Further, it is *not* expected that children memorize and "master" all questions in all subjects at any given grade level before proceeding to the next.

Knowledge gained by answering content questions is a sound learning strategy in that it is:

Specific
Measurable
Attainable
Results-oriented
Time framed by grade level
Empowering
Reinforcing

Preface

This book provides a **one-source** guide for parents/guardians/teachers to help their children learn important facts and concepts across the elementary levels that are child, grade, and age appropriate. All the grade levels are integrated together into one book to achieve a comprehensive approach that also accommodates different learning paces. It further allows for review and reinforcement based on child-readiness and retention capacity. Even though a child may learn one topic in one year does not guarantee the child will retain that same information and have the retention and recall capacity to build on that knowledge the following school year!

This oral approach is based on the premise that knowledge is acquired through the senses: sight, hearing, touch, smell, and taste. The more senses that are used in learning, the higher the retention rate will be. Children have different learning rates and different learning styles. If "speaking" is added to hearing and seeing, the learning will come even faster, and retention will be maximized. It can be concluded then, that learners have a higher retention of what they HEAR, and SAY than by what they *SEE* alone. Employing more than one sense in learning then, as this book aims to do, is what makes the learning permanent. When all is said and done, the key to long-term retention is sustained practice over time.

This book provides a vacation or summer "bridge" tool for young learners when school is not in session. "Ask Me Smarter" may also prove to be a good companion during a long road trip!

Inherent in this simple question format is building a child's self-esteem with a *low-anxiety* verbal approach, empowering him or her with essential knowledge, facts, and insights.

This book is a result of my difficulty in comprehending my son's just published 5th grade social studies textbook that was so convoluted with facts and minute details that the understanding of the main idea was completely lost. After reading a particularly wordy passage on the Civil War, my son had no clue from that reading which leader was on which side and who ultimately won the war! It further stems from my frustration in locating a resource that did not read like a textbook, or one that was not specific to just one grade level or operate like a workbook. Further, many libraries and bookstores have an abundant selection of educational psychology books, how-to books, science experiment books, how to read books, colorful trivia decks, but I was not able to locate a single resource that provides a direct and comprehensive approach to asking specific questions to young learners across all core and non-core disciplines. Trivia cards and interactive websites while fun and educational, are somewhat random and hit or miss with regard to ensuring coverage of essential facts encompassing all the necessary academic subject areas. I felt compelled to write something that might help fill a niche I felt was lacking, and one that expands on current resources. To this end, it was my intent to compile several grade levels into one book that includes both core and non-core academic disciplines.

How to Use This Book

It is important to use careful judgment in ascertaining which topics and how many questions should be asked of your child (children) at any one time. It is encouraged that questions be asked from different topics and questions that encompass different grade levels as appropriate. For example, a 1st grader may benefit from being posed "2nd grade" questions as well as being asked questions from the "kindergarten" section on any given topic. A 5th grader would similarly benefit from being asked a 3rd grade question! Some overlap with regard to the questions should be expected. Further, it is important to note that what may be deemed a "2nd grade" question in one state, may be regarded as a "3rd grade" question in another. In addition, some topics may be listed as a content standard in one state and not another. The question, "Why do you save money?" is posed as a pre-school question. That same question can be asked at any grade level. Theoretically, the older and more knowledgeable the child, the higher the level of response.

Core Questions: It is given that any one question in this book, especially in the core areas, could represent a full week lesson, many worksheets, practice, application, analysis, and hands-on experimentation. In many cases, a choice is offered after a question, but this choice could easily be eliminated if need be, or if the question is asked for the second or third time.

Language Arts: Many of these questions reflect words, spelling, sight words, readings, songs, and essential grammar facts. Many of the stories and novels mentioned are good to know, not necessarily **need** to know. What is important is that young learners be exposed to a wide variety of reading and writing experiences and genres.

Notable Literary Works Through the Ages: This chapter serves to expose children to a wide array of prominent authors and titles in world literature. Many of the books are regarded as "the classics." By no means are children expected to know every title, speech, or author. The reading of literature across all genres that is intellectually appropriate is the desired goal. The questions are arranged in chronological order by date of publication. It may behoove the interrogator to skim and scan this chapter, focusing on the questions that align with the learner's literary experiences. The first letter or words of the title are included as a prompt.

Math: These questions serve as a representation of common math topics introduced during the formative years. Math has an inherent challenge as a child's level of understanding increases. Some questions may prove difficult in a question format, especially in the later elementary grades. Allowing for paper and pencil computation, and actually *looking* at the math questions should be encouraged if need be.

Science: The questions encompass a wide array of scientific topics across all grade levels. These learning standards can easily be applied to the outside world. Exploration and experimentation is highly encouraged!

Social Studies: Many of the social studies questions encompass geography and history. While many elementary schools may focus on different early civilizations, most do cover units relating to early American heritage and history. Several of the questions related to specific states and countries are written as "mini-lessons." Further exploration of the names and places in those questions is also highly recommended!

Government and Civics: The focus of this chapter is to prompt children to think about all levels of government, the role of the citizen, and the importance of becoming contributing members of the community, the state, and the nation. The 5th grade level also includes a common version of the Practice Citizenship Test.

Economics: These questions cover foundational topics related to everyday economics.

Physical Education: Many of the questions measure a specific physical skill. It is important to keep in mind that children are not expected to demonstrate every skill. Daily physical activity is the goal.

Health and Safety: Several questions related to health and safety are designed to encourage reflection and serious discussion, as well to heighten awareness with regard to the importance of taking care of oneself.

The Arts: Some questions pertaining to the arts focus on the development of prescribed artistic skills per grade level. Other questions are designed to raise awareness of, and to develop an appreciation for all the fine arts. Children are encouraged to attend performances, and to view actual artworks in galleries, in books, or in virtual galleries online.

Environment: Many questions regarding the environment are written to prompt children to think about important environmental issues, as well as the child's role in the conservation of the planet.

Technology and Information Skills: The technology chapter serves to assess the basic proficiency outcomes with regard to using technological devices, understanding how they work, and the importance of Internet safety and etiquette. The questions also reflect the progressive expectations with gathering and evaluating information in both digital and print formats.

Timelines: Questions can easily be formulated for any of the timelines. Who invented what? Which invention came first? Which American war began in 1861? How many "Wonders of the Ancient World" can you name?

IMPORTANT: It should not be expected that children *master* a grade level before proceeding to the next! The emphasis is on the questions, *not* the grade level. As both a mother and an educator, one of the best pieces of advice I ever received was, "teach the child, not the grade or subject."

Questions are somewhat sequential and are inherently progressive as students gain knowledge. The questions are aimed to serve as a *representation* of what is listed as the prescribed "standards" or learning outcomes for the elementary grade levels in most states.

Parents/guardians/teachers are encouraged to *re-word* questions, repeat questions, and improvise. For example, if on one occasion you ask your child: "Madison is the capital of which state?" Next time ask: "What is the capital of Wisconsin?" Further, many questions have an inherent challenge in that they are posed with a choice, something that can, and should be omitted at the discretion of the interrogator.

You are also encouraged to ask questions from a wide array of topics and then go back and repeat or re-word a previous question. Or, open this book to any random page and just start "firing away!"

If questions are asked at bedtime, an ideal time for the brain to process information and store it for future retrieval, ask your child some of the **same** questions the next morning for further reinforcement and empowerment. If the question has a choice of two or more answers, leave out the choice when asking the question again.

Some questions listed as curriculum content standards will and should illicit further discussion. Many questions may be posed as yes and no or true and false questions, simply to suggest a specific learning objective. For many of the questions it is suggested that *similar* types of questions be asked to promote further competence and awareness. For example, a preschooler may be asked to name something blue in his or her bedroom. You can follow up with, "What is found in nature that is blue?" A high level question posed may ask the learner to name all the colors in the rainbow. (ROY G BIV) Many questions are asked to promote multi-cultural awareness and ideally, cultural sensitivity as well.

The intention of the author is for this book to be used as an oral and auditory approach to learning and reviewing or discussing information, but it certainly would work well for a learner to read the questions and see how many questions he or she can answer correctly. It is intended to enhance and compliment what our children are already learning in school or at home. Its all-inclusive format and oral approach is what makes it unique, I believe.

If a child seems intrigued by a particular question or answer, I would highly encourage seeking out other resources from books, the Internet, pictures, etc. (See list of further resources.) We need to expand upon our children's great capacity to learn and feed their unwavering curiosity!

My hope is that your child will be engaged and challenged, and therefore empowered through this oral questioning format.

In assessing correctness, the answers are located in the appendices organized by chapter in numerical order.

Further Resources:
Library (School and Local)
Internet
Family Members
Field Trips
Field Experts
Authentic Learning Moments (Teaching fractions while cutting and serving pizza)
Real-time applications: (Conduct a science experiment; Follow a recipe; Hand-write a thank you note.)
"Wonder" Questions (What do you wonder about?)
Have your child ask YOU a question! If you are unable to answer it, suggest that you seek out the answer together.

It needs to be stated that information expands exponentially every day. Any given topic in and of itself could easily fill a library. One war may be an entire semester of study at the University level! Neither an entire library, nor the nearly infinite information capacity of a computer could ever fit into one manageable book. Given the limits and constraints of time and space, the inclusion of any topic or question is frequently at the expense or exclusion of another. If I were remiss in any regard, I invite the reader to fill in any perceived missing questions, as you deem appropriate. What follows is a compilation of questions that encompass a wide array of essential knowledge questions aimed at children 12 and under based on traditional state learning standards. The questions loosely "cover" the learning objectives listed under the curriculum guidelines for each respective grade level. Variations and expanding upon the questions is encouraged and expected.

This book also includes good-to-know **non**-core curriculum topics. There is definite overlap between disciplines and grade levels. Because this is a question format, this approach in no way is intended to promote and develop a mastery of grade-level *skills* (socialization, cooperative learning, reading, writing, spelling, vocabulary acquisition, story-telling, math inquiry and analysis, logical thinking, scientific experimentation, observation, etc.) Nor can this format measure a child's proficiency with technology and research skills that are an integral part of learning outcomes per grade level. Any omission or perceived bias is completely unintentional. Ideally, this question and answer approach will serve to empower our children with essential and meaningful knowledge through these fact-based questions, and provide them with a strong foundation as they continue to learn, grow, and prepare for higher learning. In so doing, our children will become informed citizens and future contributing members of our global community.

Research shows that children learn in different ways and at different rates. This book is formatted to compliment the brain networks that play a key role in learning. The "Spacing Effect" is a sound strategy in that facts are learned best when they are studied at frequent intervals over a long time span. Long-term retention of facts and information is maximized through repeated retrieval. "Ask Me Smarter" aims to provide the opportunity for optimal learning to occur in that the emphasis is on the knowledge, not the grade level.

As you use this book as a supplemental learning tool, it is important to keep in mind:

1) Knowledge of **dates** is not essential in the primary grades.

2) Many of the questions, especially in grades 3, 4, and 5 have a choice of answers after the colon. The degree of difficulty is inherent in these questions in that the choice can be read or not, at the discretion of the person asking the questions, and the readiness of the learner.

3) Learners are always encouraged to learn the words to a poem or song, or seek out some new stories and novels, but are certainly not expected to be familiar with every book, poem or song mentioned.

4) Many questions are yes or no questions that reflect a specific learning standard per grade level. These questions are given the answer "Yes" if only to suggest the learning goal.

5) Many of the questions asked in the higher grades are admittedly a "stretch," but they are purposely included to challenge and engage the young learner.

6) **Important**: Many questions require the interrogator to *spell* words and to provide choices. Several of the questions have *misspelled* items and "distractors" by design.

"Knowledge is potential power?"

Now go ahead, ask them smarter!

Chapter 1 – Language Arts

Language Arts – Pre-School

1. What is your name?
2. What is your first name?
3. Do you know any of the letters in your first name?
4. Can you write any of the letters in your first name?
5. What is your middle name?
6. What is your surname, meaning your last name?
7. How old are you?
8. Who do you know that is older than you?
9. Who do you know that is younger than you?
10. Who do you know that is the same age as you?
11. When is your birthday?
12. What month are we in?
13. What day of the week is it today?
14. What day of the week is tomorrow?
15. What day of the week was yesterday?
16. Can you tell someone your needs and feelings?
17. Can you speak in sentences?
18. Can you have a conversation with an adult?
19. Can you ask me a question?
20. Can you answer my question, how do you feel today?
21. Can you describe what you did yesterday in order?
22. Can you listen to a book that is read to you out loud?
23. Can you answer questions about what is happening in a book?

LANGUAGE ARTS

24. Can you re-tell a story using pictures from the book to help you?
25. Can you show me in what direction we read a book?
26. Can you recite (say) any nursery rhymes from memory?
27. What words rhyme or sound alike in the nursery rhyme, "One two, buckle my shoe…?"
28. Can you finish the poem, "Rain, rain go away…?"
29. Can you finish the poem, "Diddle Diddle dumpling…?"
30. Can you finish the poem, "Wee Willie Winkie…?"
31. Can you finish the poem, "Peter, Peter Pumpkin Eater…?"
32. Can you finish the poem, "To market to market to buy…?"
33. Can you sing the song, "Kookaburra?"
34. Can you sing the song, "Pop Goes the Weasel?"
35. Can you sing the song, "John Jacob Jingleheimer Schmidt?"
36. Can you sing the song, "Happy Birthday to You?"
37. Can you sing the song, "Twinkle, Twinkle Little Star?"
38. Can you sing the song, "Rock-A-Bye Baby?"
39. Can you sing the song, "Row, Row, Row Your Boat?"
40. Can you sing the song, "Old MacDonald Had a Farm?"
41. Can you sing the song, "Here We Go Round the Mulberry Bush?"
42. Can you sing the song and use motion for, "Ring Around the Rosie?"
43. Can you sing the song and use motion for, "This Little Piggy Went to Market?"
44. Can you sing the song and use motion for, "The Eensy, Weensy Spider?"
45. Can you sing the song and use motion for, "Five Little Monkeys?"
46. Can you sing the song and use motion for, "I'm a Little Teapot?"
47. Can you sing the song and use motion for, "Head, Shoulders, Knees, and Toes?"
48. Can you sing the song and claps for, "B-I-N-G-O?"
49. Can you sing the song and claps for, "If You're Happy and You Know It?"
50. What is the name of the story with the character "Goldilocks?"
51. What color is the little hen in the story about a hen?

LANGUAGE ARTS

52. How many pigs are there in the story?
53. What kind of animal tried to scare the three little pigs?
54. What three materials did the three pigs use to build their house with?
55. How does "The Three Little Pigs" end?
56. What is a name of another story that you know?
57. Can you draw a straight line?
58. What is the name of the tool that you use to cut paper?
59. Do you know how to use a scissors?
60. What are some rules to follow when you are in a store? (church) (school) (pool)
61. Do you follow the rules when you play a board game?
62. What is a board game that you know how to play?
63. What is your favorite toy to play with?
64. What is your favorite food?
65. Can you name two table manners when eating a meal?
66. What is a good word to use to show politeness when asking for something?
67. What do you say to show appreciation after you are given something?
68. How do you respond to the phrase, "Thank you?"
69. How would you say hello to a neighbor who is a man or the dad of the family?
70. How would you say hello to a neighbor who is a woman or the mom of a family?
71. Is it hot or cold today?
72. Is it day or night?
73. What time of the day is it when you wake up?
74. What time of the day is it when you go to bed?
75. What time of the day is it after lunch?
76. Is it morning, afternoon, or evening right now?
77. What is the name of the meal we eat in the morning?
78. What meal do we eat in the middle of the day?
79. What meal do we eat in the evening?

LANGUAGE ARTS

80. What season of the year are we in?
81. Are you a boy or girl?
82. How many brothers/sisters do you have? (Names)
83. Do you have a pet? (Name)
84. What do we need to do to take care of a (our) pet?
85. What part of your body do you run with?
86. What part of your body do you eat and talk with?
87. What part of the body do you wave with?
88. Which of your hands is your *left* hand? (Show how holding hand up with thumb at right angle to fingers forms the letter "L.")
89. Which of your hands is your *right* hand?
90. Are you right-handed or left-handed?
91. Can you dress all by yourself?
92. Can you zipper your jacket?
93. Can you button your shirt?
94. Can you tie your shoes?
95. What part of the body do you smell with?
96. What part of the body do you hear with?
97. What part of the body do you see with?
98. On what part of your body do you wear shoes, mittens, a hat, etc.?
99. Can you point to your knee, elbow, thumb, ankle, etc.?
100. What color is the grass?
101. What things can you name that are green?
102. What color is the sky?
103. What things can you name that are blue?
104. What color are your eyes?
105. What color is your hair?
106. What color is a ripe tomato?

LANGUAGE ARTS

107. What things can you name that are red?

108. What color is a ripe banana?

109. What things can you name that are yellow?

110. What things can you name that are orange?

111. What things can you name that are black?

112. What things can you name that are white?

113. What things can you name that are pink?

114. What things can you name that are purple?

115. What color is your room? (Etc.)

116. Can you say (sing) the letters of the alphabet?

117. What do letters that are combined spell out?

118. Can you point to the cover of this book?

119. Can you point to the back of this book?

120. Can you point out a page of this book?

121. Can you "pretend" to read a book?

122. Can you turn the pages of this book?

123. What kinds of things can transport us from place to place?

124. What is the name of the vehicle that transports sick or injured people to the hospital?

125. What is the name of the truck that transports dirt or rocks?

126. What is the name of the truck that hauls broken cars in for repair?

127. What is the name of the vehicle that transports children to school?

128. What is the name of the vehicle that arrives at a fire scene?

129. What types of liquids does a tanker truck carry?

130. What is the name of a type the transportation that floats on water?

131. What is the name of a motorized bicycle?

132. Is a bicycle a means of transportation?

133. What is the name of the type of transportation that runs on railroad tracks?

134. What is the name of the transportation that travels in the air?

LANGUAGE ARTS

135. What is the name of the transportation that is used on a farm?
136. What are the names of some tools?
137. What is the name of a farm animal?
138. What is the name of a zoo animal?
139. What is the name of a sea animal?
140. What is the name of a forest animal?
141. What is an example of an insect?
142. What are some animals that are pets?
143. Can you name an animal that has stripes?
144. Can you name an animal that has fins?
145. Can you name an animal that has wings?
146. Can you name an animal that has horns?
147. Can you name an animal that has paws?
148. Can you name an animal that has claws?
149. Can you name an animal that has fangs?
150. Can you name an animal that has long neck?
151. Can you name an animal that has long trunk?
152. What sound does a bird make?
153. What sound does a dog make?
154. What sound does a cat make?
155. What sound does a frog make?
156. What sound does a horse make?
157. What sound does a bear make?
158. What sound does a monkey make?
159. What sound does a cow make?
160. What sound does a chicken make?
161. What sound does a duck make?
162. Which is bigger: an elephant or a lion?

LANGUAGE ARTS

163. Which is smaller: a mouse or a dog?

164. Who is taller: you or me?

165. Which is shorter: a skyscraper building or a house?

166. Can you point *up*?

167. What is the opposite of *up*?

168. What is *in* your bedroom?

169. What is the opposite of *in*?

170. Where is the *front* of this book?

171. What is the opposite of *front*?

172. What is *on* your bed?

173. What is the opposite of *on*?

174. Is the television on or off?

175. What is *under* your bed?

176. What is the opposite of under?

177. Can you point to the *top* of this page?

178. What is the opposite of *top*?

179. Can you point to the *middle* of this page?

180. What is your *middle* name?

181. Can you point to the *bottom* of this page?

182. What is the opposite of *bottom*?

183. What is the opposite of *sad*?

184. What is the opposite of *night*?

185. What is the opposite of *behind*?

186. What is the opposite of *above*?

187. What is the opposite of *little*?

188. What is the opposite of *low*?

189. What is the opposite of *over*?

190. What is the opposite of *more*?

LANGUAGE ARTS

191. What is the opposite of *same*?
192. Can you name someone that is the same size as you?
193. What is *beside* (next to) your bed?
194. What is *inside* your dresser?
195. What is *outside* the house?
196. Is this book right side up or upside down?
197. What is a food that is *hot*?
198. What is a food that is *cold*?
199. Can you name an animal that is *fast*?
200. What is an animal that is *slow*?
201. Do people look the same or different?
202. Can you recognize and pronounce the common sight word "a?"(Show word!)
203. Can you recognize and pronounce the common sight word "and?"(Show word!)
204. Can you recognize and pronounce the common sight word "away?"(Show word!)
205. Can you recognize and pronounce the common sight word "big?"(Show word!)
206. Can you recognize and pronounce the common sight word "blue?"(Show word!)
207. Can you recognize and pronounce the common sight word "can?"(Show word!)
208. Can you recognize and pronounce the common sight word "come?"(Show word!)
209. Can you recognize and pronounce the common sight word "down?"(Show word!)
210. Can you recognize and pronounce the common sight word "find?"(Show word!)
211. Can you recognize and pronounce the common sight word "for?"(Show word!)
212. Can you recognize and pronounce the common sight word "funny?"(Show word!)
213. Can you recognize and pronounce the common sight word "go?"(Show word!)
214. Can you recognize and pronounce the common sight word "help?"(Show word!)
215. Can you recognize and pronounce the common sight word "here?"(Show word!)
216. Can you recognize and pronounce the common sight word "I?"(Show word!)
217. Can you recognize and pronounce the common sight word "in?"(Show word!)
218. Can you recognize and pronounce the common sight word "is?"(Show word!)

219. Can you recognize and pronounce the common sight word "it?"(Show word!)

220. Can you recognize and pronounce the common sight word "jump?"(Show word!)

221. Can you recognize and pronounce the common sight word "little?"(Show word!)

222. Can you recognize and pronounce the common sight word "look?"(Show word!)

223. Can you recognize and pronounce the common sight word "make?"(Show word!)

224. Can you recognize and pronounce the common sight word "me?"(Show word!)

225. Can you recognize and pronounce the common sight word "my?"(Show word!)

226. Can you recognize and pronounce the common sight word "not?"(Show word!)

227. Can you recognize and pronounce the common sight word "one?"(Show word!)

228. Can you recognize and pronounce the common sight word "play?"(Show word!)

229. Can you recognize and pronounce the common sight word "red?"(Show word!)

230. Can you recognize and pronounce the common sight word "run?"(Show word!)

231. Can you recognize and pronounce the common sight word "said?"(Show word!)

232. Can you recognize and pronounce the common sight word "see?"(Show word!)

233. Can you recognize and pronounce the common sight word "the?"(Show word!)

234. Can you recognize and pronounce the common sight word "three?"(Show word!)

235. Can you recognize and pronounce the common sight word "to?"(Show word!)

236. Can you recognize and pronounce the common sight word "two?"(Show word!)

237. Can you recognize and pronounce the common sight word "up?"(Show word!)

238. Can you recognize and pronounce the common sight word "we?"(Show word!)

239. Can you recognize and pronounce the common sight word "where?"(Show word!)

240. Can you recognize and pronounce the common sight word "yellow?"(Show word!)

241. Can you recognize and pronounce the common sight word "you?"(Show word!)

Language Arts – Kindergarten

242. Do you know think that "kindergarten" is a German word or a Spanish word?

243. What does "kindergarten" translates to in English: Children's Garden or A Kind Garden?

244. Can you sing the letters of the alphabet?

LANGUAGE ARTS

245. What sound does "a" make and what word besides **apple** starts with the letter "a?"
246. What sound does "b" make and what word besides **ball** starts with the letter "b?"
247. What sound does "c" make and what word besides **cat** starts with the letter "c?"
248. What sound does "d" make and what word besides **dog** starts with the letter d?"
249. What sound does "e" make and what word besides **egg** starts with the letter "e?"
250. What sound does "f" make and what word besides **fish** starts with the letter "f?"
251. What sound does "g" make and what word besides **gate** starts with the letter "g?"
252. What sound does "h" make and what word besides **hat** starts with the letter "h?"
253. What sound does "i" make and what word besides **igloo** starts with the letter "i?"
254. What sound does "j" make and what word besides **jar** starts with the letter "j?"
255. What sound does "k" make and what word besides **kite** starts with the letter "k?"
256. What sound does "l" make and what word besides **lemon** starts with the letter "l?"
257. What sound does "m" make and what word besides **man** starts with the letter "m?"
258. What sound does "n" make and what word besides **nest** starts with the letter "n?"
259. What sound does "o" make and what word besides **ocean** starts with the letter "o?"
260. What sound does "p" make and what word besides **pie** starts with the letter "p?"
261. What sound does "q" make and what word besides **queen** starts with the letter "q?"
262. What sound does "r" make and what word besides **rain** starts with the letter "r?"
263. What sound does "s" make and what word besides **Sun** starts with the letter "s?"
264. What sound does "t" make and what word besides **top** starts with the letter "t?"
265. What sound does "u" make and what word besides **under** starts with the letter "u?"
266. What sound does "v" make and what word besides **vase** starts with the letter "v?"
267. What sound does "w" make and what word besides **win** starts with the letter "w?"
268. What sound does "x" make and what word besides **x-ray** starts with the letter "x?"
269. What sound does "y" make and what word besides **yellow** starts with the letter "y?"
270. What sound does "z" make and what word besides **zipper** starts with the letter "z?"
271. What images can you see on an "**x**-ray?"
272. What is a word that rhymes with hat?

LANGUAGE ARTS

273. How do you spell cat?

274. How do you spell dad?

275. What is a word that rhymes with sad?

276. Can you finish the lines to the rhyme "Hickory, Dickory, Dock?"

277. Can you finish the lines to the rhyme "Diddle, Diddle Dumpling? "

278. Can you finish the lines to the rhyme "Little Bo Peep?"

279. Can you finish the lines to the rhyme "Little Boy Blue?"

280. Can you finish the lines to the rhyme "Baa, Baa, Black Sheep?"

281. Can you finish the lines to the rhyme "One, Two, Buckle My Shoe?"

282. Can you finish the lines to the rhyme "Rain, Rain, Go Away?"

283. Can you finish the lines to the rhyme "It's Raining, It's Pouring?"

284. Can you finish the lines to the rhyme "Roses Are Red?"

285. Can you finish the lines to the rhyme "Jack and Jill?"

286. Can you finish the lines to the rhyme "Jack Be Nimble?"

287. Can you finish the lines to the rhyme "Little Miss Muffet?"

288. Can you finish the lines to the rhyme "Mary Had a Little Lamb?"

289. Can you finish the lines to the rhyme "Old Mother Hubbard?"

290. Can you finish the lines to the rhyme "Old King Cole?"

291. Can you finish the lines to the rhyme "Three Blind Mice?"

292. Can you finish the lines to the rhyme "The Three Little Kittens?"

293. Can you finish the lines to the rhyme "There Was an Old Woman Who Lived in a Shoe?"

294. Can you finish the lines to the rhyme "Star Light, Star Bright?"

295. What do combined letters form: words or sentences?

296. What do combined words form: sentences or paragraphs?

297. What do sentences related to one main idea form: paragraphs or pages?

298. What kinds of things do we read?

299. What kinds of things do we write?

300. Do you write with your right hand or your left hand?

LANGUAGE ARTS

301. What electronic machine do we use with a keyboard that allows us to type text?
302. What is the title of this book?
303. What is the title of your favorite book?
304. What is the name of a person who writes a book?
305. What does an *illustrator* do?
306. What is the opposite of true?
307. Is a *fact* true or false?
308. If something is *fiction*, is it true or false?
309. Do we also read poems, letters, articles, stories, and fairy tales?
310. When we read a newspaper, is that a work of fiction or non-fiction?
311. What things can you find in a library?
312. What do you have to do to "borrow" books from the library?
313. What is the date called when you have to return your library books?
314. What is the name of the person who works in a library?
315. What is the term used if a library book is returned past the due date?
316. Do library books have barcode labels used for identification and checkout?
317. Which section of the library would you look to find a book about frogs: fiction or non-fiction?
318. Which section of the library would you look to find the story, "Goldilocks and the Three Bears:" fiction or non-fiction?
319. When would you read a *recipe*?
320. What is the name of the season when it is snowy and cold?
321. What is the name of the season when the leaves change color?
322. What is the name of the season when the plants and flowers start to grow and the birds and butterflies come out?
323. What is the name of the season when it is very warm and many people swim and camp?
324. What is the name of a baby dog?
325. What is the name of a baby cat?
326. Is a bowling ball light or heavy?

LANGUAGE ARTS

327. Is a feather light or heavy?

328. Did you eat supper before or after school?

329. What part of the day is it now?

330. What is the common shape of a clock?

331. How many numbers are on a clock?

332. On which number is the short hand?

333. On which number is the long hand? (Show clock/watch)

334. What is another name for 12:00 in the middle of the day?

335. What is another name for 12:00 at night?

336. What is the name of the chart we use to keep track of the date and day of the week?

337. How many days are there in one week?

338. Can you name the days of the week?

339. What are the two days of the weekend?

340. What is located to the **right** of your bed?

341. What is located to the **left** of your bed?

342. What is located **between** the bed and the door?

343. Can you name an object that is **far** from you?

344. What is something that is **close** to you?

345. What is the name of the tune that you *sing*?

346. Which song would you like to sing? (London Bridge; Old MacDonald; Twinkle, Twinkle Little Star; Ring around the Rosy; Row, Row, Row Your Boat; This Old Man; The Wheels on the Bus, etc.)

347. What is the name of a famous book or story?

348. Which of the following stories are you familiar with? (The Three Little Pigs; Goldilocks and the Three Bears; The Little Red Hen; The Ugly Duckling; Cinderella; King Midas and the Golden Touch; Snow White; The Velveteen Rabbit; or Johnny Appleseed?)

349. What is the name for stories that tell a lesson: fables or fairy tales?

350. Which fable are you familiar with: "The Lion and the Mouse" or "The Hare and the Tortoise?"

351. What would come next in this series: Long, longer, _?

352. What would come after big and before biggest?

LANGUAGE ARTS

353. What would come next in this series: Good, better, _?

354. What would come next in this series: Bad, worse, _?

355. Which is correct: "We watched the movie *quiet*." or, "We watched the movie *quietly*?"

356. Which is correct: "*Hope* we will go to the zoo," "*Hopely* we will go to the zoo," or, "*Hopefully* we will go to the zoo?"

357. What is the name of the precious metal that is yellowish in color and very valuable?

358. What is the color that is also like the metal that a quarter is made of?

359. What is the metal, also a color that a penny is made of?

360. How do you finish the saying, "Better safe than _?"

361. How do you finish the saying, "It's raining cats _?"

362. How do you finish the saying, "Look before you _?"

363. How do you finish the saying, "Where there's a will _?"

364. How do you finish the saying, "A dog is a man's _?"

365. How do you finish the saying, "Do unto others as you would have them _?"

366. Can you recognize and pronounce the common sight word "all?"(Show word!)

367. Can you recognize and pronounce the common sight word "am?"(Show word!)

368. Can you recognize and pronounce the common sight word "are?"(Show word!)

369. Can you recognize and pronounce the common sight word "at?"(Show word!)

370. Can you recognize and pronounce the common sight word "ate?"(Show word!)

371. Can you recognize and pronounce the common sight word "be?"(Show word!)

372. Can you recognize and pronounce the common sight word "black?"(Show word!)

373. Can you recognize and pronounce the common sight word "brown?"(Show word!)

374. Can you recognize and pronounce the common sight word "but?"(Show word!)

375. Can you recognize and pronounce the common sight word "came?"(Show word!)

376. Can you recognize and pronounce the common sight word "did?"(Show word!)

377. Can you recognize and pronounce the common sight word "do?"(Show word!)

378. Can you recognize and pronounce the common sight word "eat?"(Show word!)

379. Can you recognize and pronounce the common sight word "for?"(Show word!)

LANGUAGE ARTS

380. Can you recognize and pronounce the common sight word "get?"(Show word!)

381. Can you recognize and pronounce the common sight word "good?"(Show word!)

382. Can you recognize and pronounce the common sight word "have?"(Show word!)

383. Can you recognize and pronounce the common sight word "he?"(Show word!)

384. Can you recognize and pronounce the common sight word "into?"(Show word!)

385. Can you recognize and pronounce the common sight word "like?"(Show word!)

386. Can you recognize and pronounce the common sight word "must?"(Show word!)

387. Can you recognize and pronounce the common sight word "new?"(Show word!)

388. Can you recognize and pronounce the common sight word "no?"(Show word!)

389. Can you recognize and pronounce the common sight word "now?"(Show word!)

390. Can you recognize and pronounce the common sight word "on?"(Show word!)

391. Can you recognize and pronounce the common sight word "our?"(Show word!)

392. Can you recognize and pronounce the common sight word "out?"(Show word!)

393. Can you recognize and pronounce the common sight word "please?"(Show word!)

394. Can you recognize and pronounce the common sight word "pretty?"(Show word!)

395. Can you recognize and pronounce the common sight word "ran?"(Show word!)

396. Can you recognize and pronounce the common sight word "ride?"(Show word!)

397. Can you recognize and pronounce the common sight word "saw?"(Show word!)

398. Can you recognize and pronounce the common sight word "say?"(Show word!)

399. Can you recognize and pronounce the common sight word "she?"(Show word!)

400. Can you recognize and pronounce the common sight word "so?"(Show word!)

401. Can you recognize and pronounce the common sight word "soon?"(Show word!)

402. Can you recognize and pronounce the common sight word "that?"(Show word!)

403. Can you recognize and pronounce the common sight word "there?"(Show word!)

404. Can you recognize and pronounce the common sight word "they?"(Show word!)

405. Can you recognize and pronounce the common sight word "this?"(Show word!)

406. Can you recognize and pronounce the common sight word "too?"(Show word!)

407. Can you recognize and pronounce the common sight word "under?"(Show word!)

LANGUAGE ARTS

408. Can you recognize and pronounce the common sight word "want?"(Show word!)

409. Can you recognize and pronounce the common sight word "was?"(Show word!)

410. Can you recognize and pronounce the common sight word "well?"(Show word!)

411. Can you recognize and pronounce the common sight word "went?"(Show word!)

412. Can you recognize and pronounce the common sight word "what?"(Show word!)

413. Can you recognize and pronounce the common sight word "white?"(Show word!)

414. Can you recognize and pronounce the common sight word "who?"(Show word!)

415. Can you recognize and pronounce the common sight word "will?"(Show word!)

416. Can you recognize and pronounce the common sight word "with?"(Show word!)

417. Can you recognize and pronounce the common sight word "yes?"(Show word!)

Language Arts – 1st Grade

418. What is your first name and can you spell it?

419. What is your middle name?

420. What is your surname (last name) and can you spell it?

421. How many total letters are there in the alphabet?

422. Can you tell me a word that begins with each letter of the alphabet?

423. What are the five vowels in the alphabet?

424. What are all the other letters called that are not vowels?

425. How do you spell hat?

426. Can you name other words from the word family ending in **-an** that rhyme with can?

427. Can you name other words from the word family ending in **-at** that rhyme with cat?

428. Can you name other words that fit under the word family ending in **–ap** that rhyme with cap?

429. Can you name other words from the word family ending in **–ab** that rhyme with lab?

430. Can you name other words from the word family ending in **–ad** that rhyme with dad?

431. Can you name other words from the word family ending in **-am** that rhyme with ham?

432. Can you name other words from the word family ending in **-ack** that rhyme with back?

433. Can you name other words from the word family ending in **-and** that rhyme with sand?

LANGUAGE ARTS

434. Can you name other words from the word family ending in **-ash** that rhyme with cash?

435. Can you name other words from the word family ending in **-ail** that rhyme with nail?

436. Can you name other words from the word family ending in **-ain** that rhyme with rain?

437. Can you name other words from the word family ending in **-air** that rhyme with fair?

438. Can you name other words from the word family ending in **-ate** that rhyme with gate?

439. Can you name other words from the word family ending in **-ake** that rhyme with bake?

440. Can you name other words from the word family ending in **-ale** that rhyme with male?

441. Can you name other words from the word family ending in **-ame** that rhyme with game?

442. Can you name other words from the word family ending in **-ay** that rhyme with hay?

443. Can you name other words from the word family ending in **-all** that rhyme with ball?

444. Can you name other words from the word family ending in **-aw** that rhyme with paw?

445. Can you name other words from the word family ending in **-ar** that rhyme with jar?

446. Can you name other words from the word family ending in **-ark** that rhyme with bark?

447. Can you name other words from the word family ending in **-art** that rhyme with cart?

448. Can you name other words from the word family ending in **-ank** that rhyme with bank?

449. Can you name other words from the word family ending in **-int** that rhyme with sink?

450. Can you name other words from the word family ending in **-ed** that rhyme with bed?

451. Can you name other words from the word family ending in **-en** that rhyme with pen?

452. Can you name other words from the word family ending in **-et** that rhyme with jet?

453. Can you name other words from the word family ending in **-eck** that rhyme with neck?

454. Can you name other words from the word family ending in **-ell** that rhyme with bell?

455. Can you name other words from the word family ending in **-est** that rhyme with best?

456. Can you name other words from the word family ending in **-in** that rhyme with pin?

457. Can you name other words from the word family ending in **-ip** that rhyme with zip?

458. Can you name other words from the word family ending in **-it** that rhyme with sit?

459. What words rhyme with Sun?

460. What words rhyme with kite?

461. What words rhyme with book?

LANGUAGE ARTS

462. What words rhyme with tree?

463. What words rhyme with best?

464. What words rhyme with sleep?

465. Can you clap out the nursery rhyme "Twinkle, Twinkle Little Star" using one clap per syllable?

466. Are all of the following fairy tales or nursery rhymes: *Mary Had a Little Lamb; London Bridge; Old Mother Hubbard; Jack and Jill; Little Jack Horner; One, Two, Buckle My Shoe; Little Boy Blue; Baa, Baa Black Sheep; Three Blind Mice; Twinkle, Twinkle Little Star; There Was an Old Woman;* and *This Little Piggy Went to Market?*

467. Are the following stories considered fairy tales or nursery rhymes: *Snow White; Little Red Riding Hood; Sleeping Beauty; Pinocchio; The Little Red Hen;* and *Jack and the Beanstalk?*

468. Do all poems have to rhyme?

469. If a fable has a moral or teaches a lesson, which of the following is **not** a fable: *The Hare and the Tortoise; The Boy Who Cried Wolf; Chicken Little; The Goose and the Golden Eggs;* or, *The Three Little Pigs?*

470. What type of story did the Greek author named **Aesop** write that included animals to teach the moral or a lesson: fables or fairy tales?

471. Can you identify all of the following written forms: A story, a poem, an article, a report, a letter, text, a recipe, a journal, a sign, a list, a logo, a poster, a caption, an address, a thank-you note, a graph, and a map?

472. Can you identify visual media like a picture, a drawing, a sketch, an artwork, a video, a DVD, an audiotape, or an artifact?

473. How do you spell hop?

474. How do you spell hope?

475. How do you spell frog?

476. How do you spell stop?

477. How do you spell trip?

478. How do you spell ship?

479. How do you spell sea, like the ocean?

480. How do you spell see as in, "I see the boat?"

481. How do you spell book?

482. How do you spell tree?

LANGUAGE ARTS

483. If you spell how h-o-w, how do you spell cow?

484. If you spell pan p-a-n, how do you spell fan? (man, tan , can, ran, van)

485. What is the first letter in the word cat?

486. What is the middle letter in the word cat?

487. What is the last letter in the word cat?

488. What combination of letters does the word *cheek* begin with?

489. What combination of letters does the word *they* begin with?

490. What combination of letters does the word *when* begin with?

491. What combination of letters does the word *ship* begin with?

492. What combination of letters does the word *singing* end with?

493. What letter does *dogs* end with?

494. What combination of letters does *jumped* end with?

495. What combination of letters does *bigger* end with?

496. What combination of letters does *biggest* end with?

497. What combination of letters does *slowly* end with?

498. Is the vowel "a" in the word **cat** long or short?

499. Is the vowel "a" in the word **play** long or short?

500. Is the vowel "e" in the word **fed** long or short?

501. Is the vowel "e" in the word **feed** long or short?

502. Is the vowel "i" in the word **kit** long or short?

503. Is the vowel "i" in the word **kite** long or short?

504. Is the last "e" of the word **kite** silent or do you pronounce it?

505. Is the vowel "o" in the word **hop** long or short?

506. Is the vowel "o" in the word **hope** long or short?

507. Can you break the word *birthday* into two syllables?

508. What is the name of a word that is made up of two words put together: single or compound?

509. Is the word sailboat a compound word or a single word?

510. What are the two words in the compound word football?

LANGUAGE ARTS

511. Can you tell me other compound words?

512. What two words make up the contraction *can't*.

513. What is the punctuation mark called before the "t" that is a substitute for one or more letters?

514. What two words make up the contraction *it's*?

515. What is the contraction for *I am*?

516. What is the contraction for *I will*?

517. What is the contraction for *we will*?

518. What are the two words that make up the contraction *aren't*?

519. Which section of the dictionary would you look to find the word *there*?

520. Which section of the dictionary would you look to find the word *quick*?

521. What letter often comes after the letter "q?"

522. What would be the alphabetical order of the words cat, ant, and dog?

523. Which word would come first in the "b" section of a dictionary: *ball* or *brother*?

524. When you write a sentence, what must you include at the end of it that looks like a dot?

525. When you write a question, what must you include at the end of it?

526. What punctuation mark may be appropriate after writing, *I won*?

527. When writing a sentence, what kind of letter do you begin the sentence with?

528. Do all names start with a capital letter?

529. Is the second letter of a word written in upper case or lower case?

530. Is a *verb* considered a thing or an action word?

531. Is a *noun* considered a thing or an action word?

532. Can a noun be a person, place, or thing?

533. What is the *verb* in the sentence: I ran to the park?

534. What is the *noun* in the sentence: The park is pretty?

535. Do *adjectives* describe nouns?

536. What is the *adjective* in the sentence: The park is pretty?

537. Can you give your own example(s) of an adjective?

538. What is an example of something that is *fiction*?

LANGUAGE ARTS

539. What is an example of something that in *non-fiction*?

540. What is an example of a *fairy tale*?

541. What part of the book on the cover lets you know what the book is about?

542. What is the name of the person that wrote the book?

543. What is the name of the person that created and drew the pictures in a book?

544. In a non-fiction book, what is the list of topics called at the beginning that lets the reader know how the book is divided: The Table of Contents or The Index?

545. Does this book have a "**jacket**?"

546. What does a publisher do?

547. What is the **copyright** of this book?

548. Is there a dedication page in this book?

549. Do books have a **title page?**

550. What part of this book is the **text**?

551. Are there any **illustrations** in this book?

552. What is on the **cover** of this book?

553. What number would this book have on its spine if it were shelved in a library: call or file?

554. What is the **main idea** or plot in the story, "Goldilocks and the Three Bears?"

555. What is the **setting** of the story, "Goldilocks and the Three Bears?

556. Which came first: when Goldilocks tasted the porridge, or when she found the beds?

557. What name next, after Goldilocks tasted the porridge?

558. Can you tell me two **details** about the house in the story, "Goldilocks and the Three Bears?"

559. How would you describe Goldilocks?

560. Is the story "Goldilocks and the Three Bears" realistic or fantasy?

561. What is your favorite book or story?

562. What is the order (sequence) of events in the story, "The Three Bears?"

563. *Who* is the person that Cinderella marries?

564. *What* does Cinderella lose when she is running home after midnight?

565. *Where* is Cinderella going to, all dressed up in her Ball gown?

LANGUAGE ARTS

566. *At what time* must Cinderella return to her coach before it turns back into a pumpkin?

567. *Why* does Cinderella have to leave the Ball so quickly?

568. *How* does Cinderella get to the Ball?

569. If you say "I think Cinderella is pretty," is that a fact or is it your opinion?

570. If you say "The story Cinderella was written by the Grimm Brothers," is that a fact or your opinion?

571. What is a *fact* that you know about butterflies?

572. What is your *opinion* about butterflies?

573. What is your *opinion* about __?

574. Which is the correct form of *look* in the sentence: "I (look, looks, looking, or looked) at the book yesterday?"

575. Which is the correct form of *look* in the sentence: "I am (look, looks, looking,) at the book now?"

576. Which is the correct form of *look* in the sentence: "He (look, looks, looking,) at the book often?"

577. Which is the correct form of *look* in the sentence: "I (look, looks, looking,) at the book often?"

578. What is the past tense of listen?

579. What is the name of a short sentence or two under a picture: a caption or a description?

580. Which is correct: She *is, am,* or *are* tall?

581. Which is correct: They *is* tall, or they *are* tall?

582. Which is correct: I *is, am, or are* tall?

583. Which is correct: We *is, am, or are* tall?

584. Which is correct: She *has* a dog, or she *have* a dog?

585. Which is correct: They *has* a dog, or they *have* a dog?

586. Which is correct: I *has* a dog, or I *have* a dog?

587. Which is correct: We *has* a dog, or we *have* a dog?

588. Which is correct: The ducks *is* in the pond, or the ducks *are* in the pond?

589. Which is the correct use of to, too, two: I am going (t-o, t-o-o, or t-w-o) the zoo?

590. Which is correct: I have (t-o, t-o-o, or t-w-o) dogs?

591. Which is correct: I have (t-o, t-o-o, t-w-o) many carrots on my plate?

592. Which is plural: dog or dogs?

LANGUAGE ARTS

593. Which is singular: cat or cats?

594. What is the plural of witch?

595. What is the plural of beach?

596. What is the singular of babies?

597. What is the antonym or opposite of in?

598. What is the antonym or opposite of wet?

599. What is the antonym or opposite of far?

600. What is the antonym or opposite of cold?

601. What is the antonym or opposite of slow?

602. What is the antonym or opposite of shout?

603. What is the antonym or opposite of sour?

604. What is the antonym or opposite of old?

605. What is the antonym or opposite of empty?

606. What is the antonym or opposite of lose?

607. What is the antonym or opposite of poor?

608. What is the antonym or opposite of night?

609. What is the antonym or opposite of strong?

610. What is the antonym or opposite of tame?

611. What is the antonym or opposite of front?

612. What is the antonym or opposite of ugly?

613. What is the antonym or opposite of end?

614. When you tell time and say that it is 10:00 a.m., is that morning or evening?

615. When you tell time and say that it is 10:00 p.m., is that morning or evening?

616. Is a.m. (from Latin ante meridiem) before or after noon?

617. Is p.m. (from Latin post meridiem) before or after noon?

618. Can you finish the saying, "An apple a day keeps the Doctor …?"

619. Can you finish the saying, "April showers bring May …?"

620. Can you finish the saying, "If at first you don't succeed…?"

LANGUAGE ARTS

621. Can you finish the saying, "Practice makes..?"

622. Can you finish the saying, "The more the…?"

623. Can you finish the saying, "There's no place like…?"

624. What is the date today?

625. What day of the week was yesterday?

626. What are the 7 days of the week?

627. What are the 12 months of the year?

628. When is your birthday?

629. Can you recognize and pronounce the common sight word "after?"(Show word!)

630. Can you recognize and pronounce the common sight word "again?"(Show word!)

631. Can you recognize and pronounce the common sight word "an?"(Show word!)

632. Can you recognize and pronounce the common sight word "any?"(Show word!)

633. Can you recognize and pronounce the common sight word "as?"(Show word!)

634. Can you recognize and pronounce the common sight word "ask?"(Show word!)

635. Can you recognize and pronounce the common sight word "by?"(Show word!)

636. Can you recognize and pronounce the common sight word "could?"(Show word!)

637. Can you recognize and pronounce the common sight word "every?"(Show word!)

638. Can you recognize and pronounce the common sight word "fly?"(Show word!)

639. Can you recognize and pronounce the common sight word "from?"(Show word!)

640. Can you recognize and pronounce the common sight word "give?"(Show word!)

641. Can you recognize and pronounce the common sight word "giving?"(Show word!)

642. Can you recognize and pronounce the common sight word "has?"(Show word!)

643. Can you recognize and pronounce the common sight word "had?"(Show word!)

644. Can you recognize and pronounce the common sight word "her?"(Show word!)

645. Can you recognize and pronounce the common sight word "him?"(Show word!)

646. Can you recognize and pronounce the common sight word "his?"(Show word!)

647. Can you recognize and pronounce the common sight word "how?"(Show word!)

648. Can you recognize and pronounce the common sight word "just?"(Show word!)

649. Can you recognize and pronounce the common sight word "know?"(Show word!)

650. Can you recognize and pronounce the common sight word "let?"(Show word!)

651. Can you recognize and pronounce the common sight word "live?"(Show word!)

652. Can you recognize and pronounce the common sight word "may?"(Show word!)

653. Can you recognize and pronounce the common sight word "of?"(Show word!)

654. Can you recognize and pronounce the common sight word "old?"(Show word!)

655. Can you recognize and pronounce the common sight word "once?"(Show word!)

656. Can you recognize and pronounce the common sight word "open?"(Show word!)

657. Can you recognize and pronounce the common sight word "over?"(Show word!)

658. Can you recognize and pronounce the common sight word "put?"(Show word!)

659. Can you recognize and pronounce the common sight word "round?"(Show word!)

660. Can you recognize and pronounce the common sight word "some?"(Show word!)

661. Can you recognize and pronounce the common sight word "stop?"(Show word!)

662. Can you recognize and pronounce the common sight word "take?"(Show word!)

663. Can you recognize and pronounce the common sight word "thank?"(Show word!)

664. Can you recognize and pronounce the common sight word "them?"(Show word!)

665. Can you recognize and pronounce the common sight word "then?"(Show word!)

666. Can you recognize and pronounce the common sight word "think?"(Show word!)

667. Can you recognize and pronounce the common sight word "walk?"(Show word!)

668. Can you recognize and pronounce the common sight word "were?"(Show word!)

669. Can you recognize and pronounce the common sight word "when?"(Show word!)

Language Arts – 2nd Grade

670. Are reading, writing, speaking, and listening important in developing language skills?

671. Are reading, writing, speaking, and listening skills important in learning a *second* language?

672. Can you print all the upper and lower case letters A-Z?

673. What words do you know in another language?

674. What kinds of books do you like to read?

LANGUAGE ARTS

675. As you read a book are you able to sound out the words to yourself?

676. *Before* reading a book, what might help you predict what the book is about?

677. *After* reading a story, is it important to identify the main ideas?

678. Do stories often have a *main character*?

679. After reading a story, are you able to re-tell the story including many of the descriptive details?

680. After reading a story, can you identify the sequence of events? (What happened first, next, etc.?)

681. After reading a book, can you identify the genre or kind of written work it is like fiction, non-fiction, poetry, etc.?

682. If someone is reading a story to you, do you have an imagery of the story and the characters?

683. Do you think that both silent reading and reading out loud are important?

684. How would you compare the story, (Cinderella) with the story (Sleeping Beauty)? How are they alike? How are they different?

685. What is the purpose of doing research?

686. Where are some resources you could use to do research?

687. What is the name of the resource you would use if you want to look up the meaning of a word?

688. In what order is a dictionary organized: numerical or alphabetical?

689. What is the order of the following words in a dictionary: stop; sound; show; sand?

690. What is the alphabetical order of the words *sand* and *same*, both beginning with s-a?

691. Do you read both fiction and non-fiction books?

692. What magazines or newspapers do you read?

693. What is the name of our local newspaper?

694. Can you always believe everything you read in a newspaper or magazine?

695. Is the "a" in **fate** long or short?

696. Is the "a" in **fat** long or short?

697. Is the "o" in **hop** long or short?

698. Is the "o" in **hope** long or short?

699. How do you spell **was**?

700. How do you spell **were**?

701. How do you spell **says**?

702. How do you spell **said**?

703. How do you spell **who**?

704. How do you spell **why**?

705. How do you spell **light**?

706. How do you spell **night**?

707. How do you spell the compound word **bedroom**?

708. How do you spell **sometimes**?

709. How do you spell **sailboat**?

710. How do you spell **happy**?

711. How do you spell **silly**?

712. How do you spell **pretty**?

713. How do you spell **know**?

714. How do you spell **wrong**?

715. Is an antonym the same or opposite of a word?

716. What is the antonym or opposite of silent?

717. Does a synonym mean the same thing or the opposite of another word?

718. What is a synonym of big?

719. What is a synonym of small?

720. What is the word for something that is spelled the same but means something different: a homonym or a synonym?

721. What is a homonym of **lock** of hair?

722. What is a homonym of **right** hand?

723. What is the beginning part of a word called: a suffix or a prefix?

724. What is the ending part of a word called: a prefix or a suffix?

725. Is the ending -er in **bigger** the suffix or the prefix?

726. What would come next: small, smaller, __?

727. Which is the correct use of slow: The turtle crawled slow, slowly, slower?

LANGUAGE ARTS

728. Can you think of a word that ends with the suffix *-less*?

729. Can you think of a word that ends with the suffix *-able*?

730. Can you think of a word that starts with the prefix *re-*?

731. Can you think of a word that starts with the prefix *un-*?

732. What are a period, an exclamation mark, and a question mark: interrogation or punctuation?

733. What is the name of the marks you see at the beginning and the end of a sentence that indicate that a character is speaking directly: punctuation or quotation?

734. What is the correct use of sleep: The baby is sleep, the baby is sleeping, or the baby is slept?

735. What is the past tense of climb: I climb the tree yesterday, or I climbed the tree yesterday?

736. What is the past tense of finish? (Can you use it in a sentence?)

737. What is the past tense of do?

738. What is the past tense of eat?

739. What is the past tense of read?

740. What is the past tense of wear?

741. What is the past tense of dry?

742. What is the past tense of see?

743. What is the past tense of come?

744. What is the past tense of he is?

745. What is the past tense of they are?

746. What is the past tense of go?

747. What is the past tense of find?

748. What is the past tense of say?

749. What would you say in a book report about the last book you read?

750. Have you ever written a letter to someone? (To whom?)

751. In the development of a fiction story, there should be a beginning, middle, and what else?

752. In a non-fiction book, what is the page called that has a list of the sub-topics that shows how the book is organized: Table of Contents or Chapters?

753. In a non-fiction book, what is the name of the alphabetical list of all the main ideas and key concepts contained in the book located at the very end: Index or Dictionary?

LANGUAGE ARTS

754. Do you have a journal or diary that you write in?

755. Do you know of anyone who wrote a famous diary or kept a journal of important information?

756. Why do you think a scientist, an inventor, or another person might keep a journal?

757. Does good writing organization include a beginning, a middle part, and an ending?

758. Can you identify all the parts of a sentence like a subject and a verb and the punctuation marks?

759. Can you write a sentence?

760. Can you write a sentence that asks a question?

761. Can you write a sentence that ends with an exclamation?

762. Can you write a letter?

763. Can you write a thank you note?

764. Can you write a report?

765. Can you write a story?

766. Can you write a poem?

767. When should you write a thank you note?

768. Can you draft a paper by first writing your ideas down on paper?

769. What does it mean when you revise your writing?

770. What does it mean when you edit your writing?

771. When a written work is published does that mean it is shared with others?

772. Is it allowable to copy what others have written without giving credit to the person who wrote it?

773. Can you print and read both upper case and lower case letters?

774. Can you write a report on a book that you have read?

775. What are some resources in a library media center that might help you gather information or do research for a report?

776. What is an encyclopedia and how is it organized?

777. Can you identify all of the following parts of a book: title, title page; table of contents, copyright, chapter, index, and the glossary?

778. Can you identify and give an example of the following literary works: poetry, legend, and fable?

779. What is the name of the non-fiction book you would look at to read about a person's life and times and significant historical events: biography or memoir?

LANGUAGE ARTS

780. Who earns the annual *Caldecott* award in children's literature: the author or the illustrator?

781. Who earns the annual *Newbery* award in children's literature: the author or the illustrator?

782. What is the name of the resource either online or in book format that gives you information regarding almost any topic, person, place or thing: encyclopedia or biography?

783. Can you turn on a computer and monitor?

784. Can you identify a computer keyboard, monitor, and mouse?

785. Is typing or word processing something on the computer a good skill to develop?

786. Are you familiar with ways of searching for library resources by conducting online computer searches?

787. Do you think that everything that you find on the internet is factual and accurate?

788. What would be an **in**appropriate use of using the internet?

789. Can you conduct a computer search in the library media center by author, title, subject, or keyword?

790. Are you able to load software (insert a CD) onto the computer?

791. Can you recognize and pronounce the common sight word "always?"(Show word!)

792. Can you recognize and pronounce the common sight word "around?"(Show word!)

793. Can you recognize and pronounce the common sight word "because?"(Show word!)

794. Can you recognize and pronounce the common sight word "been?"(Show word!)

795. Can you recognize and pronounce the common sight word "before?"(Show word!)

796. Can you recognize and pronounce the common sight word "best?"(Show word!)

797. Can you recognize and pronounce the common sight word "both?"(Show word!)

798. Can you recognize and pronounce the common sight word "buy?"(Show word!)

799. Can you recognize and pronounce the common sight word "call?"(Show word!)

800. Can you recognize and pronounce the common sight word "cold?"(Show word!)

801. Can you recognize and pronounce the common sight word "does?"(Show word!)

802. Can you recognize and pronounce the common sight word "don't?"(Show word!)

803. Can you recognize and pronounce the common sight word "fast?"(Show word!)

804. Can you recognize and pronounce the common sight word "first?"(Show word!)

805. Can you recognize and pronounce the common sight word "five?"(Show word!)

806. Can you recognize and pronounce the common sight word "found?"(Show word!)

LANGUAGE ARTS

807. Can you recognize and pronounce the common sight word "gave?"(Show word!)

808. Can you recognize and pronounce the common sight word "goes?"(Show word!)

809. Can you recognize and pronounce the common sight word "green?"(Show word!)

810. Can you recognize and pronounce the common sight word "it's?"(Show word!)

811. Can you recognize and pronounce the common sight word "made?"(Show word!)

812. Can you recognize and pronounce the common sight word "many?"(Show word!)

813. Can you recognize and pronounce the common sight word "off?"(Show word!)

814. Can you recognize and pronounce the common sight word "or?"(Show word!)

815. Can you recognize and pronounce the common sight word "pull?"(Show word!)

816. Can you recognize and pronounce the common sight word "read?"(Show word!)

817. Can you recognize and pronounce the common sight word "right?"(Show word!)

818. Can you recognize and pronounce the common sight word "sing?"(Show word!)

819. Can you recognize and pronounce the common sight word "sit?"(Show word!)

820. Can you recognize and pronounce the common sight word "sleep?"(Show word!)

821. Can you recognize and pronounce the common sight word "tell?"(Show word!)

822. Can you recognize and pronounce the common sight word "their?"(Show word!)

823. Can you recognize and pronounce the common sight word "these?"(Show word!)

824. Can you recognize and pronounce the common sight word "those?"(Show word!)

825. Can you recognize and pronounce the common sight word "upon?"(Show word!)

826. Can you recognize and pronounce the common sight word "us?"(Show word!)

827. Can you recognize and pronounce the common sight word "use?"(Show word!)

828. Can you recognize and pronounce the common sight word "very?"(Show word!)

829. Can you recognize and pronounce the common sight word "wash?"(Show word!)

830. Can you recognize and pronounce the common sight word "wish?"(Show word!)

831. Can you recognize and pronounce the common sight word "work?"(Show word!)

832. Can you recognize and pronounce the common sight word "would?"(Show word!)

833. Can you recognize and pronounce the common sight word "write?"(Show word!)

834. Can you recognize and pronounce the common sight word "your?"(Show word!)

LANGUAGE ARTS

Language Arts – 3rd Grade

835. Are reading, writing, speaking, and listening important skills as you develop your first language?

836. Are reading, writing, speaking, and listening important skills in acquiring a second language?

837. Do you read silently?

838. Do you read out loud?

839. Are you able to sound out new words you are not familiar with?

840. How many letters are there in the alphabet?

841. What are the vowels in the alphabet?

842. Can the letter "y" sometimes be a vowel?

843. What sound does the consonant blend "th" make?

844. What sound does the consonant blend "st" make?

845. What sound does the consonant blend "bl" make?

846. What sound does the consonant blend "gr" make?

847. What sound does the consonant blend "sc" make?

848. Can you say a word that begins with the consonant blend br?

849. Can you say a word that begins with the consonant blend cr?

850. Can you say a word that begins with the consonant blend dr?

851. Can you say a word that begins with the consonant blend fr?

852. Can you say a word that begins with the consonant blend gr?

853. Can you say a word that begins with the consonant blend pr?

854. Can you say a word that begins with the consonant blend tr?

855. Can you say a word that begins with the consonant blend bl?

856. Can you say a word that begins with the consonant blend cl?

857. Can you say a word that begins with the consonant blend fl?

858. Can you say a word that begins with the consonant blend gl?

859. Can you say a word that begins with the consonant blend pl?

860. Can you say a word that begins with the consonant blend sl?

861. Can you say a word that begins with the consonant blend sc?

LANGUAGE ARTS

862. Can you say a word that begins with the consonant blend sk?

863. Can you say a word that begins with the consonant blend sm?

864. Can you say a word that begins with the consonant blend sn?

865. Can you say a word that begins with the consonant blend sp?

866. Can you say a word that begins with the consonant blend st?

867. Can you say a word that begins with the consonant blend sw?

868. Can you say a word that begins with the consonant blend scr?

869. Can you say a word that begins with the consonant blend squ?

870. Can you say a word that begins with the consonant blend str?

871. Can you say a word that begins with the consonant blend spr?

872. Can you say a word that begins with the consonant blend spl?

873. Is each letter listed separately in the dictionary?

874. Which word would come first in a dictionary: derby or deputy?

875. Which word would come first in a dictionary: primary or prince?

876. In what order are words listed in a dictionary?

877. What letter is "q" almost always followed by?

878. Is a hard "c" similar to the sound of the letter "k?"

879. Is a soft "c" similar to the sound of the letter "s?"

880. Does the word "cat" begin with a hard "c" or a soft "c?"

881. Does the word "cot" begin with a hard "c" or a soft "c?"

882. Does the word "cut" begin with a hard "c" or a soft "c?"

883. What word(s) can you think of that begin with a hard "c?"

884. Does the word "cent" begin with a hard "c" or a soft "c?"

885. Does the word "cycle" begin with a hard "c" or a soft "c?"

886. Does the word "city" begin with a hard "c" or a soft "c?"

887. What word(s) can you think of that begin with a soft "c?"

888. Is a soft "g" sound similar to the "j" sound?

889. Does the word "gate" begin with a hard "g" or a soft "g?"

LANGUAGE ARTS

890. Does the word "goat" begin with a hard "g" or a soft "g?"

891. Does the word "gum" begin with a hard "g" or a soft "g?"

892. Does the word "gem" begin with a hard "g" or a soft "g?"

893. Does the word "gym" begin with a hard "g" or a soft "g?"

894. Does the word "giant" begin with a hard "g" or a soft "g?"

895. When the letter "c" or the letter "g" is followed by an "e" (cent; gem) an "i" (city; giant) or a "y" (cycle; gym) do they often have a "soft" sound?

896. Can the letter "y" be a vowel as in the word "myth," and a consonant as in the word "yoke?"

897. When the letter "y" begins a word or a syllable, is it considered a consonant?

898. In the words yes, yellow, and yogurt, is the letter "y" a vowel or a consonant?

899. When the letter "y" does not begin the word or syllable, is it a vowel or a consonant?

900. In the words, gym, baby, and sky, is the letter "y" a vowel or a consonant?

901. Do we use "a" or "an" before a word beginning with a vowel sound?

902. Which is correct: "It is **a** umbrella" or, "It is **an** umbrella?"

903. Which is correct: "It is **a** honor" or, "It is **an** honor?"

904. Which is correct: "It is **a** cat" or, "It is **an** cat?"

905. Would you use "a" or "an" before the noun **owl**?

906. Would you use "a" or "an" before the noun **bird**?

907. Would you use "a" or "an" before the noun **elephant**?

908. Would you use "a" or "an" before the noun **chest**?

909. What is the purpose of a dictionary?

910. In what order are the words listed in a dictionary?

911. Can you look up the definition of a word in a dictionary?

912. Are you able to identify the correct meaning of a word in a dictionary that has more than one meaning?

913. What would be the alphabetical order of the following words: device; defend; declare; and destroy? (Alphabetize by third letter)

914. Which word comes first alphabetically: humble, human, humor, or hum?

915. Which word comes first alphabetically: lima bean, limb, lily, or lime?

LANGUAGE ARTS

916. What letter has the shortest section in the dictionary: "y" or "x?"

917. Do words have a single definition, or can they have multiple definitions?

918. Which pair of guide words would be on the same dictionary page where **name** is found: nail net or needle nine?

919. Which pair of guide words would be on the same dictionary page where **coat** is found: coast cocoa or coconut collaborate?

920. Which pair of guide words would be on the same dictionary page where **crawl** is found: cozy crash or crate credit?

921. Are upper case letters in the alphabet the same as capital letters?

922. What are words divided into: sections or syllables?

923. Are words divided into syllables in a dictionary?

924. How many syllables does the word *happy* have?

925. How many syllables does the word *happily* have?

926. How many syllables does the word *read* have?

927. How many syllables does the word *birthday* have?

928. How many syllables does the word *Mississippi* have?

929. Can you blend syllables together to make new words?

930. What word is formed from the syllables **ta** and **ble**?

931. What word is formed from the syllables **mon** and **key**?

932. Can you divide words into syllables?

933. What are the two syllables in the word **turtle**?

934. What are the three syllables in the word **snowboarding**?

935. What are the four syllables in the word **population**?

936. Is learning the spelling of a word important in the process of developing your reading skills?

937. Are all the letters in a word always pronounced?

938. What are the silent letters in the word high?

939. How do you spell the word **half**?

940. What is the silent letter in the word **half?**

941. How do you spell **tough**?

LANGUAGE ARTS

942. What are the letters in the word **tough** that sound like the letter "f?"

943. How do you spell **hop**?

944. How do you spell **hope**?

945. Is the letter "e" at the end of the word **hope** silent?

946. Does adding an "e" at the end of the word **hope** make the vowel "o" long or short?

947. How do you spell the word **pail** from the sentence: "I shovel the sand into the pail?"

948. How do you spell the word **pale** in the sentence: "The girl looked scared and her face was very pale?"

949. How do you spell the word **quit**?

950. How do you spell the word **queen**?

951. Which letter almost always follows the letter "q?"

952. What is the rule for the order of "i" and "e" when spelling words? "I" before "e" except after _

953. Does the letter "e" come before "i" when it makes a long "a" sound like the word "*vein*?"

954. What is the color similar to tan is called: **b-_ _g-e**?

955. What is the correct spelling in this sentence: "A leader of a tribe is a c-h-_ _f?"

956. What is the correct spelling in this sentence: "The puzzle is missing one p _ _c-e?"

957. What is the correct spelling in this sentence: "They did an experiment in s-c-_ _ n-c-e class?"

958. What is the correct spelling in this sentence: "Another way to "get" is to r-e-c-_ _v-e?"

959. What is the correct spelling in this sentence: "A person who robs is called a t-h-_ _f?"

960. What are words called that have two parts to them to form one word, like **sometimes**?

961. Can you spell the compound word **everything**?

962. Can you spell the compound word **yourself**?

963. How do you spell the compound word **butterfly**?

964. How do you spell the compound word **somewhere**?

965. How do you spell the compound word **sailboat**?

966. How do you spell the compound word **grandfather**? (grandmother)

967. What other compound words can you name?

968. Is a base word one that does not have a prefix nor a suffix?

LANGUAGE ARTS

969. Are you able to recognize the base of a word?

970. Which of the following words is a base word: dangerous, thankful, listen, or speaker?

971. What is the base word of **independently**?

972. Is a *prefix* located at the beginning or at the end of a word?

973. Are you able to recognize a prefix, or the beginning letters of a word?

974. What is the prefix to the word **unable**?

975. What is the prefix to the word **reinvent**?

976. What is the prefix in the word **misunderstood**?

977. What is the prefix in the word **unintentional**?

978. What is the prefix in the word **independently**?

979. What is the prefix for this sentence: "My sister isn't old enough for kindergarten, so she will attend __school?"

980. What is the prefix for this sentence: "Kaitlyn won the spelling bee when Adam __spelled *independence*?"

981. What is the missing prefix for this sentence: "A strong wave knocked over our sand castle, so now we have to _build it?"

982. Would you use dis, in, or un for this sentence: "She is __considerate and likes to interrupt?"

983. Would you use dis, im, or un for this sentence: "Alex always __agrees with everything you say?"

984. Would you use dis, im, or un for this sentence: "It is __polite to talk with your mouth full?"

985. Would you use dis, im, or un for this sentence: "Some people feel __comfortable around babies?"

986. What is the suffix in the word **independently**?

987. What is a word called *without* a prefix or suffix?

988. What is the root or base of the word prettiest?

989. Are you able to recognize a suffix or ending letters of a word?

990. Is a suffix attached to the end or the beginning of a word?

991. Do common suffixes include "s," "ing," and "ed"?

992. What is the word when you add the suffix "s" to play?

993. What is the word when you add the suffix "ed" to play?

994. What is the word when you add the suffix "ing" to play?

LANGUAGE ARTS

995. What is the suffix in the word **mountainous**?

996. What is the suffix in the word **limitless**?

997. What is the suffix of the word **careful**?

998. What is the suffix of the word **fearless**?

999. What is the suffix of the word **happily**?

1000. What would you add to the word **care** to make it correct in the following sentence: "Callie was care_ when she carried the fish bowl?"

1001. What would you add to the word **power** to make it correct in the following sentence: "The knight lost his sword so now he feels power_ against his enemy?

1002. What suffix would you add to **e-d-i-t** to form a word that refers to a job: or, ian or ist?

1003. What suffix would you add to **a-r-t** to form a word that refers to a job: er, ian, or ist?

1004. What suffix would you add to **f-a-r-m** to form a word that refers to a job: er, ian, or ist?

1005. What suffix would you add to **d-e-n-t** to form a word that refers to a job: er, ian, or ist?

1006. What suffix would you add to **c-o-m-e-d** to form a word that refers to a job: er, ian, or ist?

1007. What suffix would you add to **p-o-l-i-t-i-c** to form a word that refers to a job: er, ian, or ist?

1008. Are synonyms words that mean the *same* thing or the *opposite* thing?

1009. What is a synonym for **big**?

1010. What is a synonym for **smart**?

1011. What is a synonym for **error**?

1012. What is a synonym for **risky**?

1013. What is a synonym for **wealthy**?

1014. What is a synonym for **completed**?

1015. What is a synonym for **stroll**?

1016. What is a synonym for **cautious**?

1017. What is a synonym for **scared**?

1018. What is a synonym for **assistant**?

1019. What is a synonym of **huge**?

1020. What is a synonym of **cry**: sob or laugh?

LANGUAGE ARTS

1021. What is a synonym of **wealthy**: poor or rich?

1022. What is a synonym of **damp**: dry or moist?

1023. Does an antonym mean the same as or the opposite of another word?

1024. What is an antonym of **wide**?

1025. What is an antonym of **smooth**?

1026. What is the antonym of **hard**: difficult or easy?

1027. What is the antonym of **hungry**: full or famished?

1028. What is the antonym of **build**: destroy or construct?

1029. What is an antonym for **deep**?

1030. What is an antonym for **sour**?

1031. What is an antonym for **over**?

1032. What is an antonym for **enemy**?

1033. What is an antonym for **dark**?

1034. What is an antonym for **poor**?

1035. What are two antonyms for **hard**?

1036. What is an antonym for **tame**?

1037. What is an antonym for **narrow**?

1038. What is an antonym for **awake**?

1039. What is the antonym for **most**?

1040. What is an antonym for **juicy**: wet, dry, tasty, or sweet?

1041. What is an antonym for **mend**: fix, sew, repair, or break?

1042. Is a homonym a word that is spelled the same, is pronounced the same, and has more than one meaning?

1043. What is the homonym of **right** and can you use each of them in a sentence?

1044. Is the word "**lock**" a homonym because it can used as" lock," as in the part of the door that you open and shut with a key, and "**lock**" as in a tuft of hair??

1045. What are the two meanings of the homonym "**bowl**?"

1046. What are the two meanings of the homonym "**yard**?"

LANGUAGE ARTS

1047. What are the two meanings of the homonym "**fly**?"

1048. What are the two meanings of the homonym "**duck**?"

1049. What are the two meanings of the homonym "**can**?"

1050. What are the two meanings of the homonym "**pitcher**?"

1051. What are the two meanings of the homonym "**ring**?"

1052. What are the two meanings of the homonym "**bat**?"

1053. What is the correct use of the word "**address**" in the following sentence according to its library definition: "The Gettysburg Address is well known by Abraham Lincoln?" A) The location of a house or building. B) The writing on an envelope that tells where it should be delivered. C) A speech

1054. What is the correct use of the word "**address**" in the following sentence according to its library definition: "When we moved, we got a new address?" A) The location of a building. B) The writing on an envelope that tells where it should be delivered. C) A speech

1055. What is the correct use of the word "**address**" in the following sentence according to its library definition: "The mail carrier couldn't read the address on the envelope." A) The location of a building. B) The writing on an envelope that tells where it should be delivered. C) A speech

1056. Is a homograph a type of homonym that is spelled the same, can be pronounced the same or differently, and has more than one meaning?

1057. Can the homograph **bass** refer to either a fish or a low, deep voice?

1058. Can the homograph **present** refer to a gift, or be used as a verb to introduce someone?

1059. Are *homophones* words that are pronounced the same but are spelled differently and mean different things?

1060. What is the homophone (and spelling) of f-l-o-w-e-r?

1061. What is the homophone (and spelling) of p-i-e-c-e?

1062. What are the two homophones of s-c-e-n-t?

1063. Are the words **by, bye,** and **buy** homophones?

1064. Which is correct: "I went to the park **b-y** the school." / "I went to the park **b-y-e** the school."/ "I went to the park **b-u-y** the school?"

1065. Which is correct: "I said **b-y** to my friends at noon." / "I said **b-y-e** to my friends at noon."/ "I said **b-u-y** to my friends at noon?"

1066. Which is correct: "I went to **b-y** an ice cream cone?" / "I went to **b-y-e** an ice cream cone?" / "I went to **b-u-y** an ice cream cone?"

LANGUAGE ARTS

1067. Are the words to, too, and two homophones?

1068. Which is correct: "I am going **t-o** the park." / "I am going **t-o-o** the park." / "I am going **t-w-o** the park?"

1069. Which is correct: "I am going **t-o**." / "I am going **t-o-o**." / "I am going **t-w-o**?"

1070. Which is correct: "I am going to the park with **t-o** friends." / "I am going to the park with **t-o-o** friends." / "I am going to the park with **t-w-o** friends?"

1071. Are the words there, their, and they're homophones?

1072. What is the homophone of r-i-g-h-t?

1073. Which is correct: "I am going t-h-e-r-e / t-h-e-i-r / t-h-e-y-'r-e tomorrow?"

1074. Which is correct: "I am going to t-h-e-r-e / t-h-e-i-r / or, t-h-e-y '-r-e house in 20 minutes."

1075. Which is correct: "T-h-e-r-e / t-h-e-i-r, / or, t-h-e-y-'r-e coming here from school?"

1076. Are the words s-e-i-z-e, s-e-a-s, and s-e-e-s homophones?

1077. Which is correct: "They are going to s-e-i-z-e, s-e-a-s, or s-e-e-s the chance to go on the ship?"

1078. Which is correct: "They are going to sail on the high s-e-i-z-e, s-e-a-s, or s-e-e-s?"

1079. Which is correct: He s-e-i-z-e, s-e-a-s, or s-e-e-s the ship on the horizon?"

1080. What is the homophone of s-c-e-n-t?

1081. What is the homophone of c-l-a-u-s-e?

1082. What is the homophone of t-a-l-e?

1083. What is the homophone of v-a-n-e?

1084. What is the homophone of p-e-e-k?

1085. What is the homophone of f-l-a-i-r?

1086. What is the homophone of p-o-l-e?

1087. What is the homophone of u-r-n?

1088. What is the homophone of b-o-u-g-h?

1089. What is the homophone of r-o-t-e?

1090. What is the homophone of b-r-e-a-d?

1091. What is the homophone of t-e-n-t-s?

1092. What is the homophone of h-e-i-r?

LANGUAGE ARTS

1093. What is the homophone of p-e-a-r?

1094. What is the homophone of t-o-a-d?

1095. Which is the correct homophone in the sentence: "How much is the plane f-a-i-r or f-a-r-e to Chicago?"

1096. Which is the correct homophone in the sentence: "I want to go to the county f-a-i-r or f-a-r-e this Saturday?"

1097. Which is the correct homophone: "The wind b-l-e-w or b-l-u-e away my hat?"

1098. Which is the correct homophone: "Sofia painted her room light b-l-e-w or b-l-u-e?"

1099. Which is the correct homophone: "I wear a belt around my w-a-i-s-t or w-a-s-t-e?"

1100. Which is the correct homophone: "It is important not to w-a-i-s-t or w-a-s-t-e paper?"

1101. Which is the correct homophone: "Mr. Anderson is the new principal: **p-a-l** or **p-l-e**?

1102. Which is the correct homophone: "Lincoln was a true man of principle: **p-a-l** or **p-l-e**?"

1103. Which is the correct homophone: "Paul t-h-r-e-w or t-h-r-o-u-g-h the ball t-h-r-e-w or t-h-r-o-u-g-h the basketball hoop?"

1104. Which is the correct homophone in the following sentence: "I will m-e-e-t or m-e-a-t you in the m-e-e-t or the m-e-a-t section of the supermarket?"

1105. Which is the correct homophone in the following sentence: "The Bears have o-n-e or w-o-n only o-n-e or w-o-n of their baseball games?"

1106. Do you know the difference between the singular form of a word and its plural form?

1107. Do you read different genres that might include fiction, non-fiction, and poetry?

1108. Can you identify fiction works like tall tales, folk tales, and fairy tales?

1109. What are "Paul Bunyan" and "Brer Rabbit examples of: tall tales or non-fiction?

1110. Is the story, "Why the Sea is Salt" an example of a folktale or a fairy tale?

1111. Is "Cinderella" an example of a fairy tale or a tall tale?

1112. Is a myth something that is real or made-up?

1113. What are the stories, "The Midas Touch" and "Helen of Troy" examples of: folktales or myths?

1114. Is it important to read a variety of materials to help build an understanding of the cultures of the United States and of the world?

1115. Are you able to make a *prediction* about what a book may be about before reading it?

1116. What part of a book can give you clues as to what the book is about?

LANGUAGE ARTS

1117. While you read a book, are you able to identify and re-tell the sequence of events like what happened first, next, last, then, and finally?

1118. After reading something in a textbook, are you able to state the main idea and other details?

1119. After reading something, are you able to write a short summary?

1120. After reading a factual reading, are you able to make a conclusion about what you read?

1121. After reading a story, are you able to identify the main idea, the characters, the setting, and the plot?

1122. What is the main idea in the story, "Cinderella?"

1123. What are the names of the characters in the story, "Cinderella?"

1124. What is the setting in the story, "Cinderella?"

1125. What is the plot of the story, "Cinderella?"

1126. When you read something, can you tell the difference between fact and opinion?

1127. Is the sentence, "A snake is a reptile." a fact or an opinion?

1128. Is the sentence, "Snakes are the scariest animals in the world." a fact or an opinion?

1129. Is a fact something that can be proven, or is it something that someone believes to be true?

1130. Is an opinion a personal judgment, or is it based on fact?

1131. When you read something in literature, are you able to understand the theme, the conflict, and the point of view?

1132. Can you identify a paragraph in a reading?

1133. How many spaces do we say that we "indent" the first sentence of a paragraph: three or five?

1134. Can you identify the major parts of a sentence like a noun and a verb?

1135. What three things can a noun be?

1136. What does the verb do in a sentence?

1137. What is the verb in the sentence: "I walked to the park today?"

1138. What are some examples of verbs?

1139. What is the noun in the sentence: "I walked to the park today?"

1140. What are some examples of nouns?

1141. What is the *proper noun* in the sentence: "Mrs. Smith walked to the park today?"

1142. What are some examples of proper nouns?

LANGUAGE ARTS

1143. Do nouns and verbs show agreement in a grammatically correct sentence?

1144. Which is correct: "The sky *are* falling." or "The sky *is* falling?"

1145. Which is correct: "The kids *have* bicycles." or "The kids *has* bicycles?"

1146. What does a pronoun do in a sentence: describes a noun or substitutes for a noun?

1147. What is the noun in the following sentence: "Maya is very pretty?"

1148. What is the subject pronoun that takes the place of the proper noun Maya?

1149. What is the subject pronoun that takes the place of the proper noun Joe?

1150. What is the pronoun that takes the place of the proper noun Chicago: it or the?

1151. What are some examples of pronouns?

1152. What does an adverb do in a sentence: describes a noun or describes a verb?

1153. What is the adverb in the following sentence: "The teacher slowly opened the door?"

1154. What two letters do adverbs often end in: ly or ty?

1155. What is the negative adverb of *always*?

1156. What are some examples of adverbs?

1157. Which of the three is the adverb: **t-o, t-o-o, or t-w-o?**

1158. What is another meaning of the adverb **t-o-o?**

1159. Which of the three is the preposition: **t-o, t-o-o, or t-w-o?**

1160. Which of the three is the adjective: **t-o, t-o-o, or t-w-o?**

1161. What is it called when you start the first sentence of a paragraph 5 spaces: invert or indent?

1162. What is the *first* sentence of a paragraph called: the topic sentence or the hook?

1163. Can you identify the punctuation marks in a sentence like a capital letter, comma, apostrophe, exclamation mark, question mark, quotation marks, colon, semi-colon, and period?

1164. What type of punctuation mark do we need to show possession: a comma or an apostrophe?

1165. How would you write the *books of John* as a possessive?

1166. How do you spell **it's** as in it is Friday?

1167. Is the word **it's** with an apostrophe "s" a contraction for *it is* or *it was*?

1168. What is the contraction for *is not*?

1169. What is the contraction for *do not*?

LANGUAGE ARTS

1170. What is the contraction for *I will*?

1171. What is the contraction for *they are*?

1172. Can you print all your letters in both upper case (capital A) and lower case (small a)?

1173. Are you beginning to write the letters of the alphabet in cursive in which you connect the letters together?

1174. When you write something, is it good practice to organize your writing with a distinctive beginning, middle, and an end?

1175. Which stage of the writing process is it if you are just jotting your ideas down on paper: drafting or revising?

1176. Which stage of the writing process is it if you are making changes to your writing: revising or drafting?

1177. Which stage of the writing process is it if you are looking for and correcting errors: editing or proofreading?

1178. What is the role of an editor of a newspaper?

1179. Is proofreading what you have written an important last step in the writing process before you submit your final piece?

1180. Which stage of the writing process is it when you are ready to share your final writing piece, or when a book is ready for the public: proofreading or publishing?

1181. What is the name of an expression that is commonly used that means something different than what it appears to mean: an idiom or a paraphrase?

1182. What does the idiom "a piece of cake" mean?

1183. Can you finish the idiom: "Actions speak louder than __?"

1184. Can you finish the idiom: "Beggars can't be __?"

1185. Can you finish the idiom: "When in Rome, do as the __?"

1186. Can you finish the idiom: "They are like two peas in a __?"

1187. Can you finish the idiom: "It cost me an arm and a __?"

1188. Can you finish the idiom: "It was a secret until Sara spilled the __?"

1189. Can you finish the idiom: "It is raining cats and __?"

1190. Can you finish the saying: "A feather in your __?"

1191. Can you finish the common saying: "Do unto others as you would have them…?"

LANGUAGE ARTS

1192. What letters in the alphabet are the same as capital letters: upper case or lower case?

1193. What is the name of the word in a sentence that tells whom or what the sentence is about: the subject or the topic?

1194. What is the *subject* in the following sentence, "Alex eats ice cream for dessert:" Alex or dessert?

1195. What is the part of the sentence that tells what the subject does, or what is done to the subject: the verb or the predicate?

1196. What is the *predicate* of the sentence, "Alex eats ice cream for dessert:" Alex or eats ice cream?

1197. What is the *predicate* of the sentence, "The cat purred softly:" the cat or purred softly?

1198. Which word of a sentence is always capitalized?

1199. Do proper nouns always begin with a capital letter?

1200. What is the proper noun in the sentence: "We live by a lake in Wisconsin?"

1201. Are titles like Doctor, Mr., and Mrs. capitalized?

1202. Are the names of places capitalized?

1203. Do you know the difference between the singular form of a word and its plural form?

1204. What is the singular form of the noun "cats?"

1205. What is the singular form of the noun "wives?"

1206. What is the singular form of the noun "teeth?"

1207. What is the singular form of the noun "geese?"

1208. What is the singular form of the noun "pennies?"

1209. What is the plural form of the noun "dog?"

1210. What is the plural form of the noun "turtle?"

1211. What is the plural form of the noun "echo?"

1212. What is the plural form of the noun "potato?"

1213. What is the plural form of the noun "tomato?"

1214. What is the plural form of the noun "hero?"

1215. What is the plural form of the noun "box?"

1216. What is the plural form of the noun "family?"

1217. What is the plural form of the noun "penny?"

LANGUAGE ARTS

1218. What is the plural form of the noun "quality?"

1219. What is the plural form of the noun "half?"

1220. What is the plural form of the noun "leaf?"

1221. What is the plural form of the noun "thief?"

1222. What is the plural form of the noun "wolf?"

1223. What is the plural form of the noun "self?"

1224. What is the plural form of the noun "knife?"

1225. What is the plural form of the noun "life?"

1226. What is the plural form of the noun "fish?"

1227. What is the plural form of the noun "deer?"

1228. What is the plural form of the noun "sheep?"

1229. What is the plural form of the noun "man?"

1230. What is the plural form of the noun "woman?"

1231. What is the plural form of the noun "person?"

1232. What is the plural form of the noun "child?"

1233. What is the plural form of the noun "mouse?"

1234. What is the plural form of the noun "foot?"

1235. What is the plural form of the noun "tooth?"

1236. What is the plural form of the noun "ox?"

1237. What is the singular form of the noun "copies?"

1238. What is the plural form of the noun "goose?"

1239. What is the singular form of the noun "flies?"

1240. What is the proper noun in the sentence: "The present is for Katie?"

1241. What is the proper noun in the sentence: "He lives in Arizona?"

1242. What is the proper noun in the sentence: "The museum will be closed on Thanksgiving Day?"

1243. How can you turn the noun **river** into a *proper* noun?

1244. How can you turn the noun **city** into a *proper* noun?

1245. How can you turn the noun **athlete** into a *proper* noun?

LANGUAGE ARTS

1246. How can you turn the noun **president** into a *proper* noun?

1247. How can you turn the noun **street** into a *proper* noun?

1248. How can you turn the noun **month** into a *proper* noun?

1249. How can you turn the noun **holiday** into a *proper* noun?

1250. How can you turn the noun **ocean** into a *proper* noun?

1251. How can you turn the noun **artist** into a *proper* noun?

1252. What is the noun in the sentence: "The leaves are turning colors?"

1253. In the sentence, "George Washington was the first President of the United States," what part of speech is 'United States?'

1254. What nouns can you name?

1255. Is a person's name a noun?

1256. What is the definition of a verb: it describes an action, or it describes a noun?

1257. What is the verb in the sentence: "The car drove by quickly."

1258. Which of the following is *not* an action verb: "run, swim, lake, collapse, walked, and saw?"

1259. What action verbs can you list?

1260. Are "is, am, are" considered verbs of *being*, or verbs of *belonging*?

1261. Which *being* verb is correct: "I **is, am,** or **are** watching television?"

1262. Which *being* verb is correct: "He **am, is,** or **are** watching television?"

1263. Which *being* verb is correct: "They **is, are,** or **am** watching television?"

1264. Which *being* verb is correct: "She **were** here yesterday" or "She **was** here yesterday?"

1265. Which *being* verb is correct: "Alyssa and Sam **was** here yesterday" or, "Alyssa and Sam **were** here yesterday?"

1266. Which verb is correct in the following sentence: "She **has** a new puppy" or, "She **have** a new puppy?"

1267. Which verb is correct in the following sentence: "Alex and Ben **has** a new puppy" or, "Alex and Ben **have** a new puppy?"

1268. Is the following sentence in the present, past or future tense: "Spencer **writes** his name on the board?"

1269. Is the following sentence in the present, past, or future tense: "Eva **jumped** on her bed?"

LANGUAGE ARTS

1270. Is the following sentence in the present, past, or future tense; "Ben **will sing** in the concert?"

1271. What is the past tense of the verb "play?"

1272. What is the past tense of the verb "cry?"

1273. What is the past tense of the verb "go?"

1274. What is the past tense of the verb "eat?"

1275. What is the past tense of the verb "buy?"

1276. What is the past tense of the verb "make?"

1277. What is the past tense of the verb "feel?"

1278. What is the past tense of the verb "hear?"

1279. What is the past tense of the verb "think?"

1280. What is the past tense of the verb "see?"

1281. What is the past tense of the verb "keep?"

1282. What is the past tense of the verb "bring?"

1283. What is the past tense of the verb "is?"

1284. What is the past tense of the verb "do?"

1285. What is the past tense of the verb "know?"

1286. What is the past tense of the verb "break?"

1287. What is the past tense of the verb "begin?"

1288. What is the past tense of the verb "have?"

1289. What is the past tense of the verb "pay?"

1290. What is the past tense of the verb "give?"

1291. What is the past tense of the verb "cut?"

1292. What is the past tense of the verb "tell?"

1293. What is the past tense of the verb "speak?"

1294. What is the past tense of the verb "send?"

1295. What is the past tense of the verb "take?"

1296. What is the past tense of the verb "meet?"

1297. What is the past tense of the verb "teach?"

LANGUAGE ARTS

1298. What is the past tense of the verb "leave?"

1299. What is the past tense of the verb "find?"

1300. What is the past tense of the verb "read?"

1301. What is the past tense of the verb "fly?"

1302. What is the past tense of the verb "get?"

1303. What is the past tense of the verb "swim?"

1304. What is the present tense of the verb "said?"

1305. What is the present tense of the verb "shook?"

1306. What is the present tense of the verb "rang?"

1307. What is the present tense of the verb "stood?"

1308. What is the present tense of the verb "found?"

1309. What is the present tense of the verb "blew?"

1310. What is the present tense of the verb "gave?"

1311. What is the present tense of the verb "froze?"

1312. What is the present tense of the verb "slept?"

1313. What is the present tense of the verb "drank?"

1314. What is the definition of an adjective: it describes a noun or it describes a verb?

1315. What is the adjective in the sentence: "Rosa has curly hair?"

1316. What is the adjective in the sentence: "The pretty lady left the salon?"

1317. What is the adjective in the sentence: "The lady that left the salon is blonde?"

1318. What would the word "*American*" be considered: a proper adjective or a proper noun?

1319. What proper adjectives that are nationalities can you list?

1320. What would appearance words like elegant, plain, and drab be considered: descriptive adjectives or descriptive adverbs?

1321. Are all colors like blue, pink, and black considered adjectives or pronouns?

1322. Are feeling words like brave, lazy, and scary considered adjectives or adverbs?

1323. Are shape words like flat, shallow, and wide considered adjectives or adverbs?

1324. Are time words like ancient, quick, and brief considered adverbs or adjectives?

LANGUAGE ARTS

1325. Would spicy and juicy be considered taste or touch adjectives?

1326. Would rough and sticky be considered taste or touch adjectives?

1327. Are quantity words like empty, numerous, and many considered adjectives or adverbs?

1328. What sensory (smell, sound, sight, touch, taste) words would you use to describe an amusement park or a fair?

1329. What part of speech is the word "those" in the sentence, "Those shoes look nice on you:" a demonstrative adjective or a demonstrative pronoun?

1330. What adjectives can you add to the following sentence to make it more descriptive: "The girl walks through the park?"

1331. What adjectives can you add to the following sentence to make it more descriptive: "The boys rode their bicycles?"

1332. What adjectives can you add to the following sentence to make it more descriptive: "The lady baked a cake?"

1333. What is the plural of the adjective "this:" these or those?

1334. What is the plural of the adjective "that:" these or those?

1335. Which sentence would convey that you are referring to something close to you: "**This** house is big." or, "**That** house is big?"

1336. Which of the following best conveys what is farthest away from the speaker: "**That** tree is big," "**That** tree **over there** is big." or, "**This** tree is big?"

1337. Is the word "big" an adjective or a noun?

1338. What comparative ending would you add to "big" to mean "more big?"

1339. What superlative ending would you add to "big" to mean "the most big?"

1340. When making comparisons and you say small, smaller, smallest, so how would you finish "tall?

1341. Using comparisons, how would you finish "happy?"

1342. Using comparisons, how would you finish "peaceful?"

1343. Using comparisons, how would you finish "friendly?"

1344. Using comparisons, how would you finish "good?"

1345. Using comparisons, how would you finish "bad?"

1346. Using comparisons, how would you finish "many?"

1347. Using comparisons, how would you finish "little?"

LANGUAGE ARTS

1348. Using comparisons, how would you finish "far?"

1349. What is the name for the figure of speech used to compare two things using "like" or "as:" a simile or a metaphor?

1350. How would you finish the simile: "It is as dry as a _?"

1351. How would you finish the simile: "Easy as _?"

1352. How would you finish the simile: "Blind as a _?"

1353. How would you finish the simile: "Busy as a _?"

1354. How would you finish the simile: "Light as a _?"

1355. How would you finish the simile: "Gone like the _?"

1356. How would you finish the simile: "Sour like an _?"

1357. How would you finish the simile: "Big as an _?"

1358. Which part of speech describes a verb to tell **how** something is done: an adjective or an adverb?

1359. What is the adverb in the sentence: "Tom walked swiftly to his house."

1360. Does an adverb always end in "-ly?"

1361. Are the words "fast" and "slow" adverbs?

1362. Are the words "often," "always," and "never" adverbs of frequency or place?

1363. Are the words "very" and "really" adverbs?

1364. Are the words "there" and "here" adverbs of place or adverbs of frequency?

1365. Are "so that" and "in order to" adverbs of frequency or adverbs of purpose?

1366. Are "next," "last," "now," and "soon" adverbs of time or adverbs of frequency?

1367. What is the name for the word or a phrase that shows the relation of a noun or pronoun to other words in the sentence: conjunction or preposition?

1368. Do examples of prepositions include above, below, around, through, toward, over, in, at, to, for, and near?

1369. What is the preposition in the sentence: "Chris looked for his cat under the bed?"

1370. What can you name in your room that is **near** the bed? (below, over; under, between the bed and door, on, for, etc.)

1371. What is the definition of a pronoun: it takes the place of a noun or it modifies a noun?

1372. What is the pronoun in the sentence: "She rode her bike to school?"

LANGUAGE ARTS

1373. What pronoun would take the place of Marissa?

1374. What pronoun would take the place of Ben?

1375. What pronoun would take the place of Sara and Ben?

1376. What pronoun would take the place of Sara and me?

1377. What pronoun would I use if I were referring to myself?

1378. Which pronoun is correct in the following sentence: "John and **I** went to the theatre" or, "John and **me** went to the theatre?"

1379. Is the sentence "John and **I** went to the theatre" correct because "I" is the subject?

1380. Which pronoun is correct in the following sentence: "John invited **me** to the theatre" or, "John invited **I** to the theatre?"

1381. Is the sentence "John invited **me** to the theatre" correct because "me" is the object?

1382. Which pronoun is correct in the following sentence: "The bike belongs to **me**" or, "The bike belongs to **I**?"

1383. What is another way of saying, "The bike belongs to me:" The bike is _ or, It is _ bike?

1384. What is another way of saying, "The bike belongs to her:" The bike is _ or, It is _ bike?

1385. What is another way of saying, "The bike belongs to him:" The bike is _ or, It is _ bike?

1386. What is another way of saying, "The bike belongs to you:" The bike is _ or, It is _ bike?

1387. What is another way of saying, "The bike belongs to Nick and me:" The bike is _ or, It is _ bike?

1388. What is another way of saying, "The bike belongs to Joey and Lucas:" The bike is _ or, It is _ bike?

1389. Is the word t-h-e-i-r a possessive pronoun that shows ownership?

1390. What is the name for the spoken word that is used to express pain, delight, or surprise: interjection or exclamation?

1391. What is the interjection in the sentence: "Ouch! I stubbed my toe?"

1392. What is the interjection in the sentence: "Hooray! We won the contest?"

1393. What is the interjection in the sentence: "Oh my! I won the drawing contest?"

1394. What is the name for the part of speech that *connects* words, phrases, or sentences: interjection or conjunction?

1395. What is the conjunction in the sentence: "I wanted to go to the pool but I had to cut the grass?"

1396. What is the conjunction in the sentence: "He will go to college and he will become a doctor?"

LANGUAGE ARTS

1397. What is the conjunction in the sentence: "He will travel to Europe if he gets the job?"

1398. What is the name of a combination of two words with an apostrophe: contraction or conjunction?

1399. What is the contraction in the sentence: "The athlete didn't give up?"

1400. What does an apostrophe take the place of in a contraction: a letter or a word?

1401. What is the contraction of "I would?"

1402. What is the contraction of "I will?"

1403. What is the contraction of "would not?"

1404. What is the contraction of "they have?"

1405. What is the contraction of "have not?"

1406. What is the contraction of "you are?"

1407. What are the two words for the contraction **wouldn't**?

1408. What are the two words for the contraction **won't**?

1409. What type of sentence makes a statement: a declarative or an interrogative?

1410. What type of sentence asks a question: a declarative or an interrogative?

1411. Is the following sentence declarative or interrogative: "He is the president of the company?"

1412. Is the following sentence interrogative or exclamatory: "Is he the president of the company?"

1413. Which is correct to make the noun agree with the verb: "The sky **is** blue" or "The sky **are** blue?"

1414. Which is correct to make the noun agree with the verb: "The boys **is** tall" or "The boys **are** tall?"

1415. Are lower case letters in the alphabet the same as small letters?

1416. Can you write your words in upper case letters?

1417. Can you write words in lower case letters?

1418. When you write using upper and lower case letters, are you *printing* or writing in *cursive*?

1419. Can you write words in *cursive*?

1420. Are most signatures written in cursive?

1421. Can you sign your name in cursive?

1422. Can you identify and write upper case letters in cursive?

1423. Can you identify and write lower case letters in cursive?

1424. What is a group of words called that express a complete thought and contain a subject and a verb?

LANGUAGE ARTS

1425. Can sentences end with a period, a question mark, or an exclamation point?

1426. What is the cause and effect of the sentence: "Maria studied her spelling words and got an "A" on the test?"

1427. What is the cause and effect of the sentence: Matt called the tow truck because he had a flat tire?"

1428. What is the punctuation mark that you need at the end of a declarative sentence?

1429. What type of punctuation do you need between a series of words: a comma or a colon?

1430. What punctuation mark do you need after the number in a date?

1431. After which words would the commas go in the sentence: "Mrs. Smith enjoys singing, dancing, and cooking?"

1432. Where does the comma go in an address: after the city name or before the city name?

1433. What punctuation mark to you need at the end of a sentence that is asking something?

1434. What punctuation mark would you write to show emotion as if a character were shouting?

1435. What kind of marks do you need when you want to indicate that someone is speaking?

1436. Where would the quotation marks go in the sentence: Do you want strawberry or chocolate ice cream? asked Ryan?

1437. Where would the quotation marks go in the following: I love my new kitten! said Brittney. He is so playful?

1438. What kind of punctuation mark do you need to show possession as in: "the **boy's** mother?

1439. Does the apostrophe in *"the girl's house"* show possession?

1440. In "the **girl's** house," does the apostrophe go before or after the letter "**s**" in girls?

1441. How would you show possession to refer to: "the bike belonging to Marcos?"

1442. In the sentence, "I bought Jack's gift yesterday," which word in the sentence needs the apostrophe?

1443. In "The **elephants'** trunks are long," does the apostrophe go before or after the "s" in elephants?

1444. How would you show possession in *"the voices of the singers?"*

1445. Which is correct on the invitation: "**Y-o-u-apostrophe r-e** invited" or, "**Y-o-u-r** invited?"

1446. What is the shortened version of a word called: substitution or abbreviation?

1447. What type of punctuation mark does an **abbreviation or abbreviated word** have?

1448. What is the abbreviation of street?

1449. What is the abbreviation of avenue?

LANGUAGE ARTS

1450. What is the abbreviation doctor?

1451. What is the abbreviation of our state?

1452. What is the abbreviation for the United States?

1453. What is the abbreviation for Washington **D**istrict of **C**olumbia?

1454. What is the abbreviation for the month of October?

1455. What is the abbreviation of average?

1456. Can you create a series of at least 4 words that rhyme with *cat*?

1457. Can you identify the word that does not rhyme from the following: bat, cat, pig, sat?

1458. Can you say words from the word family ending in "-et?" (met)

1459. Can you say words from the word family ending in "-ight?" (night)

1460. Can you say words from the word family ending in "-old?" (sold)

1461. Can you say words from the word family ending in "-eat?" (seat)

1462. Which pair of words do **not** rhyme: **A)** how, low **B)** said, bet **C)** mother, other **D)** sign, line?

1463. In the sentence, "After misspelling the word in the spelling bee, Sam put his head down and sat down dejectedly," can you **infer** the meaning of the word '*dejectedly*?'

1464. Does an *inference* draw a conclusion after considering all the facts?

1465. When you read can you use context clues to determine the meaning of unfamiliar words?

1466. What is the context clue for the word *ferocious* in the sentence: "The **ferocious** dog growled at the cat?"

1467. Using context clues, what is the meaning of *flabbergasted* in the following sentence: "She was flabbergasted when she found out she won the contest:" angry, amazed, or tired?

1468. Using context clues, what is the meaning of *somber* in the following sentence: "Justin was in a **somber** mood when he heard the bad news:" excited, sad, or happy?

1469. Using context clues, what is the meaning of *concealed* in the following sentence: "The woman's large hat **concealed** her face:" revealed, showed, or hid?

1470. Using context clues, what is the meaning of *hazardous* in the following sentence: "Eating too much sugar can be hazardous to your health:" dangerous; great; or delightful?

1471. What is it called when you read or write a series of sentences connected by one main idea?

1472. What is it called when we space the first sentence five spaces that serves to identity the beginning of a new paragraph?

1473. What is the first sentence of a paragraph called: topic sentence or a leading sentence?

LANGUAGE ARTS

1474. What part of a paragraph indicates what the paragraph will be about: topic sentence or hook?

1475. What is the term for the sentences that support the topic sentence in a paragraph: supporting sentences or related sentences?

1476. What are some words that indicate a sequence or order to a series of events?

1477. Do the words, next, then, last, finally, also indicate sequential order?

1478. Can you name a story?

1479. Can you tell a story?

1480. Can you predict how a story will end?

1481. Can you use pictures and illustrations to gather story information and predict what a story will be about?

1482. Are the characters, setting, plot, and main idea all parts of a story?

1483. Who are the characters in the story "Snow White?"

1484. What are the two main settings in the story "Snow White?"

1485. What is the plot in the story "Snow White?"

1486. What is the main idea of the story "Snow White?"

1487. Can you recall other details in the story "Snow White?"

1488. What is the main purpose for reading non-fiction: to gain information, to learn different viewpoints, or to appreciate literature?

1489. Is the statement, "There are twenty four hours in a day" a fact or an opinion?

1490. Is the statement, "There are not enough hours in the day" a fact or an opinion?

1491. When we compare two cultures, are we communicating how they are similar and how they are different?

1492. When we contrast two cultures, are we focusing on how they are alike or how they are different?

1493. What are you reading right now?

1494. What genre, or kind of literature are you reading right now?

1495. What is the name of the genre that is an imaginary creation: non-fiction or fiction?

1496. What is the name of the genre that is based on facts and reality: fiction or non-fiction?

1497. Can you distinguish between fiction and non-fiction?

1498. How are books classified in a library: the Dewey Decimal System or by the author's last name?

LANGUAGE ARTS

1499. Which books in a library are shelved in alphabetical order according to the author's last name: fiction or non-fiction?

1500. What is the term for the series of numbers and letters on the spine of a book that indicate where the book is kept in the library, or how it is organized: call numbers or decimal numbers?

1501. What types of materials might you find in the reference section of a library?

1502. What is the name for the genre of literature that conveys information about a specific time period or some event more than 30 years ago: historical fiction or science fiction?

1503. Are fiction and non-fiction located in the same or different areas of the library?

1504. Can you distinguish fiction from fantasy?

1505. Can you distinguish fantasy from realism?

1506. What is a book called that is written about a prominent (important) person: biography or bibliography?

1507. What is a book called when an author writes about his or her own life: biography or autobiography?

1508. Can you distinguish between a biography and an autobiography?

1509. What is a literary work in the form of poems: poetry or prose?

1510. What are essays and short stories examples of: prose or narrative?

1511. What is name of a story that may express the beliefs of a group of people, relates an idea that many people believe, or is a story that gives reasons for something that happens in nature: a myth or a fable?

1512. Do you know of any myths?

1513. What is the name of the genre or literary works that tell stories about life in the future, or about stars, planets, and unknown worlds: science fiction or fantasy?

1514. What is the name of a written story handed down from one generation to the next that may be based on fact but are often not entirely true: legend or fable?

1515. What is the name of an oral story that is handed down from one generation to the next: a folktale or a fable?

1516. Do you know the titles of any legends?

1517. What is the name of a story that teaches a lesson that often has talking animal characters: folktale or fable?

1518. What genre are the stories, *The Boy Who Cried Wolf*, *The Goose That Laid the Golden Egg*, and *The Tortoise and the Hare*: fables or folktales?

LANGUAGE ARTS

1519. What fables are you familiar with?

1520. What is the name of the famous storyteller from ancient Greece that is most famous for the 600 fables that he wrote in his lifetime: Aesop or Apollo?

1521. What is the name of a story that is exaggerated or not true?

1522. Can you write a fictional story?

1523. Are all of the following involved in the writing process: plan, draft, revise, edit, print, and share?

1524. Can you write a report?

1525. Can you write a poem?

1526. Can you write a letter?

1527. What is the salutation of a letter: the greeting or the closing?

1528. Does a letter include a salutation, a body, and a closing?

1529. Can you write an address on a letter?

1530. Where does the address go on an envelope?

1531. Where is the return address located on an envelope: upper left corner or upper right corner?

1532. Where does the stamp go on an envelope: upper left corner or upper right corner?

1533. Can you write an invitation?

1534. What information is included on an invitation?

1535. Can you write a thank you note?

1536. What is an occasion for writing a thank you note?

1537. Can you fill out a form or an application?

1538. When might you need to fill out an application?

1539. Does an author generally write for a purpose?

1540. What does the author's writing reflect: a point of view or a style?

1541. Does an author have a distinct style?

1542. What are some resources you could use to seek further information about a topic?

1543. What are resources of information called: reference materials or resource materials?

1544. Can you write with pen and paper?

1545. Can you use the keyboard on a computer?

LANGUAGE ARTS

1546. Can you adapt, or adjust your writing for your audience?

1547. Would a letter written to your friend be formal or casual?

1548. Would a letter written to the president be formal or casual?

1549. Does an author generally write for a specific audience?

1550. What is the name of the prestigious award that a children's author may earn for his or her book: an Emmy award or a Newbery award?

1551. What does an illustrator do?

1552. What is the name of the prestigious award that a children's illustrator may earn for his or her illustrations: Caldecott or Newbery?

1553. What does a playwright write?

1554. Can many stories be acted out and presented as a play?

1555. What is the term for a conversation between two or more people: a dialogue or a drama?

1556. What is the reason for the revising a letter, article, or report?

1557. Can you write and present a book report?

1558. What is it called when you speak in front of an audience: a debate or a speech?

1559. When talking to others, are eye contact with your audience and hand gestures both considered forms of non-verbal communication?

1560. Can you make a short speech in front of an audience?

1561. How do you introduce yourself to others?

1562. Can you introduce a friend of yours to another friend?

1563. What important information would you need to write down when taking a telephone message?

1564. What is it called when you explain the content of a story or a report in your own words: re-wording or paraphrasing?

1565. Can you briefly *paraphrase* the story "The Three Pigs?" (Etc.)

1566. What is it called when you explain the main ideas of an informative article or report: paraphrasing or summarizing?

1567. Can you summarize a book or an article that you have read recently?

1568. What is the name of a diagram that indicates value with lines or bars: a graph or an x-ray?

1569. Can you read a chart, a table, and a graph?

LANGUAGE ARTS

1570. Where might you need to read a menu?

1571. Can you read a timeline?

1572. When might a timeline be a useful reference?

1573. What is the name of a planning tool that is often used to organize information by highlighting the main points: an outline or a list?

1574. What kind of materials include a dictionary, an atlas, the Internet, an encyclopedia, and a chart: resource or reference?

1575. Can you use reference materials to search for information?

1576. What reference material would you search to find the definition of a word?

1577. What reference material would you search to find other words that mean the same as **huge**: a dictionary or a thesaurus?

1578. When you look up "big" in a thesaurus, what words would be listed?

1579. What reference material would you search to find the location of Spain: an atlas or an almanac?

1580. What information would you find if you looked in an atlas?

1581. What is the name of the resource that is published once a year that contains statistics and facts about a wide variety of subjects: an almanac or an atlas?

1582. In what print resource organized by last name would you find the address of a neighbor?

1583. What reference material(s) would you use to search for information regarding George Washington?

1584. What reference material would you use to understand the population increases of a country per year: an atlas or an almanac?

1585. What resource would be most helpful if you need to find information about how to take care of a turtle: an almanac, an atlas, the Internet, or a telephone book?

1586. Can you skim and scan for information in a newspaper article?

1587. What kind of information would you find in a newspaper?

1588. What is the purpose of a *headline* in a newspaper?

1589. Does a news story contain the facts about a person or event, and explain who, what, when, where, and why?

1590. Can you write a news story?

1591. What is the name of the description underneath a picture in a newspaper: a headline or a caption?

1592. Can newspapers have more than one edition?

LANGUAGE ARTS

1593. Can you identify the parts of a book?

1594. What is the purpose of a *title* of a book?

1595. What are the sections called that novels and textbooks are divided into: chapters or units?

1596. What section of a book would you look at to find out the starting page for the chapter on the Civil War: the index or the table of contents?

1597. What is the alphabetical section at the end of a textbook called that lists each specific subject and page number: glossary or index?

1598. In what section of a textbook would you look up the meaning of the word "suffrage:" index or glossary?

1599. In a book about insects, where would you most likely find the page numbers for all the topics related to butterflies: the index, the glossary, or the table of contents?

1600. Does personal writing include writing an imaginative story or letter?

1601. What is the term for non-fiction text that provides information about people, places, things, or events: informational text or functional text?

1602. What would you write that would be considered informational text?

1603. If you were writing to persuade, would you include your opinion of the subject along with supporting data?

1604. What is the term for the writings that are used to help people perform a task, and include recipes, schedules, memos, and directions: informational text or functional text?

1605. What *functional* text writings do you read on a regular basis?

1606. Can you recognize and pronounce the common sight word "about?"(Show word!)

1607. Can you recognize and pronounce the common sight word "better?"(Show word!)

1608. Can you recognize and pronounce the common sight word "bring?"(Show word!)

1609. Can you recognize and pronounce the common sight word "carry?"(Show word!)

1610. Can you recognize and pronounce the common sight word "clean?"(Show word!)

1611. Can you recognize and pronounce the common sight word "cut?"(Show word!)

1612. Can you recognize and pronounce the common sight word "done?"(Show word!)

1613. Can you recognize and pronounce the common sight word "draw?"(Show word!)

1614. Can you recognize and pronounce the common sight word "drink?"(Show word!)

1615. Can you recognize and pronounce the common sight word "eight?"(Show word!)

1616. Can you recognize and pronounce the common sight word "fall?"(Show word!)

1617. Can you recognize and pronounce the common sight word "far?"(Show word!)

1618. Can you recognize and pronounce the common sight word "full?"(Show word!)

1619. Can you recognize and pronounce the common sight word "got?"(Show word!)

1620. Can you recognize and pronounce the common sight word "grow?"(Show word!)

1621. Can you recognize and pronounce the common sight word "hold?"(Show word!)

1622. Can you recognize and pronounce the common sight word "hot?"(Show word!)

1623. Can you recognize and pronounce the common sight word "hurt?"(Show word!)

1624. Can you recognize and pronounce the common sight word "if?"(Show word!)

1625. Can you recognize and pronounce the common sight word "keep?"(Show word!)

1626. Can you recognize and pronounce the common sight word "kind?"(Show word!)

1627. Can you recognize and pronounce the common sight word "laugh?"(Show word!)

1628. Can you recognize and pronounce the common sight word "life?"(Show word!)

1629. Can you recognize and pronounce the common sight word "long?"(Show word!)

1630. Can you recognize and pronounce the common sight word "much?"(Show word!)

1631. Can you recognize and pronounce the common sight word "myself?"(Show word!)

1632. Can you recognize and pronounce the common sight word "never?"(Show word!)

1633. Can you recognize and pronounce the common sight word "only?"(Show word!)

1634. Can you recognize and pronounce the common sight word "own?"(Show word!)

1635. Can you recognize and pronounce the common sight word "pick?"(Show word!)

1636. Can you recognize and pronounce the common sight word "seven?"(Show word!)

1637. Can you recognize and pronounce the common sight word "shall?"(Show word!)

1638. Can you recognize and pronounce the common sight word "show?"(Show word!)

1639. Can you recognize and pronounce the common sight word "six?"(Show word!)

1640. Can you recognize and pronounce the common sight word "small?"(Show word!)

1641. Can you recognize and pronounce the common sight word "start?"(Show word!)

1642. Can you recognize and pronounce the common sight word "ten?"(Show word!)

1643. Can you recognize and pronounce the common sight word "today?"(Show word!)

LANGUAGE ARTS

1644. Can you recognize and pronounce the common sight word "together?"(Show word!)

1645. Can you recognize and pronounce the common sight word "try?"(Show word!)

1646. Can you recognize and pronounce the common sight word "warm?"(Show word!)

Language Arts – 4th Grade

1647. What is the name of the general area that includes reading, writing, spelling, and composition: English or language arts?

1648. Can you read silently?

1649. Can you read aloud?

1650. Can you summarize out loud something that you have read?

1651. What is a short story that you have read?

1652. What is a chapter book that you have read?

1653. What is the name of a poem you have read?

1654. Do all poems have rhyme?

1655. What is the term for the division of lines in poetry: a stanza or a refrain?

1656. What is the name of the verse or phrase that is repeated often in a poem or a song: a refrain or a chorus?

1657. What is the term for the ordinary language that people use in speaking or writing that does not have the repeating rhythm that is used in verse: drama or prose?

1658. What is the name of the short, lyric poem that originated in Italy: sonnet or prose?

1659. How many lines does a sonnet have: twelve or fourteen?

1660. What famous English writer wrote many sonnets: William Shakespeare or Edgar Allan Poe?

1661. What is the name of a play you have read?

1662. Can you identify the title and the author of a book?

1663. Where is the table of contents located in a book?

1664. Where is the index located in a book?

1665. What do you use an index for: to look up the meaning of a word, or to find the page number that the topic is on?

1666. What is the name of the dictionary section of a textbook: an index or a glossary?

LANGUAGE ARTS

1667. What is the name of the beginning part that is written by the author to introduce the book: the foreword or the preface?

1668. What is the name given for the written addition at the end of the book: the preface or the appendix?

1669. Do you use a dictionary to look up the meaning of a word?

1670. What is another purpose for using a dictionary besides looking up the meaning of a word?

1671. What do you say when you answer the telephone?

1672. Can you make a prediction about what a story is about before reading it?

1673. Can you put all the events of a story in the proper sequence?

1674. Can you identify the main idea in a narrative text?

1675. Can you state the author's purpose when reading text?

1676. Can you state the supporting details when reading text?

1677. Can you compare two stories and say how they are similar?

1678. How do "Cinderella" and "Sleeping Beauty" compare?

1679. Can you contrast two stories and say how they are different?

1680. How do "Cinderella" and "Sleeping Beauty" contrast?

1681. What is the name for the action that occurs in a story that makes something else happen: compare and contrast or cause and effect?

1682. Which sentence is the cause and which sentence is the effect: "Pluto is one of the coldest planets." and, "Pluto is the farthest planet from the Sun?"

1683. What is the name of the reading genre that uses characters, plots, and settings to convey events that are **not** true?

1684. What is the name of the reading genre that uses real people, plots, and settings to convey actual events that are true?

1685. What is the name of the reading genre that uses animals who act and speak like people and that teaches a moral lesson: a fable or a folktale?

1686. Which author is famous for writing the fables: "The Tortoise and the Hare," and "The Boy Who Cried Wolf:" Aesop or Shakespeare?

1687. What is the name of the reading genre that is a made-up story with folk heroes like "Paul Bunyan," and "Pecos Bill," and is passed down from one generation to the next: a tall tale or a myth?

1688. What is the name for the story that is presented with dialogue and action: drama or prose?

LANGUAGE ARTS

1689. What is the name of an account of someone's life that is written by another person: a biography or a bibliography?

1690. What is the name of a traditional story that has been passed down from person to person like "Robin Hood," and has important meaning: a legend or a fairy tale?

1691. Is "Sleepy Hollow" by Washington Irving an example of a legend?

1692. Is "King Arthur and the Knights of the Round Table" an English legend?

1693. Is "Robin Hood" an English legend or an Irish legend?

1694. What is the name of a story that often includes gods and heroes as in "Zeus," and "Pandora's Box:" a myth or a legend?

1695. Is "Hercules" an example of a Greek myth or a Roman myth?

1696. What is the name of a narrative poem that has a refrain, tells a story, and is often sung: a ballad or a limerick?

1697. What is the name of a five-line humorous poem originating from Ireland whereby lines 1, 2, and 5 rhyme as in "There Once Was a Man from Nantucket:" a limerick or a sonnet?

1698. What is the name for the literary device found in many works of literature that uses ridicule or sarcasm aimed at someone or something, and is evident in many political cartoons: satire or epic?

1699. What is the name for the story in which the events and characters are symbols that stand for truths about something in life and teach a lesson as in "Moby Dick:" an allegory or a limerick?

1700. What is the name for an extended literary poem that has been passed down from ancient civilizations that celebrates the feats of a legendary hero as in, "The Iliad," "The Odyssey," "Beowulf," and Dante's "The Divine Comedy:" lyrical poem or epic?

1701. What is the term that includes plot, theme, characters, and setting: literary elements or story line?

1702. What is the literary term called when you use the clues in the text to get a sense of what will happen next: foreshadowing or predicting?

1703. What is the name of the literary term that is an extreme exaggeration of what something really is: allegory or hyperbole?

1704. What is the term for the figure of speech that compares two unlike things as in "cheeks like roses:" a simile or a metaphor?

1705. What is the term for the figure of speech that compares two unlike things *without* using the words like or as: a simile or a metaphor?

1706. Is the phrase, "*their cheeks were roses*" a simile or a metaphor?

1707. What is the literary term for a sentence in poetry where several of the words start with the same consonant as in **P**eter **P**iper **P**icked a **P**eck of **P**ickled **P**eppers: alliteration or onomatopoeia?

LANGUAGE ARTS

1708. What is the literary term given for the sound we say something makes as in "The snake hissed," "The bee buzzed," or, "The wolf howled at the moon: onomatopoeia or alliteration?

1709. What is the literary term when human qualities are given to objects or animals as in, "this city never sleeps," "the stars winked at me," and "lightning danced across the sky:" alliteration or personification?

1710. How do you finish the saying: "Beauty is only skin _?"

1711. How do you finish the saying: "The bigger they are, the harder they _?"

1712. How do you finish the saying: "Bull in a china _?"

1713. How do you finish the saying: "Bury the _?"

1714. How do you finish the saying: "Make ends _?"

1715. How do you finish the saying: "Don't put all your eggs in one _?"

1716. How do you finish the saying: "Don't count your chickens before they _?"

1717. How do you finish the saying: "One picture is worth a thousand _?"

1718. How do you finish the saying: "Two wrongs don't make a _?"

1719. How do you finish the saying: "Can't hold a candle _?"

1720. How do you finish the saying: "Seeing is _?"

1721. How do you finish the saying: "Half a loaf is better than _?"

1722. How do you finish the saying: "Haste makes _?"

1723. How do you finish the saying: "Lightning never strikes twice in the same _?"

1724. How do you finish the saying: "Once in a blue _?"

1725. How do you finish the saying: "An ounce of prevention is worth a pound of _?"

1726. How do you finish the saying: "When it rains it _?"

1727. How do you finish the saying: "Live and let _?"

1728. How do you finish the saying: "Through thick and _?"

1729. How do you finish the saying: "You can lead a horse to water, but you can't make it __?"

1730. What is etc. an abbreviation for, that means "and so on"?

1731. What is the French abbreviation that is often included on a written invitation when the person writing the invitation wishes for a response, and is short for, "**R**epondez **S**'il **V**ous **P**lait?"

1732. Can you print using both upper case and lower case letters?

LANGUAGE ARTS

1733. Are you developing your skill in writing in cursive?

1734. Can you write a letter to a friend or to a family member?

1735. Can you write an email?

1736. Can you write a poem?

1737. Can you write a report about a topic that interests you?

1738. If you use written ideas from a source, what do you need to include in your report that gives credit to the author of that source: a biography or a bibliography?

1739. What information would be included in a bibliography?

1740. What is the alphabetical order of the bibliography: author's first name or author's last name?

1741. Can you write a book report?

1742. Can you write a description of a holiday, an object, or a person?

1743. Can you write a thank you note?

1744. Can you outline the main points from something that you have read?

1745. Can you write a written summary of something that you have read?

1746. Can you write a summary of what you did today?

1747. What is the name of the process that includes pre-writing, drafting, revising, editing, and publishing: writing or proofreading?

1748. What is the name of your first attempt to write down all of your ideas in an essay format, after you have at put together all of your thoughts: rough draft or outline?

1749. What is the first sentence of a paragraph called that tells us what the main idea of the paragraph is: a thesis statement or a topic sentence?

1750. What is the sentence called at the end of a paragraph: a topic sentence or a concluding sentence?

1751. Can you write a concluding paragraph at the end of a report?

1752. What is the name of a story that you write that includes a plot, setting, point of view, conflict, and has a closing paragraph at the end: prose or drama?

1753. Do you use transitional words in your writing like next, finally, and in conclusion?

1754. Do you using several descriptive adjectives and verbs in your writing?

1755. Can you write something to persuade, inform, and entertain?

1756. What could you write about to persuade someone to do something?

1757. What could you write about to inform someone about something?

LANGUAGE ARTS

1758. What could you write about to entertain someone?

1759. Can you write a reflective *response* to literature, making a judgment about what you read?

1760. What resources could you use if you were writing a *research* paper?

1761. What resource would you look in to find basic information about frogs: an almanac, a thesaurus, or an encyclopedia?

1762. What resource would you look in to find a synonym for delicious: a dictionary or a thesaurus?

1763. What resource would you look at to find the meaning of concave: a dictionary or a thesaurus?

1764. What resource would you look at to find the longitude of Sweden: an atlas or an almanac?

1765. What resource would you look at to find information about the Aztec culture: an almanac or an online encyclopedia?

1766. Do you have basic computer keyboard skills for typing a paper or report?

1767. Does learning grammar include being familiar with the parts of speech?

1768. What is the name of the grammatical construction in which a noun is followed by another noun, e.g., "My uncle, the doctor…" that helps to explain it: apposition or alliteration?

1769. How many parts of speech are there in the English language: eight or twelve?

1770. What major part of speech is missing in the following list: Noun, adjective, pronoun, adverb, preposition, conjunction, and interjection?

1771. What part of speech refers to a person, animal, place, thing, or idea?

1772. What is the *noun* in the sentence: "The cheetah ran swiftly?"

1773. What part of speech describes or *modifies* a noun: a pronoun or an adjective?

1774. What is the *adjective* in the sentence: "Rusty is a smart dog?"

1775. What part of speech takes the place of a noun: a pronoun or a contraction?

1776. What is the pronoun is the sentence: "He is a smart dog?"

1777. What pronoun would take the place of *Alex*?

1778. What pronoun would take the place of *Rebecca*?

1779. What pronoun would replace *the car*?

1780. What pronoun would replace *Andrew and Zachary*?

1781. Are the words I, she, he, and it considered *personal* pronouns or *possessive* pronouns?

1782. Are the words mine, yours, his, hers, ours considered *personal* pronouns or *possessive* pronouns?

LANGUAGE ARTS

1783. What part of speech describes the main action in a sentence?

1784. What is the *verb* in the sentence: "I jumped over the rock?"

1785. Do all sentences have a subject and a verb?

1786. What part of speech tells how an action occurred: an adjective or an adverb?

1787. What is the *adverb* in the sentence: "He ran quickly to the park?"

1788. What is the *adverb* in the sentence: "Emily plays the piano well?"

1789. What is the name for the part of speech that shows location and links nouns, pronouns, and phrases to the other parts of a sentence: conjunction or preposition?

1790. Are the words *in, at, around, to, through, toward,* and *above* considered conjunctions or prepositions?

1791. What is the preposition in the sentence: "The alarm clock is beside the bed?"

1792. What is the preposition in the sentence: "My jacket is on the chair?"

1793. Are the phrases, "over the hill, behind the door, and outside the house" prepositional phrases or adverbial phrases?

1794. What part of speech joins words or phrases in a sentence: an interjection or a conjunction?

1795. What is the *conjunction* in the sentence: "I sold cakes and cookies?"

1796. What is the *conjunction* in the sentence: "I wanted to go but I had to study?"

1797. What part of speech is included in a sentence for effect and emphasis: an interjection or a conjunction?

1798. What is the *interjection* in this sentence: "Wow! That was a great show?"

1799. Does a *complete* sentence include a subject and a predicate?

1800. Does a *clause* contain both a subject and a verb?

1801. What is the subject in the sentence: "Jack loves ice cream?"

1802. What is the predicate in the sentence: "Jack loves ice cream?"

1803. What kind of sentence would you have if you left out a predicate or a subject: a run-on or a fragment?

1804. Is the sentence, "Visited Disneyworld last year" a fragment or a run-on?

1805. What word could you add to the beginning of "Visited Disneyworld" to make it a complete sentence?

1806. Is the sentence, "I went to Chicago it is a big city" a fragment or a run-on sentence?

LANGUAGE ARTS

1807. How can we divide the sentence, "I went to Chicago it is a big city" into two separate sentences?

1808. How would you combine the following run-on sentence to make one sentence: "Lisa made cookies. Michael made cookies?"

1809. What is the correct verb form in the sentence: "I am /are tall?"

1810. What is the correct verb form in the sentence: "He is/are funny?

1811. What is the correct verb form in the sentence: "They is/are outside?"

1812. What is the correct verb form in the sentence: "My friend Nathan live/lives in Ohio?"

1813. What is the correct verb form in the sentence: "A pack of wolves was/were running through the woods?"

1814. What kind of sentence is in the form of a statement: a declarative or an imperative?

1815. What kind of sentence is in the form of a question: an interrogative or a declarative?

1816. What kind of sentence expresses strong feelings: declarative or exclamatory?

1817. What kind of sentence gives instructions or expresses a command: declarative or imperative?

1818. What kind of sentence is, "It is windy today:" a declarative, an imperative, an interrogative, or an exclamatory sentence?

1819. What punctuation mark does a declarative sentence end with?

1820. What kind of sentence is, "Are you going to the party:" a declarative, an imperative, an interrogative, or an exclamatory sentence?

1821. What punctuation mark does an interrogative sentence end with?

1822. How do you say the sentence, "*The game is over.*" with an interrogative voice?

1823. How do you say the sentence, "*The game is over.*" with a declarative voice?

1824. What kind of sentence is, "We won the championship:" a declarative, an imperative, an interrogative, or an exclamatory sentence?

1825. What punctuation mark does an imperative sentence often end with?

1826. What kind of sentence is similar to a command or an order: declarative or imperative?

1827. What kind of sentence is, "Go walk the dog:" a declarative, an imperative, an interrogative, or an exclamatory?

1828. What punctuation mark tells a reader when to pause in a sentence?

1829. Where is the comma placed in the date *December 7 1949?*

1830. Where is the comma placed in the sentence, "*Yes you may go the park?*"

LANGUAGE ARTS

1831. Where is the comma placed when you address an envelope to *Orlando FL*?

1832. Is a comma placed before or after the quotation marks in the dialog phrase, "I have a surprise for you," said Brian?

1833. Is a comma placed before or after the conjunctions "and" or "but," when connecting two independent clauses?

1834. Where is the comma placed in the sentence, "Sticks and stones may break my bones but words can never hurt me?

1835. What separates items that are listed in a series of two or more: periods or commas?

1836. Where are the commas placed in the sentence, "Samantha brought cookies brownies and cupcakes to sell at the bake sale?

1837. What is the correct punctuation mark when introducing a list of ideas, or setting off a quotation: a comma or a colon?

1838. What is the punctuation mark that looks like a dot with a comma underneath it that is used to separate parts of a sentence, or to separate main clauses: a colon or a semi-colon?

1839. What is the punctuation mark that looks like two dots that is used to call attention to what follows such as a list or an explanation: a colon or a semi-colon?

1840. What punctuation mark do you use after the greeting *Dear Sirs* in a business letter: a semi-colon or a colon?

1841. What punctuation mark do you use after *Dear Krista* in a personal letter: a colon or a comma?

1842. What punctuation mark do you use between the hours and the minutes when writing the time six fifteen: a comma or a colon?

1843. What punctuation mark do you use between a title and a sub-title: a colon or a semi-colon?

1844. What is the name of the punctuation mark that is used to show possession: an apostrophe or a comma?

1845. Where is the apostrophe placed in the phrase: "My friends house?"

1846. Is the apostrophe placed before or after the "s" if the noun is already plural and ends in letter "s?"

1847. Where is the apostrophe placed in the sentence: "The girls (plural) room was a mess?"

1848. Where is the apostrophe placed in the phrase: "The dogs (singular) house?"

1849. What is the name of the punctuation mark used in a contraction: a comma or an apostrophe?

1850. What can an apostrophe take the place of in a contraction: a letter or a word?

1851. Where is the apostrophe placed to make the contraction meaning we are from *w-e-r-e*?

LANGUAGE ARTS

1852. What letter is the apostrophe replacing in the contraction *we're*?

1853. What letter is the apostrophe replacing in the contraction *isn't*?

1854. What is the contraction for the words *do not*?

1855. What is the contraction for the words *I would*?

1856. What is the contraction for the words *they are*?

1857. What two words make up the contraction *she's*?

1858. What two words make up the contraction *I'll*?

1859. What two words make up the contraction *you're*?

1860. What two words make up the contraction *didn't*?

1861. What two words make up the contraction *won't*?

1862. What do you call the punctuation marks that are used in text to indicate the *exact* words of the speaker?

1863. Are the titles of poems, articles, and short stories set off in quotation marks?

1864. Where would the quotation marks be placed in the following sentence: I have a game tonight, said Jordan?

1865. What is a word called that means the same thing as another word: a synonym or an antonym?

1866. What is a synonym of spotless?

1867. What is a synonym of buddy?

1868. What is a synonym of attempt?

1869. What is a synonym of lady?

1870. What is a synonym of strange?

1871. What is a synonym of happy?

1872. What is a word called that means the opposite of another word: a synonym or an antonym?

1873. What is an antonym of fail?

1874. What is an antonym of true?

1875. What is an antonym of cheap?

1876. What is an antonym of sunny?

1877. What is an antonym of liquid?

LANGUAGE ARTS

1878. What is an antonym of out-going?

1879. What is an antonym of wet?

1880. What is an antonym of near?

1881. What is an antonym of over?

1882. What is an antonym of soft?

1883. What is an antonym of rough?

1884. What are groups of letters called that are added to the beginning of a word to form a new word that has a different meaning: a suffix or a prefix?

1885. What is the meaning of the prefixes non-, im-, and in-: *not* or *wrong*?

1886. What is the prefix of the word *impossible*?

1887. What is the meaning of the word *impossible*?

1888. What is the prefix of the word *invisible*?

1889. What is the meaning of the word *invisible*?

1890. What is the prefix of the word *nonfiction*?

1891. What is the meaning of the word *nonfiction*?

1892. What is the meaning of the prefix **mis**: *not* or *wrong*?

1893. What is the prefix of the word *misbehave*?

1894. What is the meaning of the word *misbehave*?

1895. What is the meaning of the prefix **pre**: before or after?

1896. What is the prefix of the word *pregame*?

1897. What is the meaning of the word *pregame?*

1898. What is the meaning of the prefix **en**: out or in?

1899. What is the prefix of the word *endanger*?

1900. What is the meaning of the word *endanger*?

1901. Are suffixes added to the beginning or to the end of a word?

1902. What suffix is often used to form an adverb: -ly or -ful?

1903. What is the suffix in the adverb *swiftly*?

1904. What suffix can you add to the adjective *easy* to make it an adverb: -ly or -ily?

LANGUAGE ARTS

1905. What suffix can you add to the word *sleep* to make it an adjective: -ly or -y?

1906. What is the meaning of the suffix -ful: *capable of* or *full of*?

1907. What is the suffix in the word *playful*?

1908. What is the meaning of the suffix -able or -ible: *capable of* or *full of*?

1909. What is the suffix of the word *washable*?

1910. What is the suffix of the word *flexible*?

1911. Is the suffix –*ment* used to turn a verb into a noun or a noun into a verb?

1912. What suffix is added to the verb *agree* to make it a noun?

1913. By removing the suffix, how would you change the word *achievement* from a noun to a verb?

1914. What is the name of the word that does *not* have a prefix or suffix: a stem word or a Latin word?

1915. What is the stem of the word *undeniable*?

1916. What is the term given to a word that is spelled the same in both directions, e.g. eye, pop, kayak, madam, deed, level, radar, and racecar: a palindrome or a homogram?

1917. What is the term for a phrase whose meaning cannot be directly understood from the meaning of the words contained in it as in, "You are pulling my leg:" a homophone or an idiom?

1918. Would a person who does not speak fluent English have an easy or hard time understanding idioms?

1919. Can you recognize and pronounce the common sight word "action?" (Show word)

1920. Can you recognize and pronounce the common sight word "actually?" (Show word)

1921. Can you recognize and pronounce the common sight word "alive?" (Show word)

1922. Can you recognize and pronounce the common sight word "although?" (Show word)

1923. Can you recognize and pronounce the common sight word "amount?" (Show word)

1924. Can you recognize and pronounce the common sight word "area?" (Show word)

1925. Can you recognize and pronounce the common sight word "blood?" (Show word)

1926. Can you recognize and pronounce the common sight word "cause?" (Show word)

1927. Can you recognize and pronounce the common sight word "central?" (Show word)

1928. Can you recognize and pronounce the common sight word "century?" (Show word)

1929. Can you recognize and pronounce the common sight word "charcoal?" (Show word)

1930. Can you recognize and pronounce the common sight word "chart?" (Show word)

LANGUAGE ARTS

1931. Can you recognize and pronounce the common sight word "check?" (Show word)

1932. Can you recognize and pronounce the common sight word "club?" (Show word)

1933. Can you recognize and pronounce the common sight word "colony?" (Show word)

1934. Can you recognize and pronounce the common sight word "company?" (Show word)

1935. Can you recognize and pronounce the common sight word "condition?" (Show word)

1936. Can you recognize and pronounce the common sight word "court?" (Show word)

1937. Can you recognize and pronounce the common sight word "deal?" (Show word)

1938. Can you recognize and pronounce the common sight word "death?" (Show word)

1939. Can you recognize and pronounce the common sight word "describe?" (Show word)

1940. Can you recognize and pronounce the common sight word "design?" (Show word)

1941. Can you recognize and pronounce the common sight word "disease?" (Show word)

1942. Can you recognize and pronounce the common sight word "eleven?" (Show word)

1943. Can you recognize and pronounce the common sight word "equal?" (Show word)

1944. Can you recognize and pronounce the common sight word "experience?" (Show word)

1945. Can you recognize and pronounce the common sight word "factor?" (Show word)

1946. Can you recognize and pronounce the common sight word "favorite?" (Show word)

1947. Can you recognize and pronounce the common sight word "figure?" (Show word)

1948. Can you recognize and pronounce the common sight word "hospital?" (Show word)

1949. Can you recognize and pronounce the common sight word "include?" (Show word)

1950. Can you recognize and pronounce the common sight word "increase?" (Show word)

1951. Can you recognize and pronounce the common sight word "known?" (Show word)

1952. Can you recognize and pronounce the common sight word "least?" (Show word)

1953. Can you recognize and pronounce the common sight word "length?" (Show word)

1954. Can you recognize and pronounce the common sight word "loud?" (Show word)

1955. Can you recognize and pronounce the common sight word "measure?" (Show word)

1956. Can you recognize and pronounce the common sight word "molecule?" (Show word)

1957. Can you recognize and pronounce the common sight word "national?" (Show word)

1958. Can you recognize and pronounce the common sight word "necessary?" (Show word)

LANGUAGE ARTS

1959. Can you recognize and pronounce the common sight word "noun?" (Show word)

1960. Can you recognize and pronounce the common sight word "oxygen?" (Show word)

1961. Can you recognize and pronounce the common sight word "phrase?" (Show word)

1962. Can you recognize and pronounce the common sight word "property?" (Show word)

1963. Can you recognize and pronounce the common sight word "radio?" (Show word)

1964. Can you recognize and pronounce the common sight word "receive?" (Show word)

1965. Can you recognize and pronounce the common sight word "replace?" (Show word)

1966. Can you recognize and pronounce the common sight word "rhythm?" (Show word)

1967. Can you recognize and pronounce the common sight word "serve?" (Show word)

1968. Can you recognize and pronounce the common sight word "similar?" (Show word)

1969. Can you recognize and pronounce the common sight word "southern?" (Show word)

1970. Can you recognize and pronounce the common sight word "squirrel?" (Show word)

1971. Can you recognize and pronounce the common sight word "straight?" (Show word)

1972. Can you recognize and pronounce the common sight word "subtle?" (Show word)

1973. Can you recognize and pronounce the common sight word "suffix?" (Show word)

1974. Can you recognize and pronounce the common sight word "surely?" (Show word)

1975. Can you recognize and pronounce the common sight word "though?" (Show word)

1976. Can you recognize and pronounce the common sight word "thought?" (Show word)

1977. Can you recognize and pronounce the common sight word "touch?" (Show word)

1978. Can you recognize and pronounce the common sight word "twice?" (Show word)

1979. Can you recognize and pronounce the common sight word "used?" (Show word)

1980. Can you recognize and pronounce the common sight word "usually?" (Show word)

1981. Can you recognize and pronounce the common sight word "view?" (Show word)

1982. Can you recognize and pronounce the common sight word "weight?" (Show word)

1983. Can you recognize and pronounce the common sight word "wheat?" (Show word)

1984. Can you recognize and pronounce the common sight word "whom?" (Show word)

1985. Can you recognize and pronounce the common sight word "young?" (Show word)

LANGUAGE ARTS

Language Arts – 5th Grade

1986. What are poetry, drama, music, mystery, horror, romance, fantasy, science fiction, biography, and autobiography all considered: genres, literary works, or language arts?

1987. What are the two main genres in literature, one based on reality, the other imaginary?

1988. What is the name of the genre written for children 2-12 that often has big text and pictures: children's literature or youth literature?

1989. What is the name of the genre that involves an imaginary or magical theme, setting, and characters: fantasy or unrealistic fiction?

1990. What is the name of the genre that involves an unsolved murder or puzzle that the reader tries to figure out with the clues that are given: mystery or adventure?

1991. What is the name of the genre that involves scare tactics to reach the emotions of the reader: fantasy or horror?

1992. What is the name of the genre that involves a love story and finding happiness with another person: mystery or romance?

1993. What is the name of the genre that involves extraordinary situations that are full of suspense, action, and adventure: a thriller or a western?

1994. What is the name of the genre that is the written account of a person's life written by another person: a biography or an autobiography?

1995. What is the name of the genre that is the written account of a person's life as told by that person: a biography or an autobiography?

1996. What is the name of the genre that involves speaking or oral communication: a speech or a presentation?

1997. Are biographies, historical essays, and speeches considered fiction or non-fiction?

1998. What is the name of the fiction verse or prose often used for a theatrical performance, where emotion and conflict are expressed through dialogue and action: drama or poetry?

1999. What is the name of the verse format that may contain rhythm, emotion, and imagination, and is written to appeal to the reader's emotions: fantasy or poetry?

2000. What is the name of the genre that is a story about the extraordinary or supernatural, where animals often speak as humans: fable or fairy tale

2001. What is the name of the wonder tale that may be a type of fable or folktale often about fairies or other creatures, and are aimed at children: fantasy or fairy tale?

2002. What is the name of the genre based on science that is often set in the future, or on another celestial body: realistic fiction or science fiction?

2003. What is the name of a story that can actually happen and is true in real life: realistic fiction or folklore?

2004. What is the genre name given for songs, myths, and stories that are often passed down the generations by word of mouth: folklore or fable?

2005. What is the genre name given to a story with characters and events in a historical setting: realistic fiction or historical fiction?

2006. What is the genre given to a story that is shocking or terrifying in which the characters and events create feelings of fear for the reader: fantasy or horror?

2007. What is the genre name given to a humorous story full of exaggerations, with characters that do the impossible: legend or tall tale?

2008. What is the genre name given to a fact-based story about a folk hero, and often includes imaginative details as well: tall tale or legend?

2009. What is the genre name given to a type of legend that is often based on historical events that is expressed with symbolism and the actions of gods: legend or mythology?

2010. Are narratives, essays, biographies, history, and speeches fiction or non-fiction?

2011. What is the term for a short composition on a specific topic that reflects an author's viewpoint: an essay or a narrative?

2012. What is the general term for factual text that deals with an actual subject?

2013. What is the general term for literary works that are not based on fact, and are invented or imagined stories?

2014. What is the literary term for a story or song-like poem that tells a story: a poem or a ballad?

2015. What is the literary term for a poem that tells a story from a narrative point of view: a narrative poem or a lyric poem?

2016. What is the literary term for a rhyming poem that expresses the author's feelings: a lyric poem or a narrative poem?

2017. What is the literary term for a poem that is an original work with no rhyme or pattern syllable repetition: a lyric poem or free verse?

2018. What is the term for a grouping of related lines in a poem: a paragraph or a stanza?

2019. What is the term in poetry for the pattern of rhyming words within each stanza such as ABAB or ABBA: rhyme scheme or rhyme pattern?

2020. What is the term in poetry for the regular beat that is a measure of how your voice rises and falls when you read a poem: stress or meter?

2021. What is the term in poetry for the rhyme established by a poem: stress or meter?

LANGUAGE ARTS

2022. What was the most common meter in English poetry consisting of an unstressed syllable followed by a stressed syllable, and was used extensively by Shakespeare in his poems: syllable verse or iambic pentameter?

2023. What is the term for a certain kind of stanza that was popular in England during the 17th and 18th centuries that consists of two lines that rhyme with one another: a duet or a couplet?

2024. What is the literary term for a five line humorous poem whereas lines 1, 2, and 5 rhyme and lines 3 and 4 rhyme: a limerick or a cinquain?

2025. What is the literary term for a five-line poem that does not rhyme, line 1 is a noun, line 2 has two adjectives, line 3 has three "-ing" words, line 4 has four statement words, and line 5 has a synonym for the noun in line 1: a limerick or a cinquain?

2026. What is the literary term for a four-line poem that repeats a rhyme pattern: a quatrain or a cinquain?

2027. What is the literary term given for a Japanese three-line poem that celebrates something in nature, and has a syllable pattern containing five, seven, and five syllables respectively: a limerick or haiku?

2028. What is the name of the greatest storyteller and oral poet of ancient Greece who told the two famous epics called "The Iliad" and "The Odyssey," about great heroes and famous deeds: Homer or Apollo?

2029. What is the literary term given to a work that has spoken lines, and is performed for an audience by actors: a musical or a play?

2030. Can songs that rhyme be considered a form of poetry?

2031. Do all poems have to rhyme?

2032. Was Henry Wadsworth Longfellow, author of "The Arrow and the Song" and "Paul Revere's Ride," a famous American songwriter or a famous American poet?

2033. What famous English poet is the author of "The Road Not Taken" and "Fire and Ice:" Robert Frost or Ralph Waldo Emerson?

2034. What famous American poet is the author of "The Snow Storm" and "Ode to Beauty:" Ralph Waldo Emerson or Walt Whitman?

2035. What famous American poet is the author of "I Hear America Singing," "Leaves of Grass," and "Song of Myself:" Walt Whitman or Emily Dickenson?

2036. What famous African-American poet is the author of "Narcissa" and "We Real Cool:" Gwendolyn Brooks or Emily Dickenson?

2037. What famous American poet is the author of "A Bird Came Down the Walk" and "I'm Nobody! Who are You?:" Elizabeth Browning or Emily Dickenson?

2038. What famous English poet is the author of "The Tyger" and "A Poison Tree:" William Blake or Walt Whitman?

LANGUAGE ARTS

2039. What famous English author wrote the poems "Jabberwocky" and "The Hunting of the Snark," as well as the novels, "Alice's Adventures in Wonderland" and "Through the Looking Glass:" Robert Frost or Lewis Carroll?

2040. What famous English romantic poet wrote "Ode to a Nightingale" and "To My Brother George:" John Keats or Ralph Waldo Emerson?

2041. What American writer and poet is most famous for his book "Walden," a reflection of living a simple life in natural surroundings, as well as the essay "Civil Disobedience:" Henry David Thoreau or John Keats?

2042. What American author and poet was most famous for his short stories that included *The Pit and the Pendulum, The Masque of the Red Death,* and *The Tell-Tale Heart,* as well as the poems, *The Haunted Palace* and *The Raven*: Ralph Waldo Emerson or Edgar Allan Poe?

2043. What English poet wrote "She Walks in Beauty" and "When We Two Parted," as well as his renowned narrative poem, "Don Juan:" Lord Byron or Edgar Allan Poe?

2044. What is the name of the blind 17th century English poet who is best known for his epic poem "Paradise Lost," that was originally published in 1667 in ten books, and has over 10,000 lines of verse: John Milton or Lord Byron?

2045. What is the name of one of the most prominent poets of the Victorian era who is famous for her poems and sonnets including the love sonnet, "How do I love thee? Let me count the ways:" Emily Dickenson or Elizabeth Barrett Browning?

2046. What is the name of the contemporary (1928-2014) African-American poet and author regarded as a global renaissance woman, who authored several books and poems including the poems, "And Still I Rise" and "I Know Why the Caged Bird Sings:" Maya Angelou or Elizabeth Browning?

2047. What is the name of a 14-line verse that may be Italian, English, or Shakespearean, and has a fixed rhyme scheme: a sonnet or a sonata?

2048. What is the literary term given to a short work of literature that can be read in one sitting and typically has a simple storyline: a short story or a novel?

2049. What is the literary term given for a short non-fiction work on a specific topic, written in a magazine or a newspaper that is written to inform: an essay or an article?

2050. What is the literary term given for a long story that usually involves a setting, plot, and many characters: a short story or a novel?

2051. What is the literary term given to describe the written or oral communication between at least two people, where several questions are asked and answered: an autobiography or an interview?

2052. What are the two main divisions of books in a library?

2053. What are the different formats that books can be available in?

2054. Who might benefit from books written in large print?

LANGUAGE ARTS

2055. What is the name of the classification system used in a library to shelve books according to their subject or author?

2056. What is the name of the person who writes a story, poem, article, or novel?

2057. What is the name of the person who writes a drama: an author or a playwright?

2058. What is the name of a book or story called?

2059. What is the term given either to a literary work that has a secondary title, or the printed translation of the dialog of a foreign language film: caption or sub-title?

2060. What is the name of the person who draws the pictures for a story or book?

2061. What is the name of the sections or divisions that a novel is divided into?

2062. What is the name of the section at the beginning of a non-fiction work that outlines the different topics contained in the book and their corresponding page numbers?

2063. What is the name of the section at the end of a non-fiction book or textbook that contains an alphabetical list of *terms* contained within the book along with its definition?

2064. What is the name of the section at the end of a non-fiction book or textbook that facilitates reference in that it contains an alphabetical list of names, places, and subjects in the work, giving the page or pages on which each item is mentioned?

2065. What is the name of the legal right that is granted to an author, composer, playwright, or publisher to keep the exclusive right to produce and control the content of the work?

2066. What is the name of the person or company that is listed at the beginning of a book that is responsible for printing and distributing the book, newspaper, or magazine?

2067. What is the name of the alphabetical compilation of sources cited by an author at the end of a book that were referred to in the text, giving credit to those works: bibliography or autobiography?

2068. Does a bibliography of a book source include the author's name, the book's title, the place of publication, the publisher, the date, and the page or pages where the information was found?

2069. What is the name for a reference providing an alphabetical list of words with guide words at the top of each page that may include the word's meaning, syllable divisions, pronunciation, or translation?

2070. What is the name for a reference providing an alphabetical list of synonyms, words that are similar in meaning?

2071. What is the name for the reference tool that is a collection of maps?

2072. What is the name for the annual publication that contains a calendar, weather forecasts, tides, and other weather and astronomical data: atlas or almanac?

2073. What is the name for the satellite-based electronic navigation tool: a GPS or a GSP?

LANGUAGE ARTS

2074. Does GPS stand for **G**lobal **P**ositioning **S**ystem?

2075. What is the term for "GPS," that is an abbreviation using the first letters of each word: an antonym or an acronym?

2076. Are FBI, CIA, and NCAA antonyms or acronyms?

2077. What acronyms can you name?

2078. Is ALA an acronym for the American Library Association?

2079. What is the literary term that tells the events of a story in a logical order, and includes an introduction, rising action, climax, falling action, and a final outcome: the plot or the setting?

2080. What is the name of an essential part of a plot that can be either internal or external, and may be man vs. man, man vs. society, man vs. circumstances, or man vs. himself: the storyline, the conflict, or the characters?

2081. What is the literary term for where the story takes place, and may include place, historical period, weather conditions, social conditions, and mood: the location or the setting?

2082. What is the literary term given for the people, animals, or imaginary creatures in a story: the characters or the actors?

2083. What is the name of the main character of a story: the protagonist or the antagonist?

2084. What is the name of the person that is the opposer of the main character: the protagonist or the antagonist?

2085. What is the literary term given for the angle from which a story is told: point of view or opinion?

2086. What is the point of view in a story if it is told through the eyes of the protagonist or main character, using pronouns "I," "me," and "my:" first person or third person?

2087. What is the point of view in a story that is narrated by the author in the third person using pronouns "they," "she," "he," or "it:" third person or omniscient?

2088. What is the literary term for the central or controlling idea in a piece of fiction like, "love is blind," or, "things are not always as they appear to be:" the plot or the theme?

2089. What is the literary term given for the reason an author decides to write about a specific topic either to entertain the reader, or to persuade the reader to believe in something: the author's purpose or the author's style?

2090. What is the literary term given to the thing that reveals the unique personality and voice of the author through the author's word choice, dialog, tone, mood, and either formal or informal language: the author's style or the author's point of view?

2091. What is the name of the renowned children's award in the United States that honors the author who has made the most distinguished contribution to American literature for children, and is awarded by the American Library Association: the Newbery or the Caldecott?

LANGUAGE ARTS

2092. What is the name of the literary medal that honors the best children's picture book of the year: the Newbery or the Caldecott?

2093. What is the name of the prestigious prize that is awarded annually to an outstanding contributor not only in the field of literature, but also has recognized achievement since 1901 in physics, chemistry, medicine, peace, and economics: the Pulitzer or the Nobel?

2094. What is the name of the prestigious prize that is awarded annually to the thirteen best achievements in American journalism, literature, and music: the Pulitzer or the Nobel?

2095. What is the term given to a popular, top-selling book that is recognized by many outlets, including the weekly and monthly lists provided by the New York Times newspaper?

2096. How are best-seller books divided: by language or by genre?

2097. What is it name of the process of changing the words of one language into another like English to Spanish or Spanish to English: translation or interpretation?

2098. Does a translator translate the written or spoken words from one language to another?

2099. Does an interpreter translate the written or spoken words from one language to another?

2100. What language or languages do you speak?

2101. Does the United States have an official language?

2102. What is the second most common language spoken in the United States?

2103. What is the term for a person that speaks one native language: monolingual or bilingual?

2104. What is the term for a person that can fluently speak two languages: bilingual or multi-lingual?

2105. What is the term for a person that can fluently speak more than two languages: bilingual or multi-lingual?

2106. What is the most commonly spoken language in the world: Mandarin Chinese or English?

2107. What language comes after Mandarin Chinese and Hindi in terms of how many people in the world speak that language: English or Spanish?

2108. What is the language spoken by many people of North America, South America, Central America, and Spain, that ranks right after English in terms of the amount of people that speak it?

2109. Do you think some distinct ethnic groups and tribes in the United States and the world still speak and communicate in their own native language?

2110. Do you think some languages are dying out, because fewer and fewer people speak them?

2111. What is your estimate on the number of living languages, not including dialects that are still spoken today: 3,000 or 7,000?

2112. What is the most widely published language: Chinese, English, or Spanish?

LANGUAGE ARTS

2113. What is the study of the structure of a language called: linguistics or phonetics?

2114. Do we have linguistic diversity in the United States?

2115. Do many of our English words have Greek and Latin roots?

2116. What does the Greek root "aero" mean, as in aerodynamics, aerate, or aerobics?

2117. What does the Greek root "ast" mean, as in astronaut, asteroid or astronomy?

2118. What does the Greek root "biblio" mean, as in Bible or bibliography?

2119. What does the Greek root "bio" mean, as in biography or biology?

2120. What does the Greek root "cosm" mean, as in cosmos, cosmic, or cosmopolitan?

2121. What does the Greek root "cycl" mean, as in cycle, cyclone, or bicycle?

2122. What does the Greek root "geo" mean, as in geology, geometry, and geologist?

2123. What does the Greek root "hydr" mean, as in hydrant, hydrogen and hydroelectric power?

2124. What does the Greek root "meter" mean, as in thermometer, diameter, centimeter, or barometer?

2125. What does the Greek root "mega" mean, as in megaphone or megabucks?

2126. What does the Greek root "micro" mean, as in microscope and microfilm?

2127. What does the Greek root "mono" mean, as in monologue or monarch?

2128. What does the Greek root "phon" mean, as in phoneme and telephone?

2129. What does the Greek root "photo" mean, as in photographs or photocopier?

2130. What does the Greek root "poly" mean, as in polygon and polymer?

2131. What does the Greek root "proto" mean, as in prototype or protozoan?

2132. What does the Greek root "psyche" mean, as in psychologist or psych?

2133. What does the Greek root "tele" mean, as in television or telephone?

2134. What does the Greek root "thermo" mean, as in thermometer, thermal, or thermostat?

2135. What does the Greek (and Latin) root "tri" mean, as in trilogy, triangle, and tricycle?

2136. What does the Latin root "annus" mean, as in annual and anniversary?

2137. What does the Latin root "ante" mean, as in antebellum and antecedent?

2138. What does the Latin root "aqua" mean, as in aquatic and aquarium?

2139. What does the Latin root "bi" mean, as in bicycle, bisect, and bipartisan?

2140. What does the Latin root "centum" mean, as in percent, century, and cent?

LANGUAGE ARTS

2141. What does the Latin root "decem" mean, as in decade and decimal?

2142. What does the Latin root "dico" mean, as in dictation and dictator?

2143. What does the Latin root "duo" mean, as in duo and duplicate?

2144. What does the Latin root "fortuna" mean, as in fortunate or fortune?

2145. What does the Latin root "heres" mean, as in heir, heirloom, or inheritance?

2146. What does the Latin root "labor" mean, as in laborer, laboratory, and collaborate?

2147. What does the Latin root "magnus" mean, as in magnificent or magnify?

2148. What does the Latin root "minus" mean, as in five minus two and minor?

2149. What does the Latin root "navigare" mean, as in navigate, navigator and navy?

2150. What does the Latin root "omni" mean, as in omniscient and omnipotent?

2151. What does the Latin root "post" mean, as in posterity or posthumous?

2152. What does the Latin root "pre" mean, as in prefix, predict, and preview?

2153. What does the Latin root "primus" mean, as in primary or primitive?

2154. What does the Latin root "quartus" mean, as in quarter or quartet?

2155. What does the Latin root "uni" or "unus" mean, as in unit or unanimous?

2156. What does the Latin root "video" or "visus" mean, as in video or visual?

2157. What does the Latin root "vita" mean as in vitality and vitamin?

2158. What is the name for the study of and the origin of words: etymology or lingualism?

2159. Does a dictionary often have the etymology, or origin of that word?

2160. What is the foreign origin of banana, mumbo, safari, and zombie: African or Arabic?

2161. What is the foreign origin of algebra, coffee, magazine, and zero: African or Arabic?

2162. What is the foreign origin of boomerang, dingo, kangaroo, and koala: African or Australian?

2163. What is the foreign origin of gung ho, kung fu, soy, tea, tofu, and typhoon: Chinese or Japanese?

2164. What is the foreign origin of cookie, pickle, sled, golf, snack, and wagon: Czech or Dutch?

2165. What is the foreign origin of jungle, pajamas, shampoo, cheetah, and veranda: East Indian or Chinese?

2166. What is the foreign origin of ballet, boulevard, bouquet, carousel, chic, crepe, croissant, depot, fiancé, garage, mayor, Mardi Gras, turquoise, and resume: French or Italian?

LANGUAGE ARTS

2167. What is the foreign origin of diesel, Fahrenheit, frankfurter, bratwurst, hamburger, kindergarten, sauerkraut, and strudel: French or German?

2168. What is the foreign origin of bar mitzvah, kosher, menorah, and shalom: Greek or Hebrew?

2169. What is the foreign origin of bog, clock, galore, shamrock, and leprechaun: Scottish or Irish?

2170. What is the foreign origin of bologna, carnival, confetti, fiasco, finale, gondola, macaroni, pasta, piano, spaghetti, and volcano: Spanish or Italian?

2171. What is the foreign origin of bonsai, futon, judo, karate, ninja, origami, samurai, sushi, tsunami, and tycoon: Korean or Japanese?

2172. What is the foreign origin of chipmunk, powwow, skunk, totem, and wigwam: East Indian or Native American?

2173. What is the foreign origin of aloha, hula, lei, and taboo: Polynesian or Hawaiian?

2174. What is the foreign origin of cosmonaut, czar, Kremlin, mammoth, parka, and sputnik: Russian or Polish?

2175. What is the foreign origin of kielbasa, polska, babka, and kloty: Russian or Polish?

2176. What is the foreign origin of adobe, alfalfa, alpaca, armada, avocado, bronco, burro, cafeteria, canoe, canyon, cargo, chaps, condor, conquistador, corral, Colorado, coyote, fiesta, guacamole, Florida, hacienda, hurricane, iguana, jalapeño, macho, matador, mesa, Montana, mosquito, mustang, nacho, Nevada, papaya, patio, piñata, plaza, poncho, potato, pueblo, quesadilla, quinoa, ranch, rodeo, rumba, salsa, savannah, sierra, siesta, silo, stampede, stockade, taco, tamale, tango, tapioca, tobacco, tomato, tortilla, tornado, tuna, vanilla, vigilante, and Zorro: Spanish or Italian?

2177. What is the foreign origin of coffee, kiosk, sherbet, shish kebab, and yogurt: Yiddish or Turkish?

2178. What is the English word for hallo, bonjour, hola, ciao, and shalom?

2179. What is the English word for auf wiederschen, au revoir, adios, arrivederci, and sayonara?

2180. What is the English word for bitte, s'il vous plait, and por favor?

2181. What is the English word for danke, merci, gracias, and grazie?

2182. What is the English word for ja, oui, si, and ya?

2183. What is the English word for nein, non, and nao?

2184. What is the English animal name for katze, chat, katt, and gato?

2185. What is the English animal name for kuh, vaca, and ku?

2186. What is the English animal name for hund, chien, and perro?

2187. What is the English animal name for frosch, rana and groda?

LANGUAGE ARTS

2188. What is the English animal name for cheval, caballo, or ferd?

2189. What is the English animal name for schwein, cerdo or porco?

2190. What is the English animal name for schlange, serpiente, or culebra?

2191. What is the French phrase commonly used in English writing when ordering an individual item on a menu: a la carte or a la mode?

2192. What is the French phrase commonly used in English writing that means served with ice cream: a la carte or a la mode?

2193. What is the French phrase commonly used in English writing that means goodbye, or until we meet again: adios or au revoir?

2194. What is the French phrase commonly used in English writing that means enjoy your meal: buen provecho or bon appétit?

2195. What is the French phrase commonly used in English writing that means hello: hola or bonjour?

2196. What is the French phrase commonly used in English writing that means have a good trip: bon voyage or buen viaje?

2197. What is the French phrase commonly used in English writing that means the end of a street, or a dead end: cul de sac or boulevard?

2198. What is the French phrase commonly used in English writing that means on the route, or on the way: en route or en masse?

2199. What is the French phrase commonly used in English writing that means a social mistake: faux pas or error?

2200. What is the French phrase commonly used in English writing that means appetizer: appetit or hors d'oeuvre?

2201. What is the French phrase commonly used in English writing that means the attitude or practice that we should not meddle in the affairs of others: faux pas or laissez-faire?

2202. When would you see the French acronym RSVP?

2203. What does etiquette require you to do if you see RSVP, French for *repondez s'il vous plait* on an invitation?

2204. What is the Latin phrase for *seize the day*: carpe diem or bona fide?

2205. What is the Latin phrase for *in good faith*: carpe diem or bona fide?

2206. What is the Latin phrase for *and so on*: et cetera or ibid?

2207. What is the Latin phrase for *my fault*; carpe diem or mea culpa?

LANGUAGE ARTS

2208. What is the Latin phrase for *the way things are*: quid pro quo or status quo?

2209. What is the Latin phrase for conversely, or in the reverse order: et cetera or vice versa?

2210. What is the term for a set of letters that can be attached to the front of a word to make a new word: prefix or suffix?

2211. What does the prefix *anti* mean, as in antibacterial and antibodies: away or against?

2212. What does the prefix *inter* mean, as in international, interview, and interstate: between or beneath?

2213. What does the prefix *co* mean, as in co-exist and co-captions: together or against?

2214. What does the prefix *mid* mean, as in midnight and midair: middle or high?

2215. What does the prefix *fore* mean, as in forefather and foresight: before or ahead?

2216. What does the prefix *post* mean, as in postgame and postseason: before or after?

2217. What do the prefixes *il, ir, in,* and *im* mean, as in illegal, irregular, intolerant, and immature: not or is?

2218. What does the prefix *semi* mean, as in semicircle and semiannual: whole or partial?

2219. What is the term for a set of letters that can be attached to the end of a word to make a new word: prefix or suffix?

2220. What suffixes can be added to adjectives to make them adverbs: -ly or –ness?

2221. How can you make the adjective **slow** into an adverb by adding the suffix -ly?

2222. How can you make the adjective **happy** into an adverb by adding the suffix -ily?

2223. What suffix is used to describe what somebody does or believes, like an artist or a biologist?

2224. What suffix is added to nouns to make them into adjectives, as in fool and foolish, or style and stylish?

2225. What suffix indicates the state, condition, or quality of something, as in redness or sadness?

2226. What two suffixes are often used to make verbs into nouns, as in act to action, or run to runner?

2227. What does the suffix –ish mean, that can turn a noun into an adjective, as in fool to foolish, red to reddish, or style to stylish: rather or slightly?

2228. Is a literary work built using, letters, words, sentences, and paragraphs?

2229. What do you need to do the first sentence of a new paragraph to make it stand out?

2230. What do you always need to do to the first letter of a word in a sentence?

2231. Do you always capitalize the pronoun "I?"

2232. Do you capitalize the names of specific people, places, events, dates, and documents?

LANGUAGE ARTS

2233. Do you capitalize the names of languages, races, religions, and the names of Gods?

2234. Do you capitalize titles of respect like Dr. Judge, Mr., and Mrs.?

2235. Do you capitalize the names of organizations and trade names like Nike and Coca-Cola?

2236. Do you capitalize important words in the titles of stories, books, newspapers, and magazines?

2237. Do you capitalize abbreviations and acronyms?

2238. What punctuation mark goes at the end of a sentence that makes a statement?

2239. What punctuation mark goes at the end of a sentence that asks a question?

2240. What punctuation mark goes at the end of a sentence that is exclaimed or shouted?

2241. What punctuation mark do you use when you want to separate items in a list?

2242. What punctuation mark do you use after yes and no in a sentence?

2243. Where is the comma placed when writing the month, day, and year?

2244. Where is a comma inserted when writing an address on an envelope?

2245. What is the name of the noun or noun phrase that renames another noun right beside it: an appositive or an acronym?

2246. What is the appositive in the following sentence: "My friend, Sara Smith, is visiting us from Arizona?

2247. What is the appositive in the following sentence: "Rusty, my Goldendoodle, is getting a haircut today?

2248. What punctuation looks like two periods stacked on top of one another?

2249. What punctuation mark is used in the following sentence: "I had to choose one of three clubs: dance, chorus, or jazz band," because it introduces a list?

2250. What is the term for writing letters in a word in a slant to the right: italics or bold?

2251. What should you do when you write down the title of a book: underline it, italicize it, or either?

2252. What would you use to set off a title if you're writing about a poem, a song, or a magazine article: italicize the title or place the title inside quotation marks?

2253. Where would the quotation marks be in the following sentence: "We sang The Star Spangled Banner before the game?"

2254. What is the term given for the following eight things: noun, pronoun, adjective, verb, adverb, conjunction, preposition, and interjection: language devices or parts of speech?

2255. What two parts of speech does a sentence need to be complete?

LANGUAGE ARTS

2256. What is the part of speech that names a person, place, thing, or idea?

2257. What is an example of a noun?

2258. What kind of noun names a specific person, place, or thing and is always capitalized: a common noun or a proper noun?

2259. What is an example of a proper noun?

2260. What is the proper noun in the following sentence: "Many famous monuments are located in Washington, D.C?"

2261. What kind of noun is not specific and is not capitalized unless it is at the beginning of a sentence: a common noun or a proper noun?

2262. What are the *common* nouns in the following sentence: "New York is famous for its parks, museums, restaurants?"

2263. What is an example of a common noun?

2264. What is a word that takes the place of a noun: an adjective or a pronoun?

2265. Do we use personal pronouns to make sentences longer or shorter?

2266. Does the personal pronoun agree in case, gender, and number with the noun it replaces?

2267. What pronouns can you use to refer to yourself besides "I?"

2268. Are the personal pronouns I, me, my, or mine interchangeable, or does the form of the pronoun depend on how it is used in a sentence?

2269. Does the particular form a pronoun takes called the "case" of the noun, and does it have to agree with the noun it replaces?

2270. Are nominative, objective, and possessive considered gender or cases?

2271. What pronoun would replace "the girl" in the sentence: "The girl held the doll:" the nominative case "she," or the objective case "her?"

2272. What pronoun would replace "the dolls" in the sentence: "The girl held the dolls:" the nominative case "they," or the objective case "them?"

2273. What are the personal pronouns I, we, you, he, she, it, and they: nominative or objective?

2274. What are the personal pronouns me, us, you, him, her, it, and them: nominative or objective?

2275. Which sentence illustrates the correct use of the personal pronoun: "My sister and **me** are going to the park" or, "My sister and **I** are going to the park?

2276. Which sentence illustrates the correct use of the personal pronoun: "Dad is taking Ryan and **I** to the zoo" or, "Dad is taking Ryan and **me** to the zoo?"

LANGUAGE ARTS

2277. What is an example of a pronoun?

2278. What is the part of speech that describes or modifies a noun and gives more detail?

2279. What are the adjectives in the following sentence: "The blue shirt is expensive?"

2280. Can you add adjectives to the following sentence to make it more detailed and specific: "The bike rode down the path"

2281. What is an example of an adjective?

2282. What is a word that shows action or a state of being?

2283. What is an example of a verb?

2284. Can verbs be expressed in different *tenses* like present, past, and future?

2285. How would you change the verb in the following sentence from the present to the past tense: "The dog **eats** the bone?"

2286. How would you change the verb in the following sentence from the past to the future tense: "The dog **ate** the bone?"

2287. How would you change the verb in the following sentence from the future to the present tense: "The dog **will eat** the bone?"

2288. What is the part of speech called that modifies a verb and tells how an action is performed?

2289. What is the adverb in the following sentence: "Marissa turned the key slowly?"

2290. Do all adverbs end in -ly?

2291. What is the adverb in the following sentence: "Soon the plane will land?"

2292. What is the adverb in the following sentence: "He ran very fast?"

2293. What is the adverb in the following sentence: "He played the game well?"

2294. What is an example of an adverb?

2295. Can you add an adverb to the following sentence to make it more specific: "The clerk set down the glass vase?"

2296. What are some adverbs you can name like slowly or quickly that tell us *how*?

2297. What do the adverbs like, never, and after tell us: when or where?

2298. What do the adverbs *here* and *there* tell us: when or where?

2299. What do the adverbs *quite* and *very* tell us: when or to what extent?

2300. What is the comparative adverb of *badly*: worse or the worst?

LANGUAGE ARTS

2301. What is the superlative adverb of the series: tall, taller, _?

2302. What is the superlative adverb of the series: little, less, _?

2303. What is the superlative adverb of the series: much, more, _?

2304. What is the superlative adverb of the series well, better, _?

2305. What is the part of speech called that joins words, phrases or clauses: a contraction or a conjunction?

2306. What part of speech are the words and, or, nor, for, but, yet, and so?

2307. How can you use the conjunction "so" to make a complete sentence from the following run-on: "The chicken took a long time to bake, you should start cooking it right away?"

2308. What is an example of a conjunction?

2309. What is the part of speech called that shows the relationship of a noun or pronoun to another word or words in the sentence: a conjunction or a preposition?

2310. What is an example of a preposition?

2311. What is the part of speech called that is used to express strong emotion: an exclamation or an interjection?

2312. What is the interjection in the following sentence: "Yikes! I'm late for school?"

2313. What is the interjection in the following sentence: "What! We have a test today?"

2314. What is an example of an interjection?

2315. What is the term for the part of speech that is the noun or pronoun that the verb "does" something to, the *who* or *what* that the verb is acting on: the direct object or the indirect object?

2316. What is the direct object in the following sentence: "Diego Rivera painted murals in Mexico's National Palace?"

2317. *What* was being painted in the sentence: "Diego Rivera painted murals in Mexico's National Palace?"

2318. What is the direct object in the following sentence: "Harriet Tubman led slaves to freedom?"

2319. *Who* was being led in the sentence: "Harriet Tubman led slaves to freedom?"

2320. If a sentence has a direct object, can it also have an indirect object?

2321. What is the term for the person or the thing that receives the direct object from the subject and answers *to whom* or *for whom*: the indirect object or the predicate?

2322. What is the indirect object in the following sentence: "Joe threw Zach the Frisbee?"

2323. *To whom* did Joe throw the Frisbee in the sentence: "Joe threw Zach the Frisbee?"

LANGUAGE ARTS

2324. What is the indirect object in the sentence: "Paul made his friends a pizza?"

2325. *For whom* did Paul make the pizza in the sentence: "Paul made his friends a pizza?"

2326. Is "friends" the direct or indirect object of the verb in the following sentence: "Paul made his friends a pizza?"

2327. What is the *subject* in the following sentence: "Paul made his friends a pizza?"

2328. What is the *verb* in the following sentence: "Paul made his friends a pizza?"

2329. What is the *direct object* in the following sentence: "Paul made his friends a pizza?"

2330. Can you identify the subject of a sentence by asking who or what is doing what the verb describes?

2331. What is the subject in the following sentence: "The baby smiled at his mother?"

2332. *Who* smiled at his mother in the sentence: "The baby smiled at his mother?"

2333. Is "baby' or "mother" the subject of the sentence, "The baby smiled at his mother" because it answers "who" about the verb?

2334. Do the subject and a verb always have to agree in a sentence?

2335. What form of the verb do you use if your subject is singular: singular or plural?

2336. What form of the verb do you use if your subject is plural: singular or plural?

2337. How would you say the following sentence using subject and verb agreement: "He teach science," or, "He teaches science?"

2338. How would you say the following sentence using subject and verb agreement: "The deer ran through the forest," or "The deer runs through the forest?"

2339. Which of the verbs would you use to complete the sentence: "A flock of birds **fly** or **flies** overhead?"

2340. Which of the verbs would you use to complete the sentence: "A band of musicians **was** or **were** singing for us?"

2341. Which of the verbs would you use to complete the sentence: "One of my cousins **like** or **likes** to jump rope?"

2342. Which of the verbs would you use to complete the sentence: "Two of my cousins **like** or **likes** to jump rope?"

2343. What voice is a sentence like "The dog chased the ball" written in if the subject of the sentence performs the action: active or passive?

2344. How is a sentence written if the subject of the sentence is acted upon by some other agent, and usually includes the verb form *was* or *were* as in, "The ball was chased by the dog:" active voice or passive voice?

LANGUAGE ARTS

2345. Which voice is more lively and interesting to a reader: active or passive?

2346. Is the following sentence written in active voice or passive voice: "William Shakespeare wrote *Romeo and Juliet*?"

2347. In what voice is "*Romeo and Juliet* was written by William Shakespeare:" active or passive?

2348. What is a sentence called when it is missing a subject or a verb: a fragment or a run-on?

2349. What is it called when two or more sentences are written as one sentence and are often separated by commas: a fragment or a run-on?

2350. Is the following sentence a fragment, a run-on, or a complete sentence: "I made chicken for supper?"

2351. Is the following sentence a fragment, a run-on, or a complete sentence: "Very tasty?"

2352. Is the following sentence a fragment, a run-on, or a complete sentence: "The chicken takes a long time to bake, you should start cooking it right away?"

2353. What word can you add to fix the following run-on: "The chicken takes a long time to bake, you should start cooking it right away?"

2354. What is the term for the part of a sentence that states something about the subject, always includes the verb, and can be long or short: the theme or the predicate?

2355. What is the predicate in the following sentence: "The police officer directed traffic at the intersection?"

2356. What is the predicate in the following sentence: "Evan cried?"

2357. What is the predicate in the following sentence: "I carried books in my backpack to read whenever I went on errands with my mom?"

2358. Is the predicate typically placed before or after the subject of the sentence?

2359. What is the subject in the following sentence: "The garbage left a horrible smell?"

2360. What is the predicate in the following sentence: "In the brisk wind were flying fifty kites?"

2361. Is it important to keep the rules for the parts of speech in mind when writing?

2362. What have you written a short story about?

2363. Can you write a description of a person or a place?

2364. Can you write a summary of what you did yesterday?

2365. What have you written a report on?

2366. What have you written an essay about?

2367. What is the term for the first paragraph of an essay or report: the attention-getter or the introduction?

LANGUAGE ARTS

2368. What is the term for the middle paragraphs of an essay or report: the middle or the body?

2369. What is the term for the last paragraph of an essay or report: the conclusion or the ending?

2370. What is the name of the sentence in an introductory paragraph that prepares the reader for the main focus of the paper, or the position of the author in the paper: the topic sentence or the thesis statement?

2371. When you write or say exactly what you mean, what language are you using: figurative or literal?

2372. Should a "figure of speech" be taken literally or not?

2373. Is the following sentence written in literal or figurative language: "The leaf floated in the pond?"

2374. Is the following sentence written in literal or figurative language: "The dancer floated across the stage?"

2375. What type of language do scientists often use to be as precise as they can: literal or figurative?

2376. What type of language do story-tellers and poets often use in their writings to heighten our emotions and imagination, and to help us see things in a different way: literal or figurative?

2377. What is the term for a figure of speech where there are two contradictory terms right next to each other: an octagon or an oxymoron?

2378. Which of the following would be considered an oxymoron: jumbo shrimp or baby shrimp?

2379. What would all of the following be considered: awful good, bitter sweet, civil war, icy hot, good grief, lead balloon, freezer burn, pretty ugly, steel wool, small crowd, silent scream, and wise fool?

2380. What is the term for what writers use to help the reader create pictures of images of something: imagination or imagery?

2381. What is the term for the figure of speech that makes a comparison using extreme exaggeration for emphasis or effect: imagery or hyperbole?

2382. What are the following sentences examples of: "I have a ton of homework" or, "I have a million things to do" or, "My shoes are killing me:" hyperbole or literal language?

2383. Can *you* say a phrase or a sentence that would be considered hyperbole?

2384. What figure of speech compares two unlike things using "like" or "as:" a simile or a metaphor?

2385. What is the phrase "float like a butterfly:" a simile or a metaphor?

2386. What is the phrase "quiet as a mouse:" a simile or a metaphor?

2387. What figure of speech compares unlike things *without* using "like" or "as:" a simile or a metaphor?

2388. Which of the following is a metaphor: "She is as stubborn as a mule," or, "She is a mule?"

2389. Which of the following is a simile: "The snow blanketed the field," or, "Her face was as white as a sheet?"

LANGUAGE ARTS

2390. What is the *snow* being compared to in after following sentence: "The snow blanketed the field?"

2391. What is the literary term for something that stands for or suggests something other than itself: a symbol or a stamp?

2392. What is one symbol of the United States of America?

2393. What do the 50 stars on the American flag symbolize or represent?

2394. What does a heart symbolize?

2395. What do skull and crossbones symbolize on a bottle of bleach?

2396. Can a symbol mean different things to different people?

2397. What is the symbolism of the two paths in the woods in Robert Frost's, "The Road Not Taken?"

2398. What is the literary term when a thing or an animal is given qualities or abilities of a human being: alliteration or personification?

2399. What is the literary term that is present in the following sentences: "This city never sleeps," and, "Callie heard the last piece of cake calling her name:" alliteration or personification?

2400. What is the Greek work for a special effect that writers use when a word imitates the sound that it makes: alliteration or onomatopoeia?

2401. What words related to water might be examples of onomatopoeia?

2402. What thing might produce the onomatopoeia sound of "hiss?"

2403. What is the onomatopoeia word that is often used in literary pieces when something explodes?

2404. What words might capture the sound of bacon frying?

2405. What sound does a race car make that would be an example of onomatopoeia?

2406. What sound does a dog make that would be an example of onomatopoeia?

2407. What sound does a cat make that would be an example of onomatopoeia?

2408. What sound does a duck make that would be an example of onomatopoeia?

2409. What sound does a bird make that would be an example of onomatopoeia?

2410. What sound does a sheep make that would be an example of onomatopoeia?

2411. What sound does a frog make that would be an example of onomatopoeia?

2412. What is the literary term for the special effect used by writers and poets when several words in a row start with the same sound: personification or alliteration?

2413. What literary term is "Peter Piper picked a peck of pickled peppers" an example of?

LANGUAGE ARTS

2414. What is the literary term for the genre that is essentially a play that is acted out on a stage in a theater?

2415. What is another term for the author of a drama: a poet or a playwright?

2416. What is the name of the funny, happy play first developed by the Greeks: tragedy or comedy?

2417. What is the name of the tragic, sad play first developed by the Greeks: tragedy or comedy?

2418. What symbol did the Greeks use to stand for comedy and tragedy in drama: masks or wands?

2419. What is the name of perhaps the most famous English dramatist from the early 1600's?

2420. What was the name of the theater in London where many of William Shakespeare's plays were performed: the London Theater or the Globe Theater?

2421. Where do the famous phrases "To be or not to be," and "All's well that ends well" come from: Shakespeare's plays or Shakespeare's poems?

2422. Were Shakespeare's subtle but humorous plays, "A Midsummer Night's Dream," and "Much Ado about Nothing:" comedies or tragedies?

2423. Were Shakespeare's plays "Antony and Cleopatra," "Romeo and Juliet," "Hamlet," and "Macbeth" comedies or tragedies?

2424. What does an act in a play contain: several scenes, or several acts?

2425. What is the literary term for a 14-line poem that Shakespeare was famous for writing: a sonnet or a quatrain?

2426. Do lines in poems have to be in sentence format?

2427. Do lines in poems have to rhyme?

2428. Do different kinds of poems have different rhyme patterns, like ABAB or ABBA?

2429. Can you write a poem?

2430. Can you write a letter?

2431. What is the meaning of a salutation in a letter: a greeting or a closing?

2432. What is another word for the name and return address: a greeting or a heading?

2433. What kind of a letter would include a return address, date, casual greeting, body, closing, and signature line: a personal letter or a business letter?

2434. What kind of a letter would include a return address, date, person and title to whom the letter is being addressed, greeting, body, closing, signature line, and title: a personal letter or a business letter?

2435. Can a business letter be written in either block form or indented form?

LANGUAGE ARTS

2436. Is "Dear Mr. Smith" a greeting or a closing?

2437. Is "Sincerely" a greeting or a closing?

2438. What is a closing line on a business letter besides "Sincerely?"

2439. Do different cultures have certain sayings and phrases?

2440. Does "que sera sera" mean *what will be will be* in French or Spanish?

2441. Does "asi es la vida" mean *such is life* in French or Spanish?

2442. Does "c'est la vie" mean *such is life* in French or Spanish?

2443. Do we have several sayings and idioms in our English language?

2444. How do you finish the saying: "All for one and one for _?"

2445. How do you finish this saying: "Beauty is only skin_?"

2446. How do you finish this saying: "All's well that ends_?"

2447. How do you finish this saying: "A bird in the hand is worth two in the_?"

2448. How do you finish this saying: "Don't look a gift horse in the_?"

2449. How do you finish this saying: "A fool and his money are soon_?"

2450. How do you finish this saying: "Good fences make good_?"

2451. How do you finish this saying: "He who hesitates is_?"

2452. How do you finish this saying: "He who laughs last laughs_?"

2453. How do you finish this saying: "Money is the root of all_?"

2454. How do you finish this saying: "Necessity is the mother of _?"

2455. How do you finish this saying: "It's never over till it's_?"

2456. How do you finish this saying: "Once bitten, twice_?"

2457. How do you finish this saying: "Pot calling the kettle_?"

2458. How do you finish this saying: "The proof of the pudding is in the_?"

2459. How do you finish this saying: "Rome wasn't built in a_?"

2460. How do you finish this saying that infers a guideline: "Rule of_?"

2461. How do you finish this saying: "A stitch in time saves_?"

2462. How do you finish this saying: "Strike while the iron is_?"

2463. How do you finish this saying: "There's more than one way to skin a_?"

LANGUAGE ARTS

2464. How do you finish this saying: "Truth is stronger than _?"

2465. How do you finish the saying: "Birthday _?"

2466. How do you finish this saying: "Bite the hand that feeds _?"

2467. How do you finish this saying: "Catch forty _?"

2468. How do you finish this saying: "Chip on your _?"

2469. How do you finish this saying: "Don't count your chickens before they _?"

2470. How do you finish this saying that is an idiom for humiliation: "Eating _?"

2471. How do you finish this saying: "Every cloud has a silver _?"

2472. How do you finish this saying: "Few and far _?"

2473. How do you finish this saying: "The grass is always greener on the other _?"

2474. How do you finish this saying: "Kill two birds with one _?"

2475. How do you finish this saying: "Lock, stock, and _?"

2476. How do you finish the saying: "Make a mountain out of a _?"

2477. How do you finish this saying: "A penny saved is a penny _?"

2478. How do you finish this saying: "Read between the _?"

2479. How do you finish this saying: "Steal my _?"

2480. How do you finish this saying: "Take the bull by the _?"

2481. How do you finish this saying: "Till the cows come _?"

2482. How do you finish this saying: "Time heals all _?"

2483. How do you finish this saying: "Tom, Dick, and _?"

2484. How do you finish this saying: "Vice _?"

2485. How do you finish this saying: "A watched pot never _?"

2486. How do you finish this saying: "What will be will _?"

2487. What is the word a person might say when somebody scores a point against us in a discussion: touché or andale?

2488. Can you recognize and pronounce the common sight word "ache?" (Show word)

2489. Can you recognize and pronounce the common sight word "amphibian?" (Show word)

2490. Can you recognize and pronounce the common sight word "antique?" (Show word)

2491. Can you recognize and pronounce the common sight word "audience?" (Show word)

LANGUAGE ARTS

2492. Can you recognize and pronounce the common sight word "bawl?" (Show word)

2493. Can you recognize and pronounce the common sight word "beach?" (Show word))

2494. Can you recognize and pronounce the common sight word "biceps?" (Show word)

2495. Can you recognize and pronounce the common sight word "binoculars?" (Show word)

2496. Can you recognize and pronounce the common sight word "boarder?" (Show word)

2497. Can you recognize and pronounce the common sight word "break?" (Show word)

2498. Can you recognize and pronounce the common sight word "canoes?" (Show word)

2499. Can you recognize and pronounce the common sight word "capit_a_l?" (Show word)

2500. Can you recognize and pronounce the common sight word "capit_o_l?" (Show word)

2501. Can you recognize and pronounce the common sight word "conservation?" (Show word)

2502. Can you recognize and pronounce the common sight word "cylinder?" (Show word)

2503. Can you recognize and pronounce the common sight word "deceive?" (Show word)

2504. Can you recognize and pronounce the common sight word "decimal?" (Show word)

2505. Can you recognize and pronounce the common sight word "diagnose?" (Show word)

2506. Can you recognize and pronounce the common sight word "diagonal?" (Show word)

2507. Can you recognize and pronounce the common sight word "dialogue?" (Show word)

2508. Can you recognize and pronounce the common sight word "drought?" (Show word)

2509. Can you recognize and pronounce the common sight word "earthquake?" (Show word)

2510. Can you recognize and pronounce the common sight word "equal?" (Show word)

2511. Can you recognize and pronounce the common sight word "equator?" (Show word)

2512. Can you recognize and pronounce the common sight word "equivalent?" (Show word)

2513. Can you recognize and pronounce the common sight word "exclamation?" (Show word)

2514. Can you recognize and pronounce the common sight word "expedition?" (Show word)

2515. Can you recognize and pronounce the common sight word "expense?" (Show word)

2516. Can you recognize and pronounce the common sight word "extinguish?" (Show word)

2517. Can you recognize and pronounce the common sight word "extraordinary?" (Show word)

2518. Can you recognize and pronounce the common sight word "extrasensory?" (Show word)

2519. Can you recognize and pronounce the common sight word "extraterrestrial?" (Show word)

2520. Can you recognize and pronounce the common sight word "fir?" (Show word)

LANGUAGE ARTS

2521. Can you recognize and pronounce the common sight word "guard?" (Show word)

2522. Can you recognize and pronounce the common sight word "inquire?" (Show word)

2523. Can you recognize and pronounce the common sight word "judicial?" (Show word)

2524. Can you recognize and pronounce the common sight word "knight?" (Show word)

2525. Can you recognize and pronounce the common sight word "loose?" (Show word)

2526. Can you recognize and pronounce the common sight word "microphone?" (Show word)

2527. Can you recognize and pronounce the common sight word "mourn?" (Show word)

2528. Can you recognize and pronounce the common sight word "neighbor?" (Show word)

2529. Can you recognize and pronounce the common sight word "night?" (Show word)

2530. Can you recognize and pronounce the common sight word "paraphrase?" (Show word)

2531. Can you recognize and pronounce the common sight word "pause?" (Show word)

2532. Can you recognize and pronounce the common sight word "peace?" (Show word)

2533. Can you recognize and pronounce the common sight word "petition?" (Show word)

2534. Can you recognize and pronounce the common sight word "piece?" (Show word)

2535. Can you recognize and pronounce the common sight word "pour?" (Show word)

2536. Can you recognize and pronounce the common sight word "preamble?" (Show word)

2537. Can you recognize and pronounce the common sight word "prejudice?" (Show word)

2538. Can you recognize and pronounce the common sight word "prospector?" (Show word)

2539. Can you recognize and pronounce the common sight word "punctuation?" (Show word)

2540. Can you recognize and pronounce the common sight word "usually?" (Show word)

2541. Can you recognize and pronounce the common sight word "quail?" (Show word)

2542. Can you recognize and pronounce the common sight word "qualify?" (Show word)

2543. Can you recognize and pronounce the common sight word "quality?" (Show word)

2544. Can you recognize and pronounce the common sight word "quantity?" (Show word)

2545. Can you recognize and pronounce the common sight word "quarrel?" (Show word)

2546. Can you recognize and pronounce the common sight word "quiet?" (Show word)

2547. Can you recognize and pronounce the common sight word "quite?" (Show word)

2548. Can you recognize and pronounce the common sight word "quotation?" (Show word)

2549. Can you recognize and pronounce the common sight word "quotient?" (Show word)

2550. Can you recognize and pronounce the common sight word "request?" (Show word)

2551. Can you recognize and pronounce the common sight word "retract?" (Show word)

2552. Can you recognize and pronounce the common sight word "route?" (Show word)

2553. Can you recognize and pronounce the common sight word "sequence?" (Show word)

2554. Can you recognize and pronounce the common sight word "sketch?" (Show word)

2555. Can you recognize and pronounce the common sight word "sleigh?" (Show word)

2556. Can you recognize and pronounce the common sight word "surround?" (Show word)

2557. Can you recognize and pronounce the common sight word "thermometer?" (Show word)

2558. Can you recognize and pronounce the common sight word "toe?" (Show word)

2559. Can you recognize and pronounce the common sight word "unique?" (Show word)

2560. Can you recognize and pronounce the common sight word "vertebrates?" (Show word)

2561. Can you recognize and pronounce the common sight word "veto?" (Show word)

2562. Can you recognize and pronounce the common sight word "wade?" (Show word)

2563. Can you recognize and pronounce the common sight word "weighed?" (Show word)

2564. Can you recognize and pronounce the common sight word "whether?" (Show word)

2565. Can you recognize and pronounce the common sight word "view?" (Show word)

2566. Can you recognize and pronounce the common sight word "whole?" (Show word)

2567. What is the literary term for an alternate name or pseudonym adopted by an author for various reasons: a pen name or an alias?

2568. Do most writers publish works using their own name or a pen name?

2569. What is the pen name of Samuel Clemens author of "The Adventures of Tom Sawyer:" Mark Twain or Huckleberry Finn?

2570. What was the pen name of Theodor Geisel, the author of "Green Eggs and Ham," and "The Cat in the Hat:" Dr. Seuss or Mr. Grinch?

2571. What is the name of the best-selling book of all time written in two parts, and contains chapters and verses that have been translated into more than 1200 languages?

2572. What is the term for exemplary novels that have stood the test of time, and serve as literary models in American, British, and World literature: classics or a bestsellers?

Chapter 2 – Notable Literary Works Through the Ages

1. What is the name of the ancient Greek epic poem written in approximately 800 BC by Homer that relates the battles and events during the ten-year Trojan War between Greece and Troy: "The I_?"

2. What is the name of the ancient Greek epic poem written around 800 BC by Homer that centers on the challenges facing the Greek warrior Odysseus after the fall of Troy, and his quest to return home and reestablish himself as King: "The O_?"

3. What is the name of the author and Greek storyteller of a collection of over 650 fables from 600 BC that often involve animals, and in the end teach a moral or lesson: Aesop or Hans Christian Anderson?

4. What is the name of Aesop's fable number 87 that tells a story of a goose that magically creates something gold and teaches the moral, *being greedy never pays*: "The Goose that Laid the __?

5. What is the name of Aesop's fable number 147 about two animals that attack another animal and collapse from being worn out, as another animal watching the action *grabs* this animal and runs off with it thus teaching the moral, *one might have all the work but another all the profit*: "The Lion, the Bear, and the _?"

6. What is the name of Aesop's fable number 150 that tells the story of one large animal and a much smaller one and teaches the moral, *little friends may prove to be great friends*: "The Lion and the _?"

7. What is the name of Aesop's fable number 210 that tells the story of a shepherd boy named Peter who repeatedly tricks the people of his village by convincing them that his sheep are being attacked by a dog-like animal, until one day this animal really does attack and eats his flock after his calls for help go unnoticed thus teaching the moral, *asking for help when one does not need it may result in others not believing you when you really do need it:* "The Boy Who Cried _?"

8. What is the name of Aesop's fable number 226 that centers on a turtle that challenges a rabbit to a race that teaches the moral, *slow and steady wins the race*: "The Tortoise and the _?"

9. What is the name of Aesop's fable number 352 about two rodent cousins that go to visit each that try to convince each other that its place to live is better than the others, thus teaching the moral, *better a little in safety than in abundance surrounded by danger*: "The Town Mouse and the Country _?"

10. What is the name of Aesop's fable number 373 about two insects, one of whom sings away the summer, while the other works hard to store food for the winter, thus teaching the moral, *it is best to prepare for the days of necessity*: "The Ant and the _?"

11. What is the name of Aesop's fable number 563 about a slave who escaped from his master and hid out in a cave that turned out to be an animal's den, pulled a thorn from this animal's paw, was shown

NOTABLE LITERARY WORKS THROUGH THE AGES

gratitude and friendship by this animal, was then captured by his former master but then set free when this animal refused to attack him in an open arena, thus teaching the moral, *gratitude is the sign of noble souls*: "Androcles and the _?"

12. What is the title of the Greek tragedy written by Euripides first performed in Athens in 425 BC, dramatizing the life of a slave named Andromache and her relationship with Hermoine, the wife of her master: "A_?"

13. What is the name of the Greek tragedy written by Sophocles and first performed in 429 BC and tells the life of a man named Oedipus and his path to become king of Thebes: "Oedipus the _?"

14. What is the name of the Latin epic poem from 19 BC written by Virgil that tells the story of how the Trojan Aeneas who traveled to Italy and essentially founded Rome: "The A_?"

15. What is the name of the epic Anglo-Saxon poem guessed to have existed in the year 1000, about a Scandinavian hero who fights the demon Grendel in a wrestling match: "B_?"

16. What is the name of the 1215 political charter, drafted by the powerful barons of England and signed by King John, that outlined the political and civil liberties of all classes, served to limit the powers of the King, and provided the foundation for the British constitution and English citizen's rights: "The Magna _?"

17. What is the name of 1475 collection of short stories by English author Geoffrey Chaucer, written during the Hundred Years War, that aim to showcase English society and the church as told by 29 pilgrims on their journey to a shrine in Canterbury: "The Canterbury _?"

18. What is the Latin name of the Latin narrative poem by the Roman poet Ovid, first published in English in 1498 and also called "Books of Transformations," that outlines the history of the world since its creation to the anointing of Julius Caesar: "M_?"

19. What is the title of the 1532 book by the Italian historian Niccolo Machiavelli, the most translated book from the Italian language, that serves as a guide for ruling a kingdom, attaining political power, establishing principalities, the qualities of a strong leader, and provides a perspective on what constitutes a strong Italian leader: "The P_?"

20. What is the name of the epic poem written by Italian author Dante Alighieri in 1555 about the soul's journey toward God, and the afterlife: "The Divine _?"

21. What is the title of the 1597 tragedy by William Shakespeare that centers on two feuding families in Verona, the Montagues and the Capulets, and the two main characters that are prevented from declaring their love for one another, ending tragically for both characters: "Romeo and _?"

22. What is the title of the 1599 tragedy by William Shakespeare with the famous speech by Marc Antony in Act 3, Scene 2 that begins with the often quoted opening line, "Friends, Romans, Countrymen, lend me your ears: "Julius _?

23. What is the title of the 1603 Greek tragedy by William Shakespeare, his longest play and still one of

NOTABLE LITERARY WORKS THROUGH THE AGES

the most-performed even today, set in Denmark, and tells the story of a Prince who takes revenge on his uncle Claudius for murdering his father, the King: "H_?"

24. What is the title of the 1603 tragedy by William Shakespeare that is based on an Italian story called "A Moorish Captain," and centers on a Moorish general in the Venetian army, his wife Desdemona, his lieutenant Cassio, and his infantry officer Lago, and has been adapted for film and opera: "O_?"

25. What is the name of the 1605 novel by Miguel de Cervantes about an idealist knight and his realist companion Sancho Panza and their adventures in Spain on a horse and a donkey: "Don Quixote de la _?"

26. What is the title of the 1606 tragedy written by English author William Shakespeare about an aging King who is left to divide up his kingdom among his three daughters, is ultimately betrayed by two of them, leaving the future of the kingdom in great jeopardy: "King _?"

27. What is the famous opening line of the English poet William Shakespeare's Sonnet 18, first published in 1609 as part of a collection of 154 sonnets that starts with the author comparing someone he loves to the summer season, declaring that *thou art more lovely*: "Shall I Compare Thee to a Summer's _?"

28. What is the name of the collection of books representing both Christianity and Judaism, has been translated into more than 500 languages, has a Christian version that includes the Old Testament and the New Testament, has a Hebrew version that is regarded as the sacred book of Judaism, was first published in English as the version of King James, and first printed on the Gutenberg press: "The _?"

29. What is the name of the first five books of the Hebrew Scriptures: "The Old Testament" or "The Torah?"

30. What is the name of the poem contained in William Shakespeare's comedy play *As You Like It*, first published in 1623, that gets its name from the first line in the poem: All the World's a _?"

31. What is the name of the poem first published in 1639 by Walt Whitman as part of his Holy Sonnets where the author argues against the power of death and in the end, suggests that death itself will die: "Death Be Not _?"

32. What is the name of the 1667 epic poem by John Milton, filling ten books and having over ten thousand lines, that centers on the Biblical account of the fall of man and the temptation of Adam and Eve: "Paradise _?"

33. What is the title of the 1678 Christian novel by Paul Bunyan written while the author was in prison, that follows a man named Christian and his religious journey from this world to heaven, the Celestial City: "The Pilgrim's _?"

34. What is the name of the 1697 French fairy tale by Charles Perrault about a tom cat who earns power, wealth, and a princess through trickery, ending up as a lord of his own kingdom: "Puss in _?"

35. What is the name of the 1697 French fairy tale by Charles Perrault about a little girl in a red coat who meets a wolf in the forest on her way to her grandmother's cottage, and is later saved by a lumberjack after the wolf disguises himself as her grandmother: "Little Red Riding _?"

NOTABLE LITERARY WORKS THROUGH THE AGES

36. What is the other name of the 1706 collection of 42 Asian folk stories first compiled in Arabic entitled "Arabian Nights," and include *Aladdin and the Wonderful Lamp* and *Ali-Baba and the Forty Thieves*: One Thousand and One _?"

37. What is the full title of the 1719 fictional autobiography by William Defoe about a castaway who lives on a remote tropical island near Trinidad for 28 years and his island confrontations before he is finally rescued: "Robinson _?

38. What is the full title of the 1726 novel by Irish author Jonathan Swift about the voyages and discoveries of the protagonist as he travels to several remote nations of the world, and is a satire on human nature: "Gulliver's _?

39. What is the full title of the 1729 novel by Charles Perrault that is a collection of literary fairy tales: "Tales of Mother _?

40. What is the name of the 1755 British nursery rhyme about a house that is connected to other people and other things, and shows how all these things are connected together in this progressively-told rhyme: "This is the House that Jack _?"

41. What is the full title of the 1757 fairy tale adaptation by Jeanne-Marie Le Prince de Beaumont about a girl named Belle who is obligated as part of a deal to live with a monster in a castle, leaves for a week, and sheds tears to find him near death upon her return to the castle, tears that transform him from a monster to a handsome prince: "Beauty and the _?"

42. What is the name of the 1775 speech by Patrick Henry to the Virginia Convention telling the colonists that the Revolutionary War had begun, and calling for arms and the support of all: "Give Me Liberty or Give Me _?"

43. What is the title of pamphlet written in the summer of 1776 by Thomas Paine, written in plain and simple English that served as the inspiration and motivation for the people of the Thirteen Colonies to declare and fight for their independence from Great Britain: "Common _?"

44. What is the name of the official 1776 document, drafted by Thomas Jefferson along with John Adams and Benjamin Franklin, signed by 56 members including John Hancock, was presented to the Continental Congress in Philadelphia, officially adopted on July 4, 1776, and served to explain why the colonies were choosing to separate themselves from Great Britain: The Declaration of _?"

45. What is the name of the 1794 poem by the Scottish writer William Blake about the beauty of a wild striped beast that is both beautiful and ferocious at the same time: "The T_?"

46. What is the name of the poem by the Scottish author Robert Burns in 1794 based on song of the same name, comparing the writer's love for a lady to a red flower that symbolizes love: "A Red, Red _?"

47. What is the name of the 1807 English fairy tale as told by Benjamin Tabart, about a young boy who plants a magic bean that grows to the sky, and when the boy climbs up the stalk, he meets a giant who greets him with the words *fee-fi-fo-fum*: "Jack and the _?"

48. What is the name of the 1807 poem by William Wordsworth about a cluster of lovely yellow spring

NOTABLE LITERARY WORKS THROUGH THE AGES

flowers growing alongside a lake in the English countryside, that the author admired while out on a walk with his sister Dorothy: "D_?"

49. What is the title of the 1808 tragic play by Johann Wolfgang Goethe, based on a German legend, and tells the story of a man and his quest to find true meaning and harmony in life and with nature: "F_?"

50. What is the title of the 1811 romance novel by Jane Austen set in London during the years between 1792 and 1797 that centers on the lives and romantic relationships of sisters Elinor and Marianne Dashwood: "Sense and _?"

51. What is the full title of the 1812 novel by Johann Rudolf Wyss about a family that is shipwrecked in the East Indies en route to Australia, and build a raft and a tree house during their stay on the island: "The Swiss Family _?

52. What is the name of the German authors of a collection of fairy tales published in 1812 that include the classics *Cinderella, Sleeping Beauty, Rapunzel, Hansel and Gretel, Snow White, Rumpelstiltskin, Little Red Riding Hood, and The Golden Goose*: the Grimm brothers or the Anderson brothers?

53. What is the title of the 1813 novel by Jane Austen that centers on the lives of five sisters, Jane, Elizabeth, Mary, Kitty, and Lydia Bennett in rural 19th-century England, and how their lives are affected when a wealthy man named Mr. Bingley and his friend Darcy arrive in town: "Pride and _?"

54. What is the title of the 1814 lyric poem written by Lord Byron about an elegant, beautiful lady: "She Walks in _?"

55. What is the name of the 1815 novel by Jane Austen and tells the story of a young, spoiled English woman, and the effects of her matchmaking and meddling in others' affairs: "E_?"

56. What is the name of the 1818 horror novel by Mary Shelley about a mad scientist who creates a monster while conducting a laboratory experiment: "Franken_?"

57. What is the name of the 1819 satiric poem by Lord Byron that is based on the legend of a Spanish nobleman that is easily distracted by all the women he meets: "Don _?"

58. What is the full title of the 1820 novel by Washington Irving that tells the tale of Ichabod Crane and includes a ghost that appears as a Headless Horseman: "The Legend of Sleepy _?"

59. What is the full title of the 1820 novel by Washington Irving about a man who lived near the Catskill Mountains who wandered off one day and slept for twenty years: "Rip Van _?"

60. What is the name of the historical novel from 1820 by Sir Walter Scott that portrays the tensions between the Saxons and the Normans in England during the reign of King Richard I: "Ivan_?"

61. What is the name of the 1820 poem by John Keats one of Keats's *1819 odes*, inspired by the beautiful colors he noticed while on a walk one fall evening in Winchester, England: "Ode to _?"

62. What is the name of the 1820 poem by John Keats where the author appears to be interested in the timeless drawings on a piece of classical Greek art, as well as what those pictures, forever imprinted in stone, represent: "Ode on a Grecian _?"

NOTABLE LITERARY WORKS THROUGH THE AGES

63. What is the full title of the 1823 collection by Jacob and Wilhelm Grimm that include "Snow White" and "Hansel and Gretel:" Grimm's Fairy _?"

64. What is the full title of the 1826 historical novel by James Fenimore Cooper that is set during the Seven Years War when France and Great Britain were battling for control over North America the Native American allies that helped the French, and provides a convincing portrayal of a disappearing race and way of life: "The Last of the _?"

65. What is the full title of the 1831 French Gothic novel by Victor Hugo that tells the story of Quasimodo, a deformed hunchback and bell-ringer at Notre Dame Cathedral in Paris, who falls in love with the gypsy Esmeralda, and is forever at odds with his adoptive father Claude Frollo, the Archdeacon of Notre Dame: "The Hunchback of Notre _?"

66. What is the full title of the 1837 fairy tale by Robert Southey about a young blond girl who stumbles upon a cottage belonging to a family of bears: "Goldilocks and the Three _?"

67. What is the full title of the 1837 tale by Hans Christian Anderson about two weavers to promise a new set of clothes to an Emperor that are invisible to all those unfit for their positions, and is being complimented by all the citizens at a procession before an innocent child comments that he is not wearing *any* clothing: "The Emperor's New __?"

68. What is the full title of the 1838 novel by Charles Dickens about a young orphan boy who unknowingly finds himself in London involved with pickpockets and other criminals, but rises above that life of corruption: "Oliver _?"

69. What is the name of the 1842 short story by Edgar Allan Poe that tells the story of Prince Prospero who hides in a walled abbey in order to escape a dangerous plague, holds a masquerade party with seven colored rooms, and in the end meets his fate when he encounters a mysterious masked figure in the scarlet room: "The Masque of the Red _?"

70. What is the name of the 1842 story by Edgar Allan Poe about a man who is taken prisoner during the Spanish Inquisition and his attempts to survive both a fire pit and an approaching swinging object hanging above him: "The Pit and the _?"

71. What is the name of the 1843 story by Edgar Allan Poe about the narrator who tries to convince the reader that his murder of an old man was justified, how he hid him under the floorboards of his house, and how his guilt got the better of him when he heard the heartbeat of his victim through those floorboards: "The Tell-Tale _?"

72. What is the full title of the 1843 novel by Charles Dickens that tells of the transformation of Ebenezer Scrooge after he is visited by the Ghosts of Christmas past, present, and yet to come: "A Christmas _?"

73. What is the full title of the 1843 literary tale by the Danish author Hans Christian Anderson about a homely little barnyard bird that withstands the ridicule of others, endures some challenges along the way, and is finally accepted by a flock after it transforms into a beautiful swan: "The Ugly _?"

74. What is the full title of the 1844 novel by Alexandre Dumas that is set in France, and tells of the

NOTABLE LITERARY WORKS THROUGH THE AGES

adventures of d'Artagnan after he travels to Paris to join the Guard, and his three friends Athos, Porthos, and Aramis who are bonded with the motto, *all for one, one for all*: "The Three _?"

75. What is the full title of the 1845 novel by Alexandre Dumas about a man who goes to prison, escapes, and goes after those who wrongfully put him in prison: "The Count of Monte _?"

76. What is the name of the 1845 narrative poem by Edgar Allan Poe about a man who is sad about the loss of his love Lenore, who receives a visit one night from a talking black bird that replies *"nevermore"* when he asks the bird when he will see her again: "The R_?"

77. What is the name of the 1845 short story by the Danish author Hans Christian Anderson about a poor, dying girl who tries to sell matches one New Year's Eve, uses the matches to keep herself warm, sees visions of her grandmother in heaven as she lights each match, and in the end, her soul rises to join her grandmother: "The Little Match _?"

78. What is the full title of the 1846 collection by Danish author Hans Christian Anderson that include "The Princess and the Pea;" "The Little Mermaid;" and "The Emperor's New Clothes:" "Fairy _?"

79. What is the name of the 1846 short story by Edgar Allan Poe about the narrator Montressor who tells how he took revenge on his friend Fortunado who had insulted him, by tricking him to go down to the wine cellar of an Italian palazzo to try a fine vintage of wine called Amontillado, and then traps him in a niche: "The Cask of _?"

80. What is the name of the 1847 novel by William Makepeace Thackeray that makes fun of the society in 19th century Britain, centering on themes of love and fortune as it follows the adventures of Amelia Sedley and Becky Sharp: "Vanity _?"

81. What is the name of the 1847 novel by Charlotte Bronte about the title character living in England from her childhood as an orphan, her education, her time as a governess, and her marriage to Rochester: "Jane _?"

82. What is the name of the 1847 novel by Emily Bronte about the love between Catherine Earnshaw and Heathcliff, and how their unresolved love destroys them and those around them: "Wuthering _?"

83. What is the name of the short 1848 publication by Karl Marx and Friedrich Engels, regarded as one of the world's most important political documents, that outlines the actions necessary for replacing a capitalist society with a Communist one, and asserts that only a revolution would be effective in eliminating all social classes: "Communist _?"

84. What is the full title of the 1850 novel by Charles Dickens that traces the life of a young boy who escapes an unhappy childhood in England to his adventures as an adult, his marriage, and his life as a successful author: "David _?"

85. What are the famous first lines from sonnet number 43 by Elizabeth Barrett Browning, published in 1850 as a collection of 44 love sonnets: "How do I love thee? Let me count the _?"

86. What is the name of the 1850 novel by Nathanial Hawthorne set in Puritan Boston, Massachusetts, that tells the story of Hester Prynne who committed a great sin, the red symbol she must now wear on her

NOTABLE LITERARY WORKS THROUGH THE AGES

dress for all to see as a reminder of her sin, and how she struggles to rise above it and her shame: "The Scarlet _?"

87. What is the name of the 1851 novel by Herman Melville that tells the story of Captain Ahab and his crew, and his pursuit of a ferocious great white whale that had destroyed his ship on a previous voyage off the coast of Japan, and begins with the line, *Call Me Ishmael*: "Moby _?"

88. What is the title of the 1851 romance novel by Nathaniel Hawthorne about the Pyncheon family living in a gabled house in New England that has served to provide mystery and intrigue for many generations: The House of the Seven _?"

89. What is the full title of the 1851 speech given by civil rights activist Sojourner Truth at the Women's Convention in Ohio, named for the line that she repeated throughout the speech: "Ain't I A _?"

90. What is the full title of the 1852 speech given by abolitionist Frederick Douglass to the citizens of Rochester, New York on the Fourth of July, who criticized the nation for celebrating freedom while nearly four million people were still working as slaves: "The Hypocrisy of American _?"

91. What is the title of the 1852 anti-slavery novel by abolitionist and writer Harriet Beecher Stowe, regarded as instrumental in promoting the anti-slavery movement leading to the American Civil War that depicts the life of a black slave as the *Uncle Tom*, a character portrayed as someone who is a dutiful servant to his master: "Uncle Tom's _?"

92. What is the title of the 1854 autobiography by Henry David Thoreau that is reflection of a man who immerses himself in nature, and comes to appreciate the simple things in his natural surroundings while living in a cabin near Walden pond for one year: "Walden: Life in the _?"

93. What is the name of the 1855 collection of over 400 poems by Walt Whitman that included *Song of Myself,* one of the original twelve poems in the first edition, and *I Hear America Singing*, included in one of the later editions: "Leaves of _?"

94. What is the full title of the 1856 novel by French writer Gustave Flaubert that tells the story of a doctor's wife, Emma Bovary, a romantic soul, who has grown bored with her dull life and so turns to the company of others to find fulfillment in her otherwise empty life: "Madame _?"

95. What is the full title of the 1859 novel by Charles Dickens that depicts the lives of the lower class peasantry and the upper class aristocracy in both Paris and London right before the French Revolution: "A Tale of Two __?"

96. What is the rest of the opening line of the 1859 Charles Dickens novel "A Tale of Two Cities:" *"It was the best of times, it was the _?"*

97. What is the name of the 1861 poem written by American poet Henry Wadsworth Longfellow, that celebrates the famous horseback journey of 1775 by American patriot Paul Revere from Boston to Lexington to warn Samuel Adams and John Hancock of a British attack, after leaving a code for the Sons of Liberty that lanterns were to be placed in the bell tower of the Old North Church, *one if by land, and two if by sea*: "Paul Revere's _?"

NOTABLE LITERARY WORKS THROUGH THE AGES

98. What is the full title of the 1861 novel by Charles Dickens that tells the story of an orphaned boy named Pip and the Blacksmith's family that adopts him: "Great _?"

99. What is the title of the 1862 French historical novel by Victor Hugo set during a time of political unrest in Paris, that centers on the character Jean Valjean who is imprisoned for 19 years for stealing a loaf of bread, his life on the run from a police inspector who is pursuing him, the young, motherless girl Cosette he befriends, and his continuous struggle to fit in to society as an ex-convict and attain redemption: "Les _?"

100. What is the name of the 1863 speech delivered by President Abraham Lincoln during the Civil War when he referred to the Declaration of Independence with the opening line of his speech with his words "*Four score and seven years ago:*" "The Gettysburg __?"

101. What is title of the 1865 novel by Lewis Carroll that follows the adventures of a seven-year old girl and the new world she finds herself in after falling down a rabbit hole: "Alice's Adventures in _?"

102. What is the name of the 1865 poem by Walt Whitman written as a tribute to Abraham Lincoln after his death, honoring an American President with whom Whitman shared his opposition to slavery, and his commitment to the Union: "O Captain, My _?"

103. What is the name of the 1866 novel by Russian author Fyodor Dostoyevsky and set in St. Petersburg Russia, that centers around an ex-student named Raskolnikov who plots to kill a pawnbroker for the cash, believing all along that he can justify the murder with all the good deeds he will carry out with the money, but in the end is persuaded to confess his terrible crime: "Crime and _?"

104. What is the full title of the 1868 novel by Louisa May Alcott that follows the lives of four sisters, Meg, Jo, Amy, and Beth as they mature through life, and their struggle with poverty: "Little _?"

105. What is the name of the 1869 epic novel by the Russian author Leo Tolstoy that provides an overview of the events of the 1812 French invasion of Russia under Napoleon, includes insights to the war from the perspective of five aristocratic Russian families, but illustrates the effects of the war on *all* classes of society: "War and _?"

106. What is the full title of the 1870 novel by Jules Verne that relates the adventures of Captain Nemo and his submarine Nautilus: "Twenty Thousand Leagues Under the _?"

107. What is the full title of the 1871 novel by Lewis Carroll that continues the adventures of Alice and her life compared to chess game after she looks into a mirror above the fireplace mantel: "Through the Looking _?"

108. What is the name of the 1871 nonsense poem by Lewis Carroll in his novel "Through the Looking Glass" about a boy who takes his sword and sets out to kill creatures in the woods, succeeds in killing one, and brings the head back for his dad to see: "Jabber_?"

109. What is the full title of the 1873 adventure novel by Jules Verne about an Englishman named Phileas Fogg and his French servant who makes a bet with his fellow club members that he can circle the Earth in a certain amount of days: "Around the World in 80 _?"

110. What is the name of the 1873 speech by Susan B. Anthony after being fined one hundred dollars for casting an illegal ballot in the 1872 presidential election: "Women's Right to the _?"

NOTABLE LITERARY WORKS THROUGH THE AGES

111. What is the full title of the 1876 novel by Mark Twain about a mischievous, young boy and his adventures growing up near the Mississippi River: The Adventures of Tom _?"

112. What is the full title of the 1877 autobiographical memoir by English author Anna Sewell, narrated from the perspective of a horse from the time he was a carefree colt on an English farm to his hard life pulling cabs in London, to his happy retirement in the country, and reveals how he was treated by several different masters over the course of his life: "Black _?"

113. What is the full title of the 1877 novel by Russian author Leo Tolstoy set in 19th century Russia about a woman named Anna who is miserable and bored in her marriage, and so begins a friendship with the Count Vronsky: "Anna K_?"

114. What is the full title of the 1879 three-act play by Norwegian playwright Henrik Ibsen about a housewife named Nora Helmer who becomes disillusioned with her husband Torvald, who merely regards her as his *little caged song bird*: "A Doll's _?"

115. What is the name of the 1880 novel by Johanna Spyri about a young girl raised by her grandfather in the Swiss Alps of Switzerland? "H_?"

116. What is the full title of the 1880 novel by Lew Wallace that relates the adventures of the Jewish prince of Jerusalem Judah Ben-Hur, and his choice to convert to Christianity after realizing that he is wrong in wanting to seek revenge on his childhood friend Messala, who had wrongly imprisoned he and his family: "Ben-Hur: A Tale of the _?"

117. What is the full title of the 1881 novel by American author Mark Twain that tells the story of commoner Tom Canty who lives with his father in London, and Prince Edward, the son of King Henry VIII, who decide to switch clothes one day, and how each experiences the life of the other for a time before resuming their rightful places: "The Prince and the _?"

118. What is the title of the 1881 novel by Henry James that tells the story of an American woman named Isabel Archer who inherits a lot of money, travels to Europe to find herself, marries an artist named Gilbert Osmond who does not truly love her, and in the end finds some solace when she is able to reconnect with her cousin and her soul mate Ralph: "The Portrait of a _?"

119. What is the full title of the 1883 novel by Italian author Carlo Collodi, about an animated marionette carved by a wood carver named Geppetto, and the nose that grows when the puppet tells a lie: "The Adventures of _?

120. What is the full title of the 1883 novel by Howard Pyle about an English outlaw and his men who rob from the rich and give to the poor: "The Merry Adventures of Robin _?"

121. What is the full title of the 1883 novel by Scottish author Robert Lewis Stevenson, that relates the tale of sailor Jim Hawkins who is drawn to the world of pirates when he finds Captain Flint's map in a chest, and competes with Long John Silver to be the first to find the valuable booty on Skeleton Island in the West Indies: "Treasure __?"

NOTABLE LITERARY WORKS THROUGH THE AGES

122. What is the name of the poem by Ella Wheeler Wilcox first published in 1883 in "The New York Sun," that was inspired when the author empathized with the loneliness of a sorrowful widow, with the opening lines, *laugh, and the world laughs with you, weep, and you weep alone*: "S_?"

123. What is the full title of the 1884 novel by Mark Twain that relates the adventures of the main character and his friend Jim, a runaway slave, as they journey on a raft along the Mississippi River: "The Adventures of Huckleberry _?"

124. What is the title of the 1884 short story by French author Guy de Maupassant about how the lives of Madame Mathilde Loisel and her husband who borrow a precious piece of jewelry for a social event, lose the piece of jewelry, and for years after try to raise the several thousand French francs necessary to replace it, only to find out that this lost piece of jewelry was a paste imitation: "The N_?"

125. What is the full title of the 1885 adventure novel by H. Ryder Haggard about an African adventurer, Allen Quartermain, who leads a dangerous expedition in his quest to locate a lost treasure: "King Solomon's _?"

126. What is the name of the 1885 poem by Robert Louis Stevenson from the collection "A Child's Garden of Verses," about a about a child's interest in the dark image created by the sound that follows him around: "The S _?"

127. What is the full title of the 1886 adventure novel by Robert Louis Stevenson about David Belfour and his adventures as he sets out to claim his rightful inheritance, and escape an uncle who is plotting to cheat him out of it: "Kid_?"

128. What is the title of the 1886 novella by Leo Tolstoy that tells the story of the death of a court justice named Ivan in 19th century Russia, the illness that slowly led to his slow and painful death, how he looks back on his life with regret, the greed and personal gain that consume the thoughts of his family and friends, and how in the end, he experiences acceptance and peace as he leaves one world for another: "The Death of Ivan _?"

129. What is the title of the 1892 collection of twelve short stories by Arthur Conan Doyle featuring a detective named Sherlock and his faithful assistant Dr. Watson: "The Adventures of Sherlock _?"

130. What is the full title of the 1894 by Rudyard Kipling that is a collection of fables using animals to tell a story and to teach a lesson: "The Jungle _?"

131. What is the full title of the 1895 war novel by Stephen Crane, set during the American Civil War that centers on Henry Fleming, a private in the Union Army who flees from battle in the field, but later seeks to be wounded as proof of his bravery, and to cover up his cowardice: "The Red Badge of _?"

132. What is the full title of the 1898 science fiction novel by H.G. Wells that tells of the adventures of an un-named protagonist, his brother Surray, and life on Earth after it has been invaded by Martians: "The War of the _?"

133. What is the name of the 1899 short novel by Joseph Conrad that centers on the life of ivory transporter Charles Marlow and his journey down the Congo River in Africa, his search for a man named Kurtz,

NOTABLE LITERARY WORKS THROUGH THE AGES

the corruption of the trading company at different stations in the dense jungle of the Congo, and the mistreatment of the native people in the pursuit of the valuable ivory: "Heart of _?"

134. What is the full title of the 1900 novel by F. Frank Baum about a girl name Dorothy who makes friends with a scarecrow, a tin man, and a cowardly lion as she tries to find her way back home to Kansas along a yellow brick road, but has a wicked witch from the West in her way: "The Wonderful Wizard of _?"

135. What is the title of the 1900 novel by Joseph Conrad that tells the story of a British seaman named Jim, a man who struggles to come to terms with his past because he had abandoned his ship called the Patna, and his navigation privilege is taken away from him: "Lord _?"

136. What is the name of the 1901 autobiography of Booker T. Washington that relates his experiences as a young slave during the Civil War, the challenges he faced in getting an education, and his goal to establish vocational schools for aspiring African-Americans like the Tuskegee Institute in Alabama he founded: "Up From _?"

137. What is the full title of the 1902 novel by Beatrix Potter about a curious bunny that tries over and over to sneak into Mr. McGregor's vegetable garden: "The Tale of Peter _?"

138. What is the name of the 1902 novel by Scottish author J.M. Barrie about the adventures of a boy who never ages and can fly on the small island of Neverland, his best fairy friend Tinkerbell, and his interactions with mermaids, fairies, pirates, Native Americans, and children: "Peter _?"

139. What is the full title of the 1902 horror short story by W.W. Jacobs tells the tale of how a family friend introduces the White family to the powers of a part of a monkey that can grant its owner three wishes, but those wishes may come at a high price: "The Monkey's _?"

140. What is the name of the short story in the "Just So Stories" collection published in 1902 by Rudyard Kipling, about a leopard named Sheldon and how he got the markings on his body: "How the Leopard Got His _?"

141. What is the full title of the 1903 autobiography by the deaf and blind writer Helen Keller that tells the story of her early life and her relationship with her teacher Anne Sullivan: "Helen Keller: The Story of My _?"

142. What is the full title of the 1903 novel by Howard Pyle about an English King, a lady named Guinevere, and several knights that include Sir Lancelot: "King Arthur and his Knights of the Round _?

143. What is the full title of the 1903 children's novel by Kate Douglas Wiggin about Rebecca Randall, one of seven children, who is sent to live with her two strict aunts on an English farm, and ultimately inherits the land and farm from her aunts and is able to help support the Randall family: "Rebecca of Sunnybrook _?"

144. What is the full title of the 1903 novel by Jack London about a dog named Buck that is stolen from his domestic home in California, sent to Yukon Territory, Canada to work as a sled dog during the 19th century Gold Rush, and has to learn how to survive the harsh Canadian wilderness: "The Call of the _?"

NOTABLE LITERARY WORKS THROUGH THE AGES

145. What is the full title of the 1905 historical novel by Baroness Emma Orczy set during the French Revolution in which an English aristocrat enters France and tries to save innocent people from certain death, and leaves a leaves a red flower behind as his calling card: "The Scarlet _?"

146. What is the full title of the 1906 novel by Jack London, set in Yukon Territory, Canada during the Klondike Gold Rush, about a wild wolf-dog that is raised to be vicious, is later tamed by a gold-hunter named Scott, and eventually becomes a domesticated dog: "White _?

147. What is the name of the 1906 novel by American author and politician Upton Sinclair that portrays the lives and of immigrants in the United States, and touches on themes of social inequality, poverty, corruption, and poor working conditions and wages: "The J_?"

148. What is the name of the 1906 short story written by O. Henry about a young English couple who have very little money at Christmas time, so the lady sells her long tresses to buy her husband a chain for his grandfather's watch, and the husband sells his pocket watch to buy beautiful combs for his wife: "The Gift of the _?"

149. What is the name of the 1907 fantasy novel by Edith Nesbit about three children, Jerry, Jimmy, and Cathy, who discover a tunnel that leads them to a fairy-tale castle, a princess, and the magical powers of a ring they find inside the castle: "The Enchanted _?"

150. What is the full title of the 1908 novel by Canadian author Lucy Maud Montgomery about a red-haired orphan girl named Anne Shirley that is sent to live with a family on a farm on Prince Edward Island, and how she charms the lives of everyone she meets there: "Anne of Green _?"

151. What is the title of the 1908 novel by Kenneth Grahame about the friendship of a mole, a rat, a toad, and a badger, and their adventures near a river in the English countryside: "The Wind and the _?"

152. What is the title of the 1908 novel by English author E. M. Forster that tells the story of a girl named Lucy Honeychurch who is courted by an English man named George Emerson whom she meets while staying at a pension with her cousin that overlooks a courtyard in Italy, and must choose between this man whom she truly loves and her prim and proper fiancée named Cecil back in England: "A Room With a _?"

153. What is the name of the 1908 short story by Jack London about a man and his husky who brave the bitter, winter cold while on the Yukon trail in Alaska, goes to great lengths to save himself and his dog from frostbite and hypothermia, and struggles to escape his imminent death by building something to warm them: "To Build a _?"

154. What is the name of the poem by Rudyard Kipling published in 1910 essentially giving advice and motivation to his son John: "I_?"

155. What is the full title of the 1911 novel by Frances Hodgson Burnett about an orphaned British girl born in India, who returns to England to live with her wealthy uncle in a castle, and the magical things that take place after she works to bring the neglected yard back to life: "The Secret _?"

156. What is the title of the 1912 play by George Bernard Shaw that is named for a Greek character, tells the story of professor Henry Higgins who makes a bet that he can train a flower girl named Eliza

NOTABLE LITERARY WORKS THROUGH THE AGES

Doolittle to pretend she is a duchess at an ambassador's garden party, and was the inspiration for the 1956 musical, *My Fair Lady*: "P_?"

157. What is the full title of the 1913 novel by Eleanor H. Porter about an orphan girl who goes to live in Vermont with her wealthy but strict aunt, and manages to transform the entire town to a happy place through her sunny disposition and "The Glad Game:" "Polly_?"

158. What is the name of the 1916 four stanza poem written by Robert Frost with the famous final lines, *I took the one less traveled by, and that has made all the difference*: "The Road Not _?"

159. What is the name of the 1916 novel by Irish author James Joyce that tells the story of Stephan Dedalus growing up in Ireland, from the time he was a young boy to his young adult life trying to fit it in while in college, and his decision to leave Ireland to become an artist: "A Portrait of the Artist as a Young _?"

160. What is the full title of the 1920 novel by Hugh Lofting about a poor country doctor from England who learns to talk to animals with the help of his parrot Polynesia, travels to Africa to help sick monkeys, acquires some treasures from a pirate ship on his way home, and is able to retire with his earnings from his animals in a travelling circus: "Doctor _?"

161. What is the title of the 1922 novel by Irish author James Joyce that is set in Dublin, Ireland, follows the paths of the two main characters over the course of one day on June 16, 1907, a middle-aged Jewish man named Leopold Bloom, and a young scholar named Stephen Daedalus, and is told over 18 episodes: "U_?"

162. What is the full title of the 1922 book by Margery Williams about a stuffed bunny that is given to a little boy as a Christmas present, and realizes its dream when it becomes real through the love of its owner: "The Velveteen _?"

163. What is the full title of the 1922 poem by Robert Frost describing the feelings of rider pausing to watch the snow falling in the woods, and contains the memorable last line, *and miles to go before I sleep*: "Stopping by Woods on a Snowy _?"

164. What is the title of the 1923 Newbery award- winning book by Hugh Lofting set in South America, about a doctor who meets Tommy Stubbins who learns how to speak to animals, and who helps the doctor in his quest to find a naturalist named Long Arrow: "The Voyages of Doctor _?"

165. What is the name of the 1924 collection of poems by the America poet that is a collection of 597 poems and was published long after her death in 1886: "The Poetry of Emily _?"

166. What is the name of the 1924 short story by Richard Connell about a big game hunter named Rainsford who finds himself on a remote Caribbean island after falling from his boat, and is forced by the aristocrat and game-hunter General Zaroff to participate in a human man-hunt over three days or die, with only a knife, a bag of food and a three hour head start: "The Most Dangerous _?"

167. What is the name of the 1924 novel by E.M. Forster set in India when it was ruled by the British that profiles the often tense relationships between Indians and Anglos: "A Passage to _?"

NOTABLE LITERARY WORKS THROUGH THE AGES

168. What is the name of the 1924 novella by Herman Melville about a young sailor named Billy on a merchant ship in 1797, accused of conspiracy to mutiny by a fellow sailor named Claggart whom he unintentionally kills when confronted by him, his guilty sentence, and the legacy of hope he left behind in spite of it all: "Billy _?"

169. What is the name of the 1925 novel by F. Scott Fitzgerald about the rich and glitzy lifestyles and elaborate parties of Jay, Tom, Daisy, and others living in upscale Long Island in the summer of 1922: "The Great _?"

170. What is the full title of the 1926 book by A.A. Milne about the adventures of a honey-loving teddy bear, and his friends Tigger, Piglet, Owl, Kanga, Roo, Rabbit, and Eeyore: "Winnie-the-_?"

171. What is the full title of the 1926 novel by American author Ernest Hemingway set right after World War I that tells the story of Jake Barnes and Lady Brett Ashley and their journey from Paris to Pamplona, Spain to watch the running of the bulls during the summer Festival of San Fermín: "The Sun Also _?"

172. What is the name of the fictional book series created by Edward Stratemeyer and first published in 1927 under the collective pseudonym Franklin W. Dixon, about teenage brothers and amateur detectives Frank and Joe who find themselves involved in many adventures and mysteries: "The Hardy __?"

173. What is the name of the 1927 novel by Virginia Woolf that follows the Ramsey family and their visits to their summer home off the coast of Scotland, the challenges when faced with the realities of war, sickness, and death, and how the surviving members of the family finally experience a true connection when visiting the summer house after ten years and finally taking the long-promised journey to the lighted beacon: "To the _?"

174. What is the full title of the 1929 novel by Erich Maria Remarque that describes the physical and mental stress of German soldiers during World War I, and their challenges in integrating themselves back into society upon returning home from the front lines: "All Quiet on the Western _?"

175. What is the full title of the 1929 novel by William Faulkner about the once wealthy Compson family, and the challenges they face after losing their money, their faith, family members, and the respect of their neighbors in Jefferson, Mississippi: "The Sound and the _?"

176. What is the full title of the 1929 novel by Ernest Hemingway set during World War I in Italy that centers on an ambulance driver named Frederic Henry and his love for an English nurse named Catherine Barkley whom he meets after he is wounded: "A Farewell to _?"

177. What is the full title of the 1930 book by Watty Piper about a determined little train engine that struggles, but manages to pull a train loaded with toys to the other side of a mountain for expecting children: "The Little Engine that _?"

178. What is the name of the 1930 fictional mystery series published under the pseudonym Carolyn Keene, about a 16-year-old amateur detective who spends a lot of her time solving mysteries, sometimes along with her friends Bess Marvin, George Fayne, and her boyfriend Ned Nickerson: "Nancy __?"

NOTABLE LITERARY WORKS THROUGH THE AGES

179. What is the full title of the 1930 novel by William Faulkner that is narrated by 15 different characters, and tells the story of the death of Addie Bundren and the efforts of her family to follow her wishes and have her buried in the Mississippi town of Jefferson: "As I Lay _?"

180. What is the name of the 1930 novel by Dashiel Hammett about a detective named Samuel Spade who is hired to locate the non-existent sister of Miss Wonderly, his investigation into the mysterious death of his partner Miles Archer, his pursuit to find a jewel-encrusted bird statue in order to prove his own innocence, and his discovery that Miss Wonderly herself was the real murderer of his partner: "The Maltese _?"

181. What is the title of the 1931 novel by Pearl S. Buck that tells the story of a hard-working Chinese farmer named Wang Lung, his wife O-lan, his five children, the struggles they face in buying and maintaining farm land from his family that land in their village of Anhwei, feeding their children, and in leaving behind a legacy: "The Good E_?"

182. What is the full title of the 1932 novel by Laura Ingalls Wilder that is an autobiography of her early childhood memories and pioneer life in the woods of Pepin, Wisconsin: "Little House in the Big _?"

183. What is the full title of the 1932 novel by Laura Ingalls Wilder that tells about the journey of the Ingalls family from the big woods of Wisconsin to their new home they build on the prairie, and the many challenges that come with building a house, befriending Indians, planting crops, digging a well, and surviving harsh winters and prairie fires: "Little House on the _?"

184. What is the name of the 1932 novel by Aldous Huxley set in London about an ideal society hundreds of years into the future, where science has perfected the human race: "Brave New _?"

185. What is the full title of the 1932 novel by Charles Nordhoff and James Norman about a mutiny or rebellion against the commanding officer Lieutenant William Bligh of a British Royal Navy ship in 1789: "Mutiny on the _?"

186. What is the title of the 1933 story by A.A. Milne that tells the story of a young elephant who leaves the jungle, visits the city, and upon his return is appointed king: "The Story of B_?"

187. What is the full title of the 1934 novel by P.R. Travers about an English nanny with magical powers, who flies to the Banks household with her umbrella and her carpetbag to care for Jane, Michael, and twins John and Barbara: "Mary _?"

188. What is the full title of the 1934 crime novel by James M. Cain about a man named Frank Chambers, a drifter who starts working at a California diner where he meets a waitress he ends up falling in love with, and how they plot to murder her husband to get him out of the way: "The Postman Always Rings _?"

189. What is the title of the 1934 crime novel by Agatha Christie featuring the detective Hercule Poirot who investigates the murder of a wealthy man named Ratchett, an acquaintance he met on a train he boarded in Constantinople Istanbul, discovers that everyone on the train had a motive for murdering him, and is convinced in the end, that all 12 suspects as well as the conductor himself had a hand in his stabbing as revenge for a previous murder Ratchett, alias Cassetti had committed: "Murder on the Orient _?"

NOTABLE LITERARY WORKS THROUGH THE AGES

190. What is the full title of the 1935 novel by Enid Bagnold about a fourteen-year-old girl named Velvet Brown who trains her horse and ultimately wins the Grand National Steeplechase horse race, and how she prefers to emphasize the skill and accomplishment of the horse and not the rider in winning the race: "National _?"

191. What is the name of the 1936 children's book by Munro Leaf and illustrated by Robert Lawson, about a bull that prefers to stay in his meadow and smell the flowers, rather than fight a Spanish matador in a bull ring: "The Story of F_?"

192. What is the name of the poem by Langston Hughes first published in 1936 that talks about how the American dream of freedom and equality has never been fully realized by many African Americans and other minority groups, but ends with the glimmer of hope that the dream will come true one day soon: "Let America Be America _?"

193. What is the name of the 1936 historical novel and love story set during the Civil War by Margaret Mitchell depicting the lives of southern belle Scarlett O'Hara on her Georgia plantation called Tara, her relationship with Rhett Butler and Ashley Wilkes, and her journey to re-establish her life: "Gone with the _?"

194. What is the full title of the 1937 fantasy novel by J R.R. Tolkien that tells the story of Bilbo Baggins, his quest to win a share of the treasure that is being guarded by a dragon, and his many encounters with wizards, dwarves, trolls, goblins, dragons, spiders, and eagles: "The H _?"

195. What is the title of the 1937 novel by African American author Zora Neale Hurston, that tells the story of an African American woman named Janie Crawford, as told in a flashback to her best friend Pheoby, revealing what her life has been like from the time she was a powerless, young girl, to the present time in her adult life where she finally feels in control of her destiny: "Their Eyes Were Watching _?"

196. What is the title of the 1937 memoir by Danish author Isak Dinesen, the pen name of Karen Blixen, that is a reflection of seventeen years of the author's life living on a coffee plantation in Ngog Hills near Nairobi, Kenya: "Out of _?"

197. What is the title of the 1937 novella written by John Steinbeck that tells the story George Milton and Lennie Small, migrant farm workers in California who travel from place to place during the American Depression, share the ambition of someday owning their own ranch, and the tragic ending when George kills his friend Lennie for the sole purpose of sparing him the slow death he would have suffered had he been killed by the lynch mob: "Of Mice and _?"

198. What is the name of the 1938 folktale by Esphyr Slobodkina about a hat salesman with a moustache who wears his entire inventory of hats on his head, awakens from his nap in a tree to find that all of his hats except for his own have been stolen by monkeys, and how the monkeys proceed to imitate the salesman's gestures: "Caps for Sale: A Tale of a Peddler, Some Monkeys, and their Monkey _?"

199. What is the name of the 1938 novel by T.H. White that tells of the life of King Arthur in medieval England and the lessons he learns through Merlyn, proving at the end that he is the rightful King of England: "The Sword in the _?"

NOTABLE LITERARY WORKS THROUGH THE AGES

200. What is the name of the 1938 play by American playwright Thornton Wilder that tells the story of the citizens of a small town called Grover's Corners, with the players performing scenes without scenery or props from the town's history between 1901 and 1913: "Our _?"

201. What is the full title of the 1938 children's book by Richard and Florence Atwater that relates the story of a poor house painter Mr. Popper and his family who happens to receive first one penguin, and then another, and soon find themselves overwhelmed when the creatures take over their house: "Mr. Popper's _?"

202. What is the name of the 1938 novel by Marjorie Kinnan Rawlings that tells the story of a poor farming family in Florida and their only son, Jody Baxter, who adopts the fawn of a doe that his father shoots, but the deer becomes a nuisance when it continuously eats the crops and the young boy is faced with a hard choice, and in the end this choice contributes to his coming-of-age: "The Y_?"

203. What is the full title of the 1939 book, part of a series by the Austrian author Ludwig Bemelmans, about a girl who is staying at a boarding house in Paris, and the doll house she receives from her father while recovering after having her appendix removed: "Madel_?"

204. What is the full title of the 1939 novel by Irish author James Joyce, regarded as one of the most difficult literary works in the English language that centers on the Earwicker family living in a city near Dublin, Ireland, and their efforts to disprove a rumor that was spread about HCE, the father: "Finnegan's _?"

205. What is the name of the 1939 speech of a New York Yankees player who addressed the fans at Yankee Stadium, and let them know that he was retiring from baseball after being diagnosed with a fatal disease: "The Farewell Speech of Lou _?"

206. What is the name of the 1939 novel by John Steinbeck that tells the story of Tom Joad and his migrant farming family who are forced to leave their farm in Oklahoma because of draught, their difficult journey moving the family west with the promise of jobs, and the living conditions in California given the tension between the migrants and the landowners: "The Grapes of _?"

207. What is the name of the 1940 Newbery award-winning children's book by James Daugherty about the adventurous life of a pioneer and frontiersman named Daniel, and the trail he blazed through the Appalachian mountains from North Carolina into Kentucky where he founded the village of Boonsborough.: "Daniel _?"

208. What is the title of the 1940 book based on an old Russian Folk tale that was made popular in a Little Golden Book by Margot Zemach about a hen who worked hard to plant and harvest wheat, and to bake bread, and all her friends like sleepy Cat, noisy Little Duck, and lazy Dog who only wanted to help *eat* the bread: "The Little Red _?"

209. What is the title of the 1940 novel by Eric Knight about the journey of a dog after he is sold to a wealthy man 300 miles away, and the eventual reunion of the collie and his twelve-year-old owner Joe Carraclough: "Lassie Come _?"

210. What is the title of the 1940 children's book by Dorothy Kunhardt, named for a rabbit, and is an interactive book that encourages touching different textures: "Pat the _?"

NOTABLE LITERARY WORKS THROUGH THE AGES

211. What is the name of the first 1940 speech by the British Prime Minister Winston Churchill, who in his speech, emphasized that the fight against Adolf Hitler and the Nazis of Germany was paramount to the survival of Great Britain itself: "Blood, Toil, Tears, and _?"

212. What is the title of the 1940 novel by Ernest Hemingway about an American soldier named Robert Jordan who, fighting alongside other Spanish Republicans, and is given the task of blowing up a bridge during the attack on Segovia, Spain during the Spanish Civil War: "For Whom the Bell _?"

213. What is the title of the 1940 novel by American author Richard Wright that tells the story of Bigger Thomas, a twenty-year-old African-American living in poverty in Chicago, his attempt to cover up his murder of Mary, the daughter of the wealthy family he is working for, and the challenges he faces in trying to understand white people and the world he lives in right up to the time of his own execution: "Native _?"

214. What is the full title of the 1941 story, and part of a series of children's books by H.A. Rey, about a monkey and his adventures after meeting the man with a yellow hat: "Curious _?"

215. What is the full title of the 1941 story by Walter Farley that relates the story about a wild, black Arabian horse and his young owner Alec Ramsey who are stranded on a desert island after their ship sinks, and how Alec trains the horse to race with the help of a professional trainer after they are rescued: "The Black _?"

216. What is the name of the December 8, 1941 speech given by Franklin D. Roosevelt to Congress the day after the Japanese attack of Pearl Harbor, describing it to them as *a date which will live in infamy*: "Pearl Harbor Address to the _?"

217. What is the full title of the 1942 story by Janette Sebring Lowry about a little dog that does everything different than his brothers and sisters, and ends up the only one going to bed without any dessert: "The Pokey Little _?"

218. What is the name of the 1942 children's series by Gertrude C. Warner about four orphaned children, Henry, Jesse, Violet, and Benny, who live in an abandoned old train car and encounter many adventures and mysteries, but later move in with their wealthy grandfather but keep the train car and use it as a playhouse: "The Boxcar __?"

219. What is the name of the 1942 picture book by Margaret Wise Brown about a rabbit who wants to run off and his mom who promises to run after him if he does: "The Runaway _?"

220. What is the title of the 1942 picture book by Virginia Lee Burton about a country house on a hill, and the residents who live there who are eventually crowded out over time because of city development as the roads, lights, and apartments become closer and closer: "The Little H_?"

221. What is the full title of the 1943 Newbury award-winning novel by Esther Forbes set in colonial Boston, about a promising silversmith apprentice who suffers a burn to his hand, is later introduced to the Sons of Liberty, and ends up participating in the Battles of Lexington, Concord, and the Boston Tea Party: "Johnny T _?"

NOTABLE LITERARY WORKS THROUGH THE AGES

222. What is the full title of the 1943 fable by Antoine de Saint-Exupery that tells the story of an aviator forced to land in the Sahara desert, meets someone from the planet Asteroid 612, and over the next 8 days while repairing his plane, learns about all the places this person has visited: "The Little P _?"

223. What is the title of the 1943 novel by Albert Camus about a North African named Meursault, a man portrayed as detached and unemotional, who murders a man whom he recognizes in the French province of Algiers, but comes to terms with his indifference toward the world right before he is to die: "The S_?"

224. What is the full title of the 1944 children's book by Eleanor Estes about a Polish girl named Wanda Petronski who attends a school in Connecticut, and is teased by her classmates for wearing the same blue dress every day, but claims that she has several more dresses at home: "The Hundred _?"

225. What is the title of the 1944 Newbery award-winning novel by Robert Lawson set in the countryside near Danbury, Connecticut about a group of animals that are excited that some new folks are moving into an abandoned house, and wonder how things will change and if there will be a new garden in their future: "Rabbit H_?"

226. What is the full title of the 1944 play by Tennessee Williams based on the lives of Tom Wingfield, his mother Amanda, and his two sisters Rose and Laura, and their economic, mental, and emotional struggles as they try to adapt to a life without a husband and a father in the south: "The Glass _?"

227. What is the title of the 1945 Newbery award-winning book by Lois Lenski set in Florida, that tells the story of the feuding Boyer family who raise strawberries, and the Slater family who raise cattle, and what happens when Shoestring Slater's pony ruins the strawberries at Birdie Boyer's farm: "Strawberry _?"

228. What is the full title of the 1945 fictional character featured in a series of books by the Swedish author Astrid Lindgren about the adventures of a nine year old mischievous girl whose red pigtails stick out from both sides of her head, her pet monkey and her pet horse: "Pippi _?"

229. What is the full title of the 1945 children's novel by E.B. White about a little mouse who lives in New York City with his parents, his older brother George, Snowbell the cat, and his best friend Margalo, a bird, who he sets out to save when it disappears from its nest: "Stuart _?"

230. What is the name of the 1945 satirical novel by George Orwell about a group of mistreated pigs and other animals who decide to revolt against humans, and come to realize that are not better off for trying to run a farm by themselves in order to promote progress and equality: "Animal _?"

231. What is the name of the 1946 Newbery award novel by Carolyn Sherwin Bailey about a doll made from an apple tree twig, her head made from a hickory nut, lives in a corncob doll house, and how she adapts with the animals when her family leaves her behind one winter: "Miss H _?"

232. What is the title of the 1946 political novel by Robert Penn Warren, a title that was taken from the nursery rhyme "Humpty Dumpty" that tells the story of the governorship of William Stark, a man named Jack Burdon who arrives to work for him, and the political corruption of the American South during the Depression in the 1930's: "All the Kings's _?"

NOTABLE LITERARY WORKS THROUGH THE AGES

233. What is the full title of the 1947 book by Margaret Wise Brown about a rabbit that says goodnight to everything around him: "Goodnight _?"

234. What is the full title of the 1947 Newbery award-winning book by William Pene du Bois that relates the story of Professor Sherman who sets off on a journey in a hot air balloon and ultimately crashes on the volcanic island of Krakatoa and the greedy society of the twenty families who live there: "The Twenty-One _?"

235. What is the full title of the 1947 series featuring a lady who lives in an upside-down house and has a chest full of magical cures to be used on children with bad habits: "Mrs. Piggle _?"

236. What is the title of the 1947 novel by American author John Steinbeck about a pearl diver named Kino who goes to great lengths to sell a precious pearl he has found in order to pay the doctor to treat his son Coyotito, only to be pushed to kill in his quest to preserve the pearl and in the end, tosses the pearl back into the ocean after losing the son he tried so hard to protect: "The P_?"

237. What is the name of the diary published by her father in 1947, relating the events of Anne Frank, one of the most famous Jewish victims of the Holocaust, written during the two years she was hiding in an attic in German-occupied Amsterdam during World War II: "Diary of a Young _?"

238. What is the title of the 1947 novel by English author Malcolm Lowry that tells the story of Geoffrey Fermin, a British consul living in a small Mexican town near the volcanos Popocatepetl and Iztaccihuatl, and the arrival of his ex-wife Yvonne and his half-brother Hugh on November 2, 1938, the Mexican Day of the Dead, to rescue him from the bad choices he is making: "Under the _?"

239. What is the name of the 1947 novel by Albert Camus that tells the story of doctor Rieux and his co-workers and their battle against a contagious bacterial disease inflicting the people in the Algerian city of Oran, a disease that grows to epidemic proportions, and the suffering and quarantine that result: "The P_?"

240. What is the title of a 1948 children's book by Ruth Stiles Gannett about a boy named Elmer who runs away to an island and rescues a huge fire-producing lizard: "My Father's _?"

241. What is the title of the 1948 short story by Shirley Jackson about a Bill Hutchinson's wife Tessie who picks the fateful piece of paper in a controversial drawing, sealing her fate to be stoned by the people as an act of sacrifice in order to ensure a good crop: "The L_?"

242. What is the title of the 1948 novel by Alan Paton that centers on a black Anglican priest named Stephen Kumolo who initially travels to the city of Johannesburg to help his sister Gertrude, but while there searches for his son Absalom and learns that his son will be executed because he has murdered Arthur Jarvis, the son of Kumolo's neighbor James Jarvis, leaving both fathers having to come to terms with the death of their sons: "Cry, the Beloved _?"

243. What is the title of the 1949 Newbery award-winning children's book by Marguerite de Angeli set in England during the Middle Ages, that tells the story of a boy named Robin who is sent away by his father to become a knight, his brother Luke who takes him to a monastery to care for him after Robin hurts his legs, and the advice he receives from his brother when faced with a challenge: "The Door in the _?"

NOTABLE LITERARY WORKS THROUGH THE AGES

244. What is the title of the 1949 novel by George Orwell that tells of the story of Winston Smith and the citizens of Oceania who are living under the complete control of an oppressive political party, and Smith's struggle to break free from *Big Brother* and the powerful control of this totalitarian society: "19_?"

245. What is the title of the 1949 play by the American playwright Arthur Miller that centers around an unstable and unsuccessful traveling businessman named Willy Loman living in Brooklyn with his family, his efforts to find success in his professional life and fulfillment in his personal life, and his desire to steer both of his sons Biff and Harold into the business field: "Death of a _?"

246. What is the name of the 1950 Newbery award-winning book by Elizabeth Yates about an African prince who is captured by slave traders and brought to America to become a slave, masters a trade in the town of Jaffrey, New Hampshire, and becomes a respected citizen of the community: "Amos Fortune, Free _?"

247. What is the full title of the 1950 fantasy novel by C.S. Lewis about the adventures of four children, Peter, Susan, Edmund, and Lucy in the imaginary land of Narnia, after Lucy climbs into a wardrobe and discovers a magical forest: "The Lion, the Witch, and the _?"

248. What is the full title of the 1950 book by Beverly Cleary, the first in a series of books, about a young boy named Henry and his dog Ribsy: "Henry _?"

249. What is the full title of the 1951 novel by British author Roald Dahl about a boy name James who loses his parents, lives with his two strict aunts, and has new adventures with a Grasshopper and an Earthworm after he climbs into a peach that had grown to an enormous size after he accidentally spills magic crystals on the dying peach tree: "James and the Giant _?"

250. What is the name of the 1951 Newbery award-winning children's book by Eleanor Estes set in Connecticut in 1919, about a dog belonging to Jerry Pye that he paid for with his hard-earned money, and how the entire neighborhood of Cranbury came together to find his dog after he went missing: "Ginger P_?"

251. What is the full title of the 1951 novel by J.D. Salinger about a sixteen-year-old boy named Holden Caulfield from New York City, and how he deals with the challenges of identity and alienation as he makes his way through life: "Catcher in the _?"

252. What is the name of the 1951 war novel by James Jones that deals with the struggles of a company of soldiers in Hawaii before World War II, and the challenges of Private Robert E. Lee Pruitt with his superior officers: "From Here to _?"

253. What is the title of the 1952 Newbery award-winning children's book by Ann Nolan Clark set in South American that tells the story of an Incan boy named Cusi who lives in the mountains of Peru and tends to the llamas with a herder named Chuto, and learns of the traditions of his Inca ancestors: "Secret of the A_?"

254. What is the full title of the 1952 Newbery honor novel by E.B. White about a pig named Wilbur, his friendship with a spider named Charlotte who saves his life, and a rat named Templeton, all living on the Zuckerman farm: "Charlotte's _?"

NOTABLE LITERARY WORKS THROUGH THE AGES

255. What is the full title of the 1952 fantasy novel by Mary Norton about the Clock family, a family of little people who live underneath the kitchen, who *borrow* from big people living in an old country house: "The B _?"

256. What is the name of the 1952 poem by Chilean author Pablo Neruda published in a collection of poems entitled, "The Captain's Verses," telling of his feelings after he was exiled from his homeland of Chile: "If You Forget _?"

257. What is the title of the 1952 Pulitzer-prize winning novel by Ernest Hemingway about an aging fisherman named Santiago, his struggle to catch a huge Marlin, an ordeal taking three days, catching the 18 foot fish that would feed several people, only to be unsuccessful in bringing it back whole when it is eaten to the bone by sharks: "The Old Man and the _?"

258. What is the title of the 1952 novel by John Steinbeck set in the Salinas Valley in California that tells the story of two intertwined families, the Trasks and the Hamiltons, and loosely parallels the fall of Adam and Eve, and the sibling rivalry of Cain and Abel: "East of _?"

259. What is the title of the 1953 Newbery award-winning children's novel by Joseph Krumgold that centers on the life of a 12-year-old Hispanic-American boy named Miguel whose wish of visiting the Sangre de Cristo Mountains with his father and grandfather comes true mainly because his brother is called away by the draft: "And Now M_?"

260. What is the full title of the 1953 semi-autobiography by James Baldwin that describes the role of the Christian church in the lives of African-Americans, and suggests the existence of racism in the United States: "Go Tell It on the _?"

261. What is the name of the 1953 *Little Golden Book* by Garth Williams that describes young dogs, cats, pigs, rabbits, cows, sheep, ducks, and chickens that live on a farm: "Baby Farm _?"

262. What is the name of the 1953 *Little Golden Book* by Marian Potter that tells the story of the back car of a train who wants to be as popular as the front engine of the train and have all the children wave to him, but in the end is the hero after saving the train from rolling down a hill: "The Little Red _?"

263. What is the title of the 1953 play by Arthur Miller that is a fictionalized reenactment of the Salem witch trials taking place in Massachusetts Bay in the late 1600's: "The C_?"

264. What is the title of the 1954 Newbery award-winning children's novel by Meindert DeJong, about student named Lina and her classmates who come to discover why there are no storks in their fishing village of Shora, and conclude that Storks could nest on the steep roofs of their houses if the houses had wagon wheels perched on top of them: "The Wheel on the _?"

265. What is the full title of the 1954 fantasy novel by J.R.R. Tolkien that tells the epic journey of Hobbit Frodo Baggins possessing a powerful lost ring, and teams with dwarfs and elves crossing Middle Earth, in their quest to destroy the Ring of terror belonging to the Dark Lord: "The Lord of the _?"

266. What is the title of the 1955 Newbery award-winning children's novel by Jean Lee Latham about the son of a ship captain named Nathanial Bowditch who works for a time as an indentured servant on a

NOTABLE LITERARY WORKS THROUGH THE AGES

ship, learns navigation skills on his own and through his schooling, and eventually creates a new and more accurate sailing navigation source that he eventually uses as he becomes the captain of his own ship after graduating Harvard: "Carry On, Mr. B_?"

267. What is the full title of the 1955 non-fiction book by Walter Lloyd that chronicles the devastating events of the sinking of the Titanic on April 15th, 1912: "A Night to _?"

268. What is the name of the 1955 children's book by Crockett Johnson about a mischievous four-year-old boy who has the power to create his own world just by drawing it: "Harold and the Purple _?"

269. What is the name of the 1955 novel by Vladimir Nabokov about a literature professor named Humbert who comes to live in a New England town and becomes infatuated with a young girl named Dolores and follows her everywhere: "Loli_?"

270. What is the title of the 1956 Newbery award-winning children's novel by Virginia Sorenson that centers around Marly's family who moves to the country to make things easier for her father who is suffering from the stress of the war, become friends with their neighbors Mr. and Mrs. Chirs, and return their kindness when Marly and her family help them gather maple syrup during sugaring time after Mr. Chris falls ill: "Miracles on Maple H_?"

271. What is the full title of the 1956 novel by Gene Zion about a family dog named Harry that does not like taking baths, runs away after burying the bath brush, and becomes so dirty that his own family does not recognize him when he returns home: "Harry the Dirty _?"

272. What is the full title of the 1956 children's novel by Fred Gipson that tells the story of a yellow mongrel dog who comes to stay with Travis Coates and his family at a ranch, how Travis eventually becomes attached to him, and the dog's fate at the end of the story after it is bitten by a rabid wolf: "Old _?"

273. What is the title of the 1957 Newbery award-winning historical novel by Harold Keith set west of the Mississippi during the American Civil War, that tells the story of a sixteen-year-old named Jefferson Davis Bussey, how he eventually fights for both the North and the South, and his discovery that the Union is smuggling new rifles to Indian forces of the Confederate General Stand Watie: "Rifles for_?"

274. What is the full title of the 1957 book by Theodore Geisel under the pen name Dr. Seuss, about a tall cat wearing a red bow tie and a tall red and white striped hat: "The Cat in the _?"

275. What is the full title of the 1957 book by Dr. Seuss about a grouchy Grinch with a heart two sizes too small, who decides to keep Christmas from coming to Whoville by stealing all the presents and food with his sleigh and his dog Max, but in the end understands the true meaning of the holiday: "How the Grinch Stole _?"

276. What is the pen name of Theodore Geisel whose birthday, March 2nd is the celebrated date for "Read Across America Day:" Dr. Seuss or Dr. Doolittle?

277. What is the title of the 1958 Newbery award-winning children's novel by Elizabeth George Speare about a free-spirited sixteen-year-old colonial girl named Kit who comes to live with relatives in

NOTABLE LITERARY WORKS THROUGH THE AGES

Connecticut, and finds solace in the meadows near a pond where she meets a witch named Hannah: "The Witch of Blackbird _?"

278. What is the title of the 1958 novella by Truman Capote that tells the story of Holiday Golightly living in a brownstone apartment in New York, her one year friendship with the unnamed narrator who lives in the flat above her, and her goal of marrying a rich man: "Breakfast at _"

279. What is the title of the 1959 Newbery award-winning children's novel by Joseph Krumgold set in New Jersey in the 1950's, that tells the story of twelve-year-old Rusch and his friendship with a European hermit named John who is given his name because he grows onions living near a town named Serenity, the town that wants to build a modern house to replace his simple hut, and Andy's wish to run away with him in order to be left alone: "Onion _?"

280. What is the full title of the 1959 novel by Jean Craighead George about a 12-year-old named Sam who runs away from his family's crowded New York apartment to the Catskill Mountains at his great-grandfather's abandoned farm, how he manages to survive a severe snowstorm and the harshness of the wilderness, and how he comes to realize that he needs both his family and the land to truly be happy in life: "My Side of the _?"

281. What is the name of the 1959 novel by John Knowles told from the point of view of Gene Forrester many years later, recalling his time as a sixteen-year-old student attending Devon boarding school in New Hampshire in 1942 during World War II, and reflecting on the friendship and rivalry he once shared with his roommate Finney, including his untimely death in the operating room as a result of a falling down the school's marble stairway: "A Separate _?"

282. What is the name of the 1960 rhyming children's book by Dr. Seuss about a girl and a boy and all the creatures they have as pets: "One Fish, Two Fish, Red Fish, Blue _?"

283. What is the name of the 1960 rhyming book by Dr. Seuss where "Sam-I-Am" tries to convince an unknown character to taste a specific breakfast plate: "Green Eggs and _?"

284. What is the name of the 1960 Newbery award-winning children's novel by Scott O'Dell that tells the story of a young, courageous girl named Karana, and based on the true story of Juana Maria, a Nicoleño Indian, who is left alone on an isolated island off the California coast for 18 years: "Island of the Blue __?"

285. What is the full title of the 1960 novel by Harper Lee about the injustice of prejudice with the story of Scout Finch, her brother Jem, a mysterious neighbor named Boo Radley, and her attorney father Atticus who faces a backlash after defending a black man who is wrongly accused of a crime: "To Kill a _?"

286. What is the full title of the 1960 book by Joy Adamson about how she and her husband George raised three orphaned lion cubs, the youngest of which they named Elsa, and how they eventually released her into the Kenya wilderness: "Born _?"

287. What is the full title of the 1961 novel by Scottish author Sheila Burnford that relates the story of a bull terrier, a Labrador, and a Siamese cat who travel 300 miles through the harsh Canadian wilderness

NOTABLE LITERARY WORKS THROUGH THE AGES

in search of their masters, and even though they are tired, weak, and hungry, they eventually reunite with their owners: "The Incredible _?"

288. What is the full title of the 1961 novel by the English author Roald Dahl about an orphaned English boy name James who finds himself inside a huge fruit along with a few friends, the adventures that ensue as it rolls through air, land, and water, and how James lives out his life in New York City in what was once part of this huge fruit: "James and the Giant _?"

289. What is the name of the children's novel originally published in 1961 by P.D. Eastman about a group of dogs who operate cars and scooters and ultimately have a dog party: "Go, Dog._?"

290. What is the full title of the 1961 novel by Wilson Rawls about a boy named Billy Coleman who buys and trains two Redbone Coonhounds in the Ozarks, how the dogs learn to excel at coon hunting, and how Billy finds peace when he sees a special plant growing over the graves of his beloved dogs, a plant that according to Indian legend, can only be planted by an angel: "Where the Red Fern _?"

291. What is the full title of the 1961 adventure novel filled with literary puns by Norton Juster about a boy named Milo who receives a magic tollbooth and uses his toy car to drive through it and arrives at a castle where Princess Rhyme and Princess Reason reside: "The Phantom T_?"

292. What is the name of the 1961 speech by President John F. Kennedy when he said to the American people, *ask not what your country can do for you, ask what you can do for your country*: "The Inaugural _?"

293. What is the name of the 1961 novel by Joseph Heller that is set in 1943 during World War II, and follows the events of an Air Force squadron under Captain John Yossarian and their efforts to fulfill their air mission off the coast of Italy, and their quest to return home safely: "Catch_?"

294. What is the full title of the 1962 Caldecott award-winning picture book by Ezra Jack Keats about an African-American boy named Peter who is excited to go outside and explore the neighborhood after the first major snowfall of the season: "The Snowy _?"

295. What is the full title of the 1962 science fiction fantasy Newbery award-winning novel by Madeleine L'Engle about Meg and Charles Wallace and their friend Calvin, their journey into space on a mission to find the Wallace children's father who has mysteriously disappeared, and the evil forces they find themselves up against: "A Wrinkle in _?"

296. What is the name of the 1962 series of children's books by Stan and Jan Berenstain about an animal family that include Papa, Mama, Brother, Sister, and Honey where some lesson is learned at the end: "The Berenstain _?"

297. What is the title of the 1962 novel by Ken Kesey and set in an Oregon mental institution, about an unstable man named Randle McMurphy who bands together with other patients against the totalitarian rule of nurse Ratched, along with other conflicts that emerge within the ward: "One Flew Over the Cuckoo's _?"

298. What is the title of the 1963 Newbery award-winning children's novel by Emily Cheney Neville, that centers on a fourteen-year-old boy named David Mitchell living in New York, his friendship with an

NOTABLE LITERARY WORKS THROUGH THE AGES

elderly neighbor name Kate and her many cats, and the cat he adopts that brings adventure and meaning into his life: "It's Like This, C_?"

299. What is the full title of the 1963 Caldecott Medal-winning picture book by Maurice Sendak about a boy named Max who dresses up in a wolf suit, is sent to his room without supper for misbehaving, becomes the "king" of the animals on the island he has sailed to in his bedroom that has magically transformed into a forest and an ocean, and wakes up to find a hot supper waiting for him: "Where the Wild Things _?"

300. What is the name of the children's book series first published in 1963 by Norman Bridwell about a puppy who becomes the birthday present and beloved pet of Emily Elizabeth, a puppy that grows to over 25 feet tall: "Clifford the Big Red _?"

301. What is the name of the public speech given by civil rights activist Martin Luther King Jr. in 1963 in Washington, D.C. on the steps of the Lincoln Memorial, and with a crowd of over 250,000, calling for an end to racism and discrimination in America, and outlining his hopes for freedom and equality: "I Have a _?"

302. What is the title of the 1964 Newbery award-winning children's novel by Maia Wojciechowska that centers on twelve-year-old Manolo Olivar, the son of a famous Spanish bullfighter named Juan who was killed by a bull when Manolo was very young, how Manolo comes to terms with the high expectation of the people of Spain to follow in his father's footsteps, and his realization that his true calling is not as a matador in a bullring, but as a doctor in a hospital: "Shadow of a _?"

303. What is the full title of the 1964 novel by Roald Dahl about a boy named Charlie Bucket who finds a golden ticket inside a candy bar, visits a candy factory run by Willie Wonka and singing Oommpa Loompas, and experiences all that the factory has of offer along with his grandpa Joe and four other children named Veruca, Violet, Mike, and Augustus: "Charlie and the Chocolate _?"

304. What is the full title of the 1964 children's book by Jeff Brown about a boy who is flattened by a bulletin board that falls on top of him while he is sleeping, can slide under locked doors, can be flown as a kite by his brother Arthur, and can be mailed in an envelope until the day his is re-inflated by his brother by a bicycle pump: "Flat _?"

305. What is the full title of the 1964 novel by Louise Fitzhugh about an eleven-year-old named Harriet, her friends Sport, Janie, and Rachael, and how she goes on to write stories about all the people along her spy route: "Harriet the _?"

306. What is the full title of the 1964 fantasy novel by Lloyd Alexander that tells of the adventures of an Assistant Pig-Keeper named Taran who lives with the enchanter Dallben, and his quest to escape ordinary farm life and become a hero: "The Book of T _?"

307. What is the full title of the 1964 children's picture book written by Shel Silverstein that tells the story of a young boy and his relationship with an apple tree through the years of his life: "The Giving _?"

308. What is the name of the 1964 speech by the anti-apartheid South African Nelson Mandela right now facing trial because of his opposition to the government in power: "I am Prepared to _?"

NOTABLE LITERARY WORKS THROUGH THE AGES

309. What is the title of the 1965 Newbery award-winning children's novel by Elizabeth Borton de Treviño about a half-African slave named Juan who works for and learns to paint himself from his master, the famous Spanish artist Diego Velázquez: "I, Juan de _?"

310. What is the full title of the 1965 fantasy novel by Lloyd Alexander that continues the story of Taran, the Assistant Pig Keeper, and his attempt to capture the Magical Cauldron from Arawn Death Lord: "The Black _?"

311. What is the full title of the 1965 novel by Beverly Cleary about Ralph the mouse living at the Mountain View Inn and the toy motorcycle belonging to a new guest named Keith that eventually becomes Ralph's to keep: "The Mouse and the _?"

312. What is the title of the book first published in 1965 by Charles M Schulz and based on the Christmas special, about a boy named Charlie Brown who is trying to understand the real meaning of a holiday, and celebrates the season with Lucy, Linus, and Snoopy and the gang: "A Charlie Brown _?"

313. What is the title of the of the world's best-selling 1965 science fiction novel by Frank Herbert that is set in the distant future in the year 10191, where space travel and life in the universe are dependent upon a spice called melange that only exists on the planet Arrakis, and the desire by many to control this planet: "D_?"

314. What is the name of the 1966 Newbery award-winning novel by Irene Hunt about a seven-year-old girl named Julie who goes to live with her Aunt Cordelia after her mother dies, following her life from ages seven to seventeen from elementary school through high school: "Up a Road _?"

315. What is the full title of the 1967 Newbery award-winning novel by E L. Konigsburg about a girl name Claudia Kinkaid who convinces her brother to run away with her and hide out at the Metropolitan Museum of Art in New York City, and the mystery of the famous statue they name "Angel," that leads them to the owner who allows them to search her records in order to discover the secret about the famous statue: "From the Mixed-Up Files of Mrs. Basil E. _?"

316. What is the name of the 1967 children's picture book by Bill Martin, Jr. and Eric Carle with animals of different colors that helps the reader associate colors with objects: "Brown Bear, Brown Bear, What Do You _?"

317. What is the title of the 1967 novel by Columbian author Gabriel García Márquez that tells the story of the Buendía family over seven generations in the mythical Macondo, the city founded by the family patriarch José Arcadia Buendía, and the quest for peace and truth over the span of one hundred years: "One Hundred Years of _?"

318. What is the title of the 1967 novel by Chaim Potok that tells the story of two boys named Reuven Malter and Danny Saunders who meet at a baseball game and become friends, the challenges the boys and their fathers face living Brooklyn, New York at the end of World War II, and the challenges that come with trying to live a devoted Jewish life: "The C _?"

NOTABLE LITERARY WORKS THROUGH THE AGES

319. What is the name of the 1968 Newbery award-winning fantasy novel by Lloyd Alexander that follows an Assistant Pig Keeper named Taran, who joins forces with his countrymen in the land of Prydain to defeat Arawn Death-Lord in order to rule the kingdom: "The High K_?"

320. What is the full title of the 1968 book by Don Freeman about a teddy bear that is on a display shelf in a store, how he searches the store at night for his missing button, and the girl named Lisa that buys him the next day with money from her piggy bank, takes him home, and sews a button on the strap of his overalls: "Cord_?"

321. What is the full title of the 1968 book by Beverly Cleary about a mischievous girl who manages to create trouble wherever she goes in her kindergarten class: "Ramona the _?"

322. What is the name of the 1969 Newbery award-winning novel by William H. Armstrong about a young boy living with his poor African-American sharecropper family and their dog, their fight for their survival, the reunion of the family and the dog, and the satisfaction that is felt by the young boy because he has learned to read: "Sound_?"

323. What is the full title of the 1969 picture book by Eric Carle about an insect who eats an enormous amount of unusual food, grows big and fat, and later emerges as a beautiful butterfly: "The Very Hungry _?"

324. What is the full title of the 1969 autobiography by Maya Angelou from her early years into adulthood, as she becomes transformed from a victim of racism, to a mature, dignified and capable woman: "I Know Why the Caged Bird _?"

325. What is the title of the 1969 novel by Kurt Vonnegut about the experiences of soldier Billy Pilgrim during World War II, and the effects of the bombing of Dresden, Germany: "Slaughterhouse _?"

326. What is the title of the 1970 Newbery award-winning novel by Betsy Byars that tells the story of fourteen-year-old Sara Godfrey growing up with her brother and sister, their Aunt Willie, and her search for her mentally challenged brother Charlie after he goes missing: "Summer of the S _?"

327. What is the name of the 1970 first book in a series written and illustrated by Arnold Lobel that relate the adventures of two amphibians through a series of short stories: "Frog and Toad are __?"

328. What is the full title of the 1970 novel by E.B. White that tells the story of Louis, a Trumpeter Swan that is born without a voice who learns to play a musical trumpet to earn money and to win the attention of Serena: "The Trumpet of the _?"

329. What is the name of the 1971 Newbery award-winning book by Robert C. O'Brian that relates the story of a widow mouse named Frisby and her four children, and how she manages to move her family and save her farm from a farmer's plow with the help of highly intelligent laboratory rats: "Mrs. Frisby and the Rats of N _?"

330. What is the full title of the 1971 children's book by Barbara Robinson that relates the story of Imogene, Claude, Ralph, Leroy, Ollie, and Gladys Herndon and their participation in a church holiday play: "The Best Christmas Pageant __?"

NOTABLE LITERARY WORKS THROUGH THE AGES

331. The is the name of the 1971 book by Dr. Seuss that tells about the state of the environment and a creature that speaks for the trees to protect them from the Once-ler: "The Lor_?"

332. What is the name of the 1972 Newbery award-winning children's novel by Jean Craighead George about a young girl named Julie who runs away from her Alaskan village, her acceptance by a pack of Arctic dogs, and her struggle to reconcile her old life with the Eskimos and her new one in the wilderness: "Julie of the _?"

333. What is the name of the 1972 adventure novel by English author Richard Adams about a group of rabbits including Hazel and Fiver, who engage in several adventures as they seek to establish their new warren on a hill in England: "Watership _?"

334. What is the full title of the 1972 book by Judith Viorst about a boy named Alexander who has an extremely bad day from the moment he wakes up and trips on his skateboard, to the time he goes to bed when his nightlight burns out and vows to move to Australia: "Alexander and the Terrible, Horrible, No Good, Very Bad D_?"

335. What is the name of the 1973 Newbery award-winning children's book by Paula Fox about a boy named Jesse Bollier who is kidnapped and forced to play his fife flute aboard a slave ship called *The Moonlight* for shackled slaves, and how he is affected by the inhumanity and savagery of the African slave trade: "The Slave D_?"

336. What is the title of the 1974 Newbery award-winning children's novel by Virginia Hamilton about a young boy named M.C. Higgins living on Sara's Mountain in the Appalachians with his family, the struggler he feels with regard to leaving the mountain because of the danger of sliding subsoil from mining explosions, and remaining in their home because it is the home of his great-grandmother who had escaped slavery and settled at the base of this mountain: "M.C. Higgins, the _?"

337. What is the full title of a 1974 collection of poems and drawings by Shel Silverstein that include a poem about a story about a boy that transforms into a TV set, and a girl that eats a whale: "Where the Sidewalk _?"

338. What is the name of the 1975 Newbery award-winning fantasy novel by Susan Cooper about a boy named Will Stanton who goes to live with his Welsh aunt while recovering from an illness, his quest to locate the magic golden harp with his friend Bran Davies and his dog Cafall because the harp is the last artifact needed to awaken the Sleepers, the warriors that are needed by the Light in order to defeat the king of the mountain and the Dark: "The Grey K _?"

339. What is the full title of the 1975 fantasy novel by Natalie Babbitt about ten-year-old Winnie Foster, the secret she discovers about the Tuck family who are living an eternal life after drinking from a magic spring, and a stranger that arrives who wants to take Winnie back to her home and sell the spring water: "Tuck _?"

340. What is the name of the 1976 Newbery award-winning novel by Mildred D. Taylor that reveals what life is like in the South in the 1930's after the American Civil War for a strong and proud African American family including nine-year-old Cassie Logan and her three brothers, the white Simms family, and themes of land-ownership, prejudice, and racism: "Roll of Thunder, Hear Me __?"

NOTABLE LITERARY WORKS THROUGH THE AGES

341. What is the full title of the 1976 autobiographical novel by African-American author Alex Haley that tells the story of Kunta Kinte, who grew up in Gambia, Africa, was captured and sold into slavery to American in 1767, following his harsh life through many generations including the author's, a seventh generation descendent of Kunta Kinte: "Roots: The Saga of an American F _?"

342. What is the name of the series of children's game books of 1977 by Edward Packard that are written in the second person where the reader is actually the protagonist of the story, and makes choices throughout the book that ultimately determine the outcome of the plot: "Choose Your Own _?"

343. What is the full title of the 1977 Newbery award-winning novel by Katherine Patterson about two friends, Jesse and Leslie, the imaginary world they create near a creek, and the memorial that Jesse builds in honor of Leslie after she accidentally drowns when the rope that she is swinging on breaks: "Bridge to __?"

344. What is the title of the 1977 novel by American author Toni Morrison, named for a Biblical King and the name of the great-grandfather of the main character, that tells story of an African American man named Macon "Milkman" Dead III growing up in Michigan, and includes accounts of the migration of slaves to Africa and to other parts of the United States: "Song of S_?"

345. What is the title of the 1978 Newbery award-winning novel by Ellen Raskin about the sixteen heirs of millionaire Sam Westing who come to hear the will which is actually a puzzle, divides the heirs into eight pairs, gives each pair specific clues, and promises his fortune of $200 million dollars made from his company Westing Paper Products to the person solving his murder: "The Westing _?"

346. What is the full title of the 1978 book by Judi Barrett where a grandfather narrates a story to his grandchildren about a town called Chewandswallow whereby all the residents are provided all their meals by raining food, and how an unexpected storm forces them to move to another town where they must learn to get their food in the usual way: "Cloudy with a Chance of _?"

347. What is the name of the 1978 children's picture book by English author Raymond Briggs is a wordless story about a young boy and his wintertime creation who share a magical time together: "The Snow _?"

348. What is the name of the 1978 collection of 32 short poems by Maya Angelou that are centered on the theme of hopefulness and rising above adversity: "And Still I _?"

349. What is the title of the 1979 Newbery award-winning historical novel by Joan Blos, written in the form of a journal, that provides a detailed account of the daily life of Catherine Hall living in New England with her sister and her widowed father between 1830 and 1832, with particular emphases on the events of her father's remarriage, the sudden death of her best friend, and her assistance to an escaped slave: "The Gathering of Days: A New England Girl's _?"

350. What is the name of the 1979 children series by James and Deborah Howe about the Monroe family and the bunny they find at a feature of *Dracula*, a bunny that sucks the juice out of vegetables: "Bunni_?"

351. What is the name of the German fantasy novel first published in 1979 by Michael Ende about a boy named Bastian Balthazar Bux who discovers a book in an antique store, and is transported into a fantasy world as he magically becomes part of the book while reading it: "The Neverending _?"

NOTABLE LITERARY WORKS THROUGH THE AGES

352. What is the name of the 1979 novel by American author William Styron that tells a multi-dimensional story of a southern author named Stingo and his relationship with a Polish refugee named Sophie, where he ultimately learns of the unbearable choice she was forced to make with regard to her two children while imprisoned at the Auschwitz concentration camp in Germany: "Sophie's _?"

353. What is the name of the children's 1980 book by Nadine Bernard Wescott that is based on a cumulative song that gets worse and worse after an old lady swallows a fly: "I Know an Old Woman Who Swallowed a _?"

354. What is the name of the 1981 Newbery winning and Caldecott Honor children's picture book written by Nancy Willard that is a collection of fifteen poems describing the events over a day and a half of a child's visit to William Blake's Inn, and its residents that include a Rabbit, a Rat, a Tiger, a King of Cats, and a Wise Cow: "A Visit to William Blake's Inn: Poems for Innocent and Experienced T _?"

355. What is the name of the 1981 Newbery award-winning novel by Katherine Patterson that centers on the relationships of the Bradshaw family, especially daughter Sara Louise who is always trying to escape the shadow of her prettier twin sister Caroline, and how she finally comes full circle after having twins of her own: "Jacob Have I _?"

356. What is the full title of the 1981 children's Newbery honor book by Beverly Cleary about a mischievous third grade student named Ramona and her sister Beezus in junior high: "Ramona Quimby, Age _?"

357. What is the name of the 1981 children's fantasy Caldecott Medal-winning picture book by Chris Van Allsburg that tells the story of Peter and Judy Shephard that find a jungle adventure game in a park, and after they take it home to play it, discover that all the dangers in the game like lions and monsoons suddenly come to life: "Juman_?"

358. What is the name of the 1981 children's collection of poems by Shel Silverstein, with each poem accompanied by an illustration: "A Light in the _?"

359. What is the title of the 1982 children's Newbery award-winning novel by Cynthia Voigt that tells the story of Dicey, Sammy, Maybeth, and James Tillerman who are living with their widowed grandmother on a farm in Maryland while their mother is at a psychiatric hospital in Boston, how they adjust in their new school and with their new friends, and how in the end, they come to terms with their mother's death: "Dicey's _?"

360. What is the name of the 1982 novel by Alice Walker that centers on Celie, a poor African-American girl living in Georgia who communicates her thoughts in her letters to God, the abuse she suffers at the hands of her father, the complex relationships with Sofia and a local singer named Shug Avery, her discovery that her children are alive, and the eventual reunion with her sister Nettie after believing that she had died: "The Color _?"

361. What is the title of the 1983 Newbery award-winning novel by Beverly Cleary that centers on the letters that Leigh Botts writes to his favorite author, Boyd Henshaw, and in his correspondence with the author, Leigh reveals his feelings regarding his parents' divorce, his tense relationship with his father, adjusting to a new school, and a mysterious student who keeps stealing his lunch, and in the

NOTABLE LITERARY WORKS THROUGH THE AGES

end comes to understand that there are some circumstances in his life that he cannot change: "Dear Mr. H_?"

362. What is the title of the 1984 Newbery award-winning fantasy novel by Robin McKinley that centers on Aerin Dragon-Killer and her journey from the shy daughter of the King of Damar, to the queen seeking to protect her people from Northerners, and her quest to rebuild the kingdom: "The Hero and the C _?"

363. What is the full name of the 1985 Newbery award-winning children's book by Patricia MacLachlan about a farmer whose wife has died, writes an ad in a newspaper for a wife and mother of his children Anna and Caleb, and the lady from Maine who answers his ad: "Sarah, Plain and __?"

364. What is the full title of the 1985 children's Caldecott Medal-winning picture book written and illustrated by Chris Van Allsburg about a young boy who boards a train headed for the North Pole, and while there, chooses a bell from a reindeer's harness as his gift, loses it on the train on the way home, and receives it under the tree as a gift from Santa, a bell that only he and his sister can hear: "The Polar __?"

365. What is the name of the 1985 children's series authored by Joanna Cole and illustrated by Bruce Degen that center around science teacher Mrs. Frizzle, and the exotic field trips she takes her class on in order to experience science first hand: "The Magic School _?"

366. What is the name of the 1985 children's book by Laura Numeroff that is a circular story about a little boy who gives a sweet treat to a mouse, and it asks then for a glass of milk and many more things: "If You Give a Mouse a _?"

367. What is the title of the 1986 Newbery award-winning children's novel by Sid Fleischman that centers on the events of the spoiled Prince Horace, or Prince Brat as he is sometimes called, an orphaned boy named Jemmy who that takes any punishment in place of the prince, and their challenges after they run away for a time and trade places: "The Whipping B_?"

368. What is the name of the novel series by Ann M. Martin beginning in 1986 that centers on Kristy Thomas, Mary Ann Spier, Claudia Kishi, and Stacey McGill, Connecticut middle school students who form a club to help parents with their child care needs: "The Babysitters _?"

369. What is the name of the January 28, 1986 speech by President Ronald Reagan after the space accident that occurred the day before in which all seven astronauts died, where he reassured all Americans, *the future doesn't belong to the fainthearted, it belongs to the brave*: "Address to the Nation on the Challenger _?"

370. What is the title of the 1987 Newbery award-winning biography by Russell Freedman that tells of the life of Abraham Lincoln through stories and photographs beginning with his childhood, his marriage to Mary Todd Lincoln, his Presidency, and his assassination: "Lincoln: A_?"

371. What is the name of the 1987 children's book written and illustrated by Graeme Base that contain detailed animal illustrations for each letter of the alphabet, a short poem for each letter, and a hidden picture of the author as a young boy for each illustration: "Anim_?"

NOTABLE LITERARY WORKS THROUGH THE AGES

372. What is the full title of the 1987 survival novel by Gary Paulson about thirteen-year-old Brian Robeson, and how he survives the harsh Canadian wilderness after his plane crashed with little more than the clothes on his back and the tool he managed to save: "Hat_?"

373. What is the full title of the 1987 Caldecott Medal-winning picture book by Jane Yolen that tells the story of a father and daughter who encounter a Great Horned Owl while out one cold, snowy evening: "Owl _?"

374. What is the name of the 1987 speech by President Ronald Reagan at the Brandenburg Gate near Berlin, Germany where he challenged the Soviet Union leader Mikhail Gorbachev with the words: "Mr. Gorbachev, tear down this _?"

375. What is the name of the 1987 novel by American author Toni Morrison that centers around a former slave named Sethe who had killed her young daughter and had tried to kill her other three daughters when people from her former plantation arrived to return them to the plantation in Ohio, and a woman, presumed to be the ghost of her murdered daughter, who returns to Sethe's house at 124 Bluestone Road Cincinnati years later and haunts it: "Be_?"

376. What is the title of the 1987 Newbery award-winning novel by Paul Fleishman that is a collection of fourteen children's poems intended to be read aloud by two people, with insects as the theme: "Joyful Noise: Poems for Two V_?"

377. What is the name of the 1988 children's novel by Roald Dahl about a gifted, young girl with magical powers who uses these powers against the strict headmistress at her school: "Matil_?"

378. What is the full title of the 1989 historical fiction Newbery award-winning novel by Louis Lowry, and centers on the escape of ten-year-old Annemarie Johansen's Jewish family from Copenhagen in Nazi-occupied Denmark during the Holocaust: "Number the _?"

379. What is the full title of the 1989 book by Bill Martin, Jr. and John Archambault about lower-case letters who climb a coconut tree, and the capital or upper-case letters that come to their aid after the small letters fall to the ground: "Chicka Chicka Boom _?"

380. What is the name of the 1989 children's picture book by Jon Scieszka and Lane Smith that is a variation of "Three Little Pigs" from the Wolf's point of view, as he tries to borrow a cup of sugar from three pigs to make his grandmother a birthday cake, and is finally thrown in jail trying to pound down the door of the pig living in the house made of bricks: "The True Story of the Three Little _?"

381. What is the name of the 1989 children's book by Jan Brett about a Ukrainian child named Nikki who loses one of his white articles of clothing that his grandmother had made for him, and the different animals like the mole, fox, rabbit, bear, and mouse that take up residence inside of it until Nicki finally finds it in the snow: "The M_?"

382. What is the title of the 1990 Newbery award-winning novel by Jerry Spinelli that follows an orphaned boy named Jeffrey Lionel Magee who winds up in Two Mills, Pennsylvania, and becomes known as somewhat of a legend in the town that is racially divided because of his athleticism and his efforts to unite the people: "Maniac M_?"

NOTABLE LITERARY WORKS THROUGH THE AGES

383. What is the name of the 1990 children's book, the last one published by Dr. Seuss, about a protagonist that travels through various places, suggesting all the places there are to experience and discover: "Oh, the Places You Will _?"

384. What is the name of the 1991 Newbery award-winning novel by Phyllis Reynolds Naylor about a young boy named Marty Preston and the abused beagle dog he rescues from his neighbor, and his torment because he has to lie and steal to keep him: "Shi_?"

385. What is the name of the 1991 children's picture book by David Wiesner that is named for a day of the week, and centers around frogs that rise out of a pond on lily pads and descend on the residents of a nearby town: "T_?"

386. What is the title of the 1992 Newbery award-winning novel by Cynthia Rylant about an orphaned child named Summer who finally finds happiness when she goes to live with her Aunt May and Uncle Ob in the Appalachian mountains, and the grief that she and her Uncle Ob experience after her Aunt May dies suddenly: "Missing _?"

387. What is the name of the children's horror fiction novels first published in 1992 by R.L. Stine that include stories about kids that find themselves in scary situations like "Welcome to Dead House," the first novel: "Goose_?"

388. What is the name of the 1992 children's book by Jon Scieszka that is a collection of tales making fun of the original tale like *The Ugly Duckling* and *The Gingerbread Man* as told by Jack from *Jack and the Beanstalk*: "The Stinky Cheese Man and Other Fairly Stupid _?"

389. What is the name of the 1993 Newbery award-winning novel by Lois Lowry that tells the story of twelve-year-old Jonas and other citizens that have to follow strict rules and give up many freedoms in order to live in a perfect, utopian society, but in the end, the society is revealed to be just the opposite because the people are not given basic freedoms, freedoms necessary for a happy life: "The G_?"

390. What is the title of the 1994 Newbery award-winning novel by Sharon Creech that centers on thirteen-year-old Salamanca Hiddle's car journey with her grandparents from Idaho to Ohio, telling them the story of the disappearance of her friend Phoebe's mother, a story that closely resembles the truth about her own mother's disappearance: "Walk Two M_?"

391. What is the name of the 1994 children's book by British author Sam MacBratney about two Nutbrown hares that try to outdo each other in stating how much one cares for the other: "Guess How Much I Love _?"

392. What is the title of the 1995 Newbery award-winning novel by Karen Cushman that tells the story of a homeless girl named Brat who adopts the name Alyce, becomes an apprentice to a midwife, and eventually overcomes obstacles and gains the confidence to find her own place in the world: "The Midwife's A_?"

393. What is the full title of the 1995 fantasy novel by Philip Pullman that relates the journey of Lyra to the Arctic in order to look for her missing friend Roger, and her imprisoned uncle Lord Asriel: "The Golden _?"

NOTABLE LITERARY WORKS THROUGH THE AGES

394. What is the name of the 1996 Newbery award-winning novel by E.L. Konigsburg about the life challenges of a paraplegic sixth grade teacher named Mrs. Eva Olinski, along with four of her students Noah, Nadia, Julian, and Ethan who compete in academic competitions calling themselves "The Souls," and the life lessons they all learn about the importance of hard work, family, and friends: "The View from S _?"

395. What is the title of the 1996 book by Andrew Clements about a student named Nick who invents a new word for a pen, a word that earns him national recognition: "Frin_?"

396. What is the name of the 1997 Newbery award-winning novel by Karen Hesse that tells the story in free verse format about an Oklahoma farming family during the Dust Bowl years of 1934 and 1935, focusing primarily on the challenges faced by the main character Billie Jo Kelby that include the burning accident of her mother, and the physical and mental health of the father: "Out of the D_?"

397. What is the full title of the debut 1997 novel of J.K. Rowling about a boy who discovers that he is a wizard, and experiences many new adventures at the Hogwarts School of Witchcraft and Wizardry, and how he succeeds in stopping Lord Voldemort: "Harry Potter and the Sorcerer's _?"

398. What is the full title of the 1997 novel by Dav Pilkey, the first in a series, about 4th graders Harold Hutchins and George Beard who make a comic strip with a made-up superhero: "The Adventures of Captain _?"

399. What is the name of the 1997 children's rhyming book by Deborah Guarino and Steve Kellog about a little llama that asks his friends if their moms are llamas too: "Is Your Mama a _?"

400. What is the title of the children's book series first published in 1997 by Kate McMullan about a boy named Wiglaf and his two friends Erica Von Royale and Angus du Pangus who attend a special school to learn the art of killing dragons: "Dragon Slayers' A_?"

401. What is the name of the series of realistic fiction books first published in 1997 by Jeff Kinney that serve as journals of the main character named Greg Hefley that tell the story of his daily adventures and challenges during his middle school years: "Diary of a Wimpy _?"

402. What is the name of the 1998 Newbery award-winning novel by Louis Sachar about a boy named Stanley who is caught for stealing a pair of sneakers, sentenced to 18 months at Camp Green Lake, and has to dig a hole in the desert only to find out that the warden was actually seeking to find the treasure left behind by the outlaw Kissing Kate Barlow: "H_?"

403. What is the title of the 1999 Newbery award-winning novel by Christopher Paul Curtis about a ten-year-old boy named Bud Caldwell living in an orphanage in Flint, Michigan in 1936 during the Great Depression, his relationship with his foster brother Todd, his longing to find his jazz musician father, and the journey he takes west with his friend Bugs: "Bud, Not _?"

404. What is the full title of the children series first published in 1999 by Lemony Snicket that follows the adventures of Violet, Klaus, and Sunny Baudelaire after their parents' death in a fire, and wherever they go are followed by misfortune: "A Series of Unfortunate _?"

NOTABLE LITERARY WORKS THROUGH THE AGES

405. What is the title of the 1999 children's book by Marcus Pfister about a about a sea animal with beautiful blue, green, purple, and silver scales who finds friendship with other sea animals when he learns to share: "The Rainbow F_?"

406. What is the title of the 2000 Newbery award-winning historical fiction novel by Richard Peck about fifteen-year-old Mary Alice Dowdel who leaves Chicago to go and live with her grandma in a farming community for one year, her adjustment to her new school and participation in the school's Christmas Pageant, and the boy, Royce McNabb, that she meets and eventually marries after her return to her Grandma's house in the countryside: "A Year Down Y_?"

407. What is the name of the 2000 children's picture book by Doreen Cronin about a herd of Farmer Brown's cows who find a typewriter and write letters to Farmer Brown stating their demands: "Click, Clack, Moo: Cows that _?"

408. What is the name of the 2000 fictional character and book by the same name written and illustrated by Ian Falconer about a pig who loves to sing, go to the beach, paint on walls, and build sand castles: "Oliv__?"

409. What is the full title of the 2000 novel by Pam Muñoz Ryan about a young Mexican girl, the daughter of wealthy Mexican landowners, who travels to California with her mother by train after her father was killed by bandits, and her life and the lives of other immigrants working at a farm in Depression-era America: "Esperanza _?"

410. What is the name of the 2000 children's novel by Kate DiCamillo about a ten-year-old girl named India Opal that lives with her preacher father in Florida, finds a big dog in the supermarket and names him after it, and collects stories to one day tell her mother who is not living with them at the present time: "Because of Winn-_?"

411. What is the title of the 2001 Newbery award-winning novel by Linda Sue Park that tells the story of a twelve-year-old Korean orphaned boy named Tree-ear, his fascination with pottery, his relationship with a potter named Min, his journey to transport Min's vases to Songdo after Min is granted a commission from Emissary Kim based on one broken piece or shard, and realizing his dream of making his own pottery: "A Single S_?"

412. What is the title of the 2002 Newbery award-winning novel by Avi set in 1377 England about a thirteen-year-old boy known as Asta's Son accused of a crime he did not commit, is declared a "wolf's head" meaning he may be shot by anyone at any time, and his journey through the countryside where in the end he is forced to defend himself to save his life, taking with him only the name of Crispin and his mother's cross of lead: "Crispin: The Cross of L_?"

413. What is the name of the 2002 children's books based on the Nickelodeon series like "Dora's Backpack" about the adventures of a young Latina girl named Dora and her monkey named Boots: "Dora the _?"

414. What is the title of the 2003 Newbery award-winning fantasy novel by Kate DiCamillo that is divided into four chapters, each told from the perspective of a different character, and follows the adventures of Despereaux Tilling, a castle mouse that sets out to save a beautiful human princess: "The Tale of Despereaux: Being the Story of a Mouse, a Princess, Some Soup, and a Spool of _?"

NOTABLE LITERARY WORKS THROUGH THE AGES

415. What is the title of the 2004 Newbery award-winning novel by Cynthia Kadohata about the life of a Japanese-American girl name Katie who has moved to an apartment in Georgia after her family's store is forced to go out of business, how she comes to terms with the death of her sister Lynn after a long illness, and her feelings when she hears the voice of her sister in the waves on a California beach at the end speaking their sister-created phrase meaning shiny and sparkling: "Kira-_?"

416. What is the full title of the 2004 novel by Judy Blume about nine-year-old Peter Hatcher who feels overshadowed by his spoiled two year old brother named Farley but nicknamed Fudge who gets away with everything, even swallowing his pet turtle Dribble: "Tales of a Fourth Grade __?"

417. What is the title of the 2005 Newbery award-winning novel by Lynn Rae Perkins that follows the lives of teenagers Debbie, Hector, Patty, Lenny, and Phil, revealing how their lives cross after spending one summer together in their small town of Seldem, and how each becomes more mature and confident by the end of that summer: "Criss_?"

418. What is the title of the 2006 Newbery award-winning novel by Susan Patron that centers on a ten-year-old girl named Lucky living in a California desert town named Hard Pan, how she runs away to the desert when she finds what she thinks are travel papers belonging to Brigitte, her father's first wife who has come to live with them after the death of her mother, and how after being found in the desert with two of her friends, learns that the papers were actually adoption papers: "The Higher Power of L_?"

419. What is the name of the 2006 book by Eric Carle that has pictures that can be both seen and felt, about an insect that works hard to spin her web, while other farm animals continuously try to distract her: "The Very Busy S_?"

420. What is the title of the 2007 Newbery award-winning children's book by Laura Amy Schilz that is written as a series of monologues along with two dialogues by different members of a medieval village in 1255 that include lords, ladies, millers, monks, and peasants: "Good Masters! Sweet Ladies! Voices from a Medieval V _?"

421. What is the title of the 2008 Newbery winning fantasy novel by Neil Gaiman where each of the eight chapters tells a story, beginning with a person as a small toddler who later assumes the name of Nobody, and his adventures and encounters as he grows up in a graveyard: "The Graveyard _?"

422. What is the name of the fantasy book series first published in 2008 by Stephanie Meyer about Isabella Swan who movies from Arizona to Washington and finds her life in danger after meeting a 104-year-old vampire named Edward Cullen: "Twi-?"

423. What is the full title of the 2008 trilogy science fiction series by Suzanne Collins from the voice of Katniss Everdeen in the nation of Panem, the Capitol that exercises political control over the entire nation, and the boys and girls that are selected by a lottery in each of the districts to compete in mortal battle: "The Hunger _?"

424. What is the title of the 2009 Newbery award-winning novel by Rebecca Stead about Miranda Sinclair living in New York City, who receives a mysterious note informing her to write down the location of her spare key and to document future events, events that include her mum's appearance on *The*

NOTABLE LITERARY WORKS THROUGH THE AGES

$20,000 Pyramid, when her best friend Sal suddenly stops talking to her, and the appearance of a laughing man: "When You Reach _?"

425. What is the full title of the 2010 Newbery award-winning children's novel by Clare Vanderpool about a girl named Abilene who is sent to live with a friend of her father's in Manifest, Kansas in 1936, what she learns about a boy named Jinx dating back to 1917 from the fortune teller Miss Sadie, supported with letters and news clippings found in a box, and how Abilene makes the connection of how the old life and times of Manifest somewhat fit into her current life and times: "Moon Over M_?"

426. What is the title of the 2011 Newbery award-winning autobiographical novel by Jack Gantos that tells of a boy named Jack living in Norvelt, Pennsylvania who as a punishment for firing his father's Japanese sniper rifle, has to help his neighbor Miss Volker write obituaries and her history column, and discovers that he has a great interest in historical events that he never learned about in school: "Dead End in N_?"

427. What is the title of the 2012 Newbery award-winning children's book by Katherine Applegate about a gorilla named Ivan living in a glass-walled cage at the Exit 8 Big Top Mall and Video Arcade, and how he changes his perspective of life somewhat after meeting Ruby, a baby elephant: "The One and Only I_?"

428. What is the name of the book published in 2013 by Norwegian authors Ylvis and Christian Lochstoer and illustrator Svein Nyhus, based on a popular YouTube video that tells how the cat goes meow, the dog goes woof, and the mouse goes squeak: "What Does the Fox _?"

429. What is the title of the 2014 Newbery Medal winner by Katie DiCamillo about the adventures of a young girl named Flora who loves to read comics, and her relationship with a squirrel: "Flora and Ulysses: The Illuminated _?"

430. What is the title of the 2014 Caldecott Medal winner illustrated by Brian Floca about a family's weeklong train trip from Omaha, Nebraska to Sacramento, California in 1868: "Lo_?"

431. What is the name of the reference book, first published in 1955 and every year thereafter, that contains a collection of world records, and is one of the best-selling books of all time: G__?

432. What is your favorite book?

Chapter 3 – Math

Math – Pre-School

1. Can you count to 10?
2. Which number comes after 8?
3. Which number comes before 7?
4. Which number comes between 6 and 8?
5. Can you count forward from 6?
6. Can you count backward from 8?
7. How would you complete the following sequence: 5, __, 7, 8
8. How do we make tally marks?
9. What songs do you know that have numbers in them?
10. What are 2, 3, 5, and 7 called because they are only divisible by 1 and itself: prime numbers or divisors?
11. Is 4 the sum or the difference in the equation 2 +2 = 4?
12. Is 1 the sum or the difference in the equation 2-1=1?
13. Can you complete a puzzle?
14. Is your stomach (piggy bank) etc. *empty* or *full*?
15. Which is *more*: 10 or 3?
16. Which has more people: a city or a family?
17. Which has *less people*: a country or a state?
18. Which is less: 7 or 2?
19. Is a basket of 5 apples more, less, or equal to a basket of 5 pears?
20. If I have two apples and you have two apples do we have more, less, or the same?
21. What is another word in math that means ***the same as***?
22. How do we say one plus one *is the same as* two?

MATH

23. What are some objects in your room that are large?

24. What are some objects in your room that are small?

25. What are some objects in your room that are blue? (etc.)

26. Can you name something that is square?

27. What is the shape of a coin, pizza, pie, button, or ring?

28. What are some objects in your room that are round?

29. What is the shape of a football field: a square or a rectangle?

30. What are some objects you can name that are in a rectangle shape?

31. What is the shape of a block?

32. Is a block similar to a cube?

33. What are some objects you can name that are square?

34. What do we call a baseball field and is another name for this shape?

35. Are hearts and stars also shapes?

36. Are spheres, cones, and prisms also considered shapes?

37. Is a diamond a shape, a type of precious stone, or both?

38. How would you continue the pattern, black, white, black, __?

39. How would you continue the pattern, red, white, blue: red, __?

40. How would you continue the pattern, pants, piano, scissors: pants,__?

41. What are the numbers in your phone number?

42. Can you tell me the numbers in your address?

43. Can you name something that is inside the house?

44. Can you name something that is outside the house?

45. Can you name something that is above the house?

46. Can you name something that is below the house?

47. Can you name something that is on top of your bed?

48. Can you name something that is under your bed?

49. Which side of the road do we drive on, the right or the left?

50. Which hand do you write with, your right hand or your left hand?

MATH

51. Is the neck of a giraffe long or short?
52. Is the tail on an elephant long of short?
53. Is a box of feathers light or heavy?
54. Is a box of tiles light or heavy?
55. Which holds more: a bowl or a cup?
56. Would you say that most streets are wide or narrow?
57. Would you say that a path in the woods is wide or narrow?
58. Which coin is a copper color and worth 1 cent?
59. Which coin is a silver color and is worth 5 cents?
60. Which coin is a silver color, thin, and worth 10 cents?
61. Which coin is bigger than a nickel, bigger than a dime, is silver, and is worth 25 cents?

Math – Kindergarten

62. Can you count to 100?
63. Can you count to 100 by 5's?
64. Can you count to 100 by 10's?
65. What number holds no value and is less than one?
66. Can you count forward from 7?
67. Can you count backward from 20?
68. How do you complete the following sequence, 19 _, 21, 22?
69. How many (**blue**) objects can you count in your room?
70. What number is after 7?
71. What number is before 3?
72. What number is after 79?
73. What number is between 5 and 7?
74. What is the shape of a whole pizza?
75. If a pizza is cut into 8 equal slices, and you and I eat four of the pieces, how much of the pizza is left?

MATH

76. Are four slices of an 8 piece pizza equal to half the pizza?
77. If you are sharing a big cookie with a friend, how would you divide the cookie equally?
78. Do we use measurements when we bake cookies?
79. Do we sometimes add ingredients to our cookie dough using one cup, half-cup, 1/3 cup and ¼ cup?
80. Do we measure salt and vanilla when following a recipe using teaspoons or cups?
81. Which is bigger: a tablespoon or a teaspoon?
82. When measuring ingredients for a cake is it better when following a recipe: measuring spoons or the spoons that we use for soup and cereal?
83. What is the shape of one piece of pizza or one piece of pie?
84. What is the shape of a block?
85. What is the shape of a football field?
86. What objects can you name that are round?
87. What objects can you name that are square?
88. How many sides does a square have?
89. What objects can you name that are in the shape of a triangle?
90. How many sides does a triangle have?
91. What objects can you name that are in the shape of a rectangle?
92. How many sides does a rectangle have?
93. Can you name something that is in the shape of an oval?
94. How many fingers do you have?
95. How many fingers do you have on each hand?
96. How many fingers am I holding up?
97. Can you hold up your fingers to show how old you are?
98. Can you hold up your fingers to show how ears you have?
99. Can you hold up your fingers to show how many thumbs you have?
100. Can you count backward from 10?
101. Can you count to 20 by 2's?
102. When you count by 2's, 5's or 10's is that called skip-counting?

MATH

103. Can you count to 20 by 5's?

104. Which is more 13 or 14?

105. Which is less 5 or 9?

106. What is the number that has no value?

107. What is two plus zero?

108. What is two plus two? (Use any addition facts through 10)

109. What is the sum of 5 plus 5?

110. Is 5 + 5 equal to 6+4? (Etc.)

111. Can you describe what the addition sign looks like?

112. Can you describe what the subtraction sign looks like?

113. What is 3 minus 1 equal to?

114. What is the 10 minus 5 equal to?

115. What is 3 minus 0? (Use any subtraction facts through 10)

116. Can you describe what the *equals* sign looks like?

117. How much is one penny worth?

118. How much is one nickel worth?

119. How much is one dime worth?

120. How much is one quarter worth?

121. What metal is a penny made of?

122. Is the symbol for cent(s) the letter c with one line or two lines through it?

123. Is the symbol for the dollar the letter "S" with one line or two lines through it?

124. If you have eight pennies and gave me half of them, how many would I have?

125. What is the name of the coin that is worth 5 cents?

126. What is the name of the coin that is worth 10 cents?

127. What is the name of the coin that is worth 25 cents?

128. Is there a 50 cent coin?

129. Would two quarters be equal to one half dollar?

130. Are four quarters equal to one dollar?

MATH

131. Is there a dollar coin?
132. Are all coins the same size or are they different sizes?
133. Which coin is the smallest is size?
134. Which coin is the largest: a quarter or a 50 cent piece?
135. How many sides does a coin have?
136. What is the name of the side of a coin with the imprint of a president?
137. What is the name of the other side of a coin with a picture of a building?
138. Can you describe what the symbol for cents looks like?
139. What is the name of our paper money?
140. Can you describe what the symbol for dollars looks like?
141. What are all the *red* things you can name in your room? (Classification)
142. Can you put *white* clothes in one pile and the *colored* clothes in another pile?
143. If you are making tally marks to keep track of all the red toys you have, how do you show that you have five toys?
144. What toys do you have that are big?
145. What toys do you have that are small?
146. What things are located inside a house?
147. What things are located outside a house?
148. What is located on the left side of your bed?
149. What is located on the right side of your bed?
150. What is located in the middle of your bedroom?
151. Does a boat float on the top or the bottom of a lake?
152. What part of your body is located above your neck?
153. What part of your body is located below your wrist?
154. Can you **_estimate_** how many stuffed animals you have?
155. Can you finish the pattern of red, blue: red _?
156. What is next in the series: white, green, pink: white _?
157. Which comes next in the pattern, dogs, turtles, cats: dogs, _?

MATH

158. What do we use to tell time?

159. How many numbers are on a clock?

160. Are there different kinds of clocks?

161. If the small hand is on the (**three**) and the big hand is on the twelve, what time is it?

162. Which tool measures length, how long something is?

163. What animals can you name that are long?

164. What animals can you name that are short?

165. What is the name of the tool for three rulers put together?

166. What is the name of the tool that tells us the temperature, or how hot or cold something is?

167. What is the name of the tool that can do math functions that has buttons that you press?

168. What is the name of the tool that tells us how heavy or light something is?

169. What animals can you name that are heavy?

170. What animals can you name that are light?

171. What object in your bedroom would be heavy and therefore hard to lift?

172. What object in your bedroom would be light and therefore easy to lift?

173. Did you come home from school in the morning, the afternoon, or the evening?

174. Did you eat breakfast before or after you got dressed today?

175. Did you brush your teeth before or after you ate supper?

176. If you are brushing your teeth after waking up, is it a.m. or p.m.?

177. What part of the day is it now?

178. What tool helps us to know the date and the time of year?

179. What are the days of the week starting with Sunday?

180. How many days are there in a week?

181. How many days are there in a month?

182. Are the number of days in a month always the same or are they different?

183. If today is Monday, what day is tomorrow?

184. If today is Thursday, what day was yesterday?

185. If today is Friday, what day is the day after tomorrow?

MATH

186. Which season comes after autumn?

187. Which season comes before spring?

188. Is the bathtub full or empty right now?

189. What do we say if we fill a glass half way with water: The glass is _?

190. What can you name that comes in pairs?

191. Can you show me what you would do if I said, "Simon Says put your *right* hand *behind* your head?

192. Can you show me what you would do if I said, "Simon Says put your *left* hand *between* your knees?

193. Can you show me what you would do if I said, "Simon Says put your *right* hand *under* your *left* foot?

194. Can you show me what you would do if I said, "Simon Says put your *left* hand beside your *right* knee?

195. If you are spinning a spinner that is mostly blue with a small red section, which section is the arrow most likely to point to?

196. Which is longer: a submarine sandwich or a bagel?

197. Which is shorter: a ruler or a yardstick?

198. Which is taller: a skyscraper or a house?

199. Which is lighter: a dog or an elephant?

200. Which container holds more: a tablespoon or a cup??

201. Which weighs more: a butterfly or a frog?

202. Which is the heaviest: a tiger, a monkey, or an elephant?

203. Which is the lightest: a deer, a bowling ball, or a beach ball?

Math – 1st Grade

204. Can you count to 100 by 5's?

205. Can you count to 100 by 10's?

206. Can you count to 50 by 2's?

207. Can you count back from 10?

208. If you are counting down from 18, which number comes next?

209. If you are counting up from 49, which number comes next?

MATH

210. What number would be between zero and two on a number line?
211. Which is the faster way of counting: by 5's or by 1's?
212. What is the term for things that go together and come in two's?
213. What two separate items do you have that would be called a pair?
214. What item do you have that can be called a pair even though there is just one?
215. What is the number that represents the absence of value and comes before the number one?
216. What games do you know of that help you practice math and make it fun?
217. Do you think that there are many activities and games that you could do on the computer to help you practice math?
218. What ordinal number is the opposite of *last*?
219. Which grade comes after 1st?
220. Which grade comes before 4th?
221. Which grade comes after 9th?
222. Which grade comes before 8th?
223. What is the weather like today?
224. Can you read a thermometer?
225. What does a thermometer measure?
226. What other tools can gather information about the weather?
227. Is math important in the study of weather?
228. What are some things that fly in the air?
229. What does a kite need to move in the air?
230. What do the rotating blades of windmills create?
231. What is another word for doing something *one time*?
232. What is another word for doing something *two times*?
233. What do you get when you *double* the number 2?
234. What do you get when you *double* the number 10? (1-10, etc.)
235. What number comes next: 2, 4, 6, _?
236. What is the missing number in the following sequence: 30, _, 40, 45, 50?

167

MATH

237. Are the numbers 2, 4, and 6 odd or even?

238. What number comes next: 1, 3, 5, _?

239. Can you predict what number comes next: 1, 4, 7, _?

240. Are the numbers 1, 3, and 5 odd or even?

241. Is the number 23 odd or even?

242. Which even number comes after 30?

243. Which odd number comes before 50?

244. What number comes before 30? (40,50,60,70,80,90,100)

245. If a recipe calls for *2* cups of flour, and you are making a double batch of cookies, how many cups of flour would you need to add?

246. Can you name something on a stuffed animal that come in two's?

247. Can you estimate how many stuffed animals you have? (Etc.)

248. How many sides does a square have?

249. How many sides does a triangle have?

250. How many sides does a rectangle have?

251. What is the name of the shape that is round?

252. What things in our environment are round?

253. What things can you name that are in the shape of a rectangle?

254. What things can you name that are in the shape of a square?

255. What would come next in the sequence: triangle, square, triangle, _?

256. What is the shape of a racetrack?

257. Is a piece of ice in the shape of a cube or a sphere?

258. Is the Earth in the shape of a cube or a sphere?

259. Is a cube a simple shape or a solid shape?

260. Are cylinders, cones and spheres solid shapes or simple shapes?

261. Are points, lines, and curves simple shapes or solid shapes?

262. Can you name something in the shape of a cone?

263. Do you think the crescent moon in the shape of an arc is an open shape or a closed shape?

MATH

264. Is a circle an open or closed shape?

265. What is something you know of that is straight?

266. What is something you know of that is curved?

267. What are some shapes that would look different if they were turned upside down?

268. What would you see if you looked through a prism?

269. What are some things that might be divided in half?

270. What is next in the pattern: red, green, yellow, blue: red, green _?

271. Do we use less than, greater than, and equal to when we compare numbers?

272. Which is greater: 60 or 70?

273. Which is less: 49 or 89?

274. What do say when comparing numbers: greater than, less than, equal to, or all of them?

275. Is 29 greater or less than 19?

276. What is another way of stating that 30 is greater than 20?

277. How would you compare the numbers 25 and 25?

278. Which would weigh more: one pound of feathers or one pound of stones?

279. What is 0+1 (2-10)?

280. What is 1+1?

281. What is 2 + 2?

282. What is 3+3

283. What is 4+4?

284. What is 5+5?

285. What is 6 + 6?

286. What is 7 + 7?

287. What is 8 + 8?

288. What is 9 + 9?

289. What is 10 + 10?

290. What is 20 + 10?

291. What is 30 + 10?

MATH

292. What is 40 + 10?

293. What is 50 + 10?

294. What is 60 + 10?

295. What is 70 + 10?

296. What is 80 + 10?

297. What is 90 + 10?

298. What is the sum of 15 + 3?

299. What is the sum of 12 + 9?

300. What is the sum of 16 + 8?

301. Does 3 + 2 equal 2 + 3?

302. If 5+4=9, does 4+5=9?

303. Does 3 + 0 equal 0 + 3?

304. Is 15 + 5 greater than or equal to 10 +10?

305. Is 3 + 5 =8 the same as 5 + 3 =8?

306. How many dogs were walked in all if Sam walked 4 dogs and Jason walked 6 dogs?

307. How many pieces of furniture did the store sell if it sold 3 tables, 1 couch, and 2 chairs?

308. What is 9 + 2? (Basic addition facts through 9+9)

309. What is the missing number in the following equation: 2 + __ = 6?

310. What is the sign or symbol for subtraction?

311. What is 7-3? (Basic subtraction facts)

312. What is the difference of 18-9?

313. What is 5-2?

314. What is 10-0?

315. What is 19 +1? (29,39,49,59,69,79,89,99)

316. What is 20-1? (100,70,50,60,30,90,40,80,10)

317. What is 90-10? (80-10; 70-10, 60-10, 50-10, 40-10, 30-10, 20-10, 10-10 etc.)

318. What is 40 – 20?

319. What is 23-1-?

MATH

320. What is 17-6?

321. What is 18-9?

322. How many apples are left in the refrigerator if Ann takes 2 apples out of the drawer that has 6 apples in it?

323. How would you make 4: 8-4 or 7-2?

324. How would you make 9: 6 + 2 or 2 + 7?

325. What would come next in the pattern: 5-5=0, 4-4=0, 3-3=0, _-2=0, _ - _=0?

326. How would you continue the following sequence: 10-0=10, 10-1=9, 10-2= _, 10-3=_, 10-4=__, 10-5=_, 10-6= __, 10-7= _, 10-8= _, 10-9= _, 10-10=_?

327. Can you make a subtraction equation from the following word problem: Together Pete and Sean bought 15 bags of chips for the party. If Pete bought 8 bags, how many did Sean buy? (15 -8=__)

328. What is 90 - 60?

329. What is 50 + 40?

330. How would you complete the following: _ - 3 = 6?

331. What is the related subtraction fact for **6 – 4 = 2**: 6 – 2 = 4 or 10 – 4 = 6?

332. Would you need a plus or minus sign in the following equation: 6 _ 4=10?

333. Would you need a plus or minus sign in the following equation: 10 _ 3=7?

334. In the equation 44 - 36=8, is 8 the sum or the difference?

335. Which fact is missing from the following: 5+6=11, 6+6=11, 11 - 5 = 6, __-__ = 5?

336. How many pens does Josh have all together in his supply box if he has 8 black pens and 6 blue pens?

337. What is 10 less than 31?

338. What is 10 more than 49?

339. What is the opposite of greater than?

340. What is the opposite of unequal?

341. What is the opposite of more?

342. What is the opposite of less than?

343. How would you finish the sentence using greater than, less than, or equal to: 10 is __than 8?

344. How would you finish the sentence using greater than, less than, or equal to: 6 is __than 7?

345. How would you finish the sentence using greater than, less than, or equal to: 5 is __to 5?

MATH

346. How would you finish the sentence using greater than, less than, or equal to: 82 is ___ than 72?

347. If Jordan has 6 stickers and Maddie has more stickers than Eli, how many stickers does Maddie have: 5 or 10?

348. What is the opposite of left?

349. What is the opposite of least?

350. Can you identify what happens to a plant as it grows?

351. What happens to the weather as we approach winter? (summer, etc.)

352. How does a person's weight change as they grow: increases or decreases?

353. Can you solve the equation: 2 + what number = 5?

354. What is the order of the following set smallest to largest (least to greatest): 22, 42, and 12?

355. What is the order of the following set largest to smallest (greatest to least): 22, 42, and 12?

356. In the number 76, which number is in the tens column? (26,36,46,56,66,86,96)

357. In the number 25, which number is in the ones column?

358. In the number 86 there are 8 tens and how many ones?

359. In the number 49, how many tens and ones are there?

360. Can you estimate: how many kids are in your class; how many dogs are in the neighborhood; how many stuffed animals you have; etc.?

361. Without looking at the clock, can you estimate what time it is?

362. What do we use to tell us the date and month of the year?

363. Do we use a calendar to plan family activities and events?

364. How many months are there in one year?

365. How many days (more or less) are in one month?

366. How many days are there in one week?

367. If today is Friday, what day was yesterday?

368. If today is Sunday, what day is tomorrow?

369. Which day comes before Saturday?

370. Which day comes after Tuesday?

371. If today is Monday, what day was the day before yesterday?

MATH

372. What are the two days of the weekend?

373. How many seconds are there in one minute?

374. How many minutes are there in one hour?

375. How many hours are there in one day?

376. If it is 9:00 o'clock now, what time will it be in one half hour?

377. Do you have a digital clock, an analog clock, or both?

378. When do most people go to bed: the a.m. or the p.m?

379. When you eat breakfast and get ready for your day, is it a.m. or p.m?

380. Which is the correct time unit for how long a baseball game lasts: 3 hours, 3 days, or 3 weeks?

381. How many eggs are there in one dozen?

382. Which month of the year is January: the first or the last?

383. If January is the first month of the year, what is the last month of the year?

384. What is the opposite of first?

385. Which month is second? (3rd-12th)

386. What grade are you in?

387. What grade will you be in next year?

388. What grade were you in last year?

389. What are the three months of winter in our state?

390. What are the three months of summer in our state?

391. What are the three months of autumn in our state?

392. What are the three months of spring in our state?

393. What is the name of the operation when we add things together?

394. What is the sign for addition?

395. If I have 2 books and I add 3 more, how many books do I have altogether?

396. How do you write the equation of 2 books and 3 more books amounts to 5 books?

397. What is it called when you take something away from a group?

398. What is the sign for subtraction?

399. If you have 3 books and you return 2 to the library, how many do you have left?

MATH

400. If you had 4 tacos on your plate but you only ate 3, what would the equation look like?
401. How many inches long is a ruler?
402. What is twelve inches equal to?
403. What is the name the tool that measures three feet long?
404. Are three feet greater than or equal to one yard?
405. Can we also use a tape measure tool to take measurements?
406. What is the correct order smallest to largest: yard, inches, and feet?
407. What is the appropriate unit of length of a submarine sandwich: 12 inches or 12 feet?
408. What is the name of the unit of measurement for distance when we drive a car or walk to school or the library?
409. Which tool indicates what the weight of something is?
410. What measurement of weight do we use: the pound or the kilo?
411. Which unit of weight is appropriate for a bird: 17 ounces or 17 pounds?
412. How much do you weigh?
413. If you use your hand as a measuring tool, how many hands long is your bed?
414. Which tool shows how hot or cold something is?
415. Do we in America measure the temperature in degrees Fahrenheit or degrees Celsius?
416. Is there another system of measurement used in many other places called the *metric* system?
417. What are the metric measurements for length smallest to biggest: meter, millimeter, and centimeter?
418. What would be the appropriate length of a spoon: 18 meters or 18 centimeters?
419. What is the metric measurement for temperature: Celsius and Fahrenheit?
420. What is the metric measurement for distance: the mile or the kilometer?
421. What is the metric measurement for weight: grams or pounds?
422. What would be an appropriate weight of a plastic bowl: 13 grams or kilograms?
423. What is the prefix "kilo" equal to: one thousand or one hundred?
424. What is the metric measurement for liquid volume: gallons or liters?
425. What are some things that are hot in temperature?
426. What are some things that are cold?

MATH

427. If you fill a gas tank in the car all the way, what do we say that the tank is: full or complete?

428. If you run out of gas, what is the tank now?

429. Can we measure solids and liquids?

430. What things can you name that are solids?

431. What things can you name that are liquids?

432. Which is bigger: a cup or a pint?

433. Which is bigger: a pint or a quart

434. Which is bigger: a gallon or a quart?

435. How would you put the following in order from smallest to largest: pint, cup, gallon, and quart?

436. What do cups, pints, quarts, and gallons all measure: liquid capacity or weight?

437. Do you typically drink ½ pint or one pint of milk?

438. In what capacity do most people buy milk that is equal to 4 quarts?

439. What are some things we might purchase by the gallon?

440. In liquid measurement, how many cups equal one pint: 2 cups or 4 cups?

441. In liquid measurement, how many cups equal one quart: 4 cups or 8 cups?

442. In liquid measurement, how many pints equal one quart: 2 pints or 4 pints?

443. In liquid measurement, how many quarts equal one gallon: 2 quarts or 4 quarts?

444. Which is greater: 7 cups or 1 quart?

445. What is the name of the unit of measurement when we fill up the tank with gas: quarts or gallons?

446. What is the name of the metric liquid measurement: a kilo or a liter?

447. If you just ate two hot dogs, would you say your stomach is empty or full?

448. If you fill the tank only half-way, would you say that it is half-full, or half-empty?

449. What would take *longer*: brushing your teeth or driving to school?

450. Which would be *shorter*: eating some grapes or eating supper?

451. If the red bag has 3 presents, the blue bag has 5 presents, and the white bag has 8 presents, which bag has the *most*?

452. If the red bag has 3 presents, the blue bag has 5 presents, and the white bag has 8 presents, which bag has the *least*?

MATH

453. If the green bag has 3 presents and the yellow bag has 3 presents, how would you compare them?

454. If you cut a round pizza into 8 slices, how many slices would make up half the pizza?

455. If you are baking cookies, might you need to have a measuring cups that measure ¼, ½, and 1 cup as you follow the recipe?

456. Is a fraction a part or a whole?

457. Is the top number of a fraction called a numerator or a denominator?

458. Is the bottom number of a fraction called a numerator or a denominator?

459. Which is greater: one-half or one-fourth?

460. Which is greater: one-third or one-fourth?

461. How many sides does a square have?

462. How many sides does a rectangle have?

463. How many sides does a triangle have?

464. Which shape does not have sides: a circle or an octagon?

465. How many sides does a hexagon have: 6 or 8?

466. How many sides does an octagon have: 6 or 8?

467. How many arms does an octopus have?

468. What red traffic sign is in the shape of an octagon?

469. Does a trapezoid resemble the shape of a skirt or a stop sign?

470. What shape would you call a globe: a sphere or a prism?

471. What shape would you call a flashlight or a soda can: a cylinder or a cube?

472. What is the shape of the crunchy part of an ice cream treat, a birthday hat, and an Indian tepee: a sphere or a cone?

473. What is the shape of a piece of ice or dice: a rectangle or a cube?

474. What shape would a piece of pie or a piece of pizza be: a sphere or a triangle?

475. What is the shape of an arc or a rainbow: a closed shape or an open shape?

476. Is a circle a closed shape or an open shape?

477. Is a straight line a shape?

478. What is it called when one part of a shape is a mirror image of the other part: symmetrical or bilateral?

MATH

479. In what direction would you make a tally mark to indicate 5 points: diagonally or straight?

480. What bar would be higher on a bar graph if one bar showed shirt sales of 40, and the other bar showed shirt sales of 32?

481. If you wanted to find out how many students wanted to go to the play, would you use tally marks or a graph to record your data?

482. How many wheels does a bicycle have?

483. How many wheels does a tricycle have?

484. How many wheels does a unicycle have?

485. What is the name of the coin that is worth 5 cents?

486. What is the name of the coin that is worth 10 cents?

487. What is the name of the coin that is worth 25 cents?

488. Is there a 50 cent coin?

489. Can you add coins together?

490. How many nickels is one dime equal to?

491. What three coins could you have that would equal one quarter?

492. What is the value of a quarter, a dime, a nickel, and a penny?

493. What is the value of one quarter and one dime?

494. What is the value of two quarters, one dime and one nickel?

495. What is the value of two quarters, two dimes, one nickel, and three pennies?

496. What are four quarters equal to?

497. What are two dimes and a five pennies equal to?

498. What are five dimes equal to?

499. Which coin is 25 pennies equal to?

500. Which coin are two dimes and a nickel equal to?

501. What is the value of two quarters and one dime?

502. If you have eight pennies and gave me half of them, how many would I have?

503. How many quarters are equal to one half dollar?

504. How many quarters are equal to one dollar?

MATH

505. How much money do they spend in all if Nick buys a candy bar with 5 dimes and Julia buys a candy bar with 2 quarters?

506. Do you have enough money if a bag of popcorn costs 25 cents and you have four nickels?

507. Do you have enough money if a bag of popcorn costs 25 cents and you have two dimes?

508. Does a person who is *bi*lingual speak one language or two?

509. How many languages can a person speak if he/she is *multi*lingual?

510. What is the probability that you will sleep in your bed tonight: certain, probable, unlikely, or impossible?

511. What is the probability that you will fly like a bird: certain, probable, unlikely, or impossible?

512. What is the probability that you will have 20 dogs: certain, probable, unlikely, or impossible?

513. What is the probability that you will eat breakfast tomorrow morning even though you overslept: certain, probable, unlikely, or impossible?

514. What letter is the Roman numeral for one?

515. What letter is the Roman numeral for five: V or X?

516. What letter is the Roman numeral for ten: V or X?

517. What letter is the Roman numeral for fifty: L or C?

518. What would Roman numeral XV be equal to?

519. What would Roman numeral XXX be equal to?

520. What would Roman numeral XIV be equal to?

521. What would Roman numeral LXVII be equal to?

522. How many total writing utensils does Jonathon have if he has 3 pens and 2 pencils?

523. How could you write an addition equation for the following: Rosa caught one firefly and Maya caught four, how many in all? 1 + __ = __

524. Do you find the range of numbers by subtracting the lowest number from the highest?

525. What is the range of the following numbers 10, 8, 7, 8, 6?

526. In the sequence 13,13,13,13,14,15 the number 13 is the one that is repeated the most, so is 13 the mode or the median?

527. In the numbers 5, 6, and 7, which number is the median, or the one in the middle?

MATH

Math – 2nd Grade

528. Can you count to 100 by 1's?

529. Can you count to 100 by 20's?

530. Can you count to 100 by 2's?

531. Can you count to 100 by 5's?

532. Can you count to 1000 by 100's?

533. Can you count forward by 100's from 600: 600, _, _, _, _?

534. Which number is between 979 and 981?

535. Could Brian skip count by 5's if he begins at 20 until he reached 36?

536. Can you count back from 100?

537. How do you put 44, 25, and 33 in numerical order?

538. What number is missing in the following sequence: 50, _, 60, 65, 70?

539. What number would be next on a number line to 100: 95, 96, 97, _, 99?

540. Can you count forward by twos from 26: 26, _, _, _, _?

541. What comes next in the following pattern: yellow fish, blue fish, yellow fish, __?

542. What comes next in the following pattern: blue, yellow, blue; blue, yellow, yellow; blue, yellow blue; _?

543. Is the number 37 odd or even?

544. Is the number 46 odd or even?

545. Which of the following is an even number, 2, 3, 7, and 5?

546. Which odd number comes before 3, 5, 7?

547. Which even number comes after 2, 4, 6?

548. What are the ordinal numbers? (First…)

549. What grade are you in?

550. What is the abbreviation (shortened form) for first?

551. What is the abbreviation for second?

552. What is the abbreviation for third?

553. What is the abbreviation for fourth?

MATH

554. What is the abbreviation for fifth?

555. What is the abbreviation for sixth?

556. What is the abbreviation for seventh?

557. What is the abbreviation for eighth?

558. What is the abbreviation for ninth?

559. What is the abbreviation for tenth?

560. What ordinal comes after forty ninth?

561. Which of the following are the ordinal numbers: 50th, 40, 75th, and 66?

562. How is the number t-h-i-r-t-y - n-i-n-t-h written using digits? (Etc.)

563. How is the number t-w-o h-u-n-d-r-e-d f-o-r-t-y f-i-v-e written using digits

564. In the equation 4 +2 = 6, is 6 the sum or the difference?

565. In the equation 6-2 =4, is 4 the sum or the difference?

566. Does the following equation need a plus or a minus? 5 _ 3=2

567. Does the following equation need a plus or a minus? 8 _ 4=12

568. What is the sum of 9+9?

569. What is 9 + 8? (Addition facts 0-20)

570. What is 12 + 13?

571. What is the sum of 60 + 20?

572. What is the sum of 25 + 4?

573. What is the sum of 19 + 5?

574. What is the sum of 73 + 13?

575. What is the sum of 39+ 12?

576. What is the sum of 200 + 300?

577. What is the sum of 120 + 130?

578. What is the sum of 6 + 7 + 3?

579. What is the sum of 30 + 12 + 2?

580. What is the related addition fact for 12 + 3 =15: 3 + __ = __ ?

581. What is the related addition fact for 12 + 8 = 20?

MATH

582. Which number makes the equation true: 14 + 5 = 9 + _?

583. What is the missing number in the equation: 830 + __ = 839?

584. Which number makes the equation true: 240 + 2 = 236 + __

585. If Lilly and Megan sold 12 regular lemonades and 6 strawberry lemonades at their lemonade stand, how many lemonades did they sell in all?

586. If the zoo has 7 adult lions and 6 baby lions how many lions are there in all?

587. If Alex made 24 cookies and Jack made 12, how many cookies did they make in all?

588. If 200 people bought blue T-shirts for the fundraiser and 150 bought red T-shirts, how many total shirts were bought: _+_=_?

589. What number do you get if you double the number 20?

590. What number do you get if you double the number 25?

591. What number added to 12 would equal 20?

592. What number subtracted from 15 would give you 10?

593. What is **not** a way to make 7: 6+1; 3+4; 2+7; or 5+2?

594. What is 18 –9? (Subtraction facts 0-20)

595. What is the difference in 14-9?

596. What is 6-6 equal to?

597. Which is **not** a way to make 7: 7-0; 8-1; 8-0; or 10-3?

598. What is 80 – 50?

599. What is 67 – 4?

600. What is 21– 7?

601. What is 18 – 5?

602. What is 54 – 14?

603. What is 800-500?

604. What is 750-50?

605. What is 330-130?

606. What is the missing number in the equation: _ minus one equals nine?

607. What fact is missing from this fact family: 14-2=12; 14-12 = 2; 2+12=14, __+__=___

MATH

608. Which equation does **not** equal 9: 12-2; 13-4; or 16-7?

609. What is a subtraction equation that would equal 10?

610. What number would make the equation true: 12-2 = 20 -_?

611. What is a related subtraction fact for 20 – 15 = 5: 20 - __ = __

612. What is a related subtraction fact for 30 – 10 = 20: 30 - __ = __

613. If you had 14 peas and ate 8 of them, how many would be left on your plate?

614. If you had 6 Legos and needed 20 Legos to build a bridge, how many more Legos would you need?

615. How would you write a subtraction sentence for the following: Emma had 4 cookies in her lunch but two were broken and she threw them out. How many cookies does she have now: _-_=__?

616. If there are 40 pumpkins in the pumpkin patch and Lillian's class picks out 20 of them, how many are left: __ - __ = __?

617. Drew and Marcos collected 17 leaves on their walk through the woods. If Drew collected 8 leaves, how many did Marcos collect?

618. How would you balance the following equation: 9-8 = 7-_?

619. How would you balance the following equation: 239-9 = 250 - _?

620. If the total for the homerun contest was 13 and Tommy hit 8 of them, how many did Garrett hit?

621. How can you make 70: 74-4 or 69+8?

622. What is the missing number in the following: 59-9 = 4 + _?

623. If Henry and Ashlyn read a total of 22 books for the summer library reading club, and Ashlyn reads 12 of them, how many did Henry read?

624. Is 1 +17 equal to 17 + 1?

625. What number would you add to 6 to equal the sum of 3 + 7?

626. What is 55 + 0?

627. What number would you add to 4 to equal 6?

628. How many ways can you add two numbers together to make 12 besides 12+0=12? (11+1, …)

629. What is an addition sentence for the following: If Kim bought 7 cheese pizzas and Kelly bought 5 pepperoni pizzas for the party, how many pizzas did they buy in all: _+__ = _?

630. When you add zero to any number, does it change the value of that number?

631. If an input/output table reads 2 IN and 12 OUT, 6 IN and 16 OUT, what is the rule: + __?

MATH

632. Which bar would be higher on a bar graph if the bar indicating sweatshirts purchased was 25 and the bar indicating T-shirts sold was 21?

633. Can you read a pictograph?

634. Can you read a line graph?

635. What part of a Venn diagram shows the common elements of the two things being compared?

636. Is 2 greater than, less than, or equal to 3 +1?

637. Is 6 greater than, less than, or equal to 3+2?

638. Is 6 greater than, less than, or equal to 3 +3?

639. Which is greater: 76 or 67?

640. Which is less: 58 or 49?

641. Is 92 greater than, less than, or equal to 89?

642. Is 583 greater than, less than, or equal to 583?

643. In the series 1,2,5,6, which numbers are even?

644. In the series 1,2,5,6 which numbers are odd?

645. How would you continue the sequence: 22, 24, _?

646. How would you continue the sequence: 31, 33, _?

647. How would you put the following numbers in order least to greatest: 77, 71, and 70?

648. How would you put the following numbers in order greatest to least: 92, 99, and 88?

649. In the number 704, which number is in the ones column?

650. In the number 704, which number is in the tens column?

651. In the number 612, which number is in the tens column?

652. What is the value of the digit **one** in the number 16: tens or ones?

653. What is the value of the digit **eight** in the number 81: tens or ones?

654. What is the value of each digit in the number 95: _tens and _ones?

655. What is the value of each digit in the number 345: _hundreds, _tens, and _ones?

656. What is the value of each digit in the number 3,042: _thousands, _hundreds, _tens, _ones?

657. How many thousands would 300 tens be equal to: 1 or 3?

658. Even though there are zero tens in 704, is the number zero used as a place holder?

183

MATH

659. In the number 704, which number is in the hundreds column?

660. What is the value of the digit **nine** in the number 950: hundreds or tens?

661. What is the value of the digit **three** in the number 3,421: hundreds or thousands?

662. How could you regroup tens and ones in the following equation: 2 tens and 22 ones = _tens and _ones?

663. How could you regroup tens and ones in the following equation: 6 tens and 18 ones = 7 tens, and __ones?

664. What is another way to make 65 besides 6 tens and 5 ones: 5 tens or 15 ones or 4 tens and 15 ones?

665. Is 4 tens and 20 ones the same as 6 tens?

666. What number is missing in the following: 6 tens and 15 ones = 7 tens and _ones?

667. What is the sum of 300 + 20+ 9?

668. What is the sum of 7,000 + 300 + 80 +4?

669. In the number ten point five, is the point called a decimal point or a period?

670. Can point five zero also be written as one half?

671. Is point two five written as one fourth or one half?

672. Is one point seven five written as one and seven fifths, or one and three fourths?

673. What is the ratio if there are 20 boys in a group and 10 girls: 20:10 or 2:1?

674. If there are 12 dogs at the pet shop and 3 cats, what is the ratio of dogs to cats?

675. What is the term for the answer when you multiply 2 or more numbers: the product or the quotient?

676. What is the product of 2 x 3?

677. What is the product of 3 x 2?

678. What is 1 x 15?

679. When you multiply 1 by any number, does it equal that number or a higher one?

680. What is 8 x 0?

681. When you multiply any number by zero, does it always equal zero or the higher number?

682. What is 5 x 5? (Multiplication facts 0-10)

683. What is 4 x 6?

684. What is 3 x 4?

MATH

685. What is 5 x 5?

686. What is 9 x 5?

687. What is 8 divided by 4?

688. In the equation 8 divided by 4 equals 2, is the quotient 4 or 2?

689. What is 10 divided by 2?

690. What is 20 divided by 5?

691. What is 18 divided by 3? (Division facts 0-10)

692. If 8 divided by 2 equals 4, does 2 times 4 equal 8?

693. If 9 divided by 3 equals 3, does 3 times 3 equal 9? (Inverse operations)

694. Is a fraction part of a whole number?

695. Can a fraction also be written as a percentage?

696. Is the numerator the top number or the bottom number of a fraction?

697. Is the denominator the top number or the bottom number of a fraction?

698. How would you write the fraction one fourth?

699. How would you write the fraction one half?

700. How would you write the fraction one third?

701. Which fraction is greater: ½ or ¼?

702. Which set of fractions is ordered greatest to least: 6/9, 6/8, 6/7 or 6/7, 6/8, 6/9?

703. On which color is a spinner arrow most likely to land if ¾ of it is shaded red and ¼ is shaded blue?

704. Would fractions be important in reading a recipe?

705. What is the fraction of the pizza I ate if I ate 4 slices of a pizza that was divided into 8 pieces?

706. If you eat 2 pieces of a pie that is cut into 3 slices, how much have you eaten: ¾ or 2/3?

707. What is the fraction if 8 squares are shaded in on a shape having 12 squares: ¾ or 2/3?

708. What is the fraction if there are 10 triangles and five of them are shaded in?

709. Is 2/4 the same as ½?

710. If you look at a drawing where 6 out of 7 shapes are shaded yellow, and the other is shaded red, what fraction of the drawing is shaded red?

MATH

711. If you serve tomato soup into 2 bowls and chicken soup into one bowl, what is the fraction to indicate how many bowls are filled with the tomato soup?

712. What types of fractions and ingredients do you think might be part of a recipe for cookies?

713. If a number is 5 or greater, is that number rounded up or down?

714. What number can you round 14 to?

715. What number can you round 87 to?

716. What number can you round 26 to?

717. What number can you round 32 to?

718. What is 27 rounded to the nearest ten?

719. How do you round 76 to the nearest ten?

720. How do you round 165 to the nearest ten?

721. How do you round 7,558 to the nearest thousand?

722. What number am I if I have a one in the ones place, am greater than 65, but less than 81?

723. If the price of an ice cream cone is $2.99, what would you round it to?

724. If the temperature is 88 degrees, what would you round it to?

725. Can you tell time on an analog (face) clock to the minute?

726. What time is it now?

727. How many seconds are there in one minute?

728. How many minutes are there in one hour?

729. How many hours are there in one day?

730. How many days are there in one week?

731. How many weeks are there in one month?

732. How many months are there in one year?

733. How days are there in one year?

734. What is the average number of days in one month?

735. What is the missing time word: day, _, month, and year?

736. What is the missing time: 1:00, 1:30, _, 2:30?

737. What time is it if the big hand is on the 12 and the little hand on the 9?

MATH

738. What time would it say on a digital clock if it is a quarter to 3?

739. What would it say on a digital clock if it is half past 2?

740. What time would it on a digital clock if it is a quarter after 7?

741. What time would it show on a face clock if the digital clock read 8:45?

742. Do we change the clock time by one hour in spring and fall to preserve daylight?

743. Do different areas of the world live in different time zones?

744. Do you know the name of our time zone?

745. Do most people eat supper in the a.m. or the p.m?

746. What time of day do you eat breakfast: the a.m. or the p.m?

747. If the snowstorm started at 10:00 and it snowed for 4 hours, what time was it when it stopped?

748. How many hours is Amy at work each day if she arrives at 9 in the morning and leaves at 3 in the afternoon?

749. What is the temperature on a thermometer if the red mercury is halfway between the 30 and the 40?

750. What is your height?

751. What is your weight?

752. How many ounces are in one pound?

753. How many pounds are in one ton?

754. How many pounds are in one and one half tons?

755. Can you name something that weighs over one ton?

756. What is the metric unit for weight/mass: a gram or a kilometer?

757. Which is a better estimate for the weight of a football: 16 ounces or 16 pounds?

758. What is the better estimate for the weight of a frying pan: 2 kilograms or 2 grams?

759. Which is more: 3000 grams or 4 kilograms?

760. Can you estimate the height of your dresser?

761. Can you estimate the length of your dresser?

762. What is the metric unit for length: a meter or a foot?

763. Can you put these in order from smallest to largest: kilometer, centimeter, millimeter

764. How many inches are there in one foot?

MATH

765. How many feet are there in one yard?

766. Can you estimate in inches the length of your shoe?

767. Which is the better estimate for the length of a submarine sandwich: 12 feet or 12 inches?

768. If Joey's car is 9 feet long, and Luke's car is 2 feet longer than Joey's car, how long is Luke's car?

769. Which is the better estimate for the length of a hockey skate: 25 meters or 25 centimeters?

770. Can you estimate the distance in feet between your bed and the door?

771. What is the metric unit for distance: a gram or a kilometer?

772. Which distance is greater: one kilometer or one mile?

773. Can you estimate in miles the distance between your house and your school? (Etc.)

774. Can you put the following in order from smallest to largest: foot, yard, and inch?

775. Which is longer: a yard stick or a meter stick?

776. Can you put the following in order from smallest to largest: quart; gallon; pint; cup

777. What is the metric unit for volume: a liter or a quart?

778. Which is the better estimate for the volume of a coffee pot: 2 milliliters or 2 liters?

779. Which is more: 2000 milliliters or 1 liter?

780. Which is the better estimate for the volume of a mug of hot chocolate: 12 fluid ounces or 12 pints?

781. Which is more: 4 cups or 1 pint?

782. How many cups are equal to 1 pint?

783. Which liquid measurement would you use when following a recipe: cups or pints?

784. Which tool would you use to time a 40 yard dash: a yard stick or a stopwatch?

785. What would you use a thermometer to measure?

786. What would you use a yardstick to measure?

787. What would you use a scale to measure?

788. What would you use a tablespoon to measure?

789. What would you use a cup to measure?

790. What is the date today?

791. Which month comes before November?

792. Which month comes after June?

MATH

793. How many days does July have: 28, 30, or 31?

794. How many days does December have: 28, 30, or 31?

795. How many days does February have unless it is a leap year: 28, 30, or 31?

796. How many days does February have in a leap year: 28, 29, or 30?

797. What is the date tomorrow if today is August 31st?

798. What was the date yesterday if today is May 1st?

799. What is the date tomorrow if today is December 31st?

800. What other number changes on January 1st?

801. What is the year called when there are 29 days in February?

802. What day of the week is today?

803. What day was the day before yesterday?

804. If the party is a day after tomorrow and today is Wednesday, on which day is the party?

805. If tomorrow is Monday, what day was yesterday?

806. If yesterday was Friday, what day is tomorrow?

807. Is a calendar used to measure the time of year it is?

808. What are the 3 months of winter?

809. What are the 3 months of spring?

810. What are the 3 months of summer?

811. What are the 3 months of autumn?

812. What season comes before winter?

813. What season comes after spring?

814. Can you say the specific date of a holiday we celebrate?

815. Do addresses have numbers in them?

816. What is our house number?

817. What is our phone number?

818. Do we use both metal and paper for money?

819. Do different countries use different coins and paper or currency?

820. Can you name the currency of another country?

189

MATH

821. Do you think the Canadian dollar and Australian dollar have the same value as the American dollar?

822. Do you know the name of the currency in England that is named for its weight?

823. Which coin is worth 25 cents?

824. Which coin is worth 10 cents?

825. Which coin is worth 5 cents?

826. Which coin is worth 1 cent?

827. How many cents is one quarter worth?

828. How many quarters are in one dollar?

829. Does one quarter equal one fourth or one half of a dollar?

830. How many cents is one dime equal to?

831. How many cents is one nickel equal to?

832. How many dimes and nickels would equal one quarter?

833. What coin combinations can equal 25 cents besides one quarter?

834. What coin combination is equal to 3 quarters: 6 dimes and 3 nickels or 2 dimes and 10 nickels?

835. What is the difference in the equation: 25 cents minus 10 cents?

836. How many pennies are there in one dollar?

837. How many pennies are in one quarter?

838. How many nickels would equal one dime?

839. How many nickels would equal one quarter?

840. What would 25 cents and 15 cents add up to?

841. Is there a 50 cent coin?

842. What is a 50 cent piece equal to: one quarter or to one half dollar?

843. How many quarters equal 50 cents?

844. How many 50 cent pieces would equal one paper dollar?

845. How much money would you have if you have two quarters?

846. How much money would you have if you have one quarter, one dime, one nickel, and one penny?

847. How much money would you have if you have one quarter, one dime, and 3 pennies?

848. What much money do Tim and Lisa have together if Tim has 3 nickels and Lisa has 3 quarters?

MATH

849. What is equal on one quarter: 2 dimes and one nickel, or 1 dime and 4 nickels?

850. How can you make 30 cents with the least number of coins?

851. How can you make 46 cents with the least number of coins?

852. Do you have enough money to purchase a candy bar if you have one quarter and one nickel and it costs 40 cents?

853. Do you have enough money to purchase a box of colored pencils that costs 89 cents if you have three quarters, one dime, and one nickel?

854. If you have a dollar bill, two quarters, and two nickels do you have enough to buy a jumbo muffin that costs $1.65?

855. If you have two quarters and 3 dimes, how much more do you need to equal one dollar?

856. Did you receive the correct amount of change if you received 35 cents back from your dollar bill for a cereal bar that costs 65 cents?

857. If you buy a bottle of water that costs 75 cents, and you paid with one dollar, what would you receive back in change?

858. If a daily pass to the pool costs $4 and you paid with a ten dollar bill, what would your change be?

859. If you purchase a shirt that costs $15 and a pair of shoes that cost $30, what would your total be?

860. Do we have currency in denominations of one dollar, five dollars, ten dollars, twenty dollars, fifty dollars, and one hundred dollar bills?

861. What important historical people are pictured on our American coins and dollars?

862. If you are keeping track of how many blue cars you see on the way to the park, would you make tally marks?

863. After every four *tally marks* you make, how should you write the 5th tally mark?

864. Is the 5th tally mark in a tally a slash mark straight across or on a diagonal?

865. Would a line running east and west be horizontal or vertical?

866. Would a line running north and south be horizontal or vertical?

867. What would be a good way to show the population of our city from the last 10 years: tally marks or a bar graph?

868. Do you think that the bars on the graph would be higher or lower as the years progress?

869. Would a bar graph be a good way to show an increase or decrease in the data you have collected?

870. In which sport would the score typically be the highest: soccer, baseball, football, or basketball?

MATH

871. In which sport would the score typically be the lowest: soccer, football, or basketball?

872. Would circles, squares, triangles, rectangles be considered geometric shapes or organic shapes?

873. Can you name something in the environment that is round?

874. What can you name in the environment that is rectangular in shape?

875. What can you name in the environment that might be triangular?

876. What can you name in the environment that might be oval in shape?

877. What can you name that is in the shape of a sphere?

878. What can you name that is in the shape of a cone?

879. What object is in the shape of a cylinder?

880. Do we add or multiply the length of the sides together if we want to find the perimeter of a shape?

881. What is the perimeter of a 4-sided shape where each of the sides is 5 centimeters long?

882. What is the perimeter of a triangle if the sides measure 3 feet, 5 feet, and 7 feet?

883. What is the perimeter of a tree house if it measures 6 feet wide and 10 feet long: 16 feet or 32 feet?

884. Do you find the area of a square multiplying the base times itself or the base times two?

885. What is the area of a square with a side measuring 4 inches: 8 or 16?

886. What is the area of a square with a side measuring 3 inches: 12 or 9?

887. There are 5 red M & M's and 1 yellow M &M. If you reached for one without looking, how likely is it that you would pick the yellow one: certain, probable, unlikely, or impossible?

888. How do we find the range of a group of numbers: add the highest number with the lowest, or subtract the lowest number from the highest number?

889. What is the range in the sequence of numbers 5, **1**, 3, **10** and, 8?

890. What is the term for the value that appears most often in a sequence of numbers: mode or median?

891. What is the mode of 5, 8, 5, 6, 5, 7, 5, and 9?

Math -- 3rd Grade

892. What do we call the number that has no value?

893. What do we call the highest number that suggests no end?

894. Can you count to 1000?

895. Can you skip-count to 1000 by hundreds?

MATH

896. Could Claire have been skip-counting by threes if she started at 32 and ended at 41?

897. How would you write the number ten??

898. How would you write the number fifty-six using digits?

899. How would you write the number four hundred fourteen using digits?

900. How would you write one hundred?

901. How would you write one thousand?

902. How would you write ten thousand?

903. How would you write one hundred thousand?

904. What number would come after 99?

905. What number would come after 999?

906. What number would come after 9,999?

907. What number would come after 99,999?

908. What is 2,999 + 1?

909. What is 54,099 + 1?

910. What is 234,999 +1?

911. What number would come before ten thousand?

912. What odd number comes after 55?

913. What is the even number that comes right after 178?

914. In the number 2,136, in which place is the 2: the hundreds or the thousands?

915. How many thousands, hundreds, and ones is the number 6,295 is equal to?

916. In which place is the number 7 in the number 7,528?

917. In which place is the number 5 in the number 7,528?

918. In which place is the number 2 in the number 7,528?

919. In which place is the number 8 in the number 7,528?

920. In the number 2,589, which digit is in the thousands place?

921. In the number 2,589, which digit is in the hundreds place?

922. In the number 2,589, which digit is in the tens place?

923. In the number 2,589, which digit is in the ones place?

MATH

924. Can you guess the two digit number that has a six in the tens place, and you say it when you count to 100 by tens?

925. How would you read the number *eight (comma) three two nine*?

926. How would you read the number four six (comma) eight one seven?

927. How would you read the number three *two eight (comma) five four two*?

928. How would you convert the place values of five thousand: it is equal to 50 tens or 500 tens?

929. How would you convert the place values of three thousand: it is equal to 30 hundreds or 300 hundreds?

930. What is 400 + 70 + 6 in its standard form?

931. What is 9, 325 in its expanded form: 9000+_?

932. How would you complete the pattern: 7+5=12, _+ 50=120, _+ 500=1,200, _+ 5,000=12,000?

933. Which number makes the equation true: 100 + 200 = 150 + _?

934. How can you balance the following equation: 250 +150 = 300 + _?

935. Can you add two numbers that each have three digits?

936. What is the sum of 222 and 111?

937. Is the difference in the equation 70 - 30 even or odd?

938. What number is missing in the sequence: 48, 38, 28, _?

939. On an input/output table, what is the rule if the input number reads 28 and the output number reads 38: add 10 or subtract 10?

940. How would you put the following numbers in order from least to greatest: 65, 35, and 55?

941. Is the number 736 greater than, less than, or equal to 636?

942. Is 18 + 4 greater than, less than, or equal to 16 + 5?

943. Is 78 + 3 greater than, less than, or equal to 75 + 6?

944. Is 45 + 5 greater than, less than, or equal to 25 + 26?

945. Can you add numbers that have 3 or more digits?

946. Can you subtract numbers that have 3 or more digits?

947. How can you balance the following equation: 300 -100 = 500 - _?

948. Which is the **equation**: 30+7=37 or 30 + 7?

949. When we round numbers, can we round to the nearest ten, hundred, thousand, or hundred thousand?

MATH

950. What is the rule when rounding numbers 5 or above: round up or round down?

951. What is the number 65 rounded to the nearest ten?

952. What is the number 32 rounded to the nearest ten?

953. What is 14 rounded to the nearest ten?

954. What is 97 rounded to the nearest ten?

955. What is 140 rounded to the nearest hundred?

956. What is 360 rounded to the nearest hundred?

957. What is 333 rounded to the nearest hundred?

958. What is 573 rounded to the nearest hundred?

959. What is 7,262 rounded to the nearest thousand?

960. What is 439,222 rounded to the nearest thousand?

961. What is 76,500 rounded to the nearest ten thousand?

962. What is 198,000 rounded to the nearest hundred thousand?

963. What is $8.25 rounded to the nearest dollar?

964. What is $49.99 rounded to the nearest dollar?

965. If you estimate the sum of 67 + 31, what would you round each number to and what would be the estimated sum?

966. If you estimate the difference of 49 – 22, what would you round each number to and what would be the estimated sum?

967. To help you subtract numbers mentally, is it helpful to round the number 49 to number 50?

968. How would you mentally subtract 49 - 18? (50-_ = _)

969. How would you mentally add 28 + 54? (30 + _ = _)

970. How would you estimate the product of 28 x 4?

971. How would you estimate the quotient of 32 ÷ 3?

972. Are the digits we are familiar with called Arabic numerals or Roman numerals?

973. What are the numerals called that date back to the ancient Romans?

974. What is Roman numeral I equal to?

975. What is Roman numeral V equal to?

MATH

976. What is Roman numeral X equal to?

977. What is Roman numeral L equal to?

978. What is Roman numeral C equal to?

979. What is Roman numeral D equal to: 500 or 1,000?

980. What is Roman numeral M equal to: 500 or 1,000?

981. Do you place a Roman numeral that has the same value or the lesser value to the right or the left of that numeral?

982. Do you place a Roman numeral that has the greater value to the right or left of another numeral?

983. If you have "V" and then "I" together do you add or subtract their values?

984. If you have "I" and then "V" together do you add or subtract their values?

985. Is "I" and then "V" the same as 5 - 1 =4 or is it 1 + 5 =6?

986. What is Roman numeral II?

987. What is Roman numeral XV?

988. What is Roman numeral XXX?

989. What is Roman numeral IV?

990. What is Roman numeral IX?

991. What is Roman numeral XIV?

992. What number is Super Bowl XXXVI?

993. Are Roman numerals often used to show the date that a movie was made?

994. What is the year MXMLXXX?

995. What number would MD be if M equals 1,000 and D equals 500?

996. How would you write 205 as a Roman numeral?

997. Can you say all the ordinal numbers first through tenth?

998. What is the date today using an ordinal number?

999. How would you say the king's name Louis "X", "I", "V" as an ordinal number?

1000. What ordinal is after 49th?

1001. Are there both positive and negative numbers in daily life?

1002. What kind of number is a surplus: a positive or a negative?

MATH

1003. What kind of number is a deficit: a positive or a negative?

1004. If the temperature is below zero, is that a positive or a negative number?

1005. If the number of people that are unemployed or not currently working is 8%, does that number represent a positive number or a negative number?

1006. If you owe me $5, is that a negative number or a positive number to you?

1007. If you have 300 pennies in your piggy bank, is that a positive number or a negative number?

1008. What is the fourth basic operation of arithmetic besides addition, subtraction, and multiplication?

1009. When we use the operation of multiplication, do we say two **times** or two **plus** three equals six?

1010. What letter is the symbol for multiplication?

1011. Is 3+3+3+3 the same as 4 **x** 3?

1012. Is 3x4 the same as 4x3?

1013. In the equation 2 x 3 = 6, are the numbers *two* and *three* the factors or the product?

1014. In the equation 5 x 5 = 25, which number is the product?

1015. Is the equation 9 x 7 (nine times seven) the same as 7 x 9?

1016. Can the equation 9 x 7 also be written vertically or up and down?

1017. What is the name of the table we can use to find the product of all combinations of factors?

1018. What is the product of 0 x 0? (1x0, 2x0, 3x0, 4x0, 5x0, 6x0, 7x0, 8x0, 9x0)

1019. What is the product of 1 x 1? (1x2, 1x3, 1x4, 1x5, 1x6, 1x7, 1x8, 1x9)

1020. What is the product of 2 x 1? (2x2, 2x3, 2x4, 2x5, 2x6, 2x7, 2x8, 2x9)

1021. What is the product of 3 x 1? (3x2, 3x3, 3x4, 3x5, 3x6, 3x7, 3x8, 3x9)

1022. What is the product of 4 x 1? (4x2, 4x3, 4x4, 4x5, 4x6, 4x7, 4x8, 4x9)

1023. What is the product of 5 x 1? (5x2, 5x3, 5x4, 5x5, 5x6, 5x7, 5x8, 5x9)

1024. What is the product of 6 x 1? (6x2, 6x3, 6x4, 6x5, 6x6, 6x7, 6x8, 6x9)

1025. What is the product of 7 x 1? (7x2, 7x3, 7x4, 7x5, 7x6, 7x7, 7x8, 7x9)

1026. What is the product of 8 x 1? (8x2, 8x3, 8x4, 8x5, 8x6, 8x7, 8x8, 8x9)

1027. What is the product of 9 x 1? (9x2, 9x3, 9x4, 9x5, 9x6, 9x7, 9x8, 9x9)

1028. What is the product of 10 x 1? (10x2, 10x3, 10x4, 10x5, 10x6, 10x7, 10x8, 10x9)

1029. If you are solving for "s" and s x 4 = 20, then s = ___?

MATH

1030. What is the product of 20 x 5?

1031. What is the product of 200 x 5?

1032. In computing 200 x 5, you would multiply 2 x 5 and then add how many zeros?

1033. If Adam bought 3 sets of dominos and each set had 200 pieces, how many dominos does Adam have in all?

1034. What is the product of 2,000 x 5?

1035. What is 333 x 2?

1036. What is the product of 2 x 3 x 5?

1037. If part of an equation is set off in parenthesis, would you compute that operation first or second?

1038. What is the name of the math property whereby multiplying a number by a group of numbers added together and set off in parenthesis is the same as doing each multiplication operation separately as in 3 x (2 + 4) is equal to 3x2 + 3x4, which is the same as 3 x 6: commutative or distributive?

1039. In the equation 10(3+2) = *a*, and the 3 + 2 is in parenthesis, what would *a* equal?

1040. Using the distributive property, what is two times (three plus four) equal to? 2(3+4)

1041. What is the name of the name of the algebra property whereby you can multiply and add and it does not matter how you group the numbers: the associative or the distributive?

1042. Using the associative property of re-grouping, what is 2(3x4) (*Two times three times four in parenthesis*) equal to: (2x3) times _?

1043. What is the name of the math property where changing the order of the numbers does not change the result: the commutative property or the distributive property?

1044. Using the commutative property, what is 2x3 equal to?

1045. What is the name of the math property of addition and multiplication whereby if you add any number to 0, the sum will be that number, and if you multiply any number by 1, the product will be that number: the identity property or the commutative property?

1046. In the identity property of addition, 22 plus **what** equals 22? (22 + _ = 22)

1047. In the identity property of multiplication, 6 times **what** equals 6? (6 x _ = 6)

1048. Is 1x8 = 8 an example of the identity, distributive, associative, or the commutative property of multiplication?

1049. What is the name of the math property of multiplication where it follows that 2(3x4) (*Two times, three times four in parenthesis*) equals (2x3)4 (*Two times three in parenthesis, times four*): identity, associative, or commutative?

MATH

1050. Is 2x4=4x2 an example of the associative or the commutative property of multiplication?

1051. Is 2(3+1) (*Two times, three plus one in parenthesis*) = 2 x 3 + 2 x 1 an example of the identity, distributive, associative, or the commutative property of multiplication?

1052. What is the name of the number that is the product of an integer times itself: a square number or a quotient?

1053. Can multiplication problems be represented as square numbers?

1054. In the equation 3 x 3 = 9, which number is the *square* number?

1055. Are the numbers 16 and 25 also square numbers?

1056. What is the product or perfect square of 5x5?

1057. What is the product or perfect square of 4x4?

1058. What is the product or perfect square of 7x7?

1059. What is the product or perfect square of 10x10?

1060. If 3 multiplied by itself is 9, is the number 3 the *square root* of 9?

1061. What is the square root of 25?

1062. What is the square root of 16?

1063. What is the square root of 49?

1064. What is the square root of 100?

1065. What number is 6 the square root of?

1066. Can you multiply two and three numbers together?

1067. What is another way of writing 786? (7 x__=700), + (8 x___= ___), + ___

1068. If Lucas scored 8 points in the basketball game, and Jonathon scored 3 times as many points as Lucas, how many points did Jonathon score?

1069. If the *inverse* operation of addition is subtraction, what is the inverse operation of multiplication?

1070. How many groups of 6 are there in 18?

1071. If there are 3 groups of 6 in 18, then what can we say eighteen divided by six is equal to?

1072. What does a division symbol look like?

1073. In the equation 6 divided by 3 = 2, what is the quotient: the number 2 or the number 3?

1074. In the equation 6 divided by 3 = 2, is the number 6 the dividend or the divisor?

1075. In the equation 6 divided by 3 = 2, is the number 3 the dividend or the divisor?

MATH

1076. What is 0 divided by any number?

1077. What is the quotient of any number divided by 1, like 7 ÷1?

1078. What is the quotient of 2÷2? (4÷2, 6÷2, 8÷2, 10÷2, 12÷2, 14÷2, 16÷2, 18÷2, 20÷2)?

1079. What is the quotient of 3÷3? (6÷3, 9÷3, 12÷3, 15÷3, 18÷3, 21÷3, 24÷3, 27÷3, 30÷3)?

1080. What is the quotient of 4÷4? (8÷4, 12÷4, 16÷4, 20÷4, 24÷4, 28÷4, 32÷4, 36÷4, 40÷4)?

1081. What is the quotient of 5÷5? (10÷5, 15÷5, 20÷5, 25÷5, 30÷5, 35÷5, 40÷5, 45÷5, 50÷5)?

1082. What is the quotient of 6÷6? (12÷6, 18÷6, 24÷6, 30÷6, 36÷6, 42÷6, 48÷6, 54÷6, 60÷6)?

1083. What is the quotient of 7÷7? (14÷7, 21÷7, 28÷7, 35÷7, 42÷7, 49÷7, 56÷7, 63÷7, 70÷7)?

1084. What is the quotient of 8÷8? (16÷8, 24÷8, 32÷8, 40÷8, 48÷8, 56÷8, 64÷8, 72÷8, 80÷8)?

1085. What is the quotient of 9÷9? (18÷9, 27÷9, 36÷9, 45÷9, 54÷9, 63÷9, 72÷9, 81÷9, 90÷9)?

1086. What is the quotient of 10÷10? (20÷10, 30÷10, 40÷10, 50÷10, 60÷10, 70÷10, 80÷10, 90÷10, 100÷10)?

1087. What is the quotient of 11÷11? (22÷11, 33÷11, 44÷11, 55÷11, 66÷11, 77÷11, 88÷11, 99÷11, 110÷11)?

1088. What is the quotient of 12÷12? (24÷12, 36÷12, 48÷12, 60÷12, 72÷12, 84÷12, 96÷12, 108÷12, 120÷12)?

1089. If Kristin has 3 dozen or 36 daisies, and she wants to divide them equally into 6 vases, how many daisies would she put in each vase?

1090. Is the following an example of an inverse or a reverse operation: 1 + 4 = 5, so 5 − 4 = 1?

1091. What is the inverse of 42 ÷7 = 6? (6 x 7 = __)

1092. Which of the following equations is equal to 3 x 4: 3+3+3+3, or 4+4+4+4?

1093. What is the inverse of 20-5=15? (15+ __ = __)

1094. What is the related multiplication fact for 12÷6=2?

1095. What is 100 ÷2?

1096. What is 700 ÷ 7?

1097. What is 210 ÷3?

1098. What is 320 ÷4?

1099. What is 280 ÷7?

MATH

1100. What is 810 ÷ 9?

1101. Is 2,420 divisible by 2?

1102. Is 2,425 divisible by 2?

1103. Is 250 divisible by 5?

1104. Is 256 divisible by 5?

1105. Is 240 divisible by 10?

1106. Is 223 divisible by 10?

1107. What is the math term for the amount left over after a division computation: the dividend or the remainder?

1108. In the equation 22÷7, 7 does not go into 22 evenly so would we have a *remainder*?

1109. In the equation 9÷4, what would the remainder be? (4x2=8 R __)

1110. In the equation 30÷4, what would the quotient and the remainder be?

1111. What is the name for the table that shows output values for a number of different inputs?

1112. What is the rule on an input/output table if one input number is 8 and its output number is 4, and another input number is 10 and its output number is 5?

1113. Is the inverse of 7 x 6=42 the division operation 42 ÷6=7?

1114. To finish the equation, __÷5 = 4, would you multiply or add 5 and 4?

1115. How would you finish the equation: __÷4 = 3?

1116. When you have a math equation with a letter, is that letter called the **variable** or the **integer**?

1117. What is the *variable* in the equation b÷2 = 6?

1118. What is the answer to this equation: b÷2=6?

1119. Can variables be used for all operations: addition, subtraction, multiplication, and division?

1120. What is the division equation for ½ of 28?

1121. Can you finish the following division pattern: 5÷5=__, 50÷5=__, 500÷5=__, 5000÷5=__?

1122. Solve the following word problem: Jack and his mom want to buy 24 cupcakes for Jack's birthday treat for his class. If there are 8 cupcakes in each package, how many packages of cupcakes do Jack and his mom need to buy?

1123. How would you write the division equation for 24 cupcakes, 3 packages, and 8 cupcakes in each package?

MATH

1124. What are numbers that are parts of a whole called: fractions or decimals?

1125. What are two other common fractions besides ½?

1126. What is the top number of a fraction called?

1127. What is the bottom number of a fraction called?

1128. Does the bottom number of a fraction or denominator tell how many parts the whole is divided into?

1129. If the numerator and the denominator are the same, what whole number does that fraction equal?

1130. Are 0, 1, 2, 3, 4 whole numbers or fractions?

1131. Is 13/4 a whole number or a mixed number?

1132. What two numbers is 1 ½ between?

1133. What is the denominator in the fraction 2/3?

1134. What is the numerator in the fraction ¾?

1135. Are measurements often indicated with fractions like 5 ¼ inches?

1136. What is the numerator indicating that the two fractions are equal: 2/3 = __/9?

1137. Can fractions be reduced to their lowest terms?

1138. What is the lowest term of 2/4?

1139. What can 5/10 be reduced to?

1140. What can 6/8 be reduced to?

1141. What is the equivalent fraction of 3/6: ½ or 2/3?

1142. Can you add and subtract fractions?

1143. What is the sum of ½ + ½?

1144. What is the sum of ¼ + 2/4?

1145. What is the difference of 7/8 − 4/8?

1146. Is 5/8 greater than, less than, or equal to 3/8?

1147. If a square is divided into 8 equal parts and 5 of those parts are shaded in, what is the fraction of the area that is shaded?

1148. If a pizza is sliced into 8 slices and there are 2 slices left after everyone takes a piece, how much of the pizza was eaten?

1149. If you wanted to find ¼ of 20 would you divide or multiply 20 by 4?

MATH

1150. What is division equation for 1/3 of 18? (18÷__=__)

1151. Can a fraction be represented with a decimal point?

1152. What is the number 2 and 4/10 equal to, using a decimal? (2.__)

1153. What is .25 as a fraction?

1154. What is .50 as a fraction?

1155. What is .75 as a fraction?

1156. Can we show the hundredths' place by writing 1/100 = .01?

1157. What is .08 as a fraction: 8/10 or 8/100?

1158. What would 8/100 be reduced to in lowest terms: 4/50 or 2/25?

1159. What is .6 as a fraction: 2/3 or ¾?

1160. What is 9 and 81/100 as a decimal number?

1161. What is four and three tenths as a decimal number: 4.03 or 4.30?

1162. What numbers are missing in the following pattern: 3.2, 3.3, 3.__, 3.__, 3.__?

1163. What is the sum of 2.5 and 3.1? (2+3 = __ / 5+1=__)

1164. What is the difference in 5.5 and 4.3? (5-4=__ / 5-3=__)

1165. What is the sum of 1.2 + 1.2 + 1.2?

1166. What is ¼ as a decimal?

1167. What is ¾ as a decimal?

1168. What is ½ as a decimal?

1169. Can you create and interpret bar graphs?

1170. Can you find coordinates on a graph?

1171. Can you graph points on a graph?

1172. Can you create and interpret line graphs?

1173. Can you create and interpret pictographs?

1174. Can you create and interpret a Venn diagram?

1175. In what location are the common characteristics located on a Venn diagram?

1176. How much money do you have in your (piggy) bank?

1177. What denominations of dollars are the most common?

MATH

1178. What is another name for money?

1179. Do different countries have different currencies?

1180. Does all money in all countries have the same value?

1181. What are all the coins we use and how much is each worth?

1182. How much would you have if you had one ten, two fives and three one dollar bills?

1183. How much would you have if you had two quarters, three dimes, one nickel, and four pennies?

1184. If you buy a box of cookies that costs $3.50, and you pay with a ten dollar bill, how much change would you get back?

1185. If a book you want to buy at the book fair costs $4.99 and you have four one dollar bills, three quarters, and two dimes, would you have enough money to buy the book?

1186. At the restaurant James ordered a hamburger for $4.00, Cristina ordered a chicken sandwich for $5.00, and Matthew ordered a roast beef sandwich for $7.00. What was the amount of the total bill before tax and tip?

1187. After a nice meal at a restaurant, Avery and her two friends receive a bill totaling $21.75. If they want to divide the total evenly among the three, how much would each person pay?

1188. If Katie wanted to buy 4 balloons and each balloon costs $2.00 each, how much would she pay in all?

1189. What instrument measures the temperature?

1190. What is the metric term for measuring temperature?

1191. What is the U.S. Customary term for measuring temperature?

1192. What is the temperature if the mercury is halfway between 40 and 50?

1193. What is 0 degrees Celsius equal to in degrees Fahrenheit: 32 or 98?

1194. What liquid can melt at thirty-two degrees Fahrenheit?

1195. If it is 85 degrees Fahrenheit, would the weather be hot or cold?

1196. If it is ten degrees below zero, would be weather be hot or cold?

1197. In the U.S. Customary System, what unit do we use to measure driving distance?

1198. Are there 5,280 feet in one mile or two miles?

1199. In the U.S. Customary System, what unit do we use to measure the length of a football field?

1200. In the U.S. Customary System, what unit do we use to measure the length of a 12 inch sub sandwich?

1201. How many inches is equal to one foot?

MATH

1202. How many feet are in one yard?

1203. How many inches are equal to one yard?

1204. In the U.S. Customary System what unit do we use to measure the length of a piece of wood?

1205. What kind of tools can you use make linear measurements?

1206. Can you estimate the length of an object without using any tools?

1207. In the U.S. Customary System, what unit do we use to weigh objects?

1208. What is the abbreviation of pound?

1209. What is the abbreviation of ounce?

1210. How many ounces are in one pound: 16 or 24?

1211. Does one pint equal 16 ounces?

1212. In the U.S. Customary System, what unit do we use for capacity, smallest to largest: pint, quart, cup, and gallon?

1213. How many cups are there in one pint?

1214. How many pints are there in one quart: ½ or 2?

1215. How many quarts are there in one gallon?

1216. What is the better estimate for the capacity of a can of paint: one pint or one gallon?

1217. If 2 pints equal 1 quart, and 4 quarts equal one gallon, how many pints equal one gallon?

1218. Which is more: 10 pints or one gallon?

1219. What are the Metric System units of length in order from smallest to largest: meter, centimeter, kilometer, and millimeter?

1220. What is the Metric system unit of weight: grams or pounds?

1221. Which is higher: one gram or one kilogram?

1222. What is one kilogram equal to: 1,000 grams or 2,000 grams?

1223. If the side of the balance with a ball is lower than the side of the balance with an apple, what can you conclude?

1224. What is the Metric System unit for liquid volume: the quart or the liter?

1225. What time is it?

1226. How many seconds are there in one minute?

1227. How many minutes are there in one hour?

MATH

1228. How many minutes are there in 3 hours?

1229. How many hours are there in one day?

1230. What is the abbreviation for the Latin phrase "**a**nte **m**eridiem" which means before noon?

1231. What is the abbreviation for the Latin phrase "**p**ost **m**eridiem" which means after noon?

1232. What time is it if the little hand is on the eight and the big hand is on the nine?

1233. What time is it if the little hand is on the three and the big hand is on the eight?

1234. What time is it if the little hand is on the four and the big hand is on the four?

1235. What time is it if the little hand is on the seven and the big hand is on the eleven?

1236. What is another way of saying it is twelve o'clock in the middle of the day?

1237. What is another way of saying it is twelve o'clock in the middle of the night?

1238. What is another way of saying it is 3:40?

1239. What are the clock hands on if it is 2:35?

1240. If it is 4:30, what time will it be in 45 minutes?

1241. If the class went outside for a short recess at 10:20 a.m. and returned to the classroom at 10:45 a.m., how long was the recess?

1242. Can you read a time schedule?

1243. Can you read a timeline?

1244. What kinds of events are often sequenced on a timeline?

1245. What is the date today?

1246. If today is Thursday March 2nd, what is the day on Saturday?

1247. If today is Thursday August 2nd, what was the date on Tuesday?

1248. How can you say the date for today using only numbers? (__/__/__)

1249. How can you say the date of your birthday using only numbers?

1250. What day of the week is it today?

1251. What day of the week does our calendar begin with?

1252. How many days are there in one week?

1253. How many weeks are there in one month?

1254. How many days are there in one calendar year?

MATH

1255. What is the shortest month of the year?

1256. How often are there 29 days in the month of February?

1257. How many years are in one decade?

1258. How many years are in one century?

1259. How many years is one millennia equal to?

1260. What is the study of lines, point, shapes and angles called?

1261. What saying related to geometry describes what an acorn says when it grows up?

1262. Is a square a geometric shape?

1263. What geometric shapes can you name?

1264. What are flat, closed figures called having three or more straight lines: polygons or hexagons?

1265. Is a circle a polygon?

1266. Is a diamond shape a polygon?

1267. How are polygons formed: by line segments or by angle segments?

1268. What is a line called that runs left to right or east to west: horizontal or vertical?

1269. What is a line called that runs up and down or north and south: horizontal or vertical?

1270. What are two line segments called that cross through each other like the letter X: parallel or perpendicular?

1271. What are two line segments called that stay the same distance from each other and never cross: parallel or perpendicular?

1272. How many equal sides does a square have?

1273. What can you name that is square?

1274. How many sides does a rectangle have?

1275. What can you name that is rectangle?

1276. Are polygons shapes that have many angles?

1277. How many sides does a triangle have?

1278. What can you name that is in the shape of a triangle?

1279. If a triangle has three equal angles measuring 45 degrees each, is it an equilateral or isosceles triangle?

1280. What is the name of a triangle that has two equal sides, the angles measure less than 90 degrees, and the angles opposite the equal sides are also equal: equilateral or isosceles?

MATH

1281. How many sides (or edges) does a quadrilateral have?

1282. How many sides does a pentagon have?

1283. How many straight sides does a hexagon have?

1284. How many sides does a heptagon have?

1285. How many sides does an octagon have?

1286. What is a stop sign the shape of: a hexagon or an octagon?

1287. What is a straight line called with no points at either end: a line or a line segment?

1288. What is a straight line called with two points at either end: a ray or a line segment?

1289. What is a straight line called with a point at one end and an arrow at the other: a line or a ray?

1290. What is the point called in which two line segments meet: a corner or a vertex?

1291. How are vertices named: with letters or numbers?

1292. On a four-sided polygon, could you name the figure either ABCD, DCBA, or both?

1293. Are the vertices like the points of the shape?

1294. What property does a closed shape have besides vertices: angles or rays?

1295. When two sides of a polygon meet, what does it form?

1296. What is an angle called that forms a square corner: a right angle or a left angle?

1297. How many right angles do rectangles and squares have?

1298. What are shapes called the have exactly the same size and shape: symmetrical or congruent?

1299. When a shape or figure can be folded in half and both halves match up, is the figure symmetrical or congruent?

1300. What is the name of the fold line when a shape is folded in half: the dividing line or the line of symmetry?

1301. How many lines of symmetry does a square have?

1302. How many lines of symmetry does a circle have?

1303. Can shapes be similar but not congruent?

1304. If a shape like the letter "P" is flipped over and reversed onto another grid, how has this shape been transformed: reflected, rotated, or translated?

1305. If a shape like the letter "P" stays the same but is shifted slightly to the right on another grid, how has this shape been transformed: reflected, rotated, or translated?

MATH

1306. If a shape like the letter "P" turns over on its side on another grid, how has this shape been transformed: reflected, rotated, or translated?

1307. What is the distance around a shaped called: diameter or perimeter?

1308. In order to find the perimeter around a shape, do we *multiply* or *add* the lengths of all the sides together?

1309. If a rectangle has one line segment 4 inches long, and one line segment 3 inches long, what is the distance around or the perimeter of this rectangle?

1310. If a triangle has one line segment that is 3 centimeters long, one line segment that is 4 centimeters long, and a third line segment that is 2 centimeters long, what is its perimeter?

1311. What is the perimeter of a square that shows one side measuring 5 centimeters long?

1312. What is the perimeter of a rectangle that shows the long side measuring 6 centimeters long and the shorter side measuring 3 centimeters long?

1313. What is the value of the third side of a triangle if its total perimeter is 18 inches and one side measures 9 inches and the other side measures 5 inches?

1314. What is the number of square units called that cover a surface: its perimeter or its area?

1315. If a rectangle has an area of 8 square inches, would you write that as 8 inches square?

1316. To find the area of a shape do we multiply or divide the length of its sides?

1317. What is the area of a rectangle with one side measuring 6 inches long and the other side measuring 3 inches long?

1318. What is the area of a square with each side measuring 5 millimeters long?

1319. What are three-dimensional shapes called: shapes or solids?

1320. What are cylinders, pyramids, spheres, and prisms considered: shapes or solids?

1321. What is the bottom part of a pyramid called: its base or its surface?

1322. Which three-dimensional shape has both curved surfaces and flat surfaces: a pyramid or a sphere?

1323. Is the flat surface of a solid called a front or a face?

1324. Is the line segment where two faces meet on a prism: an edge or a vertex?

1325. Do the edges come together at the face or the vertex?

1326. Is the point of a cone called a vertex or a face?

1327. To find the volume of a three-dimension object like a cube, do we multiply or add the base, the side, and the height?

MATH

1328. What is the volume of a cube that has 5 square units on its face, 2 square units on its side, and 4 square units for its height? ___cubic units.

1329. What is your favorite area of math?

1330. How do we use math concepts in our everyday lives?

Math – 4th Grade

1331. What place value comes after the ones?

1332. How many zeros are in the number 10?

1333. What place value comes after the tens?

1334. How many zeros are in the number 100?

1335. What place value comes after one hundred?

1336. How many zeros are in the number 1,000?

1337. What place value comes after one thousand?

1338. How many zeros are in the number 10,000?

1339. What place value comes after ten thousand?

1340. How many zeros are in the number 100,000?

1341. What place value comes after one hundred thousand?

1342. How many zeros are there in 1,000,000?

1343. What place value comes after one million?

1344. What place value comes after ten million?

1345. What place value comes after one hundred million?

1346. What is the next highest number place value after one thousand billion: one trillion or one quadrillion?

1347. What can you name that can be measured in the billions?

1348. If we write numbers larger than ten thousand, what do we have to write to show the correct place value?

1349. Moving right to left, how many digits do you count before inserting a comma?

1350. How would you read the number: one comma, two three four comma, five six seven?

1351. Do you *have to* use a comma for a number between one thousand and nine thousand nine hundred and ninety-nine?

1352. Is "three comma one two three" the same as "three one two three" with no comma?

MATH

1353. How many zeros are there in 1000?

1354. How many zeros are there in 100,000

1355. How many zeros are there in one million?

1356. How many zeros are there in 10,000?

1357. In the decimal system, what number are the place values based on?

1358. What do we call the time span of ten years?

1359. What do we call the time span of 100 years?

1360. How is the number "one hundred thousand five hundred" written in standard form?

1361. How is 8, 243 written in expanded form?

1362. Using digits how would you write the number five thousand, forty?

1363. Are numbers to the right of 0 on a number line positive or negative numbers?

1364. Are numbers to the left of 0 on a number line positive or negative numbers?

1365. Is 75-15 an odd or even number?

1366. Is the difference of 50-9 an odd or even number?

1367. Are negative numbers similar to having debt, or being in the "red?"

1368. Are positive number similar to showing a profit, or being in the "black?"

1369. Are the numerals zero through nine considered Arabic or Roman?

1370. Can you write the letters of the Roman numerals one through five?

1371. Can you write the letters of the Roman numerals six through ten?

1372. What Arabic number is the letter L equal to: 50 or 100?

1373. What Arabic number is the letter C equal to: 100 or 1,000?

1374. What Arabic number is the letter D equal to: 500 or 1,000?

1375. What Arabic number is the letter M equal to: 10,000 or 1,000?

1376. If smaller Roman numerals are on the left of a larger number, do we add or subtract that value?

1377. What is XL as an Arabic number?

1378. If smaller Roman numerals are on the right of a larger number, do we add or subtract that value?

1379. What is LX as an Arabic number?

1380. In Roman numerals if M=1000 and C=100 and L=50, what is MCL equal to?

MATH

1381. What is Roman numeral XVIII equal to?

1382. How would you write the year 2015 as a Roman numeral?

1383. Do some clocks have Roman numerals?

1384. What is the rule for rounding a number if it is four or less: round up or down to the nearest ten?

1385. What is the rule for rounding a number if it is five or more: round up or down to the nearest ten?

1386. What is 2,500 rounded to the nearest thousand?

1387. What is 2,200 rounded to the nearest thousand?

1388. What is 2,890 rounded to the nearest hundred?

1389. What is 2,255 rounded to the nearest ten?

1390. What is the name of a number that can only be divided by itself and by the number one: a prime number or a composite number?

1391. What is the name of a number that can be divided by at least one other number: a prime number or a composite number?

1392. If a number has only two factors, is it called a prime number or a composite number?

1393. Are zero and one prime numbers?

1394. What kind of numbers are 2, 3, 5, 7, 11, 13, and 17: prime numbers or composite numbers?

1395. What kind of numbers are 1, 2, 3, 6, 9, and 12: prime numbers or composite numbers?

1396. Is 28 a prime or composite number?

1397. Is 59 a prime or composite number?

1398. Can you add numbers up to one million?

1399. What does 50,000 and 90,000 equal?

1400. What does nine hundred thousand and one hundred thousand equal?

1401. What is the sum of six thousand, plus three hundred, plus fifty- two?

1402. What addition property is 1 + (2 + 3) in parenthesis = (1 + 2) in parenthesis + 3 an example of: the distributive or the associative?

1403. What addition property is 1 + 2= 2 + 1 an example of: the identity or the commutative?

1404. What addition property is 1 + 0 =1 an example of: the identity, distributive, or the associative?

1405. What is the approximate sum if you round to the nearest thousand and then add the following numbers together: 4,100 + 3,987?

MATH

1406. Can you subtract numbers up to one million?

1407. Do you not how to borrow from the higher place value when subtracting numbers?

1408. What is 185,000 – 84,000?

1409. What is 180,000 – 15,000?

1410. What is 1,000,000 – 650,000?

1411. Can you estimate the difference of 780 - 314?

1412. Do you know your multiplication facts up to the number up to 10 x 10?

1413. In the equation 3 x 8 = 24, which numbers are the factors?

1414. In the equation 2 x 8 = 24, which number is the product?

1415. What are some multiples of the number 2?

1416. What are some multiples of the number 6?

1417. What is the number 28 a multiple of?

1418. What is the number 81 a multiple of?

1419. What *two* numbers is 18 a multiple of?

1420. Is the number 96 a multiple of 12 or 14?

1421. What is it called when you take a number and multiply it by itself: a square or a multiplier?

1422. Is 4 x 4 = 16 the same is saying 4 squared equals 16?

1423. What is 2 x 2?

1424. What is 5 x 5?

1425. What is 6 x 6?

1426. What is 7 x 7?

1427. What is 8 x 8?

1428. What is 9 x 9?

1429. What is 10 x 10?

1430. What is the square root of 4?

1431. What is the square root of 36, or what number when multiplied by itself equals 36?

1432. What is the square root of 25?

1433. What is the square root of 81?

MATH

1434. What is the square root of 49?

1435. What is the square root of 121?

1436. What is the square root of 64?

1437. What is the square root of 144?

1438. What is the product of 3 x 4 x 2?

1439. When you are multiplying numbers by ten, what number do you add to the number that you are multiplying by: 0 or 1?

1440. What is the product of 44 x 10?

1441. What is the product of 220 x 10?

1442. Can you multiply by tens, hundreds, and thousands?

1443. What is a little trick you can use when you multiple numbers ending in zeros like 200 x 400?

1444. How many zeros would you add to find the product of 200 x 400?

1445. What is the product of 200 x 400: 8,000 or 80,000?

1446. What property is 1 x 5 = 5 an example of: the associative, distributive, identity, or zero property of multiplication?

1447. What property is 3 x (4-3) in parenthesis = 3 x 4 – 3 x 3 an example of: the associative, distributive, identity, or zero property of multiplication?

1448. What property is (1 x 3) in parenthesis x 4 = 1 x (3 x 4) in parenthesis an example of: the associative, distributive, identity, or zero property of multiplication?

1449. What property is 28 x 0 an example of: the associative, distributive, identity, or zero property of multiplication?

1450. What property is 22 x 1 and example of: the associative, distributive, identity or zero property of multiplication?

1451. How would you estimate the product of 4 x 3,120 rounding to the nearest thousand?

1452. What is the product of 7000 x 10 using the trick with adding the zeros?

1453. Is 2 x 8 greater than, less than, or equal to 15?

1454. Is 2 x 9 greater than, less than, or equal to 18?

1455. Is 5 x 8 greater than, less than, or equal to 45?

1456. What is the inverse operation of multiplication: division or addition?

1457. How would you invert the equation 10 x 2 = 20?

MATH

1458. How would you invert the equation 24 ÷ 8 = 3?

1459. What number is the *dividend* in the equation: 20 ÷ 5 = 4?

1460. What number is the *divisor* in the equation: 20 ÷ 5 = 4?

1461. What number is the *quotient* in the equation: 20 ÷ 5 = 4?

1462. What is the quotient of the problem: 72 ÷ 8?

1463. In the equation 12 ÷ 3 = 4, what does number 12 represent: the divisor or the dividend?

1464. In the equation 12 ÷ 3 = 4, what does number 4 represent: the quotient or the divisor?

1465. In the equation 12 ÷ 3 = 4, what does the number 3 represent: the divisor or the dividend?

1466. In the equation 20 ÷ 1 = 20, what number is both the quotient and the dividend?

1467. Do you remember your division facts up to 12?

1468. What is any number divided by 1 equal to?

1469. What is the product of an equation where a number is divided by itself?

1470. How would you write 12 ÷ 3 as a fraction?

1471. If there are 16 people in line for the rollercoaster and each car holds four people, how many cars will they fill up?

1472. What is a number called that divides another number evenly and does not have a remainder: a factor or a prime number?

1473. If 4 ÷ 4 = 1, 4 ÷ 2 = 2, and 4 ÷ 1 = 1, what are the *factors* of 4?

1474. What are the factors of 24?

1475. What common factors do the numbers 20 and 24 have?

1476. If Brandon has 7 cookies and he wants to divide them equally among 3 lunch boxes, how many would there be left over for him to eat? (7 ÷ 3 = __ R __)

1477. What is 26 ÷ 6?

1478. What is 246 ÷ 2?

1479. What is 246 ÷ 3? (24 ÷ 3 = __, 6 ÷ 3 = __)

1480. What is 963 ÷ 3? (9 ÷ 3 = __, 6 ÷ 3 = __, 3 ÷ 3 = __)

1481. What is a related multiplication fact for 24 ÷ 8 = 3?

1482. What is 180 ÷ 3?

1483. What is 6000 ÷ 100?

MATH

1484. What is 83 ÷ 10? __Remainder ___

1485. Is 21 ÷ 3 greater than, less than, or equal to 8?

1486. Is 24 ÷ 8 greater than, less than, or equal to 2?

1487. Is 32 ÷ 4 greater than, less than, or equal to 6?

1488. Can you divide bigger numbers on paper using long division?

1489. What is the type of math called in which letters and symbols are used to represent an unknown number?

1490. What is the value of **a** + **5** if **a** = 15?

1491. Using the order of operations and doing what is in parenthesis first, how would you simplify the following equation: 8÷(4 ÷ 2) in parenthesis, + 3?

1492. How would you solve for **a** if **a** x 5 = 30: **a** = __?

1493. Are you able to read a graph and coordinates?

1494. Are you able to read and interpret data on tables, lines, and graphs?

1495. What is the missing number in the pattern: 1, 3, 6, 12, __?

1496. What is the missing number in the pattern: 1, 2, __, 8, 16?

1497. What is the next number in the sequence: 1, 3, 6, 10, __?

1498. What is the name of the currency that we use in the United States?

1499. Can you name some currencies that are used in other countries?

1500. Can you describe the symbol we use for the dollar?

1501. Can you describe the symbol we use for cents?

1502. Which has a higher value: four quarters or $1.25?

1503. Which has the highest value: two twenty dollar bills; a ten, and a five; or a fifty dollar bill?

1504. What would $489 be rounded to the nearest ten?

1505. What would $489 be rounded to the nearest 100?

1506. What would $29.99 be rounded to the nearest ten?

1507. When we make purchases, do we have of allow extra for tax in our state?

1508. What is the total of 25 cents plus 50 cents plus 10 cents?

1509. If Jake raised $22, Megan raised $12, and Cole raised $11 selling raffle tickets, how much money did they raise all together?

MATH

1510. If you and two friends just bought a pizza for $21.00 and you divided the cost evenly, how much would each of you pay?

1511. How much change did Erin receive if she bought a bag of apples for $4.49 and she paid with a ten dollar bill? (Round 49 to __, subtract from 10.)

1512. How much would Brianna pay if she bought 4 notebooks that cost 2 dollars each?

1513. How much would Eli pay if he bought 2 packs of baseball cards that cost $2.40 each?

1514. What is the *unit price* of undershirts if a 3-pack costs $12.00?

1515. Which President is on the front of a one-dollar bill: George Washington or Abraham Lincoln?

1516. Which President is on the front of a five-dollar bill: George Washington or Abraham Lincoln?

1517. Which President is on the front of a ten-dollar bill: Alexander Hamilton or Abraham Lincoln?

1518. Which President is on the front of a twenty-dollar bill: Alexander Hamilton or Andrew Jackson?

1519. Which President is on the front of a fifty-dollar bill: Ulysses S. Grant or Alexander Hamilton?

1520. Which President is on the front of a penny: George Washington or Abraham Lincoln?

1521. Which President is on the front of a nickel: Abraham Lincoln or Thomas Jefferson?

1522. Which President is on the front of a dime: Franklin D. Roosevelt or Harry Truman?

1523. Who is the president on the front of a quarter: George Washington or Abraham Lincoln?

1524. What are the units of time, smallest to largest, starting with seconds and going up to one year?

1525. How many days are equal to one year?

1526. How do we accommodate the extra ¼ day that we have each year?

1527. If there are 365 days in one year, how many days are in ½ year?

1528. How many hours are there in one day?

1529. How many hours are there in ½ a day?

1530. How many hours are there in ¼ of a day?

1531. How many hours are there in ¾ of a day?

1532. How many seconds are there in one minute?

1533. How many minutes are there in one hour?

1534. How many hours would 90 minutes be equal to?

1535. How many minutes in ½ hour?

MATH

1536. How many minutes in ¼ hour?

1537. How many minutes would 5 quarter hours be equal to?

1538. How many minutes would there be in 3 hours and 12 minutes? (3 x 60 + 12)

1539. How many minutes and seconds would there be in 124 seconds? (124 ÷ 60)

1540. How many minutes are there in 2 ¼ hours? (2 x 60 + 15)

1541. If you went two camp for 3 weeks, how many days would you be there?

1542. What do "Pacific, Mountain, Central, and Eastern refer to with regard to time?

1543. What is the name of the time zone that you live in?

1544. Are television shows on at different times, depending on the time zone they are broadcast in?

1545. If it is now 8:25, what time will it be in one hour?

1546. What is another way of saying 9:40?

1547. If Callie started her test at 1:45 and finished 40 minutes later, what time did she finish?

1548. If the bus trip to Chicago is 8 ½ hours long and it leaves at 10:00 a.m., what time will arrive at its destination?

1549. Do you know how to read a transportation schedule in an airport or a train station?

1550. What measurement system is used in the United States: the metric system or U.S. customary units?

1551. What are the U.S. customary units of measurements smallest to largest, starting with inches?

1552. How many inches are in one foot?

1553. What fractions of an inch are also indicated on a ruler or measuring instrument?

1554. What can we do to approximate the measurement of something?

1555. How many feet are in one yard?

1556. How many feet are in 1 1/3 yards?

1557. How many inches are in one yard?

1558. How many inches are in a ½ yard?

1559. What customary unit is 5,280 feet long?

1560. If 5,280 feet equals one mile, how many feet are there in ½ mile?

1561. What customary unit has 1760 yards: a mile or a kilometer?

1562. What is the sum of 2 feet 6 inches plus 3 feet 6 inches?

MATH

1563. What are the U.S. customary units of weight smallest to largest, starting with ounces?

1564. How many ounces are there in 1 pound: 16 or 24?

1565. How many ounces are there in ½ pound?

1566. How many ounces are there in ¾ pound?

1567. How many ounces are there in 2 pounds?

1568. What customary unit do we often use to estimate weight: pounds or ounces?

1569. How many pounds would 48 ounces be equal to?

1570. What is the abbreviation of ounce?

1571. What is the abbreviation of pound?

1572. How many pounds equal one ton: 2000 or 3000?

1573. What U.S. customary unit would 6,000 pounds be equal to?

1574. What is the abbreviation for ton: t or tn?

1575. If a truck weighs 3 ½ tons, how many pounds does it weigh?

1576. What are the U.S. customary units for volume, smallest to largest, starting with one cup?

1577. What are the U.S. customary units of cooking, smallest to largest, starting with the teaspoon?

1578. How many teaspoons are equal to one tablespoon?

1579. What is the abbreviation for teaspoon?

1580. What is the abbreviation for tablespoon?

1581. How many fluid ounces are equal to 1 cup: 4 or 8?

1582. What is the abbreviation in a recipe for cup?

1583. When we measure volume when we cook, what are the common sizes of cups?

1584. How many fluid ounces are equal to one cup: 8 or 16?

1585. How many cups are there in one pint: 2 or 4?

1586. What is the abbreviation for pint?

1587. How many pints are there in one quart: ½ or 2?

1588. What is the abbreviation for quart?

1589. How many quarts are there in one gallon: 2 or 4?

1590. Which is larger: 3 pints or 4 cups?

MATH

1591. How many tablespoons are equal to 3 tablespoons and 1 teaspoon?

1592. What unit of measurement is used in many other countries?

1593. What system meaning "ten" is the Metric system based on?

1594. What number is associated with **dec**imal, **dec**agon, and **dec**ade?

1595. What number is associated with **cen**timeter, **cen**tipede, **cen**tury, and **cen**tennial?

1596. What number is associated with **mil**limeter, **mil**lipede, and **mil**lennium?

1597. How many millimeters equals one centimeter: 100 or 10?

1598. If a caterpillar is 32 millimeters long, how long is it in centimeters?

1599. What is the abbreviation for centimeter?

1600. What is the abbreviation for millimeter?

1601. How many centimeters are equal to one meter: 100 or 1000?

1602. What is the abbreviation for meter?

1603. Which is longer: a meter or a yard?

1604. How many meters are there in one kilometer: 100 or 1000?

1605. What is the abbreviation for kilometer?

1606. Which is longer: a kilometer or a mile?

1607. How many miles is 100 kilometers equal to: 620 or 62?

1608. What is the metric unit for measuring liquid capacity: liter or gram?

1609. How many centiliters are there in one liter: 10 or 100

1610. How many milliliters are there in one liter: 100 or 1000?

1611. What is the abbreviation for centiliters?

1612. What is the abbreviation for liter?

1613. If you and a friend had a one liter bottle of chocolate milk, and you both drank half of it, how many milliliters would you have left: 500 or 1000?

1614. What are the metric units of weight smallest to largest: the gram, kilogram, milligram and metric ton?

1615. How many grams are equal to one kilogram: 100 or 1000?

1616. How many milligrams are there in one centigram: 10 or 100?

1617. What is the abbreviation for milligram?

MATH

1618. What is the abbreviation for centigram?

1619. How many milligrams are there in one gram: 100 or 1000?

1620. What is the abbreviation for gram?

1621. How many centigrams are there in one gram: 100 or 1000?

1622. What is the abbreviation for kilogram?

1623. Which unit of measurement is used to conduct most science experiments: the U.S. customary system or the metric system?

1624. What is the metric unit of measurement for temperature: Celsius or Fahrenheit?

1625. What is the U.S. Customary unit of measurement for temperature?

1626. If it is 32 degrees Fahrenheit, what is the temperature in degrees Celsius?

1627. Is 0 degrees Celsius or 32 degrees Fahrenheit the temperature in which water melts or freezes?

1628. What do we call the numbers that are greater than zero but less than one?

1629. What is the numerator in the fraction 2/3?

1630. What is the denominator in the fraction 4/10?

1631. What can 2/4 be reduced to in lowest terms: ½ or ¾?

1632. What is the simplest form of the fraction 4/16?

1633. Are 1/3 and 3/6 equivalent fractions?

1634. What is the equivalent fraction of ¾?

1635. What is the equivalent fraction of 1/3?

1636. Which fraction is equal to 6/10: ¾ or 3/5?

1637. What fraction comes next in the pattern: ½, 2/4, 3/6, ___?

1638. Is 9/6 considered a proper or an improper fraction?

1639. When the numerator is the same number as the denominator, what number is that fraction equal to?

1640. What kind of a fraction is it if the numerator is larger than the denominator: mixed or improper?

1641. If you have the fraction 10/5, is that the same as 10 ÷ 5?

1642. What is an improper fraction that can be divide evenly with no remainder equal to: a whole number or a mixed fraction?

1643. What is 12/3 equal to as a whole number?

MATH

1644. What whole number is 3/3 equal to?

1645. What is 0/8 equal to?

1646. What math operation is a bar in a fraction equal to: division or multiplication?

1647. Can the fraction 4/10 be reduced?

1648. Do you need to divide both the numerator and the denominator by a common factor to reduce a fraction to its lowest terms?

1649. What is 4/16 in lowest terms?

1650. What is 18/24 in lowest terms?

1651. What do we call a number that has both a whole number and a fraction like 1 1/3: mixed or improper?

1652. How can the improper fraction 12/5 be written as a mixed number? (12 ÷ 5 = 2 R2)

1653. How would you write the mixed number 6 ¼ as an improper fraction: multiply 4 x 6 plus 1 over 4 or, add 6 + 1 over 4?

1654. How would you write the mixed number 4 and 2/3 as an improper fraction? (3 x 4 + 2)

1655. What number is ½ of 12?

1656. What number is 1/3 of 18?

1657. What number is ¼ of 16?

1658. How do we add fractions with common denominators: by adding or multiplying the numerators?

1659. What is the sum of 3/5 + 1/5?

1660. What is the sum of 4/9 + 8/9?

1661. What is the sum of 2/10 + 3/10 + 5/10?

1662. How would you write 12/9 as a mixed number in its lowest terms?

1663. What is 5/7 – 3/7?

1664. How do you add fractions with unlike denominators: find the least common denominator first, or simply add the original denominators together?

1665. What is the sum of ½ and 1/3? (3/6 + 2/6=_)

1666. How do you subtract fractions with unlike denominators: find the least common denominator first, or simply subtract the original denominators together?

1667. What is ½ - 1/6 reduced to simple terms? (3/6 – 1/6 =_)

MATH

1668. What is 7/9 – 3/9?

1669. If Alegra and Eva picked 2 pounds of strawberries and they ate ½ pound of them, how many pounds of strawberries do they have left?

1670. What is the sum of 1 and 1/3 + 1 and 1/3?

1671. If Sam is 5 ½ feet tall and Jordan is 3 ½ feet tall, how much taller is Sam than Jordan?

1672. If Sofia is 4 ½ feet tall and her sister Isabella is 4 feet tall, how much taller is Sofia than Isabella?

1673. If Sofia is ½ foot taller than Isabella, how much taller is she is inches?

1674. Is 2/5 + 1/5 greater than, less than, or equal to 4/5?

1675. Is 1/3/ + 1/3 greater than, less than, or equal to 2/3?

1676. Is ¼ + ¾ greater than, less than, or equal to 1?

1677. When following recipes, is it a good idea to use measuring cups and measuring spoons?

1678. What is the order smallest to largest of the following measuring cups: ½ 1/3, ¼, and 1?

1679. What is the order smallest to largest of the following teaspoons: ¼, 1/8, ½, and 1?

1680. If Sarah's class has 12 boys and 12 girls, how much of the class is made up of girls?

1681. What fraction would indicate how many of the fish are blue if there are 100 tropical fish in the aquarium, 75 are gold, and 25 are blue: ½, ¼, 2/3, or ¾?

1682. What is the product when you multiply the fraction ½ x 3?

1683. What is the product when you multiply 2/3 x 1/3?

1684. What is the product when you multiply ½ x 2/5?

1685. If a candy bar costs one quarter or 25 cents, and there are four quarters in one dollar, what part of a dollar is 25 cents?

1686. What fraction of a dollar is fifty cents?

1687. What fraction of a dollar is 75 cents?

1688. How do we indicate dollars and cents: with decimals or with commas?

1689. What is $4.00 + $2.75?

1690. What is $4.00 - $2.75?

1691. What number is the decimal system based on?

1692. What do we call the time span of ten years?

1693. How would you write two dollars and fifty cents using a decimal point?

MATH

1694. How is the fraction 1/10 written as a decimal?

1695. How is the fraction 1/100 written as a decimal?

1696. How is the fraction 1/1000 written as a decimal?

1697. Is 1.2 greater than, less than, or equal to 1.20?

1698. Are the decimals .9 and .90 equivalent?

1699. Is .9 greater than, less than, or equal to .09?

1700. How would you write the fraction two and four tenths as a decimal?

1701. How would point two five be written as a fraction?

1702. How would point seven five be written as a fraction?

1703. How would point five zero be written as a fraction?

1704. In the number 0.5, which digit is in the ones place?

1705. What would 3.273 be rounded to the nearest tenth if you consider the number to the right of 2?

1706. What would 4.86 be rounded to the nearest tenth if you consider the number to the right of 8?

1707. What would 4.83 be rounded to the nearest tenth if you consider the number to the right of 8?

1708. What would 3.263 be rounded to the nearest hundredth if you consider the number to the right of 2?

1709. What would 3.457 be rounded to the nearest hundredth if you consider the number to the right of 4?

1710. What would 3.248 be rounded to the nearest tenth if you consider the number to the right of 4?

1711. What is 5.612 rounded to the nearest whole number?

1712. Can you read decimals on a number line?

1713. What decimal would come next in the sequence: 1.5, 1.6, 1.7, __?

1714. What do you have to line up when you are adding decimals together: whole numbers or decimal points?

1715. What number do you need to add to 1.2 to make it line up evenly with 1.35 before you add them together?

1716. Can you *estimate* the sum of the following by rounding each number to the nearest whole number, and then adding them together: 4.8 + 2.1 = ___?

1717. What is the sum of 1.5 + 1.4?

1718. What is the sum of 2.5 + 2.5?

1719. If Andrew watched his turtle move 0.2 centimeters, then move 0.4 centimeters more, and then 0.3 centimeters more, how much distance did his turtle travel in all?

MATH

1720. Is 5/4 greater than, less than, or equal to 1.25?

1721. What is the study of points, lines, segments, and shapes called?

1722. Which can go on infinitely: a line or a line segment?

1723. What symbols are line segments often labeled with: letters or numbers?

1724. What do we draw at either end of a line to show that it can go on forever in either direction?

1725. What is the name of a line that has one end point and an arrow pointing in one direction: a segment or a ray?

1726. What point to we start with when we are labeling a ray: the end point or the point closer to the arrow?

1727. What is formed when two rays have the same end point: an angle or a line segment?

1728. What is another name for the end point: the axis or the vertex?

1729. How many sides does a triangle have?

1730. What is the name of an angle that forms a square corner?

1731. How many degrees does a right angle measure: 45 or 90?

1732. What is the name of an angle that is *less* than a right angle: acute or obtuse?

1733. What is the name of an angle that is *greater* than a right angle: acute or obtuse?

1734. Can we help ourselves remember the difference between *a*cute and *o*btuse if we think that "**a**" is a lower (or lesser) letter than "**o**" which is 'higher' in the alphabet?

1735. What is the name of a triangle that has *two* sides that are equal: isosceles or equilateral?

1736. If you have a triangle with each angle measuring 60 degrees, what kind of triangle is it: isosceles or equilateral?

1737. What is the name of a triangle that has 3 sides with different lengths: isosceles or scalene?

1738. If a triangle has one angle that measures 90 degrees, what kind of triangle is it: equilateral or right?

1739. What is the name of the tool you can use similar to a ruler for measuring angles: a protractor or a compass?

1740. If an angle measures 80 degrees and part of the angle measures 30 degrees, what is the measurement of the *adjacent* angle? (80-30= __)

1741. How many degrees is ½ turn of an angle: 90 or 180?

1742. How many degrees is ¼ turn of an angle: 45 or 90?

MATH

1743. How many degrees is ¾ turn of an angle: 180 or 270?

1744. How many degrees is 1 full turn of an angle: 270 or 360?

1745. What do we call two lines when they cross each other: intersecting or parallel?

1746. What do we call two lines that intersect each other and form right angles: perpendicular or parallel?

1747. What do we call lines that always stay the same distance apart and never intersect: perpendicular or parallel?

1748. What are lines called that run east and west like the "horizon?"

1749. What are lines called that run up and down or north and south?

1750. What are lines called that run northeast to southwest or join two opposite vertices of a quadrilateral?

1751. What is the general term of a closed plane shape with three or more line segments and angles: a polygon or a hexagon?

1752. What is the name of a polygon that is three-sided?

1753. What is the name of a polygon that has four sides: a quadrilateral or a diagonal?

1754. What two quadrilateral shapes have *two* pairs of parallel lines?

1755. What is the name of a quadrilateral with sides that run parallel: a parallelogram or a matrix?

1756. What is a quadrilateral called that has *one* pair of parallel lines: a trapezoid or a rhombus?

1757. What is a rectangle called that has four sides that are all the same exact length?

1758. What is a diamond an example of: a rhombus or a trapezoid?

1759. What is the name of any polygon with four sides: a square or a quadrilateral?

1760. What is the name of a polygon with five sides: a pentagon or a hexagon?

1761. What is the name of a polygon with six sides: a pentagon or a hexagon?

1762. What is the name of the polygon with seven sides: a hexagon or a heptagon?

1763. What is the name of a polygon with eight sides: a hexagon or an octagon?

1764. What is the name of a polygon with nine sides: a decagon or a nonagon?

1765. What is the name of a polygon with ten sides: a decagon or a pentagon?

1766. What animal are you familiar with that has 8 "arms?"

1767. Which polygon is the shape of a red stop sign?

1768. What is the name of a polygon that has 4 straight lines of equal lengths but the lines do not form right angles: a rhombus or a trapezoid?

MATH

1769. What are shapes called that have the same shape and the same size: congruent or similar?

1770. What are shapes called that have the same shape but are *not* the same size: congruent or similar?

1771. What is a shape called that has matching points on both sides of a line dividing it, and if you folded it in half, it would match up exactly: symmetrical or asymmetrical?

1772. What part of a shape would a line of symmetry run through?

1773. If you multiply the length times the width of a square or a rectangle, what would you be measuring: area or perimeter?

1774. If a rectangle measures 8 centimeters long and 4 centimeters wide, what is its area?

1775. If a square measures 3 feet by 3 feet, what is its area?

1776. Do we measure area in square units?

1777. If there are 12 inches in one foot, how many inches are there in 1 square foot? (12x12=__)

1778. What are some examples of U.S. customary units of area besides square inch?

1779. What are some examples of metric units of area besides square millimeter?

1780. Are polygons 2 or 3 dimensional?

1781. Can 2-dimensional shapes be drawn on a plane?

1782. What is the name of the <u>3</u>-dimensional shape that often has a triangular or rectangular base, and can break light into the colors of the spectrum?

1783. What is the name of the <u>3</u>-dimensional shape that has two flat circular ends and is shaped like a tube?

1784. What is the name of the <u>3</u>-dimensional shape that often has a polygon base and sides that are triangular that meet to form a point at the top, and is also the name for the buildings that the ancient Egyptians and Maya built?

1785. What is the name of the <u>3</u>-dimensional shape that has no flat surfaces and all points of the shape are the same distance from the center of the shape, similar to a globe?

1786. What is the name of the <u>3</u>-dimensional shape that has 6 square faces, similar to dice?

1787. What is the name of the <u>3</u>-dimensional shape that has a base that is round and a point at the top, similar to what you crunch on under your scoop of ice cream?

1788. What part of a 3-dimensional shape includes the top, bottom, left, right, front, and back: the perimeter or the surface area?

1789. Can you count the sides, edges, vertices, and faces on geometric figures?

1790. When we measure the amount of space or cubic units that a 3 dimensional figure takes up, what are we measuring: the surface area or the volume?

MATH

1791. If a rectangular prism has 6 cubes on one layer and there are 2 layers, how many cubic centimeters are in the prism?

1792. Is a circle a polygon?

1793. What is the name of the tool you can use to draw a circle: a compass or a protractor?

1794. What is it called when you draw a straight line from the center of a circle to any point on the outer edge of the circle: diameter or radius?

1795. What is it called when you draw a straight line from one point on the circle, through the center of the circle to the opposite end point: diameter or radius?

1796. What is it called when you draw a straight line that join two points on a curve of a circle: chord or arc?

1797. Which is longer: the radius or the diameter?

1798. What can you adjust on a compass to determine the size of the circle: the radius or the diameter?

1799. If the radius of a circle is 8 centimeters, what is its diameter: 16 or 64?

1800. What is the distance around a circle called: its radius or its circumference?

1801. Can you make a prediction about something?

1802. If a spinner has 4 blue sections, 3 red sections, and 2 yellow sections, which color would you predict that the arrow is most likely to land when you spin it?

1803. If you flipped a quarter 8 times, how many times would you predict that the quarter will land on "heads?"

1804. When we want to find the average of different numbers, what do we need to do after we add them together?

1805. What is the average of the numbers 2, 4, and 6?

1806. If you scored a 10 on your spelling test, your friend Emily scored a 7, and your friend Avery also scored a 7, what is the average score? (10+7+7 ÷3 = _)

1807. If you have a set of numbers from smallest to largest, what is the number located in the middle called: the mean, the mode, the median, or the range?

1808. What is the mean or average value of the following numbers: 2, 3, 5, and 6? (2+3+5+6÷4 = _)

1809. If you have a set of numbers, what is the number called that is listed most frequently: the mean, the mode, the median, or the range?

1810. What is the mode in the following set of numbers: 1, 3, 3, 4, 5, 3, 6, 3?

1811. If you have a set of numbers and you want to find the average of those numbers, what would you be finding: the mean, the mode, the median, or the range?

MATH

1812. What is the mean in the following set of numbers: 1, 3, 4, 4? (1+3+4+4 ÷4 = _)

1813. What are you finding if you have a set of numbers written in random order, and you subtract the smallest value that is listed from the largest value listed: the mean, the mode, the median, or the range?

1814. What is the range of the following set of numbers: 0, 1, 5, 4, and 3?

Math – 5th Grade

1815. What big number comes after a million that has 9 zeros in it?

1816. What symbol do we use to indicate the place value of thousands, millions, and billions?

1817. How many place values do you count back from the end of the number before inserting a comma?

1818. How many zeros are there in one hundred thousand: 100,000?

1819. How many zeros are there in one million: 1,000,000?

1820. How many zeros are there in ten million: 10,000,000?

1821. How many zeros are there in one hundred million: 100,000,000?

1822. How many zeros are there in one billion: 1,000,000,000?

1823. How would you write the number six hundred and twelve billion?

1824. How would you write the number five thousand four hundred eighty using digits?

1825. What is the sum of: 50,000 + 3,000 + 900 + 20 + 7?

1826. What is the number 8,145 in expanded form: 8000 + _?

1827. What is the place value of 9 in the number 9,876,543,210: 9 billion or 9 million?

1828. What is the place value of 8 in the number 9,876,543,210: 800 million or 80 million?

1829. What is the place value of 7 in the number 9,876,543,210: 70 thousand or 70 million?

1830. What is the place value of 6 in the number 9,876,543,210: 6 million or 600 thousand?

1831. What is the place value of 5 in the number 9,876,543,210: 500 thousand or 50 thousand?

1832. What is the place value of 4 in the number 9,876,543,210: 400 thousand or 40 thousand?

1833. What is the place value of 3 in the number 9,876,543,210: 3 thousand or 30 thousand?

1834. What is the place value of 2 in the number 9,876,543,210: 2 hundred or 2 thousand?

1835. What is the place value of 1 in the number 9,876,543,210: tens or ones?

1836. What is the place value of 0 in the number 9,876,543,210: tens or ones?

MATH

1837. When do we use Roman numerals?

1838. What does the letter "V" represent as a Roman numeral: 5 or 10?

1839. What does the letter "X" represent as a Roman numeral: 10 or 50?

1840. What does the letter "L" represent as a Roman numeral: 50 or 500?

1841. What does the letter "C" represent as a Roman numeral: 100 or 1000?

1842. What does the letter "D" represent as a Roman numeral: 500 or 50?

1843. What does the letter "M" represent as a Roman numeral: 100 or 1000?

1844. What number would Roman numeral CLXXVI be equal to in Arabic numbers: 100 + 50 + 20 +6?

1845. What number would Roman numeral LXXVI be equal to in Arabic numbers: L = 50 +20 +6?

1846. What number would Roman numeral MDCLXXXVI be: 1000 + 500 + 100 + 50 + 30 + 5 + 1?

1847. If M = 1000, how would you write three thousand five using Roman numerals?

1848. What digit do you look at to round a number to a certain place: the digit to the right or to the left of that place value?

1849. Are Roman numerals often used when writing an outline?

1850. What does the number have to be, or be higher than in order to round up that number?

1851. What would the number 9,821,000 be, rounded to the nearest million?

1852. What would the number 9,432,000 be, rounded to the nearest million?

1853. What would the number 3,946,000 be, rounded to the nearest hundred thousand?

1854. What would the number 3,421,000 be, rounded to the nearest hundred thousand?

1855. What would the number 3,946,000 be, rounded to the nearest ten thousand?

1856. What would the number 3,421,000 be, rounded to the nearest ten thousand?

1857. What would the number 2,689 be, rounded to the nearest thousand?

1858. What would the number 2,489 be, rounded to the nearest thousand?

1859. What would the number 59,853 be, rounded to the nearest thousand?

1860. What would the number 45,325 be, rounded to the nearest thousand?

1861. What would the number 45,526 be, rounded to the nearest thousand?

1862. What would the number 45,526 be, rounded to the nearest hundred?

1863. What would the number 45,587 be, rounded to the nearest hundred?

MATH

1864. What would the number 5,52<u>6</u> be, rounded to the nearest ten?

1865. What would the number 5,58<u>7</u> be, rounded to the nearest ten?

1866. What would the number 42<u>1</u> be, rounded to the nearest one?

1867. What would the number 42<u>5</u> be, rounded to the nearest one?

1868. Is the sum of 20 + 21 even or odd?

1869. Is the difference of 20 – 12 even or odd?

1870. Is the product of 8 x 9 even or odd?

1871. Is the quotient of 28 ÷4 even or odd?

1872. What is another term for *whole* numbers: fractions or integers?

1873. Is the number zero considered an integer?

1874. Is a *positive* number always greater than or less than a negative number?

1875. Are integers often written on a number line with *zero* in the middle?

1876. Are numbers that are the same distance from zero on a number line in opposite directions called distant numbers or opposite numbers?

1877. Do integers lose value or gain value as you move farther to the right on the number line?

1878. Do integers lose value or gain value as you move farther to the left on a number line?

1879. If the temperature is 5 degrees above zero, is that a positive number or a negative number?

1880. If the temperature is 5 degrees below zero, is that a positive number or a negative number?

1881. Are the numbers to the right of 0 on a number line positive or negative?

1882. Are the numbers to the left of 0 on a number line positive or negative?

1883. What do we write before a number to show that it is negative?

1884. Is it always necessary to write a *plus* sign before a positive number?

1885. Are the numbers +2 and –2 considered likes or opposites?

1886. What is the opposite of –5?

1887. What is the opposite of +7?

1888. What is the opposite of -20?

1889. Which integer represents winning $10 in a raffle: +10 or –10?

1890. Which integer represents earning $25 for working in the yard: +25 or –25?

MATH

1891. Which integer represents spending $5 for a turkey sandwich: +5 or –5?

1892. Which integer represents a gain of 10 yards in a football game: +10 or –10?

1893. Which integer represents a loss of 15 yards in a football game: +15 or –15?

1894. How would you indicate that a sunken pirate ship from long ago was located 200 meters below sea level?

1895. Which integer represents losing 4 pounds: +4 or –4 (negative 4)?

1896. Is the integer –1 greater than, less than, or equal to +1?

1897. Is the integer –1 greater than, less than, or equal to 0?

1898. Is the integer –1 greater than, less than, or equal to –3?

1899. Is the integer 1 greater than, less than, or equal to –1?

1900. Is the integer –8 greater than, less than, or equal to –4?

1901. Is the integer –4 greater than, less than, or equal to –8?

1902. Can we add and subtract integers?

1903. Is the sum of two positive integers positive or negative?

1904. If you are adding positive integers, in what direction do you move on a number line: to the right or to the left?

1905. Is the sum of two negative integers positive or negative?

1906. If you are adding negative integers do you keep moving to the right or to the left on the number line?

1907. What is the sum of 2 + 4?

1908. Can the sum of positive 2 plus positive 4 be written 2 + 4?

1909. What is the sum of -3 + (-2), if you start at –3 on the number line and then move 2 more units to the left?

1910. What is the sum of -10 + 6, if you start at –10 on a number line and then move 6 units to the right?

1911. What is the sum of -60 + 20?

1912. What is the sum of –20 + 25?

1913. Is the sum of opposites the same?

1914. What is the opposite of -10 + 6?

1915. What would be the sum of the opposite of 10 + (-4)?

MATH

1916. What is the sum of -5 +5?

1917. What is the sum of -27 + 27?

1918. Is the sum of an integer and its exact opposite zero?

1919. Can you also subtract integers?

1920. Is subtracting an integer the same as adding or subtracting its opposite?

1921. Is 5 –7 the same as 5 + (-7)?

1922. What is -2 – (-4), (Negative two minus negative four), if we add its opposite (-2 + 4)?

1923. What is -7 – (-4), (Negative seven minus negative four), if we add its opposite (-7 + 4)?

1924. What is 9 – 3, if we add its opposite (9 + -3)?

1925. Do you remember your times tables? (2 x 2, 2 x 3…)

1926. When you *square* a number, what do you multiply a number by: 2 or itself?

1927. What is the square of 2?

1928. Is 2 squared equal to 4 because 2 x 2 = 4?

1929. What is the square of 3?

1930. Can we say that 3 squared equals 9?

1931. What is the square root of 4?

1932. What is the square root of 9?

1933. What is the square root of 16?

1934. What is the square root of 25?

1935. What is the square root of 36?

1936. What is the square root of 49?

1937. What is 6 squared?

1938. What is 7 squared?

1939. What is the square root of 64?

1940. What is 9 squared?

1941. What is 10 squared?

1942. What is the square root of 144?

1943. When we write 4 squared, or 4 to the second power, are we using integers or exponents?

MATH

1944. What is the definition of an exponent: a small number raised up that represents how many times a number is multiplied, or the base number that is written in normal size?

1945. How would you factor the number 2 to the third power?

1946. Is the number 5 to the third power regarded as 5 cubed or 5 squared?

1947. How would 5 x 5 x 5 x 5 be written as an exponent?

1948. What is 9 to the first power equal to?

1949. What is 10 to the third power (10 cubed) equal to: (10 x 10 x 10)?

1950. If you take 10 to the fifth power, can you write its equivalent simply by writing a one with 5 zeros?

1951. How many zeros would 10 to the sixth power have?

1952. What number would 10 to the sixth power be: One million or ten million?

1953. What would one billion be written as an exponent: 10 to the 8th power, or 10 to the 9th power?

1954. What is a number called that cannot be divided evenly by any number except the number itself, or by the number one: a prime number or a multiple number?

1955. Are the numbers zero and one considered prime numbers or composite numbers?

1956. What is the name of a number divisible by 2: a prime number or a composite number?

1957. Is 2 a prime number or a composite number?

1958. What are numbers called that are not prime numbers: integers or composite numbers?

1959. What is the number 17: prime or composite?

1960. What are the numbers called that you can multiply together to arrive at a larger number: multiples or factors?

1961. What are all the factors of the number 16?

1962. What is prime factor of the number 16: 2 or 4?

1963. What is the prime factorization of the number 9?

1964. What is the prime factorization of the number 9 written as an exponent?

1965. What is the prime factorization of the number 15?

1966. What are all the factors of 20 that can by multiplied together to get 20?

1967. What is the greatest common factor, the largest factor in common between the numbers of 6 and 9?

1968. What is the greatest common factor of 6 and 8?

1969. What is the greatest common factor of 27 and 36?

MATH

1970. If multiples of 2 include 2, 4, 6, and 8, and multiples of 3 include 3, 6, 9, and 12, what is the least common multiple (LCM) of the numbers 2 and 3: 6 or 12?

1971. What is the least common multiple (LCM) of 4 and 8: 16 or 24?

1972. Do you remember your addition facts?

1973. What is the sum of 9,000 + 12,000?

1974. Which property of addition is demonstrated in 2 + 3 =5 and 3 +2 = 5: the commutative or the associative?

1975. Which property of addition is demonstrated in (4+ 2) in parenthesis + 3 =9, and 4 + (2 + 3) in parenthesis = 5: the distributive or the associative?

1976. Is 54 greater than, less than, or equal to 32 +24?

1977. Is 21 greater than, less than, or equal to 13 + 8?

1978. Is 81 greater than, less than, or equal to 32 + 47?

1979. How would you estimate the sum of 231 +179 to the nearest hundred?

1980. Can you add and compare decimals?

1981. Which is greater: 3.1 or 3.3?

1982. What is greater: .05 or .50?

1983. Is 65.450 the same as 65.45?

1984. Is .36 greater or less than .036?

1985. Can you read .36 as both point three six and 36 hundredths?

1986. Is the number 15.53 the same as 15.530?

1987. Is 12.425 greater than or less than 12.420?

1988. When adding larger decimals, what number can you add to line all the numbers up without changing the value of the number?

1989. What is the sum of .2 and .6?

1990. How much total snowfall was there if it snowed 1.5 inches in the morning, and another 2.5 inches in the afternoon?

1991. What is the name for the branch of mathematics in which relationships and operations are expressed through symbols that represent quantities, usually letters of the alphabet?

1992. When we solve an equation, what common symbol is used to stand for a number?

1993. What is the letter called in the equation 2 + b = 7: the integer or the variable?

MATH

1994. How can you solve for the variable y: (.8 − y = .5)?

1995. Is .7 + .8 greater than, lesser than, or equal to .15?

1996. What is the sum of the following if you round to the nearest whole number and then add: 10.5 + 4.3?

1997. What is the opposite operation of addition?

1998. What kinds of operations are addition and subtraction: inverse or associative?

1999. What is the related *subtraction* fact for 7 + 5 = 12?

2000. What is the related *addition* fact for 22 − 8 = 14?

2001. Do you remember your subtraction facts?

2002. What is the difference of 48 − 9?

2003. What is the difference of: 8,000 − 7,100?

2004. What is the difference of: 179,000 −78,000?

2005. What is difference of $4.75 - $2.25?

2006. What is the difference of $50.00 - $24.00?

2007. Is 65 − 15 greater than, less than, or equal to 75 - 25?

2008. What is the difference of the following if you round to the nearest whole number and then subtract: 56-31?

2009. If Elizabeth earned $986 dollars and she spend $235 of it, what is the estimated difference? (986 rounds to __, 235 rounds to __, subtracted equals __)

2010. Do you remember your multiplication tables?

2011. What is the product of 8 x 9?

2012. When multiplying two large numbers, would you add or subtract the zeros?

2013. What is the product of 10 x 1000: (One plus four zeros)?

2014. What is the product of 7,000 x 6?

2015. What is the product of 700 x 500: (35 plus four zeros)?

2016. Can you multiply two and three digit numbers on paper?

2017. Which property of multiplication is demonstrated in the equations 2 x 3 =6 and 3 x 2 = 6: commutative or associative?

2018. Which property of multiplication is demonstrated in (4x 2) in parenthesis x 3 =24 and 4 x (2 x 3) in parenthesis = 24: commutative or associative?

MATH

2019. Which property of multiplication is demonstrated in 2 x (3 + 4) in parenthesis, is equal to (2 x 3) in parenthesis, + (2 x 4) in parenthesis: associative or distributive?

2020. Which property of multiplication is demonstrated in 2 x (4 + 5) in parenthesis, is equal to 2 x 4 + 2 x 5: associative or distributive?

2021. Which property of multiplication is demonstrated in the equation 45 x 0 = 0: identity or zero?

2022. Which property of multiplication is demonstrated in the equation 7643 x 1 = 7643: identity or zero?

2023. What is the product of 3 x 10 x 4?

2024. How would you estimate the product of 59 x 33: (60x30)?

2025. Is 75 greater than, less than, or equal to 3 x 23?

2026. Is 75 greater than, less than, or equal to 3 x 25?

2027. What is the product of .7 x .3?

2028. When you multiply a decimal by 10, how many places to the right do you place the decimal point: 1 or 2?

2029. What is the product of 10 x 8.0

2030. What is the product of 10 x 2.325?

2031. When you multiply a decimal by 100, how many places to the right do you place the decimal point: 1 or 2?

2032. What is the product of 100 x 2.325?

2033. If you buy 8 bags of chips that cost .70 cents each, how much would you pay total?

2034. How would you estimate the product of 873 x 11: (900 x 10)?

2035. How would you estimate the product of 4287 x 489: (4000 x 500)?

2036. Is 6.2 greater than, less than, or equal to 2 x 3.1?

2037. What is the inverse operation of multiplication?

2038. What is the term for the number you are dividing out: the dividend or the divisor?

2039. What is the term for the number you are dividing by: the dividend or the divisor?

2040. What is the term for the number that represents the answer to a division problem: the product or the quotient?

2041. What is the quotient of 66 ÷ 3 = __?

2042. What is 144 ÷ 12?

MATH

2043. What is 77 ÷ 7?

2044. What is 1200 ÷ 3?

2045. What is the term for the number that is left over after a number is divided out evenly?

2046. Can you divide by two and three digits with remainders?

2047. When dividing large numbers, can you check your work by multiplying the quotient and the divisor and then adding the remainder?

2048. Is 45,000 greater than, less than, or equal to 92,222 ÷2 if you estimate: (90,000 ÷ 2)?

2049. What is the quotient of 18.284 ÷ 6 using estimation: (18÷6)?

2050. What is the quotient if you estimate 10.39 to the nearest ten divided by one?

2051. When you divide a number by 10, how many places do you move the decimal point to the left?

2052. What is 483.4 ÷10?

2053. When you divide a number by 100, how many places do you move the decimal point to the left?

2054. What is 483.4 ÷100?

2055. What are the two terms that make up a fraction?

2056. Is the denominator the top or bottom part of a fraction?

2057. What number of a fraction is the numerator: the top or the bottom?

2058. What is the equivalent of ¼: 2/8 or 2/4?

2059. How would you reduce 4/8 to its lowest terms?

2060. If you divide both the numerator and the denominator by its greatest common factor, what is 12/18 in its lowest terms?

2061. What is the greatest common factor or GCM of 12/18: 3 or 6?

2062. What do we need to do to find the least common denominator of two fractions: find the least common multiple or LCM of each denominator, or multiply both the numerators and the denominators?

2063. What is the least common multiple of 1/3 and 1/6: 3 or 6?

2064. What is the least common denominator or LCD of 1/3 and 1/6?

2065. What is the least common denominator or LCD of ½ and 1/8?

2066. How would you reduce the fraction 8/10 to lowest terms?

2067. What would 2 ½ be as an improper fraction: (2x2+1 =__/2)?

MATH

2068. Does a mixed number include both an integer and a fraction, or just a fraction?

2069. What is the *mixed* number of 4/3: 1 and 1/3, or 2 and 1/3?

2070. Is 1/3 greater than or less than 2/3?

2071. What do we need to find first when comparing fractions that have different denominators: a common denominator or a common numerator?

2072. When comparing the fractions 2/3 and 4/5, do we first need to find the lowest common denominators of 3 and 5?

2073. What is the lowest common multiple or LCM of 1/3 and 1/5: the number 15 or the number 20?

2074. What does the fraction 2/3 convert to if we multiply both the numerator and the denominator by 5: (2x5 and 3x5=__)?

2075. What is the fraction 10/15 in lowest terms?

2076. What does the fraction 4/5 convert to if we multiply both the numerator and the denominator by 3: (4x3 and 5x3=__)?

2077. What is the fraction 12/15 in lowest terms?

2078. If 2/3 becomes 10/15, and 4/5 becomes 12/15, which is greater: 2/3 or 4/5?

2079. What is the order of the following fractions least to greatest: ¼, 1/3, 1, ½, and 3/4"?

2080. What is the next fraction in the sequence: 1/3, 1/6, and 1/12?

2081. What is the next fraction in the sequence: 6/7, 5/7, and 4/7?

2082. What is 1 ¾ rounded to the nearest whole number?

2083. What is 90 and 1/6 rounded to the nearest whole number?

2084. How do you get the reciprocal of a fraction: multiply it by 2, or turn it upside down?

2085. What is the reciprocal of 2/5?

2086. What is the reciprocal of 4/3?

2087. What is the sum of 1/3 + 1/3?

2088. What is the sum of 1/3 + 1/3 + 1/3?

2089. What is the sum of 2/9 + 1/9 + 4/9?

2090. If you add 3/7 + 7/7, is it best to write the sum as 10/7, or as the mixed number 1 and 3/7?

2091. What is the sum of 2/3 + 2/3?

2092. How is 4/3 written as a mixed number: 1 and 1/3, or 1 and ¼?

MATH

2093. What is the sum of 1 ½ + 1 ½?

2094. What is the sum of 4 and 1/3 + 2 and 1/3?

2095. What is the sum of 2 ¼ + 2 ¼ in lowest terms: 4 and ¼, or 4 and ½?

2096. What is the sum of 10 and 1/6 + 5 and 2/6 in lowest terms? (10 + 5 and 1/6 + 2/6)?

2097. Can you subtract fractions with common denominators?

2098. What is the difference of 3/5 – 1/5?

2099. What is the difference of 6/8 – 3/8?

2100. What is the difference of 2 and 4/5 – 1 and 2/5? (2-1, 4/5 - 2/5)?

2101. Can you add and subtract fractions with unlike denominators?

2102. If Ben ate 2/8 of the pizza, and Drew ate 3/8 of the pizza, how many pieces were left?

2103. What is the missing numerator in the equation 1/8+ __/8 = ½: (1/2 = 4/8 so 1 plus what would equal 4?

2104. Is 8/9 greater than, less than, or equal to 4/9 + 3/9?

2105. Is 7/8 greater than, less than, or equal to 12/8 – 5/8?

2106. Is 3/5 greater than, less than, or equal to 2/5 + 2/5?

2107. Can you estimate the difference of the following by rounding to the nearest whole number and then subtracting: 4 and 4/5 - 2 and 1/5? (4 4/5 rounds to __, 2 and 1/5 rounds to __, 5-2=_)

2108. Can you estimate the sum of the following by rounding to the nearest whole number and then adding: 3 and 5/8 + 2 and 1/8 = _? (3 and 5/8 rounds to _; 2 and 1/8 rounds to _; 4 + 2 = _)

2109. When we multiply fractions by a whole number, do we multiply the denominator by the whole number and then divide by the numerator?

2110. Is the equation 1/3 x 6 the same as 1/3 *of* 6?

2111. What operation does 1/3 x 6 =2 which is equal to 6 x 1/3 represent: the commutative or the associative operation?

2112. What is the product of ¾ x 4? (3 x 4 =_ divided by 4 = _)

2113. When we multiply fractions do we multiply the numerators and then the denominators?

2114. How would you finish the rhyme for multiplying fractions: "Multiplying fractions, no big problem, top times top over bottom times bottom. And don't forget to simplify, before it's time to say _?"

2115. What is the product of 1/3 x 1/5?

2116. What is the product of 2/3 x 2/5?

MATH

2117. What is the product of ½ x ½ x ½?

2118. What is the product of 2/5 x 2/3?

2119. Can you estimate the product by first rounding to the nearest whole number and then multiplying the following equation: 4 and 2/3 x 6 = _? (5x6)

2120. What is the product of 1 ¼ x 8? (5/4 x 8 = 40/4 = 10)

2121. What is the product of 3 ½ x 4? (3 ½ becomes 7/2; 7/2 x 4 = 28/2, 28 ÷2=__)

2122. When we multiply by the reciprocal of a fraction, is that the same as dividing the fraction?

2123. What is the improper reciprocal 10/5 the same as: 10 ÷ __?

2124. What is the quotient of ½ ÷ 2? (½ x 2/1=2/2=_)

2125. What is the quotient of 1/2 ÷1/6? (½ x 6/1 = 6/2 =_)

2126. What is the quotient of 1/2 ÷1/3? (½ x 3/1 = 3/2 = 1 and__/__)

2127. What is the quotient of 1/3 ÷1/3? (1/3 x 3/1 = 3/3 =_)

2128. When comparing the size of two numbers, are you finding the ratio or the percent?

2129. How would you read the ratio written as one colon three?

2130. If you have 2 stuffed dogs and 5 stuffed elephants, what is the ratio of dogs to elephants?

2131. What fraction is equal to the ratio 1 to 4: ¼ or ½?

2132. How is the ratio 1 to 4 written as a percentage: 25% or 75%?

2133. How is the ratio 2 to 1 written as a percentage: 25% or 50%?

2134. How is the ratio 3 to 1 written as a percentage: 75% or 30%?

2135. Should you write ratios in lowest terms?

2136. What is the ratio 6 to 3 in lowest terms?

2137. Is the ratio 1 to 2 the same as 2 to 4 or 2 to 1?

2138. Is ½ or 1 to 2 the same proportion as 2 /4 or 2 to 4?

2139. What is the math term for the comparison of two measurements in which one of the two things has a value of one: a ratio or a unit rate?

2140. What is the unit rate of pigs per farm if there are 18 pigs at 3 farms?

2141. What is the unit rate of gumballs if 4 gumballs costs one dollar?

2142. What does a scale drawing use to represent the size of something: a ratio or a fraction?

MATH

2143. Would you likely find scale drawings maps and floor plans?

2144. If one inch is equal to 5 miles on a city map scale, and the distance from Apple Valley to Pinehurst is 4 inches long, how many miles apart are the two cities?

2145. What would be the water to concentrate ratio if you are making lemonade and need to mix 6 cans of water with 1 can of frozen concentrate?

2146. What would be the concentrate to water ratio if you are making lemonade and need to mix 6 cans of water with 1 can of frozen concentrate?

2147. What would the ratio be if the scale on the blueprints of a house is: 1 inch = 10 feet?

2148. What is the ratio called between 2 different quantities: the speed or the rate?

2149. Is speed a common form of rate?

2150. What is a common speed per hour on the highway?

2151. How do you measure the rate of speed using U.S. customary units: in miles or in kilometers?

2152. How do you measure the rate of speed using the Metric system?

2153. What are you measuring when you multiply the rate by the time: speed or distance?

2154. If you travelled by car 180 miles in 3 hours, at what speed did you travel per hour?

2155. Is percent considered a ratio?

2156. What number does a percent compare a number to: 10 or 100?

2157. If "percent" means per 100, what things besides coins ("cents") are related to the number 100 and begin with "cent?"

2158. What is 30% equal to: 30 out of 100, or 3 out of 10?

2159. How would 30% be written as a fraction?

2160. What percent is equal to ¼?

2161. What percent is equal to ½?

2162. What percent is equal to ¾?

2163. What percent is equal to the whole number 1?

2164. What fraction is 50% equal to?

2165. What fraction is 75% equal to?

2166. What fraction is 25% equal to?

2167. What fraction is 100% equal to?

MATH

2168. How would you write 75% as a decimal?

2169. How would you write 25% as a decimal?

2170. How would you write 50% as a decimal?

2171. If ¼ of the pizza had black olives, what percentage of the pizza was covered with olives?

2172. If the family ate 6 out of the 8 slices of pie for dessert, what percentage of the pie is left?

2173. What is the percentage of the following: 0.6 = 0.60 = 60/100 = _?

2174. How do you find the percent of a number: multiply or divide?

2175. If there are 200 students in the school, and 20% of them are in fifth grade, how many total students are in fifth grade? (.20 x 200=_)

2176. What is 40% of 60? (.40 x 60= _)

2177. If a jacket you like in the store has a price tag of $40, and there is a sale offering 20% off, how much will the jacket cost you after the discount? (40 x .20 = _, $40 - $8 = __)

2178. What is the mathematical term used to describe how likely it is that some particular thing will happen: probability or possibility?

2179. Is there a fifty-fifty chance that if you flip a coin it will land on "heads?"

2180. What is the probability of any one number turning up when throwing a single die: 1 in 5 or 1 in 6?

2181. What is the common phrase of probability when it is extremely remote that something will happen, like winning the lottery? (One in a __!)

2182. If you have a bag of candy with 3 red mints and 1 white mint, what is the probability that you will pick out the white mint?

2183. What is the probability that you will pick a red mint?

2184. How can one in four be written as a fraction?

2185. How can ¼ be written as a percent?

2186. How can ¼ be written as a decimal?

2187. What are you finding if you add a series of numbers together and then divide by how many numbers there are: the mode or the average?

2188. What is the average time for a rat to run through a maze if the first rat finished in 12 seconds, the second finished in 8 seconds, and the third finished in 7 seconds? (12 + 8 + 7 =__/3)

2189. What is the average score on the math test if you scored a 90%, Krista scored 80%, and Jimmy scored a 70%? (90 +80 +70 = __/ 3)

2190. What is another name for average: mean or mode?

243

MATH

2191. What is the mean of 2, 3, and 4?

2192. What is the number called that appears most frequently in a series of numbers: mode or mean?

2193. What is the mode in the following numbers: 15, 16, 14, 15, 12, 17, 15, 11, and 15?

2194. What is the name of the middle number in a series of numbers: median or mode?

2195. What should you do first to find the median in a sequence of numbers: place them in order according to their value, add them and divide by the total number?

2196. How would you order following sequence of numbers: 5, 3, 7, 9, and 2?

2197. What is the median of the number sequence: 2, 3, 5, 7, and 9?

2198. What is the mathematical term that refers to the difference between the lowest and the highest values: average or range?

2199. What is the range of the sequence: 4, 5, 3, 7, and 9? (9-3)

2200. What is the mathematical term for determining the next number in a sequence of numbers: rate of increase or growth pattern?

2201. What is the growth pattern of the following sequence: 2, 4, 6, 8, _?

2202. What is the growth pattern of the following sequence: 1, 3, 6, 10, _? (+2, +3, etc.)

2203. How would you finish the pattern if you multiply by 2 and then add 3: 1, 5, 13, __?

2204. Can you read and interpret a line graph, a circle graph, and a bar graph?

2205. How many quadrants are in a coordinate graph: 8 or 4?

2206. Are the quadrants of a graph always equal?

2207. What is the math term that refers to a pictorial representation of relationships or numerical data: a pictograph or a scale?

2208. Can you read and interpret a table and a pictograph?

2209. What is the math term that represents data on a number line, or other marks that show frequency: line plots or frequency counts?

2210. Can you create and interpret line plots?

2211. Can you plot data and interpret a frequency chart?

2212. What is the name of the graph that has horizontal or vertical rectangles to show the value of different pieces of data: a bar graph or a line graph?

2213. What is the name of the graph that shows how information is connected, or how it changes over time: a bar graph or a line graph?

MATH

2214. What kind of graph would best illustrate the relationship of several parts compared to the whole: a bar graph or a pie chart?

2215. What kind of graph or chart would best illustrate the most popular breeds of dogs: a line graph or a pie chart?

2216. What kind of graph or chart would best illustrate the number of students that earned an A, B, C, or D on a recent test: a bar graph or a line graph?

2217. What kind of graph or chart would best illustrate the change in temperature over a 24 hour period: a bar graph or a line graph?

2218. What kind of graph or chart would best illustrate the number of hot dogs that were sold per month at a year-round hot-dog stand: a pie chart or a pictograph?

2219. What are you conducting if you tally the number that represents each person's answer: a survey or a questionnaire?

2220. What are some topics you might survey your friends about?

2221. What is the specific name for the math that involves using letters and symbols to represent numbers that are unknown: geometry or algebra?

2222. What are the unknown letters called in algebra: unknowns or variables?

2223. What is the answer to the equation: $6 + 2 + 4 \div 3$?

2224. What is the answer to the following algebraic equation: $6 + b$, if $b = 3$?

2225. What is the value of "b" in the following equation: $6 + b = 11$?

2226. What are the letters called in algebraic expressions?

2227. How would you solve for **t** in the following equation: $t - 15 = 4$?

2228. How would you solve for **a** in the following: $a = b - 6$ and $b = 7$? (7-6 = __)

2229. Is 4 squared the same as 4 x 4 or 4 x 2?

2230. Which multiplication equation is equal to 4 to the third power: 3x3x3 or 4x4x4?

2231. What is 2 to the fourth power equal to? (2x2x2x2=__)

2232. How would you solve for the exponent **p** if 3 to the "p" power = 27?

2233. What two measurement systems exist for recording mass, volume, length, and temperature?

2234. What is the standard U.S. customary unit for weight?

2235. How would you order the following U.S. customary units of weight lightest to heaviest: pound, ton, and ounce?

MATH

2236. How many ounces are equal to one pound: 16 or 24?

2237. Which is more: 33 ounces or 2 pounds?

2238. How many pounds are equal to one ton: 1000 or 2000?

2239. How many pounds are equal to one half ton?

2240. How many pounds equal one quarter ton?

2241. Which is less: 3000 pounds or 2 tons?

2242. How many inches are equal to one foot?

2243. How many feet equal one yard?

2244. Which is less: 1 yard or 4 feet?

2245. What is the standard unit for mass in the Metric system: gram or liter?

2246. How would you put the Metric units of mass in order lightest to heaviest: kilogram, milligram, metric ton, and gram?

2247. How many centigrams are equal to one gram: 100 or 1000?

2248. Is the weight of a paper clip closer to one gram or one centigram?

2249. How many grams are equal to one kilogram: 100 or 1000?

2250. Approximately how many pounds are equal to one kilogram: 2 or 3?

2251. If an object weighs 2.2 pounds, how many kilograms does it weigh?

2252. What is the Metric measurement for volume: liter or pint?

2253. How many liters of water equal 1 kilogram: 4 or 1?

2254. What are the U.S. customary units in order smallest to largest: foot, yard, inch, and mile?

2255. What are the Metric units for length in order smallest to largest: kilometer, meter, millimeter, and centimeter?

2256. Which Metric unit is equal to 39.37 inches: one meter or one yard?

2257. Which is longer: a meter or a yard?

2258. How much is 1/3 of a yard?

2259. If one meter measures approximately 39 inches, how much would 1/3 of a meter be?

2260. Which Metric unit is equal to 2.5 centimeters: one inch or one foot?

2261. Would the diameter of a dime be more like a centimeter or a millimeter?

MATH

2262. Would the thickness of a dime be more like a centimeter or a millimeter?

2263. Which U.S. customary unit is equal to 1760 yards: one kilometer or one mile?

2264. Which Metric unit is equal to 0.62 miles: one kilometer or one centimeter?

2265. What is the U.S. customary unit for temperature?

2266. What is the Metric unit for temperature?

2267. If 32 degrees Fahrenheit is the melting point for water, what is the equivalent temperature in Celsius?

2268. What temperature is the boiling point for water in degrees Celsius: 100 or 200?

2269. If the boiling point is 100 degrees Celsius, what is the equivalent temperature in Fahrenheit: 212 or 112?

2270. What is the normal body temperature of a human being in degrees Fahrenheit: 108.6 or 98.6?

2271. What are the U.S. customary units for volume in order from smallest to largest: gallon, quart, pint, fluid ounces, and cup?

2272. If there are 16 cups in one gallon, how many cups are there in ¼ of a gallon?

2273. If there are 4 quarts in a gallon, how many quarts are there in ½ gallon?

2274. How many fluid ounces are equal to 1 pint: 8 or 16?

2275. If there are 8 fluid ounces in one cup, how many fluid ounces are there in 3 cups?

2276. What is a U.S. customary unit that we use to measure the area of farmland: square yards, acres, or square miles?

2277. How many pecks are there on one bushel: 2 or 4?

2278. What is a U.S. customary unit that we use to measure the quantity of farm produce: peck or bushel?

2279. If ¼ bushel or 0.25 is equal to 1 peck, how many pecks are there in 1 full bushel?

2280. What is a U.S. customary unit that petroleum is measured in: barrels or drums?

2281. What U.S. customary unit are milk and gasoline measured in: Liters or gallons?

2282. What is the standard unit of volume in the Metric System?

2283. What are the Metric units for volume in order from smallest to largest: kiloliter, milliliter, liter, and centiliter?

2284. What is a liter a little more than in U.S. customary units: a quart or a gallon?

2285. What is one meter a little more than in U.S. customary units?

2286. What is one kilometer a little more than in U.S. customary units?

MATH

2287. What time is it now?

2288. What is the next logical time: 11:00, 11:15, 11:30, _?

2289. What are the names of the time zones from west to east: pacific, mountain, central, and _?

2290. What is the name of the time zone we live in?

2291. Do television shows air at different times depending on the time zone?

2292. If you started baking a cake in the oven at 11:10 and you took it out 25 minutes later, what time would it be?

2293. If your friend's birthday party begins at 10:30 and ends two and a half hours later, what time do you need to be picked up from the party?

2294. What do you say if you are referring to a time before 12:00 noon?

2295. What do you say if you are referring to a time after 12:00 noon?

2296. What does "ante" translate to in ante-meridiem or AM: before or after?

2297. What does "post" translate to in post-meridiem or PM: before or after?

2298. What is another way of saying 12:00 at night?

2299. How many seconds are there in 1 minute?

2300. How many seconds are there in 2 minutes?

2301. How many minutes are there in 1 hour?

2302. How many minutes are there in 3 hours?

2303. How many hours are there in 1 day?

2304. How many hours are there in 2 days?

2305. How many days is 72 hours?

2306. How many hours are in ½ day? (1/2 x 24 = __)

2307. How many hours are in ¼ day? (1/4 x 24 = __)

2308. How many hours are in ¾ day? (3/4 x 24 = __)

2309. How many days are there in 4 weeks?

2310. How many weeks are in 3 months?

2311. How many months are in ½ year?

2312. How many days exactly does it take for the Earth to orbit once around the Sun?

MATH

2313. How many days are there in one Earth year?

2314. How many weeks are there in one year: 48 or 52?

2315. How many days are in a Leap year?

2316. How do we account for the extra ¼ day that we have every year?

2317. What is the month and date of the Leap year day?

2318. How many years are there in one decade?

2319. How many years are there in one century?

2320. How many years would a bicentennial celebration be?

2321. Can you read a time line?

2322. What is the name of the math that is the study of points, lines, shapes, and angles?

2323. What type of tool would be used to draw a simple line or a ray?

2324. What is the name of a line that has two points at each end: a line or a line segment?

2325. What is the name of the line that has an arrow at each end: a ray or a line?

2326. What is the name of the line that has a point at one end and an arrow at the other: ray or line?

2327. How is a ray different from a line segment?

2328. What are 2 lines called that are the same distance from each other and never cross each other: parallel or perpendicular?

2329. What are 2 lines called that form a right angle: parallel or perpendicular?

2330. What are 2 lines called that cross each other and form an X: crossing or intersecting?

2331. What is it called when there are equal parts or shapes on both sides of a dividing line, or around a figure: intersecting or symmetrical?

2332. What is formed when two lines or two line segments meet: an intersection or a right angle?

2333. What is the geometric term for the place where two lines come together: the point or the vertex?

2334. What is the name of the measuring tool that is used to measure the degrees of angles: compass or protractor?

2335. What is the name of the unit of measurement for angles: degrees or coordinates?

2336. How many degrees does a full circle measure: 180 or 360?

2337. How many degrees does half a circle measure: 180 or 90?

2338. How many degrees does one quarter circle measure: 45 or 90?

MATH

2339. What is the measurement in degrees of a right angle: 90 or 180?

2340. Is one quarter of a circle the same as a right angle?

2341. If you divided a right angle in half, how many degrees would it measure?

2342. What is the name of the angle that has a measurement of less than 90 degrees: acute or obtuse?

2343. What is the name of the angle that has a measurement greater than 90 degrees but less than 180 degrees: acute or obtuse?

2344. What is the name of an angle that measures exactly 180 degrees: a straight angle or a reflex angle?

2345. What is the name of an angle that measures more than 180 degrees: straight or reflex?

2346. Are obtuse angles greater than or less than right angles?

2347. What is the total measurement in degrees of a triangle: 180 or 360?

2348. What is the third measurement of a triangle if one angle measures 80 degrees and a second angle measures 40 degrees?

2349. What is the measurement of a straight angle: 90 degrees or 180 degrees?

2350. What are plane figures called that have straight sides and are made out of at least three line segments: polygons or octagons?

2351. What common plane figures or shapes can you name?

2352. How many angles do triangles have?

2353. What other words do you know start with the prefix "tri" meaning three?

2354. What is the name of a triangle that has three sides each measuring 60 degrees: isosceles, right, or equilateral?

2355. What is the name of a triangle that has two sides and two equal angles: isosceles, right, or equilateral?

2356. What is the name of a triangle that has no equal sides: isosceles, right, or scalene?

2357. What is the name of a triangle that has one right angle: isosceles, right, or equilateral?

2358. What is the measurement of each of the two equal angles in a right isosceles triangle if you subtract the 90 degrees of the right angle from 180? (180-90=_/2)

2359. What is the term for two triangles that have the same size and shape: equilateral or congruent?

2360. What is the name of triangle with three equal sides, each measuring 60 degrees: equilateral or right?

2361. What is the geometric term for the longest side of a triangle: the hypotenuse or the Pythagoras?

2362. What is the correct formula for finding the area of a triangle: one-half the base times the height, or the length times the width divided by 2?

MATH

2363. What is a polygon called that has four sides: a quadrilateral or a square?

2364. What is the name of the quadrilateral where the opposite sides are the same length: a trapezoid or a rectangle?

2365. What is the formula for finding the area of a rectangle: width x height or ½ width x height?

2366. What is the formula for finding the area of a square: the length of one side squared or the length of one side times 4?

2367. What is the area of a square if you know that one side equals 5 centimeters?

2368. What is the name of the quadrilateral that has four equal sides and four right angles?

2369. What is the name of the quadrilateral that has one pair of opposite parallel lines: a trapezoid or a parallelogram?

2370. What is the name of the quadrilateral where both pairs of the opposite sides are of equal length: a trapezoid or a parallelogram?

2371. Would squares, rectangles, and rhombuses be considered parallelograms or trapezoids?

2372. What is the name of the quadrilateral where all four sides are of equal length and are parallel: a square or a rectangle?

2373. How many diagonal lines does a quadrilateral have: two or four?

2374. Can a square be a rectangle, or can a rectangle be a square?

2375. What is the name of the polygon that has 5 sides: a pentagon or a hexagon?

2376. What is the name of the polygon that has 6 sides: a hexagon or a heptagon?

2377. What is the name of the polygon that has 7 sides: a heptagon or a decagon?

2378. What is the name of the polygon that has 8 sides: a nonagon or an octagon?

2379. What is the name of the polygon that has 9 sides: a nonagon or a pentagon?

2380. What is the name of the polygon that has 10 sides: a decagon or a heptagon?

2381. What is the formula for finding the area of a shape: width x height, or length squared?

2382. What is the area of a rectangle that has sides of 6 feet and 4 feet?

2383. What is the name of a flat shape that is round?

2384. What is the name of the tool that you use to draw a circle: compass or protractor?

2385. How many degrees is a full circle?

2386. What is the line segment called that connects two points on a curve: a segment or a chord?

MATH

2387. What is the line segment called that connects two points through the center of a circle: chord or diameter?

2388. What is the length of a chord equal to on a circle: the diameter or the perimeter?

2389. What is the measurement of the distance from the center of the circle to any point on the outside of the circle: the perimeter or the radius?

2390. What is the measurement of the distance around the edge of a circle: diameter or circumference?

2391. What do we multiply the diameter by in order to find the circumference of a circle: the Greek letter pi π, or the length of the chord?

2392. Does pi equal the ratio of a circle's circumference to its diameter, or to its perimeter?

2393. Does pi equal 3.14 or 2.14?

2394. What date in the calendar year do many math students recognize as "pi day?"

2395. Which figures have sides, faces, edges, and vertices: planar figures or solid figures?

2396. Which figures would have width, depth, and height: planar figures or solid figures?

2397. What common solid figures or multi-dimensional shapes can you name?

2398. Are solid figures like prisms, cones, spheres, cubes, and cylinders two or three-dimensional?

2399. How many rectangles are in a rectangular prism: 3 or 6?

2400. Is a cube considered a rectangular prism?

2401. What is the formula for measuring the volume or cubic units of a rectangular prism: length x width, or length x width x height?

2402. If a rectangular prism measures 4 inches long, 2 inches wide, and 3 inches tall, what is its volume in cubic inches?

2403. What is the word "Math" short for?

2404. What is the term for the most elementary form of mathematics?

2405. What is your favorite type of math?

Chapter 4 – Science

Science – Pre-School

1. Are people, animals, and plants living or non-living?
2. What do we call Americans, African Americans, Hispanics, Asians, and all other humans?
3. What do we call whales, bunnies, tigers, frogs, dogs, kittens, and goldfish?
4. What do we call sunflowers, roses, trees, bushes, flowers, and ferns?
5. What do people need to live?
6. What do animals need to live?
7. What small animals can you name?
8. What large animals can you name?
9. What are grasshoppers, ladybugs, butterflies, bees, and ants called: bugs or insects?
10. What does a caterpillar turn into?
11. What are some popular animals that many people have as a pet?
12. What farm animals can you name?
13. What ocean animals can you name?
14. What desert animals can you name?
15. What forest animals can you name?
16. What bugs or insects can you name?
17. How many legs does an insect have: 6 or 8?
18. How many legs does a spider have: 6 or 8?
19. Is a spider considered an insect?
20. What are some animals that have wings and feathers?
21. What are some animals that have fins?
22. What are some animals that have fur?
23. What are some animals that have a shell?

SCIENCE

24. What are some animals that fly?
25. What are snakes, turtles, alligators, crocodiles, iguanas and lizards: reptiles or mammals?
26. What liquid do mammals produce to feed their young: milk or water?
27. What are human beings and animals with warm bodies called: mammals or marsupials?
28. What animals like the kangaroo, the wallaby, and the koala bear have a pouch: mammals or marsupials?
29. What are cold-blooded animals called that live near water like salamanders, frogs and toads: reptiles or amphibians?
30. How do dogs move?
31. How do snakes move?
32. How do monkeys move?
33. What body part does a turtle use to protect itself?
34. What body parts does a lion use to protect itself?
35. What does a skunk do to warn enemies and to protect itself?
36. What does a porcupine have to protect itself?'
37. What is the term for the sharp needles on a porcupine: quills or pins?
38. What is the name of an animal that has claws?
39. What is the name of an animal with a long neck?
40. What is the name of an animal with a trunk?
41. What is the name of an animal with stripes?
42. What is the name of an animal that has a pouch to carry its young?
43. What is the name of a baby cat?
44. What is the name of a baby dog?
45. What is the name of a baby duck?
46. What is the name of a baby hen?
47. What is the name of a baby frog: a tadpole or a froglet?
48. Does a mother frog first lay an egg?
49. What does a frog egg hatch into: froglets or tadpoles?

SCIENCE

50. Does a tadpole's tail shrink or get bigger as it grows?

51. Does a tadpole start to grow legs?

52. Can a frog live in and out of water?

53. What do animals that are classified as carnivores eat: meat or plants?

54. What do animals that are classified as herbivores eat: meat or plants?

55. What do animals that are classified as omnivores eat: meat, plants, or both?

56. What do birds build together, which is the place they will live?

57. What do ants build together, which is the place they will live?

58. What is the scientific term for the different places that animals live: habitats or environments?

59. In what habitat do deer and fox live?

60. What animals can you name that live in the forest?

61. In what habitat do whales and sharks live?

62. What would be considered the largest habitat: the desert or the ocean?

63. What does ocean water have that water that you drink out of a bottle does not?

64. What is the largest fish in the ocean: the whale shark or the sea monster?

65. What is the name of the body part that fish have that let them breathe: fins or gills?

66. In what habitat do cows, chickens, and pigs live?

67. How many animals can you name that live on a farm?

68. In what habitat do many snakes, lizards, roadrunners, and Gila monsters live: ocean or desert?

69. What animals can you name that live in the desert?

70. What kind of tropical forest do many frogs, snakes, monkeys, parrots, and butterflies live: a rainforest or a thicket?

71. What needs sunlight, water, air, and soil to live: plants or animals?

72. What is the general word used for trees, flowers, weeds, grass, and bushes?

73. How do many plants start out: as a seed or as a sprout?

74. What fruit can you name that has a seed or seeds inside it?

75. What fruit grows on an evergreen tree that contains the seeds?

76. Are nuts considered seeds?

SCIENCE

77. What are some seeds that grow inside a shell?

78. What seeds can you name that grow inside a pod?

79. What red fruit do we eat in the summer that may contain many seeds?

80. Is an acorn a seed?

81. What kind of tree does an acorn seed grow up to be: an acorn tree or an oak tree?

82. What parts of a plant can you name?

83. What does a seed need in order to sprout and to grow leaves and flowers?

84. What light source in the sky do plants use to make food?

85. If the Sun is shining and it is light, what time of day is it?

86. If the Sun is not shining and it is dark, what time of day is it?

87. Does the Sun move around in the sky or does it always stay in the same place?

88. What do you use to produce light that is not natural light from the Sun?

89. How does light travel: in a straight line, or in a wave?

90. What image do we see if the sunlight is shining on us in just the right way?

91. What determines the length of a shadow: the time of day or the direction we are facing?

92. What kinds of plants do farmers grow for food, and that we buy at the grocery store or a farmer's market?

93. What kinds of products do we eat that are made from the wheat plant?

94. What important gas do we breathe that is produced by plants: oxygen or carbon dioxide?

95. Do living things need food, water, air, and space to live?

96. What natural resource covers most of our planet, and fills the oceans, lakes and rivers?

97. Does water flow underground?

98. What is the name of the structure that we build so that we can bring up water that is underground?

99. What white or gray mass in the sky contains water and contributes to our weather conditions?

100. What is the liquid called when it is frozen and is solid?

101. What is the liquid called when it is hot and creates a gas?

102. What happens when you put a boat, a beach ball, or a rubber duck on top of the water?

103. What happens when you put a stone or a rock on top of the water?

SCIENCE

104. What is the name of the invisible mixture of gases that surround the Earth that animals and people breathe?

105. Can we feel air?

106. What can we blow up that gets bigger and shows us that air takes up space?

107. What escapes from bubbles, balloons, or tires when they are popped?

108. Can moving air cause objects to vibrate or shake?

109. When we blow air into a musical instrument, what does it produce?

110. Can you name a musical instrument that we blow air into?

111. What objects need air in order to help them move or fly?

112. What do humans need to survive?

113. Are humans able to take care of themselves when they are born?

114. Are humans adaptable to their surroundings or environment?

115. What body part do humans have on the outside to help them balance: ears or eyes?

116. What body part do humans have on the outside to help them walk or run?

117. What body part do humans have on the outside to stand on?

118. What body part do humans have on the outside to touch and hold things?

119. What body part do humans have on the inside that beats and pumps blood?

120. What body part do humans have on the inside that is used to think and to reason?

121. What body part do humans have on the inside that helps us digest our food?

122. What body part do humans have on the inside that helps to hold us up, maintain structure to the body, and protects the organs?

123. What body part do humans have on the inside that is made of tissue that helps us to move, and converts chemical energy into physical energy?

124. What body part do humans see with?

125. What body part do humans hear with?

126. What body part do humans smell with?

127. What body part do humans taste with?

128. What body part do humans touch with?

129. What is the name of the planet we live on?

SCIENCE

130. Is the Earth made up of land, air, and water?
131. Is the Earth one of the planets in the Solar System?
132. What shines on us during the day?
133. What natural satellite that is white do we see in the sky on most nights?
134. What small, twinkling objects do we see in the sky at night?
135. Do you think stars are close or far?
136. What is the weather like today?
137. What is the name for the study of living things?

Science – Kindergarten

138. What are some living things?
139. What do living things need to survive?
140. Are plants living or non-living?
141. What parts of a plant can you name?
142. Can you name a plant?
143. What do plants need to live and grow?
144. What plants can you name that we eat?
145. What can you plant in a garden?
146. In what form do most plants start out?
147. How do plants change as they grow?
148. When you eat corn-on-the cob, what part of the plant are you eating?
149. When you eat bread, what is the name of the seed that is ground into flour to make the bread?
150. What small green vegetable do you eat that are seeds that grow in a pod?
151. What long, green vegetable are you eating when you eat both the pod and the seed?
152. What seeds do you eat that grow inside a shell?
153. What are some fruits that you eat that contain seeds?
154. Do we eat the seeds in apples, pears, plums, oranges, and watermelon?
155. Can you eat the seeds that you find inside of a pumpkin?

SCIENCE

156. What kind of tree grows from an acorn seed?

157. From what part of a plant are radishes, beets, onions, potatoes, and carrots: the stem or the root?

158. What part of a plant is celery and asparagus: the stem or the leaf?

159. What part of a plant are the vegetables lettuce, spinach, and cabbage: the stem or the leaves?

160. What part of a plant is broccoli and cauliflower: the stem or the flower?

161. Do all plants live on top of the Earth, or do plants also live in the ocean and lakes?

162. Can you name a flower?

163. Can you name some parts of a flower?

164. What living thing includes the seeds, flower, leaves, stem, and roots?

165. Can you name a tree?

166. Can you name some parts of the tree?

167. What living thing has leaves, branches, a trunk, and roots?

168. What kind of tree is syrup typically tapped from: an evergreen or a maple?

169. When are maple trees tapped: in the spring or in the fall?

170. Which country is the world's leading producer of syrup: Canada or the United States?

171. What kind of leaf does Canada have on its national flag?

172. What do many plants and flowers start out as?

173. What do flowers like the sunflower produce: seeds or bulbs?

174. What is the name of the orange squash that is harvested in autumn and contains seeds?

175. What breakfast food do you eat that is made from wheat, corn, oats, and rice seeds?

176. Can bulbs grow into flowers and plants, too?

177. Can you name a plant or flower that grows from a bulb?

178. Do many vegetables and flowers grow from seeds?

179. In which season do we plant flowers and crops here?

180. Do many farmers use big sprinklers to irrigate or provide water for their crops when there is no rain?

181. When do we harvest our vegetable crops here?

182. Can you name a vegetable that we eat that is actually the root and not the plant?

183. What part of the plant is the potato?

SCIENCE

184. What fried food do you eat that comes from the potato?

185. What crystalized substance do you add to a cookie recipe that comes from the sugarcane plant?

186. What are the lines on a leaf called that help carry water and food through the leaf: veins or vessels?

187. What four parts is the year divided into, each having specific weather conditions?

188. What is another name for the season of "fall?"

189. Are the seasons the same in all parts of the world?

190. In which season of the year do many leaves change color?

191. What activities do you do in the fall?

192. What activities do you do in the winter?

193. What activities do you do in the spring?

194. What activities do you do in the summer?

195. What is the name of a specific tree that stays green all year long?

196. What are trees often used for?

197. What things do we make from the wood from a tree?

198. What part of a tree does cork come from: the bark or the leaves?

199. What happens to wood when it gets wet: it shrinks or it decays?

200. What things in the house are made of wood?

201. If you sanded a piece of wood, would its surface be rough or smooth?

202. Why do you think an Evergreen is called an Evergreen?

203. Do Evergreens have leaves or needles?

204. What is the name for the spiny, leafless plant that grows in the desert?

205. What is the name for the hard material formed on the bottom of the sea that come in a variety of shapes, often form reefs, and is brightly colored?

206. What is the common name for the algae that grows in the ocean: seaweed or milkweed?

207. What is the name of the plant where you can see its large, floating leaf on top of a pond?

208. Are trees natural or man-made?

209. Does tree bark help protect a tree?

210. What color is the bark on a birch tree?

SCIENCE

211. What is the part of a tree or plant that is underground that we can't see?
212. Is pollution in the air natural or caused by humans?
213. Is pollution in the water natural or caused by humans?
214. Are buildings natural or man-made?
215. Do living things have different stages of growth?
216. What is one stage of an insect before it becomes a butterfly?
217. What does a tadpole grow into?
218. How do animals change as they grow?
219. Do some animals eat plants?
220. What is the name of the plant that eats animals: a Venus flytrap or a hemlock plant?
221. Do you have a pet?
222. What do you need to do to take care of it and help it live well?
223. Is a dog considered a wild animal or a domestic animal?
224. Is a lion a wild animal or a domestic animal?
225. What kinds of animals live in the forest?
226. What kinds of animals live on a farm?
227. What kinds of animals live in the ocean?
228. What kinds of animals live on or near a lake?
229. What do some fish have on their bodies that allow them to breathe: fins or gills?
230. What kinds of animals live in the wild in Africa?
231. Can you name an animal that lives on the continent of Australia?
232. What animals can you name that live on the continent of North America?
233. What animals can you name that have wings?
234. What animals can you name that have tails?
235. What animals can you name that have fins?
236. Which animal is known for having a spear-like snout and a large fin: a marlin or a barracuda?
237. What animals can you name that have shells?
238. What types of animals are most often considered pets?

SCIENCE

239. What do animals need to live and grow?

240. What body part does a fish have to help it move?

241. What body part does a bird have in order to fly?

242. What body part does a turtle have to help it hide or give it shelter?

243. What marking do you leave behind if you walked on wet sand?

244. When animals move on land, what marking do they leave behind?

245. What do humans need to live and grow?

246. What part of the body do humans use for the sense of sight?

247. Can we see light?

248. What part of the body do humans use for the sense of smell?

249. What part of the body do humans use for the sense of touch?

250. Can we feel heat?

251. Have you ever had a sunburn?

252. What can you apply to your skin to help prevent a sunburn?

253. What can we feel with using our sense of touch: texture or composition

254. Would the fur of a kitten feel soft or rough?

255. Would the scales on a fish feel soft or rough?

256. What part of the body do blind people use to read books in Braille, where each letter is represented by a series of bumps on the page?

257. What part of the body do humans use for the sense of hearing?

258. Can we hear sound?

259. Does sound travel?

260. Do you think that the speed of sound is faster or slower than the speed of light?

261. What is an example of a *loud* sound?

262. What is an example of a *soft* sound?

263. What part of the body do humans use for the sense of taste?

264. What foods taste sweet?

265. What foods taste sour?

SCIENCE

266. What food might taste spicy?
267. What is the weather like today?
268. What is moving air called?
269. Are there *clouds* in the sky today?
270. Are there different types of clouds?
271. What is it called when there are some clouds in the sky: overcast or partly cloudy?
272. What kind of drops are clouds made up of: ice and water, or snow and rain?
273. What weather front might be approaching if the clouds are black and it is windy?
274. What is rain called that comes down very lightly: a drizzle or a shower?
275. What is rain called that falls very heavily: a drizzle or a shower?
276. What are frozen raindrops called: sleet or hail?
277. What is the weather term when there is heavy rain, lightning, and thunder?
278. Where is a safe place to be during a lightning storm?
279. Where is a dangerous place to be during a lightning storm?
280. What precipitation falls in the winter if the temperature is low enough?
281. What is snow called when it falls very lightly?
282. What is the weather term for snow when it falls hard and heavy and it is very windy?
283. What type of flake is formed from ice crystals?
284. Are snowflakes alike or different?
285. How many sides does a snowflake have: 6 or 8?
286. Can you guess what the temperature is today?
287. What instrument do we use to measure the temperature?
288. Is the weather and temperature the same here as it is in other states?
289. What numerical measurement is measured in degrees on a thermometer changes with the seasons?
290. If the mercury in a thermometer is high, is it hot or cold?
291. If the mercury in a thermometer is low, is it hot or cold?
292. What is the weather like in our state in winter?
293. What type of clothing do you wear in the winter?

SCIENCE

294. What is the weather like in autumn?

295. What do you wear in autumn?

296. What happens to the leaves in autumn?

297. What is the weather like in spring?

298. What clothing do you wear in the spring?

299. What happens to leaves and plants in the spring?

300. What is the weather like in summer?

301. What do you wear in the summer?

302. After it rains and the Sun shines again, what spectrum of light taking the form of a multi-colored arc may be visible in the sky?

303. Can you name the colors of a rainbow? (ROY G BIV)

304. What is our principle source of energy?

305. What is the name of the energy emitted by the Sun: lunar or solar?

306. What is the name for the structure that creates energy when its blades rotate in the wind?

307. What is the name of the planet we live on?

308. Does the United States have a space exploration program?

309. What is the name given to the men and women that explore space?

310. What liquid covers 75% of the Earth?

311. What planets can you name?

312. What is the name for the large, round object that revolves around the Earth and shines at night by reflecting light from the Sun?

313. Does the Moon look the same every night, or does it take on have different shapes depending on how the Sun shines on it?

314. Which do you think is farther away: the Moon or the stars?

315. What is the name of the system that includes all objects like the moon, the planets, the stars, and galaxies that are held within the gravitational pull of the Sun?

316. What are some landforms found on the Earth's surface?

317. What covers most of the Earth: soil, water, or rocks?

318. What are the biggest bodies of water called?

SCIENCE

319. What are some things in nature that are round?

320. What are some things in nature that are hard?

321. What are some things in nature that are soft?

322. What are some things that are rough?

323. What are some things that are smooth?

324. What are some things in nature that are green?

325. What are some animals or things in nature that are heavy?

326. What are some animals or things in nature that are light in weight?

327. How does a person make a baby stroller move?

328. How does a person make a wagon move?

329. Can objects move in a straight line?

330. What is the movement of a swing: back and _?

331. If no one is on the swing of a swing set, is the swing at rest or in motion?

332. What happens to the swing if there is a breeze or wind that day?

333. What is the name for the large, round platform on a playground that goes round and round?

334. What animal or thing can you name that moves fast?

335. What animal or thing can you name that moves slow?

336. What is the name for the magnetic force that magnets produce: magnetic field or polar field?

337. What types of metals does a magnet attract: iron, nickel, and cobalt, or silver, gold, and platinum?

338. Would a magnet be attracted to paperclips or a plastic cup?

339. Would a magnet be attracted to a stainless steel refrigerator or a silver spoon?

340. Would a magnet be attracted to a metal lock or a gold bracelet?

341. What type of metal filings are often used to demonstrate the direction of a magnetic field: iron or copper?

342. How many poles does a magnet have: 2 or 4?

343. What happens when the *same* pole of two magnets are placed near each other: they will repel or they will attract?

344. What happens when the *opposite* pole of two magnets are placed near each other: they will repel or they will attract?

SCIENCE

345. Which do you think would *float* on water: a leaf or a stone?

346. Which do you think would *sink* in water: a beach ball or a bottle cap?

Science – 1st Grade

347. What is the name for the study of the land, air, and water on the Earth: Earth Science or Biology?

348. Are rocks, soil, and water the basic Earth materials?

349. What do we call rocks that have been broken down into tiny particles like dirt: soil or fertilizer?

350. What is the name for natural features on the Earth that are large rock landforms: mountains or valleys?

351. Are glaciers, cliffs, and volcanoes large rock landforms?

352. What is the name for the huge masses of dense ice that are found in the state of Alaska?

353. What are the mountains called that may emit molten lava?

354. What are some other landforms besides mountains on the Earth?

355. What is the name of an ocean?

356. What kind of water does an ocean have?

357. Do both plants and animals live in the ocean?

358. What are some other planets besides Earth?

359. What is the scientific term for the study of space: Astronomy or Astrology?

360. What astronomical objects are located in the sky?

361. Are airplanes and birds astronomical or celestial objects in the sky?

362. What are some changes that occur in the sky that you can observe?

363. Does the Earth rotate around the Sun, or does the Sun rotate around the Earth?

364. Does the Moon rotate around the Earth, or does the Earth rotate around the Moon?

365. Is the Earth flat or round?

366. What is the name of the first man to walk on the Moon: Neil Armstrong or Buzz Aldrin?

367. What is the name of an instrument that can help us see the moon more closely?

368. Can you see craters, mountains, and valleys on the Moon with a telescope?

369. What is the name of a famous scientist?

370. What is the name for the study of living things: chemistry or biology?

SCIENCE

371. What is an example of something a magnet would be attracted to?

372. Is it true that the bigger the magnet, the stronger the magnetic attraction?

373. Do like poles attract or repel?

374. Do unlike poles repel or attract?

375. What is an example of a living thing?

376. Do living things grow, develop, and reproduce?

377. Is an organism a living thing?

378. What is the final stage of human life: birth, infancy, childhood, adolescence, adulthood, Senior Citizen, and _?

379. What is the name of the third transformational stage of a butterfly, changes that we call metamorphosis: egg, caterpillar, __, and butterfly?

380. Are air, water, soil, and trees considered natural resources or landforms?

381. What are some ways to conserve these natural resources?

382. What is the natural source of heat and light for the Earth?

383. Can you sometimes see your shadow during the day?

384. When is your shadow taller: in the morning or in the late afternoon?

385. What time of day is your shadow the shortest: Noon or 3:00 PM?

386. Can a boat or any object that blocks light create a shadow?

387. What is the name of the instrument that is used to view living organisms: a magnifying glass or a microscope?

388. What is an example of a non-living thing?

389. Are plants and flowers living or non-living things?

390. What gas do plants produce that is good for the air: nitrogen or oxygen?

391. What is the effect on living things when the air becomes polluted with exhaust and factory smoke?

392. What are the parts of a plant?

393. What part of the plant helps it to gather water and other nutrients that it needs to grow?

394. What does a seed grow into?

395. What does a bulb grow into?

396. What does an acorn grow into?

SCIENCE

397. Can you name the four seasons?
398. Is the weather fairly predictable in each season?
399. Does the Sun warm the land, air, and water?
400. What is the term for the movement of air caused by differences in air pressure: breeze or wind?
401. What are breezes, gales, storms, and hurricanes all categorized as: wind or air currents?
402. What do sailboats rely on to move them forward?
403. What would a weather vane indicate: wind direction or wind speed?
404. Do kites, paper airplanes, wind socks, and wind chimes depend on land, air, or water?
405. What does windy weather help produce: electricity or solar wind?
406. What is the name of the device that weather forecasters use to help predict the weather: a radar or a sonar?
407. What might the radar tell you about the weather?
408. What might the thermometer tell you about the weather?
409. What might a severe storm turn into if a funnel cloud is present?
410. Where should you take shelter in the event of a severe storm or tornado?
411. What is the weather forecast for tomorrow, or how do you think it will be?
412. Do weather instruments like a radar, a thermometer, and a barometer help the weather people predict the weather?
413. What is matter made up of besides solids and liquids?
414. What is an example of matter that is in a solid state?
415. What is an example of matter that is in a liquid state?
416. What is an example of matter that is in a gas state?
417. How does water change properties, or turn into, when it freezes?
418. What happens to the ice on a lake when the temperature rises and it is very warm?
419. If water is boiled and the temperature increased, what vapor or gas does it form?
420. What is the term for the process by which matter may be converted from a liquid or solid state into a gas that rises into the air: evaporation or melting?
421. What do you think would evaporate quicker if left outside in the hot Sun: a dog's dish full of water, or a rain barrel full of water?

SCIENCE

422. Would you conclude that when substances are mixed, heated, or cooled, their properties change?

423. What do animals eat?

424. What sound does a cow (goat, horse, duck, chicken, cat, dog, hyena, frog, etc.) make?

425. What animals make a loud sound?

426. What animals make a soft sound?

427. Which animal makes the loudest recorded sound: the Blue Whale or the hyena?

428. Is the pitch of the sound an elephant or a hyena makes high or low?

429. Is the pitch of the sound a frog makes high or low?

430. Do you think that sound travels?

431. Which travels faster: the speed of sound or the speed of light?

432. Can you name an animal that might eat another animal?

433. Do birds eat worms?

434. Do large snakes eat rodents and other animals?

435. What is your favorite zoo animal?

436. What is your favorite farm animal?

437. What is your favorite sea animal?

438. What is your favorite circus animal?

439. Can you name two kinds of birds?

440. What is another animal besides a bird that has wings?

441. What animals can you name that have sharp teeth?

442. Do piranhas and Giant Tiger fish have razor-sharp teeth or dull teeth?

443. What kind of teeth do you think a Chainsaw Shark has?

444. Do baboons and hippos have long, sharp teeth?

445. Which animal may go through more than 2,000 teeth in its lifetime: an alligator or a crocodile?

446. Does a saber-toothed deer have two long front teeth or two short front teeth?

447. What do you think animals with flat teeth eat: plants or animals?

448. Do you still have all your baby teeth, or do you have some permanent teeth?

449. Why do you suppose you need bigger, stronger teeth as you get older?

SCIENCE

450. How many species of mammals are known to exist: more than 400, or more than 4000?

451. Can you name two mammals?

452. Are you a mammal or an amphibian?

453. Is a whale a mammal?

454. What is the name for the special kind of mammal that carries its young in a pouch like a kangaroo or a koala: marsupial or amphibian?

455. What is the name of the egg-laying mammal with a duck bill that is found in eastern Australia: the platypus or the wallaby?

456. What do dolphins, chimpanzees, pigs, and elephants have in common: they are all very smart, or they are all very large?

457. What body part does a giraffe have that is over 20 inches long and is used to clean its own ears?

458. What is the name for the class of animal that is cold-blooded, lays eggs, and its skin is covered in scales: reptiles or amphibians?

459. Can you name a reptile?

460. Which of the following is **not** a reptile: alligators, crocodiles, iguanas, snakes, frogs, turtles, and lizards?

461. What do lizards and snakes smell with: their nose or their tongue?

462. Do turtles and snakes have ears?

463. Which reptiles might someone have as a pet?

464. What is the name for the class of animal that lives part on land and part on water, hatches from an egg, and has webbed feet, gills and fins: reptiles or amphibians?

465. Can you name an amphibian?

466. Which of the following is **not** an amphibian: bullfrog, toad, snake, and salamander?

467. Can you name a fish?

468. What is the name for the animal that makes up 80% of the world's animals, has a thorax, an abdomen, and a head, has two antennae and three pairs of legs, and lays eggs: an ant or an insect?

469. Can you name an insect?

470. Which of the following is **not** an insect: butterfly, ant, grasshopper, fly, worm, bee, spider, mosquito, cockroach, and praying mantis?

471. Can you name an animal that jumps?

SCIENCE

472. Can you name an animal that slithers or slides?

473. Can you name an animal that runs fast?

474. Can you name an animal that flies?

475. Can you name an animal that swims?

476. Can you name an animal that hops?

477. Can you name an animal that hibernates, or goes to sleep during the cold months?

478. Do bumblebees, garter snakes, hedgehogs, snails, and bats hibernate?

479. What is an animal with a long neck?

480. What is an animal with a long trunk?

481. What is an animal with spots?

482. Do fawns and jaguars have spots or stripes?

483. What is an animal with stripes?

484. What is an animal with fur?

485. What is an animal with scales?

486. What is an animal with horns or antlers?

487. Do the physical features an animal help it to adapt to its environment?

488. What is the term for when a species no longer exists: extinct or endangered?

489. What is the term for when a species is in danger of no longer existing: extinct or endangered?

490. Can you name an animal that is now extinct, meaning it is no longer on Earth?

491. Are tigers, elephants, the Panda bear, American bison, and the gorilla considered endangered?

492. What is the name of the natural home where humans, plants and animals live: habitat or dwelling?

493. Are water, forest, desert, prairie, and underground examples of habitats or dwellings?

494. What liquid substance do humans, plants, and animals need to survive?

495. Besides water, what do animals need to survive?

496. Besides water, what do most plants need to survive?

497. What is the difference between day and night?

498. What is the purpose of doing an experiment: to prove something, or to collect data?

499. Is it good to always follow directions in order to be safe in a science lab?

SCIENCE

500. Are beakers, Bunsen burners, test tubes, petri dishes, microscopes, and chemicals found in a lab?

501. What would you wear in a science lab to protect your eyes?

502. Is it important to record data and observations when conducting an experiment to help you better understand the results?

503. What is a ruler used for?

504. Does looking at an organism through a microscope help you by magnifying it or shrinking it?

505. What does the red line on a thermometer tell you?

506. What is the name for the scientific device that has two pans, one for standard weights and the other to hold the mass to be weighed: a balance scale or a pendulum?

507. Does a magnifying glass make an image larger or smaller?

508. What is the name of the optical instrument that astronomers and others use to observe the stars and Moon: microscope or telescope?

509. Does the inquiry or exploring process of science involve observing, asking questions, and making predictions?

510. Can conducting experiments help you to arrive at a conclusion or hypothesis?

Science – 2nd Grade

511. Does the study of science include life science, physical science, and Earth science?

512. Is there a connection between science and math?

513. Does the study of physical science include matter and energy?

514. What state of matter is water an example of?

515. What state of matter is ice an example of?

516. What state of matter is steam an example of?

517. When water freezes, does it expand or contract?

518. What is the temperature in Celsius when water freezes: 0 or 32?

519. What is the temperature in Fahrenheit when water freezes: 0 or 32?

520. What is the temperature in Celsius when water boils: 100 or 212?

521. What is the temperature in Fahrenheit when water boils: 100 or 212?

522. What state of matter is water when it evaporates?

523. What might happen to a solid like plastic when it is heated?

SCIENCE

524. What metric liquid unit do large, plastic soda bottles often measure: 1 liter or 2 liters?

525. What metric unit of measurement is 100 centimeters equal to: 1 meter or 1 yard?

526. If the prefix centi- as in centimeters is equal to 100, how many years are in one century?

527. What is the metric unit that is close to the weight of a paper clip: 1.4 grams or 1.4 milligrams?

528. What is one thousand meters equal to: 1 millimeter or 1 kilometer?

529. Does the study of physical science include how force and motion work?

530. What object can demonstrate force and motion: weights or magnets?

531. Can magnets push and pull objects?

532. What are magnets made of that attracts metal objects: iron alloys or silver alloys?

533. What types of objects are attracted to magnets?

534. What are the names of the two poles of magnets: North and South, or East and West?

535. When two magnets attract, which two poles are pointing toward each other: the same or opposite?

536. When two magnets repel, which two poles are pointing toward each other: the same or opposite?

537. When you hold the two north poles of two magnets near each other, will they stick together?

538. What happens when you hold the south and the north poles of two magnets near each other?

539. In which direction does a needle on a compass always point: North or South?

540. Does gravity pull an object or a person toward the Earth or away from the Earth?

541. Does the Moon have gravity?

542. What is a necessary tool that you need in order to measure the length of something?

543. What tool do you need to measure the mass of something: a balance scale or a beaker?

544. What tool do you need to measure the volume of something: a graduated cylinder or a scale?

545. What do measuring cups measure: mass or volume?

546. What tool do you need to measure the weight of something?

547. What tool do you need to measure the temperature of something?

548. What is the average body temperature of a human being: 98.6 or 86.9?

549. Does life science include the study of living things that include people, plants and animals?

550. What is the term for the sequence of who eats whom within an ecosystem or a community: food chain or habitat?

SCIENCE

551. What does a food chain include besides producers: consumers or organisms?

552. How would you order the following animals based on the food chain: eagle, grasshopper, frog, and snake?

553. Can both plants and animals be part of the food chain?

554. Are most plants considered producers or consumers?

555. Are most animals considered producers or consumers?

556. What would worms, fungi, and bacteria be classified as, because they help put nutrients back into the soil: consumers or decomposers?

557. Does the life cycle of a living thing include birth, growth, reproduction, and death?

558. Do the basic needs of animals include food, shelter, and living space?

559. What are the basic needs of a plant?

560. What part of a plant are corn and peas examples of?

561. What part of a plant attracts bees because of its color and scent?

562. What part of a plant surrounds and protects the seeds while they are forming: flower or fruit?

563. What is the term for what bees do to help plants reproduce: spreads pollen or spreads nectar?

564. What gas do plants help provide, necessary for human survival: oxygen or carbon dioxide?

565. What living thing do paper, rubber, gum, and medicines originate from: plants or animals?

566. What can you name that come from plants?

567. What are some ways that adult animals protect their babies?

568. How might a bear protect its cubs?

569. Do most animals defend themselves and their young?

570. Can you give an example of a useful animal and explain why it is useful?

571. What are some examples of dangerous animals?

572. Do plants and animals all live in a specific habitat?

573. What animals might change their habitat in the winter?

574. What animals might live in a swamp or marshlands?

575. What habitat located in Central and South America is being destroyed by humans at a rapid rate: the rainforest or the marshlands?

576. What type of animals are warm-blooded and take care of their young: mammals and birds, or reptiles and amphibians?

SCIENCE

577. What is the term for the behavior that animals are born knowing how to do something: extinct or instinct?

578. Which of the following describes the body covering of mammals: skin, fur, scales, and feathers?

579. Are humans classified as mammals or vertebrates?

580. What is a bat classified as: a small mammal or a bird?

581. What insects can you name?

582. What is the third body part of an insect besides the thorax and the abdomen?

583. What do caterpillars become later in their life cycles?

584. What is the stage of a butterfly after the egg: caterpillar or chrysalis?

585. What must butterflies do to their wings after they emerge from the chrysalis before they can fly: dry them or flap them?

586. Do you know what the proper name is for the spider: anacondas or arachnids?

587. How many legs to spiders have: 6 or 8?

588. What is the term called when a bird or butterfly flies to the south to a warmer climate for the winter: migration or immigration?

589. What bird can you name that migrate to the south to a warmer climate each winter?

590. What is the name of the orange and black butterflies that migrate from Canada and the U.S. to Mexico every year?

591. What is the term for a series of events that happen in the same order with butterflies and frogs as they move through different stages of their lives: life cycle or metamorphosis?

592. What is the first stage of a frog's life?

593. What is the next stage of a frog's lifecycle after egg: tadpole or froglet?

594. What type of environment do tadpoles live in: water or land?

595. What kind of feet do frogs have that help them swim that toad's feet do not have?

596. What is the term for what frogs and bears do during the long winter: hibernate or migrate?

597. What is the place called where bears sleep in the winter: a pen or a den?

598. Which animal's dwelling is called a den: a beaver or a chipmunk?

599. What is the term for when animals blend into their surroundings: coloration or camouflage?

600. What must an animal do if the food supply is gone?

SCIENCE

601. What is the name of the big reptiles that lived millions of years ago?

602. What is the scientific term for something that is unproven, but that a scientist hopes to prove through experimentation and looking at data: theory or hypothesis?

603. What are some theories as to why dinosaurs disappeared?

604. Can you name something that might cause an animal to become extinct or die off?

605. What living things might you find in a pond habitat?

606. What living things might you find in a desert habitat?

607. What living things might you find in a forest habitat?

608. What color are many animals living in the Polar Regions?

609. What big habitats are oceans and rainforests known as: biomes or ecosystems?

610. Are biomes defined by the types of plants and animals that live there?

611. Do specific plants and animals live in a biome?

612. What are some plants and animals that live in the ocean biome?

613. What are some plants and animals that live in the rainforest biome?

614. Are some plants and animals considered producers?

615. Are some plants and animals considered consumers?

616. Does the study of Earth Science include how the Earth relates to the Sun, the Moon, the planets, the stars, and other objects in space?

617. What are some ways that scientists might explore space from the Earth?

618. What are some ways scientists might explore space away from the Earth?

619. What is the name of the tool other than binoculars that would help you see the stars or the planets more clearly, and would make them appear closer??

620. What objects in the sky can you identify?

621. Is it safe to look at the Sun with the naked eye?

622. What happens when you observe the Moon using a pair of binoculars?

623. What is a specific group of stars called: a galaxy or a constellation?

624. Can you name a constellation, a specific grouping of the stars?

625. Are the Big Dipper and the Little Dipper considered constellations?

626. Does the Earth move around the Moon, or does the Moon move around the Earth?

SCIENCE

627. Does the Earth revolve around the Sun, or does the Sun revolve around the Earth?

628. Is the Moon only visible from the Earth when it is reflecting the Sun's light?

629. What phase of the Moon would it be if the Earth is between the Sun and the Moon: New Moon or Full Moon?

630. What phase of the Moon would it be if the Moon is between the Sun and the Earth: New Moon or Full Moon?

631. Does the Earth revolve or rotate around the Sun?

632. Does the position of the Earth in relation to the Moon have an effect on the season and the weather?

633. What does the gravitational pull of the Moon create, affecting the rise and fall of the sea level in the oceans: tides or tidal waves?

634. Do the seasons affect the lives of people, animals, and plants?

635. How many hours does it take for the Earth to rotate one time on its axis: 12 hours or 24 hours?

636. How many days does it take for the Earth to revolve one time around the Sun?

637. If one side of the Earth is facing away from the Sun, would it be day or night in that part of the world?

638. If one side of the Earth is tilted toward the Sun, would it be day or night in that part of the world?

639. If the Earth's revolution around the Sun is at a point when it is farthest away from the Sun, what season would it be?

640. If the Earth's revolution around the Sun is at a point when it is closest to the Sun, what season would it be?

641. Because the Earth is revolving and rotating at the same time, do you think the seasons are the same or different in all parts of the world?

642. Do different seasons bring different kinds of weather?

643. What are some weather conditions you can name?

644. What do we call moving air?

645. What are snow, rain, sleet, and hail examples of: precipitation or condensation?

646. What is created when water changes into water vapor: condensation or steam?

647. What forms outside of windows when hot moist air rises and meets colder air: condensation or steam?

648. What is it called when there is a lack of rainfall for a long period of time?

SCIENCE

649. Can you name some instruments that help us to forecast or measure weather conditions?

650. What is the job of a meteorologist?

651. What is the name of the instrument that measures air temperature?

652. What is the name of the instrument that measures the amount of rainfall in an area?

653. What is the name of the scientific instrument that measures the amount of pressure in the atmosphere: barometer or anemometer?

654. What does an anemometer measure: rainfall or wind speed?

655. What kind of storm begins over warm ocean waters and causes a lot of damage when it moves inland bringing with it strong winds: hurricane or tidal wave?

656. Can changes in the atmosphere cause the weather to change?

657. Is the weather a temporary or permanent condition?

658. What is the weather like in our state in each of the seasons?

659. What is the term for the weather conditions that prevail in a certain region over a long period of time: climate or atmosphere?

660. Are climates defined by the weather conditions of that region?

661. Do the southern states generally have a warmer or cooler climate than the northern states?

662. What is the climate like in Alaska most of the year?

663. What is the climate like in Hawaii most of the year?

664. What is the climate like in our state for most of the year?

665. Do you think that Florida and many islands have a tropical climate?

666. Is a hurricane considered a tropical storm because it often occurs in the tropics, places with warm climates?

667. Is the date on the calendar the same even thought it might be a different season in another part of the world?

668. Is it possible to be summer here in the United States which is located in the northern hemisphere and winter in Argentina which is located in the southern hemisphere?

669. What imaginary line divides the northern and southern hemispheres?

670. Is the Earth constantly changing?

671. What is the term that describes the constant movement and change of water: life cycle or water cycle?

672. Which of the following are causes of weathering of the land: wind, water, ice, or pressure?

SCIENCE

673. What is it called when the land surface of the Earth wears away or breaks down: weathering or erosion?

674. What is the cause of most of Earth's erosion: flowing water or rainfall?

675. What could you plant that might help prevent the soil from washing away?

676. What is it term for the landform that forms at the mouth of a lake or river leading into the ocean or other large body of water: tributary of delta?

677. Are rocks and rock formations part of the study of Earth Science?

678. Are volcanoes and mountains important in the study of Earth Science?

679. What are rocks called that have an imprint of a leaf or small animal that proves the existence of plants and animals from many years ago?

680. What are wheels, levers, pulleys, wedges, ramps, axles, and screws all considered: simple machines or tools?

681. Is a hammer considered a wedge or a lever?

682. What thing on a playground that you slide down might be considered an inclined plane?

683. What is the scientific term for the process of asking and answering scientific questions through conducting research, constructing a hypothesis, conducting experiments, and drawing conclusions: scientific inquiry or scientific method?

684. Is the objective in scientific inquiry essentially the same as the scientific method?

Science – 3rd Grade

685. Does the study of science include Earth science, physical science, life science, biology, chemistry, astronomy, physics, ecology, and geology?

686. Do we often study science by testing, measuring, and experimenting?

687. Is the purpose of *scientific inquiry* to develop the ability to ask questions, investigate aspects of the scientific world around you, and use your observations in order to make reasonable explanations for the questions?

688. Are matter and energy important in the study of physical science?

689. Are force and motion important in the study of energy?

690. What are the three forms of matter?

691. What state of matter are hydrogen and oxygen examples of: liquids or a gases?

692. Can matter change from one state to another?

SCIENCE

693. How can water change from a liquid to a solid?

694. How can water change from a solid to a liquid?

695. How can water change from a liquid to a gas?

696. What is the term used when water is boiled and steam is created: vaporization or evaporation?

697. What is the smallest part of any material called: an atom or a cell?

698. What are the tiny particles called that make every object unique and are made of combinations of atoms: molecules or cells?

699. What are heat, light, and sound all forms of: energy or electricity?

700. What type of energy does the Sun provide?

701. Can sources of heat include both chemical and electrical?

702. What occurs when objects rub against each other: friction or force?

703. Can friction slow down or speed up objects that rub against each other?

704. Is friction a source of heat?

705. When you create friction by rubbing two sticks together, what heat source does it create?

706. What is created when a warmer object comes in contact with a cooler object: heat or friction?

707. Does the warm object lose heat and the cool object gain heat until both are the same temperature?

708. How does light, a form of energy, travel to reach its surroundings: in waves or in a straight line?

709. Is the speed of light 186,000 miles per minute, or 186,000 miles per second?

710. Can light waves pass through air, water, and glass?

711. Does a ray of light travel in a straight line or a curved line if it does not pass through a medium?

712. Can light create shadows?

713. Does the Sun's light create different shadows at different times of the day?

714. What is the name of the light that comes from the Sun: white light or prism light?

715. Is the white light from the Sun made up of all the colors in the rainbow or just white?

716. What is the name of the clear glass wedge that converts white light into all the colors of the rainbow: a mirror or a prism?

717. If something does not allow light to pass through it, do we consider it to be opaque or transparent?

718. What is an example of an object that is opaque: a wooden door or a window?

SCIENCE

719. What is an example of an object that is transparent: a tin can or a window?

720. What is the name of an object in which you can see yourself in and reflects light?

721. Is your image in a mirror exact or is it reversed?

722. What kind of mirrors curve inward like mirrors in a fun-house and make images appear larger: concave or convex?

723. What kind of mirrors are curved outward like Christmas tree ornaments that make images appear smaller called: concave or convex?

724. What is it called when light passes through a prism and it slows down and changes direction: reflection or refraction?

725. What colorful object in the sky is the result of raindrops in the sky refracting light and separating into all the colors of a spectrum?

726. What are the 7 colors of the rainbow?

727. What is the "name" we can give to the rainbow spectrum to help us remember all of the colors in order?

728. What are some things besides the Sun that give us light?

729. Do our eyes need light in order to see?

730. What are the cornea, pupil, iris, lens, and retina all parts of?

731. What color is your "iris" or colorful part of your eye?

732. Do we see things when light passes through the lens of ours eye and creates an image on the retina, or the back of the eyeball?

733. What might you need if the lens of your eye does not focus very sharply?

734. What is a person's eyesight if they can see things well that are close-up, but need glasses to see things far away: nearsighted or farsighted?

735. What is a person's eyesight if they can see things well that are far away, but need glasses to see things close-up or to read: nearsighted or farsighted?

736. What is the name given to the type of glasses that are used by people that help them see both close-up and far away: trifocals or bifocals?

737. What is a tool that has lenses and uses light to help us see things that are not visible to the naked eye like cells: a magnifying glass or a microscope?

738. What is the name of the tool that has special lenses that help us see celestial objects in the sky like the moon, stars, comets, and some planets: a telescope or binoculars?

SCIENCE

739. Do magnifying glasses, binoculars, and eyeglasses have special lenses that help you to see things bigger and more clearly?

740. What it is called when you use a microscope, telescope, or binoculars to make objects appear larger than they are: amplify or magnify?

741. Which is faster: the speed of light or the speed of sound?

742. What is the speed of light: 186,000 miles per hour or 186,000 miles per second?

743. What is the speed of sound: 186,000 miles per hour or 767 miles per hour?

744. Are you increasing or decreasing the sound's intensity if you turn up the volume on the radio?

745. What are sounds caused by: vibrations or sound waves?

746. What is the term for the rate at which vibrations are produced, and can be either low or high: intensity or pitch?

747. What is vibrating air called: sound waves or pitch?

748. Can sound travel through gases, solids, and liquids?

749. Does sound travel faster or slower though water?

750. What is the name of the mammal in the ocean that can sing underwater and can be heard from a mile away?

751. Is *pitch* how high or how low a sound is?

752. Can sound cause objects to vibrate?

753. What might happen to a glass if someone sings in a really high pitch?

754. What tool can you use to amplify a sound or make it louder?

755. What is the musical instrument that has a low pitch sound: the flute or the tuba?

756. What is the musical instrument that has a high pitch sound: the flute or the tuba?

757. When you make a sound, what part of your body do you feel vibrations: your larynx in your throat or your tongue in your mouth?

758. When you hear sound, what part of your ear do the sound waves travel through to reach your eardrum and make it vibrate: your outer ear or your ear canal?

759. Is your larynx also called your "voice box?"

760. What is the name for the study of sound waves: acoustics or audiology?

761. What is the term for the change in the position of an object with respect to time: motion or direction?

762. What part of a wave is the crest: the bottom or the top?

SCIENCE

763. Is the trough the opposite of the crest, the lowest part of the wave?

764. What is the name for distance between one crest to the next crest: wave length or wave height?

765. Do the three forms of motion include velocity, acceleration, and force?

766. What is the term for the measurement of the rate and direction of change of an object: velocity or acceleration?

767. What is the term for the rate of change of velocity over a period of time, as in the rate at which something speeds up or slows down: acceleration or velocity?

768. What is the term for the push or pull of an object that causes it to undergo a change in speed or direction: force or acceleration?

769. Does force cause change when you push or pull something?

770. What is the term for an object's resistance to a change in motion: inertia or resistance?

771. What is it called when force that is applied to an object moves that object: motion or work?

772. What are a hammer, a screwdriver, a pliers, and a wrench considered: simple tools or wedges?

773. What would a pulley, ramp, shovel, wedge, wheel, lever, ramp, axle, and screw be: simple machines or complex machines?

774. What would a nail, chisel, ax, and doorstop be examples of: wedges or inclined planes?

775. What would be a slide, a ramp, a ladder, and an escalator be examples of: wedges or inclined planes?

776. What would a flagpole mechanism, and a rope used to bring up well water be examples of: pulleys or axles?

777. What would a helicopter blade, a boat propeller, a hose nozzle, and a jar lid be examples of: screws or wheels?

778. What would a car tire, bike pedal, and door knob be examples of: wheel and axle, or screws?

779. What would a seesaw, crowbar, hammer, and a bottle opener be examples of: wedges or levers?

780. What are some examples of forces in nature that can change the Earth?

781. What happens to the size of rocks when they break down or are weathered by wind and water?

782. What are the solid pieces of matter called that settle to the bottom of a liquid: soil or sediment?

783. What do rocks become that have been broken down slowly over time by the freezing and melting of water: sediment or soil?

784. What is the dark, organic soil called that has completely broken down as much as it possibly can break down: humus or compost?

SCIENCE

785. What is the name of the soil that is composed of sand, silt, and clay and has a lot of nutrients: loam or humus?

786. What is the name of the small, soft plants that often grow in clumps on rocks in shady areas: sediment or moss?

787. What is the decayed matter called that becomes part of the soil: sediment or humus?

788. What do plants need from the soil to grow: sediments or nutrients?

789. What might farmers do with their crops every few years to replace any nutrients in the soil that might be lost: rotate them or fertilize them?

790. What are materials called that are used over and over again: recycled or refurbished?

791. Does energy include electrical, heat, mechanical, chemical, gravitational, and nuclear?

792. Would renewable sources of energy include water, Sun, and wind?

793. What is an example of a *wind* structure that can provide us with energy?

794. What is an example of something that would provide us with *solar* energy?

795. Can a hydroelectric plant that uses a dam to collect and preserve water be used for energy by converting the water into electricity?

796. Would non-renewable sources of energy include oil, coal, and natural gas?

797. What is the natural wearing down or breaking apart of rocks called: weathering or erosion?

798. What is the name of the force that creates the shaking of sliding of the Earth's crust: an earthquake or a hurricane?

799. What is the name of the tool that measures the intensity of an Earthquake: a scale or a seismograph?

800. Is the Earth's crust located on the outside or the inside?

801. What is the name of the layer beneath the Earth's crust: the mantle or the outer core?

802. What is the inner-most layer of the Earth called: the outer core or the inner core?

803. Which layer is the thickest layer of the Earth: the crust or the mantle?

804. Which layer is the thinnest layer of the Earth: the crust or the inner core?

805. Which layer of the Earth is make of water, basalt, granite, rocks, and soil: the mantle or crust?

806. What is it called when the Earth's crust is changed because the soil is moved by the wind: erosion or weathering?

807. What is the name of the mountain that acts as a vent in the Earth's crust, and allows hot lava, ashes, and gases to escape?

SCIENCE

808. What is the name given to the magma that has erupted from a volcano: molten lava or ash?

809. What is it called when a volcano releases lava, ash, and rocks: an explosion or an eruption?

810. Are habitats and biomes part of the study of life and environmental science?

811. What is another name for habitat that includes plants, animals, soil, and climates: biomes or communities?

812. Are biomes also considered ecosystems?

813. Which of the following would **not** be considered a biome or ecosystem: freshwater, desert, rainforest, marine, tundra, savanna, Taiga forest, Coral reef, wetland, canyon, wetlands, and grasslands?

814. Do plants and animals live in distinct biomes?

815. What is the name of the biome that is a large, flat area of land with grassy plains and scattered trees, and are especially abundant in Africa: savanna or desert?

816. Do lions, zebras, and elephants live in the savannas of Africa?

817. In which biome do turtles, fish, herons, salamanders, beavers, snakes, alligators, wrens, otter, snapping turtles, cranes, geese, falcons, marsh hawks, mink, zebra butterflies, and bullfrogs live: the wetlands or the grasslands?

818. In which biome do bison, lions, zebras, antelope, elephants, giraffes, fox, rhinoceros, wolves, ostriches, prairie dogs, hawks, grasshoppers, and monarch butterflies live: the grasslands or desert?

819. What are grasslands called in the United States: prairies or savannas?

820. What are grasslands called in Africa: prairies or savannas?

821. What are grasslands called in South America: plains or pampas?

822. Where are marshes, swamps, and bogs located: in wetlands or in grasslands?

823. Which biome is the coldest, and is the area of land that is located high in the mountains above the tree line: the Alpine tundra or the Taiga forest?

824. In what biome do butterflies, frogs, toucans, monkeys, anacondas, hummingbirds, and jaguars live: the Taiga forest or the rainforest?

825. In which biome do rabbits, coyotes, tortoises, hedgehogs, prairie dogs, roadrunners, scorpions, tarantulas, and rattlesnakes live: the tundra or the dessert?

826. In which biome do polar bears, reindeer, walruses, seals, and snowy owls live: the Arctic tundra or the Alpine tundra?

827. In which biome do penguins, seals, and killer whales live: Arctic or Antarctic?

SCIENCE

828. Is the Arctic biome located at the North Pole or the South Pole?

829. Is the Antarctic biome located at the North Pole or the South Pole?

830. In which biome do sheep, mountain goats, elk, and grasshoppers live: the Arctic tundra or the Alpine tundra?

831. In which biome do fish, coral, jellyfish, octopus, sharks, starfish, stingray, and plankton live: the Coral reef, or in lakes?

832. What is the name of the fish that is made up of over 90% water: the jellyfish or the stingray?

833. In which large biome do the Hawk owl, loon, beaver, squirrel, lynx, moose, Snowshoe rabbit, and wolverine live: the Arctic or the Antarctic?

834. In which dry biome do cacti, tumbleweeds, and yucca plants live?

835. Which is the largest desert in the desert biome: the Arabian in Saudi Arabia, or the Sahara in Africa?

836. Which polar desert is the world's largest desert with over 5.5 million square miles of snow, ice, and bedrock: the Arctic or Antarctica?

837. In which tropical biome do orchids, fig trees, ferns, bamboo, and coconut trees live: the rainforest or the Taiga forest?

838. In which biome are pond lilies, cattails, thistles, milkweed, grasses, and wildflowers abundant: the freshwater wetlands or the rainforest?

839. In which large biome do kelp, seaweed, algae, and coral live: freshwater or marine?

840. In which remote frigid biome do mosses, lichens, and algae live: the tundra or the rainforest?

841. What is the name for the permanent, frozen layer of soil that characterizes the tundra biome: frozen glaze or permafrost?

842. What is the name of the *largest* biome in the world that covers a portion of Canada, Europe, and Asia: the rainforest or the Taiga?

843. What is another name for the Taiga forest biome, so named because of the many trees that are located in this biome: coniferous forest or glacier forest?

844. Does the Taiga biome have cold winters and rainy summers, or warm winters and cold summers?

845. Are many of the trees of the Taiga conifers, which have needles and produce cones in the winter?

846. What is the name of the conifer that covers much of the Taiga and stays green all year long?

847. What is the name for the study of organisms and the environment they live in: ecology or biology?

848. Are plants and animals interdependent or dependent on one another in a specific biome?

849. What is the word, similar to biome that describes where organisms live: ecosystem or habitat?

SCIENCE

850. Could a polar bear survive in a very warm climate?

851. Could a desert iguana survive in Alaska?

852. Is an ecosystem similar to environment?

853. Does an ecosystem describe a system that provides life for a specific group of living things?

854. Can humans alter the ecosystem in that they may hunt certain animals and affect the herd numbers of that animal?

855. Does the food chain in a biome include plants and animals that are producers, consumers, and decomposers?

856. What are living things called that make their own food: producers or consumers?

857. Are plants considered producers or consumers?

858. What can plants produce by using the light energy from the Sun: food or water?

859. Are animals considered producers or consumers?

860. Are you a producer or consumer?

861. What are animals called that eat only plants: herbivores or carnivores?

862. What do you think wolves are: carnivores or herbivores?

863. Are deer carnivores or herbivores?

864. Is the word "herb" as in **herb**ivore a type of plant?

865. What are animals called that eat only meat: herbivores or carnivores?

866. Does the word "carni" sound like carne, the Spanish word for meat?

867. What are animals called that eat both plants and animals: omnivores or herbivores?

868. What are human beings, because we eat both plants *and* animals: omnivores or herbivores?

869. Are bacteria and fungi considered producers or decomposers because they eat dead plants and animals?

870. Can you name an organism that is considered a producer?

871. Can you name an organism that is considered a consumer?

872. Can you name an organism that is classified as a carnivore?

873. Can you name an organism that is classified as an herbivore?

874. What are parsley, sage, rosemary, and thyme: herbs or spices?

875. Can you name an organism that is classified as an omnivore?

SCIENCE

876. Where do all living things get their energy from: food or the Sun?

877. What do producers, consumers, and decomposers make up: the life cycle or the food chain?

878. Do food chains make a complete circle, or do they stop after a plant or animal dies?

879. In a food chain, is energy passed from plant to animal to animal to decomposer and then back to the plant again?

880. How would you explain the following food chain: grass, grasshopper, mouse, snake, and eagle?

881. Is there a "balance" in nature?

882. What do houses, burrows, holes, hives, dens, lodges, nests, caves, water, webs, and tree trunks describe?

883. What element do plants produce that animals depend on for survival: carbon dioxide or oxygen?

884. Can you name some common plants?

885. Can you name some common trees?

886. Can you name some common flowers?

887. Can you name some common birds?

888. What must many birds do because they need to change their physical environment for survival?

889. What is it called when birds fly south to a warmer climate for the cold winter: migration or immigration?

890. What do beavers, North America's largest rodent, build that may affect the physical environment: dens or dams?

891. What is the largest native land mammal in North America whose face is on a Buffalo nickel: bison or elk?

892. What is another term for American buffalo, the heaviest land animal in North America: oxen or bison?

893. What is the classification of animals that have a backbone like mammals, fish, birds, reptiles, and amphibians: vertebrates or invertebrates?

894. What is the classification of animals with no backbone like centipedes, flatworms, spiders, jellyfish, and octopuses: vertebrates or invertebrates?

895. Are vertebrates living things that have a backbone?

896. Are invertebrates living things that do *not* have a backbone?

897. Are jellyfish, crab, and sponge classified as vertebrates or invertebrates?

898. Are reptiles, amphibians, and fish cold-blooded animals where their body temperature changes

SCIENCE

depending on the temperature around them, or warm-blooded animals where their body temperature stays the same regardless of the air temperature?

899. Are mammals and birds classified as warm-blooded animals or cold-blooded animals?

900. Are you warm-blooded or cold-blooded?

901. What is the normal body temperature of warn-blooded human beings: 98.6 or 68.9?

902. What species of animals are cold-blooded, live partly on land and partly on water, have moist skin and gills, and include salamanders, toads, and frogs?

903. What is the name of the largest frog in North America that can grow up to 8 inches long, and has a deep croak: the tree frog, or the bullfrog?

904. What species of animals are warm-blooded, have wings and feathers, breathe with their lungs, can fly, lay eggs, and include cardinals, robins, eagles and chickens?

905. What kind of birds are eagles, falcons, hawks, and buzzards: birds of prey or migrating birds?

906. What species of animals are cold-blooded, breathe with their lungs, have thick skin, hatch from eggs, and include lizards, turtles, and snakes?

907. What is the name of the reptile that is the most abundant in the world today: the turtle or the snake?

908. What species of animals are warm-blooded, breathe with their lungs, have hair on their bodies, produce milk, can live on land or water, and include cats, dogs, monkeys, and human beings?

909. What are the two big ocean animals that are classified as mammals because they breathe through their lungs and swim underwater, although they come to the surface to breathe air?

910. What is a baby dog called?

911. What is a baby cat called?

912. What is a baby duck called: a goose or a duckling?

913. What is a baby goose called: a gosling or a chick?

914. What is a baby chicken called: a chick or a hen?

915. What is a baby cow called: a calf or a heifer?

916. What is a baby bear called: a cub or a kitten?

917. What is a baby kangaroo, baby koala, or baby wallaby called: a calf or a joey?

918. What class are kangaroos, possums, koalas, and the Tasmanian devil: marsupials or amphibians?

919. What is a baby whale called: a calf or a foal?

920. What is a baby horse called: a colt or a foal?

SCIENCE

921. What is a baby male horse called: a colt or a filly?

922. What is a baby female horse called: a colt or a filly?

923. What is a baby pig called: a piggy or a piglet?

924. What is a baby deer called: a fawn or a pup?

925. What is a baby lion called: a cub or a pup?

926. What is a baby turtle called: a hatchling or a tortoise?

927. What is a baby rabbit called: a bunny or a hare?

928. What is a baby ape called: a monkey or a baby?

929. What is a baby monkey called: an infant or a kid?

930. What is a baby bumblebee called: larva or wasp?

931. What is a baby fly called: a mosquito or a maggot?

932. What is a baby spider called: a spiderling or a maggot?

933. What is a baby frog or toad called: a froglet or a tadpole?

934. What is a baby goat called: a kid or a calf?

935. What is a baby sheep called: a kid or a lamb?

936. What is a baby grasshopper called: a nymph or a polliwog?

937. What is the name of the group that deer, cattle, horses, buffalo, elephants, zebras, and antelope travel in: pack or herd?

938. What is the name of the group that wolves, dogs, and coyotes travel in: pack or herd?

939. What is the name of the group that birds, ostriches, seagulls, and geese travel in: pack or flock?

940. What is the name of the group that sharks and other fish travel in: schools or groups?

941. What is the name of the group that bees and wasps travel in: droves or swarms?

942. What is the name of the group that whales travel in: a pack or a pod?

943. What is the name of a female human: a girl or a boy?

944. What is the name of a male human: a girl or a boy?

945. What is the name of a female chicken: a hen or a rooster?

946. What is the name of a male chicken: a hen or a rooster?

947. What is the name of a male pig: a sow or a boar?

SCIENCE

948. What is the name of a female pig: a sow or a boar?

949. What is the name of a male buffalo: bull or cow?

950. What is the name of female cattle and buffalo: bulls or cows?

951. What is the name of a male deer: buck or doe?

952. What is the name of a female deer: doe or stag?

953. What is the name of an adult male horse: stallion or mare?

954. What is the name of an adult female horse: mare or filly?

955. Which adult bee is the "queen:" the male or the female?

956. What is the name of the warm-blooded vertebrate animals that have feathers and hollow bones, most of which can fly?

957. Are the peacock and peahen together called "peafowl?"

958. Which is the male: the peacock or the peahen?

959. Which peafowl has the long green, blue, and yellow flowers with black in the middle: the peacock or the peahen?

960. What is the largest, and fastest-running bird two-legged bird on the Earth that lays the largest eggs: the flamingo or the ostrich?

961. What is the name of the black and white bird that has waterproof feathers, waddles rather than flies, and lives in the Antarctic biome?

962. What is the name of the bird that makes a "humming" sound, and has wings that beat up to 75 times per second?

963. What is the name of the soft-bodied animal that lives in a shell, inside of which grains of sand may be encrusted to form a pearl: oysters or crabs?

964. What is the name of the large, herbivorous mammal with a mouth that can open 4 feet wide, lives in Africa, runs extremely fast in spite of its short stature, spends much of the time in the water, and can weigh up to 10,000 pounds: rhinoceros or hippopotamus?

965. What is the tallest land animal that lives in Africa?

966. What is the fastest land animal that is spotted, lives in Africa, and can run up to 65 miles per hour: the leopard or the cheetah?

967. What animal is considered to be the biggest land animal that is either African or Asian?

968. What is the name of the animal that lives in forests or grasslands, swings by its long arms and legs, and often hangs by its tail?

SCIENCE

969. What are monkeys and apes classified as: primates or gorillas?

970. What is the name of the "clever" or "sly" hunting mammal with big ears and a bushy tail that carried the "Gingerbread Man" across the pond?

971. Are cows are herbivores or carnivores?

972. What food product do we use that comes from cattle?

973. What is the name of the fast-running omnivore that has very sharp senses, a bushy tail, is known for its singing and howling, and is similar to a wolf: a coyote or a dingo?

974. What nocturnal animal sleeps during the day while hanging upside down, eats insects, provides milk to its young, and is regarded as the only mammal capable of flight?

975. Is a bat a mammal or a bird?

976. What nocturnal animal has a large head and large eyes, hunts at night, makes a 'hooting' sound, and is considered very "wise?"

977. What is the name of the bright-colored tropical bird that lives in the rainforest, and has the ability to mimic words?

978. What is the name of the pigeon-like bird that is considered a symbol of peace: dove or seagull?

979. What is the state bird of our state?

980. What is the state animal of our state?

981. Which bird of prey is a symbol of freedom in the United States?

982. What is the name of a jet-black bird that is related to the raven and makes a "caw" sound?

983. Can you name a pink bird that has two very long legs and can stand on one leg at a time?

984. What is the name of a domestic bird that we may eat?

985. Which rodent has genes most similar to human beings: the rat or the guinea pig?

986. What is the classification of caterpillars, bees, locusts, crickets, flies, mosquitoes, beetles, and butterflies?

987. What stage does a butterfly start out as: an egg or a larva?

988. What is the second state in the butterfly cycle after the egg: a caterpillar or pupa?

989. What is another name for the pupa stage: larva or chrysalis?

990. What insect hatches out of a chrysalis?

991. What is the name of the black and orange butterflies that migrate south to Mexico?

992. How many legs do insects have?

SCIENCE

993. How many legs does a spider have?

994. Are the three body parts of insects, the head, the thorax, and the abdomen?

995. What is the name of the "buzzing" insect that eats nectar and pollen from flowers?

996. What edible product do bees produce from the nectar they collect?

997. Which bumblebee is the queen and lays the eggs: the male or the female?

998. What is the name of the "house" where bees live?

999. What is the name of the "house" that a mountain lion, fox, wolf, bear, or a beaver lives in?

1000. What is the name of the community where ants live: a colony or a hill?

1001. What is the word used to describe the group that bees travel in?

1002. Which insects may go through a metamorphosis, changing from egg, pupa, larva, and adult?

1003. Does a mosquito go through a three or four-stage life cycle?

1004. What does "mosquito" translate to in Spanish: bee or small fly?

1005. What is the name of the fly that lights up?

1006. Which amphibian that begins as a tadpole catches bugs with its long, sticky tongue?

1007. What is the name of the "wooly" animal, abundant in South America, that has its fur shaved in order to make woolen textiles, and has been known to spit at predators?

1008. What is the name of the carnivorous spotted animal living in the Sahara desert of Africa that is known for making a laughing sound: hyena or an orangutan?

1009. What is the name of the herbivorous mammal that may have one hump or two, lives in the desert, and can go up to 5 days without water which is stored in its humps?

1010. What is the name of the flat-footed mammal that lives in forests or grasslands, and include brown, black, panda, polar, sloth, and grizzly?

1011. Which bear, native to China, is on the endangered list: the Giant Panda or the Asiatic bear?

1012. What is the main food source of the Giant Panda, often eating more than 50 pounds of it per day: bamboo or eucalyptus?

1013. Which is the largest of the bears: the polar bear or the black bear?

1014. What is the term for what bears do in the winter inside caves or dens?

1015. Is hibernation a way that some animals adapt to their environment?

1016. Are koala bears, native to Australia, considered bears or marsupials?

SCIENCE

1017. What is the main food source of the koala bear: bamboo or eucalyptus?

1018. Are hibernating squirrels, ground hogs, raccoons, skunks, and bears warm or cold-blooded?

1019. Are hibernating snakes, turtles, frogs, worms, and bees warm or cold-blooded?

1020. What is the name of the nocturnal African animal that looks like a pig, has rabbit-like ears, a long nose, a kangaroo tail, and eats insects: anteater or aardvark?

1021. What is the name of the Central and South animal mammal that has short ears, a long snout, and uses its long sticky tongue to eat ants: anteater or aardvark?

1022. What is the name of the South American animal that is the only mammal covered with a hard shell, sleeps most of the day in its burrow, eats insects and ants with its sticky tongue, curls into a ball relying on its armored plated shell to protect it from danger, and is considered endangered: armadillo or tortoise?

1023. What is the name of the nocturnal animal that is known for digging tunnels, has a black and white face, a stocky body with short legs and sharp claws, sleeps most of the day in its den, digs faster than any other mammal, is a ferocious fighter, and is Wisconsin's state animal: badger or weasel?

1024. What is the name of the North American herbivore that is part of the squirrel family, is also known as a woodchuck, hibernates in the winter in its burrow, is a great digger, and is famous for predicting the arrival of spring after emerging from its den in February?

1025. What is the name of the stocky nocturnal animal that lives in woodland areas, is known for its mask-like face that makes it look like a bandit, has sharp claws and a bushy ringed tail, is an omnivore that prefers to wash its food before eating it, hibernates in the winter in its den, and has excellent night vision?

1026. What is the name of the nocturnal woodland animal that has black and white stripes, is also known as a polecat, and is commonly known for the smelly chemical that it sprays up to 12 feet when it feels threatened?

1027. What is the name of the nocturnal mammal that is similar to a hedgehog, is considered to be one of the world's largest rodents, and is known for having thousands of prickly long spikes called quills that cover its body and helps to protect it from predators?

1028. What is the name of the rodent animal that can live on land or on water, has a large flat tail that acts as a rudder in the water, has sharp front teeth that never stop growing that it uses to cut down trees, can swim underwater up to 15 minutes, and lives in a house called a lodge after building a strong dam in a canal out of mud and sticks: beaver or weasel?

1029. What is the name of the prehistoric reptiles that translate as "terrible lizards" in Greek, were hatched from eggs, and were the dominating animal on Earth millions of years ago during the "Mesozoic Era" until a mysterious mass extinction occurred?

1030. What is the name of the large plant-eating dinosaur that translates as "roofed lizard," lived near the

SCIENCE

end of the Jurassic Period, had thick legs like an elephant, a small brain, a spiked tail, and had triangular plates on its back: Stegosaurus or Brontosaurus?

1031. What is the name of the carnivorous dinosaur that translates as "king of the tyrant lizards" in Greek, lived over 70 million years ago near the end of the Cretaceous Period, had a huge head, huge tail, short but powerful arms with clawed fingers, a huge skull, long blade-like teeth, weighed up to 7 tons, was over 13 feet tall and 43 feet long, could eat over 500 pounds of meat in a single bite, and its fossil skeletal body "Sue" is on display in the Field Museum of Natural History in Chicago: Brontosaurus or Tyrannosaurus Rex?

1032. What is the name of the herbivorous dinosaur that translates as "three horned face" in Greek, lived in the United States and Canada near the end of the Cretaceous Period, weighed 12 tons, was 7 feet tall and 30 feet long, had a large head and tail, and 3 horns on one of the largest skulls of any land animal: Triceratops or Brachiosaurus?

1033. How can weather conditions like drought or flood affect the habitat of living things?

1034. What is the term for the state of the atmosphere with specific conditions: weather or climate?

1035. What is the term for the average pattern of temperature, pressure, and precipitation: weather or climate?

1036. What is the name of the person who forecasts the weather: forecaster or meteorologist?

1037. What is the general term for moisture that falls to the ground in the form of rain, hail, sleet, or snow: precipitation or condensation?

1038. What is the name for the water vapor that *condenses* on a cool surface?

1039. What visible masses of liquid droplets in the sky are formed by the condensation of water vapor?

1040. What type of high cloud looks thin and wispy, composed of tiny pieces of ice: stratus or cirrus?

1041. What is the name for the white, puffy cloud that resembles floating cotton: cumulus or cirrus?

1042. What type of cloud look like sheets or layers that are spread across the sky: stratus or cumulus?

1043. What is the name for the form of precipitation that falls when water droplets condense and become too heavy to float?

1044. What is the name given to the cirrus clouds that form very close to the surface of the Earth, reducing visibility?

1045. Where does most of the Earth's water exist: in the clouds or in the oceans?

1046. What is it called when rain is affected by industrial pollution: acid rain or black rain?

1047. What might be an environmental threat to a habitat or biome: oil drilling or a light storm?

1048. What poses a threat to the environment because it can contaminate the land and the air: chemical run-off from industry and agriculture, or deforestation?

SCIENCE

1049. What is the term for the combination of the pollutant that combines smoke with fog, found in many industrialized cities like Los Angeles?

1050. What is the effect on the environment due to car engine exhaust, factory smoke stacks, fires, and oil production: smog or black rain?

1051. If we destroy a part of the rainforest that might be the habitat of a specific plant or animal, what effect might that have on the plant or animal?

1052. How much of the Earth's surface is covered with water: 50% or 75%?

1053. If you live in the country, what might be the source of the water supply: a lake or an underground well?

1054. If you live in the city, what might be the source of the water supply: a lake or an underground well?

1055. Can water be polluted by fertilizers and other chemicals?

1056. What is the term for something found in nature that is used by people for some specific purpose: natural resources or environmental resources?

1057. Which of the following would **not** be considered a natural resource: air, water, animals, plants, weather, and fossil fuels?

1058. Which three of the following are considered **non**-renewable energy sources called fossil fuels: coal, oil, water, and gas?

1059. Is it important for us to take steps to protect the environment and our natural resources?

1060. What is the term that describes the makeup of the body, and includes skeletal, respiratory, digestive, circulatory, nervous, muscular, reproductive, and immune: structures or systems?

1061. What is the name of bone system in humans and animals?

1062. How many bones make up the human body: 106 or 206?

1063. What is the biggest bone in the human body: the tibia leg bone or the femur thigh bone?

1064. Where is the location of the smallest bone in your body, the stirrup: inside your nose or inside your ear?

1065. What is the name given to the boney framework of the head that serves to form the face and protect the brain?

1066. What is the name that refers to the backbone, and is made up of 24 vertebrae: spinal column or backbone?

1067. What is the name of the place where two bones join together in the body: joint or ligament?

1068. What is the name of the joint in the middle of your arm?

SCIENCE

1069. What is the name of the joint in the middle of your leg?

1070. What is the name of the joint that connects the arm with the hand?

1071. What is the name of the joint that connects the leg with the foot?

1072. Are shoulders and hips considered joints or ligaments?

1073. What is the name of the bone that connects your legs to your hips: pelvis or tailbone?

1074. What is the name of the stretchy tissue that help to hold bones together: muscles or ligaments?

1075. What is the name of the elastic, connective tissue that helps prevent bones from rubbing together in your knee: ligaments or cartilage?

1076. What is the name of the bone cage that helps protect your heart and lungs: the spinal column or the rib cage?

1077. What are your heart, lungs, kidneys, and liver called: organs or muscles?

1078. Which organ in your body pumps blood throughout your veins?

1079. Which organ in your body helps you breathe?

1080. Which organ serves to remove wastes and control the body's chemical balance: kidneys or liver?

1081. Which organ serves to clean your blood, and convert proteins and carbohydrates into nutrients for your body: pancreas or liver?

1082. What is the largest organ in your body: your heart or your skin?

1083. When bones are broken, are they broken forever or do they grow back together?

1084. What is the name of the picture taken of bones that is used by a doctor to examine the bones?

1085. What is the name of the tissue around the bones that you can show if you flex your arms?

1086. What are the upper muscles of your arm called: biceps or triceps?

1087. Where do you think the gluteus maximus, the human body's largest muscle, is located: the buttocks or the thigh?

1088. What is the name for the fibrous tissue that serves to connect the muscle to the bone: ligament or tendon?

1089. What is the largest tendon in your body, connecting your calf muscle to your heal bone: Achilles or hamstring?

1090. What is the name of the tendon located at the back of your knee: Achilles or hamstring?

1091. What is the name of the organ in your skull containing billions of cells, that you use to talk, listen, think, hear, smell, taste, remember and dream?

SCIENCE

1092. What system is the brain a part of: nervous or circulatory?

1093. Is the brain divided into the cerebrum, the cerebellum, and the medulla?

1094. How many hemispheres does the brain have: two or four?

1095. What side of the body does the right side of the brain control: right or left?

1096. What side of the body does the left side of the brain control: right or left?

1097. What part of the brain connects to the spinal cord: the cerebrum or the brain stem?

1098. If you touch something hot, or touch a thorn on a rose bush, will you pull your finger away because of a reflex action or a brain signal?

1099. What is the term for an involuntary movement in response to some stimulus: reflex action or brain signal?

1100. When a doctor checks your reflexes, what part of your body might the doctor tap to create a reflex?

1101. Are blinking and sneezing considered reflex actions or brain signals?

1102. What are some things we can we do to keep our bodies healthy?

1103. What is the name for the science that involves the exploration of celestial bodies in the universe and solar system other than the Earth: space science or astrology?

1104. What is the general term for the study of celestial bodies in space: astronomy or astrology?

1105. What does the prefix "**astron**" translate to in Greek: star or space?

1106. Which is bigger: the universe or the galaxy?

1107. What is the name of the galaxy that contains *billions* of stars that the Earth is located in: Andromeda or Milky Way?

1108. How many galaxies are believed to exist in the universe: millions or billions?

1109. Are asteroids, meteors, and comets also a part of the study of space?

1110. What is the name for scientists who study the universe: astronomers or astrologists?

1111. What is the name of a tool with powerful mirrors and lenses that an astronomer might use to study the planets and the stars?

1112. What is the name of a telescope that detects sound waves coming from the stars to help locate and study them: a sound telescope or a radio telescope?

1113. Where is world's largest single-dish radio telescope located, with a reflector dish measuring over 1000 feet, and covering an area of 20 acres: Arecibo, Puerto Rico or San Juan, Puerto Rico?

1114. What type of telescope will be the result of an international effort known as Square Kilometre Array,

SCIENCE

will include antennas across two continents, Africa and Australia, cover a collective area of over one million square meters, and is slated to become fully operational in the mid 2020's: the world's largest *radio* telescope, or the world's largest *reflector* telescope?

1115. What is the name of the huge, reflector telescope that was released into space in 1990, uses mirrors to collect light from stars, and then "radios" them back to Earth: the Hubble Space Telescope, or the "Rover" telescope?

1116. Based on observations through high-powered telescopes and instruments, do astronomers formulate a theory, or explanation based on evidence, regarding how objects in space were formed?

1117. What is the name of the theory that many astronomers believe explains how the universe began, and hypothesizes that an explosion occurred over 15 billion years ago, and this explosion transformed all matter that had been condensed into one giant ball into the stars and planets: Big Bang or Big Explosion?

1118. Do planetary objects that make up the solar system include planets and moons?

1119. How many planets are there in our solar system that currently have a name: 8 or 9?

1120. Which is the only planet that is not named for a god: Mars or Earth?

1121. What does the word *solar* pertain to: the Sun or the stars?

1122. What does the word "sol" mean in Spanish: solar or Sun?

1123. If "sol" translates to Sun in Spanish, what does the solar system center on?

1124. What was the name of the astronomer that theorized back in the 1500's that the Sun was the center of the Universe and not the Earth: Isaac Newton or Nicolaus Copernicus?

1125. What is the name of the nearest star to the Earth: the Sun or Alpha Centauri?

1126. Does the Sun look big and bright to us because it is relatively close to the Earth?

1127. How far away is the Sun from the Earth: 83 or 93 million miles away?

1128. How long does it take the light of the Sun to travel to the Earth given the speed of light: 8 seconds or 8 minutes?

1129. Which is bigger: the Sun or the Earth?

1130. What is the surface temperature of the Sun: 1000 degrees or 10,000 degrees Fahrenheit?

1131. What is the name of the "energy" that is produced by the Sun: solar or fusion?

1132. Does the Earth rotate and revolve around the Sun, or does the Sun rotate and revolve around the Earth?

1133. What are Mercury, Venus, Earth, Mars, Jupiter, Saturn, Uranus, Neptune, and Pluto called?

SCIENCE

1134. Is Pluto still considered an official planet?

1135. How many planets total travel around the Sun?

1136. What is Pluto now considered, and has been since 2006: a satellite or a dwarf planet?

1137. What is a way to remember the names of all 8 planets: **My Very E**ducated **M**other **J**ust **S**erved **U**s **N**oodles, **M**any **V**ery **E**lderly **M**en **J**ust **S**nooze **U**nder **N**ewspapers, or both?

1138. Which of the eight planets in our solar system is the largest: Saturn or Jupiter?

1139. Which of the eight planets in our solar system is the smallest: Mercury or Venus?

1140. Are there new planets in different galaxies being discovered and studied by astronomers?

1141. What is the term for a fixed path around the Sun: revolution or orbit?

1142. What do planets do besides orbit around the Sun: rotate or revolve?

1143. Does rotate mean to spin or to turn upside down?

1144. Would Mercury, Venus, Earth, and Mars be considered inner or outer planets?

1145. Are the inner planets solid and rocky, or are they full of liquid and gas?

1146. What is the name of the closest planet to the Sun that has extremely hot and cold temperatures, and was named for a Roman God?

1147. What is the name of the second closest planet to the Sun that shines like a bright star, and is named for the Roman goddess of love and beauty: Venus or Mars?

1148. What is the name of the fourth planet from the Sun that has a rocky surface, is sometimes referred to as the "red planet, is named for the Roman god of war, and currently has two robotic "rovers" sponsored by NASA that are canvasing this planet?"

1149. What is the name of the belt that separates the inner planets from the outer planets: the asteroid belt or the Milky Way belt?

1150. Would Jupiter, Saturn, Uranus, and Neptune be considered inner of outer planets?

1151. Are the outer planets solid and rocky, or are they full of liquid and gas?

1152. What is the name of the largest planet made mostly of hydrogen that was named for the Roman king of the gods?

1153. What is the name of the second largest planet in our solar system that has gas rings around it, and named for the Roman god of the harvest?

1154. What is the name of the eighth planet from the Sun, takes 165 years to orbit the Sun, has the strongest winds in the solar system, and is named for the Roman god of the sea: Neptune or Uranus?

SCIENCE

1155. What is the name of the smallest planet in the solar system, is now regarded as a "dwarf planet," and is named for the Roman god of the underworld?

1156. What is the name of the planet that travels around the Sun at sixty thousand miles an hour, is three-fourths covered with water, is made up of a crust, mantle, and core, and is the only known body to have life on it?

1157. What does the Earth rotate on: its equator or its axis?

1158. Is the Earth straight up and down on its axis, or is it slightly tilted?

1159. What four natural divisions of the year are created because of the tilt of the Earth on its axis?

1160. What are the four seasons of the year?

1161. Do all parts of the world have all four seasons?

1162. What season of the year is it if where you live on the planet is tilted *away* from the Sun?

1163. What season of the year is it if where you live on the planet is tilted *toward* the Sun?

1164. Are the four seasons the same or different throughout the world?

1165. If it is one season here in the Northern Hemisphere, or places north of the Equator, is it the same season or the *opposite* season in the Southern Hemisphere, south of the Equator?

1166. If it is summer here in the United States, north of the Equator, which season is it in Argentina, *south* of the equator?

1167. If it is autumn in the Southern Hemisphere, which season is it in the Northern Hemisphere?

1168. In which season are June, July, and August in the Southern Hemisphere?

1169. In which season are December, January, and February in the Southern Hemisphere?

1170. In which season are September, October, and November in the Southern Hemisphere?

1171. In which season are March, April, and May in the Southern Hemisphere?

1172. Does the date stay the same regardless of which season is it?

1173. What would the weather be like in July in Argentina?

1174. What would the weather be like in January in Argentina?

1175. Which celestial body is always in motion: the Earth or the Sun?

1176. In which direction does the Sun rise in the morning because of the way the Earth is tilted?

1177. In which direction does the Sun set in the evening because of the way the Earth is tilted?

1178. How long does it take for the Earth to complete one rotation around its axis: one day or one year?

SCIENCE

1179. How many days does it take for the Earth to complete one revolution around the Sun: one day or 365 ¼ days?

1180. Does it take exactly 365 days or 365 ¼ days for the Earth to revolve around the Sun?

1181. What is it called when we allow for the extra ¼ day every 4 years?

1182. Which month do we add an extra day, the 29th, every four years?

1183. Do you know anyone who has a birthday on February 29th?

1184. What time of the day is it when the place where you live is tilted toward the Sun?

1185. What time of the day is it when the place where you live is tilted away from the Sun?

1186. Is the Sun considered a star?

1187. What is a grouping of stars called that creates a pattern or shape: a constellation or a galaxy?

1188. How many stars make up a galaxy: millions or billions?

1189. Are two common constellations the Big Dipper and the Little Dipper because the shapes of the stars that make up this constellation resemble a *dipping spoon,* like one used for punch or soup?

1190. What is another name for the bright star Polaris, the first star in the handle of the Little Dipper: the North Star or the South Star?

1191. What direction are you facing if you are looking at the North Star?

1192. What is the North Star also known as: Polaris or Polar Star?

1193. How many moons does the Earth have?

1194. Do some planets have more than one moon?

1195. Which planet as 63 confirmed moons: Saturn or Jupiter?

1196. Which two planets do not have any moons as far as astronomers can tell: Venus and Mercury, or Uranus and Neptune?

1197. Does the Moon orbit the Earth, or does the Earth orbit the Moon?

1198. How long does it take for the Moon to orbit the Earth on average: 27 days or 24 hours?

1199. What is another name for the moon: a satellite or a constellation?

1200. Which two celestial bodies cause the tides, with their combined gravitational pull on the Earth's oceans?

1201. During a solar eclipse, what celestial body passes between the Earth and the Sun causing it to get dark in the middle of the day?

1202. During a lunar eclipse, what celestial body passes between the Sun and the Moon?

SCIENCE

1203. What is the term for what keeps the Earth and the other planets in the solar system in orbit around the Sun: force or gravity?

1204. What is the name of the force that attracts one piece of matter to another?

1205. Does the gravitational force of the Earth pull objects toward the center or away from the center of the Earth, like a magnet?

1206. Does the Earth have gravitational force?

1207. Does the Moon have gravitational force?

1208. What is the name of the scientist whose theory of relativity can be used to describe gravity: Isaac Newton or Albert Einstein?

1209. What is the force of gravity measured in: g-forces or pull forces?

1210. What is the approximate g-force of a rollercoaster: 50 g's or 5 g's?

1211. Does the force of gravity keep the Moon in orbit around the Earth and the Earth in orbit around the Sun?

1212. Would objects that are close together and big in mass have a stronger or weaker attraction than objects that are far apart and are smaller in mass?

1213. What is the name of the area in the universe where the gravitational pull is so strong that it pulls everything into it: a galaxy or a black hole?

1214. Does the Moon make its own light, or is it reflected light from the Sun?

1215. What are new moon, crescent moon, half moon, waxing moon, and full moon referred to as: stages or phases?

1216. What phase of the Moon is it when the Moon appears as a full bright circle?

1217. What is the name of the cycle when the Moon appears to have different shapes based on the way the Sun is shining on it?

1218. Does the lunar cycle cause only certain parts of the Moon to be visible from the Earth?

1219. Do recent studies reveal that the Moon has an atmosphere?

1220. How many days does it take for the Moon to go through all its phases: 29 or 33?

1221. How many moons does the Earth have?

1222. How many miles away is the Moon from the Earth: 238,855 or 832,558?

1223. Have humans ever been to the Moon?

1224. What is the name given to the scientists that fly in a shuttle or a rocket?

SCIENCE

1225. What is the name for the early space missions sponsored by NASA: Apollo or Gemini?

1226. What is the name of the first astronaut to walk on the Moon in 1969 on spaceflight Apollo 11: Buzz Aldrin or Neil Armstrong?

1227. What did Neal Armstrong communicate back to Earth after stepping on the Moon for the first time: "That's one small step for a man, one…?"

1228. What is the **N**ational **A**eronautics and **S**pace **A**dministration commonly known as?

1229. What is the instrument called that used powerful lenses and mirrors to help astronomers learn more about the planets and the stars?

1230. Would a radio telescope use sight or sound to collect signals from the universe?

1231. What means of transportation do astronauts use in the exploration of space?

1232. What is the name for the floating space station that is orbiting the Earth that serves as a space and scientific research facility with people on board: International Space Station or International Satellite System?

1233. What is the name of the celestial matter that forms a tail as it gets closer to the Sun, and is made of rock, ice, and dust: a comet or a meteor?

1234. What is the name of the comet that can be viewed from the Earth every seventy six years: Halley's Comet or Newton's Comet?

1235. What is a meteor called that is made up of rock and iron, resembles a shooting star, and often lands on the Earth's surface: an asteroid or a meteorite?

1236. What is the astronomical term for giant space bodies composed of rock and iron that orbit the Sun: asteroid or meteoroid?

1237. What is the term for an object that orbits or revolves around another celestial body: a radar or a satellite?

1238. Are artificial satellites often launched into space with the purpose of providing signals used for communications in television, internet, radio, weather, and telephones?

1239. Are Leo the Lion, Taurus the Bull, and Orion the Archer constellations or comets?

1240. What is the name of the constellation that looks like a cup with a big handle?

1241. What is the Big Dipper part of: Ursa Major or Ursa Minor?

1242. What is the name of the constellation that looks like a cup with a little handle?

1243. What is the Little Dipper part of: Ursa Major or Ursa Minor?

1244. What is the bright star you can see that is the first star in the handle of the Little Dipper: Polaris or Orion?

SCIENCE

1245. If you can locate the North Star, can you find your way south, east, or west?

1246. What is the name of the spaceship that many astronauts travel in to explore space today?

1247. What celestial body do you predict that astronauts or civilians will land on next?

1248. What is the scientific term that refers to all plants, animals, and other living things in a given area that depend on each other for survival: ecosystem or environment?

1249. Are all living things part of a cycle of nature?

1250. What are the three groups that depend on each other for maintaining the balance of nature divided into: producers, consumers, and decomposers, or plants, animals, and soil?

1251. What group of living things makes their own food: consumers or producers?

1252. What is an example of a producer: a plant or an animal?

1253. What is an example of a consumer: a plant or an animal?

1254. What is an example of a decomposer: fungi or plants?

1255. What do all living things need to give them energy?

1256. Where do plants get their energy from: the Sun or the soil?

1257. What is the name of the process by which plants use the light from the Sun, carbon dioxide, and water and convert it into sugar and oxygen that is then used by the plants for food: photosynthesis or transformation?

1258. When animals and plants die, what group of living things breaks down their remains: consumers or decomposers?

1259. If a certain species of animals or plants is reduced or killed off through hunting or gathering, is the balance of nature affected?

1260. Are water plants, fish, ducks, and frogs all part of the same ecosystem?

1261. What is something that can pollute the air and affect the pureness of the air?

1262. What is a chemical that can be added to water to kill germs in a swimming pool: bleach or chlorine?

1263. What is something that can pollute the water?

1264. What steps can we take to protect the environment?

1265. Which scientist is credited for proving that the Earth and the planets revolve around the Sun: Nicolaus Copernicus or Isaac Newton?

1266. What famous explorer of the American wilderness is credited as being one of the greatest defenders of our natural heritage, wanting to protect its parks and forests: Johnny Appleseed or John Muir?

SCIENCE

1267. What is the name of the instrument invented by Samuel Morse that worked by sending electrical pulses through wire spelling out words: the telephone or the telegraph?

1268. What is the name of the code system of dots and dashes that is named for Samuel Morse?

1269. What is the invention that started as a machine with a transmitter and a receiver that Alexander Graham Bell is most famous for?

1270. What is the invention that Thomas Edison is most famous for: light bulb or telephone?

1271. What is the name of the first woman aviator to fly solo across the Atlantic Ocean: Amelia Earhart or Jacqueline Cochran?

Science – 4th Grade

1272. Does the study of science include physical, life, environmental, Earth, and space sciences?

1273. What type of science includes magnetism, electricity, sound, matter, and energy: physical or environmental?

1274. Is the mass of an object equal to or greater than the amount of matter the object has?

1275. Can matter include both living and nonliving things?

1276. What are three most common states of matter?

1277. What fourth element is also regarded as a state matter besides solids, liquids, and gases: plasmas or fungi?

1278. Are the stars with their gases considered a type of plasma?

1279. Are fluorescent lights and neon signs types of man-made plasma of natural plasma?

1280. What type of matter is a rock that has size and shape and can be broken apart?

1281. What type of matter is water that can move freely and has no shape of its own?

1282. What type of matter is air that has no shape of its own and is invisible?

1283. What is the name of the gas that is lighter than the air and is often used in balloons and parade floats: hydrogen or helium?

1284. Can matter change into a different state of matter?

1285. How is matter changed when ice is boiled and melts: solid to gas, or solid to liquid?

1286. How is matter changed when the steam from boiling water turns into water vapor?

1287. What is another term for the water vapor that escapes from the pot of boiling water: condensation or evaporation?

SCIENCE

1288. What kind of engines were the first locomotives powered by: steam or electricity?

1289. What is the term given to water that turns into a gas: evaporation or condensation?

1290. What is the term for what may occur when warm air hits the cool surface of the window creating moisture inside the window pane and causing it to look foggy: evaporation or condensation?

1291. If the weather is extremely cold, what may form from the condensation on the inside of a window?

1292. What chemical change or reddish-brown substance results on a nail or an old bike when iron reacts with the oxygen in the air?

1293. Are mass, volume, and density visible or invisible properties of matter?

1294. Are magnetism and the ability to float visible or invisible properties of matter?

1295. What is the name of an object that would float on the water because it is buoyant?

1296. What is the name of an object that would sink in the water because it weighs more than the amount of water it is displacing?

1297. Is all matter made up of small particles called atoms and molecules that are too small to see with the naked eye?

1298. How many known elements are there of matter: 58, 118, or 218?

1299. What is the name for the smallest component of an element, is smaller than a grain of sand, and contains protons, neutrons, and electrons; an atom or a molecule?

1300. What do atoms become after they join together: molecules o protons?

1301. What is the chemical term given to matter that is made up of only one kind of atom: an element or a substance?

1302. Are elements the building blocks of all matter?

1303. What is the name of the table that lists all the elements according to the structure of their atoms: Atomic Table or Periodic Table?

1304. What is the term for matter that is made up of two or more kinds of atoms linked together: a proton or a compound?

1305. What is the fourth element that make up matter according to the Greek thinker Aristotle: Earth, air, fire, and _?

1306. Is the following statement true or false: All substances that exist in the world are made of chemicals?

1307. What is a characteristic of matter called that can be measured: a property or a mixture?

1308. Can characteristics of matter have either physical or chemical properties?

SCIENCE

1309. Would solidity, appearance, texture, hardness, density, buoyancy, conductivity, and magnetism be considered chemical or physical properties of a substance?

1310. Which properties do you think are easier to recognize: chemical or physical?

1311. What is the name of the table that is a chart of all chemical elements that are arranged according to their characteristics?

1312. What can all basic substances be divided into: metals, semi-metals, and _?

1313. Can you name something that is made of the metal copper?

1314. Can you name something that is made of the metal brass?

1315. Can you name something that is made of the metal stainless steel?

1316. Can you name something that is made of the metal bronze?

1317. Can you name something that is made of the metal nickel?

1318. Can you name something that is made of the metal gold?

1319. Can you name something that is made of the metal silver?

1320. Can you name something that is made of the metal iron?

1321. Can you name something that is made of the tin?

1322. Can you name something that is made of the metal aluminum?

1323. If you have a 2 liter bottle of Coke, is the 2 liter a measurement of mass or volume?

1324. What is the term for the total amount that something can hold: volume or capacity?

1325. What metric unit is mass measured in: grams or liters?

1326. What metric unit is volume measured in: grams or liters?

1327. What instrument would you use to measure mass: a scale or a balance?

1328. What is the term for the ability to do work: force or energy?

1329. What are the two *states* of energy: potential and kinetic, or chemical and thermal?

1330. What is the term for stored up energy: potential or kinetic?

1331. What is the term for the energy a body has once it is set in motion: potential or kinetic?

1332. Can energy be transferred from potential to kinetic?

1333. What are nuclear energy, chemical energy, electrical energy, radiant energy, mechanical energy, and thermal energy all considered: forms of energy or fields of energy?

SCIENCE

1334. When you tip the first domino, what energy is being transformed from one domino to the next: kinetic to potential, or potential to kinetic?

1335. What do wind, water, fire, sound, and light all provide: fuel or energy?

1336. Which requires more energy: pushing a wheelbarrow or watching television?

1337. What is the name of the energy that comes from the Sun: thermal or solar?

1338. What is the name of the energy that can make a kite fly, turn a mill, or power a turbine to make electricity: electrical or mechanical?

1339. Can energy be stored?

1340. What is the name of the energy that is stored in foods, batteries, and fossil fuels like coal or natural gas: chemical or potential?

1341. Which of the fossil fuels is the most widely used for energy: coal, natural gas, or oil?

1342. What is the name of the energy caused by the movement of electrons that power lights, electronics, and appliances: chemical or electrical?

1343. What point of energy do you reach if you swing back on a swing: potential or kinetic?

1344. What point of energy do you reach if you are swinging forward on a swing: potential or kinetic?

1345. What type of energy does an object have the higher it is off the ground, due to the pull of gravity: potential or kinetic?

1346. When a ball starts to fall when you let it go from the air, what does its potential energy convert to: kinetic or stored?

1347. When you are about to slide down a hill on a sled, what energy do you start out with and what does this energy become as you slide down the snowy hill?

1348. What is energy called that is caused by the movement of electrons: chemical or electrical?

1349. What is the name of the energy necessary for moving or spinning objects like a wheel gear, or the wind that turns a windmill: mechanical or electrical?

1350. What type of energy is a fire in the fireplace an example of: heat or thermal?

1351. What type of energy is cooked food an example of: chemical or electrical?

1352. What type of energy is water flowing over a waterfall an example of: gravitational or electrical?

1353. What is the name of the energy that is stored in foods, batteries, and fossil fuels like natural gas or coal: electrical or chemical?

1354. Can energy be classified as renewable or non-renewable?

1355. What type of energy source is water, wind, solar, and geothermal: renewable or non-renewable?

SCIENCE

1356. What type of energy source is petroleum, coal, natural gas, and nuclear power: renewable or non-renewable?

1357. What is the term given for a push or a pull that causes an object to move, change speed, change direction, or stop: force or motion?

1358. Can force transfer energy?

1359. What is the term for a change in position: force or motion?

1360. Will an object stay in place until some force sets it in motion?

1361. Will an object continue to move until some force slows or stops it?

1362. What describes how fast an object is moving: speed or velocity?

1363. What can a magnet create that can move an object: a force or a pull?

1364. What is the term for what causes things to fall when they are dropped: motion or gravity?

1365. Is gravity a force or a motion?

1366. Does the Earth's gravity pull the Moon, the Moon's gravity pull the Earth, or both?

1367. What is it called when two equal pushes or pulls cancel each other out: balanced forces or equal forces?

1368. If two classes are playing tug-o-war and the center flag does not move, do we say that the forces are equal, balanced, or at equilibrium?

1369. In what position is a seesaw when it is at its center of gravity in equilibrium?

1370. What is caused when two objects are rubbed together: inertia or friction?

1371. What effect does friction have on an object because of the resistance that results: slows it down or speeds it up?

1372. Would brakes against a tire or wheel be considered friction?

1373. When friction stops motion, what does it create: heat or tension?

1374. What is the term that refers to the way things resist a change in movement: force, inertia, or motion?

1375. What is the name of the principle that reads: "Objects in motion tend to stay in motion and objects at rest tend to stay at rest unless acted on by another force:" the law of inertia or the first law of motion?

1376. What is the name of the scientist that is credited for the *laws of motion* regarding objects in motion and at rest: Sir Isaac Newton or Galileo Galilei?

1377. What is said to have inspired Newton to study the effects of motion and gravity: when an apple fell out of a tree and hit him on the head, or when he threw a ball up in the air?

SCIENCE

1378. Can you finish Newton's third law of motion: "For every action there is an equal and _?"

1379. What is the cause of your body continuing to move forward, even with your seatbelt fastened, after the car you are in suddenly brakes: motion, force, or inertia?

1380. Do objects with more mass have more or less inertia?

1381. What do we call the six basic tools that use force to help us to do work: simple or basic machines?

1382. What term do we use when we are talking about a pulley, a lever, an inclined plane, a wedge, a screw, and an axle: simple or complex machines?

1383. What simple machine would describe an object with a thin, sharp edge like a knife, axe, or a nail: a wedge, a lever, or an axle?

1384. What simple machine would describe a simple machine made of a long object that rests and turns on a pivot or fulcrum like a crowbar, the back of a hammer, a hand brake on a bicycle, or a seesaw: a lever or an axle?

1385. What simple machine has a wheel attached to a thin axle like a doorknob, a wheel, a wagon, a skateboard, or a pencil sharpener: a wheel and axle, a lever, or a screw?

1386. What simple machine is shaped like a ramp that would include a ladder, a playground slide, an escalator, or a stairway: a wheel and axle, a lever, or an inclined plane?

1387. What simple machine is made of a rope wrapped around a wheel, is used to raise or lower a window blind, to hoist or lower the sails on a sailboat, or to raise or lower a flag: a lever, a wedge, or a pulley?

1388. What simple machine is an inclined plane with a winding edge called a thread, is found on a jar lid, the bottom of a light bulb, or a corkscrew: a screw, an axle, or a lever?

1389. What is the name of a machine that is a combination of two or more machines: combined or compound?

1390. What is the name given to machines that are made up of more than two simple machines: compound or complex?

1391. What kinds of machines are a bicycle, a wheelbarrow, and a pair of scissors: complex or compound?

1392. What two simple machines make the wheelbarrow a compound machine: lever, pulley, screw, or wheel and axle?

1393. What things can you name that are electric?

1394. What is the name of the pathway taken by an electric current: a circuit or a series?

1395. What type of electrons cause an electric current: positive or negative?

1396. What type of circuit allows the movement of electricity: open or closed?

SCIENCE

1397. Does electricity move through insulators or conductors?

1398. Are metals considered conductors of electricity or insulators?

1399. Are plastic, rubber, and wood considered insulators or conductors of electricity?

1400. What kind of circuit has only one pathway for the current: series or parallel?

1401. What kind of circuit has two or more pathways for the current: series or parallel?

1402. What type of circuit allows current to pass through: open or closed?

1403. What type of circuit does not allow current to pass through: open or closed?

1404. What kind of circuit will light a bulb: an open circuit or a closed circuit?

1405. What kind of circuit would a string of holiday lights be on, where the whole string will go dark if one bulb burns out: a parallel circuit or a series circuit?

1406. What is it called when the circuit has more than one pathway for the flow of electrical current, and will remain lit even if one bulb burns out: a series circuit or a parallel circuit?

1407. What type of metal are wires often made of, and is a good conductor of electricity?

1408. What type of metals do magnets attract: iron, cobalt, or nickel?

1409. What kinds of lines are created when iron filings line up with a magnetic force: electromagnetic lines or polar lines?

1410. Do dry-celled batteries generally have low or high voltage?

1411. What does a magnetic field create: current or voltage?

1412. What type of current do most electronics use: Alternating Current (AC), or Direct Current (DC)?

1413. What type of current is often used for power lines: AC or DC?

1414. What is the standard unit of measurement for current: amperes or volts?

1415. What kind of electricity would you create if you rub a balloon on a wool sweater or rub your feet on a carpet: static or friction?

1416. Is static electricity the result of either positively or negatively charged electrons that rub off on a surface?

1417. What would you create if you wrapped wire around a nail and ran electricity through it: a magnet, a magnetic field, or an electromagnet?

1418. Do some trains in the world run on guide rails that use electromagnetic energy?

1419. What kind of magnets do cranes use to move tons of steel from one place to another?

1420. What kind of electricity did Ben Franklin state that lightning was: static or electric?

SCIENCE

1421. Can electrical energy be transformed into *other* energies including heat, light, or mechanical energy?

1422. What is the name of the scientist who in 1831 demonstrated electromagnetic induction by passing a magnet through a coil of wire: Benjamin Franklin or Michael Faraday?

1423. What is the name of the scientist who in the 1870's built an electric generator and demonstrated electric lighting in America: Benjamin Franklin or Thomas Edison?

1424. What is the name of the scientist who in 1752 flew a kite with a metal tip into a thunderstorm to prove that lightning was a form of electricity, and went on to invent the lightning rod and conductor: Benjamin Franklin or Thomas Edison?

1425. Who invented the light bulb, the phonograph, the microphone, and the movie camera?

1426. What is the scientific term that refers to the visible spectrum of electromagnetic radiation, and may include ultraviolet, infrared, color, optics, speed, and the Sun?

1427. What type of light can reach a depth of 280 in the ocean: sunlight or ultraviolet light?

1428. What kind of light is a combination of different wavelengths of light traveling together: visible or invisible?

1429. Are the wavelengths of light represented by *ROY G BIV*, the colors of the visible spectrum and the colors in the rainbow?

1430. What does ROY G BIV stand for?

1431. Which color has the longest wavelength in a visible spectrum: red or violet?

1432. Which color has the shortest wavelength in a visible spectrum: red or violet?

1433. Can light be reflected, absorbed, or transmitted?

1434. Is the color of an object the color it reflects or the color it absorbs?

1435. Does an apple appear red because it reflects the color red and absorbs all other colors?

1436. How does light travel: in waves or in crescents?

1437. What is the combination of several wavelengths of light traveling together: black light or white light?

1438. What is the term for the invisible electromagnetic radiation in the ultraviolet area of the spectrum: black light or white light?

1439. Which two of the following describe the parts of a wave: a crest, a valley, or a trough?

1440. Is the crest, the top part of a wave, the same thing as a peak?

1441. What is the distance from the crest of one wave to the crest of the next wave: a frequency or a wavelength?

1442. What is the bottom of a wave called: a crest or a trough?

SCIENCE

1443. What is the top of a wave called: a crest or a trough?

1444. What kind of radio wave would be used to detect the position of objects that are far away: microwaves or radar?

1445. How long does it take for the Sun to travel 93 million miles to Earth: 8 minutes or 8 seconds?

1446. Which travels faster: light or sound?

1447. Why do you see lightning before you hear thunder?

1448. What medium can light travel through the fastest: a vacuum, a solid, a liquid, or a gas?

1449. Which needs a medium, like air or water, to travel through: light or sound?

1450. Can sound travel through solids, liquids, and gases?

1451. Which travels at a rate of 186,282 miles per second: light or sound?

1452. What kind of light is used during eye surgery: laser or neon?

1453. What living things can see ultraviolet light: insects or humans?

1454. What kind of surface reflects light: smooth or rough?

1455. Which travels in straight paths called rays: sound or light?

1456. When light hits something in its path and bounces off, is that light reflected or refracted?

1457. When light is bent, is it reflected or refracted?

1458. Can light be absorbed as heat?

1459. When light passes through a surface or an object, is it refracted or transmitted?

1460. What do the terms transparent, translucent, and opaque refer to: the amount of light that passes through an object, or the amount of light that is absorbed by an object?

1461. What type of material, such as glass, can you see through because it allows light to pass through it: transparent or translucent?

1462. What type of material, like tissue paper, allows some light to pass through, but scatters the light in different directions making it appear fuzzy: transparent or translucent?

1463. What type of material, such as wood, blocks light completely so you cannot see through it: translucent or opaque?

1464. Is light that has not been transmitted or reflected absorbed or refracted?

1465. Will a clear glass window reflect or absorb light?

1466. What kind of clothing absorbs light: dark or light?

SCIENCE

1467. Would frosted glass and tissue paper be translucent or transparent?

1468. Would window glass and air be translucent or transparent?

1469. Would a brick wall and a desk top be opaque or translucent?

1470. What is the name for the curved piece of glass or plastic that serves to refract light: lens or mirror?

1471. What do telescopes, glasses, projectors, goggles, cameras, and microscopes all have?

1472. What is it called when the light that passes through a medium like air or water bends: reflection or refraction?

1473. How are lenses classified when referring to the curve of the glass on each side of the lens: convex and concave, or convergent and divergent?

1474. How are lenses classified when referring to how the lens bends the light: convex and concave, or convergent and divergent?

1475. What kind of lens is thicker in the middle than at the edges, and focuses the light that passes through it: concave of convex?

1476. What kind of lens is thinner in the middle than at the edges, and spreads the light that passes through it: concave or convex?

1477. What kinds of lenses are used to make small things appear larger: concave or convex?

1478. What kinds of lenses are used to make objects seem smaller and farther away: concave or convex?

1479. What kind of lens does a magnifying glass have: concave or convex?

1480. What is the name of the optical instrument that uses convex lenses in order to see cells and microorganisms?

1481. What is the name of the scientific instrument that uses convex lenses to magnify stars and constellations?

1482. What is the name of the hand held instrument composed of two telescopes and a focusing device that is used to magnify objects?

1483. What is the name for the form of energy that is produced and transmitted by vibrating matter: light or sound?

1484. How does sound travel: in waves or in decibels?

1485. Can sound be described in terms of wavelength and frequency?

1486. Is the number of wavelengths in a given amount of time a measurement of the frequency of sound or the pitch of sound?

1487. What is the frequency of sound measured in: decibels or Hertz?

SCIENCE

1488. What is the distance between two compressions: the wavelength of sound or the frequency of sound?

1489. What is the term for the depth of a tone or sound: pitch or vibration?

1490. What sound waves would create a higher pitch: fast or slow?

1491. What sound waves would create a lower pitch: fast or slow?

1492. Would a big, heavy guitar string create a low pitch or a high pitch when plucked?

1493. Would a thin, lighter guitar string create a low pitch or a high pitch when plucked?

1494. Does sound travel quicker or slower through solids because the molecules of a solid are closer together?

1495. What type matter does sound travel the slowest because the molecules are the farthest apart: solids, liquids, or gases?

1496. In which medium would sound travel the fastest: air, water, or steel?

1497. Do animals make and hear ranges of sound vibrations differently than humans can make and hear?

1498. What do musical instruments do to produce sound: vibrate or compress?

1499. What is the measure of the loudness of sound: pitch or volume?

1500. What is the volume of sound measured in: decibels or Hertz?

1501. What is it called when you yell something in a canyon, and the reflection of your own sound waves comes back to you?

1502. What status do airplanes reach when they "break" the sound barrier and create a sonic boom: Mach 1 or supersonic?

1503. What part of our bodies take in sound waves?

1504. What is the name for the study of living things and life processes: Life Science or Earth Science?

1505. What are all living things made of: cells or elements?

1506. How are living things categorized: as classes or as kingdoms?

1507. What are the Monera, Protist, Fungi, Plant, and Animal all classified as: domains or kingdoms?

1508. What living things are found on land and water, have been on Earth for millions of years, contain chlorophyll, convert energy through photosynthesis, have a cell wall made of cellulose, and are stationary?

1509. What is an example of a plant?

1510. How can plants be categorized: vascular and nonvascular, or seed plants and spore plants?

1511. Do the plant groups include those that produce seeds and those that produce spores?

SCIENCE

1512. Would ferns and mosses be spore-producing or seed-producing plants?

1513. Would plants having roots, stems, flowers, and leaves be spore-producing or seed-producing plants?

1514. Do conifers like pine trees, spruces, and junipers reproduce from spores or seeds?

1515. What category do the majority of plants, trees, shrubs, vines, fruits, and vegetables belong to: flowering or non-flowering?

1516. What part of the plant is the part right under the developing flower: the leaves or the sepals?

1517. What is the process called by which green plants use chlorophyll to produce food and oxygen using carbon dioxide, water, nutrients, and sunlight: pollination or photosynthesis?

1518. What is the reproductive process of plants called by which pollen is transferred from the stamens to the stigma: pollination or photosynthesis?

1519. What process are pollination, the stamen, the pistil, the sepal, the embryo, the spore, and the seed all a part of: plant reproduction or plant photosynthesis?

1520. Are plants producers or consumers?

1521. Which part of the plant absorbs nutrients and water from the soil: the stem or the root?

1522. Which part of the plant makes food for the plant: the roots or the leaves?

1523. Which part of the plant allows for the movement of water and nutrients and is the part that supports the plant?

1524. In what female reproductive part of a flower do the seeds form, found inside the ring of petals: the pistil or the stamen?

1525. In what part of a male reproductive flower does pollen form: the pistil or the stamen?

1526. What is the name of the process when *pollen* is transferred from the stamen to the pistil?

1527. What do mosses and ferns reproduce with: spores or sepals?

1528. What is the process called whereby green plants produce their own food?

1529. What do green plants produce using chlorophyll, carbon dioxide, water, and sunlight?

1530. From what source do plants get their energy?

1531. What is the name of the substance that gives plants their green color: chlorophyll or pigment?

1532. What is the term for the plant stage in the winter, similar to some animals, when all their regular activities stop: hibernation or dormancy?

1533. What is the *variable* in an experiment to measure how different kinds of soil affect the growth of a tulip if you put a tulip bulb in four identical pots with four different kinds of soil: the pots, the soil, or the bulbs?

SCIENCE

1534. If the pots, tulip bulbs, sunlight, and water are exactly the same, would these be considered the *variables* or the *constants*?

1535. What is the name given to organisms that get their energy by eating other animals and plants: consumers or producers?

1536. What is the term used for organisms like plants that can make their own food: producers or consumers?

1537. What is the term for organisms that eat away at dead organic matter: consumers or decomposers?

1538. Would fungi that can break down organisms and recycle them back to the nutrient pool be considered a producer, consumer, or a decomposer?

1539. What is the order of the energy cycle from the following: decomposer, Sun, consumer, and producer?

1540. What is the name of the system in the environment that is made of all living and nonliving things: an ecosystem or a kingdom?

1541. What is a synonym of an ecosystem: a biome or a kingdom?

1542. What is one way that an ecosystem can be destroyed by humans?

1543. What is the name of the web that is made up of the interrelated food system in an ecosystem: food chain or life cycle?

1544. What do food chains and food webs always start with: the Sun or the plant?

1545. What is the term for an organism's role in a community: status or niche?

1546. What is the term for the environmental area inhabited by a particular species of plant, animal, or other organism: niche or habitat?

1547. What is the term that refers to the change by which a specific organism becomes better suited to its present surroundings: adjustment or adaptation?

1548. Would adaptations that some organisms do like migration, hibernation, and instinct be considered structural or behavioral?

1549. Would adaptations that some organisms have like webbed feet, long beaks, and camouflaged bodies be considered structural or behavioral?

1550. What is the name of the study of our planet below the surface, on the surface, and in space: Earth Science or Life Science?

1551. What is the name of our system of Sun and planets?

1552. What do the words *solar*, *solstice*, and *solarium* all have to do with?

1553. How many known, official planets are there?

1554. What is Pluto now categorized as: a dwarf planet or a meteorite?

SCIENCE

1555. What have astronomers recently discovered at the edge of our solar system: another dwarf planet or another galaxy?

1556. Are Earth, Venus, Mercury, and Mars inner or outer planets?

1557. Are Jupiter, Saturn, Neptune, and Uranus inner or outer planets?

1558. Is the Earth the second, third, or fourth planet from the Sun?

1559. How old is the Earth estimated to be: 2.6 billion, 3.6 billion, or 4.5 billion years old?

1560. How many million kilometers away is the Earth from the Sun: 100, 150, or 200?

1561. How many million miles away is the Earth from the Sun on average: 73, 83, or 93?

1562. What is the name of the layer in Earth's atmosphere that helps protect it from the Sun's ultraviolet rays: the ozone layer or the stratosphere?

1563. What three things does the Earth have to help it support life: atmosphere, water, and energy or water, soil, and oxygen?

1564. What did the Ancient Greeks like Ptolemy and Aristotle believe was the center of our solar system, around which the stars and the planets revolve: the Earth or the Sun?

1565. What did the scientists Galileo and Copernicus believe was the center of our solar system, around which all planets revolve: the Earth or the Sun?

1566. What is the name of the star located 93 million miles away that is over 100 times the diameter of the Earth?

1567. How many billion years old is the Sun estimated to be: 3.6, 4.5, or 5.6?

1568. How many revolutions or orbits does the Earth make around the Sun every year?

1569. How many hours does it take the Earth to make one rotation on its axis?

1570. What is the effect of the Earth's rotation on its axis: the seasons, or day and night?

1571. What season is it when the hemisphere tilted toward the Sun receives the rays more directly, and has longer days and warmer temperatures?

1572. What season is it when the hemisphere tilted away from the Sun receives the rays less directly, and has shorter days and cooler temperatures?

1573. If it is winter in the northern hemisphere, what season is it in the southern hemisphere?

1574. To what celestial body did the National Aeronautics Space Agency, known as NASA, send astronauts to on its Apollo missions?

1575. To which planet did NASA send a camera navigation rover called "Curiosity" to look for signs of life?"

SCIENCE

1576. What is the name of the rocky satellite that is about one-quarter the size of the Earth that has no water, no atmosphere, and no known life?

1577. What do "new, waxing crescent, first quarter, waxing gibbous, full, waning gibbous, last quarter, and waning crescent all refer to: Moon phases or Moon stages?

1578. What is caused and controlled by the Sun and Moon's gravitation pull, affecting the rise and fall of an ocean's water levels: tides or eclipses?

1579. What type of eclipse occurs when the Moon moves into the Earth's shadow: solar or lunar?

1580. What type of eclipse occurs when the moon passes between the Earth and the Sun: solar or lunar?

1581. How many layers does the Earth have: three or four?

1582. Which of the following is not one of the Earth's layers: crust, mantle, lithosphere, outer core, or inner core?

1583. What is the inner most layer of the Earth called, estimated to be the size of the Moon and hotter than the surface of the Sun: the crust or the inner core?

1584. What is the outer most layer of the Earth called that is about 25 miles deep: the crust or the mantle?

1585. What is the second layer of the Earth called which is 1,800 miles of hot magma or molten rock: the outer core or the mantle?

1586. What is the third layer of the Earth called which is made of hot liquid metal: the inner core or the outer core?

1587. What is the name for the innermost layer Earth, measuring nearly 4,000 feet deep, and made of solid iron and nickel?

1588. What is the name of the 30 rigid pieces making up the Earth's surface: plates or faults?

1589. What is the name of the explanation that involves the movement of the plates that make up the Earth's outer layer: plate tectonics or plate faults?

1590. What are the plates called that are moving *toward* each other: convergent or divergent?

1591. What are the plates called that are gradually pulling apart: convergent or divergent?

1592. What is the name of the theory proposed by the German scientist Alfred Wegener that the continents started as one huge land mass before moving apart: continental divergence or continental drift?

1593. What is the name of the boundary line where two plates meet in the Earth's crust: a slip or a fault?

1594. What part of the Earth's crust moves when the magma inside the Earth moves: the tectonic plates or the fault lines?

1595. What is the name of the fault under San Francisco, California: the San Francisco Fault or the San Andreas Fault?

SCIENCE

1596. What is the name of the violent shaking of the Earth's crust that most often occurs along the Earth's tectonic plates and along the fault lines?

1597. What is the name of the released energy that travels out in waves and causes the Earth to shake as a result of an earthquake or a volcano: seismic waves or tectonic waves?

1598. What is the name of the center point underground where most earthquakes start: the focus or the epicenter?

1599. What is the name of the point on the surface of the Earth directly above an Earthquake's focus point where most of the violent shaking is felt: the seismic center or the epicenter?

1600. What is the name for the scientists who study earthquakes: geologists or seismologists?

1601. What is the name of the machine that geologists use to record the vibrations of earthquakes: a seismograph or a Richter scale?

1602. What is the name given for the strength of an earthquake: intensity or magnitude?

1603. What is the name of the scale that geologists use to chart the strength of an earthquake: the Seismograph scale or the Richter scale?

1604. What is the powerful wave called caused by the energy of an earthquake that occurs on the ocean floor: a tidal wave or a tsunami?

1605. Do tsunami waves start out long and low and become bigger and higher once they reach the shore?

1606. What other force of nature may take place in a mountainous area, caused by an earthquake: an avalanche or a mudslide?

1607. What is it called when heavy rain or an earthquake cause loose soil and rocks to slide down a mountain slope: a mudslide or a landslide?

1608. What is it called when there is a slide on wet soil, and that soil becomes unstable: a mudslide or a landslide?

1609. What is it called when snow becomes unstable on a mountain, breaks free, and slides down the mountain slope: an avalanche or a snow slide?

1610. What is the name of the opening in the Earth's crust where gas, molten rock and ash is forced up to the surface of the earth erupting though a hole?

1611. What is the name of the molten rock that flows out of the volcano when it erupts: magma or lava?

1612. Where do most volcanoes occur: along the edges or along the interior of the Earth's tectonic plates?

1613. What do ash and rock that spew from the opening in the Earth and pile up over time eventually harden into: mountains or rock quarries?

1614. What is the name of a volcano that is erupting or is expected to erupt: active or dormant?

1615. What is the name of a volcano that has not erupted for a while: active or dormant?

SCIENCE

1616. What is the name of the volcano that erupted in A.D. 79 on the western coast of Italy that buried the ancient Roman city of Pompeii in ash, killing over 20,000 people: Mount Vesuvius or Mount Saint Helens?

1617. What is the name of the volcano that erupted in Washington in 1980 in which 230 square miles of forest were blown down or burned: Mount Olympus or Mount Saint Helens?

1618. What is the name given to the hot water that bubbles up to the surface and forms a pond or steam: a hot spring or a geyser?

1619. What is the name given to what forms when water collects in an underground cave and forces hot water to shoot up into the air: a hot spring or a geyser?

1620. What is the name of the famous geyser in Yellowstone National Park in Wyoming that erupts regularly, sending water and steam 160 feet into the air: Old Faithful or Old Steamboat?

1621. What was the name given to the continents that were crowded together into one landmass over 100 million years ago, gradually breaking into the continents we know today: Pangaea or Europa?

1622. What is the term for the changes in the continents and their drift away from each other, a few inches per year due to plate tectonics: continental drift or continental divide?

1623. How many categories of mountains are there, based on how they were formed: 3 or 4?

1624. What category of mountains are the Black Hills of South Dakota and the Adirondacks of New York, the result of the uplifting of tectonic plates: dome or folded?

1625. What category of mountains are the Alps in Europe, the Appalachians in the eastern United States, and the Rocky Mountains in western North America, the result of inter-continental plate collisions: dome or folded?

1626. What category of mountains are the Himalayas, the Earth's tallest mountains that include Mount Everest, that were formed over 45 million years ago: dome or folded?

1627. What category of mountains are the Grand Tetons in the western United States, and the Sierra Nevada mountains in California and Nevada, the result of a combination of tension and uplift forces: fault-block mountains or tectonic dome mountains?

1628. What are mountains made of: minerals or rocks?

1629. What are rocks made of: minerals or elements?

1630. How are rocks classified: according to how they were formed, or what they are made of?

1631. How many classifications of rock are there: 3 or 5?

1632. Are the three main classifications of rocks igneous, sedimentary, and metamorphic?

1633. What type of rock started as hot magma and cooled into rock, and include granite, pumice, and obsidian: igneous or sedimentary?

SCIENCE

1634. Is magma another term for lava?

1635. What type of rocks were formed when layer upon layer of debris and sand settled together, and include sandstone and limestone: sedimentary or metamorphic?

1636. What type of rocks have changed form over time through heat and pressure, and include marble and slate: metamorphic or sedimentary?

1637. Do processes that may change the surface of the Earth include weathering and erosion?

1638. What is the process called in which water, wind, plants, and ice take boulders and turn them into rocks, then pebbles, then sand, and finally into small particles that become part of the Earth's soil: physical weathering or erosion?

1639. What is the process called in which rocks weather after coming into contact with certain gases or plants, which results in an acid that can eat away at the surface of rocks: erosion or chemical weathering?

1640. What is the process called in which water, rocks, and soil are constantly sliding down Earth's hills and mountains due to gravity: weathering or erosion?

1641. What is the name for the layer of soil which contains small pieces of weathered rock mixed with decaying plant and animal matter called humus, replenishes itself every year, and is darker than the rest: subsoil or topsoil?

1642. What is the name of the second layer down, is made of weathered clay and rock, and takes hundreds of thousands of years for form: bedrock or subsoil?

1643. What is the name of the layer under the subsoil that is too far down to weather into the soil, and is made of solid rock: bedrock or sedimentary rock?

1644. Do wind and ice act like ice carvers?

1645. What is the name for the slow-moving masses of snow that have gradually compressed into ice, found in very cold regions like Antarctica, Greenland, Canada, and Alaska?

1646. What it the name of the time that lasted more than a million and a half years when huge glaciers covered much of North America, northern Asia, and northern Europe: the Ice Age or the Frozen Era?

1647. What did some of the water-filled, glacier-made holes become after the glaciers melted at the end of the Ice Age: Great Lakes, oceans, or rivers?

1648. What are Huron, Ontario, Michigan, Erie, and Superior: Great Lakes or Great Rivers?

1649. What are Portage, Hubbard, and Franz Josef all examples of: lakes or glaciers?

1650. Where is Glacier National Park located: Montana or Wyoming?

1651. Where is Glacier Bay National Park located: Alaska or Montana?

1652. What is the weather like today?

SCIENCE

1653. What is the study of weather called: meteorology or astronomy?

1654. What is weather the study of: the atmosphere or the environment?

1655. What is the term for the layers of air that wrap around the Earth: the atmosphere or the ozone?

1656. How many major layers of air is the Earth's atmosphere made of: 3, 4, or 5?

1657. Do the five layers of the Earth's atmosphere include the troposphere, the stratosphere, the mesosphere, and thermosphere, and the exosphere?

1658. What is the name of the outermost layer 6,000 miles beyond the Earth where the atmosphere is extremely thin and extends into space: stratosphere or exosphere?

1659. What is the name of the closest layer to the Earth's atmosphere where all living things are found, where airplanes fly, and where the weather occurs: troposphere or mesosphere?

1660. What is the name of the layer in the stratosphere that contains the gas that protects us from ultraviolet radiation from the Sun?

1661. What is the name of the coldest layer found thirty to fifty miles above the Earth that acts as a shield, burning up meteors before they reach the Earth: thermosphere or mesosphere?

1662. What is the general term that includes rain, snow, and hail, and is a part of the water cycle: precipitation or weather?

1663. What is the term for the movement of water between the surface of Earth and the atmosphere, whereby evaporated water becomes water vapor, rises to reach cooler air, condenses into tiny water droplets in the clouds, is blown across the sky by the wind, and then falls to Earth as rain: the rain cycle, the water cycle, or the life cycle?

1664. What is the term for the large droplets of water that fall to the Earth?

1665. What is formed on the ground and the grass when water vapor condenses as drops of water: dew or frost?

1666. What is formed when the water vapor in the air condenses and causes a ground-level cloud close to the Earth's surface: fog or dew?

1667. What do raindrops become when they freeze into lumps before they hit the ground?

1668. What is formed when tiny droplets in the clouds freeze to form ice crystals and then fall to the Earth?

1669. What is formed on windows and trees when the water vapor near the ground freezes into ice crystals?

1670. What is the term for the measure of how hot or cold the air is?

1671. What instrument do we use to measure the temperature?

1672. What is the metric term for the measurement of temperature?

SCIENCE

1673. What is the American term used for the measurement of temperature?

1674. What is the weather term given that refers to the distance at which things can be seen clearly: visibility or density?

1675. Can fog, mist, or rain affect visibility?

1676. What is the likely result when there is an overflow of water on land that is normally dry, affecting people, crops, and buildings?

1677. What is the likely result when there is not enough rainwater for crops, plants, or animals for an extended period of time?

1678. What is the measure of the amount of heat energy in the air: humidity or temperature?

1679. What is the term for the amount of moisture in the air: humidity or temperature?

1680. What is air pressure caused by: wind direction, or the weight of the air pushing down?

1681. Which air is denser and exerts greater air pressure: hot air or cold air?

1682. What are air balloons filled with to make them fly: hot air or cold air?

1683. Would polar air and arctic air be considered a cold air mass or a warm air mass?

1684. Would a tropical air mass be cold or warm?

1685. What are the big areas of air called that circulate around the Earth: air pockets or air masses?

1686. What is the term for the downward air current that may cause an aircraft to experience an abrupt change in altitude: air mass or air pocket?

1687. What type of system is a mass of cool, dry air that usually brings fair weather and light winds: high pressure or low pressure?

1688. What type of system is a mass of warm, moist air that usually brings stormy weather and heavy winds: high pressure or low pressure?

1689. What is the boundary called between masses of air with different densities that is usually caused by differences in temperature: a storm or a front?

1690. What kind of weather front would bring a steady rain followed by warmer temperatures: a cold front or a warm front?

1691. What kind of weather front would bring a short period of heavy rain followed by clear colder weather: a cold front or a warm front?

1692. What kind of front occurs when a warm air mass pushes out a cold air mass?

1693. What kind of front occurs when a cold air mass pushes out a warm air mass?

1694. Can the Earth's temperature be influenced by the clouds?

SCIENCE

1695. What is the name of the cloud that is made of ice crystals and are high, feathery, wispy, and thin: stratus, cirrus, or cumulus?

1696. What is the name of the cloud that is white and puffy, look like cotton balls, and usually mean fair weather: stratus, cirrus, or cumulus?

1697. What is the name of the cloud that looks like a grey blanket over the sky and often brings drizzle or a steady rain: stratus, cirrus, or cumulus?

1698. What is the name of the clouds that get larger and darker on the bottom and often bring thunderstorms or tornados: cumulus or cumulonimbus?

1699. What is the term for the huge, dark clouds that signal the approach of a storm: thunderheads or tornadoes?

1700. What is the name of the powerful white flash of electrical current that is created when the negative electrons from the cloud interact with the positive electrons of the Earth?

1701. What is the name of the loud sound that is created by the lightning bolt because after the electric current is released, the air around it expands and vibrates?

1702. How fast does a lightning bolt travel to our eyes: 186,000 miles per second or 1.8 million miles per second?

1703. What is the name of the weather instrument that measures air pressure: a barometer or a hygrometer?

1704. What is the name of the weather instrument that measures the amount of moisture in the air: a barometer or a hygrometer?

1705. What is the name of the weather instrument that measures precipitation: a rain gauge or a hygrometer?

1706. What is term for the natural movement or air across the surface of the Earth?

1707. What does the continual exchange of cool and warm air create: wind or rain?

1708. What is the term for wind that blows at 10 or 20 miles per hour: a breeze, a gale, or a hurricane?

1709. What is the term for wind that gusts up to 40 or 50 miles per hour: a breeze, a gale, or a hurricane?

1710. What is the term for the tropical cyclone that is characterized by strong winds that can travel more than 75 miles per hour: a breeze, a gale, or a hurricane?

1711. Are hurricanes, typhoons, and tropical cycles all the same kind of storm, but called different names in different regions?

1712. What is the name of the storm that forms a whirling, funnel-shaped cloud that reaches the surface of the Earth, and powerfully sucks up everything in its path?

1713. What is the name of the storm that forms over tropical oceans in low pressure areas: a hurricane or a tsunami?

SCIENCE

1714. What is the name given to the center of the hurricane spiral where the air pressure is low and the winds are calm: the epicenter or the eye?

1715. What is the name of the weather instrument that measures wind speed whereby the faster it spins, the faster the wind: a barometer or an anemometer?

1716. What is the name given to the wind pattern in tropical areas that continues its movement in the same direction and shapes big weather patterns: prevailing winds or directional winds?

1717. What is another term for prevailing winds: trade winds or jet stream?

1718. What is it called when winds are forced to the right North of the equator and forced to the left South of the equator, due to the Earth's rotation: Coriolis Effect or Trade Winds?

1719. What is the name for the fast-moving air current high in the Earth's atmosphere: a jet stream or a trade wind?

1720. What kind of ocean waves are caused by high winds?

1721. What kind of storm can high winds whip up in a desert?

1722. What is the name for the fierce snowstorm with high winds that occurs when cold, Arctic air mixes with warm, moist air?

1723. What is the name for the average weather pattern that includes the latitude, temperature, rainfall, snowfall, and humidity in a particular area: zone or climate?

1724. What would tropical, desert, semiarid, subtropical, tundra, polar, and highland all be considered on the Earth?

1725. What is the name of the climate that occurs near the equator characterized by high temperatures and high humidity: polar or tropical?

1726. What is the name of the climate that occurs near the North and South Poles where the temperatures are cold: polar or tundra?

1727. What varies among plants, animals, and humans depending on the climate they live in: habitat or weather?

1728. Have people, animals, and plants adapted to the climate in which they live?

1729. What natural division of the year is determined by the changing position of the Earth in relation to the Sun, and the part of the Earth that is tilted toward the Sun?

1730. In regions that have four seasons, is the weather different in each of those seasons?

1731. What imaginary line divides the Northern Hemisphere and the Southern Hemispheres?

1732. Are the seasons the same or the opposite in the Northern and Southern Hemispheres?

1733. Is the date on the calendar the same or different in the Northern and Southern Hemispheres?

SCIENCE

1734. What is the first day of summer in the Northern hemisphere: June 21st or September 21st?

1735. What season is it in the Southern Hemisphere beginning on June 21st?

1736. What is the first day of autumn in the Northern Hemisphere: June 21st or September 21st?

1737. What is the first day of winter in the Northern Hemisphere: September 21st or December 21st?

1738. What is the first day of spring in the Northern Hemisphere: March 21st or September 21st?

1739. What season is it in the Southern Hemisphere beginning on March 21st?

1740. Do some regions near the equator where the temperature does not vary too much have wet and dry seasons based on variations in rainfall?

1741. What is the name of the wind in southern Asia that create the wet and dry seasons: monsoon or typhoon?

1742. What is the name of a tropical cyclone in the South Pacific: monsoon or typhoon?

1743. What kind of weather do you like best?

1744. What kind of climate would you most like to live in?

1745. What is the study of the body structures of a human: anatomy or biology?

1746. What body parts can you name that are outside the human body?

1747. What body parts can you name that are inside the human body?

1748. What is the name of the structural part of a body system that is composed of tissues that allow it to perform a specific function: an organ or a muscle?

1749. What is the largest organ on your body: your stomach or your skin?

1750. What is the name of the organ that is part of the body's circulatory system that pumps blood through your body: the heart or the lungs?

1751. Is the heart organ considered a muscle?

1752. How many chambers is the heart divided into?

1753. What is the name for the top two chambers of the heart: atria or ventricles?

1754. What is the name of the bottom two chambers of the heart: atria or ventricles?

1755. How many valves does the human heart have: four or eight?

1756. What allows the ventricles and atria to open and close, allowing blood to flow through the heart: arteries or valves?

1757. What is the name of the largest artery in the human body that branches out to take the blood to all parts of the body: the aorta or the vein?

SCIENCE

1758. What is the term for the hollow, stretchy tubes that transport the blood through your body: blood vessels or capillaries?

1759. What is the name of the blood vessels that carry oxygen-rich blood *away* from your heart: capillaries or arteries?

1760. What is the name of the blood vessels that carry blood *back* to your heart for more oxygen: arteries or veins?

1761. What is the name for the smaller blood vessels delivering oxygen and nutrients that branch out and connect the veins and arteries, bringing blood in contact with the cells of the body: ventricles or capillaries?

1762. What is the term for the pushing force that moves the blood through the body caused by the pumping of the heart: pulse or blood pressure?

1763. What on your body indicates how often our heart squeezes to pump blood throughout your body: pulse or blood pressure?

1764. How many pulses per minute is the average human heart rate per minute but varies from person to person: 30 or 60?

1765. Does your heart rate go up or down when you exercise, because your cells lose oxygen and need more?

1766. What delivers nutrients from food and oxygen to the cells in organs, nerves, muscles, and bones: blood or platelets?

1767. What gas do you release when you breathe out, that blood carries back to your lungs: oxygen or carbon dioxide?

1768. What is the name of the part of the blood that is a clear, thin liquid: hemoglobin or plasma?

1769. What are the two colors of blood cells that float in the plasma?

1770. What is the name of the substance in red blood cells that carries oxygen and carbon dioxide: hemoglobin or platelets?

1771. What blood cells in your body travel in the blood and help fight disease and infection: red or white?

1772. What is the name for the tiny solids in the blood that make blood coagulate or get thinker to help stop bleeding: hemoglobin or platelets?

1773. How long is it before new red blood cells replace old blood cells: four weeks or four months?

1774. What is the rate at which your red blood cells die: 8 million per second or 2 million per second?

1775. What organ in your body helps remove dead blood cells by breaking them down and reusing what it can as nutrients: spleen or liver?

1776. What organ in your body is the cleansing organ, and helps you filter your blood and removes harmful wastes: spleen or liver?

SCIENCE

1777. What did the English doctor William Harvey theorize was the center of the circulatory system: the heart or the lungs?

1778. What may be the result when the heart does not receive enough oxygen and heart muscle cells die?

1779. What substance if eaten to excess can lead to a build-up on the inside of arteries that may lead to a heart attack: sugars or saturated fats?

1780. What is another name for a heart attack: cardiac arrest or coronary arrest?

1781. What is it called when a person receives blood from another person: a transfusion or a blood transfer?

1782. How many types of blood did an Austrian doctor conclude that there are back in 1900: three or four?

1783. What are A, B, AB, and 0 regarded as, based on the protein contained in the red blood cells?

1784. What is the name of the factor that indicates whether a blood type is positive or negative: the Rh factor or the Ra factor?

1785. What is the most common blood type and is considered the "universal donor:" Type A or Type O?

1786. Which Rh factor do 85% of Americans have: positive or negative?

1787. Can a patient receiving a blood transfusion receive any type of blood, or does the patient need to receive a blood type that is compatible with the patient's own blood type?

1788. What may be the effect if a patient receives a blood type that is not compatible with the patient's own blood type: blood clots or hardened arteries?

1789. Is your blood type inherited just like your eye color?

1790. Do you know *your* blood type?

1791. Do different animals have the same or different blood types?

1792. Are certain blood types more common than others in different countries?

1793. What system is blood a function of: respiratory or circulatory?

1794. What system is breathing a function of: respiratory or circulatory?

1795. How many times a day does the average person breathe in and out: 5,000 or 20,000?

1796. What system is your lungs part of: circulatory or respiratory?

1797. What is the name for the two inflatable sacs that expand and contract to help you breathe and are located on either side of your heart: lungs or kidneys?

1798. What part of your body does your air flow down when you take a breath through your nose or mouth: trachea or bronchi?

1799. What is the term for the tubes inside your lungs: air sacs or bronchial tubes?

SCIENCE

1800. What is the term for the air sacs at the ends of the bronchi that contain small capillaries where the circulatory and respiratory systems meet: alveoli or diaphragm?

1801. What is the term for the piece of muscle underneath your lungs that arches down to allow air in, and arches down forcing air out through the windpipe: the air sacs or the diaphragm?

1802. What can cause a person's lungs to clog with tar, cause lung cancer, and place a strain on the heart and lungs forcing them to work harder and less effectively?

1803. What things do you do to keep your body healthy?

Science – 5th Grade

1804. What different categories of sciences are there?

1805. What are Biology, Chemistry, Earth Sciences, and Physics all sub-categories of?

1806. What does the suffix -ology mean: the study of, or the science of?"

1807. What is the study of cultures and humankind past and present: anthropology or archaeology?

1808. What is the study of pre-historic peoples and their cultures: anthropology or archaeology?

1809. What is the study of hearing: ophthalmology or audiology?

1810. What is the study of life and living organisms: biology or ecology?

1811. What is the study of the heart: cardiology or hematology?

1812. What is the study of the weather: climatology or meteorology?

1813. What is the study of the skin: cosmetology or dermatology?

1814. What is the study of the universe: astronomy or astrology?

1815. What is the study of ecosystems: ecology or biology?

1816. What is the study of the origin, history, and structure of the Earth: geology or paleontology?

1817. What is the study of blood: cytology or hematology?

1818. What is the study of water: hydrology or ecology?

1819. What is the study of the climate: climatology or meteorology?

1820. What is the study of the composition of rocks and minerals: mineralogy or geology?

1821. What is the study of nerves: pathology or neurology?

1822. What is the study of tumors and cancer: oncology or neurology?

1823. What is the study of eyes: ophthalmology or audiology?

SCIENCE

1824. What is the study of fossils and prehistoric life: mineralogy or paleontology?

1825. What is the study of the mind, mental functions, and behavior: physiology or psychology?

1826. What is the study of radiation images to help in diagnoses: audiology or radiology?

1827. What is the study of earthquakes: geology or seismology?

1828. What is the study of poisonous substances and the effects of chemicals on living organisms: technology or toxicology?

1829. What is the study of viruses and viral diseases: biology or virology?

1830. What is the study of volcanoes: volcanology or geology?

1831. What is the study of animals and the animal kingdom: ecology or zoology?

1832. What is the name given for our system of planets, stars, and moons?

1833. What celestial body is the center of the solar system?

1834. What is the name of the planet we life on?

1835. How many official planets are there?

1836. Is Pluto still officially considered a planet?

1837. Which planet in the solar system is the largest?

1838. Which planet in our solar system is the smallest, and is nearest to the Sun?

1839. Which planet is surrounded by gaseous rings?

1840. Do many of the planets have multiple moons?

1841. Which planet has 63 known moons: Jupiter or Mars?

1842. How many moons does Mars have: two or five?

1843. How many moons does the Earth have?

1844. Around which celestial body do all of the planets orbit?

1845. Who was the first scientist to prove that the planets all revolve around the Sun, and that the Earth rotates on its axis: Copernicus or Newton?

1846. What is the name of the scientist that defined the orbits of the planets, and is credited for his laws of planetary motion: Newton or Kepler?

1847. Which planet is the only one to spin on its side for some mysterious reason, rotates north to south, and takes 84 years to orbit the Sun: Jupiter or Uranus?

1848. What is the name of the fourth planet from the Sun, also known as the "Red Planet?"

SCIENCE

1849. What is the name of the American program sponsored by NASA that had several space flights exploring space, and landed astronauts on the Moon?

1850. What is the name of the first person to walk on the Moon in 1960 on Apollo 11: Neil Armstrong or Buzz Aldrin?

1851. What was the name for the command module for Apollo 11: Columbia or Columbus?

1852. What was the name of the lunar module from Apollo 11: the Eagle or the Hawk?

1853. What were Neil Armstrong's first words after arriving on the Moon on July 20, 1969: "the Eagle has landed," or, "Colombia has just touched down?"

1854. Who sponsored the second manned lunar landing: the United States or Russia?

1855. Which Apollo mission had to be cut short in 1970 with James Lovell, Fred Haise, and Ken Mattingly after it suffered an explosion in its oxygen tank: Apollo 13 or Apollo 14?

1856. Which astronaut aboard Moon flight Apollo 13 is credited with the line, "Houston, we've had a problem:" James Lovell or Jack Swigert?

1857. Which astronaut was the commander of Apollo 13: Fred Haise or James Lovell?

1858. What was the name of the command module of Apollo 13: the Odyssey or the Aquarius?

1859. What was the name of the lunar module of Apollo 13: the Odyssey or the Aquarius?

1860. Which mission control center brought the three Apollo 13 astronauts home safely, six days after the launch: the Kennedy Space Center in Florida, or the Center in Houston, Texas?

1861. Have astronauts collected geological data, hundreds of pounds of Moon rocks, and used a Lunar Rover on missions since the Apollo 13 mission?

1862. What is the name of the first satellite that was launched into space in 1957 by the Soviet Union as it was known at that time: Sputnik or Soyuz?

1863. Which American President boldly proclaimed in a 1962 speech: "I believe that this nation should commit itself to achieving the goal, before this decade is out, of landing a man on the moon, and returning him safely to Earth."

1864. What is the name of the first American space station that was launched in 1973: Soyuz or Skylab?

1865. Which two countries took part in the first international space mission in 1975 called the Apollo-Soyuz Test Project: the U.S and USSR, or the U.S. and China?

1866. What is the name of the first space shuttle that was the first reusable aircraft in 1981: the Columbia or the Challenger?

1867. What is the name of the first American woman in space aboard the Challenger in 1983: Sally Ride or Kathryn Sullivan?

SCIENCE

1868. What is the name of the first American woman to walk in Space in 1984 from the Challenger space craft: Sally Ride or Kathryn Sullivan?

1869. What are the Challenger, Discovery, Atlantis, Endeavour, and Columbia all considered: space shuttles or space mission names?

1870. Did the space shuttle missions lead to more advanced study of the Moon, Mars, and space?

1871. What is the name given for specific clusters of stars: galaxies or constellations?

1872. What are many of the constellations like Aquarius, Gemini, Leo, Libra, Pisces, Sagittarius, Taurus, and Virgo named for: signs or the zodiac or Greek gods?

1873. What constellation of stars translates as "Great bear," and contains the cluster of stars known as the "Big Dipper:" Ursa Major or Ursa Minor?

1874. What constellation of stars translates as "Little Bear," and contains the cluster of stars known as the "Little Dipper:" Ursa Major or Ursa Minor?

1875. What is the name of the "North Star" that is the brightest star at the end of Ursa Minor, and is almost directly above the Earth's North Pole: Polaris or Pegasus?

1876. What is the name of the study of our planet's physical characteristics, and includes the branches of geology and oceanography: Earth Science or Physical Science?

1877. What does the name "Earth" mean in Latin: land or water?

1878. How many hemispheres is the Earth divided into?

1879. What are the two major oceans on our planet?

1880. What is the collective name for the Pacific, Atlantic, Indian, Antarctic, and Arctic?

1881. What is the name of the region at the North Pole: the Arctic or the Antarctic?

1882. What is the name of the region at the South Pole: the Arctic or the Antarctic?

1883. What is the name for the seven different landmasses on the Earth?

1884. What is the study of the placement of the continents, and includes the study of countries, cities, mountains, rivers, and lakes: geography or geology?

1885. What was the original name given to the landmass that existed over 200 million years ago that eventually broke up to form the continents we know today: Pangaea or Pegasus?

1886. How many continents are there: seven or nine?

1887. How many continents can you name?

1888. Which of the following continents is the largest: Europe, Africa, North America, South America, Asia, Australia, or Antarctica?

SCIENCE

1889. Which of the seven continents is the smallest: Europe or Australia?

1890. What is the name for the study of the Earth including its rocks and minerals: geography or geology?

1891. What are igneous, sedimentary, and metamorphic types of?

1892. What are rocks made of: elements or minerals?

1893. How many minerals in the world have been officially identified: 2,000 or 4,000?

1894. What are speck, dust, sand, pebble, stone, river rock, boulder, and mountain the common names for?

1895. Are the most common characteristics used when describing minerals, color, luster, transparency, and hardness?

1896. What did the German mineralogist Friedrich Mohs develop in 1812 to compare the relative hardness of minerals: Mohs Scale of Mineral Hardness, or Mohs Rank of Minerals?

1897. How would talc rank on Mohs hardness scale: low or high?

1898. How would a diamond rank on Mohs hardness scale: low or high?

1899. What are amethyst, garnet, emerald, topaz, ruby, sapphire, and diamond all categorized as: gemstones, minerals, or both?

1900. Which gemstone is the hardest mineral, ranking a "10" on Mohs Scale of Mineral Hardness: a ruby or a diamond?

1901. Is a diamond a crystalline form of carbon or aluminum?

1902. What is the only gemstone that can cut a diamond: a ruby or a diamond?

1903. What colors can a natural diamond be?

1904. What precious stone is often used for cutting glass?

1905. What science is the study of life and living organisms that includes structure, growth, origin, evolution, and distribution: biology or chemistry?

1906. What science is the study of the composition, structure, properties, and reactions of matter, especially regarding atomic and molecular systems: biology or chemistry?

1907. What is the name of the basic building block of matter made up of protons, neutrons, and electrons: a molecule or an atom?

1908. Do atoms also have smaller particles called nucleons and quarks?

1909. What is the term for the central region of an atom: the center or the nucleus?

1910. What sub-atomic particles exist in the nucleus of an atom: protons and electrons, or protons and neutrons?

SCIENCE

1911. Where are the electrons located in an atom: the nucleus or in orbitals around the nucleus?

1912. What sub-atomic particle has a positive electrical charge: a proton, a neutron, or an electron?

1913. What sub-atomic particle has a negative electrical charge: a proton, a neutron, or an electron?

1914. What sub-atomic particle has no charge as it is neutral: a proton, a neutron or an electron?

1915. What do all atoms have an equal number of: protons and neutrons, or protons and electrons?

1916. What is the term for the atom that has more protons than neutrons: an ion or a molecule?

1917. What is the name of a substance that is made of just one kind of atom: a property or an element?

1918. If you change the number of protons an atom has, does the element then change?

1919. What is the name for a particular element that has the same number of protons but a different number of neutrons: a molecule or an isotope?

1920. When atoms join together what do they form: an element or a molecule?

1921. Did the scientist John Dalton confirm that all matter is composed of atoms, and that the atoms of elements like gold, silver, and oxygen are identical to each other, but different from the atoms of other elements?

1922. What Russian scientist discovered that the properties of elements repeated themselves periodically, and that when you arrange the elements both horizontally and vertically, the elements have similar properties and are related: Mendeleev or Lomonosov?

1923. What is the name of Dmitri Mendeleev's chart that shows the arrangement of the similarities and differences among the elements, placed in order according to their atomic mass: timeline or periodic table?

1924. How many elements did Mendeleev's periodic table recognize in 1869: 63 or 103?

1925. How many known elements are on the most current periodic table of the elements: 100 or 117?

1926. What are two major categories of elements: metals and nonmetals, or positive and negative electrons?

1927. What category of elements are shiny and moldable into different shapes, and are good conductors of electricity: metals or non-metals?

1928. Are copper and silver good or bad conductors of electricity?

1929. What kind of metal are many electric wires made from: copper or silver?

1930. What are the elements called that are in the same vertical column on the periodic table: a set or a group?

1931. Do similar characteristics among elements include how they look, if they are shiny and good conductors of electricity, and whether they are solids or liquids?

SCIENCE

1932. What is the name of the scientist first to discover and to present an atomic model that showed the atom as a small, positively charged nucleus surrounded by electrons traveling in separate orbits: Niels Bohr or Ernest Ruthorford?

1933. What is the name of the scientist who theorized that the number of electrons in a single atom of an element gives that element its distinctive characteristics, and also determines how it combines with other elements: Niels Bohr or Ernest Rutherford?

1934. What is the name of the scientist who showed the atom having a dense, positively charged nucleus surrounded by planetary electrons, is credited with the discovery of nitrogen, and is regarded as "the father of nuclear physics:" Niels Bohr or Ernest Rutherford?

1935. What is the name of the set of abbreviations given to the 117 elements: atomic symbols or atomic signs?

1936. What is created when two or more atoms join together: a nucleus or a molecule?

1937. What is the symbol for oxygen: O_2 or H_2o?

1938. What is the name for the molecule that is made up of atoms of different elements: an isotope or a compound?

1939. What is the name for the element, one of the most important compounds of the world that can be abbreviated as H_2O?

1940. Is the water molecule H_2O formed by combining two hydrogen atoms with one oxygen atom, or one hydrogen atom with 2 oxygen atoms?

1941. What is the name of the compound that is abbreviated Co_2: carbon oxygen or carbon dioxide?

1942. Do humans breathe in oxygen or carbon dioxide?

1943. Do humans exhale oxygen or carbon dioxide?

1944. What do plants give off: carbon dioxide or oxygen?

1945. What is the Greek meaning of "photo" in the plant process of photosynthesis: picture or light?

1946. What is Greek for "synthesis" in photosynthesis: putting together or providing energy?

1947. What do plants use for the process of photosynthesis: carbon dioxide and light, or soil and oxygen?

1948. What are the changes that can happen to a substance: both chemical and physical, chemical only, or physical only?

1949. What type of change occurs when water freezes: physical or chemical?

1950. If firewood is burned in a campfire, does the wood change physically, chemically, or both?

1951. What compound is created on iron when it comes into contact with water, the iron combines with oxygen, and results in a chemical reaction: rust, erosion, or decay?

SCIENCE

1952. What is the chemical name for rust: iron oxide or iron ore?

1953. What is the chemical name for salt: sodium hydroxide or sodium chloride?

1954. What is the chemical formula for table salt: NaCl or NaOH?

1955. What are atoms called that have gained or lost electrons, giving them an electrical charge: ions or molecules?

1956. What do chemists write as a symbolic representation of a chemical reaction when elements are combined: a chemical equation or a mathematical equation?

1957. What does your body convert food into through a chemical reaction: chemical energy or potential energy?

1958. What are the scientific terms mixture, dissolve, solution, concentration, saturation, reaction, evaporation, and crystallization regarded as: chemical or biological?

1959. What is the name of the substance that is made by combining two or more different materials in such a way that no chemical reaction occurs, such as saltwater: a mixture or a solution?

1960. What is the term for making a solution by liquefying or melting: reaction or dissolve?

1961. What is the name of the process by which a gas, liquid, or solid is dispersed in a gas, liquid, or solid without a chemical change: mixture or solution?

1962. What is the measure of the relative proportions of two or more quantities in a mixture, or the abundance of a substance divided by the total volume of a mixture: concentration or solution?

1963. What is the scientific term for the degree to which something is dissolved or absorbed compared to the maximum possible: reaction or saturation?

1964. What is chemical term for when two or more molecules interact and the molecules change, or the process that leads to the transformation of one set of chemical substances to another: reaction or mixture?

1965. What is the chemical term for when two or more substances are mixed together but are not chemically combined: a solution or a mixture?

1966. What is the name of the process by which water is converted from its liquid form to its vapor form: evaporation or condensation?

1967. What is the name for the change in the state of water vapor to liquid water when it comes into contact with a cold surface, and is the opposite of vaporization: condensation or frost?

1968. What is the name of the process of forming crystals from a solution: crystallization or granulation?

1969. What is it called when we group things together based on their similarities or differences: grouping or classification?

1970. Can living things be classified?

SCIENCE

1971. Can organisms be classified?

1972. What is the name of the large groups that scientists classify living things into: kingdoms or communities?

1973. What are the organisms that include plant, animal, fungi, protest, and prokaryote categorized as: phylum or kingdoms?

1974. Can organisms be classified further within a specific kingdom?

1975. Are kingdoms, phylum, class, order, family, genus, and species grouped largest to smallest or smallest to largest?

1976. What scientific instrument would you need to view the Protista and Prokaryote kingdoms?

1977. What is the term for the tiny building blocks that make up all living things that are often only seen with a microscope: cells or organisms?

1978. What is the name of the English scientist who observed a pattern of small, boxlike squares when viewing a piece cork through a microscope, and therefore named them "cells" because they looked like little rooms: Robert Hooke or Theodor Schwann?

1979. What is the name of the German scientist who developed the cell theory, and defined the cell as the fundamental unit of animal structure: Theodor Schwann or Rudolf Virchow?

1980. What is the name of the thin covering around the cell that gives the cell its shape and protects it from its surroundings: a sheath or a membrane?

1981. What part of a cell controls what goes in and out of it like food, water, and oxygen: the cytoplasm or the membrane?

1982. What is the name of the jellylike liquid that surrounds the other cell parts: the cytoplasm or the organelles?

1983. What is the name of the cell's control center: the nucleus or the hub?

1984. What part of the cell controls what goes in and out, controls the cell growth, and contains all the instructions for running the cell: the DNA or the nucleus?

1985. What do cells do to reproduce: re-align with another cell, or split into two cells?

1986. Before a cell splits, are the instructions in the nucleus copied so that each new cell has a nucleus with a copy of the cell's instructions?

1987. What is the term for the duplication of a cell and all of its parts including the DNA of that cell: mitosis or meiosis?

1988. What is the term for the cell process where there are two cell divisions, where after the division, the cells have half the genetic material of the parent: mitosis or meiosis?

SCIENCE

1989. What is the name given to the small structures that carry out the chemical activities of the cell inside the cytoplasm: organelles or mitochondria?

1990. What part of the cell is considered the power house of the cell, enveloped by a double membrane: organelles or mitochondria?

1991. Do organelles inside the cytoplasm include vacuoles and mitochondria?

1992. What are the spherical structures that store food, water, and wastes: mitochondria or vacuoles?

1993. What are the small structures that help break food down in order to release energy for the cell and are shaped like kidney beans: vacuoles or mitochondria?

1994. Do cells in both animals and plants contain a cell membrane, cytoplasm, a nucleus, a nuclear membrane, vacuoles, and mitochondria?

1995. What is the term for organisms that take in nutrients, use energy to do work, reproduce, grow, rid themselves of wastes, and react to outside changes: cells or living things?

1996. Do cells take different shapes depending on the job they do?

1997. What type of cells are organized into tissues, organs, and systems: human or plant?

1998. What is a collection of similar cells that work together like skin and muscle: a tissue or a system?

1999. What is the term for tissues that have similar functions like the heart, brain, or stomach: organs or systems?

2000. What is the term given for organs that work together like the large intestine, the small intestine, and the stomach: tissues or systems?

2001. What are the building blocks of all tissues, organs, and systems: cells or organisms?

2002. What is the commonly known abbreviation for the nucleic acid that contains the genetic instructions used in the development and functioning of all living organism, and is the hereditary material in humans and other organisms: DNA or RNA?

2003. What is the abbreviation for deoxyribonucleic acid: DNA or RNA?

2004. What is the term for the long, single-stranded chain of cells that processes protein and sometimes plays a role in the transmission of genetic information: DNA or RNA?

2005. What is the abbreviation for ribonucleic acid: RNA or DNA?

2006. Are plant cells the same or different from animal cells?

2007. Which type of cell has a cell wall that protects and supports the cell: a plant cell or an animal cell?

2008. Which type of cell has chloroplast that contains the green substance called chlorophyll: a plant cell or an animal cell?

SCIENCE

2009. What is the name of the process in which chlorophyll traps the energy from the Sun enabling the plant to make food?

2010. Which living thing makes its own food: an animal or a plant?

2011. What is the classification of a mushroom: a fungus or a protist?

2012. What do mushroom or fungi release into the air that are cells with a protective coat which spread and start new fungi colonies: caps or spores?

2013. Is yeast used for making bread a type of fungus or protist?

2014. Is green mold that forms on bread a type of fungus or a protist?

2015. Is mildew sometimes found on shower tiles a type of fungus or a protist?

2016. Are some mushrooms and fungi poisonous?

2017. Does a puffball fungus disperse its spores into the ground or into the air?

2018. Are protists considered organisms or cells in the kingdom Protista?

2019. What is the name of the instrument that is often used to observe tiny organisms like protists?

2020. What single-celled organisms get their food from the surrounding environment: protozoa or algae?

2021. What is the name of the tiny hair-like organelles that can help an organism move about in liquids: cilia or euglena?

2022. What is the name of a protozoan that is one large cell, and can stretch its body around small organisms that it wants to eat: algae or amoeba?

2023. What is the name of the multi-celled organism that may grow and spread on a top of a lake or pond, and uses chlorophyll and sunlight to make food: algae or amoeba?

2024. Is seaweed a type of amoeba or algae?

2025. What is another term for seaweed: kelp or algae?

2026. What is the name for the single-celled protists that have both animal and plant features, can move around, can make food through photosynthesis, but also eat bacteria: euglena or protozoa?

2027. What is the name of the small, single-celled organisms that does not have an organized nuclei, and most of them are commonly known as bacteria: protists or prokaryotes?

2028. What high-powered instrument that can magnify organisms thousands of times if necessary to help scientists tell the difference between protists and prokaryotes: an electron microscope or a light microscope?

2029. What are living things called that are too small to see with the naked eye: macro-organisms or micro-organisms?

SCIENCE

2030. What is the term for the study of micro-organisms: microbiology or microscopic biology?

2031. What is the name of the Dutch scientist who is commonly known as the "father of microbiology:" Antonie Van Leeuwenhoek or Louis Pasteur?

2032. What is the term for the earliest form of an organism that may include bacteria, fungi, and viruses and protozoa that can cause disease: germs or cells?

2033. Do some bacteria cause diseases?

2034. Are certain types of bacteria like probiotics beneficial in life?

2035. What type of microorganism would fungi and bacteria be considered because they cause dead plants to rot and help to enrich the soil: constructive or destructive?

2036. What chemical compound can be added to dairy products like cheese and yogurt to aid in the fermentation process: lactic acid bacteria or protein?

2037. What is the name of the fungi used to make bread and other baked goods rise?

2038. Are there certain kinds of good bacteria that are found in our intestines that help us to digest our food?

2039. What type of disease includes meningitis, strep throat, tuberculosis, and bronchitis: bacterial or viral?

2040. What type of disease includes the common cold, chickenpox, and influenza: bacterial or viral?

2041. What is the name of the potentially serious bacterial disease that affects the lungs: tuberculosis or tetanus?

2042. What is the name of the potentially serious bacterial disease that can cause an infection through an open cut and affects the nervous system: hepatitis or tetanus?

2043. What is another name for the poisonous substance that is produced by living cells or organisms: venom or toxin?

2044. What is the term for the microorganisms that may cause diseases such as the common cold or influenza: germs or viruses?

2045. What is the name for the bacterial disease that is transmitted through fleas, ticks, and mites, and is especially common in underdeveloped regions: typhus or cholera?

2046. What is the name for the bacterial disease that affects the small intestine, and is especially common in regions where people do not have access to clean water: typhus or cholera?

2047. What is the name of the French scientist who did research in the 1800's on germs and infections in silkworms, and went on to develop vaccines and immunizations against many diseases: Louis Pasteur or Joseph Lister?

2048. What is the term for the process of heating milk that successfully kills the microbes, or germs, to keep the milk from spoiling, and is named for the French microbiologist who discovered it: sanitization or pasteurization?

SCIENCE

2049. What is the name of the British surgeon that understood the importance of having sterile conditions in hospitals, and is credited with developing antiseptics: Louis Pasteur or Joseph Lister?

2050. What is the name of the medicine that is often used to kill bacteria and cure a disease: probiotics or antibiotics?

2051. What is the name of the microorganism that can grow and reproduce only by entering the cell of another living thing, and can cause serious diseases: a germ or a virus?

2052. What is the name of the injection of a weakened form of a bacterium or virus that is used to prevent diseases: a vaccine or an antibiotic?

2053. Can a vaccine help the body to make antibodies against a disease?

2054. What is the name of the vaccine that the American scientist Jonas Salk developed in the 1950's to prevent this viral disease: tetanus or polio?

2055. What is the general name for an injection into the body of a vaccine that helps the body make antibodies against a disease: an immunization or an antibiotic?

2056. When do many people receive immunizations for mumps, measles, rubella, polio, and chicken pox?

2057. What is the cause of the common cold: a virus or bacteria?

2058. Are antiviral medications available to treat the symptoms of a viral disease like the common cold for which no cure currently exists?

2059. How are prokaryotes classified: by their cell wall shape or by their cell-count?

2060. What is the name given to the prokaryotes found in the soil or water that do photosynthesis without chloroplasts, may be bluish-green or other colors, produce oxygen in the water and in the air, and are the beginning of the food chain for many animals living in water: Cyanobacteria or Eubacteria?

2061. What is the general term for spherical or rod-shaped bacteria with rigid cell walls: Eubacteria or Cyanobacteria?

2062. What is the name for the organism that lives and feeds on other creatures: a parasite or a host?

2063. What is the name for the creature on which a parasite lives: a host or a domain?

2064. What are ticks, fleas, mosquitoes, and lice examples of that bite their hosts and feed off their blood: parasites or hosts?

2065. Can parasites spread dangerous germs that cause diseases like typhus and malaria?

2066. What is the name for the infectious disease that is spread when a mosquito bites someone whose body contains plasmodia parasites, and then bites another person passing on the plasmodia to the new host: malaria or typhus?

2067. What is the name for the bacterial disease that is spread by fleas or lice: malaria or typhus?

SCIENCE

2068. What is the name for the virus that a person can be afflicted with if bitten by an infected mosquito that has bitten an infected bird, and is named for a river in Africa?

2069. Is the best prevention of malaria and West Nile Virus the avoidance of mosquito bites?

2070. What is the name for the parasite fungus that attacks grasses and plants like wheat and barley, and can lead to dangerous diseases: ergot or typhus?

2071. What disease can result if a person consumes infected grain or rye bread infected with this fungus: Ergotism or Escherichia coli, commonly known as E.coli?

2072. What is the name of the effect of Ergotism that reduces the circulation of the blood, causing the body tissue to decay from lack of oxygen, and can lead to the amputation of limbs: gangrene or Staph Infection?

2073. How many kingdoms of organisms are there: three or five?

2074. Can living things be further classified into smaller groups?

2075. What is the system of classifying living things called: toxicology or taxonomy?

2076. Does the classification system become more specific or less specific as you move down the taxonomy?

2077. What is the last part of the classification system after kingdom, phylum, class, order, family, and genus: breed or species?

2078. Can you name the groupings of the taxonomy from the first letter of each word in the following sentence: "**K**ing **P**hilip **c**ame **o**ver **f**or **g**ood **s**paghetti?"

2079. Which is considered a sub-category of species: variety or breed?

2080. If **variety is** a poodle, is the species *familiaris* referring to a domestic dog or a wild dog?

2081. Which is bigger: phylum or species?

2082. Can phylum have subphylum?

2083. Does each kingdom contain one phylum or can it contain several phyla?

2084. Are the categories of the living organism taxonomy in Latin or French?

2085. Is *Canis familiaris* the scientific name for a dog or a cat?

2086. What species does canine refer to: a dog or a cat?

2087. What species does feline refer to: a dog or a cat?

2088. What is the scientific name for **our** species: Homo sapiens or mammals?

2089. What does *Homo* translate to from Latin: man or wise?

2090. What does *sapiens* translate to from Latin: man or wise?

SCIENCE

2091. Do the six main classes of animals include mammals, fishes, birds, reptiles, amphibians, and invertebrates?

2092. Which class has a backbone: vertebrates or invertebrates?

2093. What class of animal is a warm-blooded vertebrate with hair and lungs and produce milk to feed their babies: amphibians or mammals?

2094. What mammals can you name?

2095. What class of animal are dogs, cats, kangaroos, lions, giraffes, and humans?

2096. Are whales and dolphins mammals or fish?

2097. Which class of animal is a warm-blooded vertebrate, is born out of hard-shelled eggs, has feathers and wings, builds nests and can fly?

2098. What birds can you name?

2099. Which continent do the following birds come from and have several species worldwide: ducks, geese, swans, partridges, grouse, turkeys, quail, loons, pelicans, herons, storks, vultures, flamingos, hawks, eagles, falcons, cranes, gulls, pigeons, doves, parakeets, macaws, parrots, roadrunners, owls, hummingbirds, woodpeckers, jays, crows, magpies, ravens, larks, swallows, martins, chickadees, wrens, thrushes, mockingbirds, cardinals, blackbirds, meadowlarks, orioles, and sparrows?

2100. Which class of animal would ostriches and penguins belong to even though they cannot fly?

2101. Which class of animal is a cold-blooded vertebrate that has scales and fins on its body, and lives in water?

2102. What fish species can you name?

2103. What class of animal constitutes 95% of animals that do *not* have a backbone: vertebrates or invertebrates?

2104. Which is the largest phylum of animals that have a segmented body and jointed legs, and include shrimp, crabs, centipedes, and insects: arthropods or arachnids?

2105. Which class of animal have eight legs and include spiders, scorpions, ticks, and daddy-longlegs: arthropods or arachnids?

2106. How are earthworms, snails, clams, octopus, squid, and snails classified: vertebrates or invertebrates?

2107. Which class of animal are the vertebrates that are born in the water, breathe with gills like a fish, develop lungs, and live on land when full grown: reptiles or amphibians?

2108. How does the word *amphibian* translate from Greek: living in two places, or living in one place?

2109. What class of animal are frogs, salamanders, and toads?

2110. What is the name for the tiny tree frog that starts singing after sundown, is native to Puerto Rico, and is named for the sound that it sings: Coquí or Dumpy?

SCIENCE

2111. What class of animal are cold-blooded vertebrate that hatch from eggs on land, have scales on their skin, and breathe with lungs: amphibians or reptiles?

2112. What class of animal are anaconda snakes, boa constrictors, cobras, rattlesnakes, pythons, Gila monsters, chameleon lizards, crocodiles, alligators, iguanas, tortoises, and turtles?

2113. What is the name for the species of reptile that mostly live on the island of Madagascar, is born with special cells that give it the ability to change color, has a 360-degree arc of vision that allows it to see in two directions at once, and hits its prey with a tongue that is often twice the length of its body: a Chameleon or a Gecko Lizard?

2114. What is the only lizard that speaks: the Gecko or the Dragon Lizard?

2115. Which species of lizards is venomous: the Gila monster or the Bearded Dragon?

2116. Are Archaebacteria (ancient bacteria), Eubacteria (true bacteria), Protista, Fungi, Plantae, and Animalia considered classes or kingdoms?

2117. What is the name of the **kingdom** that a Labrador dog would belong to: *animalae* or *plantae*?

2118. What is the name of the **phylum** that the Labrador dog belongs to, because it is a vertebrate animal having this type of internal skeleton: chordata or anthropoda?

2119. What is the name of the **subphylum** of the Labrador dog, so named because it is an animal with a backbone: vertebrata or crustaceda?

2120. What is the name of the **class** of the Labrador dog: amphibea or mammalia?

2121. What is the name of the **order** of a Labrador dog: carnivora or primate?

2122. What do carnivores eat?

2123. What do herbivores eat?

2124. What do *omnivores* eat: plants, animals, or both plants and animals?

2125. What is the name of the **family** that the Labrador dog belongs to: canidae or felidae?

2126. What is a Labrador dog considered: a canine or a feline?

2127. Can canine include coyotes, wolves, and dogs?

2128. What kind of animal is a feline?

2129. Can feline include lions, tigers, and jaguars, as well as domestic cats?

2130. What is the **genus** of the Labrador dog: canis or felis?

2131. What is the **species** of the Labrador dog: familiaris or domestic?

2132. What are foxes and wolves considered: species or family?

SCIENCE

2133. What is another name that refers to the **variety** of Labrador dogs: breed or type?

2134. Which of the following animals has the longest life span: a gorilla, a parrot, or a giant tortoise?

2135. How many years have tortoises in the Galapagos Islands off the coast of Chile, South America been known to live: 85 years or 150 years?

2136. What is the term given for an animal species that is no longer in existence or has died out, like the dinosaur, the Dodo Bird, the Passenger Pigeon, the Great Auk Penguin, the Tasmanian Tiger, the Saber-Toothed Tiger, the Bali Tiger, the Baiji White Dolphin, the half-horse and half-zebra Quagga, and Steller's Sea Cow: extinct or obsolete?

2137. What is the term given for an animal species that is at risk of dying out like the Giant Panda Bear, the Amur Leopard, the Lemur, the Jaguar, the Javan Rhinoceros, the Saola Unicorn, the Leatherback Sea Turtle, the Siberian Tiger, the Galapagos Penguin, the Mountain Gorilla, the Blue Whale, the chimpanzee, and the Indian Elephant: extinct or endangered?

2138. What do habitat destruction, excessive hunting and fishing, oil spills, acid rain, and pollution all contribute to: endangerment or extinction?

2139. Can habitats be endangered?

2140. What type of habitat are the Amazon in Brazil, the Congo in Central Africa, and the Yunque in Puerto Rico: rainforests or tropical jungles?

2141. Which rainforest is considered the most endangered due to deforestation, mining, farming, logging, and road constructing: the Amazon or the Congo?

2142. Is it important to take steps to support efforts to save endangered habitats and animals?

2143. What living things are able to make their own food: plants or animals?

2144. What is the name of the molecule in leaves that makes some or all their cells appear green: chlorophyll or chlorine?

2145. What is the name of the process that plants use to make food that is the combination of "light" and "putting together:" chlorophyll or photosynthesis?

2146. What are the end products of photosynthesis: sugars, oxygen, or both?

2147. Which part of a plant transports the water and nutrients from the soil: the roots or the stem?

2148. What is the name for the plant tube that carries water and nutrients from the soil up the stem to the leaves: the phloem or the xylem?

2149. What is the name of the plant tube that carries sugars from the leaves to the roots, trunk, flowers, and fruits: the xylem or the phloem?

2150. What does the layer of cells below the surface of the leaf contain that serve to conduct the process of photosynthesis: chloroplasts or chlorophyll?

SCIENCE

2151. What are the tiny holes called on the bottom surface of the leaf where water vapor and other gases enter and leave the plant: stomata or stamen?

2152. What is the name of the gas that reaches the cells where the chlorophyll has trapped energy from sunlight, causing a chemical reaction when it combines with water to make sugar: oxygen or carbon dioxide?

2153. What is the name of the food created in the leaves and transported down the plant in the tubes that is used by the plant's cells to grow and to do work: sugars or fruits?

2154. What part of the plant are celery and asparagus: root or stem?

2155. What part of the plant are broccoli and cauliflower: flower or leaf?

2156. What part of the plant or peas and corn on the cob: seed or pod?

2157. What part of the plant are eggplant, squash, tomatoes, and cucumber: fruit or stem?

2158. What part of the plant are carrots, beets, potatoes, and radishes: leaf or root?

2159. What part of the plant are lettuce, cabbage, and spinach: leaf or flower?

2160. Do humans use stored food for energy just like plants?

2161. How many general groups of plants are there: four or eight?

2162. What are mosses, ferns, conifers, and flowers categorized as?

2163. What are the two categories that the plant kingdom is divided into: vascular and non-vascular, or chloroplasts and non-chloroplasts?

2164. Which category of plants has stems, leaves, and roots, as well as tubes that allow water and nutrients to flow through them: vascular or non-vascular?

2165. Which category of plants does not have a tube system to move nutrients, are small and low to the ground, and often grow in moist places: vascular or non-vascular?

2166. Which is an example of a vascular plant: fern or moss?

2167. Which is an example of a non-vascular plant: celery or moss?

2168. What is the process of birth, growth, and death of living things: the life cycle or reproduction?

2169. Are frogs hatched from eggs?

2170. What do tadpoles grow into?

2171. What do frogs lay to begin the life cycle over again?

2172. What do caterpillars change into?

2173. Are chicks hatched from eggs?

SCIENCE

2174. What do baby chicks grow up to be?

2175. What do hens lay to begin the life cycle over again?

2176. What do all living things do in order to keep from dying out or becoming extinct: duplicate or reproduce?

2177. What do the cells in your body do that allow you to grow bigger: divide or reproduce?

2178. What do plants make to reproduce: seeds or spores?

2179. What do mushrooms make to reproduce: seeds or spores?

2180. What is the name of the reproduction that requires combined cells from males and females: sexual or asexual?

2181. What is the name of the reproduction whereby an organism copies itself through cell division: sexual or asexual?

2182. Can bacteria reproduce by simply splitting its single cell in half?

2183. What can grow on cold foods if left out of the refrigerator too long: bacteria or germs?

2184. What keeps harmful bacteria from growing and dividing: warm temperatures or cold temperatures?

2185. What do molds, mildews, and mushrooms form to reproduce: spores or seeds?

2186. What reproduces by forming a bud on one side of its cell and separating from the original cell: yeast or mold?

2187. What is the name of the reproduction of plants whereby a stem cutting can be put into water and grow into another plant: duplication or cloning?

2188. How do simple animals such as sponges, jellyfish, and flatworms reproduce: sexually or asexually?

2189. What is the term for the ability for animals and humans to replace lost cells or lost body parts: reproduction or regeneration?

2190. What are salamanders, lizards, flatworms, spiders, sponges, and many plants all capable of?

2191. When you have a cut on your finger, can your body regenerate new skin cells to help it heal?

2192. What is the name of the fish shaped like a star that can regenerate a new arm if one of them is cut off?

2193. What is the name of an animal similar to a lizard that can regenerate a new leg if it needs to?

2194. If a worm is cut in half, what can each half of the worm grow into?

2195. What is the term for when male and female gamete cells combine to form a fertilized egg: asexual reproduction or sexual reproduction?

SCIENCE

2196. Is reproduction part of the life cycle?

2197. Where does moss grow: on shady rocks or sunny hills?

2198. In the life cycle of moss, does it grow from spores or from buds?

2199. If the buds of a moss plant are ovum or egg gametes, is the moss plant male or female?

2200. If the buds at the tips of a moss plant are sperm gametes that can swim, is the moss plant male or female?

2201. What is it called when the sperm from a male plant swims to the egg of a female plant: reproduction or fertilization?

2202. Does the fertilized egg from the female moss plant divide to form a capsule at the top of the stalk or the bottom of the stalk?

2203. What is released from the capsule when it matures to start the life cycle all over again: spores or gametes?

2204. What is the name of the initial cell formed when two gamete cells join during sexual reproduction: an embryo or a zygote?

2205. What does a fertilized egg of a plant develop into: an embryo or a zygote?

2206. What is the name of a simple seed plant meaning "cone carrier:" a pine tree or a conifer?

2207. What is the reproductive part of a pine tree: the pine needles or the pinecones?

2208. Are the small cones on a pine tree that store millions of grains of pollen male or female?

2209. What carries the pollen from the male cone to the eggs inside the larger female cone resulting in fertilization: wind or water?

2210. What drops to the ground when the cone opens: the seeds or the eggs?

2211. What happens to the conifer seed if the soil is moist and the seed germinates?

2212. Is the seed from a conifer considered naked or clothed?

2213. What group of plants do conifers belong to: gymnosperms meaning naked seeds, or angiosperms meaning covered seeds?

2214. What do angiosperms or "covered seeds" all have in common: they have needles, they have flowers, or they have cones?

2215. What are some fruits with seeds inside them that are angiosperms?

2216. Are tomatoes, cucumbers, strawberries, oranges, and green peppers considered gymnosperms or angiosperms?

SCIENCE

2217. Are flowers made up of the same parts or different parts depending on the type of plant it comes from?

2218. What is the outer ring of a flower called that is usually green, and is similar to the leaves attached to the stem at the base of the flower: the sepals or the petals?

2219. What part of a flower is located inside the sepals that are often colorful and attract insects: the leaves or the petals?

2220. What part of a flower is located inside the petal and is the male reproductive organ: the pollen or the stamen?

2221. What does each stamen have on its tip where millions of tiny pollen grains are made: an anther or a pollen tube?

2222. What is the name of the very center of most flowers that contain the female reproductive organs: the pistil or the stigma?

2223. What part of a flower does the pistil tube lead down to that contains the eggs: the stigma or the ovary?

2224. Where are the ovules produced in flowering plants: the ovary or the pistil?

2225. What is the first step of flower fertilization that moves the pollen from the anther to the top of the pistil: pollination or germination?

2226. What types of animals are credited for pollinating many flowers?

2227. What does a bee sip from a flower taking pollen along with it that it can leave on another flower: nectar or honey?

2228. What is it called when a new plant begins to sprout roots and becomes a new plant: germination or pollination?

2229. What happens when the seed from a plant reaches the soil and germinates?

2230. What part of a bean seed protects the seed and keeps it from drying out: the seed coat or the endosperm?

2231. What part of a bean seed contains food that helps to keep an embryo alive, and helps it germinate until it can make its own food: the endosperm or the nucleus?

2232. When water or rain softens the seed coat in the soil, does the embryo inside the seed begin to grow as it uses the stored food inside the seed?

2233. What part of the plant helps it make its own food for photosynthesis: the flowers or the leaves?

2234. What does an adult plant develop that produces more seeds to start the life cycle over again: cones or flowers?

2235. What are monocots and dicots: flowering plants or conifers?

SCIENCE

2236. What would grass, corn, and palm trees be considered: monocots or dicots?

2237. What would oak trees, roses, and daisies be considered: monocots or dicots?

2238. What kind of flowering plant is it when a single seed leaf breaks out of a seed and pushes through the soil: a monocot or a dicot?

2239. What kind of flowering plant sends up *two* seed leaves: a monocot or a dicot?

2240. Is a grass seed considered a monocot or a dicot?

2241. Is a bean seed classified as a monocot or a dicot?

2242. What are the flower petals on a monocot in multiples of: three or four?

2243. What are the flower petals on a dicot in multiples of: three or four?

2244. Which flowering plant typically has long narrow leaves with vines running parallel: monocots or dicots?

2245. Which flowering plants typically have broad leaves with veins that resemble nets: monocots or dicots?

2246. What are wheat, corn, rice, lilacs, and tulips classified as: monocots or dicots?

2247. What are most fruits, vegetables, and garden flowers classified as: monocots or dicots?

2248. Do plants, animals, and humans reproduce?

2249. Does sexual reproduction occur with or without another plant or animal?

2250. Does asexual reproduction occur with or without another plant or animal?

2251. Do most animals reproduce asexually meaning outside, or sexually?

2252. Do both plants and animals produce male and female gametes?

2253. What are the gametes in *male* animals called: sperm or eggs?

2254. What are the gametes in *female* animals called: sperm or eggs?

2255. What is the name of the male organ in animals where sperm are produced: the testes or the ovaries?

2256. What is the name of the female organ in animals where eggs are produced: the testes or the ovaries?

2257. Which animal has both sperm and egg-producing organs: earthworm or spider?

2258. What is the name of the process by which the sperm and the egg join together *outside* the bodies of the parents: internal fertilization or external fertilization?

2259. What is the name of the process by which the sperm and the egg join together *inside* the bodies of the parents: internal fertilization or external fertilization?

SCIENCE

2260. What is the form of external fertilization that takes place with fish: cloning or spawning?

2261. What do female fish release into the water during spawning?

2262. What do male fish release into the water that swim to the released eggs and fertilize them?

2263. Do birds, horses, and humans reproduce by internal or external fertilization?

2264. Do members of a species usually mate and produce offspring with other members of the same species, or of a different species?

2265. What is the term for a fertilized egg: an embryo or a zygote?

2266. What does a zygote develop into after several weeks of dividing and growing: an embryo or a fetus?

2267. What is the name of the female organ in mammals where the embryo develops: the fetus or the uterus?

2268. Where does the zygote travel from before it attaches itself to the wall of the uterus: the ovary or the fetus?

2269. What is an embryo called during the later stages of its development: a fetus or an infant?

2270. Is the amount of time that it takes an animal to develop the same or different for each species?

2271. How many months does it take the average human embryo to develop before it is born: nine months or eleven months?

2272. How many months does it take for a sheep embryo to develop: three months or five months?

2273. How many months does it take for a horse to develop inside its mother: nine months or eleven months?

2274. Which one of the following species look after their young after they are born: frogs, turtles, snakes, or alligators?

2275. How many years do lion cubs stay with their parents on average: two years or four years?

2276. What is the term for a group of lions: a pack or a pride?

2277. What is the term for the development of an organism from birth through reproduction, and then death: a life cycle or a life chain?

2278. What is the correct sequence of the development of a horse: embryo, fetus, foal, colt, horse **or** fetus, embryo, colt, foal, horse?

2279. What is the correct sequence of growth stages in humans: embryo, fetus, baby **or** fetus, embryo, baby?

2280. What is the name for the human growth stage after a baby: toddler or child?

2281. What is the name for the human growth stage after a toddler: adolescent or child?

SCIENCE

2282. What is the name for the human growth stage after a child: adolescent or adult?

2283. What is the name for the human growth stage after an adolescent: adult or old age?

2284. What is the name for the human growth stage after an adult: old age or middle age?

2285. What is the general term that has corresponding ages for zygote, blastocyst, embryo, fetus, neonate, infant, toddler, preschooler, elementary school age, preadolescent, adolescent, young adult, adult, middle age, old age, and death: Human Development Stages or Human Life Cycle? ?

2286. What is the name of the physical human growth stage that occurs between the ages of eight and seventeen: puberty or adolescence?

2287. What is the name of the human growth stage that includes both the physical and psychological development from puberty to full maturity: adolescence or adulthood?

2288. What is the term for the chemicals that are released into the bloodstream from glands in your body that cause mental, physical, and emotional changes: hormones or insulin?

2289. What is the term for the stage of development during adolescence when the bodies of males and females are biologically capable of producing children: adulthood or puberty?

2290. Is human reproduction similar or different to reproduction in other mammals?

2291. Can you name the reproductive organs of the human female?

2292. Can you name the reproductive organs of the human male?

2293. What is the term for what a fertilized egg develops into: a fetus or a zygote?

2294. What is the correct order of the following: fetus, zygote, and embryo?

2295. Where does the fetus grow inside the female body: the stomach or the uterus?

2296. What is the term for twins that develop from two separate eggs that are fertilized at the same time resulting in two boys, two girls, or a boy and a girl that do **not** resemble one another: identical or fraternal?

2297. What is the term for twins that develop from the same fertilized egg resulting in two boys, two girls, or a boy and a girl that resemble one another: identical or fraternal?

2298. What are the heart, lungs, spleen stomach, liver, intestine, gallbladder, pancreas, glands, kidneys, skin, and bladder classified as: organs or internal structures?

2299. Do the major organ systems include circulatory, respiratory, nervous, skeletal, digestive, endocrine, urinary, and reproductive?

2300. Which system of organs are classified as endocrine or exocrine: Glandular or Respiratory?

2301. What is the name for the substance that is secreted by the pituitary and the thyroid glands: hormones or insulin?

SCIENCE

2302. What kind of gland secretes *outside* the body like sweat: exocrine duct glands o endocrine ductless glands?

2303. What kind of gland secretes chemicals *inside* the body: exocrine duct glands or endocrine ductless glands?

2304. What is the name of the small gland known as the "master gland" located where the spinal cord meets the brain, and secretes the hormone that begins the puberty stage: the pituitary gland or the thyroid gland?

2305. What is the name of the gland located below the larynx or voice box in front of the neck that secretes a hormone that controls the rate at which the body uses food and burns energy: thyroid gland or pituitary gland?

2306. What is the name of the gland that is divided into two parts, one with ducts and the other ductless that is located behind the stomach: thyroid or pancreas?

2307. Which part of the pancreas releases chemicals that help the digestive system break down food: the part with ducts or the ductless part?

2308. What part of the pancreas secretes hormones into the blood that helps to regulate how the body uses sugar: the part with ducts or the ductless part?

2309. What is the name of the specific hormone secreted by the pancreas that regulates body sugar: adrenaline or insulin?

2310. What is the name of the disease that a person can get when the pancreas does not produce enough insulin: diabetes or influenza?

2311. What is the name of the gland located above the kidneys that releases a hormone called adrenaline that speeds up the heart: adrenal glands or the thyroid glands?

2312. What is the name of the system that transports blood throughout the body and includes the heart, arteries, capillaries, veins, blood, and blood vessels: the respiratory system or the circulatory system?

2313. What is the name of the system that brings air into the body and includes the nose, trachea, and lungs: the respiratory system or the circulatory system?

2314. What does a respirator help a patient to do in a hospital?

2315. What is the name of the system that breaks down foods into vitamins, minerals, proteins, fats and carbohydrates, and includes the esophagus, stomach, and small intestine: the digestive system or the endocrine system?

2316. What is the name of our body's defense system that helps us fight off diseases and infections in the organs, tissues, and cells: the endocrine system or the immune system?

2317. What is the name of the system that is made up of glands that release hormones that help control the body's development, growth, and metabolism: the lymphatic system or the endocrine system?

SCIENCE

2318. What is the name of the system that filters out organisms that can cause diseases, generates disease-fighting antibodies, produces white blood cells, and is made up of a network of vessels that help circulate body fluids: the immune system or the lymphatic system?

2319. What is the name of the system that sends, receives, and processes nerve impulses throughout the body that help tell your muscles and organs what to do, and includes the spinal cord, brain, and nerves: the skeletal system or the nervous system?

2320. What is the name of the system that is made up of tissues that help control the movement of your body, and includes your arms, legs, stomach, and heart: the skeletal system or the muscular system?

2321. What is the name of the system that works with the muscular system to help your body move, shapes your body, protects your organs, and includes bones, ligaments, and tendons: the skeletal system or the bone system?

2322. What is the name of the system that the skull, spinal column, ribs, sternum, pelvis, femur, tibia and patella or knee cap are part of?

2323. How many bones do adults have: 106 or 206?

2324. How many cranial and facial bones make up the human skill: 22 or 32?

2325. How many vertebrae does the human spine consist of: 23 or 33?

2326. What is the name of the layers of strong but flexible cushion that protect your vertebrae and allow you to bend: cartilage or ligaments?

2327. Where are cartilage, tendons, and ligaments located: in the muscles or in the joints?

2328. What is the name of the connective tissue that connects the muscles to the bones and allows them to move: tendons or cartilage?

2329. What are molars, wisdom, bicuspids, and incisors?

2330. How many teeth do grown adults have: 22 or 32?

2331. What is the name of the top part of a tooth that is visible: the root or the crown?

2332. What is the name of the bottom part of a tooth that is not visible: the root or the crown?

2333. What is the name of the protective white substance covering each tooth: porcelain or enamel?

2334. What is the name of the pink, fleshy part of your mouth where your teeth are located: the jaw or the gum?

2335. What can you do to ensure that your teeth and gums stay healthy?

2336. What is the name of a dentist that specializes in straightening teeth: an ophthalmologist or an orthodontist?

2337. What is the name of the fatty tissue inside your bones that produces both red and white blood cells: marrow or plasma?

SCIENCE

2338. What is the name of the system that manufactures cells that allows humans to produce children, and involves an egg from the female and sperm from the male: the regeneration system or the reproductive system?

2339. What is the name of the system that is responsible for eliminating waste from your body and involves the kidneys and the bladder: the tract system or the urinary system?

2340. What does our body produce to help fight off diseases: antibodies or antigens?

2341. What is a name of the antibiotic that helps destroy many types of bacterial diseases like pneumonia and strep throat discovered by Dr. Alexander Fleming in 1928: penicillin or ibuprofen?

2342. What can you do to ensure that your body stays healthy?

2343. What is the name of the annual award, presented in Oslo, Norway, that recognizes outstanding achievements and contributions to chemistry, physics, medicine, economics, literature, or peace: the Nobel Prize or the Pulitzer Prize?

2344. What is the name of the Polish astronomer who first theorized around 1530 that the Sun and not the Earth is the center of the solar system: Albert Einstein or Nicolaus Copernicus?

2345. What is the name of the German astronomer who is credited for contributing his three laws of planetary motion that he devised in the early 1600's: Galileo Galilei or Johannes Kepler?

2346. What was the name of the Italian scientist and astronomer who is regarded as the "Father of Modern Astronomy," who further proved the theory that supported Copernicus that the Sun is the center of the solar system, and is credited for inventing a telescope, compass, and thermometer in the early 1600's: Isaac Newton or Galileo Galilei?

2347. What is the name of the English scientist and mathematician who is credited for the invention of calculus, a new theory of light and color, the three laws of motion, the law of gravitation, and published his findings in a book in 1687: Isaac Newton or Johannes Kepler?

2348. What is the name of the German physicist who is most famous for his 1714 invention of the mercury-in-glass thermometer, and for developing a temperature scale that is named for him: Gabriel Fahrenheit or Anders Celsius?

2349. What is the name of the Swedish scientist who developed a classification system that includes kingdoms, classes, orders, and species, and published his findings in 1735 in his work, "Systema Naturae:" Carl Linnaeus or Ernest Just?

2350. What is the name of the scientist, inventor, and one of America's Founding Fathers who in 1752 determined that lightning is electrical after conducting an experiment with a key and a kite during an electrical storm in Philadelphia: Benjamin Franklin or Thomas Jefferson?

2351. What is the name of the British scientist credited for discovering hydrogen in 1766, or what he called "inflammable air:" Henry Cavendish or James Maxwell?

SCIENCE

2352. What is the name of the Italian chemist who is credited for his 1811 hypothesis that "equal volumes of gases at the same temperature and pressure contain the same number of molecules regardless of their chemical nature and physical properties," and has an honorary number named for him, 6.02 x 10 to the twenty-third, that represents the number of molecules in one mole:" Avogadro or Cannizaro?

2353. What is the name of the French science teacher who in 1820 discovered a way to measure the flow of current, and his name is a measurement of electrical current: Andre Ampere or Robert Current?

2354. What is the name of the English scientist who is credited with the discovery of electromagnetism in 1821, the invention of the electric motor, and also created the first simple burner: Robert Bunsen or Michael Faraday?

2355. What is the name of the name of the English naturalist who proposed the theory of evolution and natural selection, the notion that all species of life evolved over time from common ancestors, and conducted some of his research in the Galapagos Islands in 1835: Henry Cavendish or Charles Darwin?

2356. What is the name of the first woman to earn a medical degree in the United States in 1849: Elizabeth Blackwell or Marie Curie?

2357. What is the name of the German chemist and inventor who perfected a flame-making device called a burner in 1855, and analyzed gases: Luther Burbank or Robert Bunsen?

2358. What is the name of the scientist who studied heredity and genetics between 1856 and 1863, established that there are dominant and recessive characteristics in living things after experimenting with pea plants, and is regarded as the father of the science of genetics: Louis Pasteur or Gregor Mendel?

2359. What is the name of the Scottish physicist who was awarded a prize in 1859 for his essay "On the Stability of Saturn's Rings," created the first durable color photograph in 1861, stated the theory of electromagnetism in 1865, and contributed to developing the kinetic theory of gases: James Maxwell or Joseph Gibbs?

2360. What is the name of the Russian scientist who in 1871 discovered periodic law, and finalized a system for organizing the chemical elements known as the periodic table: Gregor Mendel of Dmitri Mendeleev?

2361. What is the name of the French chemist who developed a process of pasteurization in 1862, helped save the silk farm industry in 1865 after proving that microbes were attacking healthy silkworms, developed a vaccine for rabies in 1882 and successfully vaccinated a young boy who was bitten by a rabid dog in 1885, and has an Institute named for him in Paris, France: Louis Pasteur or Gregor Mendel?

2362. What is the name of the Austrian neurologist and researcher who presented many theories of psychiatry and the mind during the early 1900's: Sigmund Freud or Alfred Adler?

SCIENCE

2363. What is the name of the New Zealand chemist who discovered two types of radiation and coined the terms "alpha" and "beta," became one of the first alchemists when he changed nitrogen to oxygen by splitting the atoms, is known for the atomic model named for him that shows electrons circling around the nucleus, and is credited for coining the term "half-life" after devising a radioactive dating system used to date minerals, and in 1908 won a Nobel Prize for Chemistry: Ernest Rutherford or Frederick Soddy?

2364. What is the name of the first woman scientist from Poland to win a Nobel Prize in Physics in 1903 for her research on radiation, and another in Chemistry in 1911 for her discovery of elements polonium and radium: Marie Curie or Elizabeth Blackwell?

2365. What is the name of the German physicist who introduced the concepts of the Theory of Relativity and the Electromagnetic Theory of Light, won a Nobel Prize in Physics in 1921, and is known for inventing the mass-energy formula, $E=mc^2$: Galileo Galilei or Albert Einstein?

2366. What is the name of the Danish scientist who won a Nobel Prize in Physics in 1922 for his research on the structure of atoms, and the radiation that comes from them: Niels Bohr or Max Born?

2367. What is the name of the African American research scientist who in the 1920's studied the functions of individual cells and discovered that all activity not only depended on the nucleus, but on the ectoplasm, and earned an award from the NAACP: Ernest Just or Carl Linnaeus?

2368. What is the name of the scientist who contributed so much to the field of astrophysics by announcing his discoveries in 1925 regarding the law of the expanding universe and the presence of other galaxies besides the Milky Way that NASA named a space telescope for him: Johannes Kepler of Edwin Hubble?

2369. What is the name of the Scottish scientist who discovered penicillin in 1928 after he returned from vacation and discovered the presence of bacteria destroying mold in a Petri dish, proceeded to develop the world's first antibiotic that proved to be very effective in curing often fatal bacterial infections, was knighted in 1944, and earned the Nobel Prize in 1945: Alexander Fleming or Michael Faraday?

2370. What is the name of the American research chemist who discovered in 1949 how to extract a steroid called cortisone from soybeans that helps people who are suffering from arthritis, a disease that attacks the body's joints, made this substance widely available, and earned him an award from the NAACP: Percy Lavon Julian or Ernest Just?

2371. What is the name of the American medical research credited for developing the first effective vaccine against polio in 1952: Percy Lavon Julian or Jonas Salk?

2372. What is the name of the scientist, animal rights activist, and humanitarian who is most noted for her 1960 study of chimpanzees in Africa in social situations, and their parallel traits to humans: Elizabeth Blackwell or Jane Goodall?

2373. What is the name for the medieval primitive science aimed at transforming common base metals like lead into silver or gold: chemistry or alchemy?

SCIENCE

2374. What is the name for the science that focuses on the study and making of maps: cartography or geography?

2375. What is the name for the branch of biology that deals with plant life: plantology or botany?

2376. What is the name for the branch of science involving the study of animals and animal behavior: taxidermy or zoology?

2377. What is the name for the practice of preparing, stuffing, and mounting the skins, antlers, bodies, or heads of animals like bear, deer, moose, or fish for display: taxidermy or zoology?

2378. What is the name of the place where many scientists conduct their research and experiments?

2379. What is the name for a proposed explanation that is made on the basis of limited evidence that requires using the Scientific Method to prove it: a theory or a hypothesis?

2380. What is the name for the scientific principle that his based on a hypothesis and is backed up by testing and evidence: a theory or an assumption?

2381. What is the name of the process that involves asking and answering scientific questions, making observations, formulating a theory, designing experiments to test that theory, analyzing data, and communicating the results: Scientific Inquiry or Scientific Method?

2382. What experiments have you conducted where you carried out the process of the Scientific method?

2383. Are results from scientific findings more likely to be published in scientific journals or medical books?

2384. Which is your favorite field of science?

Chapter 5 – Social Studies

Social Studies – Pre-School

1. What is the name of the country that you live in?
2. Which state do you live in?
3. Which city do you live in?
4. What language(s) do you speak?
5. Do we have art, music, and dance as part of our culture?
6. What does an artist do?
7. What are the names of some musical instruments?
8. When do we celebrate America's Independence Day?
9. What holidays do we celebrate?
10. What is our nationality?
11. What is the name of the first people that lived in America?
12. Who came to America from England on the Mayflower, and met with the Native American Indians?
13. What holiday do we celebrate where we remember the first big feast that the Native American Indians and the Pilgrims had after a good harvest?
14. What is the name for the houses of the Indians: Totems or Teepees?
15. What is the name of our first President of the United States?
16. Can you name something that is named for George Washington?
17. Which American President is considered the "Father of our Country?"
18. What did President George Washington ask Betsy Ross to sew?
19. What colors are in our American flag?
20. What is the name of the American President that was born in a log cabin in Indiana and was often called "Honest Abe?"
21. During the time of President Lincoln there was a Civil war in which the North fought against whom: the South or the West?

SOCIAL STUDIES

22. What was a major cause of the Civil War pitting the North against the South: slavery or farmland?
23. What were the two main crops that were grown on the farms or plantations in the South: potatoes and tomatoes, or cotton and tobacco?
24. What is the name of the Nobel-Prize winning African American pastor who led the Civil Rights Movement in the 1950's, and gave a famous speech called, "I Have a Dream?"
25. Did Martin Luther King Jr. have a "dream" where all people of all races have equal rights?

Social Studies – Kindergarten

26. Are you a member of a family?
27. In what ways can a child become a member of a family?
28. Can you name the members of your *immediate* family?
29. What relatives outside of your immediate family can you name?
30. What is the name of the city or town we live in?
31. What is the name of the state we live in?
32. How many states are there in the United States?
33. What is the full name of the country we live in?
34. What is the name of the country above us to the north?
35. What is the name of the country below us to the south?
36. Do you think that Mexican culture is similar of different than our culture?
37. Do you think Canadian culture is similar of different than our culture?
38. Are all the people that live in America originally from America?
39. Do you think the Native Americans lived differently than we do today?
40. Does the word "native" refer to someone that was born here?
41. Are Native Americans also called American Indians?
42. How did Native Americans get their food?
43. What kinds of tools or weapons did Native Americans have?
44. What kinds of animals did Native Americans hunt for?
45. What is the name of the "house" that many Native Americans lived in, made of long poles and covered with Buffalo hide?

SOCIAL STUDIES

46. What shape are most teepees?

47. What kinds of things did Native Americans make?

48. What is the name of the shoes worn by many Native Americans?

49. What is the name of the dwelling that some early settlers like the Iroquois Indians lived in, made of wood and bark: longhouses or cliff houses?

50. What is the name of the dwelling built by Native Americans of the Southwest like the Hopi tribe, that were like small villages formed out of adobe clay bricks: cliff dwellings or pueblos?

51. What is the name of the dwelling built by Woodland Indians like the Ojibwa Tribe that were round houses with round tops made from poles, hide, and bark, and were either portable or permanent: teepees or wigwams?

52. What is the name of the boat that Native Americans carved from the bark of birch trees?

53. What is the name for the symbolic sculptures that Native Americans carved from large trees?

54. What is the nationality of our family?

55. Do all people have skin color that is the same or different?

56. What is our religion or belief system?

57. Does everyone have the same religion or belief, or can they be different?

58. Is it good to embrace and respect everyone's differences?

59. Why do you suppose the United States with its diverse population is called the "melting pot?"

60. On which continent is the United States located: North American or South America?

61. How many continents are there: six or seven?

62. Which continent is missing from the following: Asia, Europe, Africa, North America, South America, and Australia?

63. Which is bigger: a continent or a country?

64. Which continent is the largest continent in the world: Asia or Africa?

65. Can you name a large country in Asia?

66. In which continent are China, India, and Russia located: Asia or Africa?

67. What is the name of the second largest continent with 54 countries, the Sahara Desert, the Nile River, and is known for its abundant wildlife like elephants, giraffes, zebras, leopards, and cheetahs?

68. What is the name of the third largest continent with 23 countries that include the United States, Canada, Mexico, the Caribbean Islands, Bermuda, the Central American countries, and Greenland, the world's largest island?

SOCIAL STUDIES

69. What is the name of the fourth largest continent with 12 independent countries; the territories of the Falkland Islands, the Galapagos Islands, and French Guiana; where the Andes Mountains, the Amazon Rainforest, the Amazon River, Angel Falls, and the Atacama Desert are located; and is known for animals like llamas, alpacas, and parrots?

70. What is the name of the fifth largest continent that is located at the South Pole, is 98% solid ice, and is known for its abundance of glaciers, penguins, and seals?

71. What is the name of the sixth largest continent, part of the peninsula of Eurasia with 47 countries, and includes Germany, Austria, Switzerland, Spain, Italy, France, Norway, Sweden, Denmark, Finland, Belgium, England, Scotland, Ireland, Poland, Russia, Greece, and The Vatican?

72. What is the name of the smallest continent that includes an island where kangaroos, koalas and platypus live, New Zealand, many islands of the South Pacific, and is collectively known as Oceania?

73. What is the full name of the country we live in?

74. What are the two states that are located outside of the continent of North America?

75. What does the abbreviation U.S.A. stand for?

76. What is the common nickname for the symbol of our country, also called "the red, white, and blue:" Old Glory or the Stars and Stripes?

77. What are you drawing when you draw land and water shapes on a piece of paper?

78. What kind of map shows the locations of towns, cities, and highways: state or physical?

79. Can you locate where a relative lives, or where we go on vacation on a map?

80. What is a map representation called that is a three-dimensional scale model of the Earth?

81. What are the two main oceans on our planet?

82. What are the four cardinal directions that tell us where things are?

83. Which direction is the opposite of south?

84. Which direction is the opposite of east?

85. In which direction does the Sun rise: east or west?

86. In which direction does the Sun set: east or west?

87. In most cases, which direction is the top of the map: north or south?

88. In most cases, which direction is the bottom of the map: north or south?

89. Do you think Christopher Columbus used a map when he sailed here from Spain?

SOCIAL STUDIES

90. When Columbus landed after more than a month, what did he call the natives because he was so sure that he had reached the East Indies?

91. Did Columbus think that the world was flat or round?

92. What is the name of the country named for the Italian navigator Amerigo Vespucci?

93. What language or languages do you speak?

94. How do you think family life today is different now than many years ago?

95. What things do we have today that they didn't during pioneer days?

96. What kind of a school do you think that pioneer children attended?

97. Can you name some things that families of long ago had that we do not have today?

98. Which number president was George Washington?

99. Can you see George Washington's picture on a quarter and a dollar bill?

100. Who was the second president of the United States: John Adams or Thomas Jefferson?

101. Who was the third president of the United States: John Adams or Thomas Jefferson?

102. What is the name of the document that Thomas Jefferson drafted in 1776 that was written to explain to foreign nations why the colonies had decided to separate themselves from Great Britain that declared "All men are created equal: The Declaration of Independence or the Bill of Rights?

103. Who was the first to sign The Declaration of Independence: John Hancock or John Adams?

104. Did Thomas Jefferson want to declare independence from England or Spain in 1776?

105. Was Abraham Lincoln our 16th President or our 17th President?

106. Whose face is on the penny: Washington or Lincoln?

107. What was the nickname of our 26th President, Theodore Roosevelt?

108. What is the name of the stuffed animal that was named for "Teddy" Roosevelt?

109. What is the name of the famous monument in South Dakota carved in stone with the faces of Washington, Jefferson, Lincoln, and Roosevelt: Mount Rushmore or Mount Vernon?

110. Who is the President of the United States today?

111. What is the name of the house where the President of the United States lives?

112. Where is the capital and the White House located: Washington or Washington, D.C?

113. What does D.C. stand for in Washington, D.C: District of Colombia or District of Congress?

114. Are dance, theater, and music all part of American culture?

SOCIAL STUDIES

115. What is the name of a dance where the dancers wear pointed shoes?
116. What are the holidays that we celebrate?
117. What family *tradition* do we have when we celebrate Thanksgiving or some other holiday?
118. What foods are *custom* for Americans to eat on Thanksgiving Day?
119. Who were the two groups of people who gathered to eat a great feast at the first Thanksgiving?
120. Which month of the year do we celebrate New Year's Day?
121. Which month of the year do we celebrate Thanksgiving Day?
122. Which month of the year is Christmas celebrated in?
123. Do you think customs are the same or different in other countries?
124. When is America's Independence Day celebrated?
125. How would you describe the American flag?
126. Who was the first President of the United States?
127. Do we celebrate Presidents' Day in January or February?
128. Do we honor George Washington and Abraham Lincoln on Presidents' Day?
129. In which month do we honor Martin Luther King Jr: January or February?
130. What are the four seasons?
131. What holidays do we celebrate in winter?
132. What holidays do we celebrate in spring?
133. What holidays do we celebrate in summer?
134. What holidays do we celebrate in fall?
135. Do you think that other cultures have different holidays that they celebrate?
136. Do you think that there are different ways to celebrate a holiday?
137. Are homes here in America the same or different as homes in other countries?
138. Do you think we eat the same foods here as they do in other countries?
139. Is spaghetti and lasagna Mexican food or Italian food?
140. Are enchiladas and tacos Mexican food or Italian food?
141. Can you name other (ethnic) foods from another country?
142. Do you think that music is the same or different in other countries?

SOCIAL STUDIES

143. How is our family the same as other families that you know?
144. How is our family different than other families you know?
145. Do you think that each person in the world is special and unique?
146. Do people have different body shapes and sizes?
147. What are some qualities of being a responsible citizen?
148. What are some responsibilities that you have?
149. What do we use in order to buy goods and services?
150. Before money, what do you think that people long ago used in exchange for goods and services?
151. What do many people have to do in order to earn money?
152. Do we have to make choices with money?
153. Is buying food a want or a need?
154. Is buying a toy a want or a need?
155. What is the name for American currency?
156. Can you name some of the coins and bills we use as currency in the U.S?
157. Do you think that currency (money) is the same or different in other countries?
158. What do you do or can you do to earn money?
159. Is it important to save part of the money that you earn?
160. What is the name of a place that people use to keep the money that they earn?

Social Studies – 1st Grade

161. What is the difference between a map and a globe?
162. Why do we use a map?
163. Where is "North" on a direction compass: at the top or bottom?
164. Where is "South" on a direction compass: at the top or bottom?
165. Where is "East" on a direction compass: to the right or to the left?
166. Where is "West" on a direction compass: to the right or to the left?
167. Can you locate our city (town) on a map?
168. Can you locate our state on a map?

SOCIAL STUDIES

169. What is the name of the country you live in?

170. Can you locate our country on a world map?

171. Can you locate our continent on a globe?

172. How many states are in the United States of America?

173. What is the name of the state you live in?

174. Which two states are located outside the continental United States?

175. What is the capital city of the United States?

176. What is the name of the President of our country?

177. What is the name of the residence of the President and first family in Washington, D.C?

178. How do we elect the President and Vice-President to lead our country?

179. What is the capital of our state?

180. What is our state famous for?

181. What is the name of the *county* you live in?

182. Have you ever gone to the county fair?

183. Does our state have a state fair?

184. What is the name of the city we live in?

185. What is the name of the street we live on?

186. What types of things would you find in a city?

187. What types of things would you find in a small town or farm community?

188. What is the name for the total number of people living in a city, town, state, or country: residents or population?

189. How can communities around the world be different?

190. How can communities around the world be similar?

191. Do you live in a culturally diverse community with many different types of people?

192. What kind of a society do we live, whereby we follow laws and act as responsible citizens: libertarian or democratic?

193. Can you cite the Pledge of Allegiance?

194. What is the name of a song we can sing to honor our flag?

195. Does each country have its own National Anthem?

SOCIAL STUDIES

196. Can you describe how the American flag looks?

197. Do you know the colors of the Mexican flag?

198. What are the two colors in the Canadian flag?

199. What do you know about the culture (people, food, language, music, dance, holidays, Indian groups, currency, monuments, and landforms) of Mexico?

200. What do you know about the culture (people, food, language, music, dance, holidays, and wildlife) of Canada?

201. What language is spoken in Mexico?

202. What two languages are spoken in Canada?

203. What kind of wildlife is found in Canada?

204. Do you think that different countries celebrate different holidays?

205. What holiday do we celebrate the first Monday in September to honor workers and laborers?

206. What is celebrated on October 12th to remember this navigator that sailed the ocean blue on three ships from Spain?

207. What do we celebrate on October 31st when we decorate in black and orange, carve pumpkins, and wear costumes?

208. What is the name of the national holiday that falls on November 11th in which we honor military veterans, all who have served in the U.S Armed Forces: Veterans Day or Memorial Day?

209. What holiday do we celebrate on the fourth Thursday of November to give thanks, as the Native Americans and the Pilgrims did back in 1621 after a bountiful harvest?

210. How are our lives different today compared to the lives of the Pilgrims?

211. What is one of our family *traditions* for celebrating Thanksgiving?

212. What holiday is celebrated in December by many people?

213. What is a *custom* for Americans during the December holiday season?

214. Do you think all cultures share this same customs?

215. What holiday is celebrated on the first of January with food and music and parties?

216. What national holiday is celebrated the third Monday of January to honor this activist who preached to the nation in defense of the civil rights of African Americans?

217. Besides Valentine's Day, what important national holiday do we celebrate in February to honor former leaders of the United States?

SOCIAL STUDIES

218. Who was the first President of the United States whose face is pictured on the nickel: Lincoln or Washington?

219. Who was the 16th President of the United States whose face is pictured on the penny and was regarded as "Honest Abe?"

220. What is celebrated on March 17th that is a tribute to people of Irish descent?

221. Is there a holiday in spring that we celebrate as a family?

222. Do you know the name of the holiday that is celebrated in Mexico on a specific date at the beginning of May that celebrates the Mexican victory of the peasants of Puebla over the superior French army on May 5th, 1862?

223. What is the name of the national holiday at the end of May that is a day to remember and honor those who gave their lives in wars while serving in America's Armed Forces?

224. What is the date and month of America's Independence Day?

225. From where did the United States win its independence: the United Kingdom or France?

226. Do we have family photographs of holidays and celebrations?

227. What things do we have as symbols of a holiday?

228. What do many people do to earn money to purchase goods and services?

229. What is an example of a "want" that someone might purchase with the money he or she earns?

230. What is an example of a "need" that someone might purchase with the money he or she earns?

231. What are some basic needs that people have?

232. What denominations of coins are you familiar with?

233. What is the value of a penny?

234. What is the value of a nickel?

235. What is the value of a dime?

236. What is the value of a quarter?

237. What is the value of a fifty cent piece?

238. What denominations of bills or paper currency are you familiar with?

239. Can you name the currency of another country?

240. Do you think that the currency of other nations has the same value as our American dollar?

241. Why is it important to save money?

SOCIAL STUDIES

242. Before paper and coin money, how do you think people of long ago bought and sold goods and services?

243. In some shops or markets, is it possible to barter, or to go back and forth on a price for an item?

244. Who in the community do you visit when you are sick or need a check-up?

245. Who in the community wears a badge and a uniform, carries a gun and handcuffs, and can help you if you are lost or are in some kind of danger?

246. Who in the community wears a heavy coat, boots, a hard hat, and rides in a truck with ladders, water, hoses, gauges, and sirens?

247. Who in the community makes sure you have a beautiful and healthy smile by caring for your teeth and gums?

248. Who in the community delivers letters and packages to your home and wears a uniform?

249. Who in the community cares for the well-being of domestic or farm animals like dogs, cats, horses, and cows?

250. Who in the community helps young people learn in a school with their knowledge of different subjects?

Social Studies – 2nd Grade

251. What do the galaxies, stars, Sun, moon, planets make up?

252. What is the name of the galaxy we live in that also is a name for a chocolate candy bar?

253. What is the name of the planet we live on?

254. What other planets can you name?

255. What are the biggest bodies of water on the Earth called?

256. What are the names of the Earth's two biggest oceans, as referenced in the last line of the patriotic song *America the Beautiful*, from "Sea to Shining Sea?

257. Do the oceans make up most of our world?

258. Which ocean is the biggest on Earth?

259. Can you name another ocean or sea?

260. What is the name of the imaginary line that divides the Earth into the Northern and Southern hemispheres?

261. What are the pieces of land called between the oceans: regions or continents?

262. How many continents are there on the Earth?

SOCIAL STUDIES

263. What is the full name of the continent we live on?
264. Which continent are Mexico and Canada part of: North America or South America?
265. Is Mexico to the north or south of the United States?
266. Is Canada to the north or south of the United States?
267. Are the states of Alaska and Hawaii located in the *continental* United States?
268. What is the name of the spherical representation of the earth?
269. What are the two hemispheres that the Earth is divided into at the Equator?
270. Can the world be represented on a flat map?
271. Can agricultural products, languages spoken, or physical landforms be represented on a map?
272. On a physical map, what types of landforms might be indicated?
273. Can charts, graphs, and maps be used to provide specific data about a place?
274. Can symbols be used on a map?
275. What symbol does a star represent on a map: a capital or a large city?
276. What is the term for the ratio that compares a measurement on a map to the actual distance between locations: scale or legend?
277. What are the four cardinal directions located on a map compass?
278. What is the intermediate direction if a place is both north and east?
279. What is the intermediate direction if a place is both south and west?
280. In which direction does the Sun rise?
281. In which direction does the Sun set?
282. What are Northeast, Midwest, South, and West all considered: regions or areas?
283. What are regions divided into: areas or divisions?
284. What is the name of the region of the United States that you live in?
285. What is the name of the state that you live in?
286. What is the name of the city or town that you live in?
287. What is the name of the county that you live in?
288. Can you name other counties in our state?
289. What is the name of a resource book that shows different areas of the world along with facts and information about each continent: an atlas or an almanac?

SOCIAL STUDIES

290. Which of the following would likely not be included in an atlas: World map, United States map, State map, or a city map?

291. What is the name for the study of specific regions and locations: geography or geology?

292. What are Asia, Europe, Africa, North America, South America, Australia, and Antarctica the names of?

293. What is each continent is made up of: regions or countries?

294. Does each country of a continent have a name?

295. Are Canada, the United States, and Mexico located in the continent of North America or Central America?

296. Which continent are Afghanistan, Bahrain, Bangladesh, Bhutan, Brunei, Cambodia, China, East Timor, India, Indonesia, Iran, Iraq, Israel, Japan, Jordan, Kazakhstan, Korea North, Korea South, Kuwait, Kyrgyzstan, Laos, Lebanon, Malaysia, Maldives, Mongolia, Myanmar, Nepal, Oman, Pakistan, the Philippines, Qatar, Russia, Saudi Arabia, Singapore, Sri Lanka, Syria, Taiwan, Tajikistan, Thailand, Turkey, Turkmenistan, United Arab Emirates, Uzbekistan, Vietnam, and Yemen part of?

297. Does more than half of the world's population live on the continent of Asia?

298. Which is the smallest continent: Australia or Europe?

299. What is the name of the second largest continent known for its jungles, deserts, and wildlife, and includes the countries of Algeria, Angola, Cape Verde, Chad, Congo, Egypt, Equatorial Guinea, Ethiopia, Gambia, Ghana, Guinea, Kenya, Liberia, Libya, Madagascar, Malawi, Mali, Morocco, Mozambique, Namibia, Niger, Nigeria, Rwanda, Senegal, Somalia, South Africa, South Sudan, Swaziland, Tanzania, Togo, Tunisia, Uganda, Zambia, and Zimbabwe?

300. What is the name of the newest country in the world that is located in Africa: North Sudan or South Sudan?

301. What animals can you name that live in Africa?

302. Did many of our ancestors come from the continent of Africa?

303. How did many people from Asia and Africa arrive here in America, traveling between Asia and Alaska more than 12,000 years ago: on a land bridge or on a ship?

304. Do you know the names of the countries that our distant relatives or ancestors came from?

305. What is the nationality of our family?

306. What is the name of the largest non-polar desert in the world located on the continent of Africa: the Sahara or the Arabian?

307. What is the name of the longest river in the world located on the continent of Africa: The Nile or The Amazon?

SOCIAL STUDIES

308. What is the name of the third largest continent with the countries of the United States, Mexico, Central America, and Canada?

309. Which is the largest country of North America that was once covered with ice and glaciers and is divided into provinces where the people speak English and French?

310. What is the North American country that has 50 states and is covered with land, mountains, canyons, rivers, and five great lakes?

311. What is the North American country that is divided into states, is covered with mountains, lakes, volcanoes, jungles, ancient ruins and pyramids, and is Spanish-speaking?

312. What is the name for the region between Mexico and South America that includes the countries of Belize, Costa Rica, El Salvador, Guatemala, Honduras, Nicaragua, and Panama?

313. What is the name of the fourth largest continent with the countries of Argentina, Brazil, Colombia, Peru, Chile, Ecuador, Bolivia, Venezuela, Uruguay, Paraguay, Guyana, Suriname, French Guiana, and the Falkland islands, and covered with jungles and mountains and rivers?

314. What is the name of the longest mountain range in South America: The Andes or The Himalayas?

315. What is the name of the second longest river in South America that also runs through the rainforest: the Nile or the Amazon?

316. Do you know the name of the pack animal of South America that has soft fur that is sheared and made into rope, blankets, sweaters and textiles, and can even be known to spit at you?

317. What is the name of the fifth largest continent located in the polar region at the bottom of the world, is covered with ice sometimes one to two miles thick, and is the continent with an abundance of whales, penguins and seals?

318. What is the name of the sixth largest continent that includes the countries of Albania, Andorra, Armenia, Austria, Belarus, Belgium, Bosnia, Bulgaria, Croatia, Cyprus, Czech Republic, Denmark, Estonia, Finland, France, Georgia, Germany, Greece, Hungary, Iceland, Ireland, Italy, Kosovo, Latvia, Liechtenstein, Lithuania, Luxembourg, Macedonia, Malta, Moldova, Monaco, Montenegro, The Netherlands, Norway, Poland, Portugal, Romania, Russia, San Marino, Serbia, Slovakia, Slovenia, Spain, Sweden, Switzerland, Turkey, Ukraine, United Kingdom, and the Vatican City?

319. What is the name of the seventh and smallest continent that includes a mainland, New Zealand, several South Pacific islands, and is the known for the Sydney Opera House, the Great Barrier Reef, kangaroos, koala bears, and wombats?

320. What is the name for the piece of land surrounded by water?

321. What is the name of the ocean that is located south of Asia, and is the third largest ocean in the world: The Indian Ocean or the Arctic Ocean?

322. On which continent is China located?

SOCIAL STUDIES

323. What was the name given to the leader of the ancient Chinese government: king or emperor?

324. What is astronomy the study of, something the ancient Chinese and other civilizations were very advanced in?

325. Which Asian country is considered the biggest and most populated country of the world: China or India?

326. What is the capital of China: Beijing or Shanghai?

327. Are Asian countries sometimes regarded as the "far east" or the orient?

328. What language do they speak in China?

329. What do they eat in China?

330. Do they dress differently in China?

331. What is the name of the fabric that the Chinese developed made from the cocoons of worms?

332. What is the name of the only man-made object located in China that can be arguably be seen from space: the Great Wall of China or the Grand Buddha?

333. Are many items that we sell here in the United States made in China?

334. Do you think that family life is different in China than it is in the United States?

335. Is Japan a small country of Asia?

336. What is the capital of Japan: Tokyo or Osaka?

337. What language do they speak in Japan?

338. What do they eat in Japan?

339. Do they dress differently in Japan?

340. What is the name of the traditional Japanese dress: a sari or a kimono?

341. What article of clothing do the Japanese take off before entering a house: scarf or shoes?

342. Where do the Japanese and their guests sit when eating a traditional meal: on chairs or on the floor?

343. Do you think that school life is different in Japan than in our culture?

344. Which country is considered one of the most populated countries of the world after China: Indonesia or India?

345. What is the capital of India: New Delhi or Mumbai?

346. What is the principle language spoken in India: Hindi or Bengali?

347. What do you think they eat in India?

SOCIAL STUDIES

348. Do they dress differently in India?

349. What is the name of the garment that most Indian women wear: a sari or a kimono?

350. Do you think that the family life and school life is different in India than in our culture?

351. Can you name some countries on the continent of Africa?

352. What is one of the most widely spoken languages out of 2,000 in Africa: Swahili or French?

353. What are some foods they might eat in Africa?

354. What are some animals that live in the wild of Africa?

355. On which continent is Egypt located?

356. What is the name of the longest river located in Africa?

357. What is the name of the biggest desert in Africa: the Sahara or the Mojave?

358. What were built by the Egyptians that served as burial tombs in ancient Egypt?

359. What is the name for the alphabet used by ancient Egyptians: hieroglyphics or alpha beta?

360. What is the name of the plant what was used by the ancient Egyptians for paper: parchment or papyrus?

361. What is the name for the leader of the ancient Egyptian government: Emperor or Pharaoh?

362. Do they dress differently in Africa than in America?

363. Do you think that the family life and school life is different in Africa than in our culture?

364. What is the name of the continent we live on?

365. What is the name for the study that deals with the locations of places and features of the Earth?

366. Are continents, countries, states, mountain ranges, and rivers all part of geography?

367. In what area of the country is our state located?

368. Do you know the names of any states that border our state?

369. What is the name of the mountain range located in the state of Virginia that include the Allegheny Mountains and the Blue Ridge Mountains: Appalachians or Rockies?

370. What is the name of the longest river in the United States: Missouri or Mississippi?

371. What is the name of the largest salt water lake in the Western Hemisphere located in Utah: Great Salt Lake or Bear Lake?

372. What is the name of the mountain range that is located in the western part of the United States: the Rocky Mountains or the Appalachian Mountains?

SOCIAL STUDIES

373. What is the name of the 2000 mile long river that is located on the border between the United States and Mexico: the Mississippi or the Rio Grande?

374. In which the continent is Mexico located?

375. What language do they speak in Mexico?

376. What do they eat in Mexico?

377. Do they dress differently in Mexico?

378. What is the name for the type of dance from Mexico: Ballet Folklorico or Flamenco?

379. What is the name for a type of music of Mexico played with guitars, trumpets, and violins: Flamenco or Mariachi?

380. Which of the following was **not** an Indian civilization of Mexico: Aztec, Inca, or Maya?

381. What is the capital of Mexico, one of the biggest and most populated cities in the world?

382. What is the name of the country on the North American continent to the north of the United States?

383. What are Alberta, British Colombia, Manitoba, News Brunswick, Newfoundland, Nova Scotia, Ontario, Prince Edward Island, Quebec, and Saskatchewan considered: states or provinces?

384. What are Northwest Territories, Nunavut, and Yukon considered: provinces or territories?

385. What is the capital of Canada: Ottawa or Montreal?

386. What languages do they speak in Canada?

387. What do they eat in Canada?

388. Do they dress differently in Canada?

389. What types of fish and wildlife is Canada known for?

390. Do you think that the family life and school life is different in Canada than in our culture?

391. Can you name any countries in South America?

392. What language do they speak in South America?

393. Do you know of any foods that are eaten in South America?

394. Do you think that South America has its own unique music, musical instruments, and dances?

395. What language is spoken in Brazil: Portuguese or Spanish?

396. Do they dress differently in South America then here in the United States?

397. What type of clothing is South American known for: brightly-colored or dark-colored?

398. Do you know the name of an animal that is unique to South America?

SOCIAL STUDIES

399. What is the name of the ancient Indian civilization of Peru, South America: Inca or Aztec?

400. Can you name some countries on the European continent?

401. Are some countries considered part of Eastern Europe and other countries part of Western Europe?

402. Are the countries Germany, Spain, Portugal, Italy, France, Austria, and Switzerland, considered part of Eastern Europe or Western Europe?

403. What region are the kingdoms of Denmark, Sweden, and Norway collectively known as: Scandinavia or The Netherlands?

404. Are the countries Poland, the Czech Republic, Russia, Slovakia, Romania, Bulgaria, Belarus, and Ukraine considered part of Eastern Europe or Western Europe?

405. What is the name of the currency of most European countries: the Dollar or the Euro?

406. What is the currency "Euro" short for?

407. What is the official currency of England: the British Euro or the British Pound?

408. What is the official currency of Japan: the Euro or the Yen?

409. What is the official currency of China: the Yen or the Renminbi?

410. What is the capital of Germany: Berlin or Munich?

411. What language do they speak in Germany?

412. Can you name some foods that are considered German??

413. Do you think that German people dress similar to how we dress?

414. What do Lederhosen and Dirndl refer to: traditional German clothing or traditional foods?

415. Do you think Germany has music and dance unique to its culture?

416. Is Germany famous for composers like Bach, Beethoven, Schubert, and Brahms?

417. Do you think that the family life and school life is different in Germany than in our culture?

418. What is the capital of England: London or Winchester?

419. What language do they speak in England?

420. If you heard someone from England speak English, would you consider them to have an English accent?

421. What are Yorkshire pudding, Shepherd's pie, tea, and scones all considered: English cuisine or French cuisine?

422. Do you think people from England dress similar to Americans?

SOCIAL STUDIES

423. Do you think England has music and dance unique to its culture?

424. What country is also known as the "Emerald Isle:" Scotland or Ireland?

425. What is the capital of Ireland: Dublin or Waterford?

426. Does Ireland have music and dance unique to its culture?

427. Do you think that the family life and school life is different in Ireland than in our culture?

428. What is the capital of France: Marseille or Paris?

429. What language do they speak in France?

430. Can you name some foods that are considered French?

431. How do you think they dress in France?

432. Do you think France has music and dance unique to its culture?

433. Do you think that the family life and school life is different in France than in our culture?

434. What is the capital of Spain: Barcelona or Madrid?

435. What language do they speak in Spain?

436. What are churros: Spanish snacks or Spanish doughnuts?

437. What is the name of the saffron rice and seafood dish of Spain: Paella or chicken with rice?

438. Do you think that Spain has specific clothing unique to its culture?

439. Do you think Spain has music and dance unique to its culture?

440. What is the name of the traditional dance of Spain: flamenco or tango?

441. Do you think that the family life and school life is different in Spain than in our culture?

442. In which continent is Italy located?

443. What is the capital of Italy: Florence or Rome?

444. What language do they speak in Italy?

445. Can you name some foods that are considered Italian?

446. How do you think they dress in Italy?

447. Do you think Italy has music and dance unique to its culture?

448. Do you think that the family life and school life is different in Italy than in our culture?

449. What animals can be found on the continent of Antarctica?

450. What is the climate like in Antarctica compared to here in the United States?

SOCIAL STUDIES

451. Do you think anyone has ever made an expedition to Antarctica?
452. Is Australia considered both a continent and a country?
453. What is the capital of Australia: Sydney, Melbourne, or Canberra?
454. What language do they speak in Australia?
455. Do you think that Australians dress the same as Americans do?
456. Do you think Australia has music and dance unique to its culture?
457. What are some animals that live in Australia?
458. Do you think that the family life and school life is different in Australia than in our culture?
459. What cloth banner does every country of every continent have to represent their country?
460. What are the colors of our American flag and how would you describe it?
461. Can you describe out state flag?
462. What is the main city called of each state in the United States?
463. Do you know what the D.C. stands for in our capital city Washington, D. C?
464. Whom do you think our capital is named for?
465. What is the name of the study that tells a "story" of the people that lived long ago past to present: ancestry or history?
466. In our history, what is the name of some of our earliest settlers called Native Americans that hunted deer and buffalo, and lived in groups called tribes led by a chief?
467. What is the name of the first navigator to arrive here from Europe on his ship the Santa Maria?
468. What shape did Christopher Columbus believe the Earth to be?
469. What continent did Columbus sail to even though he thought that the New World he landed at was the continent of Asia?
470. What country of Europe did Columbus sail from: Spain or Italy?
471. What did King Ferdinand and Queen Isabella of Spain provide for Columbus in order for him to set sail for the New World?
472. What country did Columbus believe that he would be sailing to because he was not aware that North America existed: Africa or India?
473. What did Queen Isabella also want Columbus to bring back from the "Indies" and therefore agreed to help pay for Columbus's voyage: silk or spices?
474. Can you finish the saying: "In 1492 Columbus sailed the…?"

SOCIAL STUDIES

475. What were the names of Columbus's three ships?

476. What did Columbus call the people that he first came into contact with, thinking that he had reached the Indies?

477. What did Europeans call North and South America because it was "new" land to explore?

478. With whom did many Spaniards battle when they came here from Europe?

479. Were the Spanish successful in conquering the Indians with their superior weapons?

480. What is the name of the animal that was brought over from Spain: the horse or the cow?

481. What did the Spanish bring to the New World that included smallpox and measles: diseases or rashes?

482. What is the name for the study of peoples and cultures and their development: civilization or heritage?

483. What is the name of the Indian civilization that lived in the jungles of Central America and Mexico, and were extremely advanced in math and astronomy, the study of the universe: Maya or Aztec?

484. What were the buildings called that ancient civilizations built out of stone with tiers and steps?

485. What is the name of a later Indian civilization in Mexico, were considered great warriors, worshiped and made sacrifices to their gods, and built their capital city on a lake, Tenochtitlan?

486. Which Indian group in Mexico did the Spaniard Hernando Cortez steal gold from and ultimately conquer: the Aztecs or the Maya?

487. Which Indian group in South America lived high in the Andes Mountains and decorated everything with gold and silver: the Inca or the Zapotec?

488. What is the name of the Spanish conquistador that conquered the Inca civilization in South America in 1533: Francisco Pizarro or Vasco Nunez de Balboa?

489. What did many Indians do to provide food for their families?

490. From which continent did many of our ancestors come: Africa or Asia?

491. Did England and other European countries also want to claim some of the treasures of North America?

492. In which city in Virginia did the English colonists settle in the year 1607 right before the Pilgrims, the first important English settlement in our country: Jamestown or Williamsburg?

493. Which native people did the English continue to do battle with?

494. What is the name of the English settler who established the first permanent colony in Jamestown, Virginia in 1607: William Penn or John Smith?

SOCIAL STUDIES

495. What are groups of Indians called?

496. What do you call the leader of an Indian tribe?

497. What native Indian tribes can you name?

498. Who are the Apache, Navajo, Hopi, Potawatomi, and Sioux?

499. What is the name of the Indians of the southwest that lived in modular homes made of stone and adobe: Pueblo or Navajo?

500. What is the name for the rectangular dwellings built by some Eastern Woodland Indians like the Iroquois and Cherokee that were made from wood and bark: longhouses or wigwams?

501. What is the name of the Indians that travelled around the plains area of the U.S. following buffalo herds: Woodland Indians or Plains Indians?

502. What is the name of the poles carved and painted by Native American Indians of the Pacific Northwest that were made to represent a tribe and to tell a story?

503. What is the name for the 102 passengers that came over from England in the year 1620?

504. What were the Pilgrims seeking in the New World because they disagreed with the teachings of the Church of England?

505. What is the name for the ship that the Pilgrims sailed on from England?

506. Which ocean did the Pilgrims have to cross on the Mayflower to arrive here in America?

507. What is the name of the now famous boulder that the Pilgrims anchored their ship to, and the name for the colony that the Pilgrims established in 1620?

508. Who taught the Pilgrims how to hunt, fish, and plant crops?

509. What specific crop did the Wampanoag Indians teach the early settlers how to grow: corn or wheat?

510. With whom did the Pilgrims share their first big feast with, after a successful harvest that lasted for three days?

511. What food did the Wampanoag Indians and Pilgrims share at this first Thanksgiving feast: deer and pheasant, or turkey and stuffing?

512. Who do you think contributed the deer venison to the first Thanksgiving feast: the Wampanoag Indians or the Pilgrims?

513. What is the name of the holiday we celebrate in November to pay tribute to the union of these two important cultures?

514. What was the name of the colonist group that came after the Pilgrims and had very strict religious rules: the Puritans or the Quakers?

515. How many original English colonies were set up on the Eastern coast: 12 or 13?

SOCIAL STUDIES

516. What is the name of the American pioneer and trailblazer that led settlers to the west through the Cumberland Gap of the Appalachian Mountains, providing access to the western frontier: Davy Crockett or Daniel Boone?

517. What is the name of the famous explorer from Tennessee who was considered the "King of the Wild Frontier," and died at the Alamo in San Antonio helping the outnumbered Texans fight for their independence against the Mexican army: Davy Crockett or Daniel Boone?

518. What were early American settlers called in colonial times: pioneers or colonists?

519. Where did many early Americans settle for easy transportation and a water supply?

520. What kinds of things did pioneers have for food, shelter, work, and school?

521. Was there electricity in early colonial days?

522. What did pioneers use for light?

523. What is the name for the war that was a result of the conflicts between the thirteen colonies and the British because the colonies felt that they were not represented in the British government, a war that took place between 1775 and 1783?

524. Did the colonists have to resort to a "revolution" in order to claim their freedom from England?

525. Was one of the events that led to the Revolutionary War the French and Indian War in which the French and Indians fought against Great Britain?

526. Who won the French and Indian War 1754-1763: the French and Indians, or Great Britain?

527. After winning the French and Indian War in 1763, which country did the British win the right to keep along with several other possessions in the New World: France or Canada?

528. Which war did events like the French and Indian War, The Sugar Act, The Stamp Act, and the Boston Massacre in which 5 colonists were killed by British troops all contribute to: the Revolutionary War or the Civil War?

529. What was the name of the event in Boston, Massachusetts when the English colonists got tired of King George III and his numerous rules and new taxes, and decided to dump 342 full crates of tea into the Boston harbor on December 16, 1773?

530. Who published a pamphlet in 1776 entitled "Common Sense" that challenged the authority of the British government, and inspired the people of the thirteen colonies to declare their independence from Great Britain: Thomas Paine or Samuel Adams?

531. What was the name of the first congress that was established by the colonists who met secretly in Philadelphia in 1774 to discuss liberty from Great Britain: National or Continental?

532. What is the name of the document that came from the discussions of the Second Continental Congress, drafted in 1776 that declared the 13 American colonies independent from Great Britain?

SOCIAL STUDIES

533. Who is the principal author of the Declaration of Independence, a founding father who was also the third President of the United States: John Adams or Thomas Jefferson?

534. What did Thomas Jefferson write in the Declaration of Independence: "All men are…?"

535. Who was the second President of the United States: John Adams or Thomas Jefferson?

536. In what year did the people of the United States declare their independence from England and the King?

537. Was the Declaration of Independence signed by John Hancock, John Adams, George Washington, Ben Franklin, Thomas Jefferson, and Samuel Adams?

538. How many delegates of the Continental Congress signed the Declaration of Independence: 50 or 56?

539. What is the name of the delegate, then President of the Continental Congress, who was first to sign the Declaration of Independence: Benjamin Franklin or John Hancock?

540. What city in Pennsylvania was the site of the first reading of the Declaration of Independence, four days after it was signed in Independence Hall: Philadelphia or Harrisburg?

541. What is the name of the bronze bell in Philadelphia, Pennsylvania that serves as a symbol of American freedom?

542. What happened to the liberty bell after the first test ringing in 1752 in London, England?

543. Was the Liberty Bell rung during the first reading of the Declaration of Independence?

544. Did the British continue the war with the colonists even after the Declaration of Independence?

545. What is the name of one of the founding fathers of the United States of America; has his signature on The Declaration of Independence, The Treaty of Paris which marked the end of the Revolutionary War, The Treaty of Peace with Great Britain, and the United States Constitution; was the operator and editor of a newspaper called the "Pennsylvania Gazette;" was the publisher of "Poor Richard's Almanac;" and is credited for inventing electricity, the lightning rod, bifocal lenses, and a special stove: Thomas Jefferson or Benjamin Franklin?

546. What is the name of the famous officer who was the commander of the United States Navy during the Revolutionary War: John Paul Jones or George Rodney?

547. What is the name of the silversmith and American patriot during the Revolution who in 1775 rode on horseback to warn the American colonists that the "redcoats" or British soldiers were coming: John Hancock or Paul Revere?

548. What was Paul Revere's signal with lanterns placed in the steeple of the Old North Church in Boston to alert the colonists how the British were arriving: "One if by land, two if by…?"

549. What is the name of the Treaty that the British agreed to sign that ended the Revolutionary War on September 3, 1783: The Treaty of Versailles or The Treaty of Paris?

550. Who won the Revolutionary war in 1783: the British or the American colonists?

SOCIAL STUDIES

551. What is the name of the document that outlines America's form of government and the rights of its citizens, approved by American delegates in 1787: U.S. Constitution or the Magna Carta?

552. Which President from Virginia proposed the idea of a strong central government, and is regarded as the "father of the U.S. Constitution:" James Madison or James Monroe?

553. What kind of government do we have in America: a federal republic or a national republic?

554. What is the term that refers to the complete absence of rules and laws, a society without a publicly enforced government: democracy or anarchy?

555. What are the first 10 amendments to the United States Constitution called: the Preamble or the Bill of Rights?

556. What is the name of the purchase in 1803, considered one of the greatest real estate deals in history between the United States and France, and is regarded as one of Thomas Jefferson's greatest achievements?

557. How many millions of dollars did the United States agree to pay France in 1803 for 828,000 square miles of land west of the Mississippi: five or fifteen?

558. How much did the "Louisiana Purchase," organized by Thomas Jefferson, increase the size of the United States, expanding it by 15 states: doubled it or tripled it?

559. Who are the two explorers that were sent by Thomas Jefferson to explore and map the territory that was part of the Louisiana Purchase, and have a trail named for them?

560. Which European country still claimed the western states: England or France?

561. What name was given to the African American workers who had to work on tobacco, rice, and cotton farms in the south without pay, and were under the complete control of their masters?

562. From which continent did slaves come from that worked on the southern farms?

563. What is the term for the large farms where many slaves worked: haciendas or plantations?

564. What is the name of the war between the North or Union, and the South, known as the Confederacy, because the South wanted to break away and become its own country, and because it wanted the right to continue to use slaves on its southern plantations?

565. When did the Civil War take place: 1861-1865 or 1865-1869?

566. Who was the 16th President of the United States who saved the Union during the American Civil War, and whose face is on the penny and the five-dollar bill?

567. What was the nickname given to Abraham Lincoln because of his truthful nature?

568. What is the name of the brave woman and activist who led many slaves to freedom through a system known as the Underground Railroad: Harriet Tubman or Harriet Beecher Stowe?

569. Who become a free people as a result of the Civil War and President Lincoln?

SOCIAL STUDIES

570. Does our capital Washington, D.C. have many historical monuments?

571. What historical monument in Washington, D.C. can you name?

572. Where are the Lincoln Memorial, the White House, the Washington Monument, the Jefferson Memorial, the Pentagon Memorial, the World War II Memorial, the Vietnam Veterans Memorial, the Franklin Delano Roosevelt Memorial, the Martin Luther King Jr. Memorial, the Marine Corps Memorial known as Iwo Jima, the Korean War Veterans Memorial, and Arlington National Cemetery all located?

573. What is the name of the residence of the President of the United States?

574. Who lives at 1600 Pennsylvania Avenue in Washington D.C?

575. What is the name of the copper and iron statue in New York Harbor on Liberty Island that was a gift from France in 1886, and is recognized as a symbol of freedom and democracy?

576. What American banner is considered a historical symbol?

577. What is the Liberty Bell considered?

578. What is the name of the monumental sculpture and historical symbol in South Dakota with the faces of Presidents Washington, Lincoln, Jefferson, and Roosevelt carved into the granite?

Social Studies – 3rd Grade

579. What is the term for the study that includes history, geography, sociology, and government?

580. Does social studies include the study of geography or geology?

581. What is the name of the continent you live on?

582. What is the name of the geographic tool that is shaped like a sphere and shows all the continents and oceans?

583. What is the name for a bound collection of maps and graphs that gives detailed geographical information of different countries, continents and oceans: an atlas or an almanac?

584. What is the name of the book that is published every year that contains facts about astronomical events, the tides, weather, and includes a calendar: an atlas or an almanac?

585. What is the term for the imaginary lines that run north and south on a map or globe: latitude or longitude?

586. What is the term form the imaginary lines that run east and west on a map or globe: latitude or longitude?

587. What is the term for the imaginary east-west line that encircles the Earth midway between the North Pole and the South Pole?

SOCIAL STUDIES

588. Can you identify on a map the seven continents and the oceans of the world?

589. What are Asia, Africa, North America, South America, Antarctica, Europe, and Australia?

590. What are the Pacific, Atlantic, Indian, and Arctic?

591. Which ocean is the largest?

592. Which ocean is the smallest: the Indian or the Arctic?

593. What are the Alaska Range, the Appalachian, Blue Ridge, Alleghenies, Catskills, Coast Range, Sierra Nevada, and Rocky all considered?

594. What are the Andes, Himalayas, Alps, Pyrenees, and Ural all considered?

595. Which mountain range in the world is the tallest: the Andes or the Himalayas?

596. Which mountain is the world's longest: the Andes or the Himalayas?

597. What is the name for the tallest peak in the Himalayas standing over 29,000 feet tall: Mount Everest or Mount McKinley?

598. What is the name for the tallest peak in North America standing at just over 20,000 feet tall and located in Alaska: Mount Everest or Mount McKinley?

599. What is the name of the ancient city of the Inca high up in the Andes Mountains: Machu Picchu or Chichen Itza?

600. What are the Sahara, the Arabian, the Mojave, the Atacama, the Gobi, and the Sonoran all considered?

601. Which American desert is known for the saguaro cactus, a spiky cactus that can grow up to 50 feet tall and live for more than one hundred years: Sonoran or Mojave?

602. What are the two **polar** deserts in the world?

603. What is the term given for the region of the Earth surrounding the Equator: the tropics or the hemispheres?

604. What is the name for the type of forest characterized by very tall, densely growing trees, heavy annual rainfall, high humidity, and are located in tropical latitudes?

605. What is the name for the largest tropical rainforest in the world: the Amazon or the Congo?

606. Which country in South American has the largest tropical rainforest in the world?

607. In which habitat would you find many frogs, butterflies, birds, toucans, snakes, lizards, monkeys, ferns, orchids, waterfalls, and insects?

608. Can fire, drought, and volcanic activity have an effect on rainforests?

609. What type of storm are hurricanes, monsoons, and typhoons that may pose a threat and cause great damage to a rainforest?

SOCIAL STUDIES

610. What is the name for the piece of land that is completely surrounded by water?

611. What do Australia, Cuba, Iceland, Ireland, and the United Kingdom all have in common?

612. Are many islands part of some larger country?

613. What state are Maui, Kauai, Oahu, Molokai, and Lanai all part of?

614. What tropical storms are islands often affected by?

615. How many total states are there in the United States?

616. How many states are located in the continental United States?

617. What are the two states that are located outside of the continental United States?

618. What was the last state admitted into the union in 1959?

619. What is the name of the state you live in?

620. What is the capital of our state?

621. What state is Montgomery the capital of? Al

622. What state is Juneau the capital of? Al

623. What state is Phoenix the capital of? Ar

624. What state is Little Rock the capital of? Ark

625. What state is Sacramento the capital of? C

626. What state is Denver the capital of? C

627. What state is Hartford the capital of? C

628. What state is Dover the capital of? D

629. What state is Tallahassee the capital of? F

630. What state is Atlanta the capital of? G

631. What state is Honolulu the capital of? H

632. What state is Boise the capital of? I

633. What state is Indianapolis the capital of? I

634. What state is Des Moines the capital of? I

635. What state is Topeka the capital of? K

636. What state is Frankfort the capital of? K

637. What state is Baton Rouge the capital of? L

SOCIAL STUDIES

638. What state is Augusta the capital of? M

639. What state is Annapolis the capital of? M

640. What state is Boston the capital of? M

641. What state is Lansing the capital of? M

642. What state is Saint Paul the capital of? M

643. What state is Jackson the capital of? M

644. What state is Jefferson City the capital of? M

645. What state is Helena the capital of? M

646. What state is Lincoln the capital of? N

647. What state is Carson City the capital of? N

648. What state is Concord the capital of? N

649. What state is Trenton the capital of? N

650. What state is Santa Fe the capital of? N

651. What state is Albany the capital of? N

652. What state is Raleigh the capital of? N

653. What state is Bismarck the capital of? N

654. What state is Columbus the capital of? O

655. What state is Oklahoma City the capital of? O

656. What state is Salem the capital of? O

657. What state is Harrisburg the capital of? P

658. What state is Providence the capital of? R

659. What state is Columbia the capital of? S

660. What state is Pierre the capital of? S

661. What state is Nashville the capital of? T

662. What state is Austin the capital of? T

663. What state is Salt Lake City the capital of? U

664. What state is Montpelier the capital of? V

665. What state is Richmond the capital of? V

SOCIAL STUDIES

666. What state is Olympia the capital of? W

667. What state is Charleston the capital of? W

668. What state is Madison the capital of? W

669. What state is Cheyenne the capital of? W

670. What is the term for the administrative divisions of a state: districts or counties?

671. What is the name of the county you live in?

672. What city do you live in?

673. Is the city you live in near to or far from the capital of our state?

674. What is the name for the direction key that is located on a map: a direction legend or a compass rose?

675. What does the "N" stand for on a compass rose?

676. What does the "S" stand for on a compass rose?

677. What does the "E" stand for on a compass rose?

678. What does the "W" stand for on a compass rose?

679. What does the direction "NE" stand for?

680. What does the direction "NW" stand for?

681. What does the direction "SE" stand for?

682. What does the direction "SW" stand for?

683. Can you locate Canada on a world map or a globe?

684. What is Canada divided into: states or provinces?

685. Can you locate Mexico on a world map or a globe?

686. What is Mexico divided into: states or provinces?

687. Can you locate the United States on a world map or a globe?

688. Can you locate Central America on a world map or a globe?

689. Can you locate South America on a world map or a globe?

690. Can you locate Europe on a world map or a globe?

691. Can you locate Africa on a world map or a globe?

692. Can you locate Asia on a world map or a globe?

693. Can you locate Australia on a world map or a globe?

SOCIAL STUDIES

694. Can you locate Antarctica on a world map or a globe?

695. Can you locate the equator on a world map or a globe?

696. Can you identify the Northern Hemisphere on a world map or a globe?

697. Can you identify the Southern Hemisphere on a world map or a globe?

698. Can you locate the Pacific Ocean on a world map or a globe?

699. Can you locate the Atlantic Ocean on a world map or a globe?

700. Can you locate the Indian Ocean on a world map or a globe?

701. Can you locate the Arctic Ocean on a world map or a globe?

702. Can you locate the North Pole on a world map or a globe?

703. Can you locate the South Pole on a world map or a globe?

704. What is the name of the key on a map that explains the symbols and landmarks on a map: a compass rose or a legend?

705. What is the name of the key on a map that helps you determine distances: a legend or a scale?

706. What is the term for a large, natural stream of water that feeds into a larger body of water: a lake or a river?

707. What major rivers in the world can you name?

708. What are the Mississippi, the Missouri, the Ohio, the Colombia, the Arkansas, the Colorado, the Snake, the Hudson, and the Rio Grande?

709. What are the Ganges, the Danube, the Yangtze, the Nile, and the Amazon?

710. Which river is the largest in the world: the Amazon or the Nile?

711. Which river is the longest in the world: the Amazon or the Nile?

712. Is river water considered fresh water or salt water?

713. Is ocean water considered fresh water or salt water?

714. What is the term for the starting point of a river: source or tributary?

715. What is the term for the stream flows into another to form a river: a delta or a tributary?

716. What is the term for the landform that forms at the mouth of a river where it empties into an ocean or sea, and is often triangular in shape: a delta or a tributary?

717. What is the name of the river that has the largest delta in the world, and is located in both India and Bangladesh: Ganges or Nile?

SOCIAL STUDIES

718. What is the name of the river delta located in Africa flowing into the Mediterranean Sea, that was named by the Greek historian, Herodotus, who coined the term "delta" because the triangular shape of a river delta is similar to the Greek letter "delta:" Nile or Yellow?

719. What is the name of the river delta located in China that is known for its heavy sediment deposits and valuable arable land: Ganges or Yellow?

720. What river delta is found in the state of Louisiana, is known as the bird's foot delta, has millions of acres of wetlands, and is home to many birds and wildlife: Mississippi or Missouri?

721. What are the Missouri, Ohio, Minnesota, Wisconsin, St. Croix, Skunk, Rock, Ohio, La Crosse, and Des Moines rivers with respect to the Mississippi: deltas or tributaries?

722. What is the term for a collection of rivers and tributaries that flow together and empty into a bigger river, ocean, or sea: a river system or a river web?

723. What larger river does the Ohio River, the Tennessee River, the Arkansas River, and the Missouri River flow into: the St. Lawrence or the Mississippi?

724. What is the term for the section of land drained by a river system: a drainage basin or a reservoir?

725. Where does the Mississippi River drain into: the Pacific Ocean or the Gulf of Mexico?

726. What is the term for a narrow, navigable body of water that connects two larger bodies of water: a channel or a strait?

727. What is the name of the strait that separates Alaska from Siberia bordering on Russia, and connects the Arctic Ocean with another sea: Bering or Gibraltar?

728. What is the name of the narrow strait that connects the Mediterranean Sea with the Atlantic Ocean, and separates Spain in Europe and Morocco in Africa: Gibraltar of Magellan?

729. What is the name of the strait discovered and named for a Portuguese explorer in 1520 that separates South America from Tierra del Fuego and other islands, providing a short cut between the Atlantic and Pacific for commerce and exploration: Gibraltar or Magellan?

730. What is the term for a body of water that steams through two landmasses, or one that connects two seas: a strait or a channel?

731. What is the name of the channel separating southern England from Northern France, connects the Atlantic Ocean with the North Sea, and is one of busiest sea routes: English or French?

732. What is the name of the channel between Mexico and Cuba, connecting the Gulf of Mexico and the Caribbean Sea: Yucatan or Iberian?

733. What is the term for a man-made lake that is used for storing water like those built by the Egyptians that lived close to the Nile River: a reservoir or a channel?

734. What is the name for the large reservoir in central Missouri created by the Bagnell Dam on the Osage River that was built in 1931: Lake of the Ozarks or Lake Mead?

SOCIAL STUDIES

735. What is the name of largest reservoir in the United States located on the Colorado River in the States of Arizona and Nevada formed by the Hoover Dam: Lake of the Ozarks or Lake Mead?

736. What is the term for a high area of land with relatively flat terrain: a plain or a plateau?

737. What is the name of the highest and longest plateau in the world located in Tibet that is often referred to as the "roof of the world:" Tibetan or Andean?

738. What is the term for the long man-made waterway that is built to allow the passage of ships: canal or isthmus?

739. What is the name of the canal completed in 1825 that enabled the transportation of goods from the Great Lakes to New York City linking Lake Erie in the west to the Hudson River in the east: Panama or Erie?

740. What is the name of the waterway in Egypt completed in 1869 connecting the Mediterranean Sea and the Red Sea, separating the continents of Asia and Africa, and cutting thousands of miles from the routes of ships traveling between Europe and Asia: Panama or Suez?

741. What is the name of the 48 mile waterway completed in 1914 connecting the Atlantic with the Pacific oceans, cutting thousands of miles off voyages in that ships no longer had to sail completely around South America to reach the west: Erie or Panama?

742. What is the name of the Italian city known for its gondola boats and Italian architecture along its many canals: Florence or Venice?

743. What is the term for a narrow strip of land that connects two larger masses: isthmus or delta?

744. What is the name of the isthmus between the Caribbean Sea and the Pacific Ocean connecting North America and South America, and was first crossed by Vasco de Balboa in 1513 in his famous journey from the Atlantic to the Pacific: Panama or Erie?

745. What is the term for the piece of land that is bordered by water on three sides but connected to the mainland by an isthmus: delta or peninsula?

746. Which state is a peninsula: Texas or Florida?

747. Which state has an upper peninsula: Michigan or Wisconsin?

748. Which state has a peninsula stretching out in the northeastern part of the state having eight miles of Lake Michigan shoreline and named "Door:" Michigan or Wisconsin?

749. What is the name of the peninsula in northwest Mexico that is part of the state of California: Baja or Yucatan?

750. What is the name of the peninsula in southern Mexico that was once the home of the Maya: Baja or Yucatan?

751. What is the name of the European peninsula that includes Spain and Portugal: Iberian or Arabian?

SOCIAL STUDIES

752. What is the name of the European peninsula with the cities of Rome and Florence that makes up most of the country except for Corsica and Sicily: Greek or Italian?

753. What is the name of the peninsula in southwestern Asia that is home to many Arab people and the Islamic religion: Arabian or Iberian?

754. What is the name of the peninsula in East Asia that includes a North country and a South country, and is located between the East Sea and the Yellow Sea: Cambodian or Korean?

755. What is the term for an extension of land that extends out into a body of water like the sea: isthmus or cape?

756. What is the name of the cape on a rocky landmass in southern Africa's Cape Peninsula, first discovered by a Portuguese navigator in 1488, allowed for a route from Europe to Asia, and is known for its stormy weather and rough seas: Cape of Good Hope or Cape Horn?

757. What is the name of the cape that juts out into the Atlantic Ocean in the state of Massachusetts, and famous for its sandy beaches, rolling sand dunes, historic lighthouses, biking trails, fresh lobsters, and cranberry bogs: Cape Cod or Cape Horn?

758. What is the term for the piece of land that is completely surrounded by water: an island or a peninsula?

759. What is the largest island in the world: Greenland or Iceland?

760. What is the name of the state that is made up of many islands with Honolulu as its capital?

761. What is the name of the Polynesian island in the south Pacific, a territory of Chile, famous for its 887 Moai statues carved from solidified volcanic ash by the Rapa Nui people: Easter Island or Galapagos Island?

762. What is the name of the volcanic islands 600 miles off the western coast of Ecuador, South America famous for its tortoises, reptiles, plants, and birds and studied by Charles Darwin inspiring his theory of evolution and natural selection: Galapagos or Easter?

763. What famous rivers can you name?

764. In which Asian country can you find the Yellow river and the Yangtze River: China or India?

765. What is the name of the river that flows through India and Bangladesh, flows into the Indian Ocean, and is considered a holy river for many Hindus: the Ganges River or the Indus River?

766. What is the term for the fan-shaped deposit of sand and mud that forms at the mouth of a river, like the one located at Egypt's Nile River: channel or delta?

767. What is the name of the Asian river that flows through northern India and Pakistan and is one of the longest rivers in the world: the Indus River or the Nile River?

768. What is the name of the longest river in the world, over 4,000 miles long, located in Egypt that empties into the Mediterranean Sea: the Zaire River or the Nile River?

SOCIAL STUDIES

769. What was the Nile River often referred to as because it provided fertile soil, fresh water for drinking and bathing, provided raw materials, and was helpful to the Egyptians for trading and navigation: the Gifts of the Nile or the Presents of the Nile?

770. What is the name of the dam in southern Egypt that creates a reservoir and controls the flow of the Nile River: Hoover Dam or Aswan High Dam?

771. What is the name of the world's largest hydroelectric dam made of concrete and steel towering over the Yangtze River in China, and regarded as the world's largest power station: Three Gorges Dam or Gezhouba Dam?

772. What is the name of the river formerly called the Zaire River that flows through central Africa, is the second longest river after the Nile, and is considered the world's deepest river: the Congo River or the Niger River?

773. What is the name of the principle river that runs through western Africa, and is the third longest river in Africa after the Nile and the Congo: the Zaire or the Niger?

774. What is the name of the river that flows through four countries in western Africa: the Zaire or the Niger?

775. What is the name of the longest river in Europe that begins in Russia and flows into the Caspian Sea: the Danube or the Volga?

776. What is the name of the river that flows through Central and Eastern Europe that rises in the Black Forest Mountains of Germany and flows into the Black Sea: the Rhine or the Danube?

777. What is the name of the river that begins in the Swiss Alps, flows through several northern European countries, and empties into the North Sea: the Rhine or the Danube?

778. What is the name of the river in southern England that flows under the famous London Bridge and the Tower Bridge: the Thames or the Danube?

779. On which continent, considered the "outback," or the "land down under," are the Murray River and the Darling River located, that join together and flow into the Indian Ocean: Australia or Asia?

780. What is the name for the web-footed Australian animal that lives close to the banks of the Murray and Darling Rivers: the koala bear or the duck-billed platypus?

781. What is the name of the world's second longest river in the world located in South America that has the largest drainage basin in the world: the Orinoco River or the Amazon River?

782. What is the name of the South American river that flows through Venezuela into the Caribbean Sea and has the world's highest waterfall called Angel Falls: the Amazon River or the Orinoco River?

783. What is the name of the most famous waterfall in North America that can be seen in both New York and Ontario, Canada: Angel Falls or Niagara Falls?

784. What do Iguazu Falls in Argentina and Brazil, and Victoria Falls in Zambia and Zimbabwe have in common: are the biggest in the world, or both are located on a border?

SOCIAL STUDIES

785. Where is Yosemite Falls located in North America: Florida or California?

786. In which state is the subtropical swamp area called that is popular for its crocodiles, alligators, and tall grasses, and is commonly known as the Everglades: Florida or California?

787. What is the name of the biggest river in the United States?

788. How do you spell Mississippi?

789. What kind of boat do many people use to cruise along the Mississippi River: a canoe or a paddleboat?

790. What is the name of the river in Canada that flows north into the Arctic Ocean: the Mackenzie or the Yukon?

791. What is the name of the river that begins in the Canadian Rockies and stays frozen for nine months out of the year: the Mackenzie or the Yukon?

792. What is the term for the waterways that Venice, Amsterdam, and Panama are famous for: channels or canals?

793. What is the name of the type of boat that one may ride on in the Venice, Italy with over 150 canals: canoe or gondola?

794. How would you categorize all of the following: canoes, fishing boats, airboats, power boats, rowboats, fireboats, lifeboats, U-boats, hydrofoil boats, oil tankers, kayaks, paddleboats, pedal boats, speed boats, ships, barges, tugboats, ferries, galleons, ocean liners, submarines, gondolas, steamboats, steamships, riverboats, houseboats, rafts, cabin cruisers, vessels, yachts, jet skis, sail boats, windjammers, pontoon boats, and cruise ships?

795. What is the term that refers to the history of the world from the earliest civilization through the Roman Empire: pre-history or ancient history?

796. What is the meaning of the initials B.C. after a date that is used to refer to dates in history based on our calendar: Before Christ or After Christ?

797. What does the recent version of B.C. now written as B.C.E. mean: "Before the Common Era" or "Before the Common Epoch?"

798. What is the Latin meaning of A.D: "in the year of our Lord," or "After Christ?"

799. Is the recent version of A.D. the initials C.E. meaning Common Era?

800. If Rome was founded in the year 753 B.C.E., would that be considered 753 years before or after Christ?

801. Which ancient civilization came first: Greek or Roman?

802. Did Greek culture greatly influence Roman culture?

SOCIAL STUDIES

803. Which civilization dominated thousands of years ago in the Mediterranean, and provided the foundation for many things in Western culture today: Greek or Roman?

804. What were the time frames that include Archaic, Classical, and Hellenistic that ancient Greece was divided into: periods or eras?

805. What was ancient Greece divided into because it did not have a national government: provinces or city-states?

806. What were the two main city-states of ancient Greece: Athens and Sparta, or Corinth and Thebes?

807. Were Athens and Sparta allies or enemies?

808. Which Greek city-state was preoccupied with war and the military, and ruled by kings: Athens or Sparta?

809. Which Greek city-state was preoccupied with learning and the arts and believed in the rule of the people, or democracy: Athens or Sparta?

810. What is the name of the god of war, wisdom, and civilization that Athens is named for: Athena or Othello?

811. What is the name of the Greek fortress that was built as a retreat for the people in the event of an attack that is located high on a hill overlooking the city: the Acropolis or the Parthenon?

812. What is the name of the marble temple built as a shrine for Athena, located on a hill in the center of the city: the Acropolis or the Parthenon?

813. Which city-state was considered to have the best army and soldiers in Greece: Sparta or Athens?

814. What is the name of the series of wars between the Greeks and the Persians from 492 B.C. to 449 B.C: the Persian Wars or the Peloponnesian Wars?

815. Who did the city-states Athens and Sparta want to fight against as one force: the Persians or the Ionians?

816. Which Empire was conquered as a result of the Persian Wars: the Greek or the Persian?

817. What was the time called for the time of prosperity in Greece after winning the Persian Wars: the Golden Age or the Gilded Age?

818. What did the people of Athens watch in the theatres written by Aeschylus, Sophocles, and Euripides during the Golden Age: tragic plays or operas?

819. Were the Acropolis and the Parthenon constructed during the Greek Golden Age?

820. What artworks did many Greek artists create during the Golden Age: sculptures or portraits?

821. What do Doric, Ionic, and Corinthian refer to in Greek architecture: three types of columns, or three types of marble?

SOCIAL STUDIES

822. What is the name of the Greek General who was a leader of Athens during the Golden Age: Socrates or Pericles?

823. What is the name of the war that broke out between Athens and Sparta from 431 B.C because of conflicts regarding other city-states: the Persian Wars or the Peloponnesian War?

824. Who were Plato, Socrates, and Aristotle that became well respected after the defeat of Athens: Greek philosophers or Greek playwrights?

825. Which Greek philosopher was a student of Socrates: Plato or Aristotle?

826. Which Greek philosopher was a student of Plato: Socrates or Aristotle?

827. What is the name of the Greek poet who wrote the epic poems: the Iliad or the Odyssey: Homer or Aristotle?

828. What is the name of the King of Macedonia, a country north of Greece, who conquered vast regions of Europe and Asia and helped promote Greek culture even after his death: Alexander the Great or Peter the Great?

829. What is the name of the capital city of Egypt that is named for Alexander the Great?

830. Who were Zeus, Poseidon, Apollo, Athena, and Aphrodite in Greek mythology: Titans or Olympian gods?

831. Who were the first or elder gods who ruled during the golden age and included the parents of Zeus: the Titans or the Olympians?

832. Who was the king considered the most powerful of the Greek gods that lived at Mt. Olympus, is symbolized by a lightning rod, and rode on a horse name Pegasus: Zeus or Hercules?

833. What is the name of the mythological Greek hero who was the son of Zeus, half- man, half-god, and was famous for his strength and courage: Hercules or Apollo?

834. What is the name of the mythological Greek god of archery, light, and music, often symbolized with a bow and arrow, the Sun, and a lyre: Apollo or Artemis?

835. What is the name of the mythological Greek god of the ocean, earthquakes, and horses: Poseidon or Ares?

836. What is the name of the Greek goddess of wisdom, defense, and war, often symbolized with an owl or olive branch, and is regarded as the patron god of Athens: Aphrodite or Athena?

837. What is the name of the Greek goddess of love and beauty, often symbolized with a dove, a swan, or a rose: Aphrodite or Athena?

838. Who were Cyclopes, Medusa, Pegasus, Sphinx, and Typhon in Greek mythology: Greek monsters or Greek gods?

839. What is the name of the Greek monster that was a white horse that could fly: Minotaur or Pegasus?

SOCIAL STUDIES

840. What is the name of the Greek monster that was a one-eyed giant and was famous for making thunderbolts for Zeus: Cyclopes or Minotaur?

841. What is the name for Greek creatures that were half-man, half-horse: Centaurs or Cyclopes?

842. What ancient civilization is credited with the origins of the Olympic Games, beginning with competitions between the city-states: Greek or Roman?

843. What did the winners of the Olympic Games receive: olive branches or medals?

844. In which city were the Olympics held: Athens or Olympia?

845. Do you think the early Greek Olympics had all the events we have today?

846. What were two likely beginning Olympic competitions: running and chariot racing, or swimming and gymnastics?

847. How often are the summer and winter Olympics held?

848. Can you name an Olympic champion in a sport?

849. What did the Greeks develop for writing that includes 24 letters and symbols, begins with alpha, beta, gamma, delta, and is often used to refer to college sororities and fraternities: the Greek Numbers or the Greek Alphabet?

850. What word comes from the first two letters of the Greek letter system: alpha and beta?

851. What is the official language of Greece and Cyprus: Latin or Greek?

852. What is the name of the other ancient civilization after the Greeks: Italian or Roman?

853. How many hills was the city of ancient Rome built on: three or seven?

854. What civilization is evident in our calendar, our government, and in the design of our buildings: the ancient Roman or the ancient Mesopotamian?

855. Did Rome, Italy grow in power and go on to conquer other countries to spread its empire?

856. Who founded Rome: Romulus and Remus, or the Latins?

857. After whom is the city of Rome named after they built the city on the hills overlooking the Tiber River: Romulus or Remus?

858. In the year 753 B.C. was the city of Rome also known as "The Eternal City" and "The City of Seven Hills?"

859. Did the ancient Romans believe in several gods?

860. Who were Jupiter, Juno, Neptune, Pluto, Apollo, Diana, Mars, Venus, Cupid, Mercury, Minerva, Vulcan, Saturn, Bacchus, Janus, Uranus, and Flora: Roman Gods or Greek Gods?

861. Who did the Romans consider to be the king of all gods: Jupiter or Apollo?

SOCIAL STUDIES

862. Did the Romans engage in ceremonies and rituals to please their gods?

863. Where is Rome, Italy located: on a peninsula or on a river?

864. What is the name of the mountain range north of Rome that served to protect the Romans from invaders: the Alps or the Andes?

865. Who governed ruled Rome for hundreds of years: kings or gods?

866. What is the term for the early government of Rome after the era of kings that selected two principle leaders called consuls who were elected every year: a democracy or a republic?

867. What is the name of the Roman governmental group that gave advice to the consuls: the House of Representatives or the Senate?

868. What kind of social system did ancient Rome have which gave certain rights to certain levels: a class system or a feudal system?

869. What is the name of the land area that was conquered by the Romans: states or provinces?

870. What was the official language of the Romans: Italian or Latin?

871. What is the term for many languages spoken today that have a Latin base and include Italian, Spanish, French, and Portuguese: Germanic languages or Romance languages?

872. Do many English words have Latin roots?

873. What city located on the northern coast of Africa did the Romans want to invade and conquer in 265 B.C.E: Pompeii or Carthage?

874. Who founded Carthage: the Romans or the Phoenicians?

875. What areas of land did the Phoenicians fight to conquer: Northern Africa and Sicily, or Sardinia and Corsica?

876. What island did the Romans and the Carthaginians fight to win control of in a sea battle: Corsica or Sicily?

877. Which side was superior in winning battles at sea: Rome or Carthage?

878. What was the name of the wars between Rome and Carthage that were fought primarily at sea: the Punic Wars or the Italian Wars?

879. How many years did Rome and Carthage fight in the first Punic War: five or twenty?

880. What islands did Carthage offer Rome in a deal to end the war: Sicily, Corsica, and Sardinia, or only Corsica and Sardinia?

881. What other country did the Carthage General decide to fight in order to win back some land: France or Spain?

SOCIAL STUDIES

882. What is the name of the son that the Carthage General took with him to Spain, making him promise that he would continue the fight with the Romans as soon as he was old enough: Julius Caesar or Hannibal?

883. In which direction did Hannibal, a military genius at 26, decide to lead his 90,000 soldiers in a surprise attack against Rome: North across the Alps, or South across the Mediterranean?

884. What animal did Hannibal bring with him across the Alps that frightened the Romans: elephants or tigers?

885. Did the fight between the Romans and the Carthaginians continue for several years?

886. Who managed to win the Second Punic War in 203 B.C.E: Rome or Carthage?

887. Which side had to leave Spain, France, and Italy, reduce their warships, and pay war damages: Rome or Carthage?

888. Did Hannibal continue to spend the rest of his life fighting Rome?

889. Is Hannibal still regarded as a great military general?

890. Who won the Third Punic War winning control of Northern Africa, Spain, and the islands of Sicily, Corsica, and Sardinia: Rome or Carthage?

891. What did the Romans build to connect all the new territories, promote trade, and provide the means for transportation: canals and waterways, or roads and bridges?

892. What is the name of the man that is best known for being the leader of Rome and to ending the Roman Republic: Julius Caesar or Marc Antony?

893. Which country, now France, was Julius Caesar appointed the governor of: Gaul or Sicily?

894. What is the name of the Roman General that was a respected military leader, but soon become Julius Caesar's biggest rival: Pompey or Marc Antony?

895. Who won the civil war that came about between Caesar who had the support of the people, and Pompey who had the support of the Senate: Caesar or Pompey?

896. Who appointed Julius Caesar the dictator for life after the defeat of Pompey and his return to Rome: the Senate or the consuls?

897. What country did Pompey flee to where he was killed by King Ptolemy: Greece or Egypt?

898. Whom did Julius Caesar meet when he invaded Egypt: Ptolemy's sister, Cleopatra, or Isis?

899. Were Cleopatra and her brother Ptolemy the co-rulers of Egypt even though Cleopatra was many years older than her brother?

900. Did Ptolemy take over as the Pharaoh when he became older?

SOCIAL STUDIES

901. Whom did Cleopatra convince to help her win back the throne after she sneaked into the palace inside of a rolled carpet: Ptolemy or Julius Caesar?

902. Where did Julius Caesar defeat Ptolemy and his army making Cleopatra the ruler once again: the Battle of Alexandria or the Battle of the Nile?

903. Who uttered the famous words "I came, I saw, I conquered" after a victory in a military battle: Marc Antony or Julius Caesar?

904. Why did the Romans plot to kill Julius Caesar: they wanted a return to a republic, or they did not want to be controlled by Cleopatra and Egypt?

905. How was Julius Caesar killed on March 15th in the year 44 B.C.E on the Senate floor, in a hall next to the Pompey Theater: gunshots or stab wounds?

906. What are the names of the two men that shared control of Rome after the death of Julius Caesar: Marc Antony and Octavian, or Ramses and Caesarion?

907. Whom did Cleopatra meet in the city of Alexandria, the capital of Egypt: Octavian or Marc Antony?

908. Who came to power and ruled Rome after Marc Antony and Cleopatra lost all power and died by a sword and a snake: Octavian or Caesarion?

909. What name did the Roman Senate give to Octavian when he became the first emperor of Rome: Augustus Caesar or Emperor Octavian?

910. What month of the year is named for Augustus Caesar?

911. What month of the year is named for Julius Caesar?

912. Who is credited for making up the calendar we use today, with each month named for a god, a Latin translation, or a number: the Romans or the Greeks?

913. Which month is translated as number "7" in Latin: October or September?

914. Which month is translated as number "8" in Latin, and is similar to the words octopus, octave, and octagon?

915. Which month is translated as number "9" in Latin: November of October?

916. Which month is translated as number "10" in Latin, and is similar to the words decimal, decade, decimeter, and decathlon?

917. What is the name for the letters that the Romans used to represent cardinal numbers like I, V, X, L, C, D, and M that are still used today for outlines, Super Bowl numbering, and after kings' names: Roman numerals or Binary Numbers?

918. What was the name for the time of peace and prosperity during the 40-year rule of Emperor Augustus Caesar, and the 200 years beyond his rule: Pax Romana or Bellum Romana?

919. Were there several Roman emperors after Augustus?

SOCIAL STUDIES

920. What is the meaning of Pax Romana: Roman King or Roman peace?

921. What is the name of the downtown area in ancient Rome with its pottery, clothing shops, spice shops, markets, and temples: the Coliseum or the Forum?

922. What is the name for the temple that was built during the reign of Augustus for all the gods of ancient Rome: the Coliseum or the Pantheon?

923. What is the name for the stone structures that the Romans built that brought water from a river or stream into the city, and provided water for the public fountains and baths: aqueducts or irrigation canals?

924. Who built the famous Pont du Gard aqueduct in France and the Segovia aqueduct in Spain: the Greeks or the Romans?

925. What is the name of the largest Baroque fountain in Rome, Italy, one of the most famous in the world: the Trevi Fountain or the Tivoli Fountain?

926. Are the Romans regarded as good engineers with all their roads, bridges, aqueducts, and the Colosseum?

927. What is the name for the one-piece outer garment worn by male citizens in ancient Rome: the cape or the toga?

928. What is the name for the one-piece outer garment worn by women in ancient Rome: the stola or the tunic?

929. What was considered typical food in *ancient* Rome: spaghetti, pizza, and pasta, or bread, fish, and cheese?

930. What is the name for the open-air round arena with tiers of seats for 55,000 spectators that the Romans built for gladiator combats and other sporting events: a theatre in the round, or an amphitheater?

931. What is the name of Rome's most famous amphitheater, built over 2,000 years ago, where spectators would sit on marble seats to watch gladiators battle or animals fight, and is still the biggest landmark in Rome: the Pantheon or the Coliseum?

932. What is the name for the Roman horse races around a track called the Circus Maximus with the racer driving a team of horses several times around the track: gladiator races or chariot races?

933. What catastrophe occurred in 64 A.D. that destroyed nearly half of Rome under the reign of the unpopular Emperor Nero: the great fire or the great earthquake?

934. What is the name of the gladiator slave that led a slave revolt in 73 B.C.E: Spartacus or Olympus?

935. What is the name of the man that inspired a new religion and believed that there was just one God: Moses or Jesus?

936. What religion did many follow honoring one God, a religion that was opposed to the Romans believing in many gods: Christianity or Catholicism?

SOCIAL STUDIES

937. What is the name of the ancient city and vacation destination outside of Rome that was nearly destroyed and buried in ash after the eruption of Mount Vesuvius in 79 A.D: Sicily or Pompeii?

938. What did archaeologists discover in 1748 that they believe preserved the ancient city of Pompeii, and gave them information about the people and their way of living: sand or molten lava?

939. Under which emperor did the Roman Empire reach its peak in 117 A.D: Nero or Trajan?

940. What was the end result of Rome's excessively big empire, the plague, a weakened army, the economy, civil wars, and invasions from other tribes all contribute to over three hundred years: a divided Roman Empire or the decline and fall of the Roman Empire?

941. What is the name of the man who became the Roman emperor in 310 A.D., became the first to convert to Christianity after he had a vision, captured and ruled a united Rome, and established the new capital of Constantinople: Constantine the Great or Maxentius?

942. What artwork is Constantinople famous for that is found in many of its palaces and churches: murals or mosaics?

943. What is the modern name for Constantinople, Turkey that was the capital city of the Roman Empire in 330 A.D: Istanbul or Ankara?

944. What was the name of the western half of the Roman Empire under Constantine in 395 A.D: the Western Roman Empire or the Byzantine Empire?

945. What was the name of the eastern half of the Roman Empire under Constantine in 395 A.D: the Roman Empire or the Byzantine Empire?

946. What warrior groups invaded and conquered Rome in the 400's that marked the end of the Western Roman Empire: the Visigoths and Germans, or the Huns and the Spanish?

947. Did the eastern Byzantine Empire continue to flourish after the fall of the Roman Empire?

948. Who ruled the Byzantine Empire for forty years, is credited with compiling the laws of the Romans into ten books called a code, and now serves as a basis for our modern system of civil law: Justinian the Great or Byzantine the Great?

949. What is the name of the people that lived in Northern Europe in the Scandinavian countries of Norway, Sweden, and Denmark during the Middle Ages: the Vikings or the Visigoths?

950. What is the geographical term for a deep inlet of the sea between steep slopes in a valley that was carved by a glacier that Norway is famous for: fjord or channel?

951. Did Medieval Norway have many farming communities?

952. What were the Viking people also known as because of their numerous invasions of Northern and Western European countries and islands: imperialists or raiders?

953. What is the name of the place on the northern coast of France that was settled by the Vikings: Brittany or Normandy?

SOCIAL STUDIES

954. What is another name for Vikings: Raiders or Norsemen?

955. What did the Vikings or Norsemen wear on their heads when raiding a village or city: a horned helmet or a horned mask?

956. What things did the Vikings often steal in the late 700's when they invaded places like Iceland, Greenland, Scotland, Ireland, and England: gold and silver, or copper and steel?

957. What defenseless places, home to Christian monks, did the Vikings often burn down after they attacked and looted them: temples or monasteries?

958. What mode of transportation were the Vikings most noted for: Viking ships or Viking wagons?

959. What is the name for narrow ships that the Vikings made that were used for exploration and raiding, and were propelled by sails and oars: galleons or longships?

960. What is the name of the red-haired Viking man who fled Norway with his father to Iceland and then went on to discover and name Greenland: Eric the Red or Eric the Outlaw?

961. What is the name of Eric the Red's oldest son, a Norseman who was known as the first European explorer to arrive in North America 500 years before the arrival of Christopher Columbus: Leif Ericsson or Eric Jacobson?

962. What is the name of the large, Canadian island off the eastern coast of North America that Leif Ericson landed on early in the 11th century after a storm caused him to lose his way on his journey from Norway to Greenland: Newfoundland or Labrador?

963. What did Leif Ericson call the Canadian province where he landed because of the wild grape vines that grew there: Finland or Vinland?

964. What is the name for the strip of land that connected the continents of North America and Asia during the Ice Age that Native Americans and animals crossed: land bridge or Bering Strait?

965. What is the accepted name of the early people that made their home in the cold tundra climate of Alaska, Canada, Siberia, and Greenland: the Inuit or the Eskimos?

966. What is the Inuit name for the homes they built out of snow and ice: igloo or ice shanty?

967. What did the Inuit make their clothing from: linen cloth or animal skins?

968. What is the name for the warm boots made and worn by the Inuit: mukluks or moccasins?

969. What is the name for the warm coats with fur-lined hoods worn by the Inuit: Parkas or Minks?

970. Would the Inuit make many clothing items from the fur of rabbit, polar bear, and foxes, as well as sealskin and caribou?

971. What is the staple of the Inuit diet: corn or meat?

972. What kind of weapon would the Inuit use to hunt seals, walruses, otters, and whales: a bow or a harpoon?

SOCIAL STUDIES

973. What dog did the Inuit breed to pull their sleds: Alaskan Malamute dog or Inuit Eskimo dog?

974. What kind of boat did the Inuit often use for hunting: kayaks or canoes?

975. What is the largest state in the United States: Texas or Alaska?

976. What is the capital of Alaska: Juneau, Anchorage, or Fairbanks?

977. What is the nickname for the state of Alaska that refers to areas in the north where, during the summer, the Sun never completely disappears below the horizon, and the Sun is visible at midnight?

978. What is the common name for aurora borealis, the colorful lights that can be seen in Alaska and other places in the Northern Hemisphere: the Northern Lights or the Alaskan Lights?

979. Was Alaska known for having gold?

980. What is the name of the Alaskan gold rush that attracted more than 100,000 prospectors between 1896 and 1899, also known as the Yukon Gold Rush: the Klondike or the Skagway?

981. What other gem is abundant in Alaska besides gold: ruby or jade?

982. Is Alaska known for its wildlife like salmon, moose and bear?

983. Does Alaska have many mountains, glaciers, and fjords?

984. What kind of pipeline runs 800 miles in Alaska from wells at Prudhoe Bay to the Port of Valdez: gas or oil?

985. What is the name of the highest mountain peak in North America located in Alaska: Mt. Everest or Mt. McKinley?

986. What bears are found in Alaska besides polar bears and grizzly bears: Black or Kodiak?

987. What is the main sport in Alaska: dog sledding or snowmobiling?

988. What is the name of the famous Alaskan sled dog race: the Iditarod or the Birkebeiner?

989. What is the name of a breed of dog often used for Alaskan sled racing: Labrador or Husky?

990. What are huskies and malamutes?

991. What did some Native Americans build thousands of years ago as burial places: mounds or pyramids?

992. What is the name of the North American cliff dwellers that are regarded as the Ancient Pueblo people of Utah, Colorado, Arizona, and New Mexico: the Apache or the Anasazi?

993. What did the Anasazi use to build their multi-room homes, and built them so the overhanging cliff would serve as the roof: adobe bricks or dry rocks?

994. What is the Spanish term for the town or village that the Anasazi lived: pueblo or barrio?

SOCIAL STUDIES

995. Did the Anasazi homes have doors or windows?

996. How did the Anasazi move from level to level in their dwellings: stairs or ladders?

997. Did the Anasazi die out naturally, or did they disappear mysteriously, leaving behind their elaborate cliff dwellings?

998. What is the name of the brick that the Pueblo Indians built their houses out of in the 1500's that is a mixture of sand, clay, and straw: cement or adobe?

999. What was the name of the dance performed by the Pueblos to attract rain and good crops: the Wheat Dance or the Corn Dance?

1000. What is the name for the carved dolls of the Pueblo Indians that represent different spirits: Kachina dolls or Ancestral dolls?

1001. What is the term for the Native American tribes like the Navajo and the Apache that moved from place to place in search of food, water, and good land: wanderer or Nomad?

1002. What is the name of one kind of house built by the Apache with animal hides stretched over poles: a hut or a teepee?

1003. What is another name for a wickiup, a permanent house built by the Apache: a teepee or a wigwam?

1004. What did the Apache make many of their clothing items from: rabbit fur or buckskin?

1005. Did the Apache often decorate their clothing with beads, feathers, and fringes?

1006. What is the name for the shoes the Apache wear on their feet: moccasins or mukluks?

1007. What are the staples of the Apache diet: corn and buffalo meat, or wheat and pig meat?

1008. What weapon did the Apache use to hunt with: hatchets or bows and arrows?

1009. What did the Apache use to make the tips of their spears: flint or arrowheads?

1010. Was Geronimo the chief of an Apache tribe or a Navajo tribe?

1011. What were the Navajo Indians also known as: the Diné or the Hogans?

1012. What is the name of the dwelling built by the Navajo built with logs and clay: a wigwam or a longhouse?

1013. Which group of Native Americans are the largest in the nation: the Navajo or the Apache?

1014. What is the general term used to refer to Native American Indians that live east of the Mississippi River like the Mohican and the Iroquois: the Woodland tribes or the Mississippi tribes?

1015. What is the most important crop for the Woodland tribes: wheat or maize, a type of corn?

1016. What is the name of the language spoken by many Native American tribes: Algonquin or Cherokee?

SOCIAL STUDIES

1017. What is the name for a Native American infant or young child: a papoose or a bambino?

1018. What is the name of the structure that was built to safely carry the Native American babies: a cradleboard or a papoose?

1019. What is the modern day version of the game using sticks, balls and nets played by the Algonquin, the Iroquois, and the Huron: Cricket or Lacrosse?

1020. What did the Native Americans often cover their skin with to protect them from mosquito bites: mud and bear fat, or sand and seal fat?

1021. What is the name of the narrow boat with narrow ends that the Native Americans often built from birch trees: a kayak or a canoe?

1022. What is the name for the houses built by many Woodland Indians: teepees or longhouses?

1023. What is the name often used for the Native American religious or spiritual leader: the Medicine man or the healer?

1024. Are chiefs, headdresses, tribes, drums, dancing, war paint, jewelry, singing, and peace pipes all a part of Native American culture?

1025. What is the name for the Native American meeting and dance ritual: a powwow or a tribal dance?

1026. What is the name for the small axe used by Native Americans that is similar to a hatchet, and used as both a weapon and a tool: a tomahawk or a picket?

1027. What is the name of the symbolic wooden post carved out by the Native Americans: obelisk or totem pole?

1028. What is the name for the beads that were made from shells and used for money by many Woodland tribes: wampum or wontons?

1029. What is the name for a group of Native American families that have a common culture, language, and religion: a nation or a tribe?

1030. What is the name for the area of land that the U.S. government has set aside that is managed by a particular Native American Indian Nation or tribe: a reservation or a homestead?

1031. Which Italian explorer is remembered for his discovery of the "New World?"

1032. In what year did Columbus "discover" America?

1033. What is the name of the island that Christopher Columbus landed on in the Caribbean: San Salvador meaning "Holy Savior," or Puerto Rico?

1034. What did Columbus call the Taino natives that he met after he landed because he thought he had reached the East Indies?

1035. Who sponsored Columbus's voyages to America: Italy or Spain?

SOCIAL STUDIES

1036. What are the names of Christopher Columbus's three ships?

1037. What are the names of the Spanish monarchs who paid for Columbus's four voyages to the New World: King George and Queen Victoria, or Kind Ferdinand and Queen Isabella?

1038. What is the name of the explorer and mapmaker from Florence, Italy after whom our country is named, and because of his mapping skills, recognized that our continent truly was the "New World:" Amerigo Vespucci or Martin Waldseemuller?

1039. What is the name of the Italian explorer who sailed across the Atlantic in 1497 backed by King Henry VII of England, crossed the Atlantic with his small crew, and landed in Newfoundland, Canada: Henry Hudson or John Cabot?

1040. What is the Spanish word for "conqueror," like Hernando Cortez, Francisco Pizarro, and Vasco Nuñez de Balboa: conquistador or explorador?

1041. What were the Spanish Conquistadors searching for in the New World: gold or oil?

1042. What is the name of the Spanish Conquistador who claimed Mexico for Spain in 1519 after he conquered the Aztec Empire and killed the Aztec Emperor Montezuma: Hernando Cortez or Francisco Pizarro?

1043. What is the name of the Spanish explorer who is known for establishing the first European settlement in South America in 1511, and was the first European to see the Pacific Ocean after crossing the Isthmus of Panama in 1513: Vasco Nuñez de Balboa or Juan Ponce de León?

1044. What is the name of the Spanish conquistador who explored South America, conquered the Inca Empire in Peru in 1532, took over the Inca city of Cuzco, and established the new capital of Lima: Ferdinand Magellan or Francisco Pizarro?

1045. What is the name of the Spanish conquistador who sailed with Columbus on his second voyage, was appointed as the Governor of Puerto Rico by King Ferdinand, and led an expedition to discover the fountain of youth but somehow ended up in the state of Florida: Juan Ponce de León or Hernando de Soto?

1046. What is the translation of *Puerto Rico* in English, because of the all the gold, silver, and other minerals that are found on this island?

1047. What was Juan Ponce de León in search in the West Indies besides more gold: the fountain of youth, or silver mines?

1048. Which state did Ponce de León land on during the springtime, named this state a Spanish word that translates "place of flowers," and claimed this state for Spain: Florida or Louisiana?

1049. What is the name of the warm ocean current of the northern Atlantic Ocean, discovered by Ponce de León that helps ships sail at a higher speed: the Gulf Stream or the trade winds?

1050. On which Caribbean island did Ponce de León die because of a wound he received while fighting the Native Americans: Puerto Rico or Cuba?

SOCIAL STUDIES

1051. What is the name of the Spanish conquistador who arrived in Florida in 1539, was appointed the Governor of Florida and Cuba by the King of Spain, and was the first European to explore the territory west of the Mississippi River: Hernando Cortez or Hernando de Soto?

1052. What was Hernando de Soto main quest in exploring Florida: finding gold, or finding the fountain of youth?

1053. What animal did the Spanish bring with them to the New World: the chicken or the horse?

1054. What did the Spanish have that helped them overpower the Native Americans in the state of Florida: guns and horses, or longbows and mules?

1055. What is the name of the first permanent European settlement located on the eastern coast of Florida that Spaniard Pedro Menéndez de Avilés named for a saint: St. Angel or St. Augustine?

1056. What is "Castillo de San Marcos" that was built by the Spanish to protect the land against other invading Europeans: a fort or a castle?

1057. What is the name of the Spanish conquistador who was appointed the Governor of Spanish territories in Mexico, and traveled through the southwestern United States in 1540 in the hopes of finding the mythical Seven Cities of Gold: Francisco de Goya or Francisco Vásquez de Coronado?

1058. What natural wonder did Coronado's soldiers stumble upon in their quest to find the cities of gold: the Badlands or the Grand Canyon?

1059. What is the name of the river that the Spanish explorers discovered between the United States and Mexico that translates as "big river?"

1060. What religion did the Spanish explorers want to share with the Native Americans?

1061. What is the word used to refer to the schools and churches that the priests built close to Indian villages: cathedrals or missions?

1062. What diseases did the Spanish bring with them from Europe to the New World that many Native Americans died of during and after Coronado's exploration years?

1063. What is the name for the faster sea route that the Europeans would spend several years searching for through the icy Arctic Ocean that would lead them to Asia with all its desirable trade products like spices, tea, and silk: the St. Lawrence Seaway or the Northwest Passage?

1064. What is the name of the English explorer who sailed three times for the English and once for the Dutch in the early 1600's in his quest to discover the Northwest Passage, a shorter route between Europe to Asia by way of the Arctic Ocean: Henry Hudson or John Cabot?

1065. From which country are the Dutch: the Netherlands or Belgium?

1066. What country is regarded as a country of the Netherlands: Scandinavia or Holland?

1067. What area do Norway, Sweden, and Denmark make up: the Netherlands or Scandinavia?

SOCIAL STUDIES

1068. Which country do the Danes or Danish people call home: Denmark or Holland?

1069. What is the name of the sweet pastry that has become a specialty of Denmark?

1070. What famous explorer has a strait named for him, linking the Atlantic Ocean to a bay in Canada as well as a river in New York: St. Lawrence or Hudson?

1071. What is the name of the country, north of the United States, that extends from the Atlantic to the Pacific, and North to the Arctic?

1072. What is the largest country in the Western Hemisphere: Canada or the United States?

1073. What languages are spoken in Canada?

1074. What kind of leaf is featured on the red and white Canadian flag: oak or maple?

1075. What kind of syrup is produced from the sap of trees in Canada: maple or corn?

1076. What is Canada divided into: states or provinces?

1077. How many provinces does Canada have: eight or ten?

1078. What are Manitoba, Saskatchewan, Alberta, Ontario, British Colombia, Nova Scotia, Prince Edward Island, Quebec, New Brunswick, and Newfoundland: provinces or territories?

1079. What are Nunavut, Northwest Territories, and Yukon: Canadian provinces or territories?

1080. What is the capital of Canada, located in the province of Ontario: Montreal or Ottawa?

1081. What language is spoken in the province of Québec: French or English?

1082. What is the name of the French navigator, considered the "founder of New France," credited as the founder of the first permanent settlement and trading post near the St. Lawrence River that is now known as Québec: Henry Hudson or Samuel de Champlain?

1083. What was Champlain searching for when he came from France to Canada on his first voyage in 1603: gold mines, or animal furs?

1084. What is another name that refers to Québec: French Canada or Champlain Canada?

1085. What mountain range located in the United States extends to western Canada: the Smoky Mountains or the Rocky Mountains?

1086. What is the name of the territory where Canada connects with Alaska: Northwest Territories or Yukon Territory?

1087. Where are Québec, Toronto, Vancouver, and Montreal located: northern or southern Canada?

1088. Are moose, caribou, beaver, bear, and Canada Geese among the many animals that live in Canada?

1089. What industry and recreational sport in Canada include the following: muskellunge, salmon, and trout?

SOCIAL STUDIES

1090. What kind of hunting did the Inuit engage in while in Canada that is still a major industry today: caribou hunting or seal hunting?

1091. What are two popular sports played in Canada: lacrosse and hockey, or cricket and basketball?

1092. What age were the 1400's, 1500's and 1600's considered because it was a time when many Europeans were exploring and making new discoveries in the New World: Exploration and Discovery or conquest and invention?

1093. Where did many of the early European explorers of the 15th century come from: France and Spain, or Italy and Portugal?

1094. Which European country wanted to share in the wealth of the New World and find gold, silver, and other riches in the New World: Germany or England?

1095. What is the name of the document that was issued by King James I of England in 1606 that assigned land rights to the colonists to settle in North America: treaty or charter?

1096. Was the first journey from England to North America in 1607 an easy voyage or a difficult one?

1097. What is the name of the English navigator who founded the first English Colony in Virginia in 1607 and named it for the King of England: Captain John Smith or Captain John Cook?

1098. What is the name of the colony that the English settlers established on May 24th, 1607 that is regarded as the first permanent English settlement: Georgetown or Jamestown?

1099. Who was appointed as the leader of the Jamestown Colony: King James I or Captain John Smith?

1100. What did many settlers in Jamestown die of that first winter: starvation and disease, or frostbite and enemy attacks?

1101. What is the name of the Native Americans that Captain Smith and the settlers befriended and traded with: the Powhatan or the Patawomeck?

1102. What staple in the Powhatan diet was introduced and shared with the early English settlers: wheat or corn?

1103. What is the nickname of the Indian woman Matoaka who is credited with saving Captain Smith's life after he was visiting her village near Jamestown and captured by the Powhatan Indians: Sacajawea or Pocahontas?

1104. What is the name of the English settler that Pocahontas married, returned to England with him for a short time, and became known as the Indian Princess: John Smith or John Rolfe?

1105. Did the Native Americans and colonists have both peace and war with one another?

1106. What is the name for the period of starvation in Jamestown during the winter of 1609-1610 in which only sixty colonists survived out of five hundred: The Starving Time or The Famine?

1107. What crop did colonists raise in order to sell for profit in 1614 that helped the Jamestown economy: corn or tobacco?

SOCIAL STUDIES

1108. Who arrived on a ship in Chesapeake Bay for the first time in 1619, and paved the way for the family unit in Jamestown: slaves or women?

1109. Was Jamestown allowed to make its own laws under the governor?

1110. Who arrived on Dutch ships in Chesapeake Bay for the first time in 1619: Africans or Swedes?

1111. What is the term for the African people that came to America to work on the settlement for others for a specific period of time: slaves or indentured servants?

1112. What is the name of the 102 passengers who boarded a ship and arrived here from England in 1620 to escape religious restrictions and separate themselves from the Church of England: Puritans or Pilgrims?

1113. What is the name of the ship that the Pilgrims sailed on for sixty-six days to reach the New World?

1114. What is the name for the agreement that was signed by 41 Pilgrims that became the basis for their government in Plymouth Colony: the Pilgrim Pledge or the Mayflower Compact?

1115. What did the Pilgrims call the place where they landed in Massachusetts in 1620: Plymouth Rock or Jamestown II?

1116. What is the name of the leader of the Pilgrims that established Plymouth Colony and governed there for thirty years: John Smith or William Bradford?

1117. What did many Pilgrims die of that first harsh winter: malnutrition and exposure, or disease?

1118. What is the name for the Native American Indians that the Pilgrims met and signed a peace treaty with: the Wampanoag or the Powhatan?

1119. What is the name of the Chief of the Wampanoag: Samoset or Massasoit?

1120. What is the name of the Native American Indian who spoke English and helped to establish a treaty between the Pilgrims and local Native Americans: Powhatan or Squanto?

1121. What is the name of the three-day celebration of the first harvest in 1621 that the Pilgrims had with Chief Massasoit and ninety Native American men, organized by Governor William Bradford: the Harvest Festival or Thanksgiving?

1122. When did the Pilgrims and the Native Americans call this feast and celebration a "Thanksgiving:" the first gathering in 1621, or two years later in 1623?

1123. Did the Pilgrim and Indian Thanksgiving include goose, venison, duck, corn bread, singing, and dancing?

1124. What is the name of the people from England who started coming to the New World after the Pilgrims: the Puritans or the Calvinists?

1125. What leader guided 1,000 Puritans to America and established the Massachusetts Bay Colony in 1630: James Winthrop or Roger Williams?

SOCIAL STUDIES

1126. Why did King Charles I, the son of King James, charter the Massachusetts Bay Company, giving the Puritans the right to settle in New England: he wanted the Puritans to leave England, or he wanted the Puritans to promote the teachings of the Church of England?

1127. Who built Salem and Boston, and established more colonies in New Hampshire, Rhode Island, and Connecticut between 1630 and 1640: the Wampanoag or the Puritans?

1128. What did the Puritans build in several colonies to promote reading and knowledge for all children?

1129. Which Massachusetts University was founded by the Puritans: Boston University or Harvard?

1130. What is the name of the Puritan minister who wanted to establish a colony in Providence, Rhode Island, and believed in the separation of government and religion, commonly known as the separation of church and state: Roger Williams or John Winthrop?

1131. Did the Native Americans approve or disapprove the many Puritans that arrived here from England and claimed more and more of their land?

1132. What happened to the population of the Native Americans as more and more of them were exposed to diseases brought over by the Europeans?

1133. Did Europeans seeking religious freedom establish many English Colonies?

1134. What is the name of the religious group, known as the Society of Friends, who came to Pennsylvania to practice their faith because they were loyal to only God and not the English King: Quakers or Calvinists?

1135. What is the name of the Quaker who founded the Colony of Pennsylvania to promote religious freedom, and the Quaker belief that all men and women are created equal in the eyes of God: William Tell or William Penn?

1136. Did Pennsylvania welcome people of all religions, or only Quakers?

1137. What city did William Penn establish as the capital of Pennsylvania close to the Delaware River: Philadelphia or Pittsburgh?

1138. What is the name of the colony named for the King's wife, Queen Henrietta Maria, that was settled by many Puritans in 1634: Maryland or Maine?

1139. What was the name of the New York area and the island of Manhattan in the 1600's because for a time it was a colony of the Dutch: New Netherland or New Holland?

1140. Which English King is the colony Carolina named for: King Carlos II or King Charles I?

1141. What did many farmers in Carolina rely on to help with the crops before the 1680's: slaves or indentured servants?

1142. What two smaller colonies did Carolina divide into in the early 1700's?

1143. What new colony in the south did King George II of England in 1674 name for himself?

SOCIAL STUDIES

1144. What reached its height during colonial times with millions of slaves being transported to the European colonies in the Americas to work on the plantations: slave trade or African trade?

1145. What religious group believed in equal rights for all people and wanted to end slavery: the Amish or the Quakers?

1146. What are Judaism, Christianity, and Islam?

1147. What is the name of the monotheistic religion of the Jews, believing in only one God: Judaism or Hebrewism?

1148. What is the name of the Jewish language: Hebrew or Arabic?

1149. What is the name of the first five books of the Hebrew Bible: the Old Testament or the Torah?

1150. Who were the first two human beings, according to the Book of Genesis in the Hebrew Bible, who were driven out of the Garden of Eden when they ate the fruit of a forbidden tree?

1151. What is the name of the man that is regarded as the father of the Jewish people: Moses or Abraham?

1152. Who led the Hebrews away from the Egyptians and the Pharaoh: Moses or Abraham?

1153. What ten religious rules did God communicate to Moses on a mountaintop: the Ten Laws or the Ten Commandments?

1154. What name did the Hebrew give to the land of Canaan after they managed to conquer the whole country: Israel or Jerusalem?

1155. What is the name of the king who ruled Israel for several years: David or Abraham?

1156. What is the capital city of Israel: Canaan or Jerusalem?

1157. Who did the Jews surrender to in 66 A.D. and were shut out of Israel for nearly 2,000 years: the Romans or the Greeks?

1158. When did Israel become an independent nation again: 1848 or 1948?

1159. What is the name of the religion that is based on the life and teachings of Jesus who was believed to be the Messiah or the "anointed one:" Catholicism or Christianity?

1160. What did the Christians call the Hebrew Bible: the Old Testament or the New Testament?

1161. Do both the Old Testament and the New Testament make up the Christian Bible?

1162. What is the name for the first four books of the New Testament: the Prophets or the Gospels?

1163. Were Matthew, Mark, Luke, and John evangelists of whom the gospels were based on?

1164. What is the name of the Jewish prophet who baptized Jesus: John or Matthew?

1165. Was Jesus put to death by crucifixion because some did not believe in his teachings?

1166. Did Christianity start to spread as Christians were eager to share the gospel?

SOCIAL STUDIES

1167. What is the name given for people that are non-Jews: Prophets or Gentiles?

1168. Did the Jew Paul of Tarsus believe that Jesus was the son of God as well as the Messiah?

1169. What eventually replaced polytheism, the worship of many gods, in the Roman Empire: Judaism or Christianity?

1170. Which religion has the most followers of the three religions today: Christianity, Judaism, or Islam?

1171. Do some Christian denominations include Baptists, Catholics, Lutherans, and Orthodox?

1172. What is the dominant religion in Italy today: Roman Catholicism or Italian Polytheism?

1173. Is it a good ethic to always accept and respect religions and beliefs that are different from our own?

Social Studies – 4th Grade

1174. What is the name of the planet we live on?

1175. What is the name for the spherical representation of the Earth?

1176. How many continents are on planet Earth?

1177. What are the two main oceans on planet Earth?

1178. Which of the seven continents can you name?

1179. Can you read a map?

1180. What are climate, economic, physical, road, political, and topographic all considered?

1181. What is the name of the imaginary line that divides the globe in half and runs east to west?

1182. What is the name of the imaginary line that divides the globe in half and runs north to south: the equator or the prime meridian?

1183. What is the name for the top sphere and the bottom sphere of the Earth: pole or hemisphere?

1184. How many hemispheres is the Earth divided into?

1185. What is the geographical term given for everything above the equator: Northern Hemisphere or Southern Hemisphere?

1186. What is the geographical term given for everything below the equator: Northern Hemisphere or Southern Hemisphere?

1187. What is the geographical term given for everything to the right of the Prime Meridian: Eastern Hemisphere or Western Hemisphere?

1188. What is the geographical term given for everything to the left of the Prime Meridian: Eastern Hemisphere or Western Hemisphere?

SOCIAL STUDIES

1189. What is the name of the imaginary line that divides the globe down the middle at the poles: the equator or the prime meridian?

1190. What two hemispheres does the prime meridian divide: Northern and Southern, or Eastern and Western?

1191. What is the name for the lines that run parallel to the equator: parallels or meridians?

1192. What is the name for the lines that run from pole to pole: parallels or meridians?

1193. What is the name of the geographic coordinate that runs north to south: latitude or longitude?

1194. What is the name of the geographic coordinate that runs east to west: latitude or longitude?

1195. Do lines of latitude run north or south or east to west?

1196. Do lines of longitude run north to south or east to west?

1197. What is the name for the point where lines of longitude are measured from: the prime meridian or the equator?

1198. What is the name of the place in England that measures zero degrees longitude: London or Greenwich?

1199. Do all parallels and meridians have a number?

1200. What is the name of the unit of measurement for longitude and latitude: coordinate or degree?

1201. What is the degree number of the equator at the eastern most point and the western most point, and at the intersection with the Prime Meridian: 0 or 90?

1202. What is the degree number of the Prime Meridian from North Pole to South Pole: 90 or 180?

1203. What is another name for the 180th meridian, halfway around the globe: the prime meridian or the International Dateline?

1204. What is the name for where meridians and parallels intersect: an axis or a coordinate?

1205. How would you read the coordinates 30 degrees North 20 degrees east: 30 degrees north of the equator and 20 degrees east of the prime meridian, or 30 degrees north of the prime meridian and 20 degrees east of the equator?

1206. When given the exact coordinates of a place, can you find the location of that place on a map?

1207. Can you identify several states while looking at a map of the United States?

1208. Can you identify your city and several others on a state map?

1209. Can you follow a map inside a building?

1210. What is the term for the proportion between the distance on a map and the real distance on the Earth's surface: scope or scale?

SOCIAL STUDIES

1211. Do most maps include scales on the bottom or in the corner?

1212. What kind of map might you be looking at if the scale reads one inch equal one hundred miles: a city map or a state map?

1213. What kind of map might you be looking at if the scale reads one inch equals one mile: a state map or a city map?

1214. What kind of map might you be looking at if the scale reads one inch equals 1,000 miles: a state map or a country map?

1215. What is the name for the type of map that shows the outlines of the 48 states with their capitals in the continental United States: a political map or a relief map?

1216. What is the name for the type of map that shows the landscape like hills, mountains, and rivers: a political map or a relief map?

1217. What is the name for the type of map that shows the original 13 colonies or battles of the Civil War: a political map or a historical map?

1218. What is the name for the type of map that shows hills and valleys with contour lines, and is often three-dimensional: a relief map or a physical map?

1219. What is the name for the type of map that shows the distribution of natural resources: a physical map or a resource map?

1220. What is the name for the type of map that shows pictures of cheese in the state of Wisconsin and pictures of oranges in the state of Florida: a relief map or a product map?

1221. What is the name for the type of map that shows highways, airports, railroad tracks, cities, and points of interest: a guide map or a road map?

1222. What is the name for the type of map that shows information about the temperatures and precipitation of a region: a climate map or a topographic map?

1223. What is the name for the type of map that shows the elevations of different areas by using lines drawn close together to indicate steep terrain, and lines drawn far apart to indicate flat terrain, a political map or a topographic map?

1224. What is the name for the type of map that indicates the locations of the major mountain ranges: a relief map or a topographic map?

1225. What is the name of the mountain range in North America stretching 3.000 miles from New Mexico through Colorado and Canada, and north to Alaska: the Rockies or the Appalachians?

1226. What is the name of the tallest mountain peak in Alaska: Mount Everest or Mount McKinley?

1227. What is the name of the mountain range in North America stretching 1,800 miles from Alabama to the Gulf of Saint Lawrence that include the White Mountains, the Allegheny Mountains, the Blue

SOCIAL STUDIES

Ridge Mountains, and the Great Smoky Mountains: the Rocky Mountains or the Appalachian Mountains?

1228. Which mountain range has taller peaks: the Appalachians or the Rockies?

1229. Which mountain range is older: the Appalachians or the Rockies?

1230. What may explain why the Appalachians, over 280 million years old, are shorter and have less jagged peaks than the Rockies, over 130 million years old: erosion or weathering?

1231. What does the state of *Montana* translate to from Spanish to English?

1232. What is the name of the mountain range in South America, the longest mountain range in the world, stretching 4,500 miles from the Caribbean coast to the southern tip of the continent: the Andes Mountains or the Ural Mountains?

1233. What is the name of the highest mountain in the Andes that measures over 22,000 feet above sea level: Mount Everest or Mount Aconcagua?

1234. What ancient Indian civilization settled in the Andes of Peru with Cusco as their capital city: the Aztec or the Inca?

1235. What is the name of the city built by the Incas high in the Andes Mountains, 8,000 feet above sea level that was re-discovered by Hiram Bingham in 1911: Tenochtitlan or Machu Picchu?

1236. What is the name of the mountain range located along the northwest coast of Africa stretching 1,500 miles: the Atlas Mountains or the Eastern Highlands?

1237. What is the name of the mountain range located in Eastern Africa: the Atlas Mountains or the Eastern Highlands?

1238. What is the name of the tallest volcanic mountain in Africa: Mount Kilimanjaro or Mount Kenya?

1239. What is the name of the mountains that cover the European countries of Switzerland, Austria, France, and Italy: the Rockies or the Alps?

1240. In which mountain range was a frozen human body, estimated to be 5,000 years old, discovered by hikers in 1991 and named "Otzi," the Ice Man: the Rockies or the Alps?

1241. What is the name of the highest mountain in the French Alps in Europe meaning "White Mountain" in English: Mont Blanc or Mont Fuji?

1242. What is the name of the mountain range in Russia extending from the Arctic to the Caspian Sea: the Atlas Mountains or the Ural Mountains?

1243. What is the name of the highest mountain in Japan: Mount Fuji or Mount Kilimanjaro?

1244. What is the name of the tallest mountain range in the world: the Rockies or the Himalayas?

1245. What is the name of the world's tallest mountain, measuring over 29.000 feet tall that is located between Nepal and Tibet in the Himalayas: Mount McKinley or Mount Everest?

SOCIAL STUDIES

1246. What mountain peak was first conquered by Edmund Hillary and Tenzing Norgay in 1953: Mount McKinley or Mount Everest?

1247. Is there more oxygen or less oxygen is you climb higher above sea level?

1248. What are the two major mountain ranges in the continental United States?

1249. Can the United States be divided into geographic regions?

1250. What is the name of the region that refers to the states of Delaware, the District of Colombia, Maryland, New Jersey, New York, and Pennsylvania: Mid-Atlantic or Midwest?

1251. What is the name of the region that refers to the states of Illinois, Iowa, Indiana, Kansas, Michigan, Minnesota, Missouri, Nebraska, North Dakota, Ohio, South Dakota, and Wisconsin: the Midwest or the Northwest?

1252. What is the name of the region that refers to the states of Alaska, California, Hawaii, Oregon, and Washington: Northwestern States or the Pacific Northwest?

1253. What is the name of the region that refers to the states of Arizona, Colorado, Idaho, Montana, Nevada, New Mexico, Utah, and Wyoming: Rocky Mountain or Pacific Northwest?

1254. What is the name of the region that refers to the states of Connecticut, Maine, Massachusetts, New Hampshire, Rhode Island, and Vermont: Atlantic States or New England?

1255. What is the name of the region that refers to the states of Florida, Georgia, North Carolina, South Carolina, and Virginia: South Atlantic States or Mid-Atlantic States?

1256. What is the name of the region that refers to the states of Arizona, California, Colorado, Nevada, New Mexico, and Utah: the Southwest or the Pacific Northwest?

1257. What is the name of the country north of the United States?

1258. What is the name of the country south of the United States?

1259. What are the two states that are located outside the continental United States?

1260. What type of map can you find landforms such as rivers, channels, deltas, and peninsulas: a political map or a relief map?

1261. What is the geographical term for a wide waterway between two landmasses like the one that is located at the Columbus River in Oregon: a strait or a channel?

1262. What is the geographical term for the navigable narrow waterway between two landmasses like the Bering located between Alaska and Siberia that connects the Pacific with the Arctic, or Gibraltar connecting the Atlantic with the Mediterranean: a delta or a strait?

1263. What is the geographical term for a landform that is formed at a mouth of a river form the deposition of sediment like the one in Northern Egypt where the Nile River spreads out and drains into the Mediterranean Sea: a channel or a delta?

SOCIAL STUDIES

1264. What is the geographical term for a large expanse of grassland and flowers: a mesa or a prairie?

1265. What is the geographical term for a tableland or high plain that is relatively level, like those located in Tibet, Antarctic, and Colorado: a mesa or a plateau?

1266. What is the geographical term for a hill with steep sides and a flat top like those found in Colorado and New Mexico: a mesa or a tableland?

1267. What is the geographical term for a steep face of rock, ice, or Earth: a hill or a cliff?

1268. What is the term for a deep valley with steep cliffs cut into the terrain by running water: a basin or a canyon?

1269. What is the name of the famous canyon, considered by many to be one of the seven wonders of the natural world, located on the Colorado River in the state of Arizona?

1270. What is the geographical term for a landform in the ocean or on land that is lower in the center than at the edges: a canyon or a basin?

1271. What is the geographical term for a piece of land stretching out into water as a peninsula or a point: a cape or a gulf?

1272. What is the name of the famous cape in the state of Massachusetts: Cape Cod or Boston Cape?

1273. What is the geographical term for a large area of ocean that is partially enclosed by land: a gulf or a bay?

1274. What is the name of the largest gulf in the world that is surrounded by Mexico, the United States, and Cuba?

1275. What is the name of the gulf located between Saudi Arabia and Iran where petroleum is transferred on oil tankers: the Middle Eastern Gulf or the Persian Gulf?

1276. What is the geographical term for a small body of water that is set off from a larger body of water where the land curves like San Francisco, Chesapeake, and Hudson: a bay or a gulf?

1277. What is the geographical term for a dry, sandy area where cactus grow, tumbleweeds roll, and has very little rainfall?

1278. What is the name of the biggest desert in the world that stretches across most of North Africa: the Sahara or Death Valley?

1279. What is the name of the continent that is also considered a polar desert: Antarctica or Arctic?

1280. What is the name of the desert that is named for a Native American tribe that stretches across California, Utah, Arizona, and Nevada and includes the area known as "Death Valley:" the Sonoran or the Mojave?

1281. What is the name of the driest desert in the world that is located in Argentina and Chile in South America: the Atacama or the Arabian?

SOCIAL STUDIES

1282. What is the name of the second largest desert in the world, located in Western Asia: the Arabian or the Atacama?

1283. What is the geographical term for a part of land that extends into the water and is connected to the mainland by an isthmus, and include the Iberian, Yucatan, Italian, and the states of Florida and Alaska: a delta or a peninsula?

1284. What is the geographical term for a narrow piece of land that connects two larger land masses like the bridge located in Panama that connects Central America with South America: a fjord or an isthmus?

1285. What is the geographical term for an inlet in the sea between steep slopes carved out by a glacier, like those found in Iceland, Norway, New Zealand, and the state of Alaska: an isthmus or a fjord?

1286. What is the geographical term for a relatively still body of water that is surrounded by land: a river or a lake?

1287. What is the geographical term for a flowing body of water that typically feeds into another body of water: a river or a lake?

1288. What famous lakes can you name?

1289. What are the names of the five great lakes in the United States whose initials spell out H-O-M-E-S?

1290. What is the name of the shallow, salty lake in the state of Utah: Utah Lake or Great Salt Lake?

1291. What famous rivers can you name in the world?

1292. What famous rivers can you name in the United States?

1293. What is the name of the 1,900 mile long river that translate "Big River" in Spanish, and flows along the border between Texas and Mexico into the Gulf of Mexico?

1294. What is the name of the second largest river in the world that is 4,000 miles long, located in South America: the Nile or the Amazon?

1295. What is the name of the longest river in the world that is 4,150 miles long, flowing northward through Eastern Africa into the Mediterranean: the Yellow or the Nile?

1296. What is the name of the second longest river in that is 2,800 miles long, located in China: the Ganges or the Yellow?

1297. What is the name of the longest river in Asia that flows from Tibet into the East China Sea at Shanghai: the Ganges or the Yangtze?

1298. What river located in Asia is 1,550 miles long, flows from the Himalayas into the Bay of Bengal, and is regarded as sacred by the Hindus: the Ganges or the Yangtze?

1299. What is the name of the longest river in Europe and one of Russia's most important rivers: the Volga or the Yellow?

SOCIAL STUDIES

1300. What is the second longest river in Europe that is 1,725 miles long, borders ten countries, and flows from Southeastern Germany into the Black Sea: the Yellow or the Danube?

1301. What is the name of the major river in Germany besides the Danube: the Yellow or the Rhine?

1302. What is the name of the principle river in France: the Seine or the Thames?

1303. What is the name of the principle river in England: the Seine or the Thames?

1304. What is the name of the principle river in the United States that is 2,320 miles long and flows from Northern Minnesota to the Gulf of Mexico: the Missouri or the Mississippi?

1305. What is the name for a stream or river that flows into a main river or lake, like those found at the Colorado River and the Mississippi River: a delta or a tributary?

1306. Does the Mississippi River have several tributaries or deltas?

1307. What is the term for a landform that forms at the mouth of a river, where the river flows into an ocean or sea, like the one found on the Nile River: tributary or delta?

1308. What is the name of the continent that you live on?

1309. How many of the seven continents can you name?

1310. Which continent has the highest population in the world: North America, Asia, or Africa?

1311. Which country in Asia has the largest population?

1312. Which continent has the lowest population in the world: Australia, Antarctica, or Asia?

1313. On which continent do Spaniards, French, Italians, and Germans live: Europe or Asia?

1314. In which area of Europe do Danes, Swedes, and Norwegians live: Scandinavia or the British Isles?

1315. In which area of Europe do Irish, Scottish, and English live: Scandinavia or the British Isles?

1316. On which continent do Egyptians, Nigerians, and Moroccans live: Africa or Asia?

1317. On which continent do Chinese, Japanese, and Koreans live: Africa or Asia?

1318. On which continent do Peruvians, Argentineans, and Chileans live: North America or South America?

1319. What is Canada divided into: states or provinces?

1320. Which continent is Canada part of: North America or Asia?

1321. What are the two languages that are spoken in Canada?

1322. What is Mexico divided into: states or provinces?

1323. Which continent is Mexico part of: North America or South America?

SOCIAL STUDIES

1324. What language is spoken in Mexico?

1325. How many states is the continental United States divided into: 48 or 50?

1326. Which two states are located outside the continental United States?

1327. Which state is the "Aloha" state known for volcanoes, palm trees, Waikiki Beach, the Pearl Harbor Memorial, hibiscus flowers, pineapples, floral leis, grass skirts, luau parties, coconuts, sugar cane, has Honolulu as its capital, and was the last state to join the Union?

1328. Which state is considered the "Land of the Midnight Sun," is known for the Klondike Gold Rush, Eskimos, polar bears, forestry, wildlife, game fish, wooly mammoth fossils, husky dogs, sled-dog racing, the Northern Lights, glaciers, an oil pipeline, Mount McKinley, has Juneau as its capital, and was the 49th state to join the Union?

1329. Which state is the "Grand Canyon" state, known for Native Americans, deserts, the Saguaro cactus flower, copper mines, the Petrified Forest, Hoover Dam, London Bridge, the Painted Desert, Fort Apache, the gunfight at the O.K. Corral, has Phoenix as its capital, and was the 48th state to join the Union?

1330. Which state is called the "Land of Enchantment," is known for the Carlsbad Caverns, mining, roadrunners, adobe buildings, Navajo and Apache tribes, hot air balloons, the yucca flower, the Gila National Forest, turquoise, has Santa Fe, the oldest capital city in North America as its capital, and was the 47th state to join the Union?

1331. Which state is called the "Sooner State," was bought as part of the Louisiana Purchase, is known for oil and coal, tornados, man-made lakes, farming, mistletoe, the "Five Civilized Tribes" (Choctaw, Cherokee, Chickasaw, Creek and Seminole), the National Cowboy Hall of Fame, the Will Rogers Memorial, four mountain ranges including the Wichita Mountains, has Oklahoma City as its capital, and was the 46th state to join the Union?

1332. Which state is called the "Beehive State," is known for its mountains, skiing, prehistoric caves and ruins, rock formations, Dinosaur National Monument, mining and farming, Mormons, lilies, seagulls, Rainbow Bridge, Great Salt Lake, has Salt Lake City as its capital, and was the 45th state to join the Union?

1333. Which state is called the "Cowboy State" or the "Equality State" because it gave women the opportunity to vote in 1869, is known for sheep, cattle, bison, coal, oil, rodeos, cowboys, dude ranches, Yellowstone and Grand Teton National Parks, Old Faithful Geyser, Jackson Hole, Devil's Tower, Flaming Gorge, has Cheyenne as its capital, and was the 44th state to join the Union?

1334. Which state is called the "Panhandle State," is known for potatoes, elk, mining, the Shoshone Falls, Craters of the Moon National Monument, Hells Canyon, Sun Valley Ski Resort, the Appaloosa horse, has Boise as its capital, and was the 43rd state to join the Union?

1335. Which state is called the "Evergreen State," is known for its rain forests, apples, farming and lumber, the ferry system, rhododendron flowers, orca mammals, Mount Rainier, Mount Saint Helens, the

SOCIAL STUDIES

Space Needle, the Boeing Aircraft Company, has Olympia as its capital, and was the 42nd state to join the Union?

1336. Which state is called the "Treasure State" and is also nicknamed "Big Sky Country," is known for hunting, grizzly bears, mountain goats, fresh water springs, mining for gold, silver, agate, and sapphire and oil, the Rocky Mountains, forestry, cattle, sheep farming, Ponderosa pines, Custer's Last Stand at Little Bighorn, Glacier National Park, has Helena as its capital, and was the 41st state to join the Union?

1337. Which state is called the "Coyote State," is known for the Black Hills, Black Hills Gold, Homestake Gold Mine, the Badlands, Wounded Knee, Mount Rushmore, wooly mammoth bones, prairie dogs, bison, has Pierre as its capital, and was the 40th state to join the Union?

1338. Which state is called the "Peace Garden State," is known for wheat, sunflowers, farming, Theodore Roosevelt State Park, rodeos, the Sioux Indians, has Bismarck as its capital, and was the 39th state to join the Union?

1339. Which state is called the "Centennial State," is known for Native Americans, bighorn sheep, skiing, aquamarines, Rocky Mountain National Park, Great Sand Dunes, the Grand Mesa flattop mountain, Pike's Peak, the Mesa Verde Ancestral Pueblo, the highest paved road in North America, the world's largest rodeo, has Denver, the mile-high city as its capital, and was the 38th state to join the Union?

1340. Which state is called the "Cornhusker State," is known for underwater water reserves, mammoth fossils, cottonwood trees, Chimney Rock, Agate Fossil beds, the Lewis and Clark Trail, has Lincoln as its capital, and was the 37th state to join the Union?

1341. Which state is called the "Silver State," is known for its gambling magnets Las Vegas, Lake Tahoe, and Reno, gold and silver mining, the Comstock Lode Silver Deposits, sagebrush, wild mustangs, the Sierra Nevada Mountain Range, Hoover Dam, has Carson City as its capital, and was the 36th state to join the Union?

1342. Which state is called the "Mountain State," is known for black bears, timber and coal mining, folk music, fine glass, forests, the Golden Delicious apple, Greenbrier Resort, Harper's Ferry, the Cass Scenic Railroad, has Charleston as its capital, and was the 35th state to join the Union?

1343. Which state is called the "Sunshine State," is known for "amber waves of grain" (wheat) production, sunflowers, cattle, dust-bowls, plane-manufacturing, was the home of Dorothy in "The Wizard of Oz," has Topeka as its capital, and was the 34th state to join the Union?

1344. Which state is called the "Beaver State," is known for timber and lumber, grape flowers, thunder-egg geodes, Sea Lion Caves, Mount Hood Volcano, The Carousal Museum, ghost towns, Crater Lake, the deepest lake in the United States, the Columbia River, Tillamook Cheese Factory, the largest cheese factory in the world, has Salem as its capital, and was the 33rd state to join the Union?

1345. Which state is called the "Gopher State" or the "North Star State," is known as the "land of 10,000 lakes," boating, The Mall of America," lady's slipper orchids, loons, Green Giant vegetables, skyways, Tonka Trucks, has St. Paul as its capital, and was the 32nd state to join the Union?

SOCIAL STUDIES

1346. Which state is called the "Golden State," is known for redwood and giant sequoia trees, poppy flowers, the Gold Rush, Death Valley desert, rodeos, wine, oranges, cheese, raisons, turkeys, Disneyland, Spanish missions, The Golden Gate Bridge, The Pacific Coast Highway, the movie industry, has Sacramento as its capital, and was the 31st state to join the Union?

1347. Which state is called the "Badger State," is known for dairy, cows, fishing, 14,000 lakes, Summerfest Music Festival, robins, deer, cheese, cranberries, Muskellunge, snowmobiling, Harley Davidson motorcycles, the American Birkebeiner cross-country ski race, Noah's Ark Water Park, the Ringling Brothers Circus, the House on the Rock, the very first kindergarten, has Madison as its capital, and was the 30th state to join the Union?

1348. Which state is called the "Hawkeye State," is known for agriculture, corn, roses, Buffalo Bill, Quaker Oats, Nordic Fest, Effigy Mounds National Monument, Winnebago Motor Homes, has Des Moines as its capital, and was the 29th state to join the Union?

1349. Which state is called the "Lone Star" state, is known for The Alamo, Davy Crockett, oil, cotton, cattle farming, sheep farming, pecan trees, rodeos, cowboys, the Space Center, Dell Computers, the first hamburger, President Kennedy's assassination, has Austin as its capital, and was the 28th state to join the Union?

1350. Which state is called the "Sunshine" state, is known for oranges, grapefruit, beaches, the Everglades, the Kennedy Space Center, Disney World, Epcot Center, Sea World, Cypress Gardens, Universal Studios, the Daytona 500 auto race, Gatorade, crocodiles, pumas, the "Keys," has Tallahassee as its capital, and was the 27th state to join the Union?

1351. Which state is called the "Wolverine" state, is known for having two peninsulas, Mackinac Bridge, automobiles, Ford Motor Company, the Great Lakes, Sault St. Marie Canal, boating, navy beans, Kellogg Cereal, Petoskey Coral Stones, lighthouses, ginger ale, the world's largest weather vane, has Lansing as its capital, and was the 26th state to join the Union?

1352. Which state is called the "Land of Opportunity," is famous for its Diamond Mine, Hot Springs National Park, the Ozarks, explorer Hernando de Soto, Crater of Diamonds State Park, the first Wal-Mart, quartz crystal, spinach, duck-calling competitions, apple blossoms, has Little Rock as its capital, and was the 25th state to join the Union?

1353. Which state is called the "Show-Me" state, is known for the St. Louis Gateway Arch, Branson Country Music Shows, Bass Pro Shops, the Pony Express mail service, lead production, the Anheuser-Busch brewery, the first ice cream cones, Aunt Jemima pancake flour, Dr. Pepper, barbecue sauce, Mark Twain, caves, the Ozarks, has Jefferson City as its capital, and was the 24th state to join the Union?

1354. Which state is called the "Pine Tree" state, is known for lighthouses, lobsters, sardines, blueberries, sawmills, paper-making, moose, tourmaline stones, Acadia National Park, has Augusta as its capital, and was the 23rd state to join the Union?

1355. Which state is called the "Yellowhammer" state, is known for wild turkeys, cotton, timber, peanuts, Talladega National Forest, the Confederacy, Rosa Parks and the Montgomery Bus Boycott, the

SOCIAL STUDIES

beginning of the Civil Rights Movement, the Racking Horse, cast-iron production, rocket production, the world's first electric trolley system, Gulf Coast beaches, has Montgomery as its capital, and was the 22nd state to join the Union?

1356. Which state is called the "Prairie" state or the "land of Lincoln," is known for the Willis Tower skyscraper, John Deere machinery, the tallest man in the world (8'11"), the Dairy Queen franchise, the Windy City, the Chicago Fire, Wrigley Field, Wrigley gum, Navy Pier, The Art Institute, The Chicago Theatre, The Museum of Science and Industry, corn, pigs, has Springfield as its capital, and was the 21st state to join the Union?

1357. Which state is called the "Magnolia" state, is known for its southern magnolia trees, river boats, "Old Man River," the largest river in the United States, Theodore Roosevelt's "Teddy Bear," catfish, cotton, tree farms, "Blues" music, Pine-Sol cleaner, the first 4-H club, the International Checkers Hall of Fame, Coca-Cola, has Jackson as its capital, and was the 20th state to join the Union?

1358. Which state is called the "Hoosier" state, is known for the Indianapolis 500 auto race, corn, the first gasoline pump, basketball, the "Brain Bank of the Midwest" with many colleges and universities located there, the first Raggedy Ann Doll, interstate highways, the Saturday Evening Post, has Indianapolis as its capital, and was the 19th state to join the Union?

1359. Which state is called the "Pelican" state, is known for pelicans, Breaux Bridge, the "crawfish capital of the world," farming, frogs, alligators, tall cypress trees, Mardi Gras in New Orleans, the French quarter, jazz, the first Tarzan movie, the Superdome, Cajun descendants, "parishes" instead of counties, has Baton Rouge as its capital, and was the 18th state to join the Union?

1360. Which state is called the "Buckeye" state, is known for its buckeye trees, farming, the Pro Football Hall of Fame, the Rock and Roll Hall of Fame, rubber and bicycle tires, greenhouse plants, the first chewing gum, first cash register, first professional baseball team, first traffic light, first airplane by the Wright brothers, first police, fire, and ambulance service, has Columbus as its capital, and was the 17th state to join the Union?

1361. Which state is called the "Volunteer" state, is known for the Grand Ole Opry, Elvis's former home Graceland, Great Smoky Mountains National Park, the Country Music Hall of Fame, Bluegrass music, horses, salamanders, turtles, aluminum, zinc, caves, whitewater rafting, has Nashville as its capital, and was the 16th state to join the Union?

1362. Which state is called the "Bluegrass" state, is known for the blue grasses on the prairie, covered bridges, tobacco, whiskey, pickles, a horse derby, Mammoth Cave National Park, the long rifle, the largest amount of gold stored in the world, the Chevrolet Corvette, the first Mother's Day, has Frankfort as its capital, and was the 15th state to join the Union?

1363. Which state is called the "Green Mountain" state, is known for ski resorts, autumn colors, Morgan horses, maple syrup, Ethan Allan and his revolutionary Green Mountain Boys, dairy farming, granite and marble mines, the first Ben and Jerry's Ice Cream Store, having the lowest crime rate in the nation, the Von Trapp Family of Austria made famous in the musical "The Sound of Music," the Bing Cosby Christmas classic, "White Christmas," has Montpelier as its capital, and was the 14th state to join the Union?

SOCIAL STUDIES

1364. Which state is called the "Ocean" state, is known for red chickens, red maple trees, Newport's summer tourism, the first circus, Arkwright's "Spinning Jenny," cotton mills, textiles and electronics, silverware and jewelry, the Tennis Hall of Fame, the first National Lawn Tennis Tournament, the oldest school house in the United States, The Flying Horse Carousal, being the smallest state in the nation, has Providence as its capital, and was the 13th state to join the Union?

1365. Which state is called the "Tar Heel" or "Old North" state, is known for being the "barbecue capital of the world," the Cherokee Native Americans, Great Smokey Mountains National Park, Whitewater Falls, Pepsi, Krispy Kreme doughnuts, the Venus Fly- Trap, sweet potatoes, emeralds, furniture-making, tobacco and brick production, the first miniature golf course, Biltmore Estate, the nation's largest home, the Wright Brothers as the "First in Flight" at Kitty Hawk, has Raleigh as its capital, and was the 12th state to join the Union?

1366. Which state is called the "Empire" state, is known for Niagara Falls, the Catskill Mountains, the Adirondack Mountains, Long Island, Ellis Island, Staten Island and the Staten Island Ferry, Coney Island and the Coney Island Cyclone rollercoaster, Manhattan, Queens, the Bronx, the Bronx Zoo, Yonkers, Brooklyn, the Brooklyn Bridge, the Erie Canal, orchids, dairy farming, jazz, Yankee Stadium, Babe Ruth, The Statue of Liberty, Central Park, Radio City Music Hall, The Apollo Theatre, Times Square, Radio City Music Hall and the Rockettes, Madison Square Garden, Rockefeller Center, Lincoln Center, Broadway, The Empire State Building, The Metropolitan Museum of Art, The Museum of Modern Art, Saks 5th Avenue, Macy's Thanksgiving Day Parade, Tiffany's jewelry store, St. Paul's Cathedral, The Baseball Hall of Fame, The United Nations, the stock exchange, the first license plates, the first toilet paper, marshmallows, Jell-O, the first pizzeria, the longest running newspaper, the nation's largest public library, subways, being the most populated city in the nation, has Albany as its capital, and was the 11th state to join the Union?

1367. Which state is called the "Old Dominion" state, is known as the "birthplace of a nation" as well as for the first Colonial settlement at Jamestown, was the site of thousands of Civil War battles, the state of surrenders from both the Revolutionary and the Civil Wars, the site of Patrick Henry's speech, "Give Me Liberty or Give Me Death," home of the Blue Ridge Mountains, oysters, tobacco, the first peanuts, ship-building, Robert E. Lee, Arlington National Cemetery, the tomb of the Unknown Soldier, Chesapeake Bay Bridge Tunnel, the Pentagon, NATO headquarters, Thomas Jefferson's home Monticello, George Washington's home Mount Vernon, has Richmond as its capital, and was the 10th state to join the Union?

1368. Which state is called the "Granite" state, is known for its autumn colors, logging, leather work, farming, White Mountain National Forest, maple syrup, the first public library, the oldest pipe organ, the center for covered wagon-building, the longest covered bridge crossing 460 feet over the Connecticut River, is the home of the Clydesdales horses, poet Robert Frost, the first alarm clock, has Concord as its capital, and was the 9th state to join the Union?

1369. Which state is called the "Palmetto" state, is known for being the first state to break away from the Union at Fort Sumter, palmetto trees, the Blue Ridge Mountains, tobacco, peaches, ginkgo farms, furniture-making, basket-making, Myrtle Beach, Hilton Head Resorts, golf courses, the Thoroughbred Racing Hall of Fame, has Columbia as its capital, and was the 8th state to join the Union?

SOCIAL STUDIES

1370. Which state is called the "Old Line" state, is known for the Annapolis U.S. Naval Academy, shipping, Chesapeake Bay oysters, crabs, tobacco, John Hopkins University, the first school, the first refrigerator, the Mason-Dixon Line marking the boundary between this state and Pennsylvania, the first telegraph, wild ponies, sailing, Baltimore Oriole birds, has Annapolis as its capital, and was the 7th state to join the Union?

1371. Which state is called the "Old Colony" state, is known for the Pilgrims' arrival on the Mayflower at Plymouth, the first Thanksgiving with the Native Americans, the Revolutionary War battles at Lexington, Concord, and Bunker Hill, Boston Harbor, the Boston Tea Party, the Freedom Trail, Beacon Hill, the Old North Church, Paul Revere's House, Copley Square, Faneuil Hall, Bunker Hill Monument, the Old State House and the first reading of the Declaration of Independence, the Boston Pops, the Charles River Esplanade, Cape Cod, Nantucket Island, Martha's Vineyard, the first college now called Harvard University, the Boston Terrier, Boston baked beans, Boston Cream Pie, clam chowder, cranberries, the first Toll House chocolate chip cookies, the first Dunkin Donuts, Johnny Appleseed, Fenway Park, the John F. Kennedy Library, the John Hancock building, has Boston as its capital, and was the 6th state to join the Union?

1372. Which state is called the "Constitution" state, is known for providing goods to George Washington's Continental Army during the Revolution, the invention of Eli Whitney's cotton gin, Charles Goodyear's tire, Linus Yale's lock, Yale University, the first law school, nuclear submarine production, the first telephone book, cattle and pig branding, the first color television, the first Polaroid Camera, the first car insurance, has Hartford as its capital, and was the 5th state to join the Union?

1373. Which state is called the "Peach" state, is known for the production of peanuts, cotton, and peaches, chickens, the Okefenokee Swamps, Stone Mountain Park, the carvings of Stonewall Jackson, Jefferson Davis, and Robert E. Lee on the side of Stone Mountain making it the largest granite sculpture in the world, the Blue Ridge Scenic Railway, Ante-Bellum pre-war houses, was the location for the classic move, "Gone With the Wind," has Atlanta as its capital, and was the 4th state to join the Union?

1374. Which state is called the "Garden" state, is known for its garden vegetables, horses, the longest boardwalk in the world, seaside resorts, casinos, Princeton University, the chemical industry, shopping malls, the original "Miss America" pageant, the first Indian Reservation, Edison's inventions of the light bulb, movie projector, and phonograph, the first drive-in movie theatre, has its cities featured on the "Monopoly" board game, is home to "Lucy the Elephant" six-story building, is the most densely populated state, is almost completely surrounded by water, has Trenton as its capital, and was the third state to join the Union?

1375. Which state is called the "Keystone" state, is known for its Quaker founder William Penn, Independence Hall, the signing of the Declaration of Independence, the writing of the United States Constitution, the Liberty Bell, first American flag, Gettysburg, Valley Forge, farming, coal production, steel production, mushroom production, Hershey's chocolate, Christmas trees, the first public zoo, the world's first oil well, the first piano, the first computer, a high concentration of Amish, has Harrisburg as its capital, and was the 2nd state to join the Union?

SOCIAL STUDIES

1376. Which state is called the "First" state, is known for being the first state to ratify the U.S. Constitution, the Chesapeake and Delaware canal, chemical production, chicken farming, the blue hen chicken, ladybugs, horseshoe crabs, nylon production, processed foods, historic churches, Finnish log cabins, has Dover as its capital, and was the 1st state to join the Union?

1377. What is the largest state in the continental United States after Alaska?

1378. What is the smallest state in the continental United States?

1379. What is the capital of the United States?

1380. What do the letters "D.C." stand for as part of our capital's name?

1381. Which ocean borders the United States on the eastern coast: the Atlantic or the Pacific?

1382. Which ocean borders the United States on the western coast: the Atlantic or the Pacific?

1383. What is the name of the country that borders America to the North?

1384. What is the name of the country that borders America to the South?

1385. What are the other states that border the state you live in?

1386. Can you name any of the *counties* (or *parishes* if you live in Louisiana) that border the county (parish) you live in?

1387. Does the United States of America have symbols that represent it?

1388. What national symbol has red and white stripes, and fifty white stars on a blue background?

1389. How many stripes are there on the American Flag, representing the number of original colonies that declared independence from Great Britain and became the first states in the Union?

1390. What national oath do U.S. citizens recite while facing the flag that shows their loyalty to the United States?

1391. What is the name of the lady that is credited with making one of the original American flags: Betsy Ross or Martha Washington?

1392. What is the name of the American symbol located in Independence Hall in Philadelphia, Pennsylvania that cracked soon after it was rung?

1393. What is the national bird of the United States: the bald eagle or the hawk?

1394. What is the name of the American symbol located in New York Harbor on Liberty Island that was a gift from France, and depicts a lady holding a torch high above her head?

1395. What American national symbol is a document proclaiming the independence of the thirteen original colonies from Great Britain?

SOCIAL STUDIES

1396. What American document was approved at a Convention in Philadelphia in 1787, includes the Bill of Rights and several amendments, and is considered the supreme law of the land?

1397. What is the name of the patriotic song that was based on a poem written by Francis Scott King during the War of 1812, was adopted by Congress in 1931, and is the official national song of the United States: God Bless America or The Star-Spangled Banner?

1398. What kind of symbols do states have that represent that state?

1399. What American landmark located in South Dakota has four American presidents carved in into a mountain: Mount Rushmore or Mount Blanc?

1400. Who is the fourth president besides Washington, Jefferson, and Lincoln that is carved into the granite face at Mount Rushmore: Adams or Roosevelt?

1401. Where are the Lincoln Memorial, Jefferson Monument, National Mall, Washington Monument, World War II Memorial, Vietnam Veterans Memorial, Korean War Veterans Memorial, FDR Memorial, the Capitol Building, and the White House all located?

1402. What is the name of the memorial located at 1600 Pennsylvania Avenue in Washington, D.C?

1403. Are the following national monuments and memorials located in Washington D.C. or Virginia: Arlington National Cemetery, Washington's home Mount Vernon, Jefferson's home Monticello, Booker T. Washington Memorial, Pentagon Memorial, and Iwo Jima Memorial?

1404. What is the name of the memorial located in the National Mall that is the world's tallest stone obelisk towering 555 feet high: The Washington Monument or The Space Needle?

1405. What is another name for the memorial U.S. Marine Corps War Memorial in Virginia that honors the marines that defended America during World War II in a battle with the Japanese, and is a statue of four marines raising the American flag: Hiroshima or Iwo Jima?

1406. What is the name for the international landmark that is the collective name for three waterfalls called Horseshoe, American, and Bridal Veil that border the Canadian province of Ontario and the state of New York: Niagara Falls or Yosemite Falls?

1407. What kind of American landmark are all of the following: Rocky Mountain, Mammoth Cave, Glacier, Crater Lake, Yosemite, Badlands, Great Smokey Mountains, Everglades, Acadia, Death Valley, Grand Teton, Yellowstone, Hot Springs, Mesa Verde, and Redwood?

1408. What landmarks or monuments can you name in your state?

1409. Can history be divided into different periods?

1410. Did the Stone Age, Bronze Age, and Iron Age occur in ancient history or modern history?

1411. Does the civilization of Mesopotamia in the region in Southeast Asia fall under prehistory or modern history?

1412. Which country is referred to as the "cradle of civilization:" China or Mesopotamia?

SOCIAL STUDIES

1413. What is the name of the current country where Mesopotamia once was: Iraq or India?

1414. What ancient civilization translates in Greek as, "Land between the Rivers:" Mesopotamia or Egypt?

1415. What are the names of the rivers located in Mesopotamia: the Tigris and Euphrates, or the Nile and Danube?

1416. What type of societal system did Mesopotamia have: a class system or an estate system?

1417. What was the name of the ancient capital of the country of Babylonia, located along the banks of the Euphrates River in Mesopotamia: Babylon or Baghdad?

1418. What is the name of the ruler of Babylon, considered the greatest ruler of the first Babylonian dynasty, credited for developing a Code of Laws: Hammurabi or Herod?

1419. Which civilization was the first to develop the entity of the city, writing, government, the calendar, glass, the wheel, the potter's wheel, the aqueduct, astronomy, the 60 minute hour, the sundial, irrigation systems, and agriculture: Greece or Mesopotamia?

1420. Were Mesopotamians known for developing agriculture, government, religion, and city-states?

1421. What is the term for the first writing system of the Mesopotamian using a chisel and a clay tablet: cuneiform or hieroglyphics?

1422. Where did the empires of Sumerian, Babylonian, and Assyrian exist: Greece or Mesopotamia?

1423. What is the name for the earliest inhabitants of Mesopotamia: the Babylonians or the Sumerians?

1424. What is the name for the last race of Mesopotamia, and the first to develop iron weapons and use chariots: the Babylonians or the Assyrians?

1425. What is the name of the earliest inhabitants of Mesopotamia that invented the wheel: the Sumerians or the Assyrians??

1426. What farming machine was first invented in Mesopotamia: the seed plow or the tractor?

1427. What number did the Mesopotamians use to calculate the minutes in an hour that was based on astronomy and the moon: 24 or 60?

1428. What is the name for the sacred Sumerian structures built to honor the main god of the city, were the highest structures in the area, and resembled a step pyramid: ziggurats or temples?

1429. What is the name of one of the Ancient Wonders of the World located in Babylon: The Great Pyramid or The Hanging Gardens?

1430. What is the name given for the historical time period between Ancient and Modern: The Early Modern Era or The Middle Ages?

1431. What is the name given for the time that is associated with castles, knights, armor, King Arthur, and Joan of Arc that began after the fall of the Western Roman Empire: renaissance or medieval?

SOCIAL STUDIES

1432. What is the name for the last major group in the feudal system of people during medieval times after the king, the bishops, the barons, and the lords: the commoners or the peasants?

1433. What is the term that refers to the medieval farmer who worked the land for his lord and paid him dues in exchange for the use of the land: peasant or serf?

1434. What is the name given to the people that took control over the Western Roman Empire after Germanic tribes ruled it for a short time: the Barbarians or the Greeks?

1435. What is another name for the Eastern Roman Empire that included Greece, Turkey, and the Middle East: Byzantine or Barbarian?

1436. What is the former name of the capital of the Eastern Roman Empire: Constantinople or Istanbul?

1437. Who were the nomadic herdsmen from Mongolia, a country north of China, that destroyed much of Europe and Asia between the 3rd and 5th centuries: the Visigoths or the Huns?

1438. What is the name for the most successful king of the Huns: Herod or Attila?

1439. What is the name for what is attached to the bottom of a horse saddle that gave the Huns an advantage when fighting on horseback with their enemies: reins or stirrups?

1440. What is the name for the group of Germanic people regarded as Barbarians that are most known for conquering Rome with destruction and looting: the Vandals or the Visigoths?

1441. What is the name for the nomadic tribe who took most of southern France from the Romans but were later forced out by the German Franks, and eventually settled in Spain: the Huns or the Visigoths?

1442. What is the name of the group that England is named for that took over Britain in the Middle Ages: the Angles or the Jutes?

1443. What is the name of the group of people who merged with the Angles in Britain that the Old English language originated from: the Visigoths or the Saxons?

1444. What is the term that was created by an Italian poet that refers to the Middle Ages after the fall of the Western Roman Empire, characterized by intellectual darkness, social chaos, warfare, and poverty: Medieval Times or Dark Ages?

1445. What is the name of the official religion of the Roman Empire that experienced significant growth during the Middle Ages: Judaism or Christianity?

1446. What is the name of the leader of the Christian church in Rome: the Pope or the Bishop?

1447. What is the other main religion besides Roman Catholicism that was formed in the Middle Ages: Orthodoxy or Judaism?

1448. What is the name for the men who devoted their lives to the church in the Middle Ages and lived in monasteries: monks or friars?

1449. What is the name for the women who devoted their lives to the church in the Middle Ages and studied the writings of the ancient Romans and Greeks: postulants or nuns?

SOCIAL STUDIES

1450. Who was the King of the Franks of Germany, expanded the Frankish Empire, and was also a former Roman Emperor whose name means "Charles the Great:" Charlemagne or Carlos?

1451. What is the term given for the legal and social system in medieval times in which service was exchanged for land: feudalism or serfdom?

1452. What were the three major groups of people during medieval times: nobility, church, and commoners, or lords, ladies, and serfs?

1453. Who was more powerful: the lord or the king?

1454. Who was the person that received a piece of land, acted as a servant, and promised loyalty to the lord: the serf or the vassal?

1455. Who was the person that owned the land in a feudal system: the lord or the vassal?

1456. What was the term used for the land grant contract that a lord provided to a vassal: a contract or a fief?

1457. Could vassals promise their loyalty to more than one lord?

1458. What is the medieval term for fighters supplied to the king by the lord: warriors or knights?

1459. What is the name of the lowest member of a feudal class that performed labor on the farms and manors owned by a lord: a serf or a knight?

1460. What is the name of the medieval stone structure where the lords and kings lived that provided protection form raids and attacks: a labyrinth or a castle?

1461. What is the medieval term for a traveling musician that entertained the children: a jester or a minstrel?

1462. What is the medieval term for a clown that entertained the children: a jester or a minstrel?

1463. What is the name of a game played on the lawn that many adults and children played during the Middle Ages: croquet or lacrosse?

1464. What is the medieval term for a young boy who did simple things like waiting on tables for noblemen and knights: a page or a servant?

1465. What could a medieval page become after seven years of faithful service to a nobleman, and was considered a trainee to a knight: a squire or a page?

1466. What is the name of the poem about a squire written by the English poet Geoffrey Chaucer during the Middle Ages: "The Canterbury Tales," or "Knights at the Roundtable?"

1467. Who might have a horse, weapons, and armor: a knight or a squire?

1468. Could Noble girls train to be knights, or were they typically trained to sew, weave, and spin?

1469. What is the medieval term for battles on horseback using lances: bullfighting or jousting?

SOCIAL STUDIES

1470. What is the medieval term for the code of conduct of a knight that included bravery, courtesy, and honor: chivalry or loyalty?

1471. Did many medieval towns have craftsmen, farmers, and traders?

1472. Did merchants and craftsmen hold power in medieval towns?

1473. What is the term for the association of medieval craftsmen that regulated prices and trace: a union or a guild?

1474. What is the term for a person that is learning a new trade: a master or an apprentice?

1475. What could an apprentice be promoted to after working for a master at least seven years: a master or a journeyman?

1476. What could a journeyman be promoted to after learning the trade at an expert level: an apprentice or a master?

1477. Was religion important in medieval days?

1478. Did medieval England become stronger when the Angles and the Saxons united under King Edward the Confessor and converted to Christianity?

1479. Was Normandy, France under Duke William a weak or a strong kingdom?

1480. Where did Duke William travel to in 1066 with several hundred ships and thousands of Knights in order to defeat and conquer King Harold and his Anglo-Saxon army: England or Spain?

1481. What was the other name of the newly-crowned King William I: William the Conqueror or William the Great?

1482. Did the Anglo-Saxons object when King William promoted his Norman knights to English noblemen, built castles in England, and collected taxes from them?

1483. What is the name of the person who became the King of England after the death of William the Conqueror: William II or Henry I?

1484. Did King Henry I and King Henry II inherit the throne after William II?

1485. Did Henry II establish a strong government and new law system that is the basis of court procedures as we know them today?

1486. Is King Henry II credited for establishing English Common Law?

1487. Did King John, King Henry's son, add to England's kingdom, or did he manage to give up much of England's land to France?

1488. Who were the wealthy people of England that had to give up some of their power to King John and pay more in taxes: counts, dukes, lords, and earls, or peasants, journeymen, serfs, and knights?

SOCIAL STUDIES

1489. What is the name of the document that was created initially in 1215 to limit the rights of King John, guaranteed the rights of the average citizen from the King of England, and helped lay the groundwork for English Common Law and, later, the U.S. Constitution: the Magna Carta, the Declaration of Independence, or The Bill or Rights?

1490. What did King John's grandson Edward I create to make the royal government stronger, consisting of knights and nobles who approved the laws of the king: a Parliament or an Assembly?

1491. What was the name given for the mysterious disease, now known as the Bubonic plague that killed millions of people in Europe in the 1300's, and showed up as dark patches on the skin: Yellow Fever, Black Death, or Measles?

1492. What is the name for the string of conflicts in France between the armies of the kings of France and England that lasted between 1337 and 1453, and ended when King Edward's son, "The Black Prince," captured King John II of France: The Hundred Years' War or The French and English War?

1493. What is the name of the peasant girl from medieval France who felt that she had a calling, led a French army to several victories during The Hundred Years War, forced the English out of Orleans, and was burned at the stake at the age of nineteen: Joan of Arc or Lady Antoinette?

1494. Do many people consider the end of the Middle Ages in 1453 the same as at the end of The Hundred Years War?

1495. What major empire ended in 1453 after Turkish invaders captured the capital of Constantinople: the Byzantine Empire or the Ottoman Empire?

1496. What are Christianity, Judaism, Buddhism, and Islam all regarded as: world races or world religions?

1497. What is the name of the religion that is practiced by over one billion Muslims, believing that there is one God, and that Mohammad is the prophet: Islam or Buddhism?

1498. What is the name of the holiest place in Saudi Arabia where Muslims believe that Mohammad received the word of God whom they call Allah, and is the pilgrimage for all Islam believers: Fatima or Mecca?

1499. What is the name for the shrine and the most sacred site in Mecca where Muslims go to pray: Kaaba or Quran?

1500. What is the name of the first domed shrine to be built in Jerusalem, Israel where Mohammad is said to have begun his rise to Heaven from the top of a rock: Dome of the Rock or The Great Mosque?

1501. What is the name of the city that Mohammad and his followers moved to after being forced out of Mecca due to conflicts with traders: Medina or Jerusalem?

1502. What is the Islamic name for the journey of Mohammad and his followers from Mecca to Medina that also marks the beginning of the Muslim calendar: Hijra or Quran?

1503. What is the general term for the Muslim place of worship that has towers from which worshippers are led in prayer five times a day: a Temple or a Mosque?

SOCIAL STUDIES

1504. What is the name of the Mosque in Mecca: The Grand Mosque or the Mosque of the Prophet?

1505. What is the name of the Mosque in Medina: The Grand Mosque or The Prophet's Mosque?

1506. What is the Islamic term for a Muslim war waged by those in defense of the Islamic faith, like that led by Mohammad against non-believers in Mecca: Hijra of Jihad?

1507. What is the name of the holy book of the Islamic religion written in Arabic that Muslims believe to be the word of God: the Quran or the Makkah?

1508. What is the term for the five rules that represent the five primary obligations of Muslims that include a profession of faith, prayer, giving alms to the poor, fasting during the holy month of Ramadan, and a pilgrimage to Mecca: The Five Islamic Rules or The Five Pillars of Islam?

1509. Did the Muslims conquer other places in the Middle East, Africa, and Spain after the death of Mohammad in order to spread the Islam religion?

1510. Did the Muslims live in Spain and build many mosques and palaces there?

1511. What is the name of the Moorish palace located in Granada, Spain and named for King Alhamar with its renowned Court of the Lions, and is regarded as an elaborate example of Arabic architecture: The Alcazar or the Alhambra?

1512. What is the name of the southern Spanish city that become a center of Muslim culture and further study of the Quran: Seville or Córdoba?

1513. Do Muslims consider Jerusalem a holy city?

1514. What was the name of the military conflicts between European Christians in the 11th, 12th, and 13th centuries who wanted to win back Jerusalem (the Holy Land) from the Muslims: The Crusades or The Holy Wars?

1515. What is the term for the numbers like 1, 2, and 3 that were first introduced by the Muslims and then taught these symbols to Europeans: Roman numerals or Arabic numerals?

1516. What is the name of the people of both Arab and Berber descent from northern Africa that occupied Spain and Portugal for several hundred years: The Moors or The Moroccans?

1517. What is the second largest continent in the world: Asia or Africa?

1518. What is the name of the largest desert in the world in northern Africa: Sahara or Kalahari?

1519. What is the name of the mountain range in northern Africa: Atlas or Pyrenees?

1520. What is the geographical term for a flat area of grass in a tropical region with tall grasses and only a few trees that is the habitat for many African animals: woodlands or savanna?

1521. What is the name of the world's deepest river located in Africa that is a big economic resource for the continent, and provides parts of Africa with hydroelectric power: the Nile or the Congo?

1522. On which continent are Egypt, Ethiopia, Nigeria, and Morocco located?

SOCIAL STUDIES

1523. Which country in Africa is known for its pyramids, tombs, and kings: Egypt or Morocco?

1524. What name did Egyptians use for *king* meaning supreme ruler: Pharaoh or Chariot?

1525. Did the ancient Egyptians regard the Pharaoh as a God?

1526. Did Pharaohs have a hierarchy of rulers under them?

1527. Were the wives of the Pharaohs second or third in power?

1528. What is the term for the leader of the Egyptian government: the Vizier or the Monarch?

1529. Did citizens pay taxes to support the government?

1530. What is the term for the period of rule when Kings or Pharaohs come from the same family for several generations: dynasty or regime?

1531. Was Egypt ruled by several dynasties?

1532. Was ancient Egypt divided into Upper and Lower Egypt, or Upper, Middle, and Lower Egypt?

1533. What is the name of the first pharaoh that united Upper Egypt and Lower Egypt into one single country: King Tut or King Menes?

1534. What was the capital of Egypt during the Old Kingdom era: Memphis or Thebes?

1535. What was the capital of Egypt during the New Kingdom era: Memphis or Thebes?

1536. What is the current capital of Egypt: Cairo or Thebes?

1537. What is the name of the Great Pyramids that were built during the Old Kingdom: Giza or Sphinx?

1538. Is the Great Pyramid of Giza known as the Pyramid of Cheops or the Pyramid of Khufu?

1539. Which pyramid in Egypt is the oldest and largest of three limestone pyramids that has a perfectly square base, and is the oldest of the Seven Wonders of the ancient world: the Pyramid of Teotihuacan or the Great Pyramid of Giza?

1540. What is the name of one of the greatest monumental limestone sculptures in the ancient world from 2500 B.C. that has a lion's body and the head of a Pharaoh, is near Giza, and is a national symbol of Egypt: the Great Pyramid or the Great Sphinx?

1541. What was the purpose of the Sphinx: to honor Pharaohs or to guard the temples and tombs?

1542. How long is the Great Sphinx: 240 feet long or 20 feet long?

1543. What feature of the Sphinx's face has been mysteriously knocked off: the nose or the ear?

1544. What is the name for the natural weathering that has affected the appearance of the Sphinx thousands of years later: erosion or sand storms?

1545. What is the name for the tall, narrow monument that the Egyptians built two of near the entrance of a sacred temple: obelisk or pillar?

SOCIAL STUDIES

1546. What is the name of the Queen of Egypt, wife of King Akhenaton that reigned between 1353 and 1336 B.C., played an active role in religious life, and has a symbolic painted bust of her face because of her great beauty that is now located in Berlin's Egyptian Museum: Nefertiti or Cleopatra?

1547. What Egyptian Pharaoh became king at the age of 9, ruled Egypt between 1334 and 1325 B.C, and is known today primarily because of the 1922 discovery of his tomb in The Valley of the Kings: King Menes or King Tutankhamen?

1548. What is the name of the Pharaoh that is considered the greatest Pharaoh of Ancient Egypt that ruled from 1279 B.C. to 1213 B.C., was regarded as a great military leader, and built many temples during his reign: Ramses II or Menes?

1549. What is the name for the image on the crown of an Egyptian headdress worn only by pharaohs: cobra goddess or python goddess?

1550. Where is King Tutankhamen's tomb located in Egypt: The Valley of the Kings or The Valley of the Gods?

1551. Who discovered King Tut's tomb with over 5,000 artifacts including gold, chariots, statues, boats, jewelry, and his golden coffin: Howard Carter or Hiram Bingham?

1552. What was often found on the walls of tombs: paintings or carvings?

1553. What is the name of the book that many Egyptians wanted in their tomb that was written on papyrus or on the walls of the tomb, empowering them in the after-life and offering them protection through magic spells: the Book of Life or the Book of the Dead?

1554. Who has taken much of the valuable art and artifacts that had been buried inside Egyptian tombs: archeologists or vandals?

1555. What is the word for the Egyptian process of preserving or embalming a pharaoh or a person of wealth by wrapping the body with many layers of linen cloth in order to prepare it for the after-life: cremation or mummification?

1556. Did the Egyptians use arithmetic, algebra, geometry, and fractions in their calculations?

1557. What mathematical system did the Egyptians use to help build their pyramids and tombs, calculate time, land area, and cooking using the numbers 1, 10, and 100: the binary system or the decimal system?

1558. What is the term for the system of writing using pictures and symbols during one of the earliest dynasties: cave drawings or hieroglyphics?

1559. Did hieroglyphics use consonant sounds or vowel sounds?

1560. What is the name for the people of Egypt that could read and write hieroglyphics after years of practice, and typically came from rich families: pages or scribes?

1561. Could all ancient Egyptians read and write, or was it primarily scribes that could do this?

SOCIAL STUDIES

1562. What is the name of the stone that was discovered in Egypt by a French soldier that had the same message written in both hieroglyphics and in Greek that made it easy to translate: the Rosetta Stone or the Blarney Stone?

1563. What kind of job did most ancient Egyptians have: farmers, priests, soldiers, or craftspeople?

1564. Did the Egyptians wear make-up both for Sun protection and to make a fashion statement?

1565. What accessory did many Egyptians wear around their necks made of gold, silver, or copper?

1566. What were the houses of many ancient Egyptians made from: stone or mud bricks?

1567. What was the staple food of many commoner Egyptians: bread or meat?

1568. Who is credited for inventing locks, black ink, eye makeup, parchment paper from the papyrus plant, medicine, the ox plow, and the 365 day calendar: the Egyptians or the Ethiopians?

1569. What is the name of the people that conquered Africa in 525 B.C., ruled Africa for over one hundred years, and are renowned for their handcrafted rugs: the Persians or the Babylonians?

1570. What is the name for the ancient civilization south of Egypt known for trade and for pyramids, existing between 1000 B.C. and 300 A.D: The Kingdom of Kush or the Kingdom of Axum?

1571. What is the name of the King of ancient Greece in 336 B.C, began the dynasty that ruled Africa for 300 years after he conquered Egypt and the Persian Empire, and founded the city of Alexandria: Ibn Battuta or Alexander the Great?

1572. What is the name of the dynasty of 305 B.C. when Ptolemy I became the Pharaoh and Alexandria became the first capital: Ptolemaic or Persian?

1573. What is the name of the last pharaoh of Egypt that ruled Egypt after the death of Alexander the Great, could speak seven languages, had romances with Romans Julius Caesar and Marc Antony, and supposedly allowed a poisonous cobra snake to bite her after she heard of the death of Marc Antony: Cleopatra or Queen Nefertiti?

1574. What is the name for the valley in Egypt where tombs were constructed for the Pharaohs or Kings who ruled from 1500 B.C. to 1000 B.C: the Valley of the Kings or the Tombs of the Pharaohs?

1575. What is the name of the river that flows through Egypt south to north, is the longest river in the world, is a good place for farming wheat and papyrus because of its fertile, black soil, and provides a common means for transporting goods: the Congo or the Nile?

1576. What is the geographic term for the area where the Nile River splits into several branches before emptying into the Mediterranean: a delta or a tributary?

1577. Does Egypt have deserts, mountains, oases, and wetlands?

1578. What is the name for the plant grown near the Nile River that the Egyptians used to make parchment paper in order that they could write religious texts and important documents: Eucalyptus or Papyrus?

SOCIAL STUDIES

1579. What did the ancient Egyptians use to make ropes, sandals, and baskets: Papyrus or straw?

1580. What materials did the Egyptians build their boats with: papyrus reeds or birch bark?

1581. What kind of boats did ancient Egyptians build to navigate up and down the Nile in order to conduct trade with other countries: cargo ships or reed boats?

1582. What humped animal did traders bring back from Arabia around 400 A.D. that could go several days without water, carry a big load, and had the endurance to cross the Sahara Desert?

1583. What is the word for a group of travelers on a journey through the desert: a caravan or a convoy?

1584. What did many traders from western Africa trade their ivory tusks and gold for: salt or papyrus?

1585. Did the ancient Egyptians have an organized army?

1586. What is the name for the wheeled carriage pulled by two horses that would carry two Egyptian soldiers and their bows and arrows: a caravan or a chariot?

1587. What were the Kush, Axum, Ghana, Mali, and Songhai all considered: West African Empires or Egyptian Pharaohs?

1588. Who is the Muslim leader of Mali from Morocco who wrote about his travels that included his journey to the palace in Timbuktu: Mansa Musa or Ibn Battuta?

1589. What is the term for ancient African storytellers and entertainers who would tell a story a while singing, dancing, or playing the drum: gypsies or griots?

1590. How many independent nations are located in Africa: 54 or 82?

1591. Which continent is regarded as one of the most underdeveloped continents in the world?

1592. What disease do thousands of Africans die from every year, caused by a bite from a parasite-infected mosquito: Yellow Fever or Malaria?

1593. What is the estimated population of Africa: one billion or 500 million?

1594. What is the name of the scientist that theorized that our ancestors came from Africa: Jonas Salk or Charles Darwin?

1595. What is the biggest country in Africa: Sudan or Kenya?

1596. What is the highest point in Africa located in Tanzania: Mt. McKinley or Mt. Kilimanjaro?

1597. What is the name of the cape in South Africa on the Atlantic Ocean that explorer Vasco de Gama sailed around from Portugal in order to reach the east: Cape Cod or Cape of Good Hope?

1598. What is the name of the waterway that was built in 1869 that connects the Mediterranean with the Red Sea and took over ten years to build: The Panama Canal or The Suez Canal?

1599. What is the name of the dam across the Nile River completed in 1970 that has improved irrigation and agriculture in Egypt: the Niger Dam or the Aswan Dam?

SOCIAL STUDIES

1600. What is the name of the Egyptian President that signed a peace treaty with Israel's Prime Minister Menachem Begin in 1978: Anwar Sadat or Gamal Abdel Nasser?

1601. What is the name of the area in Africa that is named this because it was the primary source of ivory at the beginning of the 19th century: Ivory Coast or Tusk Terrain?

1602. What are the two main rivers in Africa: the Nile and the Congo, or the Nile and the Niger?

1603. What are the two main deserts in Africa: the Mojave and Atacama, or the Sahara and Kalahari?

1604. Could the Sahara desert fit into the borders of the United States?

1605. Where do many African animals live: the Sahara or the savanna?

1606. What African animals can you name that live in the savannas?

1607. What is the largest living land animal in Africa?

1608. Which animals might you see at the zoo that come from Africa?

1609. What country in Africa is famous for its jungles, safaris, wildlife preserves, and national parks where you can see many elephants, giraffes, lions, zebras, and rhinoceros: Nigeria or Kenya?

1610. Which African animal is considered the fastest land animal, running up to 60 miles per hour?

1611. What would Arabic, Swahili, French, and Portuguese be categorized as?

1612. How many different languages are spoken in Africa: 200 or 2000?

1613. Do you think that many African tribes speak their own, unique language?

1614. What is the most common language spoken in Africa: Arabic or French?

1615. What is the most common religion in Africa: Islam or Christianity?

1616. What is the name of the holiday that falls in the ninth month in the Islamic calendar, is a time of praying, fasting, and self-reflection, and is celebrated throughout the world by over one billion Muslims: Kwanzaa or Ramadan?

1617. What is the biggest island off the coast of Africa: Madagascar or the Canary Islands?

1618. What craft is Africa famous for: masks or puppets?

1619. What kind of musical instrument is Africa most famous for?

1620. What is the name of the civil rights activist that was elected President of South Africa in 1994 when the first democratic elections were held: Nelson Mandela or Muammar Gaddafi?

1621. What is the term for the racist political policy in South Africa that separated people based on their skin color, forcing blacks and whites to live apart until 1993: segregation or apartheid?

1622. What is the name of the divisive Libyan leader and dictator who ruled Libya for 42 years: Nelson Mandela or Muammar Gaddafi?

SOCIAL STUDIES

1623. Do many Africans celebrate both Muslim and Christian holidays depending on their beliefs?

1624. What is the name for the weeklong reflective holiday here in the United States that honors and celebrates African heritage and history: African Week or Kwanzaa?

1625. What is the name of the Disney movie and Broadway musical, based on an imaginary animal kingdom in Africa that included Simba, Mufasa, Nala, and Scar, and the songs "Circle of Life" and "Hakuna Matata: "Animal Kingdom" or "The Lion King?"

1626. If Africa is the second largest continent in the world, which one is the largest?

1627. How many countries make up the continent of Asia: 48 or 22?

1628. What is considered to be the smallest country in the world: Vatican City near Italy, or Monaco in the south of France?

1629. What is the largest country in the world: Canada or Russia?

1630. What is the third largest country after Russia and Canada: the United States or China?

1631. What best describes the historical time periods of China: dynasties or regimes?

1632. What is the name of the first emperor of China that founded the Qin Dynasty: Qin Shi Huang or Liu Xin?

1633. While Emperor of China, was Qin Shi Huang credited with establishing several provinces within the country, a central government, a common currency, a common system of writing, and improving the infrastructure of China with new roads and canals?

1634. What large stone structure extending 5,500 miles long and now considered one of the new wonders of the world did Qin Shi Huang begin construction on with more than one million workers, in order to protect China from northern invaders?

1635. What is the name of the baked clay that was used to build the 8,000 sculptures representing the armies of the first emperor of China, Qin Shi Huang: adobe or terracotta?

1636. What is the name of the dynasty that followed the harsh rule of the Qin Dynasty when the peasants revolted and killed Emperor Qin: Ming Dynasty or Han Dynasty?

1637. Did Liu Bang change his name to Han Gaozu when he founded and became the Emperor of the Han Dynasty?

1638. Is the Han Dynasty credited with the inventions of paper, crop rotation, and iron casting?

1639. What is the name for the social code of behavior and the philosopher whose ideas were followed during the Han Dynasty: Copernicus or Confucius?

1640. What is the name for the administrative system of the Chinese government that began with the Han Dynasty, lasted for over 2,000 years, and created educated government workers who were required to pass a difficult exam: civil service or military service?

SOCIAL STUDIES

1641. Did Confucius have a philosophy of always treating others with respect, along with other rules for good behavior?

1642. What did the Han Emperors establish in order that the people would be educated and intelligent: schools or writing tablets?

1643. What is the name of the fabric originally from China that comes from the cocoons of silkworms, and was an important trade product?

1644. Did the Chinese Emperors want to keep the silk-making process a secret and were they successful for over 1,000 years?

1645. What was the most popular embroidered design on silk clothing: birds and flowers, or animals and stripes?

1646. What was a symbol of status in China: clothing or jewelry?

1647. Would a person wearing silk more likely be from the upper class or the lower class?

1648. What was the name of the trade route between China and the East and the Mediterranean that was a great source of wealth for them: The Silk Road or the Textile Trail?

1649. Was the Silk Road important for trade and commerce, or for traveling to other parts of Asia?

1650. Were many silk paintings and sculptures created during the Han Dynasty?

1651. What was the name of the religion that many Chinese people followed during the Han Dynasty that focused on a new awakening: Buddhism or Taoism?

1652. What Chinese dynasty followed the Han and then the Sui Dynasty: Tang or Ming?

1653. What industry was important during the Tang Dynasty, transporting silk, pearls, spices, and fine porcelains from one place to another in caravans: trading or road-building?

1654. What animal would the Chinese travel on in a caravan on the trade route: a horse or a camel?

1655. What was invented during the Tang Dynasty that allowed for the mass production of a book: woodblock printing or the printing press?

1656. What is the first full-length product that was produced using Chinese woodblock printing?

1657. What product was invented in its early form during the Tang Dynasty and was used for fireworks because the Chinese beleived that it scared off evil spirits: dynamite or gunpowder?

1658. What is the name of the Chinese ceramic that was developed during the Tang Dynasty: Porcelain or Bone China?

1659. What genre of literature besides the writing of short stories became very widespread and was a very important aspect of Chinese culture during the Tang Dynasty: novels or poetry?

1660. What religion emerged after Buddhism lost its place during the Tang Dynasty: Confucianism or Islam?

SOCIAL STUDIES

1661. What hot drink became popular during the Tang Dynasty: coffee or tea?

1662. What type of paper that is used in the bathroom was invented during the Tang Dynasty?

1663. What kind of money was first developed and used during the Tang Dynasty: coins or paper?

1664. What great structure in China continued to be built and re-built to keep out northern invaders during the Tang Dynasty?

1665. Did the Song Dynasty come before or after the Tang Dynasty?

1666. What two things were invented during the Song Dynasty: the magnetic compass and the iron plow, or the clock and the wheel?

1667. What was printed in great quantities through a newly-invented process called moveable type that made it possible for more people in China to read?

1668. Was the Song Dynasty one of the most advanced civilizations in the world?

1669. What product became an import crop during the Song Dynasty, yielding two harvests per year: corn or rice?

1670. What type of architecture was popular during the Song Dynasty: imperial palaces or tall pagodas?

1671. What is the name of the country to the north of China: India or Mongolia?

1672. What is the name of the desert located in Mongolia: Mojave or Gobi?

1673. Which civilization invented writing, the magnetic compass, gunpowder, the boat rudder, moveable sails, the mechanical clock, the umbrella, porcelain, the wheelbarrow, the spinning wheel, moveable type, seismographs, stirrups, matches, acupuncture, paper money, kites, tea, and ice cream: the Mongolians or the Chinese?

1674. What is the name of the calculator that was invented by the Chinese that used sliding beads to compute equations: the abacus or the compass?

1675. When Khan from Mongolia defeated the Chinese Emperor and became the new Emperor of China, what city did he establish as his home, the city that is still the capital of China today: Hong Kong or Beijing?

1676. What did the Mongol Emperors establish to promote caravan trade over long distances whereby sellers of silks, spices, porcelains and other products could travel in a single caravan with minimal risk of losing profits: merchant associations or trade associations?

1677. What is the name of the Italian explorer and trader who traveled over 24 years throughout China trading jewels and lamp oil: Marco Polo or Lawrence of Arabia?

1678. What road did Marco Polo travel along in China: the Silk Road or the Imperial Parkway?

1679. What is the name of the dynasty after the Mongols were driven out of China, was led by a self-appointed emperor named Zhu, and lasted three centuries: Ming or Zheng?

SOCIAL STUDIES

1680. What specific handiwork is the Ming Dynasty known for: porcelain pottery or woodcarvings?'

1681. What color is Ming porcelain pottery before it is glazed: brown or white?

1682. What color was the preferred colored glaze to paint on the porcelain vases: blue or red?

1683. What did Europeans call the Ming porcelain that they traded for: pottery or china?

1684. What fabric did Chinese artists paint birds, animals, and landscapes on: canvas or silk scrolls?

1685. What is the name of the art of fancy handwriting of the Chinese that uses brushes and ink to make pictures and symbols: cursive or calligraphy?

1686. What did the Chinese consider calligraphy, poetry, and painting: the Three Perfections or the Three Arts?

1687. What did the Chinese often use in their artworks: lacquer or oil paint?

1688. What is regarded as the highest form of Chinese painting: birds or landscapes?

1689. What is the name of the 5,500 mile-long wall with over 7,000 lockout towers that the Ming Dynasty peasants helped to complete with bricks?

1690. Is the Great Wall of China considered the longest or the widest man-made structure in the world?

1691. What hauling machine did the Chinese invent to help them build the Great Wall of China: the wheelbarrow or the shovel?

1692. What is the name of the Chinese canal built during the Ming Dynasty that helped the trade industry in China, and is the world's longest artificial river: Great Canal or Grand Canal?

1693. What is another name for the imperial palace built by emperors in Beijing China, considered the largest ancient palace in the world: the Taj Mahal or the Forbidden City?

1694. What Chinese building also served as a fortress complete with a moat, lookout towers, and guards: Imperial Palace or Chinese Temple?

1695. How many Chinese Emperors lived in the Imperial Palace over 500 years: 5 or 24?

1696. Did China have a fleet of explorer ships under the Chinese Admiral Zheng He before or after Columbus and his voyages in 1492?

1697. Which countries did Zheng He help to establish trade with as the commander of his treasure ship voyages: India and Africa, or America and Canada?

1698. What were Taoism, Confucianism, and Buddhism: religions or philosophies?

1699. What is the name of the country south of China, the birthplace of Buddha in 563 BC, whose teachings emphasize the rebirth of the self: Mongolia or Nepal?

1700. What is the name for the Taoism philosophy that everything in nature has two balancing forces like hot and cold or dark and light: Yin and Yang or Feng Shui?

SOCIAL STUDIES

1701. What is the name for the Chinese system for positioning a structure or the objects within a structure in such a way as to be in harmony with spiritual forces: Yin and Yang or Feng Shui?

1702. What are the two major rives in China: the Yellow and the Yangtze, or the Tigres and Euphrates?

1703. What animal is the symbol of power and good luck in China: the panda or the dragon?

1704. What is the dragon a symbol of: imperial power or the Chinese New Year?

1705. Which holiday is the biggest holiday for the Chinese: Christmas or the New Year?

1706. What utensils do the Chinese use to eat with?

1707. What is the name of a tall grass with a hollow stem that the Chinese use to make furniture, buildings, and musical instruments: bamboo or sugar cane?

1708. What animal lives near the Yangtze River in China, eats bamboo, and is considered an endangered species: the Giant Panda or the Siberian Tiger?

1709. Where are many ginseng plants and bonsai trees grown: Nepal or China?

1710. What number is considered lucky in Chinese culture: two or four?

1711. What is each year in the Chinese calendar named after: a flower or an animal?

1712. What is the name of the major mountain range in China: the Himalayas or the Pyrenees?

1713. What is the name of the tallest mountain on Earth located between China and Nepal: Mt. McKinley or Mt. Everest?

1714. What is considered to be the second tallest mountain on Earth located on the border between China and Pakistan: Mt Everest or K2?

1715. What is the most populous country on Earth: Russia or China?

1716. What is the official name for China: the People's Republic of China or the Emperor's Republic of China?

1717. What is the name for the place on the southern coast of China that is considered a special administrative region, is an important port for exporting goods, and has several attractions including Ocean Park, Victoria Bay, Victoria Peak and Disneyland: Shanghai or Hong Kong?

1718. Is China a Communist country where the Chinese government controls all economic activity and the people are given little power to elect officials, or a Republic country where the people have the power to elect government officials?

1719. What is the current capital of China: Beijing or Shanghai?

1720. What is the name of the square in the center of Beijing that is named for the gate that is located to the north of the square, separating it from the Forbidden City: Tiananmen Square or Beijing Square?

SOCIAL STUDIES

1721. What is the most populated city of China: Beijing or Shanghai?

1722. What is the name of the official language of China: Cantonese or Mandarin?

1723. How many main groups of Chinese dialects are there in China: seven or twelve?

1724. Do many Chinese people also speak English?

1725. Is the Chinese language written with letters or with symbols?

1726. What cuisine would the following foods be categorized as: wonton soup, Peking duck, rice, noodles, egg rolls, dumplings, tofu, tea, and stir-fry prepared in a large pan called a wok?

1727. What article of clothing is traditionally removed before entering a house in an Asian country?

1728. What are the two main Chinese folk dances called: the Lion Dance and the Dragon Dance, or the Tiger Dance and the Panda Dance?

1729. What is the name of the martial art that originated in ancient China and is still widely practiced today: Kung Fu or Karate?

1730. What is the name for the twelve Chinese animal signs that symbolize when a person was born that include a rat, an ox, a tiger, a rabbit, a dragon, a snake, a horse, a sheep, a monkey, a rooster, a dog, and a pig: zodiac or horoscope?

1731. In the year 1492, who "sailed the ocean blue?"

1732. What is the century of the 1500's called because it was the time of European explorers and conquerors like Hernando Cortés, Ferdinand Magellan, Francisco Pizarro, and Sir Walter Raleigh who founded the first English colony in North America: The Reformation or the Age of Discovery?

1733. Which period is known as the time of writers like Miguel Cervantes and William Shakespeare, scientists like Johannes Kepler, Galileo Galilei, and Isaac Newton, conflicts in England regarding the monarchy and religion, the establishment of Jamestown, and the arrival of the Pilgrims on the Mayflower from England to Plymouth, Massachusetts: 1600's or 1700's?

1734. Which country ruled the American colonies in the 1700's: France or Great Britain?

1735. What is the name of the war between 1754 and 1763 that arose over a dispute regarding land in the Ohio Valley, when the British defeated the French and the Native American Indians: the French and British War or the French and Indian War?

1736. What was the French and Indian War referred to as in England: the French and Indian War, or the Seven Years War?

1737. What did Britain want to collect from the American colonists in order to help pay for the costs of the French and Indian War: land treaties or taxes?

1738. What became the rally cry of the colonists who felt that the British government did not have the right to tax them given that the colonists did not have any of their own representatives in the British Parliament: "no taxation without representation" or "unfair tax act?"

SOCIAL STUDIES

1739. What is the name of the tax law that the British government passed in 1765 that required the colonists to pay a tax on all printed materials like newspapers and legal documents, and had an official British seal on it that was proof that the tax was paid: the Tax Act or the Stamp Act?

1740. Did the colonies willingly pay the taxes to the British, or did they protest and boycott British products?

1741. What is the name of the congress formed by the American colonies that gathered in 1765 with the goal of preparing a formal protest of the British taxes: the Stamp Act Congress or the Colonial Congress?

1742. What is the name of the group that was formed by some American patriots, led by Samuel Adams, opposing the taxes on them by the British Parliament, a group that wanted to protect the rights of the colonists: the Colonies for Fair Representation, or the Sons of Liberty?

1743. What is the name for the new series of tax laws, established in 1767 by Britain on American colonists that placed a tax on paper, tea, glass, and paint: the Colonial Tax Act or the Townshend Acts?

1744. Did the colonists accept the taxes as established by the Townshend Acts, or did the colonists protest and start to rebel because they felt that these tax laws violated their rights?

1745. What is the name of the event in 1770 that occurred when the tension between 50 colonists and British soldiers that were gathered outside the Custom House in Boston became so high that the soldiers fired into the crowd killing five colonists: the Boston Tea Party or the Boston Massacre?

1746. What is the name of the protest in 1773 by the American colonists against Britain's new law that only the high priced tea of the British East India Company could be sold in America, and so they proceeded to dress up like Native American Mohawk Indians, board three ships in Boston Harbor, and throw 342 crates of valuable tea into the water: the Boston Tea Protest or the Boston Tea Party?

1747. What is the name that was given by American patriots to the new set of five laws passed by Britain's Parliament in 1774 as punishment for the Boston Tea Party that included closing Boston Harbor, and further limited the rights of the colonists: the Townshend Acts or the Intolerable Acts?

1748. What is the name of the first assembly of 12 representatives from the colonies that met in Philadelphia in 1774 to write a letter to King George III of England demanding that he repeal the new taxes of the Intolerable Acts, as well as to make a plan to meet again in May of 1775 if their demands were not met: The First Colonial Congress or the First Continental Congress?

1749. Which founding father and member of the First Continental Congress made the statement in 1775, "I am not a Virginian, I am an American," and rallied his people to join Massachusetts against the British with his famous speech that ended with, "give me liberty or give me death:" John Adams or Patrick Henry?

1750. What is the name of the famous pamphlet written by Thomas Paine in 1776 that demanded complete independence from Britain, and quickly sold over 100,000 copies in a few months: The Declaration of Independence or "Common Sense?"

SOCIAL STUDIES

1751. Who is credited for saying, "lead, follow, or get out of the way:" Thomas Paine or George Washington?

1752. What is the term for the people who wanted the American colonies to gain their independence from Britain, and included Thomas Jefferson, John Adams, Benjamin Franklin, George Washington, and Samuel Adams: loyalists or patriots?

1753. What are American patriots like Washington, Jefferson, Adams, and Franklin also regarded as: Founding Fathers or Revolutionaries?

1754. What is the term for the people who lived in the American colonies who wanted to remain British citizens and remain loyal to the king: patriots or loyalists?

1755. What are the two places in Massachusetts where the colonists concealed their guns and ammunition in preparation for the war with the British: Boston and Bunker Hill or Lexington and Concord?

1756. Were the Sons of Liberty and the colonists keeping an eye on the British in case they needed to warn other colonists of an attack?

1757. What is the name of the rider whose job it was to cross the Charles River on horseback to Charleston and then to Lexington to warn John Hancock and Samuel Adams that the British were coming during his famous "midnight ride:" Paul Revere or Patrick Henry?

1758. What is the name of the other rider that set out to warn the colonists so that they would be prepared and could better fight off a British attack: Patrick Henry or William Dawes?

1759. What did the colonist Robert Newman display in the steeple of the Old North Church on the night of April 18, 1775 as a warning to the colonists how the British would attack, "one if by land, two if by sea," the "sea" being the Charles River: candles or lanterns?

1760. What was the common way to refer to the British troops because of the bright red uniforms they wore: Redcoats or Redjackets?

1761. What did Revere and Dawes yell as a warning to their fellow patriots: "the British are coming," "the Redcoats are coming," or neither, as they did not want to risk getting caught?

1762. What are the two battles that signaled the start of the Revolutionary War: Boston and Bunker Hill, or Lexington and Concord?

1763. Did Samuel Adams and John Hancock manage to escape the British in Lexington thanks to the warnings of Paul Revere?

1764. What is another name for American militiamen, so called because they could be ready to fight with just a minute's notice: Militiamen or Minutemen?

1765. Did the American side have both a militia of ordinary citizens and a Continental Army of trained soldiers?

1766. What was the main weapon during the Revolutionary War: bows or muskets?

SOCIAL STUDIES

1767. Where was the first shot fired that later became known as "the shot heard around the world," written in a poem by Ralph Waldo Emerson: Concord or Lexington?

1768. Who was the first shot fired by in Lexington: a Redcoat, a Minuteman, or is it still uncertain?

1769. Which side won battle at the North Bridge in Concord: the British or the Americans?

1770. What is the name of the city that the British forced to retreat to: Lexington or Boston?

1771. Who led the British troops: Lieutenant Colonel Francis Smith or Captain John Parker?

1772. Who led the American troops: Lieutenant Colonel Francis Smith or Captain John Parker?

1773. What are the two hills that the British wanted to control so that they would have a tactical advantage and maintain control of the sea ports: Bunker and Breeds or Concord and Lexington?

1774. Did the Battle of Bunker Hill actually take place on that hill, or did it take place on Breeds Hill, mistakenly called Bunker Hill by the British army?

1775. Which side ultimately won the Battle of Bunker Hill in part because the other side ran out of ammunition, and claimed victory even though it had more casualties and wounded: British or American?

1776. What were the American soldiers told by their commanders because they were so low on ammunition: "Do not fire until you see the whites of their eyes," or "Do not fire until you see the reds of their coats?"

1777. Which side had 30,000 professional soldiers to the other side's 15,000 colonial farmers, and 270 navy ships to the other side's eight: the British or the Americans?

1778. What were two advantages of the American side: ammunition and weapons, or knowledge of the land and determination for freedom?

1779. What is the name of the congress, led by John Hancock that met in order to discuss further strategy to form an army, fight the British, and declare their independence: the Second American Congress, or the Second Continental Congress?

1780. Who did the members of the Second Continental Congress elect in 1775 as the General of the Continental Army: George Washington or Benjamin Franklin?

1781. What bird did John Adams and Thomas Jefferson, members of the Continental Congress, choose to symbolize the United States: the hawk or the eagle?

1782. How many African Americans fought in the Continental Army: 500 or 5,000?

1783. Which representative was chosen by the Second Continental Congress and the members of the Committee of Five to write the first draft of the letter that would declare the United States independent from Britain: Benjamin Franklin or Thomas Jefferson?

1784. What is the date that the final version of the Declaration of Independence was adopted by the Second Continental Congress: July 4, 1776 or June 11, 1776?

SOCIAL STUDIES

1785. On what date does America celebrate its independence every year?

1786. How many members of the Congress signed the Declaration of Independence: 38 or 56?

1787. Who was the first congress member to write his signature, five inches long, on the Declaration of Independence: George Washington or John Hancock?

1788. Were copies of the Declaration of Independence sent to all thirteen colonies, as well as to Britain?

1789. Does the Declaration essentially declare that all states in North America be free and independent states, and that America is its own free country moving forward?

1790. Where is the original Declaration of Independence on display today: the Smithsonian Institution or the National Archives?

1791. Was the Revolutionary war still going on after the signing of the Declaration?

1792. What did George Washington offer to encourage more people to join the troops: money, land, or money and land?

1793. What is the name of the river that George Washington crossed with his army on a snowy, Christmas night in a surprise attack on the British, was a victory for the American troops, and helped to revitalize the Continental Army: Potomac or Delaware?

1794. What did the Second Continental Congress decide that the country needed to represent the united colonies that would have thirteen red and white stripes and a blue area with thirteen stars, and passed a Resolution to accomplish this on June 14, 1777?

1795. When do we celebrate Flag Day, originally observed in Waubeka, Wisconsin at Stoney Hill School in 1885, officially approved as a day national observance by Congress, and signed into law by President John Truman: June 14th or July 4th?

1796. Has the American flag gone through many transformations since the original version of 1777?

1797. How many stars are on the American flag currently?

1798. What are "Old Glory," "The Star-Spangled Banner," and "Stars and Stripes" nicknames for?

1799. What is the name of the battle that was won by the American troops in New York in 1777 after the surrender of the British General and over 6,000 British soldiers, and was a turning point in the Revolutionary War for the American side: Yorktown or Saratoga?

1800. Which European country did Ben Franklin convince to support the American effort after the Battle of Saratoga, resulting in this country sending military aid to America: France or Spain?

1801. Which European country sent several ships to America in 1778 providing them with weapons and setting up blockades so that the British could not receive supplies?

1802. Did many women help out the Revolutionary War effort?

1803. What is the name of the war General that helped the Americans win several battles including

SOCIAL STUDIES

Saratoga, but was and is regarded as a traitor after he changed sides, acted as a spy, and sold American military secrets to the British: Benedict Arnold or Samuel Adams?

1804. What is the name of the place near Philadelphia where the Continental Army made their camp during the harsh winter of 1777-1778, and the place where the military leaders of George Washington of the American Continental Army, General von Steuben of Prussia, and General Marquis de Lafayette of France all helped to train the army: Yorktown or Valley Forge?

1805. What is the name of the last battle of the American Revolutionary War that took place in Virginia, lasted 20 days, and ended when British General Cornwallis and the out-numbered British army surrendered to Washington and the American troops with the showing of a white flag: Valley Forge or Yorktown?

1806. What is the name of the official peace treaty between Britain and the United States that was signed on September 3rd, 1783 in France that officially ended the American Revolutionary War, and was finally ratified by King George III of England in 1784: The Treaty of Trent or the Treaty of Paris?

1807. What is the name of the war in America between the British and the American Colonists that lasted from 1775-1783?

1808. Did each of the thirteen states in the United States have to create and adopt their own state constitution after the Revolutionary War?

1809. What document did the members develop that helped to establish a central government, was finally ratified by the thirteen states in 1781, and is regarded as our first constitution: the Articles of Confederation or the Bill of Rights?

1810. What is the name for the uprising that took place in Massachusetts in 1786 by farmers protesting high taxes, tax collectors, and foreclosures on farms that further emphasized the need for a strong central government: Farmers' Revolt or Shays' Rebellion?

1811. What is the name of the first plan that James Madison of Virginia and other delegates drafted in 1787 in Philadelphia proposing a strong central government while maintaining citizens' basic rights, and contained specific ideas that would become part of the U.S. Constitution: the Virginia Plan or the Constitution?

1812. What is the name for the series of 85 newspaper articles written by James Madison, Alexander Hamilton, and John Jay in 1787 that were published anonymously promoting the ratification of the U.S. Constitution: the Constitution Papers or the Federalist Papers?

1813. What is the name of the first ten amendments to the Constitution written by George Mason and James Madison, reflect the American ideals of liberty, a limited government, and the rule of law: The Preamble or the Bill of Rights?

1814. What is the name of the meeting of the delegates of colonial America in 1787 to discuss Madison's Virginia Plan and the structure of the central government, and outlined the roles of the executive branch, the legislative branch, and the judicial branch: The Constitutional Convention or the Philadelphia Convention?

SOCIAL STUDIES

1815. Which branch of government carries out the laws of the country, and is led by the President: legislative, executive, or judicial?

1816. Which branch of government includes the justices and the courts, and interprets the laws and the constitution: executive, legislative, or judicial?

1817. Which branch of government makes the laws, and includes the Senate and the House of Representatives, collectively called the Congress: legislative, executive, or judicial?

1818. What is the name of the solution to the issue of fair representation in the legislative branch of the government that would give each state equal representation in the Senate and representation in the House of Representatives based on its population: the Connecticut Compromise or the Virginia Compromise?

1819. What two bodies make up the United States Congress?

1820. How many senators does each state have in the Senate: two or four?

1821. How many total senators are in the United States Senate?

1822. How many House Representatives does each state have: the number proportional to the population of that state, or four representatives?

1823. How many total representatives are there in the U.S. House of Representatives: 400 or 435?

1824. What is the name of the compromise that was reached by the delegates in 1787 at the Constitutional Convention regarding representation based on state population and whether or not that would include slaves, agreeing that "free persons" would count as one, and slaves or "non-free persons" would count as three-fifths of a person: The Slavery Compromise or the Three-Fifths Compromise?

1825. How many years was proposed by the delegates to wait before passing any new laws that would regulate the slave trade: 10 or 20?

1826. What is considered the supreme law of the United States and the binding agreement among all people: The Bill of Rights or The U.S. Constitution?

1827. What is the name for the introduction to the U.S. Constitution that states: "We the People of the United States, in order to form a more perfect Union, establish justice, insure domestic tranquility, provide for the common defense, promote the general welfare, and secure the blessings of liberty to ourselves and our posterity, do ordain and establish this Constitution for the United States of America:" the Bill of Rights or the Preamble?

1828. What is the name for the system that the writers of the Constitution devised so that each of the three branches of the government limits the power of the others, ensuring that no one branch becomes too powerful: checks and balances, or branch monitoring?

1829. Does the President have the power to oppose or "veto" a law that is passed?

1830. In what year was the U.S. Constitution approved by all states: 1776 or 1790?

SOCIAL STUDIES

1831. What is the word for a change or an alteration: an amendment or a bill?

1832. What is the name for the first 10 amendments to the U.S. Constitution: the Preamble or the Bill of Rights?

1833. Which amendment in the Bill of Rights guarantees the freedom of religion, freedom of speech, freedom of the press, the freedom to assemble, and the freedom to petition: the First Amendment or the Second Amendment?

1834. Does each state have a government with the three different branches and a constitution?

1835. Who is the executive leader of the United States government: the President or the Congress?

1836. Who is leader of the state government: the senator or the governor?

1837. What is the name of the current governor of the state you live in?

1838. Who is the leader of the city government: the mayor or the alderman?

1839. What is the name of the current mayor of the city you live in?

1840. What do we pay to the local, state, and federal governments to run them and pay for schools, roads, and the salaries of public workers: duties or taxes?

1841. Is it important for American citizens to participate in some way in the government?

1842. Which president stated in 1863 that government should be "of the people, by the people, and for the people:" President Lincoln or President Johnson?

1843. Who became the first President of the United States in 1789 and is considered to be "the Father of the Country?"

1844. Who was the first "First Lady" of the United States, the wife of George Washington: Martha Washington or Abigail Washington?

1845. Who was the first Vice-President of the United States: John Adams or Thomas Jefferson?

1846. What is the term for the group of advisors to the President of the United States: Secretaries or Cabinet?

1847. Is the Vice-President of the United States considered a member of the President's Cabinet?

1848. What is the term for each cabinet member in the United States each of whom is in charge of a specific area of government: Secretary or Ambassador?

1849. How many executive departments make up the President's cabinet: 10 or 15?

1850. What is the name for the Secretary that handles international relations: Secretary of State or Secretary of Defense?

1851. Are there executive departments led by Secretaries for Agriculture, Education, Defense, Energy, Health, Homeland Security, Labor, State, Transportation, and the Treasury?

SOCIAL STUDIES

1852. Is the Attorney General considered part of the President's Cabinet?

1853. Who was the Secretary of State to George Washington: Thomas Jefferson or Alexander Hamilton?

1854. Who was the Secretary of the Treasury to George Washington: Thomas Jefferson or Alexander Hamilton?

1855. How many years are considered one term for a U.S. President: two or four?

1856. How many terms is a U.S. President limited to, according to the Constitution: two or four?

1857. Do candidates that run for a government typically represent a specific political party?

1858. What was the political party of Thomas Jefferson and his followers: Democratic-Republican or Federalist?

1859. What was the political party of Alexander Hamilton and his followers: Republican or Federalist?

1860. What were the country's first two political parties: Democratic-Republican and Libertarian, or Democratic-Republican and Federalist?

1861. What are the two main political parties in the United States currently: Republican and Democrat, or Federalist and Libertarian?

1862. What was the first capital of the United States: Boston or New York City?

1863. What is the present day capital of the United States of America?

1864. What is the name of the official residence of the President of the United States, located in Washington, D.C. that started with President John Adams?

1865. What is the name of Washington's home in Virginia that he retired to after his presidency: Mount Vernon or Monticello?

1866. What is the name of the office building in Washington, D.C. that houses the United States Congress: the U.S. Capitol or the White House?

1867. Who was the second President of the United States: Thomas Jefferson or John Adams?

1868. Who was the Vice-President to second President John Adams: Madison or Jefferson?

1869. What is the name of the wife of John Adams and the mother of our 6th President John Quincy Adams, who believed in equal rights for all people, including women and blacks: Martha Adams or Abigail Adams?

1870. Who was the third President of the United States and the principle author of the Declaration of Independence: Thomas Jefferson or Alexander Hamilton?

1871. Who owned the land west of the Mississippi from Canada to Mexico during the early years of Jefferson's Presidency: France or Spain?

SOCIAL STUDIES

1872. What is the name of the French territory that was named for the King of France, King Louis the Fourteenth: St. Louis or Louisiana?

1873. Whom did Jefferson ask Secretary James Monroe to talk with in France about the sale of the French territory collectively known as Louisiana: Napoleon Bonaparte or King Louis XIV?

1874. What is the name of the land deal of 1803 when President Jefferson bought Iowa, Missouri, Arkansas, Nebraska, Kansas, Oklahoma, South Dakota and parts of other states for $15 million dollars from France, nearly doubling the size of the United States: the American Acquisition or the Louisiana Purchase?

1875. What two explorers did President Jefferson ask in 1804 to explore the west, the newly purchased Louisiana Territory, and along the way met several Native American Tribes including a Shoshone Indian, Sacajawea, who helped them as an interpreter: Lewis and Clark, or Henry Hudson and Marco Polo?

1876. How many years was the expedition of Lewis and Clark, a journey that included navigating the Great Falls in Montana as well as the rugged Rocky Mountains while on foot, on horseback, and in canoes: one year or two years?

1877. How did Lewis and Clark document their findings on their expedition regarding geographical features, the Missouri River, weather, over 180 plant species, and over 120 mammals, reptiles, birds, and fish including grizzly bear, buffalo, woodpeckers, sheep, deer, prairie dogs and trout: kept detailed written journals, or shared their observations with the Indians?

1878. Who was the fourth President of the United States: James Monroe or James Madison?

1879. What is the name of the two-year war in the early 1800's between the United States and Britain that arose over trade, shipping, and naval law disagreements: the Seven Years War or the War of 1812?

1880. What is the name of U.S. naval ship nicknamed "Old Ironsides," that managed to capture 24 enemy ships during the War of 1812: USS Constitution or the USS Enterprise?

1881. What symbolic building was burned in the Battle of Washington that was re-built and painted white to duplicate the lime-based whitewash that was applied to this building in 1798: The Capitol or The White House?

1882. What is the name of the treaty that was signed in 1814 to end the War of 1812 giving the United States a victory: the Treaty of Paris or the Treaty of Ghent?

1883. What is the name for the final battle of 1812 won convincingly by the Americans, led by General Andrew Jackson, occurring 15 days after the Treaty of Ghent was signed because neither side was aware of the existing peace treaty: the Battle of New Orleans or the Battle of Louisiana?

1884. Who was the fifth President of the United States, elected in 1816, re-elected in 1820, and has a foreign policy doctrine named for him that opposed further European colonization and interference with nations in the western hemisphere: James Monroe or James Madison?

SOCIAL STUDIES

1885. Was slavery an issue in the colonial America in 1820?

1886. Which part of the country owned slaves and depended on them to work on their large plantations and farms: the North or the South?

1887. Which part of the country did not own slaves and earned a living by working in factories or managing a small farm: the North or the South?

1888. What is the term used to refer to people that wanted to abolish or do away with slavery: revolutionists or abolitionists?

1889. What is the name of the compromise that served to maintain the balance of slavery between the anti-slavery North and the pro-slavery South that allowed Missouri to enter the Union as a slave state, and Maine to enter the Union as a free state: the Missouri Compromise or the Maine Compromise?

1890. What is the name of the proclamation by President James Monroe in his address to Congress in 1823 that stated that the United States would not tolerate any European presence, intervention, or colonization in the Western Hemisphere, and that the United States would assume a neutral role in European affairs: the Monroe Plan or the Monroe Doctrine?

1891. Who was the sixth President of the United States who opposed slavery, supported freedom of speech, and only served one term: Andrew Jackson or John Quincy Adams?

1892. Who was the seventh President of the United States elected in 1828, was a commander in the war of 1812, was known as the "people's president," removed Native American Cherokees from their land, is pictured on the U.S. twenty dollar bill, and the capital of Mississippi is named for him: Andrew Jackson or Andrew Johnson?

1893. What was President's Jackson goal regarding Indian land: transfer Indian land into U.S. territory, or allow all Native American Indians to keep their land?

1894. What is the name of the bill that President Jackson convinced Congress to pass in 1830 that would allow the government to force the Native Americans to Indian Territory, more than 1,000 miles away: the Indian Removal Act or the Indian Reservation Act?

1895. What is the name given for the forced relocation of Native American Cherokee Indians from their homeland of Georgia to the Indian Territory of Oklahoma, and was so named because of the brutal journey that it was: the March of Pain or the Trail of Tears?

1896. What is the term for a person that takes action to improve social or economic conditions: reformer or revolutionary?

1897. What is the name of the lady that believed in the rights of the mentally ill, and their treatment in institutions in the early 1800's: Dorothea Dix or Clara Barton?

1898. What is the name of the reformer of American education who worked to improve public schools and the number of children attending those schools: Horace Mann or Dorothea Dix?

1899. Who are the two women who believed in equality and women's rights, and organized a convention in

Seneca Falls, New York in 1848: Lucretia Mott and Elizabeth Stanton, or Elizabeth Stanton and Amelia Bloomer?

1900. What is the name of the editor of a magazine who attended a convention in Seneca, New York promoting the right of women to wear comfortable clothing, and had bloomers, the short pants worn under a skirt, named for her: Amelia Bloom or Amelia Bloomer?

1901. Who is the African American woman, abolitionist, and women's rights activist who was born into slavery, gained her freedom in 1827, and developed a great following after her 1851 speech, "Ain't I a Woman," at the Ohio Women's Rights Convention: Sojourner Truth or Harriet Tubman?

Social Studies – 5th Grade

1902. What is the name of the study of the Earth's surface that includes the climate, vegetation, and soil: geology or geography?

1903. What is the meaning of "geo:" Earth or planet?

1904. What is the name for the sphere that is made up of all the Earth's gases: lithosphere or atmosphere?

1905. What is the name for the sphere that is the solid, rigid outer layer of the Earth, and includes physical materials like soil and rocks: lithosphere or hydrosphere?

1906. What is the name for the sphere that is made up of all the Earth's water, and includes the water on the surface, the water underground, and the water in the air: atmosphere or hydrosphere?

1907. What are two geographical reference points in the Earth to describe a location: equator and prime meridian, or the Tropics of Cancer and Capricorn?

1908. What is the name of the imaginary line that circles around the Earth midway between the North Pole and the South Pole, dividing it into the Northern and Southern Hemispheres?

1909. What do you think the South American country of **Ecuador** translates to in English?

1910. What is the reference point that refers to everything north of the equator: Northern Hemisphere or Southern Hemisphere?

1911. What is the reference point that refers to everything south of the equator?

1912. What is the climate like as you move farther away from the equator: warmer or colder?

1913. What is the name of the imaginary line that runs between the North Pole and the South Pole, passes through Greenwich, England, measures zero degrees longitude, becomes the 180 degree meridian on the other side of the Earth, and divides the Earth into the Eastern and Western Hemispheres: the equator or the prime meridian?

1914. What is another name for the prime meridian, named for the place in England that it passes through, separating east from west: London Meridian or Greenwich Meridian?

SOCIAL STUDIES

1915. What is another name for 180 degrees longitude on the other side of the earth that is designated as the place where each calendar day begins: International Date Line or prime meridian?

1916. What would change either forward or backward if you crossed the International Date Line: the clock or the date?

1917. Are the regions to the east one calendar earlier than the regions to the west?

1918. If you cross the International Date Line going west would Saturday become Sunday or Friday?

1919. If you cross the International Date Line going east would Saturday become Sunday or Friday?

1920. Could there be two different calendar days at the same time on the Earth?

1921. What is the name for the lines that run around the Earth horizontally or parallel to the equator, and measure how far north or south an object or place is on the Earth: latitude or longitude

1922. What is the name for the lines that run vertically around the Earth, are referred to as meridians, and measure how far east or west a place is from the prime meridian: latitude or longitude?

1923. Which are the lines that connect the North Pole with the South Pole: latitude or longitude?

1924. Is the prime meridian located at 0 degrees latitude or 0 degrees longitude?

1925. What is the name for the latitude and longitude numbers that indicate a specific location on the Earth: reference points or coordinates?

1926. What is the term for the line running at a north latitude that specified the boundary between Pennsylvania and Maryland, was originally surveyed by astronomers Charles Mason and Jeremiah Dixon between 1763 and 1767 who were called on to define the boundary between the free and the slave states, and later came to be known as the dividing line between the North and the South: North-South Line or Mason-Dixon Line?

1927. What is the name for the line of latitude and imaginary circle closest to the North Pole located 67 degrees north of the equator: the Arctic Circle or the Antarctic Circle?

1928. What is the name for the frozen sections of ice located at the North and South Poles: polar ice cap or frozen tundra?

1929. What is the name for the line of latitude and imaginary circle closest to the South Pole located at 67 degrees south of the equator: the Arctic Circle or the Antarctic Circle?

1930. What is the name for the line of latitude and imaginary circle located 23 ½ degrees north of the equator: Tropic of Cancer or Tropic of Capricorn?

1931. What is the name for the line of latitude and imaginary circle located 23 ½ degrees south of the equator: Tropic of Cancer or Tropic of Capricorn?

1932. What is the area within the Tropic of Cancer and Tropic of Capricorn: the tropics or the desert?

1933. What do the terms tropical, temperate, and frigid refer to: latitude zones or climate zones?

SOCIAL STUDIES

1934. Would the weather in the tropics be very hot or very cold?

1935. Would the weather in the Frigid Zone be very hot or very cold?

1936. What would the weather be like in the Temperate Zone: hot or moderate?

1937. What climate zone would the Arctic and Antarctic be in: temperate or frigid?

1938. What determines whether it is day or night: the rotation of the Earth, or the Earth's revolution around the Sun?

1939. What determines the seasons: the rotation of the Earth only, or the rotation and revolution of Earth because it creates changes in lightness, darkness, and temperature?

1940. Does latitude have a connection with the seasons?

1941. What season are the countries in the Northern Hemisphere in during the months of June, July, and August when the Earth is tilted on its axis, and the North Pole is pointed more *towards* the Sun: summer or winter?

1942. What season are the countries in the Southern Hemisphere in during the months of June, July, and August when the Earth is tilted on its axis, and the South Pole is pointed *away* from the Sun: summer or winter?

1943. What season are the countries in the Northern Hemisphere in during the months of December, January, and February when the Earth is tilted on its axis, and the North Pole is pointed *away* from the Sun: summer or winter?

1944. What season are the countries in the Southern Hemisphere in during the months of December, January, and February when the Earth is tilted on its axis and the South Pole is pointed *towards* the Sun: summer or winter?

1945. Are the seasons the same or the opposite in the Northern and Southern Hemispheres?

1946. Are the months the same or the opposite in the Northern and Southern Hemispheres?

1947. What is the term given for the two times a year, June 21st and December 21st, when the tilt of the Earth's axis reaches its maximum angle with respect to the Sun, and the rays of the Sun directly shine on one of the two tropics: solstice or equinox?

1948. What day is the longest day of the year in terms of hours of sunlight in the Northern Hemisphere: June 21st or December 21st?

1949. What day is the shortest day of the year in terms of hours of sunlight in the Northern Hemisphere: June 21st or December 21st?

1950. What is the term given for the two times a year, March 21st and September 21st, when the tilt of the Earth's axis is straight with respect to the Sun, and the rays of the Sun directly shine on the equator: solstice or equinox?

SOCIAL STUDIES

1951. What would the passage of day and night, the phases of the moon, and the revolution of the Earth in its orbit all determine: the seasons or the passage of time?

1952. How many years are there in one millennium: 100 or 1000?

1953. How many years are there in one century: 100 or 1000?

1954. How many years are there in one decade: 100 or 10?

1955. How many days are there in one year: 365 or 365 ¼?

1956. What extra day do we have every four years to match the calendar with the solar year and allow for the extra ¼ day in the year: February 29th or September 31st?

1957. What is the term we use when we have February 29th on the calendar: leap day or extra day?

1958. Who were the first people to add a leap day every four years: the Maya or the Egyptians?

1959. What Roman leader reorganized the 12 Roman months into a 365 day calendar with a leap year day added every four years, and so named the *Julian* calendar: Ptolemy or Julius Caesar?

1960. What calendar replaced the Julian calendar because it resulted in throwing the solar calendar off by one day every 128 years, was named for Pope Gregory XIII who first introduced it in 1582, and is the calendar system currently in use in most of the world today: the Mayan calendar or the Gregorian calendar?

1961. How many days are there on average in one month?

1962. How many days are there in one week?

1963. What are the two days of the weekend?

1964. How many hours are there in one day?

1965. How many minutes are there in one hour?

1966. How many seconds are there in one minute?

1967. What kind of timing device was used my many ancient civilizations before clocks: windmills or sundials?

1968. Do many towns and cities have a large clock tower?

1969. What is the reference point for measuring time: the equator or the prime meridian?

1970. How many general time zones is the Earth divided into, that are designed to match the hours it takes for the Earth to rotate once on its axis: 24 or 12?

1971. Which country would have Central Time, Mountain Time, Pacific Time, and Eastern Time?

1972. Which time zone would you be in if you lived in Wisconsin: Central or Eastern?

1973. Which time zone would you be in if you lived in Colorado: Pacific or Mountain?

SOCIAL STUDIES

1974. Which time zone would you be in if you lived in California: Eastern or Pacific?

1975. Which time zone would you be in if you lived in New York: Eastern or Pacific?

1976. What time zone are you located in?

1977. Do Alaska and Hawaii have their own time zones?

1978. What time is it when the Sun is directly overhead, and shadows are at their shortest: noon or 3:00?

1979. What is time referred to as: basic or standard?

1980. What is the term for something that many countries do to gain one more hour of sunlight, and to save energy by setting back their clocks one hour, and lasts between April and October?

1981. What do we say to refer to the time before noon: A.M. or P.M?

1982. What do we say to refer to the time after noon until midnight: A.M. or P.M?

1983. What is the English translation of the Latin term *meridiem*: medium or midday?

1984. Which abbreviation stands for the Latin words *ante meridiem*, or the hours before the Sun shines right on the meridian: A.M. or P.M?

1985. Which abbreviation stands for the Latin words *post meridiem*, or the hours after the Sun shines right on the meridian: A.M. or P.M?

1986. Are there many different maps that are used to represent the Earth?

1987. Is there a difference in how the size of a country may appear on a flat map versus a globe?

1988. What is the term for people who make maps: calligraphers or cartographers?

1989. What is the term that is used to refer to different kinds of maps: spheres or projections?

1990. What is the name of the person that is credited with creating the best-known map projection in the world in the 1500's by projecting the Earth's surface on a flat map: Gerardus Mercator or Christopher Columbus?

1991. Should the type of projection or map a person uses like globe, flat, conic, physical, or relief relate to what type of geography that person wants to learn?

1992. What are the two largest bodies of water that are easily identified on a projection or map?

1993. What is the term for bodies of water that collect in basins, or large depressions in the land: rivers or lakes?

1994. Were some lakes on the Earth formed from glaciers?

1995. Can lakes be salty?

1996. What kind of lake would the Great Salt Lake in Utah be considered: salty or freshwater?

SOCIAL STUDIES

1997. On which continent would you locate Lake Chad and Lake Victoria: Africa or Asia?

1998. On which continent would you locate Lake Maracaibo and Lake Titicaca, the world's highest navigable lake: South America or North America?

1999. On which continent would you locate the Aral Sea and the Caspian Sea: Asia or Africa?

2000. Are the Caspian Sea and the Aral Sea considered oceans or salty lakes?

2001. What lakes can you name in the United States and Canada?

2002. What are the names of the five Great Lakes located in the United States and Canada?

2003. What type of map indicates governmental boundaries of cities, counties, states, and countries: political or relief?

2004. What type of map indicates landforms like plains, deserts, and mountains often with contour lines: political or relief?

2005. Are major rivers indicated on a political map or a relief map?

2006. What major rivers in the world can you name?

2007. What major rivers can you name in the United States?

2008. Are mountain ranges indicated on a relief map or a political map?

2009. What mountain ranges in the world can you name?

2010. Are deserts often included on a political map or a relief map?

2011. What deserts in the world can you name?

2012. How many continents or landmasses can be located on a world map: five or seven?

2013. What are the three countries that make up North America?

2014. How many states make up the United States and can be located on a political map?

2015. How many geographic regions is the United States divided into: five or eight?

2016. What is the name for the region of the United States that includes the states of Maine, Massachusetts, New Hampshire, Connecticut, Rhode Island, New Jersey, New York, Pennsylvania, and Vermont: New England or the Northeast?

2017. What is the name for the division in the Northeast that includes the states of Maine, Massachusetts, New Hampshire, Connecticut, Rhode Island, and Vermont, and is known for Pilgrims, the first Thanksgiving, lobsters, and beautiful fall colors: Mid-Atlantic or New England?

2018. What is the name for the region of the United States that includes Washington D.C., New York, West Virginia, Delaware, Maryland, and Pennsylvania, is very densely populated: Northeast or Northwest?

SOCIAL STUDIES

2019. What is the name for the region of the United States that includes the states of Alabama, Georgia, Kentucky, Louisiana, Mississippi North Carolina, South Carolina, Virginia, Tennessee and Florida and is known for cotton plantations, peaches, oranges, beaches, and music: Mid-Atlantic or Southeast?

2020. What is the name for the region of the United States that includes the states of Illinois, Indiana, Iowa, Kansas, Michigan, Minnesota, North Dakota, South Dakota, Missouri, Ohio, and Wisconsin, and is known for Great Lakes and the Mississippi River: Great Plains or Midwest?

2021. What is the name for the region of the United States that includes the states of Montana, Wyoming, Colorado, Utah, Nevada, and California: West or Pacific Northwest?

2022. What is the name for the region of the United States that includes the states of Arizona, New Mexico, Nevada, Utah, and Colorado, is dry with many deserts, and borders Mexico: Southwest or Northwest?

2023. What are geographical regions further divided into: sections or divisions?

2024. What is the name for the physical region of the United States that includes the states of Alaska, Washington, Idaho, and Oregon, and borders Canada: Northeast or Pacific Alaska Region?

2025. What is the name for the physical region of the United States located in the Midwest that includes the states of Kansas, Nebraska, Iowa, and Missouri, and is rather sparsely populated with vast fields of land: Great Plains or Southwest?

2026. What is the name for the physical region of the United States located in the Midwest that includes the states or Minnesota, Wisconsin, Illinois, Indiana, and Ohio, and so named because this area includes Lakes Superior, Michigan, Huron, and Erie: North Central or Great Lakes?

2027. What is the name for the physical region of the United States that includes the states of Montana, Wyoming, Utah, Colorado, New Mexico, North Dakota, and South Dakota, and named for the mountain range that passes through these states: Appalachian Mountain or Rocky Mountain?

2028. What is the name for the physical region of the United States that includes the states of California, Nevada, and Arizona, and named for the ocean nearest to them: Pacific or Atlantic?

2029. What is the name for the physical region of the United States that includes the states of Pennsylvania, West Virginia, Virginia, Maryland, Delaware, and New Jersey, so named because these states are half way down the coast on this ocean: Mid-Atlantic or Mid-Pacific?

2030. What is the name for the physical region of the United States that includes the states of Kentucky, Tennessee, North Carolina, South Carolina, Georgia, Alabama, Mississippi, and Florida: Southeast or Lower-Atlantic?

2031. What is the name for the physical region of the United States that includes the states of Texas, Oklahoma, Arkansas, and Louisiana: Southwest or Southeast?

2032. What is the name for the physical region of the United States that includes the states of New York,

SOCIAL STUDIES

Vermont, New Hampshire, Maine, Massachusetts, Maryland, Rhode Island, and Connecticut: Northeast or Northwest?

2033. What is the name of the state outside the continental United States, is a group of islands in the Pacific, and has a warm climate?

2034. What is the name of the state outside the continental United States, has a sparse population, and has a cold climate?

2035. What state do you live in?

2036. What states border the state you live in?

2037. What is the term for the sections that a state is divided into: regions or counties?

2038. What is the term for the center of population, business, and culture: a town or a city?

2039. What city in the United States is known as the "Windy City:" Chicago or Milwaukee?

2040. What city in the United States is known as the "Motor City:" Philadelphia or Detroit?

2041. What city in the United States is known as the "Big Apple," or, "The City That Never Sleeps:" New York or Las Vegas?

2042. What city in the United States is known as the "City of Angels:" Las Vegas or Los Angeles?

2043. What city in the United States is known as the "Mile High City:" Denver or Salt Lake City?

2044. What city in the United States is known as "Bean town:" Baltimore or Boston?

2045. What city in the United States is known as "The Big Easy:" New Orleans or New York?

2046. What city in the United States is known as the "City by the Bay:" San Francisco or San Diego?

2047. What city in the United States is known "Philly," or, "The City of Brotherly Love?"

2048. What city in the United States is known as the "Gateway to the West," and is famous for its arch: St. Louis or Indianapolis?

2049. What city in the United States is known as the "Steel City:" Pittsburgh or Detroit?

2050. What city in Europe is known as "The City of Love:" Venice or Paris?

2051. What city in the world is known as the "Holy City:" Jerusalem or Fatima?

2052. What fictitious city known as the "Emerald City?"

2053. What is the term for a human settlement that is smaller than a city but larger than a village: town or municipality?

2054. What type of community or city typically has a high-density population, tall buildings called skyscrapers, public transportation, and large schools: urban or rural?

SOCIAL STUDIES

2055. What type of community typically has a low-density population, is located in the countryside, and has buildings, farms, and open spaces: suburban or rural?

2056. What type of community is often located close to cities, has residents who live in houses with yards, and has residents who drive or take a train in to the city: urban or suburban?

2057. What type of community best describes where you live: rural, urban, or suburban?

2058. What is the term for the people who live in a community and are familiar with local businesses, parks and landmarks: residents or patrons?

2059. What is the name for the central part of town or city that many cities and communities have that are often surrounded by shops, restaurants, and a city hall: the plaza or the town square?

2060. Do many city or town squares have a statue, monument, or fountain in the center?

2061. What is the name of one of the largest squares in the world that is located in the historic center of Mexico City, includes the National Palace, and has the Mexican flag in the center: the Zócalo or the Plaza Mayor?

2062. What is the name of one of the most famous city squares in England that was named for the battle that Britain won over Napoleon and the French in 1805, has a large column and statue of Lord Nelson in the middle, and is surrounded by four lions and several fountains: Plaza San Marco or Trafalgar Square?

2063. What is the name for the main square in Venice, Italy that includes a basilica and a large space in the middle: Piazza San Marco or Old Town Square?

2064. What is the name of the largest city square in the world located in Beijing, China, that is surrounded by several monuments and governments, has a flag in the center, has four marble lions guarding the gate, and was the site of a famous massacre in 1989: Trafalgar Square or Tiananmen Square?

2065. What is the name of the square in Krakow, Poland that is the largest medieval town square in Europe, is surrounded by historic palaces and churches, and has a small palace called Cloth Hall at its center: Main Market Square or Old Town Square?

2066. What is the name of the famous square in New York City near Broadway and West 42nd street, has video screens, LED signs and flashing lights, and is famous for the ball drop on New Year's Eve: Rockefeller Center of Times Square?

2067. What is the name of the square located in front of the Basilica in Vatican City, Rome, and has an Egyptian obelisk at the center of the ellipse: Plaza San Marco or St. Peter's Square?

2068. What is the name of the city square in Madrid that is surrounded by government buildings, shops, and cafes, at one time hosted bullfights, markets, and soccer games, and has a statue of Phillip III in its center: the Zócalo or the Plaza Mayor?

2069. What is the name of the square in Moscow, Russia that is surrounded by Saint Basil's Cathedral, Lenin's Mausoleum, and the State History Museum: Red Square or Main Market Square?

SOCIAL STUDIES

2070. What is the name of the statue located in Copenhagen, Denmark of a lady sitting on a rock that was built in honor of a play: the Little Mermaid or the Little Lady?

2071. What is the name of the statue in Russia that was built to symbolize the Battle of Stalingrad and was the tallest structure in the world in 1967 measuring 280 feet high: Motherland Calls or Russian Lady?

2072. What is the name of the marble statue in Florence, Italy from the renaissance that is considered the masterpiece of Michelangelo, and represents a Biblical king: David or Goliath?

2073. What is the name of the Pre-Columbian Mexican civilization that sculpted large, helmeted stone heads from basalt stone with large facial features in the lowlands of Mexico: the Olmecs or the Zapotecs?

2074. What is the name of the limestone sculpture at Giza in Egypt on the west bank of the Nile River with the head of a pharaoh wearing a headdress and the body of a lion, and is considered to be one of the oldest statues in the world: Pharaoh Khafre or Great Sphinx?

2075. What is the name of the statue of Jesus Christ on top of a mountain in Rio de Janeiro, Brazil that is a symbol of Christianity: Christ the Redeemer or Statue of Christ?

2076. What is the name of the 50 stone statues, each weighing several tons, located on Easter Island off the coast of Chile, South America that were built by Polynesians: Stonehenge or Moai?

2077. What is the name of the prehistoric group of standing stones located in England that were constructed thousands of years ago by an unknown civilization, and is believed to have been built as an astronomic observatory and religious center: Machu Picchu or Stonehenge?

2078. What is the name of the monument located in New York Harbor that was a gift from France, is a lady wearing a crown and holding a torch, and is a symbol of American freedom: the Liberty Bell or the Statue of Liberty?

2079. What is the name of the tower in Toronto, Canada built as a communication tower in 1973: the CN Tower or the Space Needle?

2080. What is the name of the observation tower over 605 feet high in Seattle, Washington that was built for the 1962 World's Fair: the Space Needle or the CN Tower?

2081. What would the Burj Khalifa in Dubai, the Makkah Royal Clock Tower in Mecca, One World Trade Center in New York City, and the Willis Tower in Chicago all be categorized as: the tallest buildings in the world, or the largest structures in the world?

2082. What is the name for the famous clock tower in London, England that has a bell weighing 13 tons, is now called Elizabeth Tower, and is the one of the largest clock tower in the world: Big Ben or Wrigley Clock Tower?

2083. What is the name for the world famous tower in Italy that began to sink after it was built in 1173 due to being constructed on an uneven foundation, and is famous for its tilt and 296 steps: the Leaning Tower of Pisa or the Tower of Italy?

SOCIAL STUDIES

2084. What is the name of the tower that is the iconic symbol of France, was constructed as an entrance for the International Exhibition of Paris in 1889, and is one of the most famous and most visited monuments in the world: the Paris Tower or the Eiffel Tower?

2085. What is the name of the famous domed building located in Washington, D.C. that is the meeting place for the Congress of the United States: the White House or the United States Capitol?

2086. What is the name of the famous cathedral in London with a large dome: St. Paul's Cathedral or Notre Dame Cathedral?

2087. What is the name of the famous domed gothic basilica in Florence, Italy called the Florence Duomo, is the symbol of the city, and is considered to be the largest brick dome ever built in the world: Santa Maria del Fiore or the Uffizi?

2088. What is the name of the largest concrete dome in the world located in Rome, Italy that was built as a temple for the Roman gods in 126 A.D: the Acropolis or the Pantheon?

2089. What is the name of the tallest dome in the world that was built on Vatican hill in Rome, Italy by several architects including Michelangelo, is considered the center for Christianity, and is the world's largest church: St. Peter's Cathedral or St. John's Cathedral?

2090. What is the name of the white marble mausoleum with a dome located in India, was built by a Muslim emperor in memory of his third wife, and is regarded as one of the eight wonders of the world: the Mausoleum of India or the Taj Mahal?

2091. What is the name of the colorful cathedral in Red Square in Moscow, Russia, was built by Ivan the Terrible in 1534, and is distinctive because of its nine colorful onion domes on top of the cathedral: the Moscow Cathedral or St. Basil's Cathedral?

2092. What is the name of the famous bridge in New York that connects Brooklyn and Manhattan over the East River, and at one time was the longest suspension bridge in the world: the Brooklyn Bridge or Manhattan Bridge?

2093. What is the name of one of the world's largest steel arch bridges located in Australia: the Sydney Harbour Bridge or the Sydney Opera House?

2094. What is the name of the bridge in London, England near Big Ben Clock Tower that has two towers connected at the top with two walkways, and is a suspension bridge over the Thames River: Tower Bridge or London Bridge?

2095. What is the name of the reddish-orange suspension bridge in San Francisco, California that was painted a bright color so it would be visible in the thick fog: the Golden Gate Bridge or the San Francisco Bridge?

2096. What is the name of the medieval stone arch bridge over the Arno River in Florence, Italy, translates as "old bridge" in Italian, and has shops, gold jewelry stores, and art galleries all along it: Ponte Vecchio or Puente Viejo?

SOCIAL STUDIES

2097. What is the name of the wall that is a national war memorial located in Washington, D.C., is dedicated to those who served and died in the Vietnam War, is made of black granite, and is engraved with the names of over 58,000 soldiers: Veterans Wall or Vietnam Veterans Memorial?

2098. What is the name of the famous wall that was built by the East Germans to divide East Germany from West Germany when each side had opposing political parties, and was finally torn down in 1989: the Iron Curtain or the Berlin Wall?

2099. What is the name of the wall in the old city of Jerusalem, Israel that is also regarded as the Wailing Wall, and is a religious center and place of pilgrimage for Jews: the Western Wall or the Holy Temple Wall?

2100. What is the name of the massive, protective walls that were built in the city-state Mesopotamia, includes the Ishtar Gate, and is one of the ancient wonders of the world: the Walls of Mesopotamia or the Walls of Babylon?

2101. What is the name of the wall in China that was initially started to protect China from the countries to the north, was built primarily during the Ming Dynasty, and is over 13,000 miles long: the Great Wall of China or the Great Border?

2102. What is the name of the rock in Massachusetts that marks the place where the Pilgrims arrived on the Mayflower, and is stamped with the date 1620: Pilgrim Rock or Plymouth Rock?

2103. What is the name of the stone in a castle in Ireland that is said to bring good luck if it is kissed: the Irish Stone or the Blarney Stone?

2104. What is the name of the limestone rock that is located in a strait south of Spain, is almost 1,400 feet high, and is under the jurisdiction of Great Britain: the Rock of Gibraltar or British Rock?

2105. What is the name of the piece of an Egyptian stone that weighs 1,700 pounds, became useful for translating Egyptian hieroglyphics into Greek because both were found on the stone, and is the most visited display in the British Museum: the Rashid Stone or the Rosetta Stone?

2106. Are many monuments and landmarks throughout the world made of stone?

2107. Which country in the world is known as the "Gift of the Nile:" Egypt or Morocco?'

2108. Which country in the world is known as the "Land of the Rising Sun:" Japan or China?

2109. Which country in the world is known as "The Boot:" Italy or Spain?

2110. Which country in the world is known as "The Land Down Under:" Australia or New Zealand?

2111. Which country has a vast, remote area called the "Outback:" New Zealand or Australia?

2112. Which country in the world is known as "The Red Dragon:" China or Japan?

2113. Which country in the world is known as the "Land of Milk and Honey:" Switzerland or Austria?

2114. Which country in the world is known as "The Emerald Isle:" Scotland or Ireland?

2115. Which country in the world is known as "The Holy Land:" Israel or India?

SOCIAL STUDIES

2116. Which country in the world is known as "The Great White North:" Canada or Greenland?

2117. Which country in the world is known as "The Melting Pot:" Canada or the United States?

2118. Which country in the world is known as "The Land of Fire and Ice:" Finland or Iceland?

2119. Which country in the world is known as "The Land of the Incas:" Bolivia or Peru?

2120. Which country in the world is known as "The Land of Hope and Glory:" England or Scotland?

2121. What is the nickname that references the American Government: "Uncle Sam" or "Melting Pot?"

2122. On which continent are China, India, Japan, Iran, Korea, and Russia: Asia or Africa?

2123. What general name is used to refer to an area of the world that includes Jordan, Iraq, Iran, Saudi Arabia, Pakistan, Afghanistan, and Israel: the Far East or the Middle East?

2124. What general name is used to refer to an area of the world that includes Indonesia, Singapore, Thailand, Korea, and Hong Kong: the Middle East or the Far East?

2125. What general name is used to refer to an area of the world that includes Russia, Poland, the Czech Republic, Hungary, Croatia, and Slovakia: Eastern Europe or Western Europe?

2126. What general name is used to refer to an area of the world that includes Spain, France, Germany, Italy, Austria, Switzerland, England, and Ireland: Eastern Europe or Western Europe?

2127. What general name is used to refer to an area of the world that includes Great Britain, Ireland, and over 6,000 smaller islands: the United Kingdom or the British Isles?

2128. What general name is used to refer to an area of the world that includes the countries of Great Britain, Scotland, Wales, and Northern Ireland: the British Isles or the United Kingdom?

2129. What general name is used to refer to an area of the world that include the countries of Denmark, Norway, and Sweden: The Netherlands or Scandinavia?

2130. What name is used to refer to the European country that is a sovereign state with twelve provinces in Western Europe, and three islands in the Caribbean: Belgium or The Netherlands?

2131. What is another term that is commonly used to refer to the seat of government in the Netherlands, with Amsterdam as its capital: Holland or The Hague?

2132. What country is famous for windmills, wooden shoes, and tulips: England or Holland?

2133. What is the nationality and language of a person living in the United Kingdom: English or Scottish?

2134. What is the nationality and language of a person living in Holland or the Netherlands: Swedish or Dutch?

2135. What is the language of a person living in Denmark, also the name for a type of donut: Kringle or Danish?

SOCIAL STUDIES

2136. What is the nationality of a person living in Denmark: Danish or Dutch?

2137. What is the nationality and language of a person living in Sweden: Swiss or Swedish?

2138. What is the nationality and language of a person living in Norway: Norse or Norwegian?

2139. What is the nationality of a person living in Belgium, also the name for a type of waffle: Swedish or Belgian?

2140. What language might a Belgian speak besides French and German: Dutch or Belgian?

2141. What is the nationality and language of a person living in Ireland?

2142. What is the nationality and language of a person living in France?

2143. What is the nationality and language of a person living in Spain?

2144. What is the nationality and language of a person living in Portugal: Spanish or Portuguese?

2145. What is the nationality of a person living in Brazil: Spanish or Portuguese?

2146. What is the nationality and language of a person living in Germany?

2147. What is the nationality and language of a person living in Italy?

2148. What is the nationality of a person living in Switzerland?

2149. What three languages are spoken in Switzerland: French, German, and Italian, or French, Spanish, and Dutch?

2150. What is the language of a person living in Austria: Austrian or German?

2151. What is the nationality and language of a person living in Poland?

2152. What is the nationality and language of a person living in Greece?

2153. What two languages are spoken in Vatican City: Latin and Italian, or Greek and Italian?

2154. What are two languages spoken in Israel: Latin and Hebrew, or Hebrew and Arabic?

2155. What is the number one language in the world that is spoken in China, Taiwan, Singapore, and Malaysia: Mandarin Chinese or Indonesian?

2156. What language is second in the world, spoken in Spain, Latin America, Mexico, and the United States?

2157. What language is third in the world, spoken in Australia, the United Kingdom, and the United States?

2158. What language is fourth in the world, spoken in India, Fiji, and Nepal: Hindi or Arabic?

2159. What language is fifth in the world, spoken in North Africa, East Africa, and the Middle East: Arabic or Hindi?

SOCIAL STUDIES

2160. What are the two official languages of Canada: French and English, or Canadian and French?

2161. What is the official language of Mexico?

2162. What is the official language of the United States: English or none?

2163. What language or languages do you speak?

2164. What is your nationality or your ethnic background?

2165. Do many people of the United States have more than one nationality?

2166. What civilizations can you name?

2167. What were three major civilizations of the Americas that existed before the arrival of the Europeans: Olmec, Zapotec, and Inca, or Maya, Aztec, and Inca?

2168. What two countries are primarily associated with the Maya civilization: Mexico and Guatemala, or Mexico and the United States?

2169. Which country is primarily associated with the Aztec civilization: Mexico or Guatemala?

2170. Which country is primarily associated with the Inca civilization: Peru or Argentina?

2171. What did the Maya develop throughout southern Mexico and Guatemala: towns or city-states?

2172. Did each Mayan city-state have its own government?

2173. Who was each Mayan city-state ruled by: a king or a priest?

2174. Did the Maya follow strict laws and have a court system?

2175. What is the name of the Maya city-state in the jungle of Guatemala with six large pyramids, and a great plaza: Tikal or Teotihuacan?

2176. What is the name of the city-state in the valley of Mexico that existed at the time of the Maya but was mysteriously abandoned by an earlier civilization, and includes the pyramids of the Sun and the Moon: Tenochtitlan or Teotihuacan?

2177. Who did the Maya build large temples in their city-states in honor of: gods or priests?

2178. What would the Mayan priests often do on the flat temples on top of the pyramids: perform sacrifices, or eat their meals?

2179. What is the name of the Mexican peninsula where the Maya established part of their civilization and built several pyramids: the Yucatan or the Iberian?

2180. What is the name of the most powerful Mayan city-state located in Mexico's Yucatan Peninsula that is dominated by the pyramid El Castillo in honor of the Mayan God Kukulkan or "Feathered Serpent," has a temple, several ball courts, and is one of the most visited tourist sites in Mexico: El Caracol or Chichen Itza?

SOCIAL STUDIES

2181. How many steps did the Maya include on the El Castillo pyramid that relate to the calendar year: 365 or 12?

2182. Which civilization built the pyramids located in the Petén in Guatemala that include El Tigre and La Danta, and were only recently discovered because they were covered by dense jungle: the Maya or the Aztecs?

2183. What did the Maya build to purposely align with movements of the Sun and the Moon: pyramids or temples?

2184. What animal appears every spring and fall equinox on the Maya pyramid El Castillo, when the Sun falls on the main stairway creating a shadow 120 feet long that joins with its serpent stone head at the bottom of the stairway?

2185. What was the name of the serpent god of the Maya: Itzamna or Kukulkan?

2186. Who was the main god of the Maya, the god of fire who created Earth: Itzamna or Kukulkan?

2187. Was religion important to the Maya civilization?

2188. Did the Maya believe that their rulers were related to their gods?

2189. Which ancient civilization had city-states that included Palenque, Uxmal, and Tulum: the Aztecs or the Maya?

2190. What was the name of the rain god of the Maya: Chac or Kukulkan?

2191. What did the Maya use to track time and religious rituals: clocks or calendars?

2192. How many calendars did the Maya have: one or three?

2193. How did the Maya use their religious calendar, the Tzolkin, their solar calendar, the Haab, and their Long Count calendar to track specific times and events: separately or simultaneously?

2194. Which Maya calendar predicted that the current cycle of life after 5126 years would end on December 21, 2012: The Long Count or the Haab?

2195. What is the name for Mayan books: codices or glyphs?

2196. Which Pre-Columbian civilization developed one of the most advanced number systems in the Americas: the Inca or the Maya?

2197. What kind of writing system did the Maya have: cave paintings or hieroglyphics?

2198. What number concept are the Maya credited for: zero or infinity?

2199. What number is the Maya math system based on: twenty or ten?

2200. What symbols did the Maya use to represent their numbers: ones and zeroes, or dots and bars?

2201. Did the Maya have a social class system?

SOCIAL STUDIES

2202. What is the correct order of the Maya hierarchy from most to least powerful: king, noble, commoner or noble, priest, and peasant?

2203. Did many of the Maya commoners work as farmers and hunters?

2204. What type of agriculture did the Maya peasant farmers practice: slash-and-burn or subsistence cultivation?

2205. What was the staple food of the Maya: wheat or maize, a type of corn?

2206. What did the Maya eat that comes from the Cacao tree: coconut or chocolate?

2207. What did the Maya often use for money: cacao beans or corn kernels?

2208. What is the name for the sinkhole that served as a source of water for the Maya, and may have been used for performing sacrifices: a cenote or a well?

2209. Which Mayan social class lived in palaces: the nobles or the commoners?

2210. Which Mayan class lived in huts made of mud with thatched roofs: the nobles or the commoners?

2211. What did the Maya use to play ball games as part of their religious ceremonies: a round stone or a rubber ball?

2212. What part of the body could not be used in the Mayan ball game: the hands or the feet?

2213. Which side might be sacrificed to the Gods as a result of the ball game: the losing side or the winning side?

2214. Did the Maya perform many dances like the "Monkey Dance" and the "Snake Dance?"

2215. What kind of art sculptures were the Maya famous for: clay or stone?

2216. Did the Maya use drums, wind instruments, and rattles to make music?

2217. What is the name of the pages that were folded like an accordion to form a book: a codex or a stela?

2218. What is the name for the large slab of stone in the shape of a pillar that is covered with carvings and hieroglyphics by the Maya: a codex or a stela?

2219. What is the name for the book or codex that contained information about Maya mythology and religion: Popol Vuh or Stela?

2220. Were wood and jade carvings also Mayan art forms?

2221. Did the Maya use a potter's wheel to make their pottery?

2222. What medium was used by the Maya to make masks: plaster or clay?

2223. What is the name of the rock that the Maya used to make tools: obsidian, a type of volcanic rock, or basalt stone?

SOCIAL STUDIES

2224. Who wore the more elaborate clothing and feathered headdresses: the Mayan nobles or the Mayan peasants?

2225. What is the name for the feathered jungle bird that the Maya used to make their headdresses: the Quetzal or the Tikal?

2226. What is the term for the peak time period or "golden age" of the Maya civilization between 250 and 900 A.D: pre-classic or classic?

2227. Is there some mystery attached to why the Maya abandoned their cities and what ultimately led to their disappearance?

2228. Did war, drought, or disease possibly contribute to the collapse of the Maya civilization?

2229. When did the Maya civilization end, also marking the arrival of the Spanish conquistadors: the 1400's or the 1500's?

2230. What is the name of another advanced civilization of Mexico: the Inca or the Aztec?

2231. What did the Aztecs observe, that they took as a sign from their god to build their city there: an eagle on a cactus holding a snake, or a hawk in a nest with a fish in its mouth?

2232. What was the name for the ancient capital city of the Aztecs that was built on a swampy island in a lake that is now modern Mexico City: Teotihuacan or Tenochtitlan?

2233. What was the Aztec Empire divided into: city-states or communities?

2234. What is the term for the raised roads that the Aztecs built in Tenochtitlan to connect with the mainland, along with the canals that served as water roads: overpasses or causeways?

2235. When might the Aztecs remove the causeways and bridges: when they wanted to navigate a boat, or when they were under attack by an enemy tribe?

2236. What is the Aztec name for the temple that was built in the center of the city: the Templo Mayor or the Temple of the Sun?

2237. Where were the palaces of the Aztec Emperors located: near the Temple, or on hill overlooking the city?

2238. Where was the Aztec government located: at Tenochtitlan or at the Emperor's palace?

2239. Who was the supreme ruler of the land in Aztec times: the Sun god or the Emperor?

2240. What were Montezuma I and Montezuma II famous for: serving as powerful Aztec Emperors, or serving as enemy warriors to the Aztecs?

2241. Did the Aztecs have a social class system of an emperor, nobles, and peasants?

2242. Were priests, judges, and military leaders considered high level or low level Aztec officials?

2243. Did the Aztecs believe that their Emperor was appointed by their gods?

SOCIAL STUDIES

2244. What did the Aztecs consider to be the most important part of their religion: honoring the Moon or honoring the Sun?

2245. What rituals did the Aztecs practice to please their gods: fasting or sacrifices?

2246. What did the Aztecs believe they needed to sacrifice to the Sun so that the Sun would rise on that day: human blood or human teeth?

2247. What kinds of animals were the Aztec gods represented with: lions and bears, or serpents and jaguars?

2248. What is the name of the most powerful Aztec god, the god of war, Sun and sacrifice: Tlaloc or Huitzilopochtli?

2249. What is the name of the Aztec god of rain and water: Tlaloc or Huitzilopochtli?

2250. What is the name of the Aztec god whose name means "feathered serpent," the god of life and wind: Huitzilopochtli or Quetzalcoatl?

2251. What was the basic unit of Aztec culture: the family or the government?

2252. What is the name of the language that was spoken by the Aztecs: Spanish or Nahuatl?

2253. What language are the words chocolate, coyote, avocado and chili: Spanish or Nahuatl?

2254. Did the Aztec men work as farmers and warriors?

2255. What is a term for the Aztec method of farming whereby the Aztecs created artificial floating islands in shallow lake beds in order to grow crops: terracing or chinampas?

2256. What was the Aztec's main crop that could be stored for a long time and ground up into flour to make tortillas and other foods: wheat or maize?

2257. What food did the Aztecs succeed in introducing the world to, made from heated corn kernels: tortillas or popcorn?

2258. What was the role of Aztec women: to cook and sew in the home, or to help on the farm and create handicrafts?

2259. Did Aztec women weave all the clothes?

2260. Was the clothing worn by the Aztec nobility the same or different as the clothing worn by the commoners?

2261. Which social class of Aztec society would wear the feathers and the jewelry: the nobles or the peasants?

2262. What did the Aztecs use to make chocolate: cocoa beans or cocoa bark?

2263. What Aztec word does chocolate come from: chocolatl or choco?

2264. What is the term for the structure that was built and used by many Pre-Columbian civilizations that brought fresh water into the city: a cenote or an aqueduct?

SOCIAL STUDIES

2265. Did the Aztecs have marketplaces to buy and sell food and crafts?

2266. How did the Aztecs use pottery, sculptures, feather-work, and jewelry: for honoring their gods, or for decorating their houses?

2267. What is one of the most famous sculptures of the Aztecs, weighs over 24 tons, and measures 12 feet in diameter: the Aztec Calendar or the Aztec Sundial?

2268. What was an important form of art for the Aztecs, passed down orally from one generation to the next: poetry or drama?

2269. Were Aztec children required by law to attend school?

2270. What is the name for the Aztec writing system of symbols: code or glyphs?

2271. What is the name of the Aztec book that was the same for the Maya: codex or slate?

2272. Did the Aztecs play a ball game on a ball court with a rubber ball as a way of preparing for war?

2273. What time measurement device did the Aztecs use to measure the passing of time according to the Sun, and as a guide for having their festivals and religious ceremonies: the Aztec Calendar or the Sundial?

2274. How many calendars did the Aztecs follow: one or two?

2275. If the Aztecs used one solar calendar to mark time, what did their other calendar calculate: weather and seasons, or festivals and ceremonies?

2276. What did the Aztecs use to cure sicknesses besides steam baths: herbs or cornhusks?

2277. Were the Spanish at an advantage or disadvantage over the Aztec warriors and Montezuma with their horses and their guns?

2278. Which country did Hernán Cortés, governor of Cuba, want to take the Aztec treasures to after hearing of the Aztec riches and gold: Cuba or Spain?

2279. What disease did the Spanish bring with them to the New World: smallpox or chicken pox?

2280. Who was the Spanish conquistador who ended the rule of the powerful Aztec empire in 1521, after 200 years in the Valley of Mexico: Francisco Pizarro or Hernán Cortés?

2281. Which Aztec city did Hernán Cortés finally succeed in capturing and conquering in 1521: Teotihuacan or Tenochtitlan?

2282. What is the new name for the capital of New Spain after Tenochtitlan was taken over by the Spanish: Madrid or Mexico City?

2283. What is the name of the Indian civilization that ruled Peru at the time that the Aztecs ruled the Valley of Mexico: the Inca or the Toltec?

SOCIAL STUDIES

2284. What is the name of the Indian group before the Incas, famous for their long lines that include images of monkeys, spiders, and fish that can be observed when flying over the plateaus along the southern coast of Peru: Moche or Nazca?

2285. What is the name for the mountains in Peru where the Incas established their cities?

2286. Did the Incas have a social class system of rulers, nobles, and peasants?

2287. Did the Inca believe that their rulers were descendants of their gods?

2288. Was the Inca ruler considered a king and the most powerful leader in the land?

2289. What is the name of the Inca ruler translated as "sole ruler:" Sapa Inca or Sola Inca?

2290. What is the name of the Sun god of the Inca: Sol or Inti?

2291. What is the name of the capital city of the Inca Empire that was established as a city-state where the Sapa Inca lived and ruled the surrounding lands: Lima or Cuzco?

2292. What is the altitude of the Inca city of Cuzco: 11,000 feet above sea level, or 4,000 feet above sea level?

2293. Did the Inca Empire extend to the countries of Ecuador, Chile, Argentina, and Bolivia at the height of its power?

2294. What is the name of the language of the Inca people: Nahuatl or Quechua?

2295. What was the job of most Inca peasants: farming the land, or weaving textiles?

2296. Did some Inca commoners work as artisans and make colorful crafts and pottery?

2297. What is the trade name for many Incas who built massive walls out of large stones that fitted together so perfectly that no mortar was necessary: bricklayers or stonemasons?

2298. Did the Incas have extensive stone roads that connected their cities?

2299. What kind of bridges did the Inca build: rope suspension bridges or stone-paved bridges?

2300. What animals did the Inca raise to make wool and colorful textiles from wool dyed with plants: sheep or llamas?

2301. What animal similar to the llama was raised by the Incas and shaved for its wool: alpaca or camel?

2302. How did the Incas turn steep hills into usable farmland: they created terraces on the steep slope, or they simply plowed and tilled the hillside?

2303. Did the Inca develop water and irrigation systems to help grow their crops?

2304. What was the most important crop of the Incas: corn or potatoes?

2305. Were corn, potatoes, beans, squash, ducks, and fish all part of the Inca diet?

SOCIAL STUDIES

2306. What did the Inca men and women wear: colorful tunics and dresses, or white linen pants and dresses?

2307. What kind of houses did the Inca families live in: adobe huts or stone longhouses?

2308. What were the Inca peasants required to pay to the government: taxes or farming dues?

2309. Which social class of the Inca attended school: the children of nobles, the children of the peasants, or all children?

2310. What were the two purposes of the Inca calendar: to mark religious occasions and the seasons for planting crops, or to monitor the movement of the Sun and to predict the solstices?

2311. What did the Inca use for medicine: herbal tea leaves or coca leaves?

2312. What is the name for the large stone city of the Inca Empire that was built as a royal estate for an Inca Emperor and other nobles, and located 8,000 feet above sea level in the Andes Mountains: Chichen Itza or Machu Picchu?

2313. What is the name of the explorer who re-discovered the lost city of Machu Picchu high in the Andes in 1911 in the deep jungle: Francisco Pizarro or Hiram Bingham?

2314. What is the name of the explorer and Spanish conquistador who joined Vasco Nuñez de Balboa and crossed the Isthmus of Panama to get to the Pacific Ocean: Hernan Cortés or Francisco Pizarro?

2315. What was Francisco Pizarro's motivation to lead his own expedition and explore South America: gold or jade?

2316. What was Francisco Pizarro's goal on his third expedition to South America: to conquer the Inca and claim all the gold, or to establish new settlements and colonize South America?

2317. Who had the advantage of guns, horses, cannons, and better weapons: the Inca or the Spanish?

2318. Who is considered the conqueror of the Inca Empire in 1533: Cortés or Pizarro?

2319. Where did many explorers come from to explore the "New World," and to increase trade opportunities: Europe or Asia?

2320. Which European country on the Iberian Peninsula explored the oceans and Africa in the 1400's under Prince Henry the Navigator and Bartolomeu Dias, in search of new trade routes: Spain or Portugal?

2321. What is the name of the famous Italian explorer who "sailed the ocean blue in 1492" on behalf of the Spanish King and Queen?

2322. What are the names of the King and Queen of Spain who agreed to fund the voyage of Columbus to the New World with the hope of spreading Christianity, opening new trade routes, and obtaining spices from the Indies to flavor up their food: Ferdinando and Isabella, or Felipe and Sofia?

2323. What land is between Europe and Asia, land that Columbus did not know existed: Australia or the Americas?

SOCIAL STUDIES

2324. Which country did Columbus believe he could sail to by traveling west: China in the East Indies, or America?

2325. What were the names of Columbus's three ships?

2326. What was the flagship or principle ship of Christopher Columbus: the Niña, the Pinta, or the Santa María?

2327. What was the name that Columbus gave to the island in the Bahamas where he and his men landed on October 12, 1492: San Salvador or India?

2328. What was the name that Columbus gave to the natives because he believed he had landed somewhere in the East Indies: Natives or Indians?

2329. What animal did Columbus bring over on his second voyage to the New World: the chicken or the horse?

2330. How many total voyages did Columbus make to the Americas: three or four?

2331. When Columbus died in 1506, did he still believe that he had successfully sailed to Asia?

2332. What is the date of Columbus Day that is celebrated in Spain and the Americas: October 10th or October 12th?

2333. What places can you name in the United States that are named for Columbus?

2334. Who is the Italian explorer, navigator, and cartographer (mapmaker) after whom the continents of North and South America are named: Amerigo Vespucci or Americus Vasco?

2335. Are there many plazas, statues, parks, subway stops, and monuments named for Columbus in Mexico, the Bahamas, Spain and Portugal?

2336. What is the name of the Portuguese explorer who wanted to find a trade route around Africa to India: Vasco de Gama or Pedro Cabral?

2337. What is the name of the Portuguese explorer who set out for India, landed in South America, and claimed the country of Brazil for Portugal: Vasco de Gama or Pedro Cabral?

2338. What is the language spoken in Brazil: Spanish or Portuguese?

2339. What tactical advantage did the Portuguese have when they landed in India that they used to help them establish a trading post, and to control trade routes that had originally been controlled by Muslims: cannons or muskets?

2340. What is the name of the Portuguese explorer that is known for leading the first expedition to sail around the world in 1519 with the support of King Charles of Spain: Vasco de Gama or Ferdinand Magellan?

2341. What was the primary goal of Magellan: to discover another route to Eastern Asia, or to bring home spices from the "Spice Islands?"

SOCIAL STUDIES

2342. What is the name for the strait located in the southern tip of South America that allows the passage of ships from the Atlantic to the Pacific, and is named for a Portuguese explorer: the Strait of Magellan or the Strait of Gibraltar?

2343. What were the Trinidad, the Santiago, the Victoria, the San Antonio, and the Concepción: the five ships of Magellan, or the names that Magellan gave to five islands he discovered?

2344. What is the name of the cape on the southern tip of Africa that the Magellan expedition sailed around on the return voyage to Spain: the Cape of Magellan or the Cape of Good Hope?

2345. Which ocean, meaning "peaceful," is Magellan credited for naming: the Atlantic or the Pacific?

2346. How long did it take Magellan to cross the Pacific once he sailed through the Strait of Magellan on the way to the east: four days or four months?

2347. Was Magellan able to see his expedition through until the end, or was he killed in a battle with natives of the Philippines?

2348. How many of the 260 sailors successfully completed the 42,000-mile voyage around the world in 1522 on the Victoria, the only surviving ship: 28 or 18?

2349. What is the name of the sailors from the Netherlands who also started to explore the sea and find new trade routes after breaking away from Spain: the Dutch or the French?

2350. What did the English have in the East Indies with the East India Company: a trade monopoly or a trade partnership?

2351. When Pizarro, Columbus, De Gama, Magellan, and other Europeans came to the Americas, where do we say they came from: the Old World or the New World?

2352. What is the name for the lands that Europeans wanted to establish in the New World while governing those lands from their own country: colonies or settlements?

2353. How many colonies did the British have in the United States that later became known as our original first states: ten or thirteen?

2354. Did the Europeans set up colonies in the New World to farm and to mine for gold and silver?

2355. What people living in the colonies were forced to work on the farms and plantations in the New World: the English or the natives?

2356. What was a principal crop grown on larger plantations that was a big industry in Portuguese colonies: corn or sugarcane?

2357. What is the term for the transportation of slaves from across the ocean from the Old World to the New World: international trade zone or transatlantic slave trade?

2358. What types of crops were grown on the large plantations in the 1600's: sugar, coffee, and cotton, or corn, wheat, and potatoes?

SOCIAL STUDIES

2359. Which continent did the European colonists import slaves from after many of the natives of the colonized lands died from European diseases: Asia or Africa?

2360. What are the names of the two coasts of Africa where many slaves were sold from: the Gold and Angolan Coasts or the Northern and Eastern Coasts?

2361. What is the term for the three-way system that took finished goods like guns and molasses from Europe to Africa, slaves from Africa to the colonies in the Americas, and raw materials like sugar, cotton and tobacco from the New World back to Europe: the Slave Passage or Triangular Trade?

2362. What is the term for the second part of the triangle trade route between the 1500's and 1800's that carried hundreds of slaves on a cramped ship from Africa to the New World on a voyage that often took over three months: the Second Leg or the Middle Passage?

2363. What is the name of the colonial city where a Dutch ship, the White Lion, released 20 slaves in 1619 that it captured, and marked the beginning of slavery in America: Jamestown or Boston?

2364. What is the estimate of the number of slaves that came from Africa to the New World to work as slaves: two million or twelve million?

2365. Did places in Europe like Italy and Greece have a renewed focus on books and learning during the time of European exploration to the New World?

2366. What languages were many Greek language books translated into by Islamic scholars: Arabic or Latin?

2367. What language were many books written in Arabic translated into: Greek or Latin?

2368. What is the name for the revival of Greek and Roman architecture, art, literature, and learning that began in the 14th century in Italy, quickly spread throughout Europe, and was regarded as a "rebirth:" Renaissance or Medieval?

2369. What was the time frame of the Renaissance: 1400-1700 or 1300-1600?

2370. What is another name for the Age of Exploration in Europe that took place at the same time as the Renaissance between the 1400's and 1600's: Age of Enlightenment or Age of Discovery?

2371. During the Age of Discovery, did the Europeans succeed in discovering new routes to Asia and the Americas?

2372. What is the name of the most powerful empire of the time that ruled the Middle East for close to 600 years from 1299 until 1923, captured the Turkish capital Constantinople and renamed it Istanbul in 1453, and forced many artists and scholars to leave the Middle East for Italy: the Ottoman Empire or the Turkish Empire?

2373. Did the start of the Renaissance mark the beginning or the end of the Dark Ages?

2374. What is the term for the way of thinking that was characterized by a renewed interest in science, art, and music: liberal arts or humanism?

SOCIAL STUDIES

2375. Are history, poetry, and philosophy considered liberal arts or humanities?

2376. What is the name of the city in Italy that the Renaissance is said to have started, around 1350: Rome or Florence?

2377. What was the inspiration for the humanists of Florence, Italy to think about life in a new way: the ancient writings of the Greeks and Romans, or the teachings of ancient philosophers?

2378. What is the name of the rich and powerful family in Florence, Italy who promoted the humanist movement by supporting and sponsoring many artists, building churches to display artworks, building a library to provide books, and making Florence the center of learning and art: Plato or Medici?

2379. Who were Michelangelo, Raphael, Botticelli, Donatello, and Leonardo da Vinci, all supported by the Medici family: Renaissance architects or Renaissance artists?

2380. Who painted the *Sistine Chapel* in Rome and sculpted the *David*: Michelangelo or Leonardo da Vinci?

2381. Who painted the *Mona Lisa* and *The Last Supper*: Michelangelo or Leonardo da Vinci?

2382. Who is Galileo Galilei, whose scientific research was supported by the Medici family: an Italian scientist or an Italian artist?

2383. What did Galileo develop during the Renaissance: the Scientific Method or the telephone?

2384. Who invented the telescope, discovered the moons of Jupiter, the phases of Venus, sunspots, and observed that the Moon is covered with craters: Galileo or Johannes Kepler?

2385. What part of the first mechanical clock did Galileo design and develop during the Renaissance: the pendulum or the second hand?

2386. What is the name of the study of stars and celestial bodies that developed during the Renaissance: Astrology or Astronomy?

2387. Did Nicolaus Copernicus theorize that the Earth and planets orbit the Sun, or that the Sun orbits the Earth and the planets?

2388. What Renaissance scientist developed the three laws of planetary motion: Johannes Kepler or Johannes Gutenberg?

2389. What is the name of the Italian author who wrote "The Divine Comedy" at the beginning of the Renaissance in Florence in the early 1300's, considered the greatest work of Italian literature: Dante or Ficino?

2390. Who is Filippo Brunelleschi: a Renaissance artist or a Renaissance archiitect?

2391. What is the name of the Italian artist who painted a mural in a convent in Milan, Italy during the high renaissance in 1495 entitled *The Last Supper*: Leonardo da Vinci or Michelangelo?

SOCIAL STUDIES

2392. What is the name of Leonardo da Vinci's portrait of a lady that hangs in the Louvre museum in Paris, and is regarded as the most famous and most visited artwork in the world?

2393. What is the name of the Italian artist and sculptor that sculpted one of the most visited sculptures in the world, the *David* in Florence in 1501, as well as the ceiling of the *Sistine Chapel* in 1508 in Vatican City?

2394. What is the name of the Italian artist famous for his fresco painting on a library wall in the Pope's palace at the Vatican entitled *The School of Athens*, a painting that includes ancient Greek philosophers like Aristotle, Plato, Socrates, Euclid, and Pythagoras, was painted in 1511, and is considered this artist's masterpiece: Raphael or Michelangelo?

2395. What was the profession of Donatello, Jan Van Eyck, Masaccio, Botticelli, Leonardo da Vinci, Michelangelo, Raphael, and Caravaggio: Renaissance architects or Renaissance artists?

2396. Which artist is known as the "father of Renaissance painting:" Donatello or Masaccio?

2397. Did the art and architecture of Florence also spread to other Italian cities like Rome, Milan, Bologna, and Venice?

2398. Did Renaissance architecture include domes, columns, and arches?

2399. What kind of architecture does the Sistine Chapel in Vatican City and St. Peter's Basilica in Rome reflect: Modern or Renaissance?

2400. Did the Renaissance spread to other parts of Europe as well?

2401. Were the courts of princes important during the time of the Renaissance?

2402. What is the name of the famous Italian author who wrote "The Prince," a story about how a prince should lead and act during times of conflict and war: Castiglione or Machiavelli?

2403. What was the main church during the Renaissance: Catholic or Protestant?

2404. What was a popular form of entertainment during the Renaissance: music and dance, or reading and cooking?

2405. Were checkers, chess, masquerade balls, and festivals all Renaissance forms of entertainment?

2406. Did the type of food, clothing, and education depend on the social status of a person during the Renaissance?

2407. What specific dance was first introduced during the Renaissance: folk dance or ballet?

2408. What is the term for the form of vocal music that became popular during the Renaissance, with singers singing in distinct voices: choir or madrigal?

2409. What musical instrument was first made in Italy in the 1500's: the flute or the violin?

2410. What was the most important invention made during the Renaissance in 1440 that made it possible for information to be communicated to many people in a timely manner: the radio or the printing press?

SOCIAL STUDIES

2411. Who invented the printing press in 1440 with moveable metal pieces that paved the way for many books to be printed in Latin, English, Italian, German, and French: Johannes Gutenberg or Johannes Kepler?

2412. What was the first book that was mass produced by Gutenberg: The Gutenberg Poems or The Gutenberg Bible?

2413. What is the name for the spreading of Renaissance ideas to France, Germany, and England: The Northern Renaissance or The Southern Renaissance?

2414. What is the name of the German priest who opposed many Catholic Church practices and thought that the Bible was the only religious authority: Martin Luther or Luther Martin?

2415. What was the name given to the German Priest Martin Luther and others who publicly objected to the teachings of the church: Reformists or Protestants?

2416. What was the name given to the followers of Martin Luther: Lutherans or Protestants?

2417. What did Martin Luther's call for a new type of Christianity become known as: the Reformation or the Inquisition?

2418. What is John Calvin known as, a French man who aligned his beliefs with his interpretation of the Bible, and developed a system known as Calvinism: a Protestant or a Lutheran?

2419. What was the result of the Reformation: Christianity sub-divided into groups that included Catholics, Lutherans, Baptists, and Mennonites, or Christianity only reflected the teachings of the Catholic Church?

2420. What is the name of the Spanish Catholic Priest who founded the Society of Priests that became known as Jesuits, and established many schools in America: Ignatius of Loyola or Martin Luther?

2421. What is the name of the English king that is most famous for separating the churches in England, and having eight wives: King Henry VIII or King Edward VI?

2422. What is the name of the church created in England by King Henry VIII after he wanted to break ties with the Catholic Church when it refused to allow him to divorce his wife because she did not produce a male heir for him: The Puritan Church or the Church of England?

2423. What era was considered the golden age, the age of peace and prosperity when art, music, theatre, literature, and exploration all flourished in the 1600's: Elizabethan or Shakespearean?

2424. Who wore, silk, velvet, and ruffled collars: the monarch, or the monarch and the nobility?

2425. What did Queen Elizabeth I, who never married claiming she was married to her country, try to convert the Church of England into: a Catholic Church or a Protestant Church?

2426. What is the term given for people that wanted to *purify* the church by doing away with some Catholic traditions: Protestants or Puritans?

2427. Was England united or divided, having both devoted Catholics and devoted Puritans?

SOCIAL STUDIES

2428. What was the Elizabethan Era most famous for: its music or its theatre?

2429. What are the "Red Lion," the "Curtain," and the "Globe:" famous theatres in England or famous plays in England?

2430. Who is considered the greatest writer in the English Language, famous for his plays, dramas, and 14-line sonnet poems?

2431. What genre were Shakespeare's works, "Romeo and Juliet," and "A Midsummer Night's Dream: poems or plays?

2432. Were Shakespeare's works, "Hamlet," "Macbeth," "King Lear," and "Othello" sonnets or plays?

2433. How many lines does a sonnet poem have: 12 or 14?

2434. Who were Shakespeare's plays often performed for: Elizabeth I and King James I, thousands of spectators, or both nobles and spectators?

2435. What did Elizabeth I do to share in the riches of the Spanish ships on their trade routes: pirate them and claim the riches for England, or send out her own ships to claim the riches?

2436. Was there tension between the King Phillip II of Spain and the Elizabeth I, the monarch of England?

2437. What is the name of the fleet of 130 Spanish ships that King Phillip II of Spain put together to take over England: The Spanish Galleons or The Spanish Armada?

2438. Whom did Elizabeth I dub a knight, and appoint as the naval captain of the British fleet: Sir Francis Drake or Sir Duke?

2439. Which side won the naval battle in 1588 due to a surprise attack and a storm, and became the most powerful naval force in the world: the English or the Spanish?

2440. Was the Spanish Armada thought to have been invincible?

2441. Did Sir Francis Drake and the British continue to dominate the seas, as well as take over other treasure ships?

2442. What is Sir Francis Drake credited for besides defeating the mighty Spanish Armada: he was the first Englishman to sail around the world, or he was the second Englishman to sail around the world?

2443. How long was the reign of Queen Elizabeth I: 44 years or 14 years?

2444. What is the name of the state that Sir Walter Raleigh named for Queen Elizabeth I because she was celebrated as England's "virgin queen:" Virginia or West Virginia?

2445. Who was Queen Elizabeth I succeeded by: James I of Scotland or Charles I of Denmark?

2446. What book did King James I develop a new translation of that had a great impact on religious life and Protestant practices: the King James Bible or the Holy Bible?

SOCIAL STUDIES

2447. What is the name of the first permanent English colony in 1607 named for King James I in Virginia: Kingston or Jamestown?

2448. Did King James I believe that he was an agent of God here on Earth and should never be disobeyed?

2449. Did King James I and his son Charles I rule England with or without an English Parliament?

2450. Did tensions escalate between Puritans and Protestants when Charles I, a Protestant, married a Catholic?

2451. Which New England state did many Puritans emigrate to: Massachusetts or Virginia?

2452. What kind of war resulted in 1642 because of the religious tension between the Parliament and Royalists, or those who supported the King: the English Civil War or the English War of Succession?

2453. Which side won the English Civil War in 1649: the Parliament or the Royalists?

2454. Who is the General who lead the Parliament known as the Roundheads, and became England's new leader: Oliver Cromwell or Charles II?

2455. Did Oliver Cromwell enforce strict Puritan rules in England, or were religious expectations loosened up?

2456. Did the English people accept the strict Puritan laws or did they want to bring back the monarchy?

2457. What is the name of the new king in 1660 that brought back the Church of England: Charles II or Charles III?

2458. Was King James II, the brother of Charles II, a Catholic King or a Protestant King?

2459. Who became the new monarchs after King James II left for France, running away from Dutch troops that wanted to restore the Protestant faith: William and Mary, or Edward and Victoria?

2460. What was the name given to the English Revolution in 1688-1689 that resulted in the peaceful overthrow of the unpopular King James II: the Protestant Revolution or the Glorious Revolution?

2461. What did the English Parliament pass in 1689 that established the powers of the Parliament, and placed limits on the powers of the monarch as proclaimed basic liberties: the Bill of Rights, or the Magna Carta?

2462. Did many Renaissance ideas spread to Western Europe during the 1400's?

2463. Did Renaissance art and architecture also influence Russian culture?

2464. What is the name of the Russian prince who was regarded as the Grand Prince of Moscow between 1462 and 1505, is credited with uniting many Russian provinces, freeing Russia from the Mongols, and even went so far as to call himself "czar:" Ivan the Great or Ivan the Terrible?

2465. What is the name of the grandson of Ivan the Great who reigned between 1533-1547, was the first crowned czar of Russian with the title Grand Prince of Moscow, had St. Basil's Cathedral built for him at the Kremlin in Moscow, and is named for his strict rule and control: Ivan the Horrible or Ivan the Terrible?

SOCIAL STUDIES

2466. What is the name of the Russian czar in the late 17th century who is best known for his reforms, helping to establish Russia as a powerful nation extending the border to the Baltic Sea, and building a new capital city, St. Petersburg that is named for him: Peter the Great or Peter the Terrible?

2467. What is the name of the longest ruling empress of Russia who increased the territory of the empire, and modernized Russia under her reign: Empress Catherine or Catherine the Great?

2468. Did emperors and empresses lead other Asian nations during the 1400's and 1500's?

2469. What is the name for the Asian country made up of four islands with Tokyo as its capital?

2470. What types of storms are common in Japan: monsoons, typhoons, and tsunamis, or tornados, blizzards, and hurricanes?

2471. What is Japan also known as: "Land of Storms," or "Land of the Rising Sun?"

2472. Did many landowners in Japan often fight each other for more power?

2473. What is the name for the four-tiered class system in Japan that included the emperor seat at the top, followed by the daimyo or landholder, the samurai warrior, and the peasants: Feudalism or socialism?

2474. In the Japanese Feudal system, were the emperor and shogun or general at the top or the bottom of the pyramid?

2475. Was the daimyo, the Japanese landowner, above or below the emperor?

2476. What is the name for the military warriors in feudal Japan that carried two swords: samurai or swordsmen?

2477. What is the correct order of importance of the Japanese feudal structure among the peasants: farmers, artisans, and merchants, or merchants, artisans, and farmers?

2478. What is the name of the religion or way of life practiced in Japan that began in India and spread throughout Asia, and is a belief system based on enlightenment: Buddhism or Shintoism?

2479. What is the name of the prince from India in the 6th century who chose to help the poor rather than keep his riches, whose name means "enlightened one," and is the person that the Japanese belief system is based on: Buddha or Shinto?

2480. What do many Buddhists practice to help them focus and become "enlightened:" Yoga or Meditation?

2481. Are their many statues, temples, and shrines throughout Asia in honor of Buddha?

2482. What works of art did the Japanese create with bridges, plants, and flowers that help the Japanese to meditate and further serve to quiet the mind: parks or gardens?

2483. Who is the French artist who painted an artwork called "Japanese Footbridge" in the impressionist style because he was greatly inspired by the beauty of Japanese gardens: Claude Monet or Edgar Degas?

SOCIAL STUDIES

2484. What is the term for the Japanese belief system that incorporates the worship of nature spirits and Japanese ancestors: Shintoism or Buddhism?

2485. What is the general term for the period of re-birth that lasted between the 1300's and the 1600's and impacted many regions of the world: Medieval Ages or Renaissance?

2486. What is the name for the American time period between 1607 and 1763: the Colonial Period or British Expansion Period?

2487. In which direction did many early settlers move: east or west?

2488. What natural barrier prevented the early settlers from moving farther west: the Rocky Mountains or the Appalachian Mountains?

2489. Did many early settlers desire more land than was available for hunting and farming in 1775?

2490. What is the name of one of the first territories settled that includes the states of Ohio, Illinois, Indiana, Wisconsin, and Michigan: Northwest Territory or Northeast Territory?

2491. What is the name of the frontiersman that led settlers through the Cumberland Gap, a narrow passage through the Appalachian Mountains and into the state of Kentucky: Daniel Boone or Davy Crocket?

2492. What is the name of the trail or road that was paved on Boone's second expedition into Kentucky: the Western Road or the Wilderness Trail?

2493. Did Daniel Boone meet up with some resistance from the Indians who did not welcome new settlers?

2494. What is the name of the transaction made by President Thomas Jefferson when he made in a deal with France to acquire land west of the Mississippi River to the Rocky Mountains, in exchange for $15 million dollars, nearly doubling the size of the country: the Treaty of Paris or the Louisiana Purchase?

2495. What are the names of the two explorers that Jefferson sent out to explore and map the Louisiana Territory and the Wild West: Lewis and Clark or Boone and Crocket?

2496. How did the Native American woman Sacagawea help them on their journey: as a cook or as an interpreter?

2497. What trade industry became popular in the early 1800's, and the Great Lakes provided passageways that helped the transport of this trade, further attracting frontiersmen and mountain men to the West: the fur trade or the gold trade?

2498. Did many American traders continue to settle lands in the Eastern States like New Mexico, California, and Oregon?

2499. What is the term that is often used to describe the early settlers who travelled from place to place throughout the west: explorers or pioneers?

2500. What is the name of the people that settled in Great Salt Lake in Utah, led by Brigham Young, where they could avoid persecution and peacefully observe the teachings of the Church of Jesus Christ of Latter Day Saints: Mormons or Christians?

SOCIAL STUDIES

2501. What attracted thousands of people to California in 1848 after a man noticed shiny flakes of this metal in the water running through his sawmill?

2502. What is the term for the influx of people to California in 1848 and 1849: the Gold Rush or the Fur Trade?

2503. What is the name that was given to the more than 90,000 gold prospectors who arrived from Mexico, China, Europe, and Australia in 1849 with the dream of striking it rich: forty-niners or prospectors?

2504. What is the name of the process of separating the dirt and gravel from the gold: sifting or panning?

2505. What is the name that referred to the camps that would grow into towns during the gold rush because of the arrival of all the miners: ghost towns or boom towns?

2506. What is the name given to the boom towns after they were abandoned, like the Californian city of Bodie: ghost towns or deserted towns?

2507. In which state are the ghost towns "Virginia City" and "Nevada City: California or Montana?

2508. What is the name that was given to the caravans of pioneers who would travel thousands of miles in covered wagons pulled by oxen or mules through rugged terrain on their journey to California, often invading Indian land and angering Native Americans in the process: wagon trains or prairie schooners?

2509. What was the greater danger to the westbound wagon trains: conflicts with Native Americans, or weather, crossing rivers, and the risk of disease?

2510. What is the name for the primary route that the pioneers took in covered wagon trains between 1841 and 1849 when migrating to the west, a journey that began in Missouri and crossed Kansas, Nebraska, Wyoming, Idaho, and Oregon: the Westward Trail or the Oregon Trail?

2511. When were "Westward Ho," and "There's Gold in Them Thar Hills" popular refrains: during the Gold Rush, or during the Lewis and Clark Expedition?

2512. What kinds of homes did many early pioneers build: log homes or longhouses?

2513. Whose role was it to cook, clean, make soap, spin wool, make clothing, wash, iron, and tend to the garden: the frontiersman, the frontier woman, or the frontier children?

2514. Whose role was it to build a cabin, build a barn, and farm the field with a plow and oxen: the frontiersman, the frontier woman, or the frontier children?

2515. Whose role was it to milk the cows, feed the chickens, chop the wood, and help out with other pioneer chores: the frontiersman, the frontier woman, or the frontier children?

2516. Which two seasons of the year would the children attend school, all grade levels in a one-room schoolhouse with one teacher, learning basic reading, writing, spelling, and history: summer and winter, or spring and autumn?

2517. Which two seasons of the year would the children stay home to help with the planting and the harvesting: summer and winter, or spring and autumn?

SOCIAL STUDIES

2518. Who would sing, dance, play fiddles, and play with simple toys for entertainment during colonial America: farmers or pioneers?

2519. Why were droughts, tornados, wildfires, and locusts a big concern to the pioneers?

2520. Who invented the plow in 1837 that made farming easier for the pioneers: John Deere or Allis Chalmers?

2521. What group of people would often help the pioneers with the planting of crops and using certain herbs for medicine: the English colonists or the Native Americans?

2522. What were the bathrooms of the pioneers called: outhouses or longhouses?

2523. What were many pioneer houses made from: log and adobe, or wood and brick?

2524. How did the pioneers put together their log cabins with the trees on their land: with nails, or with notches they would cut on the ends of the logs?

2525. What would pioneers use to seal the cracks between the logs: mortar or mud?

2526. Did many pioneer homes have a stone fireplace and a few pieces of furniture?

2527. What is the term for the belief of many people in the United States that it was their right and the country's destiny to expand west all the way to the Pacific Ocean: Westward Manifesto or Manifest Destiny?

2528. Which southern state did many Americans immigrate to in 1821 even though it was governed by Mexico: Arizona or Texas?

2529. Who won the battle between Mexico and the Texans in 1836 when Mexican General Santa Anna and his soldiers surrounded a Spanish Mission called the Alamo in San Antonio, Texas that was the fortress for 180 Texans: the Mexicans or the Texans?

2530. What two famous frontiersmen were defeated at the battle of the Alamo: Davy Crockett and Jim Bowie, or Daniel Boone and Wild Bill?

2531. What did the Texans yell six weeks later during the fight with the Mexicans: "Remember the Alamo," or "Texas belongs to America?"

2532. What did Texas become after General Santa Anna was captured and the Mexicans were defeated at the Battle of San Jacinto in 1836: the State of Texas or the Republic of Texas?

2533. When did Texas officially become a state: 1845 or 1855?

2534. What is the name of the war that was fought between the United States and Mexico over the State of Texas and the border: the Spanish-American War, or the Mexican-American War?

2535. Who is the American President that declared war on Mexico and sent troops to defend the border in 1846: James K. Polk or Abraham Lincoln?

2536. What capital city did the American army claim victory after defeating General Santa Anna and his Mexican troops in 1847: Monterrey or Mexico City?

SOCIAL STUDIES

2537. What is the name of the Peace Treaty that gave the United States the states of California, Nevada, Utah, Oklahoma, Wyoming, Colorado, Arizona and New Mexico in exchange for 15 million dollars, extending the U.S. border to the Rio Grande: the Treaty of Guadalupe Hidalgo or the Treaty of Paris?

2538. How much of its territory was Mexico forced to give up after losing the Mexican-American War: thirty percent or fifty percent?

2539. What is the name for the monument in Mexico City at Chapultepec Castle that honors the six Mexican students who defended the Castle against American troops, translates "the boy heroes," and is now a Mexican National Holiday: Los Niños Heroes or "Los Heroes Muchachos?"

2540. Did the United States now extend its territory from the Atlantic to the Pacific?

2541. Did the states in the 1800's rely on both industry and agriculture?

2542. What part of the United States relied on steel, machinery, and industry in the 1800's: North or South?

2543. What part of the United States relied on agricultural crops like tobacco and cotton and had many farms and plantations: North or South?

2544. What did the South depend on to work the farms and plantations in the 1800's: Slavery or Machinery?

2545. Did many people living in the Northern states support or oppose slavery in the 1800's?

2546. What part of the United States wanted all the new states admitted into the Union to be Free states: the North or the South?

2547. What part of the United States wanted all the new states admitted into the Union to be Slave states: the North or the South?

2548. What is the name for the boundary between Maryland and Pennsylvania that separated the Free states from the Slave states, or the North from the South in 1763, by British surveyors Charles Mason and Jeremiah Dixon: the Mason-Dixon Line or the Division Border?

2549. What is the name of the agreement that was reached in 1820 that maintained the balance of Free states and Slave states when Maine was admitted as a Free State, and Missouri was admitted as a Slave State: the Maine Compromise or the Missouri Compromise?

2550. What is the name given to many people from the Northern States like Frederick Douglass, William Lloyd Garrison, and Harriet Beecher Stowe that wanted to end slavery: revolutionists or abolitionists?

2551. What is the name of the abolitionist author who wrote a novel in 1852 entitled, "Uncle Tom's Cabin" depicting the brutality of slavery, and fueled the human rights debate before the Civil War: Frederick Douglass or Harriet Beecher Stowe?

2552. What is the name of the ruling made by the Supreme Court in 1857 that did not award a slave and his family their freedom when their owner moved back to the slave state of Missouri after living in the

SOCIAL STUDIES

free state of Wisconsin, taking the family with him to work as slaves, and ruled that slavery was legal in all U.S. Territories: the Dred Scott Decision or the Frederick Douglass Decision?

2553. What is the name given for the series of seven debates between the Republican candidate Abraham Lincoln for the Illinois Senate in 1858, and Senator Stephen A. Douglas on slavery that helped Lincoln receive national attention, and paved the road for his future presidency: the Slavery Debates, or the Lincoln-Douglas Debates?

2554. Which states believed that they had the right to stay in the Union or to leave the Union if slavery was no longer allowed based on their Constitutional rights: the Northern states or the Southern states?

2555. Which candidate opposed slavery, but stated that he did not want to interfere with the slavery practices of the Southern states, and was elected president in 1860: Stephen A. Douglass or Abraham Lincoln?

2556. What action did many Southern states take in 1861 because of their position in support of slavery: remain in the Union or secede (leave) the Union?

2557. What did the Southern states call themselves after they decided to secede from the Union in 1861 and form their own country: the Union States or the Confederate States?

2558. Was President Lincoln for or against slavery and a strong federal government?

2559. Who was the President of the Confederate States or the Confederation, as it was known: Robert E. Lee or Jefferson Davis?

2560. What is the name for the war in the United States starting in 1861 between Abraham Lincoln and the Union States of the North who opposed slavery, and Jefferson Davis and the Confederate States of the South who supported slavery: the American War of Independence or the American Civil War?

2561. What is the name of the battle near South Carolina that signaled the start of the American Civil War on April 12, 1861 where the Southern or Confederate States first started firing: the Battle of Fort Sumter or the Battle of Shiloh?

2562. What is the name of the first major land battle of the Civil War in July of 1861 when the Union army attacked the Confederate army along a creek in Virginia: the Battle of Bull Run, or the Battle of Shiloh?

2563. What is the nickname that was given to the Confederate General Thomas Jackson after he and his troops arrived at the Battle of Bull Run and held their ground similar to a "stone wall:" General Jackson Wall or "Stonewall" Jackson?

2564. What is the formal name given to the states that seceded from the Union, and had their own constitution that supported the rights of states and slavery: The Separate States or The Confederate States?

2565. Who was the President of the Confederacy: Thomas Jefferson or Jefferson Davis?

2566. Who is the leader that is credited for stopping abolitionist John Brown's raid on Harpers Ferry in 1859 to take possession of the arsenal of weapons: Robert E. Lee or Ulysses S. Grant?

SOCIAL STUDIES

2567. What is the name of the Commander and General of the Confederate Army of Virginia and the military advisor to President Jefferson Davis during the American Civil War: Robert E .Lee or Ulysses S. Grant?

2568. What is the name of the city where the Confederates established their capital: Richmond or Williamsburg?

2569. What is the name of the military leader who had his first victory in Tennessee when he captured Fort Donelson in 1863, and was appointed the Chief General of the entire Union army by President Lincoln: Robert E. Lee or Ulysses S. Grant?

2570. What was Ulysses S. Grant's nickname after he told the commanders of the Confederate army, "No terms except an unconditional and immediate surrender can be accepted:" "Unconditional Surrender" Grant, or "Immediate Surrender" Grant?

2571. What was the age range of most Civil War soldiers: 15-25 or 12-22?

2572. Did weather, fatigue, infection, disease, and lack of food and medical supplies pose challenges for many Civil War soldiers?

2573. What was the nickname that the Southerners gave to the Northerners: "Yankees" or "Rebels?"

2574. What was the nickname that the Northerners gave to the Southerners: "Yankees" or "Rebels?"

2575. What finally became the standard uniform color of the Union North: blue or gray?

2576. What finally became the standard uniform color of the Confederate South: blue or grey?

2577. What were the typical weapons of the American Civil War: muskets and rifles, or bows and swords?

2578. What did the Civil War soldiers carry their gear in: a knapsack or a duffle bag?

2579. What is the name for what the Union established to guard the eastern coastline and the ports with their ships after the start of the Civil War that was designed to prevent supplies, weapons, and the export of cotton into the Confederate States: the Union Blockade or the Anaconda Blockade?

2580. What was unique about the 1862 Confederate ship known as the "Merrimack" and the Union ship known as the "Monitor" that makes them different from their wooden ship counterparts, and would forever change the future of naval warfare: they were the first underwater ships, or they were the first ironclad ships with cannons to engage in battle?

2581. What is the meaning of emancipate: to keep someone captive against his or her will, or to set someone free?

2582. What is the name given for the order given by President Lincoln in 1862 that declared "that all persons held as slaves" within the Confederate States "are, and henceforward shall be free," and later paved the way for the Thirteenth Amendment to the Constitution: the Freedom of Slaves Act or the Emancipation Proclamation?"

2583. When did President Lincoln announce the Emancipation Proclamation that promised freedom to the slaves in the South starting on January 1, 1863: five days before or five days after the Union victory at the Battle of Antietam?

2584. Did many African Americans join the Union forces after the Union government passed a law, and as a result of the Emancipation Proclamation?

2585. What is the term used during the Civil War that referred to a network of people and hideouts that slaves used to escape the South and seek freedom in the North: the Underground Tunnel or the Underground Railroad?

2586. Where would slaves have to escape to in order to be completely safe from being returned to their owners: Canada or Mexico?

2587. What is the term given for the person that led slaves along the Underground Railroad during the Civil War: engineers or conductors?

2588. What is the term used for the hideouts for the slaves along the Underground Railroad: stations or tracks?

2589. What is the name of the African American woman and former slave that acted as a conductor in the Underground Railroad, leading many slaves to freedom, and also served as a spy for the North? Sojourner Truth or Harriet Tubman?

2590. What is the name of the battle led by Confederate General George Pickett when General Lee called on him to make a direct attack of the Union Army killing over half of the Confederate soldiers: Pickett's Charge or Pickett's Battle?

2591. What is the name of the three-day battle in Pennsylvania that is regarded as one of the most important and deadliest battles of the Civil War in July of 1863, and was a turning point after the Union was able to stop General Lee's invasion of the North: the Battle of Gettysburg or the Battle of Shiloh?

2592. What is the name of the two-minute speech given on November 1, 1863 by President Lincoln at a dedication ceremony at a cemetery in Pennsylvania, and is regarded as one of the most famous speeches in history: Lincoln's Inauguration Address, or Lincoln's Gettysburg Address?

2593. What are the words of the first line of President Lincoln's Gettysburg Address: "It was the best of times, it was the worst of times" or "Four score and seven years ago…?"

2594. What is "score" another word for: twenty or ten?

2595. Does "four score and seven years ago" equal the year 1776, when the signers of the Declaration of Independence declared "all men are created equal?"

2596. What is the name of the Union General's march in the spring of 1864 from Tennessee to Georgia, when he and his Union forces took control of Atlanta, proceeded to Savannah, and took control of the sea port, destroying everything along their way: Sherman's March to the Sea, or the March to Savannah?

SOCIAL STUDIES

2597. Was President Lincoln elected to a second term?

2598. What side was winning during the time of Lincoln's re-election after the capture of Richmond, Virginia: the Union or the Confederacy?

2599. Which side was nearly twice the size as the other: the Union or the Confederacy?

2600. Which General surrendered to the other on April 9, 1865 in Appomattox, Virginia: General Lee surrendered to the Union General Ulysses S. Grant, or General Grant surrendered to the Confederate General Robert E. Lee?

2601. Was the surrender and the terms for the surrender discussed respectfully between Lee and Grant on April 9, 1865 at Appomattox Courthouse in Virginia?

2602. Which war is still regarded as the deadliest war in American History, with a death toll of over 600,000: the American War of Independence or the American Civil War?

2603. What happened to President Lincoln five days later on April 14th while he and his wife Mary Todd Lincoln were seated in the President's box watching a play at a theatre near the White House?

2604. What is the name of the theatre where President Lincoln was shot in the back of the head: Washington's Theatre or Ford's Theatre?

2605. What is the name of the actor who silently crept up behind President Lincoln and shot him behind the head, motivated because the Confederates had all but lost the Civil War: John Wilkes Booth or General Lee?

2606. What did John Wilkes Booth break after jumping onto the stage after shooting President Lincoln: his arm or his leg?

2607. How long before John Wilkes Booth was caught and shot by soldiers after trapping him in a barn in Virginia: one day or twelve days?

2608. How is the Ford Theatre used today: as a warehouse or as a Museum?

2609. What is the name of the President who became the 17th President of the United States after the assassination of President Lincoln: Jefferson Davis or Andrew Jackson?

2610. What is the period of time called after the Civil War ended between 1865 and 1877: Expansion or Reconstruction?

2611. What had been Lincoln's vision as part of the Reconstruction process after the Civil War: to bring the Confederate states back into the Union, or to allow the Southern states to have their own government?

2612. What was the condition of many of the Southern states after the Civil War: they were in good condition, or they were largely destroyed?

2613. Was the Reconstruction period a time of rebuilding the North or rebuilding the South?

SOCIAL STUDIES

2614. What troops occupied many Southern states during Reconstruction to make sure that the laws were being followed: Federal troops or Union troops?

2615. Could people in the Southern states receive a pardon simply by pledging loyalty to the Union under President Lincoln's Reconstruction plan?

2616. What became President Johnson's nickname because he vetoed many Reconstruction laws that were passed by Congress: "The Opposition President," or "The Veto President?"

2617. What did the U.S. House of Representatives want to do to President Johnson because he had vetoed many bills and because he wanted to stop the Republican's plans regarding Reconstruction: re-elect him to office or impeach (remove) him from office?

2618. Was President Johnson found guilty or not-guilty by the Senate by one vote?

2619. What is the name given for the laws that were passed by Southern states that did not allow blacks the right to vote, own land, attend school, or other basic rights: Black Rules or Black Codes?

2620. What three amendments were added to the Constitution to protect the rights of people and to help with the Reconstruction process in that the newly passed laws would outlaw slavery, declare every U.S. citizen equal under the law, and give all people the right to vote: the 1st, 2nd, and 3rd amendments, or the 13th, 14th, and 15th amendments?

2621. Did the Southern states have to ratify or accept the new amendments to the Constitution in order to be readmitted to the Union?

2622. Which side helped the Reconstruction process by building roads, building schools, and promoting farming: the Union or the Confederacy?

2623. What is the name for Northerners who moved to the South because they wanted to help with Reconstruction, so named for what they used for travel bags: scalawags or carpetbaggers?

2624. What is the name of the agency that was set up by the federal government to fight against the Black Codes and help to distribute land and build schools: The Freedmen's Bureau or The Freedom Bureau?

2625. Was there still conflict in the South between blacks and whites during Reconstruction?

2626. What is the name for the Post Civil War society organized in the South, wore hooded garments, and aimed to suppress the newly acquired rights of blacks by means of terrorism: the Ku Klux Klan or the White Supremes?

2627. Was there still conflict between the rights of people in 1877 when Reconstruction ended?

2628. In which century were many African Americans finally able to benefit from the Thirteenth, Fourteenth, and Fifteenth Amendments guaranteeing all citizens their rights: the 19th Century or the 20th Century?

2629. Where did many people migrate to after the American Civil War: West or East?

SOCIAL STUDIES

2630. What is the name given to the West because of its reputation as being less civilized: the "Wild West" or the "Crazy West?"

2631. What is the name of the act that Congress pass in 1862 that made public lands in the West available for a low fee where a home could be built: the Homestead Act or the Farm Act?

2632. What kind of home did many pioneers build on the prairie that was cool in the summer and warm in the winter: an adobe house or a sod house?

2633. Who often worked as ranchers with cattle and cattle drives in the old west: Cowboys or Indians?

2634. What is the term for when the cowboy would work to gather all the cattle together: a round up or a cattle drive?

2635. What is the term for the process of moving a herd of cattle from one place to another: a round up or a cattle drive?

2636. Were there a lot of cattle ranches in the West after the Civil War?

2637. What did cowboys wear on their heads to protect their heads from the Sun: a ten-gallon hat or a scarf?

2638. Who would wear chaps, boots, and bandanas: Cowboys or Indians?

2639. What is the name of the sporting event that includes bull-riding, calf roping, and bareback bronco riding?

2640. What is the name of the musical instrument that a cowboy would often play: a guitar or a harmonica?

2641. Who were "Wild Bill Hickok" "Billy the Kid," "Jesse James," "Wyatt Earp," "Butch Cassidy," and "Sundance" famous for in the Old West: gunfighters, bandits, and outlaws, or cowboys, sheriffs, and ranchers?

2642. What is buffalo hunter William F. Cody who organized Wild West shows better known as: "Buffalo Bill" or "Wild Bill Hickok?

2643. Who was the star attraction and famous lady sharpshooter that performed in Buffalo Bill's Wild West Shows: Annie Oakley or Calamity Jane?

2644. What was the mail delivery service between Missouri and California that followed the Oregon Trail in 1861 and 1862, and included Buffalo Bill: the Pony Express or the Postal Trail?

2645. What means of communication replaced the Pony Express in 1861: the telephone or the telegraph?

2646. What means of transportation was built between 1863 and 1869 that replaced the wagon trains, and covered over 1,700 miles: the Transcontinental Railroad or the Continental Railway?

2647. Were there conflicts between cowboys, pioneers, and Native Americans during the time of Westward Expansion?

2648. What is another name given for the West: the American Frontier or the American Wilderness?

SOCIAL STUDIES

2649. Which state did Secretary of State William Seward purchase from Russia for seven million dollars in 1867: Hawaii or Alaska?

2650. What was discovered in Juneau, Alaska in 1868: gold or silver?

2651. Did the United States have several treaties in place with the Native Americans to settle land disputes?

2652. Did many great Native American Indian Tribes live on the American Frontier in the late 1800's and early 1900's?

2653. Were many Indian Tribes forced to live on Reservations assigned by the government?

2654. Were the Indian leaders Buffalo Bill and Crazy Horse for or against Westward expansion?

2655. What was the main cause of tension between some Native American Indians and White settlers: land rights or fishing rights?

2656. What is the name of the teacher and nurse during the American Civil War who founded the American Red Cross in 1881: Florence Nightingale or Clara Barton?

2657. What is the name of the man who married Martha, lived at Mount Vernon, led his troops across the Delaware River in 1776 on Christmas Day, supposedly cut down a cherry tree on his father's property, and helped select the site for the capital on the Potomac River that is named for him?

2658. Who is the current President of the United States?

2659. Who is the current First Lady of the United States?

2660. Who are Thomas Jefferson, J.F. Kennedy, Abraham Lincoln, Franklin D. Roosevelt, Dwight D. Eisenhower, Harry S. Truman, Richard Nixon, Ronald Reagan, Betty Ford, and George W. Bush?

2661. Who are Martha Washington, Abigail Adams, Mary Todd Lincoln, Dolly Madison, Eleanor Roosevelt, Claudia "Lady Bird" Johnson, Jaqueline Kennedy, Nancy Reagan, and Laura Bush?

2662. Who are Amelia Earhart and Charles Lindbergh: famous aviators or famous inventors?

2663. Who are Clara Barton, Elizabeth Blackwell, and Florence Nightingale: famous nurses or famous reformers?

2664. Who are Alexander Graham Bell, Thomas Edison, Samuel F.B. Morse, Eli Whitney, Benjamin Franklin, and the Wright Brothers: famous authors or famous inventors?

2665. Who are Dorothea Dix, Helen Keller, Frederick Douglass, and Lucretia Mott: famous reformers or famous military heroes?

2666. Who are P.T. Barnum, Annie Oakley, and the Ringling Brothers: famous cowboys or famous entertainers?

2667. Who are Buffalo Bill, Daniel Boone, Davy Crockett, and Kit Carson: famous frontiersmen or famous Native Americans?

SOCIAL STUDIES

2668. What famous American can you name and what is that person best known for?

2669. What country of the world is known for being a "melting pot" because of its diverse population; its colorful history; being regarded as the land of opportunity; freedom and liberty; many national parks and monuments; and for baseball, football, and hot dogs?

2670. What country of the world is known for its long river the Rio Grande; speaking Spanish; Pre-Columbian ruins and artifacts; Pre-Columbian Indian groups that include the Olmecs, the Toltecs, Maya, and the Aztecs; the pyramids of the Sun and the Moon at Teotihuacan; the Maya ruins of Chichén Itza, Palenque and Tulum; the resort cities of Cancun, Riviera Maya, and Puerto Vallarta; the cliff divers of Acapulco; Chapultepec Park; Alameda Park; The Palace of Fine Arts; The Zócalo main square; La Avenida Juarez; The National Museum of Anthropology; The Basilica of Our Lady of Guadalupe, the patron saint; The Aztec Stadium seating over 100,000 spectators; silver and copper; black pottery; serape blankets and woven textiles; food markets; chocolate; the holidays Cinco de Mayo and Dia de los Muertos; Mariachi music; colorful folk dancing; monarch butterflies; the Chihuahua; the volcano Popocatepetl; the poinsettia; bullfighting; the agave cactus; the Spanish conquistador Hernan Cortes; the Aztec God Quetzalcoatl; the priest Miguel Hidalgo; war hero Pancho Villa; the Zapotec Indian president Benito Juarez; artists Diego Rivera and Frida Kahlo; guitarist Carlos Santana; and foods that include tamales, tortillas, enchiladas, guacamole, jalepeños, enchiladas, and chicken with mole sauce?

2671. What country of the world is known for a fortress built by the Spanish to keep out invaders and pirates called Castillo de San Felipe del Morro; the Taino Indians; the tropical rainforest called El Yunque; the native tree frog called the Coquí, named for the sound that it makes; tropical birds; exotic flowers and orchids; the Cathedral of San Juan Bautista; the colonial Spanish architecture, narrow streets, and colorful buildings of Old San Juan; the largest radio telescope located in Arecibo; baseball; beaches; scuba diving; rum; salsa music; lace; hammocks; coconuts; bananas; musical instruments that include bongos, congas, guiros, and the cuatro guitar; foods that include banana turnovers called mufongo, suckling pig called lechón, and rice and beans called arroz con habichuelas; gold and silver; the Spanish explorer and first governor of this country, Juan Ponce de Leon; many baseball players including the Pittsburgh Pirate hall of famer Roberto Clemente; the Broadway actress who played the role of Anita in West Side Story, Rita Moreno; the blind singer of "Feliz Navidad," José Feliciano; and translates into English as "rich port?"

2672. What country of the world is known for being settled by the native Tainos Indians; as the first colony founded by Christopher Columbus; for sharing the island of Hispañiola with Haiti; being named for the Spanish Saint Dominic; the province of Duarte, named for one of this country's founding fathers, Juan Pablo Duarte; the tropical island of Catalina; the Punta Cana Resort and many scenic beaches; baseball and several Major League baseball players; the merengue dance and bachata music; Pico Duarte, the highest peak in the Caribbean; the Cathedral of Santa Maria in the Colonial zone of Santo Domingo, the oldest cathedral in the Americas; products like rum, stone jewelry, gold, textiles, paintings, dolls, sugar, and coffee; fashion designer Oscar de la Renta; a seven meat stew called sancocho; mashed plantains called mangú; fried bananas called tostones; and a cake called bizcocho dominicano?

SOCIAL STUDIES

2673. What country of the world is known for being the largest island in the Caribbean; the Plaza de Armas and the Spanish Morro Castle located in Havana; Fidel Castro, a polarizing socialist military leader for several decades; rum; the mojito rum cocktail; habanero hot sauce; cigars; being the birthplace of the Salsa dance; the Cha-cha-cha dance; Rumba song and dance; singers Desi Arnaz, Jon Secada, and Celia Cruz; José Martí, a revolutionary writer and leader who fought for this country's independence, and author of the poem that inspired the song, "Guantanamera;" baseball and several baseball players; the U.S. naval base of Guantanamo; the 1961 failed military invasion, supported by President John F. Kennedy at The Bay of Pigs; and beautiful beaches?

2674. What country of the world is known for Tortuguero National Park; the Monteverde Cloud Forest Reserve; the National Theatre in San Jose; rain forests; volcanoes; sea turtles; tropical birds and flowers; the Scarlet Macaw; the Quetzal bird; exports that include coffee, bananas, and sugar; soccer; a rice and black bean dish called gallo pinto; fried bananas called tostones; colorful oxcarts, canopy zip-lining; surfing; water rafting; and is a country that translates as "Rich Coast" in English?

2675. What country of the world is known for the native Maya Indians; the ruins of the Maya city El Mirador located in a tropical jungle; the island of Flores that is connected to the mainland by a causeway; the Chichicastenango Market; the Santa Catalina Arch in the colonial city of Antigua; Lake Atitlán located in the highlands; the ancient Mayan ruins of Tikal located in the lowland rainforest; the Mayan ruins of Quiriga featuring 22 carved stelae, tall sculpted stones covered with figures and glyphs; coffee; bananas; active volcanoes; women carrying giant baskets on their heads; colorful woven textiles; leather; jewelry; fruit juice drinks called licuados; tamales; the colorful chicken buses called camionetas; traditional music called marimba; fiestas; cathedrals; tropical birds; tropical animals; and exotic flowers?

2676. What country of the world is known as "the land of the volcanoes" having over 20 volcanoes; the San Salvador Volcano; world surfing competitions; the Gothic cathedral of Saint Anne; soccer; the national dish, a stuffed tortilla called pupusa; earthquakes; Mayan ruins; coffee; and translates from Spanish as, "the savior?"

2677. What country of the world is known for its mestizo population; the freshwater lake Managua where sharks live; animals like toucans, boa constrictors, wild boars, and sea turtles; exports of coffee, bananas, and sugarcane; the old Cathedral of Managua; the colorful houses, horse-drawn carriages, and Victorian architecture of Granada; the fishing village of San Juan del Sur; the Masaya volcano;; the San Sebastian Festival in January; the diving and snorkeling of the Corn Islands; the Metropolitan Cathedral in Leon; the poet Ruben Dario; and its civil wars?

2678. What country of the world is known for its location on an isthmus, and having coastlines on both the Caribbean Sea and the Pacific Ocean; the explorers Christopher Columbus and Vasco Nuñez de Balboa; indigenous native people called Kuna; exports that include bananas, coffee, rice, and beans; having over 1,400 tree species including the square tree; golden frogs; sea turtles; Miraflores Lock; and for having a 51-mile long canal that was built as an international maritime trade path connecting the Atlantic Ocean and the Pacific Ocean?

2679. What country of the world is known for the highest waterfall called Angel Falls at 3,212 feet;

SOCIAL STUDIES

Miraflores Palace; Caracas Cathedral; La Isla Margarita; Pico Bolivar, also called Mirror Peak; cornflower bread sandwiches called arepas; the Orinoco River; the giant otter called a river-wolf; large oil reserves; several Major League baseball players; politician Hugo Chavez; war hero Simón Bolivar; and is a country so named because the Italian explorer Amerigo Vespucci thought that the area around Lake Maracaibo resembled the waterways of the Italian city of Venice?

2680. What country of the world is known for having the largest Gothic basilica in the Americas located in the historic center of Quito called The Basilica del Voto Nacional; St. Francisco Church; Cotopaxi Volcano; the city of Baños at the foot of an active volcano and called the "Gateway to the Amazon;" the wood, jewelry, woven textiles, and stone carvings located in the markets of Otavalos; soccer; foods that include the yucca tortilla, potatoes, llapingacho potato pancakes, concha corn, guinea pig called cuy, locro potato soup, the aji chile pepper, shrimp ceviche and melcocha taffy; volcanic islands called The Galapagos where giant tortoises, sea lions, penguins, and iguanas are found, and served as the inspiration for Charles Darwin's Theory of Natural Selection; and is a country named for its location given that the equator runs through it?

2681. What country of the world is known for the Gold Museum of Bogotá; the beach resort city of Cartagena; the small towns called pueblos; jungles; wine; soccer; is named for the famous maritime explorer; the painter Fernando Botero, famous for his exaggerated depictions of people and animals; the Botero Musuem; author of "One Hundred Years of Solitude," Gabriel Garcia Marquez; singers Shakira and Juanes; designer Carolina Herrera; cornmeal bread called arepa; tamales; white cheese buñuelos; and world-renowned coffee?

2682. What country of the world is known for having the highest capital city La Paz; Yungas Road, considered to be one of the most dangerous in the world; Lake Titicaca; the jaguar, the titi monkey, and the 9.000 species of birds found in Madidi National Park; the llama; the historical buildings of Sucre where the liberator Simón Bolivar wrote this country's constitution; the annual Oruro Carnival, a folk festival held before Ash Wednesday involving thousands of dancers and musicians; having the largest salt flats, Salar de Uyuni; pottery; colorful woven textiles; soccer; and is the place where the American bank robbers Butch Cassidy and the Sundance Kid were killed in a shootout in 1908?

2683. What country of the world is known for Iguazu Falls; Perito Moreno Glacier; "La Boca" district of Buenos Aires with its colorful houses; Baroliche City at the foot of the Andes Mountains; the sea lions, penguins, and elephant seals in the Valdes Peninsula; the Mendoza Wine Fields; its historical buildings, outdoor cafes, and wide boulevards; the tango dance; gaucho cowboys; vast plains of grass called the pampas; foods that include grilled gaucho steak, empanadas, mate tea, roast beef called carne asado, chorizo sausage; shrimp ceviche, chipas cheese bread, and dulce de leche dessert; religious leader Pope John Francis; world leader Juan Perón; and political wife and activist Evita Perón?

2684. What country of the world is known as a landlocked country; for the colonial district of the capital city Asunción; the waterfalls in Ciudad de Este; spindle lace; having a view of Iguazu Falls; the San Blas Festival in February; as having one of the largest hydraulic complexes in the world and recognized as one of the seven modern wonders of the world, the Itaipú Dam; and the Paraguay river cruises?

SOCIAL STUDIES

2685. What country of the world is known for its beautiful beaches along the golden coast or the Costa de Oro; the fishing village of Aguas Dulces; the old city quarters of Montevideo; the popular summer destination, the beaches of Punta del Este; high consumption of beef; soccer; leather goods; mate tea; wines; gaucho cowboys; author Horacio Quiroga; and the home of the rugby team survivors of "Uruguayan Air Force Flight 571" who survived for three months after crashing into the Andes Mountains?

2686. What country of the world is known for Los Pinguinos National Monument that is home to more than 120,000 penguins; the Santiago residence of the President, La Moneda Palace; the brightly colored houses and bohemian culture of Valparaiso; the Valle de la Luna or Valley of the Moon named for its extensive sand dunes located in the Atacama Desert; the three granite peaks at Torres del Paine; the volcanoes and Lake Chungará located at Lauca National Park; foods that include corn tamales called humitas, sea bass, empañadas, and wines; soccer; poet Pablo Neruda; writer Gabriela Mistral; and the 887 statues called Moai located thousands of miles off the coast of this long, narrow country, a Polynesian island known as Easter Island?

2687. What country of the world is known for the images of monkeys, spiders, and lizards called the Nazca Lines; the group of reed islands in Lake Titicaca called Uros Islands; the Plaza de Armas in Cuzco; The Sacred Valley of the Inca located in the Andes; The Inca Trail; the walled complex of the Inca called Saksayhuaman; foods that include beef tenderloin called lomo saltado, potato croquets called papas rellenas, quinoa, fried guinea pig called cuy, and pumpkin fritters called picarones; llamas and alpacas; llama fur blankets, scarves, hats, sweaters, and mittens; brightly colored hand-woven textiles; chullo hats with ear flaps; silver jewelry; soccer; the serpent, puma cougar, and condor; pan pipes; flute music; and the ancient Inca fortress of Machu Picchu located in the Andes over 7,000 feet above sea level, and re-discovered by explorer and archeologist Hiram Bingham in 1911?

2688. What country of the world is known for the largest rainforest, the Amazon; the 4,000 mile long Amazon River; piranhas; the annual Rio Samba Parade and Carnival in Rio de Janeiro; samba music and dance; drums and percussion instruments; champion soccer teams; the majestic Iguazu Falls; Copacabana Beach; speaking Portuguese; exporting sugarcane and coffee; clay pottery and ceramics; lace; hammocks; leather sandals; Indian woodworks; cangas beachware; havaianas flip-flops; feather art; black beads; juice bars; foods that include the acai berry, bananas; shrimp stew, fried yucca sticks, black bean stew called feijoada, and candy treats called bridgardeiros; the soccer players Ronaldo and Pele; politician Jimmy Hoffa; and the statue of Jesus Christ towering over 130 feet called Christ the Redeemer?

2689. What country of the world is known for its glaciers and volcanoes, and nicknamed "the land of fire and ice;" being founded by the Vikings of Scandinavia; its location on two tectonic plates; being a land of geysers, waterfalls, and hot springs; sheep; black and white birds called Puffins; Reykjavik, the capital city where most of this country's inhabitants live; whale watching; a geothermal spa called The Blue Lagoon; the Gullfoss waterfall; believing in the existence of elves; midnight golf; handball; the soft cheese yogurt snack called Skyr; visits by the Yule Lads during Christmastime; the fishing industry; cod; the Aurora Borealis or Northern Lights; hand knit wool sweaters, blankets, and knit goods; and the birthplace of the first European to reach the New World, Leif Ericson?

SOCIAL STUDIES

2690. What country of the world is known for its long history; royalty; Stonehenge; Big Ben; London Bridge; Buckingham Palace; Windsor Castle; the River Thames, Westminster Abbey; double decker red buses; Trafalgar Square; St. Paul' Cathedral; Hyde Park; a wax museum called Madame Tussauds; William Shakespeare; Robin Hood; Isaac Newton; Charles Darwin; the Beatles; Wimbledon tennis; cricket; rugby; tea time; pubs; Oxford University; and Cambridge University?

2691. What country of the world is known as the "Emerald Isle" for its green countryside; the cliffs of Moher; sheep; Aran sweaters; foods that include potatoes, stew, soda bread, and whiskey; pubs; Guiness Beer; the Blarney Stone; Saint Patrick's Cathedral; dance and jigs; Celtic folk music; red hair; shamrocks; leprechauns; Waterford crystal; the harp; Limericks; writer Oscar Wilde; its capital city of Dublin; and the song "Molly Malone?"

2692. What country of the world is known for its medieval castles; royalty including Mary, Queen of Scots; green countryside; a 3,000 year old tree; freshwater lochs; golf courses; the Edinburgh Theatre Festival; the Glasgow Cathedral; the Loch Ness monster; the unicorn; scotch whiskey; bagpipes; kilts; having the largest population of redheads; the author of "Ivanhoe," Sir Walter Scott; Mary; Queen of Scots; the scientist and inventor, Alexander Graham Bell; the author of "Don Juan," Lord Byron; and the actor of several "James Bond" movies, Sean Connery?

2693. What country of the world is known for King Ludwig's Castle; Lichtenstein Castle; Neuschwanstein Castle; the Berlin Wall; military leader Adolf Hitler; the Holocaust; Anne Frank, The Black Forest; Cuckoo clocks; Hummel figurines; the Glockenspiel clock in Munich; the Bavarian Alps; beer; Oktoberfest; gesundheit; the waltz; the first printed book; the Edelweiss flower; gingerbread houses; composers Beethoven and Bach; Fahrenheit; the Mercedes and Volkswagen cars; ethnic clothing called Lederhosen and the Bavarian dress called Dirdnl; kindergarten; foods that include liverwurst, bratwurst, knackwurst, frankfurter, sauerkraut, sauerbraten, wiener schnitzel, pretzel, stollen fruit cake, apple streusel, and the food named for the city of Hamburg, the hamburger?

2694. What country of the world is known for the Old Market Place in Warsaw; Main Market Square in Krakow; Malbork Castle; Gdansk Old Town; Auschwitz, the Nazi concentration camp during World War II; The Wieliczka Salt Mine; the bison of the Bialowieza primal forest; the kobza bagpipe; Pope John Paul II; the composer Frederic Chopin; scientist and astronomer Nicolas Copernicus; the Russian Tsar Catherine the Great; radioactivity scientist and physicist Marie Curie; world leader Lech Walesa; the author of "Heart of Darkness," "Lord Jim," and "The Secret Sharer," Joseph Conrad; foods that include sausages, kielbasa, pierogi dumplings, and Paczki doughnuts; sharing the Oplatek Christmas wafer at Christmastime; glassware; wood carvings; Babushka scarves and shawls; paper art; stoneware; embroidery; paper art; and dolls?

2695. What country of the world is known for its rich history; the renaissance; ancient theatres; the opera; Pompeii; the Colosseum; the Pantheon; St. Peter's Basilica; the Trevi Fountain; Vatican City; the Pope; the Sistine Chapel; St. Peter's Cathedral; the Leaning Tower of Pisa; the Spanish Steps in the Piazza di Spagna in Rome; the Uffizi Gallery; the Ponte Vecchio bridge; the Piazza del Duomo; Michelangelo's "David" statue in Florence; painter and inventor Leonardo da Vinci; the gondola boats of Venice; the countryside of Tuscany; the Roman general Julius Caesar; the philosopher of nursing and social reformer Florence Nightingale; the explorer Christopher Columbus; the map

SOCIAL STUDIES

maker Amerigo Vespucci; the traveler Marco Polo; the scientist Galileo Galilee; the author of "Dante's Inferno," Dante Alighieri, the political leader Benito Mussolini; Fontanini Nativity sets; the Shroud of Turin cloth with the face of Jesus; gold; leather; the Ferarri car; the Milan fashion district; Gucci bags; designers Giorgio Armani and Yves Saint Laurent; foods that include parmesan cheese, mozzarella cheese, provolone cheese, pasta, pizza, spaghetti, fettecini, linguini, lasagna, panini, tortellini, pepperoni sausage, pistachios, olive oil, wine, risotto rice, spumoni, cannoli, bologna, antipasto, gelato, tiramisu, cappuccino, and latte; and the islands of Sardinia, Capri, and Siciily?

2696. What country in the world is known for the Lisbon Oceanarium; the Vasco de Gama Bridge; the Shrine to Our Lady of Fatima; the stone maritime fortress Belem Tower; port wine; pottery; tile paintings; the lynx; beaches; the Douro River; the first explorer to sail around the world, Ferdinand Magellan; the first explorer to discover a sea route to India, Vasco de Gama; soccer player Cristiano Ronaldo; actress Carmen Miranda; cuisine that includes cod, sardines; squid, roast suckling pig, and caldo verde soup; and has the distinction of being the world's largest producer of cork?

2697. What country of the world is known for the Eiffel Tower; Notre Dame Cathedral with its rose windows and Gothic architecture; the Seine River, the Champs-Elysees Parisian street; the Arc de Triomphe; the Louvre art museum; the Mona Lisa portrait by Leonardo da Vinci; the Palace of Versailles; the Basilica of Sacre-Coeur; the Normandy island of Mont St. Michel; the Pompidou Center, a modern art museum; D-Day and the beaches of Normandy; the island of Corsica; the castles and wine fields of the Loire Valley; the Mediterranean coastline oasis known as the Riviera; the Pere-Lachaise Cemetery with the tomb of The Doors singer Jim Morrison; the Revolution; countryside chateaus; the author of "Les Miserable" and "The Hunchback of Notre Dame," Victor Hugo; an annual 2,100 mile bike race; fashion design; perfume; wine; cuisine that includes cheese, crepes, escargot snails, onion soup, and truffles; author Alexandre Dumas; philosopher Albert Camus; military heroine Joan of Arc; the long-reigning monarch King Louis XIV; military and political leader Napoleon Bonaparte; scientists Louis Pasteur and Marie Curie; World War II general Charles De Gaulle; impressionist artists Claude Monet, Edgar Degas, Paul Cezanne, Mary Cassatt, Henri Matisse, Camille Pissarro, and August Renoir; designers Coco-Chanel, Christian Dior, Louis Vuitton, and Givenchy; and words and phrases that include a la carte, a la mode, au gratin, bon appetit, au jus, ballet, bouquet, bon voyage, boutique, café, chef, cliché, clique, cordon bleu, cul-de-sac, debut, décor, déjà vu, encore, en route, entrée, entrepreneur, façade, faux pas, fiancée, garage, genre, hors-d'oeuvres, Mardi Gras, matinee, menu, petite, potpourri, renaissance, restaurant, resume, RSVP, sauté, turquoise, and vinaigrette?

2698. What country of the world is known as an independent principality; the Monte Carlo Casino and Opera House; the Grimaldi family; the former Prince Rainer and Princess Grace; the reigning Prince Albert II; the Prince's Palace; grand prix car racing; and is considered a resort area for the rich and famous?

2699. What country of the world is known for its diverse provinces; The French and Indian War; ice hockey; freshwater lakes; Lake Ontario; the St. Lawrence River; the province of Nova Scotia; The Toronto Zoo; Niagara Falls; Glacier National Park; Banff National Park; the CN Tower; the Rockies; The Quebec Winter Carnival; Ojibwa Indians; the Inuit people of the Northwest Territories; the lumber industry; maple syrup; the maple leaf; geese; moose; beaver; caribou; lynx; fish; furs; bacon; petroleum; the Viking explorer Leif Erikson's arrival in Newfoundland in 1000 AD; free health care; and majestic scenery?

2700. What country of the world is known for The Great Barrier Reef coral system; The Sydney Opera House; The Sydney Harbour Bridge; Ayers Rock; a grand slam tennis tournament; the kangaroo, koala bear, platypus, dingo, and emus; the Tasmanian Devil marsupial; the original people of the area called the aborigines; the large sandstone structure called Ayers Rock; the crop circles of Melbourne; the collection of limestone rocks off the ocean shore called The Twelve Apostles; the beaches of Queensland; the remote inland area known as "The Outback;" the former wildlife explorer and crocodile hunter Steve Irwin; the 1986 film "Crocodile Dundee;" and is often referred to as the "land down under?"

2701. What country of the world is known for its indigenous people called the Maori; its pristine lakes, jagged mountains, volcanoes, and beaches; the southernmost capital city of Wellington; the sky tower of Auckland; Franz Josef Glacier; the geysers and hot springs of Rotorua; the penguins, whales, dolphins, and marlins at The Bay of Islands; the waterfalls and mountain scenery at Milford Sound in Queenstown; the native flightless bird called the kiwi; sheep; rugby; golf; the volcano at Lake Taupo; foods that include mussels, oysters, lamb, cheese, and fish and chips; greenstone jewelry; wood; glass; jade; the father of nuclear physics for his orbital theory of the atom, Ernest Rutherford; and the first man to reach the peak at Mount Everest in the Himalayas, Sir Edmund Hillary?

2702. What country of the world is known for royalty; King Juan Carlos and Queen Sofia; King Ferdinand and Isabella; the sponsorship of the voyages of Christopher Columbus; the Royal Palace; Madrid's Plaza Mayor; the Prado Museum; Retiro Park; La Tomatina tomato fight; bullfighting; the running of the bulls in Pamplona; the April Fair in Sevilla; the Alcazar and Aqueduct in Segovia; the "hanging houses" of Cuenca; the Sagrada Familia church in Barcelona by the architect Antonio Gaudi; El Escorial monastery; the Mezquita of Cordoba; the Alhambra Moorish palace in Granada; the prehistoric cave paintings in Altamira; the novel "Don Quixote de la Mancha" by Miguel de Cervantes; the Jai Alai court game; the Real Madrid soccer team; the FC Barcelona soccer team; flamenco music and dancing; the guitar; beaches; swords; LLadró porcelain figurines; ceramics; the hand fan; wine; the spice saffron; olives; sangria; tapas snacks; the national rice dish Paella; Iberico ham; manchego cheese; squid and churros with hot chocolate; art masters Pablo Picasso, Diego Velázquez, Francisco de Goya, El Greco, Joan Miró, and Salvador Dalí; singers Julio and Enrique Iglesias; tennis player Rafael Nadal; Barcelona soccer player Xavi; and words that include adobe, albino, alfalfa, alligator, armada, avocado, banana, barbecue, bronco, burro, burrito, cafeteria, canoe, canyon, cargo, chile, chocolate, cilantro, embargo, enchilada, fajita, fiesta, galleon, guacamole, hammock, habanero, hacienda, huarache, hurricane, iguana, jaguar, jalepeño, lasso, llama, machete, macho, maize, mariachi, matador, mesa, mestizo, mole, mosquito, mustang, nacho, nopal, ocelot, oregano, paella, papaya, patio, peso, pimento, pinto, piñata, plaintain, plaza, poncho, potato, pronto, pueblo, quesadilla, ranch, rodeo, rumba, salsa, savannah, serape, serrano, siesta, silo, sombrero, stampede, stockade, taxi, tobacco, taco, tamale, tango, tomato, tornado, tuna, vaquero, vanilla, vigilante, wrangler, and yucca?

SOCIAL STUDIES

2703. What country of the world is known for the Berbers and Arabs; the Atlas Mountains; the Sahara Desert; camels; the cities of Tangier and Casablanca; the markets of Marrakesh; the Islam religion; compacted towns called medinas; the medieval medina of Fes; fez hats; hijab headscarves; foods that include couscous rice, olives, grilled kebobs, coffee, and mint tea; the Kasbah market of Tangier; handicrafts that include textiles, jewelry, leatherwork, and ceramics?

2704. What country of the world is known for The Egyptian Museum in Cairo; the twin rock temples of Abu Simbel; the Valley of the Kings near Luxor that includes the tomb of the boy-king Tutankhamen; the Nile River; the Red Sea Reef; the ancient religious site of Karnak with its 134 massive pillars; The Pyramids of Giza; The Great Sphinx of Giza; The Underground Library of Alexandria; world leaders Anwar Sadat and Yasser Arafat; ancient pharaohs Cleopatra, Khufu, Tutankhamen, Ramses II, and Snefu; military commander Muhammad Ali; General Ptolemy; Queen Nefertiti; papyrus paper; belly dancing; the national pasta dish called koshari; couscous; beef kebobs; Anise and Hibiscus teas; alabaster ceramics; gold jewelry; cartouche personalized hieroglyphic pendants; long gowns worn by men called jallabiyas; dresses worn by women called kaftans; headscarves worn by women called hijabs; souvenir wood carvings; scarves; Stella beer; spices; and mother of pearl boxes?

2705. What country of the world is known for being regarded as the holy land for Christians, Muslims, and Jews; The Western Wall, a Jewish religious site, located in the old city of Jerusalem; the largest freshwater lake called the Sea of Galilee; the city of Nazareth where Jesus was believed to have lived; speaking both Hebrew and Arabic; the religious site known as Temple Mount; The Shrine of the Bab and its garden Terraces; the Islamic building known as The Dome of the Rock; The Mount of Olives; the Masada, an ancient fortress built by the Roman ruler Herod the great overlooking the Dead Sea; the Jewish symbol on the flag known as The Star of David; the religious leader David; Prime Minister Menachem Begin; Saint Joseph; Saint John the Baptist; Prime Minister Golda Meir; world leaders Benjamin Netanyahu, Ariel Sharon, and Yitzhak Rabin; and first books of Hebrew scripture called the Torah?

2706. What country of the world is known for being the largest Arab state; for the coral reefs of the Red Sea; as the birthplace of Islam; the Islamic holy sites of Mecca and Medina; having the largest oil reserves in the world along the Persian Gulf; the large capital city of Riyadh; having the largest continuous sand desert; camels; Persian rugs, terrorist Osama Bin Laden; and being one of the settings for the collection of Arabic folk tales as told in "One Thousand and One Nights?

2707. What is the name of the emirate located in the Persian Gulf, part of the United Arab Emirates Federation, known for having the world's tallest skyscraper called Burj Khalifa standing at 2,717 feet high with 163 stories: Dibba or Dubai?

2708. What country of the world is known as a war-torn nation; for the cave complex at Tora Bora; the Gardens of Babur; The Kabul Zoo; The Friday Mosque; The Statues of Buddha; hand-made carpets; having one of the oldest dog breeds, the Afghan Hound; and having a native of this country, a twelve-year-old girl named Sharbat Gula, as the subject of a famous photograph on the 1985 Time Magazine cover that was taken by journalist Steve McCurry while she was living as a refugee in Pakistan during the Soviet Union's occupation of this country?

SOCIAL STUDIES

2709. What country of the world is known for its long history and ancient civilizations; the number of monkeys in its capital city of New Delhi; The Kanha National Park, a wildlife reserve that served as the inspiration to Rudyard Kipling in writing his novel, "The Jungle Book;" the city of Varanasi on the River Ganges; the populous city of Calcutta; the Taj Mahal, a white domed marble mausoleum now regarded as one of the "new" wonders of the world; many ancient temples; poverty and diversity; the predominant Hindu religion; the Hindu belief that cows are sacred; camel races; the high regard for the endangered Bengal Tiger; the Himalaya mountain range; the snow-clad peaks of Kashmir; the film industry in Bombay; heavy monsoon rains; a garment worn by women called a sari; a garment worn by men called a dhoti; the game of cricket; exotic spices; fried banana chips; elaborate wedding ceremonies; henna tattoos; dances and festivals; using a social structure called the caste system; Mahatma Gandhi, the man regarded as the father of the nation; Prime Minister Indira Gandhi; nun and saint Mother Teresa; and products that include tea, incense, bangle bracelets, marble work, pottery, ceramics, shawls, silk saris, carpets, henna dye, drums, wooden flutes, leather shoes, Benkura terracotta horses, and dancing dolls?

2710. What country of the world is known for containing ten of the world's highest peaks, is landlocked between China to the north, and India to the south; the medieval and modern flair of the capital city of Kathmandu; and Mount Everest, the highest summit on earth in the Himalayas towering 29,029 feet high: Nepal or Mongolia?

2711. What country of the world is known for The Grand Palace and giant Buddha statues in the capital city of Bangkok; temples, museums, and pagodas; the Buddhist religion; the Chiang Mai Night Bazaar; the island of Ko Phi Phi; tsunami storms; lotus flowers; tigers, leopards, elephants, cobras, crocodiles, rhinoceros, exotic birds, and the black and white tapir; this country was originally known as Siam; the Siamese cat originated here; kickboxing is the national sport; golf courses; a leading manufacturer of electronics; being the largest producer of pineapples; resorts, beaches, and many islands; the three-wheeled motorbike with a cab in the back called a tuk-tuk; being the largest exporter of rice' and for the national dish of stir-fried rice noodles called Pad Thai?

2712. What country of the world is known for its long war against the North; the five royal palaces in the capital city of Seoul; the historical center of the city of Hanoi; the Cu Chi Tunnels that served as hiding places during the war; Independence Palace in Saigon, a name that was changed to Ho Chi Minh City in 1975 when it was taken over by the North, effectively marking the end of the war; the bay of dragons called Ha Long Bay; honoring the dragon, the turtle, and the horse; being the largest exporter of black pepper and cashew nuts; the Sa Pa rice terraces; having over 10,000 motor bikes on the road every day; for wearing cone-shaped hat called a non la; and engaging in the martial art of Tae Kwon Do?

2713. What country of the world is known as a collection of over 7,100 islands located off the coast of Asia; Saint Agustin Church in the capital city of Manila; mountains, volcanoes, and earthquakes;; the explorer Ferdinand Magellan who claimed the land for Spain in 1521 and named the area after the Spanish King Phillip II; The Chocolate Hills on the island of Bohol; the 2,000-year-old Banaue Rice Terraces carved into the mountains; abundant wildlife including hundreds of species of birds; the beaches and resorts on the island of Boracay; the abundance of coral species and seashells; inventing

SOCIAL STUDIES

karaoke and the yo-yo; world leaders Ferdinand Marcos and Corazon Aquino; exports that include electronics, clothing; mangoes, bananas, coconuts, and pineapples; and as having several elaborate festivals?

2714. What country of the world is known as an island nation consisting of more than 6,800 islands often referred to as "the land of the rising son;" bowing as a way of greeting; many volcanoes, earthquakes, and tsunamis; for The Hiroshima Peace Memorial, a tribute to the lives that were lost when the atomic bomb was dropped by the U.S. in 1945; launching a surprise air attack on the U.S. Naval Base at Pearl Harbor in Hawaii on December 7, 1941; The Temple of the Golden Pavilion; the active volcano with its symmetrical cone, Mount Fuji; being the only country in the world with a reining emperor; the main residence of the Emperor, the Tokyo Imperial Palace; the Great Buddha statue; being a world leader in robotics and electronics; the headquarters for companies like Sony, Toyota, Nintendo, Panasonic, Honda, Sharp, and Toshiba; not wearing their shoes inside their homes; traditional silk dresses tied with a wide belt called kimonos; a traditional coat called a happi; traditional shoes; a near 100% literacy rate; the art of shodo, a style of calligraphy; the national sport of sumo; practicing martial arts that include karate, judo, sumo, and Aikido; chopsticks; hand fans; bamboo umbrellas called wagasas; hand-painted prints; paper lanterns made of traditional wasi paper and glued onto a bamboo frame; traditional dolls; kitchen knives; pottery and porcelain; Samurai sword replicas; short, three line poems called haikus; elaborate ornamental gardens; Seiko, Citizen, and Casio watches; the art of paper folding called origami; ornamental trees grown in a pot called bonsai; foods that include rice, sushi, tofu, tempura, teriyaki, and chicken cooked on a grill called a hibachi; green tea and tea ceremonies; a rice wine drink called sake; the human-powered vehicle called a rickshaw; and words that include futon, tycoon, typhoon, gingko, honcho, ramen, soy, sushi, teriyaki, Sudoku, tsunami, yen, and wasabi, a spicy green sauce?

2715. What country of the world is known for its savannah wildlife safaris; acacia trees; forests, deserts, and plains; the Swahili language; the black rhino, leopard, hyena, cheetah, zebra, wildebeest, giraffes, and birds of Nairobi National Park; the coral reefs of Malindi; the lion, cheetah, leopard, elephant, crocodile, buffalo, and hippo of the Samburu National Reserve; the volcanic landscape of Tsavo National Park; the flamingos of Lake Nakuru; Amboseli National Park with its abundance of the elephants, giraffes, and views of Mount Kilamanjaro, Africa's tallest mountain, in Tanzania; the dense lion population and the migration of zebra and wildebeest at the Masai Mara National Reserve; foods that include ugali cornmeal, mashed peas and potatoes called irio, grilled maize, chapati flatbread, samosa pastries, coffee, and chai tea; beadwork, jewelry, bags, mango wood carvings, ebony carvings, soapstone, sisal baskets, kitengela glassware, and painted cloths called batiks?

2716. What country of the world is known for wildlife safaris; white sandy beaches; savanna animals like elephants, giraffes, and zebras at the Selous Game Reserve; the elephants, hippos, giraffes, wildebeest, flamingos, and migratory birds at Lake Mnyara National Park; Stone Town located on the Spice Island of Zanzibar; Lake Victoria; the tallest free-standing mountain and inactive volcano, Mount Kilimanjaro; and the zebra and wildebeest migration and big game safari at Serengeti National Park: Tanzania or Angola?

SOCIAL STUDIES

2717. What country of the world is known for the scenic beauty of Cape Town and the Cape Peninsula; The Cape of Good Hope, where the Atlantic Ocean meets the Indian Ocean, discovered in 1486 by the Portuguese navigator Bartholomeu Dias while searching for a sea route from Europe to India; the Victoria and Alfred Waterfront at Cape Town; the forests, mountains, lagoons, rivers, lakes, and beaches along the Garden Route; the "city of gold," Johannesburg; Blyde River Canyon Nature Preserve; the Drakensberg mountain range; the vineyards at Cape Winelands; and the largest game reserve at Kruger National Park?

2718. What country of the world is known for the scenic Alps; the Vienna State Opera; Mirabell Palace; the Hohensalzburg Castle; the Melk Abbey; the golden roof of Innsbruck; the Danube River; Vienna coffee; the Landler folk dance; the Porsche car; the composers Wolfgang Amadeus Mozart and Franz Schubert; the political leader Adolf Hitler; the psychologist Sigmund Freud; the scientist Cristian Doppler;; the chef Wolfgang Puck; Swarovski crystal; the Christmas carol "Silent Night" by author Josef Mohr and composer Franz Gruber; and the filming of the movie "The Sound of Music" with Julie Andrews and Christopher Plummer in the city of Salzburg?

2719. What country of the world is known for speaking French, German, and Italian: the Matterhorn in the Alps: villas and chateaus; clocks and watches; cows; the long alphorn; army knives; the Bank, the United Nations office in Geneva; the Red Cross; the folk hero William Tell, Johanna Spyri's book "Heidi;" billionaire Ernesto Bertarelli;, the cities of Basel, Bern, Zurich, Lucerne, and Geneva; cheese, fondue, and chocolate; tennis players Roger Federer and Martina Hingis; figure skater Denise Biellmann; and downhill skier Pirmin Zurbriggen?

2720. What country of the world is known for its ancient history; the city-states of Athens and Sparta; the Acropolis citadel and the Parthenon temple in Athens; Olympia, the home of the first Olympic games; the alphabet; the island of Crete; the philosophers Socrates, Plato, and Aristotle; the playwrights Aeschylus, Sophocles, and Euripides; the leaders Alexander the Great and Pericles; the Titan God Zeus; the Olympian Gods Zeus, Poseidon, Apollo, Athena, and Aphrodite; the heroes Hercules, Odysseus, and Achilles; the Peloponnesian War; the poet Homer, author of the epics the "Iliad" and the "Odyssey;" the author of fables, Aesop; the "father of geometry;" Euclid; the scientist and mathematician Archimedes; and foods that include Baklava, olives, wine, Spanakopita spinach pie, pita bread, hummus, baked feta, and gyros?

2721. What country of the world is known for being the home and headquarters of the European Union and NATO in Brussels; speaking Flemish and French; the Antwerp diamond center; The Museum of Cocoa and Chocolate; lace; tennis players Justin Henin and Kim Clijsters; fashion designers Diane von Furstenberg and Liz Claiborne; bicycle racing champion Eddy Merckx; and foods that include waffles, chocolate, beer, French fries, and Brussels sprouts?

2722. What country of the world is known for the Copenhagen Zoo; the Copenhagen Open Air Museum; the Tivoli Gardens; the bronze Little Mermaid Statue; as the inventor of Lego plastic bricks; the Round Tower Observatory; wind power; the Kronborg Castle, the setting for Shakespeare's "Hamlet;" the Fairy Tales of Hans Christian Anderson; the scientist Niels Bohr; Danish pastries; and for being the oldest existing kingdom in the world?

SOCIAL STUDIES

2723. What country of the world is known for having two capitals, Amsterdam and The Hague; speaking Dutch; tulips; windmills; wooden clog shoes; cheese markets; hollandaise sauce; herring; apple pie; the Anne Frank House; the Keukenhof Gardens; having the largest seaport in Europe in the city of Rotterdam; bicycling everywhere; the painter of "Starry Night," "Sunflowers," and "The Bedroom," Vincent Van Gogh; the painter of "The Night Watch" and "Self-Portrait with Beret and Turned Up Collar;" Rembrandt; and having part of this country called Holland?

2724. What country of the world is known for royalty; the Vikings; the Royal Palace of Stockholm; the Stockholm Globe Arena; the St. Lucia candle festival during Christmastime; IKEA furniture; H & M clothing; Electrolux appliances; the Volvo and Saab cars; ice hockey; Nobel prizes; the scientists Alfred Nobel and Anders Celsius; the "Pippi Longstocking" books by author Astrid Lindgren; glassworks; Absolut Vodka; meatballs; pickled herring; the musical group ABBA; tennis player Bjorn Borg; and golfer Annika Sorenstam?

2725. What country of the world is known for the Sebelius Monument in Helsinki; Helsinki Cathedral; the Santa Claus Village amusement park; the Northern Lights; saunas; Nokia phones; glass ornaments and birds; jewelry; bread cheese; lingonberry porridge; apple donuts; textile art; festivals, speaking Finnish, and having an excellent education system?

2726. What country of the world is known for Vikings and longships; the Viking Ship Museum in Oslo; fjords; the Geiranger Fjord; glaciers; the medieval wooden stave churches; having the world's longest road tunnel; telemark skiing; collecting more medals at the Winter Olympics than any other nation; soccer; reindeer, elk, and the Arctic fox; eating whale meat; consuming more coffee than any other country; waffles; trolls; the fishing industry; salmon; oil; the explorer that led the first Antarctic expedition, Roald Amundsen; the Norse explorer who was the first European to land in North America, Leif Ericson; the author of "Matilda," "The Gremlins," and "Charlie and the Chocolate Factory," Roald Dahl; the playwright and author of "A Doll's House," Henrik Ibsen; the expressionist painter of "The Scream" Edvard Munch; the figure skater Sonja Henie; the actress Marilyn Monroe; hand-knit sweaters, hats and scarves; and for hosting the annual presentation of the Nobel Peace Prize in Oslo?

2727. What country of the world is known as the largest country; for its massive export of oil; nine time zones; the ruble currency; the fortified fortress in Moscow called The Kremlin; the period of hostile relations that developed after World War II with the United States referred to as the Cold War; the distinctive architecture of the colorful Saint Basil's Cathedral located in Moscow's Red Square; the 4,000 mile Trans-Siberian Railway; The Valley of Geysers; The Hermitage Museum in St. Petersburg founded by Catherine the Great in 1764; the first artificial Earth satellite called Sputnik; the classic ballet company based at the Bolshoi Theatre in Moscow; ballet dancer Mikhail Baryshnikov; founder of the Bolsheviks and leader of a revolution Vladimir Lenin; political leader Joseph Stalin; world leaders Vladimir Putin, Boris Yeltsin and Mikhail Gorbachev; scientist Ivan Pavlov; author of "War and Peace," "The Death of Ivan Ilych," and "Anna Karenina," Leo Tolstoy; author of "Crime and Punishment," Fyodor Dostoyevsky; short story author and playwright Anton Chekhov; symphony composer of "Swan Lake," Pyotr Tchaikovsky; songwriter of "Puttin' on the Ritz" and "White Christmas," Irving Berlin; tennis players Maria Sharapova, Anna Kournikova, and

SOCIAL STUDIES

Victoria Azarenka; figure skaters Oksana Baiul and Evgeni Plushenko; Faberge jeweled eggs that were created for the Imperial Family; wooden nesting dolls; foods that include black caviar; cabbage soup; meat kebobs; smetana sour cream; Blini pancakes, and vodka; as the host country for the 2014 winter Olympics held in Sochi; and the fur cap with ear flaps called a Ushanka?

2728. What country of the world is known for its massive size and as having the largest population; a one child policy; Mandarin and Cantonese languages; over 3,500 written symbols or characters; a walled enclosure in Beijing called The Forbidden City containing the palaces of 24 emperors of the Ming and Qing Dynasties; the famous portrait of the former Communist leader Mao Zedong Tiananmen Square in Beijing; the Jade Buddha Temple and the People's Square in the populous city of Shanghai; The Great Wall that is 5,500 miles long and visible from the moon; thousands of life-size figures called The Terracotta Warriors; pottery; the Giant Panda; the international trade route called The Silk Road; the dragon; a separate administrative region called Hong Kong; the martial art kung fu; chopsticks; foods that include fried rice, white rice, chow mein noodles, potstickers, Peking duck, Kung Pau chicken, Wonton soup, tea, and soy sauce; a special calendar and New Year; a Spring Festival, a Fall Festival, a Lantern Festival, a Winter Solstice Festival, and a Dragon Boat Festival; having the highest production of electronics; over one billion dollars in exports; Feng Shui, the art of creating harmonious surroundings; silk products; calligraphy; jade and pearl jewelry; kites; paper cuttings; lanterns; silk textiles; pottery and porcelain; the teacher and philosopher Confucius; President Xi Jinping; writer Mo Yan; basketball player Yao Ming; tennis player Li Na; and the words and phrases that include chop chop, chop suey, chow, chow mein, Feng Shui, gung-ho, hoisin, ketchup, kowtow, lo mein, no can do, shih tzu, tangram, wok, and won ton?

2729. What country are Puerto Rico, Guam, the Virgin Islands, Samoa, and the Northern Mariana Islands territories of?

2730. Which countries would you like to travel to someday?

Chapter 6 – Government and Civics

Government and Civics – Pre-School

1. Do we have rules and laws?
2. Do rules and laws help keep us safe?
3. What are some rules of a school?
4. What are some rules at home?
5. What is the name of the President of the United States?
6. What are the jobs of some community helpers?
7. Do we live in a neighborhood?
8. Do we live in a community?
9. What are the names of some businesses in our community?
10. What is the purpose of having a post office?
11. What is the purpose of having banks?
12. What is the purpose of having a fire department?
13. What is the purpose of having a police station and policemen?
14. Is it our duty as a citizen to obey the laws?
15. Who enforces the laws: the police or the fire department?
16. Is it important for citizens to obey traffic signs and traffic lights?
17. What is the purpose of having schools?
18. Are some children schooled at home?
19. Is the classroom part of a school community?
20. Are churches, temples, mosques, and synagogues also part of a community?
21. What are schools, restaurants, parks, stores, movie theatres, pools, and playgrounds all a part of: a community or a village?
22. May people of the same community have different beliefs?

GOVERNMENT AND CIVICS

23. What is the name of our town or city?
24. What is the name of our state?
25. What is the name of the country we live in?
26. Do people of different cultures live here in America?
27. It is good behavior to be civic and friendly with others?

Government and Civics – Kindergarten

28. What are the names of some people that help us in our community?
29. What are the names of some people that help us in our school?
30. Is it important to obey the rules of the school?
31. Is it good to cooperate with others?
32. It is important to respect others who may be different than us?
33. How do you show responsibility in school and at home?
34. Where in the community do we go to buy groceries?
35. Where do we go to mail a letter or package?
36. Where do we go to check out a book or look for information?
37. Where do we go to deposit or take out money?
38. What are some jobs that people have?
39. What kinds of vehicles do police officers use in their job?
40. What kinds of vehicles do firemen and firewomen use in their job?
41. What are some other ways of transportation we can use to travel from one place to another?
42. Why do we follow rules at home and in school?
43. What is the name of the rule that states, "Treat others as you would want to be treated?"
44. Do rules and laws help to keep a community organized and safe?
45. Is there a consequence or something that happens to you if you break a rule?
46. Is it good citizenship to follow the rules of a game or a sport?
47. Why do we need to follow laws?
48. What does the community and state have that makes the laws: police officers or a government?
49. Who in our local community has the job of enforcing the laws?

GOVERNMENT AND CIVICS

50. What happens to someone who breaks a law?
51. Do all citizens have rights?
52. Do all citizens have responsibilities?
53. Do you think honesty and respect are important traits in being a good citizen?
54. What does our country flag look like?
55. What is the American flag of the United States of America: a symbol or a landmark?
56. Do we have a state flag?
57. What may we say if we choose to show our allegiance to our American flag?
58. Can you name a song that may show patriotism to America?
59. Do all countries have a flag that symbolizes their country?
60. What is the name of a song that represents the United States?
61. Do citizens observe national holidays?
62. What might be something you could do for a community service project?

Government and Civics – 1st Grade

63. What is the term that describes the study of the rights and duties of citizens: laws or civics?
64. What are two examples of school rules?
65. Is there a consequence if a student breaks a rule?
66. Are rules and laws in place to keep us safe?
67. Whose job is it to establish laws: the citizens or the government?
68. What is a consequence if a citizen breaks a law?
69. Are there workers in your school like a playground supervisor or a crossing guard that help keep you safe?
70. What is the name of the person whose job it is to keep you safe, and enforce the rules at swimming pools or lakes: coast guard or lifeguard?
71. Who are some people in your school who enforce the rules to help maintain safety and order?
72. Do we have a local government with elected leaders?
73. Do we have a state government with elected leaders?
74. Do we have a national government with elected leaders?

GOVERNMENT AND CIVICS

75. What do all citizens have a right to do to elect leaders into office?

76. What is the name of the process of electing a candidate: an assembly or an election?

77. Do all citizens have civic duties in their community, state, and country?

Government and Civics – 2nd Grade

78. Can you say and spell your full name?

79. Can you say your full address?

80. Can you say your home or cell phone number?

81. Can you say your parents' first names?

82. What city or town are you a resident of?

83. What is the name of the area of the community that you live: a neighborhood or a village?

84. What state are you a citizen of?

85. What are communities divided into: regions or districts?

86. What is the name of the school district where you live?

87. What is the name of the leader of a school?

88. What is the name of the leader of a school district?

89. What type of a community is typically located in the countryside: rural or urban?

90. What type of a community is typically located in the city: rural or urban?

91. Do you live in a rural or an urban community?

92. What is the name of an outlying part of a city or town: a district or a suburb?

93. What is the name of the city that our community is a suburb of?

94. What is the capital of our state?

Government and Civics – 3rd Grade

95. What is the civic term for a group of people who live in the same area and are under the same government: a county or a community?

96. What is a community also a larger part of: a global community or a national community?

97. What is the term for a person who leaves one country to permanently settle in another: immigrant or alien?

GOVERNMENT AND CIVICS

98. Is our nation a nation of immigrants or emigrants?

99. Is it good practice as a citizen to appreciate the diversity of all cultures in our nation?

100. What is the term for the practice followed among people of a particular group or place: a habit or a custom?

101. Do different cultures practice different customs and traditions?

102. What is one family custom or tradition that you have?

103. What do we follow in order to maintain order in our community, state, and nation?

104. What is the term used in which all people are treated the same: fairness, or equality under the law?

105. What is the name of the body that creates, enforces, and interprets our laws: the police or the government?

106. What is the name of the government governed by the people, where everyone is treated equally: a democracy or a liberty?

107. Is a representative democracy in which the people vote for representatives a type of republic?

108. What is the term given for the freedoms that are protected by the government: rights or responsibilities?

109. What is the term give for a citizen's duty to obey rules, laws, and the rights of others: rights or responsibilities?

110. What is the term for the person that has the rights, opportunities, and the duties of being a member of a country: a citizen or a pedestrian?

111. What is the name of the document written by our third President Thomas Jefferson and signed on July 4th, 1776 in which the 13 original colonies declared themselves free from England under King George?

112. What is the name of the document that was written in 1787 by a group of men called the "Framers" like George Washington and Ben Franklin that outlines the laws and how the government should work, and is regarded as the highest law in the land: the Declaration of Independence or the United States Constitution?

113. In which state is Independence Hall located, where the Framers met to write the Constitution: Philadelphia or Washington, D.C?

114. What is the name of the opening lines of the U.S. Constitution that begins, "We the people, in order to form a more perfect union…:" the Bill of Rights or the Preamble?"

115. What is the term for changes made to the constitution: an amendment or a revision?

116. What is the name for the first ten amendments to the U.S. Constitution that states the ten fundamental rights and liberties of all citizens: the amendments or the Bill of Rights?

GOVERNMENT AND CIVICS

117. What is the term for the rights protected by the government that include the rights of life, liberty, and the pursuit of happiness: the Bill of Rights or Inalienable Rights?

118. How many amendments are there currently to the original U.S. Constitution: 17 or 27?

119. Which amendment, added in 1791, guarantees the freedoms of religion, speech, assembly, press, and petition: the First Amendment or the Second Amendment?

120. On which day every year do Americans celebrate their independence from the British colonists under King George?

121. How many stars and how many stripes did the American flag have that represented the original number of colonies?

122. How many stars does the American flag have after the state of Hawaii was added in 1959?

123. How many horizontal stripes are there on the current American flag?

124. How would you describe the current American flag?

125. What is the term for the people who permanently settle here from another country?

126. Which group would **not** be considered immigrants: Native Americans or Latin Americans?

127. Who is the primary author of the Declaration of Independence: Thomas Jefferson or Ben Franklin?

128. What is the name of the national holiday in May in which Americans remember the people who have died for our freedoms: Memorial Day or Veterans Day?

129. What is the name of the national holiday in November in which Americans recognize the women and men who serve and have served in our armed forces: Memorial Day or Veterans Day?

130. Do all eligible citizens have the right to vote?

131. What is the minimum age that a person must be in order to vote in a public election: 18 or 21?

132. How many branches is the United States Government comprised of: three or five?

133. What are the executive, the legislative, and the judicial considered: departments or branches?

134. Do the three branches of government share the power?

135. What is the term for the ability of each branch of government to limit the powers of the other: branch equality or checks and balances?

136. What is the collective name for the two groups of people called the House of Representatives and the Senate, are stationed in Washington, D. C., and are responsible for making the laws for our country: the Assembly or the Congress?

137. How many elected members make up the U.S. Senate: 100 or 435?

138. How many elected members make up the U.S. House of Representatives: 50 or 435?

GOVERNMENT AND CIVICS

139. What is the title given to the head of the House of Representatives: the President of the House, or the Speaker of the House?

140. Which branch of the government is made up of the House of Representatives and the Senate, and is responsible for making the laws: the legislative branch or the executive branch?

141. How many national Senators does each state have: two or four?

142. What is the name of the person who is the executive leader of the United States government?

143. What is the name given to the person who is second in line to the President?

144. What is the name of the current Vice-President?

145. Which branch of the government is led by the President and the cabinet, is the leader of the Armed Forces, and has the power to veto a law: the executive branch or the judicial branch?

146. Which branch of the government is made up of Supreme Court Justices and is responsible for enforcing the laws and deciding if laws are constitutional: the executive branch or the judicial branch?

147. How many Supreme Court Justices are on the highest court: nine or twelve?

148. What is the name of the highest Supreme Court Justice: Your Honor or Chief?

149. What is the name of the place where a person goes to have their case heard when a law has been broken?

150. What is the name of the head elected official of a state: the mayor or the governor?

151. Do you know the name of the governor of our state?

152. What is the name of the head elected official of a city: the mayor or the governor?

153. Do you know the name of the mayor of our city?

154. What is the title of the head of the city police department: Lieutenant or Chief?

155. What is the title of the head of the city fire department: Lieutenant or Chief?

156. What are your responsibilities at home?

157. Is it important to have good study habits to do well in school?

158. What are some public places in our community where people work?

159. Is a museum open to the public?

160. What are some types of museums?

161. Are the library, post office, grocery store, swimming pool, and bank open to the public?

162. Can you name any private businesses in our community where people go to work every day?

GOVERNMENT AND CIVICS

163. Can you name any specific goods or services that are produced or provided in our community or in our state?

164. What are some other specialized jobs where people have to train and study in order to work in that profession?

165. What is the name of the area where people live, work, and play: a suburb or a community?

166. Can you name some civic duties of a responsible citizen in a community?

167. What is the name given to an urban area or downtown area: city or town?

168. What is the name given to a rural area of farmland: city or countryside?

169. What is the name given to the neighborhoods and communities that are located just outside of a city: suburbs or outskirts?

170. How would you describe the community you live in?

Government and Civics – 4th Grade

171. What is the term for the set of rules and regulations set up by the government of a town, city, state, and nation: statutes or laws?

172. Does America have local, state, and federal laws?

173. What are the three levels of government: executive, legislative, and judicial, or President, House of Representatives, and Senate?

174. What is the term for the national level of government: federal or local?

175. Which level of government is in charge of the military, the coining of money, highways, passports, Social Security, income tax, and interstate commerce: state or federal?

176. Which level of government is in charge of schools, automobile registration, sales tax, and welfare: state or federal?

177. Which level of government is in charge of police and fire, zoning, roads, trash collection, voter registration, school districts, and property taxes: local or state?

178. What is the name of the document that declared the United States free from English rule?

179. What are James Madison, Alexander Hamilton, Ben Franklin, and George Washington all considered: Founding Fathers or famous inventors?

180. What is the name of the introduction to the U.S. Constitution that states: "We the People of the United States, in Order to form a more perfect Union, establish Justice, insure domestic Tranquility, provide for the common defense, promote the general Welfare, and secure the Blessings of Liberty to ourselves and our Prosperity, do ordain and establish this Constitution of the United States of America?"

GOVERNMENT AND CIVICS

181. What is the name of a city law or rule: an ordinance or a treaty?

182. What is the supreme law of the land: the United States Constitution or the Bill of Rights?

183. What is a change to the U.S. Constitution called: an addendum or an amendment?

184. What is the term for the first ten amendments to the U.S. Constitution: the Bill of Rights or the Preamble?

185. Which branch of government is made up of the Congress and makes the laws: the executive branch or the legislative branch?

186. What are the names of the two chambers that make up the U.S. Congress: The House of Representatives and the Senate, or the legislative branch and the judicial branch?

187. Where does the Congress conduct their sessions in Washington, D.C: at the U.S. Capitol, or at the White House?

188. What is the capital of the state you live in?

189. What is the name of the person elected to make laws: a candidate or a legislator?

190. Which branch of government includes the President and the cabinet, and carries out and enforces the laws: the judicial branch or the executive branch?

191. Which branch of government is made up of Supreme Court Justices that interpret the law and the U.S. Constitution: the judicial branch or the legislative branch?

192. What is the name of the policy that ensures that one branch does not have more power than another: Separation of Powers, or Checks and Balances?

193. What is the name of the policy that assigns specific duties to each branch of government, Separation of Powers, or Checks and Balances?

194. Who is the leader of the executive branch: the President or the Speaker of the House?

195. What is the name of the current President of the United States?

196. Who is the current Vice-President of the United States?

197. What is the name of the President's residence in Washington D.C?

198. Who is the commander-in-chief, the person in charge of the Armed Forces: the President or the Vice-President?

199. What is the name of the avenue where the White House is located in Washington D.C.: Pennsylvania Avenue or Philadelphia Avenue?

200. What is the name of the power a President has to reject or deny a government bill: veto power or executive power?

GOVERNMENT AND CIVICS

201. What is the name of the highest court in the United States: Head or Supreme?

202. What is the name of the person who makes an official ruling in a court: a judge or a jury?

203. What is the name of a group of people who listen to a case in a courtroom and decide whether or not a person is guilty of breaking the law: a committee or a jury?

204. What two groups make up America's legislative branch called the Congress?

205. How many members are there in the House of Representatives: 435 or 100?

206. Does the number of officials elected to Congress depend on the population of each state?

207. How many elected members are there in the U.S. Senate: 435 or 100?

208. Does the number of officials elected to the Senate depend on the population of each state, or is it currently set at two per state?

209. What is the name of the leader of the House of Representatives?

210. How long is the term of a legislator, a member of Congress: two years or six years?

211. How many U.S. Senators does each state have?

212. How long is the term of a United States Senator: two years or six years?

213. What is the name of a suggested law before it becomes a law: a bill or a proposal?

214. What is the name of a bill that has been passed by a legislature and signed by an executive?

215. What is the term for the power given to the executive branch to oppose or reject a bill?

216. What is the name of the elected person in charge of a city?

217. Do you know the name of the mayor of our city?

218. What is the name of the elected person in charge of a state: a governor or a senator?

219. Do you know the name of the governor of our state?

220. Which level of government include mayors, county executives, and aldermen: local or state?

Government and Civics – 5th Grade

221. What is the study of the rights of others and the role of citizens: citizenship or civics?

222. What city or community are you a citizen of?

223. What is the term for the administrative divisions of states: counties or cities?

224. What county are you a citizen of?

225. What state are you a citizen of?

GOVERNMENT AND CIVICS

226. What country are you a citizen of?

227. What is the term for members of a community with rights and responsibilities to their community, or to their government: aliens or citizens?

228. What is the term for something that is due a person by law or nature: right or responsibility?

229. What is the term for the obligations of a person and the actions that person takes to meet them: right or responsibility?

230. What is the name of a government controlled by one person or a small group of people and hold absolute power: authoritarian or dictatorship??

231. What is the name of the legal process to obtain citizenship if a person is not a natural born citizen: naturalization or documentation?

232. What is the name for a group of people who settle far from home but still keep ties with their homeland: loyalists or colonists?

233. How many original colonies were there?

234. What is the name of the first written constitution of the colonies that created a "league of friendship" between the states: the Declaration of Independence or the Articles of Confederation?

235. What is the term for the freedom from the control and influence of others: sovereignty or independence?

236. What is the term for the right of a country to govern itself with complete independence: sovereignty or anarchy?

237. What is the term for a state of disorder and chaos due to the lack of rules, laws, authority and a central government: anarchy or monarchy?

238. Does Great Britain and other nations still recognize the monarchy and royal family?

239. What is the name of the document that declared the colonies free from Great Britain and signed in 1776?

240. What document includes the signatures of John Hancock, Thomas Jefferson, Samuel Adams, John Adams, and Ben Franklin?

241. In which state was the Declaration of Independence signed: Washington D.C. or Pennsylvania?

242. How many of the original thirteen colonies can you name?

243. Who is the principal writer of the Declaration of Independence: Samuel Adams or Thomas Jefferson?

244. What is the name of the government that manages the relationships among states: a central government or a national government?

245. What is the term for a written form of government: a Constitution or a Federal System??

GOVERNMENT AND CIVICS

246. What is the name for the supporters of the Constitution and of a strong national government: the Nationalists or the Federalists?

247. What is the name for the opponents to the Constitution who thought that it gave too much power to the Federal government: Anti-Nationalists or Anti- Federalists?

248. Can you name any of the "Framers" of the U.S. Constitution?

249. What is the name for the opening lines of the U.S. Constitution: the Preamble or the Bill of Rights?

250. What lines do you know of the Preamble?

251. What is meant by "domestic tranquility" as mentioned in the preamble: to have peace within the United States, or to have peace with others outside the United States?

252. Are "inalienable rights" rights that can be taken away, or rights that cannot be taken away?

253. How many articles is the U.S. Constitution made up of: seven or seventeen?

254. Does Article I of the Constitution reference the rules of the U.S. Congress in the Legislative Branch of government or the Executive Branch of government?

255. Does Article II of the Constitution reference the Legislative Branch of government or the rules for the President and Vice- President in the Executive Branch of government?

256. Does Article III of the Constitution reference the Executive Branch of government or the rules of the Supreme Court Justices in the Judicial Branch of government?

257. Does Article IV of the Constitution discuss the relationship between the states and the federal government?

258. What is the name of a change or an addition to a document?

259. What are the first ten amendments called that were added to the Constitution to protect individual rights?

260. Which amendment refers to freedom of religion, speech, press, assembly, petition and expression: the First Amendment or the Second Amendment?

261. What is the term for the rights or freedoms granted to the people by the First Amendment allowing individuals to speak, worship, assemble, organize, or petition without interference by the government: Civil liberties or Bill of Rights?

262. What is the term given for the suppression of speech through printed material or other media that might be considered offensive to some: censorship or freedom of the press?

263. What is the term that refers to the intentional spreading of lies through words: libel or slander?

264. What is the term that refers to the intentional false statement that may affect a person's reputation is are printed or published: libel or slander?

GOVERNMENT AND CIVICS

265. What is the term for the preference of an idea or point of view over another: bias or superiority?

266. What is the term given to an advertisement that is designed to promote a particular idea or issue: propaganda or bias?

267. Which amendment refers to the right to bear arms: the First Amendment or the Second?

268. Which amendment refers search and seizure: the Third Amendment or the Fourth?

269. When people choose to remain silent or not answer a question in order not to incriminate themselves, which amendment are they pleading: the Fourth Amendment or the Fifth Amendment?

270. What is the meaning of ratification: to formally approve a law or treaty or to formally approve an elected official?

271. Which amendment abolished slavery and involuntary servitude that was passed by Congress and ratified by the states in 1865: the Third Amendment or the Thirteenth Amendment?

272. Which amendment, ratified in 1868, granted citizenship to "all persons born or naturalized in the United States" and guaranteed equal protection of the laws: the Fourth Amendment or the Fourteenth Amendment?

273. Which amendment to the Constitution, ratified in 1870 but not fully taken advantage of until 1965 with the passage of the Voting Rights Act of 1965, granted African American men the right to vote: the Fifteenth Amendment or the Fifth Amendment?

274. What is the term that refers to the right of women to vote in public elections: suffrage or franchise?

275. Which amendment to the Constitution, ratified in 1920, recognized women's suffrage, granting women the right to vote: the Ninth Amendment or the Nineteenth Amendment?

276. How many amendments are there currently to the U.S. Constitution: 20 or 27?

277. What is the term for the fees that are required to be paid to local, state, and national government by people and businesses?

278. What is the term for the right of government to take private property for the use of the public in return for reasonable compensation: eminent domain, or search and seizure?

279. What is the name of the principle that states that the Federal Government will not pass laws that favor one religion over another: separation of church and state, or freedom of religion?

280. What is the name for a formal meeting attended by members of a group: a convention or a meeting?

281. What is the type of system in which the states and the national government share the power: a federal system or a national system?

282. What are the three branches of the Federal Government?

283. What is the term that refers to the ability of each branch of the government to check the power of the others: Balance of Power or Checks and Balances?

GOVERNMENT AND CIVICS

284. Which branch of the government has the power to pass laws by majority vote, declare war, borrow money, amend the constitution, confirm presidential nominations, tax, and regulate commerce: the executive branch or the legislative branch?

285. What are the two chambers of the legislative branch that make up the U.S. Congress?

286. What is the name of the part of the legislative branch where each state has two representatives: the House of Representatives or the Senate?

287. What is the name of the part of the legislative branch that is considered the "lower house" in which the number of representatives for each state is determined by the state's population and are elected by the people: the House of Representatives or the Senate?

288. What is the name of the leader of the House of Representatives?

289. Who is the President of the Senate: the Vice-President or the Secretary of State?

290. What is the role of the legislative branch of the government: to make the laws or interpret the laws?

291. What is the name for the time that the Congress meets that typically runs from January through November: a term or a session?

292. Does each house of Congress have Majority and Minority leaders?

293. What is the term for the legislative proposal that is draft of a law and must be voted on?

294. What is the name for a group of Senators or members of Congress that change or debate bills before passing them on to the executive branch: an assembly or a committee?

295. Who has the power to veto a law: the President or the Speaker of the House?

296. What is the name of the branch of government that enforces the laws, makes treaties, and commands the armed forces: the executive branch or the judicial branch?

297. Who is the leader of the executive branch?

298. Who is the Commander-in-Chief of the United States, in charge of: the Army, Navy, Marines, Air Force, and the Coast Guard?

299. Is the United States considered a Two-Party system or a Multi-Party system?

300. What is the name given for a group of citizens that share common ideas regarding how a government should work: a political party or a platform?

301. Can you name the two major political parties of the United States?

302. Which political party tends to be more conservative, and favors lower taxes and a smaller central government: the Republican Party or the Democratic Party?

303. Which political party tends to be more liberal, and favors higher taxes and more government programs and control: the Republican Party or the Democratic Party?

GOVERNMENT AND CIVICS

304. What is the political affiliation of the current President and Vice-president of the United States: Republican or Democrat?

305. Which animal is the political symbol for the Republican Party: the donkey or the elephant?

306. Which animal is the political symbol for the Democratic Party: the donkey or the elephant?

307. What is the term for the total number of people that vote for a candidate: popular vote or majority vote?

308. What is the name for the first election in which candidates for an office are narrowed down: the General Election or the Primary Election?

309. What is the name for the main election that is held to determine a winner of a political race: the Primary Election or the General Election?

310. What is the term for the group of people that are appointed by each state legislature to elect the President and the Vice-President: the electorate or the Electoral College?

311. How many of the 538 electoral votes does a Presidential candidate need to win: 250 or 270?

312. What is the term for the candidate that is the current holder of that office: the incumbent or the lame duck?

313. What is the term for an elected official who is near the end of his or her term or tenure and cannot be re-elected: incumbent or lame duck?

314. How old does a citizen need to be to be eligible to vote?

315. What day of the week are both primary and general elections typically held on?

316. What month does the U.S. Presidential election place?

317. In a presidential election, are the States that go to the Democratic candidate shaded red or blue?

318. In a presidential election, are the States that go to the Republican candidate shaded red or blue?

319. How long is the term of the President and Vice-President of the United States?

320. How many times can a United States President be re-elected?

321. What is the name of the event at the end of January every four years in which the elected President of the United States is officially sworn in: the inauguration or the assembly?

322. What is the name of the group of advisors to the President that includes the leaders of several departments including Agriculture, Commerce, Defense, Education, Health and Human Services, Homeland Security, Housing and Urban Development, Interior, Labor, State, Transportation, Treasury, Veterans Affairs, and the Attorney General: the U.S. Secretaries or the U.S. Cabinet?

323. What is the name of the speech given by the President that communicates the state of affairs of the United States: the State of the Union Address, or the American Status Report?

GOVERNMENT AND CIVICS

324. What is the name of the branch of government that interprets the laws and settles disputes between the states: the judicial branch or the legislative branch?

325. What is the name of the highest court in the United States?

326. How many Supreme Court Justices are there: nine or eleven?

327. What is the name of the lead Justice of the Supreme Court: the Chief Justice or the Head Justice?

328. Can you name the Chief Justice or any Supreme Court Justices currently on the bench?

329. What is the name for the group of citizens chosen to hear evidence and decide a case in a court of law: an assembly or a jury?

330. What is the name of the person or the institution that has had an action brought against him, her, or it in a court of law: a witness or a defendant?

331. What is the name of the person who sees an event and testifies in a court of law: a witness or a defendant?

332. What is the term for the written order that requires a person to attend court: a summons or a subpoena?

333. What is the term for the decision of a jury: a sentence or a verdict?

334. What is the name of the type of case in which a person has been accused of breaking a law: a criminal case or a civil case?

335. What is the name of the type of case in which a person has been involved in a non- criminal matter: a criminal case or a civil case?

336. What is the name given for the rights that a person is informed of when taken into custody by law enforcement that states, "You have the right to remain silent…:" Bill of Rights, or Miranda Rights?

337. What is the name of the person that defends the rights of the defendant in a court: an attorney or a defendant?

338. What is the term for an elected official in a county or state who conducts proceedings in a court on behalf of the government and its people: County Attorney or District Attorney?

339. What is the term for the chief law enforcement officer of the United States serving in the executive branch, is the head of the U.S. Justice Department, and represents the government in legal matters: Attorney General or Federal Attorney?

340. What is the term that states that government must follow the same rules and procedures, and be fair in all cases that are brought to trial: due process or trial by jury?

341. What protects a person's rights to life, liberty, and property: trial by jury, or due process of law?

342. What is the name for a serious crime such as murder, kidnapping, burglary, or passing counterfeit money: a felony or a misdemeanor?

GOVERNMENT AND CIVICS

343. What is the name for a less serious crime such as a traffic violation that is often punishable by fine: a felony or a misdemeanor?

344. What is the term for a formal charge by a grand jury: an indictment or a verdict?

345. What are guilty, not guilty, and no contest considered: court pleas, or verdicts?

346. What is the principle that states that the law applies to all, even those who govern: the rule of law, or fairness under the law?

347. What is the term for a formal request to someone in authority that is usually signed by several people: a declaration or a petition?

348. What is the term for the right of the government to take private property: eminent domain or implied powers?

349. What is the term for the unfair treatment of a certain group based on prejudice or bias: discrimination or segregation?

350. What is the term for a law at the local level of government: a policy or an ordinance?

351. What is the name for the gatherings of local citizens to discuss and vote on important issues: town meetings or assemblies?

352. What is the name of the governing body that is elected to make decisions on behalf of a school district: Board of Education, or School Board of Trustees?

353. What is the term given for a system of roads, bridges, sewers, and water in a community: infrastructure or incorporation?

354. Who is the head of the executive branch at the local level: the governor or the mayor?

355. Who is the head of the executive branch at the national level, and also has the title of commander-in-chief?

356. What are the names of the branches of the armed forces, besides the Coast Guard, that the President is in command of?

357. What is the term for the unmanned aerial vehicles, controlled by computers by remote control, used by the military to carry out dangerous operations or missions: robots or drones?

358. What is the term for a complex system of many departments and many rules: a democracy or a bureaucracy?

359. What is the term for the negotiations and relations between countries: diplomacy or commerce?

360. What are some civic duties that a citizen has?

GOVERNMENT AND CIVICS

Practice Citizenship Test

361. What is the supreme law of the land?

362. What does the Constitution do?

363. What are the first three words of the Constitution that suggests the idea of self-government?

364. What is an amendment?

365. What do we call the first ten amendments to the Constitution?

366. What is **one** right of freedom from the First Amendment?

367. How many amendments does the Constitution have?

368. What did the Declaration of Independence do?

369. What are **two** rights in the Declaration of Independence?

370. What is freedom of religion?

371. What is the economic system of the United States?

372. What is the "rule of law?"

373. What is **one** branch or part of the government?

374. Who is in charge of the executive branch?

375. What stops one branch of government from becoming too powerful?

376. Who makes federal laws?

377. What are the two parts of the U.S. Congress:

378. How many U.S. Senators are there?

379. We elect a U.S. Senator for how many years?

380. Who is one of your U.S. State Senators currently?

381. How many voting members does the House of Representatives have?

382. We elect a U.S. Representative for how many years?

383. Who is one of your U.S. Representatives currently?

384. Who does a U.S. Senator represent?

385. Why do some states have more U.S. Representatives than others?

386. We elect a President for how many years?

387. In what month do we vote for President?

GOVERNMENT AND CIVICS

388. What is the name of the President of the United States now?

389. What is the name of the Vice-President of the United States now?

390. If the President can no longer serve, who becomes President?

391. If the President and Vice-President can no longer serve, who becomes President?

392. Who is the Commander-in-chief in the military?

393. Who signs bills to become laws?

394. Who has the power to veto a bill?

395. What is the role of the President's Cabinet?

396. Can you name two secretaries in the President's Cabinet?

397. What is the role of the judicial branch of government?

398. What is the highest court in the United States?

399. How many Justices are there on the Supreme Court?

400. Who is the Chief Justice of the United States now?

401. What is one power of the federal government?

402. What is one power of the states?

403. Who is the current Governor of your state?

404. What is the capital of the state you live in?

405. What is the name of the current Speaker of the House of Representatives?

406. What are the two main political parties of the United States?

407. What is the political party of the current President of the United States?

408. Can you describe one amendment to the Constitution that describes who can vote?

409. What is one responsibility that is only for U.S. citizens?

410. Can you name one **right** that is only for U.S. citizens?

411. What are **two** rights of everyone living in the United States?

412. What do we show loyalty to when we cite the Pledge of Allegiance?

413. What is **one** promise you make when you become a United States citizen?

414. How old do citizens have to be to vote for President?

415. What are two ways that Americans can participate in their democracy?

GOVERNMENT AND CIVICS

416. When is the last day you can send in federal income tax forms?

417. When must all men register for the Secret Service?

418. What is one reason the colonists came to America?

419. Who lived in America before the Europeans arrived?

420. What group of people was taken to America and sold as slaves?

421. Why did the colonists fight the British?

422. Who wrote the Declaration of Independence?

423. When was the Declaration of Independence adopted?

424. Can you name **three** of the original thirteen states?

425. What happened at the Constitutional Convention?

426. When was the Constitution written?

427. Can you name **one** of the writers of the Federalist Papers that supported the U.S. Constitution?

428. What is **one** thing Benjamin Franklin is famous for?

429. Who is the "Father of our Country?"

430. Who was the first President of the United States?

431. What territory did the U.S. buy from France in 1803?

432. What is the name for **one** war fought by the United States in the 1800's?

433. What is the name for the U.S. war between the North and the South?

434. What is **one** problem that led to the Civil War?

435. What was **one** important thing that Abraham Lincoln did?

436. What did the Emancipation Proclamation do?

437. What did Susan B. Anthony do?

438. Can you name one war fought by the United States in the 1900's?

439. Who was President during World War I?

440. Who was President during the Great Depression and World War II?

441. Who did the United States fight in World War II?

442. What war was Eisenhower a General, before he became President of the United States?

443. What was the main concern of the United States during the Cold War?

GOVERNMENT AND CIVICS

444. What movement tried to end racial discrimination?

445. What did Martin Luther King, Jr. do?

446. What major event happened on September 11, 2001, in the United States?

447. Can you name **one** American Indian Tribe in the United States?

448. Can you **one** of the two longest rivers in the United States?

449. What ocean is on the West Coast of the United States?

450. What ocean is on the East Coast of the United States?

451. Can you name **one** U.S. territory?

452. What state can you name that borders Canada?

453. What state can you name that borders Mexico?

454. What is the capital of the United States?

455. Where is the Statue of Liberty?

456. Why does the flag have 13 stripes?

457. Why does the American flag have 50 stars?

458. What is the name of the National Anthem of the United States?

459. Who wrote the Star-Spangled Banner?

460. When do we celebrate Independence Day?

461. Can you name **two** national U.S. holidays?

462. Who said, "Give me liberty, or give me death?"

463. What are the 49th and 50th states of the Union?

464. What holiday was celebrated for the first time by American colonists?

465. What are some requirements to be eligible for President according to the U.S. Constitution?

466. What is the name of the residence of the President of the United States?

467. What is the name of the building where the Congress meets?

468. What are the colors of the American flag?

Chapter 7 – Economics

Economics – Pre-Sschool

1. Where do you save your money?
2. What can you buy when you save a lot of money?
3. If you borrow a book, do you need to give it back?
4. If you borrow money, do you need to pay it back?
5. What are the jobs of some community helpers?
6. What are some other jobs or professions in our community?
7. What career might you like to have some day?
8. Do family members have jobs and responsibilities in order to earn money and make a living?
9. What are some things that family members need to earn money for?
10. What American coins and bills can you name?

Economics – Kindergarten

11. Is it important to earn and save your money?
12. What can you do to earn money?
13. Where do you save your money?
14. What do you do with the money that you earn?
15. Would the purchase of food, clothing, and shelter be considered a need or a want?
16. Do people have different kinds of houses depending on where they live?
17. Would the purchase of a cell phone, a big screen television, and a bike be considered needs or wants?
18. Why do people have jobs?
19. Are all jobs important?

ECONOMICS

Economics – 1st Grade

20. What is the name for the medium we use to buy goods and services?
21. Do you save money at home?
22. Do you have a savings account in the bank?
23. How might a family living on a farm make a living?
24. How might a family living in a city or town make a living?
25. If someone works in the city, what are some means of transportation that this person might take in order to get to and from work every day?
26. Is it important to manage money well by earning it, saving it, and spending it wisely?
27. When you manage your money, is it important to budget it well as you plan how to use it?
28. Does our family have a budget or do we just spend as much money as we want to?
29. What is it called when you use a type of payment that will be paid back later: credit or debit?
30. If something is charged on a credit card, are you expected to pay the money back?
31. What is the term for the extra charge in exchange borrowing money: tax or interest?
32. Can you earn interest in a bank depending on the amount of money you have in a bank account?
33. What is the term for the money that is given to a person, often on a weekly basis, in exchange for helping out at home in some way or completing chores: salary or allowance?
34. Do you receive an allowance in exchange for some tasks?
35. Can money be used to donate to certain causes, churches, and charities?
36. If you are invited to a birthday party, is it always necessary to buy a gift, or can you make something yourself?
37. What is an example of something you could make out of raw materials to give as a gift?
38. Does each job have certain tasks and responsibilities?
39. What are your responsibilities at home and at school?
40. Is it important to have good study habits to do well in school?

Economics – 2nd Grade

41. What do people need to have in order to purchase goods and services?
42. What is the term that refers to **things** that are available to purchase: goods or services?

ECONOMICS

43. What goods and services do you think are considered "needs?"

44. What goods and services do you think are considered "wants?"

45. What is the term that refers to the **work** that is carried out to benefit others: goods or services?

46. What do Americans use to purchase or exchange for goods and services?

47. What is the name for the money that is used by a particular country: currency or bills?

48. What is the name for the currency of the United States?

49. What is the term for negotiating a price for something, or trading things without using money: sale or barter?

50. Are goods and services exchanged throughout the world?

51. What is the term for a person who uses goods and services: a producer or a consumer?

52. What is the term for a person who sells a good or service: a producer or a consumer?

53. What do natural, human, or capital, all refer to, and may contribute to the production of some good or service: resources or systems?

54. What is the term for things that come from nature like water, rock, and oil that are used by consumers: natural resources or capital resources?

55. What is the term for people that carry out some job or service like a farmer, miner, or builder: a personal resource or a human resource?

56. What is type of resources refer to tools, buildings, or machines that people use to produce goods or services: capital resources or natural resources?

57. What is the term that refers to people that work in companies that produce one specific good or service: specialization or isolation?

58. What is the term for the ability of the consumer to decide what to buy: economic choice or economic advantage?

59. What is the economic term for having more than enough of something: abundance or scarcity?

60. What is the economic term for not having enough of something: abundance or scarcity?

61. What is the term for the money a person earns while working at a job or profession: income or allowance?

62. What do families, banks, labor unions, small businesses, large corporations, and government agencies make up: an industrial system or an economic system?

63. What are the names of some businesses in your community and what kinds of goods and services to they provide?

ECONOMICS

64. What is the term for the result of labor that is produced by humans, mechanical effort, or through nature: a service or a product?

65. Can you name some major products of the state you live in?

66. What is the economic term for when products or services are brought into a country from another place to be sold: imports or exports?

67. What is the economic term for when products or services are sent to other countries to be sold: imports or exports?

68. When people make an economic decision, what is the term for weighing both the good and bad points of that decision: advantages and disadvantages, or benefits and costs?

69. What is the term for the state of working and earning an income: workforce or employment?

70. What is the term for the state of **not** working or earning an income even though a person may be actively searching for a job: unemployment or laid off?

71. What is the term for the person who starts a business and takes some risks in order to make money: entrepreneur or executive?

Economics – 3rd Grade

72. What is the economic term for the money that people use to purchase things: money or currency?

73. What is the economic term for the money people earn from work: income or compensation?

74. What is the name of the institution that provides financial services such as savings and checking accounts?

75. What is the term for the fee that people pay to the local, state, and federal government that helps to support the national economy: a tax or a fee?

76. What is the economic term for a plan to manage money: a budget or a money plan?

77. What is the economic term for a loss, a sacrifice, or a negative result: a cost or a benefit?

78. What is the economic term for a gain, an advantage, or a positive result: a cost or a benefit?

79. What is the economic term for the exchange of goods and services between countries: domestic trade or international trade?

80. What is the term for the purchase of goods or services from sellers in other countries: imports or exports?

81. What is the term for selling goods and services to other countries: imports or exports?

82. What is the economic term that refers to the way producers and consumers rely on each other: independence or interdependence?

ECONOMICS

83. What is the economic term for the amount producers will make and sell at a certain price: supply or demand?

84. What is the economic term for the amount of something consumers are willing to buy at a certain price: supply or demand?

85. What is the economic term for the money that a business makes after paying all of its workers and bills: profit or loss?

86. What is the economic term when the total of costs and expenses is more than the amount of money a business takes in: profit or loss?

87. What is the economic term for a person that has a unique idea, takes a chance or a risk, and launches a new business: an entrepreneur or an engineer?

88. What is the term for the freedom to start a business: entrepreneurship or free enterprise?

89. What is the economic term that refers to what you must give up in exchange for getting what you want: opportunity cost or sacrifice?

90. What is the economic term for promoting a good or service to convince people to purchase the good or service: advertising or marketing?

91. What is the term that refers to the efforts of two or more businesses with the same products who try to outdo one another in order to convince consumers to buy their products or services: economic choice or competition?

92. Do we sometimes need to make choices because we cannot buy everything we want?

Economics – 4th Grade

93. What is the term for how a country uses its money and resources, and reflects all the buying, selling, and producing that people do: industry or economy?

94. What is the term for the system where the people decide what to make and for whom it is made: a national economy or a market economy?

95. What is the term for activities that are performed by people or businesses to satisfy the needs of consumers: goods or services?

96. What is the term for people that use goods and services to satisfy their personal needs: producers or consumers?

97. What is the term for people that use natural, capital, or human resources in order to provide goods and services: producers or consumers?

98. What is the term for the production of products: manufacturing or building?

99. What is the economic term that describes the relationship between the amount of some good that

ECONOMICS

producers have for sale, and the amount that consumers are willing to buy: supply and demand, or imports and exports?

100. What is the term for the economic system where prices and competition are determined by the relationship of supply and demand: open economy or market economy?

101. What is the economic term that refers to the amount of goods and services that are produced related to the resources that are used: productivity or scarcity?

102. What is the economic term for the type of resources that may include machinery, tools, money, and buildings: capital or human?

103. What is the economic term for the type of resources that may include the education, skills, and values of people: capital or human?

104. What is the economic term for the type of resources that may include land and water that are used to produce something: capital or natural?

105. What is the collective economic term for the natural, capital, and human resources that are used to produce goods and services: productive resources or economic resources?

106. What is the economic term for the amount of money that people are willing to pay for some good or service, or the amount they receive when they sell some good or service: cost or price?

107. What is the economic term for something that is given up for something else: choice or opportunity cost?

108. What is the economic term that refers to the dividing up of work into smaller jobs: division of labor or assembly line?

109. What is the economic term for the money that is left over after all expenses are paid: a loss or a profit?

110. What is the economic term for the loss of money after all expenses are paid: a loss or a profit?

111. Would the money owed for some product or service be regarded as a profit or a debt?

112. What is the economic term for the reward that is offered that serves to persuade people to take specific economic actions: assets or incentives?

Economics – 5th Grade

113. What is the term that refers to the structure and management of money, goods, and services?

114. What is the economic term for the part of the economy that is not under government control: the public sector or the private sector?

115. What is the economic term for the part of the economy concerned with providing government services: the public sector or the private sector?

ECONOMICS

116. What is the term for the direct exchange of goods and services: trade or barter?

117. What is the economic term for the creation of specific goods and services produced to meet specific needs: specialization or incorporation?

118. What is the term for the service or thing necessary for survival: a need or a want?

119. What is the term for something that is not vital to survival, but is nice to have: a necessity or a luxury?

120. What is the name of the currency that is used in the United States?

121. Does our currency have value?

122. What is the term for the amount of a unit of money: currency or denomination?

123. In what denominations do our American coins come in?

124. What is the term for the service or thing necessary for survival: a need or a want?

125. What is the term for something that may be desired but is not necessary for survival: a need or a want?

126. What is the name of the currency that is used in most of Europe?

127. What is the name of the currency that is used in Canada and Australia?

128. What is the name of the currency that is used in Mexico?

129. Do you think that the Canadian dollar and the Australian dollar are valued the same as the American dollar?

130. What services does a bank offer?

131. What is the name of the box located inside a bank vault that people may keep valuables like coins, jewels, or important documents: safe deposit box or lock box?

132. What type of accounts do we have with the bank?

133. What is it called when a person adds money to a bank account: a deposit or a withdrawal?

134. What is it called when a person takes money out of a bank account: a deposit or a withdrawal?

135. What is the name of a printed promise of money issued and redeemed by a bank that can be used for the purchase of goods and services and subtracted from an account as it is spent: promissory note or check?

136. What might people use instead of a paper check to purchase goods and services that is automatically subtracted from their bank account: a debit card or a credit card?

137. What kind of market does the United States have where we can buy goods and services determined by supply and demand: a free market economy or an open economy?

ECONOMICS

138. What is the term for a long-term downturn in the economy, where spending by the government, consumers, and businesses is very low, and many people are without employment just as it was for a long time in the 1940's: a depression or a recession?

139. What is the term for an economy that suffers a short-term drop in economic growth where consumers and businesses sell fewer goods and services: a depression or a recession?

140. What is the term for the movement of the economy from one condition to another that reflects the highs and lows of the economy: business cycle or economic cycle?

141. What is the term for the phase of the business cycle when many people are working and business is productive: prosperity or surplus?

142. What is the term for the measurement of the economic strength of a nation: GDP (Gross Domestic Product) or Economic prosperity?

143. What is the term for the phase of the business cycle when demand increases for goods and services, unemployment decreases, and the GDP begins to rise again: prosperity or recovery?

144. What is the term for the increase in the general level of prices: inflation or deflation?

145. What is the term for the decrease in the general level of prices: inflation or deflation?

146. What is the name of the financial institution where you can deposit and withdraw money?

147. What is the name of America's central bank used by the government that controls the amount of money in the economy, and determines the interest rate: the FDIC or the Federal Reserve?

148. What is the term for the government agency that insures bank deposits for up to $250,000: the Federal Deposit Insurance Corporation, or the Federal Reserve?

149. What is the name of a certificate sold by the government or a company that may be cashed in with interest after a specific time: a stock or a bond?

150. Do you have any savings bonds?

151. What is the name of a banking account where people save and withdraw money?

152. What is the name of a banking account where people use checks to pay for goods and services?

153. What is the term for the fee that is charged for using somebody else's money: debt or interest?

154. What is the term for the percentage that is earned based on the amount of money saved or borrowed: interest or interest rate?

155. What is the term for what a person may borrow from a bank to purchase a house or a car that must be paid back with interest: a loan or a debt?

156. What is the economic term for the property or other assets that a borrower offers a lender in order to secure a loan: interest or collateral?

ECONOMICS

157. What is the term for the loan that is used to purchase a home or a business: a bank note or a mortgage?

158. Can mortgages be purchased for different time periods like 15 years or 30 years?

159. What does a borrower have to pay in addition to the loan and is paid for the term of the mortgage until it is fully paid: income or interest?

160. What is the term for when home owners may lose their property because they have not kept up with their mortgage payments and need to turn over the property: forfeit or foreclosure?

161. What is the term for the original amount of a loan that does not include the interest: original loan amount or principle?

162. What is the term for the ability to borrow money or pay with a card: credit or debt?

163. What is the term for the money owed to someone or a bank: credit or debt?

164. What is the economic term for using money to buy goods and services: buying or spending?

165. What is the economic term for putting money aside in a bank or another place for future use: saving or spending?

166. What is the term for what is sold by a company to raise money whereby a person may have an interest or share in that company: a stock or a bond?

167. What is the name of the market where goods and services are bought and traded every business day and may affect the economy: the bond market or the stock market?

168. What is the name of the indicator that reflects the daily average of the stock market: Dow Jones Industrial Average or Consumer Price Index?

169. What is the name of the street in New York's financial district where stocks are traded every business day: Broadway or Wall Street?

170. What rules of conduct are determined by the government for banks and stock markets to ensure that the financial system operates fairly: stipulations or regulations?

171. What other commodities besides stocks may go up or down in value depending on the market: gold and silver or diamonds and rubies?

172. What is the term for something that is purchased like stocks, bonds, or gold with the hope that it will increase in value over time: interest or investment?

173. What do citizens have that allow them to pay for goods and services in our country: employment or unemployment?

174. What is the term for the company or business that provides jobs for qualified workers: the employee or the employer?

175. What is the term for the worker that is contributing knowledge and skills for the benefit of a company in exchange for money: the employee or the employer?

ECONOMICS

176. What is the term for the salary or wages that workers earn in exchange for the knowledge and skills they provide for an employer: an income or an allowance?

177. What kind of account do many employees have that sets aside money to be used when they reach a certain age: a retirement account or an investment account?

178. Does the government have the power to determine the minimum wage a worker may earn?

179. Do you know what the current minimum wage is?

180. What is the minimum age that a worker must be?

181. What is the term for when an employer accepts a new applicant for a specific job: a hire or a recruit?

182. What is the term for when an employer terminates the position of a worker because of company finances and need: a hire or a layoff?

183. What is the term for the percentage of Americans that are seeking a job but are currently not working?

184. What is the term for the compensation that an unemployed worker may receive for a period of time: unemployment benefits or welfare?

185. What is the name for the government program that provides aid and money to people in need or out of work, providing money for food, housing, and medical costs: welfare or assistance?

186. What is the name for the government program that provides coupons for food to eligible people: food stamps or welfare?

187. What is the name for the government system that provides money and benefits to American citizens that are unemployed, retired, or disabled: Social Security or Government Assistance Program?

188. What is the name of the nine-digit number that is assigned to all citizens by the government for many identification and tax purposes among others: Government Identification Number or Social Security Number?

189. What is the term for the principle way that we pay for government services: a duty or a tax?

190. What is the general term for the total amount of money received through money or taxes: income or revenue?

191. What is the name of the tax on the salary or wages a person earns: income or compensation?

192. What is the name of the tax on a house, business, or property that helps pay for schools or public works services: a housing tax or a property tax?

193. What is the name of the tax that is paid when goods and services are purchased that helps pay for roads, schools, or the military: a state tax or a sales tax?

194. What is the name of the tax that contributes the America's social security program: FICA or FDIC?

ECONOMICS

195. What is the name of government department that manages America's money by collecting taxes and selling bonds, and is made up of 12 bureaus: the Internal Revenue Service or the Treasury Department?

196. What is the name of the bureau of the Treasury Department that is responsible for printing all the money of the United States: the U.S. Mint or the Internal Revenue Service?

197. What is the name of the bureau of the Treasury Department that is responsible for collecting all taxes owed by American citizens: the U.S. Mint or the Internal Revenue Service?

198. What is the name of the term given to either negotiate a price between buyer and seller, or something that is done like trading one thing or service for another?

199. What is the name given to people who buy and use things that are produced by other people: a producer or a consumer?

200. What is the term for goods or services purchased from other countries?

201. What is the term for goods or services sold to other countries?

202. What is the economic term for the amount producers will make and sell at a certain price: supply or demand?

203. What is the economic term for the amount of something consumers are willing to buy at a certain price: supply or demand?

204. What happens to the price if the supply of goods is limited and the demand is high?

205. What happens to the price when the demand for goods is low and the supply is high?

206. What might result if there is a high demand and limited supply: a shortage or a surplus?

207. What might result if there is low demand and an abundant supply: a shortage or a surplus?

208. What is the economic term for the imbalance between limited resources and unlimited wants: scarcity or abundance?

209. What is the term for the more than sufficient supply of a good or service: abundance or asset?

210. What is the economic term for the price someone is willing to pay for a good or service: cost or expense?

211. What would be a synonym of asset: profit or liability?

212. What would be a synonym of loss: profit or liability?

213. What is the term for a policy purchased for a product to cover repairs that usually has a time limit: a warranty or a guarantee?

214. What is the economic term for the thing that is given up in favor of another when both cannot be had at the same time: opportunity cost or economic exchange?

ECONOMICS

215. Which sector refers to the part of the economy concerned with providing government services: public or private?

216. Which sector refers to the part of the economy that is run by individuals or groups for profit: public or private?

217. What is the economic term for a group of specialized machines, equipment, and employees that all work together to make a specific product: assembly line or department?

218. What is the economic term for what goes on between buyers and sellers to get the best products at the most economical prices: supply and demand or competition?

219. What is the term for a source of support or supply: resource or capital?

220. What is the economic term that encompasses human, natural, and capital resources that serve to produce some good or service: productive resources or renewable resources?

221. What is the economic term for resources that can be replenished with the passage of time like wood or solar energy: natural resources or renewable resources?

222. What is the economic term for an abundance of money, material possessions, or resources: wealth or riches?

223. What is the economic state for a lack of money or material possessions to satisfy needs and wants: poverty or deficiency?

224. What is the term for the government's count of the total number of people in the country: population or census?

225. What is the term for buying or selling goods and services online: e-commerce or internet trade?

226. What is the economic term for wealth in the form of money or property that is used to produce more wealth: assets or capital?

227. What is the term for the "age" we are in that serves to provide more information to more people faster and easier: the technological age or the information age?

228. What is the economic term that refers to a business or company that has exclusive control of a service or a commodity in the market: free enterprise or monopoly?

229. What are community, commercial, and investment types of: banks or government agencies?

230. Is it wise to save money as well as spend money to help support our economy?

231. What is a synonym of deficit: debt or surplus?

232. What is the term for the trillions of dollars owed by the U.S. government indicated with a running clock that tallies this debt by the second: Federal Debt or National Debt?

233. What is the term for small, large, public, private, and corporations: businesses or firms?

ECONOMICS

234. What is the name of the top official of a business: president or chief executive officer?

235. What is the name for the document that highlights a person's skills, qualifications, experience, and educational background, and used to apply for jobs: application or resume?

236. What is the business-oriented online service often used for professional networking, where a person may post their employment background, credentials, and resume: LinkedIn or Twitter?

237. What is the term for the monetary compensation or money that an employee receives for the work performed per year: currency or salary?

238. What kind of salary do you believe that an employee with a strong educational background and very specialized skills would command in an organization: higher or lower?

239. What is the collective term for the total amount of money that a person may earn per year from salary, investments, interest earned, or the sale of goods: compensation or income?

240. What is the term for what many companies offer their employees in addition to a salary, and may include medical insurance, vacation, and retirement compensation: incentives or benefits?

241. What is the term for the person who receives supervised on-the-job training to acquire necessary skills in a specific field: intern or entrepreneur?

242. What is the employment term for when a person is moved to a higher, more important, and usually higher paid position in an organization: advancement or promotion?

243. What is the term for the person who starts some type of business, demonstrating both initiative and risk: intern or entrepreneur?

244. What is the term for the act of ending a working career: withdrawal or retirement?

245. What type of business would you have if you could start one right now?

Chapter 8 – Physical Education

Physical Education – Pre-School

1. Do you exercise?
2. Are you active?
3. Do you think it is important to be physically active?
4. Do people have bodies in different shapes, sizes, and colors?
5. What body parts do you have a pair of?
6. Can you walk and run?
7. Can you climb up and down stairs?
8. Can you throw and catch a ball?
9. Can you ride a tricycle?
10. Can you swing on a swing?
11. What are other things do you do for exercise?

Physical Education – Kindergarten

12. Can you run forwards and backwards?
13. Can you roll on the ground to your right and your left?
14. Can you throw a ball?
15. Can you catch a ball?
16. Can you kick a ball?
17. Can you hop?
18. Can you jump?
19. Can you launch your jump with two feet and land with two feet?
20. Can you launch your jump with two feet and land on one foot?
21. Can you launch your jump with one foot and land on two feet?

PHYSICAL EDUCATION

22. Can you gallop?
23. Can you leap?
24. Can you walk?
25. Do you look straight ahead when you walk?
26. Do you swing your arms as you walk?
27. Do you walk stepping heel to toe or toe to heel?
28. Can you run?
29. Can you play the running game "tag?"
30. Can you slide?
31. Can you skip?
32. Can you move with different forces like light, medium, or heavy?
33. Can you move at different levels like crouched down low, medium, or high?
34. Can you move at different speeds like slow, medium, or fast?
35. Can you move in different directions like forwards and backwards?
36. Can you move in different directions like clockwise and counterclockwise?
37. Can you move in different pathways like in a straight line or in a curvy line?
38. Can you move in different pathways like sideways or in a diagonal?
39. Can you move under and over other objects?
40. Can you balance on one foot?
41. Can you move your body without moving your feet?
42. Can you throw and catch a ball?
43. Can you climb a rope?
44. Can you jump rope?
45. Can you use a trampoline, hula-hoop, hoppity hop, or pogo stick?
46. What body parts can you identify?
47. Can you shake your body?
48. Can you twist your body?
49. Can you bend your body?

PHYSICAL EDUCATION

50. Can you stretch your body?
51. Can you rock your body?
52. Can you curl your body?
53. Can you sway your body?
54. Can you straighten your body?
55. Can you tense your body?
56. Can you freeze your body?
57. Can you relax your body?
58. Can you do a bear walk, a crab walk, or an elephant walk?
59. Can you stand like a flamingo with one foot up by your other knee?
60. Can you jump like a frog using your hands and feet?
61. Can you twist your body like a snake with your stomach on the floor?
62. Can you do an army crawl keeping low to the ground and bending your forearms?
63. Can you do a wheelbarrow with a partner holding your partner's legs as he or she moves forward using the arms?
64. Can you do a wheelbarrow having your partner hold your legs and you move forward using your arms?
65. Can you balance objects on your body while you move like a feather or a beanbag, keeping your arms out to the side and your eyes focused straight ahead?
66. Can you do an egg roll by squatting and wrapping your arms around your legs, dropping to one side and rolling over onto your knees?
67. Can you do a log roll by lying on your back with your arms at your sides and roll like a log in a straight line?
68. Can you do a pencil roll by lying on your back with our arms stretched out over your head and roll like a pencil in a straight line?
69. Can you walk forward on a balance beam?
70. Can you walk backwards on a balance beam?
71. Can you walk sideways on a balance beam?
72. Can you tip toe walk on a balance beam?
73. Can you climb a traverse wall?

PHYSICAL EDUCATION

74. What should be placed below a climbing wall or a rope for safety?
75. Can you use sticks or drums to create rhythm?
76. Can you use rhythm sticks and tap to the beat of the music?
77. Can you use rhythm sticks to create your own sequence of beats in a repeating pattern?
78. What kind of an activity is dance: a muscle activity or a cardiovascular activity?
79. Can you perform a dance to the beat of music?
80. Can you do a circle dance like the Hokey Pokey?
81. Can you do the circle dance called The Chicken Dance?
82. Can you do a line dance called The Macarena?
83. What kind of a dance is it called when you line dance under a stick held by two people: the duck under dance, or the limbo?
84. Is jumping rope a healthy activity for your body?
85. Can you jump rope forwards?
86. Can you jump rope backwards?
87. Can you jump a long rope that is held by two people at least 5 times in a row?
88. Can you roll a ball underhand?
89. Can you throw a ball underhand at least 10 feet?
90. Can you throw a ball overhand at least 10 feet?
91. Can you catch a ball that you throw into the air yourself without the ball bouncing?
92. Can you catch a fly ball that is thrown to you by another person?
93. Can you catch a rolling ball that is rolled to you by another person?
94. Can you bounce or dribble a ball standing in one place?
95. Can you dribble a ball as you move?
96. Can you dribble a ball with your foot?
97. Can you run away or dodge an object coming towards you?
98. Can you chase an object coming towards you?
99. Can you kick a ball coming towards you?
100. Can you kick a ball after you release it with your hands?

PHYSICAL EDUCATION

101. What is the term for fair play and respect for your opponents: fairness or sportsmanship?

102. Do you think you have good sportsmanship?

103. What is a good way to resolve a conflict during a sport activity: yell at the other team or talk it out?

104. Are flipping a coin or doing rock, paper, scissors good strategies for deciding who goes first in a game?

105. What is a good way to congratulate the winning team of any sport?

106. What is a bad way to react after losing a game in any sport?

107. Does good sportsmanship show that you follow the rules of fair play or unfair play?

108. Would arguing, complaining, and whining demonstrate good sportsmanship or bad sportsmanship?

109. Who is the person that enforces the rules in a game and makes a call if a rule is broken: a coach or a referee?

110. What is the name of the officials that call the balls and strikes in a baseball game or determines if a ball is fair or foul: a referee or an umpire?

111. Would cooperation, following directions, and respect for others demonstrate good sportsmanship or poor sportsmanship?

112. Are following the rules and using appropriate equipment for a sport important for safety?

113. What is something you should do to warm up before playing a physical activity or sport?

114. Is it good to always put forth your best effort when playing a competitive sport or doing some physical activity?

115. Can you show me your forehead?

116. Can you show me your head?

117. Can you show me your eyes?

118. Can you show me your ears?

119. Can you show me your nose?

120. Can you show me your mouth?

121. Can you show me your chin?

122. Can you show me your neck?

123. Can you show me your shoulders?

124. Can you show me your hands?

PHYSICAL EDUCATION

125. Can you show me your palms?
126. Can you show me your fingers?
127. Can you show me your thumbs?
128. Can you show me your elbows?
129. Can you show me your wrists?
130. Can you show me your arms?
131. Can you show me your legs?
132. Can you show me your knees?
133. Can you show me your ankles?
134. Can you show me your feet?
135. Can you show me your instep, the inside of your foot?
136. Can you show me your toes?
137. Can you show me your thighs?
138. Can you show me your calves?
139. Can you show me your shins?
140. Can you show me your back?
141. Can you show me your chest?
142. Can you show me your buttocks?
143. Can you show me your waist?
144. Can you show me your right side?
145. Can you show me your left side?
146. When you exercise a part of the body will the muscle become stronger or weaker?
147. What is the term for the ability of your muscles to stay strong over time without getting tired: endurance or exercise?
148. Does exercise help to circulate the blood and provide oxygen to the heart and lungs?
149. What should you do before exercising to warm up your muscles and make them more flexible: stretch or run?
150. How many seconds should you stretch a muscle: 5 or 20?

PHYSICAL EDUCATION

151. What part of your body expands and contracts: bones or muscles?

152. What uses more muscles: a smile or a frown?

153. What is the name of the large muscle located inside the upper arm: biceps or triceps?

154. What is the name of the muscle located in the back of the arm that is attached in three places: biceps or triceps?

155. What is the name of the muscle located in the front of the thigh that is divided into four parts: the triceps or the quadriceps?

156. What is the name for the five tendons that are located on the back of your knee: hamstrings or ligaments?

157. Does exercise increase or decrease your heart rate?

158. Does an increased heart rate make the heart stronger or weaker?

159. Does movement, physical activity, and sports help us to develop lifelong physical fitness?

160. What is your favorite physical activity or sport?

Physical Education – 1st Grade

161. What physical activities do you do?

162. What sports do you play?

163. Can you walk, jog, and run?

164. What movement would you use to get from point A to point B the fastest?

165. Can you hop, skip, and jump?

166. Can you leap and slide?

167. Can you gallop?

168. Can you change speeds when you move?

169. Can you travel in different directions as you move?

170. Can you travel at different levels as you move?

171. Can you jump rope?

172. Can you hula hoop?

173. Can you jump on a pogo stick?

174. Can you ride a bike?

PHYSICAL EDUCATION

175. Can you swing a bat?

176. Can you play hopscotch?

177. Can you kick a ball?

178. What part of your foot contacts the ball during a kick: the toes or the shoelace of the foot?

179. Can you kick a stationary ball with a running approach?

180. Can you dribble a soccer ball with the instep of your foot?

181. Can you keep the ball within two or four feet of you while dribbling?

182. Can you pass a soccer ball with your foot?

183. Can you trap a soccer ball with your foot?

184. Can you kick pass the soccer ball to a stationary player 20 or more feet away?

185. Do you think that footwork, leg work, and follow through affect the quality of your kick?

186. What part of your foot would you use to trap a ball?

187. Can you move your body using an arm support movement like a frog leap, army crawl, or wheelbarrow?

188. Can you move while balancing a beanbag on other object on your head with your arms out to the side?

189. Can you balance on a balance beam?

190. Can you walk forwards and backwards on a balance beam?

191. Can you walk sideways on a balance beam?

192. Can you tip toe walk on a balance beam?

193. Can you climb on a piece of climbing equipment like a rope or a net using a three point grip?

194. Can you climb a traverse wall using a three point grip?

195. What are some safety measures to keep in mind when climbing or using some tumbling apparatus?

196. Can you do an egg roll?

197. Can you do a log roll?

198. Can you do a pencil roll?

199. Can you do a forward roll?

200. What is your favorite sport?

PHYSICAL EDUCATION

201. What is your favorite physical activity?

202. What should you do to warm up before playing a sport or doing some physical activity?

203. Are muscle strength, muscle endurance, cardiovascular endurance, and flexibility all important for your health and fitness?

204. Is it important to participate in some daily physical activity?

205. If you went seven or more days without any physical activity, would your muscles get weaker or stay the same?

206. How long should a body stretch be held ideally: 5 seconds or 20 seconds?

207. Is it necessary to cool down your muscles after an intensive work out?

208. What is a good way to cool down your muscles after physical activity: running or walking?

209. Where are your biceps muscles?

210. Where are your triceps muscles?

211. Where is the group of muscles called the quadriceps located on your body?

212. Where are your hamstrings?

213. Where are your calves?

214. Where are your abdominal muscles?

215. Have you completed any kind of fitness test?

216. Are levels of fitness the same or different?

217. What are two physical activities that you do to be physically fit?

218. Is dance healthful for your body?

219. Does dance improve foot coordination and speed?

220. Would dance be more beneficial to your cardiovascular endurance or your muscle endurance?

221. Would the Hokey Pokey and the Chicken Dance be examples of line dances or circle dances?

222. Would the Macarena and the Magic Shoe Dance be examples of line dances or circle dances?

223. Can you use rhythm instruments like sticks or drums to beat to the rhythm of a song?

224. Is jumping rope healthy for your body?

225. How can you challenge yourself while jump roping?

226. In what directions can you jump a single rope?

227. Can you turn a long rope in a circular motion?

PHYSICAL EDUCATION

228. Can you jump over a long rope at least 10 times after the turners call, "ready, set, go?"
229. Can you roll a ball underhand a distance of 15 feet?
230. What kinds of balls can you catch?
231. Can you toss a ball underhand to a partner?
232. Can you catch an underhand throw?
233. Can you throw a ball overhand to a partner?
234. Can you catch an overhand ball?
235. Is it important to "absorb" the ball when catching it?
236. Is it helpful to track the flight of a ball when catching it?
237. Is there a "ready position" for catching a ball?
238. In what position is your hand when catching a ball above the waist: facing up or facing down?
239. In what position is your hand when catching a ball below the waist: facing up or facing down?
240. Can you toss and receive a ball using two different pieces of equipment?
241. Can you toss a ball underhand to yourself and catch it at least four out of five times?
242. What should you do with your opposite foot when tossing a ball?
243. If you throw a ball with the left hand, which foot should step forward?
244. If you throw a ball with the right hand, which foot should step forward?
245. Can you demonstrate a stationary dribble for 10 consecutive bounces with your right hand?
246. Can you demonstrate a stationary dribble for 10 consecutive bounces with your left hand?
247. Should you dribble a ball directly in front of your body or slightly to the side of your body?
248. Would you have better control if you dribble the ball in front of you or slightly to the side?
249. What is the best level to dribble a ball at: waist level or knee level?
250. Can you travel a court or a gym while dribbling a ball?
251. Can you chase others while playing a sport or game?
252. Can you flee others while playing a sport or game?
253. Can you dodge others while playing a sport or game?
254. How might you use chasing and fleeing skills in a sport?
255. What can you do to change up your movement if someone is chasing you?

PHYSICAL EDUCATION

256. Which hand is your dominant hand while playing a sport: your right hand or your left hand?

257. Which hand is your non-dominant hand while playing a sport: your right hand or your left hand?

258. What part of your hand should you use to dribble a ball: the palm or the finger pads?

259. Can you swing at or strike a stationary object with a paddle, a bat or a racket hitting it four out of five times?

260. Is it good practice to try to resolve conflicts on your own during competition without intervention from a parent, coach, or teacher?

261. Is it good practice for athletes to demonstrate good sportsmanship regardless if they won or lost?

262. Is it good practice to include all interested and willing players in a game?

263. Do you think it is good practice to help others in competitive activities?

264. Should winning be the only reason to participate in group activities or organized sports?

265. What are two examples of good sportsmanship?

Physical Education – 2nd Grade

266. Can you skip, hop, gallop, and slide?

267. Can you run and jump forward, backward, and sideways?

268. Can you jump and land with a one-foot takeoff and landing?

269. Can you jump and land with a two-foot takeoff and landing?

270. Can you tumble?

271. Can you do a forward roll?

272. Can you climb a rope, monkey bars, or a wall?

273. Can you bounce up and down on a trampoline

274. Can you throw a ball with one hand?

275. Can you catch a ball with one hand?

276. Can you throw a ball with two hands?

277. Can you catch a ball with two hands?

278. Can you throw a ball underhand?

279. Can you throw a ball overhand?

280. Can you catch and throw different balls like a balloon, a beach ball, a tennis ball, or a rubber ball?

PHYSICAL EDUCATION

281. Can you swing a bat?
282. Can you kick punt a dropped ball in a forward direction?
283. Can you strike a ball with a bat off a tee using the correct grip?
284. Can you bounce a ball?
285. Can you dribble a ball?
286. Can you trap a ball?
287. Can you pass a ball?
288. Can you volley a ball?
289. Can you kick a ball?
290. Can you dodge or get out of the way of a ball?
291. Can you run toward another player?
292. Can you flee or run away from another player?
293. Can you jump rope with a single rope that you turn yourself?
294. Can you walk, run, and skip to music?
295. Can you walk across a balance beam?
296. Can you go through a short obstacle course moving over, under, through, and around objects?
297. Is physical activity important to do every day to stay healthy and fit?
298. Can you dance and move to music?
299. Can you find and take your pulse?
300. What happens to your heart rate and breathing rate after you exercise?
301. Is it important to cool down after intense physical activity?
302. What happens to your heart rate and breathing rate after your body cools down?
303. What should you drink during physical activity to keep your body hydrated?
304. What physical activities do you participate in at home?
305. What physical activities do you participate in at your school or in your community?
306. Is physical activity part of a healthy lifestyle?
307. What is the likely result if a person does not eat the right foods and does not do a lot of physical activity?
308. Does eating nutritious foods help you have a healthy body?

PHYSICAL EDUCATION

309. Can you identify parts of the body?

310. Does being physically fit promote a healthy heart and strong muscles?

311. Does being physically fit promote your flexibility and range of motion?

312. What kind of physical activity is walking: low intensity or high intensity?

313. What kind of physical activity is jogging: low intensity or medium intensity?

314. What king of physical activity is sprinting: medium intensity or high intensity?

315. Are rules important when playing games and for physical safety?

316. Can you explain the rules to the game of "tag" or some other game?

317. What physical activities or games can you do or play by yourself?

318. What physical activities or games can you do or play with a partner?

319. What physical activities or games can you do or play as a team?

320. Can you follow the directions of a teacher or a coach for a physical activity?

321. Do you think it is important to encourage your teammates when playing a game?

322. Do you think it is good practice *not* to disagree with the decisions of game officials like referees or umpires?

323. Do you think it is effective to yell at a teammate when he or she makes a mistake in a game?

324. Do you think it is good practice to divide teams up as fairly and equally as possible?

325. Is it important to accept and respect others that may look different than you, or may have a higher or lower skill level in some physical activity or sport?

326. Do you show positive sportsmanship when playing a game?

327. How would you define teamwork?

328. Is it important to use appropriate equipment that each physical activity or sport requires?

329. What sports or physical activities require wearing a helmet?

330. What sports or physical activities require wearing pads?

331. What sports or physical activities require wearing a mouth guard?

332. Do you think it is good practice to win a contest fairly and without making the losing side feel bad?

333. Do you think it is good practice to lose a contest gracefully and without protesting?

334. Is it good to challenge yourself and try new physical activities?

PHYSICAL EDUCATION

335. What is necessary in order to improve a physical skill or to get better in a sport?

336. What is your favorite individual physical activity or sport?

337. What is your favorite team activity or sport?

Physical Education – 3rd Grade

338. Do you think it is important to engage in physical activity every day?

339. Can you throw and catch a ball?

340. Can you throw a ball overhand and underhand?

341. Can you throw a ball sidearm?

342. Can you throw a ball with one hand?

343. Can you throw a ball with two hands?

344. Can you dribble a soccer ball with your inside foot?

345. Can you dribble a soccer ball with your outside foot?

346. Can you dribble a ball with your right hand?

347. Can you dribble a ball with your left hand?

348. Can you hit a ball with a bat or a racquet?

349. Can you throw a ball to the rhythm of music?

350. Can you throw a ball overhand and hit a target?

351. Can you throw and catch balls of different sizes?

352. Can you hit or strike at balls of different sizes?

353. Can you kick a ball using a light, medium, and hard force?

354. Do you actively participate in physical activities or sports?

355. Are engaging in physical activities part of a healthy lifestyle?

356. Can you use a FitnessGram or fitness test to monitor your level of physical fitness?

357. What are your physical strengths?

358. What would you identify as a physical weakness, or a physical skill you could improve?

359. When is it necessary to stretch your muscles?

360. What does cardiovascular fitness include: heart and lung, or muscle and bone?

PHYSICAL EDUCATION

361. What exercise would help to develop strength in your arms?
362. What exercise would help to develop strength in your legs?
363. Do you demonstrate good sportsmanship when playing a sport or game?
364. Do you accept losing a sport or game without complaining or whining?
365. Do you follow the rules at the swimming pool?
366. What swimming pool rules can you list?
367. Do you take turns when doing physical activities?
368. Is it good practice to participate in games and sports with players of all skill levels and all cultures?
369. Is it good to give helpful advice to your teammates?
370. Is it good to encourage your teammates to perform a physical skill well?
371. Can you dance showing an emotion of sadness or joy?
372. How can you demonstrate your balancing skills?
373. What sports have you played?
374. What sport would you like to try?
375. Can you dribble, pass, and shoot a ball?
376. Can you juggle balls?
377. Can you jump rope with a short rope?
378. Can you jump rope with a long rope?
379. Can you jump high?
380. Can you jump low?
381. Can you jump a long distance?
382. Can you jump a short distance?
383. Can you perform some tumbling moves like a forward or backward roll?
384. What activity prepares your body for physical activity: warm-up or cool-down?
385. What activity is highly recommended after intense physical activity: warm-up or cool-down?
386. What helps us to monitor our exercise intensity: oxygen level or heart rate?
387. Is nutrition related to physical fitness?
388. How does practice improve performance of some physical skill or activity?

PHYSICAL EDUCATION

389. What would you say that would be considered positive feedback or praise to a teammate?

390. What is an example of something you would say that would be considered negative feedback or criticism of a teammate?

391. Do you participate in physical activity on a regular basis?

392. What does a pedometer measure: number of steps, or number of heartbeats?

393. Do you know how to use a pedometer to measure distance or the number of steps you took?

394. Do you demonstrate safe control of equipment and body?

395. Do you respectfully follow the rules of a game?

396. Do you cooperate by taking turns and respecting all equipment used for a sport or game?

397. Is it good practice to chart your skills and physical achievements and to challenge yourself to continuously improve?

398. What physical skills are you good at?

399. What physical skills do you need to improve?

400. Does exercise and physical activity help to promote positive feelings?

401. What are the benefits of engaging in physical activities every day?

402. What are all the physical activities or sports that you are involved in or do regularly?

Physical Education – 4th Grade

403. Can you catch, throw, and dribble a ball using good form?

404. Can you walk, jog, and run using good form?

405. Do you correctly use your arms when you walk or run?

406. Can you climb a rope or a traverse wall?

407. Does using your arms and legs help you to long jump your maximum distance?

408. Can you demonstrate a rhythmical movement like dance?

409. Can you demonstrate good form when throwing, catching, and batting?

410. What physical skill do you practice to improve that skill?

411. Can you pass a ball to a teammate using a chest pass?

412. Can you pass a ball to a teammate using a bounce pass?

413. Can you drop kick a football, soccer ball, or a rubber ball?

PHYSICAL EDUCATION

414. What are some physical benefits of participating in an activity or sport?
415. What physical activities and sports do you participate in?
416. Are baseball, football, basketball, and soccer considered organized sports?
417. Are hiking, dancing, and walking considered physical activities?
418. What activities besides jogging, golf, and tennis, would be considered lifelong physical activities?
419. What specific activities and skills do you engage in to demonstrate your fitness level?
420. Do you know how to assess your fitness progress by taking a fitness test?
421. How many push-ups can you do?
422. How many sit-ups can you do?
423. How many chin-ups can you do?
424. What is the greatest distance that you can run?
425. Is it good practice to always use good form when performing push-ups and sit-ups?
426. Is it important to always have good body posture at all times?
427. Are you better at running a long distance or sprinting a short distance?
428. What are some ways to warm up before participating in some physical activity or sport?
429. What does stretching help to promote: endurance or flexibility?
430. What does a gradual increase of a physical activity help to promote: endurance or flexibility?
431. What are some ways to cool down before participating in some physical activity or sport?
432. What is the best thing to drink before, during, and after any physical activity or sport?
433. What equipment is necessary when riding a bicycle?
434. What equipment is necessary when playing baseball?
435. What equipment is necessary when playing basketball?
436. What equipment is necessary when playing football?
437. What equipment is necessary when playing tennis?
438. What equipment is necessary when playing soccer?
439. What equipment is necessary when playing hockey?
440. What are some appropriate clothing articles that an athlete might wear?
441. What physical skills can you practice with a partner?

PHYSICAL EDUCATION

442. What physical skills can you practice by yourself?

443. What are three of the most popular sports played here in the United States?

444. What game, similar to baseball, is played in Australia, England, and Africa: cricket or lacrosse?

445. In what countries is soccer a popular sport?

446. What sport is popular in Puerto Rico, Cuba, and the Dominican Republic?

447. What would "kick the can," tag, dodge ball, foursquare, hopscotch, cakewalk, and jumping on a trampoline or pogo stick be described as: physical or non-physical?

448. What would playing videogames, watching television, texting, web surfing, and reading be described as: physical or non-physical?

449. Do you think it is important to have a balance with both physical and non-physical activities?

450. Is it important to recognize that some people may have limitations when it comes to demonstrating a physical skill?

451. Do you help others who may not be as capable as you are to do some physical activity?

452. What is the name for the games, originating in Athens, Greece, where athletes representing many nations compete in either winter or summer sports every four years?

453. What is the name for the program of organized sports, founded by Eunice Kennedy Shriver in 1962, that showcases children and adults with certain intellectual and physical challenges: the Special Olympics or the Paralympics?

454. What is the name for the international soccer tournament every four years in which qualifying national teams compete to determine a world champion: World Cup or Stanley Cup?

455. What is the name of the championship trophy that is awarded every year to the National Hockey Team winner: World Cup or Stanley Cup?

456. What physical activities do you participate in that you enjoy?

457. What physical activities do you participate in that you do not enjoy?

458. Have you ever participated in some type of physical contest like jump-roping, swimming, or ping pong?

459. What recreation or intramural sports do you participate in?

460. Do you prefer individual sports or team sports?

461. How can you challenge yourself with respect to physical activity?

462. What things might you say to your teammates that would be considered positive reinforcement or praise?

463. What things might you say to your teammates or your opponents that would be considered negative?

PHYSICAL EDUCATION

464. Which best demonstrates good sportsmanship: positive reinforcement or negative reinforcement?

465. Would clapping and showing a thumbs up be considered verbal or non-verbal reinforcement?

466. Is it important to bathe or shower after physical activity?

467. Why is it important to use the proper equipment when playing a sport or physical activity?

468. What are some sports or activities that are geared for younger children?

469. What are some sports or activities that are geared for older children and adults?

470. What sport or physical activity will you challenge yourself to try next?

Physical Education – 5th Grade

471. How would you define being physical fit?

472. Are you able to manage an obstacle course?

473. How many ways can you manipulate a ball?

474. Can you throw, catch, strike, kick, and rebound a ball?

475. Can you dribble a ball with your hand or your foot preventing an opponent from stealing the ball?

476. Can you keep an object continuously in the air without touching it in a group setting?

477. Can you walk, run, jump, hop, skip, slide, and gallop?

478. Can you hit a ball with a bat?

479. Can you catch a ball with a glove?

480. Can you ice skate or roller skate?

481. Would you consider a person that can ice skate well-coordinated or uncoordinated?

482. What would be considered winter sports?

483. What would be considered spring sports?

484. What would be considered summer sports?

485. What would be considered fall sports?

486. Do many sport seasons overlap?

487. What objects can you push and pull?

488. What games and sports can you explain the main rules of?

489. Can you use movements with your body with and without music?

PHYSICAL EDUCATION

490. Is it important to develop a positive attitude about yourself?

491. Is it important to understand the concept of teamwork?

492. Is competition healthy?

493. Can you move to a beat and in rhythm?

494. Can you dance or perform rhythmic movements to music?

495. Can you dance or move in formations?

496. Can you transfer your weight from your feet to your hands like a handstand?

497. Can you do a cartwheel?

498. Is one goal of physical education to increase strength and endurance?

499. Is agility, being able to maneuver your body easily, important for physical activity?

500. Do you understand game rules?

501. Do you follow rules and demonstrate fair play when engaging in physical competitions?

502. What does an athlete need to do to improve performance?

503. What personal fitness goals have you set for yourself?

504. Do you demonstrate good strength (how much) based on your age?

505. Do you demonstrate good endurance (how many times) based on your age?

506. What is the name for the exercises that are intended to improve muscle tone: calisthenics or warm-up stretches?

507. What is the name for the exercises that you do to get your muscles ready to go?

508. Do you think that bending your knees would increase or decrease your stability?

509. What is the name for the activity that you do after you do any strenuous exercise?

510. What is the term for endurance related to the heart and lungs: muscular or cardiovascular?

511. Can you find your heart rate during an aerobic activity and monitor your exercise intensity?

512. Can you run one mile and record a time?

513. Can you run a sprint and record a time?

514. What is the term for the relationship between lean muscle mass and body fat: weight or body composition?

515. What may happen to a person who eats a poor diet and engages in minimal physical activity?

PHYSICAL EDUCATION

516. Do you think that you demonstrate traits of good sportsmanship?
517. Do you accept defeat gracefully?
518. Do you choose your teammates from both genders, and of all backgrounds and skill levels?
519. What sport or activity would you like to try?
520. Is it possible for an athlete to improve as the body grows and endurance increases?
521. What is a physical advantage for a person that plays basketball?
522. Is your body more limber at the age of 10 or at the age of 15?
523. Do you think that a gymnast would be more successful at the age of 12 or at the age of 17?
524. What do you believe are your strengths with regard to performing physical activities?
525. What do you believe are your weaknesses with regard to performing physical activities?
526. What can you do to improve your physical weaknesses?
527. Do you demonstrate safe practices when playing games or sports and follow the rules and procedures?
528. Do you cooperate with others by taking turns and sharing equipment?
529. Do you encourage others when playing a game or sport?
530. What are some examples of structured physical activities?
531. What are some examples of un-structured physical activities?
532. Do you fall into a healthy fitness zone?
533. What do tennis, badminton, and volleyball have in common?
534. Why is teamwork important in invasion sports like basketball, football, and soccer?
535. How is positioning important when playing invasion sports?
536. Do players have assigned or un-assigned roles in sports like soccer, football, and basketball?
537. What are some sports that may be played in singles or in doubles?
538. Why is it important to know your body's physical limitations?
539. What are some sports where you need to have top physical skills and endurance?
540. Why is physical fitness a life-long practice?

Chapter 9 – Health and Safety

Health and Safety – Pre-School

1. Is it important to your health to eat nutritious food, to have a clean body, and to be well-rested?
2. What do you use on your head to wash your hair?
3. What do you use on your hands and body to clean it?
4. What do you use on your toothbrush for your teeth?
5. Whom do you visit for a checkup and for shots to keep you healthy?
6. Is exercise important to our health?
7. What should you do after meals to keep your teeth and gums healthy?
8. Is it an important *habit* to floss when you brush too?
9. What kinds of foods should you eat that are healthy?
10. Which is the healthier snack: an apple or a bag of chips?
11. Whom do you visit twice a year to clean your teeth and gums?
12. What should you do to remove germs from your hands before and after meals?
13. What should you do when you sneeze or cough so that your germs don't spread?
14. What should you always do before you cross the street?
15. What should you do if the orange "Don't Walk" sign is flashing?
16. What should you do when you are riding your bike on a bike path and come to a STOP sign?
17. How do you know if a train is coming?
18. What should you always wear when you ride your bike?
19. What should you always wear when riding in the car?
20. Where is a safe place to be if there is a thunderstorm?
21. Is it safe to stand under a tree if there is lightning?
22. In an emergency what is the number you should call for help?
23. Is it safe to talk to strangers?

HEALTH AND SAFETY

24. Who would you ask for help or talk to if you were lost?
25. What do you say when you would like something or are asking a favor?
26. What do you say when you are given something or someone does us a favor?
27. What rules should you follow when swimming in a pool or lake?
28. Why is it important to wear sunscreen on your skin?

Health and Safety – Kindergarten

29. Is it important to always follow the pool rules and listen to the lifeguard?
30. What should be applied on your body to protect your skin and prevent harmful sunburn?
31. In the event you should ever catch on fire, what should you do?
32. After using the restroom, what should you always do afterwards?
33. What things do we do to prevent sickness or disease?
34. What are some symptoms or how do you know you have a cold/flu?
35. Who do you tell if you feel sick or have an injury?
36. What can you spread if you don't cover your mouth or wash your hands?
37. Does washing your hands help to prevent the spread of germs?
38. What is a common cause of a broken arm?
39. Can medicines and cleaning supplies be poisonous?
40. Can you think of substances that can be dangerous (hazardous) to your health?
41. What part of your body do you use to look around?
42. What part of your body do you use to listen?
43. What body part is for your sense of smell?
44. What body part is for your sense of hearing?
45. What body part is for your sense of touch?
46. Do you know the difference between a "safe" touch and an "unsafe" touch?
47. What body part is for your sense of taste?
48. What are some foods that are good for you to eat?
49. What are some drinks that are healthy for you?

HEALTH AND SAFETY

50. Can you name any drinks that might be unhealthy for you if you drink them often?

51. Are alcohol, drugs, and smoking healthy or unhealthy habits?

52. How would you describe good eating habits?

53. What are some foods that are considered unhealthy, especially if they are eaten often?

54. How would you describe bad eating habits?

55. Is it healthy or unhealthy if you eat too many bad foods and don't get enough exercise?

56. How many hours of sleep a night are recommended for good health?

57. Besides brushing, what else should you do every day to keep your teeth and gums healthy?

58. What is the name for a hole in a tooth that is caused by decay, something that may happen to your teeth if you do not brush and floss every day?

59. How many times a year is it recommended that you visit the dentist?

60. Is it important to dress appropriately for the weather to stay healthy?

61. What diseases do you receive preventive immunizations (shots) for at the doctor's office?

62. What is the opposite emotion of happy?

63. Do people sometimes feel angry?

64. What is a good thing to do when you feel angry?

65. If you do not agree with someone about something, what is the honorable thing to do?

66. How do you take care of your body and your teeth for good hygiene?

67. What do grains, vegetables, fruits, oils, milk, and meats make up: basic food groups or diet?

68. Which foods in the 6 basic food groups should you eat more of?

69. In what shape are the food groups organized: a pyramid or a circle?

70. Does the newest version of the food pyramid provide a visual dividing the food groups from top to bottom, or in vertical divisions of the entire pyramid?

71. Is the food pyramid only a recommendation or is it a requirement?

72. Is it true that people metabolize foods differently?

73. Can you explain how diseases might be spread?

74. What are some things you can do to prevent yourself from getting sick?

75. What are some things you can do to stay safe in your neighborhood?

HEALTH AND SAFETY

76. Can you name some of your major body organs?
77. Can you name some school rules that are in place to make you safe?
78. Are respect and responsibility important in following rules in any setting?
79. How can you be safe while on the playground?
80. What are some rules regarding fire safety?
81. How many smoke alarms do we have in our house?
82. Do we have an escape plan in place in the event of smoke or fire?
83. How often is it recommended that we change the batteries in the fire alarms?
84. What are some rules regarding bus safety?
85. What are some rules to keep in mind regarding stranger safety?
86. What are some rules for bicycle safety?
87. What are the rules to follow when walking from one place to another?
88. What sign do the pedestrians need to obey before crossing a street?
89. Is it important to always walk between the lines of a crosswalk?
90. On hot days is it a good idea to rest in the shade and drink lots of water?
91. What are some other dangers to the body on a very hot day?
92. How can we protect ourselves on a hot day?
93. What might be some dangers to the body on a bitterly cold day?
94. How can we protect ourselves on a freezing cold day?
95. Are smoking and drugs dangerous to our bodies?
96. If you are offered anything from a stranger or even a friend, what should you do?
97. If you do not agree with a person about something, what is a good way to resolve it with this person?
98. Do you think watching a lot of TV is part of a healthy lifestyle?
99. Do you believe everything you see on TV?

Health and Safety – 1st Grade

100. Is it important to establish good healthy eating habits?
101. What food groups can you name?

HEALTH AND SAFETY

102. What are carbohydrates, protein, fat, vitamins, minerals, fiber, and water all categorized as: food groups or nutrients?

103. Are nutrients needed for energy and growth?

104. Are nutrition and physical exercise important for your health?

105. What is recommended that we do before eating fruits and vegetables?

106. What are some other things you can do to decrease your chances of getting sick?

107. What should you always try to do for good hygiene before and after eating, as well as after using the restroom?

108. What spreadable microorganisms can be found on handles, doors, and railings?

109. If you have a cold is it still okay to shake a person's hand?

110. What are some symptoms of a cold?

111. Do you think that the media like television and radio with its food commercials can influence our food choices?

112. Would good health behaviors include diet, sleep, fitness, and personal hygiene?

113. Can you name a way to manage your emotions?

114. To resolve conflicts or fights, which is more effective: a violent or a non-violent approach?

115. What are some good items to have in a first aid kit?

116. Is it important to call for help in the event of serious injury of yourself or another person?

117. When would you call 9-1-1?

118. In the event of a fire, what should you do?

119. What household items are considered hazardous/poisonous?

120. What is important to remember when taking medicine?

121. Should you ever accept a medicine or pills from a person other than a parent, relative, doctor, or health worker?

122. Are taking alcohol or drugs often harmful to your health?

123. Should you ever accept candy, money, or other items from a stranger?

124. If a car passed by and someone in the car asked you to help you find his or her lost dog, would you get in the car and help look for it, or what should you do?

125. If you suspect that you have been followed by a stranger, whom should you tell?

HEALTH AND SAFETY

126. Is it important to always take the same route to and from school or some other place so that you are always in familiar surroundings?

127. Is it generally safer to walk with a friend?

128. Is it okay to give your name and address to a stranger?

129. Is it okay to give your name and address to a police officer or teacher?

130. Should you ever open the door to a stranger?

131. Is it important to always let at least one other person know where you are?

132. Do you think it is safe to play in a deserted building?

133. Why is it unsafe to play on a playground by yourself?

134. Under what kind of circumstances would you seek shelter to keep you safe?

135. Is it safe to stand under a tree during a lightning storm for protection?

136. Is it ever appropriate to tease, bully, put down a person with your words, or spread rumors?

137. Is it important to always respect yourself and your body?

138. Do all people deserve respect?

139. Do you treat others with respect and dignity?

140. Is it important and respectful to listen and show full attention when others are talking?

141. Is it important in work and life to get along with others and learn to work together well?

142. Is there a relationship between effort and the quality of your work?

Health and Safety – 2nd Grade

143. How do you take care of your teeth for good dental hygiene?

144. Who should you visit at least once a year for a check-up and necessary vaccines?

145. Can you name the basic food groups?

146. In what shape are the food groups organized: a circle or a pyramid?

147. What food groups are the healthiest?

148. What types of foods are very unhealthy and should be eaten in moderation?

149. Can you explain how disease might be spread?

150. What are some things you can do to prevent yourself from getting sick?

HEALTH AND SAFETY

151. What are some things you can do to stay safe in your neighborhood?

152. Can you name some of your major body organs?

153. Can you name some school rules that are in place to make you safe?

154. Are respect and responsibility important in following rules in any setting?

155. How can you be safe while on the playground?

156. What are some rules regarding fire safety?

157. What are some other dangers to the body on a very hot day?

158. How can we protect ourselves on a hot day?

159. What might be some dangers to the body on a bitterly cold day?

160. How can we protect ourselves on a freezing cold day?

161. Are smoking and drugs dangerous to our bodies?

162. Is it always good to tell a trusted adult when something on your body hurts or you are not feeling well?

163. Is it always good to ask a trusted adult for medicine or vitamins?

164. If you are offered anything from a stranger, what should you do?

Health and Safety – 3rd Grade

165. Are health and safety important to having a good life?

166. Why is it important to see a doctor every year?

167. What is the name of your doctor?

168. Why is it important to see a dentist twice a year?

169. What is the name of your dentist?

170. What do you do to keep your body healthy?

171. Do you know the name of a medical clinic in the city where you live?

172. Do you know the name of a hospital in the city where you live?

173. Who would qualify as a health care professional?

174. Is it good to have reliable information about health services and products?

175. Can advertising sometimes influence the choices we make?

176. Are advertisements always truthful and accurate?

HEALTH AND SAFETY

177. What is an example of a "need" with regard to good health?
178. What is an example of a "want" with regard to good health?
179. What services are available in your community that provide healthy lifestyle choices for residents?
180. Does the Park and Recreation department offer swimming, sports, and activities to provide healthy lifestyle choices?
181. Does eating well and engaging in physical activity promote a healthy lifestyle?
182. Does following procedures and rules help keep you safe?
183. What would immunizations, mosquito repellant, and sunscreen be regarded as: preventative measures or reactionary measures?
184. What products are considered hazardous to your health?
185. Why is it important never to pick up a gun, even if you only want to look at it?
186. What is the purpose of a first-aid kit?
187. What would you use to treat cut, bruise, bee sting, or small burn?
188. What number would you call if you or someone you know had an accident or was in danger?
189. What are some items that you would typically find in a first-aid kit?
190. Is it important to always be prepared for a change in weather?
191. Where should you go in the event of a lightning storm?
192. What living thing should you never stand under during a lightning storm?
193. Is eating nutritious foods important to good health?
194. How many main nutrients are there: five or seven?
195. Which is **not** considered a main nutrient: carbohydrates, fat, protein, vitamins, minerals, water, fiber, or sugar?
196. Which nutrient is the main source of energy: protein or carbohydrates?
197. Which nutrient is good for building muscle: protein or carbohydrates?
198. What does "eating a balanced diet" mean?
199. What are some foods that are considered nutritious and good for your body?
200. What are some foods that are not considered nutritious?
201. What are some examples of healthy snacks?
202. What are some examples of un-healthy snacks?

HEALTH AND SAFETY

203. What exercises or physical activities do you do to stay healthy?
204. Why do you think many people take vitamins?
205. What vitamins are good for your body?
206. Are aspirin, vitamins, medicine, and prescription drugs acceptable under supervision?
207. Do you think that you make mostly good food choices?
208. Can you read a food label?
209. Are serving sizes important?
210. Does consuming too much sodium (salt) have a positive or negative effect on your body?
211. Does consuming too much sugar have a positive or negative effect on your body?
212. What do you do to keep your mouth and teeth healthy?
213. Do alcohol, tobacco, and drugs promote a healthy lifestyle?
214. What are some effects of smoking?
215. Do you have a lot of friends?
216. Does your overall health include physical, social, emotional, and intellectual?
217. What is better for your emotional health: a positive attitude or a negative attitude?
218. Is managing your emotions part of your emotional health?
219. What is the emotion of understanding how someone else feels: sympathy or empathy?
220. What is the emotion of providing comfort and assurance to someone: sympathy or empathy?
221. Is it normal to feel angry at times?
222. Are traits of loyalty and trust important in a friendship?
223. Do you have patience with others?
224. What are some behaviors that help you make friends?
225. What are some behaviors that might result in losing friends?
226. Do you show compassion for others?
227. Is it always good to treat others with respect?
228. Do you have self-respect?
229. What is it called when someone says or does something to hold power over another person: embarrassment or harassment?
230. What is considered a type of harassment: teasing or praise?

HEALTH AND SAFETY

231. Which of the following are recommended if you feel you, or someone you know, is being harassed or bullied: tell an adult, ignore it, tell the person to stop?

232. What is the name of a person who wants power over another person: a bully or a victim?

233. What is the name of a person who is the target of a bully: a victim or a bystander?

234. What is the name of a person that is witness to a bully situation: a bystander or a citizen?

235. What is something you could do if you are ever the victim of a bully situation?

236. What is something you could do if you are a bystander in a bully situation?

237. What is the term for how the body responds to the demands placed upon it: exhaustion or stress?

238. Are exercise, talking with someone, reading, and music good ways for coping with stress?

239. What is one thing that you do when you feel a little stressed?

240. If you are feeling angry or upset is it good to walk away and count to ten?

241. Can moving to a new city and starting a new school year be stressful?

242. Does stress usually lesson after you have adjusted to the new situation?

243. Do you hug your family and friends and do they hug you?

244. Are hugs and handshakes from people you know well examples of good touches or bad touches?

245. If a stranger or another adult touches you in some way that makes you uncomfortable, which of the following are good responses: say "no," do not tell anyone, or tell a trusted adult right away?

246. Do our bodies continue to grow and change?

247. Does everyone change and grow at the same rate or at different rates?

248. How many baby teeth have you lost?

249. Is losing your baby teeth a natural growing process?

250. Is it wise to speak to a stranger?

251. What would you do if a stranger offered you a ride, candy, or asked to use your phone: walk away and tell a trusted adult, or accept the offerings and lend the stranger your phone?

252. What would you do if a stranger asked you to help him or her find a lost puppy, would you get into the car?

253. What should you do if you are lost in a park or a store: tell a mom who is with her kids, tell a police officer or store manager at the front desk, or continue to wander around?

254. Why is it safer to go to places with another person and not by yourself?

HEALTH AND SAFETY

255. Would an alley, a parking lot, or a public restroom be considered safe places or an unsafe places?

256. If a stranger approaches you, what would you do?

257. Is it good practice not to tell anyone you are home alone, and to keep the doors locked?

258. What would you do if you were home alone and someone rang the doorbell or knocked?

259. Is cooking or baking when you are home alone okay?

260. What is a good treatment if you or someone you know suffered a burn from the stove or grill?

261. What is the least severe type of burn: first degree, second degree, or third degree?

262. What is the most severe type of burn: first degree, second degree, or third degree?

263. What are baking soda, butter, and egg whites used to treat: cuts or minor burns?

264. What should you do if there is a fire in the house?

265. Is it good to have an escape plan in case of fire?

266. What exercises do you do to promote good health?

267. Is having good posture important to good health?

268. What personal hygiene practices do you do to promote good health?

269. What are some safety rules to follow when at home?

270. What are some safety rules to follow when at the swimming pool or lake?

271. What are some safety rules to follow when riding the bus?

272. What are some safety rules to follow when walking by yourself?

273. What are some safety rules to follow when riding your bike?

274. What safety equipment is worn in certain sports to prevent injury?

275. Who are some people you can talk to if you have any questions about any issue regarding health or safety?

276. Is it good to develop good health and safety habits that last a lifetime?

277. Do you think you use good decision-making when it comes to health and safety?

Health and Safety – 4th Grade

278. Are you healthy?

279. What contributes to good health?

HEALTH AND SAFETY

280. Is a clean, non-hazardous environment important in maintaining good health?

281. How can polluted air and water affect your health?

282. Is it important to discard hazardous items like paint, batteries, and tires at acceptable waste material locations?

283. What household products can be potentially hazardous to your health?

284. Is eating well and exercising important to good health?

285. What are some preventative measures to avoid contracting an illness?

286. Are wearing good shoes and using required sports equipment important and necessary for your health and safety?

287. What kind of immune system does nutrition and physical activity promote: strong or weak?

288. What kind of immune system does a poor diet and minimal physical activity promote: strong or weak?

289. What would the cold, flu, and chicken pox be classified as: communicable or non-communicable diseases?

290. What would asthma, cancer, and diabetes be classified as: communicable or non-communicable diseases?

291. What are some symptoms of the cold or flu?

292. What is a symptom of chicken pox?

293. What are some treatments for communicable diseases like the cold or flu?

294. What are some treatments for a non-communicable disease like diabetes, allergies, or cancer?

295. What might someone have if that person has a negative reaction to things like cats, pollen, ragweed, latex, shellfish, eggs, or peanuts: immunities or allergies?

296. Do you know anyone who is allergic to peanuts?

297. What are you allergic to?

298. What are some symptoms of allergies?

299. Are legal drugs that are used to treat allergies and illnesses acceptable or not acceptable?

300. What affect can illegal drugs have on the body?

301. Are drugs often classified as stimulants or depressants?

302. Is the caffeine in coffee and tea a stimulant or a depressant?

303. Is alcohol a stimulant or a depressant?

HEALTH AND SAFETY

304. What are some effects of smoking or using tobacco products?

305. What is second-hand smoke?

306. How does inhaling second-hand smoke contribute to poor health?

307. Can family, friends, and the media influence your decision-making with regard to drugs and alcohol?

308. Is it always good to refuse substances from others?

309. Who are good resources at home or at school to turn to if you are feeling pressured to do or to take something that you know you shouldn't?

310. Do you believe that being active and educated increase or decrease the abuse of drugs and alcohol?

311. Have you set health-related goals for yourself that include saying NO to drugs?

312. Is it better to seek help and rescue someone you know who is involved with illegal substances, or is it okay just to remain silent?

313. What effect does the consumption of alcohol have when driving?

314. What consequences might driving under the influence of alcohol have?

315. Is the mantra, "never drink and drive" the best policy?

316. What good choices do you make every day to stay healthy?

317. Can good behaviors help avoid or reduce health risks?

318. What are some places or things where germs can be easily transmitted?

319. Can germs be spread by using another person's lip balm, or by drinking from the same glass?

320. Are germs abundant on railings and door handles?

321. What insects or pests carry germs?

322. What part of your body is better than your hand to cover your mouth with when you sneeze?

323. Can a person spread germs by openly coughing or sneezing?

324. Are germs easily spread through the hands?

325. What is a typical snack that you eat?

326. Are your meals and snacks generally nutritious?

327. Do you think that you make healthy food choices on a consistent basis?

328. Is sleep important to maintain a healthy lifestyle?

329. How many of hours of sleep do you usually get at night?

HEALTH AND SAFETY

330. What kinds of exercises do you do on a regular basis?

331. What could you put on yourself as a preventative measure to keep the bugs away in a humid area?

332. What are some preventative practices to reduce the chances of contracting the cold or flu?

333. Are there many measures that help to prevent injuries?

334. What are some preventative measures that would promote water safety in the pool?

335. Can injuries be either intentional or unintentional?

336. Can you administer first-aid to yourself or another person with a non-serious wound?

337. What do you recommend by kept inside a first-aid kit?

338. What is the best thing to do if you or another person has a serious injury?

339. What is a preventative measure to take to help avoid injury before playing a sport or engaging in some physical activity?

340. What is the abbreviation for Cardiopulmonary Resuscitation?

341. Is CPR the procedure in which the heart and lungs are made to work be systematically compressing the chest, and forcing air into the lungs?

342. In what situation would a person have to administer CPR?

343. Is it best to be formally trained and certified in order to administer CPR?

344. What is the better way to help a person that is choking: stand behind the person and administer an abdominal thrust called the "Heimlick" maneuver, or pat the choking person on the back?

345. Is it good practice to remain calm and ask for assistance in an emergency?

346. What is a common treatment for a strained muscle or knee?

347. What are some health-care services that are available in the community you live in?

348. When is it advisable to seek health-care?

349. How often is it advisable to visit the dentist?

350. What do you do to keep your teeth and gums healthy?

351. Is it important to brush and floss every day?

352. Which element helps to prevent cavities or gum disease: chloride or fluoride?

353. Are you a responsible user of the Internet?

354. Can you always believe everything you see and hear on the Internet?

355. Why do you need to be careful with regard to the personal information you provide on the Internet?

HEALTH AND SAFETY

356. What is the term for bullying that takes place on a cell phone, computer, tablet, or other electronic device: cyber-bullying or Internet harassment?

357. Should you always report online bullying and harassment?

358. Why is it important not to communicate with people you don't know through the Internet or texting?

359. Is it always good practice never to post any inappropriate picture or message online or on a cell phone?

360. Do the bodies of both boys and girls change as they develop and get older?

361. What is the term for the normal phase of development as a boy or a girl transitions from a child's body into an adult body: adolescence or puberty?

362. Do people develop at different rates and reach puberty at different times?

363. Is peace, friends, sports, and soda always the better option over violence, gangs, weapons, and drugs?

364. Is it important to stand firm, and ask for help if you are pressured into doing, possessing, or consuming something that you know is wrong?

365. Is the guidance of parents and counselors important?

366. What is an example of a high-risk behavior?

367. What short-term goals have you set for yourself with regard to your health?

368. What long-term goals have you set for yourself with regard to your health?

369. Can you name the parts of your body?

370. How do you take care of the cardiovascular system in your body, your heart and lungs?

371. How do you take care of the skeletal or bone structure in your body?

372. What is a typical treatment if you fracture or break a bone?

373. How do you take care of the muscular system in your body?

374. What are some ways that you care for your body physically?

375. What are some ways that you care for your body mentally?

376. What do you do to take care of and protect your skin?

377. What do you do to protect and take care of your eyes?

378. What do you do to take care of your ears?

379. How do you balance your activities like school, sports, and leisure time?

380. Do you think it is healthy to have a balance in life?

381. How does good food contribute to good health?

HEALTH AND SAFETY

382. How does shelter contribute to good health?
383. How does appropriate clothing contribute to good health?
384. What health services are available in your school or home?
385. What health services are available in your community?
386. Are health and safety both lifelong goals?

Health and Safety – 5th Grade

387. Do health and fitness help you to reach your full potential?
388. Do you think it is important to be confident about your body image?
389. What personal health goal have you set for yourself?
390. Is it important to adhere to safety practices and procedures regardless of your age?
391. Does health encompass physical, social, emotional, mental, and environmental?
392. How many major food groups are there: four or six?
393. Which of the following is *not* considered a food group: dairy, meats, vegetables, fruits, cakes, or grains?
394. What is the shape that the food groups are contained in: a pyramid or a circle?
395. Is the food pyramid for eating well a requirement or a recommendation?
396. Do different people of different shapes, sizes, and ages metabolize foods in their own unique way?
397. Which of the following is *not* considered one of the seven main nutrients: carbohydrates, fats, proteins, water, fiber, oils, vitamins, or minerals?
398. What are some examples of nutritious foods?
399. What are some examples of foods that are not nutritious?
400. What type of diet is recommended: varied or balanced?
401. Do portion sizes of food matter?
402. Are there recommended serving sizes?
403. What are some examples of whole foods?
404. What are some examples of processed foods?
405. Are preservatives and artificial ingredients often added to processed foods?
406. What type of food has more nutritional value: processed or whole?

HEALTH AND SAFETY

407. Is both aerobic and anaerobic exercise good your health?

408. Which activity would burn more calories: dance or golf?

409. Which activity would burn more calories: basketball or baseball?

410. Can you read and understand a nutrition label?

411. Do you think good nutrition and physical activity go hand in hand?

412. Do you think it is good practice to keep a food log and record your intake of calories?

413. Is it important to prepare foods thoroughly and correctly?

414. Is it important to have a clean and sanitary food preparation area?

415. Do you wash your hands before and after preparing food?

416. Is it important to properly wash produce and other food before preparing and serving it?

417. Is it recommended to keep sugar and salt to a minimum when preparing food?

418. What is one good way to store food?

419. Why do food products have expirations dates?

420. Which item has the longer shelf life: a gallon of milk or a can of soup?

421. Are consumable food products required to have an expiration stamped on them?

422. What is the best thing to do with food products that have expired?

423. Would it be safe to eat a piece of cheese or bread that has mold growing on it?

424. Do you eat a balanced diet?

425. Why is it important to eat breakfast every day?

426. What would be considered a nutritional breakfast that can help jump-start your day?

427. What is meant by a balanced diet?

428. What is meant by a fad diet?

429. Does a person's culture influence their food choices?

430. What are some American foods do you eat?

431. What other ethnic cuisines do you enjoy: Mexican, Italian, Chinese, Korean, Japanese, German, or Spanish?

432. Do you think that the Italian pizza made in the United States tastes the same and has the same texture as pizza hand-made in Italy and vice versa?

HEALTH AND SAFETY

433. Do people sometimes eat when they are feeling depressed or stressed?

434. What are some life experiences that can affect your stress level?

435. What are some things you can do to lessen your stress to promote your emotional health?

436. Is it important to express your emotions to a trusted friend or adult to help manage your health?

437. What are some ways you can tell how a person is feeling?

438. Can being harassed or bullied affect your emotional health?

439. What should you do if you are a victim of bullying: tolerate it or tell a trusted adult?

440. What should you do if you are a bystander and you witness someone that is clearly being bullied?

441. What effect do drugs, alcohol, and tobacco products have on the body?

442. Is there treatment for those that abuse illegal substances and confidential help available?

443. What is it called when a person takes an excessive amount of pills: intoxication or overdose?

444. What is it called when a person consumes an excessive amount of alcohol: intoxication or overdose?

445. What is the feeling that a person may experience after that person has stopped taking an illegal substance: seclusion or withdrawal?

446. Are withdrawal symptoms often temporary?

447. Are treatments available for those needing help with substance abuse or emotional issues?

448. Who are some people you can turn to if you have a problem that affects any aspect of your life?

449. Who has a greater influence regarding the choices you make: your parents or your peers?

450. Do you take responsibility for your choices?

451. Does having accurate information help us to make positive choices regarding our health?

452. Does growth and development include passing through different stages in life?

453. What would infancy, childhood, pre-adolescence, adolescence, adulthood, and old age all be regarded as: stages of life or cycles of life?

454. Do you think pre-adolescence is a rather awkward state in that it falls between childhood and true adolescence?

455. Does the life cycle include all the stages from birth to death?

456. Is it important to be aware of your family's health history?

457. Are some illnesses or conditions genetic, passed down from generation to generation?

458. Would a blood disease more likely be inherited (genetic) or contracted?

HEALTH AND SAFETY

459. What is a synonym for puberty: pre-adolescence or adulthood?

460. What does the age range of pre-adolescence generally fall between: 9-12 or 13-18?

461. Is it normal to experience many emotional and physical changes during the preteen years?

462. Can you name specific physical changes that pre-adolescents experience as it relates to puberty?

463. Is it important to understand that preteens grow and develop at very different rates?

464. Is self-esteem important at all stages of life?

465. What good grooming habits do you do every day?

466. What good hygiene habits do you do every day?

467. Does good hygiene include keeping your hair, teeth, and nails clean?

468. Is it important to bathe or shower often to keep your body fresh and clean?

469. How often do you wash your hair?

470. What is the name of the tiny insects that lay eggs in hair?

471. Is it safer to wear your own hat or is it okay to wear another person's hat?

472. How often do you brush and floss your teeth?

473. Do you wash your hands often for good hygiene, and to minimize the spreading of germs?

474. What hygiene precautions do you take in a public restroom or other public places to avoid as many germs as possible?

475. How many hours of sleep is recommended for preteens and adolescents?

476. How many hours do you sleep every night on average?

477. Are you the boss of your body?

478. Is it important to understand the boundary between appropriate and inappropriate touching?

479. Are variations of height and weight normal?

480. Do preteens often grow in "spurts?"

481. Which system of your growing body gives it support and helps it move: skeletal or muscular?

482. Which system of your growing body controls all of your actions and includes the brain and the spinal cord: circulatory or nervous?

483. Which system of your growing body helps to use food to provide energy: circulatory or digestive?

484. Which system of your growing body helps to use the air you breathe: respiratory or circulatory?

HEALTH AND SAFETY

485. Which system of your growing body helps it to move and works with your bones: muscular or respiratory?

486. Which system of your growing body helps it to move blood through it: circulatory or respiratory?

487. Does your brain continue to grow and develop during pre-adolescence?

488. Who are in your support system at home and at school?

489. Do you know that there will always an adult, a relative, a doctor, or a counselor to speak with if you have questions about growth and development?

490. Is it important to see the doctor and the dentist every year?

491. What is the name for what you show to all others: respect or compassion?

492. What is the name for thinking highly of yourself: self-absorption or self-respect?

493. Does good grooming and taking pride in you appearance help you to have a positive self-image?

494. What safety measure should you take when you are riding in a car?

495. What safety measure should you take when riding in a boat?

496. What safety measures should you take when swimming in a pool or a lake?

497. What safety measures should you take when playing soccer or skating?

498. What safety measures should you take when riding a bike?

499. Do you apply common sense with regard to dealing with strangers, keeping personal information private, and keeping yourself safe when you are home alone?

500. Do you understand the appropriate use of the Internet?

501. Is it important to make good choices and be safe with regard to texting and posting your thoughts and pictures on social media sites?

502. What are some safety rules you can cite related to the following: car safety; bike safety; water safety; home alone; strangers; sports; Sun; cold and ice; mosquitoes, ticks, or lice; walking; playground; fire; burns; fireworks; choking; guns; household products; Halloween; animals; Internet; Social Media sites; cell phone?

503. Are both health and safety lifelong and on-going?

Chapter 10 – The Arts

The Arts – Pre-School

1. Do you like to paint and draw?
2. Do you like to play with play-do, or clay?
3. Do you like to draw with chalk?
4. What is your favorite song to sing?
5. Do you know how to sing "Old MacDonald?"
6. Do you know how to sing "Bingo?"
7. Do you know how to sing "London Bridge is Falling Down?"
8. Do you know how to sing Ring Around the Rosey?"
9. Do you know how to sing "Jingle Bells?"
10. Do you know how to sing: Here We Go Round the Mulberry Bush?"
11. Do you know how to sing Twinkle Twinkle Little Star?"
12. Do you know how to sing "The Farmer in the Dell?"
13. Do you know how to sing "The Hokey Pokey?"
14. Do you know how to sing "If You're Happy and You Know It?"
15. Do you know how to sing "Row, Row, Row Your Boat?"
16. Do you know how to sing "The Wheels on the Bus?"
17. Do you know how to sing "This Old Man?"
18. Do you know how to dance?
19. Have you ever been or would you like to be in a play?
20. What musical instruments can you name?
21. What musical instruments can you play?
22. What musical instruments can a person play with their fingers?
23. What musical instruments can a person play that they blow into?

THE ARTS

24. What musical instruments can a person hold?
25. What musical instrument can a person **beat**?
26. What musical instruments have strings?
27. What musical instruments have black and white keys?
28. Which of the following have you attended: a museum, a gallery, a play at a theatre, a concert or symphony, a musical, an ethnic festival, or a medieval fair?
29. Have you ever been to an art gallery or an art museum?
30. Can art be paintings, drawings, and sculptures?
31. What is the name of the person that is the creator of a work of art?
32. What is the term given when a collection of pictures or other items are put together on a flat surface: a collage or a collection?
33. Do artists use both dark colors and bright colors in their paintings?
34. What are oils and watercolors both considered: types of pigments or types of paints?
35. What type of painting is typically created with dried paste, crayon, or chalk: a pastel painting or a chalk painting?
36. What is the name of a painting that shows views of nature and may include land or water, like hills, rivers, lakes, oceans, cities, and flowers: a portrait or a landscape?
37. What are seascapes, cityscapes, and waterscapes all considered: landscapes or naturescapes?
38. What is the name of a painting of a person: a portrait or a landscape?
39. What type of painting does an artist paint of himself or herself: solo-portrait or self-portrait?
40. What is the type of art that is very different or unrealistic: imaginary or abstract?
41. Is the Statue of Liberty a painting or a statue?
42. Have you ever seen pictures of any of the sculptures like Blue Hippo, The Little Dancer, The Discus Thrower, The Thinker, The Venus de Milo, or Michelangelo's David?
43. Can you name any famous paintings?
44. Can you name any famous artists?
45. Was Pablo Picasso a famous artist or a famous author?

The Arts – Kindergarten

46. Are music, dance, art, and theatre part of the arts?
47. Is there a fine art event that you have attended recently?

THE ARTS

48. What is the name for someone who paints, draws, designs, or sculpts something?
49. Can you create art with objects like yarn, clay, metals, buttons, or macaroni shells?
50. Can you create works of art using crayons, markers, and colored pencils?
51. Do some artists use chalk to create artworks?
52. Can an artist create an artwork with just pencil and paper?
53. Can an artist use watercolors or oil paints to create an artwork?
54. What is the name of the material that an artist uses to create an oil painting: a canvas or a palette?
55. What is the name of the tray of colors that an artist uses to dab and mix with a paintbrush to put on the canvas: a palette or an easel?
56. What is the name of the thing that might hold a canvas while an artist is painting on it: a palette or an easel?
57. Do artists often mix colors together to get just the right effect?
58. What color would you get if you mixed black paint with white paint?
59. What color would you get if you mixed red paint with white paint?
60. What color would you get if you mixed blue paint with yellow paint?
61. What color would you get if you mixed red paint with yellow paint?
62. What color would you get if you mixed red paint with blue paint?
63. What color would you get if you mixed red paint with green paint?
64. Do artists use color to create light and dark?
65. What colors would an artist use to create a light mood?
66. What colors would an artist use to create a dark, somber mood?
67. Are red, blue, and yellow considered primary colors or secondary colors?
68. Are green, orange, purple, and yellow considered primary or secondary colors?
69. What color would you get if you mixed the primary colors red, blue, and yellow?
70. Do artists use different types of lines in their artworks?
71. What type of line goes in one direction: straight or curved?
72. What type of line looks like motion with arcs: straight or curved?
73. What type of line looks like lightning and goes back and forth: curved or zigzag?

THE ARTS

74. What type of line looks like waves on a beach: straight or wavy?
75. What material might an artist use to create a pot, or a sculpture of a person or an animal?
76. What is the name of the wheel that helps an artist form a pot?
77. What is the name of the oven were clay objects are put to dry and cure: a kiln or a furnace?
78. What have you created out of clay?
79. What is the name of a *collection* of objects that are artistically put together onto one canvas or paper?
80. What is the name of the place where people can view famous artworks?
81. What is the artistic term for a painting or picture of a person: a portrait or a still-life?
82. What is the artistic term for a painting of a group of objects like flowers or fruit: a landscape or a still-life?
83. What is the artistic term for an artist who paints himself or herself on a canvas: a portrait or a self-portrait?
84. What is the artistic term for an artwork that is painted on a wall by an artist like Diego Rivera: a mural or a landscape?
85. Do you know the name of a famous art museum?
86. What famous artists can you name?
87. What famous sculptures can you name?
88. Is a sculpture flat or dimensional?
89. What is the name of the person who creates a sculpture: a designer or a sculptor?
90. Which is an example of sculpture: a totem pole or a sidewalk drawing?
91. Which one is a type of sculpture: a portrait or a monument?
92. What monuments have you visited that are examples of sculptures?
93. Are the Lincoln Memorial, Mount Rushmore, and the Washington Monument types of sculptures?
94. What color would you get if you mixed black and white paint?
95. What color would you get if you mixed red and white paint?
96. What color would you get if you mixed blue and yellow paint?
97. What color would you get if you mixed red and yellow paint?
98. What color would result if the mixed the primary colors of red, yellow, and blue?
99. Do artists often mix colors together to get just the right effect?

THE ARTS

100. What colors are the American flag?

101. Do the red and white stripes make a pattern?

102. What are some things that you have created as an artist?

103. What is the name of the artwork that hangs from something, and has a variety of objects hanging from several strings: a mobile or a chime?

104. What is **music** considered: a fine art or a sound?

105. What different types of music can you name?

106. What are some songs that you like?

107. What instruments might musicians play in a band?

108. Do you know the difference between a piano and an organ?

109. What are some examples of stringed instruments?

110. What type of instrument serves to keep the beat: cymbals or drums?

111. Can you keep a beat with your hands?

112. Can you clap hands to the beat of a song?

113. What is the name of a song that has clapping parts?

114. Can you sing "BINGO" and clap to it?

115. Can you clap along to the song, "If You're Happy and You Know It?"

116. Have you ever played a triangle, cymbals, or bells?

117. Have you ever played a xylophone with its high notes and low notes?

118. Can you sing alone?

119. Can you sing in a group?

120. What is the name of a group of singers: a band or a choir?

121. What is another name for choir: ensemble or chorus?

122. Can you sing parts LOUD and quiet?

123. Can you sing "John Jacob Jingleheimer Schmidt" with its loud and quiet parts?

124. Can you sing a song fast and slow?

125. Can you sing high notes in a song?

126. Can you sing low notes in a song?

THE ARTS

127. Do you know of any songs have other actions like skipping and moving in a circle?
128. What is the name of a song that you sing to while moving in a circle?
129. Do you know the words to "London Bridge Is Falling Down?"
130. Do you know the words to "Here We Go Round the Mulberry Bush?"
131. Do you know the words to "Old MacDonald?"
132. Do you know the words to "Twinkle, Twinkle Little Star?"
133. Do you know the words to "The Bear Went over the Mountain?"
134. Do you know the words to "London Bridge Is Falling Down?"
135. Do you know the words to "The Hokey Pokey?"
136. Do you know the words to "Jingle Bells?"
137. Do you know the words to "The Farmer in the Dell?"
138. Do you know the words to "This Old Man?"
139. Do you know the words to "The Wheels on the Bus?"
140. Do you know the words to "Pop Goes the Weasel?"
141. Do you know the words to "Row, Row, Row Your Boat?"

The Arts – 1st Grade

142. Can you move and dance to music?
143. Do you like to create art?
144. Do you like to look at art?
145. What do you like to do best: draw, paint, cut, paste, or create something out of clay?
146. What is the name of the place that houses a collection of art works?
147. What are paintings, sculptures, music, dance, musicals, and theatrical plays all considered?
148. What types of materials do artists work with?
149. Can artists create paintings, drawings, and sculptures?
150. Are you familiar with any famous artists?
151. Do some of the first paintings on the walls of caves of Spain and France date back thousands of years?

THE ARTS

152. Which of the following were animals found on the walls of caves in Spain: buffalo, deer, or butterflies?

153. Are the pyramids, Great Sphinx, and mummy cases considered to be famous artworks by the ancient Egyptians?

154. What is the name of a painting that an artist paints of a person: a portrait or a landscape?

155. What is the name of the term that represents the art style and design of a building or structure: sculpture or architecture?

156. Do artists often use imagination to create a work of art?

157. Can an artist's past experiences be reflected in his or her art works?

158. Is a historical event sometimes the subject of a work of art?

159. Can you name a famous statue, another art form?

160. In which American state is The Statue of Liberty statue?

161. What is another meaning of liberty?

162. Can you name a statue or pole that is made by Native American Indians?

163. Can you name the three primary colors?

164. What are the secondary colors?

165. Would red, yellow, orange, and red be considered warm colors or cool colors?

166. Would blue, green, and violet be considered warm colors or cool colors?

167. Which colors do you think stand out more in a painting: warm colors or cool colors?

168. What colors would be considered bright colors?

169. What colors would be considered dull colors?

170. Do some artists just use black and white in their paintings?

171. What color would you get if you mixed red paint and yellow paint?

172. What color would you get if you mixed blue paint and yellow paint?

173. What color would you get if you mixed black paint with white paint?

174. What color would you get if you mixed red paint with white paint?

175. What colors mixed together would make black?

176. What are straight, curved, wavy, zigzag, and spiral all types of?

177. Can lines by fat or skinny?

595

THE ARTS

178. What are a circle, square, triangle, rectangle, and oval all types of?

179. Do artists often use different lines and shapes in their paintings?

180. Do artists often use their favorite colors in their paintings?

181. Do artists often paint things in nature like trees, mountains, rivers, sunsets, and animals?

182. What does an artwork have if it is soft, rough, bumpy, or furry: depth or texture?

183. Do artists often paint things to appear smooth or rough?

184. Are some artists both artists and sculptors like Edgar Degas who created many artworks related to dancers?

185. What is the name of the Renaissance artist who painted the ceiling of the Sistine Chapel in Vatican City, and sculpted the *David* statue in Florence, Italy: Donatello or Michelangelo?

186. What art form is unique to both Native American and African culture: spears or masks?

187. What is the name of the artwork that is of a person, and can be a picture or a painting?

188. What is the name of one of the most famous portraits by the Italian artist Leonardo da Vinci: *Mona Lisa* or *The Dancer*?

189. What is it called when an artist paints a portrait of himself?

190. Did Vincent Van Gogh, Pablo Picasso, and Norman Rockwell paint self-portraits?

191. What is it called when an artist paints flowers, books, fruit, or other small objects: a landscape or a still life?

192. What kind of paintings were Vincent Van Gogh's *Irises* and *Sunflowers* examples of: landscape or still life?

193. Have you ever painted a "still life" of anything?

194. What is the name of the painting that is painted on a wall: a fresco or a mural?

195. What is the art of painting on fresh, wet plaster: a fresco or a mural?

196. What is the name of a famous muralist of Mexico who painted many murals in public buildings in both Mexico and the United States: Diego Rivera or Frida Kahlo?

197. What is the name of a group of people who sing as a group?

198. What is the name of a group of musicians that play musical instruments that may include drums, a keyboard, a guitar, and a tambourine?

199. What is the name of a group of musicians that play musical instruments that include violins, flutes, clarinets, cellos, harps, and bells: a band or an orchestra?

THE ARTS

200. What is the name of the musical arrangement that an orchestra plays: symphony or ensemble?

201. What type of music is a symphony regarded as: classical or traditional?

202. What are musical instruments divided into: families or groups?

203. What family would a drum, xylophone, triangle, maracas, cymbals, castanets, and tambourine belong to: the wind family or the percussion family?

204. What North American country often uses maracas to accompany their music and dance?

205. What percussion instrument made of wood are often clicked together with the thumb and fingers by Flamenco dancers in Spain: maracas or castanets?

206. What family would a guitar, a banjo, and a violin belong to: the string family or the wind family?

207. What family would a clarinet, a flute, a bassoon, a recorder, and an oboe belong to: the percussion family or the wind family?

208. What is the name of the small piece of wood on a wind instrument where you put your mouth: a horn or a reed?

209. What family would a trumpet, a saxophone, a French horn, and a tuba belong to: the percussion family or the brass family?

210. What is the name of the group of musicians who play percussion, strings, winds, and brass: a band or an orchestra?

211. What group performs a *symphony*: an orchestra or a band?

212. What is the name of the person who leads an orchestra or band: the director or the conductor?

213. What is another name for conductor that means "Master" in Spanish: Maestro or Monsieur?

214. Do you know the names of any great symphony orchestras?

215. Is the *Boston Pops* a band or a symphony?

216. Is a symphony often regarded as classical music?

217. Have you ever attended a symphony?

218. What is the name of the person who writes the music of a symphony to be played by an orchestra: a conductor or a composer?

219. What is the name of the famous Austrian composer who wrote over 600 musical pieces and 41 symphonies whose first name is Wolfgang Amadeus: Beethoven or Mozart?

220. What kind of music did the famous composers Bach, Mozart, Beethoven, and Tchaikovsky write: traditional or classical?

THE ARTS

221. What German composer wrote nine famous symphonies, with the opening notes of his Fifth Symphony one of the most famous in all of classical music, and continued to compose music even after he became deaf: Ludwig van Beethoven or Wolfgang Amadeus Mozart?

222. Are Bach, Brahms, Chopin, Handel, Schubert, and Tchaikovsky the names of famous violinists or composers?

223. Have you ever made your own instruments?

224. What musical instruments can you play?

225. What are country, jazz, rock, rap, popular, classical, and folk all categorized as?

226. Can music reflect a mood and feeling?

227. Which is *your* favorite type of music?

228. How is music written down and notated on paper: musical letters or musical notes?

229. Can you describe what a musical note looks like?

230. Can musical notes be whole, half, or quarter?

231. Do musicians read musical *notes* in order to play a song?

232. Do many songs have verses and a chorus?

233. What part of a song is often repeated: the verse or the chorus?

234. Can songs often tell a story?

235. What does the singer of "Oh, Susanna" who comes from Alabama say that he or she has on his knee: a guitar or a banjo?

236. What is the name of a musical drama where all the lines in the play are sung not spoken: a symphony or an opera?

237. Were many operas written by composers from European countries like France, Germany, and Italy?

238. Are operas often performed in languages other than English?

239. Were Mozart's *Magic Flute*, Humperdinck's *Hansel and Gretel*, and Bizet's *Carmen* symphonies or operas?

240. What is the term for the sound that is a copy of another sound when sound waves bounce off a wall or another surface: an echo or a reflection?

241. What is an instrument that keeps rhythm?

242. What is it called when you move your body to rhythm and music?

243. What are folk, ballet, ballroom, belly, clog, jazz, jig, modern, square and tap all types of?

THE ARTS

244. Are you familiar with any ethnic dances like Irish, Mexican Folk Dance, African, Indian, Spanish Flamenco, and German?

245. What type of ethnic dances are the Tango, Salsa, Samba, Merengue, Mambo, Cha Cha, Bolero, Paso Doble, Rumba, and Zumba: Spanish or Latin?

246. Can dance tell a story and reflect a *mood*?

247. What kind of dancers wear tutus and slippers and are often dancing up on their toes doing turns and leaps: tap dancers or ballerinas?

248. What is the name of the kind of dance that tells a story, and the dancers are accompanied by an orchestra: a musical or a ballet?

249. Have you ever been to a ballet or other type of dance performance?

250. What is the name of the ballet composed by the Russian composer Peter Tchaikovsky that is performed around Christmastime, about a toy nutcracker that comes to life by magic, and battles a Mouse King with the help or a girl named Clara: *Swan Lake* or *The Nutcracker*?

251. What is the name of the ballet composed by Russian composer Peter Tchaikovsky that tells the story of Prince Siegfried who falls in love with Princess Odette, who is turned into a swan by a sorcerer's curse: *Swan Lake* or *The Nutcracker*?

252. What is the name of the type of dance where eight people stand in a square and follow the directions of the "caller" who sings dance instructions like, "Swing your partner, round you go, turn to your right, yes do-si-do:" box dancing or square dancing?

253. What is the name of the music with lively rhythms and invented by African Americans, where the musicians change up the song every time they perform it: blues or jazz?

254. What is the name of one of the most renowned jazz musicians who played the trumpet and cornet: Louis Armstrong or John Phillip Sousa?

255. What type of musicians were Nat King Cole, Duke Ellington, Benny Goodman, Charlie Parker, Miles Davis, and Louis Armstrong?

256. What is the name of the city in Louisiana that is famous for the song "When the Saints Come Marching In:" New Orleans or Baton Rouge?

257. What is your favorite song?

258. When you hum a song, are you humming the melody or the harmony?

259. What is the term when different musical notes are played or sung at the same time: harmony or melody?

260. Does most music have rhythm?

261. Does Native American music have rhythm?

THE ARTS

262. Do African drummers often play music that is mainly rhythm?
263. What is a part of rhythm that helps you keep up with the music: the sound or the beat?
264. What part of your body could you use to help you "keep the beat?"
265. Is "keeping the beat" also called "keeping time" or "staying in rhythm" to the music?
266. Do you know the words to and can you sing "America the Beautiful," or other patriotic song?
267. Do you know the words and can you sing the song "For He's a Jolly Good Fellow?"
268. Do you know the words and can you sing the song "She'll Be Comin' Round the Mountain?"
269. Do you know the words and can you sing the song "The Star-Spangled Banner?"
270. Do you know the words and can you sing the song "Take Me Out to the Ball Game?"

The Arts – 2nd Grade

271. What different things are thought of as art?
272. Is art a way of communicating ideas about the world?
273. Is art a way to creatively express oneself?
274. Is imagination important in the creation of art?
275. What medium can either be oil based or water based: paints or watercolors?
276. What is the name of the tilted canvas that many artists paint on?
277. What is the name of the flat tray with circles of paints that an artist might use to create an artwork?
278. Do many artists mix the paints on the palette to create a desired color?
279. Why do artists' brushes come in different sizes and shapes?
280. What other types of materials besides paints can an artist create with?
281. Can art works be created with yarn, fabric, chalk, clay, metal, and other media?
282. Are sculptures a form of art?
283. Have you made any sculptures out of plaster or clay?
284. Are ceramics a form of art?
285. Do many ceramic pieces start out as clay?
286. Are ceramic pieces often made on a potter's wheel?
287. What is the name for the hot, brick-lined oven that ceramic pieces often dried and cured in?

THE ARTS

288. Do some ceramic pieces have a shiny glaze?

289. Have you made any ceramic work of art?

290. Are sketches and black and white drawings a form of art?

291. What have you recently made pencil sketches of?

292. Can things found in nature and the environment be considered visual forms of art?

293. Would you consider a spider web, a rainbow, and a Sun's reflection on a lake all visual forms of art?

294. What thing found in nature would you categorize as a visual form of art?

295. Are photographs taken with a camera an expression of art?

296. Can photographs be in black and white as well as in color?

297. Are many works of art as well as photographs framed?

298. Can you name a famous artist?

299. Besides paintings, what other types of art might be displayed in an art gallery or museum?

300. Can you name a famous art museum?

301. What is the name of an art museum in city close to where you live?

302. Does a work of art often incorporate color, line, shape, texture, balance, and composition?

303. What art term describes a surface as either rough or smooth: composition or texture?

304. Are blues and purples considered warm or cool colors?

305. Does an artist often incorporate light and shadow in a painting?

306. Are reds, oranges, and yellows considered warm or cool colors?

307. Can you name a famous painting?

308. What is the name of the type of painting or picture of a person?

309. Do we have any portraits in our house?

310. What are paintings in a museum often called that are worth a lot of money: priceless or valued?

311. What are the *Mona Lisa, Starry Night, The Last Supper, The Creation of Adam, Guernica, Girl with a Pearl Earring, The Scream, Night Watch,* and *Water Lilies* all considered?

312. Why do you think many art museums do not allow you take flash photographs of a painting?

313. Why do you think many art museums have security guards?

314. Do many works of art reflect and represent the life and times of the artist?

THE ARTS

315. Do many works of art represent a historical event?

316. Do you think some art is unique to a specific culture?

317. Does every person interpret art in a different way?

318. Can you draw a picture using different kinds of lines?

319. What kind of lines would you use to draw a tree trunk: vertical lines that go up and down, or horizontal lines that run side to side?

320. What kind of lines would you use to draw the ground and grass underneath a tree: vertical lines that go up and down, or horizontal lines that run side to side?

321. What kind of lines would you use that have a slant if you wanted to draw a slide, a ramp, or a hill: horizontal or diagonal?

322. What is the opposite of a thick line?

323. What is a line called that does back and forth: zigzag or spiral?

324. What is a line called that winds or circles around a center point: a zigzag or a spiral?

325. Can you draw a dog using only straight lines?

326. Can you draw a dog using only curvy or zigzag lines?

327. What is the term for a work of art made of clay, wood, metal, or stone?

328. Can you name a famous sculpture?

329. Are the "Statue of Liberty", *The Thinker* by French sculptor Auguste Rodin, the *Discus Thrower* from ancient Greece, and the *Venus de Milo* in France examples of both sculptures and statues?

330. What is a portrait a painting of?

331. What is a self-portrait?

332. What objects would be painted in a "still life?"

333. What is the name of a painting where the main focus is the sky, the land, and the trees: a still life or a landscape?

334. What is the term for the part of the picture or painting that is closest to the viewer: the foreground or the background?

335. What is the term for the part of a picture or painting that is farthest from the viewer: the foreground or the background?

336. Would you say that *View of Toledo*, a painting showing the river, bridge, and buildings under a dark sky of a city in Spain by the Spanish artist El Greco is a landscape or a still life?

THE ARTS

337. Would you say that *Starry Night*, a painting showing a town and a sky with swirly clouds and Sun in blues and yellows by Dutch artist Vincent Van Gogh is a landscape or a still life?

338. Would you say that Vincent Van Gogh's *Sunflowers* and Andy Warhol's *Campbell's Soup Cans* are landscape paintings or still life paintings?

339. Can landscapes be of imaginary places?

340. What mood is created by a landscape painting that is dark, spooky, and stormy?

341. What mood is created by a landscape painting that is bright, sunny, and peaceful?

342. Can animals and people be a part of a landscape painting?

343. When painters paint a subject in a life-like way, do we say the painting is realistic or abstract?

344. When painters paint something that doesn't look like the real thing, do we say the painting is realistic or abstract?

345. Did Pablo Picasso paint many paintings in an abstract style?

346. Are *Cat and Bird* by Paul Klee, *The Snail* by Henri Matisse, and *The Melancholic Singer* and *Constellations* by Joan Miró considered abstract art or traditional art?

347. What is the term for painting a picture in a dreamlike way: a whimsical or a dreamscape?

348. Do artists paint using both realistic and unrealistic lines and colors?

349. What kind of painting has unrealistic lines, images, and color: modern or abstract?

350. Can sculptures be abstract?

351. Have you ever created a landscape using pencil, watercolors, paint, colored pencils, crayons, or markers?

352. Have you ever created a still life using pencil, watercolors, paint, colored pencils, crayons, or markers?

353. Have you ever created a portrait using pencil, watercolors, paint, colored pencils, crayons, or markers?

354. What sculptures or figures of clay have you created?

355. Do most paintings and sculptures have titles?

356. What is the term for the art of designing and planning buildings: architecture or construction?

357. What is the name of the person that designs a house or a building?

358. Did many old buildings in Greece and Italy have distinct architecture with many columns?

359. Did Thomas Jefferson design his home "Monticello" with vertical or horizontal columns?

THE ARTS

360. What is the term for when something is the same on both sides of an imaginary line running down the middle of it: asymmetric or symmetric?

361. Is a valentine heart symmetrical?

362. What shapes can you think of that are symmetrical?

363. What is the term for two sides that do not match up: symmetrical or asymmetrical?

364. What are honeycombs, sunflowers, spider webs, crop circles, snowflakes, the Milky Way Galaxy, and the Sun and the Moon examples of: symmetry in nature or asymmetry in nature?

365. Were many old buildings in different countries like the "Great Stupa" in India, the "Dancing House" in the Czech Republic, the "Crooked House" in Poland, and Spain's "Casa Mila" by architect Antonio Gaudi designed with straight lines or curved lines?

366. What architects built the Parthenon and the Temple to Athena: the Greeks or the Romans?

367. Did the pyramids of Egypt and Mexico have a distinct architecture?

368. Did the old churches, cathedrals, and castles in Europe have a distinct architecture?

369. Who are Frank Lloyd Wright and Santiago Calatrava: famous artists or famous architects?

370. Did Frank Lloyd Wright have a modern or traditional architectural style?

371. Did Frank Lloyd Wright design the Guggenheim Museum in New York City that resembles a giant tea cup using modern or ancient architecture?

372. What museums or art museums have you visited?

373. What buildings can you name that have a very unique architectural style?

374. Do you think that the more we know about art and architecture, the more we admire and appreciate it?

375. What are jazz, rock, modern, alternative, folk, patriotic, and classical all examples of?

376. Is music a form of expression?

377. Can you name a patriotic song?

378. What is the name of the song that is often sung before an American sporting event: "The Star-Spangled Banner" or "America the Beautiful?"

379. What is our country's official song: "The Star-Spangled Banner" or "America the Beautiful?"

380. What is another term for our country's official song: The National Anthem or National Tune?

381. Can you sing the patriotic song "This Land is your Land?"

382. What is the meaning of "folk:" people or family?

THE ARTS

383. What is the name of a song that has been passed down from parents to children for many years: a family song or a folk song?

384. Which song is considered a folk song: "Home on the Range" or "America the Beautiful?"

385. What group of people brought folk music to America: the Pilgrims or immigrants from other countries?

386. Do other countries have their own folk music?

387. What stringed instrument often accompanies folk songs?

388. What is the name of the musical group that often plays wind, brass, string, and percussion instruments in a large group?

389. What is the name of a long piece of music played by an orchestra: a number or a symphony?

390. What specific instruments do orchestra members play?

391. Are members of an orchestra seated in separate sections based on the musical instrument played?

392. What kind of music do orchestras often play: traditional or classical?

393. What is the opening part of a symphony called: an overture or an introduction?

394. What instruments in an orchestra would belong to the brass family?

395. What instruments in an orchestra would belong to the wind family?

396. What instruments in an orchestra would belong to the percussion family?

397. What instruments in an orchestra would belong to the string family?

398. What instrument family do the guitar and the banjo belong to?

399. How many strings are on a violin, viola, bass, and cello: four or five?

400. Which of the following stringed instruments makes the *highest* sound: the violin, the viola, the cello, or the bass?

401. Which of the following stringed instruments plays the *lowest* pitch of all the stringed instruments: the violin, the viola, the cello, or the bass?

402. Which stringed instrument would *not* be part of an orchestra: violin, viola, banjo, cello, and bass?

403. Which instrument is smaller: a cello or a violin?

404. What is the name of the person that plays the piano: an organist or a pianist?

405. What is the name of the person that plays the violin: a violinist or a violist?

406. What is the name of the person that plays the organ?

THE ARTS

407. What is the name of the stick that a violinist uses: a wand or a bow?

408. What is the name of the stick that an orchestra conductor uses: a baton or a wand?

409. What instrument family do the drum, the triangle, the maracas, and the castanets belong to?

410. What are the bass and kettle types of: drums or violins?

411. What family of instruments helps keep the rhythm of a song: percussion or brass?

412. What percussion instrument is often used to give a big splash of sound like Georges Bizet wrote in his overture to his opera "Carmen:" cymbals or drums?

413. Can you name a famous composer?

414. Who are Mozart, Back, Vivaldi, Brahms, Handel, Chopin, Tchaikovsky, Schubert, Wagner and Beethoven: famous composers or famous musicians?

415. What is the name of the person who leads an orchestra: a director or a conductor?

416. What is the name of the European pianist and composer that became deaf while writing his Ninth Symphony: Mozart or Beethoven?

417. What is it called when one instrument group in an orchestra is featured and plays their instruments for an extended period of time: a showcase or a concerto?

418. What keyboard instrument has 52 white keys and 36 black keys?

419. What instrument that is often played in churches and cathedrals may have more than one keyboard, several foot pedals, and pipes: a piano or an organ?

420. What is the term for the person who sings or plays an instrument alone: a soloist or a featured artist?

421. What is the term for a piece of music performed by two musicians or singers: duet or duo?

422. What is the term for a piece of music performed by three musicians or singers: triad or trio?

423. Can you recognize musical notes?

424. Is reading music similar to reading a book?

425. Are the musical notes whole, half, and quarter?

426. Does each musical note stand for a sound that lasts for a different length of time?

427. How many beats make up a whole note: two or four?

428. How many beats make up a half note: two or four?

429. How many beats make up a quarter note: one or two?

430. Does the placement of the musical note represent how high or low a note is sung, or played on a musical instrument?

THE ARTS

431. What is the name of the horizontal lines that look like a ladder that musical notes are positioned on: a bar or a staff?

432. Are the musical notes positioned near the top of the staff high notes or low notes?

433. Are the musical notes positioned near the bottom of the staff high notes or low notes?

434. Do the letters in the music alphabet include A, B, C, D, E, F and G?

435. What is it called when you sing or play the musical notes in a row, usually within an octave: musical rhyme or musical scale?

436. Do you letters of the scale correlate with a specific sound?

437. Do the sounds of the following song go up or down on the musical scale: Do, re, mi, fa, sol, la, ti, do?

438. Are you familiar with a song you can sing that contains all the special sounds, and is sung in the musical "The Sound of Music," starting with "Doe, a deer?"

439. What is the name of the symbol often found at the beginning of a staff that looks like a fancy swirl with a tail:" a treble clef or a squiggle?

440. What does a composer use if he or she wants to silence part of the music: a pause or a rest?

441. What is the musical term when talking about how low or high a sound is: volume or pitch?

442. When you hum a song do you sing the rhythm or the melody?

443. When you clap out a song do you follow the rhythm or the melody?

444. Are rhythm, harmony, tempo, and melody important music skills?

445. What kinds of groups sing and perform music vocally?

446. Are musicals a combination of theatre, singing, and dancing?

447. Can you name a famous musical or musical movie?

448. What is the term for the collection of songs that come from a movie: a soundtrack or an album?

449. Can you sing with a group?

450. What is a group of singers called?

451. Can you name a popular singing group from the present?

452. Can you name a popular singing group from the past?

453. Do you know the name of the Mexican singing group and band that play guitars and trumpets and often perform in public places?

454. What is it called if you sing by yourself?

THE ARTS

455. What is it called if you sing with one other person?

456. Can people sing at different pitches, some high, some medium, and some low?

457. What musical group might be divided into sections that include soprano, alto, tenor, and bass?

458. What is your favorite song?

459. Is dance considered a performing art?

460. Can you identify different types of dances?

461. What is the name of a performing art that has dance in it?

462. When people of different countries perform dances, do they often wear the clothing that represents their country?

463. Which of the following is *not* considered a fine art: sculpture, portrait, musical, movie, or ballet?

The Arts – 3rd Grade

464. What are portraits, self-portraits, landscapes, still life, sculptures, statues, and sketches examples of?

465. What are painters of famous paintings and portraits often called: Great Artists or Great Masters?

466. Does a single artist often have an artwork that is regarded as his or her "Masterpiece?"

467. What was the masterpiece of Leonardo da Vinci: the *Mona Lisa* or *Noah's Ark*?

468. What kinds of tools does a painter use to create a piece of art?

469. What is the name of the tilted stand that an artist sets the canvas or paper on?

470. Does the manner in which artists use light in their paintings affect how you feel about the painting?

471. What emotion would you feel in viewing a painting that is warm and light?

472. What emotion would you feel in viewing a painting that is cold and dark?

473. Can an artist create light and dark effects through the use of color?

474. Did many classic artists like the Dutch artist Rembrandt show sharp contrasts between light and shade to create a desired effect?

475. What is the opposite of light in art: shadow or dark?

476. What is the opposite of shadow in art: light or bright?

477. What are the tools that a potter uses to create a sculpted piece of pottery?

478. What is the name of an artwork that is made from hundreds of pieces of glass, broken plates, tiles, jewels, or precious metals fitted together like a puzzle: a collage or a mosaic?

THE ARTS

479. Can a mosaic be created on a wall like on the walls of San Vitale, a church in Ravenna, Italy?

480. Were many great artworks created for churches during the Byzantine Empire from A.D. 400 to 1400?

481. Does a painter often start with a flat plane like a wall or a canvas?

482. How many dimensions does a painter begin with by painting the height and width of an object or a person: two or three?

483. What does an artist add to height and width to create a **three** dimensional object from a two dimensional object: depth or length?

484. Can an artist paint in such a way as to create the illusion that something is very close or far away?

485. What part of a painting features the things that are the *closest* to you: the foreground or the background?

486. What part of a painting features the objects between the foreground and the background: center, high ground, or middle ground?

487. What part of a painting features those things that are *farthest* from you: the foreground or the background?

488. Would the buildings, land, or trees in the background look big and close, or small and far?

489. Would the buildings, land, or trees in the foreground look big and close and in focus, or small, far, and fading away?

490. What colors are typically used in the foreground: bright or dark?

491. What colors are typically used in the background: bright or dark?

492. What part of a painting often has the most detail: the foreground or the background?

493. What part of a painting often makes it seem that the object or person blends in with the sky or the wall: the middle ground or the background?

494. Do artists often use lines, shapes, shadow, and colors to convey a sense of **space** and depth, as in *The Interior of the Pantheon* by Italian artist Giovanni Panini?

495. Do artists often use lines, shapes, shadow, and colors to convey a sense of movement?

496. What is the artistic term that refers to the way an artist makes the elements of an artwork work together for form the whole: composition or layout?

497. What is the first step when you draw a picture: drawing lines or drawing circles?

498. Can an artist use lines, shadow, and light in a painting to connect objects or people, like in *The Bath* by American artist Mary Cassatt?

THE ARTS

499. Do the deliberate use of specific lines, colors, shapes, shadow, light, and balance all contribute to the effect an artist wishes to achieve?

500. What is the name of the artwork created by both modern and early Americans that arranged pieces of cloth in a design and then sewed the pieces together to make a bedcover: a comforter or a quilt?

501. What is the term given for a gathering of women who would come together to make a quilt: a quilting bee or a quilt party?

502. What are *double chain* or *wedding ring* regarded as: stitches in sewing or quilt designs?

503. Are quilts often designed with colors and geometric shapes that form a pattern?

504. What does it mean if the quilt design is symmetrical?

505. What is an element other than design that makes a quilt unique: its thickness or its texture?

506. What is the name of the art form that originated among typically untrained people of a country or region, usually reflecting their traditional culture: folk art or village art?

507. Are quilts and other woven textiles a type of folk art?

508. Does the quote from African American artist Horace Pippin, "My heart tells my mind what to draw," suggest to you that his artwork *Victorian Interior* is an example of folk art or classical art?

509. What is the name for the simple machine that an artist might use for weaving thread or cloth into colorful textiles: a hoop or a loom?

510. What is the round thing called that shows six colors: a color wheel or a color ring?

511. What are the three primary colors on the color wheel?

512. What are the complementary colors on the color wheel: orange, violet, and green, or pink, brown, and black?

513. Where are the complementary colors found on the color wheel: next to each other, or opposite each other?

514. When complementary colors are used together, do they appear more or less vivid?

515. What is the term for a collection of related or unrelated shapes, pictures, or objects that are pasted together on one canvas: a mosaic or a collage?

516. Did the French artist Henri Matisse start making collages because he became too ill to stand for a long period of time at his easel?

517. When the Quaker artist Edward Hicks painted his animal picture called *The Peaceable Kingdom*, do you think he was picturing the ideal, peaceful life in America, or was he trying to tell a story about animals?

518. What is the name of a group of artists that tried to show their innermost feelings and reveal their emotions in their artworks: Impressionists or Expressionists?

THE ARTS

519. Do you think that the Norwegian artist Edward Munch was expressing his own feelings of sadness and closing out nature when he painted a figure of a person on a bridge with his hands over his ears in his painting, *The Scream*?

520. Does a painting or mural or quilt often tell a story?

521. Are hand-woven rugs considered art?

522. Did the Navajos Indians weave rugs?

523. What is the name of an animal that wool comes from?

524. What material is wool spun into after it is sheared, washed, and combed: thread or rope?

525. Where do many dyes come from to color the threads used for weaving: plants or soil?

526. What is the name of the large wooden frame that holds the spools of thread and a large, wide-toothed comb used by many native Indians and others to weave a rug?

527. Do Native American Indians follow written instructions to weave a rug, or do they do the design work in their heads?

528. What other artwork do many Navajo Indians design that incorporate symbols like cactus, feathers, animals, and rainbows: murals or sand paintings?

529. Have you ever woven a potholder or placemat?

530. What material did you use to create your weaving?

531. What can you create when you weave hair?

532. Do you think may artworks reflect life and events at the time the artist created the artwork?

533. What artists can you name?

534. What is your favorite kind of art?

535. Is a writer or singer of music also called a recording *artist*?

536. What is your favorite song?

537. Do you know the words to many songs?

538. What kind of symbols do you use to write down sounds in a song: musical notes or musical clefs?

539. What is the term for the low and high sounds of the notes?

540. What is the name of the bars you write your musical notes on: line bar or staff?

541. What are the seven musical notes from the alphabet?

542. Is the treble clef on the right or left side of the staff?

THE ARTS

543. What letter of the alphabet does a treble clef resemble?

544. What are the three kinds of musical notes?

545. Is there an eighth note in music that lasts half the time of a quarter note?

546. Which notes may be joined together when they are written: eighth notes or whole notes?

547. How many quarter notes equal one whole note?

548. What is the musical term for keeping time to music: rhythm or beat?

549. What is music divided into that is shown with a line down the staff: a series or a measure?

550. What is the name of the line on a staff that indicates the end of a measure: a rest line or a bar line?

551. What do the two thick lines on a staff indicate: the beginning or the end of the music?

552. Does every measure have the same number of beats?

553. What is the musical term given for the moments of silence in a song: stops or rests?

554. What is the musical symbol for a "rest:" a fancy letter R or a squiggly line?

555. Can "rests" and "notes" have different rhythms?

556. What is the Italian term in music for when the music is intended to be quiet: piano or forte?

557. What is the Italian term in music for when the music is intended to be loud: piano or forte?

558. What does "-issimo" mean in Italian: very or loud?

559. What does "pianissimo" mean: very loud or very quiet?

560. What does "fortissimo" mean: very loud or very quiet?

561. What are strings, brass, woodwinds, and percussion categories of?

562. What are some percussion instruments in an orchestra?

563. What percussion instrument are bass, kettle, and snare examples of?

564. What are some stringed instruments in an orchestra?

565. What is the order of stringed instruments smallest to largest: string bass, viola, cello, and violin?

566. What are some brass instruments in an orchestra that are named for the metal they are made from?

567. What brass instrument has keys used to open and close valves to change the sound?

568. What brass instrument keeps rhythm in the background with an oom-pa, oom-pa sound?

569. What is the name of a famous jazz musician?

570. What instrument family do the violin and cello belong to?

THE ARTS

571. What instrument family do the French horn and trombone belong to?

572. What is the shape of a French horn?

573. What is the largest horn in the brass family?

574. What instrument family do the triangle and xylophone belong to?

575. What instrument family do the piccolo, flute, clarinet, bassoon and oboe belong to?

576. What instrument family does an orchestra have that a band does not have: percussion or string?

577. What does the word "piccolo" mean in Italian because it is smaller than the flute and has a higher pitch: tiny or small?

578. What is the term for the flat wood mouthpiece on some woodwinds that vibrates when you blow on it: a flute or a reed?

579. Which would be considered a reed instrument: a flute, a trumpet, or a clarinet?

580. Is the clarinet the featured instrument in "Rhapsody in Blue" by American composer George Gershwin?

581. Can a harp also be part of an orchestra?

582. What is the name of the leader of the orchestra that has the baton?

583. What is the name of the person who creates the music of a symphony: a writer or a composer?

584. What famous Russian composed many pieces of music for orchestras like "1812 Overture, "Swan Lake," "Sleeping Beauty," and "The Nutcracker:" Tchaikovsky or Beethoven?

585. What famous American formed his own U.S. Navy band that toured the United States and Europe and composed his most famous march and patriotic song, "The Stars and Stripes Forever:" John Philip Sousa or Aaron Copland?

586. What famous American studied music in France and composed music for the ballets, "Billy the Kid," "Rodeo," and "Appalachian Spring" that included many folk songs: John Philip Sousa or Aaron Copland?

587. Can you sing the words to the song, "He's Got the Whole World in His Hands?"

588. Can you sing the words to the song, "My Bonnie Lies Over the Ocean?"

589. Can you sing the words to the song, "The Man on the Flying Trapeze?"

590. Can you sing the words to the song, "A Bicycle Build to Two?"

591. Can you sing the words to the song, "America" that starts out, "My country, 'tis of thee?"

592. Can you sing the words to the song, "You're a Grand Old Flag?"

THE ARTS

593. Do you know the names of any folk songs?

594. Can Medieval, Islamic, Chinese, African, and American all be types of art?

The Arts – 4th Grade

595. Is architecture a type of art?

596. What type of large structure with tall ceilings, towers, statues, and stained-glass windows was often built in the center of every city in Europe during the Middle Ages: cathedrals or palaces?

597. What medieval cathedral in Paris, France means "Our Lady" in French: Nuestra Señora or Notre Dame?

598. What is the style of architecture developed in northern France that spread throughout Europe between the 12th and 16th centuries that is characterized by stone braces called flying buttresses and by vaulted and pointed arches: Baroque or Gothic?

599. What is the name of the large, circular stained-glass window build in 1258 on the south side of Notre Dame Cathedral that has a religious significance: the South Rose Window or the South Sun Window?

600. What is the term for the sculptures of make-believe creatures on the tops of cathedrals or at the bottom of roof gutters that were designed to scare evil away from the church: buttresses or gargoyles?

601. What is the name for the hand-written books that were created by the monks in the Middle Ages with illuminated pages, added paint, and bits of silver and gold: illuminated transcripts or illuminated manuscripts?

602. Does "manuscript" come from the word *manual* meaning made or done by hand?

603. What is the name of one of the most famous illuminated manuscripts in the world created by Celtic monks in 900 A.D. that contain the four Gospels and is hand-written in Latin: "The Book of Kells" or "The Lichfield Gospels?"

604. What is the name of the thin, sheepskin paper used in medieval times that was cut and stitched together to make a book, and was also the type of paper that the *Declaration of Independence* and other historical documents were written on: wax paper or parchment paper?

605. What is the name for the pen used in medieval times by the monks: a fountain pen or a quill pen?

606. What is the name for the form of art in which pictures and scenes are woven into a fabric for a wall hanging: quilts or tapestries?

607. What kinds of buildings are tapestries often displayed in?

608. What is the name of the people that came to Spain from Northern Africa that developed a style of architecture different from Gothic: the Muslims or the Egyptians?

THE ARTS

609. What is the name of the religion of many Muslims: Islam or Arabic?

610. What is another term for the Muslim people because many of them came to Spain from Morocco, Africa: the Moors or the Africans?

611. What is the name of the ornate palace built in the 1300s by the Moors in Granada, Spain that includes a courtyard called the *Court of the Lions*: The Alameda or The Alhambra?

612. What is the name of the famous building in India built in the 1600s as a tomb for the wife of a Muslim emperor with domes and towers and a reflective pool in front of it, a great example of Islamic architecture: The Golden Temple or the Taj Mahal?

613. What is the name of the holy book of Christianity: the Bible or the Qur'an?

614. What is the name of the holy book of Islam with elegant Arabic lettering and touches of real gold: the Bible or the Qur'an?

615. What is the name of the Muslim place of worship that includes distinct architectural features like a niche in the wall that always faces Mecca, the holiest city of Islam, and located in western Saudi Arabia: a temple or a mosque?

616. How do Muslim artists and architects decorate holy books and mosques: with pictures or with geometric patterns?

617. What is the primary subject matter for most African art: the human figure or the animal figure?

618. What animal was often engraved by Africans in caves or on rock faces during prehistoric times: the buffalo or the antelope?

619. Are the different countries of Africa known for distinct forms of art?

620. What is considered Africa's greatest form of art: paintings or sculptures?

621. What metal did people of West Africa use to carve sculptures that looked like real people: brass or copper?

622. Do many Africans carve sculptures out of wood, terracotta, clay, and stone?

623. What material is used in Africa more than any other to create sculptures: clay or wood?

624. What is the name of the material that comes from the tusk of an elephant or a walrus that is used by many Africans to create masks, jewelry, and statues: ivory or jade?

625. What African art form is often created from a tiger's eye, coconut shell, or ebony wood: jewelry or mosaics?

626. What do Africans often create using terracotta and bronze: homes or sculptures?

627. Are African drums and masks an art form?

628. Which of the following are *not* associated with African art: tribal masks, sculptures, tapestries, paintings, or bronze statues?

THE ARTS

629. Are masks created by African artisans often used in dances and rituals to either attract spirits, or to scare off an enemy?

630. What theme is often reflected in African art: hunting or religion?

631. Do Africans often carve statues to honor their ancestors, Gods, and Kings?

632. What kind of African artists create blankets and other items by weaving, dying, stamping, painting, or embroidery: fabric artists or textile artists?

633. Which of the following represent a practical application of African art: basketry, body painting, or sculpture?

634. What is the architectural shape of many huts in Africa: a beehive or a cone?

635. Did the Artists Pablo Picasso and Henri Matisse often incorporate elements of African art into their works?

636. What culture believed that the spirit of nature is the cornerstone of art: the Japanese or the Chinese?

637. What is the name for the long bands of paper that the Chinese painted children, birds, flowers, and animals on at the end of the 6th century: rolls or scrolls?

638. What fabric did Chinese artists paint pictures on by the 10th century: satin or silk?

639. What is the name for the distinct handwriting that the Chinese made into an art form: calligraphy or cursive?

640. What is the name of the fine, white pottery that the Chinese began creating during the Tang Dynasty: pottery or porcelain?

641. What is another name for porcelain that was commonly used to refer to the fancy plates, cups, saucers, and pots that was being traded in Europe: Dish or China?

642. What did Chinese potters in the Ming Dynasty develop for decorating their pottery: shellac or glaze?

643. What was the favorite glaze color for Chinese pottery that was made from a chemical called cobalt: green or blue?

644. What type of art form do many wealthy or important people have taken of themselves and their families: a landscape or a portrait?

645. What type of art form did the American painter Gilbert Stuart paint of George Washington, his wife Martha, and other American Presidents?

646. Did official portraits of American patriots look serious and formal, or relaxed and informal?

647. Do paintings often capture moments in history?

648. What kind of painting was *Washington Crossing the Delaware* by the German artist Emmanuel Leutze in 1776: a painting capturing a moment in history, or a portrait?

THE ARTS

649. What is the name of Thomas Jefferson's home in Virginia, also pictured on the back of a nickel that means "little mountain" in Italian with its classical white columns, and was inspired by the temples in Greece and Rome: Mount Vernon or Monticello?

650. What do the following places all have in common: The National Gallery, The Metropolitan Museum, The Institute of Chicago, The J. Paul Getty Museum, and The Philadelphia Museum?

651. What is the term for the art of arranging sounds as to produce a unified composition through melody: harmony or rhythm?

652. What are notes, staff, treble clef, and rests all elements of: composing or musical notation?

653. What are musical notes on a staff divided into: sections or measures?

654. What language are many musical terms expressed in, including *piano* meaning soft, *forte* meaning loud, legato meaning tied together, and *staccato* meaning separated: Spanish or Italian?

655. Do the notes on a sheet of music match the notes on a piano keyboard?

656. What kind of labels do the white keys on a piano have: numbers or letters?

657. Are the black keys on keyboards sharp keys or flat keys??

658. What is the opposite of D-sharp: D-black or D-flat?

659. How is an orchestra divided: by instruments or by sound?

660. What is the typical shape of a stage in a concert hall: round or fan-shaped?

661. How many families of instruments are there: three or four?

662. What is the title of the person who helps with the timing of the symphony, and ensures that the music is played the way the composer intended?

663. What is the name of the stick that a conductor uses: a wand or a baton?

664. What part of the body are the strings played with?

665. How is sound formed from the woodwind and brass instruments?

666. What object are the percussion instrument struck with?

667. What is considered the oldest, most expressive musical instrument of all: the drum or the human voice?

668. Are the three basic elements of music rhythm, melody, and harmony?

669. Do people have a comfort zone in singing either high notes or low notes?

670. What is the term for women's voices that sing high: soprano or alto?

671. What is the term for women's voices that sing low: soprano or alto?

THE ARTS

672. What is the term for women's voices that sing in the middle range: mezzo-soprano or mezzo-alto?

673. What is the term for men's voices that sing high: soprano or tenor?

674. What is the term for men's voices that sing low: bass or alto?

675. What is the term for men's voices that sing in the middle range: mezzo or baritone?

676. What is the musical term given for the types of songs sung by the monks during the Middle Ages that had a religious meaning: carols or chants?

677. What is the musical term for a musical composition performed by an orchestra?

678. How many sections or "movements" is a symphony usually divided into: two or four?

679. What Austrian composer is sometimes called the "Father of the Symphony:" Franz Joseph Haydn or Wolfgang Amadeus Mozart?

680. What famous Austrian composer said that music came to him in his dreams, and wrote music for orchestras, singers, and operas including "The Magic Flute:" Franz Joseph Haydn or Wolfgang Amadeus Mozart?

681. Can you name another classic composer besides Mozart?

682. What night of the year would you hear the famous Scottish song "Auld Lang Syne" meaning old long since, that starts out with the line, "Should auld acquaintance be forgot?"

683. Do you know the words to the song "The Yellow Rose of Texas?"

684. Do you know the words to the song "Cockles and Mussels?"

685. Which of the following folksongs can you sing: *Bicycle Built of Two, Clementine, Home on the Range, I've Been Working on the Railroad, Oh Susannah, Row, Row, Row Your Boat, She'll Be Coming Round the Mountain, Old MacDonald,* and *Yankee Doodle*?

The Arts – 5th Grade

686. Are you both a viewer and a creator of art?

687. Can you draw, cut, paste, mold with clay, paint, and take photographs?

688. Who created some of the earliest classical art masterpieces more than 2,000 years ago: Greece and Rome, or France and Spain?

689. What is the name of the structures in Greek architecture that were called Doric, Ionic, and Corinthian: columns or domes?

690. What is the name of the temple built by the Greeks in the plain Doric style that was dedicated to the goddess Athena Parthenos, and serves as an example of balance and proportion in Greek architecture: the Acropolis or the Parthenon?

THE ARTS

691. What is the name of the fort with many ancient buildings, the highest point in Athens, Greece upon which the Parthenon was built to honor the Roman gods: the Acropolis or the Coliseum?

692. What art form did the ancient Greeks and Romans create from bronze and marble to capture the beauty of the human body?

693. What is the name of the statue by the Greek sculptor Myron around 450 B.C. that depicts one of the competitions in the original Olympics in Athens: *The Discus Thrower* or *The Shotput Thrower*?

694. What is the name of the ancient Greek marble statue from 150 B.C. that was found on the island of Milo in 1820 without her arms, is considered to be one of the most famous works of ancient Greek sculpture, and is on display in the Louvre art museum in Paris: the *Winged Victory of Samothrace* or the *Venus de Milo*?

695. What kind of art that began appearing in 12th century France was an expression of the values of the medieval church: Gothic or Classical?

696. What is the name of the cathedral in Paris, France that is an example of Gothic architecture with its arches, towers, stained glass windows, gargoyles, and huge flying buttresses that helped to support the high stone walls: Chartres Cathedral or Notre Dame Cathedral?

697. What is the French word for "rebirth" in Europe that represented the most renowned period in the history of European art, lasting from about 1400 to 1600: Renaissance or Medieval?

698. What is the name of the period in history before the Renaissance: the Middle Ages or the Stone Age?

699. What was the primary theme of art during the Middle Ages: nature or religion?

700. Did the artists of the Renaissance have a renewed interest in Gothic art or Classical art?

701. In what European country did the Renaissance begin in the early 1400's, and lasted through the 1600's when painting, sculpture, and architecture began to flourish: France or Italy?

702. What kinds of places did wealthy people pay artists to decorate during the Renaissance period: private homes or palaces?

703. What two Italian cities were the centers of the arts during the Renaissance: Florence and Rome, or Milan and Venice?

704. Were Italian artists greatly influenced by Greek and Roman art that focused on the beauty of nature and the human body?

705. Are Raphael, Sandro Botticelli, and Leonardo da Vinci regarded as French or Italian Renaissance artists?

706. What Renaissance artist is famous for the 1486 painting *The Birth of Venus* that shows a goddess on a scallop shell: Sandro Botticelli or Leonardo da Vinci?

707. What Renaissance Italian artist is famous for his paintings *Mona Lisa*, *The Last Supper*, and *Vitruvian Man* also known as *The Proportions of Man*: Leonardo da Vinci or Donatello?

THE ARTS

708. What is considered the best-known painting in the entire history of art?

709. What is considered Leonardo da Vinci's second most famous painting: *Mona Lisa* or *The Last Supper*?

710. What facial feature of the *Mona Lisa* has fascinated people for centuries: her eyes or her smile?

711. What is the name of a special type of painting applied to wet or dry plaster on a wall with water-based paints: a fresco or a mural?

712. What is the name of the artist that painted the fresco *School of Athens* that depicted the great thinkers of Plato, Aristotle, Socrates, Ptolemy, and Euclid, painted on a wall at Vatican City, and measures 19 feet tall by 27 feet wide: Raphael or Rubens?

713. What is the name of the Renaissance artist famous for painting a self-portrait and the famous painting *Madonna and Child*: Raphael or Rubens?

714. Are Donatello and Michelangelo French or Italian sculptors from the Renaissance?

715. What is the name of the famous marble statue of an unclothed man by the Italian artist Michelangelo between 1501 and 1504 that is considered a masterpiece in Renaissance sculpture, and located in Florence, Italy: the *David* or the *Venus de Milo*?

716. What is the name of the largest Christian church in the world in Rome that has a dome designed by Michelangelo: Notre Dame Cathedral or St. Peter's Basilica?

717. What is the name of the chapel in Rome where Michelangelo was asked by the Pope to paint frescos of Bible scenes onto a sixty-foot high ceiling that included *The Creation of Adam*?

718. What is the name for the architectural style of many of the cathedrals built during the Middle Ages with tall columns, stained-glass windows, and vaulted ceilings: Baroque or Gothic?

719. What type of architecture did the Renaissance architects incorporate into their designs: the ornate Gothic style, or the clean-lined ancient Greek and Roman style?

720. What bronze-colored structure did Filippo Brunelleschi design in Roman style in the early 1400's for the cathedral in Florence, Italy with simple geometric patterns, and is considered the symbol of Florence: an arch or a dome?

721. What kind of paint did Italian artists learn how to make from the Northern artists of Holland, Germany, and Belgium who made paint by mixing pigments from plant seeds: watercolors or oil?

722. What type of paint did the Flemish artist Jan van Eyck use in painting *Portrait of Giovanni Arnolfini and His Wife*, allowing him to layer colors over one another: watercolors or oil?

723. What is the term given to the type of art in which painters of Northern Europe painted scenes of the lives of common people: realistic painting or genre painting?

724. Is Pieter Brueghel, artist of *Peasant Wedding* that depicts peasant subjects in a realistic way, regarded as a genre painter or a portrait painter?

THE ARTS

725. What is the nationality of Albrecht Durer, a Renaissance artist famous for his alter pieces and self-portraits, and one of the greatest artists of the Renaissance: Italian or German?

726. What is the study of the development of art and art styles over time: art history or art movements?

727. What is the name given for the specific style of art that was used by several artists during a specific period in time: an art era or an art movement?

728. Which art movement included Byzantine art, Romanesque art, and Gothic art: medieval or Renaissance?

729. What type of medieval art focused on religious themes, symbolism, and lacked realism: Byzantine art or Gothic art?

730. What type of medieval art focused on architectural details such as murals, domes, columns, and stained-glass: Gothic art or Romanesque art?

731. What type of medieval art incorporated brighter colors, animal themes, and realism: Byzantine art or Gothic art?

732. What structure in Paris, France is a classic example of Gothic art and architecture with its tall stone walls, flying buttresses, stained glass windows, and gargoyle waterspouts: Reims Cathedral or St. Peter's Basilica?

733. Which art movement was best represented by the artists Donatello, Ambrogio Lorenzetti, Benvenuto di Guisetti, and Giotto: Medieval or Renaissance?

734. Which art movement is generally divided into two periods called early and high: Medieval art or Renaissance art?

735. Which art movement is characterized by more realistic themes, a departure from religious themes, and new painting techniques: Medieval art or Renaissance art?

736. Which art movement used more refined techniques of perspective, balance, and the use of light and dark: Renaissance art or Medieval art?

737. Which art movement was best represented by the artists Leonardo da Vinci, Michelangelo, Raphael, and Caravaggio: Medieval or Renaissance?

738. What is the period between the Renaissance period and the Baroque period called: Spiritualism or Mannerism?

739. Which art movement is characterized by more dramatic and life-like paintings with more movement, and sculptures made of marble, bronze or gilded in gold: Baroque or Gothic?

740. What is a common definition of Baroque: complex and ornate, or simple and plain?

741. What type of architecture is the Trevi Fountain in Rome, Italy considered: Gothic or Baroque?

742. What is the name of the Italian artist who introduced the world to the Baroque style with his painting *The Calling of St. Mathews*: Caravaggio or Michelangelo?

THE ARTS

743. What is the name of the Baroque artist who is famous for his work at the Church of St. Ignatius in Rome: Andrea Pozzo or Annibale Carracci?

744. What is the name of the Baroque Dutch artist renowned for his painting *Night Watch*, several self-portraits, and his use of light and shade: Peter Paul Rubens or Rembrandt?

745. What is the name of the Baroque Flemish artist who painted *Samson and Delilah* and *The Festival of Venus*, and emphasized color and movement in his paintings, landscapes, and mythological subjects: Peter Paul Rubens or Rembrandt?

746. What is the name of the Baroque Spanish artist known for his masterpiece *Las Meninas* in Madrid's Prado Museum, as well as many famous portraits: Diego Velázquez or El Greco?

747. What is the name of the Baroque and Mannerist Greek artist born in Crete but settled in Toledo, Spain for several years, is known for his masterpiece, *The Burial of the Count of Orgaz*, and is also renowned for his dramatic use of light and shade in his landscape painting *View of Toledo*: El Greco or Diego Velázquez?

748. What is the name given to the end of the Baroque period in art between 1750 and 1800 that is characterized by the use of pastel colors and light subject matter, and often portrays scenes of the lives of wealthy Europeans: Gothic or Rococo?

749. What is the name of the art movement after the Neo-classical period that focused on emotion, feelings, landscapes, nature scenes, bullfights, revolution, and beauty, and further characterized by looser brush strokes and more expressive style: Rococo art or Romantic art?

750. What is the name of the prominent Romantic artist who painted a man standing on a stone peak entitled *The Wanderer above the Sea and Fog*: Spanish painter Francisco Goya or German painter Caspar David Friedrich?

751. What is the name of the prominent Romantic artist and court painter of Charles IV who used drama and emotion is his painting *Bullfight*, and depicted a revolution and the horrors of war in his painting entitled, *The Third of May 1808*: Diego Velázquez or Francisco de Goya?

752. What is the name of the French Romantic artist who portrayed the Revolution of 1830 in Paris, France with his painting entitled, *Liberty Leading the People* based on what he saw outside his studio window: Caspar David Friedrich or Eugene Delacroix?

753. What is the name of the art movement that started in France after the Revolution of 1848 and changed the focus from emotion and romantic themes to real world people and everyday life: Classicism or Realism?

754. What is the name given for the painters who depicted the lives of regular, ordinary people and everyday subjects in their paintings: idealists or realists?

755. What is the name of the French painter who painted *The Gleaners* depicting the stark reality of the poor, as it shows three peasant women picking up grains of wheat that were left behind after a harvest: Jean-Francois Millet or Gustave Courbet?

THE ARTS

756. What is the name of the French painter who painted *Young Women from the Village* and *The Stone Breakers*, both depicting the plight of the poor and the working class: Jean-Francois Millet or Gustave Courbet?

757. What is the name of the American Realistic painter who painted *The Gross Clinic* showing a doctor teaching a class on surgery in a very graphic matter: Thomas Eakins or Henry Ossawa Tanner?

758. What is the name of the African American Realistic painter who in 1893 painted *The Banjo Lesson* showing an old man teaching a young boy how to play a banjo: Thomas Eakins or Henry Ossawa Tanner?

759. What is the name of the American Realistic painter famous for his realistic seascapes including one entitled *Northeaster*: Winslow Homer or Thomas Easins?

760. Do you think that the invention of photography in 1840 contributed to the growth of the Realism art movement?

761. What is the name of the art movement that began in France in the 1860s that captured the artist's *perception* of a subject, and is further characterized by the use of primary colors and short brush strokes that represented the appearance of reflected light: Impressionism or Realism?

762. What is the name of the French impressionist who is renowned for *Dance at the Moulin de la Galette, Girl with the Watering Can, Young Girls at the Piano, The Swing, Luncheon of the Boating Party,* and *Two Sisters on the Terrace*: Pierre-Auguste Renoir or Claude Monet?

763. What is the name of the French Impressionist with more than half of his paintings depicting dancers and included, *The Dance Class, Little Dancer of Fourteen Years*, and *The Ballet Rehearsal on Stage*: Edgar Degas or Henri de Toulouse-Lautrec?

764. What is the name of the French painter, regarded as the founder of the Impressionist movement, and famous for his paintings, *Water Lily Pond, Wild Poppies, Woman with a Parasol, Haystacks, Rouen Cathedral*, and *Impression, Sunrise*: Edouard Manet or Claude Monet?

765. What French Impressionist painter crossed over from Realism and painted *The Fifer, The Bullfight*, and *A Bar at the Folies-Bergiere*: Edouard Manet or Claude Monet?

766. What is the name of the Danish-French impressionist famous for his portrayal of the common man, and is the only artist to have displayed his artworks in all eight of the Impressionist Exhibitions: Camille Pissarro or Claude Monet?

767. What is the name of an American Impressionist whose paintings often emphasized women and the bonds between mother and child, and include the artworks, *Mother and Child, Little Girl in the Blue Armchair,* and *Children Playing on the Beach*: Camille Pissarro or Mary Cassatt?

768. What is the name of the short art movement after Impressionism that is characterized by using small dots of color to create an entire painting: Post-Impressionism or Pointillism?

769. Can pixels on a computer screen be compared to the dots of a Pointillism painting?

THE ARTS

770. Do you think that paintings that are clearer and sharper are the result of smaller dots or larger dots?

771. What is the name of the artist regarded as the founder of Pointillism, studied colors and optics, and is famous for his six foot tall by ten feet wide masterpiece entitled, *Sunday Afternoon on the Island of La Grande Jatte* that he worked on for two years: Paul Signac or Georges Seurat?

772. What is the name of the other founder of Pointillism who continued the medium of Pointillism after Georges Seurat, helping to develop Pointillist style: Vincent Van Gogh or Paul Signac?

773. What is the name of the art movement centered in France that followed Impressionism, and is characterized by artists experimenting with new subjects, perspectives, and techniques in their artworks, and developing their own unique style: Cubism or Post-Impressionism?

774. What is the name of the poor Dutch Post-Impressionist painter famous for cutting off part of his left ear, and for his masterpieces *Starry Night, Sunflowers, Self-Portrait with Straw Hat, Irises, Café Terrace at Night,* and *Bedroom in Aries*: Vincent Van Gogh or Georges Seurat?

775. What is the name of the Post-Impressionist painter known for his jungle scenes and his artwork entitled, *The Sleeping Gypsy*: Henri Rousseau or Paul Gauguin?

776. What is the name of the Post-Impressionist painter known for painting the nightlife in Paris, and includes the cabaret painting entitled, *At the Moulin Rouge, Jane Avril and the Jardin de Paris,* and *The Laundress*: Henri Toulouse-Lautrec or Henri Rousseau?

777. What is the name of the Post-Impressionist artist who is regarded as the father of modern sculpture, and famous for his French sculptures, *The Burghers of Calais* and *The Thinker*: Auguste Renoir or Auguste Rodin?

778. What is the name of the French Post-Impressionist painter who experimented with bold colors, and whose artworks include his masterpiece, *Where Do We Come From, What Are We, Where Are We Going?,* and *Breton Girls Dancing*: Paul Cezanne or Paul Gauguin?

779. What is the name of the French Post-Impressionist painter who help transition from Post-Impressionism and Cubism using repetitive brush strokes, and whose artworks include, *The Card Players* and *Basket of Apples*: Paul Cezanne or Paul Gauguin?

780. What is the name of the art movement that is considered more a philosophy than an art style, started in France and spread to Russia, Belgium, and Austria, and was a response to Realism and Impressionism in that the painters intended their artworks to have a deeper meaning using metaphors to represent something: Symbolism or Expressionism?

781. What is the name of the art movement founded in the early 1900's by Spanish artist Pablo Picasso, depicted subjects like people, glasses, and bottles in a multi-dimensional style on a flat canvas, and can be categorized as either analytical or synthetic: Cubism or Surrealism?

782. What is the name for Pablo Picasso's early stage of painting with cool colors and sad themes as represented by his artworks *The Old Guitarist, Life,* and *The Tragedy*: the Blue Period or the Sad Period?

THE ARTS

783. What is the name of Picasso's stage of painting characterized by the use of bright colors and circus themes as represented by his artworks *Harlequin with Glass* and *Family of Acrobats*: the Pink Period or the Rose Period?

784. What is the name of the art movement that would describe Picasso's geometric paintings *Three Musicians, The Weeping Woman*, and *Portrait of Daniel-Henry Kahnweiler 1910:* Expressionism or Cubism?

785. What is the name of the Picasso's masterpiece on display at the Museo Reina Sofia in Madrid, Spain, measures 11 feet tall by 26 feet wide, depicts the pain, anguish and suffering of innocent people and animals reacting to a bombing of their small city by the German and Italian warplanes during the Spanish Civil War in 1937, and is intentionally painted in somber tones of blacks, whites, and greys to further emphasize the mood of the time: *Guernica* or *Bilbao*?

786. Which artist is considered one of the greatest artists of the 20th century, having created over 1,200 sculptures and 1,800 paintings?

787. What is the name of the other founding father of Cubism and painted *Violin and Candlestick* in analytical Cubist style: Juan Gris or Georges Braque?

788. What is the name of the Cubist painter who painted a tribute *Portrait of Picasso* in Cubist style using warm browns and cool blues: Juan Gris or Georges Braque?

789. What is the name of the art movement that started in Germany, and aimed to express emotion by using vivid colors, as in the abstract artwork, *The Scream* by Edvard Munch: Expressionism or Emotionism?

790. What is the name of the art movement that began in the 1920s in France that essentially is the opposite of Realism, and aims to explore the subconscious mind: Abstract Art or Surrealism?

791. What is the name of the most famous Spanish Surrealist artist famous for his eccentric nature and trademark moustache, and known for his Surreal painting of melting clocks in a desert titled, *The Persistence of Memory*: Joan Miró or Salvador Dalí?

792. The is the name of the art movement that started in the United States in which there are not any recognizable subjects, as represented in the artworks of the founder of this art movement Wassily Kandinsky: Extreme or Abstract?

793. What is the name of the art movement, characterized by images taken from the modern world, and includes famous celebrities and singers, soup can labels, and comic books: Abstract art of Pop art?

794. What is the name of one of the most famous Pop artist whose famous paintings include *Campbell's Soup Cans, Marilyn Monroe*, and *Eight Elvises*: Keith Haring or Andy Warhol?

795. What is the name of the art form that is made up of a collection of pieces like pictures, newspaper clippings, or colored paper that is glued together: a collection or a collage?

796. What are the three primary colors?

THE ARTS

797. Do complementary colors appear on the same side of the color wheel, or on opposite sides of the color wheel?

798. What is the art term used for a painting painted on wet plaster of a wall or ceiling: fresco or mural?

799. What is the name of the oven that is used in an art room to bake the clay so it becomes permanent?

800. What is the name of the machine that is used to make a pot or other ceramic piece?

801. What is the art term used for a painting of land, mountains, rivers, oceans, and sky?

802. What is the art term for the type of material used to make an art form such as clay, paint, or marble: substance or medium?

803. What is the art term for the board that is used in painting where the different colors are mixed?

804. What is the art term for a painting that is painted on a ceiling or a wall?

805. What is the term for colors that can be made from oil or from chalk: primary colors or pastels?

806. What is the art term that refers to the way of drawing or painting that makes objects appear closer than other objects: dimension or perspective?

807. What is the art term for the part of the paint that gives it its color: tint or pigment?

808. What is the art term that is French for "open air," when painters paint outside: Plein Air or Abre Aire?

809. What is the art term for the painting of a person?

810. What is the art term when an artist paints him or herself?

811. What is the art term for a sculpture that looks that it is raised up from the background: relief or dimensional?

812. What is the art term for a three-dimensional artwork carved or chiseled from stone, wood, or marble: a model or sculpture?

813. What is the art term given for a number of artworks that are designed to go together: a sequel or a series?

814. What is the name of the paint that becomes thinner as it is mixed with water: pastels or watercolors?

815. What is the art term that refers to paintings or drawings of inanimate objects like flowers in a vase or fruit in a bowl: animate life or still life?

816. What is the art term that refers to the feel of the canvas depending on the paint applied: roughness or texture?

817. What is the term that is used to refer to a balance of materials, where one half of an image mirrors the other half exactly: asymmetry or symmetry?

THE ARTS

818. Can you name an art museum?

819. What is the name of the art museum originally a royal palace that opened in 1793 in Paris, France, and is considered the world's most famous museum, housing the *Mona Lisa* and the *Venus de Milo*: Le Louvre or El Prado?

820. What type of performances would you be able to enjoy at a Palace or Theatre of Fine Arts?

821. Which fine art would *The Barber of Seville, Madame Butterfly, Don Giovanni, La Traviata, The Marriage of Figaro, Carmen,* and *La Boheme* be categorized as?

822. Which fine art would *Romeo and Juliet, Hamlet, Macbeth, A Midsummer Night's Dream, The Crucible, Death of a Salesman, Raisin in the Sun,* and *Our Town* be categorized as?

823. Which fine art would rock and roll, pop, heavy metal, rap, jazz, blues, country, bluegrass, rhythm and blues, hip hop, classical, funk, soul, reggae, alternative, gospel, folk, salsa, disco, new wave, fusion, Christian, electronic, Latin, techno, dance, and opera all be genres of?

824. What is the name for the annual award for notable achievement in the music and recording industry: an Emmy or a Grammy?

825. What is the name for the annual award presented by the Academy of Television Arts and Sciences for notable achievement in television production and programming: an Emmy or a Grammy?

826. Which fine art would ballroom, ballet, tap, hip-hop, folk, belly, break, square, salsa, tango, merengue, samba, cha cha, paso doble, flamenco, waltz, polka, Irish, Scottish, clog, jitterbug, limbo, sword, modern, rain, robot, foxtrot, swing, twist, aerobic, and Zumba be categorized as?

827. What is the name for the person who creates and arranges the movements and formations for dancers during a performance: a cartographer or a choreographer?

828. Which fine art would *West Side Story, The Phantom of the Opera, Cats, Les Miserables, A Chorus Line, Chicago, Beauty and the Beast, The Lion King, 42nd Street, Oklahoma, The Sound of Music, Fiddler on the Roof, Grease, Mama Mia, Rent, Miss Saigon, Wicked, Hello Dolly, Guys and Dolls, Bye Bye Birdie, My Fair Lady, Cabaret, Hairspray, Annie, Annie Get Your Gun, Man of La Mancha, Jersey Boys, Pippin, Oliver, South Pacific, Hair, The Wiz, Evita, Dreamgirls, Mame," The Music Man, Funny Girl, The King and I, The Wizard of Oz, Singing in the Rain, Little Shop of Horrors, The Pirates of Penzance, Meet Me in St. Louis, Camelot, Anything Goes, Fame, Peter Pan, Godspell, Showboat, Carousel, Mary Poppins,* and *White Christmas* all be categorized as?

829. What is the name for the annual award that recognizes achievement and excellence in live Broadway theatre: a Grammy or a Tony?

830. What is the name for the annual award that recognizes achievement in motion-picture production and performance, awarded by the Academy of Motion Picture Arts and Sciences: Oscar or Emmy?

831. What famous art museums can you name?

832. What famous artworks are you familiar with?

THE ARTS

833. How are Sotheby's in New York and Chirstie's in London related to the art world: they are both fine arts auction houses, or they are both fine art museums?

834. What is the name of the famous oil painting by Grant Wood of a farmer with a pitchfork standing next to his prim and proper daughter in front of a white house, is on display in the Art Institute of Chicago, and is one of the most familiar images in American art: *Americana* or *American Gothic*?

835. What is the name of the 20th century American painter whose artworks and sketches often reflected American culture, especially the scenes he created depicting everyday life on the magazine covers of the *Saturday Evening Post*: Andy Warhol or Norman Rockwell?

836. What is your favorite type of fine art to watch or to perform?

Chapter 11 – Environment

Environment – Pre-School

1. What do we call the surroundings around us: our environment or habitat??
2. What do you think the environment is like in the desert?
3. What do you think the environment is like in the ocean?
4. What do you think the environment is like in Florida?
5. What do you think the environment is like in Alaska?
6. Do living things share the environment?
7. Are living things dependent on each other?
8. Is it good to protect and to care about our environment?
9. Is it good to care about all the plants and animals in our ecosystem?
10. What is something that is natural in our environment?
11. Does our environment include land, air, and water?
12. Is the land made up of many living things?
13. What do we depend on the soil for?
14. Is water important for living things?
15. Is it good to want to conserve and to protect our water?
16. Do all living things depend on natural resources like air, water, sunlight, plants, and animals?
17. What is something that is man-made in our environment?
18. What are some natural things in our environment?
19. What is the term for saving paper, plastic, glass, and cardboard to be used again: recycling or re-using?
20. Why do we need trees and plants?
21. How do trees change in the fall?
22. How do trees change in the winter?
23. How do trees change in the spring?

THE ENVIRONMENT

24. How do trees change in the summer?
25. Do trees have limbs, a trunk, and skin just like we do?
26. Can you imitate some sounds you hear in nature?

Environment – Kindergarten

27. What is the term for your surroundings: environment or area?
28. What are some items that we recycle?
29. Can paper be recycled?
30. What daily paper do many people read that can be recycled?
31. What metal or aluminum containers do we use that can be recycled?
32. What is the name of the glass containers that hold pickles and olives?
33. What is the name of the glass containers for soda and ketchup that can be recycled?
34. What are some resources in the environment that are important to conserve?
35. How can you conserve paper?
36. How can you conserve water?
37. How can you conserve electricity?
38. What is the name of the person that does not throw away garbage and litters in the park?
39. What are some things that you can do to help keep our Earth clean?

Environment – 1st Grade

40. How can you help conserve the environment?
41. What is it called when people do things and use products that are not harmful to the environment, and are eco-friendly: environmental practice or "going green?"
42. What is the name of the day of observation in April when we celebrate the planet: Earth Day or Green Day?
43. What is the word that refers to the collecting and processing of something in order that it may be used again: recycle or reuse?
44. Is it good for the environment to recycle and reuse?
45. What do we do in our community to recycle?

THE ENVIRONMENT

46. Can you recognize pesticides and other poisonous products in your house?
47. Is it important to keep the Earth clean?
48. Do lakes, trees, and wildlife all need protection?
49. What are some things we use that can be recycled?
50. What is the material that we can recycle that is used to make milk jugs?
51. Do we depend on the environment?
52. What are some things we can do to keep our community clean?
53. Do we have a sanitation service that picks up the garbage and recycled materials?
54. Is it good to work to contribute to a clean and "green" environment every day?

Environment – 2nd Grade

55. Is it important for us to care about our environment?
56. Are air, water, soil, humans, plants, and animals all part of our environment?
57. What are food, water, oxygen, shelter, and warmth for humans: basic needs or resources?
58. What is it called when there is too much smoke and carbon dioxide in the air: pollution or saturation?
59. Can you help the environment by using less water and electricity?
60. What are some ways you can conserve water?
61. What are some ways you can conserve electricity?
62. What things should be placed into a recycle bin in a classroom?
63. What things should be placed into a recycle bin at home?
64. Can we use recycled glass, paper, and cardboard to make other things?
65. Do you think you are making a difference by helping to keep the Earth clean and healthy?

Environment – 3rd Grade

66. How would you define the environment?
67. Is conservation a topic related to the environment?
68. Does keeping a clean and safe environment improve our lives?
69. What items are do we recycle at home?
70. What items are often recycled in a school?

THE ENVIRONMENT

71. Does recycling paper, cardboard, aluminum, glass, and plastic require more or less energy and resources?
72. Does recycling increase or reduce pollution and waste?
73. Is it important to dispose of hazardous materials like cleaners and paint properly?
74. Are many household products poisonous?
75. What is the term for the chemical that is used on crops and lawns to prevent damage from insects and other animals: pesticides or fertilizer?
76. What is the term for growing crops without using any chemicals or pesticides whatsoever: pure or organic?
77. Where is a good place to keep toxic and hazardous products?
78. Is it important to continue to preserve and protect our water, air, and soil supply?

Environment – 4th Grade

79. Do you have an awareness of issues related to the environment?
80. What are food, air, and water part of: our life cycle or our nature cycle?
81. What do all living things depend on for survival?
82. Does the term *environment* include conservation and the protection of the Earth?
83. Do you conserve and recycle in order to protect the environment?
84. Do you recycle at home?
85. Does your community have a formal recycling program?
86. Do we have specific hunting laws that are designed to preserve and protect the animal population and keep the ecosystem in check?
87. What are some ways we can protect animals from becoming extinct?

Environment – 5th Grade

88. How would you describe your environment at home?
89. How would you describe the environment of the community you live in?
90. What is the name of the independent agency that was established to promote the protection of the environment and to reduce pollution: The Environmental Protection Agency or the Pollution Prevention Agency?
91. Are all things in nature included in the environment?

THE ENVIRONMENT

92. Does our existence depend on our planet Earth and its climate?

93. What is it called when there is a change in a natural cycle forcing humans or animals to make a change as well: adopting or adapting?

94. What is the term for rain that is contaminated by chemicals and smoke from cars and factories: acid rain or smog?

95. What is the term for the form of air pollution when fog mixes with smoke, a result of dirty air produced by cars and, and usually found in cities: acid rain or smog?

96. Can acid rain and smog harm plants, animals, and people?

97. How are plants and animals affected if they are unable to adapt to a change in environment caused by pollution, water pollution, acid rain, the loss of trees, and the disposal of waste?

98. What condition would you be helping to improve if you grew your own food, conserved electricity and water, and grew your own garden and plants: pollution or the loss of trees?

99. What do increased ocean acidity, melting glaciers, higher carbon dioxide emissions, and rising global temperatures all contribute to: climate change or climate variation?

100. What greater threat is caused by car and factory emissions that create an unnatural "thermal blanket:" climate change or climate variation?

101. What is the term for the blanket of air that the Earth is wrapped up in that is made up of several layers of gases: atmosphere or oxygen?

102. What is the term for the natural process of transferring and balancing the gases between the Sun, the atmosphere, and the Earth: air transfer or the Greenhouse Effect?

103. Can human processes like the burning of fossil fuels and trees, and the increased use of aerosol sprays alter the natural Greenhouse Effect?

104. What is the name of the layer of gas that serves to absorb most of the radiation of the Sun, preventing dangerous ultraviolet rays from reaching the Earth: Ozone or Stratosphere?

105. Can new water ever be created?

106. Is it important to preserve and protect our water supply?

107. What results when acid rain falls into the water supply, or when people and factories dump trash, chemicals, and hazardous waste into lakes, rivers, and oceans: maritime pollution or water pollution?

108. What is the environmental term for the things we throw away like paper, food boxes, plastic milk cartons, and empty cleaning products: trash or waste disposal?

109. What is a great way to reduce waste disposal: renew or recycle?

110. How much oxygen do trees and marine plants produce for the Earth: 30% or 70%?

THE ENVIRONMENT

111. Do trees provide shelter, food, recreation, and homes for animals?

112. What results when more trees are cut down than are planted: a tree loss or a tree surplus?

113. What natural resource provides half of the Earth's animal and plant population: the desert or the rainforest?

114. What is the largest rainforest in the world?

115. Does supporting the effort to "save the rainforests" contribute to reducing tree loss?

116. Do you recycle in order to do your part in protecting the environment?

117. What would conserve more energy: taking a long shower or taking a short shower?

118. What would conserve more energy while brushing your teeth: letting the water run, or turning off the tap while you brush?

119. Do you conserve items like paper, plastic, and aluminum?'

120. What items can you reuse?

121. Would water, Sun, and wind be considered renewable or non-renewable resources?

122. Would coal, oil, and natural gas be considered renewable or non-renewable resources?

123. What is the term for using water to generate electricity: hydropower or wind power?

124. What renewable energy do turbines and windmills produce?

125. What would you plant to provide oxygen and to refresh and preserve the environment?

126. Do you participate in the recycling effort at home and at school?

127. What do you save when you use efficient appliances, turn off unnecessary lights, and recycle: energy or electricity?

128. What is the name of the act that protects plants and animals that may become extinct: Animal Preservation Act or Endangered Species Act?

129. What are some things that are regarded as hazardous to the environment?

130. What is the name for the layer in the Stratosphere that protects the Earth from dangerous ultraviolet light?

131. Are household cleaners, lead, smoke, pesticides, and ultraviolet rays all potentially hazardous?

132. How can you protect yourself from the rays of ultraviolet light?

133. What is the best thing to do for your health if you were standing near a person that is smoking?

134. Where is name of the potentially dangerous chemical element often found in old paint or pipes: metal or lead?

THE ENVIRONMENT

135. Can lead be found in water?

136. Is it advisable to handle hazardous materials carefully by reading labels, keeping them in their original containers, storing them in safe places, and using them only in well-ventilated areas?

137. What is the term for the radioactive gas formed from the decay of uranium in soil, rock, and water, and may cause cancer if present in excessive amounts in the air: radon or radium?

138. What is the term for the fibrous mineral that was once mixed with cement and used as a fire-retardant and insulator in older homes and buildings, but can potentially cause lung cancer if its fibers are inhaled: insulation or asbestos?

139. What would ground level Ozone, radon gas, and asbestos all be regarded as in the environment: hazardous or non-hazardous?

140. Does eating well promote a healthy body and a healthy environment?

141. What are pesticides used for: killing insects on crops or killing mold on crops?

142. What should you always make sure you do to your fruits and vegetables before eating them to ensure that all potential germs are eliminated?

143. Are pesticides often used on fruits and vegetables?

144. What is the term for fruits and vegetables that have **not** been sprayed with pesticides or insecticides: natural or organic?

145. Does washing your hands also minimize the likelihood of spreading germs?

146. Do most communities have conservation groups that encourage us to get involved?

147. What is the name for the April holiday that is observed worldwide as a day to raise awareness and demonstrate support for the protection of the environment: Earth Day or Planet Day?

148. What is the name of the National holiday in which groups and individuals are encouraged to plant and care for trees every year on the last Friday of April: Harvest Day or Arbor Day?

149. What do many people plant as a way of leaving a legacy, or to honor a special event?

150. What will you do in the future to promote a clean and healthy environment?

TECHNOLOGY AND INFORMATION SKILLS

Chapter 12 – Technology and Information Skills

Technology and Information Skills – Pre-School

1. What is the term for information that is accessed with available resources to complete some task?
2. Is technology important to progress and development?
3. Are computers, iPads, iPods, tablets, cellphones, and digital cameras all technological devices?
4. Do you have access to a computer or tablet like an iPad at home or at school?
5. What kind of information can we find using technological devices?
6. Do you think it is important to use technology in an appropriate manner?
7. Do you like to read?
8. Where can you go to check out and read books in our community?

Technology and Information Skills – Kindergarten

9. Is technology all around us?
10. Do you have access to a computer?
11. Do you have a computer in your classroom or a computer lab in your school?
12. Is it important to follow the rules for using a computer at home or in the computer lab?
13. Can you identify the computer, the monitor, the mouse, the keyboard, and the printer?
14. Are many technological devices wireless?
15. What computer programs are you familiar with for learning and for playing?
16. Do you know how to turn a computer on and off?
17. Do you know how to turn a monitor on and off?
18. What do you need to do before you turn off or shut down a computer: log off or turn the monitor off?
19. What do you need besides a user name to log into a computer: an ID number or a password?
20. Do you know how to use a mouse?
21. Can you click and drag an image on the computer?

TECHNOLOGY AND INFORMATION SKILLS

22. Are you familiar with some of the options on the tool bar like draw and paint?

23. Can you type your name on a computer keyboard?

24. What other words can you type?

25. How many hands should you learn to type with: one or two?

26. What button do you use to back up if you type an incorrect letter: the space bar or the backspace?

27. How can you make upper case letters: press the option key or press the shift key?

28. Can you find and type the numbers on the keyboard?

29. Can you open a program or game that is available on a computer?

30. Are you familiar with the Microsoft Word or other word processing program for typing text?

31. Can you open the Microsoft Word program under "File?"

32. Can you Save and Close the Microsoft Word program under "File?"

33. What is the purpose of the Microsoft Word computer program: to type sentences and text, or to chart out numbers?

34. Can you locate and use the shift, backspace, and enter keys?

35. Can you type one or more sentences in Word and then print the document with a little help?

36. Can you add a graphic or picture to a document with a little help?

37. Do you know how to change the font?

38. Do you know how to make a typed word bold?

39. Is it important to get in a good habit of using both hands when you type?

40. What can you do to get better at typing and more familiar with where the letters are on the keyboard?

41. Will practice with writing sentences and vocabulary words help you to improve your computer skills?

42. Are you familiar with some painting features like the pencil, paint bucket, and eraser tools?

43. Do you know how to delete a word or sentence that you have typed?

44. Can you write a simple letter or make a card with a graphic and then print it off?

45. Are you able to access and open the Internet?

46. Is it important to use the Internet appropriately and to never reveal any personal information over the Internet?

47. Do you know how to click on specific headings or links?

TECHNOLOGY AND INFORMATION SKILLS

48. Are many leisure and educational games available on the Internet?
49. What is the purpose of the library or the Instructional Media Center?
50. What are some rules to follow while in a school or public library?
51. What are some electronic devices that are available in a library?
52. What is the name of a type of E-reader devices that are available for use in libraries?
53. Are you familiar with the library?
54. Where do you look to search for a particular book on a specific topic in a library?
55. Can you locate and select library materials in print, non-print, and electronic formats?
56. Is fiction based on fact, or is it something invented or imagined?
57. Is non-fiction based on fact, or is it something invented using the imagination?
58. What is another name for the Instructional Media Center: library or bibliography?
59. Is a CD, an audio book, and a DVD considered media?
60. What is the time frame for checking out library materials?
61. Is a library card necessary to check out materials in a public library?
62. How many books or other materials are you allowed to check out at one time?
63. Why is it important to return library materials on time?
64. What consequence may result if you return library materials after a due date?
65. Do libraries have both electronic information devices and print information resources?
66. How would you categorize books, magazines, and newspapers: print or media?
67. How would you categorize Ebooks, CD's, and DVD's: print or media
68. Can you identify the parts of a book?
69. Do you know how to select both reading and listening materials in a library?
70. What is the general name for fiction, non-fiction, poetry, plays, and fairy tales: readings or literature?
71. Do you listen well to a story that is read out loud?
72. Do you like to listen and watch a story video?
73. Is it fun to explore all the books and the media in a library?
74. What is the name of the person that writes a book: a writer or an author?
75. What is the name of the person that draws the pictures for a book: a designer or an illustrator?

TECHNOLOGY AND INFORMATION SKILLS

76. What is the name of the award that is the highest honor earned for an American illustrator in children's literature: the Caldecott Award or the Artist's Award?

77. What is one way to know if an author or illustrator is an award-winner: the book has a subtitle, or the book will have a gold seal on the front cover?

78. Is it important to use library resources responsibly, and to follow the rules of the library?

79. Do you think that learning about new technology is a continuous learning process?

80. What technology devices do you feel capable of using?

Technology and Information Skills – 1st Grade

81. Is technology continually changing and improving in the 21st century?

82. What electronic devices do you have or are you familiar with?

83. Is it important to always follow the rules when using the computer whether you are in a library, in a computer lab, or at home?

84. Is it expected that you only use computer software that is appropriate for your age and skill level?

85. What parts of a computer can you identify?

86. Can you log on and log off a computer by yourself?

87. Are you comfortable with typing your name and a few sentences on the computer?

88. Will your typing skills continue to develop and improve as you practice throughout the year?

89. How many hands should you always use while typing?

90. What is the name for the middle row of keys where you should set your fingers as you type: the middle row or the home row?

91. Can you type at a basic level while changing fonts, color, and size?

92. Can you use graphics to create a picture?

93. Can you open a computer program, use the program, and then close the program?

94. Do you know how to save a document?

95. Do you know how to print a document?

96. Can you write a special holiday letter using Microsoft word, make font changes, add clip art or a border, save the document, and then print it out?

97. Can you open the media player program on a computer?

98. Can you manage the play, pause, volume, and stop controls on the electronic media player?

TECHNOLOGY AND INFORMATION SKILLS

99. Have you been introduced to the PowerPoint slide program?

100. Do you know how to click on the arrows to progress through the PowerPoint slides?

101. Are you able to type more things, and format your text using more features as you improve your knowledge of computer features?

102. Do you know how to insert graphics or clip art into your text document?

103. Do you use the punctuation keys correctly in your text?

104. Can you use the "cut," "copy," and "paste" options under "Edit?"

105. Are you allowed to cut text that you located using the Internet, and then paste it into your Microsoft Word document?

106. Should you believe everything you read or hear on the Internet?

107. When might you use the microphone feature on a computer?

108. When might you use headphones while working on a computer?

109. Are computer software programs available to help you improve your keyboarding skills?

110. Are computer software programs available to help you with reading, math, and music?

111. Do you understand that you should never give out any of your personal information including your name and address through an electronic device?

112. What wireless devices need to have their batteries charged?

113. What things can you do to take care of a laptop computer?

114. Is there a special cleaner that is made especially for cleaning computer monitors and TV screens?

115. How often do you use computers in the lab or in the library at your school?

116. Are you able to using the library's computer to conduct an electronic search for a book?

117. Are you familiar with both the school library and the public library?

118. What is the name of the librarian or library media specialist at your school or public library?

119. What are some things that a library media specialist does in the school library?

120. What are some rules in the library or Instructional Media Center?

121. Is it always expected to be quiet and respectful in a library?

122. Can you identify written, oral, and visual forms of literature in a library?

123. What electronic devices are available in the library or the Instructional Media Center?

124. What print materials are available in the library or the Instructional Media Center?

125. Are there computer stations in the school and public library?

TECHNOLOGY AND INFORMATION SKILLS

126. How do you locate a specific book or other library media item: by conducting an electronic search, or by looking in a card catalog?

127. Are both print books and Ebooks available for checkout or download in a library?'

128. Do you know how to locate and select print, non-print, and electronic formats?

129. Do you know how to locate and select audio books or DVDs in a library?

130. Is the school and public library organized in a systematic way with different areas that are designated for fiction, non-fiction, computers, and media?

131. What is the definition of fiction?

132. What is the definition of non-fiction?

133. Can you identify poetry?

134. Do you know the names of some fairy tales?

135. Can you choose library materials that are related to your interests and are age appropriate?

136. What specific authors and books can you name?

137. What is the name for the award given to an American illustrator for a children's book: Caldecott or Newbery?

138. What kind of books would be in the reference section of the library?

139. Are resource materials generally available for check out?

140. Are newspapers and magazines available to library patrons?

141. Are there electronic versions to many major newspapers?

142. Do you have to be careful when you are using a computer or a phone?

143. Do you understand that you should never send any pictures or video of yourself or people you know to anyone by cell phone or by computer?

144. How has technology changed our world?

Technology and Information Skills – 2nd Grade

145. Do you think that you are becoming technologically savvy?

146. What electronic devices do you have or do you have access to?

147. What electronic devices do you have that are wireless?

148. What is the name of the mobile device with several built-in applications and Internet access: cell phone or smartphone?

TECHNOLOGY AND INFORMATION SKILLS

149. What is the term for the capacity that allows computers, smartphones, and other electronic devices to connect with the Internet wirelessly in a specific area: Wi-Fi or Network?

150. What network device is necessary for Wi-Fi to be enabled, and that joins multiple networks together: a server or a router?

151. What do gaming and digital media devices like Microsoft's Xbox LIVE and Nintendo Wii require to operate: a router or a server?

152. Is technology often inter-connected?

153. Can your cell phone, your computer, and your television all by synced together?

154. Is it possible to listen to music on ITunes, or watch movies on several electronic devices?

155. What computer software programs or games are you familiar with?

156. What electronic devices are available in the Instructional Media Center or library?

157. How often do you go to your school or public library to get books, conduct research, or work on the computer?

158. What are some rules we need to follow when we are using a computer, or are in the lab?

159. What are the parts of a computer?

160. What is the function of a computer *server*: to serve the needs of a network of computers, or to provide the software for the computer?

161. What is the abbreviation for the Central Processing Unit?

162. Is it good keyboarding practice to review the letters and to reinforce where your hands should be placed on the keyboard?

163. Are you learning to type your letters with more speed and accuracy?

164. Can you identify the monitor, keyboard, mouse, and printer on a computer?

165. What do you control the curser with: the space bar or the mouse?

166. Can you log on and log off a computer by yourself?

167. Do you know how to save a document to a home directory, or other specific place?

168. Do you know how to use the web browser to access the online catalog and other databases?

169. Do you know how to use common media formats?

170. Can you access and view pre-selected sites on the Internet?

171. Can you recognize and use different tools on the toolbar?

172. Are you familiar with the desk accessories like paint or calculator?

TECHNOLOGY AND INFORMATION SKILLS

173. Are you making a good effort to keep your hands on the home row as you type?

174. Can you conduct an Internet search for information related to your report topic?

175. Do you remember how to "cut," "copy," and "paste" using Microsoft Word?

176. Can you locate and insert clipart or other graphics into your document?

177. Can you put together a short PowerPoint presentation of at least four slides on a topic of your choosing, and present it to the class with images and sound?

178. Can you type a letter or a one page report that using different fonts, clipart, and a border?

179. Can you make a simple spreadsheet using Microsoft Excel?

180. Do electronic devices often make our lives easier?

181. What is does IMC stand for?

182. What do you use the online catalog for in a library?

183. Do you know how to seek information using the Internet?

184. What information is provided in an encyclopedia?

185. Are there both print and electronic encyclopedias?

186. What is the purpose of a dictionary?

187. How is a dictionary organized?

188. Are there both print and electronic dictionaries?

189. Do you know how to use both print and electronic encyclopedias?

190. Do you know how to use both print and electronic dictionaries?

191. Can you access information from different formats including an encyclopedia, dictionary, online catalog, and pre-selected websites on the Internet?

192. What type of fiction books do you have an interest in?

193. What type of non-fiction books do you have an interest in?

194. What is the name for the list of the divisions of chapters at the beginning of a non-fiction book: the table of contents or the index?

195. Do you know how to use a table of contents to find the appropriate page?

196. What is the name for the alphabetical list of names, places, and topics with their page numbers at the end of a non-fiction book: index or glossary?

197. What is the name of an alphabetical specialized list of terms with their definitions at the end of a non-fiction book or textbook: index or glossary?

TECHNOLOGY AND INFORMATION SKILLS

198. Do you know how to use an index to find the appropriate page for a topic?

199. Do you know how to use a glossary to look up a definition of a term?

200. What is the name of the act of looking over something quickly to get an idea of the content: scanning or skimming?

201. Are you able to scan materials by looking at the table of contents or the graphics to get a sense of what information the scanned source will provide?

202. Do images and graphics convey messages?

203. What is the name of the medal that is awarded to the author of the most distinguished children's book of that year: the Caldecott Medal or the Newbery Medal?

204. What is the name of the medal that is awarded to the most distinguished illustrator of a children's book of that year: the Caldecott Medal or the Newbery Medal?

205. What is the name of the literary prize that is awarded to outstanding African American illustrators and authors of a children's book that focuses on some aspect of African American culture: The Dr. Martin Luther King Jr. Book Award or the Coretta Scott King Book Award?

206. Do award-winning books generally reflect excellence in literature and art?

207. Do you know how to locate and choose library materials that are age and level appropriate?

208. Can you choose a fiction book that is of personal interest to you?

209. Can you choose a non-fiction book that is about a subject that is of personal interest to you?

210. Do you have a favorite author?

211. What is one of your favorite books?

212. What is one of your favorite fairy tales?

213. Is it important to always take care of library materials and to return them on or before the due date?

214. What are some other services that libraries provide besides books?

Technology and Information Skills – 3rd Grade

215. Does technology help us to access and use information for specific needs?

216. What technological devices do you have?

217. What is the term for the highest and most advanced state of a device or technique: state-of-the-art, or the latest advance?

218. Is technology continuously evolving and improving?

TECHNOLOGY AND INFORMATION SKILLS

219. Are updates and sizes of computers, cell phones, and big screen televisions relatively frequent?

220. What kind of computer do you have or have access to?

221. What is an example of a tablet: an iPad or a Mac?

222. Does a PC or personal computer generally run on the Windows operating system?

223. What is the shortened and more common term for the Macintosh computer?

224. Does the Mac run on all the major operating systems?

225. What is the name for the cellular phone that has many applications built in, including Internet access: a smartphone or a mobile phone?

226. Do you have a cell phone or do you have access to one?

227. What are some basic rules to follow when using a cell phone?

228. Is it important to keep your log in information and passwords confidential for cell phones, computers, and all other electronic devices?

229. When is texting appropriate?

230. Is it safe to text or send messages to people that you do not know?

231. What are Facebook, Twitter, Pinterest, Google Plus, Tumblr, Flickr, and LinkedIn regarded as: social networking sites or free software sites?

232. What is the term for the networking device that allows users to share pictures and videos on a variety of social networking services: Instagram or Myspace?

233. What is the name of the video-sharing website where users can upload and view many thousands of videos: Facebook or YouTube?

234. Can social media sites often have content that is not appropriate for young people?

235. What can be installed or activated by parents and school officials to prevent young children from specific topics or inappropriate content: blocking software or locks?

236. What are some safety rules to follow when using social media sites?

237. Are you familiar with Microsoft Word and Excel programs on the computer?

238. Have you made it a habit to keep both of your hands on the home row on a computer keyboard?

239. What projects have you worked on using some specific computer software?

240. Are you familiar with how to do an Internet search using web browsers like Google Chrome, Mozilla Firefox, Internet Explorer, Apple Safari, or something like it?

241. What is a name of a popular Internet search engine for finding information: Google or Facebook?

TECHNOLOGY AND INFORMATION SKILLS

242. What would you use "Google Earth" for: to find 123 Lobster Street in Maine, or to view 123 Lobster Street through a variety of satellite images both close up and far away?

243. What is the abbreviation for Global Positioning System?

244. What satellite system would you use to arrive at a specific location: GPS or Google Earth?

245. Are you familiar with other features and applications on a computer?

246. What is the shorted term for *applications* that can be downloaded on an electronic device?

247. Are many "Apps" available free or for purchase either for a cell phone or a computer interface?

248. Are you improving your speed and accuracy when word processing on the computer keyboard?

249. Are you using the proper technique by keeping your hands on the home row as you type?

250. Can you access and use the Microsoft Calculator?

251. Are you becoming familiar with some of the features on the toolbar under **File** like open, close, print, or exit?

252. Are you becoming familiar with some of the features on the toolbar under **Edit** like cut, copy, and paste?

253. Are you becoming familiar with some of the features on the toolbar under **Insert** like page number or picture?

254. Are you becoming familiar with some of the features on the toolbar under **Format** like font, paragraph, and numbering?

255. Are you able to access the text formatting commands like Bold, Italic, and Underline?

256. What is the term for the process for automatically transferring a word from the end of one line to the beginning of the next: word justify or word wrap?

257. What is the term for aligning text along the right or left margins when word processing: justify or indent?

258. What documents have you processed using Microsoft Word?

259. Can you incorporate graphics and sound into a document?

260. Do you know how to delete an electronic file?

261. Is it good practice to *Save* as you go when creating a document?

262. Which command do you use to set up the file and the retrieval location of a newly created document: Save or Save As?

263. Can you save your documents in the appropriate directory?

TECHNOLOGY AND INFORMATION SKILLS

264. Can you retrieve your documents easily?
265. Have you learned how to Save and back up files on the computer hard drive or server?
266. Have you learned how to Save and back up files on an external hard drive, USB flash drive, or other computer storage medium?
267. Do you know how to send you document to the printer?
268. What is the name of the Microsoft software that allows a user to organize, format, and calculate data: Excel or PowerPoint?
269. What data have you charted using Microsoft Excel?
270. What software program would you use if you wanted to chart out a budget?
271. What software program would you use if you wanted to create a report about frogs?
272. When would you use the copy, cut, and paste features within a document?
273. Have you worked on any projects using the computer?
274. Do you know how to locate and insert clipart and images into a document?
275. Is it admissible to copy text from a site you found online and paste it into your report?
276. What is the legal term that refers to the exclusive rights given to the creator of a literary or artistic work, meaning others cannot copy or redistribute the original work: copycat or copyright?
277. Can you research a topic using a computer and find your information easily?
278. What is the name of a presentation that includes audio and video: multimedia or audiovisual?
279. Do you know how to create a multimedia presentation using PowerPoint, or some other presentational management tool?
280. Can you always trust everything you find and read on the computer?
281. Can you demonstrate the correct use of search engines like Google, Bing, or Yahoo?
282. What is the abbreviation for electronic mail?
283. Do you have an email account at home or at school?
284. Is it wise to **never** reveal your log in information and email password to anyone?
285. Can you generate and send an electronic message?
286. Can you retrieve, save, and organize email messages?
287. Why is it dangerous to correspond with people you do not know over the Internet or phone?
288. Can you locate the video camera on your computer?

TECHNOLOGY AND INFORMATION SKILLS

289. What is the name of the software that lets you make free phone calls or video calls using webcam to anyone anytime: LinkedIn or Skype?

290. Do you demonstrate proper care of electronic equipment?

291. What are the checkout procedures in the Instructional Media Center or library?

292. What is the procedure for returning books to the IMC or library?

293. What is another name for the front desk of a library: check-out desk or circulation desk?

294. What is the proper etiquette while in the IMC or library?

295. What do you utilize in the library to locate a book or other media?

296. What is the name of the classification system in a library that includes the ten main subject areas: Catalog System or Dewey Decimal System?

297. Can you locate books in a library by reading the Dewey Decimal numbers on the spine?

298. Are eBooks available in your school IMC or the library?

299. What is a Kindle: firewood or an electronic reading device?

300. Can you do a catalog search using keyword, title, author and subject?

301. Can you do an Internet search using topic, subject, or keyword?

302. Are you familiar with all the parts of a book?

303. Do many books have both titles and sub-titles?

304. What is the role of a publisher?

305. What is the symbol you see in an inside page that is evidence that the book is copyright protected?

306. Where would you likely find "Battles of the Civil War:" in the glossary or in the table of contents?

307. Where would you likely find "Fort Sumter:" in the table of contents or in the index?

308. Where would you likely find "Lincoln, Abraham:" in the index or the table of contents?

309. Where would you likely find "Abolitionist:" in the table of contents or in the glossary?

310. Can you use a table of contents or an index in order to locate specific information?

311. Is skimming a book effective in order to see if it has the information you need?

312. Can you determine if the information that a source offers is relevant to your topic?

313. Can you organize information using an outline format?

314. Do you know the difference between fact and opinion?

TECHNOLOGY AND INFORMATION SKILLS

315. Would the following be a fact or an opinion: "It is 88 degrees today?"

316. Would the following be a fact or an opinion: "It is too hot to go outside?"

317. What is your opinion about the weather today?

318. What is a factual statement regarding the weather today?

319. Can you evaluate and use different resources based on currency, genre, and the relevance to your topic?

320. Are some media resources better than others with regard to the topic?

321. What would have the most current information on phone Apps: the Internet or a print encyclopedia?

322. What is the term that refers to either a technological device or information that is out of date: obscure or obsolete?

323. What are dial-up modems, rented movies, developed film, folded maps, public pay phones, fax machines, pagers, phone books, CD's, record stores, and print newspapers all considered now?

324. Can you give me an example of something that has become obsolete?

325. Can you use an encyclopedia, a dictionary, an atlas, and an almanac in both print and electronic formats?

326. Can you find non-fiction materials in the IMC or library based on your interests?

327. Can you find fiction materials in the IMC or library based on your interests?

328. Can you identify legends, tall tales, fairy tales, and fables?

329. What is the literary term that refers to science fiction, fantasy, mystery, or realistic fiction: sub-heading or genre?

330. What is your favorite fiction genre?

Technology and Information Skills – 4th Grade

331. Do you think you are becoming technology savvy?

332. Can you use a computer, a printer, an e-reader, and a phone with relative ease?

333. Is it important to be responsible and careful when using all electronic devices?

334. Do you think you are somewhat proficient in using the basic features of Microsoft Word?

335. What is the name of the place where you position your hands as you type a Word document?

336. Can you type without looking at the keys yet?

337. How many words a minute would you guess that you could type?

TECHNOLOGY AND INFORMATION SKILLS

338. Is your keyboard typing speed and accuracy improving?

339. What key do you press to go back and change a letter or a previous word?

340. What is the name of the bar that you press that separates a word from the next word?

341. What is the name of the key that you press to start a new line or a new paragraph: shift or enter?

342. Do you know how to engage the Caps Lock feature, and disengage it when no longer needed?

343. Are you familiar with the Spelling and Grammar feature under "tools," and have you used it?

344. Have you created and saved several Word Documents?

345. Can you easily retrieve your Word Documents?

346. Do you have some documents saved on a computer either at home or at school?

347. Can you maneuver between the Internet and a Word document?

348. What is the rule regarding cutting and pasting text from an Internet document to your own Word document?

349. What is the legal term that protects an author and forbids others to copy that author's work?

350. Would you say that you understand and respect copyright law?

351. What is the name for the act of taking someone's ideas or words and presenting them as your own: copycat or plagiarism?

352. Is it both illegal and unethical to plagiarize?

353. Can you use the Internet to conduct research on a specific topic?

354. Does the website address you type in need to be completely accurate?

355. What three letters do many websites end with after the last dot?

356. Can you trust that everything you read or hear on the Internet is accurate?

357. Which search engine or engines do you use when surfing the Internet for information?

358. Do you think you are somewhat proficient in using the basic features of Microsoft Excel?

359. Do you think you are somewhat proficient in using the basic features of PowerPoint?

360. What was your subject or topic with a PowerPoint presentation that you created?

361. Can you create a basic spreadsheet using Microsoft Excel?

362. Have you been introduced to formatting templates in Word, Excel, or PowerPoint that help you with letters, reports, and projects?

363. What are the projects you have done so far using various computer programs?

TECHNOLOGY AND INFORMATION SKILLS

364. What are some specific websites that you enjoy?

365. Have you tried viewing some specific location on Google Earth?

366. What educational software programs are available on your school computer?

367. Can you log in by yourself and access pre-selected programs or sites without assistance?

368. What educational software programs are available on your home computer or iPad?

369. Have you been introduced to image software that allows you to create and manipulate visual images and pictures?

370. Have you been introduced to integrating graphics, audio, and video into your computer projects?

371. Have you created a poster, banner, song, or chart using a basic painting or graphics software?

372. Have you planned a multi-media presentation using an outline or a storyboard?

373. What is a way to back up your files after you have saved them on the computer?

374. What is a proven strategy for editing a document and checking it for accuracy before you send it to print: using the restore tool, or using the spell check tool?

375. What is one of the best ways to learn new technology, programs, or features?

376. What is the name of the unwelcome software program that is capable of reproducing itself, and can potentially cause harm to computer files or programs: viral or virus?

377. Is it highly recommended that all computers have antivirus software protection?

378. What is the term for a video that spreads and circulates rapidly over the Internet: viral or virus?

379. Do you have an email account at home or at school?

380. Is it always good to keep your personal information including your address, phone number, and passwords confidential?

381. Do you know how to access, read, and manage your email?

382. What are the initials for Carbon Copy, a feature you would use in an email if you wanted to send a duplicate copy of your message to another person?

383. It is required to fill in the subject line when sending an email?

384. Are you proficient in accessing and evaluating information in the IMC or library?

385. Is it important to use relevant resources while researching your topic, based on currency and genre?

386. Do you know how to reference a source using the standard citation format?

387. Do you believe that you are proficient in using a dictionary, an encyclopedia, an atlas, or an almanac in both print and electronic format?

TECHNOLOGY AND INFORMATION SKILLS

388. Can you distinguish between fact and opinion?

389. How can you verify that the information you found is accurate?

390. Would the publication date matter in the book you found for your report on tree frogs?

391. Would the publication date matter in the book you found for your report on Smartphones?

392. Should timeliness and validity be considered when looking at library resources?

393. Can you take notes and paraphrase information in your own words?

394. Whose name do you need to record to give credit to that person, if you copy something down verbatim, word for word?

395. What is the term for the list of books, articles, or websites you used when researching a topic for your report: a reference list or a bibliography?

396. Can you produce a basic bibliography indicating the sources where you found your information?

397. What is the literary term that refers to science fiction, fantasy, mystery, poetry, or realistic fiction: sub-heading or genre?

398. What genre would a book of poems fall under: poetry or fiction?

399. What genre would a story about Joe's first day of school fall under: realistic fiction or fantasy?

400. What genre would a collection of Greek myths fall under: folklore or science fiction?

401. What genre would the book "Alice in Wonderland" or the "Harry Potter" Books fall under?

402. What genre would a book about aliens fall under: fantasy or science fiction?

403. What genre would a book about giant tortoises fall under: realistic fiction or non-fiction?

404. What genre would a book about a crime that took place in an old mansion during a thunderstorm fall under: mystery or folklore?

405. What genre would a story about an animal with a moral be, as in "The Boy Who Cried Wolf:" fable or folklore?

406. What genre would a book about the life of Abraham Lincoln fall under: biography or fiction?

407. What genre would a story that many people believe but cannot be proven that has been handed down from earlier times be, as in "King Arthur and the Knights of the Round Table:" a legend or a tall tale?

408. What genre is an improbable story that is presented as if it were true, as in "Paul Bunyan:" fantasy or tall tale?

409. What genre would a children's story that features characters like fairies, elves, and dwarves as in "The Three Little Pigs:" fairy tale or folklore?

TECHNOLOGY AND INFORMATION SKILLS

410. Can different media promote certain viewpoints and ideas?

411. What is the literary term for when an article, newspaper, or other media is written in such a way that the author is not presenting a purely objective or neutral position on a topic: prejudice or bias?

412. What are novels, short stories, plays, poems, myths, dramas, and novellas categorized as: forms of literature or genres of literature?

413. What are tragedy, comedy, drama, satire, and romance categorized as: forms of literature or genres of literature?

414. How would the common genres like fables, fairy tales, fantasies, folklore, legends, mysteries, mythologies, poetry, short stories, and tall tales be categorized: fiction or non-fiction?

415. How would the common genres like autobiographies, biographies, essays, speeches, textbooks, and reference books be categorized: fiction or non-fiction?

416. What are autobiography, biography, fable, fantasy, poetry, folklore, legend, myth, and science fiction, all examples of: written forms of literature or media?

417. What are myths, legends, fables, tall tales, folk tales, parables, epics, and proverbs all examples of: oral forms of literature or story-telling?

418. What is the name of the highest literary honor for that year that is awarded to a children's author: The Newbery Medal or the Caldecott Medal?

419. What is the name of the highest literary honor for that year that is awarded to an illustrator of a children's book: The Newbery Medal or the Caldecott Medal?

420. What is the term for the right of an individual to have free access to information from all points of view and without any restrictions: intellectual freedom or freedom of the press?

421. What is the term for the act or process of controlling the information or ideas that are dispersed in a society: intellectual freedom or censorship?

422. What is the term for our American right to publish and to speak without interference from the government as guaranteed in the First Amendment: freedom of the press or censorship?

423. What is your favorite genre or kind of literature?

Technology and Information Skills – 5th Grade

424. What is the term for the practical application of knowledge: technology or literacy?

425. What technological devices do you know how to use?

426. What is the term that encompasses video, audio, text, animation, and graphics: digital media or multimedia?

427. What is the term that refers to sound: audio or visual?

TECHNOLOGY AND INFORMATION SKILLS

428. What is the term that refers to pictures or graphics that are placed one after another to create motion: animation or slides?

429. What is the term for the computer monitor, the keyboard, the CPU, and the mouse: hardware or software?

430. What is the term for all the programs that run the computer: hardware or software?

431. Do you know how to upload or download a desired program or App on a computer or phone?

432. What are some types of computer software?

433. Can you log on and navigate through pre-selected sites on the Internet?

434. Can you name two software programs you can open and run?

435. Can you back up your files on the computer hard drive or other storage medium?

436. Can you incorporate pictures, sound, or graphics into a document?

437. Can you operate audio and video equipment in order to listen to and view media programs?

438. Have you had the opportunity to produce a video using Microsoft Movie Maker or other software?

439. What is the name of the interactive whiteboards that are often used in schools and businesses, and have a variety of tools and features?

440. What types of activities can you do, or have you done with a Smart Board?

441. Are you familiar with image software to produce a picture book or a comic book?

442. What social media networks can you name?

443. What safety rules do you need to always keep in mind when communicating on social media networks?

444. Why is it important to protect your privacy while online?

445. What is it called when a person targets another person via computer or phone in a harassing, embarrassing, or threatening manner: cyberstalking or cyberbullying?

446. What should you do immediately if you or someone you know is a victim of cyberbullying?

447. Is there such a thing as digital etiquette?

448. What are things you do to demonstrate digital etiquette?

449. Can you power on and power off the computer without assistance?

450. Can you log on and log off without assistance?

451. What is the purpose of having a secure password?

TECHNOLOGY AND INFORMATION SKILLS

452. Can you use the mouse to click, double click, and drag objects to different places on the screen?

453. Can you use the mouse to scroll up and down on a computer?

454. Can you open, start, and close programs with ease?

455. Can you organize and save your files onto the hard drive or into your folder on a specific network?

456. Why is it important that you name your files?

457. Have you used the "help" feature to troubleshoot or help you figure something out?

458. What are the basic components of a computer?

459. Are you familiar with basic computer terminology?

460. What is the term for the process of entering data into a computer: output or input?

461. What is the term for displaying, storing, or printing the information produced by the computer: input or output?

462. What is the term that refers to the electronic memory that temporarily stores information in a computer, and has an impact on the number of programs that can run at one time: RAM or REM?

463. What does RAM stand for?

464. What is the name of the device that allows the computer to transmit and receive data through a computer or phone cable: modem or central processing unit?

465. What is the computer measurement that reflects the capacity of the computer to read signals: byte or megabyte?

466. What does one kilobyte equal: 1,000 megabytes or 1,000 bytes?

467. What does one megabyte equal: 1,000 bytes or 1,000 kilobytes?

468. What is the unit of information that is equal to one billion bytes: a megabyte or gigabyte?

469. Do different computers have different speeds and operating systems?

470. Is it important to be respectful of technological equipment?

471. Are you becoming more proficient with your word processing skills?

472. Are you familiar with many of the features on the tool bar?

473. Under what heading is the page set up option: file or tools?

474. Under what heading is the paragraph option to set up alignment and line spacing: format or edit?

475. Would you say that your word processing skills are improving?

476. How would you describe appropriate body posture and hand position while at the computer?

TECHNOLOGY AND INFORMATION SKILLS

477. Are you becoming proficient keying letters, numbers, and punctuation symbols?

478. Do you know your typing speed?

479. Do you think that 15 words per minute with 80% accuracy is reasonable for a 5th grader?

480. Do you know how to use the space bar and the enter key?

481. Do you use the shift key and the Caps Lock key when needed?

482. Can you use the backspace key and the delete key in order to delete text?

483. Do you know how to use the highlight feature?

484. Do you know how to change the font style, font type, and the color?

485. Do you know how to use the bold, italic, and underline features?

486. Do you know how to use spell check and grammar check to edit your documents?

487. What is the name of the feature that lets you choose either portrait or landscape: margins or page orientation?

488. Do you know how to use the page set up feature and adjust the margins of your document?

489. Do you know how to use the alignment tools to justify or align text left, right, or center?

490. Do you know how to format the text using bullets or numbering?

491. Do you make it a habit to revise and proofread your document before printing?

492. Are you familiar with how to insert tables or columns into your document?

493. Can you insert pictures or clipart into a document?

494. Can you move or resize images in your document?

495. Do you know how to insert headers and footers into your document?

496. Can you insert an audio file?

497. Can you insert a video file?

498. Are you familiar with paint, draw, or graphics software to create a poster, banner, or chart?

499. Can you Save your document and organize it in a file?

500. What program would you use to create a slide show presentation?

501. What PowerPoint presentations have you created?

502. Are you familiar with different design templates that you can use to customize your PowerPoint?

503. Do you know how to insert new slides and delete unwanted slides?

TECHNOLOGY AND INFORMATION SKILLS

504. What would you use to plan a multimedia presentation: storyboard or story panels?

505. Can you "publish" your presentation on PowerPoint?

506. Do you have experience presenting a PowerPoint to a class either alone or with a partner?

507. Do you know how to go from one open program to another using the task bar at the bottom?

508. Can you create, retrieve, save, move, and delete electronic files?

509. What program is popular to use when creating a spreadsheet?

510. What spreadsheets have you produced using Microsoft Excel?

511. Are you proficient in filling the cells of a spreadsheet to achieve the desired result?

512. What is the term for the facts, figures, and statistics that are entered onto the spreadsheet or other program: data or input?

513. Have you ever taken pictures with a digital camera and uploaded them onto your computer?

514. What is the name of the file extension that is created with a digital camera: a jpeg or a doc?

515. What is the term for the system of computers that are linked together to share information and programs: Internet or network?

516. What is the term for the social structure where people can connect with family and friends, and communicate with others that have similar interests: social network or interlinks?

517. What is the vast computer network that links smaller computer networks worldwide?

518. Do you participate in a social network?

519. What is the name of a portable microcomputer, usually battery-powered, that has a screen that closes over the keyboard?

520. Do you conduct research on the Internet?

521. What are Google, Ping, and Yahoo all considered: search engines or web browsers?

522. Which search engines do you use?

523. Do people and companies often display advertisements on websites?

524. What is the term that refers to Internet Explorer, Firefox, Chrome, and Safari: search engines or web browsers?

525. Which web browser do you use at school or at the library?

526. Which web browser do you use at home?

527. Can you use the Forward, Back, and Home buttons effectively to navigate the Internet?

TECHNOLOGY AND INFORMATION SKILLS

528. What is the term for the indicator on the screen, often an arrow or a hand, and is controlled by the mouse: router or cursor?

529. What is the term for the small physical device that joins several networks together: router or internet?

530. What is the term for the small picture that represents a program, a document, a hardware device, or a website: icon or tool?

531. What does the computer interface provide that cascades down when clicked on, and offers a combination of symbols and text to represent different choices: menus or icons?

532. Do you know how to use two or more computer programs at the same time?

533. Does the Internet offer many opportunities for finding information?

534. Are online educational classes offered to people of all ages and levels?

535. What is an advantage of taking an online class?

536. What might be one disadvantage of taking an online class?

537. What Internet games have you played?

538. Is the Internet useful for educational purposes?

539. Do you know how to use online encyclopedias and dictionaries?

540. Can you create projects, letters, and reports on a computer?

541. Can you successfully save and send your document to print?

542. What are checklists, rubrics, and timelines often used for with regard to technology: grading scales or assessment tools?

543. Do you think about how you can improve future productions and presentations using technology?

544. What is the name of the small, portable storage device: a flash drive or external hard drive?

545. What is the name for the round, flat, portable storage device for computer data: flash drive or compact disk:

546. What is the name for the input device that converts hard copy to electronic format: printer or scanner?

547. What is the name for the audio device worn on your head that you plug into your computer?

548. What law protects authors from others copying their work, whether in print or in digital format?

549. Do you always respect the intellectual property rights of others?

550. What is the term that outlines the conditions under which you can use copyright material: intellectual property or fair use?

TECHNOLOGY AND INFORMATION SKILLS

551. What is the term for the guidelines that you are expected to follow if you are using another person's text, graphics, or video: fair use or copyright?

552. Can you reference your sources using standard citation format?

553. Is it important to understand that some media is more relative than others?

554. Do some media outlets have a bias?

555. What do we call mail messages that are sent and received electronically?

556. Do you have an email account at home or at school?

557. Can you generate, retrieve, send, and organize electronic messages?

558. Is email an effective way of communicating?

559. When might email correspondence *not* the best option for communicating with another person?

560. What is the term for unwanted or unsolicited email: junk or spam?

561. Do you know how to manage your emails including those regarded as "Spam?"

562. What computer disease might result from an email categorized as "Spam?"

563. What is the importance of virus protection software on a computer?

564. What is the term for a computer program designed to block inappropriate website and viruses: firewall or blocker?

565. What is the name of a web application that allows the user to add, modify, or delete content, and is used collaboratively by a community of users: Facebook or Wiki?

566. What is the acronym for Hypertext Markup Language that is used to describe web pages?

567. What is the name for a website on which a person or a group of users write their opinions or provide feedback about a topic and often has links to other sites: a blog or a tweet?

568. Is it important to use all Internet sites responsibly and to know the rules of "Netiquette?"

569. What is the term for the symbolic arrangement of instructions or data in a computer program: computer programming or computer coding?

570. What are "Java," "Python," and "Ruby:" computer languages or web browsers?

571. Do you think it is good for young people to learn to devise their own unique computer games and to learn computer programming?

572. Do you think that kids who learn computer programming and coding will have an advantage for 21st century computer literacy, and will help prepare themselves for future jobs in technology?

573. Are there websites and Apps available for those interested in learning computer coding?

TECHNOLOGY AND INFORMATION SKILLS

574. Would you be interesting in looking at programs like "Scratch" or "Codespells," specifically designed to teach coding to young people?

575. Have you ever created a computer program or game using coding?

576. Would you like to create a computer game using computer coding?

577. What is the term for the development through which improved technologies are expanded: technological innovations or technological progress?

578. Do you think there will be even more technological innovations in the future with regard to computers, cellular phones, radio, satellite, medical treatments, robots, and energy?

579. Is technology continuously evolving?

580. What technological devices are now considered obsolete?

581. Which technological devices do you think will soon be obsolete?

582. What predictions can you make regarding new technological devices for the future?

583. What other services does the IMC or library offer besides technological devices?

584. How often do you go to your school or public library?

585. What two main sections is the library divided into?

586. What is the name of the system that is used in libraries to organize non-fiction publications corresponding to three digit numerals?

587. What is the term for the numbers used in libraries to classify a boy and to indicate its location on the shelves: Dewey Decimal or call numbers?

588. Can you distinguish between written, oral, and visual forms of literature?

589. Can all media, whether on a computer or in print, be used to promote certain viewpoints?

590. What authors are you familiar with?

591. What is the term for the literary composition characterized by a particular style: category or genre?

592. Do literary genres include fiction, non-fiction, and science fiction?

593. What literary genres can you name?

594. Can you identify and select fiction for class assignments and for recreational reading?

595. Can you identify and select non-fiction for class assignments and for recreational reading?

596. Can you select and use materials from all media for research purposes?

597. What is the term for the list of books, articles, and other sources you use when writing a paper or researching a specific topic: biography or bibliography?

TECHNOLOGY AND INFORMATION SKILLS

598. Can you create and begin to use a bibliography to cite your sources?

599. What is the term for free and open access to information for all citizens: intellectual freedom or free records?

600. What is the opposite of intellectual freedom, the term for restricting or repressing information: restrictive access or censorship?

601. Do all citizens have a right to their own opinion?

602. Do you acknowledge the right of your friends and classmates to express their opinions, even if they are different from yours?

603. What are some non-fiction subjects that you are interested in?

604. What notable authors can you name?

605. What notable book titles can you name?

606. Can you identify the literary genres of fiction, non-fiction, tall tales, fairy tales, and fables?

607. What is the literary term for the myths dealing with gods and legendary heroes of a group of people like the Greeks?

608. Are you familiar with any Greek myths?

609. What is the literary term for a non-fiction account of a person's life written by someone other than the subject: biography or autobiography?

610. What biographies have you read?

611. What is the literary term for a non-fiction account of a person's life as told by that person: biography or autobiography?

612. What autobiographies have you read?

613. What would you write in your own autobiography?

614. Would you say that you are technologically savvy?

615. What is the name for the world's largest online social network headquartered in California and founded by Mark Zuckerberg that connects people all over the world?

616. What is the name for the online social network and blogging service that allows users to text short, 140 character messages called "tweets?"

617. Do you use Facebook, or do you "tweet" messages on Twitter to communicate with others?

618. What is the name of the symbol used on Twitter to mark topics or keywords in a "Tweet:" hashtag or star?

619. What is the name for the telephone service, a *voice-over Internet Protocol* (voIP), that allows users to communicate over the Internet using voice, video, and instant messaging: Skype or Instagram?

TECHNOLOGY AND INFORMATION SKILLS

620. What is the name for the world's largest *business-based* social networking service that is used for professional networking: LinkedIn or Facebook?

621. What is the name of one of the largest online shopping websites in the world, is based in Seattle, Washington, and was founded in 1995 by Jeff Bezos?

622. What is the name for the multinational Internet Corporation headquartered in San Jose, California that provides an online forum for buying, selling, or auctioning goods and services: eBay or e-Auction?

623. What is the name for the website of classified advertisements that include categories such as jobs, housing, sale items, services, and personals: eBay or Craigslist?

624. It is always important to use good judgment when posting something or responding to someone on a social or business website?

625. What type of services do sites like Expedia, Orbitz, Kayak, Bing, Hotwire, and Hotels offer?

626. What is the general term that refers to the entire environment in which computer network communication occurs, the virtual world of computers: cyberspace or computerspace?

627. What is the common term used to refer to specialized internet applications that can be downloaded to run on smartphones or other mobile devices?

628. What is the name of the networking service App that allows users to take, edit, and share pictures and videos with other users on social media platforms: Vine or Instagram?

629. What is the name of the mobile App owned by Twitter that allows users to create, record, and post short six second video clips that can then be shared: Vine or Instagram?

630. What is the name for the Internet platform that provides a visual discovery tool providing ideas for food, crafts, projects, and many other items: LinkedIn or Pinterest?

631. What is the name for the set of software, hardware, networks, storage, interfaces, and servers that serve to offer computing as a service rather than a product, available on the Internet: Cloud Computing or Skype?

632. What is the name for the place on the World Wide Web that is a site of related web pages used to profile or promote a person or a business: a web map or a website?

633. What is the name for the web address that may end in dot com, dot net, dot org, or something similar that appears in the address bar of the web browser: a web address or a domain name?

634. What is the name for the Internet hosting service that allows companies and individuals to have their websites accessible on the World Wide Web: a web browser or a web host?

635. What is the term for optional software that can add more functionality to a web browser, and may include Adobe Acrobat Reader for .pdf files, Adobe Flash Player for YouTube videos, Real Audio Player, Windows Media Player, WinZip for compressing files, and Antivirus software: add-ons or plug-ins?

TECHNOLOGY AND INFORMATION SKILLS

636. Do you know how to take, download, and organize digital photographs?

637. What is the term for a picture that a person takes of himself or herself with an electronic device that is shared on a social networking website?

638. What is the term for messages that are sent and received electronically, especially from one cell phone to another?

639. What is the danger of texting while driving?

640. Does the term technology include the creation and use of innovations related to life, society, and the environment?

641. What technological devices do you have?

642. How do you think technology and libraries will change for your kids and the next generation?

Chapter 13 – Current Events

Pre-School – 5th Grade

1. What is happening now in the news? (Events; politics; natural disasters, etc.)

2. Can you explain any major events taking place right now in other countries?

3. What is happening right now in sports? (Baseball, football, basketball, tennis, golf, soccer, etc.)

4. Is there any *special* sporting event taking place right now? (FIFA World Cup, Stanley Cup, Olympics, Wimbledon Tennis Championships, Tour de France Bicycle Race, The Kentucky Derby, The Indianapolis 500, NCAA Tournament, The Masters Golf Tournament, The Super Bowl, The World Series, etc.)

5. What is the weather like right now?

6. Is there a specific weather event going on right now? (Solstice, equinox, eclipse, hurricane, etc.)

7. Is there any special holiday or celebration that is taking place some place in the world right now, (Carnaval, Mardi Gras, Chinese New Year, Independence Day, etc.), and what holiday is next?

8. What pop culture singers, dancers, musical groups, actors, or other icons are current right now?

9. Where can you receive current news information, and which news outlets, Internet sites, or cable stations are you familiar with?

10. Why do you think it is important to be informed about what is going on in local, national, and world news?

Chapter 14 – Timelines

U. S. History Timeline

12,000 B.C.
North American Indian Cultures

1000 A.D.
Leaf Ericson, a Norse seaman lands in Newfoundland.

1492
Christopher Columbus makes the first of four voyages to the New World and is financed by King Ferdinand and Queen Isabella of Spain. He lands in the Bahamas on October 12, 1492.

1513
Juan Ponce de Leon, a Spanish explorer lands on the coast of Florida.

1565
St. Augustine, Florida becomes the first permanent European colony in North America settled by the Spanish.

1607
Jamestown is established in Virginia by the London Company as the first permanent English settlement in North America.

1619
The House of Burgesses meets for the first time in Virginia as the first representative assembly in America. **The first slaves** from Africa are also brought to Jamestown.

1620
The Pilgrims arrive on the Mayflower ship from England and establish Plymouth Colony in Massachusetts.

1664
New Amsterdam is renamed New York after the English take over this city from the Dutch.

1752
The Gregorian calendar, the calendar that we still use today, is adopted by Britain and the British colonies.

1754
The French and Indian War - The war between the British and the French to gain control of eastern North America in which the British won decisively.

U.S. HISTORY TIMELINE

1763
Treaty of Paris - A Treaty signed on February 10th in which Britain gained control of Canada and all of the French possessions east of the Mississippi river.

1770
The Boston Massacre - Five men are killed when British troops fire into a mob of people in Boston and leads to many public protests.

1773
The Boston Tea Party - A group of patriots disguise themselves as Mohawk Indians, board three ships in Boston Harbor, and dump 300 crates of tea overboard in protest to the tax on Boston tea.

1774
The First Continental Congress - The first meeting takes place in Philadelphia with 56 delegates including George Washington, Samuel Adams, and Patrick Henry.

1775
The American Revolution - This war of Independence was fought between the 13 British Colonies and Great Britain on the eastern coast of North America.
The beginning of the war started in 1775 with the battles of Lexington and Concord in Massachusetts between colonial minutemen and the British army, and the "first shot that was heard around the world."
Prominent events associated with the American Revolution include the Stamp Act, the Boston Massacre, the Boston Tea Party, the Continental Congress, the Declaration of Independence, the United States Flag, Valley Forge, and the Treaty of Paris.
Prominent battles associated with the American Revolution include the Battles of Lexington and Concord, the Capture of Fort Ticonderoga, the Battle of Bunker Hill, Washington crossing the Delaware River, the Battle of Saratoga, and the Battle of Yorktown.
Prominent people associated with the American Revolution include Abigail Adams, John Adams, Samuel Adams, Benedict Arnold, Ben Franklin, Patrick Henry, Thomas Jefferson, Thomas Paine, Paul Revere, and George Washington.
The war ends when the British commander Charles Cornwallis surrenders to General George Washington in Yorktown, Virginia.
The Treaty of Paris is the agreement that is negotiated in France by John Adams, Benjamin Franklin, and John Jay and stated that Britain acknowledges the 13 Colonies as free and independent states, and Britain no longer has any claim on the government or the land.

1776
The Declaration of Independence is adopted by the Continental Congress on July 4th in Philadelphia.

1777
The first official United States flag is approved. The Continental Congress also adopts the first United States Constitution called the Articles of Confederation.

U.S. HISTORY TIMELINE

1787
The first Constitutional Convention meeting takes place in Philadelphia that is made up delegates from 12 of the 13 colonies to draft the U.S. Constitution.

1789
George Washington is elected first president of the United States.
The U.S. Constitution is successfully ratified by 9 states and goes into effect.

1790
The U.S. Supreme Court, made up of one chief justice and five associate justices, meets for the first time at the Merchants Exchange Building in New York City.

1791
The Bill of Rights, the First Ten Amendments to the Constitution are ratified.

1793
George Washington's second inauguration ceremony is held in Philadelphia.
The Cotton Gin, invented by Eli Whitney, increases the demand for slave labor.

1797
John Adams is inaugurated in Philadelphia as the second president of the United States.

1800
The U.S. capital is moved from Philadelphia, Pennsylvania to Washington D.C.
The U.S. Congress meets in Washington D.C. for the first time.

1801
Thomas Jefferson is inaugurated in Washington D.C. as the third president of the United States.

1803
The Louisiana Purchase - The United States agrees to pay France 15 million dollars in exchange for the Louisiana Territory that extends west from the Mississippi River to the Rocky Mountains (over 830,000 square miles), resulting in the United States nearly doubling in size.

1804
The Lewis and Clark Trail - Lewis and Clark begin in St. Louis, Missouri intending to explore the West and to find a route taking them to the Pacific Ocean.

1805
Lewis and Clark successfully reach the Pacific Ocean.

1809
James Madison is inaugurated as the fourth president of the United States.

U.S. HISTORY TIMELINE

1812
The War of 1812 - The United States declares war over Britain because of British interference with America's westward expansion and maritime shipping.

1814
James Madison's second inauguration as President of the United States.
The Star Spangled Banner is written by Francis Scott Key after he witnesses the British attach on Fort McHenry in Baltimore, Maryland.
The Treaty of Ghent is signed that officially ends the War of 1812.

1817
James Monroe is inaugurated as the fifth President of the United States.

1819
Spain cedes Florida - Spain agrees to give up the state of Florida to the United States.

1820
The Missouri Compromise - Maine is admitted as a free state in order for Missouri to be admitted as a slave state to maintain the balance between Free states and Slave states.

1821
James Monroe's second inauguration as President of the United States.

1822
Denmark Vesey was an African-American carpenter who purchased his freedom and planned to siege Charleston, South Carolina. After his plot was discovered, he and 32 coconspirators were hanged.

1823
The Monroe Doctrine - President James Monroe declares in his annual address to Congress that the American continents are off limits to European powers for further colonization.

1825
John Quincy Adams is inaugurated as the sixth President of the United States.
The Eric Canal opens to traffic that links the Hudson River to Lake Eric.

1828
Baltimore and Ohio Railroad - The first public railroad in the United States begins construction.

1829
Andrew Jackson is inaugurated as the seventh President of the United States.

1830
The Indian Removal Act - This act authorized the removal of Native American Indians that were living in the eastern part of the country to the lands west of the Mississippi River. More than 50,000 Indians were forced to relocate.

U.S. HISTORY TIMELINE

1831
Nat Turner, an enslaved preacher, led the biggest slave uprising in American history in the state of Virginia. The militia soon defeated him and 80 of his followers.
William Lloyd Garrison, one of the most important figures in the abolitionist movement, began publishing the "Liberator," a weekly newspaper that supported the complete abolition of slavery.

1833
Andrew Jackson's second inauguration as President of the United States.

1836
The Alamo - All Texan defenders of the Alamo are killed during a siege by the Mexican army. One month later, the Texans later defeat the Mexicans at San Jacinto and Texas declares its independence from Mexico.

1837
Martin Van Buren is inaugurated as the eighth President of the United States.

1838
Cherokee Indians are forced out from Georgia to Indian Territory in Oklahoma along the "Trail of Tears" where 4,000 of the 50,000 Indians die from disease and starvation.

1841
William Henry Harrison is inaugurated as the 9th President of the United States, dies one month later, and is succeeded by his Vice-President John Tyler.

1845
James Polk is inaugurated as the 11th President of the United States.
Texas is officially added to the United States by an act of Congress.

1846
The Oregon Treaty established the Canadian-United States border at the 49th parallel.
Oregon Territory is acquired by the United States.
Mexican War - The United States declares war on Mexico in the attempt to gain the state of California and other territories of the American southwest.

1848
Treaty of Guadalupe Hidalgo - The treaty whereby Mexico recognizes that the new border with the United States is at the Rio Grande. Mexico gives up the territory of California, Nevada, Utah, New Mexico, Arizona, and parts of Colorado and Wyoming in exchange for 15 million dollars from the U.S.
Gold is discovered in California at Sutter's Mill and the "gold rush" lasts for one year.

1849
Zachary Taylor is inaugurated as the 12th president of the United States.

1849
Harriet Tubman, a former slave, becomes one of the most significant members of the Underground Railroad.

U.S. HISTORY TIMELINE

1850
Millard Fillmore, Vice-President, succeeds President Taylor after his death.

1852
Harriet Beecher Stowe publishes an anti-slavery novel entitled, "Uncle Tom's Cabin."

1853
Franklin Pierce is inaugurated as the 14th President of the United States.

1854
The Kansas-Nebraska Act passes the Congress and establishes the territories of Kansas and Nebraska, and renews tensions between pro-slavery and anti-slavery states.

1857
James Buchanan is inaugurated as the 15th President of the United States.
Supreme Court Ruling (Scott v. Sanford) that states cannot ban slavery, and that slaves are not citizens of the United States.

1858
Abraham Lincoln debates Senator Stephan Douglas in Illinois seven times and gains popularity during this election campaign.

1859
John Brown, an abolitionist, someone wanting to do away with slavery, leads a revolt in Virginia.

1860
Abraham Lincoln is elected the 16th President of the United States.
South Carolina secedes, or separates itself, from the Union.

1861
The Confederate States of America is established.
Jefferson Davis is elected President of the Confederacy.
Abraham Lincoln is inaugurated as 16th president of the United States.

1861-65
Civil War between the North (Union) and the South (Confederacy) because of the conflict regarding the expansion of slavery.
The Confederates attack Fort Sumter in Charleston, South Carolina to start the American Civil War.

1863
Emancipation Proclamation - President Lincoln issues an executive order as Commander-in-chief proclaiming that all slaves in Confederate territory would now be forever free.
Homestead Act - The law passes that allows settlers to lay claim to land after they have lived on it for a period of five years.

U.S. HISTORY TIMELINE

The Gettysburg Address - One of the most famous speeches in American history given by President Lincoln that began with, "Four score and seven years ago our fathers brought forth on this continent, a new nation, conceived in Liberty, and dedicated to the proposition that all men are created equal." It was delivered at a dedication ceremony at Soldiers' National Cemetery in Gettysburg, Pennsylvania on November 19th.

1865
The Union armies defeat the Confederacy in Gettysburg, Pennsylvania when General Ulysses S. Grant of the Union captures Richmond, Virginia, capital of the Confederacy, and General Robert E. Lee of the Confederacy surrenders.
President Lincoln assassinated - President Lincoln is shot by John Wilkes Booth at Ford's Theatre in Washington, D.C.
Thirteenth Amendment is ratified - The amendment to the Constitution is approved abolishing slavery.

1867
The state of Alaska is purchased from Russia.

1868
Fourteenth Amendment is ratified - The amendment to the Constitution is approved defining citizenship.

1869
First Transcontinental Railroad - The Union Pacific Railroad and the Central Pacific Railroad merge in Utah.

1870
Fifteenth Amendment is ratified - The amendment to the Constitution is approved giving all blacks the right to vote.

1871
The Great Chicago Fire - This two-day fire starts in a barn in Chicago, Illinois claiming the lives of over 300 people and leaving over 100,000 people homeless.

1876
The Battle of Little Bighorn - This one hour battle took place near the Little Bighorn River in Montana and was a conflict between U.S. cavalry leader General George Custer and Chief Sitting Bull of the Sioux Indians. It is also regarded as "Custer's Last Stand" in that he had underestimated the size of the Sioux warriors along with the Cheyenne and Arapaho Indians of the Northern Plains, and consequently was killed along with his cavalry.

1877
The Statue of Liberty dedicated - The Statue of Liberty, a gift from France symbolizing freedom and located on Liberty Island in New York Harbor, is dedicated on October 28th.

1890
National American Woman Suffrage Association (NAWSA) – is founded.
Sherman Antitrust Act prohibiting commercial monopolies becomes a law.

U.S. HISTORY TIMELINE

The Battle of Wounded Knee - The last major battle between Native American Indians and the U.S. army in which the U.S. soldiers killed over 200 Sioux Indians in Wounded Knee Creek, South Dakota.

1892
Ellis Island - This small island close to New York City becomes the primary immigration center for people from overseas desiring to become U.S. citizens.

1896
Separate but Equal - Plessy v. Ferguson was a U.S. Supreme Court decision that determined that segregation, or the separation of black people from white people was legal, as long as black people were given "separate but equal" services in schools, hotels, restaurants, and on public transit.

1898
Spanish-American War - The U.S. declares war on Spain when their ship, the USS Maine is shot down near Havana, Cuba. The U.S. wants Cuba to be independent from Spain. The U.S. defeats Spain and gives up control of Cuba.
Treaty of Paris - Treaty signed that ends the Spanish-American war. Cuba becomes independent, and the U.S. takes control of the islands of Puerto Rico, Guam, and the Philippines.
The U.S. annexes (adds) Hawaii.

1899
Eastern Samoa to United States - Eastern Samoa becomes American Samoa through a Treaty with Great Britain and Germany.

1900
Galveston Hurricane - The hurricane in Galveston, Texas that is regarded as one of the deadliest in U.S. history with winds estimated at more than 145 miles an hour in which more than 6000 people died.

1903
The U.S. acquires the Panama Canal Zone through a treaty with Panama.
Wright Brothers first aircraft flight in North Carolina.

1906
The Great San Francisco Earthquake - A massive earthquake that lasts less than a minute but destroys four square miles of the city and causes many fires.

1913
Seventeenth Amendment is ratified - This amendment provides for the election of U.S. senators by popular vote.

1914-1918
World War I - The war in Europe in which the allies, France, Britain, Russia, Italy, Japan, and the United States defeated the Central Powers of Germany, Austria-Hungary, Turkey, and Bulgaria forcing them to sign an armistice ending the war.

U.S. HISTORY TIMELINE

1914
The Panama Canal - A 48 mile ship canal connecting the Atlantic to the Pacific opens to traffic.

1916
U.S. purchases the Danish West Indies that become the U.S. Virgin Islands.

1918
Worldwide influenza epidemic - This epidemic swept the world and claimed the lives of over 50 million people, more people than any other epidemic in history.

1919
Eighteenth Amendment is ratified - This amendment to the Constitution prohibits the manufacture, transport, and sale of liquor.

1919
Nineteenth Amendment is ratified - This amendment to the Constitution grants women the right to vote.

1920
The Treaty of Versailles - This peace treaty ending World War I was imposed on Germany by the Allied powers and demanded reparations from Germany and also forced it to give up land and overseas colonies.

1927
Charles Lindbergh's First Solo Flight - Lindbergh makes the first solo flight across the Atlantic in his plane, "The Spirit of St. Louis."

1929
The Stock Market crashes - The New York market crashes on October 29th, "Black Friday," devastating the economy and paving the way to the Great Depression.
The Great Depression (1929-38) was a time of worldwide economic depression and high unemployment.

1931
Star-Spangled Banner - The song, written by Francis Scott Key, is adopted as America's National Anthem.

1932
Amelia Earhart's First Solo Flight - Earhart is the first American woman to fly a plane across the Atlantic.

1933
Twentieth Amendment is ratified - This amendment to the Constitution established the presidential inauguration date as January 20th.
Twenty First Amendment is ratified - This amendment repealed the 18th amendment of the prohibition of liquor.

1939-1945
World War II - The war that started with the German invasion of Poland and ended when the Allies (the United States, Britain, and the Soviet Union) defeated the Axis powers (Germany, Italy, and Japan).

U.S. HISTORY TIMELINE

1941
Pearl Harbor - Japan attacks the United States with a surprise military strike of the naval base at Pearl Harbor, Hawaii on December 7th, bringing the U.S. into World War II.

1944
The Allies invade France - The United States invade the beaches of Normandy France on June 4th. This day, also known as D-Day which is a code word for the first day of a military attack. The goal of the Allies is to free Europe from Nazi occupation and rule.

1945
Yalta Conference - The place in the Ukraine, Russia where Franklin Roosevelt of the United States, Winston Churchill of Britain, and Joseph Stalin of Russia planned the final stages of World War II, and agreed to the division of Europe.
Postdam Conference - The city in Germany that was the site of the second conference attended by the Allied leaders, Truman, Churchill, and Stalin who gathered there to discuss the surrender of Japan and post-war issues.
Atomic bombing of Hiroshima and Nagasaki - The United States dropped a bomb on August 6th over the Japanese city of Hiroshima killing 80,000 people and destroying 90% of the city. Many more would die from the effects of radiation. Three days later, a U.S. B-29 dropped an atomic bomb on Nagasaki killing 40,000 people. Hirohito, the emperor of Japan, declared Japan's unconditional surrender on August 15th.
United Nations is established.

1946
The Philippines become an independent republic.

1947
Central Intelligence Agency (CIA) is established.

1948
Marshall Plan - The plan is named for the Secretary of State Marshall and implemented by the United States as an economic recovery plan for Western Europe after World War II.

1949
North Atlantic Treaty Organization (NATO) is established.

1950 -1953
Korean War - North Korean Communists, aided by China, invade non-Communist South Korea aided by United Nations forces. An armistice agreement is signed in 1953.

1951
Twenty-Second Amendment is ratified - This amendment to the Constitution places a limit on the office of President to two terms.

1952
Puerto Rico becomes a Commonwealth of the United States.

U.S. HISTORY TIMELINE

1953
Dwight D. Eisenhower is inaugurated as the 34th President of the United States.

1954
Brown v Board of Education of Topeka - The Supreme Court rules that racial segregation is unconstitutional in schools.

1954-1975
Vietnam War - This war is the result of the conflict between North Vietnam Communists, the Soviet Union and Communist China, and South Vietnam aided by the United States. North Vietnam wins the war by defeating the South after the United States withdraws its forces and the North captures Saigon. The North unites Vietnam under Communist rule.

1959
Alaska becomes the 49th state.
Hawaii becomes the 50th state.

1961
John F. Kennedy is inaugurated as the 35th President.
Bay of Pigs - The United States unsuccessfully invades this bay in the Caribbean Sea off the coast of Cuba in opposition to the tactics of Communist Cuban leader Fidel Castro.

1962
The U. S. Missile Crisis - This is the result of the U.S. opposition of Soviet military missile sites placed in Cuba during the Cold War. The United States sets up a naval blockade of Cuba and forces the Russian leader Khrushchev to remove the missile sites.

1963
"I Have a Dream Speech" - Reverend Martin Luther King Jr. gives this speech during a civil war march in Washington, D. C before 200,000 people.
President Kennedy is assassinated in Dallas, Texas.
Vice-President Lyndon B. Johnson is sworn in as President of the United States.

1964
Civil Rights Act is signed into law by President Johnson. This federal law authorizes action against segregation in public facilities, public accommodations, and in places of employment.

1965
President Johnson signs Voting Rights Act - This act ensures the voting rights of African Americans.
Watts Riots - These riots are the result of racial tension in a predominantly black neighborhood in Los Angeles, California. Many people were injured and 34 killed in this 6 day riot.

1966
Miranda v. Arizona - This Supreme court decision establishes "Miranda" rights that gives a person under

U.S. HISTORY TIMELINE

arrest or suspected of a crime "the right to remain silent, the right to legal counsel, and the right to be told that anything he or she says may be used against him or her in a court of law."

1967
Twenty-Fifth Amendment is ratified – This amendment to the Constitution establishes succession to the presidency in the event of the President's resignation or death.

1968
Reverend Martin Luther King Jr. is assassinated in Memphis, Tennessee. He is shot by James Earl Ray.
Robert F. Kennedy is assassinated in Los Angeles, California. Kennedy is a U.S. Senator and a presidential candidate and is shot in a hotel by Surhan Surhan.

1969
Richard Nixon is inaugurated as the 37th President of the United States.
First Lunar landing - Neil Armstrong, Michael Collins, and Edwin "Buzz" Aldrin Jr. are the first men to land on the Moon on the Apollo 11 mission. "That's one small step for man, one giant leap for mankind."

1970
Kent State shootings - Four students are shot to death at Kent State University in Ohio during a rally in opposition to the U.S. involvement to the war in Vietnam. The students are killed by Ohio National Guard members trying to restore peace after protests and riots become violent.

1971
Twenty-Sixth Amendment is ratified - This amendment lowers the voting age from 21 to 18.

1972
SALT I Treaty is signed - This strategic arms control agreement is signed by the U.S. and the Soviet Union.
Watergate break-in - Five of President Nixon's men, members of his re-election campaign, are caught breaking into and trying to wiretap the Democratic headquarters at the Watergate Hotel complex in Washington, D.C.

1973
Roe v. Wade - This Supreme Court decision makes abortion legal during the first trimester of a pregnancy.
Vice-President Spiro Agnew resigns because of income tax evasion.
President Nixon nominates Gerald R. Ford for Vice-President. His nomination is confirmed by Congress.

1974
President Nixon resigns the office of the Presidency.
Vice-President Gerald Ford succeeds Nixon as President of the United States.
Nixon is pardoned (forgiven for his crimes) by President Ford.
Nelson Rockefeller is confirmed by Congress and sworn in as Vice-President.

1977
Jimmy Carter is inaugurated as the 39th President of the United States.
Panama Canal Treaty of 1977 - This Treaty, signed by President Carter, states that control of the Panama Canal is to be turned over to Panama beginning in the year 2000.

U.S. HISTORY TIMELINE

1978
Camp David Accord - Egyptian president Anwar Sadat and Israeli Prime Minister Menachem Begin meet with President Carter at Camp David, and sign a peace treaty that ends a 30-year conflict between Egypt and Israel.

1979
The United States establishes diplomatic ties with China.
Three Mile Island Accident - This Island in southeastern Pennsylvania is the site of a nuclear accident when a meltdown releases dangerous radioactive material and forces the evacuation of thousands of residents.
Panama Canal - Panama has joint control with the United States (1979-1999) over the Panama Canal Zone.
Iran Hostage Crises - Iranian militant students take over the U.S. Embassy in Tehran, Iran where they hold 66 people hostage. They release 13 of them but hold the other 53 hostage for over a year. The hostages remain under the control of Iranian leader Ayatollah Khomeini until his conditions are met. This crisis weakens the presidency of Jimmy Carter. The hostages are finally released on President Reagan's inauguration day in 1981.

1980
President Carter announces Olympic boycott. - President Carter announces the boycott of United States in the Moscow Summer Olympics because of the Soviet Union's invasion of Afghanistan.
Iran Hostage Rescue Mission Accident - A helicopter and a cargo plane are part of a rescue mission but collide killing 8 servicemen.

1981
President Ronald Reagan is inaugurated as the 40th President of the United States.
The American hostages are released. The 53 hostages held in Iran are released after being captive 444 days.
President Reagan Assassination Attempt - President Reagan is shot in the chest by John Hinckley Jr. outside the Washington Hilton Hotel. His White House Press Secretary, James Brady, is also shot in the head, policeman Thomas Delahanty is shot in the neck, and Secret Service agent Timothy McCarthy is also shot.
Sandra Day O'Conner - First Female Justice appointed to the Supreme Court by President Reagan.

1982
Falklands War - British defeat Argentina.
Israel invades Lebanon
Prince William of England is born to Prince Charles and the late Princess Diana.
Princess Grace of Monaco dies in an automobile accident.
USA Today - The first issue is published.
Michael Jackson's "Thriller" becomes the largest selling record ever.
Tylenol capsules lined with cyanide poisin kill seven in Chicago.
First implant of artificial heart designed by Robert Jarvik.
Vietnam Veterans Memorial - The memorial is dedicated in Washington, D.C.

1983
United States Invasion of Grenada - The U.S successfully invades Grenada, a small island in the Caribbean, because of a military coup that attempted to overthrow the government.

U.S. HISTORY TIMELINE

1986
Challenger Space Shuttle Explosion - The Challenger, carrying seven crew members, explodes over the Atlantic Ocean 73 seconds into its flight.
Iran-Contra Affair - A scandal that occurs during the Reagan administration when it is discovered that some members of the executive branch sold weapons to Iran and used the profits illegally to help fund an army of rebels in Nicaragua.

1987
"Tear Down This Wall" - President Reagan gives a speech to the people of West Berlin, Germany at the Brandenburg Gate near the Berlin Wall, and challenges Soviet Union leader Mikhail Gorbachev to destroy the wall in order to promote freedom in the eastern bloc. The wall was a symbol of the Iron Curtain for 28 years when it was built by the Communist East German government. The wall was also symbolic of the Cold War division between East and West, the division between communism and capitalism.
INF Treaty Signed - The Intermediate-Range Nuclear Forces Treaty is signed by President Reagan of the United States, and General Secretary Mikhail Gorbachev of the U.S.S.R. that reduces the nuclear weapons of the two superpowers, and eliminates all land-based nuclear missiles.

1989
George H. W. Bush is inaugurated as the 41st President of the United States.
Exxon-Valdez oil tanker runs aground - The oil tanker Exxon-Valdez hits a reef at Prince William Sound Alaska rupturing the ship and leaking 11 million gallons of Alaska crude oil into the bay. This environmental disaster spreads over 500 miles, takes over three years to clean up, and costs over two billion dollars in damages.
United States invasion of Panama – The U.S. invades Panama with the intent of capturing General Manuel Noriega who is accused and found guilty of suppressing democracy in Panama, as well illegal drug trafficking. He is swiftly defeated by U.S. military forces.

1990
Iraq invades Kuwait - Iraq, under Saddam Hussein invades Kuwait due to escalating tensions involving control of oil and unpaid debts. This marks the beginning of the Persian Gulf War.

1990-1991
Persian Gulf War - This war, also called "Operation Desert Storm," is fought between Iraq and an American led coalition that freed the small Middle Eastern country of Kuwait from Iraqi invaders.

1991
START I Treaty signed - The United States and the Soviet Union sign a treaty that further reduces the arsenals of strategic nuclear arms.

1992
"Cold War" officially ends - The president of the United States George H.W. Bush and Russian President Boris Yeltsin meet at Camp David to officially declare an end to the "Cold War."
Rodney King beating and riots - Rodney King is beaten by four white police officers in Los Angeles, California during a traffic stop. The officers are acquitted of the charges. This leads to several riots causing thousands of arrests and injuries, 50 people dead, and over one billion dollars in property damage.

U.S. troops deployed to Somalia - President Bush authorizes sending troops to Somalia, Africa as part of a United Nations relief effort.

1993
William J. Clinton inaugurated - Bill Clinton is inaugurated as the 42nd President of the United States.
World Trade Center Bomb - A bomb explodes in the basement of the World Trade Center injuring 1000, killing 6, and causing an estimated $500 million in damages.
Waco, Texas compound burns -The Branch Davidian Compound burns to the ground after a 51-day standoff with federal agents, resulting in the deaths of 80 cult members.
NAFTA signed into law by President Clinton – The North American Free Trade Agreement is an agreement by the United States, Canada, and Mexico that serves to eliminate tariffs, promote trade, and increase economic activity between the three nations.

1995
Bombing in Oklahoma City - The Alfred P Murrah Federal Building was bombed in downtown Oklahoma City claiming 168 lives. Timothy McVeigh and Terry Nichols were both charged with this destructive act of domestic terrorism.
The U.S. and Vietnam - The United States establishes diplomatic relations with Vietnam.
Troops sent to Bosnia - President Clinton sends several troops to Bosnia for a peace-keeping mission.

1998
The United States launches a missile attack in Afghanistan and Sudan on specified targets after a terrorist attack on U.S. embassies in Tanzania and Kenya.
The United States and Britain launch air strikes in Iraq.
Clinton Impeachment - The House of Representatives vote to impeach President Clinton on charges of perjury and obstruction of justice. The Senate later acquits him of these charges.

1999
NATO begins an air campaign against Yugoslavia over the killing of Albanians in Kosovo.
The Columbine High School shooting - Two students kill 14 students and one teacher, and wound 23 others on April 20th in Littleton, Colorado.

2000
George W. Bush elected President - President Bush wins a slim majority in the Electoral College over his opponent Vice-President Al Gore after the U.S. Supreme Courts rules against the constitutionality of manually counting ballots in specific Florida counties.

2001
"9-11" - Two hijacked jet airplanes fly into the World Trade Center in New York City, a third hijacked plane crashes into the Pentagon, and a fourth hijacked plane crashes in a field in Pennsylvania. More than 3,000 people are killed. The United States and Britain launch air attacks on specified targets in Afghanistan with the intent of bringing down the Taliban government and Osama bin Laden, the Saudi terrorist that is the suspected mastermind behind these attacks.

U.S. HISTORY TIMELINE

2002
President Bush's First State of the Union Address - President Bush names Iran, Iraq, and North Korea an "axis of evil." He states that the United States will wage war on those places that develop weapons of mass destruction.
Homeland Security established - President Bush creates a new cabinet department called "Homeland Security" and officially signs legislation to do so.

2003
Columbia Space Shuttle explodes - Seven astronauts are killed upon re-entering the Earth's atmosphere.
The United States and Britain wage war against Iraq.

2004
The United States help achieve sovereignty in Iraq - The U.S. keep over 100,000 troops in Iraq to maintain peace.
The Big Four" of 2004 - Four hurricanes hit Florida and the southern United States.

2005
The U.S. and Iraq - The United States continues its presence in Iraq.
Hurricane Katrina - Mississippi and Louisiana are severely damaged by Hurricane Katrina, flooding 80% of the Louisiana city of New Orleans.
U.S. Supreme Court Justice – There are several changes to the Court in that Sandra Day O'Conner retires, Chief Justice William Rehnquist passes away, and John G. Roberts is promoted to Chief Justice.

2006
U.S. Census - The U.S. Census Bureau estimates the United States population to be 300 million.

2007
Nancy Pelosi appointed Speaker of The House – The House elects its first female Speaker, a Democrat representing California, as the Speaker of the House of Representatives.
Virginia Tech shooting - A man kills 30 and wounds 15 more in a classroom at Virginia Tech. This shooting is regarded as the most deadly in the history of the United States.
Bridge Collapses in Minnesota - An eight-lane interstate bridge breaks up and collapses into a river in Minneapolis killing 13 people.

2008
Barack Obama is elected president - Barack Obama becomes the first African American to be elected President. The Democrats have majorities in both the House of Representatives and the Senate.

2009
Stimulus Package - President Obama signs a $787 billion stimulus package into law.
AIG - The U.S. government loans $90 billion to the Insurance giant American International Group.
Michael Jackson dies - Pop music icon Michael Jackson dies at the age of 50.
First Hispanic appointed to the Supreme Court - Sonia Sotomayor is the first Hispanic Supreme Court Justice to serve on the Court.

U.S. HISTORY TIMELINE

Senator Edward Kennedy dies at 77.
Fort Hood army post shooting - 13 are killed and 29 injured by an army psychiatrist in Fort Hood, Texas.
"Underwear Bomber" - A Nigerian man attempts to set off an explosive advice he has hidden in his underwear on a flight from Amsterdam to Detroit. He later claims that he was following the orders of the Al-Qaeda terrorist group.

2010

Deepwater Horizon oil spill - An oil ship spills millions of gallons of oil in the Gulf of Mexico and is regarded as the largest off-shore spill in history. It seriously affects the fishing and tourism industries of the Gulf States.
Elena Kagan is confirmed as a Supreme Court Justice.
Republicans win a Massachusetts Senate seat - Scott Brown wins a special election Senate seat and is the first Republican elected to the Senate from the state of Massachusetts since 1972.
Health Care Reform bill is passed - The bill that extends health benefits and insurance to most Americans is approved.
Republicans regain control of the House - The Republicans win the majority of the mid-term elections to win back control of the House and reduce the number of Democrats in the Senate.

2011

Osama Bin Laden is killed - The mastermind behind the 9/11 2001 attacks on the World Trade Center and the Pentagon and the leader of the terrorist group Al-Qaeda is killed in his hideout in Pakistan in a raid by U.S. Navy Seals.
Final shuttle flight lands - The shuttle Atlantis lands at the Kennedy Space Center after its mission to the International Space Station ending NASA's shuttle program. It began in 1981 and sponsored 135 missions.
"Occupy Wall Street" - Many protest the big money interests on Wall Street and its contribution to the recession and the world economy.
President Obama declares the end to the war in Iraq - The last of the combat troops are ordered to leave the country.
Gabrielle Giffords shot - Arizona congresswoman Gabrielle Giffords is shot by a gunman outside a local grocery store.

2012

Record price for sale of an artwork - "The Scream" by Edwin March is sold for $120 million dollars at a New York auction house.
Terrorist attack in Benghazi, Libya - An attack on a consulate kills four Americans in Benghazi including Ambassador John Stevens because of continued conflict regarding Islamic extremism.
Hurricane Sandy - Atlantic City, New Jersey and the Long Island coasts of New York are hit by Hurricane Sandy. The storm, the largest one in recorded history with a diameter of over 1,100 miles, severely damaged many coastal cities and towns at an estimated cost of $66 billion dollars.
Barack Obama is re-elected as President of the United States. The Republicans control the House of Representatives and the Democrats control the Senate.
Sandy Hook shooting -A gunman kills 26 people including children at Sandy Hook Elementary in Newton, Connecticut.

U.S. HISTORY TIMELINE

2013
Boston Marathon bombing - Two bombs explode near the finish line of the Boston Marathon in Boston Massachusetts. Three people were killed and hundreds injured. Two brothers, reportedly affiliated with radical Islam, carried out the attack.
The Internal Revenue Service Scandal - The IRS is accused of targeting conservative groups and obtaining the phone and email records of journalists, Verizon phone customers, and other citizens.
Nelson Mandela dies – The former President of South Africa dies at 95.
Typhoon devastates the Philippines
The United States Government shuts down.
Margaret Thatcher dies – The former Prime Minister of Great Britain dies.
Pope Benedict XVI resigns - Cardinal Jorge Mario Bergoglio of Argentina becomes Pope Francis.
The Affordable Care Act – The Health Care Act is rolled out on October 1
Edward Snowdwn - The United States defense worker Edward Snowden leaks many National security Agency documents.

2014.
The Winter Olympics take place in Sochi, Russia.
The FIFA World Cup –The soccer event staged every four years takes place in Brazil.
Malaysia Airlines Flight 370 – The flight, en route to Beijing, mysteriously disappears over the Gulf of Thailand with 239 passengers on board.
Russia annexes Crimea.
ISIS - A Sunni military called the Islamic State in Iraq (ISIS) begins its attack on northern Iraq, hoping to overthrow the Shiite government led by Prime Minister Nouri al-Maliki.
Scotland Referendum - Scotland votes against becoming an independent country.
Shirley Temple dies - Child star Shirley Temple Black dies.
Sky City Tower - Work continues on the anticipated tallest building on Earth, *Sky City*, in Changsha, China.
IRS Scandal - All branches of the U.S. government are involved in issues involving the Internal Revenue Service
Immigrant Influx - A humanitarian crisis emerges with the influx of thousands of Central American immigrants, and the debate with regard to effectively controlling the U.S. border.
Obamacare health insurance glitches for Veterans – Health care issues arise for several Armed Forces Veterans because they did not receive needed health care that would have saved their lives.
Israel-Palestine Conflict - There is escalating tension between Israel and the adjoining Palestine territories of Gaza and the West Bank, and the Palestinian militant group Hamas.
Russia-Ukraine tension - There is escalating tension between Russia and the Ukraine.
Ebola - After an outbreak in West Africa, the often fatal disease arrives in the United States.
Mid-Term Elections - The Republicans win victories in November, presiding over the Senate and the House.
Civil Unrest - Protests break out in Jackson, Missouri and New York aimed at police officers as a result of court case decisions.
Ice Bucket Challenge - The campaign for ALS raises more than $100 million

2015
150th Anniversary of the American Civil War, and President Abraham Lincoln's assassination on April 15, 1865.

Timeline of Inventions, Theories, Innovations, and Discoveries

50,000 B.C.
Homo sapiens, Modern man's first appearance

20,000 B.C.
Bow and Arrow, early humans

12,000 B.C.
Domestication of animals, early humans

8000 B.C.
Agriculture, early humans

8000 B.C.
Pottery, early humans

6000 B.C.
Animal plow, early humans

5000 B.C.
Irrigation system, Middle East

4000 B.C.
Use of metals, early humans
Cosmetics, Egypt

3500 B.C.
Wheel, Mesopotamia
Bronze discovered, early humans
Writing, Mesopotamia

2800 B.C.
Calendar - 12 month, 365 day calendar, Egyptians

2737 B.C.
Tea, Shen Nung of China

2400 B.C.
Abacus (1st calculator), Babylonians

2000 B.C.
Obelisks, Egyptians

TIMELINE OF INVENTIONS, THEORIES, INNOVATIONS, AND DISCOVERIES

1550 B.C.
Medical textbook, Egyptians

700 B.C.
Sundials, Egyptians and Babylonians

650 B.C.
Coins, Greeks

512 B.C.
Cast iron, Chinese

510 B.C.
1st World Map, Greeks

400 B.C.
Catapult, Greeks

300 B.C.
Crossbow, Chinese
Geometry, Euclid of Alexandria, Egypt

312 B.C.
Appian Way (1st Roman road), Romans

300 B.C.
Binary number system, Pingala of India

210 B.C.
Archimedean screw/lever theory, Archimedes of Greece

100 B.C.
Glassblowing, Syrians

105 A.D.
Paper, Ts'ai Lun of China

300
Horse stirrups, Chinese

475
Horse collar, Chinese

TIMELINE OF INVENTIONS, THEORIES, INNOVATIONS, AND DISCOVERIES

600
Heavy plow, Slavic tribes

673.
Greek fire, Kallinkos of Heliopolis

770
Horseshoes, Europeans

810
Arabic numerals, Arabs, Persians, Egyptians, and Hindus

852
Parachute, Armen Firman of Spain

900
Horse collar, Europeans

1000
Gunpowder, Chinese

1041
Moveable clay type printing press, Bi Sheng of China

1100
Water power for making iron, Europeans

1180
Windmills, Europeans

1249
Gunpowder recipe, Roger Bacon of Europe

1284
Eyeglasses, Salvino D'Armate of Italy

1291
Venetian glass mirrors, Italians

1300
Spinning wheels, Europeans

1335
Mechanical clock, Italians

TIMELINE OF INVENTIONS, THEORIES, INNOVATIONS, AND DISCOVERIES

1350
Suspension bridge, Incas of Peru

1440
Alphabetical printing press, Johannes Gutenberg of Germany

1492
Nurnberg terrestrial globe, Martin Behaim of Germany

1500
Helicopter; calculator; ball bearing, Leonardo Da Vinci of Italy

1503
Mona Lisa **Portrait**, Leonardo Da Vinci of Italy

1510
Pocket Watch, Peter Henlein of Germany

1540
Ether, Valerius Cordus of Germany

1543
Solar System (Sun-centered), Nicholas Copernicus of Poland

1546
Contagion Theory (of diseases), Girolamo Fracastoro of Italy

1576
Ironclad Warship, Oda Nobunaga of Japan

1565
Pencil, Conrad Gesner of Switzerland

1582
Gregorian calendar, Pope Gregory VIII

1583
Pendulum, Galileo Galilei of Italy

1584
Infinity of Universe, Giordano Bruno of Italy

1590
Microscope (Compound), Hans and Zacharias Janssen of the Netherlands

TIMELINE OF INVENTIONS, THEORIES, INNOVATIONS, AND DISCOVERIES

1593
Thermometer, Galileo Galilei of Italy
Toilet (Flush), Sir John Harington of England

1600
Earth's Magnetic Field, William Gilbert of England

1608
Telescope, Hans Lippershay of Germany

1609
Microscope (With Focus), Galileo Galilei of Italy
Planetary Motion Laws, Johannes Kepler of Germany

1620
Slide Rule, William Oughtred of the United Kingdom

1628
Blood Circulation, William Harvey of England

1637
Analytic Geometry, Rene Descartes of France

1642
Adding Machine, Blaise Pascal of France

1643
Barometer, Evangelista Torricelli of Italy

1645
Vacuum Pump, Otto von Guericke of Germany

1654
Probability Theory, Blaise Pascal and Pierre de Fermat of France

1656
Pendulum Clock, Christiaan Huygens of the Netherlands

1659
Saturn Rings, Christian Huygens of the Netherlands

1665
Cells to describe cork, Robert Hooke of England
Gravitation Law, Isaac Newton of England

TIMELINE OF INVENTIONS, THEORIES, INNOVATIONS, AND DISCOVERIES

1666
Spectrum of Light, Isaac Newton of England

1668
Reflecting Telescope, Isaac Newton of England

1669
Calculus, Isaac Newton of England

1673
Microbiology, Anton von Leeuwenhoek of the Netherlands

1675
Light Speed Theory, Olaus Roemer of Denmark
Royal Observatory Greenwich, Charles II of England

1678
Light Wave Theory, Christian Huyguns of the Netherlands

1679
Pressure cooker, Denis Papin of France

1683
Bacteria, Anton von Leeuwenhoek of the Netherlands

1684
Differential Calculus, Gottfried Leibniz of Germany

1687
Motion Laws, Isaac Newton of England

1698
Steam Engine, Thomas Savery of England

1700
Piano, Bartolomeo Cristofori of Italy

1705
Halley's Comet, Edmund Halley of England
Steam Piston Engine, Thomas Newcomen of the United Kingdom

1710
Alcohol Thermometer, René Antoine Ferchault de Reaumur of France

TIMELINE OF INVENTIONS, THEORIES, INNOVATIONS, AND DISCOVERIES

1714
Mercury Thermometer, Gabriel D. Fahrenheit of Germany

1738
Kinetic Theory of Gases, Daniel Bernoulli of Switzerland

1742
Centigrade Thermometer, Anders Celsius of Sweden
Franklin Stove, Benjamin Franklin of the United States

1751
Conservation of Electric Charge, Benjamin Franklin of the United States

1752
Lightning rod, Benjamin Franklin of the United States

1760
Bifocal Lens, Benjamin Franklin of the United States

1767
Spinning Jenny, James Hargreaves of England

1769
Modern Steam Engine, James Watt of Scotland

1774
Oxygen Isolation, Joseph Priestley of England

1779
Plant Photosynthesis, Jan Ingenhausz of Holland

1781
Uranus Planet Discovered, William Herschel of England

1783
Hot Air Balloon, Montgolfier brothers of France
Silk Parachute, Lois-Sebastian Lenormand of France

1785
Loom (Power Driven), Edmund Cartwright of England

1790
Metric System, Revolutionary Government of France

TIMELINE OF INVENTIONS, THEORIES, INNOVATIONS, AND DISCOVERIES

1791
Steam Boat, John Finch of the United States

1794
Cotton Gin, Eli Whitney of the United States

1798
Vaccination (Smallpox), Edward Jenner of England

1800
Bridge (Iron Chains), James Finley of the United States
Electric Battery (Voltaic Pile), Alessandro Volta of Italy

1801
Jacquard Weaving Loom, Joseph-Marie Jacquard of France

1804
Locomotive, Richard Trevithick of the United Kingdom
Steam Engine (High Pressure), Oliver Evans of the United States

1806
Coffee Pot, Benjamin Thompson of the United States

1809
Ozone, Christian Schonbein of Germany

1810
Canned Food, Nicolas Appert of France

1811
Avogadro's Law, Amedeo Avogadro of Italy

1814
Steam Locomotive, George Stephenson the United Kingdom

1816
Matches (Phosphorus), Francois Derosne of France
Miner's Safety Lamp, Humphrey Davy of the United Kingdom
Stethoscope, Rene Theophile Hyacinche Laennec of France

1820
Arithometer (Mechanical Calculator), Charles Xavier Thomas de Colmar of France

TIMELINE OF INVENTIONS, THEORIES, INNOVATIONS, AND DISCOVERIES

1821
Electric Motor, Michael Faraday of the United Kingdom

1822
Mechanical Computer, Charles Babbage of the United Kingdom

1824
Cement, Joseph Aspdin of England
Braille (reading for the blind), Louis Braille of France

1826
Photography, Joseph Nicephore Niepce of France

1827
Microphone, Charles Wheatstone of England
Ohm's Law of Current, George Simon Ohm of Germany

1828
Induction (Electric), Joseph Henry of the United States

1829
Graham Cracker, Sylvester Graham of the United States

1830
Lawn Mower, Edwin Beard Budding of the United Kingdom

1831
Electromagnetic Induction, Michael Faraday of England
Matches (Friction), Charles Sauria of France
Mechanical Farm Reaper, Cyrus Hall McCormick of the United States

1832
Electric Carriage, Robert Anderson of Scotland

1834
Combine Harvester, Hiram Moore of the United States
Reaper (Mechanical), Cyrus McCormick of the United States
Refrigerator, Jacob Perkins of the United States

1835
Revolver, Samuel Colt of the United States

1836
Electric Telegraph (dots on paper), Samuel Morse of the United States
Gas Stoves Sold, James Sharp of England

TIMELINE OF INVENTIONS, THEORIES, INNOVATIONS, AND DISCOVERIES

1837
Electric Telegraph (pointing needles), Charles Wheatstone of the United Kingdom
Screw Propeller, Sir Francis Smith and John Ericsson of England

1839
Photovoltaics (Light for Electricity), Edmund Becquerel of France
Rubber (Vulcanization), Charles Goodyear of the United States

1840
Ice Age Theory, Louis Agassiz of Switzerland

1842
Anesthesia, Crawford Long of the United States
Thermodynamics (1st Law), Julius von Meyer of Germany

1843
Computer Programming, Ada Lovelace of England
Fax Machine, Alexander Bain of England
Rotary Printing Press, Richard March Hoe of United States
Typewriter, Charles Thurber of the United States
Vulcanized Rubber, Charles Goodyear of the United States

1844
Morse Code for Telegraphy, Samuel Morse of the United States

1845
Rubber Bands, Stephen Perry of England
Tire, Robert W. Thompson of England

1846
Neptune Discovered, Johann Galle of Germany
Nitroglycerin (Dilates Blood), Ascanio Sobrero of Italy
Sewing Machine, Elias Howe of the United States

1847
Candy Bar, Joseph Fry of Great Britain

1848
Zero (Absolute Temperature), William Thompson and Lord Kelvin of England

1849
Bullet, Claude Minie of France
Safety Pin, Walter Hunt of the United States

TIMELINE OF INVENTIONS, THEORIES, INNOVATIONS, AND DISCOVERIES

1850
Thermodynamics (2nd Law), Rudolf Clausius of Germany

1851
Converter (Bessemer), William Kelly of the United States
Lock (Cylinder), Linus Yale of the United States
Rotation of Earth, Jean Bernard Foucault of France
Sewing Machine (Continuous Stitch), Isaac Singer of the United States

1852
Elevator, Elisha Graves Otis of the United States
Gyroscope, Jean Leon Foucault of France

1853
Condensed Milk, Gail Borden of the United States

1855
Bessemer Furnace, Sir Henry Bessemer of England

1856
Dye, William H. Perkin of England

1859
Escalator, Nathan Ames of the United States
Evolution by Natural Selection, Charles Darwin of England
Oil Well, Edwin L. Drake of the United States

1860
Fermentation (Microorganisms), Louis Pasteur of France
Solar Energy, John Ericsson of the United States
Vacuum Cleaner, Daniel Hess of the United States

1862
Revolving Machine Gun, Richard J. Gatling of the United States
Submarine (Mechanical), Narcís Monturiol I. Estarriol of Spain

1863
Printing Press (Web Rotary), William Bullock of the United States

1865
Heredity Law, Gregor Mendel of Austria

1866
Dynamite, Alfred Nobel of Sweden

TIMELINE OF INVENTIONS, THEORIES, INNOVATIONS, AND DISCOVERIES

1867
Antiseptic, Joseph Lister of England
Typewriter, Christopher Sholes and Carlos Glidden of the U.S.

1868
Air Brake (for trains), George Westinghouse of the United States
Helium Observed on Sun, Sir Joseph Lockyer of England

1869
DNA, Friedrich Meischer of Germany
Margarine, Hippolyte Mège-Mouriès of France
Periodic Law and Table, Dmitri Mendeleev of Russia

1870
Chewing Gum (Chicle), Thomas Adams of the United States
Stock Ticker, Thomas Edison of the United States

1872
Electric Typewriter, Thomas Edison of the United States

1873
Barbed Wire, Joseph E. Glidden of the United States
Blue Jeans, Jacob Davis of Latvia and Levi Strauss of Germany
Light Electromagnetic Theory, James Clark Maxwell of England

1875
QWERTY Keyboard, Christopher Sholes of the United States
Steel Industry, Andrew Carnegie of Scotland

1876
Carburetor, Gottlieb Daimler of Germany
Carpet Sweeper, Melville R. Bissell of the United States
Combustion Engine (4 Cycle), Nicholaus Otto of Germany
Refrigerator, Carl von Linde of Germany
Telephone, Alexander Graham Bell of Scotland

1877
Canals of Planet Mars, Giovanni Schiaparelli of Italy
Concrete (Reinforced), Joseph Monier of France
Microphone, Emile Berliner of Germany
Phonograph, Thomas Edison of the United States
Toilet Paper, Seth Wheeler of the United States

TIMELINE OF INVENTIONS, THEORIES, INNOVATIONS, AND DISCOVERIES

1878
Cathode Ray Tube (CRT), William Crookes of the United Kingdom
Nutcracker, Henry Quackenbush of the United States

1879
Electric Light Bulb, Thomas Edison (U.S.) and Joseph Swan (England)
Ivory Soap, Harley Proctor of the United States
Saccharin (Sweetener), Constantine Fuhberg and Ira Remsen of the U.S.

1880
Photophone (Radiophone), Alexander Graham Bell of Scotland
Seismograph (Earthquakes), John Milne of England

1881
Metal Detector, Alexander Graham Bell of Scotland

1882
Christmas Lights, Edward Johnson of the United States
Electric Iron, Henry W. Seeley of the United States
Tuberculosis Bacterium, Robert Koch of Germany

1883
Cholera Bacterium, Robert Koch of Germany

1884
Bicycle, James Starley of England
Fountain Pen, Lewis Waterman of the United States
Machine Gun (Belt-fed), Hiram S. Maxim of the United States
Roll of Film, George Eastman of the United States

1885
Automobile with engine, Karl Benz of Germany
Motorcycle, Gottlieb Daimler of Germany
Rabies Vaccination, Louis Pasteur of France

1886
Coca Cola, John Pemberton of the United States
Transformer, William Stanley of the United States

1887
Disc Record Gramophone, Emile Berliner of Germany
Antibiotics, Louis Pasteur and Jules-Francois Joubert of France
Automatic Dishwasher, Josephine Cochrane of the United States

TIMELINE OF INVENTIONS, THEORIES, INNOVATIONS, AND DISCOVERIES

1888
AC Electric Power, Nikola Tesla of Croatia
Bicycle Tire, John B. Dunlap of Northern Ireland
Hand-held Camera, George Eastman of the United States
Telephone (tele-autograph), Elisha Gray of the United States

1889
Coin-operated Jukebox, Louis T. Glass and William S. Arnold of the U.S.
Automobile, Carl Benz and Gottlieb Daimler of Germany
Book Matches, Joshua Pusey of the United States

1890
Antitoxin for Diphtheria, Emil von Behring of Germany
Punch Card Machine, Herman Hollerith of the United States

1891
Zipper, Whitcomb L. Judson of the United States
Swiss Army Knife, Carl Elsener of Switzerland

1892
Diesel, Rudolf Diesel of Germany
Electric Generator (AC Current), Nikola Tesla of Croatia

1893
Modern Architecture, Frank Lloyd Wright of the United States
Motion Pictures (Movies), Thomas A. Edison of the United States
Wireless Communication, Nikola Tesla of Croatia

1894
Kellogg's Corn Flakes, Will Keith Kellogg of the United States

1895
Diesel Engine, Rudolf Diesel of France/Germany
Radio Signals, Guglielmo Marconi of Italy
Schwinn Bicycle, Ignaz Schwinn of Germany
X-rays, Wilhelm Roentgen of Germany

1896
Peanut Agricultural Science, George Washington Carver of the United States
Cracker Jack, F.W. Rueckheim of Germany
Electric Stove, William Hadaway of the United States
Radioactivity of Uranium, Henri Becquerel of France

TIMELINE OF INVENTIONS, THEORIES, INNOVATIONS, AND DISCOVERIES

1897
Aspirin, Dr. Felix Hoffmann of Germany
Jell-O, Pearl B. Wait of the United States

1898
Remote Control, Nikola Tesla of Croatia
Radioactivity, Pierre Curie and Marie Curie of France
Telegraphone, Valdemar Poulsen of Denmark

1899
Paperclip, William D. Middlebrook of the United States
Tape Recorder (Magnetic Steel), Vlademar Poulson of Denmark

1900
Hershey Bar, Milton Hershey of the United States
Tractor, Benjamin Holt of the United States
Yellow Fever (Transmission), Walter Reed of the United States

1901
Assembly Line (for autos), Ransom Olds of the United States
Lionel Hobby Train, Joshua Lionel Cowen of the United States
Razor (Disposable), King C. Gillette of the United States
Vacuum Cleaner (Motorized), Hubert Booth of England

1902
Air Conditioner, Willis H. Carrier of the United States
Electric Typewriter with Type wheel, George C. Blickensderfer of the United States
Flashlight, Conrad Hubert (Akiba Horowitz) of Russia
Teddy Bear, Morris Michtom of the United States

1903
Coat Hanger, Albert J. Parkhouse of the United States
Crayons, Edward Binney and Harold Smith of the U.S.
Electrocardiography, Willem Einhoven of the Netherlands
Powered Airplane, Wilbur and Orville Wright of the United States
Radioactivity studied, Marie Curie of Poland
Windshield Wipers (Manual), Mary Anderson of the United States

1904
Consumer Banking, Amadeo Giannini of the United States
Ice Cream Cone, Ernest Hamwi of the United States
Psychoanalysis, Sigmund Freud of Austria

1905
Intelligence Testing, Alfred Binet and Theodore Simon of France

TIMELINE OF INVENTIONS, THEORIES, INNOVATIONS, AND DISCOVERIES

Popsicle, Frank Epperson of the United States
Relativity Theory, Albert Einstein of Germany

1906
Light Bulb (Modern Incandescent), William Coolidge and General Electric Co. (U.S.)
Planters Peanuts, Omedeo Obici of Italy
Sound Radio Broadcasting, Reginald Fessenden of Canada

1907
Bakelite Synthetic Plastic, Leo Baekeland of Belguim
Color Photography, Auguste and Louis Lumiere of France
Dixie Cups, Lawrence Luellen and Hugh Moore of the U.S.
E=MC2, Albert Einstein of Germany
Helicopter, Paul Cornu of France
Outboard (boat) Motor, Ole Evinrude of Norway
Paper Towels, Arthur Scott of the United States

1908
Cellophane Plastic Wrap, Jacques Brandenberger of Switzerland
Electric Standing Mixer, Herbert Johnson of the United States
Electric Washing Machine, Alva J. Fisher of the United States
Ford Model "T," Henry Ford

1909
Radio Amplifier, Lee DeForest of the United States

1910
Conditioned Reflex, Ivan Pavlov of Russia
Neon Light, Georges Claude of France

1911
Hydrofoil Boat, Alexander Graham Bell and Casey Baldwin
Nuclear Model of an Atom, Ernest Rutherford of England

1912
Continental Drift (Plate Tectonics), Alfred Wegener of Germany
Isotopes, Frederick Soddy of England
Life Savers Candy, Clarence Crane of the United States
Liquid Fueled Rocket, Robert Goddard of the United States
Vitamins, Sir F. G. Hopkins and Casimir Frank of England

1913
Mass Production, Henry Ford of the United States
Zipper, Gideon Sundback of Sweden

TIMELINE OF INVENTIONS, THEORIES, INNOVATIONS, AND DISCOVERIES

1914
Radio Remote Control, John Hays Hammond of the United States
Tank (Military), Sir Ernest Swinton of England
Tinker Toys, Charles Pajeau of the United States

1915
Mechanical Pencil (Ever-Ready), Tokuji Hayakawa of Japan
Transcontinental Telephone Call, Alexander Graham Bell to Thomas Watson

1916
Lincoln Logs, John Lloyd Wright of the United States

1918
Rifle (Automatic), John Browning of the United States
Thermodynamics (3rd Law), Walter Nernst of Germany

1919
Proton, Ernest Rutherford of England
Toaster, Charles Strite of the United States

1920
Band-Aid, Earle Dickson of the United States
Traffic Light, William Potts of the United States

1921
Insulin, Sir Frederick Banting and Charles Best of Canada
Wheaties, George Cormack of the United States
Wonder Bread, Elmer Cline of the United States

1922
Electric Blender, Stephen J. Poplawski of Poland

1923
Automatic Traffic Signal, Garrett Morgan of the United States

1924
Frozen Food, Clarence Birdseye of the United States
Sound Film, Lee DeForest of the United States

1925
Exclusion Principle of Electrons, Wolfgang Pauli of Germany
Masking Tape, Dick Drew of the United States
Portable Metal Detector, Gerhard Fischer of the United States
Quantum Mechanics, W. Heisenberg and E. Schrodinger of Germany

TIMELINE OF INVENTIONS, THEORIES, INNOVATIONS, AND DISCOVERIES

1926
Motion Picture with Sound, Warner Bros. "Don Juan" and "The Jazz Singer"
Rocket (Liquid-fueled), Robert Goddard of the United States

1927
Big Bang Theory, George LeMaitre of Belgium
Pez Candy, Eduard Hass III of Austria
Television, Philo T. Farnsworth of the United States
Uncertainty Principle, Werner Heisenberg of Germany

1928
Bubble Gum, Walter Diemer of the United States
Penicillin (1st antibiotic), Alexander Fleming of the United States
Yo-Yo, Donald Duncan of the United States

1929
Car Radio, William Lear and Elmer Wavering of the U.S.

1929
Expanding Universe Theory, Edwin P. Hubble of the United States
Kinescope Cathode-Ray-Tube, Vladimir Zworykin of Russia.
Razor (Electric), Jacob Schick of the United States
Sunglasses, Sam Foster of the United States

1930
Scotch Cellophane Tape, Dick Drew of the United States
Toll House (chocolate chip) Cookies, Ruth Wakefield of the United States

1931
Iconoscope TV Camera Tube, Vladimir Zworykin of Russia
Microscope (Electron), Ernst Ruska and Max Knoll of Germany

1932
Defibrillator, Dr. William Kouwenhoven of the United States
FM Radio (Frequency Modulation), Edwin Howard Armstrong of the United States
Neutron, James Chadwick of England
Radio Waves, Karl Jansky of the United States

1934
Neutron Radiation, Enico Fermi of Italy

1935
Monopoly, Charles Darrow of the United States
Richter Scale (Earthquakes), Charles F. Richter of the United States

TIMELINE OF INVENTIONS, THEORIES, INNOVATIONS, AND DISCOVERIES

Telephone Answering Machine, Willy Muller
Trampoline, George Nissen of the United States

1936
Fluorescent Lamp, George E. Inman of the United States
Multi-plane Camera, Walt Disney of the United States
Radar (Radio), Sir Robert Watson Watt of Scotland

1937
Computer Science, Alan Turing of England
Jet Engine, Frank Whittle and Hans von Ohain of Europe
Shopping Cart, Sylvan Goldman of the United States

1938
Ballpoint Pen, Laszlo Biro of Hungary
Nuclear Fission, Otto Hahn and Fritz Strassmann of Germany
Nylon Stockings, Dr. Wallace Carothers of the United States
Xerox Copy Machine, Chester Carlson of the United States

1939
Atanasoff Berry Computer (ABC), John Atanasoff of the United States
Helicoptor (Single Rotor), Igor Sikorsky of the United States

1940
Blood Bank, Dr. Charles Drew of the United States

1941
Plutonium (Synthesis), Seaborg, McMillan, Kennedy and Wahl of the U.S.

1942
Duct Tape, Johnson and Johnson Co. of the U.S.
Nuclear Reaction, Enrico Fermi of Italy

1943
Aqua-Lung for Scuba Divers, Jacques Cousteau and Emile Gagnon of France
Colossus Code-breaking Computer, Alan Turing of England
Teflon, DuPont of the United States

1944
Ball-Point Pen (For writing), Laszlo Biro of Argentina
Clue Board Game, Anthony E. Pratt of the United Kingdom
Mark I Computer, Howard Aiken of the United States

1945
Microwave Oven, Percy Spencer of the United States

TIMELINE OF INVENTIONS, THEORIES, INNOVATIONS, AND DISCOVERIES

Slinky, Betty and Richard James of the United States
Tupperware, Earl Tupper of the United States

1946
Computer (ENIAC), John Mauchly and J.P. Eckert of the U.S.
Disposable Diapers, Marion Donovan of the United States

1947
Carbon Dating (Carbon 14), Willard F. Libby of the United States
Holograph, Dennis Gabor of England
Instant Photography, Edwin Land of the United States
Transistor, J. Bardeen, W. Brattain and W. Shockley of the United States

1948
Chemical Demulsifiers, Melvin De Groote of the United States
Scrabble Board Game, Alfred Butts of the United States
Velcro, George de Mestral of Switzerland

1949
Lego Bricks, Ole Kirk Christiansen of Denmark

1950
Frisbee, Walter Frederick Morrison of the United States
"Peanuts" Comic Strip, Charles Schultz of the United States
Silly Putty, Peter Hodgson of the United States

1951
Liquid Paper, Bette Nesmith Graham of the United States.
Nuclear Power Reactor, Walter Zinn of Canada
Random Access Memory (RAM), Jay Forrester of the United States

1952
Circuit (integrated), G.W.A. Dummer of England
Computer Compiler, Grace Murray Hopper of the United States
Mr. Potato Head, George Lerner of the United States

1953
DNA (Double-Helical Structure), F.H. Crick of England and James Watson of the United States
Measles Vaccine, John F. Enders and Thomas Peebles of the U.S.
Television (Color), National Television Systems Committee

1954
Geodesic Dome, R. Buckminster Fuller of the United States
Milk Carton, John Van Wormer of the United States
Robot (Programmable), George Deval of the United States

TIMELINE OF INVENTIONS, THEORIES, INNOVATIONS, AND DISCOVERIES

1955
Fiber Optics, Narinder Kapany of England
Polio Vaccine, Jonas Salk of the United States
Transistor Radio, Texas Instruments of the United States

1956
Optical Fiber and Endoscope, Dr. Basil Hirschowitz of South Africa
Play-Doh, Noah and Joseph McVicker of the United States
Transatlantic Telephone Cable, American Telephone Companies
TV Remote Control, Robert Adler of Austria
Videocassette Recorder, The Ampex Company of the United States
Yahtzee, Edwin S. Lowe of Canada

1957
Pacemaker (External), Earl Bakken of the United States
Sputnik I and II launched, Russia
Superconductivity Theory, John Bardeen, Leon Cooper, and John Sheiffer of the United States

1958
Hula-Hoop, Richard Knerr and Arthur Melin of the United States
Silicon Chip (Integrated Circuit), Jack Kilby and Robert Noyce of the United States
Van Allen Radiation Belt, James Van Allen of the United States
Video Game, William Higinbotham of the United States

1959
Barbie Doll, Ruth Handler of the United States

1960
Etch A Sketch, Arthur Granjean of the United States
Laser, Theodore Maiman of the United States
The Game of Life, Reuben Klamer of the United States

1961
Catheter (balloon) for surgeries, Thomas Fogarty of the United States
Optical Disc, David Paul Gregg of the United States

1962
Felt Tip Pens, Yukio Horie of Japan
Internal Pacemaker (Lithium), Wilson Greatbatch of the United States
Seat Belt (Three Point), Nils Bohlin of Sweden

1963
Computer Mouse, Douglas Engelbart of the United States
Easy-Bake Oven, Kenner Products of the United States

TIMELINE OF INVENTIONS, THEORIES, INNOVATIONS, AND DISCOVERIES

Home Video Recorder, Sony Company
Lava Lamp, Edward Craven Walker of England
Liquid Crystal Display (First), George Heilmeier of the United States
Push Button Telephone Service, Bell Telephone
Quasars, Marten Schmidt of the United States

1964
Holography, Emmett Leith and Juris Upatnieks of the U.S.
Smiley Face, Harvey Ball of the United States

1965
Superball, Norman Stingley of the United States

1966
Hand-held Calculator, Jack Kirby of Texas Instruments

1967
Automated Teller Machine, John Shephard-Barron of India/United Kingdom
Compact Microwaves, Amana Company of the United States
Dynamic Random Access Memory, Robert Dennard of the United States
Pulsars (Neutron Star), Antony Hewish and Jocelyn Bell Burnel of England
Quarks (Particles), Friedman, Kendall, and Taylor of the United States

1968
Microprocessor, Ted Hoff of the United States
Speakers (BOSE), Amar Bose of the United States
Videogame Console, Ralph H. Baer of Germany

1969
Arpanet (1st Internet), U.S. Department of Defense
Sesame Street, Joan Ganz Cooney and Lloyd Morrisett of the United States

1970
Bar Codes, Monarch Marking of the United States

1971
Intel 4004 Microprocessor, The world's first microprocessor is developed by Intel engineers, condensing the Central Processing Unit (CPU) into one small chip, Federico Fagan, Ted Hoff, and Stanley Mazor.
Ebooks, Michael Hart of the United States
Email (On Arpanet), Ray Tomlinson of the United States
Floppy Disc, David Noble (IBM) of the United States
Karaoke Machine, Daisuke Inoue of Japan
LCD Panal (Modern), James Fergason of the United States
Pocket Calculator, Sharp Corporation of Japan

TIMELINE OF INVENTIONS, THEORIES, INNOVATIONS, AND DISCOVERIES

1972
Compact Disc (CD), RCA of the United States
Magnavox Odyssey Game Console, Ralph Baer of Germany
Pong Videogame, Nolan Bushnell of the United States

1973
Ethernet (Links Networks), Bob Metcalfe and David Boggs of the United States
Internet, Vinton Cerf of the United States
Personal Computer, Xerox PARC of the United States

1974
Post-It Notes, Art Fry and Spencer Silver of the United States
Rubik's Cube, Erno Rubik of Hungary

1975
Microsoft Software Inc., Bill Gates of the United States
Videocassette Recorder (VCR), Sony Company (Betamax and VHS) of Japan

1976
Apple Computer, Steve Jobs and Steve Wozniak of the United States

1977
Apple II Computer, Steve Jobs of the United States
Human Powered Flight (with Bike), Paul MacCready of the United States
PC Modem, Dennis Hayes of the United States
SIMON Game, Ralph Baer of Germany

1978
Dyson Vacuum Cleaner, James Dyson of England

1979
Sony Walkman Cassette Player, Nobutoshi Kihara of Japan
Trivial Pursuit Board Game, Chris Haney and Scott Abbott of Canada

1981
IBM Personal Computer, Philip Don Estridge of the United States
Veggie Patty (Gardenburger), Paul Wenner of the United States

1982
Artificial Heart Implant, Dr. Robert Jarvik of the United States
Computer Gaming, Sid Meier of the United States
Itty Bitty Booklite, Noel Zeller of the United States

1983
Apple Macintosh, Steve Jobs and Steve Wozniak of the United States

TIMELINE OF INVENTIONS, THEORIES, INNOVATIONS, AND DISCOVERIES

Cabbage Patch Kids, Xavier Roberts of the United States
Camcorder, Sony of the United States
Mobile Phone, Richard Frenkiel and Joel Engel of the United States

1986
The Club Security Device, James Winner of the United States

1990
World Wide Web, Tim Berners-Lee of England

1993
Beanie Babies, H Ty Warner of the United States
Light Emitting Diodes (LED lights), Shuji Nakamura of Japan
Mosaic Browser for World Wide Web, Marc Andreeson of the United States

1994
Digital Camera, Steven Sasson of the United States
Bluetooth Technology, Ericsson Company of Sweden

1995
DVD (Digital Video Disk), Phillips, Toshiba, and Panasonic
Leapfrog, Michael.Wood of the United States

1997
Camera Phones, Philippe Kahn of France
Teletubbies, Anne Wood and Andrew Davenport of the United Kingdom

1998
Google, Sergey Brin and Larry Page of the United States
USB Flash Drive, Dov Moran of Israel
Wireless Keyboard and Mouse, Logitech International of Switzerland

1999
DVR (Digital Video Recorder), Anthony Wood of the United States
Webster's Online Dictionary Project, Philip Parker of the United States

2001
Abiocor Artificial Heart, Abiomed Company of the United States
Artificial Liver, Dr. Kenneth Matsumaura and the Alin Foundation
Digital Satellite Radio, Martine Rothblatt of the United States
Fuel Cell Bike, Aprilla Co. of Italy
iPod, Tony Fadell of the United States
iTunes, Steve Jobs and Apple Computer Inc.
Millennium Bridge, Wilkinson Eyre Architects and Gifford and Partners

TIMELINE OF INVENTIONS, THEORIES, INNOVATIONS, AND DISCOVERIES

Segway Human Transporter, Dean Kamen of the United States
Self-Cleaning Windows, PPG Industries of the United States
Xbox (Gaming System), Microsoft Inc. Engineers
Wikipedia online encyclopedia launched

2002
Braille Glove, Ryan Patterson of the United States
ROOMBA Robotic Vacuum, Helen Greiner of England
Solar Tower, Jorg Schlaich of Germany
Virtual Keyboard, Canesta Inc. and VK
AOL, America Online

2003
Hybrid Car, Toyota Company
Luminex Glowing Fabric, Luminex Company
Myspace, the social networking site launched
LinkedIn, the networking site for business is launched by Reid Hoffman, Konstantin Guericke, Jean-Luc
Vaillant, Allen Blue, Eric Ly
iTunes, Apple introduces the online music service

2004
Facebook (Social Media), Mark Zuckerberg of the United States
Mozilla Firefox, Dave Hyatt and Blake Ross of the United States

2005
Solar Shingles, Dow Chemical Company

2006
Blu-Ray Players, Sony Company
PSP (PlayStation Portable), Sony Engineers of Japan
Twitter, the social networking and microblogging site, by Jack Dorsey, Evan Williams, and Biz Stone

2007
Global Positioning System, Roger L. Easton of the United States
iPhone Smartphone, Apple Inc. Engineers
YouTube, Jawed Karim, Chad Hurley and Steve Chen

2008
Electric Car, Tesla Motors of the United States

2009
Nintendo Wii System, Nintendo Company of Japan
Bing, Microsoft's Bing joins Google and Yahoo as the major Internet search engines

TIMELINE OF INVENTIONS, THEORIES, INNOVATIONS, AND DISCOVERIES

2010
iPad, Steve Jobs of Apple Inc.
The Straddling Bus
The Driveless Car, Google
First synthetic cell
Lasers, lasers developed that zap malaria-carrying mosquitos

2011
The Stark hand robotic prototype, Mark Stark
The Print Brush, Alex Breton of Sweden
The Medical Mirror, Ming Zher Poh
Trip Lingo translator, Jesse Maddox
Pinterest, the visual discovery tool is launched by Ben Silvermann.

2012
Google Glass
Windows 8 is released
Vine Mobile App for Twitter Video Clips, Dom Hoffmann, Rus Yusupov, and Colin Kroll
The top ten social networks include Facebook, Twitter, Blogger, WordPress, LinkedIn, Pinterest, Google Plus, Tumblr, Myspace, and Wikia.
Blogs, videos, and podcasts prove to be popular marketing tools
3D Printer
LiquiGlide Ketchup bottle
Nike Fly-Knit racer shoe
Body armor for women
Baxter robot
The Curiosity Rover
Mayan calendar reaches the end of its current cycle

2013
The Bladeless Windmill, Mecanoo Dutch Architecture Firm
Launch of Xbox One and the PS4
New edition of Windows

2014
The Wizarding World of Harry Potter opens at Orlando's Universal.
Atlas humanoid robot
GravityLight

TIMELINE OF AMERICAN PRESIDENTS

Timeline of American Presidents

1. George Washington (1789-1797)
2. John Adams (1797-1801)
3. Thomas Jefferson (1801-1809)
4. James Madison (1809-1818)
5. James Monroe (1817-1825)
6. John Quincy Adams (1825-1829)
7. Andrew Jackson (1829-1837)
8. Martin Van Buren (1837-1841)
9. William Henry Harrison (1841)
10. John Tyler (1841-1845)
11. James K. Polk (1845-1849)
12. Zachary Taylor (1849-1850)
13. Millard Fillmore (1850-1853)
14. Franklin Pierce (1853-1857)
15. James Buchanan (1857-1861)
16. Abraham Lincoln (1861-1865)
17. Andrew Johnson (1865-1869)
18. Ulysses S. Grant (1869-1877)
19. Rutherford B. Hayes (1877-1881)
20. James A. Garfield (1881)
21. Chester Arthur (1881-1885)
22. Grover Cleveland (1885-1889)
23. Benjamin Harrison (1889-1893)
24. William McKinley (1897-1901)
25. Theodore (Teddy) Roosevelt (1901-1909)
26. William Howard Taft (1909-1913)
27. Woodrow Wilson (1913-1921)
28. Warren G. Harding (1921-1923)
29. Calvin Coolidge (1923-1929)
30. Herbert Hoover (1929-1933)
31. Franklin D. Roosevelt (1933-1945)
32. Harry S. Truman (1945-1953)
33. Dwight D. Eisenhower (1953-1961)
34. John F. Kennedy (1961-1963)
35. Lyndon B. Johnson (1963-1969)
36. Richard Nixon (1969-1974)
37. Gerald Ford (1974-1977)
38. Jimmy Carter (1977-1981)
39. Ronald Reagan (1981-1989)
40. George Bush (1989-1993)
41. Bill Clinton (1993-2001)
42. George W. Bush (2001-2009)
43. Barack Obama (2009-present)

TIMELINE OF AFRICAN AMERICAN HISTORY

Timeline of African-American History

1619
First Slaves from Africa arrive in Virginia

1787
Slavery is illegal in the Northwest Territory

1792
Benjamin Banneker - A self-educated mathematician and astronomer, Ben Banneker is renowned for the series of almanacs he wrote and published between 1792 and 1797. He is regarded as one of the first African-American intellectuals.

1793
Eli Whitney invents cotton gin, thus promoting cotton production and slavery in the south.

1800
Gabriel Prosser, an enslaved blacksmith, leads an unsuccessful slave rebellion in Virginia.

1820
Missouri Compromise - An agreement that allows Missouri to enter the Union as a slave state, and Maine to enter the Union as a free state.

1822
Denmark Vesey - The enslaved carpenter leads an unsuccessful slave revolt in Charleston, South Carolina, but is discovered and hanged along with 34 other conspirators.

1831
Nat Turner - An enslaved preacher, Nat Turner leads an effective slave rebellion in Virginia that prompts legislation further restricting the lives of slaves and free blacks.
William Lloyd Garrison - A publisher of a newspaper that pushes for abolition of slavery.

1846
Frederick Douglas - An Activist who debuts his abolitionist newspaper, and becomes a prominent figure in campaigning for the rights and conditions of Black Americans.

1849
Harriet Tubman - An influential woman who escapes slavery and becomes a leader in the Underground Railroad, leading many slaves to freedom.

1850
Fugitive Slave Act - Mandates the return of runaway slaves, and also calls for stricter punishment for those who help the slaves run away.

TIMELINE OF AFRICAN AMERICAN HISTORY

1851
Sojourner Truth - An African American former slave abolitionist who advocates for the rights of women and gives a famous speech, "Ain't I a Woman?" at a Women's Convention in Ohio.

1852
Harriet Beecher Stowe - An American abolitionist, writes her famous story depicting the harsh life of African-American slaves entitled, "Uncle Tom's Cabin."

1854
Missouri Compromise of 1820 - The Missouri Compromise is repealed by Congress, resulting in rising tensions between pro-slavery and anti-slavery groups.

1857
Dred Scot Case - The Supreme Court decision rules that the Missouri compromise is unconstitutional, that African Americans are not entitled to citizenship, and that slaves are not free even if they cross over into Free states. The decision upsets the balance between Slave states and Free states.

1859
John Brown - An abolitionist, Brown is hanged after he leads an unsuccessful revolt, attempting to capture the federal arsenal at Harper's Ferry, Virginia.

1861
The Confederate States of America - The Confederacy is founded and a government is set up with six of the seven slave states, after having declared their separation from the U.S.
The Civil War begins.

1863
Emancipation Proclamation - An executive order is issued by President Lincoln to free all slaves effective January 1, 1863.

1865
Freedman's Bureau - An agency formed to aid slaves during the reconstruction era.
Civil War ends - The Civil War ends when the Confederate General Robert E. Lee of the Southern States surrenders to the Union General Ulysses S. Grant of the Northern States.
President Abraham Lincoln is assassinated by John Wilkes Booth at the Ford's Theatre.
Thirteenth Amendment to the Constitution is ratified by Congress – This amendment abolishes slavery.
Ku Klux Klan - A Secret society that is formed in Tennessee after the Civil War, and focuses on white supremacy and terrorizing other groups.

1865-1856
Black Codes - A body of laws that are enacted by the southern states after the Civil War to regain control over the freed slaves and maintain white supremacy.

1867
Reconstruction Acts - Acts that are passed that guarantee Civil Rights to freed slaves.

TIMELINE OF AFRICAN AMERICAN HISTORY

1868
Fourteenth Amendment to the Constitution is ratified by Congress. This amendment defines citizens as those born in the United States, including those born as slaves.

1869
Howard University - First Black Law School is established for African Americans in Washington D.C.
Susan B. Anthony - An American Civil Rights Leader who is regarded as an icon in the women's suffrage movement, giving women the right to vote. This goal would finally be realized 14 years after her death with the ratification of the Nineteenth Amendment.

1870
Fifteenth Amendment to the Constitution is ratified by Congress. This amendment gives African Americans the right to vote.

1877- (Through 1950's)
Jim Crow Laws - Laws that are passed whereby whites from the south re-assert their dominance over African Americans by denying them basic civil rights, and further discriminates against blacks with regard to voting, housing, transportation, schools, and the workplace.

1879
The Black Exodus - Thousands of African Americans migrate from the south to Kansas.

1881
Spelman College founded - The first college for black women in the United States.
Booker T. Washington - An educator and Civil Rights Activist who founded the Tuskegee Normal and Industrial Institute in Alabama for African Americans.

1882
American Colonization Society founded - This society establishes the colony of Monrovia in western Africa, and paves the way for the immigration of thousands of slaves to Africa.

1896
George Washington Carver - A former slave who becomes an inventor and scientist, George Washington Carver is known for developing crop-rotation practices that serve to preserve the nutrients in soil, and for discovering many uses of the peanut. He is a professor in the agricultural department at Booker T. Washington's Tuskegee Institute.
Plessy vs. Ferguson - The Supreme Court decision that declares that racial segregation (separation) is constitutional.

1905
W.E.B. Du Bois - A political activist and Civil Rights leader who fights for the equality of Black Americans.
Madame C.J. Walker - The first American to become a self-made millionaire when she introduces her line of hair care products for African American women.

TIMELINE OF AFRICAN AMERICAN HISTORY

1909
NAACP - The National Association for the Advancement of Colored People, an African American Civil Rights organization promoting equality and social justice, was founded in New York and led by W.E.B. Du Bois.

1914
Marcus Garvey - A political leader from Jamaica who advocates for Black Nationalism, and works to promote a spirit of unity and pride among African Americans.

1915
Carter G. Woodson - An African American writer who founded the Association for the Study of Afro-American Life and History, and is regarded as the "Father of Black History."

1920's
Harlem Renaissance - An intellectual, literary, and artistic African American movement that helps to promote a renewed black cultural identify.
Louis Armstrong - Born in New Orleans, Armstrong is regarded as of the most important and influential jazz musicians in history. He was a popular singer and trumpeter.

1923
Duke Ellington - An African American composer and jazz bandleader, his career spanning more than fifty years.

1926
Carter G. Wilson - Establishes Negro History Week

1935
Mary Bethune - An educator and a Civil Rights Activist, Mary Bethune founded the National Council of Negro Women in 1935, and is also credited with establishing the Daytona Normal and Industrial Institute now known as Bethune-Cookman University.

1936
Jesse Owens - An African American Track and Field athlete who wins four gold medals at the 1936 Olympics in Berlin. His record for the long jump would stand for 25 years.

1947
Jackie Robinson - First African American baseball player to play in Major League Baseball when he signs with the Brooklyn Dodgers.

1952
Malcolm X - An African American Muslim Minister and Civil Rights Activist who serves as a spokesman for the Nation of Islam.

TIMELINE OF AFRICAN AMERICAN HISTORY

1954
Brown vs. the Board of Education of Topeka, Kansas. The Supreme Court decision that declares that racial segregation in schools is unconstitutional.

1955
Rosa Parks - An African American Civil Rights Activist who refuses to give up her seat to a white passenger on a crowded city bus in Montgomery, Alabama. She is charged for breaking the segregation law, prompting African Americans to boycott the buses for one year. One year later, the U.S. Supreme Court decides in her favor and rules that segregation laws are unconstitutional.

1960
"Greensboro Four" - Four African American students stage a sit-in at a lunch counter at Woolworth's until they are finally served.

1962
James Meredity - Is the first Black student to enroll at the University of Mississippi.

1963
Martin Luther King Jr. - An African American activist who leads the American Civil Rights Movement. He is intent on advancing Civil Rights using nonviolent civil disobedience.
March on Washington - Over 250,000 people gather at the Nation's capital to demonstrate for jobs and freedom.
"I Have a Dream" Speech - A powerful speech by Martin Luther King Jr. in Washington, D.C. in which he outlines his vision for a better future for all citizens in America, and where he voices his hope that his kids "will not be judged by the color of their skin, but by the content of their character."

1964
Civil Rights Act - President Johnson signs the Civil Rights Act that prohibits discrimination based on race, religion, color, or national origin.
Martin Luther King Jr. receives the Nobel Peace Prize.
Sidney Poitier - He is the first Black actor to win a Best Actor Oscar for "Lilies of the Field."

1965
Malcolm X assassinated - The founder of the Organization of Afro-American Unity is assassinated.
Voting Rights Act of 1965 - African-Americans in the South have an easier pathway to voting without obstacles.

1966
Black Panthers - The socialist movement is founded by Huey Newton and Bobby Seale.

1967
Thurgood Marshall - President Johnson appoints Thurgood Marshall to the Supreme Court, the first African American Supreme Court Justice.

TIMELINE OF AFRICAN AMERICAN HISTORY

1968
Martin Luther King assassinated – King is assassinated in Memphis, Tennessee.
Civil Rights Act of 1968 - President Johnson signs this act that prohibits discrimination regarding housing issues.

1969
Maya Angelou (1928-2014) - An African American activist, writer, and performer, she is regarded as a Renaissance woman having one of the most influential voices of our time. She is the author of numerous books of poetry and autobiographies. Her 1969 autobiography, "I Know Why the Caged Bird Sings," is about the early years of her life.
Shirley Chisholm - Becomes the first black congresswoman, and would become the first African American woman to make a bid for the Democratic presidential nomination in 1972.

1978
U.S. Supreme Court Case - Regents of the *University of California vs. Bakke* rules that affirmative action is constitutional.

1983
Guion Bluford Jr. - He is the first African American to fly in space aboard the Challenger shuttle.

1984
Jesse Jackson - He is a Civil Rights activist and minister, and was a candidate for the Democratic Presidential Nomination in 1984 and 1988.

1992
Race Riots - For the first time in many years, race riots erupt in Los Angeles after a jury sides with four white police officers after a brutal videotaped beating of African American Rodney King.

1993
Toni Morrison - She is the winner of the Pulitzer Prize for *Beloved* in 1988, and this year receives the Nobel Prize in literature.
Jocelyn Elders - She is the first African American woman to serve as the U.S. Surgeon General.

1995
O.J. Simpson - The former NFL football player is found not guilty of killing his wife Nicole Simpson and her friend Ronald Goldman by a jury in one of the most watched trials in history.
Minister Louis Farrakhan - The leader of the nation of Islam organizes a "Million Man March" of African American men in Washington, D.C.

1996
Michael Johnson - He is the first African American to win gold medals in the 200 and 400 meter races at the 1996 Olympic Games in Atlanta, Georgia.

1997
Tiger Woods - He is the first African American golfer to win the Masters Tournament in Augusta.

TIMELINE OF AFRICAN AMERICAN HISTORY

"Million Women March" is organized by African American women in Philadelphia.

1998
"The Little Rock Nine" - Nine African American students who were prevented from attending an all-white school are awarded the Congressional Medal of Honor.

1999
Rosa Parks - The Civil Rights activist, famous for not giving up her seat to a white passenger on a bus in 1955, is awarded the Congressional Medal of Honor.

2000
Venus Williams - She is the first African American woman since Althea Gibson to win the ladies singles tennis championships at Wimbledon. She later will win gold medals in both singles and doubles at the Olympic Games in Sydney, Australia.
Confederate Flag removed - Under pressure from the NAACP, the Confederate Flag is removed from the statehouse in South Carolina.

2001
General Colin Powell - He is the first African American to serve as the United States Secretary of State.
Condoleezza Rice - She is the first African American to be named U.S. National Security Advisor.

2002
Halle Berry - She is the first African American woman to win the Best Actress Oscar for her role in "Monster's Ball."
Denzel Washington - He wins the Best Actor Oscar for his role in "Training Day."
Vonetta Flowers - She is the first African American to win a gold medal at the Winter Olympics, winning the bobsledding event in Salt Lake.
Suzan Lori-Parks - She is the first African American to win a Pulitzer Prize in drama for her play, *Topdog/Underdog*.

2003
Vernice Armour - She is the first African American female combat pilot in the U.S. Marines Corps.

2005
Condoleezza Rice - She is the first African American woman to serve as the United States Secretary of State.

2006
Ellen Johnson-Sirleaf - She is the first African American to be inaugurated President in Liberia.

2008
Barack Obama - The first African American is elected as the 44th President of the United States.

2009
Eric H. Holder Jr - He is the first African American to serve as the Attorney General of the U.S.

TIMELINE OF AFRICAN AMERICAN HISTORY

2011

Oprah Winfrey - A prominent media proprietor, actress, producer, and philanthropist, Oprah Winfrey is regarded as a Renaissance woman and perhaps the most influential woman in the world. Her talk show aired between 1986 and 2011 and was the highest- ranking program of its kind in history.

2012

President Barack Obama is re-elected as President of the United States.

NATIVE AMERICAN FACTS

Native American Facts

Indian Tribes

Navajo, Cherokee, Sioux, Chippewa, Choctaw, Apache, Pueblo, Iroquois, Creek, Blackfeet

Famous Indian Leaders:

American Horse –Sioux (1800-1876), **Black Hawk** – Sauk (1767-1838), **Black Hoof** – Shawnee (1740-1831), **Captain Jack** – Modoc (1837-1873), **Cochise** – Apache (1812-1874), **Crazy Horse**, Lakota (Oglala Sioux) (1845-1877), **Geronimo**- Apache (1829-1909), **Hiawatha** –**Mohawk, Joseph** – Nez Perce (1840-1904), **Pontiac** – Ottawa, **Powhatan** and daughter **Pocahontas** – Algonquin, **Red Cloud** –Oglala Sioux, **Sacajawea** – Shoshone, **Sitting Bull** –Lakota (1831-1890), **Tecumsah** – Shawnee (1768-1813)

Native American Indian Tribes by Region

Southwest: Apalachee, Catawba, Cherokee, Chicasaw, Choctaw, Coushatta, Creek, Houma, Lumbee, Miccosukee, Seminole, Timucua.

MidAtlantic/Northeast: Algonquin, Iroquois, Lenape, Narragansett, Nipmuc, Pequot, Piscataway, Pokanaket, Powhatan, Rappahannock, Yaocamico, Wampanoag.

Great Lakes: Chippewa, Fox, Huron, Kickapoo, Menominee, Miami, Oneida, Onondaga, Ottowa, Potawatomi, Shawnee, Winnebago.

Great Plains: Arapaho, Blackfeet, Cheyenne, Comanche, Crow, Dakota, Kiowa, Mandan, Osage, Pawnee, Sioux, Wichita.

California/Mountain: Cahuilla, Chemihuevi, Chumash, Costanoan, Diegueno, Hupa, Luiseno, Maidu, Paiute, Pomo, Shosone, Ute.

Pacific Northwest: Aleut, Athabascan, Chinook, Colville, Coos, Nez Perce, Puget Sound Salish, Quileute, Quinault, Spokane, Tlingit, Tulalip.

Southwest: Apache, Hopi, Keres, Maricopa, Mojave, Navajo, Pima, Pueblo, Tohono O'odham, Yaqui, Yuma, Zuni.

Native American Food Contributions
Avocado, Beans, Chewing Gum, Chocolate (Cocoa) Clam Bakes, Corn, Cranberries, Jerky Maple Sugar, Peanuts, Potatoes, Popcorn, Pumpkins, Rice, Sunflower seeds, Tomatoes, Turkeys, Vanilla.

Native American Products
Adobe, Belts, Canoe, Cigars, Cotton, Cradle Board, Baby Carriers, Buckskin jacket with fringe, Dear skin clothes, Fur Parkas, Headdresses, Headbands, Jewelry (Turquoise, beaded, silver, etc.), Kayak, Lacrosse, Log Cabin/ Indian Longhouse, Moccasins, Mohawks, Mukluks Boots, Native American Flute, Poncho, Pipes (Peace Pipe), Plants – (To make medicines, dyes, soap, clothes, and baskets), Raccoon skin caps, Rubber, Smoke Signals, Snow Shoes

NATIVE AMERICAN FACTS

Symbols (Birds, animals, colors, tattoos, grave posts, etc.), Tepee, Toboggan, Tomahawk, Trading Posts, Totem Pole, War paint, Wigwam, Wickiup

Native American Tools and Weapons
Arrowheads (Made of Flint stone), Axe, Bow and Arrow, Flint (Stone), Hatchet, Knife, Lance, Musket, Poisoned Arrow, Shield, Slingshot, Spear, Tomahawk, Whip

Native American Indian Words used in the English Language
Barbecue, Caribou, Chipmunk, Chocolate, Cougar, Eskimo, Hammock, Hickory, Hurricane, Husky, Moose, Muskellunge ("Musky"), Opossum, Papoose, Pecan, Potato, Raccoon, Skunk, Squash, Squaw, Toboggan, Tomahawk, Totem, Wigwam, Woodchuck

States with Native American Indian Names
Alabama, Arizona, Arkansas, Connecticut, Dakota, Illinois, Iowa, Kentucky, Massachusetts, Michigan, Minnesota, Mississippi, Missouri, Nebraska, New Mexico, Ohio, Oklahoma, Tennessee, Texas, Utah, Wisconsin

Native American Arts Contributions
Baskets, Beadwork (jewelry, belts, purses, etc.), Ceremonies (Religious Festivals and Dances), Dream Catchers, Drums, Flutes, Headdresses and Headbands, Kachina Doll, Pottery, Pow Wows, Rattles, Rain sticks, Sculptures (Totem Poles), Silver Smithing, Turquoise Jewelry, Wampum Beadwork, Weavings

TIMELINE OF NATIVE AMERICANS

Timeline of Native Americans

1492
Christopher Columbus sails from Spain and discovers the New World.

1500
Europeans bring diseases that greatly reduce the Native Indian population.

1513
Juan Ponce de Leon of Spain explores Florida and conflicts with Native Americans.

1534
Jacques Cartier of France explores St. Lawrence River and the Great Lakes.

1539
Hernando De Soto of Spain explores Florida and the Southeast searching for silver, gold, and a passage to China. He is the first European to cross the Mississippi River.
The Spanish meet the Pueblo Indians of the Southwest.

1585
Sir Walter Raleigh of England establishes the Virginia Colony of Roanoke Island on the Outer Banks of North Carolina.

1607
Captain John Smith of England establishes the Virginia Colony at Jamestown.

1608
Henry Hudson of England explores Northeastern North America. The Hudson Bay, Hudson River, and the Hudson Strait are named for him.

1620
Pocahontas, daughter of Pohawtan, befriends the English at Jamestown and saves Captain John Smith's life. She marries Englishman and tobacco planter John Rolfe.
One hundred and one Pilgrims, seeking religious freedom, sail from England on the Mayflower for 66 days and arrive at Plymouth, Massachusetts. They establish the first permanent English settlement.
The Pilgrims and Wampanoag Indians led by Chief Massasoit celebrate the autumn harvest with a feast lasting three days that included deer, shellfish, and corn.

1621
First conflict in Virginia between the Colonists and the Indians.

1622
First recorded Thanksgiving Day. The Pilgrims are thankful for a rain after a two-month drought.

TIMELINE OF NATIVE AMERICANS

1637
The **Puritans** establish reservations in New Haven, Connecticut.

1638
The Pequot War – (1634-1638) English Colonists and Native Indian allies defeat the Pequot Tribe under Chief Sassacus.

1639
The Beaver Wars (1640-1701) - The result of conflicts between the Algonquin and Iroquois tribes due to a disagreement regarding land boundaries for hunting, and the growing demand for beaver furs.

1655
The Peach Tree War - Dutch and Indian war that started when a young Indian girl entered the orchard of Dutchman Henry Van Dyck picked a peach off a tree.

1675
King Philip's War (1675-1677) - A two-year conflict between the Colonists and the Native American Indians.

1680
The Pueblo Revolt (1680-1692) - The Pueblo Indians revolt against the Spanish and reclaim their homeland after 12 years.

1754
French and Indian Wars (1754-1763) - The French and Indians fight against the British for control of the Ohio River Valley. Great Britain defeats France and its Indian allies.

1763
French and Indian War ends with the signing of The Treaty of Paris.

1764
Chief Pontiac of the Ottawa Tribe leads a rebellion against the British in the Ohio River Valley.

1774
The Boston Tea Party - American Colonists, angry about a new tax on tea, disguise themselves as Mohawk Indians, board three British ships, and dump 342 crates of British Tea into Boston Harbor.

1775
Lord Dunmore's War - Lord Dunmore, governor of Virginia, defeats the Shawnee Indians of Kentucky who sign a treaty giving up their hunting grounds.

1785
Northwest Indian War (1785-1795) - A war between the United States and several American Indian tribes over control of the Northwest Territory. The Indian tribes are defeated and are forced to give up extensive territory in Ohio.

TIMELINE OF NATIVE AMERICANS

1790
First U.S. Census - This first population count included free African-Americans and Slaves, but it did not include Native American Indians.

1803
The Louisiana Purchase – The United States purchase 885,000 square miles of land in the American Midwest for $15 million dollars from France, doubling the size of the nation. The land extends from the Mississippi River to the Rocky Mountains and from Canada to the Gulf of Mexico.
Louis and Clark Expedition (1803-1806) - An expedition initiated by President Thomas Jefferson to explore the Northwestern Territories of the United States. Louis and Clark and forty men set out from St. Louis in 1804 and lead an expedition to the U.S. Pacific coast and back. Along the way they hire several guides including a Native American woman named Sacagawea. They keep detailed journals of other cultures, tribes, geography, and the existence of plant and animal species.

1811
Tecumsah's War and the Battle of Tippecanoe - Tecumsah is a Shawnee chief who tries to stop American expansion in the old Northwest. Indiana governor William Henry Harrison defeats the Shawnee Indians at the Tippecanoe River in northern Indiana. This ends Tecumsah's efforts to build an Indian confederacy.

1812
War of 1812 - Tecumsah and Native Americans side with the British against the United States because the British tried to interfere with American trade with France. The United States is victorious and the war ends in 1814 with the signing of the Treaty of Ghent.

1817
First Seminole War (1817-1818) - The Seminoles fight to keep their land and territory from the United States. Andrew Jackson and 3,000 soldiers invade Florida capture runaway slaves, and secure control for the United States.

1824
The Office of Indian Affairs is established in the United States.

1827
The Cherokees form their own nation.
Winnebago War

1830
Indian Removal Act - An act signed by Andrew Jackson that provides for resettlement of lands west of the Mississippi River. Over 60,000 Native Americans are forced to migrate west.

1832
Black Hawk War - The United States battle against Chief Black Hawk and the Sauk and Fox Indians to recover lost hunting grounds. The United States defeats the Sauk in Northern Illinois and Southwestern Wisconsin.

TIMELINE OF NATIVE AMERICANS

1835
The Second Seminole War (1835-1842) - This war takes place in Florida between the Seminoles under Chief Osceola and the United States. The United States is victorious and over 3,800 Seminoles are transported to Indian Territory.

1836
Osage Indian War with the Osage Indians of Missouri.

1838
Trail of Tears - The Cherokee, Choctaw, Creek, Seminole, and Chickasaw tribes are forced to leave their homelands in the Deep South, and march in harsh conditions for 116 days to "Indian Territory" in Oklahoma. Over 4,000 Cherokee, one-third of the Cherokee Nation, die of disease and exposure on the journey.

1849
The Navajo Conflicts (1846-1853) - The Navajo Indians in Arizona and New Mexico have many conflicts with the Spanish, with the Mexican government, and with the United States.

1851
Fort Laramie Treaty - An agreement between the U.S. Government and the Sioux establishing land rights, and marking the boundaries of the Lakota Sioux Tribal lands.

1854
The Sioux Wars/Plains Indians Wars (1854-1890) - A series of conflicts between the Sioux people and the government. Many Sioux, Cheyenne, Comanche, Arapaho, and Kiowa Indian tribes were angry that roads were being built on their land and that travelers were passing through on their way to California during the Gold Rush.

1855
The Third Seminole War (1855-1858) - Conflict between the United States and the Seminole Indians by Chief Billing Bowlegs because the U.S. was invading on Seminole lands in the state of Florida.

1861
American Civil War (1861-1865) - Conflict between the U.S. government and eleven Southern states that wanted to leave the Union. The issues centered on slavery, tariffs, trade, and states' rights.
Apache Wars (1861-1900) - A series of conflicts with the United States, the Confederate, and American settlers in the southwestern states of Arizona, New Mexico, and Texas. The United States ultimately won against the Apache led by the Apache chiefs Geronimo, Cochise, Chatto, Juh, and Victorio.

1862
The Homestead Act - An act that is signed into law by President Lincoln that granted 160 acres of land to heads of household who were at least 21 years old at a very low cost. The settlers had to promise to stay on that land for five years.

TIMELINE OF NATIVE AMERICANS

1865
Union Pacific Railroad Built (1865-1869) - The building of the railroad began in Nebraska and expanded west. When it was completed in 1869 it became the Nation's first transcontinental railroad connecting by rail the Pacific Ocean and the Missouri River. Many settled in the Great Plains as a result of this railroad.
The Ute Wars - Ute Chief Black Hawk wages war against Mormon settlers in Utah.

1868
Sioux vs. The U.S. Army - The Sioux led by Chief Red Cloud defeat the United States Army.

1876
Great Sioux War/ Black Hills War (1876-1877) - The Dakota Sioux and the Cheyenne Indians under Chief Crazy Horse defeat General George Crook and the U.S army at the battle of Little Big Horn. **Custer's Last Stand** - A battle between the United States Cavalry under General Custer and the Sioux and Cheyenne Indians led by Chief Sitting Bull. General Custer and the United States Seventh Cavalry are defeated at Little Big Horn, Montana.

1877
Nez Perce War - A war between the Nez Perce Indians under Chief Joseph and The United States army. Chief Joseph led his tribe 1,700 miles but surrenders his forces near the border of Canada at Bear Paw Mountain in Montana territory.

1878
Campaign against Cheyenne Indians in Dakota Territory and Montana.

1879
Sheepeater Indian War - The last Indian war of the Pacific Northwest.
White River War
Victorio's War

1881
Geronimo's War

1887
Crow War
Ute War

1890
Ghost Dance War
Wounded Knee Massacre - The last battle between the United States government and North American Indians killing almost 200 Native Americans. This battle took place on the Pine Ridge Indian Reservation in southwestern South Dakota.

1893
Navajo War against white settlers.

TIMELINE OF NATIVE AMERICANS

1895
Bannock Uprising at Jackson Hole, Wyoming

1896
Yaqui Uprising

1907
Charles Curtis - Becomes the first Native American United States Senator.

1969
Native Americans are declared citizens of the United States.

1979
American Indian Religious Freedom Act is passed.
The Seminole Tribe Bingo - The tribe enters the Bingo and Gaming Industry.

1980
The U.S. Supreme Court awards the Sioux Indians $17.5 million dollars to compensate for unjustly taking control of the Black Hills.

1981
"**The Lakota Times**" is published for the first time.

1982
The Indian Mineral Development Act - Tribes are encouraged to mine their lands.

1988
Indian Gaming Regulatory Act - Tribes have rights to have gaming on Indian lands.

1900
Native American Languages Act - Congressional Act that promotes and preserves Indian languages.
Indian Arts and Crafts Act (IACA)
Native American Grave Protection Act

1993
Foxwoods Casino of Connecticut - The Pequots open the first U.S. casino.

1994
American Indian Religious Freedom Act Amendments

1996
National American Indian Heritage Month - November
Government Support of Tribal Colleges and Universities

Timeline of Prehistoric Eras and Periods

4.5 Billion Years Ago
Formation of Planet Earth

4 Billion Years Ago
Pre-Cambrian: Cells, algae, bacteria, worms, jellyfish

540 Million Years Ago (MYA)
Paleozoic: Cambrian: fish, coral, shellfish

505 Million Years Ago
Ordovician: corals and Nautiloids (Ocean Mollusks)

438 Million Years Ago
Silurian: First land plants, fish with jaws, and sea scorpions

408 Million Years Ago
Devonian: First amphibians, spiders, insects, fish with fins

360 Million Years Ago
Carboniferous: First reptiles and swamp forests

286 Million Years Ago
Permian: First Sail back reptiles; formation of Pangaea

245 Million Years Ago
Mesozoic: Triassic, Mammals, crocodiles, turtles, frogs, and dinosaurs, First tree ferns and coniferous trees

208 Million Years Ago
Jurassic: Stegosaurus and Brachiosaurus, and Brontosaurus dinosaurs, forests, birds, gingko, and conifers.

144-88 Million Years Ago
Cretaceous: Tyrannosaurus Rex and Triceratops dinosaurs, snakes, and mammals; Continents separated; Magnolias and water lilies.
Mass Extinction / Volcanos / Flooding / Meteors / Dinosaurs Disappear

65-55 MYA (Million Years Ago)
Cenozoic-Tertiary- Paleocene Epoch: "Rise of Mammals"

55-38 MYA
Eocene Epoch: Arrival of primitive horses

38-25 MYA
Oligocene Epoch: Arrival of first Primates

25-5 MYA
Miocene Epoch: Arrival of Apes

5-2 MYA
Pliocene Epoch: First Man

2 MYA to present
Quaternary

2 MYA to 10,000 YA
Pleistocene Epoch: Rise of Man

10,000 YA to present
Holocene Epoch: Modern Man, "Ice Age;" New sea and flying animals appear, whales, flowering plants, herbs, saber-toothed cats, rhinoceros, continents are completely separated and are as we know them to be today.

Timeline of World Civilizations

Prehistoric

13.7 Billion B.C.
Formation of Universe

4.5 Billion B.C.
Planet Earth Formed

3 Billion B.C.
First Signs of Life in Oceans

100,000 B.C.
First Homo sapiens (Wise Man) in South Africa

70,000 B.C.
First Neanderthal man

15,000 B.C.
Migrations from Asia into the Americas across Bering Strait

10,000 B.C.
Developments of settlements in Mesopotamia

9000 B. C
Founding of Jericho (Earliest known city in the world)

Ancient:

3500 B.C.
Sumerians in Mesopotamia; Capital city of Ur

3100 B.C.
Egyptians in Egypt, Sudan, Palestine; Capital city of Thebes

2680 B.C.
The Great Pyramids of Giza are built in Egypt

2500 B.C.
Minoans in Greece; Capital city of Crete

2500 B.C.
Hebrews in Israel

2300 B.C.
Babylonians in Mesopotamia; Capitol city of Babylon

2200 B.C.
Olmecs in Mexico and Central America (Mesoamerica)

2200 B.C.
Chinese in Eastern Asia; Capital city of Zion

2250-1250 B.C.
Stonehenge

2000 B.C.
Mycenaeans in Greece

1327 B.C.
Death of King Tutankhamen of Egypt

1800 B.C.
Mayas in Mexico: Capital city of Tikal

1500 B.C.
Hebrews in Canaan

1500 B.C.
Phoenicians in Lebanon/Mediterranean; Capital city of Tyro

Classical:

800 B.C.
Persians in Iran; Capital city of Persepolis

800 B.C.
Greeks in Greece; Capital city of Athens

800 B.C.
Etruscans in Northern Italy

700 B.C.
Romans in the Italian Peninsula; Capital city of Rome

600 B.C.
Hanging Gardens of Babylon

TIMELINE OF WORLD CIVILIZATIONS

500 B.C.
Celts in Central and Western Europe

500 B.C.
Zapotecs in the Oaxaca Valley of Central Mexico

500 B.C.
Indians in India

480 B.C.
Pantheon build in Greece

221 B.C.
Great Wall of China begun

200 B.C.
Berbers in North Africa

200 B.C.
Unknown civilization at Teotihuacan in Central Mexico

100 A.D.
Nazca Indians in Southern Peru

200 A.D.
Huns in Europe and Asia (Eurasia)

Medieval:

500 A.D.
Byzantines in Turkey and North Africa; Capital city of Constantinople

500 A.D.
Arabs on the Arabian Peninsula: Capital city of Baghdad

600 A.D.
Anglo-Saxons in the British Isles

600 A.D.
Indonesians in Malaysia and Indonesia

700 A.D.
Moors in North Africa and Spain

700 A.D.
Anasazi in the Southwestern United States

700 A.D.
Slavs in Eastern Europe and Poland.

800 A.D.
Toltecs in Central Mexico; Capital city of Tula

900 A.D.
Mixtecs of Central Mexico

900 A.D.
French in France and Western Europe

900 A.D.
Iberians in Spain and Portugal: Capital city of Madrid

900 A.D.
Italians in the Italian Peninsula

900 A.D.
Russians in Russia

1000 A.D.
Zimbabweans in Southern Africa

1000 A.D.
Turks in Turkey

1100 A.D.
Polynesians in Hawaii and the Pacific

1200 A.D.
Balts in the Baltic Sea

1200 A.D.
Incas in Peru and Ecuador; Capital city of Cuzco

1300 A.D.
Aztecs in Mexico; Capital city of Tenochtitlan

1400 A.D.
Ottomans in Egypt and Mesopotamia; Capital city of Istanbul

1400 A.D.
Bantu in South-Central Africa

TIMELINE OF WORLD CIVILIZATIONS

Modern:

1500
Dutch in the Low Countries

1500
Ashanti in West Africa

1600
Iroquois in the Northeastern United States

1700
Cherokee in the Southeastern United States

1700
Anglo-Saxons in the Americas

1800
Sioux in the Mid-Western United States

TIMELINE OF HISTORICAL PERIODS

Timeline of Historical Periods

Prehistory

Stone Age; Bronze Age; Iron Age
3500-599 B.C. – Mesopotamia, Ancient region in Southeast Asia
3300-31 B.C. – Ancient Greece
3000-2000 B.C. – Old Kingdom in Egypt; Great Pyramids of Giza
2000-1300 B.C. – Middle Kingdom in Egypt
1600-1050 B.C. – Shang Dynasty in China
1550-1070 B.C. – New Kingdom in Egypt
1200-500 B.C. – Zhou Dynasty in China
1000 B.C.-300 A.D. – Kush Civilization in Egypt
509-476 B.C. – Ancient Rome in Italy
221-206 B.C. – Qin Dynasty in China
206 B.C.-220 A.D. – Han Dynasty in China
200-700 A.D. – Migration Period in Europe
618-907 A.D. – Tang Dynasty in China (The Golden Age of Ancient China)

Middle Ages

133-900 – Dark Ages in Europe after the fall of Western Roman Empire
300-1400 – Middle Ages in Europe
500-1000 – Early Middle Ages in Europe
700-1300 – Islamic Golden Age in the Middle East; Growth of African Kingdoms
793-1066 – Viking Age in Scandinavia. (Norway, Sweden, Denmark); The Norsemen explore the oceans and other countries of the world.
960-1279 – Song Dynasty in China
1000-1450 – High Middle Ages in Europe
Feudalism – European Political System
1279-1368 – Yuan Dynasty in China with Mongol Emperors
1300-1500 – Late Middle Ages in Europe
Renaissance (Re-birth) in Italy and Europe

Early Modern Period

1299-1923 – Ottoman Empire in Turkey
1368-1644 – Ming Dynasty in China
1400-1650 – Age of Discovery/Exploration; Europeans explore the world.
1500-1600 – Protestant Reformation; Europeans establish Protestant churches.
1526-1827 – Mahgal Empire in India
1558-1603 – Elizabethan Period in England; Queen Elizabeth I
1630-1783 – Colonial Period in the United States
1754-1753 – The French and Indian War; British defeat the French and Native Americans
1775-1783 – American Revolutionary War; The American Colonies defeat Great Britain.
1700-1800 – Age of Enlightenment; European intellectual and scientific reason

TIMELINE OF HISTORICAL PERIODS

<u>Modern Era</u>

1700-1900 – Industrial Revolution: Time of inventions and machines.
1714-1830 – Georgian Era in England; King Georg
1799-1815 – Napoleonic Era in France and Europe; Napoleon Bonaparte
1837-1901 – Victorian Era in England; Queen Victoria
1850-1920 – Romantic Era in Europe; Artistic and intellectual movement
1870-1890 – Gilded Age in the United States; Fancy Lifestyles
1880-1920 – Progressive Age in the United States; Social activism and political reform
1900-1945 – Machine Age; New machines and technology
1901-1910 – Edwardian Age in the United Kingdom; King Edward VII
1914-1918 – World War I; Allied Powers (U.S) defeat Axis Powers
1918-1939 – Interwar Period; Global Depression and Tension
1929-1939 – The Great Depression; Global Economic Collapse
1939-1945 – World War II; The Allies (U.S) defeat Germany, Italy, and Japan
1945-1989 – Cold War; United States and Soviet Union Rivalry
1945-Present – Atomic Age; Global use of Atomic Technology
1967-Present – Space Age; Exploration of Space
1975-Present – Information Age; Computerization

Present - Digital World

NOTABLE AMERICAN AND WORLD TRAGEDIES

Notable American and World Tragedies

There have been a the great number of earthquakes, hurricanes, tornados, tsunamis, landslides, typhoons, cyclones, tidal waves, avalanches, blizzards, fires, wildfires, floods, droughts, dust storms, mining explosions, flu pandemics, plagues, shipwrecks, flight disasters, train wrecks, invasions, assassinations, massacres, and wars that have greatly impacted our world. The following is a short list of noteworthy tragedies in our recent history:

1360
Black Death – A type of bubonic plague, this was one of the most devastating pandemics in human history that spread across Europe and Asia and killed an estimated 200 million people.

1865
President Abraham Lincoln assassinated by John Wilkes Booth – Ford's Theatre in Washington, D.C.

1871
Great Chicago Fire – Illinois

1900
Galveston Hurricane – Texas

1906
San Francisco Earthquake - California

1912
Sinking of the Titanic Ocean Liner - North Atlantic off the coast of Newfoundland

1915
Sinking of Lusitania Ship by German U-boat off the coast of Ireland

1918-1919
Flu Pandemic- Influenza outbreak – World-wide

1929-1940
Stock Market Crash and the Great Depression – America

1937
Hindenburg Airship Fire – New Jersey (Note: Hindenburg and Titanic disasters regarded as "Fire and Ice")

1938-1945
Holocaust, the genocide or killing of European Jews by the Nazis during World War II – Germany

1941
Pearl Harbor – Surprise air attack by Japanese on the U.S. naval base in Oahu on December 7th, as Roosevelt declared "the date which will live in infamy," and prompts the U.S. to enter World War II – Hawaii

NOTABLE AMERICAN AND WORLD TRAGEDIES

1945
Atomic Bombing of Hiroshima and Nagasaki – On August 5, 1945, during the later stages of World War II, the United States B-29 bomber, the *Enola Gay*, dropped an atomic bomb over the Japanese cities of Hiroshima and Nagasaki, immediately killing 70,000 civilians, and 70,000 more within five years from radiation.

1963
President John F. Kennedy assassinated by Lee Harvey Oswald – Dallas, Texas

1968
Civil rights activist Dr. Martin Luther King assassinated by James Earl Ray – Memphis, Tennessee
Senator Robert F. Kennedy assassinated by Sirhan Sirhan – Los Angeles, California

1970
Apollo 13 Mission to the Moon – An oxygen tank explodes soon after take-off damaging the Service Module, but all three astronauts, James Lovell, Jack Swigert, and Fred Haise are brought safely back to Earth through the efforts of many at Mission Control in Houston, Texas.

1980
Mt. St. Helens Volcano Eruption – Washington

1986
Challenger Space Shuttle Explosion – 73 Seconds after take-off from Cape Canaveral, Florida

1986
Chernobyl Nuclear Power Plant Explosion – Ukraine

1989
Exxon Valdez oil tanker spills over 11 million gallons of crude oil into Prince Edward Sound after hitting a reef – Alaska

1995
Truck bombing of the Oklahoma City Federal Building – Oklahoma

1999
Columbine High School Shooting – Colorado

2001
9-11 / Terrorist airstrike of World Trade Center, Pentagon, New York, Virginia, and Pennsylvania

2005
Hurricane Katrina – New Orleans, Louisiana and Mississippi

WONDERS OF THE WORLD

Wonders of the World

The Seven Wonders of the Ancient World

1. The Great Pyramid of Giza (Only Wonder of Ancient World still in existence!)
2. The Hanging Gardens of Babylon
3. The Temple of Artemis at Ephesus
4. The Statue of Zeus at Olympia
5. The Mausoleum at Halicarnassus
6. The Lighthouse of Alexandria
7. The Colossus at Rhodes

The Seven New Wonders of the World

1. The Great Wall of China – China
2. Petra – City that was carved into the rock in Jordan
3. Christ the Redeemer – Large statue in Brazil
4. Machu Picchu – Lost city of the Incas in Peru
5. Chichen Itza – Mayan city in Mexico
6. Coliseum – Italy
7. Taj Mahal – India

The Seven Natural Wonders of the World

1. Grand Canyon – Arizona USA
2. Great Barrier Reef – Australia
3. Harbor of Rio de Janeiro – Brazil
4. Mount Everest – Himalayas
5. Northern Lights (Aurora Borealis) – Alaska
6. Paricutin Volcano – Mexico
7. Victoria Falls – Zimbabwe, Africa

The Seven Wonders of the Underwater World

1. Great Barrier Reef – Australia
2. Lake Baikal – Siberia
3. Galapagos Islands – West of Ecuador
4. Deep-Sea Vents – Yellowstone Park in Wyoming; New Zealand; Galapagos Rift
5. Northern Red Sea – Between Africa and Asia
6. Belize Barrier Reef – Off the shores of Belize
7. Palau – Small nation near the Philippines

WONDERS OF THE WORLD

The Seven Wonders of the Industrial World

1. SS Great Eastern – Iron Steamship from England
2. Bell Rock Lighthouse – Scotland
3. Brooklyn Bridge – New York City, New York
4. London Sewerage System – England
5. First Transcontinental Railroad – Connected the eastern U.S. with the western U.S.
6. Panama Canal – Panama that connects the Atlantic with the Pacific
7. Hoover Dam – Hydroelectric dam in Arizona and Nevada

ANSWERS - LANGUAGE ARTS

APPENDICES – Answers to Questions

APPENDIX 1: Chapter 1 – Language Arts

Language Arts – Pre-School

1. Says name
2. Says first name
3. Says letters in first name
4. Says letters in last name
5. Says middle name
6. Says last name
7. Says age
8. Names person older
9. Names person younger
10. Names person of same age
11. Says birth date
12. Says current month
13. Says today's day of the week
14. Says tomorrow's day
15. Says yesterday's day
16. Can express feelings
17. Speaks in sentences
18. Converses with adult
19. Asks a question
20. Expresses how feeling today
21. Orders yesterday's activities
22. Listens carefully when being book is read aloud
23. Answers questions about book
24. Can re-tell a story
25. Shows correct direction to read a book
26. Recites a nursery rhyme
27. Rhymes two and shoe
28. Finishes poem, "Rain,Rain"
29. Finishes poem, "Diddle Diddle Dumpling"
30. Finishes poem, "Wee Willie Winkie"
31. Finishes poem, "Peter,Peter"
32. Finishes poem, "To market,to market"
33. Sings "Kookaburra"
34. Sings "Pop Goes the Weasel"
35. Sings "John Jacob"
36. Sings "Happy Birthday"
37. Sings "Twinkle Twinkle"
38. Sings "Rock-A-Bye Baby"
39. Sings "Row, Row, Row your Boat"
40. Sings "Old MacDonald"
41. Sings "Here we go round."
42. Sings/Dances "Ring around the Rosie"
43. Sings/Motions "This Little Piggy"
44. Sings/Motions "Eensey, Weensey Spider"
45. Sings/Motions "Five Little Monkeys"
46. Sings/Motions "I'm a Little Teapot"
47. Sings/Motions "Heads, Shoulders..."
48. Sings/Claps "B-I-N-G-O"
49. Sings/Claps "If You're Happy"
50. "Goldilocks and the Three Bears"
51. Red
52. Three
53. Wolf
54. Straw, sticks, and bricks
55. Pigs live in brick house happily ever after
56. Names a story
57. Draws a straight line
58. Scissors
59. Knows how to use scissors
60. Quiet, walk, observe safety rules
61. Follows rules for board game
62. Says a familiar board game
63. Says favorite toy
64. Says favorite food
65. Chew with mouth closed; use napkin etc.
66. Please
67. Thank you
68. You're welcome.
69. Hello Mr. __
70. Hello Mrs. __
71. Says if hot or cold today
72. Says if it is day or night
73. Morning
74. Night/Evening
75. Afternoon
76. Correctly states time of day
77. Breakfast
78. Lunch
79. Supper/Dinner
80. Correctly states current season
81. States gender
82. Knows number of siblings and names them
83. Says pets and their names
84. Feed/Water/Groom/Vet/Take outside etc.
85. Legs
86. Mouth
87. Hand
88. Shows left hand
89. Shows right hand
90. States correct hand
91. Can dress self
92. Can zip

ANSWERS - LANGUAGE ARTS

93. Can button
94. Can tie shoes
95. Nose
96. Ears
97. Eyes
98. Feet
99. Points and names parts of body
100. Green
101. Names green things
102. Blue
103. Names blue things
104. States eye color
105. States hair color
106. Red
107. Names red things
108. Yellow
109. Names yellow things
110. Names orange things
111. Names black things
112. Names white things
113. Names pink things
114. Names purple things
115. States color of room, etc.
116. Sings alphabet
117. Words
118. Points to the cover of this book
119. Points to back of book
120. Points out page in book
121. "Pretends" to read book
122. Can turn pages
123. Car, bike, train, plane, bus, boat, etc.
124. Ambulance/Rescue Squad
125. Dump truck
126. Tow truck
127. Bus/Car
128. Fire truck
129. Water/Milk/Oil
130. Boat/Ship
131. Motorcycle
132. Yes
133. Train/Monorail/Subway
134. Airplane/Jet
135. Tractor
136. Hammer, wrench, screw driver, etc.
137. Cow, pig, chicken, etc.
138. Elephant, Giraffe, Tiger, etc.
139. Whale, shark, octopus, etc.
140. Deer, bear, raccoon, etc.
141. Butterfly, fly, ant, ladybug, etc.
142. Dog, cat, bird, rabbit, etc.
143. Tiger, zebra, etc.
144. Dolphins, fish, etc.
145. Bird, eagle, bats, etc.
146. Deer, sheep, buffalo, moose, etc.
147. Dogs, cats, wolves, etc.
148. Tigers, lions, bears, cats, etc.
149. Wolf, bat, dog, tiger, etc.
150. Giraffe
151. Elephant
152. Imitates bird sound "Tweet-tweet"
153. Imitates dog sound "Woof"
154. Imitates cat sound "Meow"
155. Imitates frog sound "Ribbit"
156. Imitates horse sound
157. Growls like a bear
158. Imitates monkey sound
159. Imitates cow sound "Moo"
160. Squawks like a chicken
161. Quacks like a duck
162. Elephant
163. Mouse
164. States who is taller
165. House
166. Points up
167. Down
168. Mentions items in bedroom
169. Out
170. Points to front of book
171. Back
172. Mentions items on bed
173. Off
174. Says if TV on or off
175. Mentions items under bed
176. Over
177. Points to top of page
178. Bottom
179. Points to middle of page
180. States middle name
181. Points to bottom of page
182. Top
183. Happy
184. Day
185. In front of
186. Below
187. Big/large
188. High
189. Under
190. Less
191. Different
192. Names person same size
193. Names something besides bed
194. Names something inside dresser
195. Names something outside house
196. Right side up
197. Names a hot food (soup)
198. Names a cold food (ice cream)
199. Names fast animal (cheetah)
200. Names slow animal (turtle)
201. Different
202. Reads word "a"
203. Reads word "and"
204. Reads word "away"
205. Reads word "big"
206. Reads word "blue"
207. Reads word "can"
208. Reads word "come"
209. Reads word "down"
210. Reads word "find"
211. Reads word "for"
212. Reads word "funny"

ANSWERS - LANGUAGE ARTS

213. Reads word "go"
214. Reads word "help"
215. Reads word "here"
216. Reads word "I"
217. Reads word "in"
218. Reads word "is"
219. Reads word "it"
220. Reads word "jump"
221. Reads word "little"
222. Reads word "look"
223. Reads word "make"
224. Reads word "me"
225. Reads word "my"
226. Reads word "not"
227. Reads word "one"
228. Reads word "play"
229. Reads word "red"
230. Reads word "run"
231. Reads word "said"
232. Reads word "see"
233. Reads word "the"
234. Reads word "three"
235. Reads word "to"
236. Reads word "two"
237. Reads word "up"
238. Reads word "we"
239. Reads word "where"
240. Reads word "yellow"
241. Reads word "you"

Language Arts – Kindergarten

242. German word
243. Children's Garden
244. Sings alphabet
245. Says other "a" words.
246. Says other "b" words
247. Says other "c" words
248. Says other "d" words
249. Says other "e" words
250. Says other "f" words
251. Says other "g" words
252. Says other "h" words
253. Says other "i" words
254. Says other "j" words
255. Says other "k" words
256. Says other "l" words
257. Says other "m" words
258. Says other "n" words
259. Says other "o" words
260. Says other "p" words
261. Says other "q" words
262. Says other "r" words
263. Says other "s" words
264. Says other "t" words
265. Says other "u" words
266. Says other "v" words
267. Says other "w" words
268. Says other "x" words
269. Says other "y" words
270. Says other "z" words
271. Images of bones or teeth
272. Cat, bat, etc.
273. c-a-t
274. d-a-d
275. Glad, mad, dad, etc.
276. Finishes "Hickory Dickory"
277. Finishes "Diddle Diddle"
278. Finishes "Little Bo Peep"
279. Finishes "Little Boy Blue"
280. Finishes "Ba Ba Black Sheep"
281. Finishes "One, Two…"
282. Finishes "Rain, rain..."
283. Finishes "It's raining..."
284. Finishes "Roses are Red"
285. Finishes "Jack and Jill"
286. Finishes "Jack Be Nimble"
287. Finishes "Little Miss Muffet"
288. Finishes "Mary had a lamb"
289. Finishes "Old Mother Hubbard"
290. Finishes "Old King Cole"
291. Finishes "Three Blind Mice"
292. Finishes "Three Little Kittens"
293. Finishes "There was an old woman"
294. Finishes "Star light, star bright"
295. Words
296. Sentences
297. Paragraphs
298. Books, newspapers, etc.
299. Stories, letters, cards, etc.
300. States correct writing hand
301. Computer keyboard
302. "Ask Me Smarter"
303. Says title of favorite book
304. Author
305. Draws pictures
306. False
307. True
308. False
309. Yes
310. Non-fiction
311. Books, magazines, computers, etc.
312. Use library card
313. Due date
314. Media Specialist/Librarian
315. Overdue
316. Yes
317. Non-fiction
318. Fiction
319. Preparing a food or dish
320. Winter
321. Autumn/Fall

ANSWERS - LANGUAGE ARTS

322. Spring
323. Summer
324. Puppy
325. Kitten
326. Heavy
327. Light
328. After school
329. States time of day
330. Round
331. Twelve
332. States clock short hand number
333. States clock long hand number
334. Noon
335. Midnight
336. Calendar
337. Seven
338. Names days of week
339. Saturday and Sunday
340. States objects to right of bed
341. States objects to left of bed
342. States objects between bed and door
343. Names object far away
344. Names object close by
345. Song
346. Chooses song to sing
347. Says a famous story
348. Identifies familiar stories
349. Fables
350. States familiar fable
351. Longest
352. Bigger
353. Best
354. The worst
355. Quietly
356. Hopefully
357. Gold
358. Silver
359. Copper
360. Sorry
361. And dogs
362. Leap
363. There's a way
364. Best friend
365. Do onto you
366. Says word "all"
367. Says word "am"
368. Says word "are"
369. Says word "at"
370. Says word "ate"
371. Says word "be"
372. Says word "black"
373. Says word "brown"
374. Says word "but"
375. Says word "came"
376. Says word "did"
377. Says word "do"
378. Says word "eat"
379. Says word "for"
380. Says word "get"
381. Says word "good"
382. Says word "have"
383. Says word "he"
384. Says word "into"
385. Says word "like"
386. Says word "must"
387. Says word "new"
388. Says word "no"
389. Says word "now"
390. Says word "on"
391. Says word "our"
392. Says word "out"
393. Says word "please"
394. Says word "pretty"
395. Says word "ran"
396. Says word "ride"
397. Says word "saw"
398. Says word "say"
399. Says word "she"
400. Says word "so"
401. Says word "soon"
402. Says word "that"
403. Says word "there"
404. Says word "they"
405. Says word "this"
406. Says word "too"
407. Says word "under"
408. Says word "want"
409. Says word "was"
410. Says word "well"
411. Says word "went"
412. Says word "what"
413. Says word "white"
414. Says word "who"
415. Says word "will"
416. Says word "with"
417. Says word "yes"

Language Arts – 1st Grade

418. Says and spells first name
419. Says middle name
420. Says and spells last name
421. 26
422. Cites a word for each letter
423. A-E-I-O-U
424. Consonants
425. H-a-t
426. Says –an words
427. Says –at words
428. Says –ap words
429. Says –ab words
430. Says –ad words
431. Says –am words

ANSWERS - LANGUAGE ARTS

432. Says –ack words
433. Says –and words
434. Says –ash words
435. Says –ail words
436. Says –ain words
437. Says –air words
438. Says –ate words
439. Says –ake words
440. Says –ale words
441. Says –ame words
442. Says –ay words
443. Says –all words
444. Says –aw words
445. Says –ar words
446. Says –ark words
447. Says –art words
448. Says –ank words
449. Says –int words
450. Says –ed words
451. Says –en words
452. Says –et words
453. Says –eck words
454. Says –ell words
455. Says –est words
456. Says –in words
457. Says –ip words
458. Says –it words
459. Fun, bun, etc.
460. Fight, bite, sight, etc.
461. Look, took, etc.
462. Free, see, me, etc.
463. Test, west, etc.
464. Deep, weep, etc.
465. Claps to "Twinkle, Twinkle"
466. Nursery rhymes
467. Fairy tales
468. No
469. The Three Little Pigs
470. Fables
471. Identifies written works
472. Identifies visual media
473. H-o-p
474. H-o-p-e
475. F-r-o-g
476. S-t-o-p
477. T-r-i-p
478. S-h-i-p
479. S-e-a
480. S-e-e
481. B-o-o-k
482. T-r-e-e
483. C-o-w
484. F-a-n, etc.
485. c
486. a
487. t
488. ch
489. th
490. wh
491. sh
492. ng
493. s
494. ed
495. er
496. est
497. ly
498. Short
499. Long
500. Short
501. Long
502. Short
503. Long
504. Silent
505. Short
506. Long
507. Birth-day
508. Compound
509. Compound
510. Foot-ball
511. Sometimes, somewhere, etc.
512. Can and not
513. Apostrophe
514. It and is
515. I'm
516. I'll
517. We'll
518. Are and not
519. The t's or th's
520. The q's
521. u
522. Ant, cat, and dog
523. Ball
524. Period
525. Question mark
526. Exclamation point
527. Capital
528. Yes
529. Lower case
530. Action word
531. Thing
532. Yes
533. Ran
534. Park
535. Yes
536. Pretty
537. Says adjective(s)
538. Names a fiction story
539. Names a non-fiction story
540. Cinderella, Sleepy Beauty, etc.
541. Title
542. Author
543. Illustrator
544. Table of Contents/chapters
545. Depends on format
546. Publishes book to buy
547. 2015
548. Yes
549. Yes
550. Points out text
551. No

ANSWERS - LANGUAGE ARTS

552. Describes cover
553. Call number
554. Summarizes plot of Goldilocks
555. Forest, cottage, etc.
556. Tasted porridge/cereal
557. Sat in three chairs
558. House in woods; small, medium, big
559. Little girl with golden hair
560. Fantasy
561. Says favorite story
562. Sequences events of Goldilocks story
563. Prince
564. Glass slipper
565. The Ball
566. Midnight
567. Clothes and carriage will turn back
568. Glass Carriage
569. Opinion
570. A fact
571. Butterflies fly, etc.
572. Gives opinion about butterflies
573. Gives opinion about something
574. Looked
575. Looking
576. Looks
577. Look
578. Listened
579. A caption
580. Is
581. Are
582. Am
583. Are
584. Has
585. Have
586. Have
587. Have
588. Are
589. T-o
590. T-w-o
591. T-o-o
592. Dogs
593. Cat
594. Witches
595. Beaches
596. Baby
597. Out
598. Dry
599. Near/close
600. Hot
601. Fast/Quick
602. Whisper
603. Sweet
604. New
605. Full
606. Win
607. Rich
608. Day
609. Weak
610. Wild
611. Back
612. Pretty
613. Beginning or start
614. Morning
615. Evening
616. Before
617. After
618. Away
619. Flowers
620. Try and try again
621. Perfect
622. Merrier
623. Home
624. Says today's date
625. Says yesterday's day
626. Names days of week
627. Names 12 months of year
628. Says birth date
629. Says word "after"
630. Says word "again"
631. Says word "an"
632. Says word "any"
633. Says word "as"
634. Says word "ask"
635. Says word "by"
636. Says word "could"
637. Says word "every"
638. Says word "fly"
639. Says word "from"
640. Says word "give"
641. Says word "giving"
642. Says word "has"
643. Says word "had"
644. Says word "her"
645. Says word "him"
646. Says word "his"
647. Says word "how"
648. Says word "just"
649. Says word "know"
650. Says word "let"
651. Says word "live"
652. Says word "may"
653. Says word "of"
654. Says word "old"
655. Says word "once"
656. Says word "open"
657. Says word "over"
658. Says word "put"
659. Says word "round"
660. Says word "some"
661. Says word "stop"
662. Says word "take"
663. Says word "thank"
664. Says word "them"
665. Says word "then"
666. Says word "think"
667. Says word "walk"
668. Says word "were"
669. Says word "when"

ANSWERS - LANGUAGE ARTS

Language Arts – 2nd Grade

670. Yes
671. Yes
672. Yes, can print all letters
673. Says words (adios, crepe, frankfurter, etc.)
674. Articulates books of liking
675. Can sound out words
676. Looking at pictures, etc.
677. Yes, can identify main ideas
678. Yes
679. Can re-tell story
680. Can sequence events in a story
681. Can identify genre
682. Yes, can imagine story
683. Yes
684. Compares and contrasts 2 stories
685. Find information
686. Books, internet, etc.
687. Dictionary
688. Alphabetical
689. Sand, show, sound, stop
690. Same, sand
691. Yes
692. Says books and magazines read
693. Says name of local paper
694. No
695. Long
696. Short
697. Short
698. Long
699. Spells was
700. Spells were
701. Spells says
702. Spells said
703. Spells who
704. Spells why
705. Spells light
706. Spells right
707. Spells bedroom
708. Spells sometimes
709. Spells sailboat
710. Spells happy
711. Spells silly
712. Spells pretty
713. Spells know
714. Spells wrong
715. Opposite
716. Loud
717. The same
718. Large, huge, etc.
719. Little, tiny, etc.
720. Homonym
721. Key lock
722. You are right or correct
723. A prefix
724. A suffix
725. The suffix
726. Smallest
727. Slowly
728. Ageless, fearless, timeless, etc.
729. Adorable, comfortable, invisible, etc.
730. Refund, reuse, review, etc.
731. Unsafe, unbelievable, etc.
732. Punctuation
733. Quotation
734. Sleeping
735. Climbed
736. Finished; Uses word in sentence
737. Did
738. Ate
739. Read
740. Wore
741. Dried
742. Saw
743. Came
744. He was
745. They were
746. Went
747. Found
748. Said
749. Describes last book read
750. Has written letter
751. An end
752. Table of Contents
753. Index
754. Says yes or no
755. Anne Frank, et al
756. To record thoughts
757. Yes
758. Can identify sentence
759. Can write a sentence
760. Can write a question
761. Can write exclamatory sentence
762. Can write letter
763. Can write thank you note
764. Can write report
765. Can write story
766. Can write poem
767. For gift, kind gesture, party, etc.
768. Can draft ideas on paper
769. Re-write and modify
770. Check for errors
771. Yes
772. No, copyright infringement
773. Can write upper and lower case letters
774. Can write report on book
775. Books, internet, atlases, etc.
776. Informational book organized alphabetically
777. Can identify all parts of book
778. Recognizes genres with examples
779. Biography
780. The illustrator
781. The author
782. Encyclopedia
783. Can turn on computer

ANSWERS - LANGUAGE ARTS

784. Identifies keyboard, monitor, and mouse
785. Yes, keyboarding important
786. Can conduct basic search
787. No
788. Cites inappropriate use of internet
789. Can do basic computer search in library
790. Can load basic software
791. Reads word "always"
792. Reads word "around"
793. Reads word "because"
794. Reads word "been"
795. Reads word "before"
796. Reads word "best"
797. Reads word "both"
798. Reads word "buy"
799. Reads word "call"
800. Reads word "cold"
801. Reads word "does"
802. Reads word "don't"
803. Reads word "fast"
804. Reads word "first"
805. Reads word "five"
806. Reads word "found"
807. Reads word "gave"
808. Reads word "goes"
809. Reads word "green"
810. Reads word "it's"
811. Reads word "made"
812. Reads word "many"
813. Reads word "off"
814. Reads word "or"
815. Reads word "pull"
816. Reads word "read"
817. Reads word "right"
818. Reads word "sing"
819. Reads word "sit"
820. Reads word "sleep"
821. Reads word "tell"
822. Reads word "their"
823. Reads word "these"
824. Reads word "those"
825. Reads word "upon"
826. Reads word "us"
827. Reads word "use"
828. Reads word "very"
829. Reads word "wash"
830. Reads word "wish"
831. Reads word "work"
832. Reads word "would"
833. Reads word "write"
834. Reads word "your"

Language Arts – 3rd Grade

835. Yes
836. Yes
837. Reads silently
838. Reads aloud
839. Sounds out new and unfamiliar words
840. 26
841. A, E, I O, U (sometimes y)
842. Yes
843. Makes "th" sound
844. Makes "st" sound
845. Makes "bl" sound
846. Makes "gr" sound
847. Makes "sc" sound
848. Says "br" word
849. Says "cr" word
850. Says "dr" word
851. Says "fr" word
852. Says "gr" word
853. Says "pr" word
854. Says "tr" word
855. Says "bl" word
856. Says "cl" word
857. Says "fl" word
858. Says "gl" word
859. Says "pl" word
860. Says "sl" word
861. Says "sc" word
862. Says "sk" word
863. Says "sm" word
864. Says "sn" word
865. Says "sp" word
866. Says "st" word
867. Says "sw" word
868. Says "scr" word
869. Says "squ" word
870. Says "str" word
871. Says "spr" word
872. Says "spl" word
873. Yes
874. Deputy
875. Primary
876. Alphabetical
877. u
878. Yes
879. Yes
880. Hard "c"
881. Hard "c"
882. Hard "c"
883. Says hard "c" words
884. Soft "c"
885. Soft "c"
886. Soft "c"
887. Says soft "c" words
888. Yes
889. Hard "g"
890. Hard "g"
891. Hard "g"
892. Soft "g"

ANSWERS - LANGUAGE ARTS

893. Soft "g"
894. Soft "g"
895. Yes
896. Yes, Y can be both
897. Yes
898. Consonant
899. Vowel
900. Vowel
901. An
902. An umbrella
903. An honor
904. A cat
905. An owl
906. A bird
907. An elephant
908. A chest
909. Find definition, syllables, etc.
910. Alphabetical
911. Can look up word in dictionary
912. Can identify right meaning of word
913. Declare, defend, destroy, device
914. Hum
915. Lima bean
916. "X"
917. Can have multiple definitions
918. Nail net
919. Coast cocoa
920. Crate credit
921. Yes
922. Syllables
923. Yes
924. Two syllables
925. Three syllables
926. One syllable
927. Two syllables
928. Four syllables
929. Yes, can blend syllables
930. Table
931. Monkey
932. Can divide words
933. Tur-tle
934. Snow-board-ing
935. Pop-u-la-tion
936. Yes, spelling is important
937. No
938. The "g" and "h" silent
939. Spells half
940. The letter "l"
941. Spells tough
942. The letters "gh"
943. Spells hop
944. Spells hope
945. Yes, final "e" silent
946. Long
947. Spells pail
948. Spells pale
949. Spells quit
950. Spells queen
951. u
952. c
953. Yes
954. Spells beige
955. Spells chief
956. Spells piece
957. Spells science
958. Spells receive
959. Spells thief
960. Compound words
961. Spells everything
962. Spells yourself
963. Spells butterfly
964. Spells somewhere
965. Spells sailboat
966. Spells grandfather
967. Names compound words
968. Yes
969. Recognizes base of word
970. Listen
971. Dependent
972. The beginning
973. Recognizes prefix
974. un
975. re
976. mis
977. un
978. in
979. pre
980. mis
981. re
982. inconsiderate
983. dis
984. im
985. un
986. ly
987. Base or root word
988. Pretty
989. Yes
990. End
991. Yes, they are common suffixes
992. Plays
993. Played
994. Playing
995. ous
996. less
997. ful
998. less
999. ily
1000. ful
1001. less
1002. or
1003. ist
1004. er
1005. ist
1006. ian
1007. ian
1008. Same thing
1009. Large, huge
1010. Intelligent, bright
1011. Mistake
1012. Dangerous

ANSWERS - LANGUAGE ARTS

1013. Rich
1014. Finished
1015. Walk
1016. Careful
1017. Afraid, terrified
1018. Helper, aid
1019. Large, big
1020. Sob
1021. Rich
1022. Moist
1023. The opposite
1024. Narrow
1025. Rough
1026. Easy
1027. Full
1028. Destroy
1029. Shallow
1030. Sweet
1031. Under
1032. Friend, comrade
1033. Light
1034. Rich
1035. Easy and soft
1036. Wild
1037. Wide
1038. Asleep
1039. Least
1040. Dry
1041. Break
1042. Yes
1043. Right: Turn right, you're right
1044. Yes
1045. Container; sport
1046. Measurement; outdoor space
1047. Insect; verb for airborne
1048. Crouch down; animal
1049. Container; verb for ability
1050. Baseball position; container for liquid
1051. Jewelry;: phone signal; circular marking
1052. Baseball stick; nocturnal animal
1053. C, a speech
1054. A, location of a building
1055. B, the writing on the envelope
1056. Yes
1057. Yes
1058. Yes
1059. Yes
1060. Flour
1061. Peace
1062. Cent and sent
1063. Yes
1064. By
1065. Bye
1066. Buy
1067. Yes
1068. To
1069. Too
1070. Two
1071. Yes
1072. Write

1073. There
1074. Their
1075. They're
1076. Yes
1077. Seize
1078. Seas
1079. Sees
1080. Cent or sent
1081. Claws
1082. Tail
1083. Vain
1084. Peak
1085. Flare
1086. Poll
1087. Earn
1088. Bow
1089. Wrote
1090. Bred
1091. Tense
1092. Air
1093. Pair
1094. Towed
1095. Fare
1096. Fair
1097. Blew
1098. Blue
1099. Waist
1100. Waste
1101. Principal
1102. Principle
1103. Threw; through
1104. Meet; meat
1105. Won; one
1106. Yes
1107. Can identify genres
1108. Yes
1109. Tall tales
1110. Folktale
1111. Fairy tale
1112. Made-up
1113. Myths
1114. Yes
1115. Yes
1116. Cover, pictures, etc.
1117. Yes
1118. Yes
1119. Yes
1120. Yes
1121. Yes
1122. Plain lady marries prince
1123. Cinderella, prince, wicked family
1124. Home and prince's castle
1125. Lady transforms into princess etc.
1126. Yes
1127. Fact
1128. Opinion
1129. Fact can be proven
1130. Personal judgment
1131. Yes
1132. Identifies paragraph

745

ANSWERS - LANGUAGE ARTS

1133. Five
1134. Yes, can identify sentence parts
1135. Person, place, or thing
1136. Performs the action
1137. Walked
1138. Walk, run, jump, danced, etc.
1139. Park
1140. Zoo, Kansas, Sam, computer, etc.
1141. Mrs. Smith
1142. Dr. Smith, Chicago, Mozart, etc.
1143. Yes
1144. Is
1145. Have
1146. Substitutes for a noun
1147. Maya
1148. She
1149. He
1150. It
1151. I, you, he, she, it, we, they, etc.
1152. Describes a verb
1153. Slowly
1154. ly
1155. Never
1156. Quickly, easily, here, out, now, very
1157. Too
1158. Also
1159. To
1160. Two
1161. Indent
1162. Topic sentence
1163. Identifies punctuation mark
1164. Apostrophe
1165. John's books
1166. I-t apostrophe s
1167. It is
1168. Isn't
1169. Don't
1170. I'll
1171. They're
1172. Yes
1173. Yes, can write cursive
1174. Yes
1175. Drafting
1176. Revising
1177. Editing
1178. Find and correct errors
1179. Yes
1180. Publishing
1181. Idiom
1182. Easy to do
1183. Words
1184. Choosers
1185. Romans do
1186. Pod
1187. Leg
1188. Beans
1189. Dogs
1190. Cap
1191. Do onto you
1192. Upper case
1193. Subject
1194. Alex
1195. Predicate
1196. Eats ice cream
1197. Purred softly
1198. First word
1199. Yes
1200. Wisconsin
1201. Yes
1202. Yes
1203. Yes
1204. Cat
1205. Wife
1206. Tooth
1207. Goose
1208. Penny
1209. Dogs
1210. Turtles
1211. Echoes
1212. Potatoes
1213. Tomatoes
1214. Heroes
1215. Boxes
1216. Families
1217. Pennies
1218. Qualities
1219. Halves
1220. Leaves
1221. Thieves
1222. Wolves
1223. Selves
1224. Knives
1225. Lives
1226. Fish
1227. Deer
1228. Sheep
1229. Men
1230. Women
1231. Persons/People
1232. Children
1233. Mice
1234. Feet
1235. Teeth
1236. Oxen
1237. Copy
1238. Geese
1239. Fly
1240. Katie
1241. Arizona
1242. Thanksgiving Day
1243. Names specific river
1244. Names specific city
1245. Names specific athlete
1246. Names specific president
1247. Names specific street
1248. Names specific month
1249. Names specific holiday
1250. Names specific ocean
1251. Names specific artist
1252. Leaves

ANSWERS - LANGUAGE ARTS

1253. Noun
1254. Cites nouns
1255. Yes
1256. Describes an action
1257. Drove
1258. Lake
1259. Cites action verbs
1260. Verbs of being
1261. Am
1262. Is
1263. Are
1264. Was
1265. Were
1266. Has
1267. Have
1268. Present
1269. Past
1270. Future
1271. Played
1272. Cried
1273. Went
1274. Ate
1275. Bought
1276. Made
1277. Felt
1278. Heard
1279. Thought
1280. Saw
1281. Kept
1282. Brought
1283. Was
1284. Did
1285. Knew
1286. Broke
1287. Began
1288. Had
1289. Paid
1290. Gave
1291. Cut
1292. Told
1293. Spoke
1294. Sent
1295. Took
1296. Met
1297. Taught
1298. Left
1299. Found
1300. Read
1301. Flew
1302. Got
1303. Swam
1304. Say
1305. Shake
1306. Ring
1307. Stand
1308. Find
1309. Blow
1310. Give
1311. Freeze
1312. Sleep
1313. Drink
1314. Describes a noun
1315. Curly
1316. Pretty
1317. Blonde
1318. Proper adjective
1319. American, Spanish, French, etc.
1320. Descriptive adjectives
1321. Adjectives
1322. Adjectives
1323. Adjectives
1324. Adjectives
1325. Taste adjectives
1326. Touch adjectives
1327. Adjectives
1328. Fun, crowded, tasty, etc.
1329. Demonstrative adjective
1330. Pretty, big, city, etc.
1331. Young, red, new, etc.
1332. Little, old, chocolate, etc.
1333. These
1334. Those
1335. This house
1336. That tree over there
1337. An adjective
1338. Bigger
1339. Biggest
1340. Taller, tallest
1341. Happier, happiest
1342. More peaceful, the most peaceful
1343. Friendlier, friendliest
1344. Better, best
1345. Worse, the worst
1346. More, the most
1347. Littler, the littlest
1348. Farther, the farthest
1349. Simile
1350. Bone
1351. Pie
1352. Bat
1353. Bee
1354. Feather
1355. Wind
1356. Apple
1357. Elephant
1358. An adverb
1359. Swiftly
1360. No
1361. Yes
1362. Adverbs of frequency
1363. Yes
1364. Adverbs of place
1365. Adverbs of purpose
1366. Adverbs of time
1367. Preposition
1368. Yes
1369. Under
1370. Uses correct prepositions
1371. Takes place of a noun
1372. She

ANSWERS - LANGUAGE ARTS

1373. She
1374. He
1375. They
1376. We
1377. I
1378. John and I
1379. Yes
1380. John invited me
1381. Yes
1382. To me
1383. Mine; my
1384. Hers; her
1385. His; his
1386. Yours; your
1387. Ours; our
1388. Theirs; their
1389. Yes
1390. Interjection
1391. Ouch
1392. Hooray
1393. Oh my
1394. Conjunction
1395. But
1396. And
1397. If
1398. Contraction
1399. Didn't
1400. Letter
1401. I'd
1402. I'll
1403. Wouldn't
1404. They've
1405. Haven't
1406. You're
1407. Would not
1408. Will not
1409. Declarative
1410. Interrogative
1411. Declarative
1412. Interrogative
1413. Is
1414. Are
1415. Yes
1416. Yes
1417. Yes
1418. Printing
1419. Ideally yes
1420. Yes
1421. Yes
1422. Yes
1423. Yes
1424. A sentence
1425. Yes
1426. Studied; good grade
1427. Flat tire; tow truck
1428. Period
1429. Comma
1430. Comma
1431. After singing and dancing
1432. After city name

1433. Question mark
1434. Exclamation point!
1435. Quotation marks
1436. Before do and after cream
1437. All in marks except, said Brittney
1438. Apostrophe
1439. Yes
1440. Before
1441. Marcos's bike
1442. Jack's
1443. After
1444. The singers' voices
1445. You're
1446. Abbreviation
1447. Period
1448. St.
1449. Ave.
1450. Dr.
1451. Varies
1452. U.S.
1453. Washington D.C.
1454. Oct.
1455. Ave.
1456. Bat, sat, rat, mat, etc.
1457. Pig
1458. Bet, get, set, jet, etc.
1459. Sight, fight, might, bright, etc.
1460. Bold, fold, gold, told, etc.
1461. Beat, feat, heat, meat, etc.
1462. A) how, low
1463. Disappointed
1464. Yes
1465. Yes
1466. Growled
1467. Amazed
1468. Sad
1469. Hid
1470. Dangerous
1471. Paragraph
1472. Indent
1473. Topic sentence
1474. Topic sentence
1475. Supporting sentences
1476. First, second, then, last, etc.
1477. Yes
1478. Names a story
1479. Can tell a story
1480. Can predict ending
1481. Yes
1482. Yes
1483. Snow White, Seven Dwarfs, Queen
1484. Castle, Forest
1485. Snow White hides in home with Dwarfs to escape wicked Queen.
1486. Snow White living with Dwarfs, etc.
1487. Magic mirror, poison apple, Dwarf names
1488. To gain information
1489. A fact
1490. An opinion
1491. How they are similar

ANSWERS - LANGUAGE ARTS

1492. How they are different
1493. Cites what currently reading
1494. Names genre
1495. Fiction
1496. Non-fiction
1497. Yes
1498. Dewey Decimal System
1499. Non-fiction
1500. Call numbers
1501. Encyclopedia, atlas, dictionary, etc.
1502. Historical fiction
1503. Different
1504. Yes
1505. Yes
1506. Biography
1507. Autobiography
1508. Yes
1509. Poetry
1510. Prose
1511. Myth
1512. Yes
1513. Science fiction
1514. Legend
1515. A folktale
1516. Yes
1517. Fable
1518. Fables
1519. Names fables
1520. Aesop
1521. Fiction
1522. Yes
1523. Yes
1524. Yes
1525. Yes
1526. Yes
1527. Greeting
1528. Yes
1529. Yes
1530. Middle of envelope
1531. Upper left corner
1532. Upper right corner
1533. Yes
1534. Occasion, time, date, etc.
1535. Yes
1536. Birthday gift, etc.
1537. Yes
1538. Applying for job, etc.
1539. Yes
1540. Point of view
1541. Yes
1542. Internet, Encyclopedia, etc.
1543. Reference materials
1544. Yes
1545. Yes
1546. Yes
1547. Casual
1548. Formal
1549. Yes
1550. Newbery award
1551. Draws pictures
1552. Caldecott
1553. Plays, dramas
1554. Yes
1555. Dialogue
1556. Modifying in order to improve it
1557. Yes
1558. Speech
1559. Yes
1560. Yes
1561. Hello, my name is
1562. Yes
1563. Name, number, etc.
1564. Paraphrasing
1565. Paraphrases a story
1566. Summarizing
1567. Yes
1568. Graph
1569. Yes
1570. Restaurant, café
1571. Yes
1572. Find out date of event
1573. An outline
1574. Reference
1575. Yes
1576. Dictionary
1577. A thesaurus
1578. Large, huge, etc.
1579. Atlas
1580. Maps, borders, etc.
1581. Almanac
1582. Phone book
1583. Encyclopedia, Internet, etc.
1584. Almanac
1585. The Internet
1586. Yes
1587. Daily news and events
1588. Indicates what article is about
1589. Yes
1590. Yes
1591. A caption
1592. Yes
1593. Yes
1594. Indicates what book is about
1595. Chapters
1596. Table of Contents
1597. Index
1598. Glossary
1599. Index
1600. Yes
1601. Informational text
1602. Lists informational topics
1603. Yes
1604. Functional text
1605. Directions, recipes, etc.
1606. Reads word "about"
1607. Reads word "better"
1608. Reads word "bring"
1609. Reads word "carry"
1610. Reads word "clean"
1611. Reads word "cut"

ANSWERS - LANGUAGE ARTS

1612. Reads word "done"
1613. Reads word "draw"
1614. Reads word "drink"
1615. Reads word "eight"
1616. Reads word "fall"
1617. Reads word "far"
1618. Reads word "full"
1619. Reads word "got"
1620. Reads word "grow"
1621. Reads word "hold"
1622. Reads word "hot"
1623. Reads word "hurt"
1624. Reads word "if"
1625. Reads word "keep"
1626. Reads word "kind"
1627. Reads word "laugh"
1628. Reads word "life"
1629. Reads word "long"
1630. Reads word "much"
1631. Reads word "myself"
1632. Reads word "never"
1633. Reads word "only"
1634. Reads word "own"
1635. Reads word "pick"
1636. Reads word "seven"
1637. Reads word "shall"
1638. Reads word "show"
1639. Reads word "six"
1640. Reads word "small"
1641. Reads word "start"
1642. Reads word "ten"
1643. Reads word "today"
1644. Reads word "together"
1645. Reads word "try"
1646. Reads word "warm"

Language Arts – 4th Grade

1647. Language arts
1648. Yes, can read silently
1649. Yes, can read aloud
1650. Yes, can summarize
1651. Names short story
1652. Names chapter book
1653. Names poem
1654. No
1655. Stanza
1656. Refrain
1657. Prose
1658. Sonnet
1659. Fourteen
1660. William Shakespeare
1661. Names play
1662. Yes
1663. At the beginning
1664. At the end
1665. Find page number of topic
1666. A glossary
1667. The preface
1668. The appendix
1669. Yes
1670. Syllables; part of speech, etc.
1671. Hello, et al
1672. Yes, can predict
1673. Can sequence events
1674. Yes
1675. Yes
1676. Yes
1677. Yes
1678. Both have wicked stepmothers, etc.
1679. Yes
1680. Sleeping Beauty was a royal and put under a curse; Cinderella was a commoner who lived with step-family and went to a Ball, etc.
1681. Cause and effect
1682. Pluto is the farthest planet is cause, Pluto is the coldest planet is the effect.
1683. Fiction
1684. Non-fiction
1685. A fable
1686. Aesop
1687. A tall tale
1688. Drama
1689. A biography
1690. A legend
1691. Yes
1692. Yes
1693. An English legend
1694. A myth
1695. A Greek myth
1696. A ballad
1697. A limerick
1698. Satire
1699. An allegory
1700. Epic
1701. Literary elements
1702. Foreshadowing
1703. Hyperbole
1704. A simile
1705. A metaphor
1706. A metaphor
1707. Alliteration
1708. Onomatopoeia
1709. Personification
1710. Deep
1711. Fall
1712. Cabinet
1713. Hatchet
1714. Meet
1715. Basket
1716. Hatch
1717. Words

ANSWERS - LANGUAGE ARTS

1718. Right
1719. To him or her
1720. Believing
1721. None
1722. Waste
1723. Place
1724. Moon
1725. Cure
1726. Pours
1727. Live
1728. Thin
1729. Drink
1730. Etcetera
1731. RSVP
1732. Yes
1733. Yes
1734. Yes
1735. Yes
1736. Yes
1737. Yes
1738. Bibliography
1739. Author, title, publisher, date, etc.
1740. Last name
1741. Yes
1742. Yes
1743. Can write a thank you note
1744. Yes
1745. Yes
1746. Yes
1747. Writing
1748. Rough draft
1749. Topic sentence
1750. Concluding sentence
1751. Yes
1752. Prose
1753. Yes
1754. Yes
1755. Yes
1756. Cites persuasive essay
1757. Cites informative essay
1758. Cites entertaining essay
1759. Yes
1760. Internet, Encyclopedia, etc.
1761. An encyclopedia
1762. A thesaurus
1763. A dictionary
1764. An atlas
1765. An online encyclopedia
1766. Yes
1767. Yes
1768. Apposition
1769. Eight
1770. Verb
1771. Noun
1772. Cheetah
1773. Adjective
1774. Smart
1775. Pronoun
1776. He
1777. He
1778. She
1779. It
1780. They
1781. Personal pronouns
1782. Possessive pronouns
1783. Verb
1784. Jumped
1785. Yes
1786. Adverb
1787. Quickly
1788. Well
1789. Preposition
1790. Prepositions
1791. Beside
1792. On
1793. Prepositional phrases
1794. Conjunction
1795. And
1796. But
1797. Interjection
1798. Wow!
1799. Yes
1800. Yes
1801. Jack
1802. Loves Ice Cream
1803. A fragment
1804. A fragment
1805. I or we, etc.
1806. Run-on sentence
1807. I went to Chicago. It is a big city.
1808. Lisa and Michael made cookies.
1809. Am
1810. Is
1811. Are
1812. Lives
1813. Was
1814. A declarative
1815. An interrogative
1816. Exclamatory
1817. Imperative
1818. A declarative
1819. Period
1820. An interrogative
1821. Question mark
1822. Pose the words as a question
1823. Say the words as a statement
1824. An exclamatory sentence
1825. Exclamation point
1826. Imperative
1827. An imperative
1828. Comma
1829. After the number 7
1830. After yes
1831. After Orlando
1832. Before
1833. Before
1834. After bones
1835. Commas
1836. After cookies and brownies
1837. A comma

ANSWERS - LANGUAGE ARTS

1838. A semi-colon
1839. A colon
1840. A colon
1841. A comma
1842. A colon
1843. A colon
1844. Apostrophe
1845. Friend's
1846. After
1847. Girls'
1848. Dog's
1849. Apostrophe
1850. Letter
1851. We're
1852. A
1853. O
1854. Don't
1855. I'd
1856. They're
1857. She is
1858. I will
1859. You are
1860. Did not
1861. Will not
1862. Quotation marks
1863. Yes
1864. Before I, after tonight
1865. A synonym
1866. Clean, etc.
1867. Friend, etc.
1868. Try, etc.
1869. Woman, etc.
1870. Different, unknown, etc.
1871. Glad, etc.
1872. Antonym
1873. Succeed
1874. False
1875. Expensive
1876. Cloudy
1877. Solid
1878. Shy
1879. Dry
1880. Far
1881. Under
1882. Rough
1883. Smooth
1884. A prefix
1885. Not
1886. Im
1887. Not possible
1888. In
1889. Not visible
1890. Non
1891. Not fiction
1892. Wrong
1893. Mis
1894. Wrongly behave
1895. Before
1896. pre
1897. Before the game

1898. in
1899. en
1900. In danger
1901. End of a word
1902. ly
1903. ly
1904. ily
1905. y
1906. Full of
1907. ful
1908. Capable of
1909. able
1910. ible
1911. Verb into noun
1912. Agreement
1913. Achieve
1914. Stem word
1915. Deny
1916. A palindrome
1917. An idiom
1918. Hard time
1919. Says word "action"
1920. Says word "actually"
1921. Says word "alive"
1922. Says word "although"
1923. Says word "amount"
1924. Says word "area"
1925. Says word "blood"
1926. Says word "cause"
1927. Says word "central"
1928. Says word "century"
1929. Says word "charcoal"
1930. Says word "chart"
1931. Says word "check"
1932. Says word "club"
1933. Says word "colony"
1934. Says word "company"
1935. Says word "condition"
1936. Says word "court"
1937. Says word "deal"
1938. Says word "death"
1939. Says word "describe"
1940. Says word "design"
1941. Says word "disease"
1942. Says word "eleven"
1943. Says word "equal"
1944. Says word "experience"
1945. Says word "factor"
1946. Says word "favorite"
1947. Says word "figure"
1948. Says word "hospital"
1949. Says word "include"
1950. Says word "increase"
1951. Says word "known"
1952. Says word "least"
1953. Says word "length"
1954. Says word "loud"
1955. Says word "measure"
1956. Says word "molecule"
1957. Says word "natural"

ANSWERS - LANGUAGE ARTS

1958. Says word "necessary"
1959. Says word "noun"
1960. Says word "oxygen"
1961. Says word "phrase"
1962. Says word "property"
1963. Says word "radio"
1964. Says word "receive"
1965. Says word "replace"
1966. Says word "rhythm"
1967. Says word "serve"
1968. Says word "similar"
1969. Says word "southern"
1970. Says word "squirrel"
1971. Says word "straight"
1972. Says word "subtle"
1973. Says word "suffix"
1974. Says word "surely"
1975. Says word "though"
1976. Says word "thought"
1977. Says word "touch"
1978. Says word "twice"
1979. Says word "used"
1980. Says word "usually"
1981. Says word "view"
1982. Says word "weight"
1983. Says word "wheat"
1984. Says word "whom"
1985. Says word "young"

Language Arts – 5th Grade

1986. Genres
1987. Fiction and Non-Fiction
1988. Children's literature
1989. Fantasy
1990. Mystery
1991. Horror
1992. Romance
1993. A thriller
1994. A biography
1995. An autobiography
1996. A speech
1997. Non-Fiction
1998. Drama
1999. Poetry
2000. Fable
2001. Fantasy
2002. Science Fiction
2003. Realistic Fiction
2004. Folklore
2005. Historical Fiction
2006. Horror
2007. Tall tale
2008. Legend
2009. Mythology
2010. Non-Fiction
2011. An essay
2012. Non-Fiction
2013. Fiction
2014. A ballad
2015. A narrative poem
2016. A lyric poem
2017. Free verse
2018. A stanza
2019. Rhyme scheme
2020. Stress
2021. Meter
2022. Iambic pentameter
2023. A couplet
2024. A limerick
2025. A cinquain
2026. A quatrain
2027. Haiku
2028. Homer
2029. A play
2030. Yes
2031. No
2032. A famous poet
2033. Robert Frost
2034. Ralph Waldo Emerson
2035. Walt Whitman
2036. Gwendolyn Brooks
2037. Emily Dickenson
2038. William Blake
2039. Lewis Carroll
2040. John Keats
2041. Henry David Thoreau
2042. Edgar Allan Poe
2043. Lord Byron
2044. John Milton
2045. Elizabeth Barrett Browning
2046. Maya Angelou
2047. A sonnet
2048. A short story
2049. An article
2050. A novel
2051. An interview
2052. Fiction and Non-Fiction
2053. Print, eBooks, etc.
2054. Visually impaired, elderly, etc.
2055. Dewey Decimal System
2056. Author
2057. Playwright
2058. Title
2059. Sub-title
2060. Illustrator
2061. Chapters
2062. Table of Contents
2063. Glossary
2064. Index
2065. Copyright
2066. Publisher
2067. Bibliography

ANSWERS - LANGUAGE ARTS

2068. Yes
2069. Dictionary
2070. Thesaurus
2071. Atlas
2072. Almanac
2073. GPS
2074. Yes
2075. An acronym
2076. Acronyms
2077. Names acronyms
2078. Yes
2079. The plot
2080. The conflict
2081. The setting
2082. The characters
2083. The protagonist
2084. The antagonist
2085. Point of view
2086. First person
2087. Third person
2088. The theme
2089. Author's purpose
2090. Author's style
2091. The Newbery Award
2092. Caldecott Medal
2093. The Nobel
2094. The Pulitzer
2095. Best seller
2096. By genre
2097. Translation
2098. Written
2099. Spoken
2100. English, Spanish, etc.
2101. No
2102. Spanish
2103. Monolingual
2104. Bilingual
2105. Multi-lingual
2106. Mandarin Chinese
2107. English
2108. Spanish
2109. Yes
2110. Yes
2111. 7,000 languages
2112. English
2113. linguistics
2114. Yes
2115. Yes
2116. Air
2117. Star
2118. Book
2119. Life
2120. Universe
2121. Circle or ring
2122. Earth
2123. Water
2124. Measure
2125. Large, bit
2126. Small, short
2127. Single, one
2128. Sound
2129. Light
2130. Much, many
2131. First, earliest form
2132. Mind, soul
2133. Distant, far
2134. Heat, hot
2135. Three
2136. Year, annual
2137. Before
2138. Water
2139. Two
2140. Hundred
2141. Ten
2142. Speak, say
2143. Dual, two
2144. Good fate
2145. Heir
2146. Work
2147. Great, large
2148. Less, small
2149. Ship
2150. All
2151. After, behind
2152. Before, previous
2153. First
2154. Four
2155. United
2156. Vision, see
2157. Life
2158. Etymology
2159. Yes
2160. African
2161. Arabic
2162. Australian
2163. Chinese
2164. Dutch
2165. East Indian
2166. French
2167. German
2168. Hebrew
2169. Irish
2170. Italian
2171. Japanese
2172. Native American
2173. Hawaiian
2174. Russian
2175. Polish
2176. Spanish
2177. Turkish
2178. Hello
2179. Goodbye
2180. Please
2181. Thank you
2182. Yes
2183. No
2184. Cat
2185. Cow
2186. Dog
2187. Frog

ANSWERS - LANGUAGE ARTS

2188. Horse
2189. Pig
2190. Snake
2191. A la carte
2192. A la mode
2193. Au revoir
2194. Bon appétit
2195. Bonjour
2196. Bon voyage
2197. Cul de sac
2198. En route
2199. Faux pas
2200. Hors d'oeuvre
2201. Laissez-faire
2202. On an invitation
2203. Respond to event
2204. Carpe diem
2205. Bona fide
2206. Et cetera
2207. Mea culpa
2208. Status quo
2209. Vice versa
2210. Prefix
2211. Against
2212. Between
2213. Together
2214. Middle
2215. Before
2216. After
2217. Not
2218. Partial
2219. Suffix
2220. –ly
2221. Slowly
2222. Happily
2223. –ist
2224. –ish
2225. –ness
2226. –ion and -er
2227. Rather
2228. Yes
2229. Indent
2230. Capitalize it
2231. Yes
2232. Yes
2233. Yes
2234. Yes
2235. Yes
2236. Yes
2237. Yes
2238. Period
2239. Question mark
2240. Exclamation point
2241. Comma
2242. Comma
2243. After number
2244. After the city or town
2245. Appositive
2246. Sara Smith
2247. My Goldendoodle

2248. Colon
2249. Colon
2250. Italics
2251. Either one
2252. Italicize
2253. Before Star, after Banner
2254. Parts of speech
2255. Noun and verb (predicate)
2256. Noun
2257. Tree, teacher, store, etc.
2258. Proper noun
2259. Jim, Phoenix, etc.
2260. Washington, D.C.
2261. Common noun
2262. New York
2263. Store, phone, she, etc.
2264. A pronoun
2265. Shorter
2266. Yes
2267. Me, my, or mine
2268. Depends on how it is used
2269. Yes
2270. Cases
2271. Nominative case she
2272. Nominative case they
2273. Nominative
2274. Objective
2275. My sister and I
2276. Ryan and me
2277. I, she, he, they, we, etc.
2278. An adjective
2279. Blue and expensive
2280. Red bike, windy path, etc.
2281. Big, smart, loud, etc.
2282. Verb
2283. Run, see, played, is, etc.
2284. Yes
2285. Ate
2286. Will eat
2287. Eats
2288. Adverb
2289. Slowly
2290. No
2291. Soon
2292. Very
2293. Well
2294. Quietly, fast, easily, very, etc.
2295. Carefully set down
2296. Quickly, loudly, carefully, etc.
2297. When
2298. Where
2299. To what extent
2300. Worse
2301. Tallest
2302. Least
2303. Many
2304. Best
2305. A conjunction
2306. Conjunctions
2307. So you should…

ANSWERS - LANGUAGE ARTS

2308. But, and, so, etc.
2309. A preposition
2310. In, on, under, between, etc.
2311. An interjection
2312. Yikes!
2313. What!
2314. Hey, ouch, oh my, etc.
2315. The direct object
2316. Murals
2317. Murals
2318. Slaves
2319. Slaves
2320. Yes
2321. The indirect object
2322. Zach
2323. Zach
2324. Friends
2325. His friends
2326. Indirect object
2327. Paul
2328. Made
2329. Pizza
2330. Yes
2331. Baby
2332. Baby
2333. Baby
2334. Yes
2335. Singular
2336. Plural
2337. He teaches science.
2338. The deer ran
2339. Fly
2340. Was
2341. Likes
2342. Like
2343. Active
2344. Passive voice
2345. Active
2346. Active voice
2347. Passive
2348. A fragment
2349. A run-on
2350. A complete sentence
2351. A fragment
2352. A run-on
2353. Add the word "so" after bake
2354. The predicate
2355. Directed traffic at intersection
2356. Cried
2357. Carried …to mom
2358. After
2359. Garbage
2360. In the brisk wind were flying
2361. Yes
2362. Says short story topic
2363. Yes
2364. Yes
2365. Says report topic
2366. Says essay topic
2367. The introduction
2368. The body
2369. The conclusion
2370. The thesis statement
2371. Literal
2372. No
2373. Literal
2374. Figurative
2375. Literal
2376. Figurative
2377. Oxymoron
2378. Jumbo shrimp
2379. Oxymorons
2380. Imagery
2381. Hyperbole
2382. Hyperbole
2383. Says a hyperbolic phrase
2384. A simile
2385. A simile
2386. A simile
2387. A metaphor
2388. She is a mule.
2389. Her face was…
2390. A blanket
2391. A symbol
2392. Statue of Liberty, flag etc.
2393. The 50 states
2394. Love
2395. Danger; poison
2396. Yes
2397. Two paths in life
2398. Personification
2399. Personification
2400. Onomatopoeia.
2401. Drip, drizzle, splash, etc.
2402. Snake
2403. Boom, bang, pop, etc.
2404. Sssssss…pop!
2405. Vroom vroom!
2406. Woof, growl, arf etc.
2407. Meow, purr, etc.
2408. Quack quack
2409. Tweet tweet
2410. Baa baa
2411. Ribbit ribbit
2412. Alliteration
2413. Alliteration
2414. Drama
2415. A playwright
2416. Comedy
2417. Tragedy
2418. Masks
2419. William Shakespeare
2420. The Globe Theater
2421. Shakespeare's plays
2422. Comedies
2423. Tragedies
2424. Several scenes
2425. A sonnet
2426. No
2427. No

ANSWERS - LANGUAGE ARTS

2428. Yes
2429. Yes
2430. Yes
2431. A greeting
2432. A heading
2433. A personal letter
2434. A business letter
2435. Yes
2436. A greeting
2437. A closing
2438. Best Regards, etc.
2439. Yes
2440. Spanish
2441. Spanish
2442. French
2443. Yes
2444. All
2445. Deep
2446. Well
2447. Bush
2448. Mouth
2449. Parted
2450. Neighbors
2451. Lost
2452. Best
2453. Evil
2454. Invention
2455. Over
2456. Shy
2457. Black
2458. Eating
2459. Day
2460. Thumb
2461. Nine
2462. Hot
2463. Cat
2464. Fiction
2465. Wishes
2466. You
2467. Winks
2468. Shoulder
2469. Hatch
2470. Crow
2471. Lining
2472. Between
2473. Side
2474. Stone
2475. Barrel
2476. Molehill
2477. Earned
2478. Lines
2479. Thunder
2480. Horns
2481. Home
2482. Wounds
2483. Harry
2484. Versa
2485. Boils
2486. Be
2487. Touché

2488. Says "ache"
2489. Says "amphibian"
2490. Says "antique"
2491. Says "audience"
2492. Says "bawl"
2493. Says "beach"
2494. Says "biceps"
2495. Says "binoculars"
2496. Says "boarder"
2497. Says "break"
2498. Says "canoes"
2499. Says "capital"
2500. Says "capitol"
2501. Says "conversation"
2502. Says "cylinder"
2503. Says "deceive"
2504. Says "decimal"
2505. Says word "diagnose"
2506. Says "diagonal"
2507. Says "dialogue"
2508. Says "drought"
2509. Says "earthquake"
2510. Says word "equal"
2511. Says word "equator"
2512. Says word "equivalent"
2513. Says word "exclamation"
2514. Says word "expedition"
2515. Says word "expense"
2516. Says word "extinguish"
2517. Says word "extraordinary"
2518. Says word "extrasensory"
2519. Says word "extraterrestrial"
2520. Says word "fir"
2521. Says word "guard"
2522. Says word "inquire"
2523. Says word "judicial"
2524. Says word "knight"
2525. Says word "loose"
2526. Says word "microphone"
2527. Says word "mourn"
2528. Says word "neighbor"
2529. Says word "night"
2530. Says word "paraphrase"
2531. Says word "pause"
2532. Says word "peace"
2533. Says word "petition"
2534. Says word "piece"
2535. Says word "pour"
2536. Says word "preamble"
2537. Says word "prejudice"
2538. Says word "prospector"
2539. Says word "punctuation"
2540. Says word "usually"
2541. Says word "quail"
2542. Says word "qualify"
2543. Says word "quality"
2544. Says word "quantity"
2545. Says word "quarrel"
2546. Says word "quiet"
2547. Says word "quite"

ANSWERS - LANGUAGE ARTS

2548. Says word "quotation"
2549. Says word "quotient"
2550. Says word "request"
2551. Says word "retract"
2552. Says word "route"
2553. Says word "sequence"
2554. Says word "sketch"
2555. Says word "sleigh"
2556. Says word "surround"
2557. Says word "thermometer"
2558. Says word "toe"
2559. Says word "unique"
2560. Says word "vertebrates"
2561. Says word "veto"
2562. Says word "wade"
2563. Says word "weighed"
2564. Says word "whether"
2565. Says word "view"
2566. Says word "whole"
2567. A pen name
2568. Own name
2569. Mark Twain
2570. Dr. Seuss
2571. The Bible
2572. Classics

ANSWERS - NOTABLE LITERARY WORKS THROUGH THE AGES

APPENDIX 2: Chapter 2 – Notable Literary Works through the Ages

1. Iliad
2. Odyssey
3. Aesop
4. Golden egg
5. Fox
6. Mouse
7. Wolf
8. Hare
9. Mouse
10. Grasshopper
11. Lion
12. Andromache
13. King
14. Aeneid
15. Beowulf
16. Carta
17. Tales
18. Metamorphoses
19. Prince
20. Comedy
21. Juliet
22. Caesar
23. Hamlet
24. Othello
25. Mancha
26. Lear
27. Day
28. Bible
29. Torah
30. Stage
31. Proud
32. Lost
33. Progress
34. Boots
35. Hood
36. Nights
37. Crusoe
38. Travels
39. Goose
40. Built
41. Beast
42. Death
43. Sense
44. Independence
45. Tyger
46. Rose
47. Beanstalk
48. Daffodils
49. Faust
50. Sensibility
51. Robinson
52. Grimm brothers
53. Prejudice
54. Beauty
55. Emma
56. Frankenstein
57. Juan
58. Hollow
59. Winkle
60. Ivanhoe
61. Autumn
62. Urn
63. Tales
64. Mohicans
65. Dame
66. Bears
67. Clothes
68. Twist
69. Death
70. Pendulum
71. Heart
72. Carol
73. Duckling
74. Musketeers
75. Cristo
76. Raven
77. Girl
78. Tales
79. Amontillado
80. Fair
81. Eyre
82. Heights
83. Manifesto
84. Copperfield
85. Ways
86. Letter
87. Dick
88. Gables
89. Woman
90. Slavery
91. Cabin
92. Woods
93. Grass
94. Bovary
95. Cities
96. Worst of times
97. Ride
98. Expectations
99. Miserables
100. Address
101. Wonderland
102. Captain
103. Punishment
104. Women
105. Peace
106. Sea
107. Glass
108. Jabberwocky
109. Days
110. Suffrage
111. Sawyer
112. Beauty
113. Karenina
114. House
115. Heidi
116. Christ
117. Pauper
118. Lady
119. Pinocchio
120. Hood
121. Island
122. Solitude
123. Finn
124. Necklace
125. Mines
126. Shadow
127. Kidnapped
128. Ilyich
129. Holmes
130. Book
131. Courage
132. Worlds
133. Darkness
134. Oz
135. Jim
136. Slavery
137. Rabbit
138. Pan
139. Paw
140. Spots
141. Life
142. Table
143. Farm
144. Wild
145. Pimpernel
146. Fang
147. Jungle
148. Magi
149. Castle
150. Gables
151. Willows
152. View
153. Fire
154. If
155. Garden
156. Pygmalion
157. Pollyanna
158. Taken
159. Man
160. Dolittle
161. Ulysses
162. Rabbit
163. Evening
164. Dolittle
165. Dickenson

ANSWERS - NOTABLE LITERARY WORKS THROUGH THE AGES

166. Game
167. India
168. Budd
169. Gatsby
170. Pooh
171. Rises
172. Boys
173. Lighthouse
174. Front
175. Fury
176. Arms
177. Could
178. Drew
179. Dying
180. Falcon
181. Earth
182. Woods
183. Prairie
184. World
185. Bounty
186. Babar
187. Poppins
188. Twice
189. Express
190. Velvet
191. Ferdinand
192. Again
193. Wind
194. Hobbit
195. God
196. Africa
197. Men
198. Business
199. Stone
200. Town
201. Penguins
202. Yearling
203. Madeline
204. Wake
205. Gehrig
206. Wrath
207. Boone
208. Hen
209. Home
210. Bunny
211. Sweat
212. Tolls
213. Son
214. George
215. Stallion
216. Nation
217. Puppy
218. Children
219. Bunny
220. House
221. Tremain
222. Prince
223. Stranger
224. Dresses
225. Hill
226. Menagerie
227. Girl
228. Longstocking
229. Little
230. Farm
231. Hickory
232. Men
233. Moon
234. Balloons
235. Wiggle
236. Pearl
237. Girl
238. Volcano
239. Plague
240. Dragon
241. Lottery
242. Country
243. Wall
244. 1984
245. Salesman
246. Man
247. Wardrobe
248. Huggins
249. Peach
250. Pye
251. Rye
252. Eternity
253. Andes
254. Web
255. Borrowers
256. Me
257. Sea
258. Eden
259. Miguel
260. Mountain
261. Animals
262. Caboose
263. Crucible
264. School
265. Rings
266. Bowditch
267. Remember
268. Crayon
269. Lolita
270. Hill
271. Dog
272. Yeller
273. Watie
274. Hat
275. Christmas
276. Dr. Seuss
277. Pond
278. Tiffany's
279. John
280. Mountain
281. Peace
282. Fish
283. Ham
284. Dolphins
285. Mockingbird
286. Free
287. Journey
288. Peach
289. Go
290. Grows
291. Tollbooth
292. Address
293. Catch-22
294. Day
295. Time
296. Bears
297. Nest
298. Cat
299. Are
300. Dog
301. Dream
302. Bull
303. Factory
304. Stanley
305. Spy
306. Three
307. Tree
308. Die
309. Pareja
310. Cauldron
311. Motorcycle
312. Christmas
313. Dune
314. Slowly
315. Frankweiler
316. See
317. Solitude
318. Chosen
319. King
320. Corduroy
321. Pest
322. Sounder
323. Caterpillar
324. Sings
325. Five
326. Swans
327. Friends
328. Swan
329. Nimh
330. Ever
331. Lorax
332. Wolves
333. Down
334. Day
335. Dancer
336. Great
337. Ends
338. King
339. Everlasting
340. Cry
341. Family
342. Adventure
343. Terabithia
344. Solomon
345. Game

ANSWERS - NOTABLE LITERARY WORKS THROUGH THE AGES

346. Meatballs
347. Snowman
348. Rise
349. Journal
350. Bunnicula
351. Story
352. Choice
353. Fly
354. Travelers
355. Loved
356. 8
357. Jumanji
358. Attic
359. Song
360. Purple
361. Henshaw
362. Crown
363. Tall
364. Express
365. Bus
366. Cookie
367. Boy
368. Club
369. Disaster
370. Photo biography
371. Animalia
372. Hatchet
373. Moon
374. Wall

375. Beloved
376. Voices
377. Matilda
378. Stars
379. Boom
380. Pigs
381. Mitten
382. Magee
383. Go
384. Shiloh
385. Tuesday
386. May
387. Goosebumps
388. Tales
389. Giver
390. Moons
391. You
392. Apprentice
393. Compass
394. Saturday
395. Frindle
396. Dust
397. Stone
398. Underpants
399. Llama
400. Academy
401. Kid
402. Holes
403. Buddy

404. Events
405. Fish
406. Yonder
407. Type
408. Olivia
409. Rising
410. Dixie
411. Shard
412. Lead
413. Explorer
414. Thread
415. Kira
416. Nothing
417. Cross
418. Lucky
419. Spider
420. Village
421. Book
422. Twilight
423. Games
424. Me
425. Manifest
426. Norvelt
427. Ivan
428. Say
429. Adventures
430. Locomotive
431. Guiness
432. Names favorite book"

ANSWERS - MATH

APPENDIX 3: Chapter 3 – Math

Pre-School

1. Counts to 10
2. 9
3. 6
4. 7
5. Counts past 6
6. Counts backward from 8
7. 6
8. IIII with slash for five
9. Ten Little Indians, etc.
10. Prime numbers
11. The sum
12. The difference
13. Can complete puzzle
14. States empty or full
15. 10
16. A city
17. A state
18. 2
19. Equal
20. The same
21. Equal
22. Equals
23. Names large objects
24. Names small objects
25. Names blue objects
26. Names square objects
27. Round
28. Can name round objects
29. A rectangle
30. Can name rectangular objects
31. Square
32. Yes
33. Ice cube, pizza box, dice, etc.
34. A diamond
35. Yes
36. Yes
37. Both
38. White
39. White, blue
40. Piano, scissors
41. Recites phone number
42. Recites address numbers
43. Names objects inside
44. Names objects outside
45. Names objects above
46. Names objects below
47. Names objects on bed
48. Names objects under bed
49. The right
50. States correct hand
51. Long
52. Short
53. Light
54. Heavy
55. A bowl
56. Wide
57. Narrow
58. A penny
59. A nickel
60. A dime
61. A quarter

Math – Kindergarten

62. Counts to 100
63. Counts to 100 by 5's
64. Counts to 100 by 10's
65. Zero
66. Counts forward from 7
67. Counts backward from 20
68. 20
69. Names blue objects
70. 8
71. 2
72. 80
73. 6
74. Round, circle
75. One half
76. Yes
77. In half
78. Yes
79. Yes
80. Teaspoons
81. A tablespoon
82. Measuring spoons
83. A triangle
84. Square
85. A rectangle
86. Names round objects
87. Names square objects
88. 4
89. Names triangular objects
90. 3
91. Names rectangular objects
92. 4
93. An egg, rug, a racetrack, etc.
94. 10
95. 5
96. Says correct number
97. Indicates age with fingers
98. Holds up 2 fingers
99. Holds up 2 fingers
100. Counts backward from 10
101. Counts to 20 by 2's
102. Yes
103. Counts to 20 by 5's
104. 14
105. 5
106. 0
107. 2
108. 4
109. 10
110. Yes
111. A plus
112. A dash
113. 2
114. 5
115. 3
116. 2 dashes
117. One cent
118. Five cents
119. Ten cents
120. 25 cents
121. Copper
122. One line
123. Two lines
124. 4
125. A nickel
126. A dime
127. A quarter
128. Yes
129. Yes
130. Yes
131. Yes
132. Different sizes
133. Dime
134. A 50 cent piece
135. 0, it is round
136. Heads
137. Tails
138. C with line through it
139. The dollar
140. An S with two lines
141. Names red objects
142. Sorts clothes by color
143. Four lines with a fifth slash

ANSWERS - MATH

144. Names big toys
145. Names small toys
146. Names inside objects
147. Names outside objects
148. Identifies objects on left
149. Identifies objects on right
150. Identifies objects in middle
151. On top
152. Head
153. Legs
154. Estimates number of animals
155. Blue
156. Green, pink
157. Turtles, cats
158. A clock, watch, or phone
159. 12
160. Yes
161. 3:00
162. A ruler or yardstick
163. Names long animals
164. Names short animals

165. A yardstick
166. A thermometer
167. A calculator
168. A scale
169. Names heavy animals
170. Names light animals
171. Names heavy objects
172. Names light objects
173. The afternoon
174. States when breakfast was eaten
175. After
176. A. M.
177. States time of day
178. A calendar
179. Says days of week in order
180. 7
181. 30 or 31, except February
182. Different
183. Tuesday
184. Wednesday
185. Sunday

186. Winter
187. Winter
188. States empty or full
189. Half-full
190. Names paired items
191. Puts right hand on head
192. Puts left hand between knees
193. Puts right hand under left foot
194. Puts left hand beside right knee
195. The blue section
196. A submarine sandwich
197. A ruler
198. A skyscraper
199. A dog
200. A cup
201. A frog
202. An elephant
203. A beach ball

Math – 1st Grade

204. Counts to 100 by 5's
205. Counts to 100 by 10's
206. Counts to 50 by 2's
207. Counts back from 10
208. 17
209. 50
210. 1
211. By 5's
212. Pairs or twins
213. Socks, shoes, gloves, boots, etc.
214. Pants, sunglasses, scissors
215. Zero
216. States math games
217. Yes
218. First
219. Second
220. Third
221. Tenth
222. Seventh
223. States weather
224. Can read thermometer
225. Temperature
226. Rain gauge, barometer, satellite
227. Yes
228. A plane, kite, bird, etc.
229. Wind
230. Energy
231. Once
232. Twice
233. 4

234. 20
235. 8
236. 35
237. Even
238. 7
239. 10
240. Odd
241. Odd
242. 31
243. 49
244. 29
245. 4 cups
246. Eyes, ears, etc.
247. Estimates animal total
248. 4
249. 3
250. 4
251. A circle
252. Names round objects
253. Names rectangular objects
254. Names square objects
255. Square
256. Oval
257. Cube
258. Sphere
259. A solid shape
260. Solid shapes
261. Simple shapes
262. An ice cream cone, party hat, etc.
263. Open shape
264. Closed shape

265. Names straight objects
266. Names curved objects
267. A triangle, arc, etc.
268. A rainbow
269. A sandwich, an hour, etc.
270. Yellow, blue
271. Yes
272. 70
273. 49
274. All of them
275. Greater than
276. 20 is less than 30
277. They are equal
278. Equal
279. 1
280. 2
281. 4
282. 6
283. 8
284. 10
285. 12
286. 14
287. 16
288. 18
289. 20
290. 30
291. 40
292. 50
293. 60
294. 70
295. 80
296. 90

ANSWERS - MATH

297. 100
298. 18
299. 21
300. 24
301. Yes
302. Yes
303. Yes
304. Equal to
305. Yes
306. 10 dogs
307. 6 pieces
308. 11
309. 4
310. A dash
311. 4
312. 9
313. 3
314. 10
315. 20 etc.
316. 19 etc.
317. 80 etc.
318. 20
319. 22
320. 11
321. 9
322. 4
323. 8-4
324. 2+7
325. 2: 1-1
326. 8,7,6,5,4,3,2,1,0
327. 7
328. 30
329. 90
330. 9
331. 6-2=4
332. Plus sign
333. Minus sign
334. The difference
335. 11-6
336. 14
337. 21
338. 59
339. Less than
340. Equal
341. Less
342. Greater than
343. Greater than
344. Less than
345. Equal to
346. Greater than
347. 10
348. Right
349. Most
350. Gets taller; bigger
351. Gets colder; warmer; etc.
352. Increases
353. 3
354. 12, 22, 42
355. 42, 22, 12
356. 7
357. 5
358. 6
359. 4 tens and 9 ones
360. Estimates number
361. Estimates time
362. A calendar
363. Yes
364. 12
365. 30
366. 7
367. Thursday
368. Monday
369. Friday
370. Wednesday
371. Saturday
372. Friday and Saturday
373. 60
374. 60
375. 24
376. 9:30
377. States type of clock
378. The p.m.
379. a.m.
380. 3 hours
381. 12
382. The first
383. December
384. Last
385. February (etc.)
386. States grade
387. States grade
388. States grade
389. December, January, and February
390. June, July, and August
391. September, October, and November
392. March, April, and May
393. Addition
394. A plus sign
395. 5
396. 2+3=5
397. Subtraction
398. A minus
399. 1
400. 4-3=1
401. 12
402. One foot
403. A yardstick
404. Equal to
405. Yes
406. Inches, feet, yard
407. 12 inches
408. The mile
409. A scale
410. The pound
411. 17 ounces
412. States weight
413. States length using hands
414. A thermometer
415. Fahrenheit
416. Yes
417. Millimeter, centimeter, meter
418. 18 centimeters
419. Celsius
420. The kilometer
421. Grams
422. 13 grams
423. One thousand
424. Liters
425. Names hot objects
426. Names cold objects
427. Full
428. Empty
429. Yes
430. Names solids
431. Names liquids
432. A pint
433. A quart
434. A gallon
435. Cup, pint, quart, gallon
436. Liquid capacity
437. One half pint
438. The gallon
439. Gas, milk, water, etc.
440. 2 cups
441. 4 cups
442. 2 pints
443. 4 quarts
444. 7 cups
445. Gallons
446. Liter
447. Full
448. Half-full
449. Driving to school
450. Eating grapes
451. The white bag
452. The red bag
453. Equal
454. 4
455. Yes
456. A part
457. Numerator
458. Denominator
459. One-half
460. One-third
461. 4
462. 4
463. 3
464. A circle
465. 6
466. 8
467. 8
468. Stop sign
469. A skirt
470. A sphere
471. A cylinder
472. A cone
473. A cube

ANSWERS - MATH

474. A triangle	492. 41 cents	510. Certain
475. An open shape	493. 35 cents	511. Impossible
476. Closed shape	494. 65 cents	512. Unlikely
477. Yes	495. 78 cents	513. Unlikely
478. Symmetrical	496. One dollar	514. Letter I
479. Diagonally	497. One quarter	515. Letter V
480. The bar graph with 40	498. 50 cents or half a dollar	516. Letter X
481. Tally marks	499. A quarter	517. Letter L
482. 2	500. A quarter	518. 15
483. 3	501. 60 cents	519. 30
484. 1	502. 4	520. 14
485. A nickel	503. 2	521. 68
486. A dime	504. 4	522. 5
487. A quarter	505. One dollar	523. 1 + 4 = 5
488. Yes	506. No	524. Yes
489. Yes, can add coins	507. No	525. 4
490. 2	508. Two	526. The mode
491. 2 dimes and 1 nickel	509. More than two	527. 6

Math – 2nd Grade

528. Counts to 100	565. The difference	602. 40
529. Counts to 100 by 20's	566. Minus	603. 300
530. Counts to 100 by 2's	567. Plus	604. 700
531. Counts to 100 by 5's	568. 18	605. 200
532. Counts to 1000 by 100's	569. 17	606. Ten
533. Counts upwards from 600	570. 25	607. 12 + 2 = 14
534. 980	571. 80	608. 12-2
535. No	572. 29	609. States equation that equals 10
536. Counts back from 100	573. 24	
537. 25, 33, 44	574. 86	610. 10
538. 55	575. 51	611. 20 – 5 = 15
539. 98	576. 500	612. 30 – 20 = 10
540. Counts by 2's from 26	577. 250	613. 6 peas
541. Blue fish	578. 16	614. 14 Legos
542. Blue, yellow, yellow	579. 44	615. 4 – 2 = 2
543. Odd	580. 3 + 12 = 15	616. 40 – 20 = 20
544. Even	581. 8 + 12 = 20	617. 9 leaves
545. 2	582. 10	618. 6
546. 1	583. 9	619. 20
547. 8	584. 6	620. 5
548. Names ordinals	585. 18	621. 74 – 4
549. States grade	586. 13 lions	622. 46
550. 1st	587. 36 cookies	623. 10
551. 2nd	588. 200 + 150 = 350	624. Yes
552. 3rd	589. 40	625. 4
553. 4th	590. 50	626. 55
554. 5th	591. 8	627. 2
555. 6th	592. 5	628. 10 + 2 (Etc.)
556. 7th	593. 2 + 7	629. 7 + 5 = 12
557. 8th	594. 9	630. No
558. 9th	595. 5	631. + 10
559. 10th	596. 0	632. Sweatshirts
560. 50th	597. 8 – 0	633. Reads a pictograph
561. 50th and 75th	598. 30	634. Reads a line graph
562. 39th	599. 63	635. The middle
563. 245	600. 14	636. Less than
564. The sum	601. 13	637. Greater than

ANSWERS - MATH

638. Equal to
639. 76
640. 49
641. Greater than
642. Equal to
643. 2 and 6
644. 1 and 5
645. 26, 28 etc.
646. 35, 37, etc.,
647. 70, 71, 77
648. 99, 92, 88
649. 4
650. 0
651. 1
652. Tens
653. Tens
654. 9 tens and 5 ones
655. 3, 4, 5
656. 3, 0, 4, 2
657. 1
658. Yes
659. 7
660. Hundreds
661. Thousands
662. 4 tens and 2 ones
663. 8
664. 5 tens and 15 ones
665. Yes
666. 5
667. 329
668. 7,384
669. A decimal point
670. Yes
671. One fourth
672. One and three fourths
673. 2:1
674. 4:1
675. The product
676. 6
677. 6
678. 15
679. That number
680. Zero
681. Zero
682. 25
683. 24
684. 12
685. 25
686. 45
687. 2
688. 2
689. 5
690. 4
691. 6
692. Yes
693. Yes
694. Yes
695. Yes
696. Top
697. Bottom
698. One over four
699. One over two
700. One over three
701. ½
702. 6/7, 6/8, 6/9
703. Red
704. Yes
705. ½
706. 2/3
707. ¾
708. ½
709. Yes
710. 1/7
711. 2/3
712. ½ cup, etc.
713. Rounded up
714. 10
715. 90
716. 30
717. 30
718. 30
719. 80
720. 170
721. 8,000
722. 71
723. $3.00
724. 90 degrees
725. Yes, can tell time
726. States the correct time
727. 60
728. 60
729. 24
730. 7
731. 4
732. 12
733. 365 ¼
734. 30
735. Week
736. 2:00
737. 9:00
738. 2:45
739. 2:30
740. 7:15
741. Quarter to nine
742. Yes
743. Yes
744. Names time zone
745. p.m.
746. a.m.
747. 2:00
748. 6 hours
749. 35 degrees
750. States height
751. States weight
752. 16
753. 2,000
754. 3,000
755. Truck, monument, etc.
756. A gram
757. 16 ounces
758. 2 grams
759. 4 Kilograms
760. Estimates dresser height
761. Estimates dresser length
762. A meter
763. Millimeter, centimeter, kilometer
764. 12
765. 3
766. Estimates length of shoe
767. 12 inches
768. 11 feet long
769. 25 centimeters
770. Estimates distance
771. A kilometer
772. One kilometer
773. Estimates miles
774. Inch, foot, yard
775. A meter stick
776. Cup, pint, quart, gallon
777. A liter
778. 2 liters
779. 2,000 milliliters
780. 12 fluid ounces
781. 4 cups
782. 2 cups
783. Cups
784. A stopwatch
785. Temperature
786. Length
787. Weight
788. Baking powder, salt, etc.
789. Flour, sugar, etc.
790. Says date
791. October
792. July
793. 31
794. 31
795. 28
796. 29
797. September 1
798. April 30th
799. January 1
800. The year
801. A leap year
802. States today's day
803. States day before yesterday
804. Friday
805. Saturday
806. Sunday
807. Yes
808. December, January, February
809. April, May, June
810. June, July, August
811. September, October, November
812. Autumn/fall
813. Summer

ANSWERS - MATH

814. States dates of holidays
815. Yes
816. States house number
817. States phone number
818. Yes
819. Yes
820. Names other currency
821. No
822. The pound
823. A quarter
824. A dime
825. A nickel
826. A penny
827. 25
828. 4
829. One fourth
830. 10
831. 5
832. 2 dimes and 1 nickel, etc.
833. 2 dimes and 1 nickel, etc.
834. 6 dimes and 3 nickels
835. 15 cents
836. 100
837. 25
838. 2
839. 5
840. 40 cents
841. Yes
842. One half dollar
843. 2
844. 2
845. 50 cents
846. 41 cents
847. 38 cents
848. 90 cents
849. 2 dimes and 1 nickel
850. 1 quarter and 1 nickel
851. 1 quarter, 2 dimes, 1 penny
852. No
853. Yes
854. No
855. 20 cents
856. Yes
857. 25 cents
858. 6 dollars
859. 45 dollars
860. Yes
861. Former presidents
862. Yes
863. Diagonal slash
864. On a diagonal
865. Horizontal
866. Vertical
867. Bar graph
868. Higher
869. Yes
870. Basketball
871. Soccer
872. Geometric
873. Sun, moon, ball, etc.
874. Yard, football field, table, etc.
875. Pyramid, tent, pizza, etc.
876. Serving plate, stone, racetrack, etc.
877. Earth, globe, ball, etc.
878. Tepee, evergreen tree, road markers, etc.
879. Candle, flashlight, beaker, etc.
880. Add
881. 20 cm
882. 15 feet
883. 32 feet
884. Base times itself
885. 16
886. 9
887. Unlikely
888. Subtract the lowest from highest
889. 9
890. Mode
891. 5

Math – 3rd Grade

892. Zero
893. Infinity
894. Counts to 1000
895. Skip-counts to 1000
896. Yes
897. Writes 10
898. Writes 56
899. Writes 414
900. Writes 100
901. Writes 1000
902. Writes 10,000
903. Writes 100,000
904. 100
905. 1,000
906. 10,000
907. 100,000
908. 3,000
909. 54,100
910. 235,000
911. 9,999
912. 57
913. 180
914. The thousands
915. 6 thousands, 2 hundreds, 9 tens, and 5 ones
916. The thousands
917. The hundreds
918. The tens
919. The ones
920. 2
921. 5
922. 8
923. 9
924. 60
925. Eight thousand three hundred twenty nine
926. Forty six thousand eight hundred seventeen
927. Twenty eight thousand five hundred forty two
928. 500 tens
929. 30 hundreds
930. 476
931. 300 + 20 + 5
932. 70, 700, 7,000
933. 150
934. 100
935. Adds 2 three digit numbers
936. 333
937. Even
938. 18
939. Add 10
940. 35, 55, 65
941. Greater than
942. Greater than
943. Equal to
944. Less than
945. Adds numbers 3 or more digits
946. Subtracts numbers 3 or more digits
947. 300
948. 30 + 7 = 37
949. Yes
950. Round up
951. 70
952. 30
953. 10
954. 100
955. 100
956. 400
957. 300
958. 600
959. 7,000
960. 439,000
961. 80,000
962. 200,000
963. 8 dollars
964. 50 dollars
965. 70 + 30 = 100

ANSWERS - MATH

966. 50 – 20 = 30
967. Yes
968. 50 – 20 = 30
969. 30 + 50 = 80
970. 30 x 4 = 120
971. 10
972. Arabic
973. Roman numerals
974. One
975. Five
976. Ten
977. Fifty
978. One hundred
979. Five hundred
980. One thousand
981. To the right
982. To the left
983. Add them
984. Subtract them
985. 5 – 1 = 4
986. Two
987. Fifteen
988. Thirty
989. Four
990. Nine
991. Fourteen
992. 36
993. Yes
994. 1980
995. 1,500
996. CCV
997. Cites all ordinals to tenth
998. States date with ordinal
999. Fourteenth
1000. 50th
1001. Yes
1002. A positive
1003. A negative
1004. A negative number
1005. A negative number
1006. A negative number
1007. A positive number
1008. Division
1009. Times
1010. X
1011. Yes
1012. Yes
1013. The Factors
1014. 25
1015. Yes
1016. Yes
1017. Multiplication table
1018. 0
1019. 1 (2,3,4,5,6,7,8,9)
1020. 2 (4,6,8,19,12,14,18)
1021. 3 (6,9,12,15,18,21,24,27)
1022. 4 (8,12,16,20,24,28,32,36)
1023. 5 (10,15,20,25,30,35,40,45)
1024. 6 (12,18,24,30,36,42,48,54)
1025. 7 (14,21,28,35,42,49,56,63)
1026. 8 (16,24,32,40,48,56,64,72)
1027. 9 (18,27,36,45,54,63,72,81)
1028. 10 (20,30,40,50,60,70,80, 90)
1029. 5
1030. 100
1031. 1,000
1032. Two
1033. 600
1034. 10,000
1035. 666
1036. 30
1037. First
1038. The distributive
1039. 50
1040. 14
1041. The associative
1042. 4
1043. The commutative
1044. 3 x 2
1045. The identity property
1046. 0
1047. 1
1048. The identity property
1049. The associative
1050. The commutative
1051. The distributive
1052. A square number
1053. Yes
1054. 9
1055. Yes
1056. 25
1057. 16
1058. 49
1059. 100
1060. Yes
1061. 5
1062. 4
1063. 7
1064. 10
1065. 36
1066. Multiplies 3 or more numbers
1067. 100, 8 x 10=80, + 6
1068. 24 points
1069. Division
1070. 3
1071. 3
1072. Line with a dot above and below it
1073. 2
1074. The dividend
1075. The divisor
1076. 0
1077. 7 (that number)
1078. 1 (2,3,4,5,6,7,8,9,10)
1079. 1 (2,3,4,5,6,7,8,9,10)
1080. 1 (2,3,4,5,6,7,8,9,10)
1081. 1 (2,3,4,5,6,7,8,9,10)
1082. 1 (2,3,4,5,6,7,8,9,10)
1083. 1 (2,3,4,5,6,7,8,9,10)
1084. 1 (2,3,4,5,6,7,8,9,10)
1085. 1 (2,3,4,5,6,7,8,9,10)
1086. 1 (2,3,4,5,6,7,8,9,10)
1087. 1 (2,3,4,5,6,7,8,9,10)
1088. 1 (2,3,4,5,6,7,8,9,10)
1089. 6
1090. An inverse operation
1091. 6 x 7 = 42
1092. 4+4+4+4
1093. 15 + 5 = 20
1094. 6 x 2 = 12
1095. 50
1096. 100
1097. 70
1098. 80
1099. 40
1100. 90
1101. Yes (1,210)
1102. No
1103. Yes (25)
1104. No
1105. Yes (24)
1106. No
1107. The remainder
1108. Yes
1109. Remainder 1
1110. 7 and remainder 2
1111. Input/Output Table
1112. Rule: Divide by 2
1113. Yes
1114. Multiply
1115. 12 (3x4)
1116. The variable
1117. b
1118. 12
1119. Yes
1120. 28 ÷2
1121. 1,10,100,1,000
1122. 3
1123. 24 ÷ 8 = 3
1124. Fractions
1125. ¾ and ¼
1126. Numerator
1127. Denominator
1128. Yes
1129. 1
1130. Whole numbers
1131. A mixed number
1132. 1 and 2
1133. 3
1134. 3
1135. Yes
1136. 6
1137. Yes
1138. ½
1139. ½
1140. ¾
1141. ½
1142. Yes

ANSWERS - MATH

1143. 1
1144. ¾
1145. 3/8
1146. Greater than
1147. 5/8
1148. ¾
1149. Divide
1150. 18 ÷ 3 = 6
1151. Yes
1152. 2.4
1153. ¼
1154. ½
1155. ¾
1156. Yes
1157. 8/100
1158. 2/25
1159. 2/3
1160. 9.81
1161. 4.03
1162. 3.4, 3.5, 3.6
1163. 5.6
1164. 1.2
1165. 3.6
1166. .25
1167. .75
1168. .50
1169. Can read graphs
1170. Can find coordinates
1171. Can graph points
1172. Can interpret line graphs
1173. Can create pictographs
1174. Can interpret Venn diagram
1175. In the middle
1176. States money amount
1177. $1, $5, $10, $20
1178. Currency
1179. Yes
1180. No
1181. States coins with values
1182. $23
1183. 89 cents
1184. $6.50
1185. No
1186. $16
1187. $7.25
1188. $8
1189. Thermometer
1190. Celsius
1191. Fahrenheit
1192. 45 degrees
1193. 32
1194. Water
1195. Hot
1196. Cold
1197. Miles
1198. One mile
1199. Yards
1200. Ruler
1201. 12

1202. 3
1203. 36
1204. Feet
1205. Ruler, measuring tape, level, etc.
1206. Can estimate length
1207. A scale
1208. Lb.
1209. Oz.
1210. 16
1211. Yes
1212. Cup, pint, quart, gallon
1213. 2
1214. 2
1215. 4
1216. One gallon
1217. 8
1218. 10 pints
1219. Millimeter, centimeter, meter, kilometer
1220. Grams
1221. One kilogram
1222. 1,000 grams
1223. Ball is heavier
1224. The liter
1225. States time
1226. 60
1227. 60
1228. 180
1229. 24
1230. A.M.
1231. P.M.
1232. 7:45
1233. 3:40
1234. 4:20
1235. 6:55
1236. Noon
1237. Midnight
1238. Twenty to four
1239. Big hand on 2, little on 7
1240. 5:15
1241. 25 minutes
1242. Can read time schedule
1243. Can read a timeline
1244. Historical events, etc.
1245. Says today's date
1246. March 4th
1247. July 31st
1248. States dates with numbers
1249. States birthdate with numbers
1250. States day of week
1251. Sunday
1252. 7
1253. 4
1254. 365 ¼
1255. February
1256. Every 4 years
1257. 10
1258. 100

1259. 1000
1260. Geometry
1261. "Gee, I'm a Tree"
1262. Yes
1263. Names geometric shapes
1264. Polygons
1265. No
1266. Yes
1267. Line segments
1268. Horizontal
1269. Vertical
1270. Perpendicular
1271. Parallel
1272. 4
1273. Picture, table, dice, etc.
1274. 4
1275. Football field, table, etc.
1276. Yes
1277. 3
1278. Pizza, piece of pie, etc.
1279. Equilateral
1280. Isosceles
1281. Four
1282. Five
1283. Six
1284. Seven
1285. Eight
1286. An octagon
1287. A line
1288. A line segment
1289. A ray
1290. A vertex
1291. Letters
1292. Both
1293. Yes
1294. Angles
1295. An angle
1296. A right angle
1297. 4
1298. Symmetrical
1299. Congruent
1300. Line of symmetry
1301. 1
1302. Infinite
1303. Yes
1304. Reflected
1305. Rotated
1306. Translated
1307. Perimeter
1308. Add
1309. 12
1310. 9
1311. 20
1312. 18
1313. 4
1314. Area
1315. Yes
1316. Multiply
1317. 18
1318. 25

ANSWERS - MATH

1319. Solids	1324. An edge	1329. States favorite area
1320. Solids	1325. The face	1330. Explains practicality of math
1321. Its base	1326. A vertex	
1322. A pyramid	1327. Multiply	
1323. A face	1328. 40	

Math – 4th Grade

1331. Tens	1376. Subtract	1425. 36
1332. 1	1377. 40	1426. 49
1333. Hundreds	1378. Add	1427. 56
1334. 2	1379. 60	1428. 81
1335. One thousand	1380. 1150	1429. 100
1336. 3	1381. 18	1430. 2
1337. Ten thousand	1382. MMXV	1431. 6
1338. 4	1383. Yes	1432. 5
1339. One hundred thousand	1384. Down	1433. 9
1340. 5	1385. Round up	1434. 7
1341. One million	1386. 3,000	1435. 11
1342. 6	1387. 2,000	1436. 8
1343. Ten million	1388. 2,900	1437. 12
1344. One hundred million	1389. 2,260	1438. 24
1345. One billion	1390. A prime number	1439. 0
1346. One trillion	1391. A composite number	1440. 440
1347. Stars, National Debt, etc.	1392. A prime number	1441. 2200
1348. A comma	1393. No	1442. Yes
1349. 3	1394. Prime numbers	1443. Add them
1350. One million, four hundred thirty four thousand, five hundred and sixty seven.	1395. Composite numbers	1444. 4
	1396. Composite number	1445. 80,000
	1397. Prime number	1446. The identity
	1398. Yes	1447. The distributive
1351. No	1399. 140,000	1448. The associative
1352. Yes	1400. One million	1449. The zero property of multiplication
1353. 3	1401. 6,352	
1354. 5	1402. The associative	1450. Identity property
1355. 6	1403. The commutative	1451. 12,000
1356. 4	1404. The identity	1452. 70,000
1357. Ten	1405. 8,000	1453. Greater than
1358. A decade	1406. Yes	1454. Equal to
1359. A century	1407. Yes	1455. Less than
1360. 100,500	1408. 101,000	1456. Division
1361. Eight thousand, two hundred and forty three	1409. 165,000	1457. 20 ÷ 2 = 10
	1410. 350,000	1458. 3 x 8 = 24
1362. 5,040	1411. 500	1459. 20
1363. Positive	1412. Yes	1460. 5
1364. Negative	1413. 3 and 8	1461. 4
1365. Even	1414. 24	1462. 9
1366. Odd	1415. 4, 6, 8, 10, etc.	1463. The dividend
1367. Yes	1416. 12, 18, 24, 30, etc.	1464. The quotient
1368. Yes	1417. 7	1465. The divisor
1369. Arabic	1418. 9	1466. 20
1370. I, II, III, IV, and V	1419. 6 and 9	1467. Yes
1371. VI, VII, VIII, IX, and X	1420. 12	1468. That number
1372. 50	1421. A square	1469. 1
1373. 100	1422. Yes	1470. 12/3
1374. 500	1423. 4	1471. 4
1375. 1,000	1424. 25	1472. A factor

ANSWERS - MATH

1473. 1, 2, and 4
1474. 1, 2, 3, 4, 6, 8, 12, and 24
1475. 1, 2, and 4
1476. 2 Remainder 1
1477. 4 Remainder 2
1478. 132
1479. 82
1480. 321
1481. 8 x 3 = 24
1482. 90
1483. 60
1484. 8 Remainder 3
1485. Less than
1486. Greater than
1487. Greater than
1488. Yes
1489. Algebra
1490. 20
1491. 7
1492. 6
1493. Yes
1494. Yes
1495. 24
1496. 4
1497. 15
1498. Dollar
1499. Euro, Pound, Yen, etc.
1500. Letter "S" with two lines through it
1501. Letter "C" with line through it
1502. $1.25
1503. A fifty dollar bill
1504. $490
1505. $500
1506. $30
1507. Yes (No)
1508. 85 cents
1509. $45
1510. $7
1511. $5.50
1512. $8.00
1513. $4.80
1514. $4.00
1515. George Washington
1516. Abraham Lincoln
1517. Alexander Hamilton
1518. Andrew Jackson
1519. Ulysses S. Grant
1520. Abraham Lincoln
1521. Thomas Jefferson
1522. Franklin D. Roosevelt
1523. George Washington
1524. Seconds, minutes, hours, days, weeks, months, year
1525. 365 ¼
1526. Add one day, February 29th, every four years
1527. 182 ½
1528. 24 hours
1529. 12 hours
1530. 6 hours
1531. 18 hours
1532. 60 seconds
1533. 60 minutes
1534. 1 ½ hours
1535. 30 minutes
1536. 15 minutes
1537. 75 minutes
1538. 192 minutes
1539. 2 minutes, four seconds
1540. 135 minutes
1541. 21 days
1542. Time zones
1543. Names time zone
1544. Yes
1545. 9:25
1546. Twenty minutes to ten
1547. 2:25
1548. 6:30
1549. Yes
1550. U.S. customary units
1551. Inches, feet, yards, miles
1552. 12
1553. ½, ¼, 1/16, 1/8, etc.
1554. Estimate
1555. 3 feet
1556. 4 feet
1557. 36
1558. 18
1559. A mile
1560. 2,640
1561. A mile
1562. 6 feet
1563. Ounces, pounds, tons
1564. 16
1565. 8
1566. 12
1567. 32
1568. Pounds
1569. 3 pounds
1570. Oz.
1571. Lb.
1572. 2000 pounds
1573. 3 tons
1574. T
1575. 7 tons
1576. Cup, pint, quart, gallon
1577. Teaspoon, tablespoon, cup, stick (of butter)
1578. 3
1579. tsp.
1580. Tbsp.
1581. 8 fluid ounces
1582. C.
1583. ½, 1/3, ¼, 1 cup
1584. 8
1585. 2
1586. Pt.
1587. 2
1588. Qt.
1589. 4
1590. 3 pints
1591. 3 and 1/3
1592. Metric
1593. Decimal
1594. 10
1595. 100
1596. 1000
1597. 10
1598. 3.2
1599. cm.
1600. mm.
1601. 100
1602. M.
1603. A meter
1604. 1000
1605. km.
1606. A kilometer
1607. 62
1608. Liter
1609. 100
1610. 1000
1611. cl.
1612. l.
1613. 500
1614. Milligram, gram, kilogram, metric ton
1615. 1000
1616. 10
1617. mg.
1618. cg.
1619. 1000
1620. g.
1621. 100
1622. kg.
1623. Metric system
1624. Celsius
1625. Fahrenheit
1626. 0
1627. Freezes
1628. Fractions
1629. 2
1630. 10
1631. ½
1632. ¼
1633. Yes
1634. 6/8, 9/16, etc.
1635. 2/6, 3/9, etc.
1636. 3/5
1637. 4/8
1638. Improper fraction
1639. 1
1640. Improper
1641. Yes
1642. A whole number
1643. 4
1644. 1
1645. 0
1646. Division

771

ANSWERS - MATH

1647. Yes, to 2/5
1648. Yes
1649. ¼
1650. 2/3
1651. Mixed
1652. 2 and 2/5
1653. Multiply 4x6 plus 1 over 4
1654. 14/3
1655. 6
1656. 6
1657. 4
1658. Adding the numerators
1659. 4/5
1660. 12/9
1661. 10/10 or 1
1662. 1 and 1/3
1663. 4/7
1664. Find LCM first
1665. 5/6
1666. Find LCM first
1667. 1/3
1668. 4/9
1669. 1 and ½
1670. 2 and 2/3
1671. 2 feet
1672. ½ foot
1673. 6 inches
1674. Less than
1675. Equal to
1676. Equal to
1677. Yes
1678. ¼, 1/3, ½, and 1
1679. 1/8, ¼, ½, and 1
1680. ½
1681. ¼
1682. 1 and ½
1683. 2/9
1684. 2/10 or 1/5
1685. ¼
1686. ½
1687. ¾
1688. With decimals
1689. $6.75
1690. $1.25
1691. 10
1692. A decade
1693. Two point five zero
1694. .1
1695. .01
1696. .001
1697. Equal to
1698. Yes
1699. Greater than
1700. 2.4
1701. ¼
1702. ¾
1703. ½
1704. 0
1705. 3.280
1706. 4.9
1707. 4.80
1708. 3.300
1709. 3.500
1710. 3.250
1711. 6
1712. Yes
1713. 1.8
1714. Decimal points
1715. A zero
1716. 7
1717. 2.9
1718. 5
1719. .9 centimeters
1720. Equal to
1721. Geometry
1722. A line
1723. Letters
1724. An arrow
1725. A ray
1726. The end point
1727. An angle
1728. The vertex
1729. Three
1730. A right angle
1731. 90 degrees
1732. Acute
1733. Obtuse
1734. Yes
1735. Isosceles
1736. Equilateral
1737. Scalene
1738. Right
1739. A protractor
1740. 50 degrees
1741. 180 degrees
1742. 90 degrees
1743. 270 degrees
1744. 360 degrees
1745. Intersecting
1746. Perpendicular
1747. Parallel
1748. Horizontal
1749. Vertical
1750. Diagonal
1751. A polygon
1752. A triangle
1753. A quadrilateral
1754. A square and a rectangle
1755. A parallelogram
1756. A trapezoid
1757. A square
1758. A rhombus
1759. A quadrilateral
1760. A pentagon
1761. A hexagon
1762. A heptagon
1763. An octagon
1764. A nonagon
1765. A decagon
1766. Octopus
1767. An octagon
1768. A rhombus
1769. Congruent
1770. Similar
1771. Symmetrical
1772. Its center
1773. Area
1774. 32 centimeters
1775. 9 feet
1776. Yes
1777. 144 inches
1778. Square foot, acre, square mile
1779. Square centimeter, square meter, hectare, square kilometer
1780. 2 dimensional
1781. Yes
1782. A prism
1783. A cylinder
1784. A pyramid
1785. A sphere
1786. A cube
1787. A cone
1788. The surface area
1789. Yes
1790. The volume
1791. 12
1792. No
1793. A compass
1794. Radius
1795. Diameter
1796. Chord
1797. The diameter
1798. The radius
1799. 16 cm (D=Rx2)
1800. Its circumference
1801. Yes
1802. Blue
1803. 4
1804. Divide by the total numbers
1805. 4
1806. 8
1807. The median
1808. 4
1809. The mode
1810. 3
1811. The median
1812. 3
1813. The range
1814. 5

ANSWERS - MATH

Math – 5th Grade

1815. A billion
1816. A comma
1817. Three
1818. 5
1819. 6
1820. 7
1821. 8
1822. 9
1823. 612,000,000,000
1824. 5,480
1825. 53,927
1826. One thousand + one hundred + forty + five
1827. 9 Billion
1828. 800 Million
1829. 70 Million
1830. 6 Million
1831. 500 Thousand
1832. 40 Thousand
1833. 3 Thousand
1834. 2 Hundred
1835. Tens
1836. Ones
1837. Outlines; Dates, etc.
1838. 5
1839. 10
1840. 50
1841. 100
1842. 500
1843. 1000
1844. 1526
1845. 76
1846. 1686
1847. MMMV
1848. Digit to the right
1849. Yes
1850. 5
1851. 10 Million
1852. 9 Million
1853. 3,900,000
1854. 3,400,000
1855. 3,950,000
1856. 3,420,000
1857. 3000
1858. 2000
1859. 60,000
1860. 45,000
1861. 46,000
1862. 45,500
1863. 45,600
1864. 5,530
1865. 5,590
1866. 420
1867. 430
1868. Odd
1869. Even
1870. Even
1871. Odd
1872. Integers
1873. Yes
1874. Greater than
1875. Yes
1876. Opposite
1877. Gain value
1878. Lose value
1879. Positive number
1880. Negative number
1881. Positive
1882. Negative
1883. A minus
1884. No
1885. Opposites
1886. 5
1887. -7 (Negative seven)
1888. 20
1889. +10
1890. +25
1891. -5
1892. +10
1893. -15
1894. -200
1895. -4
1896. Less than
1897. Less than
1898. Greater than
1899. Greater than
1900. Less than
1901. Greater than
1902. Yes
1903. A positive
1904. To the right
1905. Negative
1906. To the left
1907. 6
1908. Yes
1909. -5
1910. -4
1911. -40
1912. 5
1913. Yes
1914. 10 + (-6)
1915. -6
1916. 0
1917. 0
1918. Yes
1919. Yes
1920. Adding its opposite
1921. Yes
1922. -2
1923. -3
1924. 6
1925. Yes
1926. Itself
1927. 4
1928. Yes
1929. 9
1930. Yes
1931. 2
1932. 3
1933. 4
1934. 5
1935. 6
1936. 7
1937. 36
1938. 49
1939. 8
1940. 81
1941. 100
1942. 12
1943. Exponents
1944. Small number raised up
1945. 2x2x2=8
1946. 5 cubed
1947. 5 to the fourth power
1948. 9
1949. 1000
1950. Yes
1951. 6
1952. One million
1953. 10 to the 9th power
1954. A prime number
1955. Composite numbers
1956. A composite number
1957. A prime number
1958. Composite numbers
1959. Prime
1960. Factors
1961. 1,2,4,8, and 16
1962. 2
1963. 3x3
1964. 3 to the second power
1965. 3x5
1966. 1,2,4,5,10, and 20
1967. 3
1968. 2
1969. 9
1970. 6
1971. 24
1972. Yes
1973. 21,000
1974. The commutative
1975. The associative
1976. Less than
1977. Equal to
1978. Greater than
1979. 400
1980. Yes
1981. 3.3
1982. .50
1983. Yes
1984. Greater than

773

ANSWERS - MATH

1985. Yes	2045. The remainder	2103. 3
1986. Yes	2046. Yes	2104. Greater than
1987. Greater than	2047. Yes	2105. Equal to
1988. Zero	2048. Equal to	2106. Less than
1989. .8	2049. 3	2107. 3
1990. 4 inches	2050. 10	2108. 6
1991. Algebra	2051. 1	2109. Yes
1992. A letter	2052. 48.34	2110. Yes
1993. The variable	2053. 2	2111. The commutative
1994. .3	2054. 4.834	2112. 3
1995. Equal to	2055. Numerator and Denominator	2113. Yes
1996. 15		2114. Goodbye
1997. Subtraction	2056. The bottom	2115. 1/15
1998. Inverse	2057. The top	2116. 4/15
1999. 12-5=7	2058. 2/8	2117. 1/8
2000. 14+8=22	2059. ½	2118. 4/15
2001. Yes	2060. 2/3	2119. 30
2002. 39	2061. 6	2120. 10
2003. 900	2062. Find the least common multiple	2121. 14
2004. 101,000		2122. Yes
2005. $2.50	2063. 6	2123. 5
2006. $26.00	2064. 6	2124. 1
2007. Equal to	2065. 2	2125. 3
2008. 30	2066. 4/5	2126. 1 and ½
2009. $800	2067. 5	2127. 1
2010. Yes	2068. An integer and a fraction	2128. The ratio
2011. 72	2069. 1 and 1/3	2129. 1:3 (One to three)
2012. Add	2070. Less than	2130. 2:5 (2 to 5)
2013. 10,000	2071. Common denominator	2131. ¼
2014. 42,000	2072. Yes	2132. 25%
2015. 350,000	2073. 15	2133. 50%
2016. Yes	2074. 10/15	2134. 75%
2017. Commutative	2075. 2/3	2135. Yes
2018. Associative	2076. 12/15	2136. 2 to 1
2019. Distributive	2077. 4/5	2137. 2 to 4
2020. Distributive	2078. 4/5	2138. Yes
2021. Zero	2079. ¼, 1/3, ½ ¾, and 1	2139. Unit rate
2022. Identity	2080. 1/24	2140. 6
2023. 120	2081. 3/7	2141. 25 cents per gumball
2024. 180	2082. 2	2142. A ratio
2025. Greater than	2083. 90	2143. Yes
2026. Equal to	2084. Turn it upside down	2144. 20 miles
2027. .21	2085. 5/2	2145. 6 to 1
2028. 1	2086. ¾	2146. 1 to 6
2029. 80	2087. 2/3	2147. 1 to 10
2030. 23.25	2088. 3/3 or 1	2148. The rate
2031. 2	2089. 7/9	2149. Yes
2032. 232.5	2090. 1 and 3/7	2150. (65) miles per hour
2033. $5.60	2091. 4/3	2151. Miles
2034. 9,000	2092. 1 and 1/3	2152. Kilometers
2035. 2,000,000	2093. 3	2153. Distance
2036. Equal to	2094. 6 and 2/3	2154. 60 miles per hour
2037. Division	2095. 4 and ½	2155. Yes
2038. The dividend	2096. 15 and ½	2156. 100
2039. The divisor	2097. Yes	2157. Century, Centimeter, etc.
2040. The quotient	2098. 2/5	2158. 30 out of 100
2041. 22	2099. 3/8	2159. 30/100 or 3/10
2042. 12	2100. 1 and 3/5	2160. 25%
2043. 11	2101. Yes	2161. 50%
2044. 400	2102. 3	2162. 75%

ANSWERS - MATH

2163. 100%
2164. ½
2165. ¾
2166. ¼
2167. 1
2168. .75
2169. .25
2170. .50
2171. 25%
2172. 25%
2173. 6/10
2174. Multiply
2175. 40
2176. 24
2177. $32
2178. Probability
2179. Yes
2180. 1 in 6
2181. Million
2182. 1 in 3
2183. 3 to 1
2184. ¼
2185. 25%
2186. .25
2187. The average
2188. 9 seconds
2189. 80%
2190. Mean
2191. 3
2192. Mode
2193. 15
2194. Median
2195. Order them by value
2196. 2,3,5,7,9
2197. 5
2198. Range
2199. 6
2200. Growth pattern
2201. 10
2202. 15
2203. 29
2204. Yes
2205. 4
2206. Yes
2207. Pictograph
2208. Yes
2209. Line plots
2210. Yes
2211. Yes
2212. A bar graph
2213. A line graph
2214. A pie chart
2215. A pie chart
2216. A bar graph
2217. A line graph
2218. A pictograph
2219. A survey
2220. Favorite color, food, etc.
2221. Algebra
2222. Variables
2223. 4
2224. 9
2225. 5
2226. Variables
2227. 19
2228. 1
2229. 4x4
2230. 4x4x4
2231. 16
2232. 3
2233. U.S. customary and Metric
2234. Pound
2235. Ounce, pound, ton
2236. 16
2237. 33 ounces
2238. 2000
2239. 1000
2240. 500
2241. 3000 pounds
2242. 12
2243. 3
2244. 1 yard
2245. Gram
2246. Milligram, gram, kilogram, metric ton
2247. 100
2248. Centigram
2249. 1000
2250. 2
2251. 1
2252. Liter
2253. 1
2254. Inch, foot, yard, mile
2255. Millimeter, Centimeter, meter, kilometer
2256. One meter
2257. A meter
2258. One foot
2259. 13 inches
2260. One inch
2261. Centimeter
2262. Millimeter
2263. One mile
2264. One kilometer
2265. Fahrenheit
2266. Celsius
2267. 0
2268. 100
2269. 212
2270. 98.6
2271. Fluid ounce, cup, pint, quart, gallon
2272. 4
2273. 2
2274. 16
2275. 24
2276. Acres
2277. 4
2278. Bushel
2279. 4
2280. Barrels
2281. Gallons
2282. Liter
2283. Milliliter, centiliter, liter, kiloliter
2284. A quart
2285. One yard
2286. One mile
2287. Says time
2288. 11.45
2289. Eastern
2290. States time zone
2291. Yes
2292. 11:35
2293. 1:00
2294. A.M.
2295. P.M.
2296. Before
2297. After
2298. Midnight
2299. 60 seconds
2300. 120
2301. 60
2302. 180 minutes
2303. 24 hours
2304. 48 hours
2305. 3 days
2306. 12 hours
2307. 6 hours
2308. 18 hours
2309. 28 days
2310. 12 weeks
2311. 6 months
2312. 365 ¼ days
2313. 365 ¼ days
2314. 52 weeks
2315. 366
2316. Leap year day every 4 years
2317. February 29th
2318. 10 years
2319. 100 years
2320. 200 years
2321. Yes
2322. Geometry
2323. Pencil or pen
2324. A line segment
2325. A line
2326. Ray
2327. It has an arrow
2328. Parallel
2329. Perpendicular
2330. Intersecting
2331. Symmetrical
2332. An intersection
2333. The vertex
2334. Protractor
2335. Degrees
2336. 360 degrees

ANSWERS - MATH

2337. 180 degrees
2338. 90 degrees
2339. 90 degrees
2340. Yes
2341. 45 degrees
2342. Acute
2343. Obtuse
2344. A straight angle
2345. Reflex
2346. Greater than
2347. 180 degrees
2348. 60 degrees
2349. 90 degrees
2350. Polygons
2351. Circle, square, triangle, etc.
2352. 3
2353. Tricycle, trio, trilogy, etc.
2354. Equilateral
2355. Isosceles
2356. Scalene
2357. Right
2358. 45 degrees
2359. Congruent
2360. Equilateral
2361. The hypotenuse
2362. ½ Base x Height
2363. A quadrilateral
2364. A rectangle
2365. Width x Height
2366. Length of side squared
2367. 25 Centimeters
2368. Square
2369. A trapezoid
2370. A parallelogram
2371. Parallelograms
2372. A square
2373. Two
2374. Square can be rectangle
2375. A pentagon
2376. A hexagon
2377. A heptagon
2378. An octagon
2379. A nonagon
2380. A decagon
2381. Width x height
2382. 24 feet
2383. A circle
2384. Compass
2385. 360 degrees
2386. A chord
2387. Diameter
2388. The diameter
2389. The radius
2390. Circumference
2391. Greek pi π
2392. Its diameter
2393. 3.14
2394. March 14th
2395. Solid figures
2396. Solid figures
2397. Cone, sphere, pyramid, etc.
2398. Three-dimensional
2399. 6
2400. Yes
2401. Length x width x height
2402. 24 inches
2403. Mathematics
2404. Arithmetic
2405. States favorite math

APPENDIX 4: Chapter 4 – Science

Pre-School

1. Living
2. People
3. Animals
4. Plants
5. Food, water, etc.
6. Food, water, etc.
7. Names small animals
8. Names large animals
9. Insects
10. A butterfly
11. Dog, cat, etc.
12. Cow, chicken, horse, etc.
13. Whale, shark, etc.
14. Scorpions, lizards, etc.
15. Deer, bear, wolves, etc.
16. Names insects
17. 6
18. 8
19. No
20. Birds, ducks, etc.
21. Fish, whales, etc.
22. Dog, bear, rabbit, fox, etc.
23. Turtles, crabs, lobsters
24. Birds, insects, bats
25. Reptiles
26. Milk
27. Mammals
28. Marsupials
29. Amphibians
30. With legs
31. Slither with body
32. Arms and legs
33. Its shell
34. Claws and teeth
35. Raise its tail and spray
36. Sharp needles
37. Quills
38. Tigers, lions, bears, etc.
39. Giraffe
40. Elephant
41. Tiger, zebra, etc.
42. Kangaroo
43. Kitten
44. Puppy
45. Duckling
46. Chick
47. A tadpole
48. Yes
49. Tadpoles
50. Shrink
51. Yes
52. Yes
53. Meat
54. Plants
55. Both meat and plants
56. A nest
57. A hill
58. Habitats
59. The forest
60. Deer, bear, fox, etc.
61. The ocean
62. The ocean
63. Salt
64. The whale shark
65. Gills
66. Farm
67. Cows, horses, pigs, etc.
68. The desert
69. Birds, lizards, toads, etc.
70. A rainforest
71. Plants
72. Plants
73. As a seed
74. Apple, peach, watermelon, etc.
75. Pinecones
76. Yes
77. Pistachio, walnut, acorn, etc.
78. Green beans, peas, etc.
79. Watermelon
80. Yes
81. An oak tree
82. Stem, leaf, flower, etc.
83. Sun, soil, and water
84. Sun
85. Daytime
86. Nighttime
87. Sun moves
88. Lamps, flashlights, etc.
89. In a straight line
90. Our shadow
91. The time of day
92. Corn, potatoes, tomatoes, etc.
93. Flour, bread, cereal, etc.
94. Oxygen
95. Yes
96. Water
97. Yes
98. A well
99. Clouds
100. Ice
101. Steam
102. It floats
103. It sinks
104. Air
105. Yes
106. A balloon
107. Air
108. Yes
109. Sound
110. Flute, clarinet, trumpet, tuba, etc.
111. Airplane, kite, windmill, etc.
112. Air, food, water, shelter
113. No
114. Yes
115. Ears
116. Legs
117. Feet
118. Hands
119. Heart
120. Brain
121. Stomach
122. Bones
123. Muscle
124. Eyes
125. Ears
126. Nose
127. Tongue
128. Hands
129. Earth
130. Yes
131. Yes
132. The Sun
133. The Moon
134. Stars
135. Far
136. States weather
137. Science

ANSWERS - SCIENCE

Science – Kindergarten

138. Names living things
139. Air, water, food, shelter
140. Living
141. Stem, leaf, flower, seed
142. Bean, tulip, fern, etc.
143. Air, water, Sun, and soil
144. Beans, corn, lettuce, etc.
145. Tomatoes, corn, etc.
146. Seeds
147. Sprout, grow taller, blossom
148. The seeds
149. Wheat
150. Peas
151. Green beans/peas
152. Sunflower, pistachio, walnuts
153. Apples, watermelon, peaches
154. No
155. Yes
156. Oak tree
157. The root
158. The stem
159. The leaves
160. The flower
161. Live on Earth and in water
162. Rose, geranium, marigold, etc.
163. Stem, petal, root, flower
164. A plant
165. Oak, evergreen, maple, etc.
166. Trunk, leaves, roots, etc.
167. A tree
168. A maple tree
169. The spring
170. Canada
171. A maple leaf
172. Seeds
173. Seeds
174. Pumpkin
175. Cereal
176. Yes
177. Tulip, daffodil, etc.
178. Yes
179. Spring
180. Yes
181. Late summer or early autumn
182. Potato, carrot, beet, etc.
183. The root
184. French fries
185. Sugar
186. Veins
187. Seasons
188. Autumn
189. No
190. Autumn
191. Sports, go to school, rake leaves, etc.
192. Sled, skate, build snowman, etc.
193. Plant flowers, walk, etc.
194. Swim, take vacation, baseball, etc.
195. An evergreen
196. Paper, lumber, etc.
197. Paper, houses, etc.
198. The bark
199. It decays
200. Names wooden objects
201. Smooth
202. Green all year
203. Needles
204. Cactus
205. Coral
206. Seaweed
207. Lily pad
208. Natural
209. Yes
210. White
211. The root
212. Caused by humans
213. Caused by humans
214. Man-made
215. Yes
216. Egg, caterpillar, chrysalis
217. A frog
218. Get bigger
219. Yes
220. Venus flytrap
221. Says yes or no to pet
222. Food, water, shelter
223. Domestic animal
224. Wild animal
225. Deer, rabbit, fox, etc.
226. Cows, chickens, pigs, etc.
227. Whales, sharks, dolphins, etc.
228. Fish, snakes, turtles, frogs, loons
229. Gills
230. Elephants, zebras, giraffes, etc.
231. Kangaroos, Koala bears, etc.
232. Bear, moose, deer, buffalo, sheep, etc.
233. Bird, etc.
234. Dog, horse, deer, lion, etc.
235. Fish, whale, etc.
236. A marlin
237. Turtles, crabs, lobsters, etc.
238. Dog, cat, goldfish, etc.
239. Food, water, air, and shelter
240. A fin
241. A wing
242. A shell
243. A footprint
244. Paw prints
245. Food, water, air, and shelter
246. Eyes
247. Yes
248. Nose
249. Hands
250. Yes
251. Yes or no
252. Sunscreen
253. Texture
254. Soft
255. Rough
256. Fingers
257. Ears
258. Yes
259. Yes
260. Slower
261. Thunder, etc.
262. Whisper, etc.
263. Tongue
264. Cookies, candy, etc.
265. Juice, limes, dill pickles, etc.
266. Tacos, salsa, hot peppers, etc.
267. States weather
268. Wind
269. States if cloudy
270. Yes
271. Partly cloudy
272. Ice and water
273. Thunderstorm or tornado
274. A drizzle
275. A shower
276. Hail
277. (Severe) thunderstorm
278. Indoors, away from windows
279. Under a tree, etc.
280. Snow
281. Flurries
282. Blizzard
283. Snowflake
284. Different
285. 6
286. Estimates temp.
287. A thermometer
288. No
289. Temperature

ANSWERS - SCIENCE

290. Hot
291. Cold
292. States winter weather
293. Coat, hat, gloves, boots, etc.
294. States fall weather
295. Jacket, hat, etc.
296. Change color and fall
297. Cool, rainy, etc.
298. Raincoat, light jacket, etc.
299. Sprout, start to grow
300. Hot, dry, etc.
301. Shorts, swim suit, etc.
302. A rainbow
303. Red, orange, yellow, green, blue, indigo, and violet
304. The Sun
305. Solar
306. Windmill
307. Earth
308. Yes
309. Astronauts

310. Water
311. Mars, Jupiter, Saturn, etc.
312. The Moon
313. Different shapes
314. The stars
315. Solar System
316. Mountains, canyons, etc.
317. Water
318. Oceans
319. Sun, Moon, water drop, etc.
320. Stones, shells, mountains, etc.
321. Sand, feathers, rabbits, etc.
322. Fish, tree bark, a gravel road, etc.
323. Skin, leaf, apple, etc.
324. Plants, trees, frogs, etc.
325. Elephants, Moose, rocks, etc.
326. Feathers, birds, leaves, etc.

327. Pushing it
328. Pulling it
329. Yes
330. Forth
331. At rest
332. Swing is set in motion
333. Merry-go-round
334. Cheetah, hares, ostriches, etc.
335. Tortoise, sloth, starfish, snail, etc.
336. Magnetic field
337. Iron, nickel, and cobalt
338. Paperclips
339. Stainless refrigerator
340. A metal lock
341. Iron
342. 2
343. They will repel
344. They will attract
345. A leaf
346. A bottle cap

Science – 1st Grade

347. Earth Science
348. Yes
349. Soil
350. Mountains
351. Yes
352. Glaciers
353. Volcanoes
354. Mountains, caves, cliffs, etc.
355. Pacific, Atlantic, etc.
356. Salt water
357. Yes
358. Jupiter, Mars, Venus, etc.
359. Astronomy
360. Moon, stars, Sun, etc.
361. No
362. Movement of Sun, Moon, etc.
363. Earth rotates around Sun
364. Moon rotates around Earth
365. Round
366. Neil Armstrong
367. Telescope
368. Yes
369. Einstein, Newton, etc.
370. Biology
371. Metal, iron, etc.
372. Yes
373. Repel
374. Attract
375. Human, animal, etc.

376. Yes
377. Yes
378. Death
379. Chrysalis
380. Natural resources
381. Ration, recycle, etc.
382. Sun
383. Yes
384. In the morning
385. Noon
386. Yes
387. A microscope
388. Sand, wood, glass, etc.
389. Living things
390. Oxygen
391. Harder to breathe
392. Stem, leaves, flower, etc.
393. Root
394. A plant or tree
395. A flower or plant
396. An Oak tree
397. Spring, summer, fall, winter
398. Yes
399. Yes
400. Wind
401. Wind
402. Wind
403. Wind direction
404. Air
405. Electricity

406. Radar
407. Rain, storm, etc.
408. Temperature
409. A tornado
410. Indoors
411. Predicts tomorrow's weather
412. Yes
413. Gases
414. Names solid material
415. Water, etc.
416. Air, etc.
417. Ice
418. It melts
419. Steam
420. Evaporation
421. A dog's dish
422. Yes
423. Animals, plants, etc.
424. Imitates animal sounds
425. Elephant, pig, cricket, etc.
426. Mouse, kitten, bird, etc.
427. The Blue Whale
428. High
429. Low
430. Yes
431. The speed of light
432. Names animal-eating animal
433. Yes
434. Yes

ANSWERS - SCIENCE

435. Elephant, giraffe, etc.
436. Cow, pig, horse, etc.
437. Whale, seahorse, octopus, etc.
438. Elephant, lion, seal, etc.
439. Robin, hawk, eagle, etc.
440. Penguins, insects, bats, etc.
441. Bats, snakes, bears, etc.
442. Razor-sharp teeth
443. Sharp
444. Yes
445. An alligator
446. Two long front teeth
447. Plants
448. Yes
449. Chew food, etc.
450. More than 4,000
451. Dog, gorilla, elephant, etc.
452. Mammal
453. Yes
454. Marsupial
455. Platypus
456. Very smart
457. Tongue
458. Reptiles
459. Alligator, snake, turtle, etc.
460. Frogs
461. Their tongue
462. No
463. Turtle, lizard, snake, etc.
464. Amphibians
465. Frog, toad, salamander, etc.
466. Snake
467. Perch, bass, walleye, etc.
468. An insect
469. Butterfly, ant, worm, etc.
470. Spider
471. Rabbit, kangaroo, etc.
472. Snake, alligator, etc.
473. Cheetah, rabbit, etc.
474. Bird, bat, butterfly, etc.
475. Fish, whale, etc.
476. Kangaroo, rabbit, frog, etc.
477. Bears, chipmunks, skunks
478. Yes
479. Giraffe
480. Elephant
481. Leopard, giraffe, dog, etc.
482. Spots
483. Zebra, tiger, skunk, etc.
484. Rabbit, fox, mink, etc.
485. Fish, snake, lizard, crocodile, etc.
486. Deer, antelope, moose, etc.
487. Yes
488. Extinct
489. Endangered
490. Dinosaurs
491. Yes
492. Habitat
493. Habitats
494. Water
495. Food and shelter
496. Sunlight
497. Light and dark
498. To prove something
499. Yes
500. Yes
501. Goggles
502. Yes
503. To measure
504. Magnifying it
505. The temperature
506. A balance scale
507. Larger
508. Telescope
509. Yes
510. Yes

Science – 2nd Grade

511. Yes
512. Yes
513. Yes
514. Liquid
515. Solid
516. Gas
517. Expand
518. 0
519. 32
520. 212
521. 100
522. A gas
523. It melts
524. 2 liters
525. 1 meter
526. 100
527. 1.4 grams
528. 1 kilometer
529. Yes
530. Magnets
531. Yes
532. Iron alloys
533. Metals, steel, etc.
534. North and South
535. Opposite
536. Same
537. No
538. They connect
539. North
540. Toward the Earth
541. Yes
542. Ruler, yardstick, etc.
543. Balance scale
544. A graduating cylinder
545. Volume
546. Scale
547. Thermometer
548. 98.6
549. Yes
550. Food chain
551. Consumers
552. Grasshopper, frog, snake, eagle
553. Yes
554. Producers
555. Consumers
556. Decomposers
557. Yes
558. Yes
559. Water, light, and soil
560. Seeds
561. Flower
562. Fruit
563. Spreads pollen
564. Oxygen
565. Plants
566. Food, flowers, etc.
567. Nests, pouches, etc.
568. Den, stays with them
569. Yes
570. Horse, oxen, etc.
571. Crocodile, Stonefish, Great White Shark, Cape Buffalo, Poison dart frog, Hyena, Puffer fish, Viper snake, etc.
572. Yes
573. Birds, butterflies, etc.
574. Alligators, frogs, fish, etc.
575. The rainforest
576. Mammals and birds
577. Instinct
578. Skin and fur
579. Mammals
580. A small mammal
581. Butterfly, ladybug, fly, etc.

ANSWERS -SCIENCE

582. Head
583. Butterfly
584. Caterpillar
585. Dry them
586. Arachnids
587. 8
588. Migration
589. Duck, geese, etc.
590. Monarch
591. Life Cycle
592. Egg
593. Tadpole
594. Water
595. Webbed
596. Hibernate
597. A den
598. A beaver
599. Camouflage
600. Travel to another place
601. Dinosaurs
602. Theory
603. Climate, asteroid, disease, etc.
604. Lack of food
605. Frog, birds, wild plants
606. Cactus, rodents, lizards, etc.
607. Deer, fox, bear, etc.
608. White
609. Biomes
610. Yes
611. Yes
612. Sharks, whales, kelp, etc.
613. Birds, frogs, parrots, butterflies, etc.
614. Yes
615. Yes
616. Yes
617. Telescope, satellites, etc.
618. Rocket, space lab, etc.
619. Telescope
620. Stars, Sun, Moon, etc.
621. No
622. It is bigger and closer
623. A constellation
624. Yes
625. Yes
626. Moon around Earth
627. Earth around Sun
628. Yes
629. Full Moon
630. New Moon
631. Revolve
632. Yes
633. Tides
634. Yes
635. 24 hours
636. 365.25 days
637. Night
638. Day
639. Winter
640. Summer
641. Different
642. Yes
643. Wind, rain, show, etc.
644. Wind
645. Precipitation
646. Steam
647. Condensation
648. Drought
649. Radar, barometer, thermometer, etc.
650. Forecast the weather
651. Thermometer
652. Rain gauge
653. Barometer
654. Wind speed
655. Hurricane
656. Yes
657. Temporary
658. Tells weather for each season
659. Climate
660. Yes
661. Warmer
662. Cold
663. Warm
664. Describes climate
665. Yes
666. Yes
667. Yes
668. Yes
669. The equator
670. Yes
671. Water cycle
672. Wind and water
673. Erosion
674. Flowing water
675. Trees
676. Delta
677. Yes
678. Yes
679. Fossil
680. Simple machines
681. A wedge
682. A slide
683. Scientific method
684. Yes

Science-3rd Grade

685. Yes
686. Yes
687. Yes
688. Yes
689. Yes
690. Solid, liquid, and gas
691. Gases
692. Yes
693. It can freeze
694. It can melt
695. It can evaporate
696. Vaporization
697. A cell
698. Molecules
699. Energy
700. Solar
701. Yes
702. Friction
703. Yes
704. Yes
705. Fire
706. Heat
707. Yes
708. In waves
709. 186,000 miles per second
710. Yes
711. A straight line
712. Yes
713. Yes
714. White light
715. All colors
716. A prism
717. Opaque
718. A wooden door
719. A window
720. A mirror
721. Reversed
722. Concave
723. Convex
724. Refraction
725. A rainbow
726. Red, orange, yellow, green, blue, indigo and violet
727. Roy G Biv
728. Lamps, candles, flashlights, etc.
729. Yes
730. The eye
731. Says eye color
732. Yes
733. Glasses or contact lenses
734. Nearsighted
735. Farsighted
736. Bifocals
737. A microscope
738. A telescope

ANSWERS - SCIENCE

739. Yes
740. Magnify
741. The speed of light
742. 186,000 miles per second
743. 767 miles per hour
744. Increasing
745. Vibrations
746. Pitch
747. Sound waves
748. Yes
749. Faster
750. Humpback whale
751. Yes
752. Yes
753. It breaks
754. Amplifier
755. The tuba
756. The flute
757. Your larynx
758. Your ear canal
759. Yes
760. Acoustics
761. Motion
762. The top
763. Yes
764. Wave length
765. Yes
766. Velocity
767. Acceleration
768. Force
769. Yes
770. Inertia
771. Work
772. Simple tools
773. Simple machines
774. Wedges
775. Inclined planes
776. Pulleys
777. Screws
778. Wheel and axle
779. Levers
780. Wind, storms, etc.
781. They break down
782. Sediment
783. Soil
784. Humus
785. Loam
786. Moss
787. Humus
788. Nutrients
789. Rotate them
790. Recycled
791. Yes
792. Yes
793. Windmill
794. Solar panels, etc.
795. Yes
796. Yes
797. Weathering
798. Earthquake
799. A seismograph
800. The inside
801. The mantle
802. The inner core
803. The mantle
804. The crust
805. The crust
806. Erosion
807. A volcano
808. Molten lave
809. An eruption
810. Yes
811. Biomes
812. Yes
813. Canyon
814. Yes
815. Savanna
816. Yes
817. The wetlands
818. The grasslands
819. Prairies
820. Savannas
821. Pampas
822. Wetlands
823. The Alpine tundra
824. The rainforest
825. The desert
826. The Arctic tundra
827. Antarctic
828. North Pole
829. South Pole
830. The Alpine tundra
831. The Coral reef
832. The jellyfish
833. The Arctic
834. The desert
835. The Sahara
836. Antarctica
837. The rainforest
838. Freshwater wetlands
839. Marine
840. The tundra
841. Permafrost
842. The Taiga
843. Coniferous forest
844. Cold winters and rainy summers
845. Yes
846. The evergreen
847. Ecology
848. Dependent
849. Ecosystem
850. No
851. No
852. Yes
853. Yes
854. Yes
855. Yes
856. Producers
857. Producers
858. Food
859. Consumers
860. Consumer
861. Herbivores
862. Carnivores
863. Herbivores
864. Yes
865. Carnivores
866. Yes
867. Omnivores
868. Omnivores
869. Decomposers
870. Green plants
871. Human, animals, etc.
872. Wolf, etc.
873. Giraffe, antelope, etc.
874. Herbs
875. Humans, pigs, squirrels, etc.
876. Food
877. The food chain
878. Complete circle
879. Yes
880. Says what eats what
881. Yes
882. Animal dwellings
883. Oxygen
884. Bean, corn, flower, etc.
885. Oak, maple, ash, etc.
886. Rose, tulip, petunia, etc.
887. Robin, sparrow, cardinal, etc.
888. Fly south; migrate
889. Migration
890. Dams
891. Bison
892. Bison
893. Vertebrates
894. Invertebrates
895. Yes
896. Yes
897. Invertebrates
898. Cold-blooded
899. Warm-blooded
900. Warm-blooded
901. 98.6
902. Amphibians
903. Bullfrog
904. Birds
905. Birds of prey
906. Reptiles
907. Snake
908. Mammals
909. Whales and dolphins
910. A puppy
911. A kitten
912. Duckling
913. A gosling
914. A chick
915. A calf

ANSWERS - SCIENCE

916. A cub
917. A joey
918. Marsupials
919. A calf
920. A foal
921. A colt
922. A filly
923. A piglet
924. A fawn
925. A cub
926. A hatchling
927. A bunny
928. A baby
929. An infant
930. Larva
931. A maggot
932. A spiderling
933. A tadpole
934. A kid
935. A lamb
936. A nymph
937. Herd
938. Pack
939. Flock
940. Schools
941. Swarms
942. A pod
943. A girl
944. A boy
945. A hen
946. A rooster
947. A boar
948. A sow
949. Bull
950. Cows
951. Buck
952. Doe
953. Stallion
954. Mare
955. The female
956. Birds
957. Yes
958. The peacock
959. The peacock
960. The ostrich
961. Penguin
962. A hummingbird
963. Oysters
964. Hippopotamus
965. Giraffe
966. The cheetah
967. Elephant
968. Monkey
969. Primates
970. Fox
971. Herbivores
972. Beef
973. A coyote
974. A bat
975. A mammal
976. An owl
977. A parrot
978. Dove
979. Names state bird
980. Names state animal
981. Eagle
982. Crow
983. Flamingo
984. Chicken
985. The rat
986. Insects
987. An egg
988. Caterpillar
989. Chrysalis
990. A butterfly
991. Monarch
992. 6
993. 8
994. Yes
995. Honey bee
996. Honey
997. The female
998. The hive
999. Den
1000. A colony
1001. Swarm
1002. Butterflies and moths
1003. Four-stage
1004. Small fly
1005. Firefly
1006. Frog
1007. Llama
1008. Hyena
1009. Camel
1010. Bear
1011. The Giant Panda
1012. Bamboo
1013. The polar bear
1014. Hibernate
1015. Yes
1016. Marsupials
1017. Eucalyptus
1018. Warm-blooded
1019. Cold-blooded
1020. Aardvark
1021. Anteater
1022. Armadillo
1023. Badger
1024. Groundhog
1025. Raccoon
1026. Skunk
1027. Porcupine
1028. Beaver
1029. Dinosaurs
1030. Stegosaurus
1031. Tyrannosaurus Rex (T-Rex)
1032. Triceratops
1033. Affects food supply, homes, etc.
1034. Weather
1035. Climate
1036. Meteorologist
1037. Precipitation
1038. Condensation
1039. Clouds
1040. Cirrus
1041. Cumulus
1042. Stratus
1043. Rain
1044. Fog
1045. The oceans
1046. Acid rain
1047. Oil drilling
1048. Chemical run-off
1049. Smog
1050. Smog
1051. Death or displacement
1052. 75%
1053. An underground well
1054. A lake
1055. Yes
1056. Natural resources
1057. Weather
1058. Coal, oil, and gas
1059. Yes
1060. Systems
1061. Skeletal
1062. 206
1063. Femur thigh bone
1064. Inside your ear
1065. Skull
1066. Spinal column
1067. Joint
1068. Elbow
1069. Knee
1070. Wrist
1071. Ankle
1072. Joints
1073. Tailbone
1074. Ligaments
1075. Cartilage
1076. The rib cage
1077. Organs
1078. Heart
1079. Lungs
1080. Kidneys
1081. Liver
1082. Your skin
1083. Grow back together
1084. X-Ray
1085. Muscles
1086. Biceps
1087. The buttocks
1088. Tendon
1089. Achilles
1090. Hamstring
1091. Brain
1092. Nervous
1093. Yes

ANSWERS - SCIENCE

1094. Two
1095. Left
1096. Right
1097. The brain stem
1098. A brain signal
1099. Reflex action
1100. Joints like the knee or elbow
1101. Reflex actions
1102. Eat well, exercise, etc.
1103. Space science
1104. Astronomy
1105. Star
1106. The universe
1107. Milky Way
1108. Billions
1109. Yes
1110. Astronomers
1111. Telescope
1112. A radio telescope
1113. Arecibo, Puerto Rico
1114. The world's largest radio telescope
1115. The Hubble Space Telescope
1116. Yes
1117. Big Bang Theory
1118. Yes
1119. 9
1120. Earth
1121. The Sun
1122. Sun
1123. The Sun
1124. Nicolaus Copernicus
1125. The Sun
1126. Yes
1127. 93 Million miles
1128. 8 Minutes
1129. The Sun
1130. 10,000 Degrees Fahrenheit
1131. Solar
1132. Earth revolves around Sun
1133. Planets
1134. NO
1135. 8
1136. A dwarf planet
1137. Both
1138. Jupiter
1139. Mercury
1140. Yes
1141. Orbit
1142. Rotate
1143. To spin
1144. Inner planets
1145. Solid and rocky
1146. Mercury
1147. Venus
1148. Mars
1149. The asteroid belt
1150. Outer planets
1151. Full of liquid and gas
1152. Jupiter
1153. Saturn
1154. Neptune
1155. Pluto
1156. Earth
1157. Its axis
1158. Slightly tilted
1159. Seasons
1160. Fall, winter, spring, summer
1161. No
1162. Winter
1163. Summer
1164. Different
1165. Opposite
1166. Winter
1167. Spring
1168. Winter
1169. Summer
1170. Spring
1171. Autumn
1172. Yes
1173. Cool, rainy
1174. Hot, sunny
1175. The Earth
1176. East
1177. West
1178. One day
1179. 365 ¼ days
1180. 365 ¼ days
1181. Leap year
1182. February
1183. Yes/no
1184. Daytime
1185. Nighttime
1186. Yes
1187. A constellation
1188. Billions
1189. Yes
1190. North Star
1191. North
1192. Polaris
1193. One
1194. Yes
1195. Jupiter
1196. Venus and Mercury
1197. Moon orbits Earth
1198. 27 days
1199. A satellite
1200. Sun and Moon
1201. The Moon
1202. The Earth
1203. Gravity
1204. Gravity
1205. Toward the center
1206. Yes
1207. Yes
1208. Isaac Newton
1209. G-forces
1210. 5 g's
1211. Yes
1212. Stronger attraction
1213. A black hole
1214. Reflected light from Sun
1215. Phases
1216. Full
1217. Lunar cycle
1218. Yes
1219. Yes
1220. 29
1221. One
1222. 238,855
1223. Yes
1224. Astronauts
1225. Apollo
1226. Neil Armstrong
1227. Giant leap for mankind.
1228. NASA
1229. Telescope
1230. Sound
1231. Rocket or shuttle
1232. International Space Station
1233. A comet
1234. Halley's Comet
1235. A meteorite
1236. Asteroid
1237. A satellite
1238. Yes
1239. Constellations
1240. Big Dipper
1241. Ursa Major
1242. Little Dipper
1243. Ursa Minor
1244. Polaris
1245. Yes
1246. Shuttle or rocket
1247. Predicts a celestial body
1248. Ecosystem
1249. Yes
1250. Producers, consumers, decomposers
1251. Producers
1252. A plant
1253. An animal
1254. Fungi
1255. Food
1256. The Sun
1257. Photosynthesis
1258. Decomposers
1259. Yes
1260. Yes
1261. Smoke, exhaust, etc.
1262. Chlorine
1263. Waste, chemicals, etc.
1264. Recycle, don't pollute, etc.
1265. Nicolaus Copernicus

ANSWERS -SCIENCE

1266. John Muir
1267. Telegraph
1268. Morse Code
1269. Telephone
1270. Light bulb
1271. Amelia Earhart

Science – 4th Grade

1272. Yes
1273. Physical
1274. Equal to
1275. Yes
1276. Solids, liquids, and gases
1277. Plasmas
1278. Yes
1279. Man-made plasma
1280. Solid
1281. Liquid
1282. Gas
1283. Helium
1284. Yes
1285. Solid to liquid
1286. Liquid to gas
1287. Evaporation
1288. Steam
1289. Evaporation
1290. Condensation
1291. Frost
1292. Rust
1293. Visible
1294. Invisible
1295. Beach ball, etc.
1296. Basketball, stone, etc.
1297. Yes
1298. 118
1299. An atom
1300. Molecules
1301. An element
1302. Yes
1303. Periodic
1304. A compound
1305. Water
1306. True
1307. A property
1308. Yes
1309. Physical properties
1310. Physical
1311. Periodic table
1312. Non-metals
1313. Penny, pipes, etc.
1314. Trumpet, bed, etc.
1315. Appliances, cookware, etc.
1316. Bells, statues, Olympic medals, etc.
1317. Buckles, keys, earrings, etc.
1318. Jewelry, coins, Olympic medals, etc.
1319. Silverware, jewelry, coins, etc.
1320. Nails, cans, pots, etc.
1321. Cans, foil, tinsel, etc.
1322. Cans, baseball bats, siding, etc.
1323. Volume
1324. Capacity
1325. Grams
1326. Liters
1327. A balance
1328. Energy
1329. Potential and Kinetic
1330. Potential
1331. Kinetic
1332. Yes
1333. Forms of energy
1334. Potential to kinetic
1335. Energy
1336. Pushing a wheelbarrow
1337. Solar
1338. Mechanical
1339. Yes
1340. Chemical
1341. Coal
1342. Electrical
1343. Potential
1344. Kinetic
1345. Potential
1346. Kinetic
1347. Potential to Kinetic
1348. Electrical
1349. Mechanical
1350. Heat
1351. Chemical
1352. Gravitational
1353. Chemical
1354. Yes
1355. Renewable
1356. Non-renewable
1357. Force
1358. Yes
1359. Motion
1360. Yes
1361. Yes
1362. Speed
1363. A force
1364. Gravity
1365. A force
1366. Both
1367. Balanced forces
1368. Balanced
1369. Balanced
1370. Friction
1371. Slows it down
1372. Yes
1373. Heat
1374. Inertia
1375. The first law of motion
1376. Sir Isaac Newton
1377. Apple fell out of tree
1378. Opposite reaction
1379. Inertia
1380. More inertia
1381. Simple machines
1382. Simple machines
1383. A wedge
1384. A lever
1385. A wheel and axle
1386. An inclined plane
1387. A pulley
1388. A screw
1389. Compound
1390. Complex
1391. Complex
1392. Lever, wheel and axle
1393. Appliances, lamps, etc.
1394. A circuit
1395. Positive
1396. Open
1397. Conductors
1398. Conductors of electricity
1399. Insulators
1400. Series
1401. Parallel
1402. Closed
1403. Open
1404. A closed circuit
1405. A series circuit
1406. A parallel circuit
1407. Copper
1408. Iron
1409. Electromagnetic lines
1410. Low voltage
1411. Current
1412. Direct Current
1413. AC
1414. Amperes or amps
1415. Static
1416. Yes
1417. An electromagnet
1418. Yes
1419. Electromagnets
1420. Electric
1421. Yes
1422. Michael Faraday
1423. Thomas Edison
1424. Benjamin Franklin
1425. Thomas Edison

ANSWERS - SCIENCE

1426. Light
1427. Sunlight
1428. Visible
1429. Yes
1430. Red, orange, yellow, green, blue, indigo, and violet
1431. Red
1432. Violet
1433. Yes
1434. The color it reflects
1435. Yes
1436. In waves
1437. White light
1438. Black light
1439. A crest and a trough
1440. Yes
1441. A wavelength
1442. A trough
1443. A crest
1444. Radar
1445. 8 minutes
1446. Light
1447. Light travels faster
1448. A vacuum
1449. Light
1450. Yes
1451. Light
1452. Laser
1453. Insects
1454. Smooth
1455. Light
1456. Refracted
1457. Refracted
1458. Yes
1459. Transmitted
1460. Light that passes through
1461. Transparent
1462. Translucent
1463. Opaque
1464. Absorbed
1465. Reflect
1466. Dark clothing
1467. Translucent
1468. Transparent
1469. Opaque
1470. Lens
1471. Lenses
1472. Refraction
1473. Convex and concave
1474. Convergent and divergent
1475. Convex
1476. Concave
1477. Convex
1478. Concave
1479. Convex
1480. Microscope
1481. Telescope
1482. Binoculars
1483. Sound
1484. In waves
1485. Yes
1486. The frequency of sound
1487. Hertz
1488. The wavelength of sound
1489. Pitch
1490. Fast
1491. Slow
1492. Low pitch
1493. High pitch
1494. Quicker
1495. Gases
1496. Steel
1497. Yes
1498. Vibrate
1499. Volume
1500. Decibels
1501. An echo
1502. Mach 1
1503. Our ears
1504. Life Science
1505. Cells
1506. Kingdoms
1507. Kingdoms
1508. Plants
1509. Says name of plant
1510. Vascular and nonvascular
1511. Yes
1512. Spore-producing
1513. Seed-producing
1514. Seeds
1515. Flowering
1516. The sepals
1517. Photosynthesis
1518. Pollination
1519. Plant reproduction
1520. Producers
1521. The root
1522. The leaves
1523. The stem
1524. The pistil
1525. The stamen
1526. Pollination
1527. Spores
1528. Photosynthesis
1529. Food
1530. The Sun
1531. Chlorophyll
1532. Dormancy
1533. The soil
1534. The constants
1535. Consumers
1536. Producers
1537. Decomposers
1538. A decomposer
1539. Sun, producer, consumer, decomposer
1540. An ecosystem
1541. A biome
1542. Waste, cut down trees, etc.
1543. Food chain
1544. The Sun
1545. Niche
1546. Habitat
1547. Adaptation
1548. Behavioral
1549. Structural
1550. Earth Science
1551. The Solar System
1552. The Sun
1553. Eight
1554. A dwarf planet
1555. Another dwarf planet
1556. Inner planets
1557. Outer planets
1558. Third planet
1559. 4.5 billion years old
1560. 150 kilometers
1561. 93 million
1562. The ozone layer
1563. Atmosphere, water, and energy
1564. The Earth
1565. The Sun
1566. The Sun
1567. 4.5 billion years
1568. One
1569. 24 hours
1570. Day and night
1571. Summer
1572. Winter
1573. Summer
1574. The Moon
1575. Mars
1576. The Moon
1577. Moon phases
1578. Tides
1579. Lunar
1580. Solar
1581. Four
1582. Lithosphere
1583. The inner core
1584. The crust
1585. The mantle
1586. The outer core
1587. The inner core
1588. Plates
1589. Plate Tectonics
1590. Convergent
1591. Divergent
1592. Continental drift
1593. A fault
1594. Tectonic plates
1595. The San Andreas Fault
1596. An earthquake
1597. Seismic waves
1598. The epicenter
1599. The epicenter
1600. Seismologists
1601. A seismograph

ANSWERS - SCIENCE

1602. Magnitude
1603. Richter scale
1604. A tsunami
1605. Yes
1606. An avalanche
1607. A landslide
1608. A mudslide
1609. An avalanche
1610. A volcano
1611. Lava
1612. Along the edges
1613. Mountains
1614. Active
1615. Dormant
1616. Mount Vesuvius
1617. Mount Saint Helens
1618. A hot spring
1619. A geyser
1620. Old Faithful
1621. Pangaea
1622. Continental drift
1623. 3
1624. Dome
1625. Folded
1626. Folded
1627. Fault-block mountains
1628. Rocks
1629. Minerals
1630. How they were formed
1631. 3
1632. Yes
1633. Igneous
1634. Yes
1635. Sedimentary
1636. Metamorphic
1637. Yes
1638. Physical weathering
1639. Chemical weathering
1640. Erosion
1641. Topsoil
1642. Subsoil
1643. Bedrock
1644. Yes
1645. Glaciers
1646. The Ice Age
1647. Great Lakes
1648. Great Lakes
1649. Glaciers
1650. Montana
1651. Alaska
1652. Says today's weather
1653. Meteorology
1654. The atmosphere
1655. The atmosphere
1656. 5
1657. Yes
1658. Exosphere
1659. Troposphere
1660. The ozone layer
1661. Mesosphere
1662. Precipitation
1663. Water cycle
1664. Rain
1665. Dew
1666. Fog
1667. Hail
1668. Snow
1669. Frost
1670. Temperature
1671. Thermometer
1672. Celsius
1673. Degrees Fahrenheit
1674. Visibility
1675. Yes
1676. A flood
1677. A drought
1678. Temperature
1679. Humidity
1680. Weight of the air
1681. Cold air
1682. Hot air
1683. A cold air mass
1684. Warm
1685. Air masses
1686. Air pocket
1687. High pressure
1688. Low pressure
1689. A front
1690. A warm front
1691. A cold front
1692. A warm front
1693. A cold front
1694. Yes
1695. Cirrus
1696. Cumulus
1697. Stratus
1698. Cumulonimbus
1699. Thunderheads
1700. Lightning
1701. Thunder
1702. 186,000 miles per second
1703. A barometer
1704. A hygrometer
1705. A rain gauge
1706. Wind
1707. Wind
1708. A breeze
1709. A gale
1710. A hurricane
1711. Yes
1712. Tornado
1713. A hurricane
1714. The eye
1715. An anemometer
1716. Prevailing winds
1717. Trade winds
1718. Coriolis Effect
1719. A jet stream
1720. Tidal waves
1721. A sandstorm
1722. A blizzard
1723. Climate
1724. Climates
1725. Tropical
1726. Polar
1727. Habitat
1728. Yes
1729. Season
1730. Yes
1731. Equator
1732. Opposite
1733. The same
1734. June 21st
1735. Winter
1736. September 21st
1737. December 21st
1738. March 21st
1739. Autumn
1740. Yes
1741. Monsoon
1742. Typhoon
1743. States weather preference
1744. States climate preference
1745. Anatomy
1746. Names outside body parts
1747. Names inside body parts
1748. A muscle
1749. Your skin
1750. The heart
1751. Yes
1752. Four
1753. Atria
1754. Ventricles
1755. Four
1756. Valves
1757. The aorta
1758. Blood vessels
1759. Arteries
1760. Veins
1761. Capillaries
1762. Blood pressure
1763. Pulse
1764. 60
1765. Goes up
1766. Blood
1767. Carbon dioxide
1768. Plasma
1769. Red and white
1770. Hemoglobin
1771. White
1772. Platelets
1773. Four months
1774. 8 million per second
1775. Liver
1776. Spleen
1777. Heart
1778. Heart attack
1779. Saturated fats
1780. Cardiac arrest
1781. A transfusion

ANSWERS - SCIENCE

1782. Four
1783. The four blood types
1784. The Rh factor
1785. Type O
1786. Positive
1787. Compatible blood type
1788. Blood clots
1789. Yes
1790. States blood type
1791. Different
1792. Yes
1793. Circulatory
1794. Respiratory
1795. 20,000
1796. Respiratory
1797. Lungs
1798. Trachea
1799. Bronchial tubes
1800. Alveoli
1801. The diaphragm
1802. Smoking
1803. Eat well, exercise, etc.

Science – 5th Grade

1804. Earth, biology, etc.
1805. Sciences
1806. The science of
1807. Anthropology
1808. Archeology
1809. Audiology
1810. Biology
1811. Cardiology
1812. Meteorology
1813. Dermatology
1814. Astronomy
1815. Ecology
1816. Geology
1817. Hematology
1818. Hydrology
1819. Climatology
1820. Geology
1821. Neurology
1822. Oncology
1823. Ophthalmology
1824. Paleontology
1825. Psychology
1826. Radiology
1827. Seismology
1828. Toxicology
1829. Virology
1830. Volcanology
1831. Zoology
1832. Solar system
1833. The Sun
1834. Earth
1835. Eight
1836. No
1837. Jupiter
1838. Mercury
1839. Saturn
1840. Yes
1841. Jupiter
1842. Two
1843. One
1844. The Sun
1845. Copernicus
1846. Kepler
1847. Uranus
1848. Mars
1849. Apollo
1850. Neil Armstrong
1851. Colombia
1852. The Eagle
1853. "The Eagle has landed."
1854. The United States
1855. Apollo 13
1856. James Lovell
1857. James Lovell
1858. The Odyssey
1859. The Aquarius
1860. Center in Houston, Texas
1861. Yes
1862. Sputnik
1863. President John F. Kennedy
1864. Skylab
1865. The U.S. and USSR
1866. The Colombia
1867. Sally Ride
1868. Kathryn Sullivan
1869. Space shuttles
1870. Yes
1871. Constellations
1872. Signs of the zodiac
1873. Ursa Major
1874. Ursa Minor
1875. Polaris
1876. Earth Science
1877. Land
1878. Four
1879. Pacific and Atlantic
1880. Oceans
1881. The Arctic
1882. The Antarctic
1883. Continents
1884. Geography
1885. Pangaea
1886. Seven
1887. Names continents
1888. Asia
1889. Australia
1890. Geology
1891. Rocks
1892. Minerals
1893. 4,000
1894. Rock
1895. Yes
1896. Mohs Scale of Mineral Hardness
1897. Low
1898. High
1899. Both
1900. A diamond
1901. Carbon
1902. A diamond
1903. White, yellow, pink, etc.
1904. A diamond
1905. Biology
1906. Chemistry
1907. An atom
1908. Yes
1909. The nucleus
1910. Protons and neutrons
1911. In orbitals around the nucleus
1912. A proton
1913. An electron
1914. A neutron
1915. Protons and electrons
1916. An ion
1917. An element
1918. Yes
1919. An isotope
1920. A molecule
1921. Yes
1922. Mendeleev
1923. Periodic table
1924. 63
1925. 117
1926. Metals and non-metals
1927. Metals
1928. Good
1929. Copper
1930. A group
1931. Yes
1932. Niels Bohr
1933. Niels Bohr
1934. Ernest Rutherford
1935. Atomic symbols
1936. A molecule
1937. O2
1938. A compound
1939. Water
1940. 2 Hydrogen with 1 Oxygen

ANSWERS - SCIENCE

1941. Carbon dioxide
1942. Oxygen
1943. Carbon dioxide
1944. Oxygen
1945. Light
1946. Putting together
1947. Carbon dioxide and light
1948. Both chemical and physical
1949. Physical
1950. Both
1951. Rust
1952. Iron oxide
1953. Sodium chloride
1954. NaCl
1955. Ions
1956. A chemical equation
1957. Chemical energy
1958. Chemical
1959. A solution
1960. Dissolve
1961. Solution
1962. Concentration
1963. Saturation
1964. Reaction
1965. Mixture
1966. Evaporation
1967. Condensation
1968. Crystallization
1969. Classification
1970. Yes
1971. Yes
1972. Kingdoms
1973. Kingdoms
1974. Yes
1975. Largest to smallest
1976. A microscope
1977. Cells
1978. Robert Hooke
1979. Theodor Schwann
1980. A membrane
1981. The membrane
1982. The cytoplasm
1983. The nucleus
1984. The nucleus
1985. Split into two cells
1986. Yes
1987. Mitosis
1988. Meiosis
1989. Organelles
1990. Mitochondria
1991. Yes
1992. Vacuoles
1993. Mitochondria
1994. Yes
1995. Living things
1996. Yes
1997. Human
1998. A system
1999. Organs
2000. Systems
2001. Cells
2002. DNA
2003. DNA
2004. RNA
2005. RNA
2006. Different
2007. A plant cell
2008. A plant cell
2009. Photosynthesis
2010. A plant
2011. A protist
2012. Spores
2013. Fungus
2014. Fungus
2015. Fungus
2016. Yes
2017. Into the air
2018. Organisms
2019. A microscope
2020. Protozoa
2021. Cilia
2022. Amoeba
2023. Algae
2024. Algae
2025. Kelp
2026. Euglena
2027. Prokaryotes
2028. An electron microscope
2029. Micro-organisms
2030. Microbiology
2031. Antonie Van Leeuwenhoek
2032. Germs
2033. Yes
2034. Yes
2035. Constructive
2036. Lactic acid bacteria
2037. Yeast
2038. Yes
2039. Bacterial
2040. Viral
2041. Tuberculosis
2042. Tetanus
2043. Toxin
2044. Viruses
2045. Typhus
2046. Cholera
2047. Louis Pasteur
2048. Pasteurization
2049. Joseph Lister
2050. Antibiotics
2051. Virus
2052. A vaccine
2053. Yes
2054. Polio
2055. An immunization
2056. As young children
2057. A virus
2058. Yes
2059. By their cell wall shape
2060. Cyanobacteria
2061. Eubacteria
2062. A parasite
2063. A host
2064. Parasites
2065. Yes
2066. Malaria
2067. Typhus
2068. West Nile Virus
2069. Yes
2070. Ergot
2071. Ergotism
2072. Gangrene
2073. Five
2074. Yes
2075. Taxonomy
2076. More specific
2077. Species
2078. Kingdom, Phylum, Class, Order, Family, genus, and Species
2079. Variety
2080. Domestic dog
2081. Phylum
2082. Yes
2083. Several Phyla
2084. Latin
2085. A dog
2086. A dog
2087. A cat
2088. Homo Sapiens
2089. Man
2090. Wise
2091. Yes
2092. Vertebrates
2093. Mammals
2094. Dog, cat, cow, human, etc.
2095. Mammals
2096. Mammals
2097. Birds
2098. Robin, sparrow, cardinal, etc.
2099. North America
2100. Birds
2101. Fish
2102. Perch, walleye, bluegill, etc.
2103. Invertebrates
2104. Arthropods
2105. Arachnids
2106. Invertebrates
2107. Amphibians
2108. Living in two places
2109. Amphibians
2110. Coquí
2111. Reptiles
2112. Reptiles
2113. A chameleon
2114. The Gecko
2115. The Gila monster

ANSWERS - SCIENCE

2116. Kingdoms
2117. Animalae
2118. Chordata
2119. Vertebrata
2120. Mammalia
2121. Carnivora
2122. Meat
2123. Plants
2124. Both plants and animals
2125. Canidae
2126. A canine
2127. Yes
2128. Cat
2129. Yes
2130. Canis
2131. Familiaris
2132. Species
2133. Breed
2134. A giant tortoise
2135. 150 years
2136. Extinct
2137. Endangered
2138. Endangerment
2139. Yes
2140. Rainforests
2141. The Amazon
2142. Yes
2143. Plants
2144. Chlorophyll
2145. Photosynthesis
2146. Both
2147. The roots
2148. The xylem
2149. The phloem
2150. Chloroplasts
2151. Stomata
2152. Carbon dioxide
2153. Sugars
2154. Stem
2155. Flower
2156. Seed
2157. Fruit
2158. Root
2159. Leaf
2160. Yes
2161. Four
2162. Plants
2163. Vascular and non-vascular
2164. Vascular
2165. Non-vascular
2166. Fern
2167. Moss
2168. The life cycle
2169. Yes
2170. Frogs
2171. Eggs
2172. Butterflies
2173. Yes
2174. Hens
2175. Eggs
2176. Reproduce
2177. Divide
2178. Seeds
2179. Spores
2180. Sexual
2181. Asexual
2182. Yes
2183. Bacteria
2184. Cold temperatures
2185. Spores
2186. Yeast
2187. Cloning
2188. Asexually
2189. Regeneration
2190. Regeneration
2191. Yes
2192. Starfish
2193. A salamander
2194. A new worm
2195. Sexual reproduction
2196. Yes
2197. Shady rocks
2198. Spores
2199. Female
2200. Male
2201. Fertilization
2202. At the top of the stalk
2203. Spores
2204. A zygote
2205. An embryo
2206. Conifer
2207. The pinecones
2208. Male
2209. Wind
2210. The seeds
2211. Grows into new tree
2212. Naked
2213. Gymnosperms
2214. They have flowers
2215. Apples and cherries
2216. Angiosperms
2217. Different parts
2218. Sepals
2219. The petals
2220. Stamen
2221. An anther
2222. The pistil
2223. The ovary
2224. The ovary
2225. Pollination
2226. Bees, butterflies, birds, etc.
2227. Nectar
2228. Germination
2229. Grows into new plant
2230. Seed coat
2231. The endosperm
2232. Yes
2233. The leaves
2234. Flowers
2235. Flowering plants
2236. Monocots
2237. Dicots
2238. A monocot
2239. A dicot
2240. A monocot
2241. A dicot
2242. Three
2243. Four
2244. Monocots
2245. Dicots
2246. Monocots
2247. Dicots
2248. Yes
2249. With
2250. Without
2251. Sexually
2252. Yes
2253. Sperm
2254. Eggs
2255. The testes
2256. The ovaries
2257. Earthworm
2258. External fertilization
2259. Internal fertilization
2260. Spawning
2261. Eggs
2262. Sperm
2263. Internal
2264. Same species
2265. A zygote
2266. An embryo
2267. The uterus
2268. The ovary
2269. A fetus
2270. Different
2271. Nine months
2272. Five months
2273. Eleven months
2274. Alligators
2275. Two years
2276. A pride
2277. A life cycle
2278. Embryo, fetus, foal, colt, horse
2279. Embryo, fetus, baby
2280. Toddler
2281. Child
2282. Adolescent
2283. Adult
2284. Middle age
2285. Human Development Stages
2286. Puberty
2287. Adolescence
2288. Hormones
2289. Puberty
2290. Similar
2291. Names female organs
2292. Names male organs

ANSWERS - SCIENCE

2293. A zygote
2294. Zygote, embryo, fetus
2295. The uterus
2296. Fraternal
2297. Identical
2298. Organs
2299. Yes
2300. Glandular
2301. Hormones
2302. Exocrine duct glands
2303. Endocrine ductless glands
2304. Pituitary gland
2305. Thyroid
2306. Pancreas
2307. The part with ducts
2308. The ductless part
2309. Insulin
2310. Diabetes
2311. Adrenal glands
2312. The circulatory system
2313. The respiratory system
2314. Breathe
2315. The digestive system
2316. The immune system
2317. The endocrine system
2318. The lymphatic system
2319. The nervous system
2320. The muscular system
2321. The skeletal system
2322. The skeletal system
2323. 206
2324. 22
2325. 33
2326. Cartilage
2327. In the joints
2328. Tendons
2329. Teeth
2330. 32
2331. Crown
2332. Root
2333. Enamel
2334. The gum
2335. Brush, floss, etc.
2336. An orthodontist
2337. Marrow
2338. The reproductive system
2339. The urinary system
2340. Antibodies
2341. Penicillin
2342. Eat well, exercise, visit doctor, etc.
2343. The Nobel Prize
2344. Nicolaus Copernicus
2345. Johannes Kepler
2346. Galileo Galilei
2347. Isaac Newton
2348. Gabriel Fahrenheit
2349. Carl Linnaeus
2350. Benjamin Franklin
2351. Henry Cavendish
2352. Avogadro
2353. Andre Ampere
2354. Michael Faraday
2355. Charles Darwin
2356. Elizabeth Blackwell
2357. Robert Bunsen
2358. Gregor Mendel
2359. James Maxwell
2360. Dmitri Mendeleev
2361. Louis Pasteur
2362. Sigmund Freud
2363. Ernest Rutherford
2364. Marie Curie
2365. Albert Einstein
2366. Niels Bohr
2367. Ernest Just
2368. Edwin Hubble
2369. Alexander Fleming
2370. Percy Lavon Julian
2371. Jonas Salk
2372. Jane Goodall
2373. Alchemy
2374. Cartography
2375. Botany
2376. Zoology
2377. Taxidermy
2378. A laboratory
2379. A hypothesis
2380. A theory
2381. Scientific Method
2382. Names experiments
2383. Scientific journals
2384. Names favorite science

ANSWERS – SOCIAL STUDIES

APPENDIX 5: Chapter 5 – Social Studies

Pre-school

1. United States (or other)
2. Names state
3. Names city
4. English, etc.
5. Yes
6. Draws, paints, etc.
7. Piano, flute, etc.
8. July 4th
9. Names familiar holidays
10. States nationality
11. Native Americans
12. The Pilgrims
13. Thanksgiving Day
14. Teepees
15. George Washington
16. The state, the capital, etc.
17. George Washington
18. The American Flag
19. Red, white, and blue
20. Abraham Lincoln
21. The South
22. Slavery
23. Cotton and Tobacco
24. Martin Luther King Jr.
25. Yes

Social Studies – Kindergarten

26. Yes
27. Born, adopted, etc.
28. Names immediate family
29. Names relatives
30. Names city
31. Names State
32. 50
33. United States of America
34. Canada
35. Mexico
36. Different
37. Different
38. No
39. Yes
40. Yes
41. Yes
42. Hunting, fishing, and farming
43. Tomahawk, spear, etc.
44. Buffalo, deer, etc.
45. A Teepee
46. Cone-shaped
47. Tools, blankets, etc.
48. Moccasins
49. Longhouses
50. Pueblos
51. Wigwams
52. A canoe
53. Totem poles
54. States nationality
55. Different
56. States religion
57. Different
58. Yes
59. Many ethnic cultures
60. North America
61. Seven
62. Antarctica
63. A continent
64. Asia
65. Names Asian country
66. Asia
67. Africa
68. North America
69. South America
70. Antarctica
71. Europe
72. Australia
73. United States of America
74. Alaska and Hawaii
75. United States of America
76. Old Glory
77. A map
78. State
79. Yes
80. A globe
81. Pacific and Atlantic
82. North, South, East, West
83. North
84. West
85. The East
86. The West
87. North
88. South
89. Yes
90. Indians
91. Flat
92. America
93. English (Spanish), etc.
94. Names differences
95. Electricity, phones, etc.
96. One-room schoolhouse, etc.
97. Clothespins, washboard, etc.
98. First
99. Yes
100. John Adams
101. Thomas Jefferson
102. The Declaration of Independence
103. John Hancock
104. England
105. 16th
106. Lincoln
107. Teddy
108. Teddy Bear
109. Mount Rushmore
110. Names current President
111. The White House
112. Washington, D.C.
113. District of Colombia
114. Yes
115. Ballet
116. Names holidays
117. Eating turkey, etc.
118. Turkey, pumpkin pie, etc.
119. Pilgrims and Indians
120. January
121. November
122. December
123. Different
124. July 4th
125. Colors, stars, stripes
126. George Washington
127. February
128. Yes
129. January
130. Names seasons
131. Names winter holidays
132. Easter, etc.
133. Independence Day, etc.
134. Halloween, Thanksgiving Day, etc.
135. Yes
136. Yes
137. Different
138. No
139. Italian food
140. Mexican food

ANSWERS - SOCIAL STUDIES

141. Names ethnic foods
142. Different
143. Names family similarities
144. Names family differences
145. Yes
146. Yes
147. Honesty, vote, etc.
148. Cleaning, care of pet, etc.
149. Money
150. Food, cattle, etc.
151. Work
152. Yes
153. A need
154. A want
155. The dollar
156. Names money bills
157. Different
158. Chores, etc.
159. Yes
160. A bank

Social Studies – 1st Grade

161. Explains map and globe
162. Help us locate and identify
163. Top
164. Bottom
165. To the right
166. To the left
167. Locates own city on map
168. Locates state on map
169. United States
170. Locates America in map
171. Locates North America on globe
172. 50
173. Names own state
174. Alaska and Hawaii
175. Washington, D.C.
176. Names current U.S. President
177. The White House
178. We vote
179. Names own state capital
180. Tells why own state is famous
181. Names county
182. States if attended a fair
183. Yes/no
184. States city of residence
185. Names street
186. Buildings, roads, stores, etc.
187. Farms, fields, cows, etc.
188. Population
189. Size, language, etc.
190. Size, language, technology, etc.
191. Yes
192. Democratic
193. Can cite Pledge of Allegiance
194. Star-Spangled Banner, etc.
195. Yes
196. Describes flag
197. Green, white, and red
198. Red and white
199. Tells about Mexican culture
200. Tells about Canadian culture
201. Spanish
202. English and French
203. Moose, fish, bears, etc.
204. Yes
205. Labor Day
206. Columbus Day
207. Halloween
208. Veterans Day
209. Thanksgiving Day
210. Cites cultural differences
211. Names a family tradition
212. Christmas (Hanukkah, Kwanzza, etc.)
213. Buy presents, decorate, sing, etc.
214. No
215. New Year's Day
216. Martin Luther King Day
217. Presidents' Day
218. Washington
219. Abraham Lincoln
220. St. Patrick's Day
221. Easter, etc.
222. Cinco de Mayo
223. Memorial Day
224. July 4th
225. The United Kingdom
226. States yes or no
227. Flag, tree, flowers, etc.
228. Work
229. Phone, vacation, etc.
230. Food, clothing, etc.
231. Food, shelter, etc.
232. Name U.S. coins
233. 1 cent
234. 5 cents
235. 10 cents
236. 25 cents
237. 50 cents
238. Names U.S. bills
239. Names foreign currency
240. No
241. Emergency, buy larger items, etc.
242. Traded with other goods and services
243. Yes
244. The doctor
245. A police officer
246. A fireman or firewoman
247. A dentist
248. Postal worker (mailperson)
249. A veterinarian
250. A teacher

Social Studies – 2nd Grade

251. The universe
252. The Milky Way
253. Earth
254. Names other planets
255. Oceans
256. Pacific and Atlantic
257. Yes
258. Pacific
259. Indian, Caribbean, etc.
260. Equator
261. Continents
262. Seven
263. North America (or other)
264. North America
265. To the north
266. To the south
267. No
268. Globe
269. Northern and Southern
270. Yes
271. Yes
272. Mountains, rivers, etc.
273. Yes
274. Yes

ANSWERS – SOCIAL STUDIES

275. A capital
276. Scale
277. North, South, East, West
278. Northeast
279. Southwest
280. The east
281. The west
282. Regions
283. Divisions
284. Names region
285. Names home state
286. Names home town
287. Names home county
288. Names other counties
289. An atlas
290. A city map
291. Geography
292. The seven continents
293. Countries
294. Yes
295. North America
296. Asia
297. Yes
298. Australia
299. Africa
300. South Sudan
301. Names African animals
302. Yes
303. On a land bridge
304. Names countries of ancestors
305. States family's nationality
306. The Sahara
307. The Nile
308. North America
309. Canada
310. United States
311. Mexico
312. Central America
313. South America
314. The Andes
315. The Amazon
316. The llama
317. The Antarctic
318. Europe
319. Australia and Oceania
320. An island
321. The Indian Ocean
322. Asia
323. Emperor
324. Stars and the Universe
325. China
326. Beijing
327. Yes
328. Chinese
329. Rice, egg rolls, etc.
330. Yes
331. Silk
332. The Great Wall of China
333. Yes
334. Yes
335. Yes
336. Tokyo
337. Japanese
338. Rice, fish, sushi, etc.
339. Yes
340. A kimono
341. Shoes
342. On the floor
343. Yes
344. India
345. New Delhi
346. Hindi
347. Rice, fish, flatbreads
348. Yes
349. A sari
350. Yes
351. Names African countries
352. Swahili
353. Rice, bread, bananas, etc.
354. Giraffes, elephants, etc.
355. Africa
356. The Nile
357. The Sahara
358. Pyramids
359. Hieroglyphics
360. Papyrus
361. Pharaoh
362. Yes
363. Yes
364. North America
365. Geography
366. Yes
367. Names area of country
368. Names bordering states
369. Appalachians
370. Missouri
371. Great Salt Lake
372. The Rocky Mountains
373. Rio Grande
374. North America
375. Spanish
376. Tacos, enchiladas, etc.
377. Yes
378. Ballet Folklorico
379. Mariachi
380. Inca
381. Mexico City
382. Canada
383. Provinces
384. Territories
385. Ottawa
386. English and French
387. Fish, bacon, ham, syrup, etc.
388. Yes
389. Trout, moose, etc.
390. Yes
391. Names South American countries
392. Spanish
393. Guinea pigs, potatoes
394. Yes
395. Portuguese
396. Yes
397. Brightly colored
398. Llama, Alpaca, etc.
399. Inca
400. Names European countries
401. Yes
402. Western Europe
403. Scandinavia
404. Eastern Europe
405. The Euro
406. Europe
407. The British Pound
408. The Yen
409. The Renminbi
410. Berlin
411. German
412. Bratwurst, sauerkraut, etc.
413. Yes
414. Traditional German clothing
415. Yes
416. Yes
417. Yes
418. London
419. English
420. Yes
421. English cuisine
422. Yes
423. Yes
424. Ireland
425. Dublin
426. Yes
427. Yes
428. Paris
429. French
430. Crepes, croissants, etc.
431. Similar to us
432. Yes
433. Yes
434. Madrid
435. Spanish
436. Spanish doughnuts
437. Paella
438. Yes
439. Yes
440. Flamenco
441. Yes
442. Europe
443. Rome
444. Italian
445. Pizza, spaghetti, etc.
446. Similar to us
447. Yes
448. Yes
449. Whales, seals, and penguins

ANSWERS - SOCIAL STUDIES

450. Bitter cold
451. Yes
452. Yes
453. Canberra
454. English
455. Yes
456. Yes
457. Koala, kangaroo, etc.
458. Yes
459. A flag
460. Red, white, and blue with stars and stripes
461. Describes state flag
462. The capital
463. District of Colombia
464. George Washington
465. History
466. Indians
467. Christopher Columbus
468. Flat
469. North America
470. Spain
471. Money
472. India
473. Spices
474. Ocean blue.
475. Niña, Pinta, and Santa María
476. Indians
477. The New World
478. The Indians
479. Yes
480. The horse
481. Diseases
482. Civilization
483. Maya
484. Pyramids
485. The Aztecs
486. The Aztecs
487. The Inca
488. Francisco Pizarro
489. Hunt and fish
490. Africa
491. Yes
492. Jamestown
493. Native Americans
494. John Smith
495. Tribes
496. The Chief
497. Names Indian tribes
498. Indian tribes
499. Pueblo
500. Longhouses
501. Plains Indians
502. Totem Poles
503. The Pilgrims
504. Religious freedom
505. Mayflower
506. Atlantic
507. Plymouth
508. The Native Americans
509. Corn
510. The Native Americans
511. Deer and pheasant
512. Wampanoag Indians
513. Thanksgiving Day
514. The Puritans
515. 13
516. Daniel Boone
517. Davy Crockett
518. Colonists
519. Near lakes and streams
520. Explains colonial lifestyle
521. No
522. Candles, oil lamps, etc.
523. Revolutionary War
524. Yes
525. Yes
526. Great Britain
527. Canada
528. The Revolutionary War
529. The Boston Tea Party
530. Thomas Paine
531. Continental
532. Declaration of Independence
533. Thomas Jefferson
534. Created equal
535. John Adams
536. 1776
537. Yes
538. 56
539. John Hancock
540. Philadelphia
541. The Liberty Bell
542. It cracked
543. Yes
544. Yes
545. Benjamin Franklin
546. John Paul Jones
547. Paul Revere
548. Sea
549. Treaty of Paris
550. The American colonists
551. U.S. Constitution
552. James Madison
553. A federal republic
554. Anarchy
555. The Bill of Rights
556. The Louisiana Purchase
557. Fifteen
558. Doubled it
559. Lewis and Clark
560. France
561. Slaves
562. Africa
563. Plantations
564. The American Civil War
565. 1861-1865
566. Abraham Lincoln
567. "Honest Abe"
568. Harriet Tubman
569. Slaves
570. Yes
571. Names monuments
572. Washington, D.C.
573. The White House
574. The President and family
575. The Statue of Liberty
576. The flag
577. A historical monument
578. Mount Rushmore

Social Studies – 3rd Grade

579. Social Studies
580. Geography
581. North America (or other)
582. Globe
583. An atlas
584. An almanac
585. Longitude
586. Latitude
587. The equator
588. Can identify places on map
589. The 7 continents
590. Oceans
591. The Pacific
592. The Arctic
593. U.S. mountain ranges
594. World mountain ranges
595. The Himalayas
596. The Andes
597. Mount Everest
598. Mount McKinley
599. Machu Picchu
600. Deserts
601. Sonoran
602. Arctic and Antartica
603. The tropics
604. Rainforests
605. The Amazon
606. Brazil
607. The rainforest
608. Yes
609. Tropical
610. An island

ANSWERS – SOCIAL STUDIES

611. All are islands
612. Yes
613. Hawaii
614. Hurricanes, monsoons, etc.
615. 50
616. 48
617. Alaska and Hawaii
618. Hawaii
619. Names home state
620. Names capital
621. Alabama
622. Alaska
623. Arizona
624. Arkansas
625. California
626. Colorado
627. Connecticut
628. Delaware
629. Florida
630. Georgia
631. Hawaii
632. Idaho
633. Indiana
634. Iowa
635. Kansas
636. Kentucky
637. Louisiana
638. Maine
639. Maryland
640. Massachusetts
641. Michigan
642. Minnesota
643. Mississippi
644. Missouri
645. Montana
646. Nebraska
647. Nevada
648. New Hampshire
649. New Jersey
650. New Mexico
651. New York
652. North Carolina
653. North Dakota
654. Ohio
655. Oklahoma
656. Oregon
657. Pennsylvania
658. Rhode Island
659. South Carolina
660. South Dakota
661. Tennessee
662. Texas
663. Utah
664. Vermont
665. Virginia
666. Washington
667. West Virginia
668. Wisconsin
669. Wyoming
670. Counties
671. Names county
672. Names city
673. States location of city
674. Compass rose
675. North
676. South
677. East
678. West
679. Northeast
680. Northwest
681. Southeast
682. Southwest
683. Can locate Canada
684. Provinces
685. Can locate Mexico
686. States
687. Locates U.S. on map
688. Locates Central America
689. Locates South America
690. Locates Europe
691. Locates Africa
692. Locates Asia
693. Locates Australia
694. Locates Antarctica
695. Locates the equator
696. Identifies N. Hemisphere
697. Identifies S. Hemisphere
698. Locates Pacific Ocean
699. Locates Atlantic Ocean
700. Locates Indian Ocean
701. Locates Arctic Ocean
702. Locates North Pole
703. Locates South Pole
704. A legend
705. A scale
706. A river
707. Names major rivers
708. American rivers
709. World rivers
710. The Amazon
711. The Nile
712. Fresh water
713. Salt water
714. Source
715. A tributary
716. A delta
717. Ganges
718. Nile
719. Yellow
720. Mississippi
721. Tributaries
722. A river system
723. The Mississippi
724. A drainage basin
725. The Gulf of Mexico
726. A strait
727. Bering
728. Gibraltar
729. Magellan
730. A channel
731. English
732. Yucatan
733. A reservoir
734. Lake of the Ozarks
735. Lake Mead
736. A plateau
737. Tibetan
738. Canal
739. Erie
740. Suez
741. Panama
742. Venice
743. Isthmus
744. Panama
745. Peninsula
746. Florida
747. Michigan
748. Wisconsin
749. Baja
750. Yucatan
751. Iberian
752. Italian
753. Arabian
754. Korean
755. Cape
756. Cape of Good Hope
757. Cape Cod
758. An island
759. Greenland
760. Hawaii
761. Easter Island
762. Galapagos Islands
763. Names rivers
764. China
765. Ganges
766. Delta
767. The Indus River
768. The Nile River
769. Gifts of the Nile
770. Aswan High Dam
771. Three Gorges Dam
772. The Congo River
773. The Zaire
774. The Niger
775. The Volga
776. The Danube
777. The Rhine
778. The Thames
779. Australia
780. The duck-billed platypus
781. The Amazon River
782. The Orinoco River
783. Niagara Falls
784. Both located on border
785. California
786. Florida
787. Missouri River
788. Spells Mississippi
789. Paddleboat

ANSWERS - SOCIAL STUDIES

790. The Mackenzie
791. The Yukon
792. Canals
793. Gondola
794. Water vessels
795. Ancient history
796. Before Christ
797. "Before the Common Era"
798. "In the year of our Lord"
799. Yes
800. Before Christ
801. Greek
802. Yes
803. Greek
804. Eras
805. City-states
806. Athens and Sparta
807. Enemies
808. Sparta
809. Athens
810. Athena
811. The Acropolis
812. The Parthenon
813. Sparta
814. The Persian Wars
815. The Persians
816. The Greek
817. The Golden Age
818. Tragic plays
819. Yes
820. Sculptures
821. Three types of columns
822. Pericles
823. The Peloponnesian War
824. Greek playwrights
825. Plato
826. Aristotle
827. Homer
828. Alexander the Great
829. Alexandria
830. Olympian gods
831. The Titans
832. Zeus
833. Hercules
834. Apollo
835. Poseidon
836. Athena
837. Aphrodite
838. Greek monsters
839. Pegasus
840. Cyclopes
841. Centaurs
842. Greek
843. Olive branches
844. Olympia
845. No
846. Running and chariot racing
847. Every four years

848. Names Olympic champion
849. The Greek Alphabet
850. Alphabet
851. Greek
852. Roman
853. Seven
854. Ancient Roman
855. Yes
856. Romulus and Remus
857. Romulus
858. Yes
859. Yes
860. Roman Gods
861. Jupiter
862. Yes
863. On a peninsula
864. The Alps
865. Kings
866. A democracy
867. The Senate
868. A class system
869. Provinces
870. Latin
871. Romance languages
872. Yes
873. Carthage
874. The Phoenicians
875. Northern Africa and Sicily
876. Corsica
877. Rome
878. The Punic Wars
879. Twenty
880. Sicily, Corsica, and Sardinia
881. Spain
882. Hannibal
883. North across the Alps
884. Elephants
885. Yes
886. Rome
887. Carthage
888. Yes
889. Yes
890. Rome
891. Canals and waterways
892. Julius Caesar
893. Gaul
894. Pompey
895. Caesar
896. The Senate
897. Egypt
898. Ptolemy's sister, Cleopatra
899. Yes
900. Yes
901. Julius Caesar
902. The Battle of the Nile
903. Julius Caesar
904. Romans wanted republic
905. Stab wounds

906. Marc Antony and Octavian
907. Marc Antony
908. Octavian
909. Augustus Caesar
910. August
911. July
912. The Romans
913. September
914. October
915. November
916. December
917. Roman numerals
918. Pax Romana
919. Yes
920. Roman Peace
921. The Forum
922. The Pantheon
923. Aqueducts
924. The Romans
925. The Trevi Fountain
926. Yes
927. The toga
928. The stola
929. Bread, fish, and cheese
930. An amphitheater
931. The Coliseum
932. Chariot races
933. The Great Fire
934. Spartacus
935. Moses
936. Catholicism
937. Pompeii
938. Molten lava
939. Trajan
940. The decline and fall
941. Constantine the Great
942. Mosaics
943. Istanbul
944. The Western Roman Empire
945. The Byzantine Empire
946. The Visigoths and Germans
947. Yes
948. Justinian the Great
949. The Vikings
950. Fjord
951. Yes
952. Raiders
953. Normandy
954. Norsemen
955. A horned helmet
956. Gold and Silver
957. Monasteries
958. Viking ships
959. Longships
960. Eric the Red
961. Leif Ericsson
962. Newfoundland

ANSWERS – SOCIAL STUDIES

963. Vinland
964. Bering Strait
965. The Inuit
966. Igloo
967. Animal skins
968. Mukluks
969. Parkas
970. Yes
971. Meat
972. Harpoons
973. Inuit Eskimo dog
974. Kayak
975. Alaska
976. Juneau
977. Land of the Midnight Sun
978. The Northern Lights
979. Yes
980. The Klondike
981. Jade
982. Yes
983. Yes
984. Oil
985. Mt. McKinley
986. Kodiak
987. Dog sledding
988. Iditarod
989. Husky
990. Sled dogs
991. Mounds
992. Anasazi
993. Adobe bricks
994. Pueblo
995. No
996. Ladders
997. Disappeared mysteriously
998. Adobe
999. The Corn Dance
1000. Kachina Doll
1001. Nomad
1002. A teepee
1003. A wigwam
1004. Buckskin
1005. Yes
1006. Moccasins
1007. Corn and buffalo meat
1008. Bow and arrow
1009. Flint
1010. Apache
1011. The Diné
1012. Longhouse
1013. The Navajo
1014. The Woodland Tribes
1015. Maize
1016. Algonquin
1017. Papoose
1018. Cradleboards
1019. Lacrosse
1020. Mud and bear fat
1021. A canoe
1022. Longhouses
1023. The Medicine Man
1024. Yes
1025. A powwow
1026. A tomahawk
1027. Totem pole
1028. Wampum
1029. A tribe
1030. A reservation
1031. Christopher Columbus
1032. 1492
1033. San Salvador
1034. Indians
1035. Spain
1036. Niña, Pinta, Santa Maria
1037. King Ferdinand and Queen Isabella
1038. Amerigo Vespucci
1039. John Cabot
1040. Conquistador
1041. Gold
1042. Hernando Cortez
1043. Vasco Nuñez de Balboa
1044. Francisco Pizarro
1045. Juan Ponce de León
1046. Rich Port
1047. The fountain of youth
1048. Florida
1049. The Gulf Stream
1050. Cuba
1051. Hernando de Soto
1052. Finding gold
1053. The horse
1054. Guns and horses
1055. St. Augustine
1056. A castle
1057. Francisco Vásquez de Coronado
1058. The Grand Canyon
1059. Río Grande
1060. Christianity
1061. Missions
1062. Smallpox, measles, etc.
1063. The Northwest Passage
1064. Henry Hudson
1065. The Netherlands
1066. Holland
1067. Scandinavia
1068. Denmark
1069. The Danish
1070. Hudson
1071. Canada
1072. Canada
1073. French and English
1074. Maple
1075. Maple
1076. Provinces
1077. Ten
1078. Provinces
1079. Territories
1080. Ottawa
1081. French
1082. Samuel de Champlain
1083. Animal furs
1084. French Canada
1085. The Rocky Mountains
1086. Yukon Territory
1087. Southern Canada
1088. Yes
1089. Fishing
1090. Seal hunting
1091. Lacrosse and hockey
1092. Exploration and Discovery
1093. France and Spain
1094. England
1095. Charter
1096. A difficult one
1097. Captain John Smith
1098. Jamestown
1099. Captain John Smith
1100. Starvation and disease
1101. The Powhatan
1102. Corn
1103. Pocahontas
1104. John Rolfe
1105. Yes
1106. The Starving Time
1107. Tobacco
1108. Women
1109. Yes
1110. Africans
1111. Slaves
1112. Pilgrims
1113. The Mayflower
1114. The Mayflower Compact
1115. Plymouth Rock
1116. William Bradford
1117. Malnutrition and exposure
1118. The Wampanoag
1119. Massasoit
1120. Squanto
1121. Thanksgiving
1122. Two years later in 1623
1123. Yes
1124. The Puritans
1125. James Winthrop
1126. Promote church teachings
1127. The Puritans
1128. Schools
1129. Harvard
1130. Roger Williams
1131. Disapprove
1132. Decreased
1133. Yes
1134. Quakers
1135. William Penn
1136. All religions
1137. Philadelphia
1138. Maryland

ANSWERS - SOCIAL STUDIES

1139. New Netherland
1140. King Charles I
1141. Indentured servants
1142. North Carolina and South Carolina
1143. Georgia
1144. Slave trade
1145. The Quakers
1146. Religions
1147. Judaism
1148. Hebrew
1149. The Torah
1150. Adam and Eve
1151. Abraham
1152. Moses
1153. The Ten Commandments
1154. Israel
1155. David
1156. Jerusalem
1157. The Romans
1158. 1948
1159. Christianity
1160. The Old Testament
1161. Yes
1162. The Gospels
1163. Yes
1164. John the Baptist
1165. Yes
1166. Yes
1167. Gentiles
1168. Yes
1169. Christianity
1170. Christianity
1171. Yes
1172. Roman Catholicism
1173. Yes

Social Studies – 4th Grade

1174. Earth
1175. Globe
1176. Seven
1177. Pacific and Atlantic
1178. Names known continents
1179. Can read map
1180. Types of maps
1181. The equator
1182. The prime meridian
1183. Hemisphere
1184. Four
1185. Northern Hemisphere
1186. Southern Hemisphere
1187. Eastern Hemisphere
1188. Western Hemisphere
1189. The prime meridian
1190. Eastern and Western
1191. Parallels
1192. Meridians
1193. Longitude
1194. Latitude
1195. East to West
1196. North to South
1197. The prime meridian
1198. Greenwich
1199. Yes
1200. Degree
1201. 0
1202. 180
1203. The International Dateline
1204. A coordinate
1205. North of equator, east of prime meridian
1206. Can find coordinates
1207. Can identify states on map
1208. Can identify city on map
1209. Can follow building map
1210. Scale
1211. Yes
1212. A state map
1213. A city map
1214. A country map
1215. A political map
1216. A relief map
1217. A historical map
1218. A relief map
1219. A resource map
1220. A product map
1221. A road map
1222. A climate map
1223. A topographic map
1224. A relief map
1225. The Rockies
1226. Mount McKinley
1227. The Appalachian Mountains
1228. The Rockies
1229. The Appalachians
1230. Erosion
1231. Mountain state
1232. The Andes Mountains
1233. Mount Aconcagua
1234. The Inca
1235. Machu Picchu
1236. The Atlas Mountains
1237. The Eastern Highlands
1238. Mount Kilimanjaro
1239. The Alps
1240. The Alps
1241. Mont Blanc
1242. The Ural Mountains
1243. Mount Fuji
1244. The Himalayas
1245. Mount Everest
1246. Mount Everest
1247. Less oxygen
1248. The Rockies and Appalachians
1249. Yes
1250. Mid-Atlantic
1251. The Midwest
1252. The Pacific Northwest
1253. Rocky Mountain
1254. New England
1255. South Atlantic States
1256. The Southwest
1257. Canada
1258. Mexico
1259. Alaska and Hawaii
1260. A relief map
1261. Channel
1262. A strait
1263. A delta
1264. A prairie
1265. A plateau
1266. A mesa
1267. A cliff
1268. A canyon
1269. The Grand Canyon
1270. A basin
1271. A cape
1272. Cape Cod
1273. A gulf
1274. The Gulf of Mexico
1275. The Persian Gulf
1276. A bay
1277. A desert
1278. The Sahara
1279. Antarctica
1280. The Mojave
1281. The Atacama
1282. The Arabian
1283. A peninsula
1284. An isthmus
1285. A fjord
1286. A lake
1287. A river
1288. Names famous lakes
1289. Huron, Ontario, Michigan, Erie, and Superior
1290. Great Salt Lake
1291. Amazon, Nile, etc.
1292. Missouri, Mississippi, etc.
1293. Rio Grande
1294. The Amazon
1295. The Nile
1296. The Yellow
1297. The Yangtze
1298. The Ganges

ANSWERS – SOCIAL STUDIES

1299. The Volga
1300. The Danube
1301. The Rhine
1302. The Seine
1303. The Thames
1304. The Mississippi
1305. A tributary
1306. Tributaries
1307. Delta
1308. North America (or other)
1309. Names continents
1310. Asia
1311. China
1312. Antarctica
1313. Europe
1314. Scandinavia
1315. The British Isles
1316. Africa
1317. Asia
1318. South America
1319. Provinces
1320. North America
1321. French and English
1322. States
1323. North America
1324. Spanish
1325. 48
1326. Alaska and Hawaii
1327. Hawaii
1328. Alaska
1329. Arizona
1330. New Mexico
1331. Oklahoma
1332. Utah
1333. Wyoming
1334. Idaho
1335. Washington
1336. Montana
1337. South Dakota
1338. North Dakota
1339. Colorado
1340. Nebraska
1341. Nevada
1342. West Virginia
1343. Kansas
1344. Oregon
1345. Minnesota
1346. California
1347. Wisconsin
1348. Iowa
1349. Texas
1350. Florida
1351. Michigan
1352. Arkansas
1353. Missouri
1354. Maine
1355. Alabama
1356. Illinois
1357. Mississippi
1358. Indiana
1359. Louisiana
1360. Ohio
1361. Tennessee
1362. Kentucky
1363. Vermont
1364. Rhode Island
1365. North Carolina
1366. New York
1367. Virginia
1368. New Hampshire
1369. South Carolina
1370. Maryland
1371. Massachusetts
1372. Connecticut
1373. Georgia
1374. New Jersey
1375. Pennsylvania
1376. Delaware
1377. Texas
1378. Rhode Island
1379. Washington D.C.
1380. District of Columbia
1381. The Atlantic
1382. The Pacific
1383. Canada
1384. Mexico
1385. Names bordering states
1386. Names bordering counties
1387. Yes
1388. The American Flag
1389. Thirteen
1390. The Pledge of Allegiance
1391. Betsy Ross
1392. The Liberty Bell
1393. The Bald Eagle
1394. The Statue of Liberty
1395. The Declaration of Independence
1396. The United States Constitution
1397. The Star-Spangled Banner
1398. Flags, birds, songs, etc.
1399. Mount Rushmore
1400. Roosevelt
1401. Washington, D.C.
1402. The White House
1403. Virginia
1404. The Washington Monument
1405. Iwo Jima
1406. Niagara Falls
1407. National Parks
1408. Names states' monuments
1409. Yes
1410. Ancient history
1411. Prehistory
1412. Mesopotamia
1413. Iraq
1414. Mesopotamia
1415. The Tigris and Euphrates
1416. A class system
1417. Babylon
1418. Hammurabi
1419. Mesopotamia
1420. Yes
1421. Cuneiform
1422. Mesopotamia
1423. Sumerians
1424. The Assyrians
1425. The Sumerians
1426. The seed plow
1427. 60
1428. Ziggurats
1429. The Hanging Gardens
1430. The Middle Ages
1431. Medieval
1432. The peasants
1433. Serf
1434. The Barbarians
1435. Byzantine
1436. Constantinople
1437. The Huns
1438. Attila
1439. Stirrups
1440. The Vandals
1441. The Visigoths
1442. The Angles
1443. The Saxons
1444. Dark Ages
1445. Christianity
1446. The Pope
1447. Judaism
1448. Monks
1449. Nuns
1450. Charlemagne
1451. Feudalism
1452. Nobility, church, and commoners
1453. The king
1454. The vassal
1455. The lord
1456. A fief
1457. Yes
1458. Knights
1459. A serf
1460. A castle
1461. A minstrel
1462. A jester
1463. Croquet
1464. A page
1465. A squire
1466. The Canterbury Tales
1467. A knight
1468. To sew, weave, and spin
1469. Jousting
1470. Chivalry
1471. Yes
1472. Yes
1473. A guild
1474. An apprentice

ANSWERS - SOCIAL STUDIES

1475. A journeyman
1476. A master
1477. Yes
1478. Yes
1479. A strong kingdom
1480. England
1481. William the Conqueror
1482. Yes
1483. William II
1484. Yes
1485. Yes
1486. Yes
1487. Gave up land to France
1488. Counts, dukes, lords, and earls
1489. The Magna Carta
1490. A Parliament
1491. Black Death
1492. The Hundred Years' War
1493. Joan of Arc
1494. Yes
1495. The Byzantine Empire
1496. World religions
1497. Islam
1498. Mecca
1499. Kaaba
1500. Dome of the Rock
1501. Medina
1502. Hijra
1503. A Mosque
1504. The Grand Mosque
1505. The Prophet's Mosque
1506. Jihad
1507. The Quran
1508. The Five Pillars of Islam
1509. Yes
1510. Yes
1511. The Alhambra
1512. Córdoba
1513. Yes
1514. The Crusades
1515. Arabic numerals
1516. The Moors
1517. Africa
1518. Sahara
1519. Atlas
1520. Savanna
1521. The Congo
1522. Africa
1523. Egypt
1524. Pharaoh
1525. Yes
1526. Yes
1527. Second
1528. The Vizier
1529. Yes
1530. Dynasty
1531. Yes
1532. Upper and Lower Egypt
1533. King Menes
1534. Memphis
1535. Thebes
1536. Cairo
1537. Giza
1538. Pyramid of Khufu
1539. The Great Pyramid of Giza
1540. The Great Sphinx
1541. To guard the temples and tombs
1542. 240 feet long
1543. The nose
1544. Erosion
1545. Pillar
1546. Nefertiti
1547. King Tutankhamen
1548. Ramses II
1549. The cobra goddess
1550. The Valley of the Kings
1551. Howard Carter
1552. Paintings
1553. The Book of the Dead
1554. Vandals
1555. Mummification
1556. Yes
1557. Decimal system
1558. Hieroglyphics
1559. Consonant sounds
1560. Scribes
1561. Scribes
1562. The Rosetta Stone
1563. Farmers
1564. Yes
1565. Necklaces
1566. Mud bricks
1567. Bread
1568. The Egyptians
1569. The Persians
1570. The Kingdom of Kush
1571. Alexander the Great
1572. Ptolemaic
1573. Cleopatra
1574. The Valley of the Kings
1575. The Nile
1576. A tributary
1577. Yes
1578. Papyrus
1579. Papyrus
1580. Papyrus reeds
1581. Reed boats
1582. The camel
1583. A caravan
1584. Papyrus
1585. No
1586. A chariot
1587. West African Empires
1588. Mansa Musa
1589. Griots
1590. 54
1591. Africa
1592. Malaria
1593. One billion
1594. Charles Darwin
1595. Sudan
1596. Mt. Kilimanjaro
1597. Cape of Good Hope
1598. The Suez Canal
1599. The Aswan Dam
1600. Anwar Sadat
1601. Ivory Coast
1602. The Nile and the Congo
1603. The Sahara and Kalahari
1604. Yes
1605. The savanna
1606. Elephants, zebras, giraffes, etc.
1607. Elephant
1608. Elephants, giraffes, lions, etc.
1609. Kenya
1610. The cheetah
1611. African languages
1612. 2000
1613. Yes
1614. Arabic
1615. Islam
1616. Ramadan
1617. Madagascar
1618. Masks
1619. Drums
1620. Nelson Mandela
1621. Apartheid
1622. Muammar Gaddafi
1623. Yes
1624. Kwanzaa
1625. "The Lion King"
1626. Asia
1627. 48
1628. Vatican City
1629. Russia
1630. China
1631. Dynasties
1632. Qin Shi Huang
1633. Yes
1634. The Great Wall of China
1635. Terracotta
1636. Han Dynasty
1637. Yes
1638. Yes
1639. Confucius
1640. Civil service
1641. Yes
1642. Schools
1643. Silk
1644. Yes
1645. Birds and flowers
1646. Clothing
1647. Upper class
1648. The Silk Road
1649. Trade and commerce

ANSWERS – SOCIAL STUDIES

1650. Yes
1651. Buddhism
1652. Tang
1653. Trading
1654. A camel
1655. Woodblock printing
1656. A book
1657. Gunpowder
1658. Porcelain
1659. Poetry
1660. Confucianism
1661. Tea
1662. Toilet paper
1663. Paper
1664. The Great Wall
1665. After
1666. Magnetic compass and iron plow
1667. Books
1668. Yes
1669. Rice
1670. Tall pagodas
1671. Mongolia
1672. Gobi
1673. The Chinese
1674. The abacus
1675. Beijing
1676. Merchant associations
1677. Marco Polo
1678. The Silk Road
1679. Ming
1680. Porcelain pottery
1681. White
1682. Blue
1683. China
1684. Silk scrolls
1685. Calligraphy
1686. The Three Perfections
1687. Lacquer
1688. Landscapes
1689. The Great Wall
1690. The longest
1691. The wheelbarrow
1692. Grand Canal
1693. The Forbidden City
1694. Imperial Palace
1695. 24
1696. Before
1697. India and Africa
1698. Religions
1699. Nepal
1700. Yin and Yang
1701. Feng Shui
1702. The Yellow and Yangtze
1703. The dragon
1704. Imperial power
1705. The New Year
1706. Chopsticks
1707. Bamboo
1708. The Giant Panda
1709. China
1710. Two
1711. An animal
1712. The Himalayas
1713. Mt. Everest
1714. K2
1715. China
1716. The People's Republic of China
1717. Hong Kong
1718. Communist country
1719. Beijing
1720. Tiananmen
1721. Shanghai
1722. Mandarin
1723. Seven
1724. Yes
1725. Symbols
1726. Chinese
1727. Shoes
1728. Lion and Dragon Dance
1729. Kung Fu
1730. Zodiac
1731. Christopher Columbus
1732. The Age of Discovery
1733. The 1600's
1734. Great Britain
1735. The French and Indian War
1736. The Seven Years War
1737. Taxes
1738. "No taxation without representation"
1739. The Stamp Act
1740. Protested and boycotted British products
1741. The Colonial Congress
1742. The Sons of Liberty
1743. The Townshend Acts
1744. Protested and rebelled
1745. The Boston Massacre
1746. The Boston Tea Party
1747. The Intolerable Acts
1748. The First Continental Congress
1749. Patrick Henry
1750. "Common Sense"
1751. Thomas Paine
1752. Patriots
1753. Founding Fathers
1754. Loyalists
1755. Lexington and Concord
1756. Yes
1757. Paul Revere
1758. William Dawes
1759. Lanterns
1760. Redcoats
1761. "The Redcoats are coming."
1762. Lexington and Concord
1763. Yes
1764. Minutemen
1765. Yes
1766. Muskets
1767. Lexington
1768. Still uncertain
1769. The Americans
1770. Boston
1771. Lt. Colonel Francis Smith
1772. Captain John Parker
1773. Bunker and Breeds
1774. Took place on Breeds Hill
1775. British
1776. The whites of their eyes
1777. The British
1778. Land and freedom
1779. The Second Continental Congress
1780. George Washington
1781. The eagle
1782. 5,000
1783. Thomas Jefferson
1784. July 4, 1776
1785. July 4th
1786. 56
1787. John Hancock
1788. Yes
1789. Yes
1790. The National Archives
1791. Yes
1792. Money and land
1793. Delaware
1794. An American flag
1795. June 14th
1796. Yes
1797. 50
1798. The American flag
1799. Saratoga
1800. France
1801. France
1802. Yes
1803. Benedict Arnold
1804. Valley Forge
1805. Yorktown
1806. The Treaty of Paris
1807. The American Revolution
1808. Yes
1809. The Articles of Confederation
1810. Shays' Rebellion
1811. The Virginia Plan
1812. The Federalist Papers
1813. The Bill of Rights
1814. The Constitutional Convention
1815. Executive
1816. Judicial
1817. Legislative
1818. The Connecticut Compromise

ANSWERS - SOCIAL STUDIES

1819. The House and the Senate
1820. Two
1821. 100
1822. Number based on population
1823. 435
1824. The Three-Fifths Compromise
1825. 20
1826. The U.S. Constitution
1827. The Preamble
1828. Checks and balances
1829. Yes
1830. 1790
1831. An amendment
1832. The Bill of Rights
1833. The First Amendment
1834. Yes
1835. The President
1836. The governor
1837. Names state governor
1838. The mayor
1839. Names city mayor
1840. Taxes
1841. Yes
1842. President Lincoln
1843. George Washington
1844. Martha Washington
1845. John Adams
1846. Cabinet
1847. Yes
1848. Secretary
1849. 15
1850. Secretary of State
1851. Yes
1852. Yes
1853. Thomas Jefferson
1854. Alexander Hamilton
1855. Four
1856. Two
1857. Yes
1858. Democratic-Republican
1859. Federalist
1860. Democratic-Republican and Federalist
1861. Republican and Democrat
1862. New York City
1863. Washington, D.C.
1864. The White House
1865. Mount Vernon
1866. The U.S. Capitol
1867. John Adams
1868. Jefferson
1869. Abigail Adams
1870. Thomas Jefferson
1871. France
1872. Louisiana
1873. Napoleon Bonaparte
1874. The Louisiana Purchase
1875. Lewis and Clark
1876. Two years
1877. Kept detailed journals
1878. James Madison
1879. The War of 1812
1880. USS Constitution
1881. The Capitol
1882. The Treaty of Ghent
1883. The Battle of New Orleans
1884. James Monroe
1885. Yes
1886. The South
1887. The North
1888. Abolitionists
1889. The Missouri Compromise
1890. The Monroe Doctrine
1891. John Quincy Adams
1892. Andrew Jackson
1893. Transfer Indian land
1894. The Indian Removal Act
1895. The Trail of Tears
1896. Reformer
1897. Dorothea Dix
1898. Horace Mann
1899. Lucretia Mott and Elizabeth Stanton
1900. Amelia Bloomer
1901. Sojourner Truth

Social Studies – 5th Grade

1902. Geology
1903. Earth
1904. Atmosphere
1905. Lithosphere
1906. Hydrosphere
1907. Tropics of Cancer and Capricorn
1908. Equator
1909. Equator
1910. Northern Hemisphere
1911. Southern Hemisphere
1912. Colder
1913. The prime meridian
1914. Greenwich Meridian
1915. The International Dateline
1916. The date
1917. Yes
1918. Sunday
1919. Friday
1920. Yes
1921. Latitude
1922. Longitude
1923. Longitude
1924. 0 degrees longitude
1925. Coordinates
1926. Mason-Dixon Line
1927. The Arctic Circle
1928. Polar ice cap
1929. Antarctic Circle
1930. Tropic of Cancer
1931. Tropic of Capricorn
1932. The tropics
1933. Climate zones
1934. Very hot
1935. Very cold
1936. Moderate
1937. Frigid
1938. Rotation of the Earth
1939. Rotation and Revolution
1940. Yes
1941. Summer
1942. Winter
1943. Winter
1944. Summer
1945. The opposite
1946. The same
1947. Solstice
1948. June 21st
1949. December 21st
1950. Equinox
1951. The passage of time
1952. 1000
1953. 100
1954. 10
1955. 365 ¼
1956. February 29th
1957. Leap day
1958. The Egyptians
1959. Julius Caesar
1960. The Gregorian calendar
1961. 30
1962. 7
1963. Saturday and Sunday
1964. 24
1965. 60
1966. 60
1967. Sundials
1968. Yes
1969. The prime meridian
1970. 24
1971. The United States
1972. Central
1973. Mountain
1974. Pacific
1975. Eastern

ANSWERS – SOCIAL STUDIES

1976. Names time zone
1977. Yes
1978. Noon
1979. Standard
1980. Daylight Savings Time
1981. A.M.
1982. P.M.
1983. Midday
1984. A.M.
1985. P.M.
1986. Yes
1987. Yes
1988. Cartographers
1989. Projections
1990. Gerardus Mercator
1991. Yes
1992. Pacific and Atlantic
1993. Lakes
1994. Yes
1995. Yes
1996. Salty
1997. Africa
1998. South America
1999. Asia
2000. Salty lakes
2001. Names lakes
2002. Huron, Ontario, Michigan, Erie, and Superior
2003. Political
2004. Relief
2005. A relief map
2006. Names world rivers
2007. Mississippi, Missouri, etc.
2008. A relief map
2009. Names mountain ranges
2010. Relief map
2011. Names world deserts
2012. Seven
2013. Canada, U.S. and Mexico
2014. 50
2015. Five
2016. The Northeast
2017. New England
2018. Northeast
2019. Southeast
2020. Midwest
2021. West
2022. Southwest
2023. Divisions
2024. Pacific Alaska Region
2025. Great Plains
2026. Great Lakes
2027. Rocky Mountain
2028. Pacific
2029. Mid-Atlantic
2030. Southeast
2031. Southwest
2032. Northeast
2033. Hawaii
2034. Alaska
2035. Names home state
2036. Names bordering states
2037. Counties
2038. A city
2039. Chicago
2040. Detroit
2041. New York
2042. Los Angeles
2043. Denver
2044. Boston
2045. New Orleans
2046. San Francisco
2047. Philadelphia
2048. St. Louis
2049. Pittsburgh
2050. Paris
2051. Jerusalem
2052. Wizard of Oz city
2053. Town
2054. Urban
2055. Rural
2056. Suburban
2057. Identifies community
2058. Residents
2059. The town square
2060. Yes
2061. The Zócalo
2062. Trafalgar Square
2063. Piazza San Marco
2064. Tiananmen Square
2065. Main Market Square
2066. Times Square
2067. St. Peter's Square
2068. The Plaza Mayor
2069. Red Square
2070. The Little Mermaid
2071. Motherland Calls
2072. David
2073. The Olmecs
2074. Great Sphinx
2075. Christ the Redeemer
2076. Moai Statues
2077. Stonehenge
2078. The Statue of Liberty
2079. The CN Tower
2080. The Space Needle
2081. Tallest buildings
2082. Big Ben
2083. The Leaning Tower of Pisa
2084. The Eiffel Tower
2085. The United States Capitol
2086. St. Paul's Cathedral
2087. Santa Maria del Fiore
2088. The Pantheon
2089. St. Peter's Cathedral
2090. The Taj Mahal
2091. St. Basil's Cathedral
2092. The Brooklyn Bridge
2093. The Sydney Harbour Bridge
2094. London Bridge
2095. The Golden Gate Bridge
2096. Ponte Vecchio
2097. Vietnam Veterans Memorial
2098. The Berlin Wall
2099. The Western Wall
2100. The Walls of Babylon
2101. The Great Wall of China
2102. Plymouth Rock
2103. The Blarney Stone
2104. The Rock of Gibraltar
2105. The Rosetta Stone
2106. Yes
2107. Egypt
2108. Japan
2109. Italy
2110. Australia
2111. Australia
2112. China
2113. Switzerland
2114. Ireland
2115. Israel
2116. Canada
2117. United States
2118. Iceland
2119. Peru
2120. England
2121. "Uncle Sam"
2122. Asia
2123. The Middle East
2124. The Far East
2125. Eastern Europe
2126. Western Europe
2127. The British Isles
2128. The United Kingdom
2129. Scandinavia
2130. The Netherlands
2131. The Hague
2132. Holland
2133. English
2134. Dutch
2135. Danish
2136. Danish
2137. Swedish
2138. Norwegian
2139. Belgian
2140. Dutch
2141. Irish
2142. French
2143. Spanish
2144. Portuguese
2145. Portuguese
2146. German
2147. Italian
2148. Swiss
2149. French, German, and Italian
2150. German
2151. Polish

ANSWERS - SOCIAL STUDIES

2152. Greek
2153. Latin and Italian
2154. Hebrew and Arabic
2155. Mandarin Chinese
2156. Spanish
2157. English
2158. Hindi
2159. Arabic
2160. French and English
2161. Spanish
2162. None
2163. Names languages spoken
2164. States nationality
2165. Yes
2166. Names civilizations
2167. Maya, Aztec, and Inca
2168. Mexico and Guatemala
2169. Mexico
2170. Peru
2171. City-states
2172. Yes
2173. A king
2174. Yes
2175. Tikal
2176. Teotihuacan
2177. Gods
2178. Perform sacrifices
2179. The Yucatan
2180. Chichen Itza
2181. 365
2182. The Maya
2183. Pyramids
2184. A snake
2185. Kukulkan
2186. Itzamna
2187. Yes
2188. Yes
2189. The Maya
2190. Chac
2191. Calendars
2192. Three
2193. Simultaneously
2194. The Long Count
2195. Codices
2196. The Maya
2197. Hieroglyphics
2198. Zero
2199. Twenty
2200. Dots and bars
2201. Yes
2202. King, noble, commoner
2203. Yes
2204. Subsistence cultivation
2205. Maize
2206. Chocolate
2207. Cacao beans
2208. A cenote
2209. The nobles
2210. The commoners
2211. A rubber ball

2212. The hands
2213. The losing side
2214. Yes
2215. Stone
2216. Yes
2217. A codex
2218. A stela
2219. Popol Vuh
2220. Yes
2221. No
2222. Plaster
2223. Obsidian
2224. The Mayan nobles
2225. The Quetzal
2226. Classic
2227. Yes
2228. Yes
2229. The 1500's
2230. The Aztec
2231. Eagle on cactus with snake
2232. Tenochtitlan
2233. City-states
2234. Causeways
2235. When attacked by enemy
2236. The Templo Mayor
2237. Near the Temple
2238. At Tenochtitlan
2239. The Emperor
2240. Powerful Aztec Emperors
2241. Yes
2242. High level
2243. Yes
2244. Honoring the Sun
2245. Sacrifices
2246. Human blood
2247. Serpents and Jaguars
2248. Huitzilopochtli
2249. Tlaloc
2250. Quetzalcoatl
2251. The family
2252. Nahuatl
2253. Nahuatl
2254. Yes
2255. Chinampas
2256. Maize
2257. Popcorn
2258. To cook and sew
2259. Yes
2260. Different
2261. The nobles
2262. Cocoa beans
2263. Chocolatl
2264. An aqueduct
2265. Yes
2266. Honoring their gods
2267. The Aztec Calendar
2268. Poetry
2269. Yes
2270. Glyphs

2271. Codex
2272. Yes
2273. The Aztec Calendar
2274. Two
2275. Festivals and ceremonies
2276. Herbs
2277. An advantage
2278. Spain
2279. Smallpox
2280. Hernán Cortés
2281. Tenochtitlan
2282. Mexico City
2283. The Inca
2284. Nazca
2285. The Andes
2286. Yes
2287. Yes
2288. Yes
2289. Sapa Inca
2290. Inti
2291. Cuzco
2292. 11,000 feet above
2293. Yes
2294. Quechua
2295. Farming the land
2296. Yes
2297. Stonemasons
2298. Yes
2299. Rope suspension bridges
2300. Llamas
2301. Alpaca
2302. They created terraces
2303. Yes
2304. Potatoes
2305. Yes
2306. Colorful tunics and dresses
2307. Adobe huts
2308. Taxes
2309. The children of nobles
2310. Mark religious occasions and crops
2311. Coca leaves
2312. Machu Picchu
2313. Hiram Bingham
2314. Francisco Pizarro
2315. Gold
2316. Conquer Inca and claim gold
2317. The Spanish
2318. Pizarro
2319. Europe
2320. Portugal
2321. Christopher Columbus
2322. Ferdinando and Isabella
2323. The Americas
2324. China
2325. Niña, Pinta, and Santa Maria
2326. The Santa Maria

805

ANSWERS – SOCIAL STUDIES

2327. San Salvador
2328. Indians
2329. The horse
2330. Four
2331. Yes
2332. October 12th
2333. Columbus, D.C., etc.
2334. Amerigo Vespucci
2335. Yes
2336. Vasco de Gama
2337. Pedro Cabral
2338. Portuguese
2339. Cannons
2340. Ferdinand Magellan
2341. Discover route to Asia
2342. The Strait of Magellan
2343. Names of five ships
2344. Cape of Good Hope
2345. The Pacific
2346. Four months
2347. Killed in a battle
2348. 18
2349. The Dutch
2350. Trade monopoly
2351. The Old World
2352. Colonies
2353. Thirteen
2354. Yes
2355. The natives
2356. Sugarcane
2357. Transatlantic slave trade
2358. Sugar, coffee, and cotton
2359. Africa
2360. Gold and Angolan Coasts
2361. Triangular Trade
2362. The Middle Passage
2363. Jamestown
2364. Twelve million
2365. Yes
2366. Arabic
2367. Latin
2368. Renaissance
2369. 1300-1600
2370. Age of Discovery
2371. Yes
2372. The Ottoman Empire
2373. The end
2374. Humanism
2375. Humanities
2376. Florence
2377. The teachings of philosophers
2378. Medici
2379. Renaissance artists
2380. Michelangelo
2381. Leonardo da Vinci
2382. An Italian scientist
2383. The Scientific Method
2384. Galileo
2385. The pendulum
2386. Astronomy
2387. Earth and planets orbit Sun
2388. Johannes Kepler
2389. Dante
2390. A Renaissance architect
2391. Leonardo da Vinci
2392. The *Mona Lisa*
2393. Michelangelo
2394. Raphael
2395. Renaissance artists
2396. Masaccio
2397. Yes
2398. Yes
2399. Renaissance
2400. Yes
2401. Yes
2402. Machiavelli
2403. Catholic
2404. Music and dance
2405. Yes
2406. Yes
2407. Ballet
2408. Madrigal
2409. The violin
2410. The printing press
2411. Johannes Gutenberg
2412. The Gutenberg Bible
2413. The Northern Renaissance
2414. Martin Luther
2415. Reformists
2416. Protestants
2417. The Reformation
2418. A Protestant
2419. Christianity sub-divided
2420. Ignatius of Loyola
2421. King Henry VIII
2422. The Church of England
2423. Elizabethan Era
2424. The monarch and nobility
2425. A Protestant Church
2426. Puritans
2427. Divided
2428. Its theatre
2429. Famous theatres
2430. William Shakespeare
2431. Plays
2432. Plays
2433. 14
2434. Both nobles and spectators
2435. Sent own ships to claim riches
2436. Yes
2437. The Spanish Armada
2438. Sir Francis Drake
2439. The English
2440. Yes
2441. Yes
2442. Second to sail
2443. 44 years
2444. Virginia
2445. James I of Scotland
2446. The King James Bible
2447. Jamestown
2448. Yes
2449. Without a Parliament
2450. Yes
2451. Massachusetts
2452. The English Civil War
2453. The Parliament
2454. Oliver Cromwell
2455. Enforced Puritan rules
2456. Bring back monarchy
2457. Charles II
2458. A Catholic King
2459. William and Mary
2460. The Glorious Revolution
2461. The Bill of Rights
2462. Yes
2463. Yes
2464. Ivan the Great
2465. Ivan the Terrible
2466. Peter the Great
2467. Catherine the Great
2468. Yes
2469. Japan
2470. Monsoon, typhoons, and tsunamis
2471. "Land of the Rising Sun"
2472. Yes
2473. Feudalism
2474. The top
2475. Below
2476. Samurai
2477. Farmers, artisans, and merchants
2478. Buddhism
2479. Buddha
2480. Yoga
2481. Yes
2482. Gardens
2483. Claude Monet
2484. Shintoism
2485. Renaissance
2486. The Colonial Period
2487. West
2488. The Appalachian Mountains
2489. Yes
2490. Northwest Territory
2491. Daniel Boone
2492. The Wilderness Trail
2493. Yes
2494. The Louisiana Purchase
2495. Lewis and Clark
2496. An interpreter
2497. The fur trade
2498. Yes
2499. Pioneers
2500. Mormons

ANSWERS - SOCIAL STUDIES

2501. Gold
2502. The Gold Rush
2503. Prospectors
2504. Panning
2505. Boom towns
2506. Ghost towns
2507. Montana
2508. Wagon trains
2509. Weather, rivers, and diseases
2510. The Oregon Trail
2511. During the Gold Rush
2512. Log homes
2513. The frontier woman
2514. The frontiersman
2515. The frontier children
2516. Summer and winter
2517. Spring and autumn
2518. Pioneers
2519. Posed threat to crops and homes
2520. John Deere
2521. The Native Americans
2522. Outhouses
2523. Log and adobe
2524. With notches
2525. Mud
2526. Yes
2527. Manifest Destiny
2528. Texas
2529. The Mexicans
2530. Davy Crockett and Jim Bowie
2531. "Remember the Alamo"
2532. The Republic of Texas
2533. 1845
2534. The Mexican-American War
2535. James K. Polk
2536. Mexico City
2537. The Treaty of Guadalupe Hidalgo
2538. Fifty percent
2539. Los Niños Heroes
2540. Yes
2541. Yes
2542. North
2543. South
2544. Slavery
2545. Opposed slavery
2546. The North
2547. The South
2548. The Mason-Dixon Line
2549. The Missouri Compromise
2550. Abolitionists
2551. Harriet Beecher Stowe
2552. The Dred Scott Decision
2553. The Lincoln-Douglas Debates
2554. The Southern States
2555. Abraham Lincoln
2556. Secede the Union
2557. The Confederate States
2558. Against slavery and strong government
2559. Jefferson Davis
2560. The American Civil War
2561. The Battle of Fort Sumter
2562. The Battle of Shiloh
2563. "Stonewall" Jackson
2564. The Confederate States
2565. Jefferson Davis
2566. Robert E. Lee
2567. Robert E. Lee
2568. Richmond
2569. Ulysses S. Grant
2570. "Unconditional Surrender" Grant
2571. 15-25
2572. Yes
2573. "Yankees"
2574. "Rebels"
2575. Blue
2576. Grey
2577. Muskets and rifles
2578. A knapsack
2579. The Union Blockade
2580. Were first ironclad ships
2581. To set someone free
2582. The Emancipation Proclamation
2583. Five days after
2584. Yes
2585. The Underground Railroad
2586. Canada
2587. Conductors
2588. Stations
2589. Harriet Tubman
2590. Pickett's Charge
2591. The Battle of Gettysburg
2592. Lincoln's Gettysburg Address
2593. "Four score and seven years ago"
2594. Twenty
2595. Yes
2596. Sherman's March to the Sea
2597. Yes
2598. The Union
2599. The Union
2600. Lee surrendered to Grant
2601. Yes
2602. The American Civil War
2603. Assassinated
2604. Ford's Theatre
2605. John Wilkes Booth
2606. His leg
2607. Twelve days
2608. A Museum
2609. Andrew Jackson
2610. Reconstruction
2611. Bring Confederate states back
2612. Largely destroyed
2613. Rebuilding the South
2614. Union troops
2615. Yes
2616. "The Veto President"
2617. Impeach him
2618. Not-guilty
2619. Black Codes
2620. 13th, 14th, and 15th
2621. Yes
2622. The Union
2623. Carpetbaggers
2624. The Freedmen's Bureau
2625. Yes
2626. The Ku Klux Klan
2627. Yes
2628. The 20th Century
2629. West
2630. The "Wild West"
2631. The Homestead Act
2632. A sod house
2633. Cowboys
2634. A round up
2635. A cattle drive
2636. Yes
2637. A ten-gallon hat
2638. Cowboys
2639. The Rodeo
2640. A harmonica
2641. Gunfighters, bandits, and outlaws
2642. "Buffalo Bill"
2643. Annie Oakley
2644. The Pony Express
2645. The telegraph
2646. The Transcontinental Railroad
2647. Yes
2648. The American Frontier
2649. Alaska
2650. Gold
2651. Yes
2652. Yes
2653. Yes
2654. For Westward expansion
2655. Land rights
2656. Clara Barton
2657. George Washington
2658. Names current President
2659. Names current First Lady
2660. Former Presidents
2661. Former First Ladies
2662. Famous aviators

807

ANSWERS – SOCIAL STUDIES

2663. Famous nurses
2664. Famous inventors
2665. Famous reformers
2666. Famous entertainers
2667. Famous frontiersmen
2668. Names famous American
2669. United States of America
2670. Mexico
2671. Puerto Rico
2672. The Dominican Republic
2673. Cuba
2674. Costa Rica
2675. Guatemala
2676. El Salvador
2677. Nicaragua
2678. Panama
2679. Venezuela
2680. Ecuador
2681. Columbia
2682. Bolivia
2683. Argentina
2684. Paraguay
2685. Uruguay
2686. Chile
2687. Peru
2688. Brazil
2689. Iceland
2690. England
2691. Ireland
2692. Scotland
2693. Germany
2694. Poland
2695. Italy
2696. Portugal
2697. France
2698. Monaco
2699. Canada
2700. Australia
2701. New Zealand
2702. Spain
2703. Morocco
2704. Egypt
2705. Israel
2706. Saudi Arabia
2707. Dubai
2708. Afghanistan
2709. India
2710. Nepal
2711. Thailand
2712. Vietnam
2713. The Philippines
2714. Japan
2715. Kenya
2716. Tanzania
2717. South Africa
2718. Austria
2719. Switzerland
2720. Greece
2721. Belgium
2722. Denmark
2723. The Netherlands
2724. Sweden
2725. Finland
2726. Norway
2727. Russia
2728. China
2729. The United States
2730. Names countries

ANSWERS - GOVERNMENT AND CIVICS

APPENDIX 6: Chapter 6 – Government and Civics

Pre-School

1. Yes
2. Yes
3. Names school rules
4. Names home rules
5. Names current President
6. Police officer, firemen, etc.
7. Yes
8. Yes
9. Names businesses
10. Mail letters, etc.
11. Place to manage money, etc.
12. Put out fires, rescue, etc.
13. Enforce laws, safety, etc.
14. Yes
15. The police
16. Yes
17. To educate; for learning
18. Yes
19. Yes
20. Yes
21. A community
22. Yes
23. Names town
24. Names home state
25. United States (or other)
26. Yes
27. Yes

Government and Civics – Kindergarten

28. Policemen, crossing guards, etc.
29. Teachers, principal, etc.
30. Yes
31. Yes
32. Yes
33. States responsibilities
34. The grocery store
35. The post office
36. The library
37. The bank
38. Names different jobs
39. Police cars or vans
40. Fire trucks, etc.
41. Boat, car, plane, train, etc.
42. For order and safety
43. The Golden Rule
44. Yes
45. Yes
46. Yes
47. For order and safety
48. Government
49. Police officers
50. Fine or jail
51. Yes
52. Yes
53. Yes
54. Describes flag
55. A symbol
56. Yes
57. The Pledge of Allegiance
58. Star-Spangled Banner, etc.
59. Yes
60. National Anthem, etc.
61. Yes
62. Suggests community project

Government and Civics – 1st Grade

63. Civics
64. Walk, listen, etc.
65. Yes
66. Yes
67. The government
68. Fine, jail, etc.
69. Yes
70. Lifeguard
71. Teachers, principal, etc.
72. Yes
73. Yes
74. Yes
75. Vote
76. An election
77. Yes

Government and Civics – 2nd Grade

78. Says and spells name
79. Cites address
80. Cites phone number
81. Says parents first names
82. Says hometown
83. A neighborhood
84. Names home state
85. Districts
86. Names school district
87. The principal
88. The Superintendent
89. Rural
90. Urban
91. Says type of community
92. A suburb
93. Names closest city
94. Names state capital

Government and Civics – 3rd Grade

95. A community
96. A global community
97. Immigrant
98. Immigrants
99. Yes
100. A custom

ANSWERS – GOVERNMENT AND CIVICS

101. Yes
102. Names family custom
103. Laws
104. Equality under the law
105. The government
106. A democracy
107. Yes
108. Rights
109. Responsibilities
110. A citizen
111. The Declaration of Independence
112. The U.S. Constitution
113. Philadelphia
114. The Preamble
115. An amendment
116. The Bill of Rights
117. Inalienable Rights
118. 27 Amendments
119. The First Amendment
120. July 4th
121. Thirteen
122. Fifty
123. Thirteen
124. Describes flag
125. Immigrants
126. Native Americans
127. Thomas Jefferson
128. Memorial Day
129. Veterans Day
130. Yes
131. 18 years old
132. Three
133. Branches
134. Yes
135. Checks and Balances
136. The Congress
137. 100
138. 435
139. The Speaker of the House
140. The legislative branch
141. Two
142. The President
143. The Vice-President
144. Names Vice-President
145. The executive branch
146. The judicial branch
147. Nine
148. Chief
149. A court
150. The governor
151. Names state governor
152. The mayor
153. Names city mayor
154. Chief
155. Chief
156. Cites responsibilities
157. Yes
158. Library, store, etc.
159. Yes
160. Art, historical, etc.
161. Yes
162. Names private business
163. Names goods and services
164. Teacher, doctor, etc.
165. A community
166. Obey laws, vote, etc.
167. City
168. Countryside
169. Suburbs
170. Describes community

Government and Civics – 4th Grade

171. Laws
172. Yes
173. Executive, legislative, and judicial
174. Federal
175. Federal
176. State
177. Local
178. The Declaration of Independence
179. Founding Fathers
180. The Preamble
181. An ordinance
182. The U.S. Constitution
183. An amendment
184. The Bill of Rights
185. The legislative branch
186. The House and the Senate
187. The U.S. Capitol
188. Names state capital
189. A legislator
190. The executive branch
191. The judicial branch
192. Checks and Balances
193. Separation of Powers
194. The President
195. Names current President
196. Names current Vice-President
197. The White House
198. The President
199. Pennsylvania Avenue
200. Veto power
201. Supreme
202. A judge
203. A jury
204. Senate and the House
205. 435
206. Yes
207. 100
208. Two per state
209. The Speaker
210. Two years
211. Two
212. Six years
213. A bill
214. A law
215. Veto
216. A mayor
217. Names city mayor
218. A governor
219. Names state governor
220. Local

Government and Civics – 5th Grade

221. Civics
222. Names community
223. Counties
224. Names home county
225. Names home state
226. United States (or other)
227. Citizens
228. Right
229. Responsibility
230. Dictatorship
231. Naturalization
232. Colonists
233. Thirteen
234. The Articles of Confederation
235. Independence
236. Sovereignty
237. Anarchy
238. Yes
239. The Declaration of Independence
240. The Declaration of Independence
241. Pennsylvania
242. Delaware, Massachusetts, etc.
243. Thomas Jefferson

ANSWERS - GOVERNMENT AND CIVICS

244. A national government
245. A Constitution
246. Federalists
247. Anti-Federalists
248. Jefferson, Madison, Franklin, etc.
249. The Preamble
250. Cites Preamble
251. Peace within United States
252. Cannot be taken away
253. Seven articles
254. The Legislative Branch
255. The Executive Branch
256. The Judicial Branch
257. Yes
258. An amendment
259. The Bill of Rights
260. The First Amendment
261. Civil liberties
262. Censorship
263. Slander
264. Libel
265. Bias
266. Propaganda
267. The Second Amendment
268. The Fourth Amendment
269. The Fifth Amendment
270. Formally approve a law
271. The Thirteenth Amendment
272. The Fourteenth Amendment
273. The Fifteenth Amendment
274. Suffrage
275. The Nineteenth Amendment
276. 27 Amendments
277. Taxes
278. Eminent domain
279. Separation of Church and State
280. A convention

281. A federal system
282. Legislative, Executive, and Judicial
283. Checks and Balances
284. The legislative branch
285. House and Senate
286. The Senate
287. The House of Representatives
288. The Speaker of the House
289. The Vice-President
290. To make the laws
291. A session
292. Yes
293. A bill
294. A committee
295. The President
296. The executive branch
297. The President
298. The President
299. A Two-Party system
300. A political party
301. Republican and Democrat
302. The Republican Party
303. The Democratic Party
304. States party in office
305. The elephant
306. The donkey
307. Popular vote
308. The Primary Election
309. The General Election
310. The Electoral College
311. 270
312. The incumbent
313. Lame duck
314. 18
315. Tuesday
316. November
317. Blue
318. Red
319. Four years
320. Once

321. The inauguration
322. The U.S. Cabinet
323. State of the Union Address
324. The judicial branch
325. The Supreme Court
326. Nine
327. The Chief Justice
328. Names Court Justices
329. A jury
330. A defendant
331. A witness
332. A subpoena
333. A verdict
334. A civil case
335. A civil case
336. Miranda Rights
337. An attorney
338. District Attorney
339. Attorney General
340. Due process
341. Due process of law
342. A felony
343. A misdemeanor
344. An indictment
345. Court pleas
346. The rule of law
347. A petition
348. Eminent domain
349. Discrimination
350. An ordinance
351. Town meetings
352. Board of Education
353. Infrastructure
354. The mayor
355. The President
356. Army, Navy, Air Force, Marines
357. Drones
358. Bureaucracy
359. Diplomacy
360. Names civic duties

Practice Citizenship Test

361. The Constitution
362. Defines government and basic rights
363. We the People…
364. A change to the Constitution
365. The Bill of Rights
366. Speech, religion, press, assembly
367. 27 amendments
368. Declared freedom from Britain
369. Life, liberty, pursuit of happiness
370. One can practice any religion
371. Capitalistic or market
372. No one is above the law
373. Legislative, executive, or judicial
374. The President
375. Checks and balances
376. The Congress
377. The House and the Senate
378. 100
379. 6 years

380. Names state Senator
381. 435 members
382. Two years
383. Names U.S. Representative
384. All of the people
385. Because of the state's population
386. Four years
387. November
388. Names current President
389. Names Vice-President
390. The Vice-President
391. The Speaker of the House

ANSWERS – GOVERNMENT AND CIVICS

392. The President
393. The President
394. The President
395. Advises the President
396. State, Defense, Energy, etc.
397. Interprets laws and Constitution
398. The Supreme Court
399. Nine
400. Names current Chief Justice
401. Print money, declare war, make treaties
402. Schools, police, fire, land zoning, etc.
403. Names current Governor
404. Names state capital
405. Names current Speaker
406. Republican and Democratic
407. Names Presidential party
408. Any citizen can vote, age 18, etc.
409. Vote, jury duty
410. Vote, run for federal office
411. Speech, worship, bear arms, etc.
412. The flag and America
413. Obey laws, loyalty, serve nation, etc.
414. At least 18
415. Vote, join civic group, run for office, etc.
416. April 15th
417. At age 18
418. Religious freedom, economic opportunity
419. Native Americans
420. Africans
421. High taxes, no self-government
422. Thomas Jefferson
423. July 4, 1776
424. Delaware, Massachusetts, Virginia, etc.
425. Founding Fathers wrote Constitution
426. 1787
427. James Madison, Alexander Hamilton
428. Inventor, diplomat, Postmaster General, etc.
429. George Washington
430. George Washington
431. The Louisiana Territory
432. 1812, Civil, Mexican-American
433. American Civil War
434. Slavery, states' rights
435. Freed slaves, preserved Union
436. Freed the slaves
437. Fought for women's rights
438. World Wars I, II, Korean, Vietnam, Gulf
439. Woodrow Wilson
440. Franklin Roosevelt
441. Germany, Japan, and Italy
442. World War II
443. Communism
444. Civil Rights Movement
445. Fought for civil rights and equality
446. Terrorists attacked
447. Cherokee, Navajo, Sioux, etc.
448. Missouri or Mississippi
449. The Pacific
450. The Atlantic
451. Puerto Rico, Guam, Virgin Islands
452. Montana, Michigan, New York, Alaska
453. California, Arizona, Texas
454. Washington, D.C.
455. Liberty Island in New York Harbor
456. Represents 13 original colonies
457. One star for each state
458. The Star-Spangled Banner
459. Francis Scott Key
460. July 4th
461. Christmas, Thanksgiving, etc.
462. Patrick Henry
463. Alaska and Hawaii
464. Thanksgiving
465. Natural born, 35 years old, etc.
466. The White House
467. The U.S. Capitol
468. Red, white, and blue

ANSWERS - ECONOMICS

APPENDIX 7: Chapter 7 – Economics

Pre-School

1. In a bank
2. Bike, iPod, House, etc.
3. Yes
4. Yes
5. Teacher, police officer, etc.
6. Librarian, postal worker, etc.
7. Names career
8. Yes
9. Food, shelter, clothing, etc.
10. Names currency denominations

Economics – Kindergarten

11. Yes
12. Make bed, take care of pet, etc.
13. Piggy bank or bank
14. Save, spend it, etc.
15. A need
16. Yes
17. Wants
18. To earn money, pay expenses, etc.
19. Yes

Economics – 1st Grade

20. Money
21. Yes
22. Confirms or denies account
23. Raising cattle, selling produce, etc.
24. Work in a business, school, etc.
25. Car, bus, subway, train, etc.
26. Yes
27. Yes
28. Confirms status of budget
29. Credit
30. Yes
31. Interest
32. Yes
33. Allowance
34. States personal allowance status
35. Yes
36. Can make something
37. Birdhouse, clay pot, etc.
38. Yes
39. States home and school tasks
40. Yes

Economics – 2nd Grade

41. Money
42. Goods
43. Food, shelter, etc.
44. Toys, dining out, big TV, etc.
45. Services
46. Money
47. Currency
48. The American dollar
49. Barter
50. Yes
51. A consumer
52. A producer
53. Resources
54. Natural resources
55. A human resource
56. Capital resources
57. Specialization
58. Economic choice
59. Abundance
60. Scarcity
61. Income
62. An economic system
63. Names local businesses
64. A product
65. Names state products
66. Imports
67. Exports
68. Benefits and costs
69. Employment
70. Unemployment
71. Entrepreneur

Economics – 3rd Grade

72. Currency
73. Income
74. A bank
75. A tax
76. A budget
77. A cost
78. A benefit
79. International trade
80. Imports
81. Exports
82. Interdependence
83. Supply
84. Demand
85. Profit
86. Loss
87. Entrepreneur
88. Free enterprise
89. Opportunity cost
90. Marketing
91. Competition
92. Yes

ANSWERS – ECONOMICS

Economics – 4th Grade

93. Economy
94. A market economy
95. Services
96. Consumers
97. Producers
98. Manufacturing
99. Supply and demand
100. Market economy
101. Productivity
102. Capital
103. Human
104. Natural
105. Economic resources
106. Price
107. Opportunity cost
108. Division of labor
109. A profit
110. A loss
111. A debt
112. Incentives

Economics – 5th Grade

113. Economy
114. The private sector
115. The public sector
116. Trade
117. Specialization
118. A need
119. A luxury
120. American dollar
121. Yes
122. Denomination
123. 1,5,10,25,50
124. A need
125. A want
126. Euro
127. Dollar
128. New Peso
129. No
130. Savings, investments, etc.
131. Safe deposit box
132. Savings, checking, etc.
133. A deposit
134. A withdrawal
135. Check
136. A debit card
137. A free market economy
138. A depression
139. A recession
140. Economic cycle
141. Prosperity
142. GDP
143. Recovery
144. Inflation
145. Deflation
146. A bank
147. The Federal Reserve
148. The FDIC
149. A bond
150. Answers yes or no
151. Savings account
152. Checking account
153. Interest
154. Interest rate
155. A loan
156. Collateral
157. A mortgage
158. Yes
159. Interest
160. Foreclosure
161. Principle
162. Credit
163. Debt
164. Buying
165. Saving
166. A stock
167. The stock market
168. Dow Jones Industrial Average
169. Wall Street
170. Regulations
171. Gold and silver
172. Investment
173. Employment
174. The employer
175. The employee
176. An income
177. A retirement account
178. Yes
179. States minimum wage
180. 16, depending on job
181. A hire
182. A layoff
183. Unemployed
184. Unemployment benefits
185. Welfare
186. Food stamps
187. Social Security
188. Social Security Number
189. A tax
190. Revenue
191. Income
192. A property tax
193. A sales tax
194. FICA
195. The Internal Revenue Service
196. The U.S. Mint
197. The Internal Revenue Service
198. Barter
199. A consumer
200. Imports
201. Exports
202. Supply
203. Demand
204. Price increases
205. Price decreases
206. A shortage
207. A surplus
208. Scarcity
209. Abundance
210. Cost
211. Profit
212. Liability
213. A warranty
214. Opportunity cost
215. Public
216. Private
217. Assembly line
218. Competition
219. Resource
220. Productive resources
221. Renewable resources
222. Wealth
223. Poverty
224. Census
225. E-commerce
226. Capital
227. The information age
228. Monopoly
229. Banks
230. Yes
231. Debt
232. National Debt
233. Businesses
234. Chief executive officer
235. Resume
236. LinkedIn
237. Salary
238. Higher
239. Income
240. Benefits
241. Intern
242. Promotion
243. Entrepreneur
244. Retirement
245. States type of business

ANSWERS - PHYSICAL EDUCATION

APPENDIX 8: Chapter 8 – Physical Education

Pre-School

1. Yes
2. Yes
3. Is important
4. Yes
5. Legs, arms, eyes, etc.
6. Can walk and run
7. Can climb stairs
8. Can throw and catch ball
9. Can ride a tricycle
10. Can swing
11. States exercises

Physical Education – Kindergarten

12. Can run
13. Can roll right and left
14. Can throw ball
15. Can catch ball
16. Can kick ball
17. Can hop
18. Can jump
19. Can jump on two feet
20. Can land on one foot
21. Can land on two feet
22. Can gallop
23. Can leap
24. Can walk
25. Can look ahead
26. Can swing arms
27. States foot motion
28. Can run
29. Can play tag
30. Can slide
31. Can skip
32. Moves with different forces
33. Moves at different levels
34. Moves at different speeds
35. Moves forwards and backwards
36. Moves in different circles
37. Moves in different lines
38. Moves sideways
39. Moves under and over objects
40. Balances on one foot
41. Moves body without feet
42. Can play with a ball
43. Climbs a rope
44. Jumps rope
45. Can play on some apparatus
46. Identifies body parts
47. Shakes body
48. Twists body
49. Bends body
50. Stretches body
51. Rocks body
52. Curls body
53. Sways body
54. Straightens body
55. Tenses body
56. Freezes body
57. Relaxes body
58. Can do animal walks
59. Stands like flamingo
60. Jumps like a frog
61. Twists like a snake
62. Can do army crawl
63. Can wheelbarrow
64. Can wheelbarrow
65. Balances objects
66. Can do egg roll
67. Can do log roll
68. Can do a pencil roll
69. Walks forward on beam
70. Walks backward on beam
71. Walks sideways on beam
72. Tiptoes on beam
73. Climbs traverse wall
74. Thick foam mat
75. Uses sticks for rhythm
76. Taps to beat of music
77. Creates sequence of beats
78. A cardiovascular activity
79. Can dance to music
80. Can dance Hokey Pokey
81. Can do The Chicken Dance
82. Can line dance
83. The limbo
84. Yes
85. Can jump rope forwards
86. Can jump rope backwards
87. Can long rope jump
88. Rolls ball underhand
89. Throws ball underhand
90. Throws ball overhand
91. Can catch own ball
92. Catches fly ball
93. Catches rolling ball
94. Dribbles ball standing
95. Dribbles ball moving
96. Dribbles ball with foot
97. Dodges a ball or object
98. Chases object
99. Kicks approaching ball
100. Can drop-kick a ball
101. Sportsmanship
102. Yes
103. Talk it out
104. Yes
105. Shake hands, etc.
106. Complaining, etc.
107. Fair play
108. Bad sportsmanship
109. A referee
110. An umpire
111. Good sportsmanship
112. Yes
113. Stretch, etc.
114. Yes
115. Shows forehead
116. Shows head
117. Shows eyes
118. Shows ears
119. Shows nose
120. Shows mouth
121. Shows chin
122. Shows neck
123. Shows shoulders
124. Shows hands
125. Shows palms
126. Shows fingers
127. Shows thumbs
128. Shows elbows
129. Shows wrists
130. Shows arms
131. Shows legs
132. Shows knees
133. Shows ankles
134. Shows feet
135. Shows inside of foot
136. Shows toes
137. Shows thighs
138. Shows calves
139. Shows shins
140. Shows back
141. Shows chest

ANSWERS – PHYSICAL EDUCATION

142. Shows buttocks
143. Shows waist
144. Indicates right side of body
145. Indicates left side of body
146. Stronger
147. Endurance
148. Yes
149. Stretch
150. 20 seconds
151. Muscles
152. A frown
153. Biceps
154. Triceps
155. Quadriceps
156. Ligaments
157. Increases heart rate
158. Stronger
159. Yes
160. Says favorite activity

Physical Education – 1st Grade

161. Names physical activities
162. Names sports
163. Can walk, jog, and run
164. Run
165. Can hop, skip, and jump
166. Leaps and slides
167. Can gallop
168. Changes speeds
169. Travels in different directions
170. Travels at different levels
171. Jumps rope
172. Hula hoops
173. Jumps on pogo stick
174. Can ride a bike
175. Swings a bat
176. Can play hopscotch
177. Kicks a ball
178. The shoelace of the foot
179. Kicks a ball running
180. Dribbles ball with instep
181. Keeps ball in front
182. Passes soccer ball
183. Traps a soccer ball
184. Can kick pass
185. Yes
186. Bottom of foot
187. Demonstrates arm support
188. Moves while balancing
189. Balances on beam
190. Walks forwards and backwards on beam
191. Walks sideways on beam
192. Can tip toe walk on beam
193. Can climb something
194. Can climb a traverse wall
195. Have a mat, spotter, etc.
196. Can egg roll
197. Can log roll
198. Can pencil roll
199. Performs a forward roll
200. Says favorite sport
201. Says favorite physical activity
202. Stretch
203. Yes
204. Yes
205. Weaker
206. 20 seconds
207. Yes
208. Walking
209. Arms
210. Arms
211. Thighs
212. Back of thighs
213. Lower leg
214. Near stomach
215. Has completed fitness test
216. Different
217. Names two activities
218. Yes
219. Yes
220. Muscle endurance
221. Circle dances
222. Line dances
223. Uses rhythm instruments
224. Yes
225. Jumping faster
226. Forwards, backwards, etc.
227. Turns rope in circular motion
228. Jumps long rope 10 times
229. Rolls a ball at least 15 feet
230. Rubber, baseball, etc.
231. Tosses ball underhand
232. Catches underhand throw
233. Throw a ball overhand
234. Catches overhand ball
235. Yes
236. Yes
237. Yes
238. Facing up
239. Facing down
240. Throws and catches ball
241. Tosses ball to self
242. Step forward
243. Right foot
244. Left foot
245. Dribbles with right hand
246. Dribbles with left hand
247. To the side of your body
248. To the side
249. Waist level
250. Travels court while dribbling
251. Chases others
252. Flees others
253. Dodges others
254. Tag, dodge ball, etc.
255. Speed up or slow down
256. States dominant hand
257. States non-dominant hand
258. Finger pads
259. Can use paddle or racket
260. Yes
261. Yes
262. Yes
263. Yes
264. No
265. Follow rules, respect others

Physical Education – 2nd Grade

266. Skips, hops, gallops, and slides
267. Runs in different directions
268. Jumps with one-foot takeoff
269. Jumps with two-foot takeoff
270. Can tumble
271. Can do a forward roll
272. Can climb an apparatus
273. Bounces on a trampoline
274. Throws ball one-handed
275. Catches ball one-handed
276. Throws a ball with two hands
277. Catches a ball with two hands
278. Throws ball underhand
279. Throws a ball overhand
280. Can throw different balls

ANSWERS - PHYSICAL EDUCATION

281. Can swing a bat
282. Can kick punt a ball
283. Can hit a ball off a tee
284. Bounces ball
285. Dribbles ball
286. Traps a ball
287. Passes a ball
288. Volleys a ball
289. Kicks a ball
290. Dodges a ball
291. Runs toward another player
292. Runs away from player
293. Jumps single rope
294. Can move to music
295. Walks across beam
296. Moves through obstacle course
297. Yes
298. Can move to music
299. Can find and take own pulse
300. Increases
301. Yes
302. Decreases
303. Water
304. Says home activities
305. Says school activities
306. Yes
307. Gains weight, health issues
308. Yes
309. Identifies parts of body
310. Yes
311. Yes
312. Low intensity
313. Medium intensity
314. High intensity
315. Yes
316. Explains "tag" rules
317. Cites solo physical activities
318. Cites paired physical activities
319. Cites team activities
320. Can follow directions
321. Yes
322. Yes
323. No
324. Yes
325. Yes
326. Demonstrates good sportsmanship
327. Playing together as a team
328. Yes
329. Riding bike, football, etc.
330. Soccer, football, etc.
331. Soccer, football, etc.
332. Yes
333. Yes
334. Yes
335. Practice
336. Says favorite physical activity
337. Says favorite team sport

Physical Education – 3rd Grade

338. Yes
339. Can throw and catch a ball
340. Throws overhand and underhand
341. Throws using sidearm
342. Throws with one hand
343. Throws with two hands
344. Dribbles with inside foot
345. Dribbles with outside foot
346. Dribbles with right hand
347. Dribbles with left hand
348. Can hit a ball with bat
349. Throws ball to music
350. Throws a ball at target
351. Can handle different balls
352. Can hit different balls
353. Kicks a ball with force
354. Yes
355. Yes
356. Can use FitnessGram
357. Lists physical strengths
358. Identifies a physical weakness
359. Before physical activity
360. Heart and lung
361. Swimming, tennis, etc.
362. Swimming, running, etc.
363. Yes
364. Yes
365. Follows pool rules
366. Lists pool rules
367. Takes turns
368. Yes
369. Yes
370. Yes
371. Dances with emotion
372. Balance beam, etc.
373. Says sports played
374. Says desired sport to try
375. Can handle a ball
376. Can juggle balls
377. Jumps with short rope
378. Jumps with long rope
379. Jumps high
380. Jumps low
381. Jumps a long distance
382. Jumps a short distance
383. Can tumble
384. Warm-up
385. Cool-down
386. Heart rate
387. Yes
388. Helps you become better
389. Good job, etc.
390. Why did you do that?
391. Yes
392. Number of steps
393. Knows how to use pedometer
394. Yes
395. Yes
396. Yes
397. Yes
398. Relates good skills
399. Relates skills needing improvement
400. Yes
401. Health and fitness
402. Names sports and activities

Physical Education – 4th Grade

403. Can handle a ball
404. Uses good form
405. Uses arms when running
406. Can climb a rope
407. Yes
408. Demonstrates a dance
409. Has good throwing form
410. Says skill in need of practice
411. Can chest pass a ball
412. Can bounce pass a ball
413. Can drop kick a ball
414. Physical fitness
415. Names activities and sports

ANSWERS – PHYSICAL EDUCATION

416. Yes
417. Yes
418. Walking, aerobics, etc.
419. Describes skills related to fitness
420. Can take a fitness test
421. States push-up count
422. States sit-up count
423. States chin-up count
424. Says running distance
425. Yes
426. Yes
427. Says long or short
428. Stretch, bend, etc.
429. Flexibility
430. Endurance
431. Walk, stretch, etc.
432. Water
433. Bike and helmet
434. Bat, ball, glove, helmet
435. Ball, hoop, etc.
436. Ball, helmet, pads, mouth guard, etc.
437. Racket, ball, net, etc.
438. Ball, shin guards, net, etc.
439. Puck, stick, pads, helmet, etc.
440. Pads, athletic shoes, etc.
441. Tennis, playing catch, etc.
442. Exercises, dancing, etc.
443. Football, baseball, basketball, etc.
444. Lacrosse
445. Brazil, Argentina, Spain, Italy, etc.
446. Baseball
447. Physical
448. Non-physical
449. Yes
450. Yes
451. Yes
452. The Olympics
453. The Special Olympics
454. World Cup
455. Stanley Cup
456. States enjoyable activities
457. States less desired activities
458. Confirms or denies participation
459. States sport involvement
460. States preference
461. Play with older kids, etc.
462. Way to go!
463. What was that?
464. Positive reinforcement
465. Non-verbal
466. Yes
467. Safety, preventing injury
468. Tag, hopscotch, etc.
469. Organized or skilled sports
470. States potential sport

Physical Education – 5th Grade

471. Have endurance, skill, etc.
472. Manages obstacle course
473. Describes ball skills
474. Can manage a ball
475. Can control a ball
476. Keeps an object in the air
477. Can move in many ways
478. Hits ball with bat
479. Catches ball with glove
480. Can skate
481. Well-coordinated
482. Basketball, hockey, etc.
483. Soccer, tennis, etc.
484. Baseball, Softball, etc.
485. Soccer, football, etc.
486. Yes
487. Wagon, swing, etc.
488. Names sport with rules
489. Moves to music
490. Yes
491. Yes
492. Yes
493. Moves to beat
494. Dances to music
495. Dances in formation
496. Can transfer weight
497. Can do a cartwheel
498. Yes
499. Yes
500. Yes
501. Yes
502. Eat well, practice, etc.
503. States fitness goals
504. Yes
505. Yes
506. Calisthenics
507. Warm-up exercises
508. Increase stability
509. Cool down
510. Cardiovascular
511. Can monitor heart rate
512. Runs mile and records time
513. Sprints and records time
514. Body composition
515. Gains weight, unhealthy, etc.
516. Yes
517. Yes
518. Yes
519. Says potential sport
520. Yes
521. Height
522. The age of 10
523. The age of 12
524. Describes physical strengths
525. Describes weaknesses
526. Practice
527. Yes
528. Yes
529. Yes
530. Organized sports, gym class
531. Running, stretching, etc.
532. Yes
533. All played with a net
534. Reliance on teammates
535. Each player has specific role
536. Assigned roles
537. Tennis, ping pong, etc.
538. So not to push body too far
539. Marathons, triathlons, etc.
540. Promotes health and wellness

ANSWERS - HEALTH AND SAFETY

APPENDIX 9: Chapter 9 – Health and Safety

Pre-school

1. Yes
2. Shampoo
3. Soap
4. Toothpaste
5. Doctor
6. Yes
7. Brush your teeth
8. Yes
9. Fruits, vegetables, etc.
10. An apple
11. The Dentist
12. Wash with soap
13. Cover mouth
14. Look both ways
15. Stay back on curb
16. Stop
17. Lights flash, bells ring, etc.
18. A helmet
19. Your seatbelt
20. In a building away from windows
21. No
22. 9-1-1
23. No
24. Police officer, mom with kids
25. Please
26. Thank you
27. Buddy system, no deep water, etc.
28. Prevent sunburn

Health and Safety – Kindergarten

29. Yes
30. Sunscreen
31. Stop, drop, and roll
32. Wash your hands
33. Eat well, get shots, etc.
34. Cough, sniffles, etc.
35. Parent, teacher, etc.
36. Germs
37. Yes
38. Fall, throw, etc.
39. Yes
40. Cleaners, pesticides, etc.
41. Eyes
42. Ears
43. Nose
44. Ears
45. Hands and fingers
46. Knows "safe" touch
47. Tongue
48. Fruits, vegetables, etc.
49. Water, milk, etc.
50. Soda, sugar juices, etc.
51. Unhealthy habits
52. Eating nutritious meals, etc.
53. Candy, chips, soda, etc.
54. Eating sweets, "junk" food, etc.
55. Unhealthy
56. Eight to ten
57. Floss
58. A cavity
59. Twice a year
60. Yes
61. Measles, mumps, chicken pox, etc.
62. Sad
63. Yes
64. Sit and count to ten, etc.
65. Respect their point of view
66. Bathe, brush, etc.
67. Basic food groups
68. Fruits and vegetables
69. A pyramid
70. Vertical divisions
71. A recommendation
72. Yes
73. Germs, touching surfaces, etc.
74. Sleep, eat well, wash hands, etc.
75. Stay close to home, etc.
76. Heart, lungs, liver, skin, etc.
77. Names school rules
78. Yes
79. Follow safety rules, etc.
80. Smoke alarm, etc.
81. Says number of smoke alarms
82. Verifies escape plan
83. Twice a year
84. Listen to driver, etc.
85. Do not talk, take bribes, etc.
86. Wear helmet, obey rules, etc.
87. Use sidewalk, crosswalk, etc.
88. The walk sign
89. Yes
90. Yes
91. Sunburn, etc.
92. Drink water, sunscreen, etc.
93. Frostbite, exposure, etc.
94. Bundle up, wear boots, etc.
95. Yes
96. Refuse, tell a trusted adult
97. Talk it out
98. No
99. No

Health and Safety – 1st Grade

100. Yes
101. Grains, fruits, vegetables, meats, etc.
102. Nutrients
103. Yes
104. Yes
105. Wash them
106. Wash hands, etc.
107. Wash hands
108. Germs
109. No
110. Cough, sniffles, etc.
111. Yes
112. Yes
113. Stay calm, etc.
114. A non-violent approach
115. Bandages, antiseptic, etc.
116. Yes

ANSWERS – HEALTH AND SAFETY

117. Emergency, injury, etc.
118. Call 9-1-1, flee, etc.
119. Cleaners, pesticides, etc.
120. Follow directions
121. No
122. Yes
123. No
124. Not believe, get away, tell someone
125. A trusted adult
126. Yes
127. Yes
128. No
129. Yes
130. No
131. Yes
132. No
133. In case of fall, etc.
134. Storm, etc.
135. No
136. No
137. Yes
138. Yes
139. Yes
140. Yes
141. Yes
142. Yes

Health and Safety – 2nd Grade

143. Brush and floss
144. The doctor
145. Names food groups
146. A pyramid
147. Fruits and vegetables, etc.
148. Candy, cakes, soda, etc.
149. Germs
150. Wash hands, etc.
151. Buddy system, stay close
152. Names body organs
153. Cites some school rules
154. Yes
155. Obey rules, supervisor, etc.
156. Says fire safety rules
157. Heat stroke, sunburn, etc.
158. Sunscreen, shade, etc.
159. Frostbite, etc.
160. Wear protective clothing
161. Yes
162. Yes
163. Yes
164. Refuse it

Health and Safety – 3rd Grade

165. Yes
166. To monitor health
167. Names doctor
168. Clean teeth, check for cavities
169. Names dentist
170. Eat well, exercise, etc.
171. Names local medical clinic
172. Names local hospital
173. Doctor, nurse, etc.
174. Yes
175. Yes
176. No
177. Nutritious food, exercise, etc.
178. Work out gym, etc.
179. Health club, vitamin store, etc.
180. Yes
181. Yes
182. Yes
183. Preventive measures
184. Cleaning supplies, pesticides, etc.
185. May be loaded
186. Provide basic aid
187. Antiseptic
188. 9-1-1
189. Bandages, antiseptic, etc.
190. Yes
191. Inside a building
192. A tree
193. Yes
194. Seven
195. Sugar
196. Carbohydrates
197. Protein
198. Eating from all groups
199. Vegetables, fruits, grains, etc.
200. Candy, potato chips, etc.
201. Apple, yogurt, carrot sticks, etc.
202. Chips, cookies, etc.
203. States physical activities
204. Supplement their diet
205. A, C, D, Calcium, etc.
206. Yes
207. Yes
208. Yes
209. Yes
210. Negative effect
211. Negative effect
212. Brush and floss
213. No
214. Lung cancer, yellow teeth, etc.
215. Yes
216. Yes
217. A positive attitude
218. Yes
219. Empathy
220. Sympathy
221. Yes
222. Yes
223. Yes
224. Friendliness, helpfulness, etc.
225. Spreading rumors, etc.
226. Yes
227. Yes
228. Yes
229. Harassment
230. Teasing
231. Tell adult, tell them to stop
232. A bully
233. A victim
234. A bystander
235. Tell a trusted adult
236. Try to stop it
237. Stress
238. Yes
239. Listen to music, etc.
240. Yes
241. Yes
242. Yes
243. Yes (or at times)
244. Good touches
245. Say no, tell trusted adult
246. Yes
247. At different rates
248. Says number of lost teeth
249. Yes
250. No!
251. Walk away and tell adult
252. No
253. Tell mom, officer, and manager
254. Buddy system
255. Unsafe places

ANSWERS - HEALTH AND SAFETY

256. Get away, tell someone
257. Yes
258. Not answer it
259. No
260. Aloe Vera, egg whites, baking soda
261. First degree
262. Third degree
263. Minor burns
264. Get out, call 9-1-1

265. Yes
266. Says exercises
267. Yes
268. Bathe, brush, wash, etc.
269. Says home safety rules
270. Says swimming rules
271. Listen to driver, stay seated, etc.
272. Stay in familiar area, daytime, etc.

273. Wear helmet, follow bike rules, etc.
274. Helmets, pads, mouth guards, etc.
275. Parent, school nurse, doctor, etc.
276. Yes
277. Yes

Health and Safety – 4th Grade

278. Yes
279. Nutritious food, exercise
280. Yes
281. Can cause diseases, etc.
282. Yes
283. Cleaners, bleach, etc.
284. Yes
285. Eat well, wash hands, etc.
286. Yes
287. Strong
288. Weak
289. Communicable
290. Non-communicable
291. Cough, headache, fever, etc.
292. Red spots
293. Rest, juice, medicine
294. Prescription medicines, etc.
295. Allergies
296. Confirms or denies
297. States any allergy
298. Sneezing, watery eyes, etc.
299. Acceptable
300. Can cause negative reaction
301. Yes
302. A stimulant
303. A depressant
304. Respiratory problems, yellow teeth, etc.
305. Smoke inhaled from another smoking
306. May affect lungs
307. Yes
308. Yes
309. Parents, teachers, and counselors
310. Decrease
311. Yes
312. Seek help
313. Greatly impairs driving
314. Accident or death
315. Yes

316. Eat well, exercise, etc.
317. Yes
318. Door handles, railings, etc.
319. Yes
320. Yes
321. Mosquitoes, flies, etc.
322. Arm
323. Yes
324. Yes
325. Says snack
326. Yes
327. Yes
328. Yes
329. Says number of sleep hours
330. Says types of exercises
331. Repellant
332. Wash hands, stay away those sick
333. Yes
334. Wear life preserver, shallower water, etc.
335. Yes
336. Yes
337. Lists first-aid items
338. Call for help, tell a trusted adult
339. Stretch
340. CPR
341. Yes
342. Person having heart attack
343. Yes
344. Apply Heimlich maneuver
345. Yes
346. Ice and heat, rest, etc.
347. Names local health-care services
348. Serious injury or illness
349. Twice a year
350. Brush and floss
351. Yes
352. Fluoride

353. Yes
354. No
355. Others my access it
356. Cyber-bullying
357. Yes
358. Dangerous practice
359. Yes
360. Yes
361. Puberty
362. Yes
363. Yes
364. Yes
365. Yes
366. Drinking, taking drugs, etc.
367. States short-term health goals
368. States long-term health goals
369. Names parts of the body
370. Exercise
371. Drink milk, exercise, etc.
372. Doctor sets bone, cast or splint
373. Stretch, eat well, etc.
374. Eat well, exercise
375. Take care of one's self
376. Washing, sunscreen, etc.
377. Wear glasses, etc.
378. Clean, keep sound level reasonable
379. No overload, good pacing
380. Yes
381. Keeps you energetic and healthy
382. Keeps you warm and protected
383. Helps regulate body temperature
384. School clinic, parent, etc.
385. Medical center, hospital, etc.
386. Yes

ANSWERS – HEALTH AND SAFETY

Health and Safety – 5th Grade

387. Yes
388. Yes
389. States personal goal
390. Yes
391. Yes
392. Six
393. Cakes
394. A pyramid
395. A recommendation
396. Yes
397. Oils
398. Apples, carrots, yogurt, etc.
399. Chips, ice cream, etc.
400. Balanced
401. Yes
402. Yes
403. Apples, broccoli, a turkey, etc.
404. TV dinners, chicken nuggets, etc.
405. Yes
406. Whole
407. Yes
408. Dance
409. Basketball
410. Yes
411. Yes
412. Yes
413. Yes
414. Yes
415. Yes
416. Yes
417. Yes
418. Air-tight containers, etc.
419. Foods only last so long
420. A can of soup
421. Yes
422. Throw them out
423. No
424. Yes
425. Breakfast charges up metabolism
426. Cereal, yogurt, etc.
427. Eating nutritiously from food groups
428. A temporary diet
429. Yes
430. Names American foods
431. States preferred ethnic cuisines
432. No
433. Yes
434. Work, school, family, etc.
435. Exercise, talk with someone, etc.
436. Yes
437. Demeanor, face, actions, etc.
438. Yes
439. Tell a trusted adult
440. Try to help the person
441. Negative effect
442. Yes
443. Overdose
444. Intoxication
445. Withdrawal
446. Yes
447. Yes
448. Parents, teachers, counselors, etc.
449. States who has greater influence
450. Yes
451. Yes
452. Yes
453. Stages of life
454. Yes
455. Yes
456. Yes
457. Yes
458. Inherited
459. Pre-adolescence
460. 9-12
461. Yes
462. Names physical changes
463. Yes
464. Yes
465. Wash body, comb hair, etc.
466. Bathe, shower, brush teeth, etc.
467. Yes
468. Yes
469. States hair-washing schedule
470. Lice
471. Your own hat
472. Every day
473. Yes
474. Wash hands, no railing, etc.
475. 8-10 hours
476. Says total sleeping hours
477. Yes!
478. Yes
479. Yes
480. Yes
481. Skeletal
482. Nervous
483. Digestive
484. Respiratory
485. Muscular
486. Circulatory
487. Yes
488. Parents, family, friends, etc.
489. Yes
490. Yes
491. Respect
492. Self-respect
493. Yes
494. Wear seatbelt, etc.
495. Wear preserver, etc.
496. Follow rules, swim with a buddy, etc.
497. Wear protective pads
498. Wear helmet
499. Yes
500. Yes
501. Yes
502. Cites specific rules for each item
503. Yes

ANSWERS - THE ARTS

APPENDIX 10: Chapter 10 – The Arts

Pre-School

1. Yes
2. Yes
3. Yes
4. Says favorite song
5. Yes
6. Yes
7. Yes
8. Yes
9. Yes
10. Yes
11. Yes
12. Yes
13. Yes
14. Yes
15. Yes
16. Yes
17. Yes
18. Can dance
19. States theatre experience
20. Names musical instruments
21. Piano, drums, flute, etc.
22. Piano, organ, clarinet, guitar, etc.
23. Tuba, clarinet, flute, trumpet, etc.
24. Guitar, clarinet, flute, etc.
25. A drum
26. Guitar, violin, base, banjo, etc.
27. Piano and organ
28. Names fine arts attended
29. Yes
30. Yes
31. An artist
32. A collage
33. Yes
34. Types of paints
35. A pastel painting
36. A landscape
37. Landscapes
38. A portrait
39. Self-portrait
40. Abstract
41. A statue
42. Yes
43. *Mona Lisa*, etc.
44. Picasso, Monet, etc.
45. A famous artist

The Arts – Kindergarten

46. Yes
47. Yes
48. An artist
49. Yes
50. Yes
51. Yes
52. Yes
53. Yes
54. A canvas
55. A palate
56. An easel
57. Yes
58. Grey
59. Pink
60. Green
61. Orange
62. Purple
63. Brown
64. Yes
65. Light, pastel colors
66. Black, brown, grey, etc.
67. Primary colors
68. Secondary colors
69. Black
70. Yes
71. Straight
72. Curved
73. Zigzag
74. Wavy
75. Clay
76. A potter's wheel
77. A kiln
78. Animals, pots, etc.
79. A collage
80. An art museum
81. A portrait
82. A still-life
83. A self-portrait
84. A mural
85. Louvre, Prado, etc.
86. Picasso, Monet, Van Gogh, etc.
87. *David, Venus de Milo*, etc.
88. Dimensional
89. A sculptor
90. A totem pole
91. A monument
92. Names monuments
93. Yes
94. Grey
95. Pink
96. Green
97. Orange
98. Black
99. Yes
100. Red, white, and blue
101. Yes
102. Names artistic creations
103. A mobile
104. A fine art
105. Names types of music
106. Names songs
107. Drums, guitar, keyboard, etc.
108. Yes
109. Guitar, violin, harp, etc.
110. Drums
111. Yes
112. Yes
113. Bingo, etc.
114. Yes
115. Yes
116. Yes
117. Yes
118. Can sing alone
119. Sings in a group
120. A choir
121. Chorus
122. Sings loud and quiet
123. Yes
124. Sings fast and slow
125. Can sing high notes
126. Can sing low notes
127. Knows movement songs
128. Ring Around the Rosey, etc.
129. Knows London Bridge
130. Yes
131. Yes
132. Yes
133. Yes
134. Yes
135. Yes

ANSWERS – THE ARTS

136. Yes
137. Yes
138. Yes
139. Yes
140. Yes
141. Yes

The Arts – 1st Grade

142. Dances to music
143. Creates art
144. Looks at art
145. Indicates art preference
146. An art Museum
147. Fine Arts
148. Paint, clay, etc.
149. Yes
150. Names artists
151. Yes
152. Buffalo
153. Yes
154. A portrait
155. Architecture
156. Yes
157. Yes
158. Yes
159. Names famous statue
160. New York
161. Freedom
162. Totem Pole
163. Red, yellow, and blue
164. Orange, green, and purple,
165. Warm colors
166. Cool colors
167. Cool colors
168. Red, yellow, orange, pink
169. Blue, grey, black, brown
170. Yes
171. Orange
172. Green
173. Grey
174. Pink
175. Red, blue, and yellow
176. Lines
177. Yes
178. Shapes
179. Yes
180. Yes
181. Yes
182. Texture
183. Yes
184. Yes
185. Michelangelo
186. Masks
187. A portrait
188. *Mona Lisa*
189. A self-portrait
190. Yes
191. A still life
192. Still life
193. Confirms or denies
194. A mural
195. A fresco
196. Diego Rivera
197. A choir
198. A band
199. An orchestra
200. A symphony
201. Classical
202. Families
203. The percussion family
204. Mexico
205. Castanets
206. The string family
207. The wind family
208. A reed
209. The brass family
210. An orchestra
211. An orchestra
212. The conductor
213. Maestro
214. Boston Pops, London, etc.
215. A symphony
216. Yes
217. Confirms or denies
218. A composer
219. Mozart
220. Classical
221. Ludwig van Beethoven
222. Composers
223. Has made instruments
224. Names instruments
225. Types of music
226. Yes
227. Reveals favorite music
228. Musical notes
229. Describes musical note
230. Yes
231. Yes
232. Yes
233. The chorus
234. Yes
235. A banjo
236. An opera
237. Yes
238. Yes
239. Operas
240. An echo
241. A drum
242. Dance
243. Dances
244. Yes
245. Latin
246. Yes
247. Ballerinas
248. A ballet
249. Has attended performance
250. The Nutcracker
251. Swan Lake
252. Square dancing
253. Jazz
254. Louis Armstrong
255. Jazz
256. New Orleans
257. Says favorite song
258. Melody
259. Harmony
260. Yes
261. Yes
262. Yes
263. The beat
264. Your foot, hands, etc.
265. Yes
266. Knows words to song
267. Yes
268. Yes
269. Yes
270. Yes

The Arts – 2nd Grade

271. Art, sculpture, dance, music, etc.
272. Yes
273. Yes
274. Yes
275. Paints
276. An easel
277. A palette
278. Yes
279. Yes
280. Clay, chalk, pencil, etc.
281. Yes
282. Yes
283. Answers yes or no
284. Yes
285. Yes
286. Yes
287. A kiln

ANSWERS - THE ARTS

288. Yes
289. Answers yes or no
290. Yes
291. House, park, etc.
292. Yes
293. Yes
294. Names art found in nature
295. Yes
296. Yes
297. Yes
298. Picasso, Van Gogh, etc.
299. Sculptures, murals, etc.
300. The "Met," Louvre, Prado, etc.
301. Names close art museum
302. Yes
303. Texture
304. Cool colors
305. Yes
306. Warm colors
307. *Mona Lisa, Starry Night*, etc.
308. A self-portrait
309. Answers yes or no
310. Priceless
311. Priceless artworks
312. Can fade pigment
313. To guard artworks
314. Yes
315. Yes
316. Yes
317. Yes
318. Yes
319. Vertical lines
320. Horizontal lines
321. Diagonal
322. A thin line
323. A zigzag
324. A spiral
325. Can draw dog
326. Yes
327. A sculpture
328. Statue of Liberty, etc.
329. Yes
330. A person
331. Painter paints self
332. Fruit, flowers, etc.
333. A landscape
334. The foreground
335. The background
336. A landscape
337. A landscape
338. Still life paintings
339. Yes
340. Somber, sad mood
341. Joy, happy mood
342. Yes
343. Realistic
344. Abstract
345. Yes

346. Abstract art
347. A dreamscape
348. Yes
349. Abstract
350. Yes
351. Answers yes or no
352. Answers yes or no
353. Answers yes or no
354. Animals, pots, etc.
355. Yes
356. Architecture
357. An architect
358. Yes
359. Vertical columns
360. Symmetric
361. Yes
362. Circle, diamond, etc.
363. Asymmetrical
364. Symmetry in nature
365. Curved lines
366. The Greeks
367. Yes
368. Yes
369. Famous architects
370. Modern
371. Modern
372. Says museums visited
373. Names unique buildings
374. Yes
375. Music
376. Yes
377. America the Beautiful, etc.
378. The Star-Spangled Banner
379. The Spar-Spangled Banner
380. The National Anthem
381. Can sing song
382. People
383. A folk song
384. Home on the Range
385. Immigrants
386. Yes
387. A guitar
388. A band or orchestra
389. A symphony
390. Flutes, violins, clarinet, etc.
391. Yes
392. Classical
393. An overture
394. Trumpet, French horn, tuba, trombone
395. Flute, clarinet, oboe, bassoon, etc.
396. Drums, cymbals, xylophone, etc.
397. Violin, cello, bass, etc.
398. The string family
399. Four

400. The violin
401. The bass
402. Banjo
403. A violin
404. A pianist
405. A violinist
406. An organist
407. A bow
408. A baton
409. Percussion
410. Drums
411. Percussion
412. Cymbals
413. Bach, Beethoven, Mozart, etc.
414. Famous composers
415. A conductor
416. Beethoven
417. A concerto
418. A piano
419. An organ
420. A soloist
421. Duet
422. Trio
423. Recognizes notes
424. Yes
425. Yes
426. Yes
427. Four
428. Two
429. One
430. Yes
431. A staff
432. High notes
433. Low notes
434. Yes
435. Musical scale
436. Yes
437. Up
438. Answers yes or no
439. A treble clef
440. A rest
441. Pitch
442. The melody
443. The rhythm
444. Yes
445. Choir, chorus, etc.
446. Yes
447. Names famous musical
448. A soundtrack
449. Can sing in a group
450. A choir or chorus
451. Names current singing group
452. Names past singing group
453. Mariachi
454. A solo
455. A duet
456. Yes
457. A choir or chorus

ANSWERS – THE ARTS

458. Names favorite song
459. Yes

460. Yes
461. Ballet, musical, etc.

462. Yes
463. Movie

The Arts – 3rd Grade

464. Art
465. Great Masters
466. Yes
467. The *Mona Lisa*
468. Brush, palette, easel, etc.
469. An easel
470. Yes
471. Happy
472. Sad
473. Yes
474. Yes
475. Shadow
476. Light
477. Wheel, clay, water, etc.
478. A mosaic
479. Yes
480. Yes
481. Yes
482. Two
483. Depth
484. Yes
485. The foreground
486. Middle ground
487. The background
488. Small and far
489. Big, close, and in focus
490. Bright
491. Dark
492. The foreground
493. The background
494. Yes
495. Yes
496. Composition
497. Drawing lines
498. Yes
499. Yes
500. A quilt
501. A quilting bee
502. Quilt designs
503. Yes
504. Both halves the same
505. Its texture
506. Folk art
507. Yes
508. Folk art

509. A loom
510. A color wheel
511. Red, yellow, and blue
512. Orange, purple, and green
513. Opposite each other
514. More vivid
515. A collage
516. Yes
517. Ideal, peaceful life
518. Expressionists
519. Yes
520. Yes
521. Yes
522. Yes
523. Llama or sheep
524. Thread
525. Plants
526. A loom
527. Design in their heads
528. Sand paintings
529. Answers yes or no
530. Names material
531. A braid
532. Yes
533. Picasso, Monet, Degas, etc.
534. Names favorite kind of art
535. Yes
536. Says favorite song
537. Yes
538. Musical note
539. Pitch
540. Staff
541. A, B, C, D, E, F, and G
542. The left
543. The letter "S"
544. Whole, half, and quarter
545. Yes
546. Eighth notes
547. Four
548. Rhythm
549. A measure
550. A bar line
551. The end
552. Yes

553. Rests
554. A squiggly line
555. Yes
556. Piano
557. Forte
558. Very
559. Very quiet
560. Very loud
561. Musical families
562. Drums, cymbals, etc.
563. Drums
564. Violin, harp, etc.
565. Violin, viola, cello, string bass
566. Trumpet, trombone, tuba
567. Trumpet
568. Tuba
569. Louis Armstrong
570. String family
571. Brass family
572. Circular
573. Tuba
574. Percussion family
575. Wind family
576. String
577. Small
578. A reed
579. A clarinet
580. Yes
581. Yes
582. The conductor
583. A composer
584. Tchaikovsky
585. John Philip Sousa
586. Aaron Copland
587. Yes
588. Yes
589. Yes
590. Yes
591. Yes
592. Yes
593. Names folk songs
594. Yes

The Arts – 4th Grade

595. Yes
596. Cathedrals
597. Notre Dame
598. Gothic

599. The South Rose Window
600. Gargoyles
601. Illuminated manuscripts
602. Yes

603. "The Book of Kells"
604. Parchment paper
605. A quill pen
606. Tapestries

ANSWERS - THE ARTS

607. Palaces, cathedrals, etc.
608. The Muslims
609. Islam
610. The Moors
611. The Alhambra
612. The Taj Mahal
613. The Bible
614. The Qur'an
615. A mosque
616. With geometric patterns
617. The human figure
618. The antelope
619. Yes
620. Sculptures
621. Copper
622. Yes
623. Wood
624. Ivory
625. Jewelry
626. Sculptures
627. Yes
628. Tapestries
629. Yes
630. Hunting
631. Yes
632. Textile artists
633. Body painting
634. A beehive
635. Yes
636. The Chinese
637. Scrolls
638. Silk
639. Calligraphy
640. Porcelain
641. China
642. Glaze
643. Blue
644. A portrait
645. Official portraits
646. Serious and formal
647. Yes
648. Capturing a moment
649. Monticello
650. American art museums
651. Harmony
652. Musical notation
653. Measures
654. Italian
655. Yes
656. Letters
657. Sharp keys
658. D-flat
659. By instruments
660. Fan-shaped
661. Four
662. The conductor
663. Baton
664. Hands and fingers
665. Blowing air
666. Sticks
667. The human voice
668. Yes
669. Yes
670. Soprano
671. Alto
672. Mezzo-soprano
673. Tenor
674. Bass
675. Baritone
676. Chants
677. A symphony
678. Four
679. Franz Joseph Haydn
680. Wolfgang Amadeus Mozart
681. Bach, Beethoven, etc.
682. New Year's Eve
683. Answers yes or no
684. Answers yes or no
685. Sings some folksongs

The Arts – 5th Grade

686. Yes
687. States art talents
688. Greece and Rome
689. Columns
690. The Parthenon
691. The Acropolis
692. Sculpture
693. *The Discus Thrower*
694. The *Venus de Milo*
695. Gothic
696. Notre Dame Cathedral
697. Renaissance
698. The Middle Ages
699. Religion
700. Gothic art
701. Italy
702. Palaces
703. Florence and Rome
704. Yes
705. Italian artists
706. Sandro Botticelli
707. Leonardo da Vinci
708. The *Mona Lisa*
709. *The Last Supper*
710. Her smile
711. A fresco
712. Raphael
713. Raphael
714. Italian
715. The *David*
716. St. Peter's Basilica
717. Sistine Chapel
718. Gothic
719. Ornate Gothic style
720. A dome
721. Oil
722. Oil
723. Realistic painting
724. A genre painter
725. German
726. Art history
727. An art movement
728. Renaissance
729. Byzantine art
730. Romanesque art
731. Gothic art
732. Reims Cathedral
733. Renaissance
734. Renaissance art
735. Renaissance art
736. Renaissance
737. Renaissance
738. Mannerism
739. Baroque
740. Complex and ornate
741. Baroque
742. Caravaggio
743. Andrea Pozzo
744. Rembrandt
745. Peter Paul Rubens
746. Diego Velázquez
747. El Greco
748. Rococo
749. Romantic art
750. German painter Friedrich
751. Francisco de Goya
752. Eugene Delacroix
753. Realism
754. Realists
755. Jean-Francois Millet
756. Gustave Courbet
757. Thomas Eakins
758. Henry Ossawa Tanner
759. Winslow Homer
760. Yes
761. Impressionism
762. Pierre-Auguste Renoir
763. Edgar Degas
764. Claude Monet
765. Edouard Manet
766. Camille Pissaro
767. Mary Cassatt
768. Pointillism
769. Yes

ANSWERS – THE ARTS

770. Smaller dots
771. Georges Seurat
772. Paul Signac
773. Post-Impressionism
774. Vincent Van Gogh
775. Henri Rousseau
776. Henri Toulouse-Lautrec
777. Auguste Rodin
778. Paul Gauguin
779. Paul Cezanne
780. Symbolism
781. Cubism
782. The Blue Period
783. The Rose Period
784. Cubism
785. Guernica
786. Pablo Picasso
787. Juan Gris
788. Juan Gris
789. Expressionism
790. Surrealism
791. Salvador Dalí
792. Abstract
793. Pop art
794. Andy Warhol
795. A collage
796. Red, blue, and yellow
797. Opposite sides of wheel
798. Fresco
799. A kiln
800. A potter's wheel
801. A landscape
802. Medium
803. Palette
804. A mural
805. Pastels
806. Dimension
807. Pigment
808. Plein Air
809. A portrait
810. Self-portrait
811. Relief
812. A sculpture
813. A series
814. Watercolors
815. Still life
816. Texture
817. Symmetry
818. Prado, Louvre, The Met, etc.
819. Le Louvre
820. Play, opera, musical, dance, etc.
821. Opera
822. Play or drama
823. Music
824. A Grammy
825. An Emmy
826. Dance
827. A choreographer
828. Musical
829. A Tony
830. Oscar
831. Louvre, Prado, Art Institute, etc.
832. Names famous artworks
833. Fine arts auction houses
834. *American Gothic*
835. Norman Rockwell
836. Names favorite fine art

ANSWERS - THE ENVIRONMENT

APPENDIX 11: Chapter 11 – Environment

Pre-School

1. Our environment
2. Hot, dry
3. Cold, dark, salty, etc.
4. Hot, humid, fun, etc.
5. Cold, dark, etc.
6. Yes
7. Yes
8. Yes
9. Yes
10. Water, land, etc.
11. Yes
12. Yes
13. Farming, plants, etc.
14. Yes
15. Yes
16. Yes
17. Houses, pools, etc.
18. Water, air, animals, etc.
19. Recycling
20. Oxygen, food, shade, etc.
21. Turn colors, loose leaves, etc.
22. Loose leaves, etc.
23. Start growing, budding, etc.
24. Bloom, grow, etc.
25. Yes
26. Yes

Environment – Kindergarten

27. Environment
28. Paper, plastic, glass, etc.
29. Yes
30. The newspaper
31. Soda cans, etc.
32. Jars
33. Bottles
34. Water, land, trees, etc.
35. Use both sides, recycle, etc.
36. Use in moderation, etc.
37. Turn off lights, etc.
38. A litterbug
39. Recycle, throw away trash, etc.

Environment – 1st Grade

40. Recycle, etc.
41. "Going green"
42. Earth Day
43. Recycle
44. Yes
45. Collect recyclables, etc.
46. Recognizes hazards
47. Yes
48. Yes
49. Paper, plastic, glass, etc.
50. Plastic
51. Yes
52. Clean, recycle, etc.
53. Answers yes or no
54. Yes

Environment – 2nd Grade

55. Yes
56. Yes
57. Basic needs
58. Pollution
59. Yes
60. Use less, etc.
61. Turn off lights, etc.
62. Paper, plastic, etc.
63. Paper, plastic, glass, etc.
64. Yes
65. Yes

Environment – 3rd Grade

66. Your surroundings
67. Yes
68. Yes
69. Paper, glass, etc.
70. Paper, plastic, etc.
71. Less energy and resources
72. Reduce pollution and waste
73. Yes
74. Yes
75. Pesticides
76. Organic
77. On high shelf or cabinet
78. Yes

Environment – 4th Grade

79. Yes
80. Our life cycle
81. Food, air, and water
82. Yes
83. Yes
84. Yes
85. Answers yes or no
86. Yes
87. Restrict hunting, etc.

ANSWERS – THE ENVIRONMENT

Environment – 5th Grade

88. Describes home environment
89. Describes community
90. The EPA
91. Yes
92. Yes
93. Adapting
94. Acid rain
95. Smog
96. Yes
97. They die out
98. The loss of trees
99. Climate change
100. Climate change
101. Atmosphere
102. The Greenhouse Effect
103. Yes
104. Ozone
105. No
106. Yes
107. Water pollution
108. Waste disposal
109. Recycle
110. 70%
111. Yes
112. A tree loss
113. The rainforest
114. The Amazon
115. Yes
116. Yes
117. Taking a short shower
118. Turning off the tap
119. Yes
120. Paper, plastic, etc.
121. Renewable resources
122. Non-renewable resources
123. Hydropower
124. Wind
125. Trees
126. Yes
127. Energy
128. Endangered Species Act
129. Pesticides, aerosols, factories, etc.
130. The Ozone layer
131. Yes
132. Sunscreen, etc.
133. Move away
134. Lead
135. Yes
136. Yes
137. Radon
138. Asbestos
139. Hazardous
140. Yes
141. Killing insects on crops
142. Wash them
143. Yes
144. Organic
145. Yes
146. Yes
147. Earth Day
148. Arbor Day
149. A tree
150. Cites examples

ANSWERS - TECHNOLOGY AND INFORMATION SKILLS

APPENDIX 12: Chapter 12 – Technology and Information Skills

Pre-School

1. Technology
2. Yes
3. Yes
4. Verifies access
5. Facts, information, etc.
6. Yes
7. Answers yes or no
8. The public library

Technology and Information Skills – Kindergarten

9. Yes
10. Verifies access
11. Yes or no
12. Yes
13. Identifies computer parts
14. Yes
15. Names computer programs
16. Yes
17. Yes
18. Log off
19. A password
20. Can use mouse
21. Can click an image
22. Familiar with tool bar
23. Can type name
24. Types words
25. Two
26. The backspace
27. Press the shift key
28. Can type numbers
29. Can open program
30. Familiar with Word
31. Can open program
32. Can Save and Close
33. To type text
34. Can locate keys
35. Can type and Print
36. Can add a picture
37. Changes font
38. Can bold words
39. Yes
40. Practice
41. Yes
42. Yes
43. Can delete text
44. Can make a card
45. Can open the Internet
46. Yes
47. Can click on links
48. Yes
49. Books, research, etc.
50. Quiet, follow rules, etc.
51. Kindle, computer, etc.
52. Kindle, Nook, Sony Reader, etc.
53. Yes
54. Online catalog
55. Yes
56. Invented or imagined
57. Based on fact
58. Library
59. Yes
60. Two weeks, etc.
61. Yes
62. Two, four, etc.
63. Obey due date
64. Fine, etc.
65. Yes
66. Print
67. Media
68. Identifies parts of a book
69. Yes
70. Literature
71. Listens to story
72. Yes
73. Yes or no
74. An author
75. An illustrator
76. The Caldecott Award
77. Gold seal on cover
78. Yes
79. Yes
80. Names devices

Technology and Information Skills – 1st Grade

81. Yes
82. Names electronic devices
83. Yes
84. Yes
85. Names parts of a computer
86. Logs on and off
87. Types simple text
88. Yes
89. Two
90. The home row
91. Can type basics
92. Can use graphics
93. Can operate computer program
94. Can save a document
95. Can print a document
96. Writes a special letter
97. Can open media player
98. Manages media player
99. Familiar with PowerPoint
100. Manipulates PowerPoint slides
101. Yes
102. Can insert graphics
103. Uses punctuation keys
104. Uses Edit features
105. No
106. No
107. Recording voice
108. While listening to audio
109. Yes
110. Yes
111. Yes
112. Cell phone, laptop, etc.
113. Use care, no beverages near it, etc.
114. Yes
115. Indicates frequency of computer use
116. Can conduct electronic search
117. Familiar with libraries
118. Names media specialist(s)
119. Describes role of media specialist
120. Quiet, no re-shelving, etc.

ANSWERS – TECHNOLOGY AND INFORMATION SKILLS

121. Yes
122. Identifies forms of literature
123. Names available devices
124. Books, newspapers, etc.
125. Yes
126. Conducting an electronic search
127. Yes
128. Can locate all formats
129. Can locate audio or DVDs
130. Yes
131. Invented or imaginary
132. Based on fact
133. Can identify poetry
134. Cinderella, Sleeping Beauty, etc.
135. Yes
136. Names books and authors
137. Caldecott
138. Atlas, encyclopedia, dictionary, etc.
139. No
140. Yes
141. Yes
142. Yes
143. Yes
144. Communication, information, etc.

Technology and Information Skills – 2nd Grade

145. Answers yes or no
146. Names electronic devices
147. Laptop, printer, cell phone, etc.
148. Smartphone
149. Wi-Fi
150. A router
151. A router
152. Yes
153. Yes
154. Yes
155. Names software programs
156. Computer, E-readers, etc.
157. Says how often
158. Use as intended, etc.
159. Names parts of computer
160. To serve computer network
161. CPU
162. Yes
163. Improving speed and accuracy
164. Identifies computer parts
165. The space bar
166. Can log on and log off
167. Can save a document
168. Can use web browser
169. Uses common media formats
170. Can access Internet sites
171. Utilizes toolbar features
172. Familiar with desk accessories
173. Yes
174. Can conduct Internet search
175. Can cut, copy, and paste
176. Can insert clipart
177. Creates and presents PowerPoint
178. Can produce report
179. Can make a spreadsheet
180. Yes, in some ways
181. Instructional Media Center
182. Search for a book or other resource
183. Knows how to search Internet
184. Facts, dates, events, etc.
185. Yes
186. Define word, syllables, etc.
187. Alphabetically
188. Yes
189. Yes
190. Yes
191. Can use various formats
192. Names fictional interests
193. Names non-fictional interests
194. The table of contests
195. Uses table of contents
196. Index
197. Glossary
198. Can use index
199. Can use glossary
200. Skimming
201. Can scan materials
202. Yes
203. The Newbery Medal
204. The Caldecott Medal
205. The Coretta Scott King Book Award
206. Yes
207. Yes
208. Can choose a fiction book
209. Can choose a non-fiction book
210. Names favorite author
211. Names favorite book
212. Names favorite fairy tale
213. Yes
214. Internet, CDs, magazines, etc.

Technology and Information Skills – 3rd Grade

215. Yes
216. Names technological devices
217. State-of-the-art
218. Yes
219. Yes
220. Names computer
221. An iPad
222. Yes
223. The Mac
224. Yes
225. A smartphone
226. Answers yes or no
227. Cites phone rules
228. Yes
229. With friends and family
230. No
231. Social networking sites
232. Instagram
233. YouTube
234. Yes
235. Blocking software
236. Cites social media safety rules
237. Familiar with basic programs
238. Yes
239. Says projects
240. Can use web browsers
241. Google
242. See street with satellite images
243. GPS
244. GPS
245. Yes
246. Apps

ANSWERS - TECHNOLOGY AND INFORMATION SKILLS

247. Yes
248. Improving at keyboarding
249. Uses proper keyboarding technique
250. Uses Microsoft Calculator
251. Yes
252. Yes
253. Yes
254. Yes
255. Accesses formatting tools
256. Word wrap
257. Justify
258. Names processed documents
259. Yes
260. Can delete a file
261. Yes
262. Save As
263. Can Save in directory
264. Can retrieve documents
265. Can Save and back up files
266. Can Save on a flash drive
267. Sends document to printer
268. Excel
269. Names data entered in Excel
270. Excel
271. A Word document
272. When adding or editing
273. Cites computer projects
274. Can insert clipart or images
275. No
276. Copyright
277. Conducts computer research
278. Multimedia
279. Can create PowerPoint
280. No
281. Yes
282. Email
283. Confirms email accounts
284. Yes
285. Can send email
286. Manages email messages
287. Dangerous practice
288. Locates video camera
289. Skype
290. Cares for electronics
291. Explains library check-out
292. Explains library's return procedure
293. Circulation desk
294. Quiet, follow rules, etc.
295. Online Catalog
296. Dewey Decimal System
297. Can locate books by Dewey
298. Confirms Ebook availability
299. An electronic reading device
300. Can conduct catalog search
301. Yes
302. Familiar with all parts of book
303. Yes
304. Publish book
305. Small "c" with circle
306. The table of contents
307. The index
308. The index
309. The glossary
310. Yes
311. Yes
312. Yes
313. Can organize with an outline
314. Distinguishes fact and opinion
315. A fact
316. An opinion
317. States opinion about weather
318. It is sunny, raining, etc.
319. Can evaluate resources
320. Yes
321. The internet
322. Obsolete
323. Obsolete
324. Names something obsolete
325. Can use resources in both formats
326. Can locate non-fiction materials
327. Can locate fiction materials
328. Can identify different genres
329. Genre
330. Names favorite fiction genre

Technology and Information Skills – 4th Grade

331. Yes
332. Yes
333. Yes
334. Yes
335. Home row
336. Can type some without looking
337. Says words typed per minute
338. Keyboard skills improving
339. Backspace
340. Space bar
341. Enter
342. Can manage Caps Lock
343. Yes
344. Has created and saved documents
345. Can retrieve documents
346. Yes
347. Yes
348. Cite others' material
349. Copyright
350. Understands copyright
351. Plagiarism
352. Yes
353. Conducts Internet research
354. Yes
355. .com
356. No
357. Cites search engine
358. Basically proficient in Excel
359. Basically proficient in PowerPoint
360. Cites topic
361. Can create spreadsheet
362. Familiar with templates
363. Cites projects
364. Reveals preferred websites
365. Has tried Google Earth
366. Cites school software programs
367. Yes
368. Cites home software programs
369. Familiar with image software
370. Familiar with media integration
371. Familiar with graphics software
372. Answers yes or no
373. External hard drive, USB flash drive, etc.
374. Using spell check tool
375. Trial and error
376. Virus

ANSWERS – TECHNOLOGY AND INFORMATION SKILLS

377. Yes
378. Viral
379. Confirms email account
380. Yes
381. Manages email
382. CC
383. No
384. Can evaluate information
385. Uses relevant resources
386. Uses citation format
387. Proficient with media
388. Yes
389. Can verify information
390. No
391. Yes
392. Yes
393. Yes
394. The author of the content
395. A bibliography
396. Can produce bibliography
397. Genre
398. Poetry
399. Realistic fiction
400. Folklore
401. Fantasy
402. Science fiction
403. Non-fiction
404. Mystery
405. Fable
406. Biography
407. A legend
408. Tall tale
409. Fairy tale
410. Yes
411. Bias
412. Forms of literature
413. Genres of literature
414. Fiction
415. Non-fiction
416. Written forms of literature
417. Oral forms of literature
418. The Newbery Medal
419. The Caldecott Medal
420. Intellectual freedom
421. Censorship
422. Freedom of the press
423. Names favorite genre

Technology and Information Skills – 5th Grade

424. Technology
425. Names familiar devices
426. Multimedia
427. Audio
428. Animation
429. Hardware
430. Software
431. Can upload and download
432. Names software
433. Navigates Internet
434. Names familiar programs
435. Can back up files
436. Incorporates multimedia
437. Operates multimedia
438. Answers yes or no
439. Smart Boards
440. Names Smart Board activities
441. Familiar with image software
442. Facebook, Twitter, etc.
443. Nothing inappropriate
444. Internet safety
445. Cyberbullying
446. Tell a trusted adult
447. Yes
448. Follow Internet rules
449. Powers on and off computer
450. Logs on and off computer
451. Privacy
452. Can use mouse
453. Scrolls up and down
454. Manages programs
455. Manages files
456. For future retrieval
457. Has used help feature
458. Monitor, keyboard, etc.
459. Yes
460. Input
461. Output
462. RAM
463. Random-access memory
464. Modem
465. Byte
466. 1,000 bytes
467. 1,000 kilobytes
468. A gigabyte
469. Yes
470. Yes
471. Improving word processing
472. Familiar with tool bar
473. File (May depend)
474. Format
475. Skills improving
476. Describes good posture
477. Yes
478. States typing speed
479. Yes
480. Yes
481. Yes
482. Yes
483. Yes
484. Yes
485. Yes
486. Yes
487. Page orientation
488. Yes
489. Yes
490. Yes
491. Yes
492. Yes
493. Yes
494. Yes
495. Yes
496. Yes
497. Yes
498. Yes
499. Yes
500. PowerPoint
501. Names PowerPoint
502. Yes
503. Manages slides
504. Storyboard
505. Can publish
506. Answers yes or no
507. Yes
508. Yes
509. Excel
510. Names spreadsheets
511. Fills cells of spreadsheet
512. Data
513. Answers yes or no
514. A jpeg
515. Network
516. Social network
517. World Wide Web
518. Answers yes or no
519. A laptop
520. Conducts research
521. Search engines
522. Names search engine
523. Yes
524. Web browsers
525. Names school web browser
526. Names home web browser
527. Navigates the Internet
528. Cursor
529. Router
530. Icon
531. Menus
532. Can use more than one program
533. Yes
534. Yes

ANSWERS - TECHNOLOGY AND INFORMATION SKILLS

535. Can work at own pace, etc.
536. Need to be self-directed, etc.
537. Names Internet games
538. Yes
539. Yes
540. Yes
541. Yes
542. Assessment tools
543. Yes
544. A flash drive
545. Compact disk
546. Scanner
547. Head or earphones
548. Copyright law
549. Yes
550. Intellectual property
551. Fair use
552. Can reference sources
553. Yes
554. Yes
555. Emails
556. Answers yes or no
557. Manages email
558. Yes
559. When face-to-face possible
560. Spam
561. Manages Spam
562. A virus
563. Protect against viruses
564. Firewall
565. Wiki
566. HML
567. A blog
568. Yes
569. Computer coding
570. Computer languages
571. Yes
572. Yes
573. Yes
574. Yes
575. Answers yes or no
576. Yes
577. Technological innovations
578. Yes
579. Yes
580. VCR, a pager, fax machine, etc.
581. Landline phone, etc.
582. Makes predictions
583. Literature, research, etc.
584. States frequency of visits
585. Fiction and Non-fiction
586. Dewey Decimal System
587. Call numbers
588. Can distinguish literature
589. Yes
590. Names authors
591. Genre
592. Yes
593. Names genres
594. Yes
595. Yes
596. Yes
597. Bibliography
598. Yes
599. Intellectual freedom
600. Censorship
601. Yes
602. Yes
603. Names non-fiction subjects
604. Names notable authors
605. Names notable book titles
606. Can identify genres
607. Mythology
608. Yes
609. Biography
610. Names biographies
611. Autobiography
612. Names autobiographies
613. Explains own autobiography
614. Answers yes or no
615. Facebook
616. Twitter
617. Answers yes or no
618. Hashtag
619. Skype
620. LinkedIn
621. Amazon
622. eBay
623. Craigslist
624. Yes
625. Travel services
626. Cyberspace
627. Apps
628. Instagram
629. Vine
630. Pinterest
631. Cloud Computing
632. A website
633. A domain name
634. A web host
635. Plug-ins
636. Manages digital photos
637. Selfie
638. Texting
639. Explains danger
640. Yes
641. Names devices
642. Forecasts technological future

ANSWERS – CURRENT EVENTS

APPENDIX 13: Chapter 13 – Current Events

1. Says what is happening in the news
2. Explains world events
3. Says what is happening in sports
4. Cites specific sporting event
5. States current weather conditions
6. Indicates specific weather event
7. Cites special holiday and next one
8. Names current pop icons
9. Names news outlets
10. Postulates rationale for being informed

Bibliography

"Ducksters: Education Site for Kids and Teachers." *Ducksters: Education Site for Kids and Teachers*. N.p., n.d. Web. Accessed 2014. http://www.ducksters.com.

"ENCHANTED LEARNING HOME PAGE." *ENCHANTED LEARNING HOME PAGE*. N.p., n.d. Web. 10 Accessed 2014. http://www.enchantedlearning.com.

"Fact Monster from Information Please." *Fact Monster: Online Almanac, Dictionary, Encyclopedia, and Homework Help*. N.p., n.d. Web. Accessed 2014. http://www.factmonster.com.

Grade Level Help at Internet 4 Classrooms." *Grade Level Help at Internet 4 Classrooms*. N.p., n.d. Web. Accessed 2014. http://www.internet4classrooms.com.

Hirsch, E. D. *What Your First grader Needs to Know: Fundamentals of a Good First-Grade Education*. New York: Doubleday, 1991. Print.

Hirsch, E. D. *What Your Third Grader Needs to Know: Fundamentals of a Good Third-Grade Education*. New York: Doubleday, 1992. Print.

Hirsch, E. D. *What Your Fourth Grader Needs to Know: Fundamentals of a Good Fourth-Grade Education*. New York: Doubleday, 1992. Print.

Hirsch, E. D. *What Your Fifth Grader Needs to Know: Fundamentals of a Good Fifth-Grade Education*. New York: Doubleday, 1993. Print.

Hirsch, E. D., and John Holdren. *What Your Kindergartner Needs to Know: Preparing Your Child for a Lifetime of Learning*. New York: Doubleday, 1996. Print.

Hirsch, E. D. *What Your Second Grader Needs to Know: Fundamentals of a Good Second-Grade Education*. Rev. Ed. New York: Dell, 1998. Print.

Hirsch, E. D., and Linda Bevilacqua. *What Your Preschooler Needs to Know*. New York, NY: Bantam Dell, 2008. Print.

"K-12 Curriculum." *Cedarburg*. N.p., n.d. Web. June 2014. http://www.cedarburg.buildyourowncurriculum.com/public/Landing_Grades.aspx.

"Make an Amazing Timeline in Minutes." *Preceden: Timeline Maker & Timeline Generator*. N.p., n.d. Web. Accessed 2014. http://www.preceden.com.

"Native Indian Tribes." *Warpaths2piecepipes*. N.p., n.d. Web. Accessed 2014. http://www.warpaths2piecepipes.com.

"Typical Course of Study." *Typical Course of Study*. N.p., n.d. Web. 10 July 2014. http://www.worldbook.com/typical-course-of-study.

BIBLIOGRAPHY

"Online Dictionary | Thesaurus." *Online Dictionary*. N.p., n.d. Web. Accessed 2014. http://www.onlinedictionary.com.

"Practice Math & Language Arts." *IXL Math and English*. N.p., n.d. Web. Accessed 2014. http://www.ixl.com.

"The Great Idea Finder - Celebrating the Spirit of Innovation." *The Great Idea Finder - Celebrating the Spirit of Innovation*. N.p., n.d. Web. Accessed 2014. http://www.ideafinder.com.

"Top Ten Lists at TheTopTens." *Top Ten Lists at TheTopTens*. N.p., n.d. Web. Accessed 2014. http://www.thetoptens.com.

"Touropia - Travel, Tours and Top Tens." *Touropia*. N.p., n.d. Web. Accessed 2014. http://www.touropia.com.

"Wikepedia.com." *Wikepedia.com*. N.p., n.d. Web. 30 Accessed 2014. http://www.wikepedia.com.

www.ingramcontent.com/pod-product-compliance
Lightning Source LLC
Chambersburg PA
CBHW060306240426
43661CB00059B/2675